A HISTORY OF
AMERICAN DEMOCRACY

A HISTORY OF

JOHN D. HICKS
University of California, Berkeley

GEORGE E. MOWRY
University of California, Los Angeles

ROBERT E. BURKE
University of Washington

AMERICAN
DEMOCRACY

THIRD EDITION

HOUGHTON MIFFLIN COMPANY · BOSTON

TO THE MEMORY OF

FREDERIC LOGAN PAXSON

Contents

SECTION FOUR

The Sectional Conflict, 1860–1877

SECTION FIVE

The New Nation, 1877–1897

SECTION SIX

World Power and Reform, 1897–1921

SECTION SEVEN

Prosperity and Depression, 1921–1939

SECTION EIGHT

The Price of Leadership, 1939–1965

APPENDIX

Preface

The first edition of this book, published in 1943 as *A Short History of American Democracy*, reflected the mood of the American people as they emerged from the Great Depression into World War II. The second edition, which appeared in 1956 with George E. Mowry as collaborator, revealed a considerable shift in emphasis to fit the postwar years of striving for peace and prosperity. The third edition, with a new title and still another collaborator, Robert E. Burke, takes advantage of another decade of perspective, and draws upon the rich harvest of historical research and reinterpretation that post-World War II scholars have made available. Few periods in the writing of American History have yielded so much by way of new information and new thinking on all historical subjects. We have made every effort to integrate into this text as far as possible the findings of the "revisionists" and to give honorable mention to those opinions with which we cannot agree. The bibliographical notes that accompany each chapter (principally the work of Burke) emphasize this new literature, even at the expense of eliminating many worthwhile older titles. To make way for the new and enlarged treatment of social and intellectual history (principally the work of Mowry), we have all joined in an effort to contract the space devoted to political and economic history, while seeking also to recognize the new scholarship in these fields. As a result of this close scrutiny, hardly a page of the earlier editions remains unchanged; this is essentially a new book.

The new *History* draws heavily upon the fourth edition of our two-volume work, *The Federal Union* (1964) and *The American Nation* (1963). The individuals whose criticisms and suggestions helped us with that undertaking have therefore helped us with this. We wish particularly to acknowledge our deep obligation to Charles A. Barker, Johns Hopkins University; Arthur Bestor and Thomas J. Pressly, University of Washington; Wesley F. Craven, Princeton University; David Cronon, University of Wisconsin; Jasper W. Cross and Edward J. Maguire, St. Louis University; Gilbert C. Fite, University of Oklahoma; Emma Beekman Gavras, Los Angeles Trade-Technical College; Dewey Grantham, Vanderbilt University; Edwin Miles, University of Houston; Richard D. Poll, Brigham Young University; Hugh Rankin, Tulane University; Madeleine H. Rice, Hunter College; Charles G. Sellers, Jr., University of California, Berkeley; David A. Shannon, University of Maryland; Wilbert H. Timmons, Texas Western College; and Frank E. Vandiver, Rice University. In addition, we have received much helpful advice on particular items from numerous teachers and students; to all these, and to the many others who have unprotestingly made use of the *History* over the years, we extend our thanks. For assistance on the bibliographies and proofreading, we are indebted to Edith Baras and Janice Steele of Seattle.

We also owe much to the very competent staff of Houghton Mifflin Company. The sales force has not only promoted the "Hicks Histories" with becoming zeal, but has also reported to us many valuable ideas for the improvement of our books. The editorial acumen of Matthew Hodgson, who assisted in the planning of the present revision, is responsible for many of the book's unique features. We wish to express our appreciation also to Ronald Murray, the Company's distinguished Art Director, for the new and handsome format; to Patricia Kindelan for yeoman service in preparing the copy for the press; to Lynn Landy for the choice and arrangement of the illustrations; and to the many others who had a part in the making of this complicated book. They all worked together without friction, and in apparent enjoyment of the task.

John D. Hicks

George E. Mowry

Robert E. Burke

Edward Hicks, "The Residence of David Twining-1787."
Courtesy of the Abby Aldrich Rockefeller Folk Art Col-
lection, Williamsburg, Virginia.

The Origins of

American Society

· 1607–1789 ·

*The foundation of authority is laid in the free consent of
the people.*

THOMAS HOOKER

I am not a Virginian but an American.

PATRICK HENRY

*The decree has gone forth, and cannot now be recalled,
that a more equal liberty than has prevailed in other parts
of the earth, must be established in America.*

JOHN ADAMS

of England. This interference, coupled with the depredations upon Spanish commerce by English seamen, led Philip to dispatch against England his "Invincible Armada" of 131 ships, manned by 8,000 sailors and carrying an invasion army of 19,000 men. The Spanish fleet reached the English coast, but its great galleons were more than matched by the smaller, more maneuverable ships of the English. The Armada was disastrously defeated (1588), many of the ships that escaped the English were destroyed by storms in the North Sea, and less than a third of Philip's great fleet ever returned to Spain. Within a short time it was England, not Spain, who was "mistress of the seas." The importance of the Armada's defeat should not be exaggerated, however, for Spain was able to maintain her American empire for well over two centuries longer.

European Rivalry for America. Since Philip had taken the Portuguese throne in 1581, his defeat revealed that the Spanish-Portuguese commercial and colonial monopoly need no longer be respected. Among the first to take advantage of this situation were the Dutch, whose "sea-beggars" helped themselves to Portuguese holdings in Africa and the East Indies, and whose traders cast covetous eyes toward the New World. In 1609 the Dutch East India Company sent Henry Hudson, an Englishman, to search for a sea route through North America to India. Hudson found no northwest passage, but he did discover an opportunity for fur trade with the Indians, and a Dutch trading post was soon established on Manhattan Island. Dutch sailors also wrested from the Spanish some valuable Caribbean Islands and a strip of the northern coast of South America. The French, with a claim to the valley of the St. Lawrence based upon the explorations of Jacques Cartier in 1534, established a trading post at Quebec in 1608, and occupied several islands in the West Indies. Even the Swedes, who for a moment had attained a place of prominence in

European affairs, planted a colony in 1638 at the mouth of the Delaware, a settlement soon absorbed by the Dutch.

England and America. Meantime the English had not been idle. A Venetian, John Cabot, sailing in 1497 under authority of Henry VII of England, had by his explorations marked off the north Atlantic coast of North America as British territory, and in the early seventeenth century there seemed to be many reasons why this long-claimed area should be exploited. The enterprise and love of adventure that had braced English seamen for the defeat of the Spanish needed some further outlet. Protestant England, with the novice's enthusiasm for her creed, regarded the New World as a legitimate missionary field, also as a desirably distant place toward which the minds of troublesome dissenters might well be turned. Hard times and overpopulation, long a nightmare to government officials, became worse following the peace of 1604 with Spain, which left many discharged soldiers and sailors unemployed, while the increasing popularity of sheepraising uprooted numerous farm laborers. The care of the poor, which before Henry VIII's dissolution of the monasteries had been a major concern of the monks and nuns, increasingly overtaxed the resources of the civilian authorities. It seemed reasonable to suppose that if the excess of English population could be drawn off to other lands, unemployment might be reduced, and economic conditions greatly improved.

English Trade and Trading Companies. All such reasons, however, were secondary to the desire of merchant and government alike to promote English trade. The importation of gold and silver from the New World had an invigorating effect upon English commerce. The well-to-do required now such table luxuries as spices, sugar, and tea, and for their new and ostentatious mansions they demanded the costliest furnishings of the East. They paid high prices cheerfully, and merchants made good profits. Capital for commercial enterprise was thus easily amassed, and ocean trade became extremely attractive. Dozens of trading companies were chartered by the government for the purpose of establishing commercial relations with some foreign region. Perhaps the most successful of these enterprises was the English East India Company, formed in 1600 to exploit the trade of India. Other companies were soon organized to make profits from the American trade.

The generous charters which trading companies received from the English crown reveal a kind of alliance between government and business. The companies' ships left England with cargoes of English manufactures to exchange for the raw materials of undeveloped regions. To the business man this meant profits; to the government, inspired by the mercantilistic theory of the age, it meant security. According to the mercantilists, the chief measure of a country's strength was the amount of gold and silver it could amass. The trading companies, by exchanging expensive English manufactures for cheap raw materials, might be counted upon to produce for England a "favorable balance of trade," by which a steady stream of precious metals would flow into the country. The urgent necessity of promoting national self-sufficiency was another reason why the government gave special privileges to trading companies. At a time when wars were regarded as the normal state of international affairs, each nation aspired to care for itself without dependence on any other.

Physical North America.   To thoughtful English officials North America, rich in timber, naval stores, potash, fisheries, sugar, and even gold, seemed ideally fitted to become an independent source of supply for the British Isles. It was free both from arctic cold and tropical heat, and since it had a wide range of climate, of rainfall patterns, of soil, its agricultural possibilities were almost limitless. It possessed some of the largest forests in the world and rich mineral resources. If flourishing colonies could be established and maintained, they would provide new and independent markets for English manufacturers. The English government, although deeply interested in having colonies founded, never seriously considered founding colonies itself. Founding colonies was regarded as a type of business, and the government, according to prevailing custom, while free to foster and regulate every type of private enterprise, might not itself engage in business, although the Crown and court favorites, acting in their private capacities, participated in numerous early colonial ventures.

From the beginning the Atlantic proved less a barrier between the Old World and the New than an artery of communication. Colonies throve because their connections with Europe could be easily maintained. The numerous sheltered bays and harbors of the coast led the British to found many colonies instead of a few. Once established, the early colonies at first found it more convenient to maintain their connections with England than to foster extensive communications with each other. Hence each colony tended to develop more or less independently. Even after the Revolution the thirteen colonies did not surrender their separate political life merely because they broke with Great Britain. They became thirteen independent states, and the common system of self-government that they worked out provided for a federal union, rather than a consolidated and centralized nation.

The Appalachians.   The Appalachian mountain barrier played an equally important part in determining the future of the American nation. While it was neither high nor difficult to penetrate, it served as a restraining influence against the too rapid extension of settlement. Because of it the English tended to settle thickly along the coast before the conquest of the interior was begun. The French, on the other hand, with easy access to the West through the Valley of the St. Lawrence and the waters of the Great Lakes, dissipated their energies over too extensive an area. When the final test of strength came, their scattered villagers were no match for the more numerous and concentrated English. The Appalachians served further to encourage the development of an American nationality. Their parallel ranges and fertile valleys bent toward the South the course of the westward movement and promoted the mingling of pioneers from the northern colonies, immigrants from Europe, and southerners to form a new people, not much concerned with former, older loyalties. From these "backwoodsmen" all future generations of western pioneers were to inherit a common legacy.

The Mississippi Valley. West of the Appalachians, the interior basin of the North American continent becomes a vast, undulating plain, bounded on the west by the Rockies, on the south by the Gulf of Mexico, and on the northeast by the Great Lakes. The great river system which drains this region gives it remarkable unity and a name, the Mississippi Valley. Here lay nearly half the land now contained within the national borders, and far more than half the arable land. Here the process of ethnic amalgamation, already begun in the troughs of the Appalachians, was long continued. Here, too, northerners met southerners, travelers from afar met those who had come from regions nearby, and foreigners met natives, all to be absorbed rapidly into one American nationality.

The Rockies. A striking physical feature of the North American continent is the great Cordillera or Rocky Mountain system of the West. The plateau from which the ranges of this system rise is everywhere from 5,000 to 10,000 feet above sea level; it spreads out within the United States to a width of a thousand miles, and its peaks rise to magnificent heights. For all their promi-

nence, however, these mountains lack the significance in American history that attaches to the Appalachians, or to most of the other great physical features of the continent. Though possessing immense mineral wealth, valuable grazing facilities, and valleys later made productive by irrigation, the Rockies were unfitted to shelter a large population, such as the Mississippi Valley naturally invited, and they were entered only when the formative period in the life of the nation was over.

The Pacific Slope. As for the Pacific slope, it too had relatively little to do with the making of early American civilization. The narrowness of the western coastal plain, the scarcity of its harbors, and its remoteness from Europe, precluded such developments as took place along the Atlantic. The Spanish established a few settlements, but these began only when the English colonies were already ripe for revolution, and they unloosed few forces of permanent significance. Man eventually conquered the obstacles to western settlement that nature placed in his way, but not until the habits of the American people were well set, and the nature of the American nation well defined.

The Call of Free Land. Why did certain Englishmen choose to become colonists? Doubtless the love of adventure, the false hope of gold, the need of a refuge from religious persecution, and the lack of employment at home all sent their quotas to America. But probably no other motive weighed so heavily as the desire for land. In England, and indeed throughout all Europe, landholding was a mark of gentility; ordinary people might not even hope to own land. But in the New World land was open to all. The younger sons of nobles, left landless by the rule of primogeniture, turned to America; the peasants and artisans, unable to advance their position at home, saw in the colonies a chance to become landed proprietors. Cheap land was the magnet that drew immigrants across the Atlantic to America, just as it was later to draw their descendants, step by step, across the continent.

The failure of two early colonial ventures — sponsored by individual promoters — made it evident that the colonizing of North America was not to be undertaken lightly. The first of these, led by Sir Humphrey Gilbert and inspired by the common illusion that there existed a northwest passage around America to the Orient, was shipwrecked in 1583 off the inhospitable shores of Newfoundland. The second, under Sir Walter Raleigh, failed twice, once in 1585 and again in 1587, to plant an enduring colony on Roanoke Island, just south of Albemarle Sound. This left the field free for the trading company, which was able to draw upon the greater resources of many investors.

The London and Plymouth Companies. In 1606, King James I was persuaded to issue a charter to some London and Plymouth merchants who wished to establish new outposts of trade in Virginia. Two companies were organized, the London Company and the Plymouth Company, and

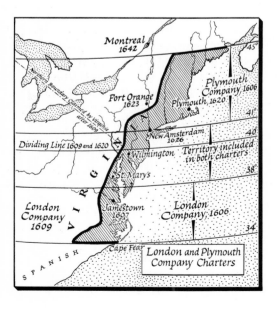

London and Plymouth Company Charters

each was promised a tract of land along the Virginia coast a hundred miles in width and extending a hundred miles into the interior. The land of the London Company was to be located somewhere between the thirty-fourth and the forty-first parallels, while the land of the Plymouth Company should lie farther north, between the thirty-eighth and the forty-fifth parallels. Neither company might establish a colony within one hundred miles of any colony established by the other.

The London merchants were the first to take advantage of this grant. In December, 1606, they sent out three shiploads of colonists, who the next spring founded Jamestown at a point thirty miles inland from the mouth of the James River. Thereafter for seventeen years the Company continued to send a steady stream of colonists and supplies to Virginia. Of profits there were none, but the stockholders hopefully invested in the project a sum which today would be reckoned at not less than $5 million. The mortality among the early colonists was frightful; by 1616, when over 1,600 emigrants had left England for Virginia, the population of the colony was only about 350. Captain John Smith, a gallant and picturesque character, stands out in these early years as the man who saved the colony from extinction. In spite of heavy odds, including an Indian attack in 1622, the number of Virginians grew, and by 1624 there were probably as many as 1,200 people in the colony.

Early Virginia. During these years the Virginia experiment was carried on as a strictly business enterprise, with local managers, or "governors," directing the work of the Company's "servants" — usually paupers or convicts who had come to Virginia under indentures that bound them to work for the Company from four to seven years in return for their passage across the Atlantic. Toward the end of the Company's rule several innovations, designed in part to keep the colonists contented and in part

THE ARRIVAL OF THE ENGLISHMEN IN VIRGINIA

Thomas Herriot, who was the geographer for Raleigh's second expedition to "Virginia," published an account of the voyage, in the 1590 edition of which this fanciful illustration appeared.

to attract new settlers, were introduced. The right to private ownership of land was conceded, and liberal grants were made to all free men and to indentured servants whose grace period of service had expired. The harsh laws deemed necessary during the first hard years of the colony were abrogated. Finally, a representative assembly "freely elected by the inhabitants," to consist of two representatives from each "plantation," was authorized to share in the making of the laws.

Charter Revisions. The original charter of 1606 was twice revised, once in 1609 and again in 1612. The new land grant gave the company a frontage along the coast of 200 miles north and 200 miles south of Old Point Comfort, while inland the Company's rights were to extend "west and northwest" from sea to sea. King James I regretted hav-

ing granted to the Company the right to govern the colony, and he especially disliked the concessions to popular rule that it had made. In 1624 he accordingly obtained from subservient judges an annulment of the charter. All governmental rights now devolved upon the King, and Virginia became a royal colony. This change deprived the Virginians of the assistance they had been accustomed to receive from the London Company, but they were permitted to retain their land titles and their representative assembly. As for the investments made by stockholders in the Company, they were a total loss.

Tobacco Culture. The success of tobacco culture was what enabled the Virginia colony to survive. The use of tobacco was already known in Europe, but it was tobacco from the Spanish colonies in America that Europeans preferred. Virginia tobacco was regarded as inferior and undesirable until about 1616, when a new method of curing it was discovered. From this time on the Jamestown colonists had a profitable product and the colony began to prosper. Land was easy to obtain under the "headright" system, by which each immigrant and each person who paid for an immigrant's passage received fifty acres. Headrights were not, however, available to indentured servants. The more prosperous planters came to own many head-rights, and the tendency toward large plantations in the South early became marked. Beginning in 1619, Negroes were brought into the colony, although in early Virginia their number was small. During the middle decades of the seventeenth century, war broke out in England between the adherents of the King, or "Cavaliers," and the supporters of Parliament, or "Roundheads." When in 1649 the "Roundheads" triumphed and executed the King, some "Cavaliers" sought safety in Virginia. By 1652 the population of the colony was estimated at 20,000.

The English Dissenters. The next successful English experiment in colony planting was at Plymouth, on the coast of Massachusetts. Here the religious motive undoubtedly assumed commanding importance. The church establishment which had been worked out in England under Queen Elizabeth occupied a place midway between Catholicism and Protestantism. Inevitably many Englishmen were dissatisfied with these halfway measures and wished to go further in the direction of Protestantism. Of these "dissenters," some, known as "Puritans," desired only to reform the existing English Church in such a way as to bring it into closer harmony with Protestant teachings; others, less numerous and influential, were called "Separatists" because they were ready to sever all connections with the established church. Neither group was seriously persecuted during the reign of James I, but there was enough threat of

persecution to make all dissenters uneasy. A little band of Separatists from Scrooby, England, furnished the nucleus for the Plymouth settlement. They went first from England to Holland and later, in 1620, some of them, after returning to England, set sail in the *Mayflower* for America. Their venture was financed by a joint-stock company in which both the emigrants and a number of London merchants owned shares. Not all who went to Holland came to America, and not all of those who came to America had been in Holland. Indeed, when the *Mayflower* set sail from England, about half its hundred passengers had never been outside their own country.

The "Mayflower Compact." On December 21, 1620, the *Mayflower* landed a scouting party at Plymouth harbor. Anticipating difficulty in controlling the action of some of the more turbulent members of the group, forty-one Pilgrim "Fathers" affixed their signatures while still on shipboard to the famous "Mayflower Compact," by which they bound themselves together into a "civil body politic" for their "better ordering and preservation." They chose John Carver as their first governor. The first winter took a toll in dead of over half the company, but the survivors persevered, and with the help of additional immigrants they were able to found an enduring settlement. Farming, fur trading, fishing, and lumbering furnished their chief occupations.

The Pilgrims soon discovered that the site of their colony lay outside the grant of the London (or Virginia) Company, from which they had obtained settlement rights, but their second governor, William Bradford, as trustee for the colony, secured title from the New England Council (successor to the Plymouth Company) to the land about Plymouth Bay. Finally, in 1641, when the debts owed to the London merchants were settled, the governor formally transferred to the people the rights he had acquired. Pure democracy at Plymouth, as practiced under the Mayflower Compact, was soon succeeded by a representative system, with a "General Court" in charge of matters pertaining to the whole colony, and local affairs in the hands of town meetings. All efforts to secure royal approval of these governmental privileges failed, but the Plymouth colony was left free to govern itself as a self-constituted commonwealth until 1686, when it became part of the "Dominion of New England." In 1691 William III joined it to Massachusetts Bay.

Massachusetts Bay Colony. The founders of the Massachusetts Bay colony, unlike the Pilgrims, were Puritans rather than Separatists. Disillusioned by the arbitrary rule of King Charles I, they not only gave up hope of "purifying" the English Church, but also despaired of England as a fit home for free men. They wished to establish in the New World an ideal Puritan commonwealth where a really "purified" church might thrive, and where the government would be wholly in their hands. They therefore secured complete control of a "Company for Massachusetts-Bay," with a charter from the King and a grant of land from the New England Council, and in 1630, led by their elected governor, John Winthrop, took the charter with them to New England. What was originally designed to be merely the articles of incorporation of a joint-stock company thus became a kind of constitution for the government of the new colony. Before the summer was over seventeen ships had landed a thousand settlers in Massachusetts, and several villages, among them Boston, Dorchester, Watertown, and Roxbury, had been founded. By 1640 no less than 25,000 refugees had found their way to Massachusetts. In that year the tide began to turn against the King in England, and the "Great Migration" came to a close.

Life on the New England frontier turned out to be a bitter struggle against unyielding soil, cruel winters, disease, and constant privation, but in spite of hardships the evidences of civilization could soon be observed. Livestock was imported and bred;

WILLIAM BRADFORD

A signer of the Mayflower Compact, William Bradford (1589–1657) took part in the landing and settlement of the Puritans at Plymouth, and served ably the new colony as its governor between 1622 and 1656.

After this they chose, or rather confirmed, Mr. John Carver (a man godly and well approved amongst them) their Governor for that year. And after they had provided a place for their goods, or common store (which were long in unlading for want of boats, foulness of the winter weather and sickness of divers) and begun some small cottages for their habitation; as time would admit, they met and consulted of laws and orders, both for their civil and military government as the necessity of their condition did require, still adding thereunto as urgent occasion in several times, and as cases did require.

WILLIAM BRADFORD: *Of Plymouth Plantation 1620–1647,* ed. by Samuel Eliot Morison.

Massachusetts, Rhode Island and Connecticut Settlements
- - - - Plymouth Colony, 1630
- - - - Present boundaries

mills to grind the grain, brick kilns and saw-mills to produce better building materials, and even ironworks to turn out a few household necessities began to appear. Trade with England developed naturally, for the colonists were quick to discover that with fish, furs, lumber, and potash to exchange, they could obtain from the mother country many of the things they needed.

Puritan Government.   All governmental power, according to the charter, rested with the stockholders, or "freemen," who were authorized to elect as a kind of board of directors a governor, a deputy governor, and eighteen "assistants," to meet four times each year. Only twelve freemen had come to America, and every one of them, as governor or assistant, was an officer of the company. This group, by neglecting to choose new freemen, at first kept all authority in its hands, but such arbitrary procedure did not long escape criticism. In the fall of 1630 heavy pressure from the settlers resulted in the creation of many new freemen, but the latter were given only an indirect voice in government. At first permitted to vote only for assistants who would then elect the higher officers, the freemen, within two years, were electing all the colony's officers

and had also acquired the right for each town to choose two representatives to act with the assistants in the levying of taxes. In 1634, after an examination of the charter had proved that the entire law-making power was vested in the freemen, the elected delegates began to participate in all the legislative activities of what they called the "General Court."

But the government of the colony was very undemocratic. Only free men who were church members could be admitted to the corporation, and not even all church members were chosen to participate in government. Since the deference of the common people to ministers and magistrates was so strong, the will of the leaders was rarely contested. Ultimately, the Massachusetts General Court divided into two houses, one composed of representatives from the various towns, and the other composed of the assistants, who together with the governor were chosen annually by the votes of the freemen.

Religious Intolerance.   In most matters of belief and conduct the Massachusetts government was decidedly intolerant. On reaching the New World the Puritans had broken away from the Church of England, referring all theological disputes to their own ministers, sitting together in synods. They held that the Church must set up standards of conduct as well as principles of theology, and believed that one of the first responsibilities of government was to punish all departures from orthodoxy in theology or from propriety in behavior. Laws were passed to make the way of the transgressor hard, and the worst offenders were punished by expulsion from the colony. Church and state worked together, each to uphold the other. Early Massachusetts was not a democracy; it was a hierarchical theocracy.

Rhode Island.   Deportations from Massachusetts for religious offenses were numerous, and two of the most famous resulted in the founding of a new colony, Rhode Island. Roger Williams was a disputatious minister who came from England in 1631, and presently became the pastor at Salem. His insistence that the state had no right to punish a man for uncommon religious views or practices was regarded as dangerous, and so in 1635 the General Court voted to expel him from the colony. With the help of a few adherents, the next spring he began the settlement on Narragansett Bay that developed into the town of Providence. Another religious rebel was Anne Hutchinson, who, according to John Winthrop, was "a woman of a ready wit and a bold spirit." Among her heresies was the belief that some ministers were definitely superior to others because they were under a "covenant of grace" rather than merely a "covenant of works." Roger Williams had few followers, but Anne Hutchinson attracted many and soon had the colony in an uproar. Finally the General Court ruled that "two so opposite parties could not contain in the same body without hazard of ruin to the whole," and banished Mrs. Hutchinson and her disciples from the colony. In 1638 they founded a settlement at Portsmouth, near Providence. Disagreements at Portsmouth led to the founding of a third settlement in 1639 at Newport, and in 1643 Samuel Gorton, another refugee from Massachusetts, founded Warwick.

The four Rhode Island communities had little love for one another, but their common fear of Massachusetts which considered them to be equally heretical drew them together. In 1644 Roger Williams secured from the English Parliament a "patent" which permitted the settlers on Narragansett Bay to govern themselves so long as their laws were in harmony with the laws of England; and in 1647 representatives from the various Rhode Island towns organized a political system not unlike that of Massachusetts. Church membership was not a qualification for voting, however, and the right of religious liberty was definitely safeguarded, "notwithstanding our different

consciences touching the truth as it is in Jesus." In 1663 a formal charter was secured from King Charles II in which the system of representative government was accorded full approval, and the principle of "liberty in religious concernments" was definitely accepted.

Beginnings of Connecticut. Meanwhile, out in the lower Connecticut Valley, another offshoot from the Massachusetts Bay colony had appeared. Fertile lands had more to do with the founding of Connecticut than religious dissensions. Thomas Hooker, minister at Newtown (later Cambridge), Massachusetts, and John Haynes, a former governor, were the chief promoters of the Connecticut project. In the years 1635 and 1636 they led about 800 settlers southeast through the forests to the Connecticut Valley. Ignoring Dutch claims to this region and their own lack of title, they founded three towns, Hartford, Wethersfield, and Windsor. Other towns were established by one group from Plymouth and another group from England under the leadership of John Winthrop, Jr., son of the Massachusetts governor. In 1639 representatives from Hartford, Wethersfield, and Windsor met at Hartford to draw up a plan of union. The result was the Fundamental Orders of Connecticut, a document usually regarded as the first constitution to be written in America. The Fundamental Orders copied the governmental practices of Massachusetts, although the prerogatives of officials were somewhat more limited.

The New Haven Colony. During this same period still another Puritan colony, New Haven, was in process of evolution along the shores of Long Island Sound. Its founders were John Davenport, an English Puritan minister, and Theophilus Eaton, a well-to-do English Puritan merchant. These men visited Massachusetts in 1637, but decided to found an ideal Bible commonwealth and trading center outside the confines of any existing colony. At New Haven

AN EARLY COLONIAL DWELLING

The Parson Capen House, Topsfield, Massachusetts, built in 1683, is typical of the period. The assumption that the overhanging second floor in such houses was designed to enable defenders to pour hot water on attacking Indians is probably pure legend.

their dreams of commercial success failed to materialize, but with this small settlement as a beginning, several other towns were soon founded. In government and religion the New Haven colony, like Connecticut, repeated with slight variations the Massachusetts experiment; indeed, no other colony was more circumspect in its Puritanism than early New Haven. In 1662 its separate existence ended when Charles II was induced, mainly through the efforts of John Winthrop, Jr., to unite the Connecticut River towns and New Haven into the colony of Connecticut under a liberal charter.

New Hampshire and Maine. As for the regions known as New Hampshire and Maine, their beginnings date back to 1623 when two English gentlemen, Sir Ferdinando Gorges and Captain John Mason, obtained from the New England Council a patent to all the land lying between the Kennebec and the Merrimac Rivers. Mason took the western half and called it New Hampshire, while Gorges took the territory along the coast and called it Maine. Both men tried to establish settlements within the confines of their grants, but success came only with the influx of settlers from Massachusetts who were reluctant to acknowledge any other authority than that of the Puritan commonwealth in which they had lived. Presently the Massachusetts government, on the pretext that its land grant really entitled it to do so, extended its authority first over the New Hampshire towns, and finally over those in Maine. New Hampshire remained a part of Massachusetts until 1679, when Charles II made it a royal colony, but Maine was not accorded a separate existence until, by the well-known Compromise of 1820, it became a state in the Union.

The New England Confederation. The advance of the New England frontier brought on at an early date trouble with the Indians, particularly the Pequots, whose tribal territory was seriously jeopardized by the founding of Connecticut. Attacks on isolated settlers resulted in a general Indian war, during which the Massachusetts colony gave valuable aid to the Connecticut pioneers. By 1637 most of the offending Pequots were either dead or enslaved, but the memory of this conflict, coupled with the thinly veiled hostility of the Dutch on the Hudson, convinced New England leaders that they must combine their forces. Accordingly, in 1643, the New England Confederation, consisting of Massachusetts, Plymouth, Connecticut, and New Haven, was formed. Two commissioners from each of the four colonies were entrusted with the management of the common business, which was mainly military defense; but the Articles mentioned also the desirability of protecting common religious interests, presumably against heretical Rhode Island. The Confederation lasted until 1684, and in 1675 it was of material assistance in waging another war against the Indians, generally known as King Philip's War.

Except for the futile efforts of Gilbert and Raleigh, and of Mason and Gorges, the colonial foundations so far mentioned owed their origins to the activities of trading companies rather than individuals. Investors put up the funds which religious enthusiasm or love of adventure alone would have been powerless to obtain. Many other colonial ventures, however, particularly those of the later colonial period, were organized and financed by proprietors, usually royal favorites who had received from the King generous grants of land. Some were mere speculators, who aimed chiefly at selling or letting out their American acres on advantageous terms. A few coveted political power such as British nobles were no longer permitted to possess, and others, while by no means indifferent to the prospects of financial and political rewards, sincerely desired to found havens of refuge for the oppressed.

The Baltimores in Maryland. The earliest of the successful proprietary provinces was Maryland. The launching of this colony was the work of George Calvert and his son Cecilius, the first and second Lords Baltimore. George Calvert was a man of means who had long been interested in colonial projects. By embracing the Catholic faith he had cut himself off from all chance of political preferment at home, but King Charles I promised him a grant of land in America. In 1632, after the death of the first Lord Baltimore, the grant of Maryland devolved upon his son. By its terms the territory from the south bank of the Potomac northward to the fortieth parallel and inland to the source of the river was given to the Baltimore family as an hereditary estate. In the making of laws and the levying of taxes the proprietor was required to consult the freemen, or landowners, of the colony, or their representatives.

A Catholic Refuge. The second Lord Baltimore greatly desired to make of Maryland a place where Catholics might worship

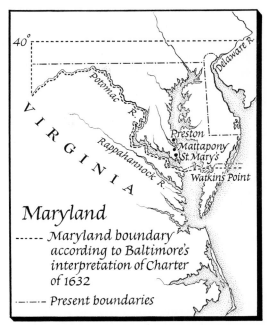

Maryland

------ Maryland boundary according to Baltimore's interpretation of Charter of 1632

-·—·— Present boundaries

without fear of oppression, and the royal charter offered no opposition to such a course. But the number of prospective emigrants among English Catholics was limited, and Lord Baltimore was too good a businessman to propose the exclusion of Protestants, who were cordially welcomed and from the first seem to have outnumbered Catholics. The *Ark* and the *Dove*, two small ships which Baltimore sent to Maryland in the fall of 1633, carried about twenty gentlemen and laborers to the new colony. Most of the gentlemen were Catholics, but most of the laborers were Protestants. Two Jesuit priests accompanied the expedition and labored with great earnestness but little success to convert the Protestant settlers and the Indians to Catholicism. In 1634 the expedition entered the Potomac and chose St. Mary's as the site of the first settlement. Lands were peacefully acquired from the Indians, and the economic life of Virginia was closely and successfully imitated.

Cecilius Calvert did not himself come to America, but sent instead as lieutenant-governor his brother, Leonard Calvert.

Small quitrents, charged in lieu of feudal dues by the proprietor against all lands granted to settlers, produced a fair revenue, but also much opposition. Furthermore, the proprietor and his lieutenant sought to hold popular participation in the government to a minimum. This was not long possible, and in Maryland, as in other colonies, a representative assembly soon developed. One of the most significant of its early measures, passed to attract Puritans then being persecuted in Virginia, was the Toleration Act of 1649. While this act threatened with death all non-Christians, Jews, and Unitarians, it guaranteed that no person "professing to believe in Jesus Christ, shall from henceforth be in any ways troubled, molested or discountenanced for or in respect of his or her religion." Persecution of Catholics, however, did break out in Maryland during the later years of the seventeenth century, and the Church of England became the established church.

The Founding of the Carolinas. The successes of the Baltimores, such as they were, inspired certain courtiers of the new king, Charles II, to emulate them. This easygoing monarch readily fell in with the plans of his friends, who were helped also by the general revival of interest in colonization that set in after the period of

North and South Carolina
--- Present boundaries

civil war. Eight prominent nobles, armed with an elaborate but unworkable plan, the "Fundamental Constitutions of Carolina," drawn by John Locke for the introduction of the feudal system into America, successfully petitioned the King for the land that lay south of Virginia and north of Florida. In what became North Carolina, pioneers from Virginia had already settled in the Albemarle region, and they paid little attention to the efforts of the Carolina proprietors to assert authority over them. In 1670, however, an expedition under Willam Sayle founded Charles-Town, or Charleston, as it was later called, and so began the settlement of South Carolina, a colony which rapidly took on a cosmopolitan tinge. French Huguenots began to arrive about 1680, and emigrants from Ireland, New England, and the West Indies were numerous. The planters used indentured servants for labor when they could, but as in Virginia and Maryland, they bought Negro slaves when the supply of white servants was deemed inadequate. They raised foodstuffs as well as tobacco, and in the eighteenth century they produced much rice and indigo. The excellent harbor at Charleston greatly facilitated trade with the outside world. In government both North Carolina and South Carolina tended to develop along the lines already marked out in Maryland.

New Netherland. The Carolina settlements were designed, in part, to act as buffers against the Spanish in Florida. But the Dutch colony of New Netherland, on the Hudson, was an even greater menace to the English than Spanish Florida. Although fur traders had been active earlier in this region, serious efforts at colonization began in 1621. The rule of this colony was in the hands of the Dutch West India Company, which among other things actively promoted the settlement of "patroons," or landlords, together with their tenants, in great estates along the Hudson. By the middle of the century a sparse Dutch population extended northward as far as the site of Albany. Many settlers from the English colonies also entered the Dutch territory. Some of them were refugees from religious persecution, others were pioneer farmers eager to accept the generous land terms offered by the Dutch, and still others were former indentured servants. Thanks to these accessions, and to the absorption in 1655 of the small Swedish colony on the Delaware, the population of New Netherland had risen before the English conquest to about 10,000.

New York. The presence of this Dutch colony in America was naturally distasteful to the English, whose holdings it cut squarely in two. Hence, in 1664, on the eve of one of the several wars of commercial rivalry between England and the Netherlands, Charles II sent an expedition across the Atlantic to take possession of New Netherland. He granted the proprietary rights over the whole province to his brother, the Duke of York, later King James II. The British occupation took place without bloodshed, and the little colony, renamed New York, exchanged without serious incident the autocratic rule of the Dutch merchants for an almost equally undemocratic system embodied in the "Duke's Laws." Throughout the seventeenth century, progress toward popular rule in New York lagged perceptibly behind that of every other English colony in America.

New Jersey. The Duke of York disposed of a part of his holdings to John, Lord Berkeley and Sir George Carteret, who were also interested in the Carolina project and hoped for riches from the sale of their lands in America. These gentlemen were given proprietary rights to the territory lying between the lower Hudson and the Delaware, a region which they called New Jersey, after Carteret's home in England. Here a few Dutch settlements had already been established, and the new proprietors, by offering land to newcomers on easy terms, succeeded in attracting many emigrants from New England and from all

parts of the British Isles. In 1665, the proprietors sent out Philip Carteret, a relative of Sir George, as governor. He promptly instituted a legislative assembly, but had considerable trouble with the settlers because the proprietors insisted, for the most part in vain, on the collection of quitrents.

Down to 1674 the two proprietors held New Jersey jointly, but in that year Berkeley sold his holdings to two Quakers. Carteret retained as his portion the settlements in the northeast adjacent to New York, or East New Jersey, while the Quakers took the region to the south and along the Delaware, or West New Jersey. After several exchanges of titles both the Jerseys emerged in Quaker hands, and with relatively democratic governmental practices.

To the Jerseys came Quakers from England and Scotland, Puritans from New England, and Scotch-Irish from the north of Ireland. The population of East New Jersey was probably twice that of West New Jersey, and in its economic character it closely resembled New England, whence so many of its settlers had come. West New Jersey, on the other hand, tended to copy the manner of life adopted by the settlers along the Chesapeake. Small holdings were the rule, but large plantations, worked in part by Negro slaves, were not unknown. By the end of the seventeenth century the two Jerseys together had a population of about 15,000.

William Penn. Among the most interested of the Quakers involved in the New Jersey project was William Penn, the son of a British admiral. Penn's father was friendly with King Charles II, with his brother the Duke of York, and with many of the nobles who had received proprietary grants of land in America. Young Penn, while still a student at Oxford, was impressed by the teachings of a Quaker preacher, and he soon became a member of the Society of Friends, as the Quakers called themselves. His father was deeply distressed by his action, for the Quakers adhered to doctrines that were much at variance with the prevailing views of the time. They rejected all the sacraments, refused to pay tithes toward the support of the established church, denounced war, declined to do military service, and in a great variety of ways put themselves entirely outside the pale of seventeenth-century respectability. Persecution under such circumstances was inevitable, and Penn, as one of the most prominent members of the sect, advanced

Pennsylvania and Delaware

the idea of founding for the oppressed members of his faith a Quaker commonwealth in America.

Pennsylvania. It was Penn's dream that the colony he would establish should be liberal in government as well as tolerant in religion. Believing that he must have a charter direct from the crown, he secured one from Charles (1681), after reminding the king of his £16,000 claim against the crown, inherited from Admiral Penn. Penn's desire to institute democratic practices was embodied in the various regulations he devised for the government of Pennsylvania, from the "Frame of Government" he issued in 1682 to his "Charter of Privileges" (1701). Full freedom of worship was guaranteed for such persons as "acknowledged one Almighty and Eternal God," although in actual practice neither Jews nor Catholics were given quite the same political privileges as Protestants. Not only Quakers, but members of various other oppressed sects also, looked upon the Quaker colony as an ideal retreat.

The growth of Pennsylvania was remarkable. Penn's advertising campaigns, which featured generous land terms, religious freedom, and a liberal government, got a ready response. From Germany, where economic conditions were bad and where minority religious groups lived under the constant shadow of persecution, came a large migration. A few Dutch and a few French Huguenots came also, and many English, Welsh, and Irish settlers, most of whom were Quakers. Some of the English settlers adhered steadfastly to the Church of England and objected strenuously, although for the most part ineffectively, to Penn's "holy experiment" in toleration. By 1689 the population of Pennsylvania was nearly 12,000, and in a short time it was larger than any other English colony in North America. Its largest city, Philadelphia, which Penn himself laid out, soon became one of the busiest in all the English overseas possessions.

Delaware. Delaware, at first a Swedish colony, became a part of New York, then later for a long time a part of Pennsylvania. Penn was determined to have for his colony free access to the sea, and he obtained from the Duke of York in 1682 the territory lying immediately to the east of the Delaware River. When the "Charter of Privileges" was issued in 1701, these "lower counties" were accorded the right to select an assembly of their own. This they soon did, but the Penns continued as proprietors, and the relations between Delaware and Pennsylvania remained close.

Georgia. Georgia was the last of the English colonies to be established on the mainland. Its founder, James Oglethorpe, wished to plant a colony in the unappropriated area between the Carolinas, Florida, and Louisiana that would act as a buffer state against the Spanish and the French. He had also a humanitarian desire to found a refuge for Englishmen who were jailed for nonpayment of debts, and for Protestants who were suffering from religious persecution on the continent of Europe. In 1732 a group of trustees, of whom Oglethorpe was the most active, secured from George II title to the land lying between the Savannah and Altamaha rivers, and westward from their headwaters to the Pacific. This grant forbade the trustees to make any profit from their venture and provided that at the end of twenty-one years their governmental privileges should revert to the crown.

In January, 1733, Oglethorpe brought over about a hundred settlers and founded Savannah. Other immigrants soon came, Salzburgers, Scottish Highlanders, Scotch-Irish, and Welsh, as well as English. At first the terms on which land could be obtained were unusual. Not more than five hundred acres could be taken by any person, and all such grants were entailed to male heirs. The proprietors also prohibited slavery and forbade the importation of rum. These provisions were extremely unpopular,

Georgia
1735

and although they were not long retained, they checked somewhat the growth of the colony. English debtors were not sent to Georgia in as great numbers as Oglethorpe had hoped, and by 1760 the total population of the colony was not more than 9,000. Of this number about one-third were Negro slaves whose presence was demanded when the economic interests of Georgia began to approximate those of the other southern colonies.

The Island Colonies. Englishmen of the seventeenth and eighteenth centuries, when they thought of the English settlements in America, included also the "island colonies," which seemed in many ways even more important than those on the mainland. Among these were the Bermudas, several hundred miles to the east of the Carolinas, Barbados and St. Christopher, together with a number of minor islands in the Lesser Antilles, and the large island of Jamaica directly south of Cuba. Together they probably contributed far more to the economic prosperity of the British Empire than did the mainland colonies. Their sugar-cane and tobacco plantations offered extraordinary opportunities for British capital, and their constant demand for slaves helped the

British slave trade prosper. Moreover, because they were eager to exchange their sugar and molasses for food-stuffs and other supplies from the continental colonies, they played an important part in making the colonies on the mainland a success.

Other British Outposts. Less important were the feeble British outposts in the Bahamas, Guiana, and Honduras; but far to the north the stations of the famous Hudson's Bay Company, chartered in 1670, tapped another important source of the fur trade. By the Treaty of Utrecht (1713) the British acquired clear title to the Hudson's Bay region, to Acadia, which they renamed Nova Scotia, and to the island of Newfoundland.

The British possessions in America were thus at the outset of the eighteenth century a far-flung empire, stretching from the northern coast of South America to the Arctic Circle. Meantime the British had acquired still other possessions in Asia, Africa, and Europe. A great variety of peoples, a wide diversity of economic interests, an immense expanse of geography confronted the British statesman who turned his attention to colonial affairs. It is not surprising that the task of integrating such an empire proved to be too great for eighteenth-century British statesmanship, and that the relatively homogeneous continental colonies of North America chose to work out their destiny apart from the rest.

SELECTED BIBLIOGRAPHY

Basic reference books for students of American history are *The Harvard Guide to American History,* edited by Oscar Handlin and others (1954); and R. B. Morris (ed.), *Encyclopedia of American History* (2nd ed., 1961). A great work of cooperative scholarship is the *Dictionary of American Biography,* edited by Allen Johnson and Dumas Malone (22 vols., 1928–1958). Single volumes compiled from this set are J. G. E. Hopkins (ed.), *Concise Dictionary of American Biography* (1964); and E. T. James (ed.), *The American Plutarch* (1964). J. T. Adams and others (eds.), *Dictionary of American History* (6 vols., 1940–1961), is another cooperative work; an abridgement is *Concise Dictionary of American History,* edited by Wayne Andrews (1962). D. H. Mugridge and B. P. McCrum, *A Guide to the Study of the United States of America* (1960), is an annotated bibliography of basic works. Among the best books of readings are *Documents of American History* (2 vols., 7th ed., 1963), edited by H. S. Commager; and *Readings in American History* (2 vols., 3rd ed., 1964), edited by J. S. Ezell and others. A useful book of readings is *The Colonial Experience,* edited by H. T. Colbourn (1966).

Another valuable tool which should be ac-

cessible to all students is a good historical atlas, such as J. T. Adams (ed.), *Atlas of American History* (1943). R. V. Coleman, *The First Frontier* (1948), describes with the aid of maps and illustrations the earliest Atlantic penetrations. On the geographic setting of American history, see E. C. Semple, *American History and its Geographic Conditions* (2nd ed., 1933). F. J. Turner, *The Frontier in American History* (1920), finds in the conquest of the continent a principal influence in the shaping of American character.

There is an abundance of excellent material on the American Indians. H. E. Driver, *Indians of North America* (1961), sets forth the basic facts in an encyclopedic fashion. An excellent brief survey is W. T. Hagan, *American Indians* (1961). Other general works of interest include J. C. Collier, *Indians of the Americas* (1947); and Clark Wissler, *Indians of the United States* (1940). G. E. Hyde, *Indians of the Woodlands: From Prehistoric Times to 1725* (1962), treats the northern tribes east of the Mississippi.

The essential background may be found in E. P. Cheyney, *European Background of American History, 1300–1600* (1904), and *The Dawn of a New Era, 1250–1453* (1936). W. P. Webb, *The Great Frontier* (1952), is a provocative and controversial attempt to en-

* Throughout the bibliographies in this book, items starred are available in paperback form.

large the concept of the frontier by presenting European expansion in that context. Other valuable studies include two by the English scholar J. H. Parry, *The Establishment of the European Hegemony: 1415–1715* (1949), and *The Age of Reconnaissance: Discovery, Exploration and Settlement, 1450–1650* (1963).

Outstanding general works on exploration are J. B. Brebner, *The Explorers of North America, 1492–1806* (1933); and H. I. Priestley, *The Coming of the White Man* (1929). The Portuguese activities are described in H. V. Livermore, *A History of Portugal* (rev. ed., 1947); and S. E. Morison, *Portuguese Voyages to America in the Fifteenth Century* (1940). The best biography of Columbus is S. E. Morison, *Admiral of the Ocean Sea* (2 vols., 1942); see also Morison's edition of *Journals and Other Documents on the Life and Voyages of Christopher Columbus* (1964). E. G. Bourne, *Spain in America, 1450–1580* (1904), is a convenient and durable survey; see also C. H. Haring, *The Spanish Empire in America* (1952). A lively book on the Spanish conquests is F. A. Kirkpatrick, *The Spanish Conquistadores* (1934). R. B. Merriman, *The Rise of the Spanish Empire in the Old World and the New* (4 vols., 1914–1934), is a monumental work of lasting worth. A. P. Newton, *The European Nations in the West Indies, 1493–1688* (1933), concentrates on one vital area.

Notable books on the background for English expansion include A. L. Rowse, *The Expansion of Elizabethan England* (1955), and *The Elizabethans and America* (1959); and Wallace Notestein, *The English People on the Eve of Colonization, 1603–1630* (1954). F. W. Maitland, *The Constitutional History of England* (1908), is a classic. Helpful also are the works of the prolific English scholar J. A. Williamson, which include *A Short History of British Expansion* (2 vols., 4th ed., 1955); *The Voyages of John and Sebastian Cabot* (1937); *The Age of Drake* (4th ed., 1960); and *Sir Francis Drake* (1962). On reasons behind English colonization see G. L. Beer, *The Origins of the British Colonial System, 1578–1660* (1908); and K. E. Knorr, *British Colonial Theories, 1570–1850* (1944).

Useful surveys are C. L. Ver Steeg, *The Formative Years, 1607–1763* (1964); and L. B. Wright, *The Atlantic Frontier: Colonial American Civilization (1607–1763)* (1947). Lead-

ing textbooks include Max Savelle and Robert Middlekauff, *A History of Colonial America* (1964); and C. P. Nettels, *The Roots of American Civilization* (2nd ed., 1963), especially strong on the economic side. A provocative new work which emphasizes American differences from the Old World is D. J. Boorstin, *The Americans: The Colonial Experience* (1958). Older works of merit include Edward Eggleston, *The Transit of Civilization from England to America in the Seventeenth Century* (1901); Carl Becker, *Beginnings of the American People* (1915); M. W. Jernegan, *American Colonies, 1492–1750* (1929); and C. M. Andrews, *Our Earliest Colonial Settlements* (1933). Excellent on the beginnings of settlement is T. J. Wertenbaker, *The First Americans, 1607–1690* (1927). A work which treats early movements of people to America is M. L. Hansen, *The Atlantic Migration, 1607–1860* (1941).

H. L. Osgood, *The American Colonies in the Seventeenth Century* (3 vols., 1904–1907), is packed with detail on political and constitutional matters. C. M. Andrews, *The Colonial Period of American History* (4 vols., 1934–1938), concentrates on the seventeenth century. The first two volumes of Edward Channing, *A History of the United States* (6 vols., 1905–1930), provide an admirable synthesis of historical opinion; for a contrast see the early parts of the survey by C. A. Beard and M. R. Beard, *The Rise of American Civilization* (2 vols., 2nd ed., 1949).

An excellent general treatment of the early southern settlements is in W. F. Craven, *The Southern Colonies in the Seventeenth Century, 1607–1689* (1949). T. J. Wertenbaker, *The Old South* (1942), is a well-rounded survey. The most readable and generally satisfactory work on its subject is F. B. Simkins, *A History of the South* (2nd ed., 1953), which is useful for any period. Brief and documentary is W. H. Stephenson, *A Basic History of the Old South* (1959).

Two valuable works by a leading authority are T. J. Wertenbaker, *The Planters of Colonial Virginia* (1922), and *The Shaping of Colonial Virginia* (1958). R. L. Morton, *Colonial Virginia* (2 vols., 1960), is a recent and monumental work. The classic work of Robert Beverley, *The History and Present State of Virginia,* is now available in a new edition by L. B. Wright (1947). P. L. Barbour, *The*

Three Worlds of Captain John Smith (1964), is a lively account of a dramatic life. Conflicting points of view on Bacon's Rebellion are presented in T. J. Wertenbaker, *Torchbearer of the Revolution* (1940); and W. E. Washburn, *The Governor and the Rebel* (1957), which sees Bacon as a disorderly land-grabber. Excellent on indentured servitude is A. E. Smith, *Colonists in Bondage* (1947), which helps to set the record straight on a complex subject. Two important monographs are J. C. Robert, *The Story of Tobacco in America* (1949); and A. P. Middleton, *Tobacco Coast; A Maritime History of the Chesapeake Bay in the Colonial Era* (1953).

The mood of historians toward the Puritans has softened considerably in the past thirty years. An interesting collection which gathers conflicting viewpoints is G. M. Waller (ed.), *Puritanism in Early America* (1950). J. T. Adams, *The Founding of New England* (1921), is brilliant and militantly anti-Puritan in point of view. E. S. Morgan, *The Founding of Massachusetts* (1963), brings together the accounts of the event by four historians — Cotton Mather, George Bancroft, J. T. Adams, and S. E. Morison. The background of Puritanism is discussed in the works of William Haller, *The Rise of Puritanism* (1938), and *Liberty and Reformation in the Puritan Revolution* (1955); and in Alan Simpson, *Puritanism in Old and New England* (1955). An interesting work by a leading authority is L. B. Wright, *Religion and Empire* (1943).

A sympathetic modern account of the Pilgrims is G. F. Willison, *Saints and Strangers* (1945); but no serious student should miss the classic by William Bradford, *Of Plymouth Plantation* (1856). Short and dispassionate is C. M. Andrews, *The Fathers of New England* (1919); fuller and less sympathetic is T. J. Wertenbaker, *The Puritan Oligarchy* (1947). Two important works are S. E. Morison, *Builders of the Bay Colony* (2nd ed., 1963); and E. S. Morgan, *The Puritan Dilemma; The Story of John Winthrop* (1958). Other outstanding biographies include L. S. Mayo, *John Endicott* (1936); and R. S. Dunn, *Puritans and Yankees; The Winthrop Dynasty of New England, 1630–1717* (1962). On Williams, see S. H. Brockunier, *The Irrepressible Democrat* (1940); Perry Miller, *Roger Williams* (1953); and T. P. Greene (ed.), *Roger Williams and the Massachusetts Magistrates* (1964). Edith Curtis, *Anne Hutchinson* (1930); and Emery Battis, *Saints and Sectaries; Anne Hutchinson and the Antinomian Controversy in the Massachusetts Bay Colony* (1962), are useful.

Among the helpful localized studies are G. L. Clark, *A History of Connecticut* (1914); W. H. Fry, *New Hampshire as a Royal Province* (1908); and H. S. Burrage, *The Beginnings of Colonial Maine, 1602–1658* (1914). Recent and stimulating are J. B. Hedges, *The Browns of Providence Plantations: Colonial Years* (1952); and S. C. Powell, *Puritan Village* (1963). For the beginnings of Maryland, M. P. Andrews, *The Founding of Maryland* (1933), is still the most satisfactory book. An important special study is T. O. Hanley, *Their Rights and Liberties; The Beginnings of Religious and Political Freedom in Maryland* (1959).

T. J. Wertenbaker, *The Middle Colonies* (1938), is a useful survey. Christopher Ward, *The Dutch and Swedes on the Delaware, 1609–1664* (1930), is a satisfactory summary. Two interesting works on Dutch activities are S. G. Nissenson, *The Patroon's Domain* (1937); and H. H. Kessler and Eugene Rachlis, *Peter Stuyvesant and His New York* (1959). G. T. Hunt, *The Wars of the Iroquois* (1940), covers an aspect of New York history often neglected. Two scholarly works by J. E. Pomfret tell the story of early New Jersey: *The Province of West New Jersey, 1609–1702* (1956); and *The Province of East New Jersey, 1609–1702* (1962).

William Penn has excited much interest among historians; among his biographers are S. G. Fisher (1932); W. W. Comfort (1944); and C. O. Peare (1957). An interesting survey is S. G. Fisher, *The Making of Pennsylvania* (1932). Quaker doctrines are treated by R. M. Jones, *The Faith and Practice of the Quakers* (1927). An important monograph is E. B. Bronner, *William Penn's "Holy Experiment"* (1962). The vexing problem of quitrents is treated fully in B. W. Bond, Jr., *The Quit-Rent System in the American Colonies* (1919).

A reliable modern survey on North Carolina is H. T. Lefler and A. R. Newsome, *North Carolina* (1954). On South Carolina, see R. L. Meriwether, *The Expansion of South Carolina, 1729–1765* (1940). The best life of Oglethorpe is still A. A. Ettinger, *James Edward Oglethorpe, Imperial Idealist* (1936). Other major works on the South include V. W. Crane, *The Southern Frontier, 1670–1732* (1929); and T. R. Reese, *Colonial Georgia* (1963).

2

COLONIAL LIFE

* è The Plantation Area • Slavery and Servitude • New England • Occupations • West Indian Trade • Calvinism • The Middle Colonies • Quakers on the Delaware • The "Pennsylvania Dutch" • The Scotch-Irish • Other Nationalities • Cities in the Wilderness • The Frontier • Differences between Frontier and Coast • Amusements • The Self-made Man*

Although each of the thirteen colonies had an important and distinctive history, a parallel development and a unity of interest are discernible even from the days of their founding. From the earliest days down through the Revolution most of the colonial population was of British stock and was English speaking. A modern study of family names in the first census of 1790 indicates that at that date only 17 per cent of the white population seemed to stem from non-British sources. While much has been made of the religious differences in the colonies, the similarities were actually more important than the diversities. By the time of the Revolution, small communities of Jews were to be found in every colony, especially in the larger towns and the cities. Though their numbers were small, they lived without persecution and made important contributions to the commercial and intellectual life of the community. By 1755

only 20,000 to 25,000 Roman Catholics lived in all the colonies. Colonial America was overwhelmingly Protestant, and though colonial Protestantism was divided into numerous sects, their differences were on the whole more apparent than real. The Puritans of New England, the Dutch Reformed Church in the Middle Colonies, and the Presbyterians from the frontier and the Piedmont South all had the same Calvinistic inspiration. Anglicanism established in the southern colonies was a religion of compromise, and though in seventeenth-century Britain it became briefly intolerant of dissenters, its accommodating spirit survived.

The first colonists had a common economic and social British background. Most of them were of yeoman or lower middle-class stock and came from the countryside and the provincial towns. Wherever they landed, they faced much the same problems. Their responses to the demands of their new environments were remarkably similar.

Yet despite these similarities, many factors soon divided the colonies into four ultimately well-defined sections. The British settlements in North America extended from a region of long winters and short summers to a region of short winters and long summers. They embraced great areas of mountains and high hills, and other extensive areas of broad valleys and fertile plains. The plantation country came early to be recognized as a section apart. The

TOBACCO PRODUCTION

Steps in the process of producing tobacco, as pictured in An Historical and Practical Essay on the Culture and Commerce of Tobacco *by Wm. Tatham (London, 1800).*

spacious bays, many harbors, and wide-mouthed, navigable rivers. Near the banks of the rivers a rich alluvial soil made for successful agriculture, although a little distance in from the waterline the soil was less fertile. Because the tides swept far up the rivers, the coastal plain was known as the Tidewater. At varying distances into the interior, waterfalls blocked navigation, and the Falls Line — that is, an imaginary line drawn from north to south through these waterfalls — marked approximately the end of the Tidewater. Between the falls and the mountains lay a hilly country, known as the Piedmont.

Tobacco became the staple crop in most of the Tidewater area, although in the Carolinas rice and indigo were also important. Experience proved that the easiest way to prosperity was to raise these crops, particularly tobacco, for an outside market. In exchange for them the planter could obtain from Europe articles to make his life agreeable. The Virginians and their neighbors raised all the tobacco they could, loaded it at their own or nearby wharves for shipment, usually to England, and in return brought in all the goods they could buy.

Tobacco culture led naturally to the development of large plantations. It was soon discovered that, however fertile the soil might be, the constant growing of tobacco exhausted it. More and more acres must therefore be acquired if the yield was to be kept up, although lands allowed to lie fallow for a time could again be put in cultivation. This the large landowner could manage much more easily than the small landowner. Moreover, the fall in the price of tobacco that followed inexorably as the supply increased, did its share to promote expansion in the size of plantations. The only way to make good the loss in income was to acquire more acres and raise more tobacco, and this the planter promptly did if he could. If he could not, he sold out to those who could afford to buy his land and possibly dropped into the small farmer class.

colonies of New England also had an identity that separated them from the rest. The Middle Colonies — New York, New Jersey, Pennsylvania, Delaware — had much in common with the sections northeast and south of them, but were yet different. Finally to the west of the more thickly settled areas lay the frontier, where new settlements were constantly being made, and where the conditions of life did not vary much from north to south.

The Plantation Area. The civilization which developed in the plantation area was due in considerable part to the existence there of a wide coastal plain, indented with

28

The great planter could have his own wharf, which the small planter had to use on whatever terms he could obtain. Nor could the small planter compete with the great in the possession of indentured servants and slaves; as the price of tobacco went down, the prices of servants and slaves went up.

But it must not be thought that Virginia in either the seventeenth or the eighteenth century was primarily a land of large-scale tobacco planters. Only one Virginian in fifteen owned more than a thousand acres. Many small farmers, even in the Tidewater region, worked their fields alongside a few slaves or indentured servants, and the great majority had no help save from their own families. To the west, on the frontier, the one-man farm was all but universal. The great planter with his thousands of acres has become the remembered figure of the early South because he belonged to an economic, intellectual, social, and political elite which furnished many of the nation's leaders in the Revolution and the years immediately after. But always the planters remained a small minority surrounded by common farmers whose lives were not much different from those of northern or western farmers.

Plantation Life. The successful southern planter usually had frontage on some winding stream, and if he were fortunate he might own a whole neck of land jutting out into the river. The average size of the great planter's holding was about three thousand acres, but many planters held more. The headquarters of each plantation made a little village. The planter and his family lived in a large and well-appointed house, near which were clustered the workhouses where cooking, weaving, carpentry, blacksmithing, and other activities were carried on. Other buildings were dwellings for the servants and slaves, or shelters for livestock. In so far as it was possible, each plantation was a self-sufficing economic unit. Such articles as tools, which could not easily be manufactured locally, and

luxuries — fine clothes, expensive wines, furniture, and even building materials — were imported. Once a year exchanges were made, ships bringing from England the orders sent over by the planters the year before, and taking back with them the annual salable tobacco output of the plantation. Nearly always the planter overestimated the value of his crop, and in consequence overordered. Debts to British merchants accumulated almost everywhere in the plantation area, and on the eve of the Revolution had become a major source of irritation.

Slavery and Servitude. During the eighteenth century slavery came to play a more important role in the life of the southern plantation. Adequate numbers of indentured servants were hard to obtain, and with an inviting wilderness to the west, harder still to keep. Negro slaves were fairly cheap and were kept with little difficulty in a servile position. In the rice-growing regions of South Carolina, where the climatic conditions were bad and whites quickly succumbed, Negro laborers were able to survive. By the close of the colonial

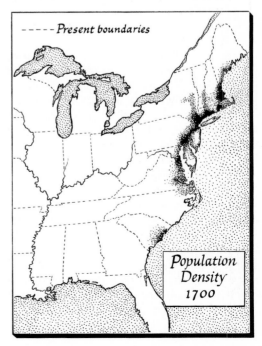

----- *Present boundaries*

Population Density 1700

INDIGO CULTURE IN SOUTH CAROLINA

From a map of the Parish of St. Stephen, in Craven County, after a drawing by Henry Mouzon. The scene supposedly depicts Mulberry, a plantation on the Cooper River.

period there were about 400,000 Negro slaves in the colonies. Three-fourths of them lived in the South, where they constituted two-fifths of the entire population. In South Carolina they outnumbered the white population two to one. Slaves were treated with extreme harshness at first, but as time went on relations between masters and slaves improved.

The plantation system left little chance for urban development in the South. Colonial capitals were hardly more than villages, except when a legislature met or a court convened. Norfolk and Baltimore attained some importance as ports, and Charleston became a thriving little city, but these were exceptions. The life of the South was decidedly rural in character.

Local Government in the South. In the establishment of local political units in the South, the example offered by rural England was followed. The parish was the smallest political division, and its boundaries were drawn to include the residences of all communicants of the parish church. A vestry, in practice consisting of the more

important planters, governed the local church, cared for the poor, levied taxes to obtain necessary public funds, and looked after the affairs of the parish generally. In each county eight to twenty justices of the peace were appointed by the governor from among the planters, and these justices held county court. They administered the laws, chose constables and highway surveyors for the various precincts, ordered the building of roads and bridges, and assessed taxes. Orders of the county court were executed by the sheriff, who was appointed by the governor, usually only on nomination of the county court.

Once in two years, ordinarily, the voters of the county assembled to choose members of the colonial legislature. In Virginia each county was entitled to two representatives in the House of Burgesses. Property tests for voting were universal, but the holdings of most small farmers were sufficient to qualify them for the suffrage. While small farmers probably outnumbered the great planters ten to one, representatives were almost invariably chosen from the latter class.

Religion. In religion, as in government, the plantation area of the South was not unlike rural England, where the strength of the established church was always great. In every southern colony, from Maryland to Georgia, the Church of England was established by law, and its ministers were held to be as much entitled to their pay as any other officers of the state. Dissenters existed in sizable numbers in every southern colony, especially away from the Tidewater, but there was little religious persecution in the South. The American Anglican Church was more tolerant than the English one, in part because it was not so well organized. There was no bishop of the English Church in America, and the Bishop of London, under whose spiritual guidance the American Church was placed, never visited his trans-Atlantic communicants. Moreover, the fact that Anglican clergymen had to be ordained in England held down their number. In such an atmosphere Presbyterians, Quakers, and others lived in relative peace with the established church, especially toward the west. Yet the great bulk of the population remained loyal Anglicans. Because of the vestrymen's local control, practices differed rather widely from parish to parish, and occasionally English officials complained about the "low Church" ritual practiced in Virginia, but little was done to press for conformity.

Education in the South. Schools were a rarity in the South, and only the children of planters were adequately educated. Frequently these children were taught at home by tutors, who were often indentured servants. Further education was open only to those who could afford it, in England or at William and Mary College, founded at Williamsburg, Virginia, in 1693. A few "free grammar schools" and more "pay schools" existed, but since true public schools were unknown even in Charleston, the poor got what education they could from the parish clerics and from their families. The extremely slow growth of public education in the South helps to explain the power of the planting and commercial elite.

With a virtual monopoly on education, and "to the manner born," the great planters of the South played the principal role in southern history. They managed the affairs of their great estates and used the talents thus sharpened in discharging the political duties that fell to their lot. Naturally averse to governmental interference in their private affairs, they were quick to resent injustices, especially when the source of trouble lay as far away as England. They fancied themselves extremely democratic because they were very sociable among themselves, given to much visiting back and forth, and fond of showing hospitality. Their charm of manner and distinction of bearing marked them off clearly even from the elite of the northern colonies.

Throughout the colonial period the upper class in the South was never a closed one. Its members had made their way up in colonial society by their work and their wits at planting and at trade. Nor did the great planters consider commercial transactions as demeaning, as might their English counterparts. For the man who could make money, land was always available, and with money and land social status could soon be won. Many a one-time indentured servant made his way to the top of southern society.

New England. In New England, as in the South, physiographic conditions had much to do with shaping the course of development. The early settlers of New England found the topography exceedingly irregular, with high hills or mountains rising in clusters rather than ranges not far from the sea. The surface, even in the level places, was apt to be covered with boulders, and the soil, where it could be found, required infinite patience and endurance to work. At frequent intervals along the coast rapidly flowing rivers plunged into the sea, and waterfalls made penetration into the interior difficult. Natural harbors dotted the coast line, while heavy forests were everywhere available to furnish naval stores, masts, spars, and timbers for the builders of ships.

The inhabitants of this "stern and rock-bound coast" were a fairly homogeneous group. Probably 95 per cent of the migrants to colonial New England had come from England. Most of them had come from little peasant villages, where they had worked as artisans or from which they had gone out each day to till their land. If they were not always Puritans on coming to America, as a rule they or their children soon fell in with the dominant religious faith.

Emigration to New England proceeded usually in groups. A congregation, led by its minister and financed by some wealthy Puritan, would come to America as a unit, establish a new town, and continue to live in much the same fashion as before. This procedure was generally followed in the extension of settlements into the interior. Actuated perhaps by some minor political or religious difference, and interested at the same time in seeking out new economic opportunities, a large number of families would put out together to found another town on another site. In the formative period New Englanders showed little disposition to settle as individuals upon separate farms. Long-established custom, aided by the great desirability of having a church easily accessible and the necessity of protecting themselves against hostile Indians, kept the settlers together in villages. The New England town thus came to be the social and economic unit on which all New England life tended to center.

The town was also a natural self-governing political unit. The practice among the Puritans with respect to church government was to allow each congregation the complete right to choose its minister, its deacons and elders, its tithing men. Even in matters of doctrine, the decision of the congregation was final. In the government of the town these same ideas of democracy prevailed. Matters of local importance were brought before the town meeting, to which usually all church members or perhaps even all citizens were entitled to come. The levying of taxes, the distribution of land, the establishment of schools, the passing of local ordinances of government, all were brought before this meeting. Between meetings "selectmen," duly elected for the purpose, carried on the government. As time went on the unwieldy nature of the town meeting made it necessary to hand over to this smaller group many of the duties first performed by the meeting itself. The town was also the unit from which members were chosen to the lower house of the colonial legislature.

Occupations. New England's climate and topography prevented the development of staple money crops imported by England, comparable to the tobacco, rice, and indigo raised in the South. Fields were cleared of timber and of stones, the latter being used extensively for the construction of stone walls to serve as fences, and crops of many sorts were planted. Individual land holdings were early introduced, and generally each farmer tilled his own land. Labor was scarce, for virtually anyone might acquire land of his own; hence the holdings tended to be no larger than one man could work. Lacking money with which to buy manufactured goods from Europe, farmers fashioned for themselves the tools they used, the shoes they and their families wore, the furniture they needed, the very houses in which they lived. The women spun wool or flax into yarn, wove cloth, and made the clothes the family wore. Habits of thrift and frugality were thus established.

Agriculture was supplemented by fishing and commerce. The New England coasts were rich in fish, and the banks of Newfoundland were not far away. Fishing led directly to commerce, for far more fish could be taken than could be consumed locally. According to reliable estimates not less than 300,000 cod were exported by New England fishermen in 1641, and by the year 1675 no less than 600 vessels and 4,000 men were engaged in the cod fisheries alone. New England fishermen found ready markets for their wares in the West Indies and in Southern Europe.

West Indian Trade. Commerce became rapidly diversified. Foodstuffs of various kinds were carried to the West Indies, not only from New England, but also from ports farther down the coast where the Yankee traders stopped to complete their cargoes. In return for these commodities, molasses, sugar, ginger, and other insular products were obtained, and in addition bills of exchange which could be used in the purchase of manufactured articles in England. At first the West Indian trade was confined mainly to the British islands, but by the eighteenth century trade with foreign islands was also common. From these sources came a good share of the money that found its way to the colonies. The Spanish *peso* or "piece of eight," called the *peso duro* or "hard dollar," circulated throughout the thirteen colonies.

In 1697 the slave trade, which had for some time been monopolized by a few English trading companies, was opened to all British subjects, and an interesting "triangular trade" developed. Molasses, brought from the West Indies to New England, was manufactured into rum, which was shipped to the African coast, where it was used in the purchase of slaves. The slaves were then brought to the West Indies and there exchanged for more molasses, which was then brought back to New England to make more rum, to acquire more slaves, to exchange for more molasses, and so on. Many other trading routes, however, some with England and the continent and some with Mediterranean countries, brought money, goods, and slaves to the North American mainland, and not all of the rum was exported. The New England fishermen used it liberally, and other New Englanders soon developed a keen taste for it. Rum was useful also in the prosecution of the fur trade, which furnished yet another item for export.

Shipbuilding. Shipbuilding went hand in hand with fishing and commerce. Skillful craftsmen early contrived to build ships which not only withstood the battering of the elements, but frequently outran revenue vessels, and made an art of smuggling. Especially was this the case after the British began to collect duties under the Navigation Acts. Indeed, on the eve of the American Revolution smuggling became an industry in itself. Timbers for shipbuilding were plentiful, and such items as barrel-staves, clapboards, and naval stores were soon available for export. Yankee ships and seamen came to be seen and known all over the world, while the shrewdness of Yankee salesmen received widespread recognition. Many New England merchants, owners of ships and dealers in foreign wares, made comfortable fortunes; and the active business life that centered in the principal ports caused the villages so located to grow into sizable cities. Before the Revolution, Boston, with less than 30,000 inhabitants, was the largest city in New England and the second largest in America, but many other villages had become towns.

Calvinism. The theology of John Calvin made a profound impression upon the New England character. At the heart of Calvinism was the dualism between God and man. God, the supreme sovereign of the universe, was the essence of good, while man by nature was evil. Although God had originally created man in His own image, and thus had endowed him with His own purity, Adam's fall had forever destroyed that pristine goodness. Thereafter every man carried the mark of evil from his birth; Calvin said that sin was in the very seed of man. Since God, the eternal embodiment of good, could do no evil, He could not accept sinful man into His bosom. Therefore, every man was condemned to eternal punishment. But God took pity on man and, through the suffering of His Son, Jesus Christ, on earth, opened the way for the salvation of the righteous elect. Since God was both omnipotent and omniscient, the elect were inevitably predestined, but man, not being omniscient, could not be certain whether he was of the elect. The best he could do to escape eternal damnation was to follow the divine injunctions and seek to know the ways of God by joining His church, taking the sacraments of baptism and Holy Communion, reading the Scriptures, being repentant of his sins, and leading the righteous life. In the end only the few, the elect, were to be saved. All the rest of mankind, including even unborn infants, were "elected" to be damned.

The hard aspects of Calvinistic theology, at times tenaciously dwelt upon by Puritan divines, were driven deeply into the marrow of the New Englander. Was he of the elect whom God had chosen to be saved? One could never know, and yet the behavior of a man should show to some degree at least whether or not he had been deemed by God worthy to be saved. Those who were religiously inclined watched their conduct and searched their souls for evidences of the divine will toward them; hence the development of the "New England conscience." They displayed also a very great interest in the spiritual welfare of their neighbors. Who of those they knew were to be saved, who were to be damned? Village life with its intimate associations gave ample opportunity for observation. The injunction to be one's brother's keeper was carefully obeyed, and buttresses against temptation were erected in the shape of "blue laws" that regulated closely the behavior of the individual. Church attendance in some of the New England colonies was long required by law.

No people with as earthy a tradition and temperament as the early New Englanders could be expected to follow all the strict Calvinist tenets faithfully over the years. Indeed, a great many inhabitants of New England were not Calvinist church members at all. The temptation to delight in the things of the world and to forget the spiritual side of life was great. The worldly spirit grew rapidly as wealth and opportunity increased, especially in the rising cities and towns. Nevertheless, the Calvinist tradition and spirit were never altogether eradicated, and their manifestations have been numerous down through the history of the section.

The Witchcraft Delusion.   Toward the end of the seventeenth century, preoccupation with what Cotton Mather called the "wonders of the invisible world" swept the little settlement of Salem Village, Massachusetts. At this time the existence of persons endowed with supernatural powers of evil was still taken for granted on both sides of the Atlantic. The Hebraic law had accepted the idea, and in the Old Testament (Exodus xxii:18) there was a direct command: "Thou shalt not suffer a witch to live." During the sixteenth and seventeenth centuries secular courts, first in Europe and then in America, had sentenced to death persons convicted of being witches. The "witchcraft delusion" was thus based on long-standing tradition. During the spring of 1692 some Salem children, insisting that certain individuals had bewitched them, began to act queerly, having, or perhaps feigning, fits. Soon ministers and magistrates were giving serious attention to these accusations and were demanding that something be done about them. Finally the governor appointed a special court of distinguished judges to try the cases, and the whole colony debated the evidence. Arrests multiplied, convictions were obtained, and no less than nineteen persons were hanged and many others imprisoned. Then a reaction set in, and soon even among the leaders of the frenzy there was abject repentance. A few years later one of the judges before whom the trials had been held, and a number of the jurymen, openly confessed their error, and asked forgiveness. The Salem executions were not actually the last for witchcraft in America, but there was never again a comparable outburst.

The New England Conscience. The New England conscience endured long after some of the Calvinistic tenets that produced it had lost their binding force. Scrupulous observance of the moral law, rigid self-control carried even to the length of self-denial, earnestness of purpose, and firm belief in the righteousness of God's way with man set the conscientious New Englander apart from other Americans. His conscience was apt to carry over into business and politics. In these realms the contract idea, so firmly embedded in Calvinistic theology, was not without its helpful side. Since good Puritans believed that God had made the original contract with man to live by His terms, all contracts carried with them a moral and even a religious sanction. A bargain was a bargain, and a contract once signed had to be obeyed. It behooved the maker of business contracts to watch carefully the terms laid down, and mercy was not always vouchsafed to the careless. Governmental charters and constitutions were likewise held to be sacred covenants, and the principals, whether kings, lords, or commoners, might justly be held to their plighted word. Nor was the law of the land, duly made and recorded, to be lightly ignored.

Education in New England. Education was taken more seriously in New England than elsewhere. This was due to the heavy emphasis which the Puritans placed upon individual reading of the Scriptures, to their well-educated lay and clerical leadership, and to the existence of towns. Six years after Boston was founded, the Boston Latin School started its long and distinguished history. In 1642 the General Court of Massachusetts required the selectmen of every town to inquire whether every New England child was able to obtain instruction in the common subjects. Three years later it resolved that universal education be afforded to all youths to prevent "that old deluder Satan" from withholding from any man a "knowledge of the Scriptures." "Free schools" were far more numerous in New England than elsewhere, and they were supplemented by numerous "Dame Schools" for the training of girls, and by vocational schools with instruction in such subjects as navigation and bookkeeping. By 1700 the great majority of New Englanders of both sexes could probably read and write.

The common schools taught reading, writing, and arithmetic; Latin or grammar schools prepared boys for college; and academies, which admitted both boys and girls, offered a wider course of study. Pupils were taught the catechism at an early age, they read selections from the Bible, and such textbooks as came into use were strongly impregnated with Scriptures and theology. Discipline was extremely severe, and any tendencies toward self-expression were promptly suppressed.

Since Massachusetts Bay had been founded not alone for economic gain but also as "a City upon a Hill" to justify God's ways to man, the New Englander clung to his views and institutions wherever he went. As the population expanded, emigrants carried with them the institutions New Englanders held dear. The typical New Englander was exceedingly intolerant of customs that diverged to any great extent from his own. In eighteenth-century New England, however, the narrowness in religious matters that had been so characteristic of the formative period was much less in evidence. By this time Anglicans, Catholics, and Jews were treated with consideration, and many such, particularly Anglicans, were to be found in all the urban centers.

The Middle Colonies. The Middle Colonies rested upon a geographic foundation that combined the chief characteristics of New England and the South. Here there was a coastal plain and a piedmont, but the plain was narrower than in the plantation area, and the piedmont wider. In New York, the mountains were in great glacial-ground clusters, but in Pennsylvania the long parallel ridges of the Alleghenies began to rise. The rivers of the central area were fewer in number than in the other sections, but they were longer and furnished more convenient highways into the interior. Indeed, three great river systems, the Hudson, the Delaware, and the Susquehanna furnished the chief key to the development of the region. Each of these rivers flowed from north to south, each was entered through a spacious harbor, and each was navigable by ocean-going vessels for a considerable distance into the interior. In each river valley a distinctive civilization developed, and in due time a city marked the point where each river reached the sea. New York commanded the trade of the Hudson Valley, Philadelphia of the Delaware, and Baltimore of the Susquehanna. Even in colonial times the spirit of rivalry between these growing towns was much in evidence.

Dutch Influence. The Dutch influence left a lasting impression upon the people of the Hudson Valley. The hopes of those who invented the patroon system were never fully realized, but the pretensions of the system tended to mark off an aristocratic caste of landowners from the other elements of society. On some of the large estates of the lower Hudson tobacco was raised much as in Virginia. In a country where free land was so plentiful, however, and where emigrants were practically given all the land they could improve, it was difficult to maintain a tenant class. The estates might exist, but many of their acres remained unworked. Nevertheless, their owners came to constitute a distinguished upper class of "Vans" and "velts," who exerted a preponderant influence in the affairs of the colony.

Dutch governmental practices also left some traces upon New York. During the period of Dutch control very little was permitted the colonists by way of a voice in their government; except for a limited amount of local self-government permitted in the villages, the English conquest found the colony wholly lacking in democratic political institutions. Under the rule of the reactionary Duke of York the introduction of self rule was still delayed. Richard Nicolls, the tactful first British governor, managed to keep discontent at a minimum. His successor, Edmund Andros, an able soldier and administrator, was also successful in New York, but later ran into trouble in New England.

In 1683 the proprietor felt obliged to yield to the pressure for a representative assembly, but the charter of Liberties and Privileges adopted by the Assembly nettled him, and when he became King James II in 1685, he went back on his bargain. New Yorkers ultimately won the right to participate in the control of their colony, although only a privileged minority were granted the right to vote, and the government of the colony was distinctly less democratic than that of any other. New York politics tended to be little more than a series of factional fights among the important families.

Some Dutch religious survivals may also be noted. The Dutch Reformed Church was as definitely Calvinistic in its teachings as even the Puritan congregations of New England could have asked. The Dutch, however, fed their souls less upon the doctrine of election than did the Puritans, and were a little more content to rely upon God's abounding grace. With them religion played no such dominant role as in New England. Religious toleration, moreover, was a Dutch tradition. After New Netherland became New York, the Church of England supplanted the Dutch Reformed Church in six parishes as the official church, but the number of Anglicans remained small for a long time. Furthermore, there were many Puritans from New England, Quakers, Catholics, and Jews. Inasmuch as the proprietor was known to be a Catholic, it seemed expedient to carry over the Dutch spirit of toleration into the new regime. Well before the Revolution New York City had both Catholic churches and a Jewish synagogue.

Quakers on the Delaware. The Delaware Valley became the seat of a culture quite as distinctive as that found along the Hudson, for it was here that the Quaker influence was preponderant. Democracy was inherent in the Quaker teaching. Quakers believed that God spoke to men directly by a voice that reached their hearts, and this "inner light" was denied to no man or woman. Since anyone might thus be in direct contact with the divine will, there was no necessity for ministers, or bishops, or ecclesiastical foundations. Even the Bible as a guide of faith and conduct suffered somewhat, for the "inner light" furnished quite as convincing an authority. All men were equal before God, so why should there be the distinctions in dress and manners that marked the aristocracy apart from the common run of men? Good Quakers called no man master, and used simply the word "Friend" by way of address. They objected to the use of the formal "you" when speaking to an individual, and employed instead the democratic "thee." They kept their hats on their heads even in the presence of kings, and they wore a plain, standardized garb that was designed to deny all social distinction. Since the "inner light" came to women as well as to men, women were accorded the same religious privileges that men enjoyed. Women spoke their minds freely "in meeting," notwithstanding the injunction of Saint Paul to "let the women keep silence in the church." Slavery the Quakers deeply deplored.

Faith in such principles as these markedly affected the development of the Quaker colonies. Their tolerance of many varieties of religion, their unwillingness to propagandize in the Puritan fashion, and their generous land terms attracted great numbers of settlers. The valley of the Susquehanna, quite as much as the Delaware, was to profit from these inviting practices. To the Susquehanna came a mixed population, including many colonials from other regions, but in far greater numbers emigrants from Europe, in particular the "Pennsylvania Dutch" and the Scotch-Irish.

The "Pennsylvania Dutch." The "Pennsylvania Dutch" were actually Germans. The wars of Louis XIV of France made of the adjacent German states a periodic battlefield. For emigrants from this region, the Quaker doctrine of pacifism had a special attraction. Economic pressure furnished another motive for emigration. Petty feudal lords exacted heavy dues, required annoying services, and collected burdensome tithes for the support of state churches. Religious persecution also played a part, for each prince was left free to determine the religious faith of his people. Particularly oppressed were sects such as the Mennonites, who objected to military service. Penn's agents advertised persistently the advantages of America among the distressed Germans, and in 1709 the British Parliament passed a law for the naturalization of foreign Protestants.

Some German immigration reached the colonies late in the seventeenth century but the great bulk of the German invasion came toward the middle of the eighteenth century. Some Germans settled in North Carolina, New York, New Jersey, Maryland, and Virginia, but most found their way to Pennsylvania, where they picked for themselves choice lands usually well up the valley of the Susquehanna, for the English colonists already had the Delaware. From there they worked their way westward, and goodly numbers turned south into Maryland and the Valley of Virginia. They came in such numbers that the provincials began to be alarmed. It is estimated that by 1775 about one third of the inhabitants of Pennsylvania were German. Living together, they retained their own language, established their own schools, printing presses, and newspapers, and continued for many years to be a people apart. Indeed, some of their descendants in central Pennsylvania still speak and write a patois known as "Pennsylvania Dutch."

The Scotch-Irish. The Pennsylvania Germans were soon followed by the Scotch-Irish, with somewhat similar reasons for migration. These newcomers were from the north of Ireland, but most of their ancestors had been lowland Scots, some of whom had settled on lands taken from the Irish during the reigns of Queen Elizabeth I and King James I, and others on Irish lands confiscated by Oliver Cromwell. As Presbyterians they could not get on well with the Catholic Irish, to whom they seemed to be mere trespassers. As dissenters, they resented the requirement that they pay tithes to the Anglican Church. The tenant system was peculiarly harsh upon them, since most of their landlords were absentees, who were not only unconcerned about the oppressive rentals, but were also often unaware of the still more oppressive methods of collecting them. The English government passed laws against the importation of vital Irish products, such as dairy cattle and woolen goods, and placed discouraging regulations upon the production of linen. Bad harvests and frequent famines added to Scotch-Irish discontent.

Like the Pennsylvania Germans, some Scotch-Irish colonists reached America before 1700, but the great majority did not arrive until toward the middle of the next century. Some of the Scotch-Irish settled in New England, New York, and New Jersey, but most of them penetrated into the back country of Pennsylvania by way of the Susquehanna and its tributaries. Coming a little later than the Germans, the Scotch-Irish went a little farther into the interior to find lands. They spoke English, and hence were not bothered in their relations with the native Americans by the language barrier that so often perplexed the Germans, but they were harder to deal with than the Germans. When some of them were accused of holding lands without legal title, they replied that it was "against the laws of God and Nature, that so much land should be idle while so many Christians wanted it to labor on." There were fully as many Scotch-Irish as German emigrants to America, probably more. At the time the American Revolution broke out, Pennsylvania was no less than one-third Scotch-Irish.

Other Nationalities. Diversity of population was an important characteristic of the Middle Colonies. In addition to the Dutch, the Quakers, the Germans, and the Scotch-Irish, although in no such numbers, there were here French Huguenots, southern Irish, Scots, a few Welshmen, and a few Jews. The Jews were most numerous in New York, where they had come from South America, Holland, Germany, and Poland. Coupled with variety in population was variety in religion. The Middle Colonies were thus a rich soil for factional politics. This region gave rise to a group of astute politicians, quick to compromise and ready to shift their ground as the occasion required.

Local Government in the Middle Colonies. Local government in the Middle Colonies borrowed a little from New England and a little from the colonies to the south. Counties appeared after the fashion of the plantation area, but were usually subdivided into townships reminiscent of New England. In New York the influence of New England was more marked than elsewhere in the Middle Colonies, but well before the end of the seventeenth century a county board of supervisors, composed of representatives from the various towns, had absorbed many of the important functions of local administration. In Pennsylvania the townships were even less important than in New York. The combination of town and county government in the Middle

Colonies proved to be of greater than local significance, for it was this example that most of the states of the West were to follow later.

Public education in both New York and Pennsylvania came slowly. As early as 1658 the citizens of New Amsterdam petitioned for a Latin school, but thereafter there was little educational growth despite repeated attempts to pass school legislation in the New York legislature. In his original design for the founding of Pennsylvania, William Penn had included a system of free schools in order to encourage "mechanical, physical or natural knowledge." Although Philadelphia did establish a grammar school in 1689, little else was accomplished in public education for over 125 years. As in New York, educational institutions were left in the hands of the various religious denominations, with the consequence that educational opportunities were far below those in New England.

Occupations. Farming was the chief occupation in the Middle Colonies, where the production and exportation of foodstuffs gave rise to the name of "bread colonies." Grains, livestock (particularly among the Germans who understood how to care for domestic animals in winter), and vegetables, most of which were native to America and did not need to be acclimated, were produced in ever-increasing quantities. Hemp and flax were also grown.

Manufacturing quickly sprang up, especially in Pennsylvania and New Jersey after the coming of the Germans, among whom there were many skilled workmen. Iron, textiles, glass, and paper were among the articles commonly made in these regions. Weavers, tanners, metal workers, and printers plied their trades successfully. Sawmills furnished excellent lumber, and good bricks were made in Philadelphia and New York. Mills were numerous, and the flour they produced was excellent.

In commerce the Middle Colonies were not far behind New England, and the mer-

NORTHERN SAWMILL

This sawmill, and the adjacent Block House which afforded it protection, were located on Fort Anne Creek, on the New England frontier.

chants of Philadelphia and New York prospered. Philadelphia, toward the close of the colonial period, came to exceed Boston in size. Grain, flour, and other provisions were exported, mostly to the West Indies. New York by the middle of the eighteenth century exported no less than eighty thousand barrels of flour a year. Here the fur trade, which had been fostered by the Dutch, continued under the English as an important incentive to commerce. Shipbuilding was a natural accompaniment of overseas trade.

Cities in the Wilderness. Until recently the importance of the cities to colonial life was underemphasized. During the seventeenth century Boston, Newport, New York, Philadelphia, and "Charles Town" were relatively small and insignificant compared to their much larger European prototypes. In America they contained but a small fraction of the total population. As late as 1790 the first census designated only twenty-four urban places in the United

States, with a total population of about 200,000, as against a total rural population of 3.7 million. However, these small "cities in the wilderness," in the later seventeenth century and especially in the eighteenth, played an important part in the making of American life. The city became one of the first areas wherein varying European peoples and cultures met and associated in a start toward the slow evolution of an American people and culture. Historians have usually identified the melting pot process with the frontier and the "back country," as the western settlements were then generally called. But there is now good evidence to indicate that one of the first thorough amalgamations of European stocks took place in such cities as New York and Philadelphia. Commercial and industrial changes evolved most rapidly in the city. With the fast growth of trade and capital, specialization soon appeared. Merchants wholesaling to the interior soon became distinct from importers. A growing trade demanded better interior communications and initiated the establishment of the first postal system and the construction of early post roads. Excess capital from trade stimulated manufacturing, which was largely carried on by artisans who, working with apprentices, produced for the local market, or by merchant capitalists using the "putting out system" then common in England. In this system, a merchant desiring the fabrication of articles would purchase raw materials, carry them to the homes of workingmen, and return at a specified time to collect the finished product.

The colonial city, as the center of foreign trade and domestic distribution and collection, became also the focal point through which European influences and ideas were channeled to the struggling colonies. Cities naturally became the centers of culture where newspapers were published and where artistic and cultural life appeared. But to the degree that they were cosmopolitan they were also European, a semi-European fringe, as it were, on the American cloth. For some of the more distinctive traits which were to characterize American society one had to look at the back country or the frontier.

The Frontier.   Inland from the seacoast, cutting across the boundaries of every other section and of most of the colonies, lay the colonial "West" — the frontier. Its limits were necessarily shifting; indeed, at some time every settled area in America had been frontier. But by the end of the colonial period the "back country" could be marked off rather distinctly from the rest. Fur traders, who almost invariably led the English advance upon the West, cattle-growers, who especially in the South were attracted by the free grazing lands of the interior, and soldiers, who in one or another of the wars against the Indians had seen the western country, revealed the possibilities of the regions they had visited, and presently settlement followed.

Various conditions worked together to promote the rapid extension of the frontier. Colonial families were large, and the natural increase in population provided many pioneers. The exhaustion of the eastern lands by poor methods of farming, particularly in the tobacco-growing areas, provided others. Still others came from the ranks of the indentured servants. Frequently, religious dissenters sought homes in the West, where they would not be looked down upon because of their religious faith. Immigrants, who found themselves unpopular when they tried to settle in the older American communities, turned quickly to the more hospitable frontier.

Westward also went men who could not get along in the East, either because of their predilection for breaking the law, or because they found the competition of a settled society too strenuous. On the frontier one was accepted without much inquiry into one's background. Unoccupied land abounded, and one could squat on a clearing for a long time without being dislodged by an eastern owner. A lean-to could be constructed with little effort, a small clearing served for planting grain, the forest and the streams afforded meat and fish. Although the frontiersman has traditionally been pictured as ambitious and energetic, there was at least a sizable minority which exhibited less admirable traits. William Byrd's description of a North Carolina frontier settlement has the ring of authenticity. In his diary he noted that the settlement was peopled with slovenly, lazy, dirty families, the women doing most of the manual labor. Most families raised just enough for their own subsistence. Indian style, they cut down wild fruit trees to get their fruit instead of picking the fruit and tending the trees for next year's crop.

For the ambitious, however, conditions on the frontier were hard. Practically all the land was heavily timbered, and the "clearings" on which crops could be planted were made only through infinite labor. The difficulty of transporting goods from the East held down such trade to the barest necessities. Along the frontier, Indians were usually in evidence. Here pioneer families were accustomed to select some well-located farmhouse for a "station," and to build about it a stockade, duly equipped with shelters and storehouses, to which they could flee when an Indian attack seemed imminent. All good frontiersmen were adept with the axe and the rifle. The pioneer cabin was usually on the farm that the pioneer owned, or hoped to own, and at a considerable distance from any other dwelling. Pioneer life was therefore lonely, particularly for the housewife, and the opportunities for such privileges as church and school were decidedly limited.

Differences between Frontier and Coast. The society thus established in the back country differed markedly from that of the older and more settled coast. For one thing, it was extremely heterogeneous. Here English emigrants from the colonial East met a variety of foreigners and mingled freely with them. The frontier thus became another melting pot out of which a new and distinctively American people was to come. Furthermore, the frontier settlements, cutting across colonial lines, tended to break down local peculiarities. The mountain valleys from Pennsylvania south lay parallel to the coast and access to them was difficult except at favored points. In the Carolinas not only mountains, but eighty miles of pine barrens, separated the frontier outposts from the settled areas. People entered the mountains mainly from Pennsylvania, and, spreading slowly southward, presented everywhere the same characteristics, often in striking contrast to the institutions and traditions that bound the colonists who lived closer to the coast.

The genuine equality of conditions that existed among the northern frontiersmen and southern mountaineers bred a vigorous spirit of democracy. The movement of plantations west in the lowland South helped maintain the class distinctions of the seaboard. But in the northwest woods, in the Piedmont, and in the southern mountains one man owned about the same amount of land, lived in the same kind of house, worked with the same primitive tools, dressed in the same crude fashion as his fellows. Whatever ancestry and education he possessed was not important in the West.

This emphasis upon equality in the West was paralleled by an equally marked emphasis upon individual freedom. The pioneer came to set high store by the privilege which the wilderness gave him of managing his own affairs in any way he chose. Interference by government in anything that seemed to him his own business was apt to be met by wrathful opposition. He objected to regulations which hampered the acquisition of land, and he resented bitterly every attempt to impose upon him a religious establishment to which he did not subscribe. The Scotch-Irish, so many of whom found their way to the West, added a contentious note to frontier individualism.

The contrasts between the people of the

back country and the people of the coast led inevitably to some antagonisms. Men of the East still valued class distinctions and were careful to safeguard the rights of property. Men of the West had foresworn aristocracy, and to them the rights of the debtor were more a matter of concern than the rights of the creditor. The strong foreign infusion in the West was another source of difficulty. The older elements of society feared that their institutions would not be safe in the hands of such people. The westerners resented the suspicions of the East. Differences of opinion developed also on such matters as religious freedom, the right to hold slaves, the assessment of taxes, the control of the Indians. Distrustful of the political wisdom of the backwoodsmen, colonial legislatures under eastern control rarely accorded the frontier counties their proportionate share of representatives.

Everyday Life in the Colonies. Transportation was difficult in colonial America. The colonies were at least six weeks from Europe, and often, with contrary winds, the ship passage was longer. Coast towns communicated with one another most easily by sea; indeed, the Atlantic Ocean and the navigable rivers which emptied into it furnished the strongest of the ties that bound the colonies together. Even so, coastwise travel was slow and sometimes dangerous. Roads existed between the principal cities, but elsewhere they were rare, and usually they were incredibly bad. But the growing trade between colonies demanded better communications, and by 1750 transportation facilities were probably not much inferior to those existing in provincial Britain. Packet boats sailed on regular schedules between the New England ports, New York, and Philadelphia. From late summer

A native of Italy, Father Giovanni Antonio Grassi (1775–1849) served as president of Georgetown College near Washington from 1812 to 1817. A sympathetic — but not uncritical — observer of the new republic, his description of early American cities is typical of those of foreign sojourners who both preceded and followed him.

The American cities have the rare advantage of being built according to well-designed and uniform plans. The streets are wide and straight, with poplars now and then along the way. Along the sides are convenient walks which spare the pedestrians the inconveniences they meet in most European cities from wagons, carriages, and horses. Except for some government buildings, and a few banks, the architecture is simple and monotonous. The facades of the houses are of red brick, with little intervals of white. In the rooms there are few pictures, statues or decorated furniture; instead they prefer mahogany furniture and fine carpets on the floors. If these lack magnificence, they have, in general, an air of ease, of simplicity, and of cleanliness.

In the cities the window glass, the floors, and the thresholds of the doors are washed at least once a week. The buildings seem rather weak and always are built with a very large amount of wood, which accounts for the frequency of fires. But the safeguards for extinguishing them are effective, since each quarter has its night watchmen, and there are also men appointed to appear at first sound of the alarm, bringing pumps, ladders, pails, axes, and other instruments that may be needed.

Excerpt from *Notizie varie sullo stato presente della repubblica degli Stati Uniti dell' America* (1819) by G. A. Grassi. From O. Handlin, *This Was America*, Harvard University Press.

---

through the winter months, when the roads were either dry or frozen hard, stage coach lines maintained regular schedules between the major cities in the North. During wet seasons, however, even the best roads were often impassable except by foot or on horseback. In 1753 a major advance was made in communications when Benjamin Franklin and William Hunter of Virginia were appointed deputy postmasters general for all the colonies. By instituting post riders who rode day and night, Franklin reduced the time of mail delivery between Philadelphia and New York to just over twenty-four hours and between Philadelphia and Boston from ten days to three. By the middle of the eighteenth century roads were also reaching into the interior. By far the most important of these was the Philadelphia Wagon Road which ran from Philadelphia to Lancaster to York, then south into the Valley of Virginia. On this road traders and drovers mingled with a stream of immigrants intent upon settling in the South and the West. At convenient distances were taverns and inns, where travelers found lodging and local patrons found diversion. These inns were in a sense the social clubs of the time, and in them public opinion took form.

Colonial Houses. The houses in which colonial citizens lived ranged from the crude thatch-roofed shelters of wattle or planks stood on end to roomy dwellings usually of Georgian design. The log house or cabin was probably introduced by the Swedes settling along the Delaware River. By 1750, however, the notched log house had become almost the universal dwelling of the frontier. Most houses were of wood, although the wealthier citizen often used brick or native stone. In the cities and towns rows of wooden houses were built closely together. Most of the wooden structures, comprising great sections of the larger cities, were eventually destroyed, leaving the mistaken impression today that colonial construction was mostly of brick or stone. Within even the most sumptuous houses there were few conveniences. Fireplaces rarely provided enough heat for comfort in severe winter weather, and adequate screening against flies and insects in summer was impossible. Water was obtained from springs or surface wells that were easily contaminated, and this accounted for much of the disease common in colonial times. Candles were the principal source of light, although whale-oil lamps were not uncommon in the fashionable circles. Food was obtainable everywhere in great abundance and even in the cities at low prices, but often the fare was severely plain. Corn bread, hominy, and salt pork furnished the chief items of subsistence for the poor, particularly in the South. Whiskey, beer, hard cider, and rum were manufactured locally and were available in great profusion, but only the upper classes could afford the finer imported wines and brandies.

Colonial cities compared fairly favorably with cities of similar size in Europe. Philadelphia was built on a plan worked out by William Penn, with wide paved streets crossing at right angles. Here the houses were mostly of brick, and sometimes as many as three stories high. Sidewalks were plentiful, and street lamps made the lot of the night traveler easy. Both Boston and New York were noted for their general planlessness and their narrow crooked streets, but some of the more important streets in both cities were paved, and they were usually kept clean. In all the cities ashes and garbage were dumped into alleys and on vacant lots, and in most of them hogs running at large served as scavengers.

Since sanitary conditions were universally bad, repeated plagues swept through all colonial cities, causing most people to flee until the contagion had passed. Physicians were scarce and most of them were self-taught. The first public hospital, in Philadelphia, was not founded until 1755. Around this institution a group of physicians soon established a center for the study of medicine which, first as the College of Philadelphia and then as a part of the University of Pennsylvania, became the first colonial medical school. Even so the popular practice of medicine until well into the nineteenth century relied upon folk remedies and such dubious techniques as bleeding. In colonial times the death rate was appalling, and there were few families which did not suffer the loss of a child or a parent.

Amusements. Attendance at church, public meetings, "Thursday lectures" in New England, and — in the less strait-laced communities — dances and theaters furnished a large share of the amusement the people were permitted to enjoy. Lavish hospitality was a point of honor with the southern planters. Dancing was a favorite amusement with all classes in the South and was a common pastime nearly everywhere. Theaters existed in the large cities only, but by the time of the Revolution the American stage was definitely established. Gambling, horseracing, cockfighting, and foxhunting were major activities with the young bloods, especially in the South, but lotteries to raise money for churches, public works, and even college endowments were conducted without censure in Puritan New England. In the rural districts, particularly along the frontier, "logrollings," house-raisings, husking bees, weddings, and funerals furnished relief from the ordinary tedium of life. Courtship was officially surrounded with many hampering conventions, but the habit of marriage was strong with the colonials. Bachelors and widowers were under great social pressure to marry, and sometimes laws discriminated against the unmarried.

The Colonial Aristocracy. There was no such thing as a colonial nobility, but throughout the colonial period a well-recognized aristocracy existed which held itself above the common run of men. To this class belonged most of the English officials resident in America, the ministers and magistrates, the well-to-do merchants, the bankers, the owners of great estates in the Middle Colonies, and the great planters of the South. Members of the aristocracy sought to distinguish themselves from the lower classes by their manners, their superior education, and particularly their mode of dress. Wealthy men wore silk stockings, breeches of velvet, silk, or other expensive goods, and frock coats made of imported broadcloth richly trimmed. Wigs were generously worn during the eighteenth century. The colonial dames were equally gorgeous in dresses of costly silk, duly amplified by hoopskirts. The garb of the lower classes more closely resembled the simplicity of the garments universally worn today. Homespun fabrics were in general use, although on the frontier the men preferred leather jackets and breeches. The slow breakdown of class distinctions reflected the essential conservatism of the people who emigrated to America.

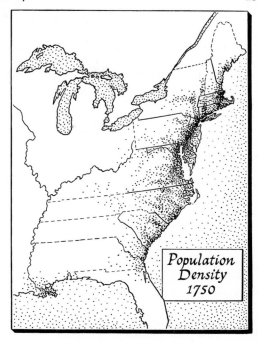

Population Density 1750

The Self-made Man. If there were strong aristocratic tendencies in colonial society, contrary influences were also at work from the time of the earliest settlements. Since most colonials were of middle- or lower-class stock, no great disposition existed anywhere to look down on either trade or work. Most of the great planters engaged in trade, while in New England shrewd dealing was accounted a virtue. Idleness was frowned upon and material success was esteemed, and often won entrance into the upper classes. Opportunities abounded everywhere for men to raise themselves economically. The family which produced John Hancock, wealthy merchant of Boston and signer of the Declaration of Independence, was founded by a shoemaker of Cambridge. Henry Laurens, great planter and Revolutionary patriot of South Carolina, was a saddlemaker's son, and

Benjamin Franklin rose from the obscurity of a little printing office to colonial and indeed European eminence. Some wealthy individuals of course tried to ape the aristocratic traditions of Europe. Had there been only a few such self-made men in America perhaps upper-class lines might have congealed into an aristocracy resembling that of Europe. But opportunities afforded by trade, the professions, manufacturing, and farming were so abundant that the large numbers of once-poor citizens who joined the wealthier classes during the eighteenth century and after effectively prevented the formation of a static aristocracy, with its exclusive pretensions to property and privilege. Although some aristocratic forms, especially those of dress and elaborate etiquette, existed in America for years after the Revolution, the prime colonial virtues of hard work, thrift, and material success, plus the willingness to honor the self-made man, were middle-class in origin. Though the aristocratic urge never entirely disappeared, these humbler attributes became in time almost inextricably entwined in the American scale of social virtues.

SELECTED BIBLIOGRAPHY

General works on American social history sometimes contain rich material on the colonial period; especially notable are H. J. Carman, *Social and Economic History of the United States* (2 vols., 1930–1934); and C. N. Degler, *Out of Our Past* (1959). Harvey Wish, *Society and Thought in Early America* (1950), is detailed and stimulating. Marshall Davidson, *Life in America* (2 vols., 1951), is excellent pictorial history, rich for all periods. C. M. Andrews, *Colonial Folkways* (1919), is entertainingly written and based on first-rate scholarship. J. T. Adams, *Provincial Society, 1690–1763* (1927), does not neglect the colonial frontier. S. H. Sutherland, *Population Distribution in Colonial America* (1936), is a standard work. Urban history is treated with great distinction by Carl Bridenbaugh, *Cities in the Wilderness* (1938), and *Cities in Revolt; Urban Life in America, 1743–1776* (1955). See also the beautifully illustrated study by J. W. Reps, *The Making of Urban America* (1965). Interesting sidelights are given by W. L. Sachse, *The Colonial American in Britain* (1956).

On the plantation South, P. A. Bruce, *The Colonial Period, 1607–1763* (*History of Virginia*, I, 1924), is excellent. Carl Bridenbaugh, *Myths and Realities; Societies of the Colonial South* (1952), is stimulating and controversial in its effort to debunk the cavalier "myth," and should be compared with another lively recent work by W. R. Taylor, *Cavalier and Yankee; The Old South and American National Character* (1961). J. C. Spruill, *Women's Life and Work in the Southern Colonies* (1938), deals with a subject all too frequently neglected. E. L. Goodwin, *The Colonial Church in Virginia* (1927), treats an interesting theme adequately. A. H. Hirsch, *The Huguenots of Colonial South Carolina* (1928), deals with a small but important immigrant group. Significant works on Virginia social history include P. A. Bruce, *Social Life of Virginia in the Seventeenth Century* (2nd ed., 1927); E. S. Morgan, *Virginians at Home; Family Life in the Eighteenth Century* (1952); Carl Bridenbaugh, *Seat of Empire: The Political Role of Eighteenth Century Williamsburg* (1950); and Robert McColley, *Slavery and Jeffersonian*

*Available in paperback

Virginia (1964). Several diaries of William Byrd II have been published; see especially *The Secret Diary of William Byrd of Westover, 1709–1712*, edited by L. B. Wright and Marion Tinling (1941). One of the best works on eighteenth-century Maryland is A. C. Land, *The Dulanys of Maryland* (1955).

On New England, J. T. Adams, *Revolutionary New England, 1691–1776* (1923), is strongly anti-Puritan. More sympathetic are Perry Miller, *Orthodoxy in Massachusetts, 1630–1650* (1933), and *Errand into the Wilderness* (1956); and O. E. Winslow, *Meetinghouse Hill, 1630–1783* (1952). K. B. Murdock, *Increase Mather* (1925), is absorbing; but see also *Selections from Cotton Mather*, edited by K. B. Murdock (1926). Other biographies of important clergymen include J. K. Morse, *Jedidiah Morse* (1939); and Larzer Ziff, *The Career of John Cotton* (1962). E. S. Morgan, *The Puritan Family* (1944), is a collection of essays dealing with the seventeenth century. An interesting special study is Emil Oberholzer, Jr., *Delinquent Saints; Disciplinary Action in the Early Congregational Churches of Massachusetts* (1956). On the perennially interesting problem of witches, see G. L. Kittredge, *Witchcraft in Old and New England* (1929); M. L. Starkey, *The Devil in Massachusetts* (1949); and a documentary collection edited by David Levin, *What Happened in Salem* (2nd ed., 1960). W. B. Weeden, *Economic and Social History of New England* (2 vols., 1891), is a work of enduring merit. D. E. Leach, *Flintlock and Tomahawk* (1958), treats New England at the time of King Philip's War. L. J. Greene, *The Negro in Colonial New England* (1942), deals with a neglected subject.

On the Middle Colonies, a major work of lasting importance is Percy Bidwell and J. I. Falconer, *History of Agriculture in the Northern United States, 1620–1860* (1925). Significant works on Philadelphia include Carl and Jessica Bridenbaugh, *Rebels and Gentlemen* (1942); F. B. Tolles, *Meeting House and Counting House* (1948), and *George Logan of Philadelphia* (1953). A great classic is J. H. St. John de Crèvecoeur, *Letters from an American Farmer* (1782). An interesting chapter dealing with immigration is in A. M. Schlesinger, *New Viewpoints in American His-*

tory (1922). T. J. Wertenbaker, *The Golden Age of Colonial Culture* (2nd ed., 1949), centers on the six leading colonial cities.

Of the histories of the frontier, R. A. Billington, *Westward Expansion* (2nd ed., 1960), is fullest on the colonial period, but see also F. L. Paxson, *A History of the American Frontier, 1763–1893* (1924); R. E. Reigel and R. G. Athearn, *America Moves West* (4th ed., 1964); and T. D. Clark, *Frontier America* (1959). The great collection of basic documents of the frontier is R. G. Thwaites (ed.), *Early Western Travels, 1748–1846* (32 vols., 1904–1907). An interesting and well-illustrated monograph is C. P. Russell, *Guns on the Early Frontiers* (1957). On the frontiers of the southern colonies an entertaining account is Archibald Henderson, *The Conquest of the Old Southwest, 1740–1800* (1920). Dale Van Every, *The Frontier People of America* (4 vols., 1961–1964), is a lively treatment of the frontier from 1754 to 1845. Books dealing with non-English frontiersmen include: J. G. Leyburn, *The Scotch-Irish: A Social History* (1962); W. F. Dunaway, *The Scotch Irish of Colonial Pennsylvania* (1944); G. S. Klett, *The Scotch-Irish in Pennsylvania* (1948); Frederic Klees, *The Pennsylvania Dutch* (1950); and I. C. C. Graham, *Colonists from Scotland* (1956).

Perhaps the best general treatise on economic aspects of American colonial life is to be found in the first volume of Joseph Dorfman, *The Economic Mind in American Civilization, 1606–1865* (2 vols., 1946). Other general treatments include E. C. Kirkland, *A History of American Economic Life* (3rd ed., 1951); Stuart Bruchey, *The Roots of American Economic Growth* (1965); and H. U. Faulkner, *American Economic History* (8th ed., 1960). Useful collections are G. D. Nash (ed.), *Issues in American Economic History* (1964); and H. N. Scheiber (ed.), *United States Economic History* (1964). For descriptions of manufacturing see V. S. Clark, *History of Manufactures in the United States* (3 vols., 1929); Carl Bridenbaugh, *The Colonial Craftsman* (1950); Caroline Ware, *The Early New England Cotton Manufacture* (1931); E. N. Hartley, *Ironworks on the Saugus* (1957);

and Esther Forbes, *Paul Revere and the World He Lived In* (1942). Among the significant treatments of businessmen are Bernard Bailyn, *The New England Merchants in the Seventeenth Century* (1955); W. T. Baxter, *The House of Hancock* (1945); G. M. Waller, *Samuel Vetch, Colonial Enterpriser* (1960); Glenn Weaver, *Jonathan Trumbull, Connecticut's Merchant Magistrate* (1956); and P. L. White, *The Beekmans of New York in Politics and Commerce* (1956). Important special studies include H. A. Innis, *The Cod Fisheries* (1940); Richard Pares, *Yankees and Creoles* (1956); and Bernard and Lotte Bailyn, *Massachusetts Shipping, 1697–1714* (1959). M. W. Jernegan, *Laboring and Dependent Classes in Colonial America, 1607–1783* (1931), is a major work of colonial period history. R. B. Morris, *Government and Labor in Early America* (1946), breaks new ground.

Two books by W. W. Sweet provide useful surveys: *Religion in Colonial America* (1942), and *The Story of Religion in America* (2nd ed., 1950). E. S. Gaustad, *Historical Atlas of Religion in America* (1962), is a superb piece of work. Three brief treatments are W. S. Hudson, *American Protestantism* (1961); J. T. Ellis, *American Catholicism* (1956); and Nathan Glazer, *American Judaism* (1957). An exciting new monograph is Carl Bridenbaugh, *Mitre and Sceptre; Transatlantic Faiths, Ideas, Personalities, and Politics, 1689–1775* (1962); it is a supplement to A. L. Cross, *The Anglican Episcopate and the American Colonies* (1902). Important works on the relationship of government to religion are E. B. Greene, *Religion and the State* (1941); and A. P. Stokes, *Church and State in the United States* (2nd ed., 1964). Special studies of particular groups include J. R. Marcus, *Early American Jewry* (2 vols., 1951–1953); G. S. Klett, *Presbyterians in Colonial Pennsylvania* (1937); R. W. Albright, *A History of the Protestant Episcopal Church* (1964); and G. G. Atkins and F. L. Fagley, *History of American Congregationalism* (1942). Interesting studies of religion on the frontier are T. S. Miyakawa, *Protestants and Pioneers* (1964); and W. B. Posey, *Religious Strife on the Southern Frontier* (1965).

3

COLONIAL THOUGHT

In the early seventeenth century, superstition and the supernatural still loomed large in the European mind. Because of the lower-class origin of most colonials, the belief in witches and malignant spirits was probably even more pervasive among Americans than among Europeans. The good Puritan not only believed that he could commune with God, he was also convinced that he could be tempted into sin and eternal damnation by the devil himself. For the early colonists the world was frightening and unpredictable, full of dread signs and portents, in which God, the devil, and evil spirits constantly intervened in the affairs of men. In considering the physical world, the average Puritan had no doubt that God Himself directed its daily operation, and that both the bountiful harvest and the killing frost were manifestations of His pleasure or His anger. And since God's ways were inscrutable, so also were the ways of nature and the universe.

Rise of Rationalism and Science. In Europe, however, a gradual revolution in thought had begun. At its base was the spirit of rationalism, which held that there were logical explanations for most physical phenomena and that man's mind was capable of understanding them. Rationalist thought at first envisioned the possible existence of "natural laws," then slowly evolved an even more revolutionary idea: that once man understood the workings of nature, he could by scientific methods shape and possibly even harness its forces. The first great contributions to this philosophical revolution were the astronomical discoveries of the Polish scientist Copernicus (1473–1543), followed by those of such men as Kepler and Galileo, which undermined man's long-held belief that the earth was the center of the universe and that man was its most important creature. In England, the writings of Francis Bacon (1561–1626), in defense of the scientific method, the experiments of Robert Boyle (1627–1691) with gases, and the discovery by William Harvey (1578–1657) of the circulatory system in the human body, gave further impetus to English science. But the discovery of the law of gravity by Sir Isaac Newton (1642–1727) had the most revolutionary impact upon man's view of the world and universe. From Newton's concept of a universe in which all heavenly bodies were held together by the force of gravitation that varied exactly in proportion to the sum of their mass and inversely to the square of their distance, there evolved a picture of a "world machine" in which all parts of the universe were geared together, the whole functioning like a gigantic clock. The popularity of the new scientific attitude among the educated classes of Europe was attested to by the foundation in the 1660's of both the British Royal Society and the French Academy of Sciences. By 1700 rationalism had become a major force in western European thought, and the scientific revolution which inspired it and was nourished by it became dominant during the eighteenth century. Both the scientific revolution and the new spirit of rationalism had a profound impact upon all areas of social thought. Both had measurable influence upon the thirteen colonies which were formed and grew to adulthood during the two centuries in which science and rationalism made their great advances.

American Colleges. New England was well disposed to receive the rationalistic and scientific impulses emanating from Europe. Puritan anxiety to perpetuate an educated clergy and lay leadership led early to the founding of institutions of higher learning. In 1636 a group of Bostonians, most of whom had been educated at Cambridge University in England, founded Harvard College. Though theological and classical studies composed the core of the curriculum, the new sciences were immediately welcomed. So liberal in its outlook had Harvard become by 1701, that a group of its more conservative graduates founded in defense of traditional religion the Collegiate School at New Haven, Connecticut, which became Yale University. Eight years before, through gifts from English merchants and from the colonial government of Virginia, William and Mary College at Williamsburg had been founded. The first three colonial colleges were followed around the middle of the eighteenth century by what were later to become Princeton, Co-

lumbia, Pennsylvania, and still later Brown and Rutgers. King's College, later Columbia, was of particular importance to the new secularism, since from its start it had no prescribed course of study leading to the ministry. One-third of the first curriculum of the Philadelphia Academy (later the University of Pennsylvania), which was largely inspired by the interest of Benjamin Franklin, was devoted to mathematics and the sciences. Although far inferior to their British counterparts in size and facilities, these struggling colleges did much to keep Americans abreast of European intellectual advances.

Science in America. In the introduction of the new scientific studies, Harvard College led its rivals. By 1640 it offered courses in arithmetic, geometry, astronomy, physics, and botany. The first American fellow of the British Royal Society was John Winthrop, Jr. (1605–1676), son of the first governor of Massachusetts Bay Colony, and the perennial governor of Connecticut. Winthrop had become an enthusiastic supporter of Harvard when a young graduate, Zechariah Brigden, in 1659 published an almanac of the Copernican system of astronomy which refuted Ptolemaic views then held as orthodox by the church. Winthrop was a considerable scientist. He corresponded with Newton and Boyle and predicted the discovery of Jupiter's fifth satellite, although at the time no telescope was powerful enough to confirm his hypothesis. Another member of his family, John Winthrop IV (1714–1799), became in his day the country's most noted and honored academic scientist. Elected a member of the Harvard faculty in 1738, Winthrop taught both physics and mathematics, but his reputation derived mainly from his studies in astronomy.

The growing interest in science was not confined to New England. In the South William Byrd II, educated in England, brought back to his native Virginia inquiring habits of mind that led him to publish

a series of papers that won his election to the Royal Society. The custom of southern planters to send their sons to England for their higher education kept the southern upper classes familiar with trans-Atlantic scientific developments. This stimulus, together with a traditional close feeling for the land, probably accounts for the development of a number of first-rate southern botanists. John Bartram, a Philadelphia Quaker, was the foremost colonial botanist. Appointed royal botanist for America, Bartram roamed the colonies in search of new specimens, which he sent to London. His greatest service to his native land was his establishment near Philadelphia of a botanical garden which was at once one of the nation's first parks and the center for the study of its natural flora.

Benjamin Franklin. In the eighteenth century Philadelphia became the country's busiest seaport and its largest city. With its Quaker tradition of tolerance and its diverse population, it also became the intellectual center of North America and numbered among its citizens several noted scientists, whose work achieved international recognition. David Rittenhouse, a clockmaker with little formal education, constructed a telescope and an orrery which mechanically illustrated the relation between the planets of the solar system. Philadelphia's chief claim to scientific eminence, however, lay in the fact that Benjamin Franklin decided to settle and make a career there.

Franklin (1706–1790), a Bostonian by birth, had little formal education, having spent only a few years at a Boston grammar

BENJAMIN FRANKLIN ON RELIGION

The religious beliefs of Benjamin Franklin solicited by his close friend, the Reverend Ezra Stiles (1727–1795), then president of Yale College, display Franklin's honest yet tolerant skepticism of the Christian dogma of his day.

You desire to know something of my Religion. It is the first time I have been questioned upon it. But I cannot take your Curiosity amiss, and shall endeavour in a few Words to gratify it. Here is my Creed. I believe in one God, Creator of the Universe. That he governs it by his Providence. That he ought to be worshipped. That the most acceptable Service we render to him is doing good to his other Children. That the soul of Man is immortal, and will be treated with Justice in another Life respecting its Conduct in this. These I take to be the fundamental Principles of all sound Religion, and I regard them as you do in whatever Sect I meet with them.

As to Jesus of Nazareth, my Opinion of whom you particularly desire, I think the System of Morals and his Religion, as he left them to us, the best the World ever saw or is likely to see; but I apprehend it has received various corrupting Changes, and I have, with most of the present Dissenters in England, some Doubts as to his Divinity; tho' it is a question I do not dogmatize upon, having never studied it, and think it needless to busy myself with it now, when I expect soon an Opportunity of knowing the Truth with less Trouble. I see no harm, however, in its being believed, if that Belief has the good Consequence, as probably it has, of making his Doctrines more respected and better observed; especially as I do not perceive, that the Supreme takes it amiss, by distinguishing the Unbelievers in his Government of the World with any peculiar Marks of his Displeasure.

BENJAMIN FRANKLIN to EZRA STILES: Philadelphia, March 9, 1790

---

school. The son of a chandler, he was apprenticed at an early age to his half-brother James, a printer. Soon he was mainly responsible for the publication of his brother's newspaper, the *New England Courant*, which was so politically indiscreet that in 1722 James was jailed for a month. Shortly afterward Benjamin left Boston for Philadelphia where he became a printer and in due time began to publish many of his own writings. His *Poor Richard's Almanack*, which appeared from 1732 to 1757, presented in homely garb the wise sayings of all ages and won wide recognition in Europe as well as universal acclaim in America. The *Pennsylvania Gazette*, with which Franklin was long associated, furnished another outlet for his pen, and it was in this journal that some of his earliest scientific observations were set down. He was interested in a great variety of natural phenomena, but won recognition as a scientist chiefly through his experiments with electricity. Author, diplomat, inventor, philanthropist, scientist, and statesman, Franklin was a true son of the eighteenth century. His curious and far-ranging mind continually probed the phenomena of nature with a view to their utilization for the benefit of humankind. Skeptical of much of the religious dogma of his time, he concentrated his genius on this world rather than the hereafter, thereby symbolizing the spirit of secularism that had invaded English and American religion.

Deism. Although most early English scientists supported religious orthodoxy, the conflict between the new science and traditional mysticism was soon apparent. If the universe resembled a vast machine or a master clock whose operations could be explained by scientific law, obviously there was no place for divine interposition, to say nothing of the earthly seductions of Satan and his imps. Consequently, among the educated eighteenth-century elite in Europe, Deism, or "natural religion," spread rapidly. Fundamental to Deism was the belief that God was the originator of the universe and the essence of reason. Obviously such a God could not do violence to His own nature and to His logical universe despite human supplications and prayers. Nor could Satan or witches interfere with the ordered measures of the earth or cosmos, all attuned to the rationality of the Godhead.

Many Puritan New England divines regarded the new scientific findings with consternation. Cotton Mather, grandson of John Cotton, a member of the Royal Society, sought unsuccessfully to reconcile his religious views with those emanating from the new science. Less notable preachers wrestled with even less success to save their godly Commonwealth of Massachusetts from invasion by Deists, secularists, and devotees of other sects. Part of their problem was political. Under Governor Andros, Anglican services were held in Boston for the first time in 1687, and within a few years an Anglican Church, King's Chapel, was erected. Following the Glorious Revolution of 1688, the New Charter not only provided for the toleration of Anglicans but also granted them the vote, thus breaking the connection between the suffrage and Puritan church membership. Their material success also contributed to the Puritan difficulties, for with wealth came the desire to enjoy it, and the old Puritan restraints against worldly pleasures became irksome. Respect for intellectual achievement also drew the Puritans toward Anglicanism, and their congregational form of church organization encouraged the proliferation of doctrines. By the early decades of the eighteenth century both Deism and secularism had done much to undermine the old faith. Even some of the Puritan ministry were now inclined to minimize or dismiss the doctrines of predestination and election. Peter Bulkeley, for one, believed that if a man lived a moral life, abided by the injunctions of the Scriptures, and performed good works, God would be inclined to accept him into heaven. Elsewhere in the colonies, the new movements developed at an even more rapid pace. Benjamin Franklin's thinking was strongly tinctured by deistic beliefs, as was that of a host of illustrious American statesmen and philosophers who followed him.

Jonathan Edwards. As a reaction against the rising wave of secularism and the new rationalistic faith, a revivalist movement swept the colonies about 1740. This "Great Awakening," as it was called, was a complex religious phenomenon. One of its beginnings was in Northampton, Massachusetts, where in 1733 Jonathan Edwards fervidly admonished his flock to turn away from the new doctrines and embrace again the Calvinism of the early Boston Bay Colony. So much has been written about Edwards' "hell and damnation" sermons that proper perspective on the man has been all but lost.

Edwards (1703–1758) was a philosopher and theologian of the first rank. Before he was ten years old he had written an essay on the soul. In college he had been fascinated by the writings of both Newton and Locke, and for the rest of his life he kept abreast of the new scientific and social thought coming from Europe. Too much a Calvinist logician to accept the religious formulations flowing from the new doctrines, Edwards, through sermons, essays, and books attacked both Deism and Arminianism, the doctrine that man could be saved by the regeneration of his own spirit. His most noted work, *Freedom of the Will* (1754), rejected the concept of an autonomous will as inconsistent with the spirit of the new science and repugnant to the concept of an omnipotent and omniscient God. In his other major theological tract, *Original Sin* (1758), Edwards spoke strongly against belief in the innate goodness of man.

For a time Edwards was extremely successful as a preacher. Outraged by the rational and secular attacks against pristine Calvinism, he sought to shock his congregation into an awareness of their dereliction. So vividly eloquent was he about the damnation and hell that awaited the sinner at the hands of a just but stern God that his congregation experienced veritable paroxysms of fear and repentance. For a time church attendance swelled mightily. But an unfortunate suicide ascribed to the violence of his preaching, plus a theological dispute occasioned by Edwards' refusal to allow all church members to take communion, led to his resignation. He continued to champion old-fashioned Calvinism, but thereafter he played less on the emotions of his audience. His forceful but dignified farewell sermon at Northampton underlines the stronger pull of his nature toward reflection and speculation. Edwards was the most forceful speculative defender of Calvinism in America. As such he was recognized in his day, a recognition which won for him brief tenure as president of the Presbyterian college that was later to become Princeton University.

The Great Awakening. More directly responsible for the "Great Awakening" was George Whitefield, the noted English preacher and disciple of John Wesley, who made numerous trips to America between 1739 and 1744. Everywhere he preached between Georgia and New England, Whitefield captivated his audiences with his eloquence, but his flair for the dramatic eventually affronted many conservatives. Edwards and Whitefield were joined by other preachers, notably Theodorus Frelinghuysen of the New Jersey Dutch Reformed Church and Gilbert Tennent, a Pennsylvania Presbyterian.

Whitefield and Tennent were orthodox Calvinists, but their methods soon occasioned a growing breach between Calvinist sects. Harvard College, which had at first welcomed Whitefield, censured him in 1744 for the extreme emotionalism of his appeals. Disgusted by the growing injection of emotionalism into church services, some of the more dignified Congregationalists entered the Anglican Church, while others later helped to found the movement that eventually led to Unitarianism. Even more pronounced was the split among the Presbyterians. Whereas the "Old Side" or "Old Light" Presbyterians adhered to the sober ways of the Church, Tennent and his New Lighters demanded that ministers and parishioners alike give visible proof of conversion in the revival meetings. Congregations were split asunder over the issue, and the New Light Presbyterians not only rebelled against their own church government but also grew increasingly antagonistic toward the Anglican establishment, a political issue of some importance to the growth of anti-British sentiment in the colonies. Although the revivalist spirit among the Calvinists seemed to wane after 1744, the appetite of humbler folk for a more emotional religion was not satisfied until the Methodist and Baptist churches were established. Both of these creeds stressed the possibility of universal conversion and regeneration through the movement of the Holy Spirit. Thus the movement which had aimed originally at re-emphasizing the sober Calvinist tenets of the universality of evil and election resulted indirectly in the growth of emotional religions which promised that all men could be born again and saved.

John Woolman and Pietism. Colonial religious and ethical thought was not entirely dominated by Calvinism and its critics and defenders. The Quakers and other pietistic groups believed that from the human heart might come persuasive expressions that could prompt men to strive for the betterment of existing institutions. In John Woolman (1720–1772) the humanitarian spirit had its finest colonial flowering. Woolman was born in a New Jersey Quaker community, and his life exemplified frugality, gentleness, tolerance, charity, and a consciousness of the worth and dignity of every human being. His refusal to sign a legal document arranging for the transfer of other people's slaves, although it would have meant for him an economic gain, illustrates the ethical considerations that guided his conduct. Woolman was the author of numerous essays in which he urged his fellow citizens to cease their exploitation of the poor and even to moderate their harsh treatment of working animals. One of his essays inspired the beginning of the antislavery movement in America. Another work, "A Plea for the Poor," was reprinted over a century later by the British Fabians as one of the best arguments for socialism. John Woolman's *Journal*, simple in style and gentle in tone, remains one of the great testaments to the best efforts of the human spirit.

Colonial Culture.   Faced with the necessity of creating a livelihood in the wilderness, and endowed with little capital and relatively few tools, the very early colonists had little time or energy for the cultivated life. But colonial America was by no means a cultural desert.

A level of culture had developed in most of the colonies which by the Revolution was as vigorous and viable as that afforded by the provincial cities and countryside in Great Britain. By 1750 more children probably went to the common schools in Massachusetts than in any comparable area in Old England, and the New England literacy rate was probably higher than that across the Atlantic. One sure measure of the cultural growth of the colonies was the increased expenditure for the founding of newspapers and the collection of books. The first continuously published newspaper in the colonies, the *News-Letter*, was started in 1704 by John Campbell, who was also the official postmaster of Boston and who

was allowed to use the posts for the delivery of his newspaper. This was an important advantage, since newspapers were not officially considered to be acceptable mail, and the pattern of postmaster as newspaper proprietor was soon widespread throughout the colonies. Anxious to retain their unique and profitable postal privileges, most postmaster-editors were careful not to criticize constituted authorities. Still other editors were deterred by the readiness of British officialdom to prosecute its newspaper critics.

It was not, in fact, until the passage of the Stamp Act of 1764, which imposed a direct tax on newspapers, that colonial editors in significant numbers began to attack the policies and leaders of the British government. There were, however, earlier exceptions. In 1734 a New York editor, John Peter Zenger, was jailed for being too outspoken in his *Weekly Journal*. The Zenger trial in 1735 has often been cited as a landmark in the long struggle for the freedom of the press, for after a memorable and eloquent defense by Zenger's attorney, Andrew Hamilton, the jury returned a verdict of not guilty to the official charge of seditious libel. Despite this precedent there was little relaxation of the close censorship of American papers. Still, by 1750 almost every American town had its local paper, and the support given by it to the patriotic cause, especially during the decade preceding the Revolution, was one of the major reasons for the extent of colonial resistance to British policy.

During the first century of colonial life books were a scarce commodity. The largest libraries in the thirteen colonies, each housing no more than three to five thousand books, were owned by Harvard College and by a few individuals. By 1700, both William Byrd II of Virginia and Cotton Mather of Boston possessed such libraries, mostly devoted to theology, the classics, and science. James Logan, Secretary to William Penn, collected an impressive scientific library which at his death in 1751 he left to Philadelphia as a start toward a public library. Still other public or semi-public libraries were founded by Royal Governors or by gifts from British religious societies. Numerous private subscription libraries also were organized, the most famous being the one in Philadelphia which was largely the work of Benjamin Franklin.

Although some libraries were devoted to special subjects, most were general and heavily weighted with the classics. Since colonial higher education tended to follow the British pattern, a knowledge of Greek and Roman literature was considered the mark of the cultivated mind, and many American political leaders embellished their political observations with examples drawn from classical sources. The reading of humbler men was, of course, much more confined. The Bible, John Foxe's *Book of Martyrs*, as it was popularly called, a few practical books on cures for "man and beaste," the inevitable almanac, together with occasional newspapers and political or religious tracts, often comprised their total reading.

In 1640 the first colonial press at Cambridge, Massachusetts, published the first American book, *The Whole Book of Psalms*, or, as it has come to be known, the *Bay Psalm Book*. The first real textbook, the famous *New England Primer* (1690), began its alphabet: "In Adam's fall we sinned all." Generations of New England children learned by heart the verses of the *New England Primer* and Michael Wigglesworth's *The Day of Doom* (1662), and these books had much to do with sustaining the vitality of the Puritan tradition. On a much higher level was Cotton Mather's *Magnalia Christi Americana* (1702), which sought to record the workings of Providence in the New World. Composed of the history of the early settlements, the lives of the leading ministers and governors, together with much mystical and esoteric information, the volume is an important source of New England history as well as a mirror of the early New England mind. The religious literary

tradition was brought to a climax, however, by the numerous writings of Jonathan Edwards.

Many colonial literary figures turned their attention to writing the history of the American venture. William Bradford's *Of Plymouth Plantation,* written in simple prose and full of realistic detail about the Pilgrim band, was a sterling beginning for the nation's historical tradition. Other contemporary historical works of interest and merit are John Winthrop's *Journal,* Thomas Hutchinson's *History of the Colony of Massachusetts Bay* (1764), and Robert Beverley's *The History and Present State of Virginia* (1705). Benjamin Franklin's only book, the *Autobiography,* written at various times when he was past middle age, gives a sharp picture of his extremely practical and idealistic strains. His essays on a great variety of subjects, his "how to do it" tracts, and his scientific writings all repay reading. His chief conveyor of advice and counsel, to the common man at least, was *Poor Richard's Almanack,* which appeared annually and was filled with pithy advice, inspirational messages, and didactic folk sayings culled from many sources. Simply written, materialistic, and practical, the *Almanack* appealed to an enormous audience.

The Arts. Since both the Calvinists and the Quakers opposed the theater on religious grounds, it is not surprising that the earliest stage presentations appeared in Williamsburg and New York. Not until 1754, when the Quaker influence in Philadelphia had waned, was a permanent theater opened in that city. Practically all the plays performed were the works of Shakespeare, Dryden, and Addison, and most of the actors came from England. According to the scanty records no native work appeared on the American commercial stage until 1767.

More noteworthy among the fine arts was the development of architecture. As early as 1720 a British traveler observed that in Boston the merchant and the banker had displaced the preacher and the civil official as owners of the finest domestic establishments. Most of the designs were copied by colonial carpenters from English builders' manuals. Brick and stone were often used for public buildings and for a few of the more sumptuous private dwellings, especially in Pennsylvania. Elsewhere, even in the larger cities, wood was the dominant material. By 1700 the Georgian revival was well under way in Britain, and colonial architecture tended to follow this prevailing style. In its simplest form Georgian architecture consisted typically of a rectangular two-story brick structure with white wood trim. In its more elegant forms, the Georgian residence followed the same plan, greatly enlarged, often ornamented with a columned porch or portico. An elaborate staircase rising from a central hall, decorated plaster ceilings, and walls panelled with wood or hung with damask or imported Chinese wall papers achieved a formal and aristocratic decor. Williamsburg, with its superb restorations, is a showplace of Georgian examples.

Colonial craftsmen flourished, particularly in the Middle Colonies and in New England. In the South the inclination of the planters to import their furniture and housewares from England retarded the development of native crafts. German and Dutch cabinet makers in Philadelphia and New York early acquired a reputation for the excellence of their work. Paul Revere was the most noted silversmith, but his fellow craftsmen turned out excellent work in both silver and pewter. The Pennsylvania Dutch craftsmen in Lancaster, Pennsylvania, early acquired a reputation as gunsmiths and perfected the excellent "Kentucky rifle." These graceful firearms became the prized possessions of the colonial frontiersman, who depended upon his rifle for much of his food and, on occasion, for his very life. From the same Pennsylvania region also came the Conestoga covered wagon with its high wheels and raised bed designed to negotiate the roughest terrain.

Most colonial products were made and designed for use rather than ornament. Consequently, functionalism became ingrained, and the less utilitarian arts tended to lag. Except in New York, where Dutch fondness for landscapes and interiors persisted, most early American painting consisted of portraits by anonymous wandering artists. By the eighteenth century, however, a few colonial portrait-painters had acquired competence, even excellence, and their likenesses of prominent contemporaries revealed with striking insight the character and personality of their subjects. Both John Singleton Copley and Benjamin West, born in 1738, began to paint early; and both men eventually settled in London, then the mecca for portraitists, where they achieved fame and success.

Political Thought. The roots of practically all colonial political thought lay across the Atlantic. At the core of seventeenth- and eighteenth-century European political theory were the concepts of *nature* and *law.* From these came the belief in natural rights, the existence of which was attested by the social compact or contract. Obviously, the development of the idea that natural laws existed for man and society was closely linked with the discovery of those laws that seemed to govern the inanimate universe. If there were natural and unvarying laws governing the movement of planets, the nature of gases, and even the circulation of the human blood, why not, the seventeenth-century man asked, similar laws for man and his relations with both God and his earthly society? The rise of Deism was largely the result of the attempt to discover by rational means the natural laws governing man's relation to the Godhead. Paralleling the search for natural law in religion was a similar quest in politics. This effort to substitute reason and law for mysticism and an authoritarian tradition in human affairs was known as the Enlightenment.

The Enlightenment. Among the many English thinkers of the Enlightenment who had a profound effect upon colonial political and social ideas were Thomas Hobbes (1588–1679) and John Locke (1632–1704). Hobbes sought to fashion a political theory as rational and exact as the laws supposedly governing the physical universe. Troubled by Puritan attacks upon the Stuart monarchy, and the resulting civil war, Hobbes in his *Leviathan* (1651) argued that man's original state was one of complete freedom and anarchy from which he had escaped only by entering into a social compact, thereby giving up his original freedom for the opportunity to secure order and social peace. Hobbes defended absolute monarchy — an increasingly unpopular position — but his concepts of man's original state of freedom and of a social contract were eagerly taken up by successors who were to use them against the monarchy which Hobbes had so vehemently defended. The idea that all earthly government was based upon an original social contract between men was especially acceptable to the Puritans, whose own religious ideas contained the concept of a contract between God and man. The Pilgrims had already fashioned the Mayflower Compact before landing in America, and the leaders of the Massachusetts Bay Company regarded their charter granted by the English King as just that sort of lasting contract.

More revolutionary than Hobbes was James Harrington, who in his *Oceana* (1656) supplied a good many ideas that stimulated American readers. Although his belief in democracy, a written constitution, and the secret ballot were much too advanced for his time to be fully acceptable either to British or Americans, his argument that political power must follow economic power influenced the thinking of many Americans.

John Locke. Far more influential in America than Hobbes was John Locke, the philosopher of the Glorious Revolution of 1688. Locke, whose father had been a Puritan who had fought with Cromwell against the royal forces, was all of his life interested in religious and political freedom. In his *Two Treatises of Government* (1690) he accepted Hobbes's ideas of man's original free state and of the social compact, but he also argued trenchantly against any authoritarian government. According to Locke, man in his original state had by natural law certain rights which he could not give up to government. Thus the right to hold property, the right of free thought and free speech, the right to worship as he pleased, were not to be violated. The only rights man had given up to government in the original social contract were the rights to keep the peace and to judge and punish his fellow men. Governments were therefore severely limited in their just powers, and the use of such powers was defensible only on the ground that it served the public interest. When governments ceased to serve the public interest or perverted it, they broke the social compact, and thus the citizens of the state had the right to change the government if necessary. The parliamentary acts following the Glorious Revolution were premonitory of Locke's concepts and became important precedents which were honored by Britons everywhere.

The works of John Locke were read and discussed in America, and as early as 1717 they found their way into a controversy which was primarily religious in origin. By the end of the seventeenth century the various independent congregations of the Massachusetts Puritan church showed a wide latitude in their interpretation of Calvinism. Consequently a group of leading Boston divines organized a central authority to regulate dogma and forms of church service. The Reverend John Wise (1652–1725) of Ipswich defended the freedom of his congregation to worship God as it chose, citing the ideas and words of Locke. Wise argued that man is by nature free and equal and that the duty of government is to defend these principles. Although Wise conceded that once a government is established by a "Publick Vote" of the majority individual men are bound to acquiesce in the results, he left no doubt that "The first Humane Subject and Original of Civil Power is the

People." Some thirty years after Wise won his argument another minister, Jonathan Mayhew (1720–1766) of Martha's Vineyard, argued that government existed only to promote the "common safety and utility." When governments failed to do so, or if they enjoined things such as the legal establishment of a religion, it was the citizen's duty to disobey.

By 1750–1770 the ideas of Hobbes, Locke, and others were widely disseminated, and in the looming debates over the nature of the British Empire, they were used often and effectively. Of all the intellectual concepts which colonial America inherited from the English Enlightenment, they were, perhaps, the most pervasive, lasting, and meaningful.

SELECTED BIBLIOGRAPHY

Excellent summaries of colonial cultural and intellectual History may be found in Max Savelle, *Seeds of Liberty* (1948), and *The Colonial Origins of American Thought* (1964); and L. B. Wright, *The Cultural Life of the American Colonies* (1957). The first volume of V. L. Parrington, *Main Currents in American Thought* (3 vols., 1927–1930), contains much of interest, but it is marred by the author's anti-Puritan bias. Standard general treatments of American intellectual history include Merle Curti, *The Growth of American Thought* (3rd ed., 1964); Stow Persons, *American Minds* (1958); and A. M. Schlesinger, Jr., and Morton White (eds.), *Paths of American Thought* (1963). An interesting attempt to broaden American cultural history is Michael Kraus, *The Atlantic Civilization: Eighteenth-Century Origins* (1949). An interesting group of essays is R. M. Gummere, *The American Colonial Mind and the Classical Tradition* (1963). An absorbing treatment of a neglected subject is L. B. Wright, *The First Gentlemen of Virginia: Intellectual Qualities of the Early Colonial Ruling Class* (1940); the same author's *Culture on the Moving Frontier* (1955) is a delightful series of essays emphasizing the efforts of westerners to maintain ties with the East and with England. One strain of political thought is traced carefully by L. W. Labaree, *Conservatism in Early American History* (1948); more general is Clinton Rossiter, *Conservatism in America: The Thankless Persuasion* (2nd ed., 1962). In a class by itself is the erudite and provocative treatment of political thought by Louis Hartz, *The Liberal Tradition in America* (1955).

Old but of major importance is M. C. Tyler, *A History of American Literature during the Colonial Period* (2 vols., 2nd ed., 1897); a single-volume abridgement is entitled *A History of American Literature: 1607–1765* (1962). Major cooperative works are W. P. Trent and others (eds.), *The Cambridge History of American Literature* (2nd ed., 1943); and R. E. Spiller and others (eds.), *Literary History of the United States* (3 vols., 3rd ed., 1964), which contains superb bibliographies. A valuable reference work which can be consulted with profit for any period is J. D. Hart, *The Oxford Companion to American Literature* (3rd ed., 1956). J. B. Hubbell, *The South in American Literature, 1607–1900* (1954), treats a rather neglected aspect of colonial literary history. Some useful anthologies are R. H. Pearce (ed.), *Colonial American Writing* (1956); M. R. Stern and S. L. Gross (eds.), *American Literature Survey; Colonial and Federal to 1800* (1962); Perry Miller and T. H. Johnson (eds.), *The Puritans* (2 vols., 1938); and Perry Miller (ed.), *American Puritans: Their Prose and Poetry* (1956). Other major works on intellectual aspects of Puritanism include Perry Miller, *The New England Mind* (2 vols., 1939–1953); R. B. Perry, *Puritanism and Democracy* (1944); H. W. Schneider, *The Puritan Mind* (1930); K. B. Murdock, *Literature and Theology in Colonial New England* (1949); and S. E. Morison, *The Intellectual Life of Colonial New England,* formerly entitled *The Puritan Pronaos* (2nd ed., 1956).

A rewarding major work in American cultural history is S. E. Morison, *Three Centuries of Harvard, 1636–1936* (1936). A distinguished group of studies by H. M. Jones

* Available in paperback

ranges from *America and French Culture, 1750–1848* (1926) to *O Strange New World* (1964). Important recent biographies of educators include E. S. Morgan, *The Gentle Puritan; A Life of Ezra Stiles* (1962); and L. L. Tucker, *Puritan Protagonist: President Thomas Clap of Yale College* (1962). T. J. Wertenbaker, *Princeton, 1746–1896* (1946), is an interesting survey. Valuable monographs include Robert Middlekauff, *Ancients and Axioms: Secondary Education in Eighteenth Century New England* (1963); and Bernard Bailyn, *Education in the Forming of American Society* (1960). C. L. Becker, *The Heavenly City of the Eighteenth Century Philosophers* (1932), has deservedly become a classic.

Colonial science has been attracting the attention of scholars in recent years. Some of the more important results are Theodore Hornberger, *Scientific Thought in American Colleges, 1638–1800* (1945); I. B. Cohen, *Some Early Tools of American Science* (1950); D. J. Struik, *Yankee Science in the Making* (1948); Brooke Hindle, *The Pursuit of Science in Revolutionary America, 1735–1789* (1956); and *David Rittenhouse* (1964). J. W. Oliver, *History of American Technology* (1956) is a basic survey. See also the collection edited by H. G. Cruickshank, *John and William Bartram's America* (1957). Among the contributions of R. H. Shryock, leading historian of American medicine, are *Medicine and Society in America, 1660–1860* (1960); and *American Medical Research, Past and Present* (1947). Popularly written and entertaining is J. T. Flexner, *Doctors on Horseback; Pioneers of American Medicine* (1937). Recent monographs of importance include John Duffy, *Epidemics in Colonial America* (1953); and O. T. Beall, Jr., and R. H. Shryock, *Cotton Mather, First Significant Figure in American Medicine* (1954).

Benjamin Franklin has captured the attention of many scholars. One of the major editorial tasks of our time has been assumed by L. W. Labaree; six volumes of his *Papers of Benjamin Franklin* (1959 —) have appeared so far. Franklin's *Autobiography* is available in many editions; see also *The Benjamin Franklin Papers*, edited by Frank Donovan

(1962). Among the many biographies are V. W. Crane, *Benjamin Franklin, Englishman and American* (1936); Carl Van Doren, *Benjamin Franklin* (1938); and V. W. Crane, *Benjamin Franklin and a Rising People* (1954), brief but rich. An interesting collection illustrating how Franklin has been interpreted by various writers is C. L. Sanford (ed.), *Benjamin Franklin and the American Character* (1955). Special studies of Franklin include I. B. Cohen, *Benjamin Franklin: His Contribution to the American Tradition* (1953), and *Franklin and Newton* (1956); A. O. Aldridge, *Franklin and His French Contemporaries* (1957); and W. S. Hanna, *Benjamin Franklin and Pennsylvania Politics* (1964).

E. S. Gaustad, *The Great Awakening in New England* (1957), is an interesting modern survey. Principal works on the leading character in this episode are O. E. Winslow, *Jonathan Edwards* (1940); and Perry Miller, *Jonathan Edwards* (1949). Studies of the great Methodist evangelist include A. D. Belden, *George Whitefield, the Awakener* (1930); and S. C. Henry, *George Whitefield, Wayfaring Witness* (1957). A monumental collaborative effort is Emory Bucke (ed.), *The History of American Methodism* (3 vols., 1964). Recent significant monographs include Conrad Wright, *The Beginnings of Unitarianism in America* (1955); and C. C. Goen, *Revivalism and Separatism in New England, 1740–1800: Strict Congregationalists and Separate Baptists in the Great Awakening* (1962).

On journalism see two interesting works by Sidney Kobre, *The Development of the Colonial Newspaper* (1944), and *Foundations of American Journalism* (1958). Another useful book is C. S. Brigham, *Journals and Journeymen; A Contribution to the History of Early American Newspapers* (1950). General works on journalism include B. A. Weisberger, *The American Newspaperman* (1961); F. L. Mott, *American Journalism; A History, 1690–1960* (3rd ed., 1962), and *A History of American Magazines* (4 vols., 1938–1957). L. W. Levy, *Legacy of Suppression; Freedom of Speech and Press in Early American History* (1960), is both exciting and somewhat disillusioning.

4

ENGLAND'S
COLONIAL PROBLEM

ɜ► *British and Colonial Governments Compared · British Trade and Currency Regulations · Evolution of Colonial Governments · Colonial Benefits from the Empire · Defense and New France · The French and Indian War · The Proclamation Line and the New Western Settlements*

Few early settlers came to America with unique political ideas or a burning desire to set up new forms of government. Familiar — and for the most part comfortable — with the British type of government, the colonists sought to adapt its institutions to the conditions and problems with which the New World soon confronted them.

At the time the colonies were founded, the role of the sovereign in government was conceived to be far greater than in recent times. The King, with his claim to rule by "divine right," was, in effect, the executive branch of the government. With the advice of a Privy Council consisting of from twenty to forty high officials, he watched over the affairs of the realm, sometimes issuing orders that were virtually legislative in character. The principal lawmaking body, however, was Parliament, which consisted of the House of Lords and the House of Commons. Membership in the former

was based on heredity or high ecclesiastical office. In the Commons, which was supposed to represent the common people of the realm, each shire, or county, was entitled to two members and some three hundred towns elected one or two members each. This distribution of seats was historic rather than proportionate to population, and many large cities were left wholly without representation. Although suffrage excluded most of the non-propertied classes, in theory Parliament represented "all the men of England," and its right to a voice in the levying of taxes and the making of laws was conceded during most of the colonial period. All judicial officers were appointed by the crown, but were guided in their decisions not only by statute law but also by the precedents of the common law. Such rights as trial by jury and freedom from arbitrary arrest they defended stoutly, and in general they maintained their independence of both King and Parliament.

The Colonial Governments. The colonial governments, although they followed the English model, were not all alike. Some operated under charters that were little constitutions in themselves; others had proprietors into whose hands governmental authority had been placed; still others were royal colonies under the direct supervision

60

of the English government. But the types of government did not differ so much from one another as the names used to describe them (corporate, proprietary, royal) would seem to indicate. A single executive, a two-house legislature, and a judicial system, roughly on the English plan, eventually appeared in every colony. Colonial citizens, moreover, enjoyed the personal rights that would have been theirs in the mother country.

Many Americans felt it only natural to think of their colonies as practically separate and independent units of the British nation and to look upon their charters as constitutions and their legislative bodies as "little Parliaments." On the other hand, most English officials felt it just as natural, and with more justification, to consider the colonial plantations as little more than dependencies of the home government and subject to such regulations as the home government chose to establish. But for many reasons the British were slow to develop a definite policy of colonial control. The English government lacked experience in dealing with colonies. Moreover, during much of the seventeenth century English governmental machinery was itself in bad order. The attempts of the early Stuarts to expand the royal prerogative were bitterly resisted by Parliament, and for many years the boundaries between the rights of the King and the rights of Parliament in respect to colonial affairs were in dispute. Civil war in England during much of this period also paralyzed such feeble efforts at control as the English authorities attempted. The colonies were thus left comparatively free during the formative period to work out their own destinies.

Efforts to Establish Control. With the restoration of the Stuarts to the throne of England in 1660 it was possible to give more definite attention to the colonial problem. A group of administrative experts was assembled, known at first as the Council for Foreign Plantations, but later as the Lords of Trade. This body inquired into colonial affairs and recommended such legislation and such administrative policies as it saw fit. One of its primary functions was to suggest ways in which the overseas possessions could be directed to make England economically independent of other nations. Holding to the principles of mercantilism, the Lords of Trade recommended that the colonists should sell all their products to England and should purchase most of their manufactures from or through England only. The colonists were not to engage in competition with the mother country, but instead should be guided by considerations of the common imperial good, rather than the colonies' individual welfare.

The much-discussed Navigation Acts were enacted by Parliament as a part of this policy. The first of these measures, passed in 1660, had as its primary purpose the encouragement of English shipping. Only English ships with English captains and crews three-fourths English might engage in the colonial trade. Sometime later it was further stipulated that ships engaging in colonial trade be built either in England or the colonies (not including Ireland). These provisions were not seriously damaging to the colonists, who were themselves included under the term English. The Navigation Acts also contained a list of "enumerated articles" — sugar, tobacco, cotton-wool, indigo, ginger, dyewoods — that might be sold only to England or to another colony. These products were all items that England had to obtain either from her colonies or from other nations. Later expanded, this original list at first contained only one item, tobacco, that seriously affected any continental colonies. As compensation, however, the growing of tobacco in England and the purchase of tobacco from foreign countries for use in England were forbidden.

The Staple Act. The Staple Act of 1663 affected the continental colonies more directly than the earlier law. This legislation, designed to prevent the colonies from trading with other nations, contained the provision that most imports from Europe to the colonies must first pass through England before transshipment to the colonies. Duties, both import and export, were collected by the English government, but an elaborate system of rebates allowed the colonists to purchase foreign goods through England almost as cheaply as Englishmen themselves could buy them. And, through resort to smuggling, the colonists managed to minimize the restrictions.

The Plantation Duty Act of 1672 was designed to bear directly upon the colonists. A duty, equal to the basic English duty, was to be collected *in the colonies,* unless the ship's captain would give bond that he would carry the cargo directly to England. This law called for the appointment of a number of colonial collectors who were directly responsible to the English commissioner of customs. These collectors, stationed in the colonies, were so underpaid that the Americans soon found bribery effective and continued their smuggling with little opposition. Others, attempting to perform the duties of their office, made themselves so obnoxious to the colonists that they were virtually ineffective in their positions.

The tendency of the colonists to ignore unpopular British regulations was responsible for the determination of James II and his advisers to reform the colonial governments. The attitude of New England, whose elected officials had made little or no effort to enforce the disagreeable laws, was regarded as particularly reprehensible. Finally the Attorney General brought suit for the annulment of the Massachusetts charter, and in 1684 won his case. The way now lay open for a series of radical reforms. In the interest of efficient imperial control, royal colonies were to supplant corporate or proprietary colonies, small colonies were to be consolidated with their larger neighbors, and royal officials were to have their powers strengthened.

Dominion of New England.   Between 1684 and 1688 the eight northernmost colonies were joined into the "Territory and Dominion of New England," with Sir Edmund Andros as its governor. All the New England colonies were included in the combination and, in addition, New York, East New Jersey, and West New Jersey. Colonial assemblies were abolished in favor of rule by a council, quitrents were demanded of land owners, taxes were levied without the consent of any representative assembly, and religious worship according to the rites of the Anglican Church was given official encouragement.

The Glorious Revolution.   These drastic changes, enforced as they were by a stubborn and tactless governor, might well have led to revolt in the colonies had there not been a "Glorious Revolution" in England. But the efforts of James II to free himself of the control of Parliament had aroused deep resentment in the mother country. In 1688, without bloodshed, James was deprived of his royal rights, and, by act of Parliament, William and Mary of Orange were invited to become joint sovereigns. The kings of England thereafter owed their title solely to the will of the English people as expressed by Parliament. To leave no doubt in the matter this doctrine was recorded in the Bill of Rights (1689) and also in the Act of Settlement (1701). As for the "Dominion of New England," it promptly collapsed, and Andros was thrown into prison.

Governmental Changes.   When the English government was free to turn its attention once more to America, it abandoned the principle of consolidation, but it did not hesitate to establish royal colonies in preference to any other type wherever that could conveniently be done. New Hampshire was again cut off from Massachusetts and given a royal governor. Massachusetts was given a new charter (1691), which provided for a governor appointed by the crown instead of elected by the people as formerly. Connecticut and Rhode Island were allowed to keep their old charters, but the Plymouth Bay Colony and the settlements in Maine were annexed to Massachusetts. Maryland became a royal colony with a Protestant governor, and the rights of the proprietor were not restored until 1715. Penn's friendship with the fallen Stuarts was held against him, and he did not regain his proprietary rights until 1694. In 1702 the Jerseys were united as the royal colony of New Jersey. Misgovernment in the Carolinas gave an excuse to withdraw the privileges of the proprietors there in 1728. When Georgia became a royal colony in 1752, only Connecticut and Rhode Island were left of the corporate colonies, and of the proprietorships only the holdings of the Penns in Pennsylvania and Delaware, and of the current Lord Baltimore in Maryland.

These changes in America registered far less progress toward democracy than did the Glorious Revolution in England. Before many years the English King reigned, but ministers, responsible to Parliament rather than to the King, really ruled. For America, however, no such transformation was in sight. It made little difference whether royal governors were appointed on the recommendation of the English ministers or at the whim of the English monarch. In either event the source of constituted authority lay outside the colony. Colonial assemblies, however, could and sometimes did sway royal governors by refusing to grant funds unless specific grievances were abated.

Neither did the Glorious Revolution mean any abatement of the English determination to control the trade of the colonies in the interest of the mother country and of the empire as a whole. In 1696 William III replaced the old Lords of Trade with a new colonial agency, commonly known as the Board of Trade. A new Navigation Act (1696) required that all colonial governors take a strong oath to uphold the English regulations, and in case they failed to live up to their oaths, they were liable to a heavy fine and removal from office. Soon afterwards admiralty courts were established in the colonies to enforce the English customs regulations. These courts were not embarrassed by the necessity of holding jury trials; hence colonial juries, notorious for their leniency towards offenders against the trade laws, could be avoided.

New Trade Regulations. The determination to enforce commercial regulations in the colonies continued unabated during the early years of the eighteenth century. The list of enumerated articles was lengthened by the addition of rice, molasses, naval stores, ship timbers, copper, and beaver skins. Colonists were forbidden to transport wool from one colony to another. The Molasses Act of 1733 was aimed at the profitable trade carried on between the mainland colonies and the French West Indies. To ensure that the former should buy West Indian produce from the English islands exclusively, practically prohibitive duties were placed on all sugar, molasses, rum, and spirits imported from foreign plantations. This was a shortsighted piece of legislation, for the continental colonies had more to sell than the markets of the English West Indies could absorb, and much of the hard money that found its way to the mainland ultimately went to England to redress an unfavorable balance of trade. The Molasses Act, however, did little harm, for from the first it was ignored both by the colonists and by local English authorities, who saw that the empire would be damaged by its enforcement.

In various other ways the English government undertook to control the economic life of the colonies. Manufacturing, it was assumed, could best be done in England, and colonial manufactures were, therefore, discouraged. A law of 1732 placed a limit upon the number of apprentices that colonial hat makers might employ, and a law of 1750 restricted the right of the colonists to manufacture iron goods. All paper-money issues by colonial legislatures were prohibited either by law of Parliament or by disallowance of the colonial laws involved.

However, English trade laws were not all detrimental to the colonies. Colonial production was encouraged by generous bounties on such items as indigo and on naval stores and ship timbers when the latter two products were placed on the enumerated list. Colonial agents (each colony was required to be so represented) lobbied against proposed measures considered damaging to American interests, and argued the American cause before the Board of Trade. Colonial governors, whose salaries were appropriated by colonial assemblies, tended to interpret unpopular regulations as loosely as possible. Many Americans could see, too, that the protection given to colonial trade by the English navy and by English treaties far outweighed the commercial restrictions; and for this protection the Americans were taxed not a cent.

"Salutary Neglect."   Finally, the will of the mother country to maintain restrictions on the colonies often lagged seriously. Sir Robert Walpole, the virtual head of the English government for more than two decades (1721–1742), believed that more was to be gained for England by encouraging colonial trade than by restricting it, since trade of any sort would make the colonies prosperous and better able to buy English goods. This opinion was shared by the Duke of Newcastle, who had much to do with colonial affairs during Walpole's supremacy and continued powerful even after Walpole's fall. Indeed, Newcastle's frankly admitted policy of "salutary neglect" was not seriously amended until the close of the French and Indian War.

A clearly understood principle of British colonial policy was that the colonies, in return for the regulation of their trade, could rely upon the mother country for military protection. This was a matter of great importance, for the English settlements were hemmed in by the Indians, the French, and the Spanish. While the threat of independent attack from the Spanish empire was slight, the danger from the French and their Indian allies was often very real. By the middle of the eighteenth century, indeed, it was clear that a struggle was impending to determine which nation, England or France, would dominate the world's seas, and thus a major part of the world's colonial empire. On the continent of Europe both nations sought alliances, and in India, in the Mediterranean basin, on the Atlantic, in the West Indies and America their land and sea forces eyed each other nervously. In North America the ambitions of the contending nations centered upon the lands beyond the Appalachian barrier.

New France.   The French settlements in North America dated back to 1608, when Samuel de Champlain founded Quebec on the St. Lawrence River. By the end of the seventeenth century, French outposts had advanced by way of the Great Lakes and the Mississippi to the Gulf of Mexico. The French in America, most of whom were concentrated along the St. Lawrence with a few villages in the "Illinois country," numbered only 80,000 in 1750, when the English population stood at 1.5 million. For the most part, the French *habitants* came to America not for reasons of their own but because the French government was determined to build up an American colony. The French were relatively unprogressive, except in the fur trade, at which they excelled and upon which their economy was based. The situation might have been somewhat different had the French government permitted the Huguenots, who were driven from France after the revocation of the Edict of Nantes (1685), to come to Canada. Many of the exiled French Protestants went instead to the English colonies where, because of their intelligence and industry, they soon became prominent.

The French colonials remained in a state of semi-dependence upon their mother country. Their government, like that of

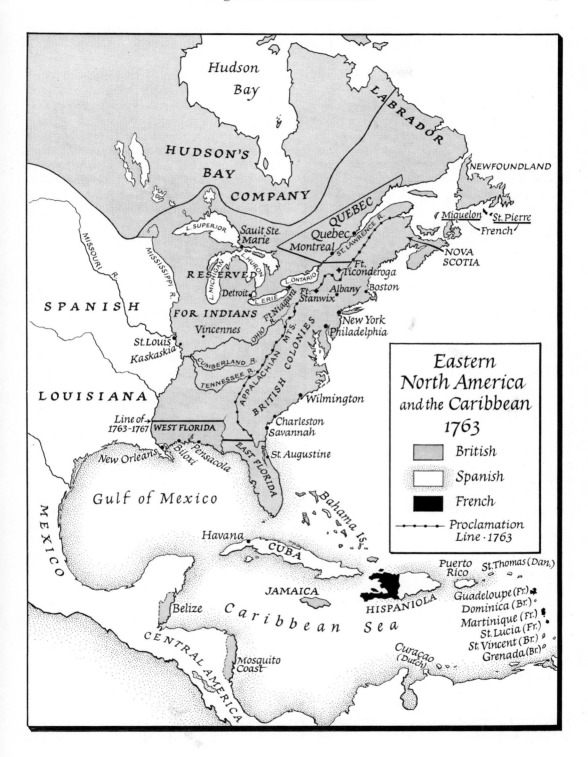

Eastern
North America
and the Caribbean
1763

British
Spanish
French
Proclamation
Line · 1763

France, was concentrated in the hands of the governor, the intendant, and the bishop. The system of landholding imitated as closely as the proximity of the wilderness would permit the feudal practices to which the French settlers had been accustomed in the Old World. French industries were very tightly controlled and compared unfavorably with those of their English neighbors.

The Forks of the Ohio

Agriculture was sickly and fishing was not notably successful. Only in fur trading did the French really excel.

Military Efficiency.   In military defense, however, the French in America possessed a decided advantage over the English. Unhampered by a multiplicity of authorities, they had unity of command and unity of action. The French government likewise kept French ships and soldiers available for the protection of their colonists, while England, although ready at all times to guard the seas with the English navy, relied upon the colonial militia, which was of very uneven quality, to take care of land fighting in their own defense, except in case of great emergency.

The struggle for world empire between the French and the English lasted many years and involved the two countries in numerous wars. The earlier of these struggles, "King William's War" (1689–1697), "Queen Anne's War" (1701–1713), and "King George's War" (1744–1748), left the status of French and English rivalry in America relatively unchanged. The decisive contest, however, the French and Indian War, actually began in America two years before its counterpart in Europe, the Seven Years' War, got under way.

Rivalry with the English.   The struggle for the continent was precipitated when a group of Virginian and English land speculators formed the Ohio Company, which hoped to establish settlements beyond the Appalachians. In 1749 royal consent was obtained to a grant of 200,000 acres of land below the "forks" of the Ohio. Next year the noted surveyor, Christopher Gist, prepared the way for the coming of settlers, upon whose purchase of lands the company hoped to realize a handsome profit. This project alarmed the French who recognized at once the peril to their Ohio Valley fur-trade interests which the new settlements entailed. Accordingly, the governor of New France dispatched an agent, Celéron de

Blainville, to the contested area to claim the region. Also, Indians friendly to the French were induced to attack Indians friendly to the English, and French forts made their appearance in the disputed area.

The French Warned by Washington. When Governor Robert Dinwiddie of Virginia, a stockholder in the Ohio Company, received word from the British government that he was at liberty to "repel force by force," he sent the youthful George Washington to the nearest French outpost to warn the French that they must withdraw from the Ohio Valley. Washington delivered the ultimatum in the fall of 1753; the French ignored it, and the Virginians had no choice but to back down or prepare for war. Next year Washington was again sent across the mountains, this time with a small detachment of troops, to aid a British outpost lately established at the forks of the Ohio. After some preliminary skirmishing, Washington was attacked and defeated at Great Meadows, July 3, 1754, and compelled to withdraw, while the British fort on the Ohio had already been captured and as Fort Duquesne became the headquarters for further French operations in the West.

The Albany Plan. One of the greatest of the disadvantages the English colonials suffered was their lack of unity in government and in command. A plan to remedy this situation had been proposed in 1754 by Benjamin Franklin at the Albany Congress, held to discuss the Indian menace, and attended by representatives of seven colonies. Franklin's "Albany Plan" proposed an intercolonial council, composed of forty-eight representatives apportioned among the colonies according to their wealth and population and elected by the several colonial legislatures. A president-general for all the colonies, appointed and paid by the crown, would direct its activities. Subject to veto by the president-general, the council would have the right to control Indian affairs, raise and pay armies, build forts, and levy

LOUIS JOSEPH, MARQUIS DE MONTCALM

Montcalm was the outstanding leader of the French in their final struggle with the English for control of North America. An able and gallant soldier, he was mortally wounded while trying to rally his troops against the British during the assault on Quebec.

the taxes necessary for these purposes. But this plan was promptly rejected by the colonial assemblies, who objected to any curtailment of their prerogatives and who possibly feared that any such intercolonial organization would transfer too much responsibility for the winning of the war from England to the colonies.

French and Indian War. Although the events of 1754–1755 marked the beginning of hostilities in North America, the European governments chose to postpone a general war as long as possible. Nevertheless, the British government soon sent General Edward Braddock with two regiments of regulars to cooperate with the Virginians in the capture of Fort Duquesne. With over 2,000 troops and a long baggage train, Braddock slowly cleared a way through the wilderness. He was within ten miles of his goal, when on July 9, 1755, he was ambushed and utterly defeated by a party of

67

WILLIAM PITT

Later created the Earl of Chatham, Pitt was the resourceful British political leader who persuaded both the British Parliament and the British people to wage relentless war against the French, both in America and elsewhere.

French and Indians. Braddock was mortally wounded in the battle, and for a long time thereafter frontier fighting went badly for the English. By 1756 England and France were openly at war, with the Canadian forces under the able Marquis de Montcalm nearly everywhere in the ascendancy. The road Braddock had built, however, was eventually to become the highway for the English migration that finally was to conquer the Ohio Valley.

Colonial Support of the War. The failure of the Albany Plan left each colony free to support the war as it chose. The colonies that were in greatest danger did most; those that were farthest removed from the scene of conflict did least; and in general there

was much waiting to see what the other planned to do. The leading British minister, William Pitt, who virtually took charge of the war, worked out a requisition system which secured as much colonial assistance as was possible under existing circumstances. He left to the colonies the responsibility of levying, clothing, and paying provincial soldiers. The English government undertook to furnish the colonial troops with arms, ammunition, and provisions, and promised to compensate the colonies later for their outlays in accordance with the vigor of their actions. The amount of compensation actually paid by England to the colonies was equal to about two-fifths of the expenditures the colonies made. Spurred on by this appeal, as well as by the real menace of the French and Indian attacks, the New England colonies strongly supported the war; in New York and Pennsylvania, however, quarrels between governor and legislature prevented anything like adequate support; Virginia did only fairly well, and most of the other colonies scarcely participated at all.

The British Victory. William Pitt's vigorous prosecution of the war in the end turned the tide of battle in favor of the English all around the world. Abler and younger officers were dispatched to America to replace those proven to be incompetent. Their communications cut by a British victory on the shores of Lake Ontario, the French abandoned Fort Duquesne, which was quickly occupied by the British under General Forbes. The crowning event of the war came the next year when Admiral Saunders and General Wolfe successfully advanced up the St. Lawrence and forced General Montcalm to fight a decisive battle (September 19, 1759) on the Plains of Abraham overlooking Quebec. Both Wolfe and Montcalm lost their lives as a result of the battle, but the English victory was complete. Next year Montreal surrendered to Lord Jeffery Amherst and Canada was secured for the English crown.

Other spectacular victories for the British, in the West Indies and in the Orient, and the success of their Prussian ally in Europe emphasized the decisiveness of the French defeat.

By 1763 the French gave up the struggle and signed the humiliating Peace of Paris. Canada and all the French possessions east of the Mississippi River, most of the French stations in India, and some of the French West Indies were ceded to England. Some of the English leaders would have been willing to return Canada to France in exchange for a cleaner sweep of the rich sugar islands of the French West Indies. From the Spanish, who had entered the war on the French side in 1761, the British demanded and received Florida. This Spanish loss was made good by the cession of Louisiana and the Isle of Orleans from France to Spain; and thus the French possessions on the continent of North America were entirely wiped out.

In bringing about this happy solution of

THE DEATH OF GENERAL WOLFE

This painting by Benjamin West in 1771, set a pattern for romantic historical painting that influenced American artists for many generations to come. From an engraving of the original.

their difficulties with New France the colonies had played a considerable part; and yet to Englishmen it seemed that the Americans had done far less than their duty. They had depended upon British regulars when colonial levies might well have been materially increased; they refused to unite for their common defense; and they had been guilty of almost wholesale trade with the French, which had appreciably prolonged the war.

The Proclamation Line. Early in 1763 a violent outbreak against British rule by the pro-French Indians of the northwestern frontier, known as Pontiac's Conspiracy, led the British authorities to issue the Proclamation of 1763, which forbade colonial settlement beyond the sources of the rivers flowing into the Atlantic. The colonists were outraged, since the opening of the transmountain region to settlement seemed to them to have been the principal reason that the war had been fought. Furthermore, the

JEFFERY AMHERST

General Amherst (after 1776 Baron Amherst) commanded the British expedition that took Louisburg in 1758. Later, as commander of all the British forces in the American theater, he brought the war to a successful conclusion.

69

Proclamation utterly ignored the western land claims of those seaboard colonies whose original charters had contained "sea to sea" grants. However, it soon became apparent that the British government had no intention of forever withholding the region west of the Proclamation Line from settlement. In 1764 two strong expeditions were dispatched into the Indian country. As a result, Pontiac and his allies were defeated and in July, 1766, at Oswego, Pontiac agreed with Sir William Johnson to a treaty of peace. Other treaties with the Iroquois and the Cherokees gave the English title to a wide strip of land west of the mountains. Probably the government hoped to establish a neutral zone from which both whites and Indians should be temporarily excluded. But that some of the lands so acquired would be opened to new settlement was clear from the official support given a project which contemplated the creation of a new colony to be known as Vandalia. For this purpose a British-American syndicate was formed and much pressure was brought upon the Board of Trade to agree to the necessary land grant. After considerable dissension a patent was granted to the petitioners which would have handed over to them most of what is now West Virginia and eastern Kentucky. But by the time consent to this grant had been won, the American Revolution had started and the project lapsed.

The Upper Ohio Frontier. Nevertheless, the settlement of the Vandalia region had already begun. Even before the French and Indian War thousands of pioneers had ventured into the eastern part of this district, and although most of them had been compelled to leave during the war, many promptly returned as it came to an end. With the help of Braddock's road from Fort Cumberland to the Ohio and the road Forbes had cut through Pennsylvania to Fort Pitt (the British name for Fort Duquesne), migration into the upper Ohio region was made relatively easy. As early as 1767 permanent settlements in the upper

Ohio and its tributaries had appeared, and before the revolution broke out both Pittsburgh and Wheeling were sizable villages.

The Watauga Settlements. During these years other irregular settlements were being made beyond the crest of the mountains farther to the south. In 1769 pioneers from Virginia pushed southwestward across the watershed into the Watauga Valley, which they supposed to be within the limits of Virginia, although actually it was a part of North Carolina. Two years later they were joined by a number of "Regulators" from the back country of North Carolina, who were compelled to seek safety in flight because of an unsuccessful revolt they had waged against the domination of the colony by the eastern propertied class. Two resolute and resourceful Virginians, James Robertson and John Sevier, furnished the little settlement with effective leadership. When the Wataugans found themselves practically without a government, they adopted "Articles of Association" as a basis for self-government and through a convention of thirteen delegates chose a court of five members to rule the community. The Watauga Association lasted until 1778.

Kentucky. In 1774 the punitive Lord Dunsmore's War again taught the Indians the futility of trying to stay the white man's advance across the mountains, and paved the way for the settlement of Kentucky. That same year Judge Richard Henderson of North Carolina formed the Transylvania Company, and purchased from the Cherokees their claim to the region between the Kentucky and Cumberland rivers. To promote settlement he sent Daniel Boone, a frontier hunter who had visited Kentucky as early as 1769, to cut a road through from the back country of North Carolina to the bluegrass region. By April, 1775, Boone's party of thirty men had cleared their "Wilderness Road" from the Holston River through Cumberland Gap to the Kentucky River, and had begun the settlement of Boonesborough. Nearby at Harrodsburg other settlers, led by James Harrod of Pennsylvania, were already on hand, and the Kentucky pioneers were soon numbered by the hundreds. Henderson tried to organize a government for "Transylvania," as he proposed to call the colony, and held a convention of delegates for the purpose. But his land title was defective and he failed to obtain recognition of his claims, either from the British government or from the American Continental Congress. In December 1776, the Virginia legislature recognized Kentucky as a county of Virginia.

The impunity with which the English colonists pushed their settlements across the mountains in complete disregard of the Proclamation Line is only one of the many indications that they had come to think of themselves as almost entirely independent. They obeyed only such British restrictions on their trade as they cared to recognize. They magnified their governmental privileges at every opportunity, and did their best to minimize the role of British representatives in America. They helped in the war they themselves had made on the French only to such an extent as they cared to help. It should have been obvious to keen observers on both sides of the Atlantic that the attachment of the colonies to the mother country was in delicate balance, and any major changes in the existing relationship might endanger the unity of the empire.

SELECTED BIBLIOGRAPHY

Among the many treatises on various aspects of the English constitution, the following are particularly useful here: A. F. Pollard, *The Evolution of Parliament* (1920); C. H. McIlwain, *The High Court of Parliament and its Supremacy* (1910); and Wallace Notestein, *The Winning of the Initiative by the House of Commons* (1924). H. L. Osgood, *The American Colonies in the Eighteenth Century* (4 vols., 1924–1925), is richly detailed. Merrill Jensen has edited a superb documentary collection, *American Colonial Documents to 1776* (1955). L. W. Labaree, *Royal Government in America* (1930), may now be supplemented by J. P. Greene, *The Quest for Power* (1963). Useful monographs on certain aspects of colonial government include: Ella Lonn, *The Colonial Agents of the Southern Colonies* (1945); R. B. Morris, *Studies in the History of American Law* (1930); G. L. Chumbley, *Colonial Justice in Virginia* (1938); and E. S. Griffith, *History of American City Government: The Colonial Period* (1938). An important monograph is Gilman Ostrander, *The Rights of Man in America, 1606–1861* (1960).

Many of the works listed in earlier bibliographies treat the political and constitutional developments within the colonies. On New England see the following works: G. L. Haskins, *Law and Authority in Early Massachusetts* (1960); J. A. Schutz, *William Shirley* (1961); and Oscar Zeichner, *Connecticut's Years of Controversy, 1750–1776* (1949). Important monographs on Middle Colony politics include L. H. Leder, *Robert Livingston, 1654–1728* (1961); Irving Mark, *Agrarian Conflicts in Colonial New York, 1711–1775* (1940); and Theodore Thayer, *Pennsylvania Politics and the Growth of Democracy, 1740–1776* (1953). Politics in the colonial South are treated in W. E. Dodd, *The Old South: Struggles for Democracy* (1937); D. M. Owings, *His Lordship's Patronage: Offices of Profit in Colonial Maryland* (1953); C. S. Sydnor, *Gentlemen Freeholders; Political Practices in Washington's Virginia* (1952); T. J. Wertenbaker, *Give Me Liberty: The Struggle for Self-Government in Virginia* (1958); and W. W. Abbott, *The Royal Governors of Georgia, 1754–1775* (1959).

On the crucial subject of the relations between the mother country and the colonies, the leading authority is G. L. Beer, whose *The Commercial Policy of England toward the American Colonies* (1893) opens a series which includes also: *The Old Colonial System, 1660–1754* (1912); and *British Colonial Policy, 1754–1765* (1907). Another significant old monograph is C. M. Andrews, *British Committees, Commissions, and Councils of Trade and Plantations, 1622–1675* (1908). R. L.

* Available in paperback

Schuyler, *Parliament and the British Empire* (1929), represents an effort to put an old problem in new perspective. An important new work is D. M. Clark, *The Rise of the British Treasury* (1960). See also L. B. Namier and John Brooke, *Charles Townshend* (1965).

The senior imperial historian of today is L. H. Gipson, whose great work, *The British Empire before the American Revolution* (12 vols., 1936 —) is now close to completion. Gipson handles his details meticulously, while keeping his whole work in perspective; the result is masterful history. L. A. Harper, *The English Navigation Laws* (1939), is an influential revisionist work. Abortive efforts at "reform" are treated in M. G. Hall, *Edward Randolph and the American Colonies, 1676–1703* (1960). C. P. Nettels, *The Money Supply of the American Colonies before 1720* (1934), is an excellent treatment of a vital subject.

The great historian of New France was Francis Parkman (1823–1893), whose *France and England in North America* (9 vols., 1865–1892) remains the starting-point for all seriously interested in the subject. Parkman's works, based upon multi-archival research, have real literary distinction. Several individual volumes are now readily available to the student, including *Discovery of the Great West: La Salle;* *The Jesuits in North America;* *A Half-Century of Conflict;* and *The Conspiracy of Pontiac.* An excellent sampler is *The Parkman Reader,* edited by S. E. Morison (1955). The activities of the French missionaries who played so large a part in the early history of New France are reported in great detail in *The Jesuit Relations, 1610–1791,* edited by R. G. Thwaites (73 vols., 1896–1901).

R. G. Thwaites, *France in America, 1497–1763* (1905), is a useful summary by a leading American scholar. G. M. Wrong, *The Rise and Fall of New France* (2 vols., 1928), should be supplemented by Gustave Lanctot, *A History of Canada . . . to 1663* (1963). Other useful accounts include H. I. Priestley, *France Overseas through the Old Regime* (1939); G. L. Nute, *Caesars of the Wilderness* (1943); L. P. Kellogg, *The French Régime in Wisconsin and the Northwest* (1925); and W. B. Munro, *The Seigneurs of Old Canada* (1941). H. H. Peckham, *Pontiac and the Indian Uprising* (1947), restudies to good advantage the famous Indian uprising; and H. A. Innis, *The Fur Trade in Canada* (2nd ed., 1956), is an

excellent general account. Recent important works include W. J. Eccles, *Frontenac* (1959).

On the British side, C. W. Alvord, *The Mississippi Valley in British Politics* (2 vols., 1917), has long been a standard work. But see also J. M. Sosin, *Whitehall and the Wilderness, 1760–1775* (1961). Studies of individual parts of the Middle West in this period include: C. W. Alvord, *The Illinois Country, 1673–1818* (1920); L. P. Kellogg, *The British Régime in Wisconsin and the Northwest* (1935); and N. V. Russell, *The British Régime in Michigan and the Old Northwest* (1939). A major work is T. P. Abernethy, *Western Lands and the American Revolution* (1937). Recent military studies include E. P. Hamilton, *The French and Indian Wars* (1962); and H. H. Peckham, *The Colonial Wars, 1689–1762* (1964). Washington's early exploits are treated in detail in the first three volumes of the monumental work of D. S. Freeman, *George Washington* (7 vols., 1948–1957); and in C. H. Ambler, *George Washington and the West* (1936). Maritime problems are explored in two interesting works by Richard Pares: *War and Trade in the West Indies, 1739–1763* (1936); and *Colonial Blockade and Neutral Rights, 1739–1763* (1938). Max Savelle, *The Diplomatic History of the Canadian Boundary, 1749–1763* (1940), is an admirable study by a leading historian. An important special study is J. J. Malone, *Pine Trees and Politics* (1964).

On American expansion into the West, see J. A. Caruso, *The Appalachian Frontier; America's First Surge Westward* (1959). Theodore Roosevelt, *The Winning of the West* (4 vols., 1889–1896), grasps the spirit of the frontier advance; a single-volume abridgement is available in paperback. R. G. Thwaites, *Daniel Boone* (1902), is the best biography. A durable classic now readily available is John Filson, *The Discovery, Settlement and Present State of Kentucke* (1784). Notable biographies include C. G. Talbert, *Benjamin Logan, Kentucky Frontiersman* (1962); N. B. Wainwright, *George Croghan* (1959); K. P. Bailey, *Thomas Cresap* (1944); and J. R. Alden, *John Stuart and the Southern Colonial Frontier* (1944). Important monographs include W. S. Lester, *The Transylvania Colony* (1935); and D. H. Corkran, *The Cherokee Frontier, 1740–1762* (1962). Great classics are L. H. Morgan, *League of the Iroquois* (2 vols., 1851); and Cadwallader Colden, *History of the Five Indian Nations* (1866).

5

THE AMERICAN REVOLUTION

On both sides of the Atlantic there were those who mistakenly believed that the expulsion of the French from North America would draw England and her colonies into a closer unity. Many Englishmen, looking back over the critical world struggle with the French, felt that the ties of the Empire needed to be greatly strengthened. British officials denounced freely the hesitancy with which many Americans supported a war fought in their defense. Americans freely criticized the British conduct of the war and denounced the Proclamation Line. The colonies, with the French menace removed, saw little reason to submit to further British interference in their affairs. With the war won and the French ousted, why should the colonials trouble further about conciliating the British? Instead of promoting unity, the French and Indian War in reality paved the way for the American Revolution.

The Grenville Reforms. When the war ended it fell to the lot of George Grenville to deal with the colonies. Grenville had long been a member of the Cabinet, but in April, 1763, as Chancellor of the Exchequer, he became its head. He was a mediocre man of great obstinacy who made a fetish of efficiency. Incensed by the evasions of the tariff laws, he relentlessly prosecuted smugglers and, to avoid colonial juries, authorized their trial by admiralty courts, whose verdicts could be rendered without a jury. He pushed through Parliament the Sugar Act of 1764, which substituted for the unenforceable duties of the Molasses Act of 1733 new and more reasonable rates that were meant to be collected. He also induced Parliament to pass a Currency Act which placed restrictions upon the use of paper money in the colonies, a particularly serious blow to debtor communities who were trying to solve their currency problem in spite of an inadequate supply of hard money.

The Stamp Act. But the most objectionable of the Grenville measures to the Americans was the Stamp Act of 1765, which was devised to make them pay a part of the cost involved in protecting their western frontier from Indian attacks. Since, according to Grenville, colonial troops had been found unreliable in the French and Indian War, a permanent British garrison of 10,000 regulars should be stationed in America. The British officials also thought it only reasonable that the Americans themselves should pay about

PATRICK HENRY

A fiery militant during the decade of controversy that preceded the American Revolution, Patrick Henry played a leading role in persuading the American colonials to resist British tyranny. The likeness is from an engraving of the original painting by Alonzo Chappel.

one-third of the £300,000 that this service would cost. Estimating that about £45,000 of the American contribution would come from the new duties under the Sugar Act, the ministers planned to raise the remainder by a stamp tax levied upon newspapers and upon the various official and legal documents through which colonial business was transacted.

Colonial Opposition. It took some time for American sentiment on the Grenville acts to crystallize, but the reaction, when it came, was forthright. Grenville's program seemed admirably designed to cripple in the most effective manner the economic life of the colonies.

The colonies were poor, and the debts that some of them had incurred during the French and Indian War seemed heavy.

Yet this was the time the English government selected to impede their westward movement, restrict their trade, remodel their monetary system, and tax them for a protection that they did not want and thought they did not need. The most vulnerable part of the Grenville program, and that which drew the heaviest fire, was the Stamp Act. From the colonial point of view, this was a clear case of taxation without representation. So Patrick Henry, in his famous speech, argued in the Virginia House of Burgesses, and so the Virginia Resolutions, which he supported, plainly stated. Some colonists were willing to admit that external taxes in the shape of duties on imports might legally be levied on the colonies by Parliament in the course of regulating imperial trade. But most Americans believed that in imposing internal taxation without the direct sanction of popular representatives the British Parliament had clearly exceeded its authority and its right.

The Stamp Act Congress. Some of the northern merchants agreed that they would cease importations from England as long as the law held, and the General Court of Massachusetts sent out a circular letter inviting all the colonies to participate in a protest conference at New York in October. With nine colonies represented, the Stamp Act Congress agreed that the only persons who might legally represent the colonies were those "chosen therein by themselves." Since not a single American sat in the British Parliament, that body was wholly without authority to enact such a measure as the Stamp Act. Further, the Congress denounced the use of admiralty courts as a device to circumvent trial by jury and bitterly denounced restrictions on colonial commerce. Thus led, the American public defiantly refused to buy the offensive stamps and began also to discriminate against British-made goods. Non-importation agreements multiplied, and English merchants suffered great loss of trade.

Faced by both colonial and domestic protests, there seemed nothing for the British government to do but back down. While some Englishmen agreed with William Pitt, who felt free to "rejoice that America has resisted," the surrender of Parliament was occasioned less by the American arguments than by political and economic expediency. Most Englishmen, themselves accustomed to an inequitable system of representation, accepted the argument advanced by Lord Justice Mansfield that the colonists had "virtual representation" in Parliament, although they directly elected not a single member. When repeal was finally accomplished (1766), it was accompanied by a Declaratory Act which stated that the King and Parliament had "full power and authority" to legislate for the colonies "in all cases whatsoever."

The repeal of the Stamp Act was received with much enthusiasm in America, and the menacing portent of the Declaratory Act was scarcely noted. Loyalty to the mother country ran high, and only a little tact might have avoided further dissension. But unfortunate circumstances told heavily against the preservation of good relations. George III hoped to acquire great personal power and by every means at his disposal added to the number of the "King's friends" in Parliament. On the subject of America the King was both ignorant and prejudiced. The illness of William Pitt (now the Earl of Chatham) deprived the government of its only outstanding leader and left each minister free to do about as he pleased within his own domain. The result so far as America was concerned was one blunder after another. The Chancellor of the Exchequer, Charles Townshend, to whom fell the task of finding adequate revenue, was distinctly hostile to the colonies. He continued the unpopular war that Grenville had begun against the smugglers, and he formally authorized the use of writs of assistance, or general search warrants, which did not require that the premises to be searched be specifically mentioned.

The Townshend Duty Act. Townshend also proposed to raise a revenue from the colonies by an act imposing duties upon all tea, paper, glass, painters' colors, and lead to enter American ports. Ostensibly, the Townshend Duty Act was a strictly external tax; but the preamble stated that the law was designed to raise revenue rather than to regulate trade, and that the revenue so obtained might be used at the discretion of the government to pay the salaries of colonial governors and colonial judges. In reality, however, the law was a direct challenge to the American theory of taxation and to the colonial practice of disciplining

GEORGE III

Succeeding to the British throne in 1760, George III sought with great temporary success to enhance his influence over Parliament. He had no sympathy with the rebellious Americans and did all he could to bring about their defeat. Their victory greatly lessened his power in the government, and led him twice to consider abdication.

governors and judges by withholding salaries. Townshend died soon after the acts that bore his name were passed, but his successor, Lord North, attempted for three years to enforce them.

The hated Townshend Acts did much to inflame public opinion in America. Besides the new duties, they included a law suspending the New York legislature, and another creating a Board of Commissioners of Customs to be located at Boston with ample authority to enforce the Navigation Acts. The threat to self-government implicit in the attack on the New York legislature was deeply resented throughout the colonies, while the colonial merchants believed that rigorous enforcement of the long-neglected Navigation Acts would ruin them. The Duty Act was denounced generally as an unwarranted and unconstitutional measure. Many agreed with John Dickinson of Pennsylvania, whose *Letters from a Farmer in Pennsylvania* were widely read, that an external tax designed primarily to raise a revenue was no less an instance of taxation without representation than an internal tax such as the Stamp Act had been. Others held that all legislation by the British Parliament for America was unconstitutional. For the slogan, "No taxation without representation," these extremists would substitute the slogan, "No legislation without representation."

Samuel Adams. It fell to Samuel Adams (1722–1803), the astute leader of the popular party in the Massachusetts legislature, to lead the colonial assault upon the Townshend Acts. Under his guidance all classes of malcontents were united in opposition to the Duty Act. He cleverly maintained that the British constitution, like the constitutions of all free peoples, was "fixed in the law of Nature and of God," and that "neither the supreme legislature nor the supreme executive" could alter it. In a *Circular Letter,* which he drafted, all the colonial assemblies were invited to join with Massachusetts in resisting the policies of the British government. Soon legislative halls throughout the colonies began to ring with resolutions supporting the position of Massachusetts.

Non-importation agreements. Once more non-importation agreements were entered into by the merchants of the leading cities, a program that many southern colonies also chose to adopt. British trade began to fall off; British merchants began to protest; and the British government had little choice but to back down once again. Moreover, time had demonstrated that it cost more to collect the Townshend duties than the amount of revenue they brought in. Accordingly in March, 1770, Lord North moved the repeal of the duties except the tax on tea "to keep up the right." On this very same day the "Boston Massacre" proved conclusively the wisdom of the British retreat. Their nerves rubbed raw by the constant harassment of the local citizens, and goaded to desperation by the conduct of a mob of jeering men and boys, a few British soldiers from the two regiments then stationed in Boston had opened fire, killing five Americans. John Adams, a young lawyer distantly related to Samuel Adams, acted as counsel for the British in the trial that followed. The British officer in command, unfairly accused of giving the order to fire, was acquitted, but two of the men were given light sentences for manslaughter.

Good Relations Restored. The news that the Townshend duties had been repealed tended once more to restore harmony between the colonies and Great Britain. Non-importation agreements were either rescinded or reduced in scope to oppose merely the importation of tea from England. The fact that the British government had not backed down on the right of Parliament to tax the colonies troubled very few, for in practice the British attempt to tax the colonies had failed. It would not be correct to say, however, that the fires of discontent had gone out; they were merely burning low. In June, 1772, a mob of colonists overpowered the crew of the *Gaspee,* a British revenue cutter grounded on the Rhode Island coast, and burned the vessel. That same year Samuel Adams organized "committees of correspondence" throughout the colony to inform one another of the current state of affairs. Soon, at the instigation of back-country militants in the Virginia House of Burgesses, intercolonial committees of correspondence were also established.

The Tea Act. At this point the British government made one of its worst blunders. In May, 1773, to help out the East India Company, which had an oversupply of tea on hand, it agreed to remit the twelve-pence-a-pound duty charged on all tea imported into England, and to allow the tea to be reshipped to America, where the duty would be only three pence. It was hoped that the Americans would be willing to buy the tea at the exceptionally low price for which it could be sold, a price lower than they were accustomed to pay for smuggled Dutch tea. However, the Tea Act was extremely annoying to colonial merchants who had grown rich from smuggling, and it gave the agents of the company a monopoly on the sale of tea. It furnished Adams and his following with a new and attractive grievance. Confronted with opposition to their landing, the ships sent to New York and Philadelphia returned to England with their cargoes intact. Tea landed at Charleston remained unsold and was long stored in government warehouses. At Boston, on December 16, 1773, fifty or sixty men, faintly disguised as Indians, boarded the ships and threw the tea into the harbor, while some months later, at Annapolis, another tea-ship was burned.

The Intolerable Acts. The Boston Tea Party was regarded by nearly all English-

BOSTONIANS PAYING THE EXCISE MAN

By such irregular — even brutal — methods as the one here portrayed the colonists emphasized their objection to taxation without representation.

men as an outrage. Why Americans should refuse to buy tea for even less than Englishmen could buy it was beyond comprehension. Moreover, the seizure of the tea was an outright attack upon the private property of the greatest trading company of the day. With full public approval Parliament early in 1774 passed five measures, usually called by the Americans the "Intolerable Acts." One act ordered that the port of Boston should be closed to all commerce until the tea destroyed had been paid for. Another reformed the government of Massachusetts by increasing the power of the governor, by making the council appointive instead of elective, and by suppressing town meetings except as the governor might permit. Another measure enabled royal officials who were accused of capital offenses in Massachusetts to be sent for trial to England or to another colony whenever, in the opinion of the governor, a fair trial in the local courts would be difficult to secure. The Quartering Act authorized colonial governors to requisition such buildings as might be needed for the use of royal troops stationed within the boundaries of a given colony.

The Quebec Act. The Quebec Act, which to the Americans seemed quite as "intolerable" as any of the rest, was not designed by the British government as a punitive measure. It was based upon several years' experience in attempting to govern Canada, and showed a spirit of accommodation toward the French subjects of Great Britain that was all too rarely in evidence when the British government dealt with its English colonists. The French, unaccustomed to participation in the affairs of government, were given the kind of government they could understand. French rather than English legal traditions were authorized in the trial of civil suits; and Roman Catholicism, the religion of the *habitants,* was accorded full recognition. Also, in complete disregard of the western land claims of the seaboard colonies, the boundaries of Quebec were extended to include the territory south to the Ohio River and west to the Mississippi.

These five measures at once aroused the spirit of resistance in America. Four regiments of troops under General Thomas Gage, the British commander-in-chief and newly appointed Governor of Massachusetts, appeared in Boston, and apprehension was rife in other colonies lest they suffer the same suppression of their liberties that Parliament had decreed for Massachusetts. The Quebec Act was interpreted as threatening the English-speaking colonies with an end to self-government, a limitation of the colonists' legal rights as Englishmen, and the encouragement of Roman Catholicism. Small wonder that the network of committees of correspondence began to function, and that Massachusetts was speedily assured of sympathy and support from the growing anti-British element throughout the colonies. A Virginia resolution called upon all the colonies to send delegates to a Continental Congress, to meet in Philadelphia the following September, and the militants everywhere took into their own hands the selection of these delegates. In most colonies provincial assemblies were also elected.

Militants vs. Moderates. The years of controversy with Britain had divided colonial society more or less definitely into two schools of thought. The militants were determined never to yield to the British pretensions. They meant to stand firmly by the rights Americans had traditionally enjoyed and to gain new rights if they could. But the moderates, who saw the great benefits of British trade and protection, favored conciliation. In general the lower and middle classes inclined more toward the militant point of view, while the upper classes were moderate. There were, however, numerous deviations from this division, and the war cannot be viewed as a class struggle. Many rich colonial merchants, outraged by the tax policies of the British government, were willing to make common cause with the militants. So also were the bulk of great planters, intense individualists who regarded with extreme disfavor both the regulations of the British government and their own embarrassing indebtedness to British merchants. Class lines were still further shifted by the fact that to many Americans, particularly those of the interior and the back country, "home rule" was of rather less consequence than "who should rule at home." In New England and some of the Middle Colonies, revolt against English control and revolt against the local governing aristocracy were practically one and the same, for local governors were often themselves appointees of the Crown. In Virginia, back-country farmers and tidewater planters postponed their local differences to make common cause against the more pressing dangers of British misrule. But in the Carolinas many pioneer farmers generally took the British side, for they could see little good in a cause supported by so many tidewater aristocrats.

First Continental Congress. The First Continental Congress, which opened in Philadelphia on September 4, 1774, was attended by fifty-six delegates representing every colony except Georgia, where anti-British sentiment had been slow to develop. Although the militants were clearly in the majority, a plan of compromise proposed by Joseph Galloway of Pennsylvania came within one vote of adoption. It would have created a grand council of delegates, chosen by the various colonial assemblies, to deal with imperial relations, subject to the veto of a president-general appointed by the crown. Regulations touching America would have required the consent of both the British Parliament and the colonial council. But the militants, although professing their loyalty to the British crown, preferred instead to push through a Declaration of Rights and Grievances, which stated the case against taxation without representation, and demanded the repeal of the Intolerable Acts. The delegates set up a "Continental Association" designed to prevent the importation of all British goods. Local committees, to be popularly elected, were charged with the enforcement of this measure, and after the lapse of a year a second Continental Congress was to meet and observe the progress of events. These actions were essentially revolutionary; to the British they were rebellious. Without any constitutional authority whatever, the First Continental Congress had passed a law and provided the means for its enforcement. Even so, only a minority of voices in the Congress spoke out for independence.

The Association proved to be highly effective. In nearly every colony radical committees resorted to such acts of violence as tarring and feathering to secure obedience to the regulations of the Congress. Spokesmen for the militants urged also with some success that home industries be patronized and that militia companies be formed and munitions of war collected. These measures had much the same effect upon British opinion that Americans had

learned by previous experience to expect. Edmund Burke and other Whigs urged that the various repressive acts be repealed, while British merchants, who had lost heavily by the American boycott, petitioned Parliament to conciliate the Americans and reopen trade. But this time the ministry, strongly supported by the King and by a majority in Parliament, refused to yield to the clamor and voted instead to send more troops to America.

Meantime party lines in America became more and more definite. For some time, however, even the militants were not precisely of one mind. All were agreed that no concessions should be made to the British point of view, but the more moderate viewed with some misgivings the military preparations under way. Some moderates thought that peaceful resistance might well be continued in the hope of ultimate success; others were eager for conciliation and compromise. Most moderates, like some militants, were against the use of outright force, not only from principle, but because they were afraid that once force was used the control of the movement might drift into the hands of the extreme militants,

A PATRIOT BROADSIDE

The First Continental Congress was composed of delegates chosen by provincial congresses, or by popular conventions called together by broadsides.

ADVERTISEMENT.

THE Committee of Correspondence in New-York, having on Monday Night last proceeded to the Nomination of five Persons to go as Delegates for the said City and County, on the proposed General Congress at Philadelphia, on the 1st of September next; the five following Persons were nominated for that Purpose,

Philip Livingston,
James Duane,
John Alsop,
John Jay,
Isaac Low.

The Inhabitants, therefore, of this City and County, are requested to meet at the City-Hall, on THURSDAY next, at 12 o'Clock, in order to approve of the said five Persons as Delegates, or to choose such other in their Stead, as to their Wisdom shall seem meet.

By Order of the Committee,

ISAAC LOW, CHAIRMAN.

TUESDAY, 5th July, 1774.

BOSTON

CHARLES TOWN

whom they regarded as demagogic radicals. Those who preferred the British connection to anything that resistance to the mother country had to offer became the "Tories" or "Loyalists" of the American Revolution. Other conservatives gradually drifted over to the militants, and finally joined them as "Whigs" or "Patriots" to take up arms and to win independence. Doubtless a minority in the beginning, the militants through their effective organization and aggressive tactics ultimately won over a majority to their way of thinking. John Adams was to estimate, however, that one-third of the population were Whigs, another one-third Tories, and the final third remained neutral.

Lexington and Concord. Colonial resistance was at its stiffest in Massachusetts. Minutemen, reacting to British pressure, drilled openly and collected munitions with which to defend themselves. Neither side wished to precipitate hostilities, but finally General Gage felt obliged to seize the military supplies that had been accumulated at Concord. For this purpose a small

detachment of British troops left Boston on the night of April 18, 1775. Through the activity of Paul Revere and others the whole countryside was aroused. At Lexington the British felt obliged to disperse by force a small detachment of militia drawn up to oppose them. They then marched on to Concord and destroyed the American supplies. When they retired back toward Boston, however, the "redcoats" were fired upon by farmers and militiamen from the roadsides so effectively that their march became a humiliating rout. Greatly heartened, armed militiamen from all over New England collected around Boston to lay siege to the city.

On May 10, 1775, the Second Continental Congress began its sessions at Philadelphia. It was a far more militant body than its predecessor. Although enough moderates were present to induce the delegates to appeal once more to the King for a redress of grievances, the tide of revolt could not be stemmed for long. On June 15 Congress, at the solicitation of Massachusetts, constituted the troops gathered near Boston as

THE BATTLE OF BUNKER HILL

Actually fought on Breed's Hill, this sharp action between entrenched American militiamen and advancing British regulars resulted in heavy casualties among the latter until the colonials, their ammunition exhausted, were forced to retreat.

. . . it was resolved to force General Gage to an action; with this view it was determined to seize possession of the height on the peninsula of Charles-Town, which General Gage had occupied . . . and erect some batteries on Banhin-hill (Bunker Hill), to batter down the town and General Gage's camp on the common and his entrenchment on Boston neck (which you know is only about three fourths of a mile across); . . . When the enemy were landed, to the number of 2500 . . . they marched to engage 3000 provincials, arrayed in red worsted caps and blue great coats, with guns of different sizes, few of which had bayonets, ill-served artillery, but of invincible courage! The fire from the ships and artillery of the enemy was horrid and amazing; the first onset of the soldiers was bold and fierce, but they were received with equal courage; . . . The King's troops . . . made their push against Charles-Town, which was then set on fire by them, our right flank being then uncovered, two floating batteries coming in by the mill dam to take us in the rear, more troops coming from Boston, and our ammunition being almost expended, General Putnam ordered the troops . . . to retreat . . .

Letters on the American Revolution 1774–1776, edited by Margaret Wheeler Willard (1925), Houghton Mifflin Company

---

the Continental Army, and assumed authority for the direction of the war. At the suggestion of John Adams, command of all forces was given to George Washington. While this selection was designed in part to secure southern support, no wiser choice could have been made.

The First Year of Fighting. Washington was present in uniform as a delegate to the Congress from Virginia when he was chosen to head the army. He set out at once to join his command, but before he could complete his journey, another battle had been fought. On June 17, 1775, General Gage, reinforced to about 10,000 men, sent a detachment under General William Howe to drive the Americans from Bunker Hill (in reality Breed's Hill) overlooking Charlestown, only to be thrown back twice before the colonials, for lack of ammunition, were obliged to give way. Fortunately Fort Ticonderoga, on distant Lake Champlain, had fallen on May 10, 1775, to Ethan Allen and Benedict Arnold, thus providing the army with the necessary artillery to batter the enemy. Washington faced a difficult task in making an army out of his militiamen, and he was not ready to move until March, 1776. Then, with cannon dragged overland from Ticonderoga, he occupied Dorchester Heights, to the south of Boston, and trained his artillery on the city. General Howe, who had succeeded Gage in command, recognizing that he had been outmaneuvered, quickly embarked his troops, together with about 1,000 Loyalists, for Nova Scotia, and without bloodshed the Americans occupied the city. In November, 1775, colonial troops under Richard Montgomery had taken Montreal and then, bolstered by the troops Benedict Arnold had marched through the wilderness, attacked Quebec. But the assault, made December 31, 1775, was unsuccessful, and cost Montgomery his life. The French Canadians showed no inclination to help the Americans, the winter siege proved futile, and Montreal had to be abandoned. A British invasion force, which attacked both Wilmington and Charleston, met stiff resistance and had to withdraw.

Thus the first year of the war ended in a kind of stalemate, with the Americans repulsed in their effort to conquer Canada, and the British equally unable to secure a foothold anywhere in the colonies.

Movement for Independence. Nevertheless, American opinion during this period had by no means remained stationary. At the outbreak of hostilities the great majority thought of the conflict as merely an armed debate within the Empire. But the events of the year seemed to make an imperial settlement impossible. George III had rejected the American petition, apparently with the full consent of Parliament, and had even begun to hire German mercenaries — "Hessians" — to augment the British forces in America. Revolutionary governments had replaced the old colonial foundations. American trade with Great Britain was now completely cut off, and new outlets were desperately needed. Military help was needed also from the enemies of Great Britain, particularly France, and to get it Americans clearly must avow their independence. Under these circumstances public opinion veered sharply toward the militants who wished to sever all connections with the mother country and to transform the rebellion into a revolution. Such was the opinion stated by Thomas Paine in his widely circulated pamphlet, *Common Sense*, which made innumerable converts to the idea of independence.

Declaration of Independence. Congress was soon in a mood to respond to the shift in public opinion. On the seventh of June, 1776, Richard Henry Lee, acting on instructions from the Virginia Convention, moved "that these United Colonies are, and of right ought to be, free and independent states." Lee's resolution also contained the suggestion that foreign alliances be made and that a plan of confederation be drawn up. On July 2 every state except New York, whose provincial assembly gave its assent a week later, voted for independence. On this same day a committee headed by Thomas Jefferson reported its carefully drawn Declaration of Independence, which, after some minor amendments, was adopted July 4.

The Declaration of Independence, which was written almost entirely by Jefferson, borrowed heavily from Locke and asserted in already familiar terms the natural rights of men, including the right of revolution. It differed markedly from earlier protests in that it directed its attack primarily against the King rather than Parliament, for by this time the rebels were unwilling to concede that Parliament had any authority over the colonies. They even blamed the King for some of the offensive acts of Parliament and held that the long list of grievances they were able to recite constituted a kind of breach of contract on the part of the monarch which gave the colonies the right, if they chose, to become free and independent states. This justification of the right of revolution against an allegedly arbitrary king was well conceived to unite sentiment at home as well as to gain support among the English Whigs. But of equal importance was the radical social theory embedded in the preamble of the great document. For Jefferson's phrases demanding the equality of men, the right of every individual to life, liberty, and the pursuit of happiness, the protection of these rights against arbitrary power, and government by the consent of the governed, constituted a charter of human liberty which was nowhere accepted in the world of 1776. It was a program for which men could fight and die if necessary. Not only did the Declaration of Independence sustain Americans through the dark years of the Revolutionary War; but it immediately became — and has since remained — an instrument of almost incalculable influence upon the political thought of the western world.

Loyalists vs. Patriots. The appearance of unanimity which accompanied the Declaration quite belied the facts, for in the course of the next few years probably as many as 50,000 "Loyalists" joined with the British forces to fight against the "Patriots." Many saw their property destroyed or confiscated, they often suffered great personal violence, and they were driven by the thousands to take refuge in Canada, Florida, the West Indies, or England. It is also noteworthy that the thirteen separate state governments, although in full control of the Patriots, were themselves imperfectly united. The new states did indeed cooperate through Congress in a way they had never done before, but Congress was an extra-legal body, lacking in real authority, and often proved to be a debating society when what was needed was a powerful and efficient central war office.

The mother country was hardly more united than the rebellious colonies. The King's party, which commanded a majority in Parliament, strongly favored the war, but the opposition, long schooled in the tolerant doctrines of Burke and Chatham, were unenthusiastic at taking up arms against the Americans. Many Whigs even hoped to see the King discredited by failure in America; merchants desirous of retaining American trade were for peace at almost any price; and the common people showed their sentiments by refusing to enlist for fighting their kinsmen overseas. Furthermore, many of the King's friends were poor administrators, and British governmental incompetence often rivaled or surpassed that of the inexperienced Continental Congress.

Comparison of Armed Forces. In the comparison of armed forces the odds were heavily against the Americans. Washington rarely had as many as 16,000 men at any one time, and at Valley Forge his forces dwindled to two thousand effectives. Poor and uncertain pay together with inadequate supplies made it difficult to obtain enlistments. Local legislatures seldom filled their quotas in the Continental line, and placed a great reliance upon the state militia, who sometimes fought well in de-fending their own homes and firesides, but were otherwise exceedingly unreliable. To oppose these troops the British had a well-trained army of perhaps 60,000 men, most of whom were needed, however, on garrison duty somewhere in the far-flung empire. Shortages were made up by the employment of Hessians, Loyalists, and Indians. The British armies in America were well equipped, well fed, and more frequently adequate in numbers. They were backed also by strong naval power; but even so their superiority was not sufficient to enable them to win. The British soldiers operated 3,000 miles from home; their attack had to be delivered along a thousand miles of seacoast; and they were confronted, once they had penetrated into the interior, with a trackless wilderness, often short on forage and supplies, into which the Americans could melt at will.

Washington, The General. In military leadership, thanks mainly to the steadfast qualities of Washington, the Americans were more nearly equal to the British. By no means a military genius, and not even thoroughly versed in military tactics, Washington might have had great difficulty in commanding a large modern army. But whatever the limits of his ability, he proved equal to the emergency. His integrity, courage, and determination inspired his men with confidence and paved the way to ultimate victory. He was a master of the strategy of retreat and understood thoroughly that while he had an army in the field the Patriot cause was not lost. However, few of Washington's immediate subordinates were of comparable ability. Probably Nathanael Greene was the best of them, although he had had virtually no military experience before the war. The contributions of a number of European volunteers were highly creditable — particularly those of the German, Steuben, who as a drillmaster at Valley Forge whipped Washington's mob into a respectable fighting force, and of the youthful Frenchman, the Marquis de Lafayette,

GEORGE WASHINGTON

This portrait, painted from life by Charles Willson Peale in 1783, is thought to resemble Washington more than the better-known likenesses by Gilbert Stuart. Peale did more than a dozen portraits of Washington between 1772 and 1795.

whose lack of experience was overcome by his zeal for the Patriot cause and by his talent for battlefield leadership.

The British commanders were notably ineffective. Neither Sir William Howe, who was placed in command at the outset of the war, nor Sir Henry Clinton, who succeeded him, could be classified as first-rate, but even so both men might have done better than they did had they been given adequate support from England. Howe's lack of vigor was due to his penchant for procrastination while Clinton, hampered both by his inability to get along with his subordinates, and by lack of consistent naval support after the French entered the war, was unable to take full advantage of his opportunities. In technical knowledge the British commanders far outmatched the Americans, but the unusual character of the fighting in America sometimes turned this seeming advantage into a liability.

In the matter of finances the picture was one-sided. British gold was available at all times in America to purchase supplies for the British forces, while Washington usually had only paper money and promises with which to pay. Congress lacked the power to tax, and the millions of dollars in "continental currency" that it issued fell rapidly in value — by 1780 a continental dollar was worth only two cents in gold. State issues were only a little better. Robert Morris, upon whom Congress placed the chief burden of financing the war, was compelled to borrow upon his own personal credit. Haym Salomon, a Polish refugee, advanced specie and invested heavily in government securities, and thus lost his fortune.

After General Howe abandoned Boston, he decided to take New York, where by controlling the Hudson Valley he could separate New England from the rest of the colonies, and perhaps establish connections with Canada. With a formidable army — 25,000 British and 8,000 Hessians — he moved by sea late in the summer of 1776. Anticipating Howe's movements, Washington abandoned Boston and with some 18,000 men prepared to defend New York. In a series of battles, the well-trained British regulars soon routed the shaky Americans. Defeated on Long Island, August 27, 1776, Washington was barely able to escape with his army to Manhattan, and after the actions at Fort Washington, White Plains, and Harlem Heights, pulled his men back across to New Jersey. During the winter of 1776–1777 his army dwindled to some 3,000 men, and the Patriot cause seemed near collapse. Still Washington was twice able to defeat isolated British detachments, at Trenton on Christmas Eve night, where he captured most of the Hessian garrison, and at Princeton in January, where he inflicted a stinging defeat upon British troops under Lord Cornwallis.

The British Occupy Philadelphia. The year 1777 saw two major movements by the British: Howe's shift of his base from New

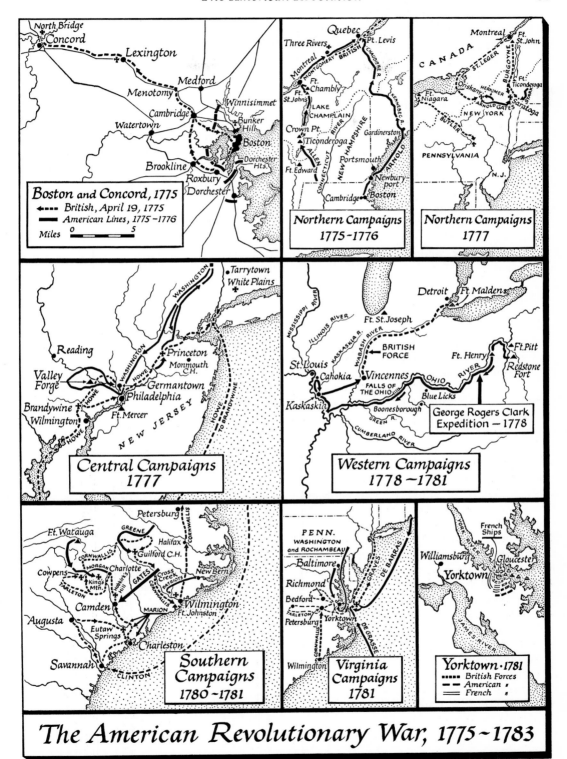

Boston and Concord, 1775
- - → British, April 19, 1775
─── American Lines, 1775–1776
Miles 0 5

Northern Campaigns 1775–1776

Northern Campaigns 1777

Central Campaigns 1777

Western Campaigns 1778–1781

George Rogers Clark Expedition – 1778

Southern Campaigns 1780–1781

Virginia Campaigns 1781

Yorktown · 1781
····· British Forces
- - - American
═══ French

The American Revolutionary War, 1775–1783

York to Philadelphia, and General Burgoyne's advance down the Lake Champlain-Hudson Valley route. Howe chose not to proceed directly overland against the rebel capital, but sent his troops most of the way by sea. After defeating Washington at Brandywine, Howe entered Philadelphia in September, 1777, and repulsed Washington's attack on his outpost at Germantown. The capture of the American capital was a serious blow to the Patriot pride, but of little real military importance. Howe has since been subject to much criticism on the grounds that he should instead have sent aid to Burgoyne, whose position was rapidly becoming desperate. With the American forces under General Horatio Gates swollen to unusual size by accretions from local militia, Burgoyne suffered a disastrous defeat near Saratoga, and on October 17, 1777, with his army of 5,800 men entirely surrounded, he surrendered. This was the first notable victory that either side had yet won, and it gave renewed hope to the faltering Patriot cause.

The French Alliance. The surrender of Burgoyne made possible the consummation of the greatly desired alliance with France. With the news of Burgoyne's defeat to support their argument, American agents led by Benjamin Franklin pressed successfully for an alliance. On February 6, 1778, a treaty was signed between France and the United States uniting the two countries in a military alliance to effect the independence of the United States. France agreed, when peace with England should be made, not to ask for additional territory on the mainland of North America, and the United States in turn promised to guarantee to France indefinitely the French West Indies. Neither party was to make peace without the full consent of the other. Thus the rebelling colonies won the support of Britain's traditional continental enemy, while Great Britain now faced the threat of a two-front war and even the possibility of invasion.

The value of the alliance to the American cause was enormous. French loans kept the American army intact, and French officers helped with its training. Above all, French sea power supplied a vital need. The exploits of John Paul Jones, whose *Bonhomme Richard* defeated the *Serapis* (September, 1779) in a famous naval battle, would have been impossible but for the backing of the French. Even though British superiority on the high seas was at no time fully overcome during the war, French fleets hampered the British movements of troops, threatened an attack on England that drew attention from America at critical times, and held the British fleet at bay during the later phases of the war.

Other Aid to America. The Franco-American alliance against Great Britain was in due time heavily reinforced. The entrance of France into the war practically assured the entrance of her ally, Spain. Secretly some financial aid was given the Americans before the outbreak of war between Spain and England in 1779; and after that event, the Spanish navy cooperated intermittently with the French. In 1781 the allies gained another recruit in Holland. Dutch sea power, together with the helpful loans that John Adams was able to negotiate, had much to do with the outcome of the war. Great Britain had also to deal with the "Armed Neutrality," a combination of nations effected in 1780 by Catherine II of Russia, which included Russia, Denmark, Sweden, Portugal, and Prussia, all of which were earnest opponents of the regulations which the British navy imposed upon neutral trade. Thus the British had to meet a powerful combination of nations which might at any time become still more powerful by the addition of new members.

Valley Forge. Meantime Washington, who held his army in winter quarters at Valley Forge, near Philadelphia, during the winter of 1777–1778, wondered how long resistance could be maintained. During these terrible months, the Patriot army almost vanished; for the handful of soldiers who remained the suffering and privations were incredible. But fortunately for the Patriots, Howe remained inactive in Philadelphia, and Washington's little army, in spite of its tribulations, managed to exist through the winter. The next spring the British government, visibly shaken by the French alliance, was ready to offer the Americans any terms short of independence, but Congress, inspired with the hope of victory, spurned suggestions that two years before would have been regarded as highly satisfactory.

The British Return to New York. Fearful of French naval power, the British government granted Howe's request to be relieved and replaced him with General Clinton. When 5,000 of his troops were ordered to the West Indies, Clinton was forced to abandon Philadelphia and concentrate his forces at New York. Accordingly, the British began a march across New Jersey, with Washington in close pursuit. At Monmouth, June 28, 1778, the Americans might have won a victory but for what Washington considered to be the "disobedience" of General Charles Lee. Clinton's army made good its retreat, and once more Washington's army stood guard

WASHINGTON AT MONMOUTH

This painting (1854), by Emanuel Leutze, shows Washington rallying the troops after rebuking General Charles Lee (on the white horse), whose order to retreat had precipitated the confusion. Behind Washington are Lafayette (hatless) and Alexander Hamilton. Leutze is also known for his Washington Crossing the Delaware.

SIR HENRY CLINTON

This British officer, who superseded General Howe in 1778, had served in America ever since Bunker Hill. Had Lee obeyed Washington's orders at Monmouth, Clinton's army might have suffered the same fate as Burgoyne's.

before New York. From this time on no major military movements took place in the North, although the British conducted many exasperating raids along the coast adjacent to their headquarters. Marauding bands of Tories and Indians also laid waste the northwestern frontier. In 1778 the Wyoming Valley of Pennsylvania and the Cherry Valley of New York were the scenes of terrible massacres; and well before that date constant fighting had brought the pioneer outposts in Kentucky to the verge of extinction.

George Rogers Clark. It was at this point that George Rogers Clark, a young Kentucky land speculator, obtained the support of Governor Patrick Henry of Virginia to organize a retaliatory expedition against Fort Detroit, then the British headquarters in the West. Clark realized that the old French towns in the Illinois country, although seemingly indifferent to the

outcome of the war, were actually breeding places for conspiracies of Indians and British. He planned to capture them, and if possible also the British post at Detroit. After much delay he succeeded in organizing a few hundred frontier militia, with which in the summer of 1778 he set out down the Ohio for the Illinois towns. From the mouth of the Cumberland he marched overland, and taking the inhabitants by surprise, he captured Kaskaskia and Cahokia without a blow. Vincennes, also, with the connivance of the French residents in the captured towns, readily accepted Clark's control.

News of these events greatly incensed Colonel Henry Hamilton, British commander at Detroit and Lieutenant-Governor of Canada, who determined to repossess the French towns. He succeeded without difficulty in retaking Vincennes, but he was surprised by Clark, who marched his troops overland through midwinter cold and ice to attack and capture Vincennes once again (February, 1779). Hamilton himself was sent as a prisoner to Virginia. This exploit greatly cheered the frontiersmen who detested Hamilton, since, as it was commonly reported, he had made presents to the Indians in return for American scalps. Clark never succeeded in capturing Detroit, but his action curbed the activities of the British and their Indian allies along the frontier, and probably saved the Kentucky settlements. In order to punish the Indians for their part in the Wyoming and Cherry Valley massacres of 1778, Washington sent a successful expedition under John Sullivan the following year into the Iroquois country. Thereafter, while frontier fighting did not cease, the menace from this quarter was distinctly lessened.

From 1778 to the close of the war practically all other important fighting took place in the South. In this region were many Loyalists whose services the British wished to enlist. Late in 1778 Clinton dispatched an expedition by sea which captured Savannah, and with the aid of troops from Florida, the whole of Georgia. In May, 1780, the British took Charleston, making prisoners of practically the entire southern army of General Benjamin Lincoln. When Horatio Gates, Lincoln's successor was defeated by Cornwallis at Camden (August 16, 1780), South Carolina, like Georgia, seemed lost to the enemy, but Patriot bands under such partisan leaders as Thomas Sumter, Francis Marion, and Andrew Pickens constantly harassed the invaders and seriously impeded their movements. The British met their first major reverse in the South when a force under Major Patrick Ferguson, whom Cornwallis had sent through the back-country to recruit Loyalists and protect his left flank on a proposed invasion of North Carolina, was annihilated at King's Mountain in October, 1780, by Wataugans who had swarmed across the mountains to defend their homes. Nathanael Greene now replaced Gates as commanding general in the southern department. After Daniel Morgan's defeat of Banastre Tarleton at the Cowpens, Cornwallis, who had planned an invasion of North Carolina, began a premature pursuit of the forces of Greene and Morgan, and soon saw his army reduced by a costly victory at Guilford Courthouse. In order to bolster his forces, Cornwallis now marched north to make a junction with other British troops in Virginia.

Benedict Arnold. During these gloomy days, when most of the news from the South was bad, Washington's army stood watch over Clinton around New York. With American morale almost at the breaking point, word came that Benedict Arnold, a man who had won a reputation as a daring and gallant battlefield leader, had gone over to the enemy. After a court-martial had sentenced him to receive a reprimand for his excesses as commandant of Philadelphia, he turned informer, and from the early summer of 1779 on kept Clinton fully apprised of American plans. His plot to ob-

LORD CORNWALLIS

Marquis Cornwallis was second in command to Sir Henry Clinton, with whom he quarreled constantly. In charge of the southern theater from 1780 on, he won victories at Camden and Guilford Courthouse, but lost the war at Yorktown.

tain the command of West Point in order to surrender it was foiled when Major John André, through whom the negotiations were being conducted, was captured within the American lines with incriminating papers on his person. Arnold promptly fled to the British, and André was executed as a spy.

Yorktown. Nevertheless, the tide of the war was soon to turn. Early in 1781 Cornwallis had entered Virginia, in giving chase to a small force of Americans under Lafayette. But Lafayette escaped, and Cornwallis, at Clinton's suggestion, fortified himself in the village of Yorktown on the tip of the peninsula made by the James and York Rivers, where, with the Royal Navy controlling the vital Chesapeake waterway, he could be reinforced from New York. This mistaken strategy, which left the way open for a combined Franco-American sea and land attack, was not lost on Washington. The American commander, who had hoped to attack Clinton in New York, changed his plans when the French admiral, Comte de Grasse, notified the allies that he would operate for a short while in the region of Chesapeake Bay. The American army, strengthened by the French regulars under Rochambeau, marched south to join Lafayette in Virginia. After the "Battle of the Capes" — near the mouth of Chesapeake Bay — in which de Grasse drove a British fleet back to New York, Cornwallis found himself not only cut off from retreat by sea, but hemmed in also by an allied army of 16,000 men, more than twice the number of his own. He held out for several weeks, but on October 19, 1781, surrendered his entire command.

Although the war ran on several months longer, Washington's victory at Yorktown assured the ultimate independence of the United States. In March, 1782, the British Prime Minister, Lord North, bowed to the inevitable and resigned, an event which marked also the end of George III's experiment in personal rule. The new ministry contained many former friends of the colonies and favored peace with all the enemies of England. The colonies would be welcomed back within the British Empire on their own terms if they would come; but if they would not come they might have their independence.

Treaty of Paris. Three Americans took part in the negotiation of peace: John Adams, Benjamin Franklin, and John Jay. Congress instructed the commissioners to work for — but not to demand — the Mississippi River boundary and to be governed in all matters of consequence by the advice of the French. Fortunately John Jay, who played the leading role for the Americans when peace negotiations were opened at Paris in 1782, refused to consider himself bound by these instructions, and on November 30, 1782, won a notable diplomatic triumph when the British and American delegations approved a separate preliminary agreement to be incorporated into the final treaty of peace. By the terms of this agreement, Britain's former colonies were granted their independence and the boundaries of the United States were to be the Great Lakes, the Mississippi River, and the thirty-first parallel in case Spain received Florida, but a line nearly a degree and a half farther north in case Great Britain retained it. The final treaty, signed September 3, 1783, accepted the terms of the preliminary treaty, and since Spain later received Florida, the United States regarded its southern boundary as thirty-one degrees. When the English ceded Florida to Spain without definition of boundaries, the setting was arranged for a boundary dispute that was to last for many years. Vergennes, the French Foreign Minister, was flabbergasted at the liberality of the British terms. "The English," he wrote, "buy peace rather than make it. Their concessions . . . exceed all that I could have thought possible."

Other provisions agreed upon at Paris included the retention of fishing rights for Americans off the coasts of Newfoundland, equal rights of navigation for the United States and Great Britain in the Mississippi River, the right of British subjects to sue for the collection of debts unpaid at the outbreak of the war, and a recommendation to the several states that confiscated Loyalist property be restored to its owners. The last two provisions caused much difficulty. Ultimately the central government agreed to pay off such debts still outstanding, but laws discriminating against Loyalists remained on the statute books of some states until after the War of 1812. Although the lack of adequate commercial agreement with Great Britain was felt long afterward, the treaty as a whole was a magnificent victory for American diplomacy.

SELECTED BIBLIOGRAPHY

Two recent surveys by leading historians provide excellent introductions to this period: L. H. Gipson, *The Coming of the Revolution, 1763–1775* (1954); and E. S. Morgan, *The Birth of the Republic, 1763–89* (1956). C. H. Van Tyne, *The Causes of the War for Independence* (1922), is sympathetic to the British position. Other useful general works include E. B. Greene, *The Revolutionary Generation, 1763–1790* (1943); and Esmond Wright, *Fabric of Freedom, 1763–1800* (1961). Clinton Rossiter, *Seedtime of the Republic* (1953), is the interpretation of a leading political scientist; part of it is available as *The First American Revolution*. The varying pattern of interpretation of causation may be traced in such works as C. L. Becker, *The Eve of the Revolution* (1918); C. M. Andrews, *The Colonial Background of the American Revolution* (2nd ed., 1931); J. C. Miller, *Origins of the American Revolution* (2nd ed., 1957); and Bernhard Knollenberg, *Origin of the American Revolution: 1759–1776* (2nd ed., 1961). See the very useful collection, *The Causes of the American Revolution,* edited by J. C. Wahlke (2nd ed., 1962). An important documentary collection is Bernard Bailyn, (ed.), *Pamphlets of the American Revolution* (1965 —); the first volume covers 1750–1765. A. M. Schlesinger, *The Colonial Merchants and the American Revolution* (1918), brings out clearly the motives that actuated the merchant class.

The constitutional aspects of the Revolution have attracted much attention. On this subject see especially C. H. McIlwain, *The American Revolution; A Constitutional Interpretation* (1923); and R. G. Adams, *Political Ideas of the American Revolution* (1922). Incomparable on the English situation are L. B. Namier, *Structure of Politics at the Accession of George III* (1929), and *England in the Age of the American Revolution* (2nd ed., 1961). Other valuable works include Reginald Coupland, *The American Revolution and the British Empire* (1930); G. H. Guttridge, *English Whiggism and the American Revolution* (1942); and G. S. Brown, *The American Secretary: The Colonial Policy of Lord George Germain, 1775–1778* (1963). Important monographs include Lynn Montross, *The Reluctant Rebels: The Story of the Continental Congress, 1774–1789* (1950); E. S. and H. M. Morgan, *The Stamp Act Crisis* (1953); O. M. Dickerson, *The Navigation Acts and the American Revolution* (1951); and Carl Ubbelohde, *The Vice-Admiralty Courts and the American Revolution* (1960). The war of words may be traced in A. M. Schlesinger, *Prelude to Independence; 1764–1776* (1958); and Carl Berger, *Broadsides and Bayonets* (1961).

There are many biographies of men who had a part in the making of the Revolution, including J. C. Miller, *Sam Adams, Pioneer in Propaganda* (1936); M. C. Tyler, *Patrick Henry* (1917); R. D. Meade, *Patrick Henry: Patriot in the Making* (1957); and D. R. Gerlach, *Philip Schuyler and the American Revolution in New York* (1964). The prominence of Washington in these events is the theme of C. P. Nettels, *George Washington and American Independence* (1951); Bernhard Knollenberg, *George Washington: The Virginia Period* (1964), and *Washington and the Revolution* (1940); Esmond Wright, *Washington and the American Revolution* (1957); and Marcus Cunliffe, *George Washington* (1958). On John Adams, see C. D. Bowen, *John Adams and the American Revolution* (1950); and the first volume of Page Smith, *John Adams* (2 vols., 1963).

Individual colonies in this period have attracted the attention of scholars. J. T. Adams, *Revolutionary New England, 1691–1776* (1923), has no counterpart for other regions. R. E. Brown, *Middle-Class Democracy and the Revolution in Massachusetts, 1691–1780* (1955), is an important work which establishes that the suffrage was more broadly based than tradition has held. Excellent monographs which deal at least in part with the crises of the immediately pre-revolutionary period include D. S. Lovejoy, *Rhode Island Politics and the American Revolution, 1760–1776* (1958); B. W. Labaree, *Patriots and Partisans; The Merchants of Newburyport, 1764–1815* (1962); C. A. Barker, *The Background of the Revolution in Maryland* (1940); R. M. Brown, *The South Carolina Regulators* (1963); Richard

* Available in paperback

91

Walsh, *Charleston's Sons of Liberty* (1959); and B. W. Labaree, *The Boston Tea Party* (1964). An important early work of one of America's greatest historians is C. L. Becker, *The History of Political Parties in the Province of New York, 1760–1776* (1909).

Excellent, accessible general treatments by leading American historians are J. R. Alden, *The American Revolution, 1775–1783* (1954); and R. B. Morris, *The American Revolution; A Short History* (1955). *American Revolution through British Eyes* (1962), is an interesting collection edited by Martin Kallich and Andrew MacLeish. Strongly sympathetic to the American cause is the work of the distinguished British writer G. O. Trevelyan, *The American Revolution* (4 vols., 1905–1912); a one-volume abridgement by R. B. Morris (1964) contains the heart of this work. C. H. Van Tyne, *The American Revolution, 1776–1783* (1905); *The Loyalists in the American Revolution* (1902); and *The War of Independence* (1929), have done much to rehabilitate the reputation of the Loyalists. J. F. Jameson, *The American Revolution Considered as a Social Movement* (1926), is a controversial classic. A collection of conflicting interpretations on this theme is *The American Revolution*, edited by G. A. Billias (1965). Interesting special studies of phases of the Revolution include E. P. Douglass, *Rebels and Democrats; The Struggle for Equal Political Rights and Majority Rule during the American Revolution* (1955); David Hawke, *In the Midst of a Revolution* (1961); and Benjamin Quarles, *The Negro in the American Revolution* (1961). An old work which is of enduring interest is M. C. Tyler, *The Literary History of the American Revolution, 1763–1783* (2 vols., 1897). *The Era of the American Revolution*, edited by R. B. Morris (2nd ed., 1965), is a series of scholarly essays by the students of E. B. Greene.

The Declaration of Independence has been subject to the closest scrutiny. No student of the history of ideas should miss the brilliant study by C. L. Becker, *The Declaration of Independence* (1922). A monograph by the editor of the Jefferson Papers is J. P. Boyd, *The Declaration of Independence* (1945); but see also David Hawke, *A Transaction of Free Men* (1964). Adrienne Koch, *The Philosophy of Thomas Jefferson* (1943), is useful in this connection. The best study of Jefferson is the

still incomplete work of Dumas Malone, *Jefferson and His Time* (3 vols., 1948–   ). A useful collection of the works of Tom Paine is *Common Sense and Other Political Writings*, edited by N. F. Adkins (1953).

Three convenient summaries of the military aspects of the Revolution are H. H. Peckham, *The War for Independence* (1958); E. S. Miers, *The Great Rebellion* (1958); and H. F. Rankin, *The American Revolution* (1964). On crucial aspects, see Harrison Bird, *March to Saratoga; General Burgoyne and the American Campaign, 1777* (1963); M. F. Treacy, *Prelude to Yorktown* (1963); and T. J. Fleming, *Beat the Last Drum* (1963). On General Clinton, see his narrative, *American Rebellion*, edited by W. B. Willcox (1954); and Willcox's biography, *Portrait of a General* (1964). The character of the Patriot army is well portrayed by Allen Bowman, *The Morale of the American Revolutionary Army* (1943). For the other side see E. E. Curtis, *The Organization of the British Army in the American Revolution* (1926); Piers Mackesy, *The War for America, 1775–1783* (1964); and P. H. Smith, *Loyalists and Redcoats* (1964). On naval aspects see A. T. Mahan, *The Influence of Sea Power upon History* (1890), and *The Major Operations of the Navies in the War of American Independence* (1913); W. B. Clark, *George Washington's Navy* (1960); and Harold and Margaret Sprout, *The Rise of American Naval Power, 1776–1918* (1939).

Diplomatic aspects of the war are comprehensively covered in S. F. Bemis, *The Diplomacy of the American Revolution* (1935); and more briefly treated in P. A. Varg, *Foreign Policies of the Founding Fathers* (1963). Relations with France are covered in Gerald Stourzh, *Benjamin Franklin and American Foreign Policy* (1954). The principal general works on American diplomatic history are S. F. Bemis, *A Diplomatic History of the United States* (5th ed., 1965); T. A. Bailey, *A Diplomatic History of the American People* (7th ed., 1964); J. W. Pratt, *A History of United States Foreign Policy* (2nd ed., 1965); R. W. Leopold, *The Growth of American Foreign Policy* (1962); and Alexander DeConde, *A History of American Foreign Policy* (1963).

Biography furnishes a convenient vehicle for much excellent history of the Revolution. A trilogy by Louis Gottschalk, *Lafayette Comes to America* (1935), *Lafayette Joins the Amer-*

ican Army (1937), and *Lafayette and the Close of the American Revolution* (1942), presents an intimate view. Two excellent biographies by J. A. James are *The Life of George Rogers Clark* (1928), and *Oliver Pollock* (1937). Meritorious biographies include C. L. Ver Steeg, *Robert Morris* (1954); S. E. Morison, *John Paul Jones* (1959); North Callahan, *Daniel Morgan* (1961), and *Henry Knox* (1958); R. D. Bass, *Swamp Fox; The Life and Campaigns of General Francis Marion* (1959); Theodore Thayer, *Nathanael Greene* (1960); C. P. Whittemore, *A General of the Revolution, John Sullivan of New Hampshire* (1961); J. R. Cuneo, *Robert Rogers of the Rangers* (1959); and J. T. Flexner, *Mohawk Baronet: Sir William Johnson of New York* (1959). A collection of essays is G. A. Billias (ed.), *George Washington's Generals* (1964).

A superb regional study is J. R. Alden, *The South in the Revolution, 1763–1789* (1957). R. J. Taylor, *Western Massachusetts in the Revolution* (1954), is a careful study of an important locality. State and local studies of significance include T. J. Wertenbaker, *Father Knickerbocker Rebels: New York City during the Revolution* (1948); R. L. Brunhouse, *The Counter-Revolution in Pennsylvania, 1776–1790* (1942); P. A. Crowl, *Maryland during and after the Revolution* (1943); and Kenneth Coleman, *The American Revolution in Georgia* (1958).

6

THE CONFEDERATION

❧ The New State Constitutions • State Sovereignty • The Articles of Confederation • The Revolution as a Social Movement • The Confederation and the West • The Western Ordinances • Diplomatic Failures • Financial Troubles • Debtor versus Creditor • The Movement for a New Government

The outbreak of war not only brought into existence a new and revolutionary central government, but also resulted in the establishment of new and equally revolutionary governments within the former colonies, soon to be called states. Only in Rhode Island and Connecticut, where liberal charters of self-government already existed, were the old forms of government retained. Elsewhere substantial changes were effected, although in Massachusetts an effort was made for a time, in spite of the absence of a royal governor, to adhere to the terms of the colonial charter.

Constitutional Conventions. While these transformations placed the revolutionists in control everywhere, political leaders in several of the states were concerned about procedural regularity and petitioned the Continental Congress for advice. After some hesitation Congress in May, 1776,

urged the adoption of permanent constitutions, a course which Virginia had assumed even before the decision of Congress had been learned. During the next few years all the other states except Rhode Island and Connecticut followed the advice of Congress. Procedures varied widely, but the Massachusetts method became something of a model. The existing legislative body postponed the calling of a constitutional convention until it had asked and received from the towns the authority for such a course, while the convention itself, although directly chosen by the people, felt obliged to submit the constitution it had drawn to the towns for approval.

It was natural enough that the Americans should wish to have written constitutions. In the past most of the colonies had been able to point to some specific document according to which their government had been carried on, and the new states were merely following precedent when they replaced the old document with a new one. Furthermore, the generally accepted contract theory of government seemed to call for a written instrument, which would clearly define the relationship between the people and those who were to be placed in authority over them. There seems to have been no disposition whatever to follow the English example and permit an accumulation of precedents to grow into an unwritten constitution.

The New State Governments. Far from being ultra-radical, the structure of the new constitutions relied heavily upon colonial experience, and because the colonial governments had been remarkably alike so also were the new state governments. In their bills of rights, many of them emphasized the Declaration of Independence doctrine that man had certain inalienable rights upon which government might not trespass. The theory that governmental powers were unlimited was thoroughly distasteful to Americans, both before and after the Revolution. The framers of the first constitutions assumed also that there should be three branches of government, executive, legislative, and judicial, and that each should be kept as distinct as possible from the others. Late unpleasant relations with royal governors tended to hold the powers of the chief executives of the new states to a minimum, while the prerogatives of the more trusted legislative branch were generally amplified. Pennsylvania and Georgia experimented for a time with single-chamber legislatures, but soon adopted the two-house system common to the other states. Judicial systems were complicated and varied, but most state constitutions affirmed the independence of this third department of government.

The conservative character of the American Revolution was modified somewhat by a broadening of the suffrage in several states, as well as by a reapportionment of some state legislatures. Property qualifications as a prerequisite for voting were maintained in every state, and sometimes far higher property qualifications were prescribed for office holders than for voters. Indirect elections, particularly for such high officials as governors and judges, were common, although the upper house of the legislature was invariably so constituted as to represent the elite. Only in the irregularly organized and officially unrecognized state of Vermont, formed out of territory claimed by both New Hampshire and New York, was the right of suffrage granted to all men over twenty-one years of age. Furthermore, the new constitutions made quite inadequate provisions for amendments.

Yet in other respects the new constitutions made substantial political advances. The new bills of rights listed many individual and group rights that had not been recognized either in the colonies or in England. Specific provisions guaranteeing freedom of speech, of the press, of assemblage, and of bearing arms, for example, were to be found in several of the new documents. And while governors and other elected officers continued to be wealthy men by reason of high property qualifications, the severe limitations upon executive power, the principle of rotation in office, and the very short terms of most officials prescribed in the new constitutions, all emphasized the drift away from aristocratic government.

State Sovereignty. The Revolution evoked little disposition in the states to submerge their separate identities into a national whole. Instead the various states assumed for themselves without question all rights of sovereignty and paid scant attention to the Continental Congress. Loyalty to state was probably far stronger than loyalty to nation, although the exigencies of the war required a certain unity of action. The problem of union, evaded in colonial times, now had to be faced. The Continental Congress was quick to recognize that it had little if any legal authority for the powers it exercised, and in June, 1776, with a declaration of independence imminent, it appointed a committee headed by John Dickinson of Pennsylvania to draft a plan of confederation. Dickinson's committee made no effort to introduce innovations. The sufficiency of the existing *de facto* central government was mostly taken for granted; all that was deemed necessary was to describe its character, and then to obtain the necessary grant of powers from the states. Congress was to be clothed only with such authority as might be necessary to deal with problems common to all the states.

The Articles of Confederation. It was not until November 15, 1777, that the Articles of Confederation were recommended to the states for adoption. In spite of the pleas of some who wanted a stronger central government, the Articles provided for just such a Congress as already existed. It was to be composed of delegates from each of the thirteen states, who were more like diplomatic agents than representatives, for they were paid by their states, were chosen annually, and were subject to recall at any time. Although a state could send from two to seven delegates, it had only one vote. One provision, unfortunate as it turned out, required that any delegate might serve only three years out of each six. A still worse provision required the consent of two-thirds of the states to pass any measure of importance. To cast the vote of a state at least two delegates must be present and in agreement. If a state delegation divided equally on any matter, then the state lost its vote. Otherwise, a majority of the delegation determined the vote of the state.

Powers of Congress. The listed powers of Congress gave it complete control over foreign affairs and some control over interstate relations. Congress might make peace or war, send and receive ambassadors, make treaties and alliances, govern trade relations with the Indians, determine the standards of coinage (the states might still coin money) and of weights and measures, and organize a postal service. Conversely, the states might not, without the consent of Congress, make treaties with foreign powers, send or receive ambassadors, or engage in war. Yet the Articles of Confederation pointedly declared that each state retained its "sovereignty, freedom, and independence." Congress could exercise only such limited powers as were assigned to it; the states had all the rest, including the all-important right of taxation. If Congress wanted money, it might requisition it from the states. The regulation of commerce was another power fully reserved to the states.

Only through the incidental provisions of treaties could Congress in any way control commerce with foreign nations, and it was given no authority whatever over interstate commerce. Changes in the Articles could be made only after the approval of Congress and ratification by every state legislature.

The Problem of Ratification. But for the objections of Maryland, the Articles of Confederation might have been quickly adopted. That one state, however, speaking up in behalf of the "small" states (and for certain land speculators, as well) insisted that the states with claims to western lands — Massachusetts, Connecticut, Virginia, North Carolina, South Carolina, Georgia, and perhaps New York — should surrender their claims to a "common stock, to be parceled out by Congress into free, convenient, and independent Governments, as the wisdom of that body shall hereafter direct." Not until Virginia, the neighbor whose potential greatness Maryland feared, had agreed to surrender her claim to Congress was Maryland content. Her ratification came on March 1, 1781, more than two years after every other state had agreed to the Articles, and only then could they go into effect.

The Revolution, Socially Considered. While the leaders of the American Revolution were chiefly interested in bringing about political changes, the transformation of life in this eventful period was not confined to politics. It is a fact that "many economic desires, many social aspirations were set free by the political struggle, many aspects of colonial society profoundly altered by the forces thus let loose." Nor was this social revolution ended with the conclusion of the war. The old colonial aristocracy was weakened by the departure of British officials and many Loyalists. Yet it is an exaggeration to say that the Revolution was a social leveler. Class distinctions based on wealth and position persisted, and many Loyalists never went into exile. Still, the revolutionary doctrine did have important effects, even if it took time for them to be observed. Many read into the Declaration of Independence, with its emphasis upon equality of men, a demand for the emancipation of the slaves, and in all the northern colonies abolition closely followed independence. Even in the South emancipation societies were common, and the gradual disappearance of slavery was generally expected.

Land Ownership. The trend toward small independent holdings of land, which was marked even in colonial times, was probably accelerated by the Revolution. While many of the largest estates, the property of Loyalists, were confiscated and sold in small tracts to free farmers, some of these lands were absorbed into large Patriot estates. The old feudal rules of primogeniture, which provided that property in land should descend to the eldest son, and of entail, which held such property in the family by prohibiting its owner from selling it or giving it away, were quickly abolished. Quitrents, always regarded as a nuisance and rarely paid without protest, became a thing of the past. Moreover, British restrictions upon the advance of the agricultural frontier were removed, and cheap lands in the West were available, particularly for those veterans of the war who had been granted land bounties as an inducement to enlist.

Industry and Commerce. American manufactures, always hampered by British restrictions and still more by the habit of buying manufactured articles from England, were immensely stimulated by the war. Far more attention than formerly was given to the making of such necessary articles as firearms, gunpowder, nails, salt, paper, and cloth. Commerce, on the other hand, suffered acutely from the war, although much successful privateering kept seamanship alive. Freedom from British restrictions on colonial trade was probably more than offset by the loss of trade privileges that the colonies had once enjoyed as a part of the British Empire.

Religious Adjustments. Independence served also to force a series of readjustments in the religious life of Americans. The union of church and state that existed in nine of the colonies was promptly attacked, although with varying results. In the South, where the state church was the Church of England, disestablishment was early accomplished, although not without a vigorous struggle in Virginia. In New England where, except for Rhode Island, the Congregational Church was supported by the state, patriotism could not so easily be invoked on the side of religious freedom, and the struggle lasted far into the nineteenth century.

After the Revolution most of the American denominations undertook to reorganize their systems of church government. The American Anglicans, when they failed to obtain the cooperation of English church officials, persuaded the non-juring bishops of Scotland to consecrate in 1784 an American bishop, Samuel Seabury. Thus the Protestant Episcopal Church of the United States was organized. About the same time the separate status of the American Catholic Church was recognized by a decree from Rome, and in 1790 Father John Carroll was made Bishop of Baltimore. At the close of the Revolution John Wesley, the English founder of Methodism (who himself never left the Church of England), sent Thomas Coke to the United States as general superintendent of the American Methodists. Coke promptly associated himself with Francis Asbury, the leading spirit among the American Methodists, and in 1784, at a conference held in Baltimore, the two were designated joint superintendents. Asbury and his successors, contrary to Wesley's wishes, assumed the title of bishop, and the denomination over which they presided became officially known as the

Methodist Episcopal Church. Other denominations, although freer from overseas connections than these three, generally redefined and elaborated their systems of church organization.

Revolution in Thought and Feeling. Of still greater significance was the revolution in thought and feeling that came over the American people during the war. While religious ties were loosened, standards of morality lowered, and traditional beliefs swept away, the revolutionary ideals of liberty and equality were deeply impressed upon the minds of the people. The inhuman penal codes, including imprisonment for debt, of the eighteenth century were more frequently denounced. The colonial schools, such as they were, had been virtually destroyed by the years of Revolution, and new systems had to be devised. In an age that exalted the rights of the common man, pressure upon the state to accept the obligation of popular education steadily increased. Prophetic of the future was the provision in the first constitution of the unrecognized state of Vermont that a school system, beginning with the towns and including a state university, should be established. Systems of this sort were slow to develop, but when the American school system did take form, it was under secular, not religious, control, and its right to public support was still defended on the grounds Jefferson had stated years before. "Above all things," he had written, "I hope the education of the common people will be attended to; convinced that on their good sense we may rely with the most security for the preservation of a due degree of liberty."

The Confederation and the West. The spirit that had permeated the American Revolution manifested itself again in the efforts made by Congress under the Confederation to deal with the problem of the West. All thought of establishing a western

THE RESTLESS FRONTIER

Timothy Flint (1780–1840), a native of Massachusetts and a Harvard graduate, served as a missionary in several of the new Western states. His melodramatic accounts of life on the frontier won him a wide reading public.

From some cause, it happens that in the western and southern states, a tract of country gets a name, as being more desirable than any other. The imaginations of the multitudes that converse upon the subject, get kindled, and . . . the hills of the land of promise, were not more fertile in milk and honey, than are the fashionable points of immigration. During the first, second, and third years of my residence here, the whole current of immigration set towards this country . . . It was the common centre of hopes, and the common point of union for the people . . . I conversed with great numbers of these people, affording just samples of the great class of frontier or backwoods people, who begin upon the retirement of the Indians, and in their turn yield to a more industrious and permanent race who succeed them, and they in turn push on still farther, with their face ever toward the western sea . . . Thus the frontier still broadens . . . the range is almost beyond the stretch of imagination . . . Nothing can or will limit the immigration westward, but the Western Ocean. Alas! for the moving generation of the day, when the tide of advancing backwoodsmen shall have met the surge of the Pacific. They may then set them down and weep for other worlds.

TIMOTHY FLINT, *Recollections of the Last Ten Years* (1826)

---

colonial empire dependent upon the East was brushed aside; and there was general agreement that the rights of statehood and local self-government won by the Revolution were to extend across the mountains. The new United States would clearly not repeat the mistakes of the British Empire. The cessions of western lands to Congress by the states claiming them were not completed until 1802, when Georgia at last surrendered her claim, but after the adoption of the Articles of Confederation in 1781 it was apparent that the nation rather than the states must deal with the West. Here a number of permanent settlements had already been made. Farthest in the interest lay the French villages that Clark had conquered, which together with Detroit and other centers of fur trade had a population numbering several thousands. On the upper Ohio around Pittsburgh, in the valleys of the Holston and Watauga Rivers, in the bluegrass region of Kentucky, and now also along the Cumberland in central

Tennessee were other growing settlements.

That these settlements would require the attention of the central government was soon made evident. New western states that might willingly acknowledge the supremacy of a national government, but would not remain content to be merely western divisions of eastern states, were in the making. When the Wataugans found in 1784 that the state of North Carolina had ceded the region in which they lived to the central government, they promptly established the State of Franklin, and with John Sevier as governor, applied for admission to the Union. Ultimately the North Carolina legislature repented of its action, and the Wataugans returned reluctantly to their former allegiance. Their example, meantime, had been followed by pioneers from Watauga and from Virginia whom Judge Richard Henderson had induced to settle in the vicinity of Nashborough (or Nashville) in the valley of the Cumberland. For a few years a temporary government functioned smoothly, but in 1782 the Assembly of North Carolina recognized the new region by the creation of Davidson County. In Kentucky, which thousands of new pioneers had entered during the closing days of the Revolution, an insistent demand for separate statehood set in. Although Virginia was agreeable, the Confederation Congress failed to make Kentucky a state.

The Northwest.   Nevertheless, the strong sentiment in the Southwest for separate statehood and the willingness of its residents to rely upon the national government for protection and support were not lost upon Congress. In the territory northwest of the Ohio River, where the title of the national government to the land was already clear, some provision for the future had to be made, and with this end in view Congress passed a series of "Northwest Ordinances" which showed a sympathetic appreciation of the problems of the West. Whether the attitude of Congress was directly affected by the situation in the Southwest is not entirely clear, but the Ordinances safeguarded in a most satisfactory way the right of settlers to venture into the West and to establish new states with the same privileges enjoyed by the old.

Ordinance of 1784.   The initiative in this matter was taken by Thomas Jefferson, who realized more fully than most men of his time that provision must be made for the development of the western country. In 1784 he introduced into Congress a loosely-drawn plan for the organization of the West into new states that should remain forever a part of the United States, subject to the central government only as other states were subject, and guaranteed a government republican in form. As originally drawn the Ordinance of 1784 also proposed that slavery should not exist in the West after 1800, and that the region should be gridironed into ten states with fantastic classical names. Congress eliminated both the anti-slavery clause and the pedantic names, but passed the rest of the ordinance

as a kind of declaration of intention. In most of the territory under consideration the Indian titles had not yet been extinguished, and north of the Ohio River, except in the French villages, white settlers had not yet begun to come in.

Ordinance of 1785.   Congress, again at Jefferson's instigation, laid out a plan for the systematic survey and sale of western lands. Instead of permitting the location of tracts as the whims of purchasers might direct, the Ordinance of 1785 provided for the "rectangular" or "rectilinear" system of survey. Parallel lines were to be drawn at six-mile intervals, both north and south, and east and west, as nearly as the sphericity of the earth would permit. Each of the squares so described was to be called a township, and each north and south tier of townships was to be called a range. Further subdivisions of the townships were to be made by east and west as well as north and south lines surveyed at intervals of one mile, so that each township would be marked off into thirty-six "sections." The sections, each of which was thus a mile square and contained approximately six hundred and forty acres, might then be divided into "halves" and "quarters," the "quarters" into "half-quarters" and "quarter-quarters," and so on indefinitely. The Ordinance of 1785 made provision for the sale as well as for the survey of the public domain. In accordance with a New England precedent, section sixteen of each township was to be reserved as a bounty to public schools, but the rest of the land was to be offered for sale to the highest bidder in lots of a section or more. The minimum price was fixed at one dollar per acre, but it was hoped that by holding auctions in each state competitive bidding would result in a considerably higher price being paid. From these sales Congress hoped to obtain a steady and much-needed source of revenue.

Land Companies.   With the way further prepared by the signature of treaties with Ohio Indians, Congress authorized the survey of seven ranges of townships west of Pennsylvania and sent out surveyors to proceed with the work. Those in charge saw the boundless possibilities for land speculation and were instrumental in creating the Ohio Company of Associates. Each participant was permitted to subscribe up to five thousand dollars in the company, the subscription to be paid in the certificates of indebtedness — now considered worthless — which Congress had issued to soldiers in lieu of pay. Congress was then to be persuaded to sell to the company perhaps as much as a million dollars' worth of land at an extremely low price, and to take its own worthless certificates in payment. The Reverend Manasseh Cutler, a Massachusetts clergyman, was sent as lobbyist to New York to push the project through. He succeeded, after agreeing that a group of congressmen and their friends, to be known as the Scioto Company, should be let in on the deal. To the Ohio Company, Congress would sell a million and a half acres of land at two-thirds of a dollar an acre; to the Scioto Company it would give an option on the purchase of an additional three and a half million acres. When a quorum could be assembled, Congress promptly chartered both companies.

Ordinance of 1787. Meantime Congress was at work on the Ordinance of 1787 for the government of the territory northwest of the Ohio River. Much more cautious than Jefferson's superseded Ordinance of 1784, the new act provided for three stages in the evolution of government. During the first stage a governor, a secretary, and three judges, all appointed by Congress, were to adopt and enforce such laws of the older states as might seem appropriate to the new territory. Whenever the district could show five thousand free male inhabitants of voting age, however, the freeholders might choose a representative assembly, which on coming together would nominate ten persons, from whom Congress would choose five to be a legislative council, or upper house. The two-house legislature thus established might then enact whatever laws it chose, subject to the governor's veto. Furthermore, a delegate to Congress might be chosen, who could speak and introduce bills, but could not vote. The Ordinance presumed that ultimately the territory northwest of the Ohio River would be divided into not less than three nor more than five states, and whenever a given district had attained a population of sixty thousand free inhabitants it should be admitted "on an equal footing with the original states in all respects whatsoever," and with full "liberty to form a permanent constitution and state government."

Certain declarations were set apart from the rest of the Ordinance as "articles of compact between the original states and the people and states in the said territory." Freedom of religious worship, freedom from arbitrary imprisonment, and the right of trial by jury were thus guaranteed; public education was to be forever encouraged; the utmost good faith was always to be observed toward the Indians; the settlers in the new territory were to pay their share of the federal debt and the expense of federal government; the prospective territorial or state legislatures were never to interfere with the administration of the public lands; the navigable waters of the West were to remain forever free for use without tax or duty by all citizens of the United States; and there should be "neither slavery nor involuntary servitude in the said territory, otherwise than in punishment of crimes whereof the party shall have been duly convicted." Jefferson's plan to exclude slavery from the Northwest, which had barely failed of adoption in 1784, was now revived and accepted, doubtless as a lure for New England settlers.

The Ohio Settlements. In the spring of 1788, forty-seven colonists from New England floated down the Ohio River from Pittsburgh to Marietta. Marietta was soon a village of many log cabins, surrounded by numerous "clearings," and possessed of the customary "block-house" for defense against

A KEELBOAT DESCENDING THE OHIO

Boats of this type were the fastest on the river before steamboats came into use, and were common on all inland waterways. Sketch by Charles Leseuer.

the Indians. The Ohio Company never became profitable, but it did stimulate colonization and was able to redeem a small fraction of the land to which it was entitled. The Scioto Company, except for the settlement of a few hundred forlorn French colonists at Gallipolis, down the river from Marietta, accomplished nothing whatever of note and was unable to take up any part of its option. Another settlement was made at what came to be known as Cincinnati by John Cleves Symmes of New Jersey, who in 1788 obtained a grant of land from Congress. By 1790 the Northwest Territory had nearly 4,300 inhabitants as well as an acute Indian problem, which taxed to the limit the resources of General Arthur St. Clair, the first governor.

Relations with Britain. Aside from its decisions with respect to the West, the Congress of the Confederation had apparently few successes to its credit. Immediately after the war the country enjoyed a period of prosperity during which hard money accumulated from sales to British and French armies was spent for long-denied foreign goods. When the supply of hard currency ran out, a depression followed in 1784 that lasted for at least two years. American trade had always flowed naturally to Great Britain, and once the interruption of war was at an end it tended to resume its normal channels. But American shippers soon found that they could not count on the same privileges in British ports that they had enjoyed before the war, and that in the British West Indies, where their ships had once been free to come and go, they were confronted by exasperating restrictions. And even though some of these restrictions were circumvented by smuggling, a trade treaty with Britain became highly desirable.

Another problem arose out of the fact that many of the British posts in the Northwest, despite the treaty of peace which gave the region south of the Great Lakes to the United States, were still held by British troops. The British were loath to withdraw the protection they had always given the Canadian fur trade; furthermore, it was important from the fur traders' point of view that the settlement of the Northwest be held back, for whenever settlers came in, fur-bearing animals became extinct. Americans believed, with good reason, that the British posts were centers of anti-American influence among the Indians. To deal with these problems of commerce and of the frontier, John Adams was dispatched to England in 1785, but his mission failed miserably. It was apparent that the British could count on whatever American trade they wanted without the commercial treaty, and they had good excuses to offer for the retention of their Northwest posts. In spite of the terms of the treaty of 1783, British subjects found it practically impossible to collect debts owed them by Americans since before the war, and the promised restoration of Loyalist property failed also to materialize. If the Americans themselves broke the treaty, why should they expect the British to keep it?

Jay-Gardoqui Negotiations. The Confederation government was equally unsuccessful in its efforts to solve its problems with Spain. The United States needed to make trade agreements with Spain, particularly for the easy exchange of commodities with the Spanish West Indies. Furthermore, there was difficulty about the location of the Florida boundary, and about the American claim to free navigation of the Mississippi River. In 1785 Don Diego de Gardoqui arrived in the United States with power to negotiate on these matters and proposed to John Jay, who in 1784 had been charged by Congress with the conduct of American foreign affairs, that the United States give up for twenty-five or thirty years its claim to the right of navigation of the lower Mississippi, in return for a favorable trade treaty. Jay was tempted by this bargain, for he knew that the agreement would be of great value to the northeastern states, while the West, as he saw it, would grow slowly. But representatives from the southern states, who were vitally interested in the welfare of the West and saw little to gain from the proposed treaty for their section, blocked the agreement. Thus Confederation diplomacy failed with Spain as completely as it had with Great Britain.

Confederation Finance. Good relations between the United States and her former allies were continually imperiled by the inability of the American government to pay its foreign debt. The financial embarrassment of the Confederation government was always acute. To meet its ordinary expenditures it required an income of about $500,000 a year, even without provision for payments on the public debt. Altogether the United States had incurred an indebtedness of well over $40 million during the war. About $6 million had been borrowed from France, and perhaps another $2 million from other foreign sources. The remainder was owed to citizens of the United States.

The means by which the government could raise money to discharge its financial obligations were strictly limited. It might resort to paper-money issues, but these had already been overused. Some funds were borrowed in Holland for use in paying the interest on the foreign debt. A small sum was realized from the sale of public lands, and the post office brought in a little revenue. In the main, however, Congress had to rely upon requisitions levied upon the states. The requisition system proved to be just as inadequate as it had been when proposed by the British during the French and Indian War. Requests for funds were honored by the states only in so far as they chose to honor them, and probably not more than one-tenth of the sums asked for by Congress was ever paid in. Much of the money that was obtained, moreover, was of uncertain value. In 1781 and again in 1783 Congress sought to obtain a limited right to levy tariffs, but in each instance the proposition failed to be ratified.

Confusion in the States. The state governments were confronted by problems almost as difficult as those which Congress faced. They possessed the power to levy tariffs that Congress so much coveted, but its exercise by thirteen different agencies resulted in serious complications. Imports tended to arrive at the ports of low-tariff states rather than high-tariff states, with smuggling as an inevitable by-product. Endless confusion and much bad feeling were added when the states levied duties against each other.

The power of the states to issue paper money was another source of trouble. During the Confederation period the lack of gold in the United States, always a chronic complaint of the mainland colonies, became an acute menace.

The debtor classes, more articulate than ever as a result of the Revolution, urged the wholesale printing of paper money because of the blessings that an inflated currency would bring to them; and in some states the propertied classes, who opposed inflation, were outvoted. In Rhode Island the paper-money faction got the upper hand in the legislature, multiplied issues until the currency was almost valueless, and lent this depreciated money to debtors on extremely easy terms. Subsequently, when this "legal-tender" paper money was refused by merchants and creditors, the legislature passed a law making its refusal a punishable offense without so much as requiring a trial by jury for the offender. The attempt to enforce this law led to one of the most important judicial decisions in American history, for in the case of *Trevett* v. *Weeden* (1786) the state supreme court held that the law was out of harmony with the Rhode Island charter and therefore unconstitutional. This decision was attacked by the legislature, and at the next election three out of the four judges concerned were retired. But the precedent set was not overthrown, and the later power of the courts over legislation which they deemed unconstitutional owed much to this decision.

Shays' Rebellion.   In Massachusetts the contest over paper money took the form of a test of strength between the coastal towns, which were relatively prosperous, and the small farmers of the interior, who found it difficult during the prevailing hard times to pay their debts and taxes. As a measure of debt relief the rural classes demanded liberal paper-money issues, but the legislature was under the control of the coastal towns and refused to comply with their demands. Instead, heavy taxes were levied to pay off the war debt, and sheriffs' sales were multiplied. In the summer of 1786 open rebellion broke out. Bands of insurgents, composed of farmers, artisans, and laborers, marched on the courts in several districts and prevented them from sitting. Shays' Rebellion, as this outbreak was called, after its leader, Daniel Shays, was put down by militia led by General Lincoln and paid by means of a loan to which property-minded citizens subscribed generously. But the enduring power of the debtor classes was demonstrated in the next state election when the incumbent governor who had suppressed the "rebellion" was defeated by John Hancock, still the idol of the populace.

AN AMERICAN HOMESTEAD

An early New England farm was the scene of many homely activities, such as laundering and the making of cider, maple-sugar, and soap.

The Economic Chaos Overdrawn. Government under the Articles of Confederation has been traditionally described as impotent, unable to secure respect either at home or abroad. Recent research, however, indicates that the adverse conditions were overdrawn by those who wanted a strong national government. By 1786 the country was rapidly recovering from the postwar depression. Foreign trade was expanding and domestic production was increasing. The financial condition of the government was never completely desperate. Congress maintained interest payments on Dutch loans, and a good many foreign investors were always willing to purchase the indebtedness of the new nation. Considering the very large war debt the states had incurred, some of them were in a sound financial condition. What then explains the rising demand for a revolutionary change in the national government?

Some of the demand for a new government was clearly actuated by a fear on the part of the elite for the new social and political position of the masses. The Society of Cincinnati, an organization of Revolutionary War officers, was charged with desiring a change in government so that the lower classes could be put in their place. Many other elements in the states undoubtedly agreed with the Society. Other groups wanted a stronger national government for economic reasons. The manufacturers, chiefly individual and often poor artisans, wanted a nationwide protective tariff. And while the merchants were against a tariff, they hoped for a stronger national government that would discriminate against foreign ships in domestic trade and would obtain treaties favorable to American merchants abroad.

But of all the many issues involved, probably the paper money question and the specter of a popular rebellion most strongly impelled leading citizens to support a change. In practically all the states, substantial citizens were alarmed by the weakening of governmental authority. To check the democratic and inflationary tendencies so painfully evidenced, a stronger government was needed, one further removed from the will of the masses, one that could tax and pay its obligations, maintain order at home, and also protect American rights abroad. Clearly the state governments could not be trusted to do these things, while the central government lacked the power. The Confederation was without an effective executive, and its gropings in that direction had so far proved ineffectual; it had no judiciary whatever; it could not regulate commerce; it had no taxing power; and it was at best a mere creature of the states, utterly incapable of acting directly upon individuals. Worst of all, amendments to the Articles of Confederation required a unanimous vote, and experience seemed to prove that on this account any strictly legal change would be impossible.

A Closer Union Foreshadowed. The movement for a closer union was soon given added impetus by two significant interstate gatherings. The first of these was a conference of Maryland and Virginia delegates, held at Alexandria and charged with the duty of reconciling certain conflicting regulations with regard to the navigation of Chesapeake Bay and the Potomac River. On the particular points at issue the two states reached an agreement, but the need of a general conference on all matters of commerce was evident. As a result the Virginia legislature invited all the states to send delegates to a convention to be held at Annapolis in September, 1786. The Annapolis Convention was actually attended by delegates from only five states, but it adopted a report by Alexander Hamilton which pointed out some of the conspicuous defects in the Articles of Confederation and called upon the states to send delegates to a new convention through which a remedy should be sought. The date set for the new convention was May, 1787, and the place of meeting suggested was Philadelphia. This proposal was transmitted not only to the various state legislatures, but also to Congress, and on February 21, 1787, the latter body joined in the call. In doing so, however, Congress stated that the purpose of the convention was merely to propose amendments to the existing Articles of Confederation. The clear inference was that only by the subsequent ratification of all the thirteen states could any such amendments be adopted.

Forces Making for Union. Forces had long been at work to ensure that ultimately the hope of a stronger union would be realized. The very isolation from the rest of the world that the thirteen American states shared with one another tended to bring them together. Their inhabitants were for the most part of a common nationality, spoke a common language, read mostly the same books, and had inherited practically the same traditions. Every part of the new nation had, at some time not far removed, gone through the frontier process — a process which did not differ markedly from place to place or from time to time, and tended therefore to supply a common mold for the formation of American attitudes. Furthermore, in the mountain valleys of the Appalachians and in the new communities still farther to the west there was a continual mingling of settlers from many different states and even from the Old World.

Moreover, the problems that faced the American states were increasingly national in character. The conflicting interests of debtors and creditors cut across state lines. In the back country the debtor point of view dominated; along the coast the creditors tended to maintain their control. Commerce vied with agriculture, but most of the states were neither strictly commercial nor strictly agricultural; the commercial classes everywhere tended to present a solid front against an almost equally united agricultural interest. Even in matters pertaining to religion there was a tendency to divide along national rather than along state or local lines. In the East adherents of the old settled faiths found themselves drawn together in defense of the old ways against hordes of upstart Presbyterians, Methodists, and Baptists, who challenged church establishments wherever they found them, overturned time-worn customs, and demanded complete religious freedom as the right of every man. Such common problems as these revealed lines of cleavage within the nation as a whole rather than within the individual states. As the issues became essentially national ones, efforts to solve them tended to draw together the like-minded from every state and section, and to prophesy the speedy formation of a closer union, or — less likely — a split at the mountain barriers.

SELECTED BIBLIOGRAPHY

On the transition from colonies to states the standard general work is Allan Nevins, *The American States during and after the Revolution, 1775–1789* (1924). Two valuable regional studies are J. T. Adams, *New England in the Republic, 1776–1850* (1926); and F. M. Green, *Constitutional Development in the South Atlantic States, 1776–1860* (1930). Important books dealing with individual states in this period include: W. C. Abbott, *New York

* Available in paperback

in the American Revolution* (1929); R. E. and B. K. Brown, *Virginia 1705–1786* (1964); M. B. Jones, *Vermont in the Making, 1750–1777* (1939); J. A. Munroe, *Federalist Delaware, 1775–1815* (1954); R. J. Purcell, *Connecticut in Transition, 1775–1818* (2nd ed., 1963); and R. P. McCormick, *Experiment in Independence: New Jersey in the Critical Period, 1781–1789* (1950).

The Confederation Period remains an area of sharp controversy among historians. John Fiske, *The Critical Period of American History*

(2nd ed., 1916), generally viewed as the best of Fiske's many books, takes a very dim view of the accomplishments of the Confederation. A strongly differing interpretation emerges from the major works of the leading contemporary scholar of the period, Merrill Jensen. No student of this period should miss Jensen's *The Articles of Confederation* (1940), and *The New Nation: A History of the United States during the Confederation, 1781–1789* (1950). B. F. Wright, *Consensus and Continuity, 1776–1787* (1958), is an important discussion; the same author's *American Interpretations of Natural Law* (1931), has a brief section on legal thought in the Confederation era. A. C. McLaughlin, *Confederation and Constitution* (1905), the work of a distinguished constitutional historian, is particularly good on the problem of union. Interesting new studies are P. C. Nagel, *One Nation Indivisible; The Union in American Thought, 1776–1861* (1964); and W. H. Bennett, *American Theories of Federalism* (1964). R. R. Palmer, *The Age of the Democratic Revolution* (2 vols., 1959–1964), places the American events of the period in the context of European developments in a highly stimulating way. Dixon Wecter, *When Johnny Comes Marching Home* (1944), explores the postwar activities of veterans, beginning with those of the American Revolution. On the growth of American liberties, see R. A. Rutland, *The Birth of the Bill of Rights, 1776–1791* (1955). An important work which opens new terrain for historians is Oscar and Mary Handlin, *Commonwealth; A Study of the Role of Government in the American Economy: Massachusetts, 1774–1861* (1947).

On the western settlements, F. J. Turner, *The Significance of Sections in American History* (1932), has a chapter on "Western State-making in the Revolutionary Era." S. C. Williams, *History of the Lost State of Franklin* (1924), tells of the political transformations that befell the Watauga settlements. T. P. Abernethy, *From Frontier to Plantation in Tennessee* (1932), is a major work. Valuable on cultural aspects are H. L. S. Arnow, *Seedtime on the Cumberland* (1960), and *Flower-*

ing of the Cumberland (1963); and A. K. Moore, *The Frontier Mind* (1957). For the region north of the Ohio River see: F. A. Ogg, *The Old Northwest* (1919), a short treatment; and B. W. Bond, Jr., *The Civilization of the Old Northwest, 1788–1812* (1934), which includes social history. An excellent state history that begins with this period is *The History of the State of Ohio*, edited by Carl Wittke (6 vols., 1941–1944). Among the many special accounts see particularly two works by R. C. Downes, *Council Fires on the Upper Ohio* (1940), and *Frontier Ohio, 1788–1803* (1935). Of major importance is the monumental collection edited by C. E. Carter, *The Territorial Papers of the United States* (25 vols., 1934–1962).

Two general accounts deal with the whole history of our national land policy: B. H. Hibbard, *A History of the Public Land Policies* (1924); and R. M. Robbins, *Our Landed Heritage* (1942). A fine collection of scholarly monographs is *The Public Lands*, edited by Vernon Carstensen (1962).

On Spanish-American relations during this period, consult A. P. Whitaker, *The Spanish-American Frontier, 1783–1795* (1927); F. A. Ogg, *The Opening of the Mississippi* (1904); E. W. Lyon, *Louisiana in French Diplomacy, 1589–1804* (1934); and C. M. Burson, *The Stewardship of Don Esteban Miró, 1782–1792* (1940). For diplomatic relations with Great Britain, see A. L. Burt, *The United States, Great Britain, and British North America from the Revolution to the Establishment of Peace after the War of 1812* (1940). W. E. Stevens, *The Northwest Fur Trade, 1763–1800* (1928); and I. A. Johnson, *The Michigan Fur Trade* (1919), treat one important aspect.

A rich over-all treatment of economic history is C. P. Nettels, *The Emergence of a National Economy, 1775–1815* (1962). D. R. Dewey, *Financial History of the United States* (12th ed., 1936), is a useful work; on this subject see also W. J. Shultz and M. R. Caine, *Financial Development of the United States* (1937). A recent and lively treatment of Shays' Rebellion is M. L. Starkey, *A Little Rebellion* (1955).

Charles Willson Peale, "Peale Family Group."
Courtesy of The New-York Historical Society,
New York City.

The

Federal Era

· 1789–1828 ·

Governments, like clocks, go from the motion men give them, and as governments are made and moved by men, so by them they are ruined, too. Therefore government rather depends upon men than men upon government.

WILLIAM PENN

The General Government, though limited as to its objects, is supreme with respect to those objects. This principle is part of the Constitution, and none can deny its authority.

JOHN MARSHALL

But every difference of opinion is not a difference of principle. We have called by different names brethren of the same principle. We are all Republicans, we are all Federalists.

THOMAS JEFFERSON

7

THE CONSTITUTION

The problem of why men act as they do
is one of the most difficult tasks facing the
historian. The motives of the delegates to
the Philadelphia Convention have been
much disputed by twentieth-century historians. Charles A. Beard concluded that
the delegates represented the well-born,
the well-educated, and the economically
prosperous elements in American society;
also, that they made use of their talents to
restrain democracy in the interest of the
privileged upper classes, and, in the process, to make personal gains through the
strengthening of the public credit. Some
recent historians, finding Beard's scholarship questionable and his interpretation too
doctrinaire, have argued that the delegates
were essentially men of principle, less influenced by the personal factors stressed by
Beard than by their desire to promote the
general welfare. Recent experiences, in
Rhode Island and elsewhere, had convinced
them that they must devise some means
whereby the basic interests of the people
as a whole could be protected, even from

transitory popular majorities. They also
feared that, if matters were allowed to drift,
the United States might break up into two
or three sectional sovereignties, might become a monarchical dictatorship, or might
even be added to the possessions of one of
the great powers of Europe.

Character of the Delegates. Delegates
to the Philadelphia Convention were not
popularly elected, but instead were chosen
by various methods. The radical Rhode
Island legislature refused to send delegates,
but from the other states a total of seventy-
three men were chosen, of whom fifty-five
put in an appearance at the convention. Almost without exception these were men of
financial and social standing, well prepared
for their labors by education and by previous governmental experience. Among
them were many of the most distinguished
Americans of the time. It is noteworthy
that the small farmers and artisans were
not represented at all.

Philadelphia Convention. On May 25,
1787, twenty-nine delegates met in Independence Hall and chose George Washington to preside. For three and a half months
the sessions continued, usually with not
more in attendance than appeared the first
day. The Convention at once decided that
to promote freedom of discussion and to
avoid outside interference, its sessions must

be held behind closed doors and all proceedings carefully guarded from the public. This decision was strictly adhered to and only the barest details of business were recorded in the official journal. For an account of what went on, one must turn to notes kept by individual members. The problem the delegates faced was how to construct a government popular enough to be adopted, but not so democratic as to allow a majority to trample upon the rights of minorities. As to the fundamental ends that the new government was to accomplish, the delegates were in remarkably close agreement; they accepted with little debate many of the precedents set by the English constitution and by the constitutions of the new states; and they evinced a commendable willingness to arrange compromises on matters of minor detail.

The Virginia Plan. It was not easy, however, to adjust the relative weight of states and nation in the new government. The most nationalistic point of view was embodied in the Virginia Plan, which had resulted from the daily meetings of that state's delegation. This plan proposed a two-house legislature, the lower house to be chosen by the people of the several states in such a manner as to give small states only one representative and large states like Massachusetts and Virginia sixteen or seventeen representatives; the upper house was to be chosen by the lower house. The Virginia Plan satisfied the large states fairly well, and was supported also by states in which the possibilities of growth were great. But the small states were profoundly agitated at the prospect and feared that with such a plan they might even lose their separate identity. Their point of view found expression in a report by William Paterson, commonly called the New Jersey Plan, which proposed to retain the states as equal, and perhaps sovereign, units.

Ultimately a solution was found, sometimes called the "Great Compromise," which in a measure, at least, satisfied both sides.

In accordance with the Virginia Plan the convention voted to establish a bicameral legislature, with the membership of the lower house to be apportioned according to population, and with an upper house in which the states should be equally represented. It was decided also that the representatives who were to sit in the lower house should be elected directly by the people, for two-year terms, while the senators, two from each state, were to be chosen for six-year terms by the various state legislatures.

The "Three-Fifths" Compromise. There remained, however, many adjustments to be made, and one may say that almost every line of the Constitution that was written came as the result of some compromise. Even on the matter of representation in the lower house a serious dispute arose. Should the slaves, so numerous in some of the southern states, be counted in apportioning the number of representatives to which the states were entitled? Or should these slaves be regarded as property rather than persons? These questions were the more perplexing in view of the fact that the convention had already agreed to assess direct taxes upon the states in accordance with the population. The northern states were unwilling to allow the South to count its slaves in determining the representation a state should have in the lower house of Congress, but desired to count them when direct taxes were to be assessed; the South, on the other hand, wished to count its slaves when the question of representation in Congress was up, but not when taxes were to be levied. An acceptable, if utterly illogical, solution was found in the decision to count five slaves as equal to three whites both in the apportionment of representatives and in the assessing of direct taxes.

During the debate that led to the "Three-Fifths" Compromise the question of the part that new western states were to be allowed to play in the new government was also discussed. Gouverneur Morris argued earnestly that the rule of representation ought to be so fixed as to secure to the Atlantic states a prevalence for all time in the national councils. The new frontier states, he said, would know less of the public interest than the old, and in particular might involve the nation in wars with the Indians and with neighboring nations that would have to be paid for by the maritime states. Fortunately, the narrow view expressed by Morris did not prevail. Possibly many members of the convention comforted themselves with the thought, to which Roger Sherman gave expression, that the number of future states would probably never exceed that of the existing states anyway.

Commerce. The divergent views of the northern and the southern states, already apparent in the discussion of the "Three-Fifths Compromise," were revealed again in the debate on the powers to be given Congress to regulate commerce. The northern states, in which commerce was a dominant interest, favored a generous grant of authority, but some of the southern states, whose prosperity depended mainly upon agriculture, feared that this power might be used to stimulate northern commercial prosperity at their expense. Some of the southern states, particularly Georgia and South Carolina, were also concerned lest Congress might tax heavily or even forbid the importation of slaves, and thus strike at what in their section was still believed to be an essential labor supply; consequently they insisted that there should be no tax on exports or upon "such persons" as the several states should "think proper to admit," and they demanded that navigation acts should be passed only by a two-thirds vote of both houses of Congress. To resolve these differences, the northern states yielded to the South on the prohibition of export duties, and agreed also that the importation of slaves should not be forbidden before the year 1808, although Congress might levy a tax of ten dollars per head for each person imported. The southern states, thus re-

assured, gave up their insistence on a two-thirds vote in Congress for the passage of navigation acts.

The Powers of Congress. The convention early decided that the national government should have only "enumerated powers"; hence one of the most important sections of the Constitution was that which listed the powers of Congress. In this enumeration many provisions of the old Articles of Confederation were taken over almost intact. Such, for example, were those which authorized Congress to borrow money on the credit of the United States, to declare war, to maintain an army and navy, and to establish post offices and post roads. Extremely significant, however, were the new powers, especially those which gave Congress authority to levy and collect taxes, duties, imposts, and excises, to regulate commerce with foreign nations and among the several states, to pass naturalization and bankruptcy laws, and "to make all laws which shall be necessary and proper for carrying into execution the foregoing powers"—the famous "elastic clause." Congress was also authorized to provide for a militia to execute the laws of the Union and to suppress insurrections and repel invasions.

Limitations on the States. Hardly less important than the delegation of powers to the national government was the withdrawal of certain powers from the states. States were forbidden to coin money, to emit bills of credit, to make anything but gold and silver legal tender in payment of debts, to have direct relations with foreign countries, to levy duties on imports or exports (without the consent of Congress), "to pass any bill of attainder, *ex post facto* law, or law impairing the obligations of contracts, or grant any title of nobility." Most of these provisions were designed to protect private property against attack by popular majorities within the separate states. For example, while the national government was left free to print paper money, and even to declare it legal tender, the states were expressly forbidden to exercise these powers. Clearly, the delegates felt that popular (and, to their minds, dangerous) majorities would find it impossible to get control of the central government.

The Executive.   While the convention had little difficulty in deciding to establish the customary three departments of government, there were many opinions as to the most desirable make-up for the executive branch. Some wished a plural executive, but the majority stood by the traditional idea of an individual to head the government. Divergent views had to be reconciled, however, before the convention decided that the executive should be called the President, that he should be chosen for a term of four years, and that he should be eligible for indefinite re-election. In providing for the election of the President, the convention sought to avoid on the one hand delegating to Congress the right to choose the executive, and on the other assigning to the people directly so important a duty. The result was the creation of an "electoral college," roughly analogous to Congress, but composed of different individuals. As many electors were to be named in each state as the state had senators and representatives, and the method of choosing the electors was to be left for each state to determine. The electors were to vote for two candidates for President, and if anyone should receive the vote of a majority of the electors he was to be declared elected, while the candidate receiving the next highest number of votes, whether a majority or not, was to become Vice-President. In case no one person should receive a majority, a situation that the constitution-framers expected to recur repeatedly, then the election of the President should be the prerogative of the House, voting by states. Needless to say, delegates failed completely to foresee the subsequent practice of popular presidential elections.

Powers of the President.   There was little hesitation about granting extensive powers to the President. He was made the commander-in-chief of the army and navy and also of the state militia whenever it was called into national service; he had the power to make treaties with foreign nations "by and with the advice and consent of the Senate . . . provided two-thirds of the Senators present concur"; he could with the consent of the majority in the Senate name ambassadors, ministers, consuls, judges of the federal courts, and all the other officers of the United States not otherwise provided for; he might call Congress into extraordinary session when he believed such a session necessary; he must "take care that the laws be faithfully executed"; and he had the right to veto bills passed by Congress, with the qualification that a two-thirds vote of both houses might make the bill a law without the President's signature. As a safeguard against executive usurpation or other misbehavior by federal officials a method of impeachment was devised, with the House bringing the indictment and the Senate sitting as a court. A two-thirds majority of the Senate was required to convict and remove from office.

The Judiciary.   The importance of a federal judiciary was apparently underestimated, for there was surprisingly little debate on the subject during the convention, and the section on the judiciary that was finally written was very brief. That there should be a supreme court was generally agreed, but many believed that the existence of state courts made inferior federal courts unnecessary. This difference of opinion was compromised by providing merely that Congress might establish inferior courts if it chose to do so, but nothing was put into the Constitution to require their establishment, and Congress was free to substitute state courts if it chose. The Supreme Court was given original jurisdiction over cases affecting foreign ministers and cases to which a state was party; other-

JAMES MADISON

"The father of the Constitution," James Madison proposed also the first ten Amendments, or "bill of rights," and wrote twenty-nine of the famous Federalist papers. As a member of the national House of Representatives, he broke with the Federalists over Hamilton's financial policies, and became one of Jefferson's chief lieutenants. Later he was Jefferson's Secretary of State, then President. Portrait by Gilbert Stuart.

wise its jurisdiction was appellate only. While the judicial power of the federal courts was so defined as to extend to all cases arising under the Constitution, the laws of Congress, and the treaties to which the United States was a party, the Constitution itself says nothing with regard to the power which the judiciary soon assumed of declaring invalid such laws as in its opinion were contrary to the Constitution. It is probable, however, that many members of the convention took this more or less for granted. Indeed, a proposition to give the Supreme Court a qualified veto over laws of Congress was voted down partly because it was assumed that the federal judges would probably exert some such authority anyway.

Checks and Balances. The three-headed system of government, with its separate legislature, executive, and judiciary, provided numerous opportunities for preventing those abuses of power which were so much feared by the framers of the Constitution. The judiciary was designed to act as a check on the President and Congress, while the executive would also check the legislature, and the legislature the executive. A number of provisions for the direct operation of this principle were adopted, such as the power given the Senate to reject treaties and appointments made by the President, and the right of the President to exercise a qualified veto over the acts of Congress. The right of the people to representation was never seriously questioned, but the delegates hoped that the people would select able and independent-minded men. Indeed, the Convention vested certain governmental functions in individuals once or twice removed from the popular choice. The only officers of the central government elected directly by the people were the members of the House of Representatives.

Radical Features. The American Constitution was, for its time, a radical document. It reaffirmed the doctrine of popular sovereignty that had formed the philosophic background of the American Revolution. Thus in a day when nearly every other government adhered to the principle of monarchy, with its implied belief in the divine right of kings, the American government was strictly republican in form. Unique also was the effort to establish a dual or federal type of government, but the experiment turned out to be as successful as it was unusual. Further, although the Constitution in its original form contained no formal bill of rights, it did include such guarantees as that the privilege of the writ of habeas corpus should not ordinarily be suspended, and that bills of attainder and *ex post facto* laws should not be passed. The first ten amendments — introduced at the insistence of George Mason of Vir-

ginia and known as the Bill of Rights —
stated even more definitely the various
"rights of man" upon which government
was forbidden to transgress. The ease with
which these amendments could be accomplished constituted another radical innovation. Alternative methods were provided,
but ordinarily an amendment could be
adopted when proposed by two-thirds of
the members of Congress and ratified by
the legislatures of three-fourths of the states.

Debate on the Constitution. The last
article of the Constitution provided that as
soon as the document was ratified in nine
states by conventions called for the purpose, it should go into effect for those states.
This was out of harmony with the method
of amendment under the Articles of Confederation, and therefore revolutionary, but
the Congress of the Confederation did not
protest the procedure, and itself submitted
the Constitution to the states. Ratification
was not accomplished without a struggle.
The Philadelphia document was regarded
with much suspicion by such popular leaders as Patrick Henry, Richard Henry Lee,
and Samuel Adams. They criticized the
"artful" way in which the Constitutional
Convention had been proposed and the
secret character of its meetings. In particular they feared the proposed curtailment of
the rights of the states by the "consolidat-
ing" features of the new document, and
especially the absence of a bill of rights.
But most of all, they attacked the Constitution for its "aristocratical tendencies."
Richard Henry Lee could see "very little
democracy" in it and predicted that the
new government would be run by the "natural aristocracy of the country." But the
Federalists, as those who favored the Constitution came to be called, made a strong
case for adoption. They did not defend
every clause in the Constitution, but asserted that it was the only alternative to the
chaos of the Confederation. Among the
numerous articles written in support of the
Constitution, a series by Hamilton, Jay,

GEORGE MASON

*A Virginia planter and Revolutionary
statesman, George Mason was one of the
most active members of the Federal Convention, but in the end said he "would
rather chop off his right hand than put
it to the Constitution as it now stands."
A true disciple of the Enlightenment, he
objected to the compromises on slavery,
the lack of a bill of rights, and the inadequate restrictions on the power of
Congress. He died in 1792.*

and Madison, signed *The Federalist*, attracted much attention. These documents,
collected to form a book, still constitute the
best commentary on the Constitution as its
framers intended it to be interpreted.

Ratification. While the opponents of
the Constitution, or Antifederalists, stated
their side of the argument fully and well,
the advantage from the first lay with the
Federalists. Nearly everywhere the Federalists included the ablest politicians, men
who knew how to make the most of their
opportunities. Restrictions on the suffrage
told heavily in their favor, and in some
states the back country, which was especially hostile to the Constitution, was hardly

represented in the ratifying conventions. By the end of the year the ratifications began to come in. Equality of representation in the Senate seemed to satisfy most of the small states, and on December 7, 1787, Delaware ratified by a unanimous vote. By June 21, 1788, when New Hampshire ratified, nine states had adopted the Constitution, enough to put it into effect. But these nine included neither Virginia nor New York, without whose support the Constitution could hardly be expected to succeed. Only three states had ratified unanimously; in each of the others there had been determined opposition. Finally, on June 25, 1788, Virginia ratified by a vote of 89 to 79, and a month and a day later New York, convinced that the Constitution would be given a trial anyway, voted its half-hearted participation. Five states had ratified only with reservations, most of which demanded a bill of rights. North Carolina and Rhode Island did not ratify until after Congress had submitted to the states a bill of rights, in the form of the first ten amendments to the Constitution.

There was great relief that the long dispute over the form of government was at an end, and among the bitter opponents of ratification many were ready, now that the Constitution was actually adopted, to give it a fair trial. The old Congress of the Confederation, even before ratification by New York, acknowledged that its authority had been supplanted by ordering the states to choose presidential electors, senators, and representatives, and set the first Wednesday in March, 1789, as the date for the new Congress to convene.

George Washington.   Much remained to be done, nevertheless, before the new government should really go into effect. In this crisis the talents of George Washington, whom everyone knew would be the first President, were invaluable. Few public leaders have captured the confidence of their contemporaries with such completeness, and the fact that his solid judgment and rugged honesty would be at the command of the new government during its experimental period allayed many misgivings. In the first and second presidential elections Washington received every electoral vote, an honor that would no doubt have been accorded him for a third time also had he been willing to accept it.

Washington was born, February 22, 1732, in Westmoreland County, Virginia, the son of a moderately well-to-do planter who owned several estates. His father had gone to school in England, but this privilege was denied George, whose education was somewhat limited. He took an interest in mathematics, and at an early age knew the rudiments of surveying. When only sixteen he accompanied a surveying party into the Shenandoah Valley, and upon his return became surveyor-general for Fairfax County. His career as surveyor was cut short when his elder brother Lawrence died in 1752, and left him the management of the estate at Mount Vernon. A few years later Washington married Martha Custis, the widow of a wealthy planter, and her property, added to his own, made him a very rich man. For many years he lived the usual life of the prosperous southern planter, entertained lavishly, participated actively in parish affairs, and sat for his county as a member of the House of Burgesses.

The greatness of Washington is as apparent now as it was at the time of his election. He was most exceptional for his many-sided talents. No doubt his knowledge of military tactics was defective, but it was sufficient to meet the needs of the situation he faced, and to win the admiration of such a master-strategist as Frederick the Great. As an administrator he was wise in his choice of advisers, acted decisively, kept abreast of his duties. As a statesman he was farsighted and sagacious. He saw clearly the important part that the West was to play in the history of the nation, he recognized the dangers in a growing sectionalism, he understood better than most men of his time the menace of slavery, and he realized fully the wisdom of diplomatic isolation from Europe until the nation he had helped to create could get securely upon its feet. Washington's genius was not of the spectacular sort, but his sound judgment and plain common sense saved his country many trials, and may have saved its life.

Launching the New Government. Not until the sixth of April, 1789, were majorities in both houses of Congress present in New York, the temporary capital. Thereupon, quorums being obtained, the electoral votes were counted, and the election of Washington to the Presidency and John Adams to the Vice-Presidency was announced. By April 30 the President-elect had reached New York, traveling part of the way by horseback, and the inauguration took place.

But the new government was not even then fully launched. The Constitution was a relatively short document, and much legislation had to be passed in order to make it effective. Laws had to be enacted, for example, to create departments of state, of war, and of the treasury, and most important of all to provide for the levying and collection of taxes. The Judiciary Act of 1789 established not only a Supreme Court but also inferior federal courts, although the original jurisdiction of the latter was strictly limited. Once the essential laws were enacted the President still had to select the officials to carry them into effect, and the Senate had to pass on the President's appointees. In many important matters, also, significant precedents had to be set, and new practices given time to develop. For example, there was no provision in the Constitution for the use of the Cabinet as an official board of advisers to meet with the President from time to time. This custom, however, grew naturally out of the clause which provided that the President might ask for the opinions of heads of departments *in writing* whenever he so desired.

Alexander Hamilton. The Confederation had failed largely because it was unable to solve the problem of finance. If the new government was not also to founder, its financial policy must be wisely conceived. Washington recognized this fact when he chose as his Secretary of the Treasury Alexander Hamilton, a young man only thirty-four years of age who had already displayed remarkable financial talent. Hamilton (1755–1804) was a West Indian by birth, the son of a Scottish father and a mother of English descent. He was sent to school in New Jersey and later attended King's College in New York. Here, although New York was a Loyalist center, he embraced the American point of view in the quarrel with England and when war broke out joined

FEDERAL HALL

At the corner of Wall and Nassau Streets, New York, this was the first national Capitol. Here Washington was inaugurated. Formerly the New York city hall, it was extensively remodeled through the generosity of private donors.

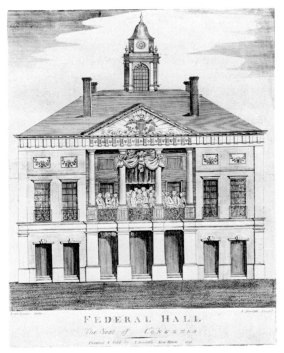

FEDERAL HALL
The Seat of CONGRESS

the army. A Federalist, Hamilton believed that a strong central government was necessary alike to protect property and to preserve civil liberties. He thought that the nation had more to fear from powerful states, such as Virginia, than from any overuse of power by the central government.

Funding the Debt.   As Secretary of the Treasury, Hamilton concerned himself first with the establishment of the nation's credit. He had long feared the effects of continued inflation, and was determined to put the country's finances on a sound basis. To make sure that there could be no doubt about the determination of the United States to pay its debts, he proposed that all outstanding loans be funded at their face value. The United States, during and after the Revolution, had borrowed from abroad about $12 million, and against the meeting of this obligation in full there could be no valid complaint. But the domestic debt, which now amounted to nearly $42 million, seemed to many honest men a totally different matter. Since these securities were worth on the market about twenty-five cents on the dollar, many thought that for the government to purchase them back at that price, or a little above, with a new and valid issue would be an entirely respectable procedure. But Hamilton was determined to win the enthusiastic approval of the moneyed class and insisted that the entire debt be funded at par. As a result many speculators, including some members of Congress, reaped a rich harvest.

Assumption of State Debts.   Hamilton's plan did not end merely with the funding of the debts owed by the United States. He wished also to take over such of the debts incurred by the states themselves for the cause of independence as they had not yet paid. His object, again, was to place the creditor class under deep obligation to the central government, and thus to win its hearty support. But the assumption of state debts by the central government was not

accomplished without a struggle. It was all very well to argue that these debts were incurred for a common cause and should be paid out of the common treasury, but the fact remained that some states had large obligations to pass over and some did not. Virginia, for example, had financed the war to a great extent with paper-money issues that had either been redeemed in western lands or had ceased to have any value. The South in general opposed the scheme, and it was finally put through Congress only after Hamilton, working through Jefferson, the Secretary of State, had struck a notable bargain. The South was exceedingly desirous of securing the site for the national capital, and Hamilton now offered to use his influence in favor of a southern site if Jefferson would help find the votes to pass the funding-assumption bill. The bargain worked, Congress agreed that the new capital should be located at Philadelphia for a period of ten years, and thereafter on the Potomac. The Funding-Assumption Act of 1790 included a provision for the assumption by the federal government of $21.5 million worth of state war debts.

Bank of the United States.   Still further to bind the financial interests to the government, Hamilton proposed, in December, 1790, that Congress should authorize the establishment of a Bank of the United States similar to the Bank of England. He could give many sound arguments in favor of such a measure, but he was unable to point to any specific grant of authority in the Constitution to warrant its passage. James Madison, who as the most active member of the Constitutional Convention knew the motives of the framers as well as any man, said that the Constitution was not meant to give Congress authority to create such a bank. But Hamilton was willing to interpret the "necessary and proper" clause broadly enough to meet the situation, and against heated opposition he induced a majority in Congress to accept his view. The Bank of the United States to which

Congress now granted a charter was to have a capital stock of $10 million, a very large sum for the time. Of this amount one-fifth was to be subscribed by the United States, and the other four-fifths by private individuals. Into the bank normally went the deposits of the United States, and this fact, coupled with the fact that the national government also owned a large part of the stock, tended to win public confidence for the institution. The bank had the right to issue paper money, and these notes were made receivable for public dues. Investors were quick to take advantage of the opportunity offered them, and the bank was soon doing business.

Tariff and Excise. Hamilton's plan for funding the debt cost money, and the modest tariff that Congress had levied was unequal to the emergency. In consequence, he offered yet another solution. Congress clearly had constitutional authority to levy an excise tax, and Hamilton now proposed to place one on distilled liquor. This would spread the tax burden widely, although it would fall especially on the West. Thrifty farmers who lived far from markets turned their surplus grain into whiskey in order to solve the problem of transportation, and the sale of this commodity brought them about the only ready cash they knew. For westerners the whiskey tax was a direct one; unlike eastern distillers, they were unable to pass it on to the consumer. Hamilton knew that the whiskey tax would mean trouble, but he was convinced that the government should demonstrate that it could collect the taxes it had levied even if by force. Although the whiskey excise was offensive to Madison and Jefferson, they regarded themselves as bound not to oppose it because their bargain with Hamilton on the assumption of state debts made it necessary. Congress passed the bill early in 1791. However, Congress refused to give its assent to Hamilton's proposal for a high protective tariff, outlined in his celebrated Report on Manufactures of December, 1791.

ALEXANDER HAMILTON

The first Secretary of the Treasury, Alexander Hamilton left an indelible imprint on the government of the United States. A conservative and a nationalist, he put the finances of the new nation in order, and won for it the warm support of most men of substance. Portrait by John Trumbull.

His nationalism outstripped that of his commercial supporters who, in the main, were still traders rather than manufacturers.

Opposition to Hamilton. Washington had hoped to prevent the growth of political parties, and he purposely had chosen men of such divergent views as Jefferson and Hamilton for his Cabinet. But the financial program was so clearly designed to benefit the commercial elements that other groups were soon in opposition. A central government which at all times could be counted on to serve the businessman aroused the deep resentment of the farmers. The merchant, the manufacturer, the shipbuilder, and their dependents might profit, directly and indirectly, by Hamilton's policies; but

119

the land owner and the small farmer would not. For them the Hamiltonian system meant the multiplication of taxes and the curtailment of liberty no less than the British government had once planned. The agrarian interests tended, therefore, to join hands under the leadership of Jefferson and Madison. Hamilton's friends called themselves Federalists, so their opponents were often called Antifederalists. But before long the opposition took for its party label the more significant term, Republican.

Whiskey Rebellion.   The attempt to enforce the excise tax soon brought on trouble. The chief center of opposition lay in the Pittsburgh area, where "Whiskey Boys" raided stills that paid the tax, roughly handled the tax collectors, and successfully nullified the law in a number of western counties. On August 14, 1794, a convention was held to remonstrate, and an attack by local militia on some regulars stationed at Pittsburgh was narrowly averted. Washington now called out fifteen thousand state militia from Virginia, Maryland, and Pennsylvania, and ordered them to march to the scene of the trouble. As the troops approached their destination, the enthusiasm of the rebels abated, and the moderate counsels of Albert Gallatin, a highly respected resident of the affected area, were accepted. All that the army could find to do when it arrived was to arrest a number of the leaders and send them for trial to Philadelphia. Of eighteen so brought to trial, only two were convicted, and these the President pardoned. The "Whiskey Rebellion" was over, and the tax thereafter was collected, but the residents of frontier areas were aghast at the power the Federalists in control of the central government had chosen to wield.

The Southwestern Frontier.   The revolt in western Pennsylvania was not the only western problem that the new government was called upon to solve. As the West grew in population, the uncertainty of trade

down the Mississippi became constantly more serious. The Spanish remained unwilling to open the river freely to trade from the United States, they continued to urge their claim to a boundary for Florida much farther north than the United States was willing to concede, and they placed no obstacles in the way of Indians under their control who moved to attack the southwestern frontier. In the Northwest the English continued to hold their posts south of the Great Lakes, and Canadian fur traders gave aid and encouragement to the Indian tribes of the Northwest who had already gone on the warpath against the pioneers in Ohio. Washington realized fully that the loyalty of the West, and even the prestige of the nation, were at stake.

Unwilling to fight two wars at once, Washington tried diplomacy on the Indians of the Southwest, and through money payments to Alexander McGillivray, a halfbreed Creek of great influence, obtained a somewhat undependable promise of peace. Ultimately the Tennesseans were obliged to take matters in their own hands; their extensive raids into the Indian country during 1793–1794 were far more effective than Washington's diplomacy. In the Northwest the central government did not hesitate to use force. By two treaties, Fort Stanwix (1784) and Fort McIntosh (1785), the Indians had given up a large section of land west of the western boundary of Pennsylvania and north of the Ohio. With the tacit approval of the British in the forts and furtrading posts, the Indians had committed so many depredations by the time Washington took office that drastic retaliatory measures seemed necessary.

War in the Northwest.   Three separate expeditions against the Northwest Indians were required before they could be brought to terms. After General Harmar and Governor St. Clair each had led groups of untrained militiamen into disastrous Indian ambushes, Washington turned to "Mad" Anthony Wayne, a hero of the Revolution.

Wayne insisted upon regular enlisted troops, and he spent nearly two years in training them for battle. At the Battle of Fallen Timbers, August 20, 1794, Wayne's forces overwhelmed the Indians. Next year at Fort Greenville they signed a treaty which opened vast stretches of land in central Ohio to settlement. So stinging was their defeat that they gave the United States no further trouble for many years to come.

New States. Not less gratifying to the people of the West was the willingness of the new government to admit frontier states into the Union. In 1791, Congress finally agreed to accept Vermont as the fourteenth state. In 1792, with Virginia's permission, Kentucky was admitted to statehood. In 1796, Tennessee, once part of North Carolina and then a separate territory, became the sixteenth state of the union. The constitutions of these new states were markedly democratic, for Vermont and Kentucky provided universal manhood suffrage, and Tennessee closely approximated it.

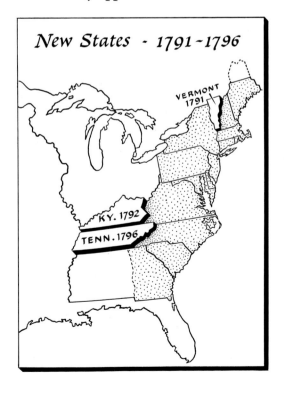

New States - 1791-1796

VERMONT 1791

KY. 1792

TENN. 1796

Land Policy. Another concern vital to the West was the national land policy. Hamilton's idea was to sell the land primarily to raise revenue for the federal government. But westerners resented the idea of using the land to produce a revenue, and eventually had their way. Congress long delayed action on the subject, but in the Land Law of 1796 finally set the price at $2 an acre, with a minimum purchase by an individual of 640 acres, both figures too high for the ordinary settler. When sales lagged, Congress, by the Harrison Land Law of 1800, established four local land offices in the Northwest, reduced the size of minimum tracts to 320 acres, and extended credit for four years to all who wished to purchase, one-fourth of the purchase price to be paid down, and one-fourth with interest each succeeding year. As a concession to those who wished to obtain the maximum revenue from the lands, the law provided that auctions should be held for a period of three weeks whenever a new tract was opened for sale, but after the auction was over unsold lands were to be equally open to all at the minimum price, two dollars per acre. Except that it did not incorporate the right of "preemption," according to which the trespasser on government land claimed that he should have the first chance to purchase the land he held, this law satisfied the westerners fairly well.

Election of 1792. Meantime the new government had survived a test of strength at the polls. It was the good fortune of the Washington administration to take office at a time when prosperity was returning. The public tended to believe that the adoption of the Constitution was responsible. By the end of Washington's first administration there were few who regretted the establishment of the new government. There were many, however, who felt that the Federalists had gone too far in the direction of centralization and had granted unreasonable favors to the commercial interests. To remedy this defect they were already considering the wisdom of placing the government in other hands. Had Washington retired at the end of his first term, as he wished to do, undoubtedly there would have been a hard fight between the Hamiltonian and Jeffersonian factions over the choice of his successor. But Washington was persuaded to stand for re-election, and there was none to oppose him. When it came to the Vice-Presidency, which John Adams held, the

Republicans asserted their independence by giving their votes to George Clinton. In the election of 1792, Washington again received a unanimous vote, but Clinton, who carried New York, Virginia, North Carolina, and Georgia, and took one vote in Pennsylvania, received a total of 50 votes to 77 for Adams. It was clear that the time was not far off when a real party struggle for control of the government would be waged.

SELECTED BIBLIOGRAPHY

Excellent documentary collections are *The Federal Convention and the Formation of the Union of the American States, edited by W. U. Solberg (1958); and Merrill Jensen, *The Making of the American Constitution (1964). See also the monumental Records of the Federal Convention of 1787, edited by Max Farrand (4 vols., 1911–1937). *The Declaration of Independence and the Constitution, edited by Earl Latham (2nd ed., 1956), brings out conflicting interpretations of major themes of this period.

Carl Van Doren, *The Great Rehearsal (1948), is a readable account of the making and ratifying of the Constitution. Authoritative works include Max Farrand, *The Framing of the Constitution of the United States (1913); Charles Warren, The Making of the Constitution (1928); R. L. Schuyler, The Constitution of the United States (1923); and A. C. McLaughlin, *The Foundations of American Constitutionalism (1932). H. C. Hockett, The Constitutional History of the United States, 1776–1876 (2 vols., 1939), traces the evolution of the Constitution during the formative years. The standard general surveys of American constitutional history are: A. C. McLaughlin, A Constitutional History of the United States (1935); C. B. Swisher, American Constitutional Development (2nd ed., 1954); and A. H. Kelly and W. A. Harbison, The American Constitution: Its Origins and Development (3rd ed., 1963).

Many members of the constitutional convention have attracted biographers, among the best of whom are: E. M. Burns, James Madison, Philosopher of the Constitution (1938); R. S. Boardman, Roger Sherman, Signer and

Statesman (1938); C. P. Smith, James Wilson (1956); and R. A. Rutland, *George Mason (1961). A popular collective biography is Nathan Schachner, *The Founding Fathers (1954). Important studies by leading historians are W. F. Craven, *The Legend of the Founding Fathers (1956); and Adrienne Koch, *Power, Morals, and the Founding Fathers (1961).

A great classic in American politics is *The Federalist (2 vols., 1788), a collection of essays by Madison, Hamilton, and John Jay which put the case for ratification. A major recent monograph is J. T. Main, *The Antifederalists; Critics of the Constitution, 1781–1788 (1961). Several works study the situation in the crucial state of New York: E. W. Spaulding, New York in the Critical Period, 1783–1789 (1932); and His Excellency, George Clinton (1938); and C. E. Miner, The Ratification of the Federal Constitution by the State of New York (1921).

C. A. Beard, *An Economic Interpretation of the Constitution of the United States (2nd ed., 1935), is important. While Beard could scarcely be called an opponent of the Constitution, he contended that the founding fathers were motivated by selfish economic interests. Although many people were troubled by what they felt was Beard's irreverence, scholars were slow to attack his central thesis. But with the publication of R. E. Brown, *Charles Beard and the Constitution (1956), a short but outspoken attack; and Forrest McDonald, *We the People (1958), a large study which impugns Beard's scholarship as well as his conclusions, there began a major controversy which still rages. J. A. Smith, The Spirit of American Government (1915), depicts the Constitution

* Available in paperback

as reactionary. This interpretation has been set forth again recently by A. A. Ekirch, *The Decline of American Liberalism* (1955).

The best general introduction to the new regime may be found in J. C. Miller, *The Federalist Era, 1789–1801* (1960). On the social side, J. A. Krout and D. R. Fox, *The Completion of Independence, 1790–1830* (1944), is outstanding. The only really satisfactory regional history of the period is T. P. Abernethy, *The South in the New Nation, 1789–1819* (1961). Standard studies of elections are Edward Stanwood, *A History of the Presidency* (2 vols., 2nd ed., 1916); and E. H. Roseboom, *A History of Presidential Elections* (2nd ed., 1964).

Much that was of lasting significance in the Washington Administration involved the setting of precedents. A superb guide to these developments is L. D. White, *The Federalists* (1948). On the Presidency, see E. S. Corwin, *The President, Office and Powers; 1787–1957* (4th ed., 1957); and L. W. Koenig, *The Chief Executive* (1964). An excellent history of public finance in the period immediately before Hamilton's assumption of power is E. J. Ferguson, *The Power of the Purse* (1961). A readable general treatment of American military policy is Walter Millis, *Arms and Men* (1956). Important recent monographs include Marshall Smelser, *The Congress Founds the Navy, 1787–1798* (1959); and H. M. Ward, *The Department of War, 1781–1795* (1962). Rich for this period is G. H. Haynes, *The Senate of the United States: Its History and Practice* (2 vols., 1938).

On economic developments of this period, see *Documentary History of American Economic Policy Since 1789*, edited by William Letwin (1961). A great work of important scholarship is Bray Hammond, *Banks and Politics in America, from the Revolution to the Civil War* (1957). One of the best works on a single bank is N. S. B. Gras, *The Massachusetts-First National Bank of Boston, 1784–1934*, (1937).

R. G. McCloskey, *The American Supreme Court* (1960), is a brief survey of a complicated history. The standard general treatment is Charles Warren, *The Supreme Court in United States History* (2 vols., 2nd ed., 1937). A monograph dealing especially with the establishment of precedents is C. G. Haines, *The Role of the Supreme Court in American Government and Politics, 1789–1835* (1944). Other important works on this subject include

C. A. Beard, *The Supreme Court and the Constitution* (2nd ed., 1938); and E. S. Corwin, *The "Higher Law" Background of American Constitutional Law* (1955).

An interesting recent work by a leading student is Clinton Rossiter, *Alexander Hamilton and the Constitution* (1964). A full biography is Broadus Mitchell, *Alexander Hamilton* (2 vols., 1957–1962), very friendly to its subject. Nathan Schachner, *Alexander Hamilton* (1946); and L. M. Hacker, *Alexander Hamilton in the American Tradition* (1957), are both by admirers. More critical is J. C. Miller, *Alexander Hamilton* (1959). Understanding of the first Secretary of the Treasury will certainly be advanced by the monumental collection, *The Papers of Alexander Hamilton* (7 vols., 1961–), edited by H. C. Syrett and J. E. Cooke. Accessible source collections include *The Reports of Alexander Hamilton* (1790–1791), edited by J. E. Cooke; and *Alexander Hamilton Reader*, edited by M. E. Fuller (1957). *Hamilton and the National Debt*, edited by G. R. Taylor (1950), is a selection of materials on one crucial theme.

Other Federalists are now beginning to receive the attention of biographers; see C. M. Destler, *Joshua Coit* (1962); D. J. Mays, *Edmund Pendleton* (1952); and Frank Monaghan, *John Jay* (1935). A great source on the thinking of a leading Antifederalist is *The Journal of William Maclay*, edited by E. S. Maclay (2nd ed., 1927).

There are books on a great variety of special subjects pertaining to the period. On diplomacy, see especially Alexander DeConde, *Entangling Alliance; Politics and Diplomacy under George Washington* (1958). L. B. Dunbar, *A Study of "Monarchical" Tendencies in the United States from 1776 to 1801* (1923), reveals the strength of conservative thought in the new nation. The evolution of political parties in a single state is the theme of H. M. Tinkcom, *The Republicans and Federalists in Pennsylvania, 1790–1801* (1950). Of interest particularly on problems of the West is J. R. Jacobs, *The Beginning of the U.S. Army, 1783–1812* (1947). L. D. Baldwin, *Whiskey Rebels* (1939), is both standard and colorful. Other interesting books on western themes in this period include: H. E. Wildes, *Anthony Wayne* (1941); W. H. Masterson, *William Blount* (1954); and F. P. Prucha, *American Indian Policy in the Formative Years: The Indian Trade and Intercourse Acts, 1780–1834* (1962).

8

FEDERALISTS
AND REPUBLICANS

ঽঌ The French Revolution • Problems of Neutrality • The Jay and Pinckney Treaties • The Election of 1796 • The Alien and Sedition Acts • The Kentucky and Virginia Resolutions • Jefferson's Victory • The United States in 1800 • Jefferson's Domestic Policies • Louisiana Purchase • Expeditions to the West • The Burr Conspiracy

The American colonies had never been isolated from Europe. As outlying parts of the British Empire, they had been dependent on ties with the mother country for their livelihood, and they had fought in all the wars that involved the Empire. As a new nation, the United States was still closely bound to Europe, and was seriously affected by any events that deeply affected the Old World.

The French Revolution. The outbreak of the French Revolution was thus a matter of tremendous interest and concern to the people of the new American nation. A week after Washington's inauguration, the French Estates-General met to place limitations on the arbitrary powers of government. Americans naturally sympathized with the French struggle for individual rights and saw in it a close analogy with the American Revolution. But the mounting excesses of the French Revolution soon alarmed many leading Americans. When in April, 1792, France declared war on Austria, it became clear that the French Revolution was no longer an internal affair. Even so, most Americans continued to sympathize with France until after the French declarations of war against Great Britain and Spain. Then many of them began to be deeply concerned. The United States was bound by a treaty of alliance to France. Would another war with England have to be fought, and perhaps also a war with Spain? Any such development might mean the death of American commerce, which was mostly with England and Spain, and it might mean the loss of American independence as well.

It was not long before public sentiment in the United States on the war in Europe began to divide along party lines. To Hamilton and most of the Federalists it now seemed that England was fighting for the preservation of civilization while France had become a public enemy. But Jefferson and the Republicans took a very different view, seeing the Revolution as carrying into effect their own principles. Representing mainly the agrarian interests, they had little concern for American commerce. England, the traditional enemy of American democracy, still unlawfully held the northwest posts; Spain, an even older antagonist, still controlled the mouth of the Mississippi, thus barring that vital waterway to western farmers. Many Republicans, now organized into pro-French Republican clubs, were ready to join France in a war against the English in Canada and the Spanish on the Gulf of Mexico.

Citizen Genêt. Washington received with understandable misgivings the news that the revolutionary government had dispatched a minister, "Citizen" Edmond Charles Genêt, to the United States. The Genêt mission sought to obtain the assistance of the United States in the war against England and Spain. The President at once laid the matter before his Cabinet, and although there was sharp disagreement between Hamilton and Jefferson, particularly on the validity of the treaties of alliance, all agreed that for the time being, at least, neutrality was the only possible course. The government recognized Genêt as the rightful minister of France, but made clear to him by a proclamation of neutrality that the United States did not intend to participate in the war.

Washington, who knew the pro-English sentiment of the commercial sections of the nation, received the French representative coolly, and made it clear to him that the American declaration of neutrality meant exactly what it said. Nevertheless the Frenchman tried to obtain funds for financing his schemes by offering to discount the debts owed by the United States to France in return for immediate repayment. If only the money could be found, American ships could be outfitted as French privateers, and George Rogers Clark, whose services Genêt had enlisted, could be sent on an expedition down the Mississippi River to attack the Spanish at New Orleans. But Washington forbade such a fund-raising

scheme as a clear breach of neutrality, so Genêt found himself without financial resources. He managed, however, to convert a French prize ship into an armed commerce destroyer and permitted it to sail without notice from an American port. Since Genêt had expressly promised not to do this, Washington asked the French government for his recall. By this time the French Revolution had progressed another step in the direction of radicalism, and Genêt was already out of favor at home. A new minister, Fauchet, was appointed, who was instructed to send his predecessor home under arrest. Washington, however, mercifully granted political asylum to Genêt.

Thus began the American doctrine of nonintervention in European affairs. For the moment, even though it might be argued that the nation had ignored its treaty obligations, this policy was wisely conceived. The United States was as yet a tiny nation, none too certain of survival. It was almost surrounded by two great empires, the British to the north, and the Spanish to the south and west. Its ally, France, had once had American colonial possessions, and French imperialism might easily turn again toward the New World. Moreover, sentiment in the United States on the European conflict was badly divided, and, worse still, was divided along party lines. To save its life the infant nation had no alternative but to tread the precarious path of rigid neutrality.

The Profits of Neutrality. It soon became apparent that neutrality was not altogether without its rewards. American shipping prospered, for neutral vessels were safer than the merchant vessels of nations flying enemy flags. Particularly lucrative was the trade between the French West Indies and France, which was now opened to vessels from the United States. Congress established by a law of 1794 definite rules of neutrality, emphasizing particularly the duties of neutrals, and it appropriated $75,000 to be used if needed in enforcing the law.

While the public increasingly came to understand and appreciate the policy of neutrality, serious diplomatic problems soon arose. For the most part these involved disputes with the British, whose navy controlled the high seas. Particularly vexatious to the United States was the "rule of 1756," invoked by Great Britain to prevent neutral ships from trading with the French West Indies. According to this rule, trade not open to a nation in time of peace could not be opened to that nation in time of war. Under this rule hundreds of American ships were taken, and American seamen and passengers were subjected to indignities. The United States protested that the British had no international sanction whatever for their actions; while the British contended that it was unfair for France to monopolize trade with her colonies in time of peace, and then to expect that the same trade in time of war could enjoy immunity under a neutral flag.

Disagreements with England. As time went on the disagreements multiplied. The United States maintained that "neutral ships made neutral goods," but the British flouted this doctrine. The United States held that foodstuffs were not to be regarded as contraband of war. The British argued otherwise and held that such cargoes might lawfully be seized if paid for. The United States contended that a blockade to be legally binding must be effectively enforced by a blockading squadron off port, but the British did not hesitate to establish paper blockades of many French ports, or to capture neutral ships, bound for a forbidden destination, anywhere on the high seas. There were complications, too, with regard to the rules of visit and search, the United States insisting that search be confined merely to the examination of the ship's papers and the British holding that search really meant search. Impressment presented another problem. The British in-

sisted that every Briton owed naval service to his country, and press gangs made a practice of "impressing" sailors into the royal navy from British merchant ships. When, in the course of searching American ships, British sailors were found serving in American crews, they were taken off and made to serve under British colors. Naturalization, although recognized by the United States, meant nothing to the British, who still adhered to the rule, "Once an Englishman, always an Englishman." Mistakes occasionally occurred, also, and some American-born sailors were impressed into the British service, to the intense indignation of most Americans.

Republicans, supported by public opinion, demanded drastic reprisals against the British for these alleged violations of American neutrality. As a result, Congress in 1794 placed a two months' embargo on all foreign trade. This embargo was meant primarily as a threat; what the Federalists wished to do was to come to an understanding with Great Britain whereby American trade might continue on tolerable terms. They finally persuaded Washington to send Chief Justice John Jay to London with instructions to negotiate a treaty with the British. Jay's instructions explicitly required him to obtain (1) evacuation by the British of the military posts they held south of the Great Lakes, (2) compensation for their illegal seizures of American ships, (3) a satisfactory commercial treaty, which must embody, among other things, the American position on disputed points of international law. If such a treaty seemed unattainable, Jay was told to seek the cooperation of the northern nations of Europe in a joint effort to maintain neutral rights.

Jay's Treaty. Jay paid little heed to these admonitions, but succeeded in arranging in a fairly satisfactory way the disputes that had arisen out of the settlement of the Revolutionary War. The news of the battle of Fallen Timbers had made a deep impression in England, and the British now agreed to withdraw their military posts from south of the Great Lakes. Plans were also made for a settlement of the disputes over the non-payment by Americans of their pre-Revolutionary War debts to British subjects, and over the boundary between Canada and Maine. Ultimately Congress was obliged to assume the debts, while a compromise boundary was drawn. On commercial matters Jay, totally ignoring his instructions, agreed to a series of halfway measures. The treaty he signed called for a commission to determine what damages should be paid for the illegal seizure of American ships, and set up a trade agreement between the two nations that was to last for a period of twelve years. On this basis the treaty finally went into effect, although the American public, as a whole, heartily condemned it. Nevertheless, the British lived up to their agreement to abandon the northwestern posts, thus opening the way for a new advance of settlement into the Northwest. Also, on the commercial side, the treaty eased somewhat the obstacles confronted by American trade. Perhaps equally important, its adoption greatly facilitated negotiations between the United States and Spain for the settlement of their long-standing difficulties over the southwestern frontier.

Pinckney's Treaty. By 1795 Spain had withdrawn from her alliance with England and had revived her normal friendship with France. To offset Jay's Treaty, which was regarded on the Continent as a kind of forerunner to an alliance between Great Britain and the United States, the Spanish government suddenly determined to sign an even more generous treaty with the Americans. The result was the Treaty of San Lorenzo, or "Pinckney's Treaty," as it was sometimes called, after its American negotiator. Spain now consented to the thirty-first parallel as the northern boundary of Florida, conceded to Americans the navigation of the Mississippi "in its whole breadth from its source to the ocean," and agreed to allow citizens

of the United States the right to deposit at New Orleans, duty-free, such merchandise as they planned to export. This "right of deposit" was to run for three years; thereafter the Spanish monarch promised renewal, but, if he chose, at some suitable site other than New Orleans. Thus, within a few months' time the most critical problems of the Northwest and the Southwest seemed to be solved.

The French reaction to Jay's Treaty was far different from the Spanish. Assuming that the American negotiations with England amounted to a virtual repudiation of the French treaties with the United States, the French government authorized French sea captains to interfere with American trade as nearly as possible after the British pattern of behavior. This order soon brought a series of French violations of American neutral rights that were about as offensive as anything ever suffered from the British. Washington recalled James Monroe, the pro-French American minister, but the French government refused to receive the Federalist, C. C. Pinckney, as his successor. The French government also ordered its minister to the United States to withdraw his credentials, although it allowed him to stay in the United States and work for the election of Thomas Jefferson to the Presidency.

Election of 1796. The election of 1796 thus turned to some extent upon foreign affairs. Since Washington refused a third term, the Republicans supported Jefferson, who had been out of the Cabinet since 1793, and felt free to criticize the policy of the government. The Federalists did not nominate their ablest leader, the conservative Hamilton, who like Jefferson had left the Cabinet, but unlike him had retained a powerful voice in the Administration. They turned instead to the more moderate John Adams, who had made fewer enemies, with Thomas Pinckney as their candidate for Vice-President. By this time Jefferson had built up a strong following among the common people, who considered the Federalists pro-British, disliked thoroughly every item of the financial program Hamilton had forced through Congress, and were appalled at the vigorous suppression of the Whiskey Rebellion. The states'-rights element was also with Jefferson, for the Supreme Court, in one of its first important decisions, *Chisholm* v. *Georgia* (1793), had held that a state might be sued by a citizen of another state. No more complete denial of the doctrine of state sovereignty could have been devised, and the decision was promptly recalled by the submission and ratification of the Eleventh Amendment. By a narrow majority, 71 to 68, Adams was chosen over Jefferson, but some New England electors refused to vote for Pinckney, with the result that Pinckney received fewer votes than Jefferson, who thus became Vice-

JOHN ADAMS

John Adams of Massachusetts was the first distinguished member of a family which, through four generations, contributed spectacularly to the making of American history. Short of stature and plump, Adams as Vice-President, according to one sarcastic senator, might well have been addressed as "His Rotundity."

President in spite of the fact that he was the leader of the defeated party.

Washington's Farewell Address. Washington left office far less popular than when he assumed it. His dream of avoiding the formation of political parties in the United States had been shattered, and he had been forced, by both his temperament and his convictions, to ally himself with the Federalists. His Farewell Address, published on the eve of the election of 1796, urged loyalty to the Union, cautioned against an "irregular opposition" to government, and warned his countrymen "to steer clear of permanent alliances with any portion of the foreign world," but to trust instead "to temporary alliances for extraordinary emergencies." From the time of his retirement until his death in 1799, Washington devoted himself mainly to his Mount Vernon plantation.

John Adams. The new President, John Adams (1735–1826), was one of the ablest men ever to occupy the presidential chair. He had been a well-known lawyer of fame before the Revolution, and his role during that struggle was always an important one. He served as minister to England during the Confederation period, and it was no fault of his that his mission did not succeed. While he served Washington faithfully as Vice-President, he did not fully trust Hamilton even though he supported Hamilton's financial policies. John Adams was never anybody's man but his own. Vain, and often irritable when crossed, he was nevertheless, in the words of Jefferson, "as disinterested as the being who made him." His decisions with regard to national policy were invariably the result of his best judgment, and were wholly disregardful of his own political fortunes.

"X Y Z" Affair. Adams was soon called upon to show his mettle. The result of the election of 1796 still further alienated the French, who continued their spoliation of American commerce, and even ordered the rejected American minister, Pinckney, to leave the country. Many Federalists were ready by this time to sever all relations with France, even at the cost of war, but Adams knew that the United States was in no position to take such a stand and urged instead that a mission be sent to France to treat for the restoration of good relations. As a result two Federalists, C. C. Pinckney and John Marshall, and one Republican, Elbridge Gerry, were dispatched to Paris. Talleyrand, the French foreign minister, quite in keeping with the corrupt times, instructed three of his subordinates, later known as X, Y, and Z, to demand a bribe of the Americans as a condition of negotiations. There followed an exchange of statements, known to history as the "X Y Z dispatches," which revealed fully the contemptuousness of the French towards America.

Armed Neutrality. Adams still hoped for peace and did not reveal the "X Y Z dispatches" in full until called upon by Congress to do so. For a time thereafter it looked as if an open declaration of war could not be averted. Congress voted liberal appropriations to strengthen the national defense, and by repealing the treaties with France brought the alliance between the two countries to an end. Three powerful frigates, the *United States,* the *Constellation,* and the *Constitution,* were made ready for battle, and soon began to give a good account of themselves in action against French men-of-war. Merchantmen were permitted to carry guns for use in their own defense, and over four hundred privateers were commissioned. Naval vessels were ordered to seize French privateers wherever found and to take whatever measures necessary for the protection of American commerce. For over two years this period of "armed neutrality" continued, although neither nation formally recognized the existence of a state of war.

Federalists versus Aliens. The victory of the Federalists over the Republicans in 1796 was won by a narrow margin, and Adams was always sensitive to the taunt that he was "President by three votes"; but the threat of war with France tended both to strengthen his hand and to give courage to the diminished Federalist majority in Congress. In part to guard against the danger of antiwar activities within the United States, and in part to ensure against a Republican victory at the polls, the Federalist leaders pushed through Congress during the summer of 1798 an extensive program of legislation known as the Alien and Sedition Acts. Unhappily for the Federalists, most of the foreigners who came to the United States during this period joined the Republican Party. Some of them were refugee Frenchmen who had been thoroughly indoctrinated with the theories of the French Revolution. Others were Irishmen or Englishmen whose radicalism had made it expedient for them to emigrate. Among the newcomers were many highly educated men who, as pamphleteers or editors of newspapers, gave no quarter to Adams and the party he represented.

Alien and Sedition Acts. Three of the Federalist measures are generally referred to as the Alien Acts. Under their provisions, the period of residence before naturalization was lengthened to fourteen years; the President was authorized to order dangerous aliens out of the country; and in certain cases he might imprison aliens almost at will. Never seriously enforced, the Alien Acts were probably intended mainly to frighten pro-Republican Frenchmen out of the country, and undoubtedly they served their purpose well. A fourth repressive measure, the Sedition Act, was designed to subdue scurrilous criticism of the administration by Republican editors. Under penalty of heavy fines and imprisonment, conspiracy to oppose or interfere with the legal measures of the government was forbidden, and the publication of any false or malicious writing directed against the President or Congress was made a misdemeanor. The act was frankly partisan, and was to expire with the term of the administration on March 3, 1801. The Sedition Act accomplished more by threat than by actual enforcement, but a few persons were brought to trial and convicted. Since the victims were ordinarily well-known Republicans, it seemed plausible to charge that the persecution was primarily a party affair, and that those being punished were martyrs to the cause of free speech.

The Kentucky and Virginia Resolutions. To offset the Alien and Sedition Acts, Jefferson and Madison soon put forward their famous Kentucky and Virginia Resolutions. These measures proposed that the states should assume the right to decide when Congress had exceeded its powers under the Constitution. The resolutions of the Virginia legislature, which Madison had drafted, merely asserted that the states might properly "interpose" their authority against such "palpable and alarming infractions of the constitution" as were contained in the Alien and Sedition Acts, but those which the Kentucky legislature adopted, and which had secretly come from the pen of Jefferson, went much further. They called upon the other states to join Kentucky in declaring the Alien and Sedition Acts "void and of no force, and . . . in requesting their repeal at the next session of Congress." The chief purpose of the resolutions was to furnish Jefferson a platform on which to make his race for the Presidency in 1800. He meant to drive home to the electorate the dangers of Federalist rule. If the Federalists chose to violate the Constitution in one way, why not in another? And if a halt were not called soon, how long would it be before some Federalist administration would choose to obliterate the rights of the states themselves as well as the rights of individuals? But the remedy that Jefferson had in mind was not really nullification. It was the election of Thomas Jefferson to the Presidency.

Had John Adams yielded to the demand of extremists within his party for a vigorous war policy, he would probably have been re-elected in spite of Jefferson's plans, for under the stimulus of war enthusiasm the Federalists in 1798 had increased their majorities in Congress. But Adams never gave up his hope of avoiding outright war, and when he learned in 1799 that the French government was ready to receive a new American minister, he promptly sent to the Senate a nominee for the post. The more warlike Federalists were deeply shocked, but by this time the war fever had abated and they dared not oppose the President. They urged a commission of three, however, instead of a minister, and on that the President gave in.

Peace with France. By the time the envoys reached Paris, Napoleon Bonaparte headed the French government, and had chosen to play the role of peacemaker. The task of the Americans was thus an easy one. By a convention signed September 30, 1800, France agreed to the abrogation of the earlier treaties and accepted the principle that neutral ships make neutral goods. The United States, on the other hand, waived indemnities for illegal seizures by the French of American shipping. When the treaty reached America, the country was entirely over its war mood, and however much some Federalists disliked the prospect of peace, the treaty could not be turned down.

John Adams was much criticized by some members of his party for keeping the country out of war, but his policy was clearly in the national interest. By his course those embarrassing entanglements with European nations that Washington had advised against were avoided, and the policy of permanent American neutrality with regard to European wars was given an added impetus. Years later he said that as his epitaph he could ask nothing better than "Here lies John Adams, who took upon himself the responsibility of peace with France in the year 1800."

As he had feared, Adams lost the election

of 1800 to Thomas Jefferson. The Federalists, instead of being united in the support of a popular war, again found themselves handicapped by factional strife. When the returns were in, it appeared that seventy-three Republican electors had been chosen against sixty-five Federalists. The strength of the Republicans lay mainly to the south of Mason and Dixon's line, but they also carried New York, thanks to the activities of their candidate for Vice-President, Aaron Burr, and they won eight votes out of fifteen in Pennsylvania. It was significant that the new western states, Kentucky and Tennessee, voted for Jefferson, and that nearly every state with a considerable frontier element either voted for Jefferson or gave him more votes than it gave Adams.

Unfortunately, the election was not decided when the electoral college had registered its will. The provision in the Constitution which permitted each elector to vote for two candidates for the Presidency had made Jefferson Vice-President in 1796 when a majority of the electors were against him, and it now almost cost him the Presidency. A thoughtful New England Federalist threw away a vote on Jay, so that Pinckney got one less vote than Adams, but the Republican electors with greater zeal than foresight voted unanimously for Jefferson and Burr. These two having, therefore, an equal number of votes, it fell to the strongly Federalist House of Representatives, elected in 1798, to choose between them. Although a Federalist caucus decided for Burr, Hamilton used his influence on behalf of Jefferson, who finally won the Presidency. Once in power, the Republicans secured a constitutional amendment providing that each elector should thereafter vote separately for President and Vice-President.

Judiciary Act of 1801. The Federalists sought to salvage what they could following their defeat. On February 27, 1801, President Adams signed a new Judiciary Act, increasing the number of district courts, creating a new system of circuit courts, and providing for the reduction of the number of Supreme Court justices (after the first vacancy) from six to five. The Judiciary Act of 1801 had merit, for it strengthened the federal court system. But the Federalists who passed it undoubtedly hoped that the twenty-three new federal judges Adams could now appoint would ensure Federalist domination of the judiciary for many years to come. The Republicans who opposed the act denounced it as an effort on the part of a defeated party to retain control of one branch of the government after losing the other two.

Why the Federalists Lost. It is not surprising that the Federalists went down to defeat. They failed to recognize that in a democracy the opinions of the masses must be considered. They persisted too long in their assumption that government could be monopolized by an elite. Proceeding too rapidly in their endeavor to build up a powerful centralized government, they paid too little attention to the strong state loyalties that had grown so naturally out of the separate status of the various colonies. Led by men who were for the most part commercially minded, they ignored the fact that the vast majority of the American people got their living from the soil. Finally, they were split into factions, one group looking to Hamilton for leadership, and the other faithful to Adams.

Nevertheless, the Federalists in many important ways had served their country well. They had succeeded in making the new government work. They had successfully avoided entanglements in European affairs when a contrary policy might well have been fatal to the new nation. They had established the credit of the United States at home and abroad and had given to the future a praiseworthy example of honest and frugal administration. Their Republican successors thus had much to thank them for, although there is no evidence that they did so at the time.

Jefferson. Thomas Jefferson (1743–1826), whose election to the Presidency ushered in what he was pleased to term the "Revolution of 1800," was, like Washington, a Virginia planter, but there the similarity ends. Jefferson's father was from Albemarle County, "back country" at the time Thomas was born. Jefferson's mother was a Randolph, and hence from one of the first families of Virginia, but this alliance did not prevent the development of her son into perhaps the outstanding theoretical democrat of all time. Unlike Washington, Jefferson had had the advantage of an excellent formal education. His knowledge of ancient and modern languages, mathematics, the natural sciences, music, and the arts was far more than elementary. He had studied and practiced law, but preferred the management of his estate and the practice of politics.

Jefferson had succeeded Patrick Henry as governor of Virginia, and made it his business then and later to promote such innovations as complete religious liberty and church disestablishment, the outlawry of medieval legal survivals, such as primogeniture, and even the abolition of slavery. Jefferson respected Washington, but he left his Cabinet to organize the opposition to Hamilton's policies. Even as Vice-President he kept at this work. Jefferson understood the popular whims and fancies better than most politicians and possessed great talent as an organizer. He was not an orator, but he wrote with exceptional skill. If Hamilton's sympathies were with the commercial classes, Jefferson's were as definitely agrarian. A society consisting exclusively of small free farmers would, from Jefferson's point of view, have very closely approximated the ideal.

This was the man who became President on the fourth of March, 1801, in a setting of extreme simplicity. The new President even walked from his boardinghouse to the Capitol to deliver his inaugural address. Jefferson was the first President to take the oath of office in the new capital city on the Potomac, appropriately named Washington. An admirable plan for the city had been devised by a Frenchman named L'Enfant; but the streets were unpaved and most of them unopened, the public buildings were as yet unfinished, and only the distances between them were magnificent.

Census of 1800. And yet the capital city, in which great possibilities were only faintly realized, was not unlike the nation as a whole. The United States, with a population of 5,308,473, according to the census of 1800, was still a small nation. Nine-tenths of these people lived to the east of the mountains; the other tenth occupied the territory on the upper Ohio and its more important tributaries in Kentucky and Tennessee. Nor had American society as yet shown many signs of sophistication.

But the new nation was growing with phenomenal rapidity. In 1790 the population had been listed at 3,929,214; hence the total increase during the decade had

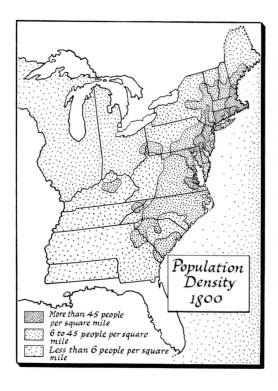

Population Density 1800

More than 45 people per square mile

6 to 45 people per square mile

Less than 6 people per square mile

amounted to about thirty-five per cent. This is the more important in view of the fact that the number of Europeans who had come to America had been relatively insignificant since before the Revolution. The increase in population was thus due almost exclusively to increase in the native stock. Marriages were early and families were large.

The mingling of European peoples in America was beginning to develop a distinctively American type. The English furnished the dominant strain, and except in a small part of Pennsylvania, where the "Pennsylvania Dutch" still clung to their patois, the English language was practically universal. But the absorption of the Hudson Valley Dutch, the French Huguenots, the Scotch-Irish, the Scottish Highlanders, and the Pennsylvania Germans, not to mention the "Hessians" whom the British had hired to fight the Americans in the Revolution, but many of whom remained in America to found American families, was producing a new, distinctly American people, no longer purely English, and not wholly uninfluenced by the minor ingredients. English political ideas, legal concepts, notions of literary and cultural excellence generally won out, but only rarely without modification. Particularly in the West the variation from the original English type was becoming more and more marked.

Economic Conditions. Economic conditions had not changed greatly from colonial times. New England still devoted her chief energies to agriculture, the fisheries, shipbuilding, commerce, and merchandising. Her greatest profits came from her overseas trade, and the wealth of some of her merchants and traders was considerable. The middle states, once called the "bread colonies," still produced great quantities of foodstuffs, and because of the protracted Napoleonic wars in Europe these commodities brought good prices. Here, too, were carried on nearly all the activities upon which the prosperity of New England

THOMAS JEFFERSON ON CONSTITUTIONS

The most gifted of Presidents, Jefferson turned his brilliant intellect to almost every aspect of human endeavor. A competent musician, architect, and naturalist, his theories of government, education, and philosophy greatly influenced the course of American Democracy.

Some men look at constitutions with sanctimonious reverence, and deem them like the arc of the covenant, too sacred to be touched. . . . I am certainly not an advocate for frequent and untried changes in laws and constitutions. I think moderate imperfections had better be borne with; because, when once known, we accommodate ourselves to them, and find practical means of correcting their ill effects. But I know also, that laws and institutions must go hand in hand with the progress of the human mind. As that becomes more developed, more enlightened, as new discoveries are made, new truths disclosed, and manners and opinions change with the change of circumstances, institutions must advance also, and keep pace with the times.

The Writings of Thomas Jefferson, edited by PAUL L. FORD (1899)

depended, and "infant industries," such as the manufacture of iron, grew increasingly numerous. In the South only the large planters made money. The old colonial staples, tobacco and rice, produced by the labor of over a million slaves, were still the chief sources of prosperity. In 1793 Eli Whitney invented the cotton gin, and the resulting change in the status of cotton was already slightly in evidence. By 1800 the country exported 25,000 bales of cotton, but the later significance of cotton growing in southern economy was as yet hardly foreseen. Free farmers in the West made a living for themselves and enjoyed a little prosperity from trade down the Mississippi in flatboats, or, in spite of Hamilton's tax, from the distilling of whiskey. Numerous speculators in western lands sometimes took good profits. Many easterners were interested in this business, and on account of their western holdings often became the most ardent champions of western rights.

Americans still lived in the country rather than in the city, and the danger that Jefferson most feared, a city proletariat, seemed too far away for any but theorists to worry about. Philadelphia with 70,000 people was the most populous of American cities. New York came next with 60,000; Baltimore had 26,000; Boston, 24,000; Charleston, 20,000. These cities still lacked what would today be called "all modern conveniences." Sewers were conspicuously absent, and as in colonial times, hogs ran loose in the streets to dispose of the garbage. The country was as primitive as the city, and the farmers' tools were much the same as in Biblical days.

The West. The West was already "the most American part of America." Here the melting pot had fused national elements more completely than elsewhere, and made the difference between American and European ways most pronounced. Cheap lands almost literally opened opportunity equally to all. Here democracy was practiced as well as preached, and each citizen believed himself the equal of any other. People looked out for themselves, and the ideal of individual freedom held universal sway. The society of the West was crude and rough, and the "men of the western waters" were mostly uncouth and illiterate, but they had begun the conquest of a continent, and they had little time for anything else.

Crowninshield's Wharf, Salem. High adventure and great wealth attended the shipping trade that sailed from Salem to every part of the world. Long panel painting by George Ropes, 1806.

Salem is, next to Boston, the lagest (*sic*) town in Massachusetts, and one of the earliest settled in the state. It is situated on a peninsula formed by two branches of the sea, called North and South Rivers, and consists of about 1500 houses, and contained in 1800, 9547 inhabitants. The houses are built partly of wood, and partly of brick; and many of them are uncommonly elegant. The principal public buildings are a court-house, five congregational churches, and one each for quakers and episcopalians. Salem carries on a very extensive shipping trade, more business being done here in that line than in any town in the New England states, Boston excepted. There is a ship-yard in Salem, and a considerable manufactory of sail-cloth. A bank has long been established. The inhabitants are said to be industrious and frugal, and the appearance of the town indicates a considerable accumulation of wealth.

JOHN MELISH, *Travels through the United States of America, in the Years 1806 & 1807, and 1809, 1810, & 1811* (1818)

"Revolution of 1800." Jefferson was at pains to introduce democratic simplicity into all the affairs of state, but he did not surround himself with men from the lower walks of life. For example, he chose as his Secretary of State James Madison, the "father of the Constitution," and like himself a Virginian of good position. For Secretary of the Treasury he picked another man of consequence, Albert Gallatin of Pennsylvania, a Swiss by birth who had taught at Harvard. In general, the "Revolution of 1800" meant the transfer of leadership in government from representatives of business to those primarily interested in agriculture. Jefferson's concept of an ideal government might perhaps be put as one of the people and for the people, but by an educated elite. Jefferson really hoped to win over the rank and file of the Federalists to his party and asserted in his inaugural address, "We are all Republicans, we are all Federalists." When it came to the removal of Federalist officeholders, he acted with extreme caution. Nevertheless, by the end of Jefferson's first administration a majority of the federal officeholders were Republicans.

The Republicans wasted little time in reversing many outstanding Federalist policies. The excise tax, so offensive to back-country distillers of whiskey, was promptly repealed. The period of naturalization was set again at five years, and the Alien and Sedition Acts were allowed to lapse. Appropriations for public expenditures, particularly the army and navy, were mercilessly pruned down. The Judiciary Act of 1801, under the terms of which President Adams had made many "midnight appointments" just before leaving office, was replaced by another which restored in the main the old judicial system. As for the new judges that Adams had appointed, they were left without duties and without salaries.

It was not long, however, before the Supreme Court, which was still predominantly Federalist and headed by the extremely able John Marshall, found a way to impress upon the Republicans the necessity of keeping their "revolution" within reasonable bounds. In the famous case of *Marbury* v. *Madison* (1803), Marshall stated the doctrine that the Court could, if it chose, declare a law of Congress unconstitutional.

135

The case itself, except for the rule of law it provoked, was insignificant. A commission as justice of the peace, designed for one William Marbury, had been signed by Adams before leaving office, but was still undelivered when Jefferson became President. After inauguration, Madison, the Secretary of State, refused to deliver the commission, whereupon Marbury asked the Supreme Court to issue a mandamus requiring its surrender. This, Marshall, in his momentous opinion, refused to do. The law, he admitted, gave the Court abundant authority to take such action, but in granting this authority to the Supreme Court, Marshall held, Congress had exceeded its powers under the Constitution, which permitted the Court to exercise original jurisdiction only in "cases affecting ambassadors, other public ministers and consuls, and those in which a state shall be a party." With the law and the Constitution thus in direct conflict, the Chief Justice maintained that the Constitution must be followed and the law disregarded. This "doctrine of judicial review" placed a powerful weapon in the hands of the Federalist judiciary, but the Court wisely kept the weapon in reserve for many years.

Gallatin succeeded with the reduction of the national debt. The growing wealth and population of the country led to increased purchases abroad and to corresponding increases in the tariff revenues. Also, except for a brief interlude, the European war raged on, and with British consent in the case of the *Polly* (1800), American ships were permitted to carry goods from the French West Indies to France, provided they first landed their cargoes at an American port and paid the duty. Before the end of Jefferson's administration Gallatin, aided by the advantages of American neutrality, had retired as much of the national debt as was due and payable.

The Tripolitan War. The Tripolitan War (1801–1805) probably saved the American navy from extinction. It had long

been the habit of European nations to pay tribute to the piratical rulers of the maritime states of northern Africa — Morocco, Algiers, Tunis, and Tripoli — sometimes known as the Barbary States. In this practice the new United States, whose trade relations in the Mediterranean were of some consequence, soon joined. To Jefferson, however, the idea of paying tribute money to pirates was particularly offensive, and much as he deplored the expense attached to a navy, he felt obliged to support this arm of the national defense as a means of dealing with the corsairs. Open warfare broke out with Tripoli, whose ruler was particularly insolent in his demands. Finally, after the United States had lost one of its best ships, a small overland expedition from Egypt, headed by a pretender to the Tripolitan throne and backed by an American citizen, William Eaton, cooperated with the navy to bring the Pasha to terms. But for many years an American squadron had to be retained in the Mediterranean, and the practice of paying tribute did not wholly disappear until 1815.

Napoleon Acquires Louisiana. To Jefferson the purchase of Louisiana was as unexpected a development as the Tripolitan War. But he understood the people of the Mississippi Valley far better than had his predecessors, and he regarded the purchase as a necessity in order to retain western loyalty to the Union. In a letter dated April 18, 1802, Jefferson expressed to Robert R. Livingston, the American minister to France, his deep concern over Bonaparte's apparent intention to acquire Louisiana from Spain:

> There is on the globe one single spot, the possessor of which is our natural and habitual enemy. It is New Orleans, through which the produce of ⅜ of our territory must pass to market, and from its [the West's] fertility it will ere long yield more than one half of our whole produce, and contain more than half of our inhabitants. France, placing herself in that door, assumes to us the attitude

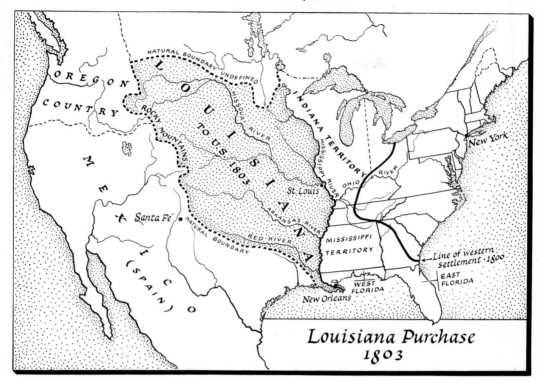

**Louisiana Purchase
1803**

of defiance. The day that France takes possession of New Orleans . . . we must marry ourselves to the British fleet and nation.

Jefferson's worst fears seemed confirmed when he learned a few months later that the "right of deposit" at New Orleans had been suspended. Since most western products were brought down the Mississippi in small boats, the denial of deposit was tantamount to closure of the river. Actually Bonaparte had secretly acquired title to Louisiana in 1800, but had chosen not to take possession until a long-standing revolt against French authority in the island of Santo Domingo could be suppressed. The Spanish officials were thus left in control at New Orleans, and the closing of the Mississippi to American trade seems to have been the idea of the Spanish governor. But westerners, aware at last of the secret treaty, were convinced that the French government had ordered the action, and meant

to cut off their life-line to the sea. To prevent such a calamity, they were capable, as Jefferson well knew, of taking drastic action.

Purchase of Louisiana. Faced with this situation, Jefferson ordered Livingston to open negotiations for the purchase of the Isle of Orleans and West Florida, and he sent James Monroe as special envoy to France with authority to offer as much as ten million dollars for the coveted territory. Meantime Bonaparte, discouraged by the lack of success of his forces in Santo Domingo, had decided to abandon his colonial empire in favor of continental expansion, and as a step in that direction to sell Louisiana to the United States. He knew that his plans would precipitate war with Great Britain, and since the British would have control of the sea, he could not hope to protect Louisiana. With war in prospect, the French treasury needed money. Even before Monroe arrived, the French foreign minister, Talleyrand, had asked Livingston what he would give for the whole of Louisiana. Once Monroe arrived, the bargain was quickly struck. For about $15 million the United States acquired title to whatever territory in America Bonaparte had obtained from Spain.

Jefferson was greatly astonished when he learned what his ministers had done; indeed, he seriously doubted whether the Constitution authorized the central government to add so much new territory to the Union. But he quickly stifled his doubts, and submitted the treaty to the Senate, where it was ratified by a vote of 26 to 5. The House authorized the funds necessary to carry the treaty into effect by a vote of 90 to 25. Some of the Federalists were alarmed at the prospective growth of the agricultural West, which, they feared, might join with the South to tyrannize over the commercial Northeast. When they were unable to prevent ratification of the treaty,

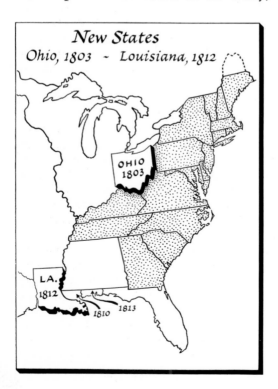

New States

Ohio, 1803 - Louisiana, 1812

OHIO 1803

LA. 1812

1810   1813

they urged that Louisiana should at least be kept in a perpetual state of dependency. It was decided, however, to adapt the Northwest Ordinance to the territory acquired from France, and to permit the formation from its area of new western states. The process of subdivision into territories and states was soon begun. In 1812 the state of Louisiana, with its present boundaries, was admitted to the Union.

Admission of Ohio. Meantime the Jeffersonian regime had been at pains to seek solutions for other problems of the West. The Republican Congress, in 1804, further liberalized the public land laws. It reduced the minimum unit of sale to 160 acres, so that thereafter a man with eighty dollars in cash could make the first payment on a frontier farm. The administration also showed its willingness to establish new governmental units in the West. The population of the Northwest Territory, stimulated by the Land Law of 1800, increased so rapidly that in 1802 Congress voted to admit the new state of Ohio. The "enabling act" by which this decision was effected set two important precedents: (1) national aid to public education, and (2) national aid to road building. The law redeemed the promise of the Ordinance of 1785 by handing over to the new state one section of land out of every township in aid of education; and it provided also that five per cent of the proceeds of the sales of public lands within the state should be "applied to laying out and making public roads" in Ohio, and from Ohio to the "navigable waters emptying into the Atlantic." Under a constitution that included many democratic provisions, Ohio was formally admitted in 1803.

Yazoo Claims. A more difficult problem of territorial development appeared during these years in the Southwest, where in 1798 the new territory of Mississippi had been created out of what was left of the national domain on the admission of Tennessee.

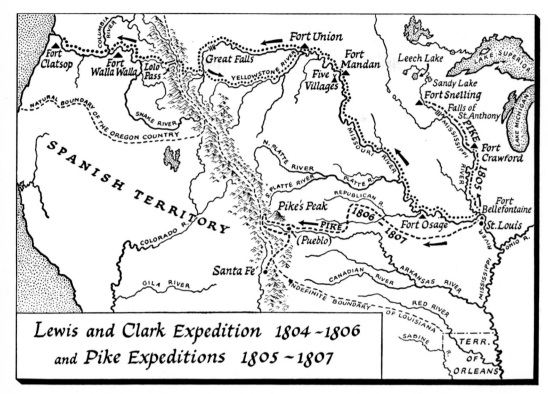

Lewis and Clark Expedition 1804~1806
and Pike Expeditions 1805~1807

Here the land claims of the United States and of Georgia were in confusion, but in 1802 a satisfactory agreement was reached, and Georgia formally ceded her holdings to the national government. A part of this agreement called for the indemnification of certain claimants to lands in the Yazoo district whose title had been obtained from the state of Georgia by corrupt means. This bargain was steadfastly opposed by John Randolph of Roanoke, a fiery Virginian, whose differences with the Jefferson administration led a small faction of the Republican Party into open revolt. The "Quids," as these insurgents were sometimes called, claimed that Jefferson had in reality become a Federalist. In 1810 the Supreme Court in the case of *Fletcher* v. *Peck* upheld the Yazoo claimants; and in 1814, $8 million was voted for the settlement of their claims.

Lewis and Clark Expedition. The Lewis and Clark Expedition, which Jeffer-

son dispatched into the West in 1804, revealed the President's interest in the territory he had purchased, and perhaps an interest in further expansion. Led by Meriwether Lewis, the President's private secretary, and William Clark, the brother of George Rogers Clark, the explorers left St. Louis in the spring of 1804, ascended the Missouri River far toward its source, crossed the Continental Divide, and reached the mouth of the Columbia. Then, by approximately the same route they returned, arriving in St. Louis in September, 1806, after an absence of nearly two and one-half years. Their published journals recorded with meticulous detail the doings and discoveries of the party, and furnished much new information for scientists and map makers. As for the future of the country, Lewis and Clark held that not much of it would ever be fit for white men, but their explorations nevertheless gave the United States whatever claim it wished to

LEWIS AND CLARK

Lewis and Clark Holding a Council with the Indians. Illustration from Patrick Gass, Journal of the Voyages and Travels under Lewis and Clark (1812).

assert to the region beyond the Rocky Mountains.

Expeditions of Pike. Similar explorations by Zebulon Montgomery Pike in 1805–1807 sought to locate the source of the Mississippi River and to penetrate into the Spanish-held Southwest. On the latter expedition, Pike was picked up by the Spanish, his papers taken away from him, and he and his men conducted by a circuitous route back to the United States. His verdict, like that of Lewis and Clark, showed much skepticism as to the habitability of the arid West.

Jefferson's manifold interests, and particularly his success in purchasing Louisiana, insured his re-election in 1804. Some northeastern Federalists, rather than face the prospect of continued agricultural control of the government, were ready to break up the Union. In the Vice-President, Aaron Burr, they found a willing tool for their plots. Jefferson never forgave Burr for refusing to withdraw from the contest for President in 1800, and his influence with the members of the Republican Party soon faded. When, therefore, a number of Federalists suggested that he become their candidate for governor of New York in 1804, he agreed. Their plan was to elect Burr, and then under his leadership to take New York and New England out of the Union. Fortunately Hamilton learned of the plot and exposed it. Burr, now completely discredited, challenged Hamilton to a duel and on July 11, 1804, mortally wounded him. In the election the Federalists, compelled now to defend themselves against the charge of treason, were overwhelmed. George Clinton, Burr's chief rival in New York politics, became the Republican vice-presidential candidate and helped to carry that state for Jefferson. Even New England, with the exception of Connecticut, went Republican. The electoral vote stood 162 for Jefferson to 14 for C. C. Pinckney, the Federalist candidate.

Aaron Burr. Unfortunately the last had not yet been heard of Aaron Burr. Discredited everywhere in the East, and in two states indicted for murder, he determined to carve out for himself a new career somewhere in the troubled borderland between the United States and Spain. As he well knew, the boundaries of Louisiana were only vaguely defined, and Jefferson had promptly opened a dispute with Spain over West Florida. Already hostile Indians were using Florida as a base of operations against the American frontier, and as a haven of refuge. The Creole population of Louisiana was restive under the American rule. An admirable foil for Burr's ambitions was available, also, in the person of General James Wilkinson, in charge of American troops in Louisiana. Wilkinson had long been in the pay of Spain.

As to what Burr really intended to do, there is no agreement among historians. He himself told one treasonous story to the British minister, and quite another to the Spanish minister. He made a trip to the West and talked freely of his plans. To some he said merely that he was going out west to make a new start in politics. To others he spoke of carving a Mississippi

Valley Confederacy out of the possessions of Spain, or of the United States, or both. With consummate skill he suited the degree of treason to the taste of each listener.

Burr's "conspiracy" was well received by many westerners. Some were interested merely because of the excitement that the project promised. Wilkinson, a past master at intrigue, was easily attached to the scheme. Open plans were made for an expedition to start down the Ohio River on November 15, 1806, and plans were laid for Wilkinson to be with his troops far to the west of New Orleans when Burr's boats should arrive. But everything went wrong. Burr was delayed temporarily; Wilkinson, true to his record, turned informer and gave the plot away. When the "expedition" finally started, it consisted of only thirteen flatboats carrying sixty men. Before it reached Natchez, Burr learned of Wilkinson's duplicity and fled, only to be caught and sent to Richmond, Virginia, for trial.

Burr's Trial. When the case came to trial, it took on more the aspect of a test of strength between Thomas Jefferson and John Marshall than a trial for treason. Jefferson sent a notable array of legal talent to prosecute Burr, but the Chief Justice, before whom the trial was set, circumvented their best arguments by ruling that to be guilty of treason a man had to be present when the overt act was committed. Since the overt act was held to be the starting of the expedition, and since Burr was not present at that time, but joined the expedition later, his acquittal followed as a matter of course. Marshall was interested in demonstrating that the President of the United States could neither coerce the courts nor use them as a means of political persecution. Nevertheless, Jefferson was not wholly bested. When the Court summoned him to appear during the proceedings, and to bring certain papers with him, Jefferson ignored the summons and sent only such papers as he chose. The President could not be at the command of the courts. It was a drawn battle in which each department of the government stoutly and successfully maintained its independence of the other.

SELECTED BIBLIOGRAPHY

An interesting documentary collection is N. E. Cunningham, Jr. (ed.), *The Making of The American Party System, 1789 to 1809 (1965). Adams scholarship is being greatly advanced by the publication of *The Adams Papers, under the editorship of L. H. Butterfield (6 vols. to date, 1961–   ). The volumes in this series published so far contain John Adams' diary and autobiography. Convenient documentary collections are *The Selected Writings of John and John Quincy Adams*, edited by Adrienne Koch and William Peden (1946); and *Political Writings of John Adams, edited by G. A. Peek (1954). Interesting recent monographs are Zoltán Haraszti, *John Adams and the Prophets of Progress (1952); S. G. Kurtz, *The Presidency of John Adams (1957); and Edward Handler, *America and Europe in the Political Thought of John Adams* (1964).

* Available in paperback

Political historians have recently published a number of important monographs which help to explain the development of the two-party system. Two extremely interesting treatments are W. N. Chambers, *Political Parties in a New Nation, 1776–1809 (1963); and J. E. Charles, *The Origins of the American Party System (1956). M. J. Dauer, *The Adams Federalists* (1953), treats a previously neglected subject. Monographs which present differing interpretations of the rise of the Republican Party are E. P. Link, *Democratic-Republican Societies, 1790–1800* (1942); and N. E. Cunningham, Jr., *The Jeffersonian Republicans, 1789–1801* (1957); and *The Jeffersonian Republicans in Power, 1801–1809* (1963). No student of the period should overlook C. A. Beard, *Economic Origins of Jeffersonian Democracy* (2nd ed., 1949), even though its conclusions are disputed by many historians. Claude Bowers, *Jefferson and Hamilton* (1925), a lively work, votes for Jefferson on almost every page. The Alien and Sedition Acts are given full treatment in J. C. Miller, °*Crisis in Freedom* (1951); and J. M. Smith, *Freedom's Fetters* (1956). A reliable general survey of politics is W. E. Binkley, *American Political Parties, Their Natural History* (3rd ed., 1958); for one party, see W. N. Chambers, °*The Democrats, 1789–1964* (1964). *The American Secretaries of State and their Diplomacy*, edited by S. F. Bemis (10 vols., 1927–1929), is a cooperative work that covers in detail the history of American foreign relations. Illuminating studies are Felix Gilbert, *To the Farewell Address* (1961); and Julian Boyd, *Number 7: Alexander Hamilton's Attempts to Control American Foreign Policy* (1964). S. F. Bemis, °*Jay's Treaty* (2nd ed., 1962), and °*Pinckney's Treaty* (2nd ed., 1960), are durable works. Important recent monographs include Bradford Perkins, *The First Rapprochement; England and the United States, 1795–1805* (1955); and L. M. Sears, *George Washington and the French Revolution* (1960). On maritime problems, see J. F. Zimmerman, *Impressment of American Seamen* (1925). An important theme is treated in Merle Curti, *The Roots of American Loyalty* (1946).

Brief surveys which provide useful introductions to the Jefferson period are C. M. Wiltse, °*The New Nation, 1800–1845* (1961); Raymond Walters, Jr., °*The Virginia Dynasty* (1964); and Max Beloff, °*Thomas Jefferson and American Democracy* (1949). A lively pro-Jefferson treatment of politics is Claude Bowers, *Jefferson in Power* (1936); but a powerful antidote to this is L. W. Levy, *Jefferson and Civil Liberties: The Darker Side* (1963). In a class by itself is Henry Adams, *History of the United States of America during the Administration of Thomas Jefferson and James Madison* (9 vols., 1889–1891), detailed critical history on the grand scale by a master stylist; a two-volume abridgement is available in paperback. An extract which contains Adams' famous social section is published as °*The United States in 1800*. W. H. Jordy, °*Henry Adams: Scientific Historian* (1952), is a careful analysis of Adams and his methods.

While Jefferson has attracted many biographers, most of them adulatory, we do not yet have a full-length scholarly study. Nathan Schachner, *Thomas Jefferson* (2 vols., 1951), is heavily factual and not overly-sympathetic to its subject. Of the many single-volume biographies, Gilbert Chinard, °*Thomas Jefferson* (2nd ed., 1939); and A. J. Nock, °*Jefferson* (1926), are both interesting and readily available. A great work of scholarship still in process is *The Papers of Thomas Jefferson*, edited by J. P. Boyd (9 vols., 1950–　　). Collections of Jefferson's writings include °*The Autobiography of Thomas Jefferson* (1829); °*Political Writings of Thomas Jefferson*, edited by Edward Dumbauld (1955); °*Notes on the State of Virginia* (1801); and *The Adams-Jefferson Letters*, edited by L. J. Cappon (1959).

Special studies of Jefferson and his influence are numerous, and only a few can be listed here. Two important and broad-gauged works are C. M. Wiltse, °*The Jeffersonian Tradition in American Democracy* (1935); and Merrill Peterson, °*The Jefferson Image in the American Mind* (1960). The mind of Jefferson is probed by D. J. Boorstin, °*The Lost World of Thomas Jefferson* (1948); E. T. Martin, °*Thomas Jefferson: Scientist* (1952); and Karl Lehmann, °*Thomas Jefferson, American Humanist* (1947). Other significant works include F. L. Mott, *Jefferson and the Press* (1943); Adrienne Koch, °*Jefferson and Madison: The Great Collaboration* (1950); and Dumas Malone, *Thomas Jefferson as a Political Leader* (1963). A monograph on southern conservatism in this period is N. K. Risjord, *The Old Republicans* (1965).

A masterly work on administrative history is L. D. White, *The Jeffersonians* (1951). On problems of politics and administration, see C. R. Fish, *The Civil Service and the Patronage* (1905); and S. H. Aronson, *Status and Kinship in the Higher Civil Service* (1964). On Jefferson's Secretary of the Treasury, see Raymond Walters, Jr., *Albert Gallatin* (1957); and A. S. Balinky, *Albert Gallatin: Fiscal Theories and Policies* (1958). George Dangerfield, *Chancellor Robert R. Livingston of New York* (1960), is a first-rate biography of a neglected figure. Studies of other Jeffersonians include W. B. Hatcher, *Edward Livingston* (1940); E. T. Mudge, *The Social Philosophy of John Taylor of Caroline* (1939); and Henry Adams, °*John Randolph* (2nd ed., 1917). Interesting treatises on politics include S. W. Higginbotham, *The Keystone in the Democratic Arch: Pennsylvania Politics, 1800–1816* (1952); P. J. Coleman, *The Transformation of Rhode Island, 1790–1860* (1963); Alvin Kass, *Politics in New*

York State, 1800–1830 (1965); and Paul Goodman, *The Democratic-Republicans of Massachusetts* (1964). A fine study of the leader of the opposition is Morton Borden, *The Federalism of James A. Bayard* (1955).

The expanding power of the Supreme Court is dealt with in great detail in A. J. Beveridge, *The Life of John Marshall* (4 vols., 1916–1919). See also David Loth, *Chief Justice; John Marshall and the Growth of the Republic* (1949); and B. W. Palmer, *Marshall and Taney* (1939). Most of Marshall's colleagues have been neglected, but see D. G. Morgan, *Justice William Johnson* (1954). H. S. Commager, *Majority Rule and Minority Rights* (1943), expresses doubts on the constitutional justification of the doctrine of judicial review.

The Barbary Wars are treated in C. O. Paullin, *Diplomatic Negotiations of American Naval Officers* (1912). Standard works include A. P. Whitaker, *The Mississippi Question, 1795–1803* (1934); and J. K. Hosmer, *The History of the Louisiana Purchase* (1902). The character of Aaron Burr has long fascinated students of this period. On the critical side is T. P. Abernethy, *The Burr Conspiracy* (1954). More friendly to its subject is Nathan Schachner, *Aaron Burr* (1937). Interesting documentary

collections are H. C. Syrett and J. G. Cooke (eds.), *Interview in Weehawken* (1960); and V. B. Reed and J. D. Williams (eds.), *Case of Aaron Burr* (1960). Wilkinson biographies include J. R. Jacobs, *Tarnished Warrior* (1938); and M. R. Werner, *The Admirable Trumpeter* (1941). A study of a rather neglected western leader is A. B. Sears, *Thomas Worthington* (1958).

On exploration, see the survey by W. H. Goetzmann, *Army Exploration in the American West, 1803–1863* (1959). J. E. Bakeless, *Lewis and Clark* (1947), is a clearly written narrative; see also Richard Dillon, *Meriwether Lewis* (1965). *Original Journals of the Lewis and Clark Expedition,* edited by R. G. Thwaites (8 vols., 1904–1905), is both a prime source and fascinating reading. A single-volume abridgement is Bernard De Voto (ed.), *The Journals of Lewis and Clark* (1953). See also *The Lewis and Clark Expedition* (1814), edited by Nicholas Biddle and published over Lewis' name; it is now available in a new edition (3 vols., 1961). Another great source is *Letters of the Lewis and Clark Expedition,* edited by Donald Jackson (1962). On Pike, see the biography by W. E. Hollon, *The Lost Pathfinder* (1949).

9

THE WAR OF 1812

&ᐳ British-French-American Relations · Armed Action at Sea · Jefferson's Embargo · Substitution of Non-Intercourse · Failure of Economic Weapons · Causes of the War of 1812 · Course of the War · Peace of Ghent · Subsequent Agreements

For all the growing interest in the West, the United States during Jefferson's administration was still bound by close commercial ties to Europe, especially to England. The era of American self-sufficiency had not yet arrived. Great quantities of manufactured articles still had to be imported, and raw materials, particularly foodstuffs, exported. During part of Jefferson's first administration, Europe was at peace, and this trade went on in normal fashion. But war between England and France was resumed in 1803, and from that time on the twofold task of American diplomacy was to keep the United States out of the war, and at the same time to defend her commercial rights as a neutral.

Revival of Difficulties with England. The customary difficulties with England were soon in evidence. By 1805 Napoleon's bid to control the seas had been frustrated by Lord Nelson's defeat of a combined French and Spanish fleet off the Cape of Trafalgar, and the Royal Navy was free to tighten its control over commerce. The British government now found inconvenient the decision that Sir William Scott had handed down in the case of the *Polly*, and another judge, Sir William Grant, held in the case of the *Essex* (1805), that a French-owned West Indian cargo could not be shipped by way of the United States to Europe unless the owners could show that their original intent had been to leave the goods in the United States. Thenceforth the British used their judgment as to what part of the West Indian trade in neutral ships to permit, and what part to restrain.

Napoleon's Continental System. The struggle in Europe had now reached a degree of intensity in which neither side cared much for neutral rights. Napoleon saw the English as a nation of shopkeepers, whose livelihood depended upon their trade with the outside world. Europe was England's chief customer, and Napoleon thought that he could control most of Europe. His Continental System was devised to stop all imports into European ports from England. He would rob England of her markets and by an unfavorable balance of trade drain her of her gold supply. He would also, in so far as he could accomplish it by threats or violence, prevent trade between England and her customers outside of Europe, particularly the United States. The Berlin and Milan Decrees, issued respectively in 1806

144

and 1807, laid a paper blockade around Great Britain, forbade all trade in British merchandise, and ordered the confiscation of all neutral ships bound to or from a British port. Napoleon knew that he could not enforce his decrees fully, but he believed that he could stop much trade to the continent of Europe, and, even with the limited sea power he possessed, he thought that he might interfere somewhat with trade between England and the neutral nations.

British Orders in Council. The English replied to Napoleon's decrees with a series of Orders in Council that were quite as careless of neutral rights as the decrees themselves. All trade between ports in the possession of France or her allies was forbidden, and these ports placed under a further blockade against trade with the outside world. This meant that all neutral trade with Europe was outlawed, although the British blockade was also a "paper" blockade which could at best only hamper the movement of goods to and from continental ports. The British hoped that a shortage of foodstuffs would develop, which would induce Napoleon to withdraw his obnoxious decrees. The plight of American shipping was now a sorry one indeed. Ships destined to France or to any of the nations controlled by France, which meant most of Europe, were subject to seizure by the English, while ships sailing for any English port were threatened with confiscation by the French.

Both the French and the British enforced their illegal blockades by captures on the American side of the Atlantic, where privateers and warships took what prizes they could. The French naturally took fewer, for their ships were less numerous and were themselves in danger of capture by the British. Admiralty courts in the West Indies, both French and British, decided against captured American ships. British impressments of sailors from American ships occurred more and more frequently, and were sometimes carried out with brutality. American resentment against this practice, particularly among the people along the coast whose friends and relatives had been victimized, grew steadily more intense.

The *Chesapeake* Affair. The supreme outrage occurred in June, 1807, when a British man-of-war, the *Leopard*, attacked an American frigate, the *Chesapeake*, and took off four members of her crew. This incident followed shortly after the escape of a boatload of sailors from the sloop *Halifax*, which, together with several other British warships, had put in at Lynnhaven Bay, near the mouth of the Chesapeake. The commander of the British squadron had noted that an American warship, the *Chesapeake*, was preparing to leave the harbor for a cruise in the Mediterranean. Having reason to believe that some of the deserting British sailors must be upon it, he gave orders that the *Chesapeake* should be searched. When the American man-of-war finally put to sea, she was followed by the *Leopard*, which insisted on exercising the right of search, quite as if the American ship had been a merchant vessel instead of a warship. When Commodore Barron of the *Chesapeake* refused to submit to the proposed indignity, the *Leopard* promptly opened fire, and forced the unready *Chesapeake* to strike its colors. The British then boarded the *Chesapeake* and took off four deserters, only one of whom turned out to be an Englishman.

The Embargo. The news of this outrage put the country in a belligerent mood. But the President chose to keep the peace if he could. After forbidding British warships the use of American ports and harbors, and demanding reparations from the British government, he laid before Congress as his chief weapon of retaliation an Embargo Act of December 21, 1807. This measure prohibited all ships, except foreign ships in ballast, to depart from the United States for any foreign port. Ships engaged in the coasting trade were required to give heavy bond that they would land their cargoes in the United States.

Jefferson had hoped that the warring nations of Europe, rather than suffer the loss of American trade, would withdraw their obnoxious regulations, but in this he was disappointed. In the first place, the embargo could not be perfectly enforced, and many American ships continued to sail the seas. In the second place, the law hurt the United States at least as much as, and probably more than, the European belligerents. Shippers, shipowners, and shipbuilders suffered sizable losses; sailors, sailmakers, and other artisans were thrown out of work; articles of trade that were normally imported became scarce and high priced; farm prices dropped as the crops of 1808 found their normal gateways to market closed.

The Election of 1808. The election of 1808 showed clearly that the temper of the country had changed. Jefferson was importuned to stand for re-election again, but he declined with such emphasis as to set a precedent that long remained unbroken. He did not hesitate, however, to throw the succession to his Secretary of State, James Madison. The Federalists supported C. C. Pinckney, and by emphasizing the unpleasant features of the embargo, they won back many voters who had deserted them for Jefferson four years before. In the electoral college Madison received 122 electoral votes to 47 for Pinckney. Congress remained Republican, although by a much-reduced majority.

Repeal of the Embargo Act. The results of the election made it abundantly clear that the Republicans must repeal their embargo or witness an even more embarrassing revival of Federalist strength. Undoubtedly the English were also greatly distressed by the embargo, but they were willing to put up with it as a necessary accompaniment of the war with Napoleon. But the United States lacked any such effec-

tive motive, and was unwilling to continue its self-inflicted punishment. After the election, Jefferson left the determination of future policy to his successor, and with Madison's approval, a few days before he left office, he signed a bill to repeal the embargo.

James Madison. James Madison (1751-1836), the fourth President, was another representative of the Virginia planter class. When he was only a few years out of Princeton and still undecided as to his life work, the outbreak of the American Revolution determined his course for him. Successively he served as a member of the local committee on public safety, of the convention that drew up the first Virginia constitution, of the Continental Congress, of the Virginia House of Delegates, of the Convention that framed the Constitution of the United States, and of the national House of Representatives. For eight years he was Jefferson's Secretary of State and close adviser. Certainly his political apprenticeship had been ample.

Non-Intercourse. As a substitute for the embargo, Madison gave his approval to what was called the Non-Intercourse Act, a measure which closed American ports to the ships of England and France and forbade the importation of goods into the United States from either of those nations, or from their colonies or dependencies. American ships were permitted to leave American ports, provided only that their destinations were not French or British. The act also carried with it an offer to the offending belligerents. In case England withdrew her Orders in Council, the President was authorized to suspend non-intercourse with England, and in case Napoleon withdrew his decrees, to suspend non-intercourse with France.

It would be quite inaccurate to assume that the Embargo and Non-Intercourse Acts had no effect whatever upon British policy. Shortly after the *Chesapeake* affair, a special British envoy was sent to the United

States to seek a satisfactory settlement of that unhappy episode, but neither side would yield, and the mission failed. Another effort to restore good relations was made by David M. Erskine, the regular British minister to the United States, who was instructed by the British government to prepare the way for a general treaty of amity between the two nations. It appeared that Canning, the British foreign minister, was even ready to consider the withdrawal of the British Orders in Council in return for the opening of American trade and some other favors. Madison easily reached an agreement with Erskine, and thinking that the troubles with the British were now over, issued a proclamation restoring intercourse with Great Britain and permitting American ships to sail for British ports. Unfortunately, however, Canning held that Erskine had exceeded his instructions, and repudiated his agreement at sight, leaving Madison no alternative but to issue another proclamation, this time restoring non-intercourse with Great Britain.

Macon's Bill Number 2.   Non-intercourse was of course a transparent fraud. It was impossible to tell, once a ship had cleared from an American port, what its destination might be. At the end of a year's trial, even the most ardent Republicans were willing to admit that the policy, although responsible for a great revival of American trade, was well-nigh worthless as a weapon of economic coercion. Accordingly, non-intercourse was succeeded by a new measure, sometimes called Macon's Bill Number 2, which repealed the Non-Intercourse Act outright, and tried to bargain with the contending European powers for their favor. If England would repeal her obnoxious Orders in Council, the United States would revive non-intercourse with France; if France would withdraw her offensive decrees, the United States would revive non-intercourse with England. On May 1, 1810, this bill became a law.

The embargo had fitted in well with Napoleon's policy of crippling British trade, and non-intercourse, while far less satisfactory to the Emperor, was still better than nothing. But the abandonment of commercial coercion by the United States, as embodied in Macon's Bill Number 2, suited Napoleon not at all. He therefore proposed to take advantage of the offer that the United States would resume non-intercourse with England in case France withdrew her decrees. Accordingly, his foreign minister, the Duke of Cadore, wrote a letter to the American minister to France stating that the Berlin and Milan Decrees would be withdrawn beginning November 1, 1810, provided that the United States "shall cause their rights to be respected by the English." Thereupon Madison, who could not possibly have overlooked the conditions Napoleon specified, reinstituted non-intercourse with England. Perhaps the President, whose foreign policy to date had been so full of failures, could not resist the temptation to display one slight success. But Madison's triumph was short-lived, for Napoleon, having accomplished his purpose, laid down new regulations against American shipping in French ports that were quite as distressing as the decrees he had repealed.

The *President* and the *Little Belt*.   But if the relations between the United States and France were bad, those between the United States and Great Britain were worse. Diplomatic interchanges had, at least for the time being, come to an end. When on May 16, 1811, an American frigate, the *President,* charged with the duty of protecting American commerce, attacked and defeated the British *Little Belt*, the American public rejoiced that the *Chesapeake* had been avenged. Convinced at last that failure to withdraw the offensive Orders in Council might mean war, the British sent a new minister to the United States, and finally, on June 16, 1812, announced that the Orders in Council had been withdrawn. Obviously the British people had no stomach for an American war at a time when their nation was engaged in a life-and-death struggle with Napoleon. Furthermore, British manufacturers had suffered grievously from the loss of American markets, and the British people were in desperate need of American food.

War Declared. Unfortunately, the British concession came too late. On the very day that the British foreign secretary, Lord Castlereagh, told Parliament that the Orders in Council were being withdrawn, the American government was pushing a declaration of war through Congress. On June 1, 1812, Madison sent in his war message; on June 4, the House by a vote of 79 to 49 declared for war; and on June 18, just two days after Castlereagh's announcement, the Senate, by a vote of 19 to 13, concurred.

The War of 1812 merged with a long-pending Indian war in the West. For many years the tribes had been obliged to retreat before the ever-advancing frontier of white settlement. The time for another stand against the aggressors had come, and the Indians had found a leader in Tecumseh. According to tradition, the blood of northern and southern tribes had been united in Tecumseh for his father was a Shawnee and his mother was a Creek. Tecumseh did not wish for war against the whites, but he did hope to unite the Indians into a confederacy strong enough to stop the unending cessions of Indian land that the American government demanded. In 1808 he joined with his brother, a medicine man generally spoken of as the "Prophet," to found near the mouth of Tippecanoe Creek on the banks of the Wabash a headquarters soon known as "Prophet's Town."

Indian War in the Northwest. When in 1811 Tecumseh made a visit to the South to secure greater support from the tribes in that section, William Henry Harrison, governor of Indiana Territory, could wait no longer. With a strong force of militia he set out for Prophet's Town with the avowed intention of destroying it. But on November 6, 1811, he stopped to treat with the Indians, and next morning, before day broke, he was ambushed. Finally the Indians were driven off, but Harrison had lost sixty-one killed and one hundred and twenty-seven seriously injured. The battle of Tippecanoe, as this engagement was called, was hailed nevertheless as a great victory for the whites. The Indians did not return to the attack, and Prophet's Town, which they had abandoned, was destroyed. Even after this incident Tecumseh still counseled peace, but the war had in truth begun.

When Harrison reported the battle of Tippecanoe, he complained bitterly that the Indians were well supplied with powder and guns obtained from the British in Canada. That Tecumseh was in close touch with the British authorities was a matter of common knowledge. Almost the same situation existed in the Northwest that had confronted Washington when he entered the Presidency. To be sure, the British had removed their military posts to the Canadian side of the boundary, but these posts still existed. Tecumseh's plan for organized Indian resistance to the advance of the farmers' frontier fitted in well with Canadian needs. Should the Indians make good their efforts, the northward flow of pelts from the unsettled western lands of the United States might still continue. To the westerner it appeared that the Canadian fur trader and the Indian, with identical interests, were merely preparing once more to join forces for the protection of those interests.

Western Desire for War. It was only natural under these circumstances that the people of the West should applaud vigorously each step taken by the national government in the direction of war with England. They knew, certainly as early as 1811, that a war with the Indians was sure to come, and they believed implicitly that to make war against the Indians without fighting an accompanying war against the allies of the Indians in Canada was to leave the task half-done. If war with the British was to come, why not make it a war for the conquest and annexation of Canada? In Congress John Randolph of Roanoke remarked that the westerners, like the whippoorwill, knew only one song, and that, "Canada, Canada, Canada."

The Southwestern Frontier. In the Southwest there was less certainty of immediate war than in the Northwest, but the preaching of Tecumseh had aroused the latent forebodings of the southern tribes and had bolstered their will to resist. In this region, despite the cession of Louisiana to the United States, the Spanish were still the logical enemies of the Americans and the natural allies of the Indians, for Florida remained in Spanish hands, and the boundary dispute was still alive. As the southwestern frontier expanded, its residents saw with increasing clarity the necessity of ousting the Spanish from the adjacent seacoast. Through the Florida panhandle ran many of the rivers by which the produce of the new Southwest could most easily find access to the sea. Along the coast of Florida were nests of dangerous pirates that the enfeebled rule of Spain was powerless to destroy. Hostile Indians took refuge in Florida, and with the runaway Negroes and renegade whites there formed bands of unsavory ruffians. In 1810 Madison, carrying out Jefferson's policy of acquiring West Florida, ordered the governor of Louisiana to extend his territory peacefully over that portion of the Spanish province adjacent to the Mississippi River, but the southern expansionists wanted still more.

The "War Hawks." Thus from the interior, whether to the north or to the south, every strongly anti-British stand of the administration in Washington was received with unbounded enthusiasm. In the elections of 1810 and 1811 the moderate policy embodied in Macon's Bill Number 2 received a thoroughgoing rebuke. Nearly half the congressmen who had voted for that measure were left at home, and a new generation of politicians seized the reins of power. Among them were John Sevier and Felix Grundy from Tennessee, John C. Calhoun from the back country of South Carolina, and Henry Clay from Kentucky, whom the newcomers banded together to make Speaker of the House. These young patriots and their followers were eager for war and quickly won for themselves the designation, "War Hawks." They defended more stoutly than any easterner the rights of American sailors and American commerce on the high seas; they denounced in unmeasured terms the assistance that the British in Canada were giving to marauding bands of Indians on the frontier; and they pointed out as the chief prize to be won from the war, the easy acquisition of Canada.

The Vote for War. Madison was by now convinced of the necessity for a declaration of war, but the vote that he obtained from Congress was far from unanimous. The commercial interests of the Northeast were desperately opposed to the measure, and their sentiments were reflected by a majority of the congressmen from that section. Nor were the opponents of the war all Federalists, for a large section of the Republican Party either voted against the declaration or refused to vote at all. The vote for war was delivered mainly by representatives of the West and the South. From the four frontier states, Vermont, Ohio, Kentucky, and Tennessee, every vote but one was cast for war. Most of the rest of the majority came from the South.

The Election of 1812. The election of 1812, which was held before much fighting had occurred, constituted a kind of popular referendum on the decision that the President and Congress had made. Should the war be fought, or should it be called off? As a candidate to oppose Madison, peace men among the Republicans advanced

DeWitt Clinton of New York, whom the Federalists were also induced to support. The issue was clear-cut: a vote for Madison meant a vote for war, and a vote for Clinton meant a vote for peace. The results of the election seemed to place upon the West the main responsibility for the war. New England, with the exception of Vermont, cast 43 electoral votes for Clinton and peace, while the middle states (including Maryland and Delaware) preferred Clinton over Madison by a vote of 46 to 31. The South voted solidly, 59 to 0, for Madison and war. Thus the seaboard states — the original thirteen — were as nearly equally divided as possible, with a vote of 90 for Madison to 89 for Clinton, certainly too narrow a margin upon which to wage a war. But the five states that had been admitted to the Union by act of Congress cast their entire vote for Madison, who was thus elected, 128 to 89. It was another victory of the West, aided by the dominantly agricultural South, over the commercial Northeast.

Unpreparedness for War. Financially speaking, the country could hardly have been less prepared for war. Failure to renew in 1811 the charter of the Bank of the United States had deprived the country of both a stable currency and the machinery needed for floating loans. The doubling of tariff rates hardly compensated for the loss in revenue sustained as a result of the restrictions on trade that were laid down before the war and tightened by its advent. Internal taxes, although finally accepted as a necessity, were at first spurned as "unrepublican." A direct levy on the states in 1813 brought only the most meager results. Most of the cost of the war had, therefore, to be met by loans, but in order to attract investors, government securities had to be sold at a heavy discount, with interest rates sometimes as high as seven and one-half per cent. Even so, New England capital practically refused to support the war. It was small wonder that by the

time peace was restored the government was virtually bankrupt.

In the all-important matter of military preparedness, the country was not much better off. The regular army consisted of about 7,000 men, all of whom were needed on garrison duty. Presumably the states could muster some 700,000 militia, but requisitions by the federal government on the states were halfheartedly filled, and sometimes flatly refused. At no time during the war did the government have in service more than 35,000 men, and on occasion whole detachments of militia refused to fight outside the boundaries of their state. Commanding officers, some of whom had fought well in the Revolution, were now overage and often "utterly unfit for any military purpose whatever." Even the Canadians were better off than the Americans. They were far more ably commanded, they had a small nucleus of British regulars to start with, and they had more success enlisting an army to resist an invasion than the Americans had to make one. On the high seas the odds against the Americans were overwhelming. The American navy numbered sixteen frigates, together with a fair number of smaller craft, but against these the British could count about one thousand ships of the line, of which nearly a hundred were assigned to duty on the western side of the Atlantic. Apparently the War Hawks were counting more heavily on the victories that Napoleon was expected to win than upon anything that the Americans could hope to do.

Attack on Canada. And yet, the American attack on Canada, to which all other considerations were subordinated, was planned with complete confidence and undertaken with full expectation of success. Three separate, but more or less simultaneous, blows were to be delivered. Henry Dearborn was to advance northward by the Lake Champlain route toward Montreal; Stephen Van Rensselaer, relying mainly upon New York militia, was to attack the

British at Niagara; and William Hull, the governor of Michigan Territory, was to launch from Detroit an invasion of Upper Canada. Unfortunately not one of the three officers mentioned was in the least fitted to cope with the situation that confronted him.

Throughout the year 1812 the news from the northern front was uniformly bad. On July 12, 1812, Hull crossed the Detroit River and marched timidly toward the British post at Malden. His doubts and fears multiplied as he observed the hostility of the inhabitants, the poverty of their country, and the evidence that a strong force was concentrating at Malden to oppose him. When finally the news came that Tecumseh and a band of Indian warriors had joined the British, Hull's nerve failed completely, and he fell back to Detroit. There he was surrounded by British and Indians under General Isaac Brock, and on August 16 was induced to surrender. For his conduct he was later court-martialed and sentenced to be shot, but because of his creditable record in the Revolution the President pardoned him. A month before Hull's surrender, the American garrison at Michilimackinac had been forced to capitulate, Detroit was lost, and only the day before the little American garrison at Fort Dearborn (Chicago) had been massacred by the Indians. Meantime the attacks on Niagara and Montreal had failed to get under way. At Niagara some fighting occurred in October, but the unwillingness of the New York militia to cross the border destroyed all hope of invasion. The senior major general, Dearborn, delayed his advance on Montreal until November, but when still twenty miles from the Canadian border he turned back to his headquarters at Plattsburg.

The High Seas. Fortunately for American morale, the fighting on the high seas was going far better. The men who manned the American ships were well-paid and competent volunteers, and the captains who

THE NATIONS BULWARK.

AN EARLY MILITIA MUSTER

Military training was required by law of all able-bodied citizens both in colonial times and during the days of the early republic. Militia musters were often accompanied by politicking, preaching, and general socializing. The inexpertness at drill of both officers and men was often ludicrous and occasionally fatal, as the following account suggests.

This day our regement paraded and went through the manuel exesise then we grounded our firelocks and every man set down by their arms and abial Petty axedently discharged his peace and shot two Balls through the Body of one asa cheany through his Left side and rite rist he Lived about 24 hours and then expired he belonged to Walpole and he was carried their and Buried on the 30 day of April.

The Military Journals of Two Private Soldiers, published by ABRAHAM TOMLINSON of the Museum, POUGHKEEPSIE (1855)

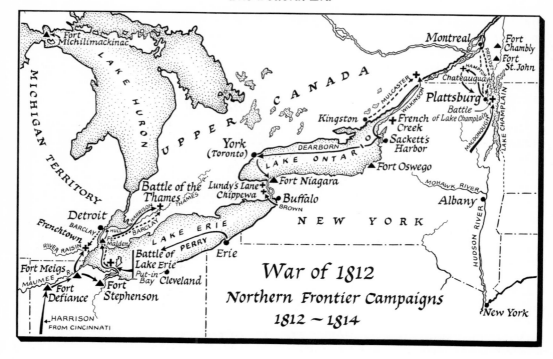

War of 1812
Northern Frontier Campaigns
1812 – 1814

commanded them were veterans of the Tripolitan War. American ships, moreover, were carefully constructed to carry more guns and sail than the corresponding units of European navies. Thus in ship-for-ship engagements the Americans scored a series of spectacular victories. On July 11 the *Essex* captured the *Minerva* and two days later forced the *Alert* to surrender. On August 19, the *Constitution,* Captain Isaac Hull commanding, outfought the *Guerrière* in what was probably the most brilliant American sea-victory of the war. On October 18, the *Wasp* took the *Frolic.* On October 25, the *United States* defeated the *Macedonian,* and brought her as a prize into an American port. On December 29, the *Constitution* ("Old Ironsides") now under William Bainbridge, destroyed the *Java.* On February 24, 1813, the *Hornet* sank the *Peacock* after a combat that lasted only fifteen minutes. Meantime American warships and privateers were also taking a heavy toll of British commerce.

The uninterrupted series of naval victories

tremendously lightened the gloom that the military blunders along the northern frontier had cast over the American people, but the effect on the British public was even more marked. For centuries British sea captains had been accustomed to win against all odds, and the defeats by Americans seemed beyond comprehension. However, the American naval successes were only temporary. With the spring of 1813 the British established a tight blockade of the American coast, and from that time on American ships of war scarcely dared to leave port. Four or five American warships managed to operate intermittently on the high seas until the war was over, and American privateers continued to take prizes to the very end; but as a fighting weapon for either offensive or defensive purposes, the American navy had ceased to function. New England, which from New London northward was exempted by the British from the blockade because of its notorious opposition to the war and its readiness to sell to the enemy, could still carry on a fair export trade, but elsewhere shipments from American ports were held down to nearly nothing. In 1814 not more than $200,000 worth of goods left the ports of New York, and hardly $17,500 worth left the ports of Virginia.

Battle of Lake Erie. Before attempting another invasion of Canada, American war-makers wisely decided that the control of the Great Lakes must be wrested from the British. With this end in view a small fleet was constructed on Lake Erie, and on September 10, 1813, with Captain Oliver Hazard Perry in command, it won a significant victory. Perry's terse report, "We have met the enemy and they are ours," lives deservedly. When, shortly afterward, the British felt obliged to retreat from Detroit and Malden, they were followed by William Henry Harrison with a far larger army than Hull had commanded. In the ensuing battle of the Thames, fought on October 5, 1813, Tecumseh was slain, and the British command put to flight. The American invasion did not proceed much further, but the war ended with the Indians completely humbled, and the northwestern border in American hands. Meantime, fighting on the Canadian frontier had produced nothing more startling than the burning of the parliament buildings at York (Toronto) by the Americans, and the capture of Fort Niagara by the British.

British efforts during the year 1814 to invade the United States were similarly inconclusive. In the Niagara area, where most of the fighting took place, the Americans scored a considerable victory at Lundy's Lane, but were compelled to fall back when the news came that the British had received reinforcements. The Lake Champlain invasion route was rendered useless to the British when a small flotilla of American ships, Lieutenant Thomas Macdonough commanding, defeated a

THE BATTLE OF THE THAMES, OCTOBER 5, 1813

This highly imaginary and stilted print attempts to include everything the artist knew, or thought he knew, about the battle. He gives the spotlight to Colonel Richard Mentor Johnson, commander of a Kentucky mounted regiment, who is shown here "heroically defending himself against the attack of an Indian chief." Frontispiece from Henry Trumbull, History of the Discovery of America *(1819).*

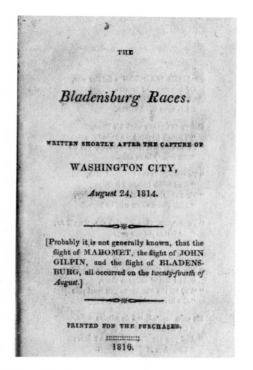

THE BLADENSBURG RACES

The title page of a pamphlet present- ing a satirical poem to celebrate the pre- cipitous flight of the Madison adminis- tration from Washington, following the disastrous defeat of the American forces at Bladensburg, August 24, 1814. From the William L. Clements Library, Ann Arbor.

British squadron off Plattsburg Bay. This victory somewhat softened the blow that American pride had just received, when a landing party of British marines and sailors had marched into Washington (August 24), had burned the Capitol and the White House, and had returned to their ships without serious loss.

The War in the Southwest. The final phase of the war was fought in the South- west, where on August 13, 1813, an Indian massacre at Fort Mims had precipitated hostilities. At Horseshoe Bend General Andrew Jackson in command of Tennessee troops thoroughly avenged the white dis- aster, and in the Treaty of Fort Jackson he forced the chastened tribes to hand over to the United States thousands of acres of the choicest Indian lands. Jackson was now placed in command of all the American forces in the Southwest and given the task of beating off the British offensive being mounted against New Orleans. Balked along the northern border because of Amer- ican superiority in the lake fighting, the British had decided to send an overwhelm- ing force of nearly 10,000 troops, many of whom were veterans of the Napoleonic wars, to capture New Orleans. The in- vaders were met by Jackson and his frontier militia, and on January 8, 1815, from im- provised defenses, consisting partly of cot- ton bales, were cut to pieces in the most astounding victory of the war. But the battle of New Orleans should really never have been fought, for on December 24, 1814, a treaty of peace had been signed by British and American plenipotentiaries at Ghent.

The Hartford Convention. During the dark days of 1814 commercial New Eng- land's loyalty to the Union had been put to a severe test. To the inevitable losses suf- fered in trade were added British raids along the coast, raids which seemingly aroused more resentment against the gov- ernment at Washington than against the British themselves. Finally the legislature of Massachusetts voted to call a convention to meet at Hartford, Connecticut, for the purpose of giving voice to New England opinion. The Convention met on Decem- ber 15, condemned the "multiplied abuses of bad administrations" and "acts of Con- gress in violation of the Constitution." In language definitely reminiscent of the Ken- tucky and Virginia Resolutions, the Con- vention maintained "the right and duty of a state to interpose its authority" in cases of "deliberate, dangerous, and palpable infrac- tions of the Constitution," but insisted also that it would be unwise "to fly to open resistance" upon every offense. The Con- vention then went on to list for the consid-

THE BATTLE OF NEW ORLEANS, JANUARY 8, 1815

From a colored engraving of a drawing made on the field of battle by H. Laclotte.

eration of the states it represented seven amendments to the national Constitution which, had they been adopted, would have limited the power of Congress to make war, to admit new states, to lay embargoes, and to restrict commerce. Other provisions were aimed at the "Virginia dynasty" and the "three-fifths" compromise. Successive Presidents might not come from the same state and a President would be ineligible for re-election, while in the apportionment of representatives to Congress only whites might be counted. The speedy termination of the war and the subsequent prosperity of New England made the proponents of the Hartford measures eager to forget what they had done, but since the Convention had been primarily the work of Federalists, the Republicans were able to charge the party of Washington and Adams with treason, and virtually to force it from the political scene.

Treaty of Ghent. Peace negotiations had meantime begun through the good offices of the Tsar of Russia, and since August, 1814, commissioners representing the two warring governments had been in session at Ghent. The American delegation consisted of five exceptionally able men: James A. Bayard, Albert Gallatin, John Quincy Adams, Henry Clay, and Jonathan Russell. The British government, with its best talent engaged in a European settlement at Vienna, was less effectively represented, and partly for this reason the Americans were able to score a notable diplomatic triumph. The British, had they so desired, could have carried on the war indefinitely, although British public opinion leaned strongly in the direction of calling the war off and favored a speedy resumption of normal trade relations with America. As finally signed, the Treaty of Ghent reflected well the existing military situation and ignored totally the potentialities of British might. It provided, according to Adams, for "a truce rather than a peace. Neither party gave up anything; all the points of collision which had subsisted between them before the war were left open. . . . Nothing was adjusted, nothing was settled — nothing in substance but an indefinite suspension of hostilities was agreed to."

Subsequent Agreements. While the Peace of Ghent merely restored for the time being the *status quo ante bellum*, it did make provision for the future settlement of some of the outstanding differences between England and America. Stimulated in part by these clauses in the treaty and in part by the mutual desire to clear up misunderstandings, the two nations came to several important agreements. On July 3, 1815, a commercial convention was signed by which trade discriminations, except for the exclusion of American trade from the British West Indies, were mutually withdrawn. On April 28, 1817, the justly famous Rush-Bagot Agreement provided for complete disarmament by both nations on the Great Lakes, except for a few gunboats permitted for police purposes. The difficult question of the northeastern fisheries was treated in a convention signed October 20, 1818, which acknowledged the right of American citizens to fish along the coasts of Newfoundland and Labrador, and to dry and cure their fish on unsettled shores. This same convention also determined the boundary line between the possessions of the United States and Great Britain in the Northwest. The Treaty of 1783 had described a line "on a due west course" from the Lake of the Woods to the Mississippi River. Such a line could not be drawn. The Convention of 1818 worked out a new line and sensibly adopted the forty-ninth parallel as the dividing line between the United States and Canada as far west as the "Stony" mountains. Beyond the mountains neither side was willing to acknowledge the other's pretensions, and the dispute was left open by an agreement that the subjects of both nations might occupy the region jointly.

American Impression of Victory. It is not surprising that the War of 1812, which was at best a drawn battle, settled into the American consciousness as a telling victory. The news of Jackson's magnificent triumph at New Orleans was quickly followed by the news of peace, and the public assumed that between these two impressive events there was the relation of cause and effect. Furthermore, the defeat of the Indians, both in the Northwest and in the Southwest, together with the death of Tecumseh, opened the way for an unprecedented advance of the frontier. No real need had ever been felt for the lands of Canada, and the failure of the War Hawk program of conquest and annexation was quickly forgotten. With peace in Europe restored, American commerce on the high seas was no longer molested, and American patriots were not above imputing to the battle of New Orleans a happy situation that was in reality the result of Leipzig and Waterloo. Pride in the achievements of the American frigates during the early part of the war soon obscured their helplessness in the face of British superiority at its close. American manufacturers, moreover, had benefited greatly by the trade restrictions that preceded and accompanied the war, and their successes had promoted a degree of economic independence from England that the United States had never known before. From the political point of view it is absurd to speak of the War of 1812 as the "Second War for Independence," for political independence had been won in fact no less than in theory by the American Revolution; but from the economic point of view it is abundantly clear that the second war with England markedly accentuated the divorcement of the two countries.

SELECTED BIBLIOGRAPHY

A fine survey of the diplomatic background of the War of 1812 may be found in Bradford Perkins, *Prologue to War; England and the United States, 1805–1812* (1961). Among the numerous special studies see: L. M. Sears, *Jefferson and the Embargo* (1927); F. E. Melvin, *Napoleon's Navigation System* (1919); and Harry Bernstein, *Origins of Inter-American Interest, 1700–1812* (1945). An interesting monograph by a British scholar is Frank Thistlethwaite, *The Anglo-American Connection in the Early Nineteenth Century* (1959). S. E. Morison, *The Maritime History of Massachusetts, 1783–1860* (1921), is a rich work by our leading naval historian.

Causation of the War of 1812 has long been debated by historians, and there has recently been a striking revival of interest in the subject. Conflicting viewpoints may be explored in *The Causes of the War of 1812*, edited by Bradford Perkins (1962); and *The War of 1812; Past Justifications and Present Interpretations*, edited by G. R. Taylor (1963). J. W. Pratt, *Expansionists of 1812* (1925), is the now-classic argument for the western and southern causes of the war. It can be contrasted with such recent studies as Reginald Horsman, *The Causes of the War of 1812* (1962).

The standard work on Madison is Irving Brant, *James Madison* (6 vols., 1941–1961), of which the fifth and sixth volumes deal with his presidency. While Brant, like most biographers, is partial to his subject, his is a great work of scholarship. In process is the compilation of *The Papers of James Madison*, edited by W. T. Hutchinson and W. M. E. Rachal (4 vols., 1962–   ). Since Madison was exceedingly prolific, it will be many years before this set reaches Madison's period as Secretary of State and President. A brief biography is A. E. Smith, *James Madison, Builder* (1937).

On Clay, the standard biographies are Bernard Mayo, *Henry Clay, Spokesman of the New West* (1937); and G. G. Van Deusen, *The Life of Henry Clay* (1937). An excellent brief study is Clement Eaton, *Henry Clay and the Art of American Politics* (1957). A major work of scholarship is *The Papers of Henry Clay*, edited by J. F. Hopkins (3 vols., 1959–   ); this set now reaches in time to 1824. J. H. Parks, *Felix Grundy, Champion of Democracy* (1940), is the biography of another "War Hawk." The views of a leading opponent of the war may be found in full detail in S. E. Morison, *The Life and Letters of Harrison Gray Otis, Federalist, 1765–1848* (2 vols., 1913).

A colorful large-scale history of the War of 1812 is Glenn Tucker, *Poltroons and Patriots* (2 vols., 1954). Henry Adams, *The War of 1812* (1944), an extract from his great history, is a splendid general treatment of the war years. See also F. F. Beirne, *The War of 1812* (1949); H. L. Coles, *The War of 1812* (1965); and R. R. Brown, *The Republic in Peril: 1812* (1965). For the Canadian point of view, see William Wood, *The War with the United States* (1915). The military situation in the Northwest is treated in A. R. Gilpin, *The War of 1812 in the Old Northwest* (1958); Glenn Tucker, *Tecumseh* (1956); and D. B. Goebel, *William Henry Harrison* (1926).

On naval aspects of the war, A. T. Mahan, *Sea Power in its Relation to the War of 1812* (2 vols., 1905), is both standard and detailed. The same can be said about Theodore Roosevelt, *The Naval War of 1812* (1882). A lively modern account by a brilliant stylist is C. S. Forester, *The Age of Fighting Sail* (1956). Interesting popular biographies include C. L. Lewis, *The Romantic Decatur* (1937); and Fletcher Pratt, *Preble's Boys: Commodore Preble and the Birth of American Sea Power* (1950). General works on the history of the American navy include Fletcher Pratt, *The Navy: A History* (1943).

On the peace negotiations, see Bradford Perkins, *Castlereagh and Adams: England and the United States, 1812–1823* (1964). See also the appropriate sections in R. B. Mowat, *The Diplomatic Relations of Great Britain and the United States* (1925); and E. W. McInnis, *The Unguarded Frontier; A History of American-Canadian Relations* (1942).

* Available in paperback

157

10

NATIONALISM AND
SECTIONALISM

The War of 1812 marks a definite turning
point in the history of the United States.
Before it the American people, while politically independent, were still tributary to
Europe and especially England in their
economic life. The factory system was slow
to take root in America, for it was cheaper
to import goods from England, where manufacturing on a large scale was already well
established. Moreover, the commercial
connections of colonial times had been
promptly resumed at the close of the Revolution, and there were no stronger vested
interests in the country than those concerned with the importation and distribution of foreign goods. Planters and farmers,
likewise, were accustomed to depend heavily upon foreign trade. Their excess pro-

duce was sent to Europe as consistently as
during colonial times, while the continual
European wars forced up the prices of
American raw materials and foodstuffs.
With a steady trade flowing both ways,
there was little difficulty in making exports
balance imports in value.

The embargo, non-intercourse, and the
War of 1812 upset completely this scheme
of things. American commerce was for the
time being almost destroyed, and the opportunity to import foreign goods was reduced to a minimum. Much capital that
had formerly been invested in commerce
turned now to manufactures, for which the
existing situation was equivalent to a high
protective tariff. Manufacturing, moreover,
became a patriotic duty which states,
counties, municipalities, and societies sought
to encourage by offering attractive bounties.
As early as 1810 Gallatin reported to the
House of Representatives a surprisingly
long list of manufactured items in which
the United States was already self-sufficient.
Throughout the period textile mills for the
production of cotton, linen, and woolen
cloth increased rapidly in number, and
even more rapidly in the volume of their
output. Facilities for the manufacture of
paper, leather goods, iron, and iron goods
multiplied until the most urgent needs of

the American market were fully met. By the end of the war American manufacturing was well established, and the shortage of European imports was no longer keenly felt.

New England Factories. New England early led in the shift toward manufacturing. In several important ways New England was ideally fitted to assume the manufacturing role. Power to turn the wheels of the new machinery was abundantly supplied by the swift-flowing streams and their numerous waterfalls; shippers and shipping were available to send the products down the coast to the other American states; an abundant labor supply was at hand. Workers in the New England factories were mainly farmers and their families, who were quite willing to give up the unequal struggle with the hard climate and unyielding soil to accept the more certain financial rewards of the mills. They brought with them a degree of dexterity and ingenuity that placed them among the most capable factory employees anywhere in the world.

But the interest in manufacturing was by no means confined to New England. As far south as the Chesapeake the new opportunity for American manufacturers was producing results. If New England led in the production of textiles, Pennsylvania, New York, and New Jersey excelled in the production of iron ore and the manufacture of iron goods. By 1815 in this region bituminous and anthracite coal, which could be obtained cheaply, was being used successfully by manufacturers. In the South there was talk of building factories and putting the slaves to work in them; however, few such enterprises were actually established. Instead the South turned to cotton growing and became a heavy purchaser of northern goods.

American Agriculture. The period of enforced isolation from Europe had witnessed many changes also in American agriculture. The growth of the woolen industry

THE ELI WHITNEY GUN FACTORY

Whitney received little or no remuneration from his invention of the cotton gin, but as a manufacturer of fire-arms he foreshadowed the idea of interchangeable parts, and made a fortune. At what came to be called Whitneyville, near New Haven, he erected a mill, and a row of houses for the use of his employees — another innovation. From an oil painting by William Giles Munson.

made sheep-raising profitable as never before, especially in the back country of New England and in the Middle Atlantic states. In the South the production of cotton took on ever-increasing significance. Before Eli Whitney's invention of the cotton gin in 1793, only the long-staple cotton grown in the lowlands could be profitably raised. But the cotton gin, by reducing greatly the cost of separating the seed from the cotton, made profitable the growing also of the short-staple cotton which throve well in the uplands. The results were revolutionary. The output of southern cotton, which in 1791 had amounted only to about 2 million pounds, had grown by 1810 to 40 million, and by 1811 to 80 million pounds. Once the war was ended, both foreign and domestic manufacturers clamored for cotton, and the spread of cotton culture was more rapid than ever before. The increasing cultivation of sugar cane in the South, particularly

ELI WHITNEY'S COTTON GIN

From a model presented to the National Museum in 1884 by Whitney's son.

in Louisiana, added another commodity to the list of articles that could be supplied within the United States.

An American Type. Much was therefore achieved toward that national self-sufficiency which economists of the eighteenth century had regarded as so vital to the life of a nation. Accompanying this development the discerning observer might have noted also the rapid emergence of an American national type. When the Revolution ended, the typical American was still essentially an English colonial. By 1800 some notable changes were already in evidence, but in the years following the War of 1812 a new nationality, with new and different characteristics, was clearly in the making. The decline of commerce, and the consequent lessening of contacts between Americans and Europeans, undoubtedly stimulated the divergence of American from European ways, but probably the unique opportunities of the New World, now better realized than ever before, account for most of the changes. America had become

preeminently a land of "opportunity." To the resident of the Northeast the factory system brought to employers and employees alike new avenues to prosperity. To the southern planter, and to the southern small farmer who hoped to become a planter, the revolutionary possibilities of cotton culture seemed to point the way to sure success. To the restless of every section came the call of the West. Almost for the first time the boundless possibilities of the new nation were fully realized. Now anyone could see that future generations of Americans had before them a task no less inviting than the conquest and exploitation of half a continent. The lure of rich rewards, whether in industry, in cotton culture, or in the development of the West, captured the imaginations of Americans and determined their characteristics. Thus they saw little reason to imitate or esteem the ways of an Old World where opportunity was limited, but paid deference instead to whatever qualities in themselves seemed best calculated to insure success in the new undertakings.

Postwar Legislation. President Madison in his annual message to Congress of December 5, 1815, divined clearly the nationalistic trend of the times. He urged that steps be taken to provide for a stronger military establishment, a uniform national currency, a tariff to protect the new American industries, and a national system of roads and canals. Speedy action was taken on each of these items. A standing army of 10,000 men was authorized, and an appropriation of $8 million was voted for the construction of fifteen new naval units. The Military Academy at West Point, which had been established in 1802, was reorganized with a view to greater efficiency and was given increased support. A second Bank of the United States, patterned after the first Bank, was created to provide the national currency Madison had requested, and to end the inflationary activities of the numerous state-chartered banks that had taken over the entire banking business of the country in 1811. The new Bank was stronger than Hamilton's Bank, with a capital stock of $35 million instead of $10 million, but it was almost identical in character and privileges. A tariff, passed in 1816, maintained or increased the special wartime duties and made every effort to protect the "infant industries," built up during and just prior to the war. Finally, Congress showed clearly that it was ready to go ahead with internal improvements when it appropriated the funds necessary to continue construction of the Cumberland Road by means of which East and West were to be joined along the route of the old Braddock Road. By 1818 the new highway was completed to Wheeling, on the Ohio River.

Sectionalism in New England. These momentous additions to the nation's powers were not accomplished without opposition. The strongest protests came from New England, where the commercial interests still feared the growing strength of the representatives of agriculture. Many New Englanders, led by Daniel Webster, objected to a protective tariff on the ground that it would interfere, as indeed it would, with their foreign trade. Webster also opposed the rechartering of the Bank. The banks of his section were safe and sound, and he reflected their fear that a national bank under western and southern management might become a source of danger rather than of strength. New England opponents of internal improvements also advanced the argument that those states which would profit most from the building of roads should pay for them. But the chief obstacle to an expanded program of road building turned out to be President Madison himself, who doubted the constitutionality of all such measures except when a specific national interest was involved. A so-called Bonus Bill, which pledged to the promotion of internal improvements the "bonus" of $1.5 million that Congress had required of the second Bank of the

United States as a condition of its charter, was killed by a presidential veto. Many southern disciples of the states'-rights dogma, ably led by John Randolph of Roanoke, joined the New Englanders in protest against the further eclipse of the states by the nation, a development which others found quite acceptable. "The Constitution," said John C. Calhoun as he defended the Bonus Bill, "was not intended as a thesis for the logician to exercise his ingenuity on [and] ought to be construed with plain good sense."

The Election of 1816. The election of 1816 seemed to put the stamp of popular approval upon the nationalistic program that Congress had adopted. The Federalists, whose leaders had furnished the principal opposition to the new measures and whose war record was a bad one, were hopelessly defeated. Their candidate for President, Rufus King of New York, carried only three states. The Republicans, amidst considerable grumbling, permitted the "succession" to go to James Monroe. The custom had developed of making party nominations by a "congressional caucus," composed of all the members in Congress of the party concerned, and the Republican caucus chose Monroe over W. H. Crawford of Georgia by the vote of 64 to 44. The final electoral vote stood 183 for Monroe to 34 for King.

Like three of his predecessors, James Monroe (1758–1831) was a Virginia planter. His family, however, was of the western, small planter class, and included in its family tree many Scottish and Welsh ancestors. By the time he reached the Presidency, Monroe's political experience had already been considerable. He had served in the Virginia Assembly, in the Congress of the Confederation, and in the United States Senate; he had represented his country on important missions to France, Spain, and England; he had been governor of Virginia for several terms; and he had been both Secretary of State and Secretary of War. In most respects, Monroe was able to keep abreast of the nationalistic trend his party had taken, although, like Madison, he saw little justification in the Constitution for an unrestricted program of internal improvements. He allowed the Cumberland Road to be finished, but in 1822, when a bill passed Congress to provide funds for its repair by establishing toll gates and collecting tolls, he interposed a veto. The exercise of such power by Congress, he claimed, implied a "power to adopt and execute a complete system of internal improvements," and for this he found no constitutional warrant. He believed, however, that a change in the Constitution to permit the United States to build "great national works" would be desirable, provided that "all minor improvements" were left to the states.

Marshall and the Supreme Court. In the meanwhile, the Supreme Court was making its contribution to the new nationalism. Chief Justice John Marshall (1755–1835) was another Virginian, born far out on the frontier. He fought in the Revolution as a member of his father's regiment, but toward the end of the war he attended lectures on law at William and Mary College and in 1781 began to practice. He was soon recognized as the leader of the Virginia bar, and as a shrewd and successful politician. He was one of the three commissioners sent to make peace with France in 1797, served a term in Congress, became Secretary of State during the last year of the Adams administration, and was elevated to the Chief Justiceship early in 1801. Curiously, he continued as Secretary of State until the end of the Adams administration, although he accepted a salary only as Chief Justice. For thirty-four years he guided the Supreme Court in a thoroughly Federalist interpretation of the Constitution. So great was the power of his personality and so convincing his logic that, to the despair of Republican Presidents, the new judges they appointed were soon following Marshall's

lead. The growth of the national spirit during and after the War of 1812, however, served to bring the Court and the dominant political party more closely together. The nationalistic decisions of Marshall and his colleagues now aroused approval, rather than disapproval, even among the young Republicans.

Marshall's Opinions. Marshall's decision in the case of *Marbury* v. *Madison*, already noted, and the utter failure of the Republicans to undo it, added greatly to the prestige of the Court. Its power to declare null and void an act of Congress out of harmony with the Constitution was frequently asserted, although the authority was not again utilized in an important case until 1857. By then, the doctrine of judicial review had won general acceptance.

Gradually, as occasion offered, the Court built up its own, and the nation's, prerogatives. In the case of *United States* v. *Judge Peters* (1809), it found opportunity to show that its power, in case of conflict, transcended that of a state legislature. Neither was a legislature to be left free to void a contract it had made with individuals. In the case of *Fletcher* v. *Peck* (1810), already noted, the Court held that even so dishonest an act as that by which the state of Georgia had granted lands to the Yazoo companies could not be repealed without "impairing the obligation of contract." Nor could a legislature go back on its contracts with corporations. In the case of *Dartmouth College* v. *Woodward* (1819), the Court maintained that a charter of incorporation was also a contract within the meaning of the Constitution. Two notable decisions, *Martin* v. *Hunter's Lessee* (1816) and *Cohens* v. *Virginia* (1821), completed the picture by asserting that the Supreme Court was superior to the state courts whenever federal rights were involved. As a result of these two decisions, the federal courts obtained much new business. Litigants preferred them over the state courts whenever they would accept jurisdiction, in part because the finality of the state decision was less certain.

National Supremacy Approved. In the two Virginia decisions and in others also the Court was at pains to defend not only its own prerogatives as a court, but also the supremacy of the national government over the states. The classic expression of this point of view came in the case of *McCulloch* v. *Maryland* (1819). The state of Maryland had attempted to tax out of existence the Baltimore branch of the Bank of the United States, and the bank had refused to pay the tax. The state courts naturally found against the bank and ordered it to pay, but an appeal was taken to the Supreme Court of the United States. Here was a clear-cut issue between state and nation, and Marshall made the most of it. He upheld the constitutionality of the act of Congress by which the Bank was created, and in so doing gave the approval of the Court to Hamilton's doctrine of implied powers. "Let the end be legitimate, let it be within the scope of the Constitution, and all means which are appropriate, which are plainly adapted to that end, which are not prohibited, but consist with the letter and spirit of the Constitution, are constitutional." He held also that the state of Maryland had exceeded its authority in attempting to tax the notes of the Baltimore branch. "The power to tax," he reasoned, involved the "power to destroy." Marshall took the occasion to speak out plainly against the theory that the Constitution emanated from the states, and that the government established by it was therefore merely a creature of the states. "The government of the Union," he maintained, "is emphatically, and truly, a government of the people. In form and in substance it emanates from them. Its powers are granted by them, and are to be exercised on them, and for their benefit. . . . If any one proposition could command the universal consent of mankind, we might expect it would be this — that the government of the Union, though limited in

JOHN MARSHALL

The fourth Chief Justice of the United States, with a rare gift for "putting his own ideas into the minds of others, consciously or unconsciously," dominated the Supreme Court during his thirty-five years of leadership.

its powers, is supreme within its sphere of action. . . ."

The Supreme Court majority made no secret of their desire to exalt the power of the nation whenever warrant could be found for such action in the Constitution. They attempted, however, to draw a reasonable line between powers granted exclusively to the national government and powers reserved wholly or in part to the states. In the case of *Gibbons* v. *Ogden* (1824), the Court held unconstitutional a monopoly of the state waters of New York that the state legislature had granted, an obvious trespass upon the interstate-commerce powers of Congress; but in the case of *Ogden* v. *Saunders* (1827), the Court upheld a state bankruptcy statute in spite of the fact that Congress had similar authority. It has been many times charged that Marshall's decisions were designed not merely to exalt the power of the nation, but also to prevent the states from restricting the rights of property holders. This in a measure is true. It should be remembered, however, that opportunities for the acquisition of property in Marshall's time were not limited to the few, but could be enjoyed by the many. Marshall's decisions fitted in well with the temper of the American people in the years immediately following the War of 1812. The country was young and growing, conscious of its strength, confident of the future. Americans were property-minded men, as full of optimism for themselves as for their country.

The Monroe Doctrine. While at home Marshall was laying the foundations for national sovereignty, events abroad were preparing the way for a significant statement of American foreign policy. Absorbed primarily in their own affairs, Americans were less concerned than formerly with what was going on in Europe, but in their new nationalism they were willing to challenge instantly any tendency of European nations to limit the development of the United States. The diplomatic background of the Monroe Doctrine lay both in the New World and the Old. During the years 1807–1808, when the armies of Napoleon had overrun Spain and Portugal, the American colonies of these now satellite nations began to revolt. In this endeavor they were greatly aided by the English, who were also at war with Napoleon and were eager at the same time to take advantage of the better trade relationships that must surely follow independence for the former colonies. While the Spanish-American revolutionists at first professed allegiance to Ferdinand VII, whom Napoleon had dethroned, Ferdinand's subsequent restoration found them unprepared and unwilling to resume the Spanish yoke, and the movement for independence continued. The Spanish Empire in the New World had dwindled by 1822 to little more

than the Caribbean islands of Cuba and Puerto Rico. In Brazil the separatist movement was also clearly manifest. There the Portuguese royal house had taken refuge from Napoleon, but at the insistence of the Brazilians an independent empire was proclaimed in 1822, with Dom Pedro I as ruler.

Latin America. The successful revolt of the Spanish-American colonies was viewed with undisguised approval by the people of the United States, who saw in the actions of their neighbors to the south full vindication of the principles enunciated in their own Declaration of Independence. Moreover, the Spanish-American republics, while unable to combine into a single union, copied in other respects the form of government which had been developed in the United States. Public opinion in the United States called so strongly for recognition of the Spanish-American governments that John Quincy Adams, Monroe's Secretary of State, was able only with great difficulty to postpone such action until after his negotiations with Spain for the purchase of Florida were completed.

Florida. By this time Spanish occupation in Florida had dwindled to little more than a few garrisons, and disorder among the Indians, runaway Negroes, and ruffians who inhabited the region made it virtually a "no man's land." When in 1816 the American government sent General Andrew Jackson with troops to police the Florida border, the General construed his orders to include the right of "hot pursuit," invaded Spanish territory, took St. Marks and Pensacola, executed two white troublemakers, and sent the Spanish governor and all his soldiers to Havana. Secretary of War John C. Calhoun would have censured Jackson for exceeding his orders, but Adams defended the General and persuaded the Spanish government to cede the region to the United States, on condition that the United States should meet claims for damages made by American citizens against

Spain, amounting in all to about $5 million. On these terms the United States acquired Florida by a treaty signed in 1819. It took some time to effect the transfer, but with Florida at last safely in hand, President Monroe announced in March, 1822, that the time for recognition of the new Spanish-American governments had come.

The European System. European nations also were interested in the course of events in Spanish America, although with the exception of England they were far from pleased with what had happened. Following the defeat of Napoleon, the great powers of Europe — England, Austria, Russia, Prussia, and, after 1818, France — were closely associated in what came to be called the European Concert. Representatives of these powers met from time to time to discuss international relations and the best means of preserving peace. The leading European statesman of the period was Prince Metternich of Austria. In his opinion democracy and nationalism were kinds of communicable diseases that must be stamped out wherever found, if the peace of the world was to be maintained. When, therefore, revolutionary outbreaks occurred in Spain, and in the two Italian kingdoms of Naples and Piedmont in 1820, Metternich persuaded Russia and Prussia to agree to the principle that revolution in any European state might properly be suppressed by the great powers. England strongly dissented from this view, and France at first held aloof, but in 1821 Austria was commissioned in the name of Austria, Russia, and Prussia to suppress the revolutions in Italy; and a year later, France was authorized to do the same for Spain. England's opinion of this "doctrine of intervention" was plainly stated. It was the privilege of all nations, her foreign secretary insisted, "to be left free to manage their own affairs, so long as they left other nations to manage theirs." But this protest was unavailing. Austrian troops in Italy, and French troops in Spain, stamped out the revolutions and revived the old system of autocracy.

Intervention in America? While the doctrine of intervention was confined specifically to European countries, the possibility of the use of European military power to suppress the revolts in Spanish America was a subject of much speculation. It was an open secret that Ferdinand VII sought such aid, and it was supposed that he might be generous to any nation or nations from which aid might come. France had actually proposed intervention in Spanish America as well as in Spain. To England the possibility that the Spanish-American republics might be restored to Spain was alarming, for such a development would mean in all probability the revival of the old colonial trade barriers. Moreover, if France should help subdue Spanish America, she could hardly be expected to do it for nothing. What pay could Ferdinand give other than an American colony for France?

All this diplomatic gossip in due time reached the United States, where it produced a reaction somewhat similar to that in England. Furthermore, if European rivalries were once more let loose in America, could the United States hope to hold aloof from them? Seeking to take advantage of the similarity between British and American views, George Canning, the British foreign minister, suggested to Richard Rush, American minister to England, that the two nations issue a joint statement disclaiming any intention of acquiring Spanish-American territory, and insisting firmly that other nations, with the possible exception of Spain, also keep their hands off America.

Monroe's Decision. Rush promptly referred this communication to President Monroe, who recognized its importance and gave it immediate attention. At the outset he felt inclined to accept the British proposal, although this departure from the policy set by Washington and Jefferson against entangling the United States in European affairs gave him much concern. On this matter, however, the counsel he received was divided. Jefferson and Madison both urged him to join forces with the British; with England "on our side," said Jefferson, "we need not fear the whole world." But Monroe's Secretary of State, John Quincy Adams, voiced a contrary opinion. He maintained that the United States should issue a wholly independent statement. He had no desire to see the United States appear merely as a "cockboat in the wake of a British man-of-war"; he had caught, perhaps from Henry Clay, the vision of a Pan-American system in which the United States would play a leading part. He was by no means certain that the United States should bind itself not to add more American territory to its boundaries; and he knew that Great Britain would do as much to prevent European intervention in Spanish America without an alliance with the United States as with one.

Monroe at length came around to the point of view of Adams. He was perhaps influenced by the fact that, although several months had elapsed, he had received no further word from Canning on the subject. As a matter of fact, although Monroe could probably have had no definite information to this effect, Canning's interest in American cooperation had declined. He had hoped originally that Rush might join him, without referring the matter to President Monroe, in an immediate declaration, and when Rush refused had turned to other expedients. From the French ambassador to England Canning now sought and obtained assurance that the French government had no idea of using force against the rebellious Spanish colonies, and this statement, privately communicated to the other European powers, completely eased his mind on the subject.

In two widely separated statements the President set forth what was to become a major cornerstone of American foreign policy. The first statement, directed particularly at Russia, whose colonizing efforts had already brought forth protests from this nation, flatly asserted that the American continents "are not to be considered subjects for future colonization by any European power." The second addressed itself to the European Concert of powers and to Metternich's doctrine of intervention. The political systems of Europe and America, Monroe wrote, were essentially different and antagonistic, the one based upon autocratic monarchy and the other upon constitutional principles. The United States had not intervened in the internal affairs of European nations and would not do so. In return the United States would consider any European attempt to extend its system "to any portion of this hemisphere as dangerous to our peace and safety." With existing colonies the United States would not interfere. But as to the newly created republics of Latin America, it should view "any interposition for the purpose of oppressing them, or controlling in any other manner their destiny . . . as the manifestation of an unfriendly disposition toward the United States."

Enforcement of the Doctrine. Canning's subsequent claim to authorship of the Monroe Doctrine — "I called the New World into existence to redress the balance of the Old" — was an obvious exaggeration. In fact, no country probably was more annoyed at the Doctrine than Great Britain, whose own claim to pre-eminence in American affairs it summarily denied. But Monroe's contention that Europe had one system of government and America another was also far fetched in view of the constitutional governments existing in several European nations, while Brazil, the largest country in South America, was still a monarchy. Moreover, the Monroe Doctrine had no immediate consequences. Even before it was announced Russia had stopped her expansion in the Northwest, and France had given up all thought of intervention in Spanish America. Furthermore, for many years to come the United States could not possibly have enforced against serious European attack the doctrine it had declared. But thanks to the similarity of British and American interests in most instances, the British navy would do what the United States for the moment could not do. And since Britain was a sea power primarily interested in commerce and constantly threatened from the rear by the large continental powers of Europe, her own threat to the Americas was small. Thus this nation obtained in the days of its youth exactly what it most needed, isolation and time to expand to the Pacific, to develop its farms and factories, to nurture its strength. The relatively unmolested development of the United States can be explained in good part by the lack of aggressive competitors throughout the western hemisphere. Small wonder then that Americans through the years were so devoted to Monroe's doctrine of hands off.

The New West. The growth of American nationality after the War of 1812, so clearly revealed in the postwar legislative program, the decisions of the Supreme Court, and the Monroe Doctrine, was nevertheless accompanied by an almost equal emphasis on sectionalism. The United States was not only a nation; it was also a nation of sections. The admission to the Union of six new states in as many years — Indiana (1816), Mississippi (1817), Illinois (1818), Alabama (1819), Maine (1820), and Missouri (1821) — all of them frontier, and five definitely western — called attention to "the rise of the New West," and to the sectional complications it involved. Part of the New West gradually aligned itself with the South, but the rest of it took on the character of a new and different section, sometimes called the Northwest, and sometimes, less accurately, just "the West."

The opening up of the new western states and the rapid growth of the older ones were undoubtedly promoted by the war itself, which served both to advertise the region

and to end the Indian menace. Reviving business conditions stimulated western migration, while the completion of the Cumberland Road made the trip to the west fairly easy, even for residents of the Atlantic seaboard. Tall tales of the frontier, told with especial delight by European travelers in America, tended to promote the westward movement. The journals of Lewis and Clark, and of Zebulon Pike, provided good publicity for the newly opened areas and stimulated many readers to leave their old homes for lands that the great explorers never saw.

The phenomenal growth of cotton culture in the years following the War of 1812 added a strong southern element to the stream of westward migration. The lands of the new Southwest were in large part ideally fitted for the production of cotton, whereas the cotton lands of the Southeast soon showed signs of wearing out. Sometimes well-established planters sold their eastern lands in order to purchase more

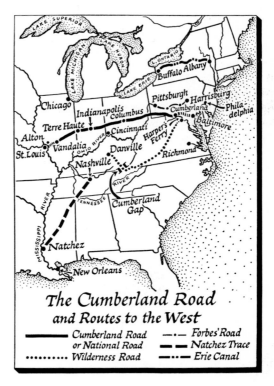

The Cumberland Road
and Routes to the West

————— Cumberland Road or National Road
·········· Wilderness Road
—·— Forbes' Road
—■—■ Natchez Trace
—·■·— Erie Canal

fertile lands farther west, but more often planters preferred to enlarge their holdings at home as the yield per acre declined. Both groups helped populate the West, for the planter who bought out his neighbors left them little alternative but to migrate. Members of the non-slaveholding class often displayed great eagerness to flee from a region where only the great planters made money, and where manual labor was esteemed by the well-to-do as beneath the dignity of free men. Most of the poorer southern whites went directly west and laid the foundations of such states as Alabama and Mississippi, but many of them, like the father of Abraham Lincoln, crossed the Ohio River to swell the population of such free states as Illinois and Indiana. Still others crossed over into Missouri, where slavery was legalized, but for climatic reasons could never flourish.

The "B. U. S." This rapid assault upon the West was not without its unfortunate aspects. Pioneers were usually short of funds, and they developed the habit of borrowing a large part of the money they needed from banks. After the disappearance of the first Bank of the United States in 1811, all such business for the next six years fell to the state banks. In the West these institutions were so careless in their banking habits that they came to be known, appropriately, as "wildcatters." Because money was easily

obtainable from them, western farmers and speculators made purchases of land far in excess of their needs. This unhealthy situation was ended by the second Bank of the United States, chartered in 1816. At first the "B. U. S." was itself inclined to do a "wildcat" type of business, and as a result some of its branches were soon in serious financial straits. But by 1819 it had sobered up, and was requiring a similarly conservative course of the state banks. Notes of a given state bank would be accumulated by the "B. U. S." and then suddenly presented for payment in specie. Thereupon the bank so attacked would be compelled to call in its loans, while individuals who had borrowed from it would be forced in turn to raise what they owed by selling their property for whatever it would bring. With such a policy generally pursued, speculation was effectively arrested, and the general liquidation which followed precipitated the Panic of 1819. For more than two years the people of the United States were caught in the throes of a serious economic depression.

The political power of the New West was made manifest during these years by the success which attended its efforts to secure a change in the land policy of the United States. The Harrison Land Law of 1800 had permitted the purchaser of government land to pay only one-fourth of the purchase price in cash, and the remainder in three annual installments. In practice the collection of these debts owed to the government had proved exceedingly difficult. Land purchasers had frequently used up all their resources in making their first payment and had trusted to the future for the funds with which to meet later payments. Congress passed "relief bills" almost annually, postponing the date of payments due, while the westerners, as their arrears accumulated, easily convinced themselves that they ought not to have been charged for the land at all. During the Panic of 1819 Congress put an end to the unworkable credit system. A law passed in 1820 reduced the size of the tract that an individual might buy to

GROWTH OF THE WEST, 1810–1830			
	1810	*1820*	*1830*
Kentucky	406,511	564,317	687,917
Tennessee	261,727	422,823	681,904
Ohio	230,760	581,434	937,903
Louisiana	76,556	153,407	215,739
Indiana	24,520	147,178	343,031
Illinois	12,282	55,211	157,445
Mississippi	40,352	75,448	136,621
Alabama		127,901	157,445
Missouri	20,845	66,586	140,455

eighty acres and fixed the price per acre at $1.25 cash. Next year a final Relief Act was passed which permitted purchasers who were behind with their payments to return a proportionate part of their land to the government in lieu of cash. Purchasers who wished to keep all their land, however, were allowed to do so, with one of two alternatives, either a cash payment with a discount of 37.5 per cent, or eight annual installments instead of four, with all interest remitted. These acts gave much satisfaction to the people of the West and facilitated materially the ending of the depression.

Slavery and Sectionalism. The rapid expansion of the West soon made the country acutely aware of an impending conflict between the North and the South. Fundamentally the issue upon which these sections came to divide was whether slavery in the United States was to be a temporary or a permanent institution, but for the moment the difference of opinion was restricted to the question of what limits, if any, should be set for the expansion of slavery in the territory west of the Mississippi River. Under French and Spanish rule slavery had been legal in the whole of Louisiana, a situation which the American occupation did not at first disturb. Most of the pioneers who crossed the Mississippi came from the southern states, and while the newcomers, particularly in the St. Louis area, were rarely slaveholders, they were accustomed to slavery and showed no disposition whatever to interfere with it. Once northerners fully realized, however, that the entire trans-Mississippi West was in danger of being pre-empted for slavery, they were ready to call a halt.

Statehood for Missouri. When Jefferson purchased Louisiana from France, he acquired for the United States not only a vast area of land but also about 15,000 new citizens, most of whom were of French or Spanish descent. The chief center of Louisiana settlement was along the lower Mississippi in the vicinity of New Orleans, but a smaller population was located near the confluence of the Missouri and the Mississippi, with St. Louis as its principal city. Soon after the purchase had taken place, American settlers began to enter the lower Mississippi region in appreciable numbers, and by the time of the War of 1812 thousands of them each year were crossing also in the vicinity of St. Louis to thrust a firm wedge of settlement up the valley of the Missouri. With the admission of the lower region as the state of Louisiana in 1812, the upper region received the name of Missouri, and by 1817 was an applicant for statehood. Since there were many slaves in Missouri, the people had no thought except to become a slave state, but Representative James Tallmadge of New York expressed a sentiment strongly held by many of his section when he proposed to set limits to the expansion of slavery. As an amendment to the bill before Congress to make possible statehood for Missouri, he advocated that the further introduction of slavery into Missouri should be forbidden, and that all children born to slave parents after the admission of the state should be free on reaching the age of twenty-five years.

Until the introduction of the Tallmadge amendment, the slavery question had played little part in national politics. The three-fifths compromise of the Constitution had received general acceptance, and the law contemplated by the Constitution to forbid the importation of slaves after 1808 had been duly passed. In most of the country slavery was for many years far from profitable, and by 1804 all the states that lay to the north of Mason and Dixon's line had made provision for emancipation. Active emancipation societies existed in the South as well as in the North. But the discovery that cotton could be grown profitably by slave labor served to revive the institution just when it seemed destined to disappear. Cotton growing was a simple process that the uneducated slaves could comprehend; it was a long-continued activity that kept the workers busy almost the whole year round; it could make use of women and children as well as men; and it could be easily supervised. Suddenly the South discovered that it could not readily give up slavery.

Balance of the Sections. When the question of admitting Missouri came up, there were eleven free states and ten slave states, but the impending admission of Alabama would soon restore the balance of the sections that Americans had come to regard as normal. Of the original thirteen states, seven had abolished slavery and six had retained it, while of the new states four had been admitted without slavery and five (counting Alabama) were slave. This would mean an equal number of United States senators from each section, a balance which the South, always sensitive on the slavery question, wished to maintain.

In the House of Representatives there was no such equality. In population the

SLAVE AND FREE STATES, 1820	
Original Thirteen	
SLAVE	FREE
Delaware	New Hampshire
Maryland	Massachusetts
Virginia	Rhode Island
North Carolina	Connecticut
South Carolina	New York
Georgia	New Jersey
	Pennsylvania
New States	
SLAVE	FREE
Kentucky (1792)	Vermont (1791)
Tennessee (1796)	Ohio (1803)
Louisiana (1812)	Indiana (1816)
Mississippi (1817)	Illinois (1818)
Alabama (1819)	

South had lagged far behind the North; in fact, the Northwest had been peopled to some extent by emigrants from the South. Whereas in 1790 the two sections had been almost equal in population (1,968,000 for the North to 1,925,000 for the South), by 1820 the North had forged far ahead (5,144,000 to 4,372,000). This difference was reflected in the number of representatives which the free and the slave states sent to the lower house of Congress, a difference made even more marked by the fact that five slaves counted only as three free men in making the apportionment of seats. Thus in 1790 there had been 57 representatives from the states north of Mason and Dixon's line to 48 south of it, but by 1820 there were 123 representatives from the free states to only 89 from the slave states. It was because of this situation that the South became so excited over the Tallmadge amendment. Should Missouri and all other states admitted from the Louisiana Purchase become free states, then the balance of the sections in the Senate would be lost, and future Congresses might act, not only to exclude the slaveowner from the West in favor of the free farmer, but even

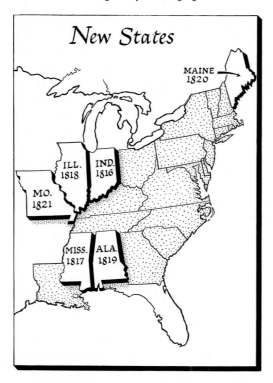

New States

MAINE 1820

ILL. 1818 IND. 1816

MO. 1821

MISS. 1817 ALA. 1819

to interfere with the now profitable institution of slavery where it had long existed. Not for years had there been so heated a debate in Congress. Both sides resorted to elaborate constitutional arguments, but the real issue at stake, as everyone knew, was the control of the Union. During the closing days of the session the House passed the amendment by a small majority, but the Senate rejected it, 22 to 16, five northern senators voting with the South.

The Missouri Compromise. When during the next session of Congress Maine, with the consent of Massachusetts, sought admission to the Union, the chance of maintaining the historic equality of representation for slave and free states became at once apparent, and presently bills for the admission of Missouri as a slave state, and Maine as a free state, became law. This, of course, was in itself a kind of compromise, but the Missouri Compromise proper concerned the disposition of the slavery question in the Louisiana Purchase outside Missouri. A resolution introduced by Senator J. B. Thomas of Illinois proposed that in this region the line of 36°30' should divide free from slave territory. Although much of the land north of that line was then deemed uninhabitable, and hence ineligible for statehood, more northerners in Congress than southerners favored this measure, which became a law March 6, 1820.

The Second Missouri Compromise. The Missouri Compromise in principle offered a natural solution to the problem of slavery expansion. East of the Mississippi River, Mason and Dixon's line and the Ohio River had long been accepted as the proper dividing line between slave and free states, and the idea of continuing such a line west of the Mississippi could readily be accepted. The specific line, however, located at the southern boundary of Missouri, was in the light of later developments to prove most unfavorable to the South. A quick glance at the map will indicate that the great bulk of the remaining unorganized territory of the

Louisiana Purchase lay to the north of that line. Soon men were to learn that much of this territory was good farming land, and some, indeed, excellent. To counter these potential free state senators and representatives, the South could only look forward to the certain development of Arkansas. Thus the long-term implication of the Missouri Compromise to the South was the alternative choice between a permanent minority status or an aggressive policy of expansion to the West and Southwest. Even as the compromise was passed, the Missourians were somewhat irritated that Congress had even considered limiting their rights to control slavery within their borders, and in defiance included in their state constitution two aggressively proslavery clauses. One forbade the state legislature ever to pass a law emancipating slaves without the consent of their masters, and another forbade the entrance of free Negroes into the state on any pretense whatever. For a time it seemed that the debate would break out anew in Congress, and the admission of Missouri would have to be postponed. Finally through the efforts of Henry Clay a second Missouri Compromise was arranged. By its terms the state was admitted under the constitution it had written, but the Missouri legislature was required to pledge itself never to deny citizens of any state the privileges which they enjoyed under the Constitution of the United States. This meant, of course, that free Negroes, if citizens of another state, might migrate to Missouri. With Missouri at last a state, the dispute again died down, but far-seeing men were deeply disturbed. The sectional conflict was only quiescent, not settled. John Quincy Adams wrote that he regarded the dispute as "a mere preamble — a title page to a great tragic volume."

Election of 1820. Despite the acute sectional differences over slavery that immediately preceded the election of 1820, that event found the country almost completely free of partisan strife. The Federalist Party, which in its day had ministered

15.

Buffalo skin coats
dark buff.—

9.

Fur collar & trimming

primarily to the needs of the commercial classes, was by this time well on the way toward becoming merely a memory. Manufacture now mattered more to the Northeast than commerce, and Republicans, not Federalists, had enacted the protective tariff law of 1816. In 1820 the Federalists made no effort to oppose the re-election of President Monroe, who won every vote but one in the electoral college. The complete triumph of Republicans for the next few years led contemporaries to describe the period as an "era of good feelings," but the phrase was misleading, for bitter factionalism within the dominant party would soon split it apart.

The Southwest Boundary. Indeed, the scene was already being set for future sectional disputes by the increasing interest of Americans in the trans-Mississippi West. The Adams-Onís Treaty that transferred Florida from Spain to the United States marked off also the boundary line between the United States and Spanish-American possessions west of the Mississippi River. Adams believed that the boundary line should have been placed at the Rio Grande, but the administration was eager to make sure of the Florida cession and forced him to make an offer more favorable to Spain. As a result, all of what later became Texas was left in Spanish hands, and the western boundary of the United States was placed at the Sabine River, "up that river along the western bank to the thirty-second parallel, thence due north to the Red River, up that river to the one-hundredth meridian, thence due north to the Arkansas, up that river along its southern bank to its source, thence due north to the forty-second parallel, and then along that parallel to the South Sea." This article clearly gave over to the United States whatever claim Spain had previously held to the Oregon country, and it furnished for the first time since the purchase of Louisiana an authentic southwestern boundary.

The exploits of the fur trappers of the early decades of the nineteenth century entranced Americans, as did later the life of the cowboy. Hiram Martin Chittenden (1858–1917), an engineer and historian, has remained the authoritative chronicler of the Rocky Mountain fur trade.

The free trappers, or freemen, as they were commonly called, were the most interesting and enviable class in the mountains. Bound to no company, free to go where they pleased, they were held in higher repute than any other class. Moreover, they were men of bold and adventurous spirit for none other would have the courage to follow so hazardous a business. . . . The nature of service in the wilderness produced its effect in the physiognomy, language, habits, and dress of the hunter. The hard life which he was compelled to follow left a deep impression upon his physical appearance. He was ordinarily gaunt and spare, browned with exposure, his hair long and unkempt, while his general make-up, with the queer dress which he wore, made it often difficult to distinguish him from an Indian. The constant peril of his life and the necessity of unremitting vigilance gave him a kind of piercing look, his head slightly bent forward and his deep eyes peering from under a slouch hat, or whatever head-gear he might possess, as if studying the face of the stranger to learn whether friend or foe. On the whole he impressed one as taciturn and gloomy, and his life did to some extent suppress gaiety and tenderness.

H. M. CHITTENDEN, *The American Fur Trade of the Far West* (1902)

Long's Expedition. Curiosity about the unsettled portions of the trans-Mississippi West led to another great exploring expedition, this time under the command of Major Stephen H. Long, who had gained some experience on a trip up the Mississippi River in 1817. With a Pittsburgh-built steamboat, the *Western Engineer,* Long left St. Louis in June, 1819, and arrived at the mouth of the Platte the following September. Here the expedition halted until the next spring, when, reinforced by a detachment that had marched overland from St. Louis, it advanced westward along the Platte River and its southern branch to the Rockies. After sighting and naming Long's Peak, the expedition skirted the mountains to the Arkansas, and a small party pushed on to the Canadian River. The return trip was one of great hardship, and Long's report was pessimistic. Most of the country he had visited he regarded as wholly unfit for white habitation. His report did more than any other single document to fix in the American mind the legend of the "Great American Desert."

The Northwestern Fur Trade. Meantime the region north and west of the route taken by Long was being penetrated with singular completeness by fur traders rather than by official explorers. As early as 1808 agents of the Missouri Fur Company, operating from St. Louis, planned to exploit the fur trade of the upper Missouri. They gained more experience than profits, but their knowledge was inherited by the Rocky Mountain Fur Company, which in 1823 began a series of brilliant explorations by sending Jedediah S. Smith to the Green River Valley and the Great Salt Lake. Other fur-trade activities of the period centered on John Jacob Astor, whose Pacific Fur Company, a subsidiary of his American Fur Company, sent out two expeditions in 1810 to the Oregon country, one by sea, the other by land, and founded Astoria. This outpost was sold to the British fur-trade interests during the War of 1812, to be known thereafter as Fort George. When the war was over, Astor induced Congress to prohibit aliens from carrying on the fur trade within the United States. This law did not permit him to recover Astoria, but it did give him a chance to purchase at his own price many British trading posts south of the international border. Astor's traders made good profits, but they were less responsible for the exploration of the West than the adventurous employees of the Rocky Mountain Fur Company.

Americans of Monroe's time might well have asked themselves two significant questions. What would be the destiny of this vast new area that their explorers were opening up? What changes would they wish to make in the national borders that their diplomats were marking out?

SELECTED BIBLIOGRAPHY

An excellent synthesis is provided by George Dangerfield, *The Awakening of American Nationalism, 1815–1828* (1965). But no student should overlook F. J. Turner, *Rise of the New West, 1819–1829* (1906). Companion volumes which provide syntheses of economic history are G. R. Taylor, *The Transportation Revolution, 1815–1860* (1951); and P. W. Gates, *The Farmer's Age: Agriculture, 1815–1860* (1960). On the tariff, see the standard works: F. W. Taussig, *The Tariff History of the United States* (8th ed., 1831); and Edward Stanwood, *American Tariff Controversies in the Nineteenth Century* (2 vols., 1903). An important recent monograph is M. N. Rothbard, *The Panic of 1819: Reactions and Policies* (1962). On the crucial subject of transportation, A. B. Hulbert, *The Paths of Inland Commerce* (1920), is brief and to the point.

A superbly written survey of the politics of this period is George Dangerfield, *The Era of Good Feelings* (1952). W. P. Cresson, *James Monroe* (1946), remains the best modern biography; students of the period await the publication of the results of the long study of Harry Ammon. The standard biography of Webster is C. M. Fuess, *Daniel Webster* (2 vols., 1930); but see the brief, discerning treatment by R. N. Current, *Daniel Webster and the Rise of National Conservatism* (1955). On the decline of Federalism, see D. R. Fox, *The Decline of Aristocracy in the Politics of New York* (1919); and Shaw Livermore, Jr., *The Twilight of Federalism; The Disintegration of the Federalist Party, 1815–1830* (1962). Other

political studies of importance include P. S. Klein, *Pennsylvania Politics, 1817–1832: A Game Without Rules* (1940); J. A. Kehl, *Ill Feeling in the Era of Good Feeling; Western Pennsylvania Political Battles, 1815–1825* (1956); and L. W. Turner, *William Plumer of New Hampshire, 1759–1850* (1962). J. T. Horton, *James Kent, A Study in Conservatism, 1763–1847* (1939), examines the reasoning of a prominent state jurist.

On the Monroe Doctrine, the standard survey by the foremost authority is Dexter Perkins, *A History of the Monroe Doctrine* (2nd ed., 1955). Other studies by Perkins include *The Monroe Doctrine, 1823–1826* (1927); and *The Monroe Doctrine, 1826–1867* (1933). An interesting collection of varying interpretations is *The Monroe Doctrine*, edited by Armin Rappaport (1964). On the Latin American situation the best work is A. P. Whitaker, *The United States and the Independence of Latin America, 1800–1830* (1941). An interesting book which challenges Perkins' interpretations at some points is E. H. Tatum, Jr., *The United States and Europe, 1815–1823; A Study in the Background of the Monroe Doctrine* (1936). An important recent monograph is J. A. Logan, Jr., *No Transfer; An American Security Principle* (1961). The activities of leaders of American diplomacy are described and analyzed in J. H. Powell, *Richard Rush, Republican Diplomat, 1780–1859* (1942); and S. F. Bemis, *John Quincy Adams and the Foundations of American Foreign Policy* (1949). See also *John Quincy Adams and American Continental Empire*, edited by Walter LaFeber (1965).

On the Missouri Compromise, see F. C. Shoemaker, *Missouri's Struggle for Statehood,*

* Available in paperback

1804–1821 (1916); and Glover Moore, *The Missouri Controversy, 1819–1821* (1953). Useful background may also be found in M. S. Locke, *Anti-Slavery in America, 1619–1808* (1901); A. D. Adams, *The Neglected Period of Anti-Slavery in America, 1808–1831* (1908); and W. F. B. DuBois, *The Suppression of the African Slave Trade to the United States of America, 1638–1870* (1896). See the essays by F. J. Turner, *Frontier and Section,* edited by R. A. Billington (1961).

On the South, see the important survey by Clement Eaton, *The Growth of Southern Civilization, 1790–1860* (1961). Lively accounts of southern expansion are Everett Dick, *The Dixie Frontier* (1948); and J. A. Caruso, *The Southern Frontier* (1963). L. J. White, *Politics on the Southwestern Frontier* (1964), concerns Arkansas Territory. The notable career of the master inventor whose device altered the course of southern history may be traced in Jeannette Mirsky and Allan Nevins, *The World of Eli Whitney* (1952); and C. McL. Green, *Eli Whitney and the Birth of American Technology* (1956).

On transportation, Seymour Dunbar, *A History of Travel in America* (4 vols., 2nd ed., 1937), is particularly valuable because of its excellent illustrations. L. C. Hunter, *Steamboats on the Western Rivers: An Economic and Technological History* (1949), follows its theme in abundant detail. L. D. Baldwin, *The Keelboat Age on Western Waters* (1941), deals effectively with the pre-steamboat age. J. T. Flexner, *The Story of the Steamboat; Inventors in Action* (1944), records the early steamboating experiments. The connection between transportation and urbanization is traced in Richard Wade, *The Urban Frontier* (1959), a pioneering and highly successful effort at synthesis. G. M. Capers, *The Biography of a River Town; Memphis: Its Heroic Age* (1939), is an interesting case study. Major works on the Old Northwest in this period include J. D. Barnhart, *Valley of Democracy* (1953); R. C. Buley, *Old Northwest: Pioneer Period, 1815–1840* (2 vols., 1950); and P. C. Henlein, *Cattle*

Kingdom in the Ohio Valley, 1783–1860 (1959). One fascinating theme is explored in abundant detail by M. E. Pickard and R. C. Buley, *The Midwest Pioneer: His Ills, Cures, Cares and Doctors* (1945).

On economic history, see L. M. Hacker, *The Triumph of American Capitalism* (1940). W. B. Smith and A. H. Cole, *Fluctuations in American Business, 1790–1860* (1935), is particularly useful. See also H. E. Miller, *Banking Theories in the United States before 1860* (1927). In addition to the books on public land policy already listed, see H. S. Zahler, *Eastern Workingmen and National Land Policy* (1941); and P. W. Gates, *Frontier Landlords and Pioneer Tenants* (1945).

On the Far West, a dependable survey is L. R. Hafen and C. C. Rister, *Western America* (2nd ed., 1950). Bernard De Voto, *The Course of Empire* (1952), is a vivid and highly personal account by a brilliant stylist. Other interesting general treatments are E. W. Gilbert, *The Exploration of Western America, 1800–1850* (1933); and Dorothy Gardiner, *West of the River* (1941). Detailed surveys of a major subject are H. M. Chittenden, *The American Fur Trade of the Far West* (3 vols., 1902); and P. C. Phillips and J. W. Smurr, *The Fur Trade* (2 vols., 1961). A great classic is Washington Irving, *Astoria* (1836); see also the standard biography by K. W. Porter, *John Jacob Astor, Business Man* (2 vols., 1931). On British competition, see J. S. Galbraith, *The Hudson's Bay Company as an Imperial Factor, 1821–1869* (1957). D. L. Morgan, *Jedediah Smith and the Opening of the West* (1953), is a superb biography of the greatest "mountain man"; see also Morgan's *The West of William H. Ashley* (1964).

The principal work on the Adams-Onís Treaty is P. C. Brooks, *Diplomacy and the Borderlands* (1939). On Florida, see Marquis James, *Andrew Jackson: The Border Captain* (1933); S. W. Martin, *Florida during the Territorial Days* (1944); and R. W. Patrick, *Aristocrat in Uniform: General Duncan L. Clinch* (1963).

11

THE RISE AND DECLINE
OF FEDERAL CULTURE

ટ્ર *Crèvecoeur · The Federal Spirit · Education · Higher Education and Science · Deism · Unitarianism · Architecture · Painting · Literature · Poetry · Irving · Cooper · Romanticism · Cultural Nationalism · Deism Attacked · Religion in the West · American Traits · Democracy · Individualism*

The years from the adoption of the Constitution through the War of 1812 have usually been called the Federal period of American history. Dominated politically by men who had fought in the Revolution and helped frame the Constitution, these years were distinct from those that followed in several significant ways.

Crèvecoeur. Even before the Revolution, Michel Guillaume St. Jean de Crèvecoeur had raised the question which Europeans were to ask persistently during the next century: What is an American? This well-disposed Frenchman, who spent fifteen years as a gentleman farmer in New York, answered first that the American was an Englishman with Scottish, French, Dutch, German, or Swedish blood in his veins, who had brought with him the British traditions of liberty but not the British "aristocratical families," or the court, the king, the bishops and "ecclesiastical dominion." Moreover, he was a freeman who for the first time in history found that he could work for himself on his own land and pay no quitrents or tithes to a landlord class. As a freeholder he was industrious, sagacious, litigious, proud, and obstinate, given to good living, and quick to criticize his government and its officials. Europe, Crèvecoeur concluded, held no counterpart. "The American is a new man, who acts upon new principles; he must therefore entertain new ideas, and form new opinions."

The Federal Spirit. At the time Crèvecoeur wrote, however, it was not clear just how different from its European models American society was to become. The leaders of the Revolutionary generation were in most respects still British and European in their attitudes. The Constitution they fashioned was inspired by British precedent and European political thought, and the republican society they envisioned was one whose values were not unlike those held by liberal upper-middle-class society in England. Some leaders of the Federal period

176

knew Europe well, and not a few felt at home among the cultural elite of Britain and the Continent. Most of them, whether self-taught or college-trained, were well-educated men who knew science and politics and enjoyed an easy familiarity with the classical literatures of Greece and Rome. Their tastes in modern literature and the arts were similar. Like the upper classes of England and the Continent, they embraced the neoclassical movement, the artistic counterpart to rationalism. With reason rather than emotion as a guide, their preferences were for order, symmetry, and restraint, whether in literature, painting, sculpture, or architecture.

By and large, the leaders of the Federal period were greatly influenced by the ideas of the Enlightenment. Their political, scientific, and social thinking was strongly infused with the ideas of Newton, Locke, Montesquieu, and Rousseau. Rationalists, for the most part, they believed in an ordered world, in natural law for the universe, and in natural rights for man. Although they agreed with Locke and Jefferson that all men were created equal before God and before the law, they were no less convinced that men were born with vast differences between them. Both Adams and Jefferson believed that only a fortunate few in each generation were endowed with great capabilities, and that these constituted a natural aristocracy. The mark of good government was its ability to discover and make use of the talents of this natural elite. Where Adams and Jefferson disagreed was how such an elite came into being. While Adams believed that the aristocracy of ability arose mainly from circumstances of wealth and genteel breeding which could be perpetuated from one well-founded generation to another, Jefferson held that such an assumption was fallacious and that the result would be an artificial aristocracy without special virtue or talent, sustained only by hereditary privileges.

What Jefferson sought was a natural aristocracy "of virtue and talents" unrelated to family or wealth. This objective could only be accomplished, Jefferson argued, through the creation of a free public school system which would select and educate the able. Subsequently, this elite would be elected to office by an enlightened electorate whose natural intelligence was strengthened by the moral and social instincts implanted in them by God. Adams, in opposition, took a more pessimistic view of human nature. Politics, he felt, would always be a contest between the ignorant, resentful masses of the poor and the wealthy and rapacious upper classes. One group, he argued, could only be restrained from infringing upon the rights of the other by a system of checks and balances, and by the elevation to public office of those men of wealth and culture who by added reason of their morality and ability belonged to the real aristocracy.

Whatever their differences about the character of a natural aristocracy, both Adams and Jefferson, along with most of the leaders of their time, strongly believed that such an intellectual and cultural elite did in fact exist and that the only chance for a reasonably effective government came from promoting the ablest, best educated, and most cultured representatives of such a "natural aristocracy" to positions of power.

Education. For these reasons — a belief in rationalism and the existence of a natural aristocracy of talent, no matter its origin — the leaders of the Federal period were concerned with the furtherance of education and educational facilities in the new nation. By acts of 1784–1787, lands for the support of public education were set aside, and during the Constitutional Convention Charles Pinckney attempted to persuade that body to found a national university. But despite support from such men as John Adams and James Madison, the delegates, fearful of centralized government in any manifestation, defeated the proposals. After the Convention proponents of public education renewed their efforts. Jefferson in particular drew up a school plan for Virginia which comprehended several levels of free public schools, which would be capped, he hoped, by a state or even a national university. But the fear of the conservatives that public schools might implant radical Jeffersonian ideas in their pupils, and the opposition of the churches, which still maintained almost a monopoly of education, prevented early and widespread public support.

In 1800 three types of common schools existed. For the children of the wealthier classes there were a number of "tuition schools" where college preparatory courses, including foreign languages, classics, religion, and science were taught. Ranking below them, but still requiring tuition, were the "apprentice schools" in which trade and commercial subjects predominated. At the lowest level in most communities were the "charity" or free schools, often indifferently maintained by public taxation, where the rudiments of reading, mathematics, and moral studies were taught.

Despite the earlier encouragement of public grammar schools by the Massachusetts legislature, little even there had been done to provide free high schools. For a quarter of a century after 1800, in fact, the only appreciable growth in secondary education was in the private academies, most of which were associated with religious sects. By 1830, Massachusetts had sixty-eight such institutions, and though the academy movement was not as pronounced elsewhere in America, in every state there were a few such institutions where for a price students might be prepared for college entrance. Not until 1821 were the first two publicly supported high schools established, one in Boston, the other in Portland, Maine. Three years later, however, the Massachusetts legislature passed a law requiring each town of more than five hundred families to support a high school. In time this law became the pattern for the creation of public high schools in many other states.

Higher Education and Science. More impressive gains in education were made in the establishment of colleges. Before 1795 six states had chartered state colleges. But these were far outnumbered by the sectarian institutions founded by churches to train ministers and to provide the youth of the country with higher education based on Christian ethics and denominational beliefs. Methodists and Presbyterians in particular were active all through the period. Catholics, although still comparatively few in numbers, displayed a like activity. Georgetown College, in the District of Columbia, for example, was founded in 1789. Religious antagonism, prompted by grave suspicion of public, and thus, secular, institutions, kept appropriations for the new state colleges at a minimum level, while the relative poverty of most church-supported institutions resulted in inadequate facilities and faculties of small distinction. But the men of the Revolutionary generation at least had attested their faith in education and provided some promise for its future.

The post-Revolutionary years were also marked by increased interest in the new sciences. Inspired by the example of Benjamin Franklin's American Philosophical Society, John Adams helped found the American Academy of Arts and Sciences in 1780. State and medical societies were formed during the period and played an important part in establishing the first standards for the profession. The Chemical Society of Philadelphia, organized in 1792, was the first of its kind in the world. Although laboratories were maintained by Dr. Benjamin Rush and Joseph Priestley, the discoverer of oxygen, the country produced few scientists of note for the next quarter century. Most branches of science were rapidly becoming specialized, and Americans without the superior facilities and technical training of the great European universities were at a serious disadvantage.

Deism. The continuing interest in European science and the devotion of the generation to the spirit of Enlightenment did, however, encourage the spread of deism until its rationalist approach had tinctured the spiritual beliefs of many of the country's leading citizens. Most scientists, like Benjamin Rush, were deists, while several of the nation's budding writers, like Joel Barlow and Philip Freneau, also embraced its tenets. Freneau's description of the universe paid poetic tribute to the ultimate rationality of the Creator and to the impossibility of change in such a perfectly thought-out design:

"All in its proper place arranged
Immortal, endless, and unchanged."

Many of the Founding Fathers themselves, including Benjamin Franklin, James Otis, James Wilson, and Thomas Jefferson, were deists. Unlike Jefferson and others, who were content to believe what their minds dictated without attacking their neighbors' more conservative faiths, a few radical deists launched an open attack against all organized religion. Among them was Ethan Allen, the leader of the "Green Mountain Boys," who wrote part of *Oracles of Religion,* published in 1781. But the most notable of all deist tracts was Thomas Paine's *Age of Reason* (1794–96). Though a firm believer in God, in life after death, and in Christian ethics, he scornfully castigated all ceremony or ritual, and much of the creeds of organized religions. His *Age of Reason* was a phenomenally successful book, running through seventeen editions in three years. But its assault upon formal worship provoked a vigorous counteroffensive by orthodox religionists which helped to bring about the "Second Great Awakening," and which contributed to the death of deism as a strong religious movement.

Unitarianism.   The glorification of rationalism also fostered movements in Calvinist churches which led, especially in New England, to the founding of new denominations and sects. The increasingly

benevolent view of man's status and capabilities as exemplified in the Declaration of Independence and the Bill of Rights was the source of a conflict between liberal and conservative Calvinists over the whole question of literal versus liberal and rational interpretation of the Bible. William Ellery Channing, a leading Boston minister, put the case for rational interpretation by declaring that since God had endowed man with rational powers, "the ultimate reliance of a human being is and must be his own mind." To Channing and his followers the traditional Calvinist concept that man was a creature of iniquity and doomed to perdition was unthinkable. They believed that virtue was an innate human quality and that man was capable of great improvement. The Unitarians, as this group came to be called, also believed in the unity of the Godhead, and that the Almighty "was by nature not the stern and Righteous Creator of Calvin, but rather a God of mercy, love, and benevolence." By 1806, Harvard College was a center of Unitarianism.

The appeal to reason as the final arbiter in religious matters, and the growing belief in man's essential goodness, also resulted in an increased toleration of minority religious sects. Before the Revolution every colony had discriminatory laws against both Roman Catholics and Jews. Even after the adoption of the new state constitutions, six states still required adherence to Protestantism as a qualification for office, and all except two, Virginia and New York, disqualified Jews. But the discounting of traditional religious views by rationalist leaders led to the repeal of most such laws by 1800, and the last of them was repealed by Rhode Island in 1842.

Architecture.   The Federal period left its mark on architecture and the arts as it did on thought and religion. In fact, the style of Charles Bulfinch of Boston, the leading architect of New England, has often been called Federal. Drawing his inspiration from the great British neoclassical designers, whose buildings he had seen and admired, Bulfinch combined their architectural ideas with delicate and simple lines reminiscent of the classical period. Until the construction of the Federal capitol in Washington (the completion of which Bulfinch supervised), his notable Boston State House (1800) was generally considered to be the most imposing building in the country. Although Jefferson was a friend and an admirer of Bulfinch, he derived his architectural enthusiasms from other models. Seeking to depart from the British tradition and to initiate a purely American style of building, Jefferson borrowed heavily from Roman sources for his own designs. Inspired by the Pantheon in Paris, which he greatly admired, Jefferson gave his own home at Monticello and the Virginia state capitol the prominent heavy dome and pillars that characterize the original Pantheon in Rome.

Of more influence than either Bulfinch or Jefferson on the American architectural tradition was Benjamin Latrobe (1764–1820), who was born in England and emigrated to Virginia in 1796. Latrobe supervised the completion of Jefferson's Virginia capitol. Soon thereafter he moved to Philadelphia where he developed his own individual style. Feeling that buildings suggestive of ancient Rome were ostentatious and grandiose for a young republic, Latrobe became attracted to the dignified simplicity of classical Greek buildings. His Bank of Pennsylvania (1799), designed after the Erechtheum on the Acropolis in Athens, started the Greek revival in the United States, and its style was reflected in innumerable other banks and public buildings throughout the country. Made surveyor of public buildings by President Jefferson, Latrobe designed the new Federal capitol and employed his considerable architectural and engineering skills in other important works, including the Chesapeake and Ohio Canal.

Painting. "I would not give a sixpence for a picture of Raphael or a statue of Phidias," John Adams once wrote. The utilitarian and unaesthetic spirit that prompted the second President's remark was common in the young nation which for years was apathetic to the development of painting and sculpture. Nevertheless, the

BANK OF PENNSYLVANIA

An example of the style of Benjamin Latrobe, the leading exponent in America of the Greek revival style.

AN AMERICAN PRIMITIVE

An eighteenth-century portrait, probably of Timothy Swan, by an unknown painter.

work of such artists as John Singleton Copley, Benjamin West, Charles Willson Peale, Gilbert Stuart, and John Trumbull inaugurated a national tradition of painting. Four of these men were born before the Revolution. All of them were strongly influenced by the British neoclassical movement, and all spent most of their time painting portraits, an economic necessity for the artist in America. Copley's portraiture ranged from the dramatically elegant study of Nicholas Boylston to the realistic portrayal of Paul Revere in a profound revery over one of his silver teapots. West's paintings were more flamboyant, perhaps as the result of three years' study in Italy and his subsequent residence in England, then artistically dominated by Sir Joshua Reynolds. Under George III, West became the court painter and was elected the second president of the Royal Academy. Although West painted in a

style then fashionable in England, many of his subjects were American, such as "Penn's Treaty with the Indians," in which the noble savages are arranged in classic juxtaposition to Penn's more somber delegation.

Charles Willson Peale (1741–1827) was subsidized by a group of admiring Maryland businessmen to study under West in London. He returned in 1776 to fight for his country, but so loathed what he saw of war that he became a lifelong pacifist. Nevertheless, he painted such martial figures of the Revolutionary period as Washington and John Paul Jones, as well as Madison, Hamilton, Adams, and Franklin, with artistic honesty and considerable skill. Peale organized the first public art exhibition in the United States, and in 1805 helped found the Pennsylvania Academy of Fine Arts.

Undoubtedly, the most notable of all American portraitists was Gilbert Stuart (1755–1828). Like Peale, he studied under West in London, and after a successful

A CLASSIC OF AMERICAN PORTRAITURE

The Gilbert Stuart portrait of Mrs. Perez Morton, c. 1802.

sojourn in England returned in 1792 to the United States, where he was soon acknowledged as a master of his medium. Among the very large number of Stuart paintings are likenesses of the first five Presidents of the United States. Although most of his portraits were done in the neoclassical style, his experiments with color showed an original mind. Stuart's Washington is familiar to generations of Americans who until recently saw it daily on their postage stamps. John Trumbull (1756–1843), a Revolutionary War hero, was another student of West, and is best known for his many canvases depicting battle scenes of the Revolutionary War, including the well-known "Surrender of Cornwallis."

Literature.   America's writers labored under much the same difficulties as did her painters. The reading public with a taste for anything more substantial than newspapers was small, and a good portion of this group preferred British authors and publications to American ones. Moreover, many Americans disdained native writers as idlers who contributed nothing useful to the public weal. Leisure reading, especially of novels, was frowned upon by many of the pious as a frivolous — and possibly sinful — waste of time. Because the absence of a copyright treaty between the United States and Great Britain permitted the inexpensive publication of "pirated" foreign works, American authors found it difficult to have their works published. It is little wonder then that the three leaders of America's first literary circle, the Hartford or Connecticut Wits, eventually turned their energies to other pursuits: Timothy Dwight to the presidency of Yale College, John Trumbull to the legal profession, and Joel Barlow to public life.

Poetry.   None of the Hartford Wits possessed great talent, and perhaps their propagandizing, through verse, of Federalist politics contributed to their failure. Adopting the neoclassical style, they could not compete with their models in either poetic skill or imagination. Joel Barlow's *The Columbiad* (1807) was patriotically conceived as a large-scale national epic, but Barlow's abilities were not equal to his theme. America's first genuinely gifted poet was Philip Freneau (1752–1832), a Princeton graduate, Revolutionary patriot, journalist, and ardent Jeffersonian. During the first part of his career Freneau's poetry, like that of the Hartford Wits, was largely concerned with political themes and the celebration of nationalist thought. He had this to say in his *On False Systems of Government:*

> How can we call those systems just
> Which bid the few, the proud, the first,
> Possess all earthly good;
> While millions robbed of all that's dear
> In silence shed the ceaseless tear,
> And leeches suck their blood.

So sharp were his political attacks on the Federalists that Washington referred to him as "that rascal Freneau." But his best poetry was innocent of both politics and deistic professions. Under the influence of the rising Romantic movement, Freneau, in his maturity, turned his back on political contention and wrote of nature, as in his memorable poem, "The Wild Honeysuckle." Fitting his life to his poetry, he renounced his career in journalism and spent his last years as a seaman and a farmer.

Although much younger than Freneau, William Cullen Bryant (1794–1878) also first attracted public attention with his political poems. When only thirteen, he wrote "Embargo," an attack upon Jefferson's attempt to secure American rights by non-intercourse in trade with foreign powers. The son of a western Massachusetts clergyman, Bryant parted with Federalism to become one of the nation's most consistent liberals. After a short legal career he turned to journalism and for decades was the editor of the New York *Evening Post*, in whose pages he supported such reforms as free trade, antislavery, and labor unions. He was instrumental in establishing the city's Central Park and the Metropolitan Museum. Throughout his long life Bryant continued to write poetry, sometimes expressing himself in the English Romantic tradition in poems which celebrated nature. Bryant's Puritan background and his preoccupation with social and political reform, however, never permitted him to become a full-fledged Romantic. In "Thanatopsis," his best-known poem, written when he was sixteen, Bryant revealed a stoic concern with the "silent halls of death." His mature poetry was characterized by a neoclassic spareness and a cool restraint not found in the great poets of the Romantic movement.

Washington Irving. For all their talent Freneau and Bryant were little known outside of America. The honor of being the first American to be widely read and appreciated in Europe went to Washington Irving (1783–1859). Irving was born of a New York family wealthy enough to provide him with a legal education and with the means for a leisurely tour of Europe. Returning to New York, he soon turned to letters, and with the publication of his *History of New York* by "Diedrich Knickerbocker," in which he satirized local history and displayed his not inconsiderable knowledge of the past, he soon gained an American reputation. His European fame came after 1815, however, with the publication of his *Sketch Book* (1820), *Tales of a Traveller* (1824), and *The Alhambra* (1832). Irving not only was the young nation's first man of letters, acknowledged as such abroad, but made America aware that its own history could be used as literary material. In Rip Van Winkle and Ichabod Crane, Irving created two characters from the American soil who have remained familiar to the literate wherever English is read.

James Fenimore Cooper. More exclusively American than Irving in his use of locale and characters was the country's first major novelist, James Fenimore Cooper

THE LEATHERSTOCKING TALES

This first illustration of James Fenimore Cooper's hero, Natty Bumppo, is scarcely faithful to the winter dress of the frontier.

(1789–1851). Cooper came from a well-to-do New York family. He spent his youth in western New York in Cooperstown, which his father had founded. After attending Yale College and spending three years as a midshipman in the navy, Cooper returned to Cooperstown to manage the family estate. There he started writing fiction in the romantic historical style which the tales of Sir Walter Scott had made popular in England and America. Cooper wrote especially of the epic American conquest of the wilderness. *The Spy* (1821), a tale of the Revolution, was his first success, but Cooper's name will always be most closely associated with the rugged and guileless frontiersman, Natty Bumppo, whom a modern critic has aptly described as "the democrat's idea of the democratic man." Bumppo was the hero of the Leatherstocking Tales, of which *The Last of the Mohicans* (1826) is probably the best. Full of derring-do and lively forest clashes between frontiersmen and Indians, Cooper's tales appealed to the rising interest of Europeans in the American West. Most of his thirty-two novels were quickly translated into French and German, and captured a reading audience which has persisted to the present. Ironically, as Cooper's fame spread in Europe, his reputation in America steadily declined. After a long stay in Europe, during which he constantly extolled American institutions, he came home in 1834 and was soon disillusioned by the changes that had taken place during his absence. Cooper was a gentleman, a man of taste and discernment, and a member of that aristocratic elite which both John Adams and Thomas Jefferson hoped might govern the country and set its ethical and cultural standards. Leaving the United States during the administration of John Quincy Adams, he came home to be confronted with Jacksonian democracy at its zenith. The admiration for excellence and the veneration of Europe's great cultural achievements had been swept away, or so it seemed to Cooper, by the adulation of the common man and a narrow and provincial nationalism. Embittered, Cooper wrote a series of works attacking the age's mediocrity, the vulgarity, parochialism, and the assault on culture to which, ironically enough, the development of his own much-admired frontier had contributed most.

Romanticism. Change was prevalent at the beginning of the nineteenth century, and not the least important force affecting the future of America was the European cultural and intellectual movement known as Romanticism. The Romantic movement was in essence a revolt against some of the prevailing ideas of the Enlightenment and against the neoclassic vogue in the arts. Diffused, in part, through the writings of Rousseau, Goethe, Lamb, and Coleridge, Romanticism rejected the idea that the world was built on a logical pattern, and conceived of it instead as an ever-growing and ever-changing cosmos. Nature, in its scenic splendors, became a profound source of inspiration for the romanticist, and natural man, Rousseau's "noble savage," who relied upon his impulses, his intuition, his feelings, and his conscience rather than upon the cultivated power of reason, became an object of veneration.

To the extent that Romanticism prized the emotional and intuitive over the rational powers of man, it was democratic rather than aristocratic. Its emphasis upon change in nature had its effect on contemporary political thought, thus speeding the wave of nineteenth-century nationalism. Its veneration of natural or primitive man gave new luster to the common man. After the War of 1812, large numbers of Americans either visited or were educated in Germany, where they were exposed to the rising German Romantic movement, and subsequently brought its impulse across the Atlantic. Stay-at-homes fell under the same influence, since American newspapers and magazines published the writings of Goethe and Schiller. Even though all manner of British things were unpopular with the American populace immediately after the War of 1812, such British Romantic writers as Coleridge, Wordsworth, Byron, and Scott probably were most influential in disseminating Romantic ideas in America. Scott's historical romances were particularly popular in the United States for at least a generation.

Cultural Nationalism. Everywhere in Europe the nineteenth century was an age of intensified nationalism. In this respect the United States was no different from Italy, Germany, or even Russia. But the American preoccupation with its steadily expanding West gave American nationalism an even more striking particularism than marked similar movements in Europe. Ever since Patrick Henry uttered his famous remark in 1774 that he was "not a Virginian, but an American," the tide of nationalistic sentiment had been rising. But the rapid development of the new West after 1800, the passions aroused by the War of 1812, and the lack of a substantial leavening of immigrants from Europe until the 1840's gave the United States a parochial quality and even a disdain for European influences that had not marked it before. Evidences of this intense cultural nationalism were plentiful. Paralleling Jefferson's search for an American style of architecture was Noah Webster's plea for a simplified American spelling of English words. In his subsequently published *Speller,* which he hoped would develop "an American tongue," and in his *Compendious Dictionary of the English Language* (1806), Webster not only made wide changes in traditional English orthography but added many words coined in the New World. "Theatre" thus became "theater" and words like "skunk cabbage" and "stinkweed" colored the new compilation. The intensified interest in American things was also attested by the increased popularity of books of American history and biography, often of the most patriotic and even vainglorious content. Numerous accounts of the life and exploits of Daniel Boone were published, thus creating the first western American hero. Such fanciful concoctions of truth and legend as "Parson" Mason Locke Weems's *Washington* found thousands of avid readers. First published in 1800, the book went through many changes, the now familiar cherry tree episode appearing first in the 1806 edition.

Deism Attacked. The influence upon the American mind and character of the rise of the Romantic movement and the soaring spirit of a nationalist democracy is best seen perhaps in religious developments. Deism, "the religion of reason," was at its height in popularity and influence when Thomas Paine published his *Age of Reason.* But Paine's views were angrily attacked from both the pulpit and the press. By 1800 more than a score of printed broadsides had

appeared in which Paine was variously described as a revolutionist, a French radical atheist, and a conspirator who would destroy all religion and government, were he permitted his way. In most such publications, reason was asserted to be utterly incapable of understanding the solemn mysteries of traditional religion. "The heart and only the heart," it was argued, could comprehend God's benevolent plan for the universe and for man.

Religion in the West. Throughout the 1790's ministers even in New England had made use of emotional sermons and revivalism as weapons against deism. But nowhere did the new movement catch on as it did along the frontier. Throughout the West no such formal connections existed between the new states and the church as there were in the East. Moreover, there were in the West few buildings especially designed as churches and few ministers trained to conduct religious services according to traditional rituals and doctrines. Most western preachers substituted fervor, imagination, and emotion, which they had in plenty, for the traditional religious learning which they lacked. These sects, whether old or newly founded, responded to emotional appeals more readily than to reasoned sermons. Sects and splinter groups proliferated, some of which served but a small region or even a single community. Consequently, even before the influence of the Second Great Awakening hit the West, the section was ripe for the "camp meeting," the most characteristic phenomenon of an awakened and loosely directed religious impulse.

James McGready was probably responsible for the first great camp revival meeting in the West. A Presbyterian preacher in South Carolina, he was asked to move when his hell fire and damnation sermons created a furor among his parishioners. Settling in Logan County, Kentucky, McGready began a series of outdoor meetings, welcoming all comers whatever their religious affiliations. So successful were his efforts that McGready

soon had many imitators. The camp meeting revival became a regular institution, as social in appeal, perhaps, as it was religious, and attracted frontier families from as far as 150 miles away who came equipped with tents and food for a stay of four or five days. Although the revivalists resorted to extreme emotion in their appeals, their religion was strictly orthodox inasmuch as they usually accepted the Bible as the literal word of God. These men and their followers soon dominated religion in the West, and their influence continued to prevail when later generations of settlers pushed across the continent.

"Campbellites" and Perfectionism. Although the camp meeting was most popular among Baptists and Methodists, many Presbyterian and Congregationalist ministers, despite the disapprobation of their church leadership, also employed strong emotional appeals in their sermons. Without traditions or a trained ministry, the West was the natural home of splinter religions, the number of Methodist and Baptist sects reaching

an awesome total. Even among the more disciplined Presbyterians frequent schisms occurred, the most important of which led to the establishment of the Disciples of Christ or the Campbellites, as they were popularly known after their founders, Thomas Campbell and his better-known son, Alexander Campbell. Disgusted by interminable arguments over Presbyterian dogma, and alive to the results of revivalism, the Campbells argued against the doctrines of original sin and election and predestination, and in favor of a return to the Bible. The Campbells also practiced immersion in baptismal rites and held mammoth revival meetings. When their efforts were denounced by conservative Presbyterians, they established their own church. Its great success in the West was undoubtedly due as much to the democratic spirit that infused its doctrine as to its colorful and emotional practices.

The Congregationalists, already split by the movement that was to become Unitarianism, were also affected by the trend toward an emotional and more democratic

A "CAMP MEETING"

Religious revivalism, during both colonial times and the early decades of the republic, was manifested most strikingly in services held outdoors, or "camp meetings." Captain Marryat (1792–1848), a peripatetic English naval officer and journalist, here chronicles his impressions of one such meeting held near Cincinnati.

. . . in the centre was a long form, against which were some other men kneeling, . . . as if occupied in prayer. Gradually the numbers increased . . . an elderly man gave out a hymn, which was sung with peculiar energy . . . As the din increased so did their enthusiasm . . . sobs were intermingled with prayers . . . Every minute the excitement increased; some wrung their hands and called for mercy; some tore their hair; there was sobbing . . . and hysterics and deep agony. One young man clung to the form, crying: "Satan tears at me, but I would hold fast. Help — help, he drags me down!" It was a scene of horrible agony and despair; and when it was at its height, one of the preachers came in, and raising his voice high above the tumult, intreated the Lord to receive into his fold those who now repented and would fain return . . . I quitted the spot and hastened away into the forest, for the sight was too painful, too melancholy. Its sincerity could not be doubted, but it was the effect of over-excitement, not of sober reasoning . . .

Frederick Marryat, A Diary in America (1839)

---

religion. Charles G. Finney, inspired by movements abroad, began to preach Perfectionism throughout New England. Although retaining the concept of punishment for sin after death, Finney's Perfectionism eschewed eternal damnation and offered the hope that mankind was capable of perfection and thus of "free and full salvation." These doctrines appealed especially to the New England workingmen, but were no less enthusiastically received in the West, where Finney held many revivals. He subsequently became President of Oberlin College.

Even a sketchy comparison of the deism of the 1790's with the Campbellite and the Perfectionist doctrines of thirty years later reveals striking differences. Deism was a rational religion which appealed mostly to an intellectual elite. It was an intensely personal belief in that it was without organized churches and a priesthood. The new emotional religions of the 1820's were group religions which relied upon the fervor of the mass meeting to inspire their communicants. By inference, at least, they were democratic in that they assured salvation to all who would respond to their appeals and in many instances relied upon lay preachers instead of a trained and educated ministry. Also, perhaps because of their unsophisticated adherents, they were on the whole strict in their doctrines and dogmatic in their spirit. To a degree, the difference between deism and frontier revivalism characterized the great change in the spirit of the nation between 1790 and 1830. During the next century, at least, the American character was to be closer to the spirit of the frontier camp meetings than it was to that of Tom Paine's *Age of Reason.*

Fortunately for the historian, there came to America during the years following the War of 1812 a procession of foreign travelers who wrote down freely what they saw — or what they thought they saw. Some of these visitors, as the official or unofficial agents of European governments, were in search of an outlet for European emigration. The Napoleonic wars had produced widespread economic distress, and most European nations were faced by an acute unemployment problem. Why not send their excess population to America?

American Traits. One of the ablest and most perceptive commentaries ever written on the American character was by Alexis de Tocqueville, a Frenchman, who traveled in the United States in 1831–1832. It is significant that he chose to entitle his great work *Democracy in America* (1835–1840). De Tocqueville's and all other accounts agree that the typical American was very "provincial." To some extent this was only another way of saying that he differed from the typical Englishman or Frenchman, or other European. But it was also a fact that most Americans knew little or nothing about the world outside America, and usually cared even less. Somewhat on the defensive because of this ignorance, Americans were inclined to be boastful, both about themselves and about their country. "For two generations," de Tocqueville observed, "they have been convincing themselves they are the only religious, enlightened and free people." They were particularly proud of the American experiment in democratic government, and they would admit neither that mistakes had been made, nor that any other form of government was half so good. Patriotism became almost a national obsession.

In one respect, at least, even irritated or disdainful foreigners were quick to agree that some American boastfulness was justified. The ordinary American was remarkable for his ingenuity. He could turn his hand with considerable skill to almost any problem that confronted him. He was not precisely inventive, but he was a born jack-of-all-trades whose adaptability rarely left him baffled by a new situation or defeated because of an unanticipated need.

American ideas of good manners did not always conform to European standards. Such crudities as normally accompanied the unrestrained use of chewing-tobacco excited the amazement of travelers, and sometimes, for good reason, their anxiety as well.

The American's habit of bolting his meals in record time also induced comment. The restlessness and nervousness of Americans annoyed foreigners. Americans resented delay and were forever in a hurry. This quality, incidentally, marks a pronounced change from the habits of colonial Americans — habits for which their descendants could have found no more appropriate adjective than "lazy." Probably the chief reason why Americans were such "hustlers" was that they were so keenly aware of the challenging opportunities that confronted them. With riches a seemingly sure reward for enterprise, the typical American felt that he had no time to waste. He took it for granted that to get his share he must work hard; indeed, he idealized work, and had great disdain for those who sought to avoid it. De Tocqueville particularly noticed this passion for work — for "commercialism" he called it. "The whole country," he observed, "is simultaneously engaged in productive industry and commerce." Nor did the utilitarian bent of the American people escape him. No other people, he wrote, held "practice in more honor than theory." De Tocqueville noted that Americans were the least philosophical people on the face of the globe, and the least creative of all civilized peoples in science, literature, and the arts. They required nothing of science, he concluded, "but its special application to the useful arts and the means of rendering life comfortable." Americans, he predicted, would "make the taste for the useful predominate over the love of the beautiful in the heart of man."

Optimism and Equality. Optimism was another by-product of opportunity. America had neither slums nor poor in the European sense, and the most worthless person could at least make a living. Faith in the future sometimes overshot the mark and tempted men to speculation. "Stock-watering" was often not so much a matter of fraud as of great expectations — the profits of the company were sure to grow. The misrepresentations of land speculators were more frequently than not a fair statement of what they genuinely believed. Overissues of bank currency were not all made with dishonest intent—more money was needed to care for the natural demands of a growing country.

Equality of. opportunity had much to do with the turn that democracy was taking in America. The equalitarian doctrine of the Declaration of Independence was in its day merely the statement of an ideal: fifty years later it was not far from a correct description of American society.

De Tocqueville noted that equality of status had prevailed even among the first immigrants to America and had subsequently been furthered by a more equitable division of landed property than anywhere else on earth. The same spirit existed, he argued, in educational opportunities; in no other country were there so few people without some formal instruction and at the same time so few who were really learned. Americans, he concluded, were more equal in social status, wealth, and education — "in other words more equal in their strength, than any other country in the world, or in any age of which history has preserved the remembrance."

To be sure, a kind of aristocracy existed in every part of the country, except perhaps in parts of the West, but it was basically an economic one to which even the lowliest might aspire. Social lines were more loosely drawn, and family trees counted for less and less. Material success, not birth, marked one as a member of the upper class, and the road to success was open to all. The old distinction between the dress of the aristocrat and the common man disappeared, but it was the aristocrat who gave up his furbelows, not the common man who put them on. The status of women in the new democracy seemed also to be rising toward a frank admission of equality with men. In place of the obsequious and condescending chivalry which Europeans of the better class were accustomed to exhibit toward their own class of women only, Americans, to the consternation of some foreign observers, tended to treat women of whatever class with marked respect and courtesy.

Democracy. For a people that set great store by its government, this democratic trend was certain to be reflected in politics. The new western states on admission to the Union unhesitatingly established universal manhood suffrage, and the older states of the East soon did the same. In the latter it did not follow at once that the ordinary people held offices, for the old colonial tradition that candidates should be chosen only from the elite died hard. In the West, however, there was no authentic upper stratum from which to choose, and the plain people themselves held the offices. It was not long before this excess of democracy was in evidence throughout the land. Travelers could observe even then a growing intolerance of superiority which in time would turn into a kind of worship of mediocrity. Noting this "passion for equality," de Tocqueville observed that equality and not freedom was the American idol, and he wondered whether at some future time this burning spirit of equalitarianism might not only stamp out individual excellence but also tend to crush true freedom. Majority opinion so dominated American life in 1830, he commented, that there was "little true independence of mind. . . ."

Individualism. Whatever the state of intellectual freedom in 1830, there was no doubt that the almost endless economic opportunity opened the way to an almost unrestrained economic individualism. With the chances for success everywhere so great, anyone with an ambition to fulfill rushed forward to achieve his goal by whatever means he could. He asked only to be let alone. Fortunately, there was room enough for all. The New England manufacturer who expanded his mills need not necessarily destroy his competitor; with abundant markets the two might expand and prosper side by side. If new machinery threw employees out of work, more likely than not other jobs, equally good, would soon appear. As for the increasing number of farmers and farm laborers, cheap lands and a fertile soil beckoned them to the West, where as pioneers they might achieve a greater success and a greater degree of independence than they could ever have known anywhere else. Throughout the West individual freedom was a frontier heritage much prized by all. Pioneers made their way in the world by their own efforts, and they took pride in their work. They made a fetish of their freedom, and would brook few restraints, whether of government or of society. All this was possible, of course, only because of the abundant opportunity in America.

SELECTED BIBLIOGRAPHY

An excellent introduction to the themes treated in this chapter is R. B. Nye, *The Cultural Life of the New Nation, 1776–1830* (1960); its bibliography is a reliable guide.

On education, the important recent study by Rush Welter, *Popular Education and Democratic Thought in America* (1962), gives emphasis to the 1820–1840 period. A rich collection is *American Higher Education: A Documentary History*, edited by Richard Hofstadter and Wilson Smith (2 vols., 1961). Lawrence Cremin, *The American Common School, an Historic Conception* (1951); and R. F. Butts, *The American Tradition in Religion and Education* (1950), are stimulating books by leading historians of education. R. D. Mosier, *Making the American Mind* (1947), is a study of the McGuffey readers. Richard Hofstadter and W. P. Metzger, *The Development of Academic Freedom in the United States* (1955), is already the standard treatment of that important subject. G. P. Schmidt, *The Liberal Arts College* (1957); and Frederick Rudolph, *The American College and University* (1962), are excellent syntheses. A valuable special study is W. F. Norwood, *Medical Education in the United States before the Civil War* (1944).

W. W. Manross, *The Episcopal Church in the United States, 1800–1840* (1938) is a standard work on one major church. On William Ellery Channing and his work, consult D. P. Edgell, *William Ellery Channing* (1955); A. W. Brown, *William Ellery Channing (Always Young for Liberty)* (1956); and M. H. Rice, *Federal Street Pastor* (1961). An interesting biography of another important figure is

B. M. Cross, *Horace Bushnell: Minister to a Changing America* (1958). For church policy toward Indians, see C. B. Goodykoontz, *Home Missions on the American Frontier* (1939); and R. F. Berkhofer, Jr., *Salvation and the Savage* (1965).

There are a number of books dealing with the growth of evangelical religion. R. G. Torbet, *A History of the Baptists* (1950), is concerned with an important denomination on both sides of the Atlantic. A good scholarly study is W. C. Barclay, *Early American Methodism, 1769–1844* (1949). W. B. Posey has done a number of important works on religion in the West, including: *The Development of Methodism in the Old Southwest, 1783–1824* (1933); *The Presbyterian Church in the Old Southwest, 1778–1838* (1952); and *The Baptist Church in the Lower Mississippi Valley, 1776–1845* (1957). A monumental collection of source materials is W. W. Sweet (ed.), *Religion on the American Frontier, 1783–1840* (4 vols., 1931–1946). Important special studies are C. I. Foster, *An Errand of Mercy; The Evangelical United Front, 1790–1837* (1960); C. C. Cleveland, *The Great Revival in the West, 1797–1805* (1916); and C. A. Johnson, *The Frontier Camp Meeting* (1955). B. A. Weisberger, *They Gathered at the River* (1958), is a lively study of great American revivalists. Richard Hofstadter, *Anti-Intellectualism in American Life* (1963), finds that evangelical religion was a major factor in the development of his subject.

A rich picture history of art and architecture is O. W. Larkin, *Art and Life in America* (2nd ed., 1960). On architecture alone, see T. E. Tallmadge, *The Story of Architecture in Amer-*

* Available in paperback

ica (1927); John Burchard and Albert Bush-Brown, *The Architecture of America; A Social and Cultural History* (1961); and Harold and James Kirker, *Bulfinch's Boston, 1787–1817* (1964). Christopher Tunnard and H. H. Reed, *American Skyline* (1955), is brief and accessible. On sculpture, see Lorado Taft, *The History of American Sculpture* (3rd ed., 1930); and A. T. Gardner, *Yankee Stonecutters: The First American School of Sculpture, 1800–1850* (1945). A good survey of painting is Virgil Barker, *American Painting: History and Interpretation* (1950). J. T. Flexner has published a number of works on this subject, among them: *America's Old Masters* (1939); *American Painting: First Flowers of Our Wilderness* (1947); the brief but excellent *Pocket History of American Painting* (1957); and *That Wilder Image; The Painting of America's Native School from Thomas Cole to Winslow Homer* (1962). Studies of important artists include C. C. Sellers, *Charles Willson Peale* (2 vols., 1947); J. C. Taylor, *William Page* (1957); and C. M. Mount, *Gilbert Stuart* (1964).

On literature, Van Wyck Brooks, *The World of Washington Irving* (1944), is a richly detailed survey of the 1800–1840 period. George Boas (ed.), *Romanticism in America* (1940), is a valuable collection. An accessible short anthology is *American Literature Survey, The American Romantics, 1800–1860*, edited by M. R. Stern and S. L. Gross (1962). An interesting biography of Joel Barlow is James Woodress, *A Yankee's Odyssey* (1958). Dorothy Waples, *The Whig Myth of James Fenimore Cooper* (1938), is a substantial study of Cooper's political ideas. Early American drama has not received much attention from historians, but see R. D. James, *Cradle of Culture, 1800–1810; The Philadelphia Stage* (1957); and A. H. Quinn, *A History of the American Drama from the Beginning to the Civil War* (2nd ed., 1943). Other important cultural themes are explored in R. H. Pearce, *The Savages of America; A Study of the Indian and the Idea of Civilization* (1953); Morton and Lucia White, *The Intellectual versus the City* (1962); and R. B. Davis, *Intellectual Life in Jefferson's Virginia* (1964). L. L. Hazard, *The Frontier in American Literature* (1927), is a notable pioneering study. J. M. Miller,

The Genesis of Western Culture: The Upper Ohio Valley, 1800–1825 (1938), is a suggestive volume. On folklore, especially west- (1956); and T. D. Clark, *The Rampaging* (1959); J. A. Shackford (ed.), *David Crockett* (1956); and T. D. Clark, *The Rampaging Frontier* (1939).

The classic portrait of American democracy in the early Jackson period is Alexis de Tocqueville, *Democracy in America* (4 vols., 1835–1840); a fine modern edition by Philips Bradley (2 vols., 1945) is available in paperback. The notebooks of de Tocqueville have been edited by J. P. Mayer and published with the title *Journey to America* (1959). The standard account of de Tocqueville's visit is G. W. Pierson, *Tocqueville and Beaumont in America* (1939); an abridgement by D. C. Lunt is entitled *Tocqueville in America* (1959). Harriet Martineau, *Society in America* (3 vols., 1834–1836), is available in a single-volume abridgement. Impressions of other foreign visitors may be found in such works as J. L. Mesick, *The English Traveller in America, 1785–1835* (1922); G. E. Probst (ed.), *The Happy Republic* (1962); Charles Dickens, *American Notes* (1842); Frances Trollope, *Domestic Manners of the Americans* (1832); Allan Nevins (ed.), *American Social History as Recorded by British Travellers* (2nd ed., 1931); and F. J. Grund, *Aristocracy in America, From the Sketch-Book of a German Nobleman* (1839). An important synthesis dealing with the reverse of the usual subject is Cushing Strout, *The American Image of the Old World* (1963).

The attempt to define American traits, and to seek their origins, has long been a favorite activity of writers. D. M. Potter, *People of Plenty: Economic Abundance and the American Character* (1954), is an influential effort. *Sources of Culture in the Middle West*, edited by D. R. Fox (1934), presents the interpretations of a number of authorities. H. N. Smith, *Virgin Land; The American West as Symbol and Myth* (1950), is based in part upon literary and sub-literary materials, and has excited much interest. A perennial American theme is explored in depth in I. G. Wyllie, *The Self-Made Man in America, The Myth of Rags to Riches* (1954).

George Caleb Bingham, "Verdict of the People."
Courtesy of The Boatmen's National Bank of
St. Louis.

The Road to

Division

· 1828–1860 ·

During my stay in the United States nothing struck me more forcibly than the general equality of condition among the people.

ALEXIS DE TOCQUEVILLE

Slavery can be limited to its present bounds, it can be ameliorated; it can and must *be abolished, and you and I can and must do it.*

WILLIAM H. SEWARD

The advice nearest my heart and deepest in my convictions is, that the Union of the states be cherished and perpetuated. Let the open enemy of it be regarded as a Pandora with her box opened, and the disguised ones as the serpent creeping with his deadly wiles into paradise.

JAMES MADISON

12

THE REVOLUTION OF 1828

The Election of 1824.   As already noted, the strongly nationalistic spirit that developed in the United States after the War of 1812 was accompanied by an equally determined emphasis on sectionalism. The beginning of a three-cornered sectional struggle among Northeast, South, and West was plainly in evidence. Boundary lines between these sections could not always be clearly drawn, but their points of view, determined respectively by the needs of the northern manufacturer, the southern cotton planter, and the western farmer, were fairly obvious. The election of 1824 served to throw these divergent interests into bold relief. By that time the Republicans were the only party that counted. President Monroe, in keeping with the already established "no-third-term" tradition, was not a candidate to succeed himself. Four eager

aspirants, William H. Crawford of Georgia, John Quincy Adams of Massachusetts, Henry Clay of Kentucky, and Andrew Jackson of Tennessee, each claiming to be a good Republican, had long hoped for the succession. Each candidate was a kind of incarnation of the prejudices and special interests of his section, Crawford representing the South, Adams the Northeast, Clay and Jackson the rising West. John C. Calhoun of South Carolina, who was also interested, had decided to wait, and was generally acclaimed as the proper person for the Vice-Presidency.

Ordinarily a congressional caucus would have reduced the number of candidates to one, but this means of making nominations had fallen into ill repute, and only 66 of the 216 Republican members of Congress attended the caucus. Its endorsement of Crawford was thus of little consequence, and state legislatures took it upon themselves to name candidates. Prophetic of the future, however, were some resolutions passed by a meeting in Lancaster County, Pennsylvania, which asserted that "the best and most unexceptional method" of nominating a candidate would be by "a convention of delegates from all the States of the Union." Of the four candidates mentioned, Crawford was soon at a hopeless disadvantage because of a paralytic stroke. The other three not only remained in the race to the end; they also became the outstanding leaders in American politics for a generation.

John Quincy Adams. John Quincy Adams (1767–1848) was the son of the second President, and in some respects an even abler man. In addition to his rare inheritance, he had received a rigorous training for public life. At eleven he was taken by his father to Europe, where he was educated by private tutors in a variety of countries. At twenty he was graduated from Harvard, and soon after began the practice of law. At twenty-seven he began a diplomatic career that took him on important missions to England, Holland, Russia, and Sweden. On returning to the United States after the election of Jefferson, Adams served in the Massachusetts legislature, and was elected in 1803 to the United States Senate. This seat he resigned in 1808 because his conscience bade him approve the embargo, while the legislature of Massachusetts opposed it; and thereafter he became a member of the Republican Party. After notable service as Monroe's Secretary of State, he was eager to crown his career by becoming President, but his cold and forbidding demeanor alienated public support. Belligerently incorruptible in all his dealings, Adams was inclined to ascribe the worst motives to all who disagreed with him.

Henry Clay. The education of Henry Clay (1777–1852), son of a back-country Virginia Baptist preacher, was as limited as Adams' was extensive. But Clay had a warm, magnetic personality and won friends as easily as Adams lost them. He made the most of his meager opportunities, and when he was twenty years old opened a law office in Lexington, Kentucky. His legal career was successful from the start because of a native shrewdness that proved to be of greater value in the frontier courts than any amount of intellectual accomplishment. Within a few years he was a member of the state legislature, then, for a short time, of the United States Senate. On the eve of the War of 1812 he entered the House, where he was repeatedly chosen Speaker.

He served with Adams on the commission that made peace with Great Britain after the war, and acquired from the experience an acquaintance with Europe. Likable, and desiring to be liked, Clay could usually be counted on to reflect his surroundings. In his youth he was a man of the West, tempestuous and aggressive — a leading "War Hawk" when the West wanted war. As he grew older, contacts with the East and with Europe had a sobering influence upon him, and a discreet moderation took the place of his former recklessness. He saw intuitively the need of a political program that would satisfy all sections — a national program. He saw, too, the necessity of compromise when conflicting interests were involved, and he soon won the title of the "Great Compromiser." His persuasive oratory, once it was enlisted in any cause, was a potent influence in shaping public opinion. Few American statesmen have ever maintained, through victory and defeat, a larger or more devoted personal following.

Presidential Election of 1824

Adams Clay Jackson Crawford

JOHN QUINCY ADAMS

As ex-President Adams represented a Massachusetts district for seventeen years in the House of Representatives, where he was known as "Old Man Eloquent," and wielded tremendous influence.

Andrew Jackson. Andrew Jackson (1767–1845), like Henry Clay, was a product of the upland South, a South Carolinian whose parents had emigrated from the north of Ireland to the American frontier. He saw service during the later years of the American Revolution, and out of this experience acquired a bitter hatred of England. He began the practice of law in western North Carolina when he was only twenty years of age, but within a year he followed the course of migration into Tennessee and settled at Nashville. Here he was soon public prosecutor, then in turn a member of the national House of Representatives and of the United States Senate, then a judge of the Tennessee Supreme Court. But it was as a warrior that he won his chief renown. His successful campaign against the Creeks in 1814, his triumph the next year at New Orleans, and his subsequent exploits in Florida made him the out-

standing military hero of the time. In 1823 he was again chosen to represent the state of Tennessee in the United States Senate. The pride of the West in Jackson was especially strong because he possessed in marked degree those qualities that the West most highly esteemed. He personified the democratic ideal which held that the plain people were just as good as those who considered themselves to be the elite. He exhibited, too, the contentious individualism of the frontier, its unreasoning hatreds, its rashness, and its resourcefulness. An ardent patriot, he identified with patriotism the westerner's desire to obtain expanded boundaries for the nation and unlimited opportunities for its citizens. Jackson was not at first politically ambitious, but a few designing politicians saw the powerful intersectional appeal his candidacy would make, and pushed him into the race.

While the election of 1824 turned to a great extent upon the personalities of the candidates, it showed also the interplay of sectional forces. Adams won the electoral votes of New England and most of the votes of New York. Crawford led only in Virginia and Georgia. Clay carried Kentucky, Ohio, and Missouri. Jackson alone had a large enough following to win electoral votes outside his own section. He divided the West with Clay, the South with Crawford, and made an excellent showing in the Middle Atlantic states. The electoral vote stood: Jackson 99, Adams 84, Crawford 41, Clay 37. No candidate having received a majority, the choice went to the House of Representatives, where Adams, with Clay's support, won an easy victory. Thereupon Adams chose Clay as his Secretary of State — a matter of "bargain and corruption," the Jacksonians charged, but never proved.

The Democratic Party Foreshadowed. Out of the election there emerged a new political division. The supporters of Jackson had appealed to the more democratic elements of American society. The government of the United States, they maintained, had been ever since its inception in the hands of a relatively small elite, and the time had come for the introduction of new blood. Jackson to a considerable extent became the candidate of the ordinary people, while those who opposed him were branded as tools of the upper classes. Westerners imbued with frontier ideals of democracy, easterners of the farmer and laborer classes who were just beginning to be conscious of their political power, and back-country southerners who had long struggled within their respective states against the domination of the ruling planters, all rallied enthusiastically to the Jackson standard. Ably led, they made of the Adams administration one prolonged campaign for the election of Jackson to the Presidency in 1828.

The National Republicans. The forces opposed to Jackson, now united under the leadership of Adams and Clay, were held together by strong bonds. In 1824 Clay alone had had what today would be called a platform — his "American System." The War of 1812 had made him deeply conscious of the need of economic self-sufficiency for the United States, an end which he believed could best be promoted by a protective tariff and internal improvements. The tariff could be used to build up American manufactures, while internal improvements, paid for out of tariff receipts, would provide the roads and canals over which the products of eastern factories could reach the West and South, and western and southern agricultural commodities could reach the East. This program, which contained many principles of the deceased Federalist party, suited Adams — and New England — as well as it suited Clay and such of the West as would follow him. It laid firm foundations for a new intersectional party, dependent upon voters from the Northwest no less than from the Northeast, and soon to be known as the National Republican Party. The Jacksonian adherents, disdaining subtleties, were presently pleased to be called Democrats.

The "Tariff of Abominations." Sectional differences on the tariff question had become acutely apparent well before Adams entered the White House. The tariff of 1816 had received some support from every section, although the commercial elements in the Northeast and a majority of the southern planters had opposed it. The depression of 1819–1820 led to a movement, emanating chiefly from the Middle Atlantic states, for increased duties as an aid to languishing manufacturing interests, and a bill drawn along these lines failed in 1820 for the lack of a single vote in the Senate, only to pass in 1824. Still unsatisfied, the protectionists pressed on for higher duties, and in 1827 saw another bill they had sponsored defeated by the vote of the Vice-President, John C. Calhoun. When the tariff question came up again, a few of the Jacksonian leaders determined to make political capital of it. They knew that Jackson must win support from the South, which opposed a protective tariff, and from the Northeast and the West, where a strong majority favored it. Their plan was to present a bill placing such excessively high rates on raw materials that some of the manufacturers of the Northeast would join with the commercial interests and the South to defeat the measure. Amendments which would make the bill more satisfactory to the manufacturers were to be voted down, and thus the Jackson men could claim credit in the North for having supported a high-tariff measure, and in the South for having defeated it. But the proposed strategy for defeating the bill came to naught when the manufacturing interests of the Northeast decided to accept it as the best they could get, and in the end gave the bill votes enough to secure its passage. In this manner the "Tariff of Abominations," as it was widely called, became law.

Among those who unexpectedly favored the measure was Daniel Webster of Massachusetts. In preceding tariff debates as late as 1824, Webster had led the fight against protection. His change of front reflected the growing importance of manufacturing in New England, just as Calhoun's reversal had indicated the complete conversion of the South to low-tariff principles. The Northwest was still impressed by the arguments Clay presented for an American system, and particularly by the high duties proposed on such items as wool, flax, and hemp.

TARIFF VOTES IN THE HOUSE OF
REPRESENTATIVES

	1816		1820		1824		1828	
	For	*Against*	*For*	*Against*	*For*	*Against*	*For*	*Against*
New England	17	10	18	17	15	23	16	23
Middle Atlantic° ...	42	5	55	1	57	9	56	6
South Atlantic° ...	16	35	5	49	4	56	4	47
Southwest ...	3	3	0	7	2	14	0	16
Northwest† ..	10	1	12	3	29	0	29	1

° Includes Delaware.
† Includes Kentucky and Missouri.

Road Building. Adams was an enthusiastic believer in internal improvements at national expense, and, unlike his immediate predecessors, he considered them constitutional. In 1824 Monroe had given his approval to a General Survey Act which authorized the President to conduct such surveys of canal and turnpike routes as would serve an important national interest. Adams hoped to use this power to lay out a great national system of transportation. During his term army engineers were detailed freely to survey protective transportation routes, and the sums actually expended in aid of internal improvements grew rap-

idly. But almost the only strictly national project that the administration was able to carry on was the continuation westward of the Cumberland Road. The National Road, as it came to be called, progressed slowly across central Ohio, then on through Indiana and Illinois, with Jefferson City, Missouri, as its intended western terminal. By 1838 construction reached Vandalia, Illinois, but was discontinued because of the Panic of 1837, and was not resumed because of the increasing evidence that railroads, not turnpikes, would soon carry the commerce of the country.

The Erie Canal. Undoubtedly the most spectacular development in transportation during this period was the building of the Erie Canal, a project which DeWitt Clinton, governor of New York, persuaded his state to undertake in 1817. By 1825 this waterway was open for business. A lock canal, costing $7.6 million, it extended from Troy on the Hudson to Buffalo on Lake Erie, a distance of 363 miles. Thanks to a lucrative local traffic that soon made cities of such points along the route as Syracuse, Rochester, and Utica, the canal was a financial success even before it was finished, and a branch canal to Lake Champlain was similarly successful.

The through traffic that began at once to make use of the Erie Canal was of immense significance in linking the East to the West. Before it was built the cost of transporting a ton of freight from New York City to Buffalo had been about $100, and the time required, about twenty days. The canal at once reduced the cost to $10 and the time to eight days, and as the volume of business increased, the cost of transportation went steadily down. Steamboats on the Great Lakes made possible a cheap all-water route to the shores of Lake Huron and Lake Michigan as well as Lake Erie. Pioneers by the tens of thousands took up vacant lands in the northern parts of Ohio, Indiana, and Illinois, as well as in western New York. Michigan Territory

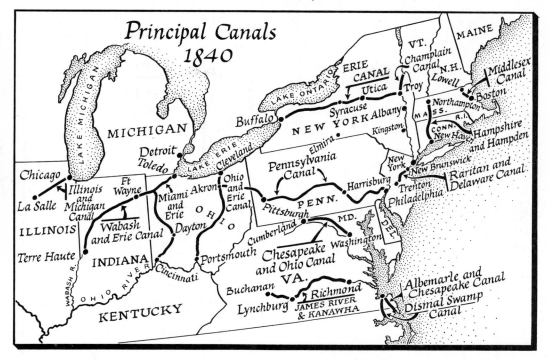

Principal Canals 1840

grew so rapidly in population that by 1836 the eastern half was ready for statehood, while the western half, known later as Wisconsin, seemed likewise destined to an early admission to the Union. Moreover the tremendous volume of trade that flowed through the Erie Canal–Great Lakes route to and from the West paid a generous tribute to New York City. In population New York grew from less than 125,000 in 1820 to over 200,000 by 1830; during the same time the value of its real and personal property rose 60 per cent; and the increasing volume of its trade soon made it the leading American city.

The Pennsylvania System. The success of New York led to quick emulation by her chief rivals, Philadelphia and Baltimore. The legislature of Pennsylvania in 1825 authorized the construction of an elaborate system of canals to unite the various sections of the state. By 1834 the "Pennsylvania System" stretched all the way to Pittsburgh, but a portage railway was necessary to carry the canal traffic across the mountains. This new route to the West did a flourishing local business, but it never became a serious rival to the Erie Canal, and Philadelphia never seriously challenged the lead of New York in the race for the western markets. Baltimore, meantime, began in 1828, with state backing, the Chesapeake and Ohio Canal, which for engineering reasons could never reach its goal. But the Baltimore and Ohio Railroad, projected at the same time, finally reached its destination in 1853.

The Canal Age. The craze for canals that began while Adams was President went to unreasonable lengths. In the East feeders to the main canals, and connecting links between arms of the Atlantic, were built with little regard to costs involved. In the new western states the task of connecting the Ohio–Mississippi River system with the Great Lakes was eagerly undertaken. Ohio led the way in 1825 by authorizing the building of two such canals, one from

Portsmouth to Cleveland, and the other from Cincinnati to Toledo. The former was completed in 1832, and for a little while did a thriving business; but by the time the latter was completed in 1845, railroads were rapidly making canals obsolete. Not to be outdone by Ohio, Indiana began in 1832 and completed in 1843 the Wabash and Erie Canal, while Illinois between 1832 and 1848 built the Illinois and Michigan Canal. In the fifties Wisconsin succeeded in opening a waterway from Green Bay to the Mississippi by way of the Fox and Wisconsin Rivers, and Michigan, by building a canal around St. Mary's Falls, greatly facilitated through traffic on the Great Lakes. Except for Maryland, there was little canal construction in the South, where the mountain barriers were obstacles and the highways of the rivers and the ocean still furnished fairly adequate means of transportation. Charleston was eager for connections with the West that would give her a better chance to compete with her new western rival, New Orleans, but for topographical reasons she was compelled to turn to a railroad rather than to a canal. By 1850 the total canal mileage in the United States had reached 3,200.

Adams and Clay. Ironically, President Adams, with his wide experience in foreign affairs, faced few diplomatic problems. Secretary of State Clay had visions of supplementing the Monroe Doctrine by actively promoting Pan-American cooperation. But the Senate blocked the principal effort of the administration in this direction when it refused, purely for reasons of party advantage, to confirm until too late the appointment of delegates from the United States to attend the Panama Congress called by Bolívar in 1826.

The Adams administration was unfortunate also in its dealings with the South. Clay's linking of the obnoxious protective tariff with the program of internal improvements tended to make the two equally unpalatable to a section that was coming more and more to see in the high duties on manufactured articles a drain on its prosperity. Adams also aroused much antagonism by his handling of Indian affairs. The expansion of the cotton South led to an insistent demand from the Southwest that the lands held by the now semi-civilized Creeks, Cherokees, Choctaws, and Chickasaws be made available for settlement. In response to this demand a treaty was signed at

SCENE ON THE ERIE CANAL

Before the advent of the railroad, the canal traffic between larger American waterways was of great importance in the development of inland commerce. The Duke of Saxe-Weimar Eisenach (1792–1862) traveled on the Erie Canal soon after it was opened.

The canal is thirty-five feet wide on the surface, twenty-eight feet at the bottom, and four feet deep, so that none but flat vessels and rafts can sail on it. The packet-boat which took us to Schenectady, was seventy feet long, fourteen feet wide, and drew two feet of water. It was covered and contained a spacious cabin, with a kitchen, and was very neatly arranged. On account of the great number of locks, the progress of our journey was but slow: our packet-boat went only at the rate of three miles an hour, being detained at each lock, on an average, four minutes. The locks are fourteen feet wide above the surface, and have a fall from seven to twelve feet. The packet-boat was drawn by three horses, which walked upon a narrow tow-path leading along the canal, and beneath the numerous bridges that are thrown over it. . . . I spent an uncomfortable night, on account of my constrained posture, the insects which annoyed me, and the steersman, who always played an agreeable tune upon his bugle whenever he approached a lock.

BERNHARD KARL, Duke of Saxe-Weimar Eisenach, *Travels through North America* (1828)

Indian Springs, just before Adams took office, by which the Creeks gave up all their holdings in Georgia. This treaty was duly ratified by the Senate, but it was promptly repudiated by the great majority of the Creek nation, and one of its chief negotiators was put to death. Adams, on investigation, found that the treaty had been obtained by fraud, refused to proclaim it in effect, and ordered that new negotiations be begun. Balked temporarily in obtaining the lands they coveted, the planters were deeply offended, and the governor of Georgia, who championed their cause, quarreled heatedly with the President over what he deemed to be a violation of states' rights. Long before Adams left office it had become abundantly clear that the Adams-Clay National Republicans could not count on any support from the lower South.

The defeat of Adams and the election of Jackson to the Presidency in 1828 were long foreseen, even by Adams himself. The President and his chief advisers were representatives of the old federal culture that had always dominated in the government of the country. Jackson's candidacy was a challenge to this type of governmental control. A new concept of democracy was abroad in the land. No longer were the people satisfied, as Jefferson had supposed they would be, to fill the offices from among their betters. Popular rule had come to mean that the common people should choose their rulers from among themselves, and by 1828 the extension of the suffrage had gone so far that such a man as Adams in a contest with such a man as Jackson had little chance to win.

Democratic Trends. Although all of the original thirteen states had placed certain restrictions upon the suffrage, the new states had with one accord either granted manhood suffrage outright, or else had put up such slight barriers against it as amounted to almost the same thing. Gradually the older states fell into step with this march of democracy. By 1828, three of the original states, New Hampshire, Maryland, and Connecticut, had abolished all property qualifications for voting, while two others, Massachusetts and New York, had made them only nominal. Thus by 1828 the ordinary people in a good majority of the states had the ballot, and they had acquired the will to use it. In Pennsylvania, for example, only 47,000 votes were cast in the election of 1824; with no significant changes in the election laws 150,000 votes were cast in 1828.

The agitation against property qualifications for voting, and other undemocratic practices, continued throughout the next two decades. Constitutional conventions, held between 1820 and 1850 in nearly every state, generally enfranchised all white males over twenty-one years of age, and in keeping with the growing spirit of democracy they also increased the number of popularly elected officials, often including even judges among those so chosen. Guided by experience, the conventions gave greater powers to the governors, and limited more closely the prerogatives of the legislatures, for which they ordinarily stipulated biennial rather than annual sessions. An extremely important step in the direction of popular rule, taken during this period, was the substitution of popular for legislative election of presidential electors. By 1828 the old system of permitting the legislatures to choose the electors had disappeared in all but two states, Delaware and South Carolina.

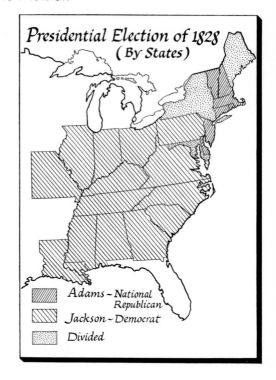

The Election of 1828. In the campaign of 1828, personalities rather than issues held the center of the stage. Arguments in favor of Clay's American System had far less appeal to the public than the popular prejudices to which Jacksonian orators catered. Even in the Northeast the rising tide of industrialism had created a large class of daily wage workers, many of whom had already turned against Adams and Clay. Jackson's election was not accomplished, however, without the assistance of many voters to whom an excess of democracy did not appeal. Calhoun, as the Jacksonian candidate for the Vice-Presidency, hoped to wield a great influence in the new administration and to succeed the General after four years, or perhaps sooner, since Jackson's health was supposed to be frail. This consideration weighed heavily with the cotton planters of the South, to

whom, in any case, Adams was anathema because of his well-known attitude on the tariff. Former adherents of Crawford also tended to vote for Jackson, while in New York the "Albany Regency," a powerful political machine dominated by Martin Van Buren and William L. Marcy, was able to swing a majority of the state's electoral vote to the hero of New Orleans. An alliance of the West, the South, and the discontented elements in the Northeast won the election for Jackson. Every western state supported him, and every southern state except Maryland, which divided its vote. The total electoral vote stood 178 to 83, and the popular vote, as nearly as it could be ascertained, 647,276 to 508,064.

The day of Jackson's inauguration brought to Washington a "noisy and disorderly rabble" bent on celebrating the rescue of the government from the hands of the aristocrats. The capital city was taxed to the limit to care for the huge crowd of celebrants that overflowed the boarding-houses, lined the streets to cheer the President-elect uproariously as he walked to the capitol, followed him in frenzied droves as he rode down the Avenue after taking the oath of office, surged through the White House, upset the presidential punch, and trampled under muddy feet the presidential carpets.

Jackson's Advisers. Jackson's Cabinet, headed by Martin Van Buren, showed that he was quite aware of the revolution that had taken place. Instead of the men of distinction who had usually been chosen to such positions, he selected men who were as new to national politics as the President himself, and who represented primarily the factions that had made his triumph possible. Two cabinet appointments went to the friends of Calhoun, but the other four went to Jackson and Van Buren henchmen. Once he had organized his cabinet, however, the President made little use of it as a group, expecting from its members only the administrative duties for which each was legally responsible. For advice he leaned principally upon a "kitchen cabinet" of intimate friends. Ablest among these men was Amos Kendall of Kentucky, whose facile pen phrased many Jacksonian state papers. William B. Lewis of Tennessee was probably the President's closest friend and lived at the White House to offer sagacious counsel on the ways of practical politics. Others connected with the "kitchen cabinet" included Senator Isaac Hill of New Hampshire; Andrew Jackson Donelson of Tennessee, the President's nephew and secretary; Duff Green of the *United States Telegraph;* and Francis P. Blair, who after 1830 edited a new administration organ, the *Globe.*

The Spoils System. More has been made of Jackson's introduction of the "spoils system" — "to the victor belong the spoils" — than the facts warrant. It is true that removal of appointive officers for purely party reasons was rare before his time, but

replacement after death or resignation had ordinarily been made from members of the dominant political party. Owing to the long tenure of the Republican Party it was probably a fact, as Jackson charged, that the efficiency of the public service was crippled by the presence within it of many incompetent relics of an earlier day. The novelty of Jackson's action lay in the speed with which he got results. Immediately after his inauguration he began a proscription of officeholders that soon eliminated hundreds of men who had supposed that they were to retain their positions indefinitely. Naturally their outcries were loud, but Jackson's conduct was hardly as ruthless as they tried to pretend. During his first year and a half in office he made only about 900 removals from among civil servants numbering about 10,000, and some of his removals could be accounted for on grounds that were not strictly partisan. Most of the men who lost office, however, were Adams men, and all of their successors were Jackson men. Even so, many more office seekers appeared than there were positions. Hence the doctrine of "rotation in office" was devised. Politicians argued that the valuable training in citizenship acquired in holding public office ought to be widely diffused by passing around the same positions among several faithful party men during a single presidential term.

Already the practice of rewarding the victors with the "spoils of office" had been tried out by local politicians in New York and Pennsylvania with phenomenal results. The hope of obtaining office spurred party workers to far greater endeavor than could have been expected of them out of mere devotion to principle. The fear of losing an office, once obtained, proved likewise a powerful incentive to fighting the party's battles. On the basis of carefully distributed spoils, it was possible to build up a party "machine" that could raise money, wage campaigns, reward loyalty, punish disobedience, and perpetuate itself in power for long periods.

ANDREW JACKSON

*The first President not from Virginia
or Massachusetts, Jackson lived the life
of a southwestern frontiersman in his
early years, but eventually became the
owner of a fine estate, "The Hermitage,"
near Nashville.*

Jackson's View of the Presidency.   Jackson's interpretation of the Presidency also offered something new to American politics. His decisive majority, coupled with the fact that the American people themselves were directly responsible for the result, gave rise to the theory that the executive was endowed with greater authority than any other branch of the government. Jackson sought actively to secure the passage of the laws he favored, and he lectured Congress with regard to its duties in a fashion that Washington and Jefferson would have regarded as unbecoming, if not actually unconstitutional. Moreover, he made more extensive use of the veto power than any other President had seen fit to do. All six of his pre-

decessors in office together had vetoed only nine bills, whereas Jackson during his two terms vetoed twelve measures, and used freely also the "pocket veto," a device which no previous President had dared to invoke. The pocket veto was made possible by a provision in the Constitution that unless the President vetoed a bill within ten days after it reached him, the bill would become a law anyway, "unless Congress by their adjournment prevent its return, in which case it shall not be a law." Since many important measures were passed in the closing days of a session, the President might, if he chose, defeat legislation by a mere failure to act, or in popular parlance "pocketing" the bill. Jackson's concept of presidential authority extended even to his relations with the Supreme Court. After the Court had sided with some Indians against the state of Georgia, he is reported to have said: "John Marshall has made his decision; now let him enforce it."

Sectional Interests.   By the time Jackson became President sectional interests in the United States had reached the explosive point. Each of the three major areas had made up its mind about its political objectives. The Northeast, increasingly dependent on manufactures, was wedded to the idea of a protective tariff; the South, dependent upon export markets for its cotton, was as firmly convinced that tariffs must be lowered; the West, growing prodigiously in area and population, craved nothing so much as cheap lands. Standing alone, not one of the three sections could hope to win complete victory, but by combining forces, any two sections could out-vote the third. Since the clash between the Northeast and the South was principally over a single issue, the tariff, the battle between them inevitably took the form of each seeking the support of the West.

The Land Question.   Western representatives, following the victories they had won in the Land Law of 1820, were soon

204

pressing new demands on Congress. Many of them felt particularly aggrieved that the government insisted on collecting a minimum of $1.25 for each acre of land it sold. While the best lands in a newly opened area were quickly sold, the poorer lands were apt to remain vacant for many years. Some cheap land advocates argued that the price of these left-over acres should be reduced each year by twenty-five cents until taken. Any lands still unsold after four or five years might then be donated outright, either to the settlers themselves, or to the states. Some even urged that all public lands be turned over to the states in the first place, for easy and liberal allocation to the settlers.

Pre-emption. Pre-emption voiced another standard western demand. With increasing frequency pioneers rushed far out into the West and selected for themselves the best lands they could find. Such foresight and energy the West was eager to reward, and it resented, sometimes to the point of armed resistance, the attempts of speculators and others to acquire for little or nothing the improvements that a "squatter" had made on his "claim." Westerners urged that the government should grant to the man who had braved the dangers of the far frontier first chance at the purchase of the land he had appropriated. One proposition, rejected in 1820 but by no means forgotten, was that the squatter should be given the chance, up to two weeks before land sales in any particular district began, to purchase at the prevailing minimum price 160 acres adjacent to his house and improvements. The long-continued failure of Congress to recognize the right of pre-emption, or as it was more frequently called in the West, "squatters' rights," led to the formation in many frontier communities of "claims clubs." Groups of settlers in a given community banded themselves together and, when land sales began, prevented by force the purchase of a member's land by anyone other than the squatter who lived upon it.

The Foot Resolution. Western insistence on the further liberalization of land terms met firm resistance from the manufacturers of the Northeast. If eastern factories were to grow and prosper, they needed a dependable supply of cheap labor close at hand. Ever more favorable terms for western lands, the manufacturers argued, tended to drain off the surplus population of the East into the West. They even contended that laborers could, and did, demand higher wages than they could have hoped to receive had they not had the alternative of a move to the West with which to threaten their employers. To correct this situation some easterners were ready to see the sales of western land discontinued entirely. One such was Senator Samuel Augustus Foot of Connecticut, who in a notable resolution proposed "That the Committee on Public Lands be instructed to inquire into the expediency of limiting for a certain period the sales of the public lands to such lands only as have heretofore been offered for sale, and are subject to entry at the minimum price. And also, whether the office of Surveyor General may not be abolished without detriment to the public interest." In other words, had the time not come when the growth of the West must be checked, "for who would remove to a new country if it were not to get new lands?"

Here was too good an opportunity for southern politicians to miss. Northeastern policies threatened both West and South; why should the two sections not stand together against their common enemy? Why, some southerners argued, should they not both embrace the doctrine of nullification, according to which any state might claim to nullify within its limits any federal legislation that it deemed unconstitutional? If this theory could only win acceptance, the western states could invalidate any new land legislation that they disliked, while the southern states could eliminate protective tariffs.

The idea of nullification soon came to be

intimately connected with the name of the Vice-President, John C. Calhoun (1792–1850), whose leadership in South Carolina politics was not seriously questioned. Although a member of the planter class, Calhoun had long been an ardent nationalist. He had helped bring on the War of 1812, and had strongly supported the nationalistic legislation that followed it. His career as a politician lay primarily in the national arena. From 1811 to 1817, he was a member of Congress; from 1817 to 1825, he was Secretary of War in Monroe's Cabinet; now he was Vice-President with a strong title to the succession. Under the circumstances he viewed with great alarm the talk of secession, so prevalent in South Carolina after the hated tariff acts of 1824 and 1828. If South Carolina should leave the Union, not only the nation but also the career of John C. Calhoun would be ruined.

The Cotton South. That South Carolina as a cotton-exporting state was seriously hurt by the protective tariff policy of the national government, few South Carolinians doubted. The real trouble, however, both with South Carolina and the whole Southeast, was that in cotton growing the Southwest had completely outdistanced it. The lands of the Southeast were wearing out; the lands of the Southwest were still rich. Slavery in the Southeast was fast becoming an uneconomic system of labor; slavery in the Southwest still made slaveowners good money. As the total production of cotton rose, the price of cotton fell, a disaster to the Southeast, but not to the Southwest where the planters raised more and more cotton and continued to prosper. Unwilling to recognize the real cause of their troubles, and convinced that the national tariff policy, which made them buy on a protected market and sell on a free market, was wholly to blame, some South Carolinians and other southerners had begun to urge secession as their only remedy.

Secession or Nullification? Despite Marshall's decisions, many students of the Con-

stitution still adhered to the theory that sovereignty resided wholly with the states. The United States, they contended, was a partnership of sovereign and independent states, joined together only to accomplish certain specified ends; and therefore if any state chose for any reason to withdraw at any time from the partnership, it had full power to do so. There was nothing necessarily southern about the doctrine of secession, for many New England Federalists had once regarded it as their last defense against the tyranny of Jeffersonian democracy. The Hartford Convention had been restrained with difficulty from asserting secessionist views. Now some of the southern leaders, because they thought their states were destined to remain forever an oppressed minority section, were boldly reasserting the right of a state to secede.

While Calhoun did not disagree in theory with the doctrine of secession, he took steps to prevent it from having to be put into practice. Following in part the arguments of the Kentucky and Virginia Resolutions, he insisted that the several states, acting individually and separately through conventions called for the purpose, might decide whether and to what extent the federal government had exceeded the authority originally conferred upon it. Should such a convention find the federal government guilty of an unconstitutional act "so deliberate, palpable, and dangerous, as to justify the interposition of the State to protect its rights," it might declare the act "null and void within the limits of the State; which solemn declaration, based on her rights as a member of the Union, would be obligatory, not only on her citizens, but on the General Government itself; and thus place the violated rights of the State under the shield of the Constitution." The new doctrine of nullification, with which Calhoun contended he was seeking to save the Union, was first authoritatively stated in a document known as the "South Carolina Exposition," which the legislature of South Carolina adopted in December, 1828, as part of a protest against the Tariff of Abominations. Calhoun's connection with the Exposition was not known at the time, but later he elaborated his arguments in various speeches and documents, particularly in an essay entitled *A Disquisition on Government*.

Webster-Hayne Debate. Calhoun's doctrine might with sufficient reiteration be made acceptable to the South, but the support, or at least the tolerance, of a majority of the states had to be obtained if nullification was to be anything more than an empty gesture or a prelude to secession. Nothing, certainly, was to be hoped for from the industrial Northeast, to which the advantages of a strong central government were increasingly obvious. But the West, although it in part favored a protective tariff, now had a well-developed grievance against the Northeast on the land question. During the debate on the Foot Resolution, Senator Robert Y. Hayne of South Carolina seized the opportunity to set forth to the irritated westerners what advantages the doctrine of nullification might offer them. He was answered by Senator Daniel Webster of Massachusetts, who upheld brilliantly the supremacy of the Union. In a sense, the doctrine of nullification was on trial, and the West was to be the jury.

Daniel Webster (1782–1852), the son of a New Hampshire pioneer farmer, had surmounted many obstacles to obtain an education and had won distinction as a lawyer because of his superb rhetoric, impassioned oratory, and able reasoning. For two terms, 1813–1817, he served as a New Hampshire representative in Congress, and devoted himself to the defense of the commercial interests with which his home city, Portsmouth, was then closely identified.

The Webster-Hayne debate was not an affair of a few hours, but, following some preliminary skirmishing, occupied the attention of the Senate from January 18, 1830, when Senator Benton of Missouri undertook to expound the views of the West, until the end of the month. Vice-President Calhoun could take no part in the debate,

but he heard his views admirably set forth by Hayne. Webster's oratory rose to new heights; indeed, his orations on this occasion are generally conceded to be the greatest ever delivered in an American forum. He attacked the theory that the states were sovereign under the Constitution, or were ever meant to be. The Constitution, he maintained, was created primarily to impose certain restrictions on state sovereignty, and the states were left sovereign only "so far as their sovereignty is not affected by the supreme law." He cited the historical fact that if once the thirteen states had created the nation, the nation had since that time created nearly as many new states, and might yet create many more. He pointed out the impracticability of a doctrine that left to each of the twenty-four states individually the right to pass on the constitutionality of an act of Congress, and to the eminent practicability of leaving this power where, as he contended, the Constitution placed it, in the hands of the federal courts, with a right of appeal to the Supreme Court. He warned the South that the nation could never admit that its laws might constitutionally be defied by a state, and that nullification, if attempted, could lead only to a fratricidal war or the disruption of the Union.

Jackson's Stand. The states'-rights South had spoken through Hayne, the nationalistic Northeast through Webster. What would be the judgment of the West? Throughout the long debate Benton had been the chief exponent of western opinion, but when the western verdict came in, it was voiced by the President himself. At an anniversary dinner set for April 13, 1830 — Jefferson's birthday — at which members of every Democratic faction were present, Jackson offered a toast: "Our Federal Union — it must be preserved!" Calhoun countered: "The Union — next to our liberty, the most dear!"

But the President's speech had made it clear that his states'-rights views went to no such lengths as those of Calhoun and

Hayne. Time was to prove that he had represented also the views of the West with rare accuracy. Southern leaders, who had hoped to achieve a political union of the South and the West that would make Calhoun the next President, were completely discomfited. The ties that bound the West to the Northeast were stronger than the ties that bound the West to the South.

The new sectional alliance was accomplished, however, only at the expense of a rift in the Democratic party. Following a squabble among the Cabinet wives over the social recognition to be accorded to Peggy O'Neale, daughter of a Washington tavernkeeper, but now the wife of John H. Eaton, Secretary of War and close friend of the President, the entire Cabinet resigned, and when their successors were appointed, the Calhoun element in the party was ignored. An open rupture between the President and Calhoun occurred after Jackson learned that Calhoun, as Secretary of War under Monroe, had warmly advocated the censure of Jackson for the course the latter had pursued in Florida after the War of 1812. The chief political significance of this break was that Martin Van Buren, who had helped bring it about, would receive the President's support for the succession when Jackson's term of office came to a close.

Indian Policy. Jackson entered the Presidency with many prejudices, but with few considered policies. As a result the program for which he came to stand was to a considerable extent improvised. Probably he had firmer convictions on the Indian question than on most others. No friend of the Indian, he sided with the State of Georgia in its contention that it had full authority over the Cherokee Indians living within its borders. When the matter came to the Supreme Court in the case of the *Cherokee Nation* v. *Georgia* (1831), the Court, although complimenting the Indians on their successful efforts at self-government, refused to take jurisdiction on the grounds that the Cherokees were a "domes-

tic dependent nation," rather than a "foreign state," as the suit contended. Later, however, in the case of *Worcester* v. *Georgia* (1832), the Court held that the laws of Georgia were of no effect within the Cherokee borders. This decision was openly flouted by the Georgians, and the President, as already noted, made no effort to enforce it.

Jackson also supported the policy of Indian removal to the trans-Mississippi area, a policy that Calhoun and Monroe had urged upon Congress in 1825. In the Jackson administration this policy was successfully carried through. On May 28, 1830, he signed an Indian Removal Act that gave legal sanction to the transfer. Under Jackson, ninety-four Indian treaties were signed, most of which were treaties of cession; and under the steady pressure of the United States government even the civilized Cherokees were forced to move West. Two wars had to be fought in order to subject the Indians wholly to the white man's will. The Black Hawk War with the Sauks and Foxes, whose departure from northern Illinois was too slow to satisfy the frontiersmen, was fought in 1832; the Seminole War was an unhappy legacy that Jackson left to his successor, Van Buren, and that ended in the forties only when most of the Seminoles had been hunted down and killed. Jackson's Indian policy aroused considerable criticism, particularly from humanitarians like the Quakers, but the West approved it heartily, and the country as a whole offered no effective objection to it.

Internal Improvements. Perhaps many of those who supported Jackson in 1828 could have predicted the nature of his handling of the Indian problem, but they could less easily have foreseen his stand on federal assistance to public works. As a westerner he might be expected to favor them, but as a southerner, to oppose them. Perhaps a shrewd observer might easily have foreseen that his position would be as much at variance as possible with the views of Adams and Clay. While Adams was President, Congress, with much encouragement from the executive, granted federal aid liberally for the building of roads and canals, the improvement of ports and harbors, and the clearing of obstructions from the channels of navigable streams. But Jackson was not long in concluding that many such expenditures were neither constitutional nor expedient. An opportunity to state his position came in May, 1830, when Congress sent him a bill which authorized federal assistance for the building of a road in Kentucky from Maysville to Lexington. Although this road was in reality only a link in the once famous Natchez Trace, during the eighteenth century the main overland route from Kentucky to the lower Mississippi, the measure as it stood provided merely for a strictly intrastate road. Half the stock in the turnpike company that was to do the work was to be subscribed by the United States government, and the other half in equal parts by the state of Kentucky and by private individuals.

HENRY CLAY

Although a representative of what in his time was regarded as the West, Clay understood that to achieve any national policy western interests must be reconciled with those of other sections.

The Maysville Veto. Much to the disgust of its proponents, Jackson refused to sign the Maysville Road Bill. In defense of the position he had taken, he questioned the bill's constitutionality and stated his belief that a constitutional amendment should be adopted if federal aid to roads and canals was to be continued; but his chief objection to the measure was the local character of the internal improvement it proposed to aid. He pointed also to the drain on the treasury entailed by lavish expenditures for internal improvements, and suggested that Congress might better reduce the revenue if it could spare the funds, or use its surplus to pay off the national debt.

The Maysville veto was the subject of acrimonious debate in Congress and in the country at large, but it was sustained. Other vetoes and pocket vetoes of similar measures soon followed. It should not be assumed, however, that Jackson's vetoes ended all national aid to improvements in transportation. The President showed no disposition to interrupt work on the National Road, he signed many bills for federal assistance to road building in the territories, and he offered little opposition to federal grants in aid of river and harbor improvement. But the cessation of appropriations for the construction of roads and canals within and among the several states was actually of even greater significance than Jackson knew. Before his administration ended, canals and turnpikes were giving place to railroads, and the enormous capacity of this new variety of internal improvements for absorbing federal funds was not hard to see. Jackson's policy, however, set a strong precedent against such expenditures, and for many years the railroads were unable to induce Congress to aid them, even by grants of land.

Distribution. The President's stand on internal improvements was undoubtedly meant as a blow against Henry Clay's American System. Ever alert for a promising issue that would serve further to bind East and West together, Clay soon adopted into his American system the idea of "distribution," as applied to the revenue from the public lands. Why not distribute these funds among the several states? The United States Treasury did not need the money as long as the high tariff rates were continued, for the duties on imports alone brought in enough revenue to pay the cost of the national government. To make distribution more palatable to the West, Clay, in April, 1832, suggested that a small portion (later set at one-eighth) of the revenue from the public lands be given to the states in which the sales were made, and that the remainder be divided among all the states in accordance with the congressional ratio. The South showed little interest in distribution, in part because it meant a too generous subsidy to the populous eastern states, and in part because what Clay really intended to accomplish by distribution, as Thomas Hart Benton took pains to point out, was to divert "the land revenue from the support of the Government," and thus "to create a vacuum in the treasury, which must be filled up by duties on imported goods." If distribution meant high tariffs, the South would oppose it.

The Tariff and Nullification. In the end it was the tariff controversy that brought on the test of the doctrine of nullification. In December, 1831, Jackson urged Congress, in view of the rapid reduction of the national debt that the heavy revenues had made possible, to undertake a revision of the tariff. The South insisted upon radically lower duties, but the Northeast and the Northwest, standing together under the leadership of John Quincy Adams, now a member of the House, and Henry Clay, now a member of the Senate, achieved in July, 1832, another victory for protection. The

response of South Carolina to this challenge was all that Calhoun could have hoped for. The newly elected legislature, upon the recommendation of the governor, promptly called a convention to deal with the emergency. Delegates were chosen, the convention met, and on November 18, 1832, by a vote of 136 to 26, it declared the tariffs of 1828 and of 1832 "null, void, and no law, nor binding upon this State, its officers, or citizens." Furthermore, federal officers were forbidden to collect customs in South Carolina after February 1, 1833, and any federal action designed to coerce the state into obedience of the nullified laws was declared to be not only null and void, but also "inconsistent with the longer continuance of South Carolina in the Union." Calhoun now resigned as Vice-President, was promptly elected to the Senate, and made ready to defend the course of action that he had led his state to pursue.

The Tariff of 1833. Jackson did not hesitate to accept the challenge of the nullificationists. He reinforced the garrisons in Charleston Harbor, issued a proclamation denouncing nullification, asked, and obtained, from Congress authority to use force, if necessary, in the collection of the duties. But he also urged the South Carolinians to reconsider their action, and in the interest of harmony he encouraged his friends in Congress to seek a downward revision of the tariff. Finally, under the leadership of Henry Clay, a compromise tariff bill was rushed through Congress early in 1833. This measure, which even Calhoun supported, somewhat enlarged the free list, and provided for the gradual reduction of such duties as remained until at the end of nine years no rate should exceed 20 per cent. A peaceful solution was now in sight, for with the obnoxious tariff of 1832 repealed, the nullification ordinance could be withdrawn. On March 11, 1833, this action was taken.

Both sides claimed the victory. The nullificationists pointed out that their firm stand had won a concession on the tariff that could otherwise never have been obtained. The nationalists maintained that through Jackson's firm course the doctrine of the supremacy of the Union had been singularly vindicated. In a sense both contentions were correct. But it was the threat of secession and the danger of civil war rather than the resort to nullification that had led to the passage of the Compromise Tariff. Jackson, in spite of his strict interpretation of the Constitution, had proved to be an ardent defender of the Union.

SELECTED BIBLIOGRAPHY

Since individuals tended to reflect the attitudes of the sections they represented, biographies are of great importance. The principal works on Clay and Webster have already been listed. S. F. Bemis, *John Quincy Adams and the Union* (1956), is a superb book, by far the best on its subject. But see also B. C. Clark, *John Quincy Adams* (1932); and G. A. Lipsky, *°John Quincy Adams, His Theory and Ideas* (1950). *The Diary of Charles Francis Adams* (2 vols., 1964–   ) is being edited by A. D. and David Donald; the volumes published cover 1820–1829. J. E. D. Shipp, *Giant Days; or, The Life and Times of William H. Crawford* (1909), is of some value.

On Calhoun, the major biography is C. M. Wiltse, *John C. Calhoun* (3 vols., 1944–1951). Wiltse is strongly sympathetic with his subject, as is M. L. Coit, *°John C. Calhoun* (1950). More critical is G. M. Capers, *John C. Calhoun, Opportunist* (1960). An accessible collection of Calhoun's writings is *°Disquisition on Government and Selections from the Discourse,* edited by C. G. Post (1953). A. O. Spain, *The Political Theory of John C. Calhoun* (1951), is an interesting monograph. A major scholarly project now in progress is the publication of *The Papers of John C. Calhoun* (2 vols., 1963–   ). Volume I, edited by R. L. Meriwether, reaches to 1817; Volume II, edited by W. E. Hemphill, covers 1817–1818.

Sectional differences on one major subject are brought out in a good collection, *°The Great Tariff Debate, 1820–1830,* edited by G. R. Taylor (1953). Other important works with a strong sectional implication include R. G. Albion and J. B. Pope, *The Rise of New York Port, 1815–1860* (1939); E. C. Kirkland, *Men, Cities and Transportation; A Study in New

England History, 1820–1900* (2 vols., 1948); and Julius Rubin, *Canal or Railroad?* (1961). Major state studies include S. J. Folmsbee, *Sectionalism and Internal Improvements in Tennessee, 1796–1845* (1939); Louis Hartz, *Economic Policy and Democratic Thought: Pennsylvania, 1776–1860* (1948); Nathan Miller, *The Enterprise of a Free People: Aspects of Economic Development in New York State during the Canal Period, 1792–1838* (1962); J. H. Krenkel, *Illinois Internal Improvements, 1818–1848* (1958); M. S. Heath, *Constructive Liberalism; The Role of the State in Economic Development in Georgia to 1860* (1954); and A. G. Smith, *Economic Readjustment of an Old Cotton State: South Carolina, 1820–1860* (1958).

The Canal Age is surveyed in A. F. Harlow, *Old Towpaths* (1926); and M. S. Waggoner, *The Long Haul West* (1958). Carter Goodrich, *Government Promotion of American Canals and Railroads, 1800–1890* (1960), is a useful summary of a complex subject. See also *Canals and American Economic Development,* a cooperative work edited by Carter Goodrich (1961). N. E. Whitford, *History of the Canal System of the State of New York* (2 vols., 1906), remains the major work on the Erie Canal. W. S. Sanderlin, *The Great National Project* (1947), deals with the Chesapeake and Ohio Canal. For the part played by the Great Lakes waterways, see Harlan Hatcher, *The Great Lakes* (1944). Individual volumes in a worthy series are M. M. Quaife, *Lake Michigan* (1944); Fred Landon, *Lake Huron* (1944); G. L. Nute, *Lake Superior* (1944); Arthur Pound, *Lake Ontario* (1945); and Harlan Hatcher, *Lake Erie* (1945).

An excellent recent survey is G. G. Van Deusen, *°The Jacksonian Era, 1828–1848* (1959); its bibliography is full and highly

° Available in paperback

useful. Rich but incomplete is F. J. Turner,* *The United States, 1830–1850* (1935). H. R. Fraser, *Democracy in the Making; The Jackson-Tyler Era* (1938), is an interesting work. Claude Bowers, *The Party Battles of the Jackson Period* (1922), which votes for Jackson on nearly every page, gives an unrestrained account of the inauguration, and of the events that succeeded it. A lively short study is R. V. Remini, *The Election of Andrew Jackson* (1963). L. D. White, *The Jacksonians; A Study in Administrative History, 1829–1861* (1954), serves as a useful corrective to the frequent charge that the spoils system seriously damaged public administration in this period. M. I. Ostrogorski, *Democracy and the Organization of Political Parties,* II (1902), is a great classic, highly critical of the Jacksonians.

The major biographies of Jackson are J. S. Bassett, *The Life of Andrew Jackson* (2 vols., 2nd ed., 1916), scholarly and sympathetic; and Marquis James, *The Life of Andrew Jackson* (2 vols., 1933–1937), brilliantly written, and especially useful on the personal side, if somewhat lacking in original research. An excellent short and objective treatment is Harold Syrett, *Andrew Jackson* (1953).

An important study of the broadening of the franchise is Chilton Williamson, *American Suffrage; from Property to Democracy, 1760–1860* (1960). Political behavior in New York state has long interested scholars; major works on this subject include Henry Christman, *Tin Horns and Calico* (1945); D. M. Ellis, *Landlords and Farmers in the Hudson-Mohawk Region, 1790–1860* (1946); and Lee Benson, *The Concept of Jacksonian Democracy: New York as a Test Case* (1961). Another valuable state study is A. B. Darling, *Political Change in Massachusetts, 1824–1848* (1925).

On the Indian problem, particularly with reference to Indian removal, the following are useful general works: W. C. Macleod, *The American Indian Frontier* (1928); Angie Debo, *The Road to Disappearance* (1941); and G. D. Harmon, *Sixty Years of Indian Affairs* (1941). An excellent collection of materials is *The Removal of the Cherokee Nation: Manifest Destiny or National Dishonor?* (1962), edited by Louis Filler and Allen Guttmann. Individual tribes are studied in M. L. Starkey, *The Cherokee Nation* (1946); H. T. Malone, *Cherokees of the Old South* (1956); and E. C. McReynolds, *The Seminoles* (1957). A leading authority on Indian removal was Grant Foreman, whose works include: *Indians and Pioneers* (1930); *Indian Removal* (1932); *Advancing the Frontier* (1933); and *The Five Civilized Tribes* (1934).

On the public lands, the general histories already cited may be supplemented by a special study: R. G. Wellington, *The Political and Sectional Influence of the Public Lands, 1828–1842* (1914), a book which reveals how greatly sectional interests and jealousies affected the course of events. See also T. D. Jervey, *Robert Y. Hayne and His Times* (1909); and A. M. Sakolski, *The Great American Land Bubble* (1932). T. H. Benton, *Thirty Years' View; or A History of the Working of the American Government, 1820–1850* (2 vols., 1854–1856), presents the western view on the land question, and nearly every other. Biographies of Benton include two modern treatments: W. N. Chambers, *Old Bullion Benton, Senator from the New West* (1956); and E. B. Smith, *Magnificent Missourian* (1958).

On nullification, see C. S. Boucher, *The Nullification Controversy in South Carolina* (1916); and Frederic Bancroft, *Calhoun and the South Carolina Nullification Movement* (1928). The German historian, H. E. von Holst, gives a pronounced anti-southern interpretation in his monumental *The Constitutional and Political History of the United States* (8 vols., 1876–1892).

13

THE PANIC OF 1837

The Bank of the United States. Almost as spectacular as his conflict with the nullificationists was Jackson's war on the Bank of the United States. This institution, operating after 1822 under the presidency of Nicholas Biddle, a wealthy and aristocratic Philadelphian, was in a flourishing condition when Jackson took office. Its conservatism satisfied the eastern industrialists and silenced the criticism of many states'-rights southerners. Its charter rights would last until 1837, and the chances that the privileges it enjoyed would be renewed for another twenty years seemed excellent. The Bank, however, did not lack for critics, particularly in the West. It had unhesitatingly made use of its powerful position to restrain banks chartered by the various states from indulging in dubious practices, such as issuing more paper money than their resources warranted, and lending freely on insufficient security. It thus won the resentment not only of all state bankers with "wild-cat" tendencies, but also of the many disappointed customers of state banks, who were given to understand that the real reason they could not renew old loans or negotiate new ones lay in the policy of the Bank of the United States. The Bank was itself a good collector, and by its numerous foreclosures had acquired numerous enemies. There were those, too, who had begun to think that the whole banking business was essentially dishonest and ought to be outlawed.

Jackson's War on the Bank. Jackson's known hostility to the B. U. S., as it was generally called, although at first not much in evidence, was a matter of great concern to Biddle, whose peace of mind was by no means improved when the President's henchman, W. B. Lewis, hinted broadly that places for good Jacksonian Democrats should be found on the Bank's payroll. Biddle did not hesitate to make a number of Jackson men directors of branch banks, but he was unwilling to subject the welfare of the Bank more fully to the hazards of the spoils system. His apprehension, however, led him to seek the favor of Congress in a way almost equally open to question. Before the election of Jackson, the Bank had lent to congressmen only when such a course seemed warranted as a strictly business proposition; but, beginning with 1829, this policy was relaxed. Also, it lent

THE DOWNFALL OF MOTHER BANK

This cartoon, "draw'd off from Natur by Zek Downing," is the work of a popular pro-Jackson cartoonist.

with similar freedom to powerful newspaper editors, and it paid a generous retainer each year to its leading attorney, Senator Daniel Webster.

A New Charter Vetoed. Jackson's war on the Bank was precipitated by the ill-advised action of Webster and Clay, who persuaded Biddle to bring forward a request for the recharter of the Bank along existing lines well before the election of 1832. They knew that Congress would pass such a bill, and they thought it shrewd politics to force upon Jackson the alternative of signing a measure he disliked, or taking the responsibility for what, in their opinion, would be an unpopular veto. Clay was early in the field as the candidate of the National Republican Party in 1832, and he felt especially confident of victory in case he could make an issue of the President's antagonism to the Bank. All went substantially as the

conspirators had planned. In the summer of 1832 the Senate, by a vote of 28 to 20, and the House by a vote of 109 to 79, passed the Bank bill, and Jackson's veto was quickly forthcoming. The Bank, he argued, was un-American because of its large number of foreign stockholders; it was undemocratic because it concentrated vast and monopolistic "power in the hands of a few men irresponsible to the people"; and it was unconstitutional because its charter was neither a "necessary nor proper" exercise of the authority delegated by the states to Congress.

Jackson's message was couched in language well calculated to appeal to the patriotism and self-interest of the masses, and it showed deliberate deference to the states'-rights prejudices of the South. It may have shown a complete lack of understanding of banking and finance, but it was far shrewder politics than the more elaborate schemes of Webster and Clay. The issue in the election

214

became for the ordinary voter not so much the success or failure of the Bank, as Clay had intended, but rather the success or failure of Andrew Jackson, champion of the common man. Jackson and his advisers had grasped the fact, far more clearly than their opponents, that elections were won by the votes of the people rather than by the good opinion of the elite. Issues, to be effective, must be dramatized and simplified.

Anti-Masonry. In this campaign, for the first time in American history, an organized third party put in its appearance. The Anti-Masonic Party originated in western New York, a region still distinctly frontier in character. Secret societies in this democratic community were regarded with much disfavor, partly, no doubt, because only a few could afford the membership fees, and partly because of the fantastic rumors regarding the rituals and oaths of such organizations. After the disappearance of a man who had allegedly revealed the secrets of the lodge, Anti-Masonry spread through the Northeast. For a time it was a social upheaval rather than a political movement, but shrewd anti-Jackson politicians — such men as Thurlow Weed and William H. Seward in New York, and Thaddeus Stevens in Pennsylvania — soon found ways to make Anti-Masonry serve their purposes, since the President himself was a Mason. They appealed to religious prejudice, and saw in even the small number of Catholic immigrants who were coming to the United States (most of whom voted the Democratic ticket) a menace to the liberties of the Republic. Finally, they widened their program to include practically all of Henry Clay's American System. With the election of 1832 in sight the Anti-Masonic leaders took the unprecedented step of calling a national nominating convention to select their candidate for the Presidency, and in September, 1831, their convention at Baltimore chose William Wirt of Virginia to lead them. Wirt's friendship and admiration for Clay were well known, and it was the Anti-Masonic hope that all anti-Jackson men would support him.

The Election of 1832. But the Anti-Masonic movement failed completely to divert attention from the main contest, which was between the National Republicans, with Clay as their candidate, and the Democrats, with Jackson as theirs. Both parties, however, followed the Anti-Masonic precedent in calling together national nominating conventions. Such a direct consultation of the popular will was quite in line with the current conception of democracy, and neither party dared overlook the opportunity of thus cultivating the favor of "King Numbers." In December, 1831, the National Republicans nominated Clay for President. In May, 1832, the Democrats endorsed the "repeated nominations" which Jackson had received "in various parts of the Union," and chose Martin Van Buren of New York as their candidate for Vice-President. The nomination of Van Buren was in strict accordance with Jackson's desires, but was so lacking in popular appeal that in the hope of giving a contrary impression, a rule was devised whereby a candidate to be nominated must receive "two-thirds of the whole number of votes in the convention." For a hundred years the "two-thirds rule" remained the practice of Democratic national conventions.

Jackson's Victory. The election resulted in a decisive victory for Jackson. In New York, Ohio, and elsewhere the National Republicans and the Anti-Masons supported the same electoral tickets, and in general the Wirt candidacy was used to promote Clay's chances of victory. Nevertheless, in the popular vote Jackson triumphed by 687,502 to 530,189 for Clay and Wirt combined, while in the electoral college the vote was 219 for Jackson to 49 for Clay. Only half the states of New England stood by Clay; Vermont cast her seven votes for Wirt, while Maine and New Hampshire gave comfortable majorities to

Jackson. In South Carolina, where the legislature still chose presidential electors, the nullificationists retained their majority and gave the votes of the state to John Floyd of Virginia. Jackson's re-election was essentially an endorsement of the popular principles of government for which he stood. The Bank issue received much attention during the campaign, but in general the people voted for or against Jackson rather than for or against the Bank of the United States.

The Removal of Deposits. It was natural, however, that the President should interpret his re-election as a mandate against the recharter of the Bank. But he was far too impatient to await its orderly demise, and determined to cripple it at once by withdrawing from its possession the deposits of the United States government, some $10 million to $12 million. Power to withdraw the deposits was vested in the Secretary of the Treasury, who was authorized to take such action only in the event that he considered the Bank an unsafe place for the government's funds. To get his way Jackson found it necessary to promote Secretary of the Treasury, Louis McLane, to be Secretary of State, and to remove his successor outright. But the next Secretary of the Treasury, Roger B. Taney of Maryland, had come to accept the states'-rights theory that the Bank was unconstitutional, and did not hesitate to issue the order which Jackson desired. Thereafter the United States drew upon its deposits in the Bank to meet its obligations, but placed all newly collected tax money in selected state banks — "pet banks," as they were called — whose importance increased as that of the Bank of the United States declined. Later, on the death of Marshall, Jackson made Taney Chief Justice.

State Banking Methods. Jackson's war on the Bank ushered in a period of great financial uncertainty. In the Northeast a money famine occurred, partly promoted

by Biddle in the hope of forcing a recharter, and partly because the number of pet banks located in the agricultural South and West was proportionately too large, and in the industrial Northeast much too small. But the West, which was already on the verge of a boom, seemingly prospered as never before. Here the declining power of the Bank of the United States emboldened state bankers of wildcat tendencies to indulge their long-suppressed desires to issue more currency and extend their loans. Eastern state bankers remained for the most part conservative, but the number of wildcatters in the West steadily increased. What was happening can best be set forth as follows:

STATE BANKING IN THE UNITED STATES				
YEAR	NUMBER OF BANKS	CAPITAL*	CIRCU-LATION*	LOANS*
1829	329	110.2	48.2	137.0
1834	506	200.0	94.8	324.1
1836	718	251.9	140.3	475.5
1837	788	290.8	149.2	525.1

  * In millions of dollars.

So marked an inflation of money and credit was certain to result in some form of speculation, and with the chief incidence of inflation in the West, this meant primarily speculation in land. Purchases of government land far outran any reasonable demand, and the same plots were often sold and resold several times without once being held by anyone who expected to till them. Government sales of public lands rose from 4 million acres in 1834 to 15 million in 1835, and to 20 million in 1836. It was during this period that the phrase "doing a land-office business" entered the American vernacular. The changed banking habits of the United States government added unneeded fuel to the flames. Receipts from the public lands rose from $4.8 million in 1834 to $24.8 million in 1836, and most of this money was deposited promptly in pet banks. These institutions then lent the money out again, all too frequently to speculators who bought more land, only to increase thereby the surplus in the Treasury, which had to make still more deposits in the pet banks, to be lent out again for speculation, and so on in a vicious circle.

The "Specie Circular." The unhealthiness of this situation was not lost on Jackson, who finally decided that the practice of accepting bank notes in payment for public lands must stop. Jackson's decision was embodied in the "Specie Circular," issued in July, 1836, to take effect after the election of that year. From that time on all payments to the United States for public lands had to be made in gold or silver. Since the state banks had little or no hard money available, the Specie Circular meant an end to the speculation, and, as matters turned out, a beginning of depression. Congressmen railed violently at the President's policy, and particularly in the West there was much opposition to this move that meant the end of easy money.

Labor and Jacksonian Democracy. Whatever support Jackson lost in the West by the Specie Circular was partially compensated for by gains in the eastern cities. There the workingmen were delighted by the President's hard-money policy, because they believed that inflation was seriously reducing their weekly paycheck. By 1832 workingmen in the larger cities had organized city federations. Two years later the National Trades Union was formed in New York City. Jackson had already won labor's admiration by his support of the 1832 act outlawing imprisonment for complaints of debt in the federal courts. The unions also warmly supported the President's efforts to make the public lands of the West more accessible to easterners who wished to settle there. In national politics labor constituted an important wing of the radical faction of the Democratic party throughout the east-

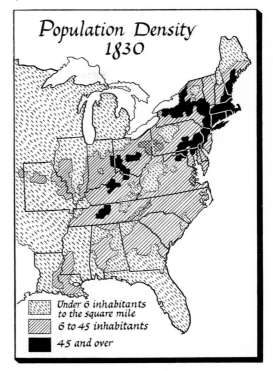

Population Density 1830

Under 6 inhabitants to the square mile

6 to 45 inhabitants

45 and over

ern states, a faction that became known as the "Loco-Focos." And while the main support for Jacksonian democracy probably came from the West, some of the inspiration for Jackson's and Van Buren's policies came from the Loco-Focos.

Meantime, the Treasury was seriously embarrassed by its mounting receipts. In 1835 the last dollar of the public debt was paid off, and the Treasury needed only enough money to pay current expenses. At the peak of the speculation, however, the revenues from the public lands were alone sufficient to meet the entire cost of the national government, and by that time the tariff was also bringing in startlingly large sums. The Compromise Tariff of 1833, because it provided for a gradual scaling-down of rates, was expected to produce less rather than more revenue as time went on; but the exact reverse proved to be true. The huge speculative profits that were being made in western lands, and the stimulating effects of inflation on business generally, fostered heavy purchases of foreign goods. Tariff receipts which had stood at only about $16 million in 1834 were half again as large by 1836, and, like the receipts from the public lands, sufficient in themselves to pay the full cost of the national government.

Distribution of the Surplus. Various projects were brought forward to rid the Treasury of its surplus revenue. Most debated was Clay's plan for the distribution of the proceeds of the sales of public lands among all the states, but the President's antagonism to such a measure prevented its adoption. Finally, it was agreed that the money should be distributed among the states as a loan rather than as a gift, and in June, 1836, such a bill became law. According to this act, whatever money in excess of $5 million was in the Treasury on January 1, 1837, was to be apportioned among the states in accordance with their representation in the electoral college, and paid over to them during the year in four quarterly installments. The hazards involved in this course of action were very great, but they did not become fully apparent until after Jackson left office, and his successor, Van Buren, took over. Later it could be said with some reason that "Jackson sowed the wind and Van Buren reaped the whirlwind."

"Shirt-sleeve" Diplomacy. Jackson's administration was primarily concerned with domestic affairs, but in the handling of American foreign relations it witnessed an abrupt break with the past. The men whom Jackson appointed to office were little schooled in the niceties of European diplomacy, and their "shirt-sleeve" methods proved most exasperating to Europeans. Nevertheless, the results were usually gratifying. Determined to end once and for all British discriminations against American trade in the West Indies, Jackson asked and received from Congress authority to admit British ships bound from the West

Indies to American ports, on whatever terms West Indian ports were open to American ships. As a result of this direct move, an agreement was soon reached that permitted the same freedom of trade between the United States and the British West Indies that existed between the United States and Great Britain, although the right of American ships to trade between these islands and Great Britain was still withheld. Another problem that confronted Jackson was the non-payment by France of the "spoliation claims," long demanded in consideration of the losses which Napoleon, in his vain effort to enforce the Continental System, had inflicted upon American shipping. Under strong pressure from Jackson, a settlement was agreed upon in July, 1831, whereby the United States was to be paid 23.5 million francs in six equal installments, beginning in February, 1833. But the French Chamber of Deputies refused to appropriate the funds, and Jackson denounced in brutally plain words this violation of a solemn agreement. For a time feeling between the two countries was at white heat, but at length the Chamber was induced to vote the necessary sums on condition that the President would apologize for his blunt threats. When Jackson said that he had meant no insult, the money was finally paid over.

Texas. Jackson also was confronted with the difficult task of maintaining peaceful relations with Mexico while Texas was becoming independent. In Spanish times Moses Austin of Missouri sought and obtained permission to lead a group of colonists to Texas. After Moses Austin's death, his son Stephen won from the new revolutionary government of Mexico confirmation of the privileges the Spanish had extended to his father. A nucleus of settlement from the United States speedily appeared at San Felipe de Austin, and in 1824 a general colonization law welcomed other American settlers. By 1830 about 20,000 former citizens of the United States, owners of perhaps 1,000 Negro slaves, were residents of Texas.

Inevitably trouble developed between the Texans and their Mexican overlords. The former were constantly irritated by the fact that Texas was not a separate and self-governing state of Mexico, but was joined to the neighboring state of Coahuila on terms that ensured to the native Mexicans a permanent majority in the state legislature. They were skeptical, too, of the semi-feudal land titles they had received; they were not all Catholics, as the law required them to be; and they longed sentimentally to be within the boundaries of the United States. Both before and after Jackson became President the American government tried repeatedly to purchase Texas, but the Mexicans, both officially and unofficially, resented warmly all such suggestions. In 1830 further immigration into Texas was prohibited and the importation of Negro slaves was forbidden. Practically prohibitive duties were placed on imports from the United States, and Mexican officials sup-

ported by Mexican soldiers were sent to the border to enforce these regulations.

Almost inevitably the Texans were soon involved in revolutionary activities. At first they took sides with a Mexican rebel, Santa Anna, but when he triumphed, they found themselves no better off than before. Finally, they decided to follow the precedent of the American Revolution, and in March, 1836, declared their independence of Mexico. By this time war had already begun, and Santa Anna was sweeping northward with so many troops at his command that the Texans should have been easily overwhelmed. The Alamo at San Antonio fell on March 6, 1836, and its entire garrison was massacred. But at San Jacinto, on April 21, 1836, the Mexicans were disastrously defeated by a Texan army under the command of General Sam Houston, and from this time on Mexican authority in Texas was at an end.

As long as the Texan revolution was in progress, the government of the United States preserved an air of neutrality,

THE ALAMO

An abandoned mission at San Antonio fortified against attack, the Alamo was held by a handful of Texans against a large Mexican force until the entire garrison was overwhelmed and massacred. Among those who died at the Alamo was Davy Crockett.

although it made little effort to restrain the American public from supporting the Texans. With Texas as an independent republic, however, Jackson would gladly have favored annexation, had it only been feasible politically. But many northerners were by this time on record against the acquisition of any new territory open to slavery, while the Mexican government threatened war in case annexation should be attempted. Under the circumstances, the Jackson administration did as little about Texas as possible; not until the day before Jackson left office was the Republic of Texas recognized by the United States.

The Election of 1836. The election of 1836 found the opposition to Jackson strong, but divided. The National Republicans, led by Henry Clay, included within their membership the business leaders of the Northeast, most of whom were interested, directly or indirectly, in manufactures, and therefore in favor of a protective tariff. They deplored Jackson's war on the Bank and welcomed the support of westerners offended by his Maysville veto. The Anti-Masons very generally went over to the National Republicans, bringing to the party an enthusiastic rural following and an atmosphere of democracy that it otherwise would have lacked. Southerners who opposed Jackson still thought of themselves as Democrats, but they could have little sympathy with National Republicanism as long as its cardinal tenets were a national bank, a protective tariff, and a national program of internal improvements. Lacking all other bonds of unity, anti-Jackson men could at least agree in their denunciation of the "Tory" policy of vesting too much authority in the President, whom they sometimes characterized as "King Andrew I." It became the fashion in some circles for the opponents of Jackson to speak of themselves as "Whigs."

The weakness of the Whigs lay in their lack of cohesion. Although they were essentially conservative and nationalistic, their party differences were such that they did not dare to have a national convention, for their leaders doubted that they could agree either on candidates or platform. To oppose Martin Van Buren, whom Jackson forced the Democrats to nominate as his successor, the Whig leaders decided that there should be as many candidates as the various sections might choose to support. The election of 1836 was thus a kind of free-for-all. Tennessee presented Judge Hugh L. White; Massachusetts nominated Daniel Webster; a Pennsylvania state convention presented William Henry Harrison; and South Carolina, where the legislature still chose electors, cast her vote for Willie P. Mangum. But in the fall of 1836 the country was still prosperous, and all four candidates were not enough to defeat Van Buren, who received 170 electoral votes to 73 for Harrison, 26 for White, 14 for Webster, and 11 for Mangum. Jacksonian Democracy had triumphed, but the margin of victory was uncomfortably narrow.

Martin Van Buren. Martin Van Buren (1782–1862), to whose lot fell the task of guiding the United States government through a period of depression, was by no means lacking in political experience. He was of Dutch descent, but not of the Hudson Valley aristocracy, for his father was a poor farmer and tavernkeeper of Kinderhook, New York. Young Van Buren's formal education was limited, but in spite of this handicap he won success both in the law and in politics. Unusually adroit in his dealings with men, he was the recognized leader of the Albany Regency which directed the policies of the Democratic Party in New York. By 1828 Van Buren had achieved the governorship, but he resigned to enter Jackson's Cabinet as Secretary of State. He was far more conciliatory than his chief in his personal relationships, but he lacked popular appeal, and it was only because of the President's support that the "Little Magician" won the succession.

Van Buren had barely taken office when

the Panic of 1837 broke upon the country. The distribution of the surplus had turned out to be a blunder of vast magnitude. Many of the states, particularly the new states of the West, in receiving this bounty had embarked upon extensive programs of internal improvement and had borrowed heavily for that purpose, frequently from foreign investors who were soon to learn that the credit of the United States and of the various American states were two different things. Dazzled by the prospect of receiving further subsidies from the national government, some states redoubled their extravagance; by 1837 the total state indebtedness had reached the prodigious sum of $170 million.

Panic of 1837. English exporters, who noted as early as 1836 that the balance of trade was running strongly against the United States, were among the first to foresee a collapse of American prosperity. As a result of their fears, the Bank of England raised its discount rates, and English merchants refused new credits to American customers. Thereupon American importers, since the foreign balance could be met only in hard money, deluged their bankers with requests for specie, requests that could not possibly be met in full, for American specie in great quantities had already been drained out of the country. By this time speculators in land, whose efforts to secure the withdrawal of the Specie Circular had proved unavailing, were also frantically demanding gold from the hard pressed bankers. To make matters still worse, the pet banks were given a body blow by the Distribution Act, which required them to return the surplus government funds they held on deposit. Payment of the first installment, January 1, 1837, caused them great embarrassment, and the second, on April 1, brought almost immediate disaster. Bank failures now came thick and fast, and in May, 1837, every bank in the United States suspended specie payment. Notes of the failed or failing banks became virtually worthless, and

KING ANDREW THE FIRST

Accused by his opponents of autocratic actions, Jackson is portrayed here in the trappings of royalty, with one foot on the torn Constitution of the United States and the other on the shredded remnants of the B.U.S. and internal improvements.

the public took enormous losses. Meantime, many English exporters, unable to collect on the debts owed them by Americans, had also been forced into bankruptcy. Their failure brought down, in turn, the English merchants and manufacturers who furnished goods for the American market. Soon both England and the United States were plunged into the depths of a profound economic depression.

Causes of the Panic. It would not be fair to say that Jackson's war on the Bank of the United States was alone responsible for the Panic of 1837. Doubtless the West would have developed with dangerous rapidity under any circumstances; internal improvements, particularly the building of canals, were already an obsession when the "war" began; overexpansion of cotton planting in the South and of manufacturing in the Northeast could hardly have been forestalled. But Jackson's crude handling of public finance certainly stimulated the boom and accentuated the crash. Fortunately for his popularity, he left office a few weeks before the Panic broke. As for the Bank of the United States, it secured a charter from the state of Pennsylvania, and continued in operation until 1841, when it failed.

Van Buren realized that the Panic of 1837 was a political as well as an economic calamity, but in conformity with the thinking of his time he considered that the depression was an affliction of the business world, and business would have to work out its own salvation. Van Buren did feel obliged, however, to try to put the government on a sound financial basis, and with this in mind he called a special session of Congress for September, 1837. He urged first that the law calling for the distribution of the surplus be repealed, and in this Congress promptly followed him. But his most cherished plan, the establishment of an independent treasury, was violently opposed, and its adoption long delayed. Van Buren recommended that for the future the United States Treasury should have no dealings whatever with banks, whether national or state. Sub-Treasuries should be constructed in the various cities and placed in the charge of government officials, who should receive and disperse government funds on a strictly specie basis. Thus the government would run no risk of losing its money by depositing it in banks, nor would it contribute indirectly and unintentionally to such an overexpansion of bank credit as had preceded the Panic of 1837. It was not until 1840 that the advocates of the Sub-Treasury succeeded in obtaining the required majorities in both houses of Congress. The Sub-Treasury debate served to emphasize the existence within the Democratic Party of two diametrically opposed

factions, the "Loco-Focos," who particularly in New York were noisily opposed to banks and rejoiced to see the United States sever all connections with banking institutions, and the more conservative Democrats, who resented Jackson's ignorance of finance and believed banks of some kind to be a necessity. The debate also gave the Whigs that rare thing, something they could agree upon.

State Banking Methods. With the national government completely divorced from the banking business, it became necessary for the states and private individuals to work out a banking system that would meet the needs of the country. Several western states experimented with state-owned banks, but with a few exceptions these banks soon met disaster. Better results were obtained by instituting reforms in the existing banking system. In New England a kind of clearinghouse was devised which made possible the redemption in Boston at par of notes issued by sound rural banks. In New York state-chartered banks were obliged to contribute a certain percentage of their incomes to a common safety fund, the purpose of which was to ensure that all bank notes should be redeemed at par. More important still was the adoption in the same state of the principle of "free banking"; that is, the enactment of a state banking law under the terms of which any individual or group was free to start a bank so long as the stipulations of the law were met. This eliminated the chance for political jobbery, by means of which so many unsound banks had previously been chartered. By following such precedents the various states were soon able to provide a banking system which, if not wholly satisfactory, at least enabled the country to carry on its business.

Repudiation of State Debts. Many of the states, however, were long troubled by the debts they had incurred during the boom period. Little of the money they had so freely lavished upon canals and other works of internal improvement had been raised by taxation; most of it had been borrowed on the assumption that profits from the works undertaken would ultimately pay off the debt. Also, some western and southern states, notably Louisiana, Alabama, and Mississippi, had borrowed the capital for their state-owned banks. Overwhelmed by the depression, and unable to meet their obligations by taxation or by further borrowing, several states frankly repudiated their indebtedness. The blow which this action dealt to American credit abroad was long felt. Some of the defaulting states repented and paid off their obligations in whole or in part, but others remained obdurate, and their debts were never paid. Urgent pleas that the federal government save American credit by assuming all state debts came to nothing.

State Withdrawal from Business. The reverses experienced by the states in their efforts to finance banks and internal improvements made a lasting impression upon the public mind. One after another the projects so initiated found their way into private hands or were abandoned altogether. The conviction grew that the state might better withdraw completely from the field of business and leave the carrying-out of even such expensive enterprises as canals and railroads to private initiative. Many of the new state constitutions of this period limited closely the amount of indebtedness the state might incur. Also, general laws of incorporation, in which the privilege of limited liability for stockholders was reluctantly conceded, encouraged private corporations to take over much of the work that states had previously felt obliged to do.

Attack on Van Buren. The political effect of depression is usually adverse to the party in power, whichever it is and whatever it does. The Whig orators, led by Clay, Adams, and Webster, pointed to the hundreds of closed factories, the thousands of unemployed men, the collapse of cotton prices in the South and of land prices in the West as evidence of the mistaken policies that the Democratic Party had pursued. Not an opportunity was lost to discredit the unfortunate Van Buren, who was held responsible not only for his own faults, but also for those of his subordinates. The Seminole War was branded as a proslavery extravagance, while the President's failure to work for the annexation of Texas was cited as unmistakable proof of his antislavery views. It was no surprise to anyone when the administration lost control of both houses of Congress in 1838, and the Whigs were confident of victory if they could only hold together during the campaign of 1840.

The Election of 1840. The experience of 1836 had made it obvious that a single candidate would have to be agreed upon, so a Whig convention was called to meet at Harrisburg, Pennsylvania, in December, 1839. Henry Clay was the outstanding Whig leader, but his political principles were disliked by many, and the party finally nominated William Henry Harrison of Ohio (1773–1841), who owed his popularity to his military service in the War of 1812 and his demonstration in the election of 1836 that he could win support. Harrison's long association with the West was deemed an advantage, for he could be played up as the representative of the common man. The observation of a disappointed adherent of Henry Clay, that if Harrison could only be given a pension and a barrel of hard cider he would gladly retire to a log cabin for the rest of his days, gave Whig orators the chance to portray Harrison as the "log-cabin, hard-cider candidate" of the masses against the "aristocratic" Van Buren. For Vice-President the Whigs nominated John Tyler of Virginia, not only as an appropriate concession to the South, but also as a gesture of good will to his close personal friend, Henry Clay, whose disappointment at being passed over in favor of Harrison was extreme. The Whigs presented

LOG CABIN AND HARD CIDER CAMPAIGN

In this cartoon General Harrison is shown giving a hearty welcome to a wounded soldier. Note the barrel of cider on one side of the cabin, and the "Beautiful Ohio" on the other.

no platform, for their leaders knew full well that they could never agree upon one. In a campaign of hokum never since surpassed, they succeeded completely in their undertaking. Van Buren lost by an electoral vote of 234 to 60. The popular vote, however, was close, for Harrison received less than 150,000 majority out of over 2.4 million votes cast.

Death of Harrison. The Whig leaders, particularly Webster and Clay, took it for granted that they would be called upon to guide the new administration, and all started off well enough. Harrison chose Webster to be Secretary of State and gave most of the other places in his Cabinet to the friends of Henry Clay. Clay himself retained his seat in the Senate and prepared to push through Congress his American System. Unfortunately for Clay, however, the President, who was more than sixty-eight years of age at the time of his inauguration, did not long survive that event. Thousands of Whig office seekers, bent upon replacing the "rascally Democrats" at once, thronged into the capital and gave him no peace. With his

strength thus overtaxed, he failed to throw off a severe cold contracted the day of his inauguration, and a month later he was dead.

John Tyler. John Tyler (1790–1862) was a Virginia planter who had long been known for his pronounced and strongly held views. As a member of the Virginia legislature, of the national House of Representatives, and finally of the United States Senate, he had gone on record repeatedly on all the important issues of the day. Despite his friendship with Clay, he was uncompromisingly opposed to a protective tariff, to a national bank, and to internal improvements at national expense; and he was equally ardent in his defense of states' rights, slavery, nullification, and expansion. Few politicians could have represented the views of Webster and Clay less well. He had, too, a kind of vanity in his views and a touchiness about them that made it extremely difficult for him to compromise. He retained Harrison's Cabinet, however, and tried to be conciliatory toward the Whig leaders.

When Congress met in special session the last of May, 1841, Henry Clay was on hand as a member of the Senate with a series of demands that in the main satisfied the Whig majority: (1) repeal of the Sub-Treasury Act, (2) a third Bank of the United States, (3) a higher tariff, and (4) the distribution among the states of the proceeds from the sales of public lands. Tyler agreed to the repeal of the Sub-Treasury Act, but twice vetoed a plan to establish a new Bank of the United States, and Congress refused to override his vetoes. He signed the distribution bill, but only after an amendment had been attached to it which stipulated that in case the tariff duties were raised above the 20 per cent maximum set by the Tariff of 1833, distribution should cease. Then he approved a bill to raise the tariff because he believed that the treasury required the money — an act that totally nullified distribution. The tariff of 1842, which restored duties to about the level of the act of 1832, was in reality protective in character — the only important success that Clay achieved. Two other measures were designed primarily to alleviate the existing economic distress. One was a Bankruptcy Act which debtors promptly used so freely that the same Congress which enacted it also repealed it. The other was a Pre-emption Act, which western members succeeded in attaching to Clay's distribution bill before it became law. After its passage the "pre-emptors" of Indians lands, or lands of the United States not yet opened to settlement, were assured that in case they were actual residents on their claims and had made slight improvements, they might, when the government offered the land for sale, buy as much as 160 acres at the minimum price.

Growth of the West. The West as a haven of refuge was discovered, however, long before it received this legislative blessing. During the boom period two new western states, Arkansas (1836) and Michigan (1837), were admitted to the Union, and in the next few years their population rapidly increased. So also did the population of all the western states where cheap lands were still available. But the most startling development occurred in the territories that were soon to become the states of Wisconsin, Iowa, and Minnesota. Here land was still to be found that government surveyors had not entered, and here squatters by the thousand took claims which for the time being cost them nothing. Here many of the unemployed found jobs and at the same time created by their efforts a new market for the goods which the older sections so much needed to sell.

Whig Dissensions. The conflict between Tyler and Clay wrecked all hope of Whig harmony. At Clay's behest the entire Tyler Cabinet, with the exception of Webster, resigned, and the President was formally read out of the party. Naturally this dis-

sension at Washington had an adverse effect on the voters, and in the elections of 1842 the Whigs lost their majority in the House of Representatives, although they still controlled the Senate. Clay himself dramatically retired to private life. His farewell speech to the Senate moved many of his auditors to tears, even though everyone knew that he would be a candidate for the Presidency in 1844. Meanwhile legislation, except on routine matters, was at a standstill.

The Webster-Ashburton Negotiations. Webster's decision to remain in Tyler's Cabinet was due in part, no doubt, to his unwillingness to have it appear that Clay could tell him what to do; but he also believed that he was well fitted to effect a settlement of the serious difficulties that had arisen between the United States and Great Britain. Fortunately the British Prime Minister, Sir Robert Peel, was equally interested in maintaining good relations between the two countries and sent as special envoy to Washington Lord Ashburton, a man well versed in American matters with whom Webster found it easy to cooperate.

New States —

MICHIGAN 1837

ARK. 1836

The Canadian insurrection of 1837 was responsible for a part of the trouble, for many Americans had sympathized with the insurrectionists and had tried to help them. On one occasion some Canadian rebels had chartered a small steamship, the *Caroline,* to bring them supplies and volunteers from the American side of the Niagara River. The British, perhaps owing to a misunderstanding, seized the offending vessel when it was in American waters, and sent it in flames over the falls. In this action one member of the *Caroline's* crew was killed, and several were injured. The matter was further complicated when in November, 1840, a Canadian named Alexander McLeod boasted that he was the member of the boarding party who had killed the American. Thereupon McLeod was promptly arrested and brought to trial for murder in the New York state courts. By the time Webster became Secretary of State, threats of war quite out of keeping with the importance of the episode had been freely exchanged. Webster, however, kept a watchful eye on the trial of McLeod, and was not surprised when the prisoner was acquitted on an alibi. The international tension was further eased by concessions on both sides. The United States officially agreed that the British were right in contending that in military affairs individuals were not responsible for carrying out orders issued by their government, and Congress, at Webster's request, passed a law which provided that in the future the accused in all such cases should have the right of appeal to the federal courts. The British, while maintaining that their part in the *Caroline* affair was strictly defensible, expressed regret that it had ever occurred.

Boundary Disputes.   The vagueness of the Treaty of 1783 on the northeastern, or Maine, boundary of the United States had also bred trouble, for about 12,000 square miles of territory could reasonably be claimed by both Canada and the United States. Clashes between American and Canadian lumberjacks in the disputed area led by the end of the 1830's to what was called the "Aroostook War." Early in 1842 Webster and Ashburton negotiated a settlement that gave the United States a little more than half of the territory in dispute. Two other minor boundary disputes were settled in the same treaty. The northern boundary of New York had been incorrectly surveyed, but Webster and Ashburton wisely agreed to accept as the international boundary the old line, which had been marked off originally in 1774. Also, the boundary west from Lake Superior through the Lake of the Woods, which had been inadequately defined in earlier negotiations, was reconciled with existing geographic information. West of the Lake of the Woods to the Rockies the Canadian-American boundary took the form that it still retains, but Webster and Ashburton felt no call to settle the Oregon question.

Probably as a result of the *Caroline* affair, it was decided to include in the treaty an article on extradition, something wholly lacking in Anglo-American relations since the expiration of the Jay Treaty. Seven crimes were listed, "murder, or assault to commit murder, or piracy, or arson, or robbery, or forgery, or the utterance of forged paper," for which extradition was to be required. Embezzlement, unfortunately, was not included, and for a long time the phrase "gone to Canada," implied in the American vernacular that the traveler was guilty of this crime. Later, however, the list of extraditable offenses was greatly extended.

The Slave Trade.   Another subject that the treaty dealt with was the international slave trade. In 1807 Great Britain, and the following year the United States, had declared this trade illegal, and in a short time practically all the other civilized nations of the world had done likewise. But as long as slavery existed anywhere, there were bound to be those who were willing to take the risk of breaking the law. Great Britain took the lead in efforts to suppress this nefarious traffic and succeeded in obtaining from many countries permission to visit and search suspected vessels, regardless of the flag they happened to fly. However, when American ships were so molested the United States entered vigorous protests. Webster and Ashburton at length agreed that both powers should keep strong naval forces off the coast of Africa, the two squadrons to cooperate whenever occasion demanded. This agreement was reasonable enough, but the United States failed to maintain its quota of ships in African waters, and until the time of the Civil War the American flag continued to be used freely by ships engaged in the slave trade.

The *Creole* Affair. Webster and Ashburton were also forced by circumstances to try to smooth out irritations that had arisen because of the practice, common along the Atlantic seaboard, of transporting slaves by sea from one part of the United States to another. On several occasions ships engaged in this maritime domestic slave trade were compelled because of storms or other exigencies to put in at some British West Indian port, whereupon the slaves they carried were promptly set free by the British authorities. In 1841 the *Creole* case brought this matter to a dramatic head. The *Creole* was an American ship bound from Virginia to New Orleans with a cargo of 135 slaves. During the voyage the slaves engaged in a successful mutiny, killing one person and wounding several others, and then took the ship into the British port of Nassau, where, with the exception of those held responsible for murder, they were given their freedom. On this case Webster and Ashburton were unable to reach a final agreement, but Ashburton accepted the principle that there should be "no officious interference with American vessels driven by accident or by violence" into British ports, and in 1853, a British umpire, Joshua Bates, to whom the case had been submitted for arbitration, awarded the United States damages of $110,330. Thirty years before, any one of these controversies with Great Britain might have been the prelude to war. But gradually the two nations were developing the habit of settling quarrels by negotiation.

SELECTED BIBLIOGRAPHY

For Jackson's war with the Bank of the United States, see the excellent collection of materials brought together by G. R. Taylor in *Jackson versus Biddle* (1949). The standard work on its subject remains R. C. H. Catterall, *The Second Bank of the United States* (1903), strongly pro-Biddle. An excellent critical biography is T. P. Govan, *Nicholas Biddle* (1959). On Taney's role as Secretary of the Treasury, see C. B. Swisher, *Roger B. Taney* (1936). The financial unsettlement that followed Jackson's overthrow of the Bank is treated with commendable directness and brevity in R. C. McGrane, *The Panic of 1837* (1924). See also M. S. Wildman, *Money Inflation in the United States* (1905); M. G. Madeleine, *Monetary and Banking Theories of Jacksonian Democracy* (1943); and L. C. Helderman, *National and State Banks* (1931). David Kinley, *The Independent Treasury of the United States and its Relations to the Banks of the Country* (1910), deals effectively with the national situation. On state banking, D. R. Dewey, *State Banking before the Civil War* (1910), is particularly good on banking methods. On state debts, see W. A. Scott, *The Repudiation of State Debts* (1893); and R. C. McGrane, *Foreign Bondholders and American State Debts* (1935). On land, see G. M. Stephenson, *The Political History of the Public Lands from 1840 to 1862* (1917); and A. G. Bogue, *Money at Interest* (1955).

The attempt to define "Jacksonian Democracy" has led to much controversy among historians, especially during the present generation. Two recent collections illustrate the varying interpretations: *Jacksonian Democracy; Myth or Reality?*, edited by J. L. Bugg, Jr. (1962); and E. C. Rozwenc (ed.), *The Meaning of Jacksonian Democracy* (1963). Richard Hofstadter has a stimulating essay on the subject in his *The American Political*

* Available in paperback

Tradition and the Men Who Made It (1948).
A. M. Schlesinger, Jr., °*The Age of Jackson*
(1945), is a brilliant reevaluation, which finds
the sources of Jackson's power in the urban
working classes rather than in the frontier
farmers. This line of argument was earlier advanced by the socialist writer A. M. Simons in
Social Forces in American History (1911);
and by A. M. Schlesinger, Sr., in one of the
chapters of *New Viewpoints in American History* (1922). A number of labor historians
strongly dissent from this interpretation; see
Walter Hugins, *Jacksonian Democracy and the
Working Class, A Study of the New York
Workingmen's Movement, 1829–1837* (1960).
Two recent efforts to get at the essence of
Jacksonian Democracy are J. W. Ward,
°*Andrew Jackson, Symbol for an Age* (1955);
and Marvin Meyers, °*The Jacksonian Persua-
sion* (1957). Useful anthologies are: *The
Leaven of Democracy*, edited by Clement
Eaton, (1963); and E. C. Rozwenc (ed.),
°*Ideology and Power in the Age of Jackson*
(1964).

For new political developments, see Charles
McCarthy, *The Antimasonic Party* (1903);
and S. R. Gammon, *The Presidential Campaign
of 1832* (1922). In recent years a number of
state studies of Jacksonian Democracy have
appeared, including H. R. Stevens, *The Early
Jackson Party in Ohio* (1957); W. S. Hoffman,
°*Andrew Jackson and North Carolina Politics*
(1958); C. M. Snyder, *The Jacksonian Heritage; Pennsylvania Politics, 1833–1848* (1958);
and E. A. Miles, °*Jacksonian Democracy in
Mississippi* (1960). W. D. Burnham, *Presidential Ballots, 1836–1892* (1955), is a highly
useful compilation of election statistics. Important biographies of Jackson men include
J. A. Garraty, *Silas Wright* (1949); C. G. Sellers, Jr., *James K. Polk, Jacksonian, 1795–1843*
(1957); and I. D. Spencer, *The Victor and the
Spoils; A Life of William L. Marcy* (1959).

On diplomacy and expansion, see especially
two broad-gauged interpretations: A. K. Weinberg, °*Manifest Destiny* (1935); and R. W.
Van Alstyne, *The Rising American Empire*
(1960). Interesting monographs include G. A.
King, *The French Spoliation Claims* (1912);
and Henry Blumenthal, *A Reappraisal of Franco-
American Relations, 1830–1871* (1959).

On Texas, see the excellent brief treatment
in R. A. Billington, °*The Far Western Frontier,
1830–1860* (1956), a very sprightly synthesis.

Two good books by the leading Texas historian
E. C. Barker are *The Life of Stephen F. Austin*
(1925), and *Mexico and Texas, 1821–1835*
(1928). Two recent books by J. M. Nance,
After San Jacinto (1963), and *Attack and
Counterattack* (1964), treat Texas from 1836
to 1842. On Sam Houston, see Marquis James,
°*The Raven* (1929); and M. K. Wisehart, *Sam
Houston* (1962). Works on the Lone Star
Republic include: W. R. Hogan, *The Texas
Republic* (1946); J. W. Schmitz, *Texas State-
craft, 1836–1845* (1941); Stanley Siegel, °*A
Political History of the Texas Republic, 1836–
1845* (1956); and E. D. Adams, *British Inter-
ests and Activities in Texas, 1838–1846* (1910).

On Van Buren, see *The Autobiography of
Martin Van Buren*, edited by J. C. Fitzpatrick
(1920), rich although incomplete. An excellent recent monograph is R. V. Remini, *Martin
Van Buren and the Making of the Democratic
Party* (1959). Excellent on the election of
1840 is R. G. Gunderson, *The Log-Cabin Campaign* (1957). On the Whigs, see E. M. Carroll, *Origins of the Whig Party* (1925); G. R.
Poage, *Henry Clay and the Whig Party* (1936);
and A. C. Cole, *The Whig Party in the South*
(1913). The Harrison and Tyler administrations are covered by O. D. Lambert, *Presidential Politics in the United States, 1841–1844*
(1936). Biographies of Harrison include Freeman Cleaves, *Old Tippecanoe* (1939); and
J. A. Green, *William Henry Harrison* (1941).
The standard life of the second Whig President
is O. P. Chitwood, *John Tyler* (1939), scholarly but sympathetic; but see also *And Tyler
Too*, by Robert Seager, II (1963). R. J. Morgan, *A Whig Embattled* (1954), is a careful
study of the Tyler administration. See also
G. G. Van Deusen, *Thurlow Weed* (1947).

J. S. Reeves, *American Diplomacy under
Tyler and Polk* (1907), is a competent survey.
On Anglo-American relations during this period
there have been a number of important mono-
graphs, among them: A. B. Corey, *The Crisis
of 1830–1842 in Canadian-American Relations*
(1941); J. F. Sprague, *The Northeastern
Boundary Controversy and the Aroostook War*
(1910); and H. G. Soulsby, *The Right of
Search and the Slave Trade in Anglo-American
Relations, 1814–1862* (1933). An able study
of a subject unknown to most Americans is
G. D. Lillibridge, °*Beacon of Freedom; The
Impact of American Democracy upon Great
Britain, 1830–1870* (1954).

14

THE FLOWERING OF
THE AMERICAN MIND

The New Democratic Culture. By 1830 the intellectual and emotional bases for the old Federal culture had largely been eroded away. The vigorous and often narrow spirit of nationalism bred by the War of 1812, the rampant democratic and egalitarian creed of Jacksonianism, the steadily developing sense of confidence which accompanied the material progress of the new country, and a new way of looking at the world which can perhaps best be described as Romantic — all these things had created a new culture. The elitist and aristocratic sentiments of the European-centered Federalists had been submerged in a society both more democratic and more provincial in tone. Romanticism rather than Classicism was the dominant intellectual attitude of this new society between 1830 and 1860.

Man's emotional and intuitive powers were emphasized rather than his rational faculties, his "natural" goodness rather than the cultivation of intellect and taste. The artistic bent of Romanticism was toward complexity and ebullience rather than Classical balance and restraint. The Romantic age was characterized by a quickening of the American mind and resulted in a remarkable literary flowering, in a vigorous growth of popular culture, in diverse religious developments and, except for the South, in an impulse toward reform.

Emerson. Ralph Waldo Emerson (1803–1882) reflected much that was close to the mind and spirit of his age. Descended from a long line of New England preachers, he attended Harvard and studied for the ministry. But after brief service in the Unitarian pulpit he resigned because he had lost faith in the tenets of Unitarianism and found himself unable to perform its sacraments and prayers. After an extended trip to Europe, Emerson returned to Concord, Massachusetts, where he devoted the remainder of his life to writing and public lecturing. Within a few years he became not only the nation's most eminent man of letters, but also its reigning popular philosopher. He encouraged the American taste for individualism, for curtailing the power

RALPH WALDO EMERSON

Few American intellectuals have so impressed their age as did this Concord, Massachusetts poet, essayist and philosopher.

of the state, and for reform. He firmly believed that the individual was uniquely able to move the world toward perfection, while the state represented the restraint of custom and the past. But individualism to Emerson did not imply hostility to social reform. Essentially, however, he argued for the substitution of individual self-discipline and control for the coercive power of the state.

Transcendentalism. Emerson never achieved a systematic philosophy, but at the core of his thoughts was a group of doctrines which came to be known as Transcendentalism. Its roots lay in the thinking of the German idealist, Kant, in the writings of the English Romantics, in neo-Platonic ideas of perfectibility, in several strains of Oriental philosophy, and certainly in the developing New England religious spirit. It was based upon the assumption that while the world of man and nature was made up of a bewildering variety of separate entities, the great unifying reality was the spiritual power of God, or the Over-Soul, and that every individual and all parts of nature were infused with this spiritual element and could strengthen their contact with it. Consequently there was much to be learned from nature, for whose teachings Emerson sought to be a "transparent eyeball." The Transcendentalists believed that great truths came less from minute observation than from intuitive contemplation and mystical perception. The fundamental truth about man was that he contained within his soul a part of the spiritual power of the Over-Soul. Thus he was capable of continuous improvement until he neared the perfection in goodness, truth, and beauty which characterized the Godhead.

Emerson was not alone in spreading the word of the new Transcendentalist gospel. In Boston, from 1836 to 1843, a small group of like-minded men, Emerson among them, met together informally. In 1840 they began publication of *The Dial*, through which many of Emerson's writings reached the public. Nearly all the original Transcendentalists became nationally prominent: Henry Thoreau as one of the masters of American prose; Bronson Alcott, Theodore Parker, and James Freeman Clarke as preachers and lecturers; and George Ripley and Margaret Fuller as editors and literary critics. The Transcendentalists dreamed of an America which should live up to its opportunities, and, because they thought it so often failed to do so, they criticized it scathingly. In 1840 some of them, hoping to substitute "a system of brotherly cooperation" for "one of selfish competition," took part in the establishment of Brook Farm, near West Roxbury, Massachusetts. Here they labored in common and allotted much time to social and literary activities. The experiment lasted several years and, because of its originators, attracted wide attention.

Thoreau. Emerson once noted that he could not recall a single individual who had "defied the authority of the laws, on the simple ground of his own moral nature." But his young admirer, Henry David Thoreau (1817–1862), went to jail in 1846 for refusing to pay a poll tax to a government that countenanced the institution of slavery. On the basis of this experience Thoreau wrote his famous essay "Civil Disobedience," which a century later inspired Mohandas Gandhi to inaugurate his campaign of passive resistance against the British for the freedom of India. Thoreau is best known, however, for his nature writings, and his description of life at Walden Pond near Concord, Massachusetts, is a classic. Thoreau exemplified the romantic and rebellious individual of his age. He never married, never held a regular job, and despised material wealth. Property, he wrote, was easier to inherit than to dispose of. He was content to spend his life reading and writing, lecturing when he could, and living close to nature.

Longfellow and Whittier. New England produced also a number of writers in the romantic, optimistic tradition. However modern critics may estimate him, Henry Wadsworth Longfellow (1807–1882) was a great poet to those of his own age. In 1835 he was appointed to a teaching position at Harvard, and from that time on he was closely identified with the intelligentsia. In his poetic forms Longfellow followed European models and often made use of European themes; indeed, some of his best work is in his translations. But he also used American motifs, as in "Evangeline," "The Courtship of Miles Standish," and "Hiawatha," although in such a restrained and genteel manner that the originals would hardly have recognized themselves. Longfellow's romanticism, his aloofness from the sometimes painful realities of life, and his gentle, soothing rhymes appealed greatly to the American masses.

Less popular than Longfellow, but more indigenous, was John Greenleaf Whittier (1807–1892). He was born in Massachu-

setts, of Quaker parents. His first publication of consequence, *Legends of New England* (1831), exploited themes with which he had a natural intimacy, but he was soon caught up in the antislavery crusade, and turned his talent toward that cause. He advocated the overthrow of slavery by pacific means, but he portrayed its evils in verse vivid enough to gratify the most fervent abolitionist. His "Ichabod," a scathing denunciation of Webster for supporting the Compromise of 1850, clearly reveals his intransigence. His output was more limited than Longfellow's, and his poetic competence less marked, but his influence upon the course of events was far greater.

Holmes and Lowell. Among the other major figures of the New England Renaissance were Oliver Wendell Holmes (1809–1894) and James Russell Lowell (1819–1891). Holmes is known for his poetry no less than for his prose, but for his wit and humor most of all. He hated Calvinism cordially, and could celebrate its collapse in the amusing "Wonderful One Hoss Shay." His *Autocrat of the Breakfast-Table* showed him to be a master of the worldly lore and native drollery of the Yankees. Lowell, like Holmes, was remarkable for his versatility. A New England Brahmin, he expressed himself admirably in dialect poems, such as the *Biglow Papers*, many of which, like the poems of Whittier, had definite antislavery views. But Lowell was also a political essayist of note, a professor at Harvard, editor of the *Atlantic Monthly,* and later one of the editors of the *North American Review.*

Whitman. Although many of the New England writers chronicled some of the dominant themes of American life, none really reflected the lusty, robust, democratic vigor and aspiration of the masses. That remained for Walt Whitman (1819–1892), who caught the democratic spirit of his time and echoed it in vigorous free verse. Born in Brooklyn of a radical Jeffersonian carpenter father and a Quaker mother, Whitman had acquired the optimism and faith in the individual which characterized the Transcendentalists. But, unlike them, he was of the people. His *Leaves of Grass,* a volume of poems in free verse, registered a more complete break with the forms of poetic tradition than anything that had come out of New England. The book teemed with hymns to democracy, to the pioneers, to the flesh, to the characters of the New York City underworld, and to the American experiment. He was an authentic voice of the people, speaking in the native idiom of his country.

Hawthorne. Literature was not entirely dominated by optimism and confidence. Nathaniel Hawthorne (1804–1864) wrote of a world full of dark forces in which evil and a sense of guilt tinged the lives of most men whose chief hope was the leaven of the human heart. Much of Hawthorne's greatest writing was about his stern Puritan ancestors. In *The Scarlet Letter* (1850) and in numerous superb short stories, he drew up a powerful indictment against their system of moral values. He dealt just as darkly and soberly with his contemporaries. The characters in *The House of the Seven Gables* (1851) were as powerless against the evil forces surrounding them and as guilt-ridden as were his Puritan characters. His preoccupation with moral values, his haunting symbolism, his artistry with words, and his deep psychological insight gave his writings permanent value which only a later age, less confident of its individual and collective future, could properly appreciate.

Melville. Another great literary objector to the confident assumptions of the age was Herman Melville (1819–1891). Born in New York City of poor parents, Melville early became a sailor and saw much of the South Seas. Returning to the United States in 1844, he began to write novels, which were widely read as a mixture of travel and romance. The greatest of these was *Moby Dick* (1851), the story of a "strange fierce

white whale" and his remorseless pursuer, Captain Ahab. Read either as a tale of the sea or for its symbolic statement of the human condition, the book is a masterpiece, epic in conception, universal in theme, poetic in language. Yet, at the time of its publication it was rejected by a public baffled at its depths and disquieted by its melancholy tone. In the last year of his life he completed *Billy Budd,* another profound comment upon the nature of good and evil, guilt and innocence, and the ironies of justice and law. But Melville had been so completely forgotten that the book could not be published until 1924. Only a later generation, assaulted by misfortune and tragedy, could appreciate his deeply pessimistic and tragic view of life.

Poe. Edgar Allan Poe (1809–1849) was another writer of stature and a profound influence on writers of a later time. Poe was born in Boston, was brought up by foster parents in Richmond, Virginia, and worked as a journalist in New York and Baltimore. He was intensely interested in literary theory, and was a stylist of a high order. Best known for a few melodic poems such as "The Raven," "The Bells," and "Annabel Lee," and for short stories, Poe's principal contributions to literature are in the advances he made in the short story as a form, and in the stimulus he gave to a group of late nineteenth-century French poets who called themselves symbolists.

The Historians. Any survey of middle period literature would be incomplete without mentioning its able group of historians. Foremost among those who treated upon North America were George Bancroft (1800–1891) and Francis Parkman (1823–1893), both natives of Massachusetts and Harvard graduates. Bancroft, after postgraduate study in Germany, returned to the United States where he soon became involved in politics. He was for a time Secretary of the Navy under James K. Polk, and later became minister to Great Britain (1846–1849) and to Germany (1864–1874).

His most notable work was a ten-volume *History of the United States* (1834–1876), written in a strongly patriotic vein, which achieved great popularity.

The career of Parkman was vastly different. At the age of twenty-three he undertook a journey to Wyoming, which he recounted in *The California and Oregon Trail* (1849) This strenuous trip overtaxed his health, and he remained thereafter a semi-invalid, rarely venturing from his Boston home. Parkman fixed his attention upon the struggle between the British and French for the domination of North America, a theme he developed with great success and genuine literary distinction in his monumental series *France and England in North America* (1865–1892). Two other New England historians, William H. Prescott (1796–1859) and John Lothrop Motley (1814–1877), combined keen historical perception with a literary flair. Both looked beyond the United States for their subjects, and both won enviable reputations at home and in Europe. Prescott centered his interest in the history of Spain and in the Spanish empire in America, while Motley dealt with the early history of the Dutch nation.

The Arts. It is a curious fact that the literary activities of the years following 1830 were not paralleled by similar successes in the realm of the arts. Indeed, the period witnessed a decline in such fields as painting and architecture. The blame for this state of affairs is usually placed on the triumph of democracy — a triumph which exalted the taste of the ordinary man. But this explanation is not entirely satisfying, for by the same reasoning a dearth of good literature should also have developed. One might rather suppose that the artists found it more difficult than the men of letters to keep abreast of the Industrial Revolution. The traditions that bound them were more rigid than literary forms; the materials they worked with were less plastic than words. Not only in the United States, but throughout the western world, the arts were at low ebb during the middle decades of the nineteenth century.

American architecture throughout this period was strikingly devoid of originality. The classical vogue still flourished, and replicas of early Greek temples were everywhere in evidence. For public buildings the favorite design was a combination of dome and portico. Dwelling houses were apt to reveal the old Georgian influence of the colonial period, although there was a tendency to copy anything that anybody had ever done anywhere. About the middle of the century American builders began to follow European architects in a sharp revolt against classicism. Gothic forms were revived, and excessive ornamentation replaced simplicity.

Buildings are a necessity, and architecture of a kind is therefore indispensable in any age, but the same can hardly be said of painting and sculpture, which throughout the period were almost nonexistent in the United States. Portrait painters there were, but they exhibited little of the distinction shown by the post-Revolutionary artists; the beginnings of photography soon also threatened their craft. A group of landscape painters — the "Hudson River School" — called attention to the beauty of American scenes, but their technique was European, not American, and their achievements were mediocre. American sculptors had even less to their credit. What few of them there were clung tenaciously to classical models and did their best to make American politicians look like Roman statesmen.

Music. In music, too, dependence on Europe remained marked. Musical societies were common in the larger cities, European artists often made American tours, a few symphony orchestras were organized, and some attempts to produce opera, mainly Italian, were made. But American composers were neither numerous nor of profound ability, although some of their work lives on. The hymns of Lowell Mason (1792–1872) are familiar to many American churchgoers. Mason also introduced the teaching of music into the public schools. Stephen C. Foster (1826–1864), a native of Pennsylvania who knew little of the South, or, for that matter, of formal music, wrote both the melodies and the words of dozens of popular songs which reflected the tempo of southern plantation life. Foster's songs, and many others like them, frequently reached the public first through blackface minstrel shows, which then enjoyed a great vogue. A few American virtuosi gained prominence, most notable among them the New Orleans-born and Paris-trained pianist-composer, Louis Moreau Gottschalk.

The Theater. Owing partly to frontier conditions and partly to the hostility of New England Puritanism, the American theater was slow to develop. During the colonial period, both plays and players were English, and the response to their efforts was not always cordial. But by the thirties and forties, most of the cities had stock companies that also used the talents of well-known actors or actresses on tour. The tendency to rely mainly upon English actors was a serious handicap to the development of native talent, but a few Americans, Edwin Forrest, Edwin Booth, and Charlotte Cushman, rivaled the best of the visitors in popularity.

The theater of this period was more famous for its actors than for its playwrights. People accustomed to the resonant oratory of Daniel Webster and Henry Clay asked nothing better than to listen to the long declamations of Shakespearean actors, and the steady devotion of theatrical patrons to the classics tended to discourage the writing of new plays. But there were a few exceptions. George Henry Boker's *Francesca da Rimini* won a place in contemporary literature, and Cora Mowatt's *Fashion, or, Life in New York* burlesqued so successfully the social pretensions of the times that it has had numerous popular revivals. Current English plays also enjoyed a considerable popularity. One of them,

Tom Taylor's *Our American Cousin,* ran one hundred and forty nights in New York.

Religious Experiments. Far more inventive than the artistic impulse was the religious mind of the period, which produced many new sects and reinvigorated older religious groups such as the Shakers. The story of the Mormons and their migration to Utah is told elsewhere in this volume. But it should be noted that their founder, Joseph Smith, was in complete accord with the thought of his day about man and his destiny. It is probable that he never read Emerson, but he could declaim "As God was, man now is. As God is, man may become."

For the Millennialists, or Millerites, the time required for man to reach the state of full heavenly grace was to be short indeed. This sect was started by William Miller, a Vermont farmer, who prophesied on the basis of a Biblical interpretation that the Second Coming of Christ would occur in 1843. When that year passed, a recalculation by Miller set the date of October 22, 1844, for the end of the world. With many enthusiastic followers spreading the word of the Second Coming throughout the country, excitement mounted as the fateful day drew near. Most of the Adventists, as they came to be known, bought ascension gowns and many gave away their earthly property. When October 22 had passed without incident, Miller was discredited, but some of his followers, insisting that the great advent was still immediate, continued to proselytize and formed the Seventh Day Adventist Church.

The Shakers originated when Mother Anna Lee, after a disastrous marriage and the death of her four children, joined the Shaking Quakers in 1758 in England. Subsequently she was enjoined by a revelation to found a new sect which would be devoted to equality and celibacy for both men and women. With eight female followers Mother Lee immigrated to America where she founded a cooperative community dedicated to the principles of celibacy, equality, neatness, simplicity, and charity. By 1830 at least fifteen Shaker communities were flourishing, housing communicants of both sexes who met each other only at meal times, in the fields when at work, and at their peculiar dances. Since celibacy continued to be a guiding principle of Shaker communities, the sect was doomed unless it could win new converts.

This preoccupation with the non-material world was again reflected in the growth of many fringe groups, which often combined in their doctrines religious, scientific, pseudoscientific, and medical strains. Among the many sects given to such occult practices as phrenology, hypnotism, and animal magnetism, the most popular perhaps was the cult of spiritualism. Of the mediums who suddenly appeared, claiming they could communicate with the spirits of the dead, the most famous were two sisters, Maggie and Katie Fox of upstate New York. As their fame spread, Syracuse became the spiritualist center of America. The impetus of the spiritualist movement was diminished by the confessions of the Fox sisters that their rappings had not come from souls from outer space and time but were faked. Still, the cult continued to interest many Americans and has lasted down to the present.

The Press.   As could be expected, popular culture also flourished during the period. Scores of new magazines and newspapers appeared in every decade, chiefly patterned to the taste of the rising masses. Among the best and most successful were the *Southern Literary Messenger* (1834); *Godey's Lady's Book* (1837) which set the standard for feminine style and manners throughout most of the nineteenth century; *Harper's New Monthly Magazine* (1850); and its Boston rival, *The Atlantic Monthly* (1857). The most significant change in journalism came with the publication of the penny dailies, the first such being the *New York Sun* (1833), followed by the

LOUIS MOREAU GOTTSCHALK (1829–1869): *American Pianist-Composer*

A native of New Orleans, Gottschalk studied under Hector Berlioz in Paris, where his brilliant musicianship also won the praise of Frederic Chopin. The following extract from his Journal *describes some tribulations of the touring artist.*

What singular audiences I meet with! . . . The other evening before the concert, an honest farmer, pointing to my piano, asked me what that "big accordion was." . . . Lately a gentleman among the audience did not cease repeating during the whole concern, "When then are they going to play an air?" . . . after my five or six solos, he repeated, "I have not yet heard one air," and he went away perfectly disgusted. . . . A general . . . loves to repeat to his friends that he can recognize on hearing them but two airs — the one "Yankee Doodle," and the other which is not!

Louis Moreau Gottschalk, *Notes of a Pianist* (1881)

235

New York Herald (1835) and the *New York Tribune* (1841). The *Sun* and the *Herald* both devoted themselves to crime and sensation. But the *Tribune* under Horace Greeley became a national vehicle for education and reform. Greeley, together with his rival New York editors, set the style for an age of personal journalism. They were joined by other great editors all over the country who dominated their papers and strongly influenced all public matters.

The Lyceum. Scarcely less influential than the newspapers and magazines in providing information, education, and entertainment to the public was the lyceum movement. Begun in 1826 by Josiah Holbrook at Millburg, Vermont, as a "Society for Mutual Education," the idea spread rapidly to all parts of the country. In most towns and cities the lyceum was supported informally by groups of public-spirited citizens, but in a few large eastern cities, lyceums had independent endowments. Since its programs were made up in good part by traveling lecturers, the lyceum movement, like the national circulation of weekly newspapers, grew apace with the

development of the railroads. By 1835 there were probably more than 3,000 cities and towns scheduling a series of winter lectures and discussions. Although most lecturers devoted themselves to literature, science, morality, and health — politics and religion were too controversial — many reform ideas, including the antislavery cause, were furthered from lyceum platforms. Such eminent figures as Emerson, Webster, Louis Agassiz, the scientist, and Frances Wright, the fighter for women's rights, appeared before small town audiences throughout the East, the Middle West, and the upper South. The effect the lyceum movement had on the formulation of public opinion cannot be measured with exactitude, but certainly it created a new channel through which ideas could flow from one part of the country to another. Undoubtedly, it contributed significantly to the diversity of ideas and cultural trends.

Educational Advances. The public schools underwent great changes during this period. That each community was obligated to maintain a system of public schools was a principle first enunciated by Massachusetts, and a task carried into gen-

LECTURER AND HIS AUDIENCE AT CLINTON HALL, ABOUT 1838

A pen and ink drawing by an unknown artist with a sense of humor.

eral practice by Horace Mann, who was secretary of the State Board of Education from 1837 to 1848. Elsewhere the establishment of free schools was more difficult. In some cities, such as Philadelphia, the free-school movement gained strong support from the young labor unions which argued that public schools would decrease the number of child laborers and thus deprive fewer adults of the opportunity to work.

Generally, however, the strongest support for public schools came from humanitarian reformers who argued that every child in a democracy had the right to an education. Led by such men as Mann and Henry Barnard of Connecticut, the campaign to provide elementary education at state expense had been won well before the Civil War in every northern state. In the South the movement generally failed. The politically powerful planting families were loathe to tax themselves for public schools. In 1839, however, North Carolina provided for a system of common schools, although few such were actually instituted until the 1850's. But free public schools did not mean universal education. In some communities the law was given only a token observance, many teachers were themselves almost illiterate, and few communities required school attendance. It is probable that in the North not more than one-quarter of the white children attended the elementary schools, while in the South the comparable figure was possibly 10 to 15 per cent.

Teacher Training. The campaign for better schools prompted new efforts to secure better teachers. Teaching was often looked upon as either a temporary job or as a haven for individuals unfit for other work. Consequently, many teachers were either students preparing for the ministry or the law who carried out their teaching duties during vacations and spare time, or disabled war veterans.

By 1830, however, women began to invade the teaching field. Since at the time neither coeducational nor women's colleges existed, the educational level of teachers fell even lower. To remedy this situation, Mann, in 1839, induced Massachusetts to organize the first state-supported teacher-training school. Other states soon established similar institutions, invariably named "normal" schools after their French models.

The movement for state-supported education also promoted the establishment of tuition-free high schools and colleges. Massachusetts again led the way and by 1860 could boast of over 100 public schools, with New York not far behind. But until well after the Civil War, private academies far outnumbered public high schools, with the result that few children of the poorer class managed to obtain a high school education.

Higher education also felt the influence of reform and progress. State universities were established, especially throughout the Middle West and the South. Following the pattern already set, the great majority of the transmountain states established colleges or academies as soon as they had achieved statehood. Since these institutions were uniformly handicapped by the lack of financial support from the state legislatures, the teaching staffs were poor, facilities inadequate, and libraries almost nonexistent. One of the principal reasons for the poor support was the long-lived opposition of the denominational colleges and their affiliated churches.

Some progress was made in both private and state institutions toward improving the opportunities for women's education. In 1837 Oberlin College in Ohio enrolled four women, and before 1860 the State University of Iowa also became coeducational. In the East, during the same period, Mount Holyoke was rapidly developing into a woman's college, an example soon followed by other eastern institutions for women. All colleges offered the traditional classical curriculum. Classes in Latin, Greek, and mathematics absorbed the bulk of the student's time, although modern languages and natural science were gradually being introduced in some eastern institutions.

SAMUEL F. B. MORSE

A noted painter, sculptor, and the inventor of the telegraph, Samuel F. B. Morse was also the first instructor of the well-known photographer, Mathew Brady, in the daguerreotype process.

College students sometimes learned more from the debates and oratorical contests which literary societies and fraternities delighted to sponsor than from their classroom exercises. Few went to college except those who wished to enter one of the three learned professions, the ministry, the law, and medicine; and many entered these professions without the benefit of college, or even secondary, training. Separate divinity, law, and medical schools were fairly common among the older colleges and universities by the middle of the century, but the instruction offered, particularly for the medical students, was extremely meager. Students with a real thirst for advanced learning found it necessary, as a rule, to spend some time in Europe.

Science and Technology. With the colleges and universities almost exclusively devoted to training the learned professions, America's contributions to science could not compare with those of Europe. Still, American science was not entirely negligible. Of importance was the use of anesthetics in surgery by a Georgia physician, Dr. Crawford W. Long, in 1842. He did not publish his findings for some years, however, and in the meantime two New England dentists, Dr. Horace Wells of Hartford, Connecticut, and Dr. W. T. G. Morton of Boston, achieved similar results. American scientists also made available much descriptive data. During these years Louis J. R. Agassiz, a French-Swiss immigrant who became a Harvard professor, made important contributions to the world's knowledge of geology and zoology. John James Audubon, born in Haiti, the son of a French naval officer, and educated as an artist in France, made the United States his home and devoted his life to the classification of birds and animals, which he painted with realistic skill and high artistry. Notable also was the work of Joseph Henry, a physicist and the first head of the Smithsonian Institution, a foundation made possible by an Englishman's eccentric bequest of a half-million dollars to the United States government "for the increase and diffusion of knowledge among men." Other American scientists who won distinction were Asa Gray in botany, James Dwight Dana in mineralogy, Ormsby M. Mitchell in astronomy, and Benjamin Silliman in geology. Silliman, a professor at Yale, was not content merely with his teaching and research, but spread through popular lectures information about the work the scientists were trying to do.

More significant than the nation's scientific discoveries were its contributions to the rapid evolution of technology. In 1832, as Samuel F. B. Morse was returning to the United States from a trip abroad, he talked with his fellow passengers about some electrical experiments then being made in France and conceived the idea of the electromagnetic telegraph. He became a professor at the University of the City of New

York, where he spent much of his time in experimentation. By 1835 he had constructed in a room at the University a mile of telegraph wire over which he was transmitting messages successfully. In 1843 he obtained an appropriation of $30,000 from Congress to build an experimental line from Washington to Baltimore. On May 1, 1844, with the line completed to Annapolis, the first news message was sent over the wires. By 1850 the settled portions of the country were well supplied with telegraphic communications, and in 1858 a cable was successfully laid across the Atlantic.

The McCormick Reaper. Of major importance to agriculture was the work of Cyrus Hall McCormick, a back-country Virginian of Scotch-Irish descent, who in 1831 produced a successful reaper. His father had long sought to invent an improved harvesting machine, and had made extensive experiments which his more successful son had been able to utilize. In 1834 young McCormick patented his device. He succeeded ultimately in marketing a machine which contributed greatly to the revolution in methods of farming that characterized the middle years of the nineteenth century. The reaper was not the only new tool during this period that inventors provided for the farmer. Dozens of other useful devices were constructed, but the full effect of these inventions was long delayed.

The Sewing Machine. Another American invention of great importance was the sewing machine, which Elias Howe, a manufacturer of cotton-mill machinery at Lowell, Massachusetts, patented in 1846. By the early fifties the manufacture of sewing machines was being carried on extensively, and a decade later the extraordinary demands of the Civil War made the industry extremely prosperous. But the sewing machine, like the reaper, was of far greater benefit to a subsequent generation than to the one that produced it.

Several other products of the American inventive genius deserve to be mentioned. In 1830 Samuel Colt, a sixteen-year-old

McCORMICK REAPER

Through his invention of the reaper, Cyrus H. McCormick became one of the first to advocate the use of machinery in agricultural production.

Connecticut lad, whittled out a wooden model of a revolving pistol. In 1835 he patented his "revolver" in England, and next year in the United States. By 1838 a company at Paterson, New Jersey, had begun its manufacture. It is difficult to imagine what the history of the Great Plains, just then beginning, would have been like without Colt's invention. In 1836, another Connecticut Yankee, Charles Goodyear, made his first important discovery of an improved treatment for the surface of India rubber products. Some years later he perfected the vulcanizing process. In 1846, Richard M. Hoe, a New York City manufacturer of printing materials, produced the first steam cylinder press. Faster presses were an absolute necessity if the demand for more and more newspapers was to be met, and improvements upon Hoe's invention made during the next few years enabled the publishers to print an almost incredible number of papers in a minimum length of time.

Americans also showed great resourcefulness in improving and adapting inventions introduced from abroad. The English locomotive had to be made lighter and speedier to meet American needs, and railroad equipment was changed in many details. Most of the machinery used in American factories and foundries, the photograph developed from the French "daguerreotype," the "loco-focos," or friction matches, were invented in Europe but first patented and developed in America. Heating and cooking stoves, which had ancestors on both sides of the Atlantic, were made sufficiently practical during the period to cause the closing-off of many handsome fireplaces. By the middle of the century furnaces and plumbing fixtures were being installed, whale-oil lamps were replacing candles, gas lighting systems were spreading from city to city, tinware was being substituted for costlier copper and iron kitchen utensils, woven carpets superseded the old-fashioned rag rugs, and wallpaper was coming into general use. At least for the city dweller, life was becoming increasingly comfortable.

The Labor Problem. By far the best evidence of the vigorous creative qualities of American society in the prewar years was the widespread demand for social and humanitarian reform. The rapid industrialization of the country had, as in Europe, created dissatisfactions that unquestionably contributed to the demand for change. The rapid advance of the factory system in the American Northeast created a serious labor problem. Under the vanishing domestic system apprentices and journeymen could hope ultimately to become master craftsmen and employers, but only rarely was it possible under the new system for a workman to climb into the capitalist class. As the number of employees under a single management grew, the line of cleavage between the two classes deepened. Competition among manufacturers was keen, and the need of keeping down labor costs led frequently, especially in the textile mills, to the employment of women and children. Long hours of labor were required in the early factories — "from dawn to dark," or from thirteen to fifteen hours a day, was not unusual. Since most of the original "hands," or operators, had been recruited from the farms, where these long working hours had been the rule, the laborers at first saw no reason to protest. But bad lighting and poor ventilation were only two of the abuses which made the factories dangerous

to life and limb. Children were given little if any opportunity for schooling, women were kept away from the duties of the home, and heads of families were often unemployed because of the competition of women and children.

As the lot of the laborer grew harder, the strength of the employer grew greater. During the decade of the twenties American manufacturers increased their output six times over, while by 1830, with a total investment about one-fifth as great as that of all the southern plantations combined, they were turning out goods worth one and one-half times as much. To the wealthy manufacturers the lawyers looked for fees, the ministers for salaries, the colleges for endowments, the shopkeepers for goods on credit. Even the farmers, who supplied the foodstuffs to the factory towns, and the laborers themselves, who had no other means of subsistence than their factory jobs, generally accepted the manufacturer's point of view. His will became the will of the community.

Such a denial of the democratic tenets of the age should have aroused criticism sooner than it did. But the right of individual freedom was a heritage no less prized by Americans than democracy itself. An employer, according to this tradition, must be left free to conduct his business as he chose; an employee must be equally free to accept or reject the contract he was offered. When, early in the nineteenth century, artisans in some of the larger cities sought through unions to force their employers to raise wages, public opinion rallied strongly to the support of the employers. Courts that made use of the English common law to punish strikers for "conspiracy to raise wages" were applauded.

Trades Unions. In spite of these obstacles the country witnessed during the decade before the panic of 1837 a well-defined and relatively successful labor movement. Its leadership came from the artisans rather than from the factory hands, but the benefits were shared quite generally by all types of laborers. Prior to 1827 the few labor organizations formed in the United States were merely local trades unions. But in the year mentioned the failure of a carpenters' strike in Philadelphia led to the formation of the Mechanics' Union of Trade Associations, a federation of many trades unions. By thus combining forces the Philadelphia workingmen found that their power was enormously increased. Strikes, when supported by the city federation, had a good chance to win, and the political influence of so large a group of voters was not to be despised. Soon other cities were similarly organized, and from 1830 to 1837 a national federation held annual meetings.

The city federation revealed a strong penchant for political action. The recent widening of the suffrage had made voters of the workingmen, and the possibility of turning this newly won weapon to good purpose was too obvious to be overlooked. Mechanics' lien laws, free schools supported by public taxes, the abolition of imprisonment for debt, and the abolition of chartered monopolies were among the demands of the Philadelphia workingmen, who for four years, beginning in 1828, regularly nominated candidates for office. During the same period, a Workingman's Party was active in New York. Workingmen's parties existed in many other cities, and steps were even taken toward the formation of a national labor party. This movement was undermined and defeated by the old parties only at the cost of taking over and putting into effect many of the reforms which the workingmen demanded.

To supplement their political activities the workingmen resorted also to strikes. These were particularly numerous during the four years of lush prosperity, 1833–1837, when there were no less than 168 such conflicts. Of this number 103 were held to secure higher wages, and twenty-six for a ten-hour day. Strikers also demanded what came later to be called the "closed shop";

that is, the employment of union men only. Even the factory operatives, who had at first taken little part in the labor movement, now began to strike. Through these direct methods the workingmen gained some victories, although the courts remained on the whole hostile. In 1842, however, the Massachusetts Supreme Court relaxed the rule of conspiracy to the extent of holding that labor organizations might legally seek to advance wages "by rules binding solely on members." By this time, however, the labor movement was at low ebb; indeed, lack of employment after the panic of 1837 led to the disintegration of many unions.

Labor Reforms. The untimely decline of this first American labor movement did not prevent it from winning many substantial victories. A number of the strikes for a ten-hour day were successful, and the demand for shorter hours attracted much favorable comment, even outside labor circles. In 1840 President Van Buren proclaimed the ten-hour day in effect on all public works conducted by the national government. In 1847 the state of New Hampshire legalized the ten-hour day "except in pursuance of an express contract requiring greater time." Other states followed this precedent, employers reluctantly swung into line, and by 1860 the ten-hour day was general throughout the country, although longer hours were by no means unknown, particularly in New England. In nearly all the states new mechanics' lien laws were passed which gave the claims of laborers for wages precedence over the claims of those who merely furnished materials. Imprisonment for debt was abolished throughout the North by 1840, although in the South it still continued. Also, laws designed to safeguard the life and health of factory workers were enacted with increasing frequency.

Reform Leadership. Even though the developing labor unions and the labor reform measures passed in the period signified the rise of a new social class which in the future would vitally affect reform movements, neither the unions nor their well-wishers contributed markedly to the social agitation that characterized the period. Nor did the Jacksonian Democratic leaders who had led the recent movement for political reforms. Most of the reform leaders who gave impetus to the numerous social changes, as distinguished from political ones, were Whigs instead of Democrats, and came from New England, New York, and northern Ohio. Stoutly opposed to the collective efforts of the labor unions, they preferred to emphasize the creative, ethical, and spiritual powers of the individual. Socially most reformers were middle-class intellectuals, professionals, farmers, and merchants. The essence of their creed was a confident spirit of individualism which was largely based upon their theological and ideological heritage. There was also a strong religious basis for reform. The Quaker faith had long contended that even in the humblest of men there resided an inner light, a spark of the divine spirit. The developing Unitarian theology agreed, as did the Transcendentalists who held forth the possibility that man could approach divine perfection. The optimism about human destiny was likewise reflected in Perfectionism, in Millerism, and in Mormon thinking. Long before the publication of Darwin's *The Origin of Species* in 1859, the idea of evolution enlisted able advocates on both sides of the Atlantic. Reform ideas born in Europe and Britain found an enthusiastic reception in America. In an age that believed so intensely in the capacity of mankind for improvement, society could not fail to become increasingly aware of the evils with which it was afflicted, and to seek for remedies. But during the first half of the nineteenth century these "heaven stormers" found their solution to society's ills in an intense individualism which was ethical and spiritual in nature and which had little in common with the economic individualism that developed after 1860.

Communitarian Settlements. Paradoxically, in such an individualistic age, the most comprehensive efforts for social reform in the prewar period were centered around the establishment of communitarian settlements where property was held in common and where all work was cooperative. The belief that most human ills came from the environment created by traditional social and economic institutions, particularly those brought into sharp focus as a result of industrialization, was chiefly responsible for the establishment of these communities. Orestes Brownson, the Transcendentalist, felt that the only solution was the abolition of hereditary property. Horace Greeley, surveying the misery among the unemployed in the cities, concluded that every individual's right to work had to be assured by new types of social institutions.

Although some of the early socialist experiments were inspired by Americans, most of them traced their origins back to Europe. The writings of theorists like the Frenchman Charles Fourier, the activities of such men as Robert Owen, the benevolent Scottish industrialist, and the leaders of small religious sects who sought to find a better spiritual and earthly home for their followers were all influential. Although some communitarian groups existed in Europe, America was the site of most of their experiments. Not only was cheap land easily obtainable, but the New World was still comparatively free of the old inhibiting social institutions of Europe. Thus it offered the best chance for the success of such radical experiments. The communitarians' ultimate hope was that they would establish in their small communities a new life so attractive that all of mankind would be impelled to follow their example.

Fourier Phalanxes. During the first fifty years of the nineteenth century, about 100 experimental colonies were founded in the United States, most of them located in western New York and in the Middle West. Religious groups, including the Shakers, the

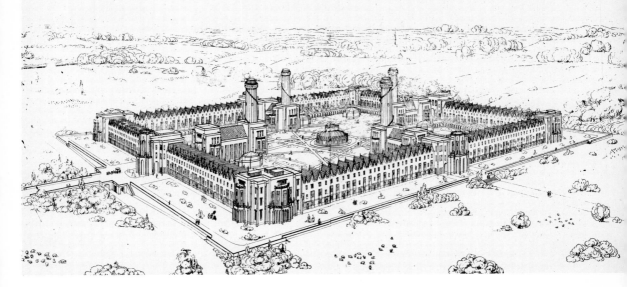

NEW HARMONY: *From the architect's drawing*

The building, it was claimed, was so located and constructed "as to form a new combination of circumstances, capable of producing permanently greater physical, moral, and intellectual advantages to every individual, than have ever yet been realized in any age or country."

Rappites, the Moravians, and the Amish, some emigrating in a body directly from Europe, accounted for many of these communities. Most of the rest were organized either by Owenite groups or followers of Fourier. Of the Owenite colonies, New Harmony, Indiana, was the most famous, attracting intellectuals, tradesmen, and artisans, as well as numerous cranks and unworldly visionaries.

Of all the early socialistic experiments those inspired by Charles Fourier were perhaps the most interesting. An eccentric French philosopher, Fourier had concluded that the only way to improve society radically was to establish self-sufficient communities, or phalanxes, each having 1,600 people, each owning three square miles, with a great phalanstery in the center where all were to live in common. Fourier's system was based upon an analysis of personality types, each of which was to be represented in the phalanx, where labor tasks would be assigned to correspond with psychological inclinations. In this way the laborious quality of "work" would be removed. Believing routine deadly and the division of labor inimical to the human personality, Fourier insisted that everyone should work at several tasks. Harmony would replace the class conflict which pervaded his own age, Fourier believed, if only his system were established. But the Fourier communities in America were soon rent by internal squabbles and tended to disappear, as did those established by the Owenites. For all of their unhappy experiences and short lives, the communitarian experiments were striking manifestations of intense reform spirit.

Temperance Reform. Other reform crusades of the period were no less intent upon freeing the individual from harmful forces. One of the most spectacular was that dedicated to temperance. Hard drinking was an English tradition transplanted to America which flourished in the new environment. Whiskey and hard cider were popular drinks, and public drunkenness, at least for men, was no disgrace. At first the movement was directed against obvious excesses. A few humanitarians connected drunkenness with poverty and crime, and sought by promoting temperance to effect a more fundamental reform. Even before 1830 many local temperance societies had been formed and by 1833 a United States Temperance Union joined these locals into one national organization. During the 1830's the temperance movement was practically taken over by the teetotalers. For more than twenty years orators denounced drinking as a crime against society; and writers such as Timothy Shay Arthur, with his highly effective *Ten Nights in a Bar-Room*, portrayed the decay of the individual who indulged in drink. This campaign of education was strikingly successful. Individuals by the tens of thousands gave up the use of liquor, churches set more rigorous standards of conduct for the clergy and often also for the laity, and excessive drinking fell into general disrepute.

Efforts to diminish the temptation that led to the downfall of so many youths suggested naturally an appeal to the power of the state. To the New Englanders, who stood in the vanguard of the movement, such an appeal was no confession of failure. Brought up, as most of them were, on the tradition that the state was properly charged with the duty of protecting the morals of the people, they could not overlook so effective an ally. Laws were demanded, and were frequently obtained, to license the liquor traffic, to hamper it with heavy taxation, and even to prohibit it altogether. State-wide prohibition of a sort was first adopted by Maine in 1846. Ohio followed in 1850, and perhaps a dozen other northern states had enacted prohibition laws before the Civil War. None of these laws was as effective as its advocates had hoped, and most of them were repealed during the Civil War period. The South was totally uninterested.

Penal Reform. Not only in the United States, but throughout the western world, the "man of sensibility" was at the crest of his power, seeking out wrongs, striving earnestly to right them. Many reform movements came to America from Europe; others originated on both sides of the Atlantic at about the same time. The rigors of penal codes, although much modified since colonial times, were still open to attack by reformers, who objected to the long sentences meted out for trivial offenses, and to the overfree use of the death penalty. The barbarities common to prisons, insane asylums, and almshouses needed only to be revealed to arouse a feeling of horror and a demand for change. Probably Dorothea L. Dix, the leading advocate in the United States of this type of reform, saw more of her ambitions realized than any other reformer of the period. New plans for dealing with convicts, designed not so much to punish as to reform them, were tried with some success, and the idea that the mentally afflicted were entitled to hospitalization and medical treatment gained support.

The Peace Movement. The sufferings incidental to war were also recognized, and the problem attacked at its source by concerted efforts to prevent the outbreak of war. As early as 1815, the formation of local organizations devoted to the cause of peace had begun in the United States. In 1828 about fifty of them joined hands to found the American Peace Society, which for decades not only carried on within the United States a steady propaganda for peace, but cooperated also with similar organizations abroad. An American peace plan was formulated which called for regular world congresses to codify international law, and a world court to apply it. Unhappily the peace movement was unable to sustain the shock of the wars which soon engulfed both Europe and America, and naturally the interest of reformers turned during the war-torn decades of the 1850's and 60's from the problem of world peace to the more pressing necessity of ameliorating the horrors of the battlefield.

Women's Rights. Of the many reform movements, the cause of women's rights was one of the most colorful. The emancipation of women enlisted the efforts of a notable company of American reformers. On both sides of the Atlantic custom had long decreed that woman's place was in the home. The education of women, therefore, except insofar as it might be of use in better fitting them for their domestic duties, was regarded as unnecessary, and even unwise. Before the 1830's not a college or university in the United States had opened its doors to women, and every other approach to the learned professions was similarly restricted to men. Also, the legal status of woman was definitely inferior to that of man: she could not vote; control of her property passed at the time of marriage to her husband; in certain matters the husband answered to the law for the conduct of his wife; legal responsibility for the children of a marriage was vested exclusively in the father.

Women as Reformers. While American men treated women with a deference that excited the comment of European travelers, the women themselves had to take the lead in the crusade for women's rights. And of these women many were led to embrace the feminist cause mainly through their interest in other reforms. So deep-seated was the prejudice against women in any public capacity that male reformers sometimes refused to accept the assistance of women, except in a definitely humble and secondary capacity. Women delegates to a World's Anti-Slavery Convention, held in London in 1840, were denied admission solely because of their sex. Two of them, Lucretia Mott and Elizabeth Cady Stanton, then realized that if women were ever to accomplish anything as reformers they must first achieve a more honorable status for themselves. In this sentiment they were supported strongly by other able women such as Frances Wright, a Scotswoman who had remained in America to work against slavery and on behalf of the emancipated slave; Lucy Stone, one of the first to demand equal suffrage; Margaret Fuller, who in 1844 published a frank book, *Women in the Nineteenth Century*; Dr. Elizabeth Blackwell, who won admission to the medical profession against almost insuperable obstacles; Dorothea L. Dix; and Mrs. Antoinette Louisa Brown Blackwell, pioneer woman preacher.

For a time almost every woman who had the temerity to address a public meeting was met with rough and raucous masculine laughter. Despite opposition and ridicule, these earnest and stouthearted women persisted, and soon a few were licensed to preach. Many others eventually won toleration and even approval as lecturers, and their contributions to many of the reform causes, especially those of temperance and anti-slavery, were not insignificant. A few states at length permitted married women to hold property separately from their husbands. And though women failed to win the vote in any state or make much of a dent in the almost total masculine monopoly of the professions, the feminine reformers did at least plant the seed for more sweeping reforms after the Civil War.

Slavery a Natural Target. In arguing for women's rights Margaret Fuller wrote that men "had the same feeling toward women as toward slaves. . . ." With the spirit of humanitarian reform so thoroughly unleashed, it was unthinkable that the continued existence of slavery in the South could long be overlooked. Ever since the French Revolution slavery had been generally frowned upon by world opinion, and its extinction had proceeded with such rapidity that by the middle of the nineteenth century the southern states of the United States, Brazil, and the Spanish colonies were the last strongholds of slavery in the civilized world. That many people in the United States were opposed to slavery became obvious during the debate on the admission of Missouri. *The Emancipator,* published monthly by Elihu Embree in Jonesboro, Tennessee, from April to October, 1820, was probably the first periodical devoted wholly to doing away with slavery. Benjamin Lundy, a New Jersey Quaker, published from 1821 to 1836 a magazine known as *The Genius of Universal Emancipation.* Lundy's gentle tactics and mild manners, however, did not satisfy William Lloyd Garrison, a young enthusiast of New-

buryport, Massachusetts, who proposed instead a crusade "as harsh as truth" and "as uncompromising as justice." With the first issue of Garrison's newspaper, the *Liberator,* published in Boston on January 1, 1831, the abolitionist movement may properly be said to have begun. So completely did this reform take the center of the stage that all other reforms soon seemed insignificant in comparison. The slavery issue was destined to shape the course of American politics for more than a generation.

SELECTED BIBLIOGRAPHY

A general introduction to most of the themes treated in this chapter may be found in C. R. Fish, *The Rise of the Common Man, 1830–1850* (1927). H. S. Commager, °*The Era of Reform, 1830–1860* (1960), is a useful short survey and collection of documents. R. H. Gabriel, *The Course of American Democratic Thought* (2nd ed., 1956), is useful from this point onward. See also Yehoshua Arieli, *Individualism and Nationalism in American Ideology* (1964); and A. A. Ekirch, *The Idea of Progress in America, 1815–1860* (1944).

On literature, a general work of great importance is F. O. Matthiessen, *American Renaissance* (1941). Provocative interpretations are R. W. B. Lewis, °*The American Adam* (1955); and Leo Marx, *The Machine in the Garden* (1964). See also two works by Van Wyck Brooks, °*The Flowering of New England* (2nd ed., 1940), and *The Times of Melville and Whitman* (1947). Interesting anthologies are Perry Miller (ed.), °*American Transcendentalists* (1957); and G. F. Whicher, (ed.), °*The Transcendentalist Revolt against Materialism* (1949).

On the principal authors of the period the literature is vast and can only be touched upon here. On Emerson, see S. E. Whicher, °*Freedom and Fate* (1953); °*Selections from Ralph Waldo Emerson,* edited by S. E. Whicher (1957); and °*The Portable Emerson,* edited by Mark Van Doren (1946). On Thoreau, see

H. S. Canby, °*Thoreau* (1939); and °*The Portable Thoreau,* edited by Carl Bode (1947). On Whitman, see H. S. Canby, *Walt Whitman* (1943); and °*The Americanness of Walt Whitman,* edited by Leo Marx (1960). On Hawthorne, see Randall Stewart, °*Nathaniel Hawthorne* (1948); and °*The Portable Hawthorne,* edited by Malcolm Cowley (1948). On Melville, see Lewis Mumford, °*Herman Melville* (1929); Newton Arvin, °*Herman Melville* (1950); and °*The Melville Reader,* edited by R. W. B. Lewis (1952). On Poe, see William Bittner, *Poe* (1962); and °*The Portable Poe,* edited by P. van D. Stern (1945). Ferris Greenslet, *The Lowells and Their Seven Worlds* (1946), is an interesting family study.

General works on historiography include Michael Kraus, *The Writing of American History* (1953); and Harvey Wish, *The American Historian* (1960). D. D. Van Tassel, *Recording America's Past; 1607–1884* (1960), narrates the development of the study of history. David Levin, °*History as Romantic Art: Bancroft, Prescott, Motley, and Parkman* (1959), is a distinguished monograph. Studies of individual historians include R. B. Nye, °*George Bancroft* (1944); and Howard Doughty, *Francis Parkman* (1962).

Many cultural topics are treated by Carl Bode, *The Anatomy of American Popular Culture, 1840–1861* (1959); note also his *The American Lyceum* (1956), an excellent monograph. A. M. Schlesinger, Sr., *Learning How*

° Available in paperback

to Behave: *A Historical Study of American Etiquette Books* (1946), is a sprightly work. Dixon Wecter, *The Saga of American Society* (1937), is lively and well-informed. Two interesting works on the book trade are David Kaser, *Messrs. Carey & Lea of Philadelphia* (1957); and Walter Sutton, *The Western Book Trade* (1961), a study of Cincinnati. On notable journalists, see Oliver Carlson, *The Man Who Made News, James Gordon Bennett* (1942); and W. H. Hale, *°Horace Greeley; Voice of the People* (1950). A standard survey is J. T. Howard, *Our American Music; Three Hundred Years of It* (3rd ed., 1954). Works on art include Nathalia Wright, *Horatio Greenough* (1963); Robert Taft, *Artists and Illustrators of the Old West, 1805–1900* (1953); and Alice Ford, *John James Audubon* (1964).

On education, basic works include Paul Monroe, *Founding of the American Public School System* (1940); and S. L. Jackson, *America's Struggle for Free Schools* (1941). *°The Republic and the School* is a selection from Horace Mann's reports, edited by L. A. Cremin (1957). A stimulating work is Merle Curti, *°The Social Ideas of American Educators* (1935). In addition to the histories of individual institutions already cited, see R. S. Fletcher, *A History of Oberlin College from its Foundation through the Civil War* (2 vols., 1943); and Frederick Rudolph, *Mark Hopkins and the Log; Williams College, 1836–1872* (1956).

A. H. Dupree, *°Science in the Federal Government* (1957), is a fine survey by a leading authority. Individual scientists have begun to attract biographers. Among the best published so far are: A. H. Dupree, *Asa Gray* (1959); Edmund and D. S. Berkeley, *John Clayton* (1963); Talbot Hamlin, *Benjamin Henry Latrobe* (1955); and Edward Lurie, *Louis Agassiz* (1960). W. T. Hutchinson, *Cyrus Hall McCormick* (2 vols., 1930–1935), is a richly detailed life of a leading inventor and promoter. Carleton Mabee, *The American Leonardo: A Life of Samuel F. B. Morse* (1943), is a lively treatment of a fascinating character. On the development of the telegraph system see R. L. Thompson, *Wiring a Continent* (1947).

An excellent survey of reform movements is A. F. Tyler, *°Freedom's Ferment* (1944). Sympathetic biographical sketches are in C. A.

Madison, *Critics and Crusaders* (2nd ed., 1959). R. E. Riegel, *Young America, 1830–1840* (1949), touches at least briefly on nearly all reform movements of the period. R. H. Bremner, *°American Philanthropy* (1960), is a short survey. Important monographs tracing the connection between religion and reform are T. L. Smith, *Revivalism and Social Reform in Mid-Nineteenth Century America* (1957); and C. S. Griffin, *Their Brother's Keepers* (1960). The standard work on the temperance movement of this period is J. A. Krout, *The Origins of Prohibition* (1925). Blake McKelvey, *American Prisons* (1936); and W. D. Lewis, *From Newgate to Dannemora* (1964), are careful treatments of one important aspect of the reform movement. Arthur Bestor, *Backwoods Utopias: The Sectarian and Owenite Phases of Communitarian Socialism in America, 1663–1829* (1950), is a superb study. The literature on the feminist movement is huge; recent surveys are Eleanor Flexner, *Century of Struggle* (1959); and R. E. Riegel, *American Feminists* (1963). On the peace movement, see Merle Curti, *Peace or War; The American Struggle, 1636–1936* (1936).

Biographies of reformers are numerous but of uneven quality. Among the best are: R. W. Leopold, *Robert Dale Owen* (1940); H. E. Marshall, *Dorothea Dix* (1937); A. J. G. Perkins and Theresa Wolfson, *Frances Wright* (1939); A. M. Schlesinger, Jr., *Orestes Brownson* (1939); H. S. Commager, *°Theodore Parker* (1936); Otelia Cromwell, *Lucretia Mott* (1958); Alma Lutz, *Emma Willard* (1929), and *Created Equal; A Biography of Elizabeth Cady Stanton* (1940); K. S. Anthony, *Margaret Fuller* (1920); and Frank Freidel, *Francis Lieber* (1947).

Good surveys of one major subject may be found in H. J. Pelling, *°American Labor* (1960); F. R. Dulles, *Labor in America* (2nd ed., 1961); and Philip Taft, *Organized Labor in American History* (1964). A great cooperative work is J. R. Commons and others, *History of Labour in the United States* (4 vols., 1918–1935). P. S. Foner, *History of the Labor Movement in the United States* (3 vols., 1947–   ), is a Marxist interpretation. Two valuable monographs are N. J. Ware, *°The Industrial Worker, 1840–1860* (1924); and W. A. Sullivan, *The Industrial Worker in Pennsylvania, 1800–1840* (1955).

15

SLAVERY AND ABOLITION

The opening of the abolitionist crusade
found the institution of slavery more deeply
entrenched in the South than ever before.
The insatiable world demand for American
cotton had produced a like demand in the
South for slaves to cultivate it. Under pressure of rapidly expanding markets, the
South produced nearly twice as much cotton
in 1830 as in 1820, fully twice as much in
1840 as in 1830, and more than three times
as much in 1860 as in 1840. Cotton exports
showed similar gains. By 1860 well over
half the value of American goods shipped
abroad was in cotton, and the South was
supplying three-quarters of the world's supply of the staple. A broad belt, ranging in
width from about 500 miles in the Carolinas and Georgia to 600 or 700 miles in the
Mississippi Valley, was devoted primarily
to cotton.

In this region, too, most of the slaves were
concentrated. Virginia had more slaves in
1860 than any other state, but with Kentucky, she depended chiefly upon tobacco

growing and general agriculture for her
prosperity. Slaves were employed, although in smaller numbers, in the Carolina-
Georgia rice fields, in the production of
Louisiana sugar cane, in hemp growing,
and in many of the small textile mills and
tobacco factories which were beginning to
appear.

Growth of Slavery. The demand for
slaves in the lower South led both to an increase in the slave population and in the
price of slaves. Between 1820 and 1860 the
number grew from about 1.5 million to
nearly 4 million, while the price of a good
field hand rose from $300 or so to over
$1,000. So great was the demand for slaves
that their importation, although illegal, was
carried on surreptitiously. Even freed Negroes, living either in the North or the
South, were in danger of being kidnaped
and sold back into slavery.

The ownership of slaves was confined to
a relatively small number of whites. In
1860, more than 72 per cent of the white
population of North Carolina, 65 per cent
of that of Tennessee, and perhaps 40 per
cent of the farmers of Alabama held no
slaves. There were extensive regions in the
South where the number of slaves was negligible. By 1860 probably fewer than 400,-
000 families — approximately one-fourth of
the South's population — held slaves. Furthermore, at least two-thirds of these fami-

lies held fewer than ten slaves each. The number of great planters — men who owned fifty or more slaves and large holdings of land — was probably not above 6,000 or 7,000.

The small farmers who lived in the cotton belt raised a considerable part of the crop; but the chief profits of the industry went to the big planter. He was in a far better position to practice scientific agriculture, and he generally owned the most fertile lands. Except in the mountain districts the small farmers, however, tended to agree with the planters in most matters connected with slavery. Poor men looked forward to the time when they would become slave-holders; and the owners of a few slaves aspired to own many. The abolition of slavery was thus opposed by the yeomen, not only because it would create a problem of control of the freed Negroes, but also because it would threaten their own superior status as free men. Thus the great planter and his customs occupy a place in the history of the South quite out of proportion to the numerical strength of his class.

The Plantation System. The plantation owner was primarily a manager. Ordinarily a single plantation, which rarely exceeded 1,000 acres, commanded his entire energies. If he owned several plantations, or if he preferred to live away from his plantation a good share of the time, he delegated authority to stewards and overseers. Practically all of the manual labor of a plantation was done by the slaves. Most of them were field hands, but every sizable plantation had its quota of skilled workers, while a favored few were selected for domestic service about the master's house. Sometimes Negro foremen, or "slave drivers," were placed in charge of small gangs of slaves. Field labor was accomplished by the gang system, in which a driver kept a group of slaves at work on a given task under fear of the lash, or by the task system, in which each individual was given a certain amount of work to do in a given period of time.

The Slave. Because the slave was valuable property, his health was a matter of considerable consequence to his owner, although the self-interest of the master was no automatic guarantee of the slave's welfare. A typical slave ration for a week consisted of three or four pounds of salt pork, a peck of corn meal, and a jar of molasses. This basic diet was often supplemented by garden vegetables from a patch of ground worked by each slave, by fish and small game, and perhaps from the master's leftovers. In the matter of food, the slave probably fared about as well as the poor white farmer. Slave living quarters, usually located near the big house of the planter, were generally primitive, but they afforded some protection, and were ordinarily provided with fireplaces although not with glazed windows. The slave's clothing was coarse but adequate. When he became ill the slave was cared for by the same physician that attended the master and his family. The life expectancy of the slave was only a few years shorter than that of white southerners.

The planter usually provided for his sick and aged slaves; layoffs and unemployment did not exist. Between the master and some of his wards, especially the house servants and artisans, a mutual affection often developed and lasted over the years. Small children, regardless of color, played together freely, and the affection of white boys and girls for their Negro nurses, or "mammies," was proverbial. The slaves were deeply religious and almost universally accepted Christianity, usually as interpreted by one of the more emotional denominations, such as the Methodists and the Baptists, whose camp meetings, revivals, and baptizings were the occasion for the slave to express himself through his own songs. A few Negroes were taught to read, but most of them acquired by word of mouth rather than by reading a considerable knowledge of the Bible and of Christian theology. Negroes sometimes worshiped separately from the whites, and

sometimes they were assigned seats in the galleries of the white people's churches. More or less formal marriages among slaves were encouraged by some masters, although a certain amount of promiscuity was taken for granted. Slave women were at the mercy of predatory white males, as their numerous mulatto progeny abundantly attested.

Slave Discipline. Although the Negro may have derived some benefits from slavery in exchange for his labor, he was also subject to some terrifying restrictions. He was a chattel of his master who, according to the Alabama legal code, owned his time, labor, services, and obedience. He was also a person to whom the master by the same law was obliged to furnish food and clothing and to provide for in sickness and old age. By the slave code of most southern states the slave was required not only to submit to his master but also to respect all white people. He could not sue in court or even give witness against white men. He was not permitted to leave the plantation without a pass which he had to show to any white person upon demand. Nor was he allowed to meet with more than a limited number of his race away from the home plantation. He was legally prohibited from owning firearms, from purchasing or possessing liquor, from owning or raising large animals such as horses, pigs, or cows, and in several states even from raising cotton. Some state codes forbade teaching a Negro to read or write. Local municipal rules often obliged him to lift his hat and to step aside when meeting whites and to refrain from swearing or smoking in the presence of white people. While in most communities these rules were never strictly enforced, they were on the books and were always enforceable if the dominant whites so desired.

Even minor slave offenses were punishable by law, but in all save the most exceptional cases, the master usually chose to mete out punishment himself. Whippings by the master or his agents were permissible by law. Although it was a punishable crime to beat a slave to death, few white men thus accused were found guilty by white juries. Most planters felt that whippings were necessary to maintain discipline, and at times a new overseer on an absentee-held plantation might whip all the field hands upon his arrival merely for the purpose of estab-

A popular English actress, Frances A. Kemble (1809–1893) was for a time the wife of a southern planter. Her revulsion over Negro slavery resulted in her Journal of a Residence on a Georgia Plantation (1863) *which had a powerful effect upon British public opinion during the Civil War.*

The habitual harsh tone of command towards these men and *women*, whose labor is extorted from them without remorse, from youth to age, and whose hopeless existence seems to me sadder than suffering itself, affects me with an intolerable sense of impotent pity for them. . . . Not a few of these slaves know and feel that they are wronged, deplore their condition, and are perfectly aware of its manifold hardships. . . . They are worked hard, poorly clothed, and poorly fed; and when they are sick, cared for only enough to fit them for work again. The only calculation in the mind of an overseer being to draw from their bones and sinews money to furnish his employer's income, and secure him a continuance of his agency.

FRANCES A. KEMBLE, *Records of Later Life* (1882)

---

lishing his authority. Some masters, and not a few of their subordinates, were exceedingly cruel, although punishment so severe as to unfit the slave for labor was an expensive indulgence which not many masters would either practice or permit. A consistently rebellious slave was usually sold. Community pressure also helped to curb cruelty; an owner with a reputation for such conduct was often ostracized by his fellow planters. A few slave owners were mean, tyrannical, and cruel; others, in common with most mankind, were subject only occasionally to the baser passions. The most damaging count against slavery, aside from the fact that it completely subjected one man to the will and power of another, was not the occasional cruelty involved, but rather the almost absolute barrier the institution placed against the slave's ability to develop his intelligence and capabilities.

The Slave Trade. Undoubtedly the most brutal aspect of slavery was the slave trade. As already noted, the international slave trade was outlawed in 1808, and after 1820 it was punishable as piracy, but the right to buy and sell slaves within the United States was unimpaired. During the

years that the cotton lands of the newer South were being opened up, the domestic slave trade throve. Because Gulf state planters needed more and more slaves at a time when the upper South was confronted by an oversupply of slaves, planters of the upper South frequently sold their slaves down South to work in the cotton fields. Except in the case of difficult slaves, however, some masters hesitated to dispose of their human property, and in many cases planters allowed themselves to become "slave poor." Others were not so squeamish, and bankruptcy or death often accomplished what masters hoped to avoid. Sometimes planters went as emigrants to the new South, taking their slaves along; but far more frequently the slaves were transported to the new region by slave traders. In 1836, the peak year, the number of slaves sold South, or taken there by their masters, from Virginia alone reached the astounding figure of 120,000. In the forties and fifties an agricultural revival took place in the upper South, due in part to the discovery of better methods of curing tobacco, and in part to the introduction of new and superior varieties. This served to check the domestic slave trade to some

251

extent. But down to 1860 there were many planters in the upper South who were engaged primarily in the business of raising slaves for sale.

The Slave Trader. The slave trader was nevertheless an object of disdain throughout the South. His business involved both the separation of families and the disciplining of slaves who had often been selected for sale because of their recalcitrance. Few high-minded men would engage in the trade, although a good many "gentlemen" were silent partners. In 1860 fifty slave trading firms operated in Charleston and at least eighteen in Richmond. To succeed among ruthless competitors, the slave trader learned to drive close bargains. He was rarely accepted into polite society; indeed, he was often treated as an outcast even by those with whom he dealt.

The collection of a group of slaves and their shipment to the lower South afforded many painful spectacles. Frequently they were marched overland in coffles to their destination, although the trader also made use of river steamers and ships engaged in the coastwise trade. Slaves were most frequently sold at auction, but the slave trader availed himself of every opportunity to sell, and stops along the route of march, or at wharves, were utilized for the cultivation of purchasers. Sometimes slaves were hired out for long or short periods of service, in which case the employer succeeded to the disciplinary authority of the master. Hired slaves were more frequently overworked and mistreated than slaves directly under the control of their masters.

Negro Attitudes. Since few slaves were literate, there is little direct written evidence to indicate the attitude of the slaves themselves toward their condition of bondage. Indirect evidence points to the conclusion that most of them disliked the institution intensely and took every safe opportunity to express their sentiments.

Early in the century three slave con-

SLAVERY RECORD.

INSURRECTION IN VIRGINIA!
Extract of a letter from a gentleman to his friend in Baltimore, dated

'Richmond, August 23d.

An express reached the governor this morning, informing him that an insurrection had broken out in Southampton, and that, by the last accounts, there were seventy whites massacred, and the militia retreating. Another express to Petersburg says that the blacks were continuing their destruction; that three hundred militia were retreating in a body, before six or eight hundred blacks. A shower of rain coming up as the militia were making an attack, wet the powder so much that they were compelled to retreat, being armed only with shot-guns. The negroes are armed with muskets, scythes, axes, &c. &c. Our volunteers are marching to the scene of action. A troop of cavalry left at four o'clock, P. M. The artillery, with four field pieces, start in the steam boat Norfolk, at 6 o'clock, to land at Smithfield. Southampton county lies 80 miles south of us, below Petersburg.'

From the Richmond Whig, of Tuesday.

Disagreeable rumors have reached this city of an insurrection of the slaves in Southampton County,

spiracies alarmed the South. In 1800 the Prosser plot to destroy Richmond, Virginia, was disclosed by a slave. As a consequence, a permanent armed guard was established there to protect the white citizens against slave rebellion. Twenty-two years later a sizable insurrection was thwarted in Charleston, South Carolina, by the execution of thirty-seven Negroes including their leader, Denmark Vesey, and the deportation of thirty-four more. In 1831 apprehension ran through the white South at the news of Nat Turner's Rebellion in Southampton County, Virginia, where in two days Turner's band of seventy Negroes murdered fifty whites. As a response to the 1831 insurrection, most southern states increased the severity of their slave codes and many established permanent patrols to guard against uprisings. No major slave uprising occurred from that time until the Civil War, although in every black belt community there were periodic rumors of slave plots. The grim possibility of a black rebellion always preyed upon the minds of the southern whites, especially in those areas where they were outnumbered by slaves.

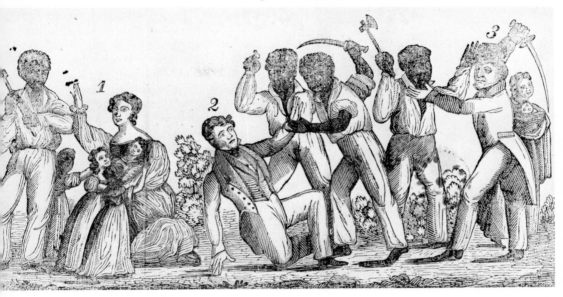

The almost universal acceptance of freedom when offered to slaves, even though it meant migration to Africa, would also argue the unpopularity of slavery among the slaves. Every southern newspaper was full of advertisements for runaway slaves. It has been estimated that each year at least 1,000 runaway slaves tried to make their way to freedom.

The Abolitionist Attack. Such was the institution upon which Garrison and the abolitionists opened their attack. They knew little about it at first hand, but they found an abundance of ammunition to use. Stories of atrocities committed against slaves, such as brutal whippings, the breaking up of slave homes, enforced immorality, and the like were constantly drifting northward. These tales were picked up by abolitionist editors and orators who were eager to believe the worst about slavery. The abolitionists regarded the institution at its best as morally indefensible. Slaves were men, and no man, they felt, had the right to hold a fellow man in bondage. On this ground the abolitionists rejected totally the idea of compensated emancipation.

The abolitionist doctrines struck a responsive chord in many northern hearts. Many New Englanders, angered by the vicious attacks upon their section that nullificationist orators delighted to make, retaliated, perhaps unconsciously, by going over to the abolitionist camp. The Quakers had always regarded slavery as immoral, and great numbers of them found the transition from passive to active opposition extremely easy to make. Most of the northern evangelical churches, particularly the Methodist and the Baptist, began to lean toward abolition. Among the abolitionist orators, Wendell Phillips, scion of an aristocratic Boston family, was preeminent. Not since the days of Patrick Henry had American audiences been treated to such fervid appeals. Two South Carolinians, Sarah and Angelina Grimké, went to Philadelphia, joined the Society of Friends, and devoted their lives to the antislavery crusade. Theodore Dwight Weld, a westerner who married Angelina, is thought by some to have done more for the cause of abolition than Garrison himself. Lucretia Mott, a Philadelphia Quaker, lectured far and wide in behalf of abolition. Gerrit Smith, an upstate New Yorker of

WILLIAM LLOYD GARRISON

A native of Newburyport, Massachusetts, and a printer and editor by trade, Garrison was an outstanding abolitionist. Lowell wrote of him:

"There's Garrison, his features very Benign for an incendiary."

considerable wealth, devoted both his time and his fortune to the cause. Escaped slaves, such as Frederick Douglass and Harriet Tubman, lifted up eloquent voices on behalf of freedom. Unnamed hundreds of workers spread the abolitionist doctrines among their neighbors and established lines of secret stopping places, or "underground railroads," by means of which fugitive slaves could be passed along from the southern states to Canada and freedom. Probably more slaves were aided on their way North by free Negroes than by the abolitionists, however..

One curious fact about many of the abolitionists is that for all their devotion to the cause of the freeing of the southern slaves, few of them did much to help the northern Negro gain equal political and civic rights. Throughout great sections of the North there was widespread discrimination against the free Negro. By 1860, only three states gave him suffrage. In some states he was not permitted to serve on juries; in others he was barred from holding civic and state offices. Years before the South enacted segregation laws, Jim Crow had made its appearance in the North with segregated schools, restaurants, and hotels. The fact that five major anti-Negro riots broke out in Philadelphia between 1832 and 1849 indicates that the doctrine of white supremacy was not a monopoly of the South.

Abolitionist Organization. The first local abolitionist society was formed in 1831, after which little time was lost in perfecting an organization extending throughout the North. In 1833 a convention at Philadelphia launched the American Anti-Slavery Society. A division in this society occurred in 1840, however, mainly because Garrison and a few other extremists were unwilling to use political methods. Slavery was recognized by the Constitution of the United States, a fact which, according to Garrison, made that document "a covenant with death and an agreement with hell." Theodore Parker, the most eminent preacher of his time, prided himself on his unwillingness even to cast a vote under the authority of such a government. But to the rank and file of abolitionists, the obvious way to promote their cause was through united political action. The actual abolition of slavery was conceded to depend upon the individual states where antislavery majorities could not soon be achieved, but the national government had authority to abolish slavery in the District of Columbia and to put an end to the interstate slave trade. To promote these ends, as well as to work toward the eventual abolition of slavery in every state, the Liberty Party was formed shortly before the election of 1840, and James G. Birney was selected as its candidate for President. Birney was a Kentuckian by birth, who, after spending many years as a

254

planter in Alabama, had freed his slaves and come North to work against slavery. For a time he published an abolitionist paper, *The Philanthropist,* at Cincinnati, but in 1837 he became secretary of the American Anti-Slavery Society and moved to New York. In the election of 1840 he polled a total of about 7,000 votes.

The abolitionists had made greater progress, however, than this small vote seemed to indicate. Their arguments had stirred up much feeling against slavery throughout the North and had convinced many people that the slavery system must ultimately be overthrown. Furthermore, the prestige of the southern planters was seriously damaged. Northern farmers came to suspect southern leadership of working against the interests of the small free farmer and solely for the interests of the slaveholding planter. More and more the conviction grew that the newly opened lands of the West should be reserved for the use of free farmers and should be denied forever to slaveholders.

The abolition of slavery in the District of Columbia won perhaps more support than any other abolitionist tenet. Northern members of Congress were increasingly sensitive to the existence of slavery in the national capital and to the necessity of witnessing day by day the public buying and selling of slaves. Floods of abolitionist petitions, most of them praying that slavery be abolished in the District, descended upon them. The southern members, however, were deeply offended by these memorials, and in 1836 they persuaded the House to pass a "gag rule" that required all such petitions to be laid on the table without debate. This action was construed by Representative John Quincy Adams as a direct violation of the constitutional right of petition, and he fought against it with all his might. While the ex-President was not himself an abolitionist, his constant appearance as a defender of abolitionist petitions tended to identify him with the antislavery movement and to clothe it with increasing respectability. In 1844 his efforts were successful,

and by a vote of 108 to 80 the obnoxious rule was repealed. In 1850 the slave trade was abolished in the District of Columbia, but slavery itself was allowed to remain.

Opposition to the Abolitionists. Regardless of the headway they made, the abolitionists were cordially disliked in the North as well as in the South. The indifference of the extremists to the Constitution and their willingness to see the South outside the Union were thoroughly resented by a generation which held both the Constitution and the Union in reverence. Business interests took fright at the abolitionist propaganda, for northern manufacturers were making profits from southern trade and they feared that abolitionist activities might imperil trade relations with the South. Many northerners, moreover, agreed wholeheartedly with the southern contention that the only proper status for the Negro was slavery. In fact, many of the antislavery crusaders, particularly in the early years, were subjected to frequent outrages. One abolitionist editor, Elijah P. Lovejoy of Alton, Illinois, was put to death by a proslavery mob.

The unpopularity of the abolitionists in the North was mild compared with the venomous hatred they provoked in the South. Losses from runaway slaves became increasingly serious, and for these the masters held the abolitionists responsible. Abolitionist literature, some of which deliberately suggested to the slaves the possibility of escape, flooded the South. Whatever the efficiency of the underground railroad, abolitionists naturally boasted its success and southerners believed their stories. They were convinced also that the abolitionists were trying to provoke slave insurrections. Nat Turner's Rebellion, which occurred at about the time that the abolitionist crusade began, served to confirm this belief. But even more galling than property losses or the fear of insurrection were the abolitionist denunciations of slaveholders as the lowest types of criminals.

The South on Slavery. Coincident with the rise of abolitionism came the almost complete subsidence of southern interest in emancipation. However, the increasing profits of slavery had already sapped the vitality of southern emancipationism. Such projects as compensated emancipation and the return of freed Negroes to Africa no longer received southern approbation. The last significant southern debate on the subject of slavery occurred in the Virginia legislature of 1832, immediately following Nat Turner's Rebellion. During the debate the institution of slavery was subjected to the most searching criticism; slavery, according to one member, was "the heaviest calamity which has ever befallen any portion of the human race," and according to another was "a curse upon him who inflicts as upon him who suffers it." But on the motion for the passage of a bill for gradual abolition the slaveholders from the eastern part of the state won by a wide majority. Within a few years hardly a southerner of consequence could be found who would openly criticize the institution of slavery.

Furthermore, every possible effort was made throughout the South to suppress all agitation in favor of emancipation, and in particular to prevent the delivery of the abolitionist tracts that the mails brought in. The Postmaster General ruled that local postmasters might refuse to deliver such mail if they believed it to be of an incendiary nature. Although this ruling was soon rescinded, many southern postmasters continued the practice, and many other obstacles to the spread of abolitionist propaganda in the South were devised.

The Proslavery Argument. At length, arguments were adduced to prove that slavery, far from being an evil, was actually a positive good. Of all the proslavery philosophers probably Thomas Roderick Dew, professor in the College of William and Mary, and afterwards its president, was the most systematic. Dew had obtained his education in Germany, where he was im-

pressed by the open recognition of the inequalities of man and the inevitability of a stratified society. Instead of apologizing for what he found in the South, he defended it. The great planters, because of their superior education, ability, and property, stood at the head of southern society; next to them in rank were the small landowners, the traders, and free laborers; at the bottom of the ladder were the slaves. "It is the order of nature and of God," he claimed, "that the being of superior faculties and knowledge, and therefore of superior power, should control and dispose of those who are inferior. It is as much the order of nature that men should enslave each other as that other animals should prey upon each other." Dew was ably seconded by Chancellor William Harper of the Supreme Court of South Carolina, who published in 1838 a *Memoir on Slavery* that was quoted as authority throughout the South. Professional men of every kind, particularly the preachers and the politicians, took up the argument and boldly proclaimed the virtues of the South's most distinctive institution.

The idea that slavery was ordained by God was particularly comforting to the people of the South, most of whom were devoutly orthodox in their religious views. The Fourth and the Tenth Commandments, which referred to man-servants and maid-servants as of the same status as slaves, clearly gave the stamp of divine approval to slavery. Abraham, Isaac, and the other patriarchs had held slaves. The apostle Paul had enjoined servants to be obedient to their masters. Moreover, it was a particularly happy dispensation of Providence which brought heathen Africans to America, where they might learn the truths of Christianity. But for the institution of slavery they might still be outside the pale of Christian influence.

Slavery was also defended as a benevolent institution in which the relationship between capital and labor was more kindly than could be found anywhere else in the world. The master must care for the slave in sickness as well as in health, in childhood and old age no less than in his prime. The master must not overwork his slave, for to do so would impair the slave's value. Compared with the wage-slave system of the industrial North and of Europe, where, it was asserted, men, women, and children were worked to death in mines and factories, and where the aged, the ill, and the incompetent were ruthlessly discharged, the slavery system could be made to appear as "a beautiful example of communism, where each one receives not according to his labor, but according to his wants." George Fitzhugh, a Virginia lawyer who defended this line of argument, was nothing if not consistent. In his book *Cannibals All! or Slaves Without Masters* (1856) he argued that the industrial system of the North would inevitably bring on a gigantic class struggle and earnestly advocated that the slave system be adopted there before such a disaster should occur.

Another proslavery argument claimed that the plantation system was essentially a school to civilize the Negro and thus was to his benefit. Still another argument claimed that only the Negro, by virtue of his black skin and curly hair, was fitted for strenuous labor in the hot rice and sugar plantations. Finally, in 1854, so-called scholarship was brought to bear to prove the southern proslavery thesis. In *Types of Mankind*, a book written by Dr. Josiah Nott and George Glidden, an archaeologist, it was seriously argued that instead of deriving from a common source, the various races of mankind had had diverse origins and that of all the types and races of mankind the Negro was obviously the lowest, and thus destined to a life of labor. By the 1850's, after two decades of heated interchange, the great majority of southerners had made up their minds about slavery and agreed with Calhoun that it "was the most safe and stable basis for free institutions in the world."

The Economics of Slavery. Whether slavery was economically profitable was ar-

HINTON R. HELPER

A native of North Carolina, Hinton R. Helper used statistics taken from the Census of 1850 to prove that slavery was nothing short of a disaster to many southern whites. Southern reaction to the book was violently hostile.

gued vigorously before the Civil War even among southerners. Edmund Ruffin, the eminent southern agriculturist, thought it was decidedly so — principally because of the economic advantage in large-scale production and in the wholesale purchasing of supplies made possible by the plantation system. Ruffin also argued that the planter could specialize his labor force, allotting tasks in accordance with the special aptitudes of individual slaves. Among free farmers, this was not possible. He contrasted the relatively peaceful labor relations under slavery with the expensive struggles between capital and labor that he contended had come to be characteristic of the northern factory system. On the other hand, a North Carolinian, Hinton R. Helper, in *The Impending Crisis* (1857) not only attacked slaveholding interests but condemned the slavery system for bringing economic backwardness and even destitution to the South.

Modern scholars have continued the argument, and the truth of the matter in narrow economic terms is still difficult to judge. Unquestionably, the slaveholder had a lot of his capital tied up in slaves and land. But, in turn, he received very cheap labor over a lifetime, even though slave labor was perhaps only about half as efficient as the free labor of the North. Moreover, with field hands selling for about $1,000, the natural increase of his slaves augmented the master's property considerably. Perhaps the conclusion of one scholar that slave labor returned on capital invested about 12 per cent if employed on good land, 5 per cent on average land, and 4 per cent on poor, and that such returns on the average were about as remunerative as capital invested in alternative uses in the South, is not far from the mark.

When one turns from the economic effects of the slave system on individual planters to its effect on the section as a whole, the results are much clearer. The South, thanks in considerable part to the limitations of the slave, was overspecialized. It produced only what the slave could produce profitably, and to an increasing extent this meant cotton. Even foodstuffs, which could be, and ordinarily were, grown on every southern farm and plantation, were frequently produced in such meager quantities that importations from the North had to be made. The prosperity of the South thus rose and fell with the proceeds from its money crops. An off year or a serious drop in the price of cotton meant widespread disaster.

Effect of Slavery on the Whites. Doubtless the worst feature of the system of slavery, from the economic point of view, was that its profits were absorbed by so small a number of planters. Edmund Ruffin was

right in his contention that large-scale production was more profitable economically than small-scale production. But the bulk of the people of the South belonged to the small planter and the farmer class. They had no choice but to compete with the large planter on terms that made him comfortable, but kept them permanently poor. It was on this account that tens of thousands of southerners who had no slaves or only a few slaves fled to the free states of the old Northwest, or to such portions of the slave states where the plantation system was unable to follow them. Not only did the South lose a steady stream of emigrants to the North; it failed also, because of slavery, to attract immigrants in large numbers, as the North was doing, from outside the United States. The effect of slavery upon the rank and file of the native southern whites was also unfortunate. They tended to regard physical labor, because it was the customary lot of slaves, as essentially menial and degrading. The leisure class thus came to include many who might have fared far better had they been less opposed to work, and who made little or no contribution to the welfare of their section.

The Southern Mind. Culturally and psychologically the slave system also produced profound consequences for the section. The plantation way of life set the social and cultural values for the entire South. With few large cities, most sections of the South remained more provincial than even the Middle West, where burgeoning towns and cities acted as a cultural leaven for the surrounding countryside. As the slavery controversy intensified, the section also sought to isolate itself culturally. Each year fewer southern students attended northern universities, and during the fifties a campaign was launched throughout the cotton belt to induce southern students to enroll in southern institutions. Progressively, the southern inclination was to read southern magazines, talk with southern-minded people, and worship in churches staffed by a southern ministry. The old cultural and intellectual ties with Europe and the North which the Virginian gentry nurtured and sustained in the days of Jefferson and Madison were being severed. In 1824, a northern traveler reported that the love of literature and new ideas that had characterized many of the planter class in earlier days had now been replaced by an almost total involvement in hunting and outdoor sports. Thirty years later, a southerner visiting plantation families throughout the section remarked that he had not seen one piano, one work of art worthy of the name, nor one library in all his journey from the seacoast to the Mississippi. Thus isolated from the world, the South sacrificed that intellectual and cultural leadership which had given so much to the Revolutionary War generation. Most southerners were never able to understand or appreciate the full force of the progressive and reform mentality that had come to dominate northern and western European thought.

In some respects, social and political thought in the South actually began to regress. The defense of slavery against the mounting criticism of the North caused southern whites to violate the free movement of the mails, and eventually the traditional American right of free speech. In many communities mob action quieted all criticism of the dominant institution. Of more importance, its rabid defense of slavery forced the South to give up a part of its political birthright. When southern representatives in Congress voted down a home-stead bill providing free land for every adult male citizen, and when Calhoun maintained that the American form of government was not democratic, but representative, the great southern-inspired traditions of democracy were denied. Slavery was thus not only embroiling the present and imperiling the future; it was also nullifying a great past.

Undoubtedly, the social liabilities inherent in the slave labor system were too numerous and too serious for slavery to have survived indefinitely. In the 1840's and 1850's, however, the leaders of southern opinion were deceived by the booming cotton economy, and came boldly to the defense of the South's "peculiar institution." The attacks of the abolitionists had transformed earlier southern apologies for slavery into a belligerent insistence on its righteousness. And a near monopoly of the world's cotton market had given the leaders of the section a distorted impression of southern strength. On the floor of the Senate James H. Hammond of South Carolina viewed an imaginary world for three years deprived of southern cotton: "England would topple headlong and carry the whole civilized world with her save the South. No, you do not dare to make war on Cotton. No power on earth dares to make war on it. Cotton is King." With this southern spirit of defiance set squarely against the intense reform mentality which had possessed the North, many thoughtful Americans sensed that an "irrepressible conflict" was in the making — a conflict that would rock the Union to its foundations.

SELECTED BIBLIOGRAPHY

Two valuable survey volumes are C. S. Sydnor, *The Development of Southern Sectionalism, 1819–1848* (1948); and Clement Eaton, *A History of the Old South* (1949). L. C. Gray, *History of Agriculture in the Southern United States to 1860* (2 vols., 1933), is a standard

° Available in paperback

work. Among the notable attempts to define southern character are W. J. Cash, °*The Mind of the South* (1941); R. G. Osterweis, *Romanticism and Nationalism in the Old South* (1949); and J. H. Franklin, °*The Militant South, 1800–1861* (1956). Social history is treated in such works as F. L. Owsley, °*Plain Folk of the Old South* (1949); and Lewis

Atherton, *The Southern Country Store, 1800–1860* (1949). Accessible first-hand accounts include J. G. Baldwin, °*The Flush Times of Alabama and Mississippi* (1854); and °*The Slave States (before the Civil War)*, a selection from the works of F. L. Olmsted, edited by Harvey Wish (1959). Important special studies include F. H. R. Floan, °*The South in Northern Eyes, 1831 to 1861* (1958); and J. W. Hurst, *Law and the Conditions of Freedom in the Nineteenth-Century United States* (1956).

K. M. Stampp, °*The Peculiar Institution* (1956), is an important modern synthesis, based upon a wide study of manuscript materials, sympathetic to the Negro and strongly revisionist in its treatment of the economic aspects of slavery. Stanley Elkins, °*Slavery* (1959), stresses the factors which degraded the Negro. U. B. Phillips argued that there were mitigating factors which kept slavery from being an unqualified evil, even for the Negro; see his °*Life and Labor in the Old South* (1929). A modern documentary collection is °*Slavery in the South*, edited by Harvey Wish (1964). The best history of the Negro in the United States is J. H. Franklin, *From Slavery to Freedom* (2nd ed., 1956). A rich anthology is °*A Documentary History of the Negro People in the United States: From Colonial Times Through the Civil War*, edited by Herbert Aptheker (1951). An important theme is developed in R. C. Wade, *Slavery in the Cities* (1964). On the slave trade, see D. R. Mannix, *Black Cargoes* (1962); and W. S. Howard, *American Slavers and the Federal Law, 1837–1862* (1963). See also Herbert Aptheker, °*American Negro Slave Revolts* (1943); P. J. Staudenraus, *The African Colonization Movement, 1816–1865* (1961); and P. S. Foner, *Business and Slavery: The New York Merchants and the Irrepressible Conflict* (1941).

Studies of slavery and related problems in individual states are numerous. Among the more important are J. B. Sellers, *Slavery in Alabama* (1950); O. W. Taylor, *Negro Slavery in Arkansas* (1958); J. C. Bonner, *A History of Georgia Agriculture, 1732–1860* (1964); J. W. Coleman, *Slavery Times in Kentucky* (1940); R. W. Shugg, *Origins of Class Struggle in Louisiana* (1939); J. G. Taylor, *Negro Slavery in Louisiana* (1963); C. S. Sydnor, *Slavery in Mississippi* (1933); J. H. Moore, *Agriculture in Ante-Bellum Mississippi* (1958);

C. O. Cathey, *Agricultural Developments in North Carolina, 1783–1860* (1956); R. H. Taylor, °*Ante-Bellum South Carolina* (1942); and C. C. Mooney, *Slavery in Tennessee* (1957).

The most convenient introduction to the abolitionist movement is in Louis Filler, °*The Crusade Against Slavery, 1830–1860* (1960). D. L. Dumond, *Antislavery: The Crusade for Freedom in America* (1961), is a monumental compilation. A collection of sources is °*Slavery Attacked*, edited by J. L. Thomas (1965). Varying interpretations are gathered in Hugh Hawkins (ed.), °*The Abolitionists* (1964); and R. O. Curry (ed.), °*The Abolitionists* (1965). An interesting psychological study is H. H. Simms, *Emotion at High Tide: Abolition as a Controversial Factor, 1830–1845* (1960). The significance of the western abolitionists is set forth by G. H. Barnes, °*The Anti-Slavery Impulse, 1830–1844* (1933); and D. L. Dumond, °*Antislavery Origins of the Civil War in the United States* (1939). The role of the New England abolitionists is described in Lawrence Lader, *The Bold Brahmins* (1961). The role of the "underground railroad" is treated, perhaps with overemphasis, in Henrietta Buckmaster, °*Let My People Go* (1941). Two important special studies are R. B. Nye, *Fettered Freedom: Civil Liberties and the Slavery Controversy, 1830–1860* (2nd ed., 1964); and T. E. Drake, *Quakers and Slavery in America* (1950). J. C. Furnas, °*Goodbye to Uncle Tom* (1956), is critical of many abolitionists because of their Negrophobia, a point well brought out by R. F. Durden, *James Shepherd Pike: Republicanism and the American Negro, 1850–1882* (1957). The difficult lot of the free Negro is well described in L. F. Litwack, °*North of Slavery; The Negro in the Free States, 1790–1860* (1961).

Biographies of abolitionists are useful for getting the feel of the movement. On Garrison, see the brief study by R. B. Nye, *William Lloyd Garrison and the Humanitarian Reformers* (1955); and the full-length biographies by J. L. Thomas, *The Liberator* (1963); and W. M. Merrill, *Against Wind and Tide* (1963). On Phillips, see Oscar Sherwin, *Prophet of Liberty* (1958); and I. H. Bartlett, *Wendell Phillips* (1961). Other good biographies of significant figures include B. L. Fladeland, *James Gillespie Birney* (1955); M. L. Dillon, *Elijah P. Lovejoy* (1961); F. O. Gatell, *John*

Gorham Palfrey and the New England Con- *science* (1963); R. V. Harlow, *Gerrit Smith* (1939); R. F. Wilson, *Crusader in Crinoline: The Life of Harriet Beecher Stowe* (1941); and B. P. Thomas, *Theodore Weld* (1950). An interesting collection of essays, sympathetic to the abolitionists, is *The Antislavery Vanguard,* edited by M. B. Duberman (1965). *The Life and Writings of Frederick Douglass,* edited by P. S. Foner (4 vols., 1950–1955), is an important source for the great Negro leader. Douglass' °*Autobiography* (1881) is accessible in a new edition. See also P. S. Foner, °*Frederick Douglass* (1964).

On the proslavery side, a useful anthology is °*Slavery Defended: The Views of the Old South,* edited by E. L. McKitrick (1963). Two of the basic works by George Fitzhugh are available in °*Ante-Bellum,* edited by Harvey Wish (1960); see also Wish's, *George Fitzhugh* (1943). W. S. Jenkins, *Pro-Slavery Thought in the Old South* (1935); and Clement Eaton, °*The Freedom of Thought Struggle in the Old South* (2nd ed., 1964), are monographs of basic importance. A recent series of lectures by Clement Eaton, *The Mind of the Old South* (1964), provides a stimulating survey.

16

MANIFEST DESTINY

Until the early 1840's, most American citizens took it for granted that the growth of the populated area of their country would be limited by certain geographical factors. They had foreseen for some time that the frontier of population would advance into the upper Mississippi Valley and that it would reach, and perhaps cross, the international border to the southwest, but they had no idea that the supposedly barren region west of Missouri, labeled on the maps the "Great American Desert," would ever be desired for settlement. The only significant changes they anticipated were in the international boundaries. They expected the United States to acquire sole title to at least a part of the Oregon country, and they recognized also that the southwestern boundary, set in 1819, might have to be revised. But they never dreamed that the distant regions of the farther West would ever be settled by whites. Yet within a few years responsible American statesmen were talking of the nation's "manifest destiny" to expand westward in all directions until only the Pacific Ocean stopped their

progress. More expansive citizens dreamed of acquiring not only the land directly west of the old Louisiana Purchase, but the entire Pacific shore from Russian Alaska to the Isthmus of Panama.

New Mexico. One of the circumstances that served to provide Americans with a new vision of expansion was the opening of the Santa Fe Trail. On the upper Rio Grande, separated by a long desert trip from Mexico City, the Spanish had established outposts at about the same time the English were founding Jamestown. Early efforts of Americans to trade with New Mexico were thwarted by Spanish officials, but the Mexican Revolution brought a change of policy. After 1822, when an American returned to the Missouri settlements from the first profitable trip to Santa Fe, caravans of American traders crossed the "Desert" each year for more than two decades. Sometimes their profits were excellent although the volume of trade remained small.

The Santa Fe Trail. The opening of a new trail into the Far West was, at least to the people of the Mississippi Valley, an event of real significance. Traders who were often also farmers observed that the land along the first lap of the journey was good, and that heavy rainfall sometimes impeded their progress. They persuaded

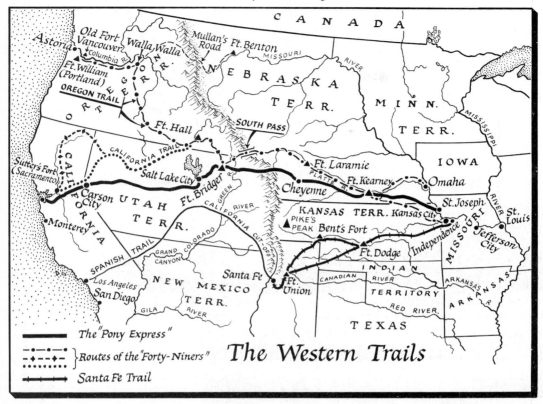

The "Pony Express"

Routes of the "Forty-Niners"

Santa Fe Trail

The Western Trails

Congress to survey the trail, and they sometimes obtained military escorts to accompany and protect their caravans. When in 1843 Santa Anna, the Mexican leader, put a temporary end to the trade, they and the whole country were deeply shocked.

The Oregon Trail. Meantime, the Oregon Trail had opened to American eyes a new vision of the possibilities of the Pacific Northwest. The origins of this route to the West are obscure, but by the 1830's Indian traders had settled upon it as the easiest way through to the coast. It led, not without many variations, from the bend of the Missouri to the bend of the Platte, out the latter stream and its north fork to what is now southern Wyoming, through South Pass, an easy divide in the mountains, to the Snake Valley, then by a cutoff to the Columbia. The region in which it terminated was in

dispute between Great Britain and the United States. Whatever claims Spain might once have had the United States had acquired by the Florida Treaty of 1819; and whatever rights Russia might once have had the British had acquired by an agreement on the Alaskan boundary in 1825. Eventually the Oregon country must all go to the United States or to Great Britain, or be divided between the two. But with settlement almost nonexistent and with traders sparse, the problem of political jurisdiction could wait.

Rivalry in Oregon. Rivalry between British and American fur traders, however, was immediate and intense. The British interests, united after 1821 under the exclusive control of the Hudson's Bay Company, were ably commanded by Dr. John McLoughlin, and carried on a profitable trade. But McLoughlin's agents on their adventures into the Rockies were soon reporting contacts, and even conflicts, with American traders. So strenuous was the competition for the fur trade that by the year 1832 it was abundantly evident that "joint occupation" was soon to be given a real test.

Missionaries to Oregon. And yet the conflict, when finally it came, was less the work of traders than of missionaries. By the 1830's most American religious denominations had developed a keen interest in missions, and had recognized that the Indian tribes offered a suitable field for such labors. The Methodists in 1833 sent out their first missionary to the Oregon country, Jason Lee. Close on the heels of the Methodists came the Presbyterians, whose ablest representative, Dr. Marcus Whitman, appeared on the scene in 1836. By the end of the decade the American Catholics also were represented in the person of Jesuit

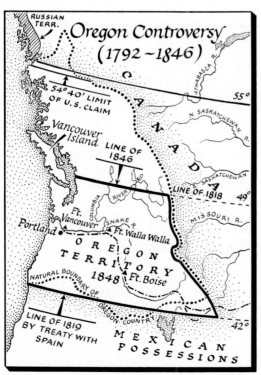

Father Pierre Jean de Smet. Conflict among the rival denominations was at first avoided, for the Methodists chose the Willamette Valley as their headquarters, the Presbyterians the region where the Snake enters the Columbia, and Father de Smet the mountains and plains still farther inland. The great majority of McLoughlin's traders, however, were Catholics, and the French-Canadian priests who came out at about this same time to minister to their needs worked at will among all the Indians. Religious rivalry began to take on a nationalistic bias.

The real trouble came, however, from the fact that many of the Methodist and Presbyterian missionaries became so actively engaged in agriculture that they almost forgot the spiritual needs of the Indians. The news that there was good farming land in Oregon had spread to the East, and after 1841 hundreds of emigrants gathered each spring at Independence, Missouri, to make the long journey by covered wagon into the new frontier. To watch over the growing American colony, the government of the United States in 1842 sent out Dr. Elijah White, ostensibly as an Indian agent, and that year Lt. John C. Frémont, of the United States Army, began an official survey of the Oregon Trail. A year later the Americans in Oregon held a convention to inaugurate self-government. It was evident that the issue whether Oregon should be British or American would soon have to be faced.

California. Even in California, where Spanish outposts antedated by many years the American occupation, the workings of manifest destiny were becoming apparent. Spanish penetration had begun here when the officials of New Spain sought, by sending missionaries, soldiers, and a few colonists to California, to forestall British and Russian advances down the Pacific coast. The civilians were mostly ranchers who, with the aid of a rich soil and a favorable climate, could produce great herds, but could find no way to market them. The missionaries, conscientious Franciscan friars, were content to establish self-sufficient communities. They converted the Indians, taught them various arts and crafts, and from a score of picturesque centers ruled benevolently. Unfortunately both the Spanish and the Mexican overlords insisted on regarding the missions as merely temporary affairs to be broken up whenever the Indians were sufficiently civilized. Soon after the revolt from Spain the Mexican government attempted to put this policy into effect, but the disorder that followed was so great that an abortive effort was made to restore the old system.

The uneasiness of California society was increased by the presence of a constant influx of non-Mexican residents. One such was Thomas O. Larkin, an American, who in 1822 opened a store in Monterey. Occasionally, also, seamen deserted from ships that put into California harbors, and more important still, a few immigrants began to trickle in from the American frontier, lured on by the spreading tales of California's unclaimed fertile acres. By 1845 there were 700 Americans in California out of a total white population of about ten times that number. Sutter's Fort on the American River furnished a convenient haven of refuge for these newcomers from the "States." Here a German-Swiss named John A. Sutter had established himself in 1839, and had gathered about him a considerable group of Indians and other retainers. With their aid he had created on a large land grant obtained from the Mexican authorities a kind of feudal barony.

The interest of the American government in California became clear in 1842 when Commodore Thomas Ap Catesby Jones, in command of the American Pacific squadron, landed a force at Monterey, took possession of the public property, and ran up the American flag. Jones had acted on the assumption that the British were about to seize California, which he had orders to prevent. When he learned that there were no British about he withdrew, but his act revealed clearly the ultimate goal of his government. Two years later Larkin was designated American consul at Monterey.

Texas. Much as the American public was interested in New Mexico, Oregon, and California, the place where manifest destiny was most clearly at work was Texas. Here lived far more Americans than in all the other coveted regions combined. Furthermore, the United States had had a shadowy claim to Texas before 1819, and had renounced it only in order to obtain Florida. The issue could therefore be made to appear not so much annexation as reannexation. Texas had made good its independence, and had been recognized by foreign governments as well as by the United States. Texans, with few exceptions, were ready to accept annexation on any reasonable terms. If, however, the United States were to hesitate longer the Texans might be forced into an alliance with Great Britain, who, it was feared, might persuade Mexico to acknowledge the independence of Texas in return for a British guarantee of Mexico's northern boundary. But far worse was a parallel suggestion that Texas in return for England's favor might abolish the institution of slavery. This proposal raised before southerners the dread possibility of a free, cotton-growing state immediately next to the heart of the slave-holding South. And to American patriots everywhere it offered the much grimmer specter of powerful and perhaps permanent European intervention in the affairs of continental America.

Only the growing distaste in the North for the addition of more slave territory to the Union and the threat of a Mexican war stood in the way of the annexationists, and neither President Tyler nor Secretary of State John C. Calhoun felt obliged to conciliate antislavery men anywhere. As a result a treaty was signed on April 12, 1844, between the United States and the Republic of Texas which provided that Texas should become a territory of the United States. The

Senate rejected this treaty, but the election of 1844 was at hand, and annexation became at once a dominant issue in the campaign.

The Election of 1844. This was no fault, however, of Henry Clay, prospective Whig candidate, and Martin Van Buren, prospective Democratic candidate, both of whom came out openly against annexation. But the Whigs, although nominating Clay unanimously, made no mention of Texas in their platform, while the Democrats passed over Van Buren and nominated instead James K. Polk of Tennessee, an annexationist. Further, the Democratic platform urged "the reoccupation of Oregon and the reannexation of Texas," while the possibility of acquiring New Mexico and California, if unmentioned, was by no means overlooked. Clay attempted to qualify his prenomination statement during the campaign, but Polk was under no such handicap, and it became increasingly plain as the campaign

wore on that the public had little disposition to impede manifest destiny. The slogan "Fifty-four-forty or fight" was apparently of post-election origin, but the expansionist issue seemed to outweigh in importance the antislavery argument against adding slave territory to the Union. Polk won a narrow, but complete, victory. Relatively unknown, the first "dark horse" candidate had defeated the outstanding politician of his time and carried with him into office a Democratic majority in both houses of Congress. The mandate of the electorate in favor of expansion was perfectly clear.

Annexation of Texas. With this reassuring popular verdict, steps were taken toward the annexation of Texas even before Polk became President. In accordance with a scheme long advocated by Tyler, a joint resolution, passed in the House by a vote of 120 to 98 and in the Senate by a vote of 27 to 25, Texas was invited to become a state in the Union on condition that it should

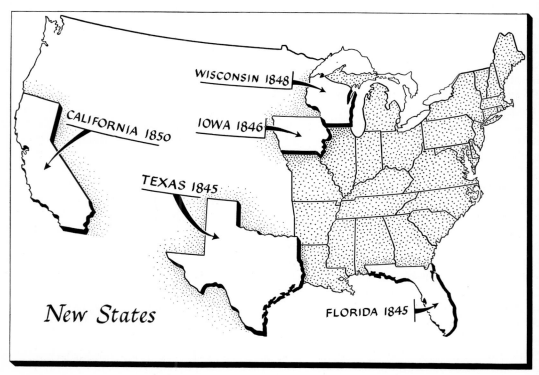

WISCONSIN 1848

CALIFORNIA 1850

IOWA 1846

TEXAS 1845

FLORIDA 1845

New States

(1) present a constitution acceptable to Congress, (2) agree that at some future time it might be subdivided into as many as five states, (3) pay its own war debt, and (4) retain its own public lands. Assurance that the institution of slavery would not be disturbed was given by extending the terms of the Missouri Compromise to apply to Texas as well as to the new states formed from the Louisiana Purchase. Three days before he left office, March 1, 1845, Tyler signed this resolution, and at once dispatched a courier to notify the Texan authorities. It was not long before the Lone Star State had signified its willingness to exchange independence for membership in the American Union, but formal admission was not accomplished until December 29, 1845.

James K. Polk. The new President, James K. Polk (1795–1849), was a North Carolinian by birth, but had served seven terms in the House as a representative from Tennessee, and one term as governor of the same state. During the time he was President he kept a diary which reveals him as a prodigiously hard-working, conscientious executive who believed his foremost duty was to carry out the will of the people. Even before the election he regarded the annexation of Texas as both a necessity and a right. As for Oregon, he declared pointedly that "to us belongs the duty of protecting" our emigrants "wherever they may be upon our soil." But as a practical necessity Polk hoped to settle the Oregon question peacefully. To this end he suggested that the United States would be willing to accept the forty-ninth parallel as the international boundary. After some diplomatic sparring a treaty was signed on June 15, 1846, which accepted the line Polk had proposed, except that all of Vancouver Island went to the British.

Even if the President had no further ambitions, there still remained the problem of Mexico. With this in mind, in July, 1845, after the Texans had voted their approval

"YOUNG HICKORY"

James K. Polk, of Tennessee, owed his nomination in 1844 to Van Buren's open opposition to the annexation of Texas. This attitude greatly offended many southern Democrats, who threw their support to Polk, an ardent annexationist. Photograph by Mathew Brady.

of annexation, he ordered General Zachary Taylor and regular army troops to the Neuces River to guard against a possible attack. But by this time Polk had a wider vision. Why not seize the opportunity to obtain all the territory west of Texas, including Upper California, and thus round out the boundaries of a continental United States? American naval officials had long since eyed San Francisco harbor as a most desirable naval station. In June, 1845, Commodore John D. Sloat received orders to take San Francisco if Mexico declared war.

The Slidell Mission. But Polk did not want a war if it were possible to achieve his ends by other means. Consequently, on

November 10, 1845, he sent John Slidell as his representative to Mexico with the offer that the United States would assume all the claims of its citizens against Mexico if the latter recognized the Rio Grande as the southern border of Texas. For the rest of New Mexico, the United States would pay $5 million, and as for California, "money would be no object." No Mexican official, however, dared to treat with Slidell. Even so, the ambitious rebel, General Mariano Paredes, accused the government of bargaining with the hated Yankees and managed to overthrow the existing regime and install himself and his war-minded followers as the *de facto* government.

Meantime, acting on Polk's orders, American troops under General Taylor had occupied territory near the Rio Grande in order to be able to "protect what, in the event of annexation, will be our western frontier." The region between the Neuces and the Rio Grande had long been disputed by Texas and Mexico, but Mexico had the better claim to the territory. All that Polk could reasonably hope for was an incident. But nothing happened, even after the troops, at Polk's insistence, had advanced in January, 1846, to the banks of the Rio Grande. Impatient of further delay, Polk prepared a message to Congress early in May, 1846, in which he recited the failure of the Slidell mission and recommended war to bring the Mexicans to terms. Before this message was sent, news arrived in Washington that fighting had broken out between Taylor's troops and the Mexicans along the border. Polk, therefore, rewrote his message placing the blame for starting hostilities upon the enemy. On May 11, 1846, he told Congress that "war exists, and, notwithstanding all our efforts to avoid it, exists by the act of Mexico herself." Thus encouraged by the President, Congress promptly put through a declaration of war by a vote of 174 to 14 in the House, and 40 to 2 in the Senate, authorized the raising of a volunteer army of 50,000 men, and appropriated $10 million to pay the costs of the military venture upon which the country now embarked.

For a time the war spirit remained high, but presently strong opposition began to develop. The attack upon a weaker neighbor was criticized as unworthy of the national honor. The Democrats were charged with fomenting war in order to gain glory enough to enable them to win the next election. Antislavery men, already deeply distressed at the annexation of Texas, were sure that a southern conspiracy existed to extend still further the area open to slavery. The Whig Party, always in danger of dissolution because of the discordant views of its members, found a new source of dissension. The "cotton" Whigs, mostly from the West and South, supported the war now that it had begun, while the "conscience" Whigs, mainly from the Northeast, branded it as an inexcusable blunder that ought to be abandoned at once, with apologies and reparations to Mexico.

Campaigns of the Mexican War. Perhaps an even more potent cause of opposition came from the fact that the war was by no means easy to win. Advancing southwestward into Mexico, General Taylor captured Matamoras, but was held up by three days' hard fighting (September 21–23) before he could take Monterrey. Pushing forward slowly, he was presently confronted by a large Mexican army under Santa Anna, which he defeated with considerable difficulty at Buena Vista (February 22–23, 1847). Taylor's tactics, probably for good reason, had not pleased Polk, but "Old Rough and Ready," as the General was called, had captured the American public, and could not be superseded. Polk therefore determined to shift the main attack on Mexico to Vera Cruz on the eastern coast. With General Winfield Scott in command, an American expeditionary force successfully invested Vera Cruz in March, 1847, and after six months of hard marching and fighting captured the Mexican capital. Meantime a small military force from the Missouri border under Colonel Stephen W. Kearny had taken Santa Fe and had advanced into southern California. There

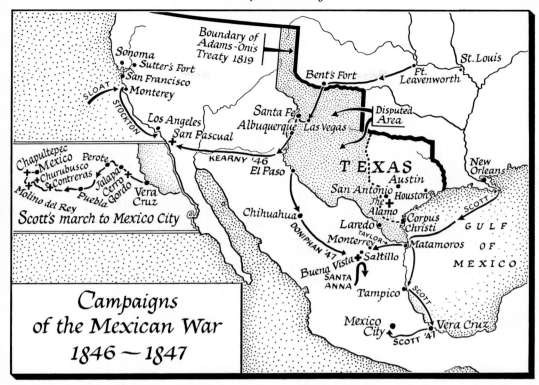

Campaigns
of the Mexican War
1846 — 1847

Kearny saw some hard fighting, although farther north American naval units under Sloat's successor, Commodore R. F. Stockton, with some assistance from John C. Frémont, the explorer and son-in-law of Senator Thomas Hart Benton, had virtually put an end to Mexican rule. Frémont furnished American leadership to the so-called "Bear Flag Revolution," staged by American residents of California, but he was accused by Kearny of insubordination, and taken back to Washington virtually a prisoner, court-martialed, and ordered dismissed from the army. Although pardoned by the President, he resigned his commission.

Treaty of Guadalupe Hidalgo. During his advance on Mexico City, Scott had been accompanied by the chief clerk of the American State Department, Nicholas P. Trist, who was authorized to negotiate for peace. Trist's talents proved to be decidedly limited, and Polk finally deprived him of all authority and ordered him to return

to the United States. But with the war won, Trist, in cheerful disregard of his instructions, negotiated the treaty of Guadalupe Hidalgo, February 2, 1848. By its terms Mexico accepted the Rio Grande boundary, and ceded New Mexico and California, including all the territory that lay between them, to the United States. The United States, in return, promised a cash payment of $15 million to Mexico, and agreed to the cancellation of all claims due from Mexico to American citizens, claims which the United States government itself now undertook to satisfy to the extent of $3.25 million. It was an expensive peace, considering that the United States was in position to demand what it liked, but Polk accepted it, and sent the treaty to the Senate, where it was ratified by a vote of 38 to 14.

The Mormons. While General Scott was advancing on Mexico City, another invasion of Mexican territory was launched by a group of religious refugees who cared

less about the politics of manifest destiny than they did about being unmolested. The Mormons had originated in western New York during the late 1820's when that region was booming under the impact of the recently completed Erie Canal. The prophet of the new religion, Joseph Smith, claimed divine authority to re-establish the original and complete form of Christianity. His "Church of Jesus Christ of Latter-Day Saints" accepted the teachings of the Bible, but received added inspiration from the Book of Mormon, to which Smith attributed a miraculous origin, and from other revelations which he announced from time to time. The chief distinction of the church was its centralized civic and economic life, which contrasted markedly with the "rugged individualism" of the Jacksonian West. Moving repeatedly because of strong public antagonisms, the Mormons first made Kirtland, Ohio, their residence, then Independence, Missouri, then Clay County, Missouri, and then Nauvoo, Illinois, a Mississippi River town. Here they prospered until 1844, when

Smith's political ambitions, coupled with talk of polygamy among the church leaders, led to further persecution. Eventually Smith was arrested and shot by a mob which broke into the jail that held him. Brigham Young, to whom most of the Mormons now looked for leadership, decided that their only hope of peace lay outside the populated area of the United States.

The Mormon migration is one of the outstanding episodes of American frontier history. During the spring and summer of 1846, about 15,000 Mormons crossed Iowa to Council Bluffs, a name then given to the region on both sides of the Missouri River adjacent to the present city of Omaha. Early in 1847 Young and a small company of his associates pushed west to the Great Salt Lake Valley, which had been selected as the best available site for the colony they meant to establish. Two larger groups followed, and a number of members of the "Mormon Battalion," which had accompanied Kearny to California a year before, also reached the valley before winter.

The Mormon Trail, traversed by upwards

A View of Salt Lake City, 1853, as sketched by Frederick J. Piercy and published in Linforth's From Liverpool to the Great Salt Lake Valley. *What the Mormons accomplished within the next decade is apparent from the following:*

The city revealed itself, as we approached, from behind its screen, the inclined terraces of the upper table-land, and at last it lay stretched before us as upon a map. At a little distance the aspect was somewhat Oriental, and in some points it reminded me of modern Athens without the Acropolis. None of the buildings, except the Prophet's house, were whitewashed. The material — the thick, sun dried adobe, common to all parts of the Eastern world — was of a dull leaden blue, deepened by the atmosphere to a gray, like the shingles of the roofs. The number of gardens and compounds . . . the dark clumps and lines of bitter cotton-wood, locust, or acacia, poplars and fruit-trees, apples, peaches, and vines — how lovely they appeared, after the baldness of the prairies! — and, finally, the fields of long-eared maize and sweet sorghum strengthened the similarity to an Asiatic rather than to an American settlement.

RICHARD F. BURTON, *The City of the Saints and Across the Rocky Mountains to California* (1862)

---

of 60,000 Latter-Day Saints prior to the completion of the transcontinental railroad, followed the north bank of the Platte River to Fort Laramie, continued westward through the South Pass, and then turned southward to the Great Salt Lake. Salt Lake City grew rapidly and soon became, to the profit of the Mormons, a convenient stopping-point for migrants on their way to California. The success of the colony, however, was due in large measure to the sound judgment and extraordinary executive ability of Brigham Young. He planned the migration, supervised the settlement of the newcomers and the introduction of irrigation which made the arid desert fertile, and in many other ways warded off the misfortunes that might otherwise have befallen so large a company in so difficult an environment. His vigorous, occasionally arbitrary, leadership was virtually unquestioned by his followers, and he enjoyed the respect even of his enemies.

Polk's Achievement. Polk's policy of expansion was carried through well before

his term of office was over, and without a serious failure. He obtained all of Oregon to which he could reasonably lay claim, insured the permanence of the annexation of Texas, and by taking one-third of the territory of Mexico advanced the boundary of the United States to the Pacific in the Far Southwest, as it had already been advanced in the Far Northwest. Important settlements had been made in every section of the new acquisitions — in Oregon, in California, in New Mexico, and, thanks to the Mormon migration, in what was soon to be known as Utah. Well-defined trails crossed the continent to the Southwest, to the Northwest, and in between. Much of the western country was still regarded as uninhabitable, but such guides as Kit Carson, who accompanied Frémont on some of his explorations and showed Kearny the way from Santa Fe to California, and Jim Bridger, who discovered the Great Salt Lake, were fast dispelling its mysteries.

While Polk's main concern as President was expansion, he was able during the first half of his administration to redeem two of his party's pledges on domestic affairs. On July 30, 1846, he signed the Walker Tariff, a measure that again turned the country away from protection and toward the principle of a tariff for revenue only. Enactment of the lowered rates met much opposition from the industrial interests of New England and the Middle Atlantic states, but significantly it won support from the West as well as from the South. The second of the Democratic pledges which Polk carried through was the reestablishment by act of Congress, signed August 6, 1846, of the independent, or Sub-Treasury, system that had been discontinued early in the preceding administration.

The Wilmot Proviso. Far more exciting than either the tariff or the Sub-Treasury was a question that began to be raised as soon as war broke out with Mexico. Should slavery be permitted to expand into the territory soon to be acquired? This issue was formally presented to Congress as early as August, 1846, when David Wilmot, an antislavery Democrat from Pennsylvania, proposed an amendment to a bill appropriating money for the purchase of territory from Mexico. According to the Wilmot Proviso, which failed of passage, "neither slavery nor involuntary servitude" was ever to be permitted in any territory so acquired. The Wilmot Proviso was debated, not only in Congress, where for years it was proposed, but throughout the country at large. Northern antislavery men maintained that Congress was legally competent to exclude slavery from the territories of the United States, and should exercise its right at once. Southern extremists took the opposite view and held that the Constitution, because it recognized and protected slavery in some of the states, must be construed to protect slavery also in the territories, for otherwise the property rights of slaveowners would be discriminated against in a region which was the joint possession of all the states. Still others were ready to compromise. Some said that the Missouri Compromise

line should be extended all the way to the Pacific; others, that the new territories to be formed in the West should decide for themselves whether they would be free or slave. This latter idea, known generally as "squatter sovereignty," was suggested first by Lewis Cass of Michigan, but it was later taken up by Stephen A. Douglas of Illinois, who renamed it "popular sovereignty," and won for it many adherents.

The obvious determination of the northern antislavery forces to keep the South's "peculiar institution" out of the Mexican cession drove southern extremists to a frenzy of anxiety. They knew that in population the North was drawing further and further away from the South, while unless new territory open to slavery could be acquired, the balance of the sections in the Senate would soon be broken. Iowa and Wisconsin, admitted in 1846 and 1848, respectively, would serve as offsets to Florida and Texas, admitted in 1845, but Minnesota could not long be kept out of the Union, and the Oregon country offered an additional opportunity for the creation of new free states. Southern members of Congress, in a vain attempt to extend the Missouri Compromise line to the Pacific, held up the organization of a free territorial government in Oregon until 1848.

The Election of 1848. The issue raised by the Wilmot Proviso was so fraught with peril to the Union that both the Whigs and the Democrats evaded it during the campaign and election of 1848. The Democrats turned to the West for their presidential candidate, Lewis Cass. The Whigs presented as their candidate General Zachary Taylor, the "hero of Buena Vista," who by a lucky chance happened to be from Louisiana and to own over a hundred slaves. For second place on their ticket, the Whigs chose Millard Fillmore, an obscure politician from western New York. But this flouting by the older parties of the most significant issue before the country led to the union of many antislavery men, of all gradations of opinion, in support of a new "Free Soil" Party, which called eloquently for "Free Soil, Free Speech, Free Labor, and Free Men." To win the votes of the strong anti-Polk faction among the northern Democrats, the third party leaders chose as their standard-bearer ex-President Van Buren. His refusal to countenance the annexation of Texas had not only lost him the Democratic nomination in 1844, but had also won the enthusiastic applause of many antislavery men. During the campaign the Free Soilers emphasized primarily the necessity of keeping the lands of the West out of the clutches of the southern slaveholders in order to make them available for the use of small free farmers. The strength of the Free Soil movement was revealed when it polled nearly 300,000 votes, won the balance of power in a dozen states, and drew enough votes from the Democratic column in New York to throw that state, and the election, to Taylor. The thirteen Free Soilers chosen to the House of Representatives were a power to be reckoned with, for no party had a majority in that branch of Congress.

Gold in California. The discovery of gold in California early in 1848, and the subsequent gold rush, introduced a new element into the situation. Immediately thousands of men from every part of the United States left for California. Gold seekers who could not afford anything better took the long journey overland by covered wagon; others took ship around Cape Horn; still others went expensively and with great danger to their health by way of the Isthmus of Panama. Agitation at once began for the building of a Panama Canal, and to promote this venture the United States and Great Britain, in the Clayton-Bulwer Treaty of 1850, accepted joint responsibility for any such undertaking. Meantime, not the United States alone, but the whole world caught the gold-fever, and a huge polygot population descended upon California. San Francisco, a city of tents and shacks, grew

A FORTY-NINER

This sketch is by John Woodhouse Audubon (son of John James Audubon), who went to California in 1849 by way of Mexico.

prodigiously. The temporary military government was totally inadequate to handle so bewildering a situation. The need of an adequate and authoritative civil government was obvious, and was keenly felt.

Zachary Taylor. It devolved naturally upon the new President, Zachary Taylor (1784–1850), to take the initiative in seeking a solution for this pressing problem. Taylor was a Virginian by birth, but he grew to manhood in frontier Kentucky, and from his youth was an officer in the regular army. He was in no sense a politician, but was honest and forthright, well accustomed to meeting emergencies, and unembarrassed by the necessity of making a sudden decision. His solution for the problem of government in the newly acquired territory was simple. Let the people of California and New Mexico organize state governments and decide for themselves whether to be slave states or free states. Heedful of the President's advice, the Californians in 1849 drew up a constitution, elected state officers, and took over the government of their self-created state. New Mexico, with less occasion for haste, was not ready with its constitution until a year later. Even the Mormons caught the contagion, drew up a

273

constitution, discreetly silent on slavery, for a proposed state of Deseret, and with Brigham Young as their duly elected governor, applied for admission to the Union. But to the immense chagrin of the proslavery politicians, none of the prospective states showed any disposition to establish slavery within its borders.

Had Taylor been more experienced in politics, he might have known that Congress would never permit him, unaided, to resolve the dispute over slavery in the newly acquired territory. The Congress that convened late in 1849 was one of the ablest ever chosen, because it was a kind of meeting-point of two generations. In it sat the three great statesmen of the preceding era: Daniel Webster, John C. Calhoun, and Henry Clay. But its roster contained also the names of many men whose careers were before them, such as Salmon P. Chase, William H. Seward, Thaddeus Stevens, Stephen A. Douglas, Jefferson Davis, Alexander H. Stephens, and Robert Toombs. Naturally such a Congress proposed to have a hand in the slavery question, and all eyes turned for leadership to the aged Henry Clay, whose reputation as a compromiser was justly deserved. Throughout his life he had never held so tenaciously to any principle that under sufficient pressure he had found himself unable to give it up.

The Compromise of 1850. It is not fair, however, to assign the whole credit for the Compromise of 1850 to Henry Clay. Other men, notably Stephen A. Douglas, had an important part in its making, and during the long debate over the Wilmot Proviso a multitude of political theorists had set forth the various possibilities of compromise. It was Clay, however, who presented to the Senate the elaborate resolutions that were to form the basis of compromise, and it was Clay's well-established reputation that won for them an instant hearing. Sensibly, his resolutions did not stop with the question of slavery extension, but included also all the other phases of the slavery problem

with which the public mind was vexed. Clay hoped that his plan would restore "the peace, concord, and harmony of the Union" for another thirty years, the length of time that the Missouri Compromise had lasted. On January 29, 1850, he asked the Senate to consider (1) permitting California to enter the Union as a free state, but setting no restrictions on slavery in the rest of the territory acquired from Mexico, (2) defining the western boundary of Texas, (3) abolishing the slave trade (but not slavery) in the District of Columbia, (4) enacting a more stringent fugitive slave law, and (5) asserting that Congress had no right to interfere with the interstate slave trade.

The debate that these resolutions precipitated in the United States Senate ranks as one of the greatest in American legislative history. Clay led off in a defense of the Compromise that was less an exposition of its provisions than an appeal to Congress and the country to quiet the clamor over slavery, and thus to save the nation from the unnecessary chaos of civil war. To his support came his old rival for preferment within the Whig Party, Daniel Webster, who argued that the prohibition of slavery in New Mexico was an unnecessary taunt and reproach to the South, for slavery could never survive in that alien soil. Why "re-enact the will of God"? Webster's "Seventh of March" speech on the Compromise justly ranks as among the most memorable of American orations. But neither of these giants, nor the lesser men who followed in their train, were able to win over the extremists. John C. Calhoun, so old and ill that his address had to be read by a colleague, accused the North of intending to destroy "irretrievably the equilibrium between the two sections." William H. Seward, the young Senator from New York, denounced with equal vehemence the transplantation of slavery into new soil, asserted that emancipation was both inevitable and near, and urged that its peaceful consummation should not be impeded by new proslavery laws.

THE WEBSTER-HAYNE DEBATE

Daniel Webster Addressing the Senate during the Great Debate on the Compromise of 1850. The artist includes many recognizable portraits of Webster's contemporaries, but packs over a hundred persons on the Senate floor, whereas the Senate membership then numbered only sixty.

Sentiment for the Compromise. Meantime, sentiment throughout the country began to assert itself unmistakably in favor of some sort of compromise. Businessmen, thanks to the flow of gold from California and the increasing demand for railways, enjoyed a degree of prosperity unparalleled since the panic of 1837. Farmers benefited materially from the strong foreign demand for American grain that followed the repeal of the Corn Laws in England, and commercial interests, already flourishing because of the pre-eminence of the American-built clipper ship, were still further stimulated by the low rates of the Walker Tariff. Workers drew high wages and could count on steady employment. Such prosperity was far too precious to be disturbed by an academic dispute over slavery. Northern manufacturers were particularly eager to insure the permanence of their southern markets by conciliating the South; while southern producers were by no means happy at the prospect of secession, with its inevitable disruption of their normal lines of trade.

Millard Fillmore. As the favorable reaction of the country made itself felt, Congress became increasingly willing to accept some form of compromise. Even so, serious obstacles had to be surmounted. Most baffling was the unrelenting opposition of President Taylor, who seemed determined to pursue his own course without regard for the wishes of Congress. But in July, 1850, the President was taken suddenly ill, probably of cholera morbus, and died within a few days. The new President, Millard Fillmore (1800–1874), was known only as a successful lawyer from Buffalo, New York, who had served several terms in the state legislature and in Congress. Early in his career he had won some distinction by pushing through the New York legislature an act for the abolition of imprisonment for debt; later, as a member of Congress, he had much to do with the writing of the Tariff of 1842. When nominated for the Vice-Presidency he was generally regarded as an antislavery man, but the debates in the Senate on the Compromise measures, to

275

which he listened as presiding officer, seem to have impressed upon him the urgent necessity of conciliating the South. On succeeding to the Presidency he at once put himself into the hands of Clay, formed a new Cabinet with Webster at its head, and gave his undivided support to the proposed plan of compromise.

The Compromise Adopted. Most of Clay's original proposals found their way first into three, and finally into five, separate measures, a device which permitted each measure to pass with a different majority. It thus came about that the Compromise of 1850, as finally passed by Congress and signed by the President, was complete in five laws: (1) California was admitted as a free state; (2) New Mexico was created a territory without the Wilmot Proviso, and the claim of Texas to New Mexican territory was indemnified by the payment of $10 million from the federal treasury; (3) Utah was created a territory without the Wilmot Proviso; (4) more stringent provision was made for the return of fugitive slaves; and (5) the slave trade was abolished in the District of Columbia. Actually only four senators voted for every one of the five measures, although several others, including Clay and Douglas, would have done so had they not been unavoidably absent when some of the votes were taken. Indeed, in both houses of Congress the majorities in favor of the various compromise bills were in no two instances identical.

For a time it seemed that the Compromise, which by the admission of California at last upset the balance of sections in the Senate, might fail to satisfy the South. In four states, Georgia, Mississippi, Alabama, and South Carolina, special state conventions were held to consider the advisability of immediate secession, but only in South Carolina were the secessionists able to command a majority. On second thought the people of the South made up their minds to accept the Compromise, and even the South Carolinians were unwilling to risk secession without the support of other southern states.

The "Georgia Platform," which looked upon the Compromise as a "permanent adjustment of the sectional controversy," probably best expressed the southern point of view. But the North was warned that the preservation of the Union depended on the "execution of the Fugitive Slave Bill."

The Fugitive Slave Act was gall and wormwood to the antislavery people of the North. It denied the right of trial by jury to the fugitive, refused him the privilege of testifying in his own behalf, and virtually required that he be turned over to anyone who claimed him. Federal marshals and their deputies were enjoined, under threat of heavy penalties, to make unusual exertions to capture fugitives, and anyone aiding in the escape of a slave was liable to a fine of not more than $1,000 or imprisonment not to exceed six months, in addition to civil damages of $1,000 to the owner of the slave. These terms, quite obviously, were not dictated merely by the desire to secure the return of fugitive slaves. They were, and they were meant to be, as Rhodes says, "a taunt and reproach to that part of the North where the antislavery sentiment ruled supremely." But even this thoroughly obnoxious act did not keep the North from rallying to the support of the Compromise. Business interests were enthusiastically for it, able lawyers defended it as if it were constitutional throughout, and the promise of the politicians that it had settled the issue of slavery with finality was accepted with a feeling of great relief. Peace and prosperity lay ahead.

The Election of 1852. The presidential election of 1852 served as a kind of popular referendum on the Compromise. The Democratic nominee, Franklin Pierce of New Hampshire, another "dark horse," had given his unqualified endorsement to the Compromise, while the convention which nominated him had announced its determination to "resist all attempts at renewing, in Congress or out of it, the agitation of the slavery question." The Whigs, on the other hand, because many of their ablest leaders had opposed the Compromise, were unable to take so bold a stand. They "acquiesced in" the Compromise, but they refused to renominate Millard Fillmore, the President whose signatures had made it possible, and turned instead to General Winfield Scott, whose reputation, like Taylor's, grew out of the Mexican war, and whose views on the Compromise were unknown. The issue before the electorate was thus primarily Franklin Pierce and the Compromise, or General Scott and uncertainty. A third alternative was offered by the Free Soil candidacy of John P. Hale, but four years of Whig supremacy had brought the Van Buren Democrats back into the party fold, so that the Free Soilers polled little more than half the votes in 1852 that they had polled four years before. The popular verdict was plain. The Democrats carried twenty-seven states, and the Whigs only four: Massachusetts, Vermont, Kentucky, and Tennessee. Pierce's electoral vote was 254 to Scott's 42. Indeed, the Whig Party, which throughout its existence had rarely been more than an "organized incompatibility," collapsed under the blow, and was never again strong enough to contest a presidential election. For the time being an overwhelming majority, both in the North and in the South, chose to believe that the slavery question was permanently settled.

SELECTED BIBLIOGRAPHY

Several recent documentary collections on the West are useful here. See especially, R. V. Hine and E. R. Bingham (eds.), *The Frontier Experience* (1963); R. A. Billington, *The Westward Movement in the United States* (1959); and Bayrd Still (ed.), *The West* (1961). A stimulating reinterpretation which stresses the desire of statesmen for ports on the Pacific is N. A. Graebner, *Empire on the Pacific* (1955). Bernard De Voto, *Year of Decision, 1846* (1943), is an exciting book by a colorful and opinionated western enthusiast. An influential study of the trans-Mississippi environment is W. P. Webb, *The Great Plains* (1931). Bernard De Voto, *Across the Wide Missouri* (1947), is a lively treatment of the Rocky Mountain fur trade, magnificently illustrated. See also J. E. Sunder, *The Fur Trade on the Upper Missouri, 1840–1865* (1965). R. G. Cleland, *This Reckless Breed of Men* (1950), covers the mountain men of the Southwest. A clear summary of a complex subject is G. G. Cline, *Exploring the Great Basin* (1963). An interesting regional survey is R. G. Athearn, *High Country Empire; The High Plains and Rockies* (1960). One great post is dealt with by David Lavender, *Bent's Fort* (1954).

On New Mexico and the Santa Fe trail, Josiah Gregg, *Commerce of the Prairies: or, The Journal of a Santa Fe Trader* (1844), is a classic. A competent regional history is W. E.

* Available in paperback

Hollon, *The Southwest* (1961). H. E. Bolton was a leading authority on the Spanish Southwest; see especially his *The Spanish Borderlands* (1921), and *Coronado* (1949). Other important books on this period include G. P. Hammond, *Don Juan de Oñate and the Founding of New Mexico* (1927); and A. B. Thomas, *After Coronado* (1935). A classic account of the fur trade in this region is L. H. Garrard, *Wah-to-yah, and the Taos Trail* (1850).

On Utah and the Mormons, H. H. Bancroft published an immensely detailed two-volume history in his *Works*, cited below. L. H. Creer, *The Founding of an Empire* (1947), is meticulous and detailed. A lively popular account is R. B. West, Jr., *Kingdom of the Saints* (1957). A valuable source collection is *Among the Mormons*, edited by William Mulder and A. R. Mortensen (1958). L. J. Arrington, *The Great Basin Kingdom: An Economic History of the Mormon People* (1958), is one of the finest pieces of scholarship in western history. See also: F. M. Brodie, *No Man Knows My History; The Life of Joseph Smith* (1945), highly critical; D. L. Morgan, *The Great Salt Lake* (1947); T. F. O'Dea, *The Mormons* (1957); and Wallace Stegner, *The Gathering of Zion* (1964). On the "Utah War," see Juanita Brooks, *The Mountain Meadow Massacre* (2nd ed., 1962); and N. F. Furniss, *The Mormon Conflict* (1960).

On the Pacific Northwest, good surveys are D. O. Johansen and C. M. Gates, *Empire of* the Columbia (1957); and O. O. Winther, *The Great Northwest* (2nd ed., 1950). Francis Parkman, °*The Oregon Trail* (1849), is a great classic. Also valuable for this trail is David Lavender, *Westward Vision* (1963), a popular history of the Pacific Northwest. On the solution of the Oregon crisis see Frederick Merk, *Albert Gallatin and the Oregon Problem* (1950). C. M. Drury, *Marcus Whitman, M.D.* (1937), is an excellent biography of an important figure. A well-written account of missionary activities is Nard Jones, *The Great Command* (1959). A useful monograph about the Indians of this region is Philip Drucker, °*Indians of the Northwest Coast* (1955).

On California, the best survey is J. W. Caughey, *California* (2nd ed., 1953), especially rich on the Spanish period and containing a full bibliography. H. H. Bancroft, *The Works of Hubert Howe Bancroft* (39 vols., 1874–1890), is a great compendium, of which seven volumes comprise a history of California and several others treat California themes. Bancroft's interest in western history spread from California to the regions north, south, and east of it. Much of his writing was done for him by the staff members in his "history factory," and it is unequal in value. See the excellent biography by J. W. Caughey, *Hubert Howe Bancroft* (1946). On the overland trails, see I. D. Paden, *The Wake of the Prairie Schooner* (1943); and G. R. Stewart, *The California Trail* (1962). On the Gold Rush, J. W. Caughey, *Gold is the Cornerstone* (1948), is judicious and well written; and R. W. Paul, °*California Gold* (1947), is especially well-informed on technology. One of the most important recent works in western history is D. L. Morgan (ed.), *The Overland Diary of James A. Pritchard* (1959). Other valuable California studies include J. H. Kemble, *The Panama Route, 1848–1869* (1943); and J. A. B. Scherer, *Thirty-First Star* (1942). A classic legal work is C. H. Shinn, °*Mining Camps* (1885).

On Texas, see the good general history by R. N. Richardson, *Texas* (2nd ed., 1958). J. H. Smith, *The Annexation of Texas* (2nd ed., 1941), is a full treatment of a basic problem. A biography of the last Texas president is Herbert Gambrell, *Anson Jones* (1964).

On the Mexican War, see the excellent collection of conflicting interpretations, °*The Mexican War; Was It Manifest Destiny?*

edited by R. E. Ruiz (1963). J. H. Smith, *The War with Mexico* (2 vols., 1919), is richly detailed; it argues that the United States was not wholly to blame for the outbreak of hostilities. Short and objective are R. S. Henry, *The Story of the Mexican War* (1950); and O. A. Singletary, °*The Mexican War* (1960). On Polk see E. I. McCormac, *James K. Polk* (1922); and C. A. McCoy, *Polk and the Presidency* (1960). A vital source is James K. Polk, *The Diary of a President, 1845–1849*, an abridgement edited by Allan Nevins (1952). Biographies of value include C. W. Elliott, *Winfield Scott* (1937); Brainerd Dyer, *Zachary Taylor* (1946); Holman Hamilton, *Zachary Taylor* (2 vols., 1941–1951); Allan Nevins, *Frémont* (1939); and Lloyd Lewis, *Captain Sam Grant* (1950). An excellent short study of political factionalism in the Polk era is J. C. N. Paul, °*Rift in the Democracy* (1951).

Allan Nevins, *Ordeal of the Union* (2 vols., 1947), reviews in great detail the events of the decade following the war with Mexico. A brief treatment by another leading scholar is R. F. Nichols, °*The Stakes of Power, 1845–1877* (1961). A. C. Cole, *The Irrepressible Conflict, 1850–1865* (1934), is excellent social history. °*The Compromise of 1850* is a useful anthology edited by E. C. Rozwenc (1957). An interesting analysis by a major authority is Holman Hamilton, *Prologue to Conflict* (1964). A. O. Craven takes an essentially pro-southern position; see his *The Repressible Conflict, 1830–1861* (1939); *The Growth of Southern Nationalism, 1848–1861* (1953); *The Coming of the Civil War* (2nd ed., 1957); and *Civil War in the Making, 1815–1860* (1959).

Biographies of the principals in the Compromise of 1850 are important. See again those of Clay, Calhoun, Webster, and Taylor, listed earlier. On Douglas, consult G. F. Milton, *The Eve of Conflict* (1934), a full-length study by a strong admirer; and G. M. Capers, *Stephen A. Douglas* (1959), a brief biography whose subtitle, "Defender of the Union," indicates its thesis. U. B. Phillips, *The Life of Robert Toombs* (1913), is a good study of an important southern leader. Other works on major political figures include R. J. Rayback, *Millard Fillmore* (1959); F. B. Woodford, *Lewis Cass* (1950); R. F. Nichols, *Franklin Pierce* (1931); and C. H. Hall, *Abel Parker Upshur* (1963). R. F. Nichols, *The Democratic Machine, 1850–1854* (1923), is a work of lasting importance.

17

PEACE AND PROSPERITY

The prominence of the slavery dispute in American politics during the two decades preceding the Civil War has tended to divert attention from other subjects of great significance. During these years railway construction revolutionized transportation, industry and commerce expanded phenomenally, agriculture began its far-reaching shift from traditional to more mechanized methods, a new flood of European immigrants swept over the country, and the final conquest of the Far West was assured.

The Railroad. Undoubtedly the greatest factor in transforming American society during this period was the railroad. Until about 1840 this means of transportation was still in the experimental stage, and the building of a railroad was a choice of desperation, resorted to only where engineering difficulties made a canal impossible. The Baltimore and Ohio railroad line opened a few miles to traffic in 1830, and the Charleston and Hamburg, in 1833, with its 137 miles

of track across the state of South Carolina, was the longest railroad in the world. Short lines were built to facilitate trade between the principal cities and their outlying districts. By 1840 the total railroad trackage of the country had reached 2,818 miles.

Horses and sails for motive power, used by some of the earliest railroads, were quickly discarded in favor of steam locomotives similar to those built by George Stephenson, the English inventor, but lighter and speedier. Wooden rails, bound by thin iron straps, gave way to far more durable iron rails. Improved engineering knowledge eliminated the dizzy curves and steep grades, characteristic of the early road-beds, while wooden cross-ties, designed to insure that the two lines of rails remained at all times equidistant, replaced the more uncertain separate foundations. Low four-wheeled trucks, pivoted beneath each end of a freight or passenger car, made the rounding of curves less hazardous, and pointed the way to a complete abandonment of the stagecoach and rail-wagon appearance of the first "rolling stock." Coal began to replace wood as fuel, partly to save the time consumed in "wooding up" at frequent intervals, partly to allay the irritation of passengers whose clothing caught fire from the steady stream of sparks that a wood-burner always emitted. Also, the necessity of railroad companies to own the equipment and manage the traffic was

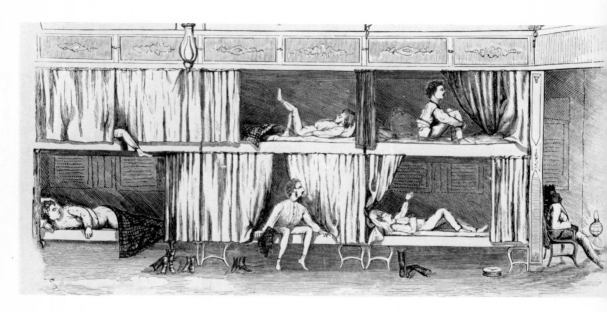

THE COMFORTS OF RAIL TRAVEL

Interior view of a sleeping car, about 1850, presumably on a warm night.

quickly demonstrated. For this service they exacted whatever charges they saw fit, but as "common carriers" they were under obligation to accept for shipment anything within reason presented to them.

Through Routes. The public, at first suspicious of the privately owned and operated railroads, soon became enthusiastic about them. Connections, such as those making possible all-rail transportation from Boston to Albany after 1841, added tremendously to the business of the connecting lines, and pointed the way to future development. The significant part that the railroads might play in linking the East and the West became apparent in 1842, when a series of seven or eight local lines furnished an alternative route to the Erie Canal across the state of New York. The combinations of all such roads into one through route, delayed in this case until the emergence of the New York Central in 1853, was a logical next step. By that year three other lines connected the eastern seaboard with the West: the Erie, completed through southern New York in 1851; the Pennsyl-

vania, opened all the way to Pittsburgh in 1852; and the Baltimore and Ohio, which reached the Ohio River at Wheeling in 1853. Within the West itself the railroad was hailed as the long-sought solution to the problem of land transportation, and innumerable ambitious projects were begun. Such cities as Memphis, Chicago, and St. Louis, eager to become important as railroad centers, held railroad "conventions" to arouse enthusiasm. Hastily built local lines were soon succeeded by through routes, such as the Michigan Central and the Michigan Southern, which reached Chicago in 1852, and the Rock Island and Chicago, which connected the Great Lakes with the Mississippi River in 1854. The next year through rail connections were established between New York and St. Louis.

Railroad Finance. The task of providing funds for these extensive enterprises taxed the resources of the railroad promoters to the limit. The earlier roads, when not actually owned and operated by some state, could ordinarily depend upon a loan of the state's credit or a generous state subscription to railroad stock. But as already noted, this policy was very generally discredited after the financial disasters that overtook the states during the panic of 1837. Railroad lobbyists were able, however, to get direct aid from a few states, and they became extremely adept at securing from all the states valuable privileges and immunities for the companies they represented. They also induced cities and counties that lay along the route of a proposed line to vote large sums to the coveted railroad, either as outright gifts, or as loans, or as subscriptions to stock. Skillful if none too scrupulous salesmen persuaded private investors, foreigners as well as Americans, to buy large blocks of railroad securities. Finally, the politicians who sympathized with the aims of the railroads won from Congress grants of federal land to be used in aid of railroad building. The first such grant was obtained in 1850 for the Illinois Central Railroad by Senator Stephen A. Douglas. According to this act, about 2.6 million acres of land in alternate blocks on each side of the proposed line were granted to the state of Illinois for transfer to the railroad as fast as construction was completed. To secure the necessary political support for this measure, similar grants had to be made available for a railroad from the Ohio River to Mobile; and thereafter land grants were generally allotted to any railroad projected in a region where the government still owned land. Between 1850 and 1860 about 20 million acres of public land were handed over in this manner to the railroads.

Railroad Expansion. Under these circumstances the conquest of the country by the railroads proceeded with astonishing rapidity. The amount of trackage increased from 2,818 miles in 1840 to 9,021 miles in 1850, and to 30,626 miles in 1860. By the last-mentioned year the Northeast alone had 9,500 miles of railroads, more than the whole country had possessed ten years before. Practically all the important eastern cities were connected by rail, and many of them also had direct connections with the West.

The most feverish building, however, had taken place in the Northwest. Before the panic of 1837, this section had hardly a mile of railroad in effective operation; by 1860 it had 11,078 miles, more than one-third of the total trackage of the country. Chicago, mainly because of its natural advantages as a railroad center, had grown from a town of 4,000 inhabitants in 1840 to 29,000 in 1850, and to 109,000 in 1860. Inland cities, such as Indianapolis, had achieved an importance that without the railroads could scarcely have been imagined. Railroad connections between the Great Lakes and the Ohio-Mississippi River system put the western canal virtually out of business and greatly stimulated the growth of such cities as Cleveland, Cincinnati, and Milwaukee, which could serve as links between the waterways and the rails. By 1855 the Mississippi River had been bridged; by 1857 the railroad frontier had reached the Missouri River at St. Joseph.

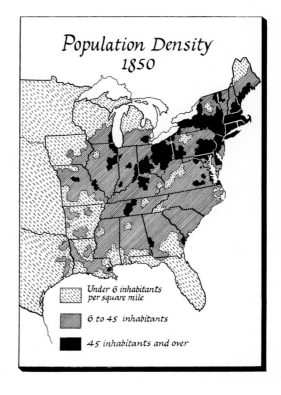

Population Density 1850

Under 6 inhabitants per square mile

6 to 45 inhabitants

45 inhabitants and over

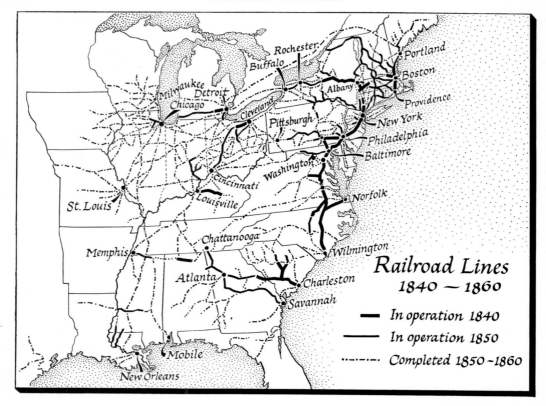

**Railroad Lines
1840 — 1860**

—— In operation 1840

—— In operation 1850

·—·—· Completed 1850~1860

North and South Compared. In the South, railroad building lagged perceptibly. This section, with its extensive coastline and its numerous navigable rivers, stood far less in need of railroads than the Northwest; moreover, whatever surplus capital the South could command was generally invested in plantations and slaves. Nevertheless many short lines were built, and a few achieved sectional importance. By 1860, both Norfolk, Virginia, and Charleston, South Carolina, were connected through Chattanooga, Tennessee, with the Mississippi River at Memphis; and the Mississippi itself was paralleled from the Ohio to the Gulf. With 10,048 miles of railroads the South was only slightly ahead of the Northeast in total mileage, although, in view of its greater distances, the effectiveness of its railroads was far less marked. On the eve of the Civil War the Northeast had about twice as much railroad

trackage per square mile of land as the Northwest, and four times as much as the South.

One of the most striking developments that a railroad map of 1860 reveals is the drawing together of the Northeast and the Northwest. So closely connected, indeed, were the railroads of these two sections that they appeared to be, as to all practical purposes they were, one network. With ever-increasing ease the produce of the Northwest found its way to the consumers of the East and to the eastern seaports for transshipment to Europe. Similarly the eastern manufacturers found in the expanding Northwest a gratifying market for the output of their factories. The southern railroads, on the other hand, were not yet integrated with the railroads of the rest of the country. Because so many of them had been built primarily as a means of supplementing waterways, they lacked even sectional unity, and they made contact with the northern railroad system at only three widely separated points.

YEAR	MILES	YEAR	MILES
RAILROAD MILEAGE IN THE UNITED STATES, 1830–1865			
1830	32	1850	9,021
1835	1,098	1855	18,374
1840	2,818	1860	30,626
1845	4,663	1865	35,085

Western Steamboating. In spite of the mounting significance of the railroads, the western waterways long remained a major factor in the communications system of the country. Until the railroads appeared, the river steamboats had no transportation rivals in the West, and for years after the coming of the roads the Mississippi River continued to carry an enormous volume of traffic. Great shipyards, located at Cincinnati, St. Louis, and Louisville, turned out huge speedy craft to carry grain and merchandise downstream, cotton, rice, and sugar upstream, and a steady flow of passengers both ways. By means of these boats the northern farmers found a needed outlet for their produce in the South; southern cotton planters saved money by buying foodstuffs from the Northwest instead of raising their own; and both farmers and planters had more funds to use in the purchase of eastern manufactured goods. Some of the boats were incredibly swift — the best of them made the trip of about 1,300 miles from New Orleans to St. Louis in four days or less. By the fifties well over a thousand steamboats plied the Mississippi and its tributaries, and since the cost of the larger boats ran to about $50,000 each, this represented a sizable investment. Cargoes valued at $250,000 were not unknown. To the upper Mississippi and its tributaries steamboats brought the benefits of swift transportation long before the railroads arrived, and on the upper Missouri fur traders, too, had their steamboats. Indeed, this elaborate system of river communications seemed so essential to the life of both the Northwest and the South that the prospect of its separation from New Orleans, the head of the river traffic, was one of the worst of the nightmares associated with secession. But the steamboats not only solved a problem of transportation for the West; they created also a way of life and a cast of characters that Mark Twain's *Life on the Mississippi* (1874) has preserved intact for posterity.

Ocean Transportation. The revolution in means of communication that took place during this period also extended to the high seas. American shipbuilders contributed during the 1840's the fleet clipper ship, which with a fair breeze could make better time than the early steamships, and under normal circumstances could make three trips to Europe while an ordinary ship made two. Partly because of the superiority of these clippers, partly because of recurring wars both in Europe and in Asia, American ships for a few years carried a far greater proportion of the world's commerce than they ever had before. During the 1850's, about 70 per cent of the total foreign trade of the United States was carried in ships that flew the American flag, while in the year 1853 alone, according to a reliable estimate, the total tonnage carried by American ships exceeded that of the British by no less than 15 per cent. About 1855, however, the American clipper ship began to be superseded by the British-built iron steamer, which could cross the Atlantic in less than two weeks. From the point of view of efficiency in transportation, it mattered little whether the commerce of the United States was carried in British or American ships. What was of far greater significance was the fact that ocean lanes were being multiplied, and the time of transit was being lessened.

Manufacturing. Easier means of communication had much to do with the growth of industry in the United States during this same period. Not until the advent of the steam locomotive did the full effects of the Industrial Revolution begin to be felt in the United States. Factories that had previously depended on serving only a local market began suddenly to expand, while others, less fortunately situated, began to decline, and even to disappear. Regardless of the number of factories, the total amount of manufactured goods mounted rapidly. By 1850, the first year in which the federal census attempted to ascertain accurately the amount of manufacturing in the country, the total value of manufactured goods was over $1 billion, exceeding slightly the total value of agricultural products, $994 million. Ten years later the figures were $1.88 billion for manufacturing and $1.91 billion for agriculture. But the ascendancy that agriculture seemed to have regained during the fifties proved short-lived, for all subsequent census statistics showed manufacturing far in the lead.

Not only improved transportation, but many other factors tended to promote the growth of American industry. The liberal patent system of the United States, which guaranteed to patent-holders a long-time monopoly upon the manufacture, use, and sale of their inventions, encouraged American inventors to devise many labor-saving machines for use in the factory or on the farm, as well as a great variety of articles for the comfort and satisfaction of individuals. A rising standard of living meant also the manufacture and sale in quantities to the ordinary man of the one-time luxuries of the rich. Moreover, the United States was growing rapidly in population, both from natural increase and from a new wave of immigration; hence the needs of ever greater numbers of people had to be met. Prosperity meant that nearly everyone had the means to buy. Wages were good; agricultural products, thanks in part to the repeal of the Corn Laws in England and in part to the mid-century European wars, brought high prices; newly mined gold and silver paid the bills of the Far West and

Although at times critical of travel facilities in mid-nineteenth century America, European visitors, of whom the Reverend David Macrea was a typical example, were enthusiastic about the steamboats which plied the nation's waterways.

. . . these steamers are admirably contrived for comfort. That one from New Orleans to Vicksburg — the *Robert E. Lee* — was the largest and finest I saw on any American river except the St. Lawrence and the Hudson. Her accommodation was immense; her gorgeous saloon, extending without a break from end to end of the steamer . . . was richly carpeted, and had tables, reading-desks, and luxurious lounges without number. The very spittoons were richly silvered . . . The greater part of the saloon aft of the center tables is fitted up in even more luxurious style, and is reserved for ladies . . . River traveling in America, in these first-class steamers, free as it is from all danger of storm and sea-sickness, is the most delicious and luxurious kind of traveling of which I have ever had experience.

DAVID MACRAE, *The Americans At Home* (1866)

---

helped to provide a stable currency for the United States.

Manufacturing Practices. American manufacturing, in spite of its rapid growth, still showed many immature characteristics. The concentration of factories at strategic centers had only begun. While New England and the Middle Atlantic states maintained their early lead in manufacturing, small factories of one kind or another could be found in any part of the country, even in the South and along the frontier. Another mark of immaturity was the close restriction of American manufacturing to the use of the raw materials produced within the country: comparatively little was imported to be processed. American grain was turned into flour and meal, American forests into sawed lumber, American cotton into cotton goods, American wool into woolen goods, American iron ore into iron products, and so on. Also, with some minor exceptions, the entire output of the American factories was consumed in the United States, and that without fully satisfying the demand. American cotton mills turned out enough cotton goods of the coarser grades, and a little to spare, but the finer grades still had to be imported from Europe. American woolens fell still further short of supplying the domestic demand, for the American manufacturers were handicapped not only by their inability to compete with the English in producing fine fabrics, but also by an inadequate American supply of raw wool. The use of anthracite coal and of coke as fuel greatly stimulated the iron industry and pointed the way to a phenomenal development, but the heavy demands of the railway age long remained greater than the American supply could meet. In many minor industries the situation was not far different.

The Tariff. The high degree of prosperity that American manufacturers enjoyed during these years was achieved in spite of the relatively low duties of the Walker Tariff. Naturally, the fact that importers were able to throw upon the

AN EARLY IRON WORKS

The Nashua Iron Company, in New Hampshire, promised "the best quality and every form used . . . for Steam Marine Work, for Ship Work, and upon Railroads."

American market a plentiful supply of foreign-made goods was not relished by manufacturers. However, demands for higher duties to promote the more rapid expansion of American industry, while persistent, were unsuccessful. Both the South and the West profited from the low duties, as did the commercial and shipping interests of the East. Indeed, in 1857 the rates of the Walker Tariff were still further reduced.

The Profits of Cotton Growing. Circumstances conspired to make this period one of extraordinary prosperity for the cotton growers of the South. The steady fall in the price of cotton that had at first accompanied the expansion of cotton growing was arrested in the forties and reversed in the fifties. From an all-time low of less than six cents a pound in 1845, cotton rose to an average of ten to eleven cents through the fifties, and to nearly fourteen cents in 1857. Nor was this change in price due to any curtailment of production, for each year saw a sizable increase in the acreage devoted to cotton culture. Rather, the world demand for cotton had been im-

mensely accelerated. Improvement in textile machinery now made possible the manufacture of cotton goods for sale at so low a price that even primitive peoples could buy it. Manufacturers everywhere turned to the American South for their raw cotton, for nowhere else could they find an abundant supply of comparable quality. To meet this tremendous demand practically all the land of the South that was suited to cotton culture was used for that purpose. Except for cotton and tobacco the production of every important crop in the South failed during the fifties to keep pace with the growth of the population. But the cotton crop, which had risen from 1.5 million bales in 1840 to 2.5 million bales in 1850, reached the enormous total of 5.3 million bales in 1860 — seven-eighths of the world's supply.

Tobacco Growing. Less frequently noted is the fact that during these same years a renaissance of tobacco growing made the states of the upper South more prosperous than they had been for years. This was due in part to the increased demand of a growing world population, in part to the introduction of new species, and to improved methods of cultivation and manufacture. In 1849 the tobacco crop of the United States amounted to less than 200 million pounds; ten years later it was nearly 430 million pounds. Virginia and Kentucky were the greatest tobacco-growing states, but Maryland, Tennessee, and Missouri also contributed large quotas. Indeed, every state in the Union, North as well as South, grew some tobacco, although the cotton states during this decade grew proportionately less tobacco than they had ever grown before.

While tobacco was second in value only to cotton among the crops of the South, it was a rather poor second. Throughout that section the saying that "Cotton is King!" went unchallenged. Southerners were proud of the fact that the world depended upon them almost exclusively to supply one of the primary necessities of civilization; they relished the thought that without their help the wheels of industry in the North and in England would scarcely turn; they never forgot that the export of cotton paid more than half the bills contracted by the United States abroad. On one score, however, they confessed some embarrassment. The world's need for cotton would continue to mount, but by the end of the fifties the South's ability to meet that need would be taxed to the limit. Practically all available cotton-growing land was already in use, and in the older states continual planting of the same crop had almost exhausted the soil. New cotton lands must be found. If they did not exist within the United States, why not expand the national borders to include them?

The Northwest Farmer.   In the general reign of plenty, the small farmer of the Northwest was not forgotten. The steady growth in population meant for him, too, an increased demand. Eastern farmers were unable to meet in full the needs of their new industrial centers for foodstuffs, but the western farmer, thanks to improved means of transportation, was able to flood the eastern markets with his produce. By mid-century he had become the nation's most important producer of wheat, corn, and hogs. Southerners also, owing to their increasing concentration upon cotton and tobacco, consumed an ever-growing quantity of northwestern farm products. For this intersectional trade the Mississippi and its tributaries still furnished a cheap and easy means of transportation; and it is worth noting that nearly all the northern goods sent down the river in the years immediately preceding the Civil War found a market in the South itself. The export of northern grain and flour from New Orleans, once deemed so important a factor in the economic life of the Northwest, dwindled to insignificance in comparison to the domestic trade. This did not mean, however, that exports of northwestern products were

not being made, for during the middle years of the century the need of Europe for American foodstuffs was considerable. But grain and flour destined for a foreign market now generally went by rail to the eastern ports for transshipment, instead of by river boats, as formerly, to New Orleans. These overseas sales, while only a small part of the total output of the American farms, were sufficient most of the time to absorb the excess not needed for domestic consumption. Particularly during the Crimean War (1853–1856), the European demand was great and the prices paid were correspondingly high. Stimulated by the new prosperity, the population of the Northwest grew with amazing rapidity. Frontier conditions quickly disappeared in central Illinois, Missouri, Iowa, and southern Wisconsin, and in 1858 a new northwestern state, Minnesota, was added to the Union.

The Revolution in Agriculture.   That a revolution in agriculture had begun — a revolution soon to be particularly significant for the new Northwest — was perhaps less apparent to contemporaries than to later generations. The farmer was no longer so strictly concerned, as once he had been, that his own farm should produce all the necessities of life for himself and his family. New agricultural machines, such as the reaper, enabled him to produce far more of certain commodities than he could hope to use. New means of transportation, especially the railroads, enabled him to ship his excess to market. With the proceeds from the sale of his crop he could now buy many of the things he formerly had to make for himself or go without. He could, and did, begin to specialize in farming, even to the extent of producing only one kind of crop. His farm became a kind of factory upon whose profits he lived. No longer was he independent of the rest of the world, for he must sell to it and buy from it. His purchases stimulated manufacturing, and the growth of manufacturing provided him with new markets. Northwestern

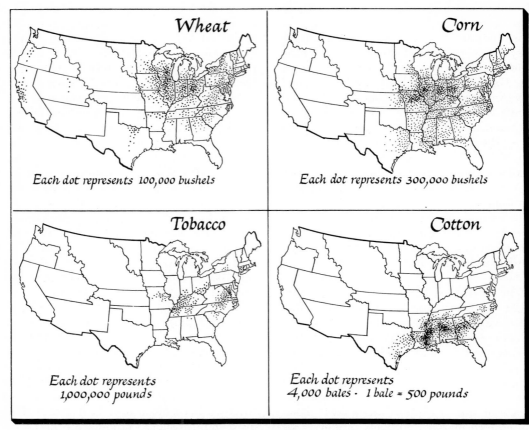

Agricultural Products in the United States in 1859

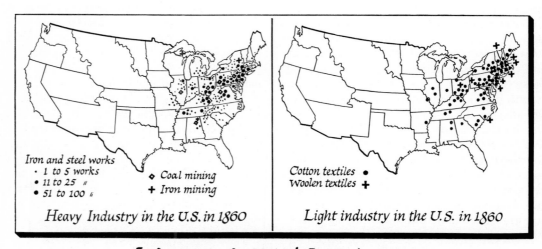

Industry in the United States in 1860

farmers, while grateful for the markets that the cotton- and tobacco-growers of the South were also providing, were increasingly conscious of the greater purchasing power of the industrial Northeast. The bond of union that was being cemented between these two sections would soon be strong enough to meet the test of civil war.

Exploitation of Mineral Resources. The rich natural resources of the United States were already contributing generously to what President Franklin Pierce chose to call "the light of our prosperity." Precious metals had much, although by no means everything, to do with making the population of California four times as large in 1860 as it had been in 1850. Magnificent virgin forests in the upper Mississippi Valley furnished an enormous supply of lumber to the prairie states below. The lead mines of northwestern Illinois and southwestern Wisconsin, once worked by the Indians, now made profits for the new settlers. Coal and iron ore were found conveniently close together in central and western Pennsylvania. The first oil well was drilled in 1859, near Titusville in northwestern Pennsylvania.

Immigration. It is not surprising that the United States, as "the land of opportunity," attracted during these prosperous years a host of European immigrants. The impact of the Industrial Revolution upon Europe had not been without its unfortunate aspects. Those left unemployed by the introduction of labor-saving devices found difficulty in obtaining re-employment. Also, political disturbances, such as the Chartist movement in England and the revolutions of 1848 on the Continent, accompanied the changing economic order. For those who wished to flee this turmoil, Europe had no adequate outlet of its own, but this defect the United States was fortunately in good position to remedy. Its industries were new and could profitably absorb both skilled and unskilled European workmen. Its frontier, seemingly capable of almost indefinite

expansion, could give homes not only to its own millions, but to millions of Europeans as well. Before 1840 the number of immigrants who came to the United States each year was almost negligible, 23,000 in 1830, and 84,000 in 1840; but between 1845 and 1855 the average number of newcomers admitted annually had risen to not less than 300,000. They came from many lands, but, owing to special circumstances, from Ireland and Germany far more than from all other countries combined.

The Irish. The new Irish immigrants came from the southern counties; they were Celtic in origin and Roman Catholic in religion. Their incentives for leaving Ireland were numerous: political oppression, absentee landlordism, overpopulation, and above all a series of devastating famines that began with the failure of the potato crop in 1845. The Irish landed virtually destitute at Boston, New York, and other

AERIAL VIEW OF BOSTON, 1860

This early photograph was taken from a captive balloon.

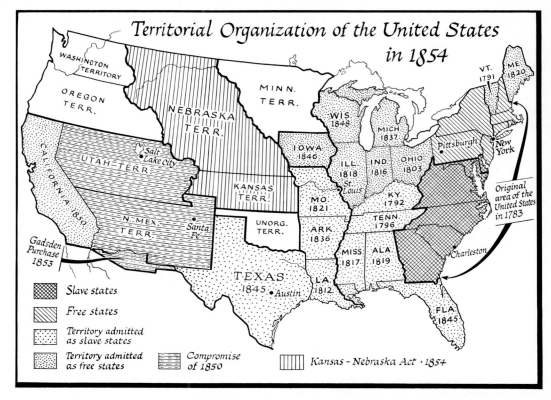

Territorial Organization of the United States in 1854

Slave states

Free states

Territory admitted as slave states

Territory admitted as free states

Compromise of 1850

Kansas - Nebraska Act · 1854

eastern ports, and went to work at small wages in the factories, on the railroads, or wherever their help was needed. Thousands of Irish girls found employment as domestics. Soon nearly every city had its "Shantytown" where the newly arrived Irish lived in quarters even more squalid than those they had known in Ireland, and prospered on incomes that to the native Americans seemed pitifully inadequate.

The Germans. In the vanguard of the German migration were the political refugees, liberals who had taken a part in the revolutions of 1848, only to lose to what they considered to be the forces of reaction. Some men of this type, such as Carl Schurz, soon achieved a greater prominence in their adopted land than they had ever known in Germany. Still others left to avoid the compulsory military service required by most German states, and others to escape distressing economic conditions for which they

saw no hope of improvement. The success of the British manufacturers with factory-made textiles brought ruin to the numerous German household producers of linen, while crop failures in the Rhine Valley and a losing struggle to hold the English grain market meant critical times for German agriculture. Unlike the Irish, the Germans rarely settled in the East, but went instead to the Middle West, where lands were cheaper and opportunity more abundant. For a generation or more they continued to speak the German language, and clung tenaciously to the manners and customs of their native land.

Certain politicians, in search of new issues after the Compromise of 1850 had effected at least a temporary truce over the issue of slavery, were quick to discover in the immigrant a menace to American institutions. Some citizens in the port cities and the districts adjacent to them complained bitterly of the pauper population created by the immigrant tide. Certain religious zealots professed alarm at the presence of a rapidly growing Roman Catholic element in a country that before had always been predominantly Protestant. Some workmen complained that their wages were being lowered and their jobs taken away from them by aliens. Southerners were deeply concerned because the foreigners, antagonistic to slavery and aware that the South provided few opportunities for the European immigrant, helped to swell the already alarming population lead of the North.

The Know-Nothings. The first impulse of many politicians, however, was to cater to the foreign vote. Aliens were permitted to exercise the suffrage after an extremely short period of residence, German and Irish names appeared on almost every ballot, and naturalized citizens were showered with political favors. In this contest for foreign support the Democrats completely outdistanced the Whigs, whose well-established conservatism repelled both the poverty-stricken Irish and the liberal-minded Germans. Indeed, the Whigs might well have seized upon the antiforeigner issue, but their party was already too moribund to take a pronounced stand on anything. Thus it was that a new party was formed precisely for this purpose. Its origins lay in a succession of antiforeigner and anti-Catholic secret societies, culminating in the Order of the Star-Spangled Banner, and finally in the "Know-Nothing," or American Party. The Know-Nothings, careful always to keep their decisions secret, and professing to "know nothing" about what they intended to do, carried many local elections in the early 1850's in such immigrant centers as Massachusetts, Pennsylvania, and New York.

Expansion as a Political Issue. In their search for an attractive issue to keep the mind of the public off the slavery question, the Democrats tried repeatedly to rekindle the interest in expansion that had brought them such success in the election of 1844. President Pierce apparently hoped to make the acquisition of Cuba the outstanding achievement of his administration, even at the cost of war with Spain. His ministers to Great Britain, France, and Spain (James Buchanan, John Y. Mason, and Pierre Soulé), when charged with the task of formulating the American program, brought forth the famous "Ostend Manifesto," stating that the United States should first seek to buy Cuba from Spain, but failing that, should take it by force. But this bit of international bad manners came to nothing. Indeed, the sole tangible result of all the expansionist activities was the purchase in 1853 from Mexico for $10 million of a sandy triangle south of the Gila River. Surveyors claimed that this territory, generally called the "Gadsden Purchase," would be needed in case the United States ever wished to construct a railroad along a southern route to California.

MATTHEW CALBRAITH PERRY

The American naval officer Matthew Calbraith Perry, who negotiated the opening of Japan to western trade, as he looked to a Japanese artist. From a Japanese wood block, about 1853.

Commerce with the Orient. More successful were the efforts of the administration to smooth the way for American traders in the Far East. Ever since 1784, when the *Empress of China* set sail under the Stars and Stripes from New York for Canton, a small but lucrative oriental trade had been maintained, and in 1844, following the Opium War between England and China, the United States had been accorded by formal treaty the same commercial privileges that the English had won by force. But in China the Americans furnished only weak competition for the better-established Europeans, so the American government determined to open a new field for commercial activities in the "Hermit Kingdom"

of Japan. With this end in view, and also to persuade the Japanese not to mistreat American seamen shipwrecked on their shores, Commodore Matthew Perry visited Japan in 1854 with the largest fleet the United States had ever assembled in Asiatic waters. Overawed by so great a show of force, the Japanese government agreed to open two ports to American traders, to permit an American consul to reside at one of them, and to accord protection to American seamen in distress upon Japanese shores. A trade treaty with Siam (Thailand), concluded in 1856, and an unsuccessful project for the annexation of Hawaii called further attention to the Pacific interests of the United States.

SELECTED BIBLIOGRAPHY

Excellent for many of the subjects treated in this chapter is T. C. Cochran and William Miller, °*The Age of Enterprise; A Social History of Industrial America* (2nd ed., 1961). An interesting general treatment of urbanization is C. McL. Green, *American Cities in the Growth of the Nation* (1957); on the rise of one great industrial city, see B. L. Pierce, *A History of Chicago* (3 vols., 1937–   ). Important monographs include J. W. Cadman, Jr., *The Corporation in New Jersey; Business and Politics, 1791–1875* (1949); and A. D. Chandler, *Henry Varnum Poor, Business Editor, Analyst, and Reformer* (1956).

On railroads, a good brief survey is J. F. Stover, °*American Railroads* (1961). Among the many special works, note especially B. H. Meyer and others, *History of Transportation in the United States before 1866* (1917); U. B. Phillips, *A History of Transportation in the Eastern Cotton Belt to 1860* (1908); Edward Hungerford, *The Story of the Baltimore and Ohio Railroad, 1827–1897* (1928); and F. W. Stevens, *The Beginnings of the New York Central Railroad* (1926). Political ramifications are dealt with in R. R. Russel, *Improvement of Communication with the Pacific Coast as an Issue in American Politics, 1783–1864* (1948);

° Available in paperback

and Lee Benson, *Merchants, Farmers, and Railroads; Railroad Regulation and New York Politics, 1850–1887* (1955).

On river transportation, see W. J. Peterson, *Steamboating on the Upper Mississippi* (1937); and W. E. Lass, *A History of Steamboating on the Upper Missouri River* (1962). On ocean-going shipping, the following are useful: A. H. Clark, *The Clipper Ship Era, 1843–1869* (1910); C. C. Cutler, *Greyhounds of the Sea* (1930); and R. G. Albion, *Square Riggers on Schedule* (1938). The role of the federal government is discussed in J. G. B. Hutchins, *The American Maritime Industries and Public Policy, 1789–1914* (1941). A colorful biography is W. J. Lane, *Commodore Vanderbilt* (1942).

On agriculture, see the excellent anthology, *Readings in the History of American Agriculture*, edited by W. D. Rasmussen (1960). Joseph Schafer, *The Social History of American Agriculture* (1936), approaches the subject from an interesting point of view. Leo Rogin, *The Introduction of Farm Machinery in its Relation to the Productivity of Labor in the Agriculture of the United States during the Nineteenth Century* (1931), is excellent. Among the other significant special studies see especially W. C. Neely, *The Agricultural Fair* (1935); and A. L. Demaree, *The American Agricultural Press, 1819–1860* (1941). Valuable regional studies include B. H. Clark, *The Tennessee Yeoman, 1840–1860* (1942); A. G. Bogue, *From Prairie to Corn Belt* (1963); J. P. Pritchett, *The Red River Valley, 1811–1849* (1942); and P. W. Gates, *The Illinois Central Railroad and its Colonization Work* (1934).

On industrial development, there are a number of special studies, such as M. T. Copeland, *The Cotton Manufacturing Industry of the United States* (1912); J. V. Woodworth, *American Tool Making and Interchangeable Manufacturing* (1905); and J. M. Swank, *History of the Manufacture of Iron in all Ages* (1892). Fascinating social history is contained in Hanna Josephson, *The Golden Threads; New England's Mill Girls and Magnates* (1949).

The problems of transportation and communication which arose in the West in the wake of mining rushes are dealt with by numerous books, among the best of which are L. R. Hafen, *The Overland Mail, 1849–1869* (1926); O. O. Winther, *Via Western Express and Stagecoach* (1945); R. P. and M. B. Conkling, *The Butterfield Overland Mail, 1857–1869* (1947); Edward Hungerford, *Wells Fargo* (1949); and W. T. Jackson, *Wagon Roads West; A Study of Federal Road Surveys and Construction in the Trans-Mississippi West, 1846–1869* (1952).

On immigration, a brief overview by a British scholar is M. A. Jones, *°American Immigration* (1960). An excellent collection of readings gathered by our leading authority is *°Immigration as a Factor in American History,* edited by Oscar Handlin (1959). Standard surveys of the subject are: G. M. Stephenson, *A History of American Immigration* (1926); Carl Wittke, *°We Who Built America* (1939); and M. L. Hansen, *°The Immigrant in American History* (1940). But no serious student of American history should miss Oscar Handlin, *°The Uprooted* (1951), an impassioned study, rich in insight. See also his *Boston's Immigrants, 1790–1865* (1941); and *°Race and Nationality in American Life* (1957). Among the important studies of groups are Carl Wittke, *The Irish in America* (1956); W. F. Adams, *Ireland and Irish Emigration to the New World from 1815 to the Famine* (1932); T. C. Blegen, *Norwegian Migration to America* (2 vols., 1931–1940); and R. T. Berthoff, *British Immigrants in Industrial America, 1790–1950* (1953). Cecil Woodham-Smith, *°The Great Hunger; Ireland, 1845–1849* (1962), is a horrifying account of the great potato famine. Excellent social studies are Robert Ernst, *Immigrant Life in New York City, 1825–1863* (1949); and D. B. Cole, *Immigrant City: Lawrence, Massachusetts, 1845–1921* (1963). The standard account of the nativist reaction to immigration is R. A. Billington, *°The Protestant Crusade, 1800–1860* (1938).

On the proposal to annex Cuba, see J. M. Callahan, *Cuba and International Relations* (1899); and Basil Rauch, *American Interest in Cuba: 1848–1855* (1948). An interesting monograph is Te-kong Tong, *United States Diplomacy in China, 1844–60* (1964).

Victor Nehlig, "Infantry Fighting Hand-to-Hand." Courtesy of the George Walter Vincent Smith Art Museum, Springfield, Massachusetts.

The
Sectional Conflict

· 1860–1877 ·

We will hold as a brother, him who stands by the Union; we will hold him as an enemy, who would strike from its constellation a single star.

BENJAMIN F. BUTLER

Sir, the time has not come for amnesty. You must be just to the colored race before you are generous to former rebels.

CHARLES SUMNER

All should unite in honest efforts to obliterate the effects of war, and to restore the blessings of peace.

ROBERT E. LEE

18

THE SECTIONAL CRISIS

Despite the soothing effects of prosperity, the impossibility of keeping the vexatious slavery question in abeyance became increasingly apparent as the 1850's wore on. Know-Nothingism won a strong following in the South where there were few foreigners, because immigration increased the population of the North and thus became a potential threat to slavery. Expansion was denounced in the North as a subterfuge to add more slave territory to the Union. Abolitionists contended that the Fugitive Slave Act was a legal sham used to kidnap northern free Negroes and sell them South into slavery. Southerners in turn were convinced that many northerners were aiding in the escape of runaway slaves. The evangelical churches, long split over the morality of slavery, continued, in spite of the political truce, to debate the issue. Of almost equal importance was Harriet Beecher Stowe's *Uncle Tom's Cabin,* which appeared in book form in 1852, and swept the North. Three thousand copies were sold the first day, and 300,000 copies before the end of a

year. As a novel, it had many flaws, but as a moral indictment of slavery it was devastating. Dramatized, and played before enthusiastic audiences throughout the North, it made converts for the antislavery cause even among the illiterate. But nowhere in the South was *Uncle Tom's Cabin* played. Below Mason and Dixon's Line it won only fiery denunciations.

Twice before, in 1820 and in 1850, the threat of slavery expansion had precipitated sectional conflicts, and now the old dilemma seemed to be rising again. What disposal was to be made of the still unorganized territory lying to the west of Iowa and Missouri? It was now known that along the western bank of the Missouri River the land was both fertile and well-watered; demands for its opening to settlement could therefore not long be postponed. Indeed, during the year 1853 the Commissioner of Indian Affairs began negotiations for the removal of the Indians from the coveted areas, and a bill for the creation of a vast new Nebraska Territory passed the House of Representatives. There was the further problem of building through to the Pacific a transcontinental railroad, and survey parties sent out in 1853 under authority of an act of Congress revealed that several feasible alternative routes existed. The railroad to connect California with the rest of the Union could be built, but where? Should it follow a northern, central, or southern route?

Stephen A. Douglas. It fell to Stephen A. Douglas (1813–1861) of Illinois, Chairman of the Senate Committee on Territories, to try to resolve these difficult problems. Douglas, born in Vermont, had come to Illinois when twenty years of age, and was now the idol of the boastful, expansionist Illinois democracy. In the Senate since 1847, he had won his greatest victory in 1850, when he had persuaded Congress to adopt the policy of liberal grants of land to the states in aid of railroad building. The resultant rapid construction of the Illinois Central and other roads made Chicago the "metropolis of the West," and put into the heads of its enterprising citizens the idea of a still more ambitious project, a land-grant railroad west from Chicago all the way to the Pacific. But if any such grants were to become available, the western territory would have to be organized.

The Kansas-Nebraska Act. Douglas' efforts to devise a strategy that would make possible the opening of another West have been subjected to the most intensive criticism. Some contemporaries claimed that he deliberately reopened the slavery question in order to further his ambitions for the Presidency. That he wished to become President, and that he hoped to reconcile the contending elements within the Democratic Party, can scarcely be doubted, but it is unjust to charge him with full responsibility for breaking the sectional truce. Circumstances forced his hand. He knew that settlement was certain to cross the Missouri River, and that territorial governments in the now unorganized Indian country would become a necessity. Missourians, in particular, were insistent on this course.

His first intent was to go along with the idea of a single new territory, Nebraska, but to substitute for the Missouri Compromise, with its prohibition of slavery north of 36° 30′, his "great principle" of popular sovereignty. For years he had argued that the people of a territory should be free to decide for themselves whether to accept or reject slavery. Even if the Nebraska settlers voted slavery down, as he believed they would, the proslavery elements would have had their chance. But to win support for his measure he had to make two fundamental concessions. On January 23 he proposed that instead of one new territory there should be two, Kansas to the west of Missouri, and Nebraska to the west of Iowa, with the fortieth parallel as the dividing line. Those who demanded the second territory included proslavery elements who felt that they would have an excellent chance to win the southernmost one (Kansas). And Douglas was obliged also to include a specific provision for the repeal of the Missouri Compromise, something he would have preferred merely to take for granted. So amended, the Kansas-Nebraska Act passed Congress, and on May 30, 1854, received President Pierce's signature.

The debate over this measure revived all the bitterness of the years that had preceded the Compromise of 1850. Practically all the northern Whigs and many northern Democrats opposed it. In defense of the act Douglas argued that the formula of popular sovereignty would "withdraw the question of slavery from the halls of Congress and the political arena," and by solving the slavery question once and for all would perpetuate the unity of the nation and the Democratic Party. But whatever Douglas may have hoped, he had, in fact, started once again the raging fires of sectional controversy. The Democratic Party of the North was torn violently apart. Those who defended the act were known as Pro-Nebraska Democrats; those who opposed it as Anti-Nebraska Democrats. The Whig Party lost its last vestige of unity. Northern Whigs were almost unanimously anti-Nebraska; southern Whigs were quite as unanimously pro-Nebraska. Even the Know-Nothings were forced to take sides, and anti-Nebraska and pro-Nebraska factions brought discord to their lodges. Division of opinion, however, was for the time being confined to the North. Southerners, whether Whigs, Democrats, or Know-Nothings, stood solidly for the act.

Birth of the Republican Party. The united front achieved by the opponents of slavery extension during the debate on the Kansas-Nebraska Act led almost immediately to the formation of the Republican Party. At Ripon, Wisconsin, February 28, 1854, an Anti-Nebraska mass meeting revived the name Republican; and at Jackson, Michigan, July 6, 1854, the first state-wide Republican organization was launched. By November, Republican tickets, or their equivalent under a different name, challenged the Democrats in every northwestern state, and won far more often than they lost. In the Northeast the emergence of the new party was not quite so speedily accomplished, for there both the Whigs and the Know-Nothings clung tenaciously to life. But by the fall of 1855, when Seward, the leading antislavery Whig, came over to the Republicans, the new party was safely out of the third-party status. Eastern Republicans, while embracing within their numbers many former abolitionists, were often quite as much pro-tariff as antislavery. They believed that the influence of the agrarian-minded southern leaders on the national government should be lessened, and since new slave states meant more pro-southern votes in Congress, they felt obliged to oppose their creation.

Everywhere in the North the rise of the Republicans did serious damage to the Democrats. States that had once been safely Democratic began to elect Republican legislatures and state officers. Douglas himself, the outstanding leader of the Democrats and the author of the Kansas-Nebraska Act, suffered considerable loss of popularity. In Chicago he was greeted with groans and hisses by an unruly audience that finally drove him in a temper from the platform. In the South, however, his popularity increased, and the Democratic Party gained notably at the expense of the Whigs. Some of the latter, unable to join hands so suddenly with their former adversaries, became "Know-Nothings" for a season. The Democrats could not yet count upon a "solid South," but obviously it was in the making.

Kansas. The real test of popular sovereignty as a remedy for the sectional controversy over slavery came in Kansas. The middle westerners who were moving into Nebraska were certain to exclude slavery from that territory at the first opportunity, and did so; but Kansas was no sooner organized as a territory than rivalry broke out between antislavery northerners and proslavery southerners to see who should settle it. Normally Missourians, generally in favor of slavery, would have furnished the greater proportion of the settlers, but antislavery groups throughout the North, even in New England, organized to send men to Kansas. Soon a stream of determined free-soilers began to descend upon the new territory. With instinctive common sense, the bona fide proslavery and antislavery immigrants to Kansas settled at a considerable distance from each other. Most of the proslavery men settled close to the Missouri River, and founded such towns as Atchison and Leavenworth. The antislavery men, on the other hand, went farther into the interior, where they founded Lawrence and Topeka.

Franklin Pierce on Kansas. The situation in Kansas could hardly have been more completely mishandled. President Franklin Pierce (1804–1869) was not suited for such an emergency. A good lawyer and a polished public speaker, he had entered the Presidency with the hearty good will of almost the entire American public. Judging from his record as a member for short terms each in both houses of Congress and as a volunteer officer in the Mexican War, there was good reason to suppose that, in spite of his relative obscurity, he would rise to the requirements of his high office. But these expectations were doomed to quick disappointment. It soon developed that he was at the mercy of the strongest-willed of his advisers, among whom proslavery extremists were usually dominant. Andrew H. Reeder of Pennsylvania, the first territorial governor that Pierce appointed for Kansas, turned out to be more interested in land speculation than anything else, but the two elections held during his term of office were won by the proslavery faction with the assistance of large numbers of Missourians who temporarily crossed the border just for the purpose of voting. Disgruntled because the legislature would not locate the capital at a town site in which he had a speculative interest, Reeder eventually went over to the antislavery side, and was removed from office by Pierce. The second governor, William Shannon of Ohio, was strongly proslavery in his sympathies. It was clearly apparent that to him "popular sovereignty" in Kansas meant a proslavery Kansas.

The Topeka Constitution. When the antislavery Kansans realized the hopelessness of trying to win a territorial election, they decided to follow the precedent recently set by California for establishing a state government in advance of congressional permission. Accordingly they elected delegates to a convention which met at Topeka, October 23, 1855, and drew up a free state constitution. Before the end of the year this document was submitted to the people at the polls, and, since the proslavery faction did not participate in the election, was adopted by a one-sided vote. Under its terms a governor and legislature were promptly chosen, and Congress was petitioned to admit Kansas as a free state. This action President Pierce denounced as treasonous. The proslavery territorial government, he told Congress, was the only lawful government in Kansas, and as such was deserving of the full support of the United States.

Brooks's Attack on Sumner. Douglas had claimed that popular sovereignty would

exile the debate over slavery from the halls of Congress and put it where it belonged, in the territories themselves. But this theory did not work out in practice, for Congress had now to decide whether to recognize the proslavery territorial government or admit Kansas as a free state. The debate was hot in both houses, and on May 19, 1856, it reached a climax in the Senate when Charles Sumner of Massachusetts spoke at length on "The Crime against Kansas." During this address he cast aspersions upon the name of Senator Andrew P. Butler of South Carolina and upon the reputation of his state. These remarks were avenged three days later by Representative Preston Brooks, a relative of Butler and also a South Carolinian, in a singularly brutal attack. While Sumner was sitting at his desk in the Senate, Brooks beat him over the head with a heavy cane until he fell insensible to the floor. Because of his injuries, Sumner was absent for several years from his seat in the Senate, but Brooks, after resigning his seat in the House, was not only promptly re-elected, but was also showered with gifts of canes from southerners.

"Bleeding Kansas." In Kansas, meantime, "border ruffians" from Missouri bent on violence were being met in kind by free-state men from the North. Henry Ward Beecher had counseled sending rifles to the antislavery emigrants, and such weapons, generally known as "Beecher's Bibles," were soon in use. When a proslavery mob, called by courtesy a "posse," assisted in the arrest of the free-state officers at Lawrence by sacking that city, John Brown of Osawatomie, an abolitionist fanatic, brought about the murder of five proslavery settlers in reprisal. The "Civil War in Kansas" that followed possibly cost the lives of 200 citizens. It was ended by a new governor, John White Geary, who invoked the aid of federal troops to restore order, but not until "Bleeding Kansas" had become the leading issue in the presidential campaign of 1856.

Election of 1856. Despite the turmoil that popular sovereignty had produced in Kansas, the Democratic National Convention declared that this principle furnished "the only sound and safe solution of the slavery question." For its nominee, however, it chose James Buchanan of Pennsylvania, whose absence from the country as minister to England had saved him from the commitments that Pierce and Douglas had been obliged to make. The Republicans, no less devoted to expediency than the Democrats, overlooked the claims of Seward and Chase, their best-known leaders, to choose John C. Frémont, the glamorous "Pathfinder of the West." Their platform revived the Free-Soil doctrine that Congress had the constitutional right and the moral duty to prohibit the expansion of slavery into any of the territories of the United States. The Know-Nothings and a remnant of the Whigs held separate conventions, but nominated the same candidate, ex-President Fillmore, and adopted platforms, that sought in the main to avoid sectionalism by an insistent demand for the preservation of the Union. The Republicans made a whirlwind campaign, patterned on the Whig tactics of 1840, but the country was frightened by the specter of disunion, and the Democrats won an unexpectedly easy victory. Eleven northern states cast 114 votes for Frémont, but five northern states and every southern state but one cast a total of 174 votes for Buchanan. While the Know-Nothings furnished strong opposition to the Democrats in the South, Fillmore carried only one state, Maryland, with 8 electoral votes. Both houses of Congress remained safely Democratic.

James Buchanan. James Buchanan (1791–1868), unlike Pierce, had ample experience in politics. Before he became minister to England, he had served for ten years in the House of Representatives, had been

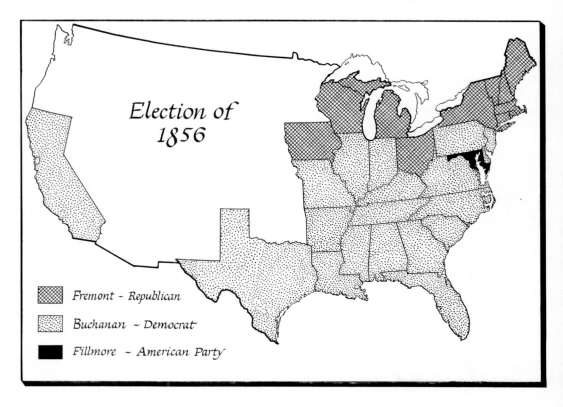

Election of 1856

Frémont – Republican
Buchanan – Democrat
Fillmore – American Party

minister to Russia, member of the United States Senate for two decades, and Secretary of State under Polk. His opposition to the Wilmot Proviso and his ardent championship of expansion marked him as a "dough-face," that is, a "northern man with southern principles." Beyond a doubt he was devoted to the Union, but at sixty-five the conservatism of old age tended to confirm him in the belief that the only way to preserve the Union was to permit the southern leaders to have their way.

Dred Scott Case. Two days after Buchanan's inauguration the Supreme Court of the United States handed down a decision in the case of *Dred Scott v. Sanford* that put a new aspect upon the dispute over slavery in the territories. This decision did not come unsolicited. Congress, when it passed the Kansas-Nebraska Act, had assumed that the Supreme Court might have to review the measure; and southerners, confident that the Court would be on their side, were eager for its pronouncement. Seven of the justices were Democrats, one was a Whig, and one a Republican; and of the seven Democrats five were from the South. Surely such a Court would decide against the Republican contention that Congress had a right to exclude slavery from the territories. No doubt the justices themselves felt that the weight of their opinion would be sufficient to bring the heated controversy to an end.

The Dred Scott case offered a satisfactory opportunity for the Court to declare itself. Dred Scott was a Negro who until 1834 had legally been held in bondage in the slave state of Missouri. After that date his master, an army surgeon, moved, taking Scott with him, first to Illinois, a free state, and then to Wisconsin Territory (later Minnesota) where, under the terms of the Missouri Compromise, slavery was also forbidden. Ultimately Scott was brought back to Missouri. Here he was induced by some individuals who wished to make a test case of his experience to bring suit for his freedom on the ground that his residence in free territory had set him free. The case attracted much attention, and eventually Scott was sold to a New Yorker named Sanford so that the litigation could be transferred to the federal courts. By 1856 the case was before the United States Supreme Court, where it was twice argued. When Buchanan was inaugurated in March, 1857, he referred to the forthcoming opinion with the hope that it would settle with finality the status of slavery in the territories.

Chief Justice Taney spoke for the seven Democratic justices. He denied emphatically the right of the lower federal court to assume jurisdiction in the case. Dred Scott, said the Chief Justice, was not a citizen of Missouri within the meaning of the Constitution; hence he could neither sue nor be sued in the federal courts. The Court, as some of the assenting justices would have preferred, need have gone no further, but Taney argued also that Negroes of slave descent, as legally an inferior order of beings, were not and could not possibly become citizens in the sense in which the word was used in the Constitution. He pointed out further that Dred Scott's residence in territory north of the Missouri Compromise line could not have made him free, for Congress, he said, had exceeded its authority in forbidding slavery in that part of the Louisiana Purchase north of 36° 30′. Slave property in the territories was as much protected by the Constitution as any other kind of property. The Missouri Compromise had therefore been unconstitutional, and Dred Scott was no less a slave in a supposedly free territory than in Missouri. Southern extremists could ask no more. It is worth noting, however, that the reasoning of Taney was questioned, even by some of his Democratic associates, while the two other justices filed vigorous dissenting opinions.

It was idle to suppose that a decision so partisan from a Court so divided could settle anything with finality. The Republicans refused to concede that the status of slavery in the territories had actually been before the Court at all. If Dred Scott was not a citizen, that fact alone required demonstration. All the rest of the argument was ir-. relevant and gratuitous, or as the lawyers put it, *obiter dicta.* Southern Democrats, on the other hand, were greatly elated by the stand that the Court had taken, and they insisted it had settled this matter for all time. Slavery must now be allowed to spread freely into all the territories. The northern Democrats were in a sorry plight. Those who thought the matter through realized that Douglas' doctrine of popular sovereignty, to which they had pinned their faith, could not easily be reconciled with Taney's opinion. If slavery could not be excluded from a territory by a law of Congress, how then could the legislature of a territory, which owed its authority to Congress, exclude slavery? For the moment, however, they refused to admit the contradiction and said little about it.

Events in Kansas.   Once more the attention of the country turned to Kansas. Eager to prevent a recurrence of trouble there, Buchanan persuaded Robert J. Walker of Mississippi, a man of real ability, to accept the governorship of the new territory. Walker promptly called an election for delegates to a constitutional convention, and urged the free-state men to participate. This, however, they refused to do, for they felt little confidence in the Buchanan administration and doubted the fairness of its appointee. In consequence, the proslavery element carried the election overwhelmingly, and in October, 1857, a convention held at Lecompton framed a proslavery constitution. Determined to take no chances, the Lecompton convention failed to give the voters an opportunity to reject the document it had framed, but provided merely that they might vote for or against the further introduction of slaves. Whichever way the vote went, slavery in Kansas would be fully protected. The free-state men again refused to vote, so that the constitu-

tion was carried with the proslavery clause. In the fall elections for the territorial legislature, however, the free-state men not only voted, but thanks to the rejection by Governor Walker and the territorial secretary of many fraudulent votes, they won. Thereupon the legislature resubmitted the Lecompton constitution, this time with the full alternative of adoption or rejection. Now the proslavery men refused to vote, so that the constitution that had just been so easily ratified was almost unanimously rejected. But the relative strength of the two sides was clearly revealed. In support of the Lecompton constitution the proslavery forces had cast only 6,226 votes, whereas the free-state men only a few weeks later had cast 10,226 votes against it. That Kansas wished to become a free and not a slave state was now fully apparent to any unprejudiced observer.

Douglas on Kansas.   Unhappily, President Buchanan could not be so described. His most trusted advisers were southerners, and ordinarily he reflected their views. In November he forced Walker out of office because the governor's rejection of fraudulent proslavery votes had given the legislature of Kansas to the free-state men. Moreover, in December, 1857, when Congress convened, the President made clear his desire to see Kansas admitted promptly as a slave state. Two months later he submitted to Congress the now thoroughly discredited Lecompton constitution, and urged its acceptance. All this was too much for Douglas. His doctrine of popular sovereignty rested upon the assumption that a majority had the right to decide for or against slavery, and now the President proposed to make Kansas a slave state against its clearly expressed will. This travesty upon popular sovereignty Douglas denounced with all the vigor at his command. Many other northern Democrats agreed with him, and while the President was able to force his policy upon the Senate, he failed in the House. Eventually a compromise measure, the English bill, offered Kansas immediate statehood under the Lecompton constitution in case a majority of the voters approved that document, but once again the Kansans voted the constitution down.

The Panic of 1857. Meantime the Panic of 1857 had burst upon the country, and had left in its train a trying period of economic depression. The success of the railroads had tempted them to unreasonable overexpansion. Lines were built into unsettled areas where for years to come there could be little hope of profits. Manufacturers, eager to keep pace with the ever-growing markets, were soon well ahead of them. Producers of foodstuffs were misled by the abnormal demand of a war-torn and famine-wracked Europe for American grain. At best the prices that the farmers received were none too good, and the loss of the European market when the Crimean War ended was calamitous. Moreover, the boom period, like every other of its kind, was accompanied by an enormous amount of land speculation. Town sites along the lines of projected railroads, city lots in the rapidly growing industrial centers, desirable farm lands everywhere, but particularly in the West, tempted investors to over-buy. The situation was seriously aggravated by the weakness of the state banking system upon which, ever since the destruction of the Bank of the United States, the country had been forced to depend. Credit was overextended, and the currency was seriously inflated. When in August, 1857, a supposedly powerful financial house, the Ohio Life Insurance and Trust Company, closed its doors, the panic, soon to be followed by a long period of depression, had begun.

The economic depression accentuated to an extraordinary degree the bitterness of sectional controversy. Because of the hard times, the proslavery administration of President Buchanan lost ground throughout the North. Particularly aggrieved were the northeastern industrialists, whose demand for a higher tariff went unheeded. More and more northern businessmen, regardless of their opinions on slavery, swung their support to the new Republican Party. But the South too drew more closely together. Because of the continuing world demand for cotton, the South was less seriously affected by the panic and depression than the North. Southerners, therefore, claimed for the "Cotton Kingdom" an economic stability that the North did not possess. And yet the South was uneasy in the fact that the North, despite the depression, continued to outstrip the South, both in population and in number of states. Minnesota won admission to the Union in 1858, statehood for Oregon could not long be postponed, and antislavery majorities seemed destined to prevail in both Kansas and Nebraska. In the elections of 1858 the tightening sectional lines became clearly apparent. Republicans, Know-Nothings, and anti-Lecompton Democrats drew closer together, and gave the Buchanan administration a sharp rebuke. While the Senate remained safely Democratic, the House returned twenty-three fewer Democrats than Republicans, with no party having a majority.

The Senatorial Election in Illinois. Undoubtedly the most spectacular contest of the campaign took place in Illinois, where Stephen A. Douglas fought desperately to retain his seat in the United States Senate. Douglas' break with Buchanan over Kansas had rehabilitated his reputation in the North to the extent that even many Republicans had begun to say that his election to the Senate ought not to be opposed, while a few of them, mostly easterners, had begun to think of him as a possible Republican candidate for the Presidency in 1860. But the Illinois Republicans held no such sentiments. To oppose Douglas they settled upon Abraham Lincoln, a Springfield lawyer who was well known throughout the state for his political sagacity and his forceful public speaking. Lincoln had served one term in Congress during the Polk administration, had barely missed election to the United States Senate by the Illinois legislature in 1855, and had received strong support for the vice-presidential nomination in 1856. He was the best man the Republicans of Illinois could put forward against Douglas, as the Senator himself well knew. In accepting the nomination, Lincoln made a prophetic statement:

"A house divided against itself cannot stand." I believe this government cannot endure permanently half slave and half free. I do not expect the Union to be dissolved — I do not expect the house to fall — but I do expect it will cease to be divided. It will become all one thing or all the other.

STEPHEN A. DOUGLAS

Known to his admirers as the "little Giant," Douglas was an effective public speaker and a resourceful politician. He saw clearly the disruptive forces unleashed by the slavery dispute, and fought valiantly for a compromise solution that would save the Union and keep the peace.

Then, as if to defend this radical doctrine, he promptly challenged Douglas to a series of joint debates, a challenge that Douglas was delighted to accept.

The Lincoln-Douglas Debates. The Lincoln-Douglas debates attracted widespread notice, not only in Illinois, where eager throngs attended them, but throughout the nation at large. Douglas was the outstanding northern Democrat, and his political life was at stake. More than that, if he lost, the northern Democracy had little chance to retain a place in the party councils; if he won, his chances for the Democratic nomination in 1860 would be strong indeed. Lincoln was hardly known outside of Illinois, but his bold words, and his temerity in challenging the able Douglas to a joint debate, awakened an interest in him that grew as the debates progressed. Lincoln succeeded in making two points effectively. One was that Douglas, to use his own words, did not care "whether slavery was voted down or voted up." The Republican Party, on the whole, did care, and by emphasizing Douglas' lack of interest in the morality of slavery, Lincoln disqualified him for Republican support. The other telling point was the essential contradiction between Douglas' doctrine of popular sovereignty and the Dred Scott decision. Douglas attempted to reconcile the two in his Freeport speech by asserting that a territorial legislature could refuse to enact a slave code without which slavery could not exist, and so might effectively exclude slavery regardless of the Supreme Court. This clever dodge, which Lincoln had not failed to foresee, cost Lincoln the election, for it satisfied the Democracy of Illinois. But whatever lingering hope Douglas might have had of southern support was not long in disappearing. Completely convinced by Taney's reasoning, the South was ready to demand the last measure of "protection for our slave property in the territories." The wedge between the northern and southern wings of the Democratic Party was thus driven deeper than ever.

John Brown Again. After the elections, the sectional dispute raged on with ever-increasing acrimony. Whatever the North desired, Congress was at great pains to deny. Buchanan would have liked a higher tariff to please the Pennsylvania manufacturers, but the southern leaders would have none of that. The Pacific railroad project, upon which the North had now set its heart, and the Homestead Bill, long demanded by western farmers and eastern laborers, were both rejected. Southern orators assailed the lax enforcement of the Fugitive Slave Act and denounced vehemently the "personal-liberty laws" by which some northern states circumvented it. Northern orators railed at the repeated violations of the federal law against the importation of slaves. As if matters were not bad enough already, John Brown of Osawatomie re-emerged, this time in western Virginia, with a plot to capture the Harpers Ferry Arsenal and secure the arms necessary for a slave insurrection. On October 16, 1859, with eighteen followers, he took the Arsenal, only to be captured a little later by Colonel Robert E. Lee, in command of a detachment of United States Marines. After a fair, if somewhat hasty, trial for treason, Brown was found guilty, condemned, and hanged. Responsible Republican leaders were quick to denounce his mad act, but many northerners agreed with Emerson that Brown had made "the gallows glorious like the cross."

Helper's *Impending Crisis*. Three days after the execution of John Brown, on December 5, 1859, the Congress elected in 1858 convened for its first session, and plunged into a long contest over the speakership. During this struggle, which resulted eventually in the choice of a Republican, the Democrats made much of the fact that a book by Hinton R. Helper, *The Impending Crisis of the South*, had received official endorsement by the Republicans in the campaign of 1858. Helper was a non-slaveholding North Carolinian whose book attempted to demonstrate that the deep poverty of his class was due to slavery, which he therefore

JOHN BROWN OF OSAWATOMIE, KANSAS

Financed by a group of wealthy New England abolitionists, Brown organized and led the raid on Harpers Ferry which lighted the torch of Civil War.

opposed on economic grounds. The Republicans had claimed that they would not attack slavery where it already existed, but had they not done just that in approving Helper's book? Sectional feeling became increasingly tense.

The Congress that began so tempestuously enacted few measures of consequence. Only a presidential veto, however, prevented the passage of a homestead act. With the election of 1860 in sight, the southern Democrats hesitated to antagonize further the northern wing of their party, which was as fully committed to the homestead policy as the Republicans themselves. Senator Andrew Johnson of Tennessee, in fact, had long been the most ardent backer of the measure because he believed it would benefit the poor whites of his section. But Johnson was a man of very humble antecedents and not a representative of the controlling plantation class. During the summer of 1860 both houses agreed to a measure permitting citizens or aliens who had declared their intentions of becoming citizens to occupy 160 acres of public land for five years, and then buy it at the nominal price of twenty-five cents per acre. But Buchanan promptly vetoed the bill in a message reciting all the traditional arguments against it. Buchanan's real reason — apparent to most observers — lay in the planters' fear of a rapidly expanding free farming West. By vetoing the measure, Buchanan had not only reversed the historic position of the Democratic party on public lands, but had also gone a long way to alienate the small farmer, the worker, and the recent immigrant, groups which had traditionally been the backbone of the northern Democratic party.

Election of 1860. Under the circumstances the presidential campaign of 1860 aroused an intense interest throughout the country. Meeting at Charleston in April, the Democratic National Convention failed after ten days of balloting to make a nomination. Douglas had a clear majority of the delegates, but not the required two-thirds. The convention adjourned to meet in Baltimore two months later. There, after a few preliminaries, it divided. One faction, composed mainly of northern delegates, nominated Douglas and stood by popular sovereignty. The other, composed almost exclusively of southerners, nominated John C. Breckinridge of Kentucky, and called for the protection of slavery in all the territories. On May 16 the Republicans met at Chicago, with William H. Seward of New York as the leading candidate. But the West was regarded as far more uncertain ground for Republicans than the East, and in recognition of this situation the nomination went on the third ballot to Abraham Lincoln of Illinois. The Republican plat-

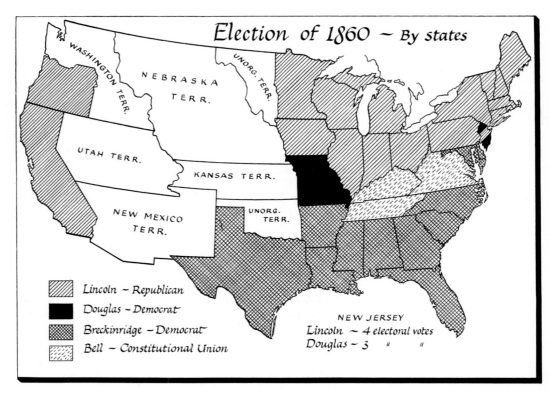

Election of 1860 ~ By states

Lincoln ~ Republican
Douglas ~ Democrat
Breckinridge ~ Democrat
Bell ~ Constitutional Union

NEW JERSEY
Lincoln ~ 4 electoral votes
Douglas ~ 3   "   "

form was intensely nationalistic, not only in its denunciation of southern threats of disunion, but also in its advocacy of national action to satisfy the demands of its adherents. The authority of Congress or any other power to legalize slavery in the territories was denied, but the power of each state to control its own domestic institutions was fully affirmed. The Republicans further pledged new tariffs "to encourage the development of the industrial interests," a satisfactory homestead law, the continuation of the existing liberal naturalization policy, and a railroad to the Pacific (advocated also by both Democratic platforms). All of this was to be done by authority of the national government. Still a fourth ticket was placed in the field by the Constitutional Union Party, which was composed of the Whig-Know-Nothing remnants that had nominated Fillmore four years before. Recognizing "no political principle other than the Constitution of the country, the union of the States, and the enforcement of the laws," theirs was primarily a party of conciliation and compromise. To emphasize their intersectional appeal, they offered a southerner, John Bell of Tennessee, for President, and a northerner, Edward Everett of Massachusetts, for Vice-President.

The Contest in the North and South. The campaign and election served only to emphasize how deep the line of cleavage between the sections had become. For all practical purposes two separate contests were being held, one in the North and another in the South. The only candidates to figure seriously in the northern balloting were Lincoln and Douglas, and the issue between them was clearly: should the North use its numerical majority to force upon the South the nationalistic program called for in the Republican platform? On this issue, Lincoln won every northern state except New Jersey, and there he received four out of the seven electoral votes. With the admission of Oregon in 1859, the free states numbered three more than the slave states and cast half again as many electoral votes. Thus Lincoln was elected, although he had received not a single electoral vote from a southern state. In ten southern states his name had not even appeared on the ballot.

In the South the contest lay between Breckinridge on the one hand and either Bell or Douglas on the other. Here the question at issue was should "southern rights" be maintained, even at the cost of secession and possible civil war? The election of Lincoln, southern extremists contended, would in itself constitute so flagrant an invasion of "southern rights" as to justify the southern states in seceding immediately from the Union. The party that supported Lincoln lay wholly in the North, and its triumph, they genuinely believed, would be but a prelude to the complete domination of the South by the North. Against this radical point of view, the adherents of Bell and Douglas urged an intermediate course that would save the Union, but in the South as in the North the more aggressive policy won. Eleven out of the fifteen slave states voted for Breckinridge; only four, all in the upper South, for his opponents.

With so many candidates in the field, and the North and the South holding virtually separate elections, it was inevitable that the popular vote should be badly divided. Lincoln received a total of 1,866,452 votes, Douglas 1,376,957, Breckinridge 849,781, and Bell 588,879. Thus Lincoln's clear majority in the electoral college, 180 to 123 for all his opponents combined, was obtained with only forty per cent of the popular vote being cast for the Republican candidate. Lincoln's opponents actually received altogether nearly a million more popular votes than their successful rival.

It would be a mistake, however, to assume that a majority of the voters, either in the North or in the South, were ready to force the issue of secession. Many Republicans refused to believe that the southern threat need be taken seriously. While it is true that secession was exactly what some of the southern extremists desired, probably the majority of southerners wished to preserve the Union. Presumably the supporters of Bell and Douglas were against secession. Breckinridge was from a border state, and was known to favor the Union, despite the fact that all the extremists flocked to his standard. Many southerners who voted for him did so in the conviction that his election would allay the crisis and preserve the Union; indeed, a few northerners also voted for him on precisely this ground. The Republicans had failed to capture a majority in either house of Congress, and the Supreme Court still had its southern majority. Thus the North was not yet in a position to force its views upon the South.

Secession of the Lower South. But for the action of South Carolina, the long-threatened appeal to secession might again have been postponed. There the legislature, in order to be able to take prompt action in case Lincoln won, had remained in session until after the election. Without the slightest hesitation it summoned a convention which, at a meeting held in Charleston December 20, unanimously decided to secede from the Union. For leaders of the other southern states this precipitate decision tended to identify the theory and the practice of secession. They knew full well that one state, standing alone, could not hope to maintain its independence. Further, if a seceding state should be forced back into the Union, the whole doctrine of secession would be correspondingly discredited. By February 23, therefore, the remaining six states of the lower South, Mississippi, Florida, Alabama, Georgia, Louisiana, and Texas, had followed South Carolina out of the Union. In every one of these states, however, a determined minority had urged insistently that the time for secession was not yet.

Secession was but a means to an end, and the desired end was a united southern confederacy. Early in February a congress of delegates, chosen for the purpose by the several secessionist conventions, met at Montgomery, Alabama, to establish the new nation. On February 8 this congress adopted for the Confederate States of America a hastily devised provisional constitution; next day it chose as provisional President and Vice-President, respectively, Jefferson Davis of Mississippi and Alexander H. Stephens of Georgia; and thereafter it remained in session long enough to act as a legislature for the provisional government and to draw up a permanent constitution. The Confederate constitution, closely resembling that of the United States, was submitted in March and ratified in April. Throughout the convention proceedings the delegates had been acutely conscious of the parallel between their actions and those of their revolutionary forefathers in severing the ties that had bound the colonies to Great Britain. They issued no common declaration of independence, but they found the real justification of their course in the right of an oppressed people to revolt.

Jefferson Davis. Jefferson Davis (1808–1889), the newly elected Confederate President, was a Kentuckian by birth, a graduate of West Point who had seen active military service on the frontier and in the war with Mexico, and a Mississippi cotton planter long active in national politics. He was regarded as less radical than many of his southern compatriots, as for instance, R. B. Rhett of South Carolina, whose states'-rights views outlasted secession. Davis was essentially a southern nationalist, and immediately set himself the task of building a new nation.

Northern Opinion on Secession. Most northerners showed little realization of the seriousness of the situation. Some said that the South would soon return to the Union; others that a "reconstruction" of the Union by means of such a compromise as had been worked out in 1850 should be undertaken; still others, including most of the abolitionists, that it was probably a good thing to have the lower South out of the Union. Above all else the North seemed determined that there should be no civil war. President Buchanan held that while secession was unconstitutional, so also was the coercion of a state. Therefore, he could never lead the North into war to conquer the South. The President told Congress that the blame for the existing sectional controversy rested entirely with the North, and urged the adoption of an "explanatory amendment" to the Constitution which would yield every disputed point to the South.

Fort Sumter. Nevertheless, the President faced a most embarrassing situation in Charleston Harbor. There Major Robert Anderson, in command of a small federal garrison, had removed his troops from the mainland to an island fortification in the mouth of the harbor, Fort Sumter. Buchanan at first sought only to maintain the *status quo,* but the withdrawal of many southerners from his Cabinet brought to the fore a group of strong Unionists who finally persuaded him to reinforce Sumter. On January 8, 1861, he sent the *Star of the West,* a merchant steamer, to Charleston Harbor, with 200 soldiers aboard. But when three days later the vessel attempted to enter the harbor, she was met by the fire of state batteries, and turned back to New York without discharging her errand. This attack was in reality an act of war, but the President chose to ignore it, and during the remainder of his administration he made no further effort to aid Anderson.

The Crittenden Compromise. Congress, meantime, was hard at work on a plan of compromise by which the Union might be preserved. The leadership of this movement was assumed, appropriately, by Senator John J. Crittenden of Kentucky, the successor to Clay's seat in the Senate. Two days before the secession of South Carolina, Crittenden introduced into the Senate an elaborate set of resolutions which provided for the prohibition of slavery in all territory

of the United States, "now held or hereafter acquired," north of 36° 30′, and protected it south of that line; set drastic limits on the right of Congress to abolish slavery in the District of Columbia and in other territory under its control; guaranteed the preservation of the domestic slave trade; and required the federal government to compensate the owners of rescued fugitive slaves. These and all other plans of compromise were now brought before a Senate committee of thirteen, headed by Crittenden, and so selected as to represent every section and party. For a time it seemed as if the Crittenden plan would be endorsed by the committee, but Seward, the leading Republican member, quite properly sounded out Lincoln and found the President-elect opposed to any compromise that would permit the spread of slavery. Thereafter, the Republicans voted unanimously against the proposed 36° 30′ dividing line, and the committee reported back to the Senate that it could not agree.

Other Efforts at Compromise. Other efforts to devise a satisfactory compromise also failed. A House committee proposed (1) an amendment to the Constitution that would safeguard slavery where it already existed, (2) a recommendation that the northern states repeal the "personal-liberty laws" by means of which they interfered with the capture of fugitive slaves, and (3) the admission of New Mexico, "with or without slavery." But this plan was as unsatisfactory to the representatives of the cotton states as the Crittenden plan had been to the Republicans. Both houses of Congress, however, voted to submit a thirteenth amendment to the Constitution for the protection of slavery in the existing slave states — a far cry from the Thirteenth Amendment that eventually was adopted. With the failure of compromise in Congress, the Virginia legislature invited the states to send delegates to a great peace convention to open in Washington, February 4. Twenty-one states responded favorably, but the convention found little new to suggest, and its recommendations were promptly rejected by the Senate. While many important differences existed in all the compromise efforts, the most stubbornly contested point seemed to center on the extension of slavery into the federal territories. The North remained adamantly opposed to its slightest expansion, whereas the Confederacy demanded its recognition south of some such line as that drawn by the Missouri Compromise. Upon this critical point the impasse of the sections seemed complete.

SELECTED BIBLIOGRAPHY

Allan Nevins, *The Emergence of Lincoln* (2 vols., 1950), begins where his *Ordeal of the Union* leaves off; it is valuable for its great mass of well-documented detail. A useful source collection is R. W. Johannsen (ed.), *The Union in Crisis, 1850–1877* (1965). H. H. Simms, *A Decade of Sectional Controversy, 1851–1861* (1942), blames the war mainly on political factors. R. F. Nichols, *Blueprints for Leviathan: American Style* (1963), is a rather sweeping interpretation of constitutional history, with its focus on this period. G. H. Mayer, *The Republican Party, 1854–1964* (1964), is a convenient modern survey. The first Republican campaign is well described in R. J. Bartlett, *John C. Frémont and the Republican Party* (1930); and J. A. Iseley, *Horace Greeley and the Republican Party, 1853–1861* (1947). P. S. Klein, *President James Buchanan* (1962), is a thorough and scholarly biography. W. N. Brigance, *Jeremiah Sullivan Black* (1934), gives a good account of one of Buchanan's most loyal advisers. R. F. Nichols, *The Disruption of American Democracy* (1948), is a richly detailed account of the split during the Pierce and Buchanan administrations.

The situation in Kansas and Nebraska is treated in the standard state histories: W. F. Zornow, *Kansas* (1957); and J. C. Olson, *History of Nebraska* (1955). Interesting attempts to revise traditional interpretations are G. R. Gaedert, *The Birth of Kansas* (1940); and J. C. Malin, *The Nebraska Question, 1852–1854* (1953). On the role of the New England Emigrant Aid Society, two works help to set the record straight: J. C. Malin, *John Brown and the Legend of Fifty-Six* (1942); and S. A. Johnson, *The Battle Cry of Freedom* (1954).

On Brown the literature is extensive. Biographies include W. E. B. DuBois, *John Brown* (1909); and O. G. Villard, *John Brown* (1910). Substantial biographies of key figures in the Kansas struggle are W. E. Parrish, *David Rice Atchison of Missouri* (1961); and J. P. Shenton, *Robert John Walker* (1961). A careful study of one important problem is P. W. Gates, *Fifty Million Acres: Conflicts over Kansas Land Policy, 1854–1890* (1954).

On the rise of Lincoln, see A. J. Beveridge, *Abraham Lincoln, 1809–1858* (2 vols., 1928); and Carl Sandburg, *Abraham Lincoln: The Prairie Years* (2 vols., 1926). Important recent monographs include D. W. Riddle, *Lincoln Runs for Congress* (1948), and *Congressman Abraham Lincoln* (1957); and D. E. Fehrenbacher, *Prelude to Greatness; Lincoln in the 1850's* (1962). The debates are collected in *Created Equal?*, edited by P. M. Angle (1958); and *The Lincoln-Douglas Debates*, edited by R. W. Johannsen (1965). An interesting analysis of these famous debates is H. V. Jaffa, *Crisis of the House Divided* (1959).

Hinton Helper's famous work, *The Impending Crisis of the South* (1857), is readily available in two modern editions. Important scholarly biographies of significant leaders include: J. H. Parks, *John Bell of Tennessee* (1950); D. E. Fehrenbacher, *Chicago Giant; a Biography of "Long John" Wentworth* (1957); David Donald, *Charles Sumner and the Coming of the Civil War* (1960); and A. D. Kirwan, *John J. Crittenden* (1962). On Davis, the best modern biography is Hudson Strode, *Jefferson Davis* (3 vols., 1955–1964). Davis' own memoir, *The Rise and Fall of the Confederate Government* (2 vols., 1881), is an important source. William and Bruce Catton, *Two Roads to Sumter* (1963), follows the careers of Lincoln and Davis in the 1850's.

° Available in paperback

Important studies of the 1860 election include: W. L. King, *Lincoln's Manager, David Davis* (1860); R. H. Luthin, *The First Lincoln Campaign* (1944); and Ollinger Crenshaw, *The Slave States in the Presidential Election of 1860* (1945). See also the interesting collection of essays edited by N. A. Graebner, *Politics and the Crisis of 1860* (1961). Major studies of the North during the final crisis are D. M. Potter, °*Lincoln and His Party in the Secession Crisis* (2nd ed., 1962); W. E. Baringer, *A House Dividing* (1945); K. M. Stampp, °*And the War Came* (1950); and R. N. Current, °*Lincoln and the First Shot* (1963). Henry Adams, °*Great Secession Winter of 1860–61 and Other Essays*, edited by George Hochfield (1958), contains the impressions of one of America's great historians. An excellent collection of conflicting interpretations is °*Lincoln and the Coming of the Civil War*, edited by Norton Garfinkle (1959). R. G. Gunderson, *Old Gentlemen's Convention; The Washington Peace Conference of 1861* (1961), is a fine study of an abortive endeavor.

On secession, an excellent scholarly treatment is D. L. Dumond, *The Secession Movement, 1860–1861* (1931). An important recent monograph is R. A. Wooster, *The Secession Conventions of the South* (1962). Useful older special studies include R. R. Russel, *Economic Aspects of Southern Sectionalism, 1840–1861* (1924); and J. T. Carpenter, *The South as a Conscious Minority, 1789–1861* (1930). Of the seceding states, South Carolina has properly received the fullest scholarly attention; see J. G. Van Deusen, *Economic Bases of Disunion in South Carolina* (1928); H. S. Schultz, *Nationalism and Sectionalism in South Carolina, 1852–1860* (1950); and C. E. Cauthen, *South Carolina Goes to War, 1860–1865* (1950). Other state studies include C. P. Denman, *The Secession Movement in Alabama* (1933); W. M. Caskey, *Secession and Restoration of Louisiana* (1938); P. L. Rainwater, *Mississippi, Storm Center of Secession, 1856–1861* (1938); W. H. Ryle, *Missouri: Union or Secession* (1931); J. C. Sitterson, °*The Secession Movement in North Carolina* (1939); and H. T. Shanks, *The Secession Movement in Virginia* (1934).

The problem of causation of the Civil War has long concerned historians. On this theme see the excellent documentary collection, K. M. Stampp (ed.), °*The Causes of the Civil War* (2nd ed., 1965). Conflicting interpretations are brought out in two "problems" volumes edited by E. C. Rozwenc: °*The Causes of the American Civil War* (1961), and °*Slavery as a Cause of the Civil War* (2nd ed., 1963).

19

THE APPEAL TO ARMS

Lincoln. As the time for Lincoln's inauguration approached, the attention of the nation focused upon the ungainly westerner whose duty it had become to confront and, if possible, resolve peacefully the coming crisis. Abraham Lincoln (1809–1865) was born in Kentucky, the descendant of several generations of frontiersmen. His father, Thomas Lincoln, was only a child when his father, Abraham Lincoln, was killed by Indians. Grown and married, Thomas Lincoln made two typical pioneer moves to the West, first to Indiana, and later to Illinois. Thus repeatedly transplanted, the boy Abraham obtained little formal schooling, but he was intelligent, he read widely, and he ultimately learned enough law to meet the modest requirements of the West for admission to the bar. He possessed a native shrewdness and developed a remarkable capacity for logical thinking and for the accurate — even eloquent — expression of his thought. A thoroughgoing westerner, he

instinctively idealized both nationalism and democracy, and he resented deeply those southern leaders who, with or without a majority, were determined to rule the nation or else ruin it. Tall and homely, stoop-shouldered, and with a loose-jointed shambling gait, Lincoln knew little of the polite usages of eastern society, and to sophisticates the essential gentility of his nature was often obscured by his uncouth manners, his crude jokes, and his easy familiarity.

Lincoln's Inaugural Address. During his months as President-elect, Lincoln had studiously avoided any public expression of opinion, and the country awaited eagerly his announcement of policy. This statement he properly decided to reserve for his inaugural address, but when crowds gathered around his train on the long journey to Washington he unwisely resorted to ambiguous and sentimental remarks that made some men wonder if he really understood the situation at all. But his inaugural address presented a calm, cogent argument against the constitutional right of secession that could scarcely have been improved upon. More than that, he left the South no alternative but to return to the Union, or else fight to stay out. He declared his intention to execute the federal laws in all the states, to "hold, occupy, and possess the property and places" belonging to the

United States, and to collect as usual the duties and imposts. "In doing this," he reasoned, "there needs to be no bloodshed or violence; and there shall be none, unless it be forced upon the national authority."

Lincoln had stated his policy with candor, but for the first few weeks his administration was in too chaotic a condition to do more than mark time. The President, never an efficient administrator, was hampered by the preponderance of new and inexperienced men among his subordinates. Some members of his Cabinet were not fully loyal to their chief. Four out of the seven, Secretary of State Seward, Secretary of the Treasury Chase, Secretary of War Cameron, and Attorney-General Bates, had hoped for the nomination that Lincoln had won; and two of them, Seward and Chase, were convinced that in ability they far outranked the new President. Seward, in an amazing document written four weeks after the inauguration, actually offered to take over the government. Fortunately, Lincoln did not choose to abdicate his duties, and with that extraordinary magnanimity for which he soon became noted, made no effort to discipline his presumptuous Secretary.

Sumter Fired On. It was the Sumter situation that finally forced Lincoln to act. Either he would have to furnish Major Anderson with supplies, or else permit the evacuation of the fort. Approximately the same situation existed at Fort Pickens in the harbor of Pensacola, Florida. To relieve these garrisons might mean war; failure to do so would amount to a tacit recognition of the Confederacy. At length Lincoln, in spite of the disapproval of most of his Cabinet, ordered relief expeditions to both garrisons. The one sent to Fort Pickens was entirely successful, but the news that Sumter was to be reprovisioned led the Davis government to order its bombardment. On the morning of April 12 this order was executed, and after defending his post gallantly for more than a day, Major Anderson surrendered. On Sunday after-noon, April 14, with the relief expedition standing helplessly by, he abandoned the fort "with colors flying and drums beating, bringing away company and private property, and saluting my flag with fifty guns." No one had been killed on either side, but the South had served notice by the incident that it meant to accept Lincoln's challenge, and would fight to stay out of the Union.

Temporary Unity in the North. Whatever the earlier sentiments of the North may have been, the reception of the news from Fort Sumter made it clear that an overwhelming majority of the people in the free states were ready to fight to save the Union. Such prominent Democrats as ex-Presidents Pierce and Buchanan and Senator Stephen A. Douglas came out unqualifiedly for union, and the common people of all parties echoed their sentiments. Not every individual had been swayed to a decision by the same considerations. Abolitionists saw in the coming struggle a long-awaited opportunity to destroy African slavery. Northeastern industrialists feared the loss of southern cotton for their mills and southern markets for their goods, both of which might be imperiled if the South were permitted to leave the Union. Northwestern farmers believed, probably without foundation, that the Mississippi outlet was essential to their prosperity. Thoughtful men in every section saw that secession would create more problems than it could possibly settle. Who should have the territories? What should be done about fugitive slaves? Would secession stop with the withdrawal of the South, or would there eventually be a Pacific confederacy and a northwestern confederacy? How would a divided nation maintain the Monroe Doctrine and the policy of isolation? Could a democracy such as existed in the United States endure?

The Border Slave States. Before the bombardment of Sumter the eight slave states of the upper South had steadfastly refused to leave the Union. Ties of kinship and of interest bound them no less to the North than to the South; war, if it came, would surely make them a battleground. From their point of view the retention of the Union as it was, or its "reconstruction" in such a way as to satisfy the seceding members, was far preferable to dismemberment. In all of them, however, the right of secession was generally conceded, and a strong minority favored testing the principle by practice. When war between North and South became a certainty, this minority was quickly transformed into a majority in Virginia, North Carolina, Tennessee, and Arkansas. Three others — Delaware, Maryland, and Missouri — decided definitely to remain with the North. Kentucky for a time attempted neutrality, but Lincoln, with excellent judgment, allowed the Confederacy to invade the state first, whereupon Kentucky also fell to the Union. Another important victory for the North was won when a block of mountain counties in northwestern Virginia refused to follow the rest of the state out of the Union, and by somewhat irregular methods became the independent loyal state of West Virginia, which Congress in June, 1863, belatedly admitted to the Union. In all the border states, however, sentiment remained divided, and most of them furnished regiments for the armies of both North and South.

The Division of Forces.   In the division of forces the North fared far better than the South. Eleven states left the Union; twenty-two (or counting West Virginia, twenty-three) remained loyal to it. Of the territories, only New Mexico and the Indian country to the west of Arkansas fell to the South, and this whole region was quickly reconquered. The North got all the rest, and from it admitted Kansas (1861) and Nevada (1864) to statehood. In population the North outnumbered the South, 22 million to 9.5 million, while the relative fighting power of the South was still further lessened by the fact that about 3.5 million of its population were slaves. Most of the slaves remained loyal to their masters, and, although they were not recruited by the South as soldiers until the waning days of the war, their labor, both at home and at the front, released a far larger proportion of southern white population for military service than could otherwise have been available.

A disproportionately large share of the economic resources of the nation also lay in the North. The known mineral deposits of the country — coal, iron, copper, precious metals — were located almost entirely there. Ninety-two per cent of the manufacturing of the country was carried on in the North, and its iron foundries, textile mills, tanneries, etc., had only to be expanded to meet the unusual demands of war. The South, on the other hand, expected to import the greater part of its manufactures, including the matériel of war, a task that would have been easy enough had the North done nothing to prevent the exportation of cotton in payment. Neither side suffered for lack of foodstuffs, although southern armies and southern cities often went hungry because of transportation difficulties. Of tremendous importance was the railroad supremacy of the North. With nearly two and a half times as many miles of railroad as the South, and with northern railroads far more strategically located, the advantage of the North in this all-essential factor was decisive.

Nearly all government property of any military value went to the North. The South seized the Norfolk Navy Yard, Harpers Ferry, and the other southern arsenals, the sub-treasury and mint at New Orleans, and a few coastal defense installations; but the North got practically all the rest, including almost every ship in the United States Navy. As for munitions, neither side possessed enough reliable weapons at the outbreak of the war to constitute a real menace to the safety of the other. In 1861, the personnel of the United States Army numbered about 16,000 men, while the navy had 90 ships manned by a total of perhaps 9,000 men. The enlisted men in both branches of the national defense remained, with few exceptions, loyal to the North, but at least one-fourth of the officers resigned their commissions and tendered their services to the South. Unfortunately for the North, the officers who resigned were as a group superior in ability to the rest, for southern planters had long been proud to send their sons to West Point or Annapolis, while among northerners the military life was but little esteemed. Southern officers, moreover, accepted commissions in the regiments of their native states, thus providing a leavening of professional military leadership throughout the entire Southern army. Northern officers, on the other hand, tended at first to remain grouped together in the old regiments of the regular army.

Any assessment of the relative strength of North and South would be incomplete without an evaluation of the personal characteristics of the men who were to do the fighting. The southerners were convinced that their men far outshone their adversaries. The statement that "any Southerner could lick five Yankees" was sincerely believed. Southerners were more habituated to outdoor life, better skilled in the use of firearms, superior as horsemen, and in a much shorter space of time produced good cavalry. On neither side did the common soldiers take kindly to discipline, but the northern privates were as a whole far better educated than their southern opponents, were drawn from a wider range of occupations, and possessed greater mechanical skill. All of which was hardly sufficient to overcome the handicap of fighting in an alien climate and over unfamiliar terrain. The "preponderating asset of the North" turned out to be Lincoln himself. This was not because he possessed any intuitive military understanding that was of use to his generals. Nor was he at first a notably good judge of military men. His strength lay in his extraordinary understanding of the feelings and prejudices of the masses, without whose support the war could never have been won. He realized, more fully than most of his advisers, that when a democracy goes to war military efficiency is of no avail without the backing of public opinion. Every such war has, therefore, its political no less than its military side; and it was in the management of the political side of the struggle that Lincoln's genius was most clearly manifest.

Lee. What Abraham Lincoln, the politician, was to the North, Robert E. Lee (1807–1870), the soldier, was to the South. The two men could hardly have stood in greater contrast to each other. Lee was of the Virginia gentry, and a military genius. The son of General Henry Lee, who had served under Washington during the Revolution, he entered West Point in 1825, where four years later he was graduated, second in his class. As Captain Lee, he was General Scott's chief of staff in Mexico, and out of that campaign he won no less than three promotions for gallant service in the field. Always a favorite with General Scott, who considered him the ablest officer in the army, he was the first choice of both Scott and Lincoln for the active command of the United States Army. A week before the bombardment of Fort Sumter, Francis P. Blair, speaking unofficially for the President, actually offered Lee this post. But Lee declined the offer. Although deeply distressed at the thought of fighting against the United States, he regarded it as his duty, in the event that Virginia should secede, to defend his native state. Handsome, chivalrous, and quick to give battle, he was the perfect embodiment of the role he was chosen to play.

Lack of Preparedness. In a military sense neither side was ready for war. Except for some eleventh-hour activities in the South, neither side had given any very serious consideration to the military problem. The regular army of the United States was insignificant in size and scattered along the Indian frontier. The organized state militia, which was the second line of defense

JEFFERSON DAVIS

The only President of the Confederacy, Jefferson Davis was a devoted southern nationalist, but he was far less skillful than Lincoln in getting the best from his subordinates.

for the North and the beginning and end of southern preparedness, consisted of a few companies of volunteers in each state, imperfectly armed and inadequately drilled. Probably the total number of militiamen in the loyal states on the eve of the war was less than 10,000, and in the seceding states even less than that. When Lincoln, on April 15, 1861, issued his call for 75,000 state militia, and Davis shortly afterward countered with a request for 100,000, both men knew that they were asking for units that did not exist. Before there could be any war, volunteers had to be obtained, armed, and organized into armies. This situation, more than anything else, accounts for the slow beginning of military operations and the uncertainty and delay that characterized the first campaigns. Not until well toward the middle of the war did the armies of North and South confront each other as dependable fighting machines.

How the Armies Were Raised. Lincoln's first call for troops, issued under an antiquated militia law, asked for a specified number of regiments from each state. Since none of the states had nearly enough organized militia to fill its assigned quota, each loyal governor was forced in turn to issue his own call for troops. He was in no better position, however, than the President to accept individual volunteers, so he as well passed on this task to the various communities of the state. There local leaders called patriotic mass meetings where "muster-rolls" were started, and as soon as a company was filled offered its services to the state. Company officers were invariably elected by the volunteers themselves, but regimental officers were usually chosen by the governor, and general officers by the President, by and with the advice and consent of the Senate. Within a short time the troops thus raised far exceeded the number called for; but in spite of frantic purchases abroad by both the state and national governments, the supply of arms was totally inadequate, and the uniforms, when they existed at all, presented an astonishing variety of colors and patterns. Few recruits knew even the rudiments of military drill, and the officers, selected usually because of their political or social prominence, were almost as ignorant of military matters.

Encouraged by the response of the country to his first call, Lincoln issued another on May 3, 1861, which asked for 42,000 volunteers to serve for three years, and directed an increase of 18,000 men in the regular army. Since the Constitution gives Congress rather than the President the right to raise armies, this second call can scarcely have been constitutional. Lincoln himself was under no illusions about his action, and when Congress met on July 4 he asked (and subsequently received) its official ratification of what he had done. He asked also for a volunteer army of at least 400,000 three-year men. Congress granted him 500,000. In raising and organizing these troops, the precedents already set in calling out the state militia were closely followed.

Merrimac at length withdrew, never again to figure in the war. The engagement marked a turning point in naval history, for it proved that the old-fashioned wooden ships were obsolete. But it did nothing to aid the Confederacy, for the North was able to multiply the number of *Monitors* at will, while the South could not produce another *Merrimac*.

Commerce-destroyers. The South succeeded, however, in harassing the trade of the North by means of commerce-destroyers. Nineteen of these vessels, of which the best known was the *Alabama*, put to sea. Nearly all of them were British-built, manned chiefly by British subjects and outfitted from British ports, but they were officered by the Confederacy, and, acting on its authority, they destroyed over 250 northern merchant ships. Their exploits struck an almost fatal blow to the American merchant marine, for the risk of destruction and the consequent high insurance rates led American shipowners to dispose of the bulk of their holdings to foreigners, whereupon the ships were transferred to foreign registry. Commerce between the United States and the outside world was not seriously interrupted, but such trade tended increasingly to be carried on under a foreign flag.

The War in the West. For the North, the war in the West got off to a somewhat better start than the war in the East. Here the first objective was to clear the Confederates from the state of Missouri. This was almost accomplished by General Nathaniel Lyon, who about a month before Bull Run defeated a small secessionist force under General Sterling Price at Boonville. But Lyon's defeat and death at the battle of Wilson's Creek, August 10, 1861, left southern Missouri in Confederate hands until the following spring. Then Union forces at Pea Ridge, Arkansas, May 5–8, 1862, won a victory that drove the Confederates far south of the Missouri-Arkansas border.

After the death of Lyon, General John C. Frémont was placed in charge of the war in the West, but Frémont's incompetence soon led to his replacement by General Henry W. Halleck, a West Point graduate who had left the army to become a lawyer. Halleck was far from brilliant, but he was soon able to report advances along the Mississippi, Tennessee, and Cumberland Rivers, which almost parallel each other for 100 miles south of the Ohio. At Columbus and Island No. 10 on the Mississippi, at Fort Henry on the Tennessee, and at Fort Donelson on the Cumberland, General Albert Sidney Johnston, the Confederate commander, had made every effort to prepare for the Union attack. Early in February General Ulysses S. Grant, supported by a Union flotilla of gunboats under Flag Officer Andrew H. Foote, advanced against Fort Henry. On February 6, after hard fighting, the fort surrendered to Foote shortly before Grant's army arrived on the scene. On February 16 another joint army and gunboat attack under the same officers brought about the fall of Fort Donelson. These victories forced Johnston to abandon his northernmost hold on the Mississippi River at Columbus, as well as his headquarters at Nashville on the Cumberland. The way seemed well prepared for a Union invasion of western Tennessee.

Ulysses S. Grant. Ulysses S. Grant (1822–1885) was the son of an unprosperous Ohio tanner. Accident rather than ability won him an appointment to West Point in 1839, where, to use his own words, he "never succeeded in getting squarely at either end of my class, in any one study, during the four years." Among the thirty-nine members of the graduating class of 1843, he ranked twenty-first. Commissioned a second lieutenant of infantry, he emerged from the Mexican War only a first lieutenant, and in 1854, as a captain, resigned his commission rather than face a court-martial on the charge of drunkenness. The years of poverty and failure that followed sapped

Grant's confidence, but in 1861 his military experience was too valuable to be overlooked, and he became brigadier-general in command at the strategic point of Cairo, Illinois. There his good judgment in occupying Paducah on the Kentucky side of the Ohio, and his success in ousting the Confederates from Belmont on the Missouri side of the Mississippi, marked him as the man to lead the attacks on Forts Henry and Donelson. Time proved that Grant had qualities of great importance to the Union cause. He knew sound advice when he heard it, and was willing to accept it. He had a dogged determination never to turn back once he had decided on a given course of action. He chose his subordinates with skill, and accepted without hesitation every new responsibility that was thrust upon him. Grant's victory at Donelson, where he refused to consider any terms except "unconditional surrender," won him a sobriquet that followed him all through the war. In Grant the North had found its first and most authentic hero.

The River War. Grant's triumph at Donelson was soon somewhat eclipsed by his close escape from defeat at Shiloh, or Pittsburg Landing, near the Tennessee-Mississippi border, where his troops were surprised and attacked by the Confederates on the early morning of April 6, 1862. During the first day of the battle, Grant's army was almost driven into the Tennessee River, but the arrival of reinforcements the second day enabled the Federal troops to recover their lost ground and to force the Confederates back into Mississippi. The battle of Shiloh cost the Confederates the life of their commanding officer, General Albert Sidney Johnston, whom southerners esteemed no less than Lee. His successor, General Beauregard, made Corinth, Mississippi, his headquarters, but was forced to abandon that point in May when the Union army, with Halleck now in personal command, advanced in overwhelming numbers. Fortunately for Grant, of whom Halleck

seemed to be jealous, Halleck was rewarded for his success in the western theater by being made general-in-chief of all the Union armies. Meantime there had been spectacular fighting on the Mississippi River. Union troops and gunboats had taken Island No. 10 from the Confederates and had defeated a Confederate flotilla near Memphis, where Grant promptly established his headquarters. On the lower Mississippi, Captain David Glasgow Farragut ran the strong defenses at the mouth of the river, occupied New Orleans on April 25, and penetrated upstream as far as Vicksburg. By the end of the year it was apparent that Grant would move against that stronghold in the coming spring.

Northern Defeats in the East. While the North was scoring these moderate successes in the West, the South was piling up victory after victory in the East. McClellan's plan of campaign was to transport his army by water to the peninsula that lay between the York and James Rivers, and then to advance westward to Richmond. This was no doubt sound strategy, but it worried the politicians in Washington, who insisted that a part of McClellan's army be kept directly between Washington and the enemy. Obliged against his better judgment to thus divide his forces, McClellan, with nearly twice as many men as the Confederates failed to take Richmond, although he came within four and a half miles of the city. In the famous Seven Days' Battles, Lee, who succeeded General J. E. Johnston in field command when the latter was wounded, decisively defeated McClellan and forced him to withdraw to the protection of the Union gunboats on the James River. McClellan then proposed, again with sound strategy, to remove his army to the south bank of the James River, and, by threatening the railroads that brought supplies from the south to Richmond, to force the Confederates to abandon their capital. Later, Grant was to follow precisely this plan through to success, and with the full

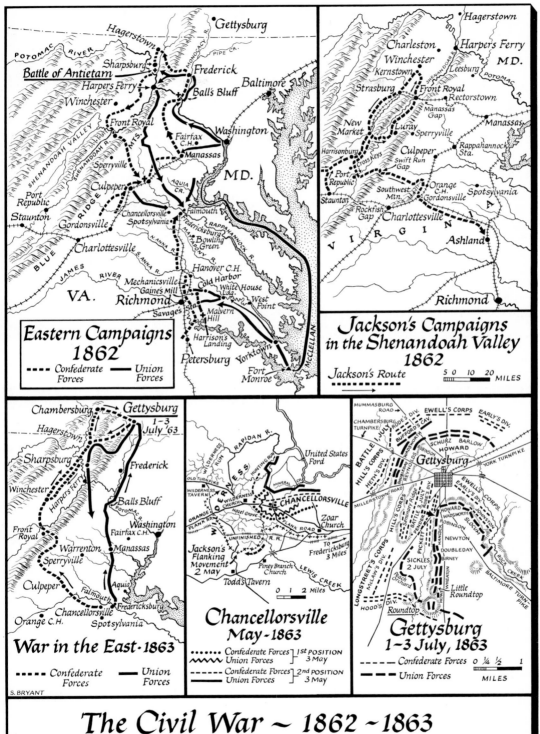

Eastern Campaigns 1862

- - - - Confederate Forces — Union Forces

Jackson's Campaigns in the Shenandoah Valley 1862

Jackson's Route

5 0 10 20 MILES

War in the East · 1863

- - - - Confederate Forces — Union Forces

S. BRYANT

Chancellorsville May · 1863

⋯⋯ Confederate Forces 1ST POSITION 3 May
⌇⌇⌇ Union Forces
- - - - Confederate Forces 2ND POSITION 3 May
—— Union Forces

0 1 2 Miles

Gettysburg 1~3 July, 1863

- - - - Confederate Forces
━ ━ Union Forces

0 ¼ ½ 1 MILES

The Civil War ~ 1862 ~ 1863

support of Lincoln. However, Halleck was by this time in Washington as general-in-chief, and his advice, rather than McClellan's, was followed. McClellan was not actually removed from command, but Halleck brought General John Pope from the West to head a new venture directly toward Richmond from Washington, built up Pope's army at the expense of McClellan's, and ordered McClellan back to the Potomac. Thereupon, Lee turned his attention to Pope, whom he completely outmaneuvered and defeated at the second battle of Bull Run, August 30, 1862. The rout of the Union forces was almost as complete as that which McDowell's army had suffered at the same place the year before.

Antietam to Gettysburg. Pope's disaster brought McClellan back into favor again, but before the Union forces could be fully reorganized, Lee crossed the Potomac from Leesburg, Virginia, to Frederick, Maryland, and headed toward Pennsylvania. McClellan gave chase, and at the costly battle of Antietam, September 17, turned Lee back

to Virginia. Had McClellan been as good a field commander as he was a drillmaster and organizer, Lee's defeat at Antietam would have been a rout. This Lincoln knew, and he therefore began his long and disheartening search for a general whom he could trust. His first choice, General Ambrose E. Burnside, proved his incompetence at Fredericksburg, December 13, in one of the bloodiest and most disastrous defeats of the war. Burnside was then succeeded by "Fighting Joe" Hooker, an able soldier whom the men liked. At Chancellorsville, early in May, 1863, Lee defeated Hooker as decisively as he had defeated Burnside, but Lincoln delayed making another choice until Hooker himself precipitated matters by resigning the command. This happened shortly after Lee had again crossed the Potomac heading northward into Pennsylvania with Hooker paralleling his movements somewhat to the east. Lincoln then gave the command to General George G. Meade just as the greatest battle of the war was shaping up, at Gettysburg, Pennsylvania. Here, after three days of intense

> *A Union officer in the famous "Iron Brigade," Frank Aretas Haskell (1828–1864) won the praise and admiration of his superiors for gallantry during Pickett's Charge at Gettysburg. Within two weeks, while the white heat of battle still lingered, he wrote the following classic account.*

Now came the dreadful battle picture . . . Upon the front and right flank of Sickles came sweeping the infantry of Longstreet and Hill. Hitherto there had been skirmishing and artillery practice — now the battle began; for amid the heavier smoke and larger tongues of flame of the batteries, now began to appear the countless flashes and the long fiery sheets of the muskets, and the rattle of the volleys, mingled with the thunder of the guns. We see the long gray lines come sweeping down upon Sickles' front, and mix with the battle smoke; now the same colors emerge from the bushes and orchards upon his right, and envelope his flank in the confusion of the conflict.

O, the din and the roar, and these thirty thousand Rebel wolf cries! What a hell is there down that valley!

FRANK ARETAS HASKELL, *The Battle of Gettysburg* (1908)

---

fighting, July 1–3, 1863, the Union army won a signal victory. The most spectacular phase of the fighting came the third day, when Lee sent General George E. Pickett with 10,000 men directly against the Union center. Three-fourths of Pickett's men fell dead or wounded and next day Lee began his retreat to Confederate soil. Meade's forces were too badly mauled to take full advantage of the victory they had won, and Lee escaped, but with this battle the tide seemed definitely to have turned in favor of the North.

Vicksburg. From the West also came news of a Union triumph. There Grant had been wrestling for months with the difficult problem of taking Vicksburg. After several hard-fought battles, Grant settled down in May, 1863, to a siege of that fortress city, which ended in its surrender, July 4, while Meade was winning the great battle at Gettysburg. On July 8 following Port Hudson surrendered. Shortly afterward, the safe descent of a commercial steamboat from St. Louis to New Orleans justified Lincoln's observation that "the Father of Waters again goes unvexed to the sea." More important than the opening of the Mississippi was the fact that the Confederate states to the west of the river were now virtually out of the war.

Chattanooga and Chickamauga. The fighting now shifted to eastern Tennessee, where the Union objective was to take Chattanooga, and so cut squarely in two the only continuous railroad from the East to the West that the Confederacy possessed. At Murfreesboro, on the last day of 1862 and the first two days of 1863, a Confederate army under General Braxton Bragg successfully halted the Union advance under General William S. Rosecrans. But the next spring and summer, Rosecrans drove Bragg out of Chattanooga, and on September 9 occupied the city. A little later, however, on September 19–24, Bragg badly worsted Rosecrans at the battle of Chickamauga, and cut off Union communications with Chattanooga except for a narrow mountain wagon road. General Grant,

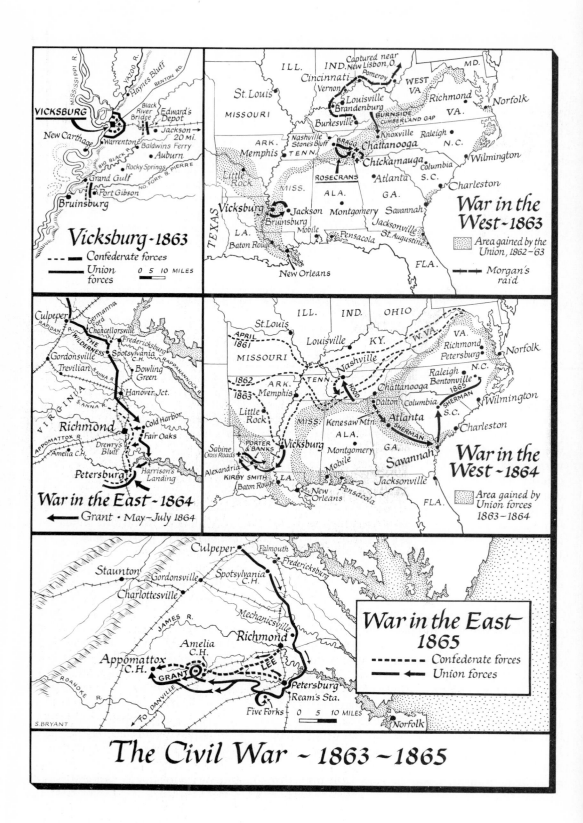

Vicksburg - 1863

MISSISSIPPI R. • VAZOO R. • Haynes Bluff • BENTON RD. • Black Bluff • Edward's Depot • Black River Bridge • Jackson 20 MI. → • VICKSBURG • New Carthage • Warrenton • Baldwins Ferry • BIG BLACK • Auburn • Rocky Springs • Grand Gulf • NO. FORK B. PIERRE • Port Gibson • Bruinsburg

- - - Confederate forces
―― Union forces

0 5 10 MILES

War in the West ~ 1863

ILL. • IND. • Captured near New Lisbon, O. • MD. • Cincinnati • Pomeroy • WEST VA. • Vernon • Louisville • Brandenburg • Richmond • Norfolk • St. Louis • MISSOURI • Burkesville • BURNSIDE CUMBERLAND GAP • VA. • ARK. • Nashville • Stones Bluff • BRAGG • Knoxville • Raleigh • Memphis • TENN. • Chattanooga • N.C. • Little Rock • ROSECRANS • Chickamauga • Columbia • Wilmington • MISS. • ALA. • Atlanta • S.C. • Charleston • Vicksburg • Jackson • Montgomery • Savannah • GA. • TEXAS • Bruinsburg • Mobile • Jacksonville • St. Augustine • LA. • Pensacola • Baton Rouge • FLA. • New Orleans

Area gained by the Union, 1862–63

―― Morgan's raid

War in the East - 1864

Culpeper • Germanna Ford • RAPIDAN R. • Chancellorsville • THE WILDERNESS • Fredericksburg • Gordonsville • Spotsylvania C.H. • RAPPAHANNOCK R. • Trevilian • N. ANNA R. • Bowling Green • Hanover Jct. • VIRGINIA • S. ANNA R. • Richmond • Cold Harbor • APPOMATTOX R. • Fair Oaks • Amelia C.H. • Drewry's Bluff • Harrison's Landing • Petersburg

← Grant · May–July 1864

War in the West ~ 1864

ILL. • IND. • OHIO • APRIL 1861 • St. Louis • Louisville • KY. • W. VA. • Richmond • Petersburg • Norfolk • MISSOURI • Nashville • 1862 • 1863 • ARK. • TENN. • HOOD • Raleigh • Bentonville 1865 • N.C. • Memphis • Chattanooga • Dalton • Columbia • SHERMAN • Wilmington • Little Rock • MISS. • Kenesaw Mtn. • Atlanta • S.C. • Charleston • Sabine Cross Roads • PORTER & BANKS • Vicksburg • SHERMAN • Alexandria • KIRBY SMITH • Montgomery • GA. • Savannah • Baton Rouge • LA. • Mobile • Jacksonville • New Orleans • Pensacola • FLA.

Area gained by Union forces 1863–1864

War in the East 1865

Culpeper • Falmouth • Staunton • Gordonsville • Fredericksburg • Spotsylvania C.H. • Charlottesville • Mechanicsville • JAMES R. • Richmond • Amelia C.H. • Appomattox C.H. • LEE • GRANT • Petersburg • Ream's Sta. • ROANOKE R. • TO DANVILLE • Five Forks • Norfolk

S. BRYANT

- - - Confederate forces
← Union forces

0 5 10 MILES

The Civil War ~ 1863 ~ 1865

whose exploits at Vicksburg had by this time led to his being made supreme commander in the West, now appeared in Chattanooga and assumed command. The battle of Chattanooga, which followed on November 24–25, was a decisive Union victory, and Bragg was sent in full retreat toward Atlanta.

Grant in Supreme Command. Grant's victories at Vicksburg and Chattanooga marked him as the man so sorely needed to take supreme command of all the Union armies, East as well as West. Congress, therefore, revived the grade lieutenant-general, and Lincoln as promptly nominated Grant for the place. By March, 1864, the new commander-in-chief was in Washington to assume his responsibilities. His modesty and tact won him many friends. Halleck was consoled for the loss of his title as general-in-chief by being made Grant's chief of staff, and Meade, who had little success after Gettysburg, was left in command of the Army of the Potomac. Grant made it clear, however, that he had no intention of remaining in Washington as an "armchair" general, and the first hard fighting of the spring found him beside Meade directing the operations of the Army of the Potomac. If the war was to be won, Lee must be beaten, and Grant rightly concluded that his first duty was to match his wits with Lee's.

The first results were far from reassuring. Grant with an army twice the size of Lee's began an advance directly toward Richmond, but early in May, 1864, at the bloody battle of the Wilderness he was fought to a standstill. Undismayed by his defeat, he wheeled his columns to the left and began again his southward march. Again Lee blocked his way, and at Spottsylvania, May 8–12, again prevented a Union breakthrough. Grant's determination to "fight it out along this line if it takes all summer" led to still another terrible repulse at Cold Harbor, June 1–3, after which he adopted McClellan's strategy, and began an advance on Richmond south of the James River by way of Petersburg.

Sherman in Georgia. Meanwhile the western army, now under General W. T. Sherman, was advancing southward from Chattanooga to Atlanta. The Confederates, commanded by General J. E. Johnston, who had succeeded Bragg after the battle of Chattanooga, artfully delayed the invader's progress. But Johnston, like Lee, was badly outnumbered. Sharp fighting occurred at many points along the route, and it was not until September 2 that the Confederates, now under the command of John B. Hood, abandoned Atlanta. Sherman, believing "war and individual ruin" to be synonymous terms, left a trail of desolation wherever he went. Atlanta was burned, and on November 15 Sherman began an advance

ULYSSES S. GRANT

Although he did not enjoy West Point nor military life after graduation, General Grant became the ablest northern officer of the war.

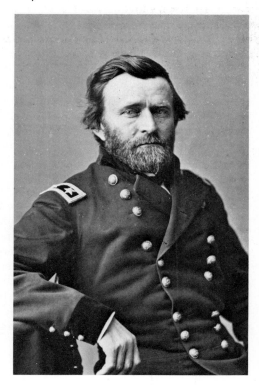

"from Atlanta to the sea" that devastated an area in central Georgia 300 miles long and 60 miles wide. On December 10 he arrived at Savannah, there to begin a march northward through the Carolinas to join Grant. Meantime, as a diversionary tactic, the remnants of the Confederate army commanded by Hood had moved northward into Tennessee, where, at the battle of Nashville (December 15–16, 1864), they were disastrously defeated by the Union forces under General George H. Thomas. The final phase of the war was at hand.

Appomattox. Ever since the summer of 1864, Grant had been engaged in the dreary business of besieging Petersburg and Richmond. For a while Lee successfully used the Shenandoah Valley for diversions, but victories won by General Philip Sheridan over General Jubal Early in the fall of 1864 put an end to that. By the spring of 1865, Lee's position had become extremely precarious. Finally, following the battle of Five Forks, April 1, 1865, Lee abandoned both Petersburg and Richmond, only to discover that Sheridan's cavalry was on one side of him and Grant's infantry on the other. By this time his army had dwindled to less than 30,000 men, whereas Grant had more than 100,000, and Sherman with still other thousands, having defeated Johnston (whom Lee had restored to command) at Bentonville, North Carolina (March 19–20), was approaching from the south. There was nothing left for Lee to do but to surrender, and this he did at Appomattox, April 9. Grant's terms were magnanimous. All the Confederate troops, officers as well as men, were to be paroled under promise not to serve against the United States again until exchanged; all military stores and arms, except the sidearms of officers, were to be surrendered; the mounted Confederates, who unlike the Union cavalry owned their own horses, were to be allowed to keep their mounts. Learning that Lee's men were desperately short of food, Grant also ordered that rations for 25,000 men, approximately the number of troops Lee had surrendered, should be sent to the former enemy at once. Johnston, whose army was now "melting away like snow before the sun," realized that further resistance was useless and soon surrendered to Sherman on similar terms. One by one the lesser armies of the Confederacy laid down their arms, and on May 10 Jefferson Davis himself was captured. The Confederate States of America had ceased to exist.

Losses of the War. The Union was saved, but at a fearful cost. For four years great numbers of men had been taken by both sides from productive employment and had been turned into efficient engines of destruction. The armies of the Civil War were not large, judged by present-day standards, for only rarely did a general have mobile units of as high as 100,000 men under his command. But considering that the combined population of North and South approximated only about 32 million, the manpower that had been mobilized was impressive. The total number of enlistments in the Union army had been about 2.9 million; in the Confederate army about 1.3 million. But because these figures take no account of short-term enlistments they fail to give an accurate picture of the relative strength of the two armies. Thomas L. Livermore computes that the Union army was equivalent to about 1.5 million men serving for three years, and the Confederate army on the same basis, to about 1 million men. These statistics are mere estimates, because the confused state of the records makes it virtually impossible to be sure of the actual number of individuals who served on one side or the other. The casualties were very heavy. For the Union army, counting those killed or mortally wounded in battle, and those who died from sickness or other causes, Livermore sets the figure at about 359,000, and for the Confederate army at about 258,000. Among the survivors were thousands who were maimed for life, and other thousands whose health was permanently undermined.

Behind the Lines. While over 600,000 men were dying, the war and the forces it unleashed were making vast changes on both sides. To the North the war brought an unparalleled wave of prosperity to both agriculture and industry. Mass government purchases of foodstuffs, woolen goods, and leather more than made up for the northern farmer's loss of the southern market. Moreover, extraordinary British imports of wheat from the United States, over three times the normal amount because of bad crop years, swelled the demand for agricultural goods. The northern farmer rapidly increased his land under cultivation and by the extensive introduction of labor-saving farm machinery steadily boosted his production. The corn planter, the two horse cultivator, the mower, the reaper, and the steam thresher had all been invented before the Civil War, but their high cost prohibited their widespread use. It took the war-induced labor shortage, huge demands, and high prices for farm produce to persuade the average farmer to give up his old-fashioned methods and make use of the new tools. A reaper operated by one man could cut ten or twelve acres of grain in a day, whereas the best a man could do with the old back-breaking cradle was an acre and a half. By 1865 it was estimated that not less than 250,000 reapers were in use.

Two important pieces of legislation to stimulate agricultural expansion were passed by Congress in 1862, the Homestead Act and the Morrill Land Grant Act. Both had been opposed by the South and vetoed by President Buchanan, but with the southern representatives absent their speedy passage was assured. The homestead law offered to any adult citizen of the United States, or to aliens who had declared their intention of becoming citizens, 160 acres of public lands virtually free. And under the Morrill Act each state was given huge tracts of public lands as an endowment for agri-

ROBERT E. LEE

"The grey knight of the Confederacy," Robert E. Lee earned from winners and losers alike respect and devotion accorded to few losing generals.

cultural colleges or agricultural departments in state-supported universities. Both acts played important parts in the settlement of the Far West during subsequent decades. Probably of far greater significance in boosting agricultural production during the war years was the weather. Year after year ideal climatic conditions prevailed over the greater part of the North. The total wheat production of the loyal states and territories rose from 142 million bushels in 1859 to 187 million in 1862, and to 191 million in 1863. The general level of production for all agricultural commodities remained high throughout the entire war. With inflated prices, and with adequate transportation, the American farmer enjoyed a degree of prosperity such as he had never known before.

Wartime Manufacturing. Much as the war profited agriculture, the stimulus it gave to manufacturing was even greater.

The armies required huge quantities of manufactured goods of every sort and kind — clothing, boots and shoes, hats and caps, blankets, wagons, arms and ammunition, ready-to-eat rations. To meet these needs old factories were expanded and new factories built. The manufacturer had only to make use of inventions already at hand in order to increase his output. Possibly of all machines the sewing machine helped him most. By use of it whole uniforms, and many other types of garments, could be turned out in far greater quantity and with far less hand labor than had ever been possible before. The war, indeed, changed the clothing habits of masculine America. For the average male, ready-made suits largely replaced suits made at home or at the local tailor shop. Out of the war, too, came the habit of using such factory-made items as shoes, caps, socks, and prepared foods. Manufacturers whose fortunes were founded on government contracts saw their wealth continue to increase after the war, for the changes in customs that the war promoted enabled them to sell with equal advantage to the civilian population.

Heavy industry expanded rapidly during the war. Purchases of munitions abroad practically ceased after the first year because of the rapidity with which American factories supplied the government's needs. The new iron works, gun factories, and powder plants that came into existence were for the most part the results of private initiative, but the government itself went as deeply into the business of manufacturing war materials as public opinion would permit. Railroad building, which was resumed in the North after the outbreak of the war, and the continued need for railroad repairs did much for the manufacturers of iron and steel. They were helped, also, by the demand for ironclads.

The Morrill Tariff Act. High tariffs ensured the northern manufacturers against the dangers of European competition. A protectionist policy had been demanded by the Republican national platform in 1860, and a higher schedule of tariffs, sponsored by the same Justin S. Morrill who gave his name to the act for the stimulation of agricultural education, was placed upon the statute-books two days before Buchanan left office. This speedy answer to the demands of the protectionists was made possible by the withdrawal from Congress of the delegations from the seven seceding states of the lower South, and by the fact that President Buchanan finally conceded to the demands of the manufacturers within his home state. The original Morrill Tariff Act was repeatedly revised upward during the war, until by 1864 the average of duties levied on imports had reached 47 per cent, the highest thus far in the history of the nation.

Business Activities. From whatever angle the subject is viewed, the wartime prosperity of the North was phenomenal. Its railroads, overbuilt during the fifties, were turned into profitable investments by the heavy traffic of the war, and the railroad mileage of both the Northeast and the Northwest had to be substantially increased to carry the load. Internal waterways — the Great Lakes, the western rivers, and the canals — did an enormous volume of business. Financial institutions, which at the outset of the war had seriously missed the patronage of the South, found a more than adequate compensation in the expanding commercial activity of the northern states. Millions of dollars worth of gold and silver flowed into the nation's mints from the mines of California and the Rocky Mountains. The northern merchant marine, as already noted, was virtually ruined by the war; but this involved little loss of capital, for most of the ships were sold, not sunk, and the proceeds from their sale were invested in such lucrative securities as government bonds, manufacturing concerns, and railroads. From a narrow point of view, American shippers were fortunate in leaving the field of transportation at this particular time. Wooden ships were soon to be replaced by ships of iron and steel, and many American firms sold out just in time to escape the cost of extensive replacements.

Northern Wartime Finance. Once prosperity had arrived, the North had little difficulty in financing the war. At the outset, however, the credit of the northern government was at low ebb, the treasury was empty, and the banks soon suspended specie payments. Secretary of the Treasury Chase had little acquaintance with finance, and was so fearful of the political effects of taxation that he proposed to pay the cost of the war mainly from loans. At first he was compelled to pay ruinous rates to obtain money — on one occasion as high as 7.3 per cent — but with the assistance of Jay Cooke, a Philadelphia banker, he succeeded in floating loans that totaled by the end of the war well over $2 billion. Cooke, for a consideration, popularized the bond issues, and besides making the public see that they were a good investment, he played up the patriotic motive. People bought bonds to help the government as well as to help themselves.

Northern Taxation. While relying mainly upon loans, the government resorted also to far heavier taxation than the people of the United States had ever before been called upon to pay. In 1862 excises were levied upon a remarkable variety of articles, businesses, occupations, and activities. Even lawyers, physicians, and dentists were required to buy licenses, and such articles as liquor, tobacco, carriages, yachts, and billiard tables carried heavy duties. Manufacturers were required to pay a tax for the privilege of manufacturing, and the articles they manufactured were also taxed. Railroads, steamboats, toll bridges, savings banks, and insurance companies paid a 3 per cent duty on their gross receipts. Multifold as these taxes were, they did not produce a great revenue. Even with the help

of increased rates, levied in 1864, the total receipts from all such sources during the war barely passed the $300 million mark. An income tax, which began in 1861 as a 3 per cent tax on all incomes above $800, and was later so modified as to tax incomes between $600 and $5,000 at the rate of 5 per cent, and all higher incomes at the rate of 10 per cent, was even less successful as a revenue measure, for it brought in a total of only $55 million. Still these were large sums to a people quite unused to federal taxation.

Greenback Issues. But neither the loans nor the taxes sufficed to keep the government supplied at all times with ready cash, and as a result several issues of paper money were authorized by Congress. Between February, 1862, when the first of the "legal tender" acts was passed, and March, 1863, the date of the last, a total of no less than $450 million in fiat money was ordered printed. Of this sum $431 million was outstanding at the close of the war. Back of the "greenbacks," as the public promptly dubbed these notes, there lay no gold reserve, but only the good faith of the government. They were by law made legal tender for all debts, public and private, except duties on imports and interest on the public debt.

The National Bank Act. A National Bank Act, passed in 1863 and amended in 1864, provided the nation with yet another type of paper money, the national bank note. According to this measure, any association desiring to do a national banking business and possessed of the minimum capital was entitled to a national charter of incorporation. Partly as a means of stimulating the market for United States bonds, the law provided that one-third of the capital of such a bank must be invested in national securities, but it was also stipulated that, by depositing these bonds with the United States Treasurer as security, the bank should be entitled to receive in exchange circulating notes equal in amount to 90 per cent of their market value. It was hoped at first that the state banks would quickly convert themselves into national banks, but when they failed to do so, Congress levied in 1865 a 10 per cent tax on all state bank notes. While this law did not destroy state banking, it did, as was intended, almost tax state bank notes out of existence, so that one of the legacies of the Civil War was a national currency, composed in part of greenbacks and in part of national bank notes. By the end of 1865 the national bank note circulation had reached more than $200 million. The bank notes were not "legal tender," as were the greenbacks, but both types of paper money depended in the last analysis upon the credit of the national government and circulated at the same value.

Currency Depreciation. Since the government had been forced to suspend specie payments early in the war, none of this paper money was worth its face value in gold. During the dark days of 1864, when it appeared that even the tenacity of Grant might prove insufficient to win the war, the value of the paper dollar, as expressed in terms of gold, dropped to thirty-nine cents, and even at the close of the war it stood at only sixty-seven cents. Even small-denominational coins were driven out of circulation as the premium on precious metals mounted, and the Treasury was forced to issue paper half-dollars, quarters, dimes, five-cent and three-cent "shin-plasters," as the small-sized notes were called. The changing value of paper money caused an equivalent fluctuation in prices that netted huge fortunes to speculators. While the wages of laborers rose slowly to meet the new price levels, the salaries of "white collar" workers proved to be extremely resistant to change. Soldiers, also, fought on at $13 a month until late in the war, when their pay was raised to $16. The generous bounties paid for enlistments served somewhat to correct this inequality.

Downfall of "King Cotton." If the war brought prosperity to the North, it brought little but adversity to the South. With the welfare of the section so intimately bound up with cotton culture, the failure of southern cotton to find a normal market was catastrophic. The southern government, gambling on the hope that European nations would come to the aid of the South whenever the European mills faced a serious cotton shortage, tried in the early months of the war to prevent the shipment of cotton abroad. Cotton-planters were even urged to destroy their crops as the best insurance against exportation, and it is estimated that this mistaken policy cost the South about a million bales of cotton. Had exportation been stimulated rather than discouraged, the South might have built up credit abroad for subsequent use, but faith in the power of "King Cotton" clouded the judgment of the southern leaders. By 1862 the southern government was ready to reverse its cotton policy, but by that time the northern blockade held shipments to a minimum. The effectiveness of the blockade may be estimated from the fact that the price of cotton in Liverpool rose from fourteen cents in 1861 to fifty cents in 1865. Trade between the lines helped the South and the cotton-planter to some extent, especially after the union armies had penetrated far into the southern states. In exchange for cotton and tobacco, southern traders received salt, clothing, foodstuffs, and even war materials.

Southern Manufacturing. The break with the North, followed by the blockade, forced the South to attempt a far greater diversity of economic life, both agricultural and industrial, than it had known before the war. Foodstuffs were grown instead of cotton, salt works were established, and cotton mills, boot and shoe factories, munitions plants, and the like were started up in spite of inadequate capital, defective machinery, and poorly trained workers. The difficulties experienced by the South in its effort to achieve self-sufficiency, however, were too great to be overcome in a short time, and as the war wore on, both soldiers and civilians were frequently called upon to endure the greatest extremes of privation. While the North was pushing forward relentlessly to the factory system, the South was compelled to resort more and more to household manufacture. The breakdown of southern transportation, particularly the railroads, which the South was utterly unable to keep in repair, served to compound the confusion. The suffering endured by northern prisoners in southern prison camps was due far more to this confused economic situation than to any deliberate intent on the part of the jailers.

Southern Finance. The South, in its efforts to finance the war, was driven rapidly from one makeshift to another. The United States mint at New Orleans and the United States customhouses that were seized provided the Confederacy with perhaps $1 million in greatly needed specie, and the confiscation of private debts owed by southern citizens to northern creditors also helped. Bond issues were floated, both by the Confederacy and by the several Confederate states, but the limited credit resources of the South were soon dried up. The best results were obtained when the bonds were made payable in produce. In this fashion the southern government came into the possession of large quantities of cotton, tobacco, and other staple commodities, some of which it was able to market, and some of which it pledged as security for a small loan floated in Europe in 1863. Taxation turned out to be almost as fruitless as borrowing. An attempt to levy a direct tax through the instrumentality of the states netted little real money. Thereafter, the example set by the northern government of levying excises, licensing occupations, and taxing incomes was tried, but with comparatively slight success. One unique feature of the southern taxation program, a 10 per cent tax on farm produce,

to be paid in kind, proved to be of great assistance to the Confederate armies. It was excessively unpopular, however, and the charge of unconstitutionality was persistently hurled at this and all other effective means of taxation. The total receipts of the Confederacy from all tax sources has been estimated at about $100 million.

The inadequacy of the sums realized from bond issues and taxation drove the Confederacy early in the war to a chief reliance upon printing-press money. Notes were issued by the Confederate Treasury in a steadily increasing volume until before the end of the war more than $1 billion of such money was in circulation. In addition, states, municipalities, and private corporations also put out issues of paper that passed for money. The depreciation that inevitably set in as the amount of fiat money increased, and the prospect of Confederate victory dimmed, far outran the depreciation of the northern greenback. By the summer of 1863 the Confederate dollar was worth only twenty-five cents in gold; a year later it was worth less than five cents; by the end of the war it was valueless.

"King Cotton" Diplomacy. The confidence of the South that European intervention on behalf of "King Cotton" would be the decisive factor in the war made diplomacy a major concern of both belligerents from the very beginning. Every move of the southern government was designed to promote intervention, while the fondest hope of the northern government was to prevent it. Jefferson Davis' two secretaries of state, R. M. T. Hunter and Judah P. Benjamin, were quite outmatched by Seward. William L. Yancey, the first Confederate commissioner to England, quickly lost heart and came home. He was succeeded by James M. Mason, who was well received by the British aristocracy, but made little headway with the British government. In France, John Slidell did better, but there was little that France could do to aid the Confederacy without the approval of England, who, as "mistress of the seas" and the chief foreign consumer of southern cotton, had to make the decision for or against European intervention in the war.

English Attitude toward the American Civil War.

English sympathy at the outset of the war seemed definitely to lean toward the South. The Tory aristocracy, which understood and appreciated the kindred southern planter class, looked forward with satisfaction to the possible downfall of democracy anywhere. Many English liberals also favored the South, for their favorite doctrine was then free trade, and the South seemed to be definitely committed to a free-trade policy, while the North had just inaugurated a program of protection. Diplomats of both parties saw a probable advantage for England in the division of the United States into two contending powers.

The North, however, was not without its friends in England. Such reformers as John Bright and Richard Cobden, although distressed at the newly adopted tariff policy of the United States, saw clearly that a northern victory would result in the abolition of slavery. With the issue thus reduced to a struggle between free labor and slave labor, their sympathies could lie only with the North. Lincoln's early insistence that the war was one for the preservation of the Union, and not for the abolition of slavery, was somewhat confusing to many Englishmen, but when at last he issued his Emancipation Proclamation, the number of northern sympathizers was greatly increased, particularly among the lower classes. To some extent, perhaps, British sympathy for the North was purchased by the greater need for northern wheat than for southern cotton; and there can be no doubt that the profits of neutrality were widely regarded as preferable to a hazardous war on behalf of southern independence. At all events, well before the end of the war the weight of British opinion had shifted to the side of the North.

British Recognition of Southern Belligerency.

Northern anxiety about the course Great Britain meant to pursue became acute as early as May, 1861, when the British government issued a proclamation of neutrality. This action, because it accorded to the South the status of a belligerent, was regarded by the North as deliberately unfriendly. However, Lincoln himself, in ordering a blockade of the southern coast, had already unwittingly recognized the belligerency of the South. Nevertheless the fact that the British proclamation was issued just before the arrival in England of Charles Francis Adams, whom Lincoln had sent as minister from the United States, confirmed northerners in their suspicion that the sympathies of the British government lay with the South. But northern fears that the recognition of southern belligerency would ultimately be followed by the recognition of southern independence proved to be unfounded.

The *Trent* Affair.

An incident that occurred late in 1861 almost precipitated war between Great Britain and the United States. When the news reached Captain Charles Wilkes of the United States frigate *San Jacinto* that the two Confederate commissioners, Mason and Slidell, were aboard a British mail steamer, the *Trent,* bound from Havana to Southampton, he promptly intercepted the neutral ship, arrested the Confederate commissioners, and took them to Boston. Wilkes's action was totally without official authorization and was much the same sort of high-handed procedure that the United States had protested against when practiced by Great Britain before the War of 1812. But the northern public went wild with joy at the news, and Congress voted Wilkes the thanks of the nation for his exploit. British reaction was similarly excited, and the demand of the British government that Mason and Slidell be released and a suitable apology made was fully supported by public opinion. To emphasize the gravity of the situation, the British navy was put on a war footing and 8,000 troops were sent to Canada. In reply Seward failed to make a very emphatic apology, but he surrendered the prisoners, and lessened the tension.

Destruction of Northern Commerce. The blockade of the southern coast that the North maintained caused far less friction with the British government than might have been expected. Even the American doctrine of continuous voyages, which led at times to the capture of British ships bound from one British port to another, was allowed to pass unchallenged. Great Britain wisely offered little objection to practices that she herself might use to advantage as a belligerent. But the British idea of neutral duties sorely taxed the patience of the United States. The Confederate commerce-destroyers were British-built and operated from British ports. For their depredations the American government proposed to collect damages, and after the war succeeded in doing so. The heavily ironclad Laird rams, had they been permitted to sail, might have raised the blockade, but when it became clear that their departure from British waters would mean war between the United States and Great Britain, they were not permitted to leave port. The British government may also be credited with having restrained Napoleon III of France from interference in the war. Napoleon did offer mediation, significantly right after Fredericksburg, and he took advantage of the division of American forces to invade Mexico and install a puppet emperor, Maximilian of Austria, on a Mexican throne. But he never dared recognize the independence of the South, and he was compelled to content himself with the working out of his project for the virtual acquisition of Mexico. A more complete violation of the Monroe Doctrine could scarcely have been imagined, but as long as the United States was torn by civil strife Napoleon knew that he had nothing to fear from north of the Rio Grande. Secretary Seward

did not fail to register a vigorous protest, however, and after the defeat of the South, Napoleon found it expedient to recall his troops from Mexico. The fall of Maximilian's government then followed as a matter of course.

Other European nations showed comparatively slight interest in the American Civil War. Spain did indeed attempt to reannex Santo Domingo, but by 1865 active local opposition had forced her to abandon the project. Russia and Great Britain were on bad terms, and the appearance of two Russian fleets in American waters during 1863 was generally interpreted in the United States as a gesture of friendship toward the North. More probably the Russians were simply stationing their ships where they could most damage British commerce in case war should break out.

Politics in the South. More important to the governments of both North and South than problems of diplomacy were the political dissensions that existed within their own borders. While the South was far more united than the North, the Davis administration lost steadily in popularity. Extreme states'-rights advocates saw in Davis' southern nationalism nothing less than an organized effort to establish a centralized despotism upon the ruins of the states. Conscription, because it was an act of the central government, was denounced for its encroachments upon the reserved rights of the states. Each effective tax measure produced more enemies who took refuge behind the well-worn screen of unconstitutionality. And finally, the horrors of war and the increasing probability of a northern victory brought forth not only critics of the government, but also a large number of defeatists who were always about ready to give up. Party lines were not clearly drawn in the Confederacy, but the congressional elections held in the fall of 1863 placed the Confederate Congress definitely in the hands of the anti-administration forces.

Politics in the North. In the North discontent with Lincoln's administration and dismay at the prospect of a long war had become abundantly apparent before the summer of 1861 was over. To hold a maximum number of northern Democrats to the support of the war, the Republicans in the fall of 1861 quite generally gave up their party name and nominated state and local tickets under the Union label. That year satisfactory Union majorities were attained, but by 1862 opposition to the war in the North was open and active. Lincoln was accused of ordering arbitrary arrests, and of suspending the writ of habeas corpus without adequate constitutional warrant. Military courts took action against civilians even when regular civil courts were open for business. In May, 1863, Lincoln approved the arrest and conviction by court-martial of Clement L. Vallandigham of Ohio, leading Democratic critic of the war measures. In this case, however, Lincoln commuted the sentence of close confine-

ment until the end of the war to banishment to the Confederacy, and so branded Vallandigham with treason. On the question of freedom of the press the President's course was less open to criticism. When the military authorities attempted to suppress the New York *World* and the Chicago *Times,* he promptly reversed their orders.

Emancipation. Radical Republicans who wished for a more vigorous prosecution of the war were almost as great a trial to the President as pacifist Democrats. A Joint Committee on the Conduct of the War, created by Congress in April, 1862, and dominated by the "radicals," did its best to take over the actual direction of military affairs. One policy on which the "radicals" were extremely insistent was the emancipation of the slaves, but this Lincoln refused at first to countenance because of the damage it would do the Union cause in the loyal slave states, and in Democratic

Although his formal schooling probably amounted to less than one year, Abraham Lincoln became a master of the English language — whether spoken or written. His almost ruthless dedication to the preservation of the Union and the humanity which gave lustre to his thoughts and acts are reflected in the following excerpts from a letter to Major-General Hooker and from the Gettysburg Address.

. . . I have heard, in such a way as to believe it, of your recently saying that both the army and the government needed a dictator. Of course it was not for this, but in spite of it, that I have given you the command. Only those generals who gain successes can set up dictators. What I now ask of you is military success, and I will risk the dictatorship. . . . And now beware of rashness. Beware of rashness, but with energy and sleepless vigilance go forward and give us victories.

. . . It is rather for us to be dedicated here to the unfinished work remaining before us — that from these honored dead we take increased devotion to that cause for which they gave the last full measure of devotion — that we here highly resolve that these dead shall not have died in vain — that this nation, under God, shall have a new birth of freedom — and that government of the people, by the people, for the people, shall not perish from the earth.

ABRAHAM LINCOLN, *Complete Works* (1905).

---

circles generally. His "paramount object," he told Horace Greeley, was to save the Union, and not to free the slaves. Nevertheless, the time came when Lincoln was obliged to yield to abolitionist pressure. Runaway slaves fled to the Union armies, where according to General Benjamin F. Butler they became "contraband of war." What should be done with them? Were they slave or free? Two of his generals issued premature emancipation proclamations for the regions under their military command, orders which Lincoln felt obliged to reverse, but knew that he could not long oppose. Lincoln would have preferred to work toward some system of gradual emancipation, but the time came when he must either free the slaves or alienate the majority of his own party. He knew, too, that if freedom for the slaves were made one of the northern objectives in the war, there would be an immediate end to the danger of foreign intervention. His mind made up, he waited two full months longer before he acted, so that a Union victory (Antietam, September 17, 1862) could be cited as proof that his course was not a choice of desperation. Then, on September 22, 1862, he issued his preliminary Emancipation Proclamation. Claiming the right as commander-in-chief of the army and navy, he promised that "on the 1st day of January, A.D. 1863, all persons held as slaves within any state or designated part of a state the people whereof shall then be in rebellion against the United States shall be then, thenceforward, and forever free."

The "Copperheads." Lincoln, like Davis, was soon obliged to confront a Congress steadily less friendly to his administration. "Union" tickets in 1862 drew many war Democrats into collaboration with the Republicans, but many others refused either to leave their party or to permit it to remain dormant for the duration of the war. Some Democrats objected to Lincoln's dictatorial course and criticized his lack of military success. Others held that the Emancipation Proclamation had turned a war to save the Union into a war to free the slaves, something they were utterly unwilling to fight for. Unfortunately Douglas, who had loyally supported the war, died unexpectedly in June, 1861, and left the northern Democrats virtually leaderless. This permitted the rise of such "Copperhead" leaders as Vallandigham, whose extreme opposition to the war was notorious. Helped along by the lack of Union victories, the Democrats in 1862 won the ascendancy in many states that had supported Lincoln two years before, and came within a few votes of winning the national House of Representatives. Strongly Copperhead legislatures chosen that year in Indiana and Illinois almost withdrew those states from support of the war, but the resourcefulness of the two governors concerned, Oliver P. Morton of Indiana and Richard Yates of Illinois, was equal to the emergency.

The Effect of Union Victories. However, the elections held in the fall of 1863 revealed an unmistakable trend back to the support of the administration. In nearly every instance the Unionists showed greater strength than the Democrats, although by majorities that were not always large. This change of sentiment was due primarily to the victories at Gettysburg and Vicksburg, but even these successes were insufficient to quiet the peace-at-any-price men, whose numbers, particularly in the states that bordered on the Ohio River, were very great. In Ohio a governor had to be chosen, and Vallandigham himself, still an exile but by that time in Canada, won the Democratic nomination. But he was decisively defeated by the Unionist candidate, John Brough, a former Democrat.

Election of 1864. The Presidential campaign of 1864 began during the darkest days of the war when long casualty lists and infrequent victories made the Lincoln administration extremely vulnerable. Some Republicans would have been willing to discard Lincoln, and supported a movement that culminated in the nomination of John C. Frémont by a mass convention held in Cleveland, May 31, 1864. But the renomination of Lincoln was decided upon as the sounder strategy, and Frémont withdrew. For Vice-President, at Lincoln's insistence, the Union Party (the name Republican was still carefully avoided) named Andrew Johnson of Tennessee, a War Democrat who had no Republican connections whatever. The Democrats made an undignified straddle. For President they chose General McClellan, while at the same time writing a peace-at-almost-any-price platform. McClellan accepted the nomination, but denounced the platform. "No peace," he asserted, "can be permanent without union." For a while it seemed that surely Lincoln would lose, but military victories changed the situation, and the Union ticket won. The electoral vote showed 212 for Lincoln to 21 for McClellan, but the popular vote was very close. In New York, for example, Lincoln's majority was less than 7,000 out of a total of 730,000.

Death of Lincoln. By Inauguration Day, March 4, 1865, the war was nearly over, and Lincoln promised, "with malice toward none, with charity for all . . . to bind up the nation's wounds." But he was not permitted to have a part in the work of reconstruction, for on April 15, less than a week after Lee's surrender, he was dead. His assassination, coming as it did at the very hour of victory, forced a reappraisal of his capacities, with the result that his name and fame were soon coupled in the public mind with Washington's.

Significance of the Civil War. Lincoln and his contemporaries interpreted the victory of the North as primarily a triumph of nationalism over states' rights. That the

Union was now in fact "one and indivisible," whatever theoretical views some individuals might continue to hold, was generally acknowledged, even by the defeated South. Incidentally, the institution of slavery, which had made the doctrine of states' rights its chief constitutional defense, was also brought to an end. While the Emancipation Proclamation had applied only to those states and parts of states that on January 1, 1863, were still at war with the United States, the momentum that Lincoln's action gave to the abolition movement was too great to be stopped. State action in Missouri, West Virginia, Maryland, Tennessee, and Louisiana had abolished slavery within their respective borders by the time the war was over. Meantime, a movement to write abolition into the national Constitution had gathered headway, and in January, 1865, Congress submitted to the states the Thirteenth Amendment, which forbade slavery or involuntary servitude, except as a punishment for crime, within the United States, or any place subject to its jurisdiction. By the end of the year this amendment had become a part of the Constitution.

Industrial Supremacy. A factor not fully understood at the time, and possibly overemphasized later, was the commanding importance that the new industrial interests won during the course of the struggle. War profits compounded the capital of the industrialists and placed them in a position to dominate the economic life, not only of the Northeast where they were chiefly concentrated, but also of the nation at large. With the southern planters removed from the national scene, the government at Washington tended more and more to reflect the wishes of the industrial leaders. The protective tariff became the cornerstone of the new business edifice, for by means of it the vast and growing American market was largely restricted to American industry. Transcontinental railroads, designed to complete the national transportation system, were likewise accorded the generous assistance of the government, while a national banking act and a national currency facilitated still further the spread of nationwide business.

The Northwest, where industry was definitely subordinate to agriculture, profited less from the war than the Northeast, but westerners applauded the passage of the Homestead Act, and they were for a time as eager as the easterners to accelerate the expansion of the railroads. By assisting in the defeat of the South, however, the Northwest had unknowingly sacrificed a valuable ally. Before the war the two agricultural sections had repeatedly stood together, first against the commercial, and later against the industrial, Northeast. Now, with the weight of the South in the Union immensely lessened, the Northwest was left to wage its battles virtually alone. For more than a generation after the war, with eastern policies in the ascendancy, American industry steadily consolidated the gains it had made.

SELECTED BIBLIOGRAPHY

J. G. Randall and David Donald, *The Civil War and Reconstruction* (2nd ed., 1961), is the most convenient survey and guide. It is thoroughly abreast of the latest scholarship and contains a magnificent critical bibliography. A model study of historiography is T. J. Pressly, *Americans Interpret Their Civil War* (1954). Allan Nevins, *The War for the Union* (2 vols., 1959–   ), is a major work in progress.

On Lincoln, the chief scholarly biography is J. G. Randall, *Lincoln, the President* (4 vols., 1945–1955); the final volume was finished after Randall's death by R. N. Current. Carl Sandburg, *Abraham Lincoln: The War Years* (4 vols., 1939), is a richly detailed labor of

* Available in paperback

love. The best single-volume lives of Lincoln are B. P. Thomas, *Abraham Lincoln* (1952); and R. H. Luthin, *The Real Abraham Lincoln* (1960). A major source is the *Collected Works of Abraham Lincoln,* edited by R. P. Basler (9 vols., 1953–1955). Shorter collections are °*Abraham Lincoln: His Speeches and Writings,* also edited by Basler (1946); °*The Lincoln Reader,* edited by P. M. Angle (1947); and °*Selected Speeches, Messages and Letters of Abraham Lincoln,* edited by T. H. Williams (1957). Stimulating essays on various aspects of Lincoln's career may be found in J. G. Randall, °*Lincoln, the Liberal Statesman* (1947); R. N. Current, °*The Lincoln Nobody Knows* (1958); N. A. Graebner (ed.), *The Enduring Lincoln* (1959); and David Donald, °*Lincoln Reconsidered* (2nd ed., 1961). B. P. Thomas, *Portrait for Posterity: Lincoln and His Biographers* (1947), is an interesting evaluation. Lloyd Lewis, °*Myths After Lincoln* (2nd ed., 1941), is fascinating. Frederic Bancroft, *The Life of William H. Seward* (2 vols., 1900), has long been standard. On Stanton, the best biography is B. P. Thomas and H. M. Hyman, *Stanton* (1962).

The literature on military aspects of the Civil War is enormous and can only be touched on here. Bruce Catton, *The Centennial History of the Civil War* (2 vols., 1961–   ), is a vivid treatment by our most popular military historian; the volumes so far published reach November, 1862. The same author's °*This Hallowed Ground* (1956) is a powerful account of the Union side. Other works on Union military history by Catton are °*Mr. Lincoln's Army* (1951); °*Glory Road* (1952); °*A Stillness at Appomattox* (1953); and *Grant Moves South* (1960). T. H. Williams, *Lincoln and His Generals* (1952), is a fine analysis by a leading authority. W. W. Hassler, *Commanders of the Army of the Potomac* (1962), makes some interesting comparisons. Stimulating essays are gathered together in David Donald (ed.), °*Why the North Won the Civil War* (1960). Interesting collections of first-hand accounts include *The Blue and the Gray,* edited by H. S. Commager (2 vols., 1950); *The Confederate Reader,* edited by R. B. Harwell (1941); and *The Union Reader,* also edited by Harwell (1958). On the creation of the armies that fought the war, see F. A. Shannon, *The Organization and*

Administration of the Union Army (2 vols., 1928); and A. B. Moore, *Conscription and Conflict in the Confederacy* (1924). The lot of the common soldier is vividly described in two works by B. I. Wiley, °*The Life of Johnny Reb* (1943), and °*The Life of Billy Yank* (1952).

The best picture of Grant's military career is given in his own *The Personal Memoirs of U. S. Grant* (2 vols., 1885–1886); an abridgement is available in paperback. K. P. Williams, *Lincoln Finds a General; A Military Study of the Civil War* (5 vols., 1949–1959), is a monument of painstaking scholarship. An excellent brief biography is Bruce Catton, °*U. S. Grant and the American Military Tradition* (1954). On Sherman, see Lloyd Lewis, *Sherman* (1932); and E. S. Miers, °*William Tecumseh Sherman* (1951). On Thomas, see F. F. McKinney, *Education in Violence* (1961); and Wilbur Thomas, *General George H. Thomas* (1964). Biographies of other northern generals include F. H. Harrington, *Fighting Politician: Major General N. P. Banks* (1948); Stephen Ambrose, *Halleck* (1962); W. H. Hebert, *Fighting Joe Hooker* (1944); W. W. Hassler, Jr., *General George B. McClellan* (1957); Freeman Cleaves, *Meade of Gettysburg* (1960); and Joseph Hergesheimer, *Sheridan* (1931). The background for the freeing of the slaves may be found in Benjamin Quarles, *Lincoln and the Negro* (1962); and J. H. Franklin, °*The Emancipation Proclamation* (1963). Important case studies of emancipation are W. L. Rose, *Rehearsal for Reconstruction: The Port Royal Experiment* (1964); and C. L. Wagandt, *The Mighty Revolution* (1964), which deals with Maryland.

On the naval side, two important recent surveys are J. M. Merrill, *The Rebel Shore; The Story of Union Sea Power in the Civil War* (1957); and Robert Carse, *Blockade; the Civil War at Sea* (1958). Naval affairs in the North are treated in two works by R. S. West, Jr., *Gideon Welles* (1943), and *Mr. Lincoln's Navy* (1957). On Farragut, see C. L. Lewis, *David Glasgow Farragut* (2 vols., 1941–1943). On the naval activities of the Confederacy, see J. T. Durkin, *Stephen R. Mallory* (1954); and E. C. Boykin, *Ghost Ship of the Confederacy; The Story of the Alabama and her Captain, Raphael Semmes* (1957).

The trans-Mississippi West during the Civil

War is the subject of many books. On Confederate efforts in that area, see S. B. Oates, *Confederate Cavalry West of the River* (1961); and R. S. Brownlee, *Gray Ghosts of the Confederacy* (1958). *Destruction and Reconstruction* (1956), the memoirs of Lt.-General Richard Taylor, C.S.A., chronicles the Red River Campaign — and much else. See also R. H. Jones, *The Civil War in the Northwest* (1960); and R. C. Colton, *The Civil War in the Western Territories* (1959). Excellent state studies are W. E. Parrish, *Turbulent Partnership: Missouri and the Union, 1861–1865* (1963); and Albert Castel, *A Frontier State at War: Kansas, 1861–1865* (1958). Ex-Confederates in the West are treated in D. A. Brown, *The Galvanized Yankees* (1964).

R. V. Bruce, *Lincoln and the Tools of War* (1956), is an interesting treatment of an important theme. On the Negro, see Benjamin Quarles, *The Negro in the Civil War* (1953); D. T. Cornish, *The Sable Arm; Negro Troops in the Union Army, 1861–1865* (1956); J. M. McPherson, *The Struggle for Equality* (1964), and *The Negro's Civil War* (1965). War reporting is discussed in three recent works: B. A. Weisberger, *Reporters for the Union* (1953); J. C. Andrews, *The North Reports the Civil War* (1955); and L. M. Starr, *Reporting the Civil War* (1954). Railroads are treated in a number of works, including G. E. Turner, *Victory Rode the Rails* (1953); Thomas Weber, *The Northern Railroads in the Civil War* (1952); R. C. Black, *The Railroads of the Confederacy* (1952); and A. J. Johnston, *Virginia Railroads in the Civil War* (1961).

Lincoln's difficulties on the home front are treated in a number of works. On his relations with the Joint Committee on the Conduct of the War, see T. H. Williams, *Lincoln and the Radicals* (1941). H. J. Carman and R. H. Luthin, *Lincoln and the Patronage* (1943), is a detailed study of an important subject. W. B. Hesseltine, *Lincoln and the War Governors* (1948), treats an especially difficult problem of wartime administration. Important themes are treated by R. S. Harper, *Lincoln and the Press* (1951); and Dean Sprague, *Freedom under Lincoln* (1965). J. B. McMaster, *A History of the People of the United States during Lincoln's Administration* (1927), is again in print, with the title *Our House Divided* (1961). Shrewd appraisals are in

Allan Nevins, *Statesmanship of the Civil War* (1953). Long a standard work is J. G. Randall, *Constitutional Problems Under Lincoln* (2nd ed., 1951); but see also D. M. Silver, *Lincoln's Supreme Court* (1956). Other significant books on political themes include B. J. Hendrick, *Lincoln's War Cabinet* (1946); W. F. Zornow, *Lincoln & the Party Divided* (1954); C. A. Jellison, *Fessenden of Maine* (1962); H. B. Hancock, *Delaware during the Civil War* (1961); and G. E. Moore, *A Banner in the Hills; West Virginia's Statehood* (1963). General treatments of Copperheadism are Wood Gray, *The Hidden Civil War* (1942); and G. F. Milton, *Abraham Lincoln and the Fifth Column* (1942). Scholarly regional studies include F. L. Klement, *The Copperheads in the Middle West* (1960); K. M. Stampp, *Indiana Politics during the Civil War* (1949); and R. O. Curry, *A House Divided* (1964), which treats West Virginia. C. F. Dunham, *The Attitude of the Northern Clergy toward the South, 1860–1865* (1942), shows the part played by the clergy in the formation of war aims.

On the Confederate side, excellent survey histories are Clement Eaton, *A History of the Southern Confederacy* (1954); and E. M. Coulter, *The Confederate States of America, 1861–1865* (1950). Useful documentary selections are included in *The Confederacy*, edited by A. D. Kirwan (1959); and in F. E. Vandiver, *Basic History of the Confederacy* (1962). C. P. Roland, *The Confederacy* (1960), is a brief survey. Important political studies include W. B. Yearns, *The Confederate Congress* (1960); L. B. Hill, *Joseph E. Brown and the Confederacy* (1939); J. K. Bettersworth, *Confederate Mississippi* (1943); and B. H. Procter, *Not without Honor; The Life of John H. Reagan* (1962). Recent state studies of value include J. G. Barnett, *The Civil War in North Carolina* (1963); J. E. Johns, *Florida during the Civil War* (1963); and J. D. Winters, *The Civil War in Louisiana* (1963). On southern governmental leadership, see B. J. Hendrick, *Statesmen of the Lost Cause* (1939); and R. W. Patrick, *Jefferson Davis and His Cabinet* (1944). A discriminating portrait of the Confederate Vice-President is Rudolph Von Abele, *Alexander H. Stephens* (1946). J. B. Ranck, *Albert Gallatin Brown* (1937), shows the attitude of the southern small farmer toward division. Constitutional aspects of the Confederacy are dealt with in F. L. Owsley, *State Rights in the Confederacy* (1925); and C. R. Lee, Jr., *The Confederate Constitutions* (1963).

On Lee, the standard life is D. S. Freeman, *R. E. Lee: A Biography* (4 vols., 1934–1935). Sir F. B. Maurice, *Robert E. Lee, The Soldier* (1925), is useful on the military side. An important new study is Clifford Dowdey, *The Seven Days; The Emergence of Lee* (1964). See also D. S. Freeman, *Lee's Lieutenants* (3 vols., 1942–1944). On Jackson, the major works are G. F. R. Henderson, °*Stonewall Jackson and the American Civil War* (2 vols., 1898); F. E. Vandiver, *Mighty Stonewall* (1957); and J. I. Robertson, Jr., *The Stonewall Brigade* (1963). Biographies of other southern generals include T. H. Williams, °*P. G. T. Beauregard* (1955); J. P. Dyer, *The Gallant Hood* (1950); C. P. Roland, *Albert Sidney Johnston* (1964); G. E. Govan and J. W. Livingood, *A Different Valor, The Story of General Joseph E. Johnston, C.S.A.* (1956); J. H. Parks, *General Leonidas Polk* (1962), and *General Edmund Kirby Smith* (1954); and J. P. Dyer, *"Fightin' Joe Wheeler"* (1941). Military monographs on the Confederacy are numerous; among the best are F. E. Vandiver, *Rebel Brass: The Confederate Command System* (1956); Archer Jones, *Confederate Strategy from Shiloh to Vicksburg* (1961); F. E. Vandiver, °*Ploughshares into Swords; Josiah Gorgas and Confederate Ordnance* (1952). The last phases of the war are treated in B. I. Wiley, *The Road to Appomattox* (1956); and °*The Defeat of the Confederacy*, edited by H. S. Commager (1964).

One significant subject is the theme of °*Europe Looks at the Civil War*, edited by B. B. Sideman and Lillian Freedman (1960). E. D. Adams, *Great Britain and the American Civil War* (2 vols., 1925), is one of the great studies in American diplomatic history. On relations with France, see M. A. Clapp, *Forgotten First Citizen: John Bigelow* (1947). On relations with Russia, see A. A. Woldman, °*Lincoln and the Russians* (1952). On Confederate diplomacy, see F. L. and H. C. Owsley, *King Cotton Diplomacy* (2nd ed., 1959). Problems of the northern border are treated in R. W. Winks, *Canada and the United States: The Civil War Years* (1960).

Certain aspects of social history have been well covered. Margaret Leech, °*Reveille in Washington, 1860–1865* (1941), gives a vivacious account of Washington society during the war; but see also the major history of the city by C. McL. Green, *Washington: Village and Capital, 1800–1878* (1962). On the situation in Richmond, see A. H. Bill, *The Beleaguered City* (1946); and M. B. Chestnut, °*A Diary from Dixie*, edited by B. A. Williams (1949). W. Q. Maxwell, *Lincoln's Fifth Wheel: The Political History of the United States Sanitary Commission* (1956), is an excellent monograph. W. E. Barton, *The Life of Clara Barton* (2 vols., 1922), is the major biography of the founder of the American Red Cross. Among the several important social histories are B. I. Wiley, °*Southern Negroes, 1861–1865* (1938); and °*The Plain People of the Confederacy* (1943); and M. E. Massey, *Refugee Life in the Confederacy* (1964). On the moot question of southern treatment of war prisoners, see W. B. Hesseltine, *Civil War Prisons* (1930). On hospitals and surgery, see G. W. Adams, °*Doctors in Blue* (1952); and H. H. Cunningham, *Doctors in Gray* (1958).

20

RECONSTRUCTION

Postwar Problems. The arrival of peace in 1865 introduced difficulties perhaps more appalling than the nation had ever faced before. The South, after four years of war, was not only defeated; its whole social organization lay in hopeless ruin. How were the people of the New South to live? What was to be the status of the freedmen? When and how were the normal processes of government to be resumed? Nor were the problems of the day confined wholly, or even mainly, to the South. In the North a million men were under arms. How could their speedy reabsorption into civilian life be best facilitated? A huge national debt, an inflated currency, an overgrown system of taxation were parts of the inevitable legacy of war. What course should the new governmental financial policy take? Manufactures stimulated by war orders and war profits had reached a phenomenal development. Could their prosperity be preserved

with the nation at peace? Agriculture had expanded abnormally. How were the farmers to find markets for their produce? Less tangible, but no less important, was the feeling of hatred, nurtured by four years of fighting, between the peoples of North and South. How could they learn to forgive and forget?

Reconstruction. "Reconstruction" is the label that historians have generally applied to these postwar years. As a descriptive term it leaves much to be desired. Neither the prewar South nor the prewar Union could ever be rebuilt or restored. Out of the ordeal of war and its aftermath emerged a new nation, a nation so different from the old that the term "revolution" might more properly be applied. But reconstruction has the sanction of long usage, and properly redefined, it may still be permitted to serve. In a narrow sense, reconstruction means the process by which state government was revived in the South; broadly speaking, it must include all the drastic transformations of the period, both North and South.

Conditions in the South. The war had left much of the South in ruins. For four years, armies had marched, camped, foraged, and fought in practically every southern state, and in some of them almost continuously. As Sherman's army turned from

Georgia northward into South Carolina, it vented its fury upon the state that most northerners held responsible for starting the war. Carl Schurz reported, from observations made six months later, that the countryside along the track of Sherman's march looked for many miles like a broad black streak of ruin and desolation — the fences all gone; lonesome smoke stacks, surrounded by dark heaps of ashes and cinders, marking the spots where human habitations had stood; the fields along the road wildly overgrown by weeds, with here and there a sickly-looking patch of cotton or corn cultivated by Negro squatters. Traveling through Virginia in October, 1865, Alexander H. Stephens wrote in his diary: "The desolation of the country from Alexandria to near Charlottesville was horrible to behold." Around Petersburg, where the forces of Grant and Lee had fought under conditions resembling modern trench warfare, farmers were stopped in their plowing by the weight of metal they found in the ground, and the stench of death ended only with the autumn frosts. The Shenandoah

Valley was so thoroughly denuded that, in accordance with Sheridan's promise: "a crow could not fly over it without carrying his rations with him." Several years after the war an English traveler in America found the Valley of the Tennessee little better, while great parts of Charleston, according to Schurz, looked "like a vast graveyard with broken walls and tall blackened chimneys for monuments, overtopped by the picturesque ruins of the cathedral." Many another southern city had been despoiled.

Transportation. The havoc that the war had wrought on the South's transportation system was appalling. Columbia, South Carolina, had been a railway center before the war, with five lines converging upon it. By the time Sherman's troops had departed, the tracks had been torn up for thirty miles in every direction. Rolling stock, left standing in the fields, was used by the homeless as dwellings. Rails were heated in the middle and twisted fantastically around trees. Similar thoroughness

344

Struck by the devastation left in the wake of the Civil War, David Macrae, an English visitor to the United States in the late 1860's, wrote the following description of the ruins that once were Richmond.

. . . we found ourselves about four in the morning entering the far-famed capital of the Confederacy . . . The ghostly houses standing in the cold weird moonlight, the empty streets, the profound stillness over all, made it seem as if we were entering a city of the dead. Great shells of buildings gutted with fire glided past, looking at us with their eyeless sockets. On one side of the valley, rising alone from what seemed to me a wilderness of gray tombs, a ghastly wall like the gable of a ruined cathedral towered into the frosty sky. Here and there from amongst the seeming tombs a cold light would gleam out for a moment and disappear — probably some fragments of pottery or broken glass reflecting the moonlight as we passed.

DAVID MACRAE, *The Americans at Home* (1870)

---

had characterized railroad destruction in Georgia, Mississippi, and various other parts of the South, while the wear and tear of wartime usage without adequate repairs had made the railroads outside the devastated regions almost as worthless as those within. Before the war, river traffic had played a large part in moving the produce of the South. Now river channels were blocked, steamboats were destroyed, and wharves were missing. Seaports, so essential to the trade of the prewar South, were inoperable. Country roads and bridges were gone; many horses, mules, oxen, carriages, wagons, and carts had been commandeered by the troops of North or South.

Southern Losses from War. Property losses suffered in the states of the Confederacy were of many other kinds. Confederate bonds, both state and national, into which much southern capital had gone, were valueless. So also was Confederate currency. Banks were closed; factories were idle; land values toppled to nearly nothing; business in general was at a standstill. Property in slaves, which before the war accounted for much of the South's wealth, was completely wiped out. Worse still, northern confiscation of private property, contrary to a common opinion, took a heavy toll from the scanty resources of the defeated states. President Johnson tried to prevent this by ordering, in an amnesty proclamation issued May 29, 1865, that no further seizures of private property be made, and his Attorney-General ruled that private property already seized must be restored to anyone who had received a presidential pardon. But it was generally agreed that the property of the Confederate government now belonged to the United States, and that all such property must be seized.

From the attempts to seize this public property the South came to know what confiscation meant. Agents of the Treasury Department, sent South on a 25 per cent commission basis to locate the 150,000 bales of cotton that the Confederate government was supposed to have had on hand, developed a tendency to take whatever cotton they saw, and to turn over to the United States only such of their takings as they saw fit. "I am sure I sent some honest cotton agents South," Secretary of the Treasury McCulloch admitted ruefully, "but it sometimes seems doubtful whether any of them remained honest for long." Not only cotton, but livestock, tobacco, rice, sugar, and anything else of value was seized by individuals who represented themselves as agents of the United States. The total sum realized by the Treasury from seizures was $34 million, a considerable part of which was later returned. But this sum represents only a fraction of the southern losses.

The Southern People.   In an assessment of the damage done the South by the war, the personal element must not be ignored. Perhaps 250,000 soldiers and an untold number of civilians lost their lives. Among these were a large portion of the natural leaders of the South. For the Negroes the boon of freedom was not without its unfortunate consequences. Before the end of the war about 180,000 of them had been enrolled as soldiers in the federal armies; others were camp followers and refugees. The downfall of the Confederacy plunged all the rest into freedom — a state of society for which most of them were ill-prepared. As slaves, they had depended upon their masters for food, shelter, and protection. As free men they had little idea how to provide such things for themselves. Freedom to many ex-slaves meant freedom from work, and the right to leave the home plantation at will; that it might carry with it onerous responsibilities few were able to understand. Some stayed with the old masters and worked on as if nothing had happened; others wandered about aimlessly. During the spring and summer of 1865, they could be found in bands like gypsies, roving the country and emulating Sherman's "bummers" in their search for food.

National Policy.   At the present time the people of the United States, or of any other great power, if confronted with such a condition as existed in the South of 1865, would take it for granted that the government must play the principal part in restoring the economic life of the war-stricken section. In the middle of the nineteenth century, however, "the less government the better" was still the dominant philosophy, not only of the Democrats, but also of the great majority of the Republicans. Indeed, the doctrine of rugged individualism, whether derived from the experience of the American frontier or from the writings of European savants, was never more universally accepted. The economic problems of the South, therefore, were regarded as the concern of individuals, rather than of the government, and in their solution the government gave only incidental assistance.

The Freedmen's Bureau.   The necessity of direct aid for the freedmen, however, was something that could not easily be overlooked. The power of the national government had been used to free the slaves; hence the Negroes, now that they were free, had become in a sense the wards of the nation. The freedmen themselves were by no means unaware of this obligation. That Congress was ready to accept such responsibility, at least for a limited time, was shown by the passage in March, 1865, of an act creating the Freedmen's Bureau. This organization, which was to last for a year after the close of the war, was to be set up in the War Department under a commissioner appointed by the President. It was authorized to distribute "such issues of provisions, clothing, and fuel" as might be necessary to relieve the "destitute and suffering refugees and freedmen and their wives and children." It had also the right to take over any land within the designated states that had been abandoned by its owners or confiscated by the United States, and to distribute it in tracts of forty acres or less, on a three-year rental basis, to "loyal refugees and freedmen."

Under the leadership of General Oliver O. Howard, an able and conscientious man,

A FREEDMAN'S SCHOOL

The Freedmen's Union Industrial School of Richmond, Virginia. Glimpses of the school as sketched by an illustrator for Frank Leslie's Illustrated Newspaper, *September 22, 1866.*

the Freedmen's Bureau went promptly to work. Its agents soon penetrated to every part of the South, and were kept busy, for a time, distributing the bare necessities of life to hundreds of thousands of needy, white as well as black. Without this assistance there can be no doubt that many more would have starved to death. The Bureau also made a laudable effort to provide its dependents with medical care and hospitalization, but among the Negroes, who knew so little about how to take care of themselves, illness took a frightful toll.

"Forty Acres and a Mule." The plan to distribute abandoned land to the freedmen led to an unfortunate misunderstanding. It was inferred at first that all land "abandoned" because its owners had left it for Confederate service would be available for distribution, but President Johnson's policy permitted the pardoned owners of such property to recover it. The result was that the Bureau had comparatively little land

of value to give away. The Negro, however, got the impression, often deliberately spread by unscrupulous agents, that each freedman would soon be given "forty acres of land and a mule." Some included, for good measure, a white man to do the work. With so rosy a prospect for the future, and an abundance of free rations for the present, many of the Negroes found it difficult to see why they should do more than await the day of "jubilee."

The Army of Occupation. The army of occupation played an important role in assisting the crippled section toward economic health. For several years detachments of federal troops were not far away in any part of the South, and there were regions in which the hated "blue-bellies," as they were inelegantly termed, were very numerous. The northern army, always abundantly provided with rations, clothing, and other supplies, shared its plenty with the destitute. This was the more natural because some of the federal troops were themselves Negroes, although General Grant, out of deference to the wishes of the southern whites, removed practically all the Negro troops from the South by the end of 1866. The soldiers, whether white or black, had money to spend, and the government spent still larger sums for their maintenance. Directly or indirectly, the army thus contributed an appreciable amount to the economic rehabilitation of the South.

One other item of governmental aid to the South deserves mention, that given to the southern railroads. While northern troops accounted for an enormous amount of railroad destruction, wherever the operations of the federal army required the reconditioning of the railroads, that, too, was done. In those portions of the upper South that the North had long held, the railroads were actually left in better condition than they were found. At the end of the war the United States War Department even went so far as to reorganize some of the bankrupt railroad companies, and then, with "loyal" boards of directors assured, to return them to their owners.

Private Benevolence. Private benevolence added a little to the aid given by the government. Even before the end of the war the American Missionary Association, for example, had begun a work among the Negroes that led to expenditures after the return of peace of about $100,000 annually, mostly on education. The churches of the North sent a sizable army of missionaries, preachers, and teachers into the South, zealously determined to help the Negroes adjust themselves to freedom. They induced most of the ex-slaves to separate from the churches of their former masters, and to form new churches of their own. They used northern missionary money to build and maintain Negro churches and schools, and to care for the needy. Among the most active in this respect were the agents of the Freedmen's Aid Society of the Methodist Episcopal Church, but sim-

ilar work was supported by the Baptists, Presbyterians, and many other denominations.

Philanthropy, although then in its infancy, furnished another source of outside income to the South. The most notable donation of money came from George Peabody, who gave the income from a fund of $2 million or more "to the suffering South for the good of the whole country." The Peabody Education Fund was wisely administered, and proved to be an effective aid. to the establishment of better common schools in the South. Many Negroes were eager for book learning and flocked into whatever schools were provided for them.

Scarcity of Capital. Southerners were at first hopeful that a great outpouring of northern capital would aid in the rehabilitation of the South, but in this they were to be sadly disappointed. Northern investors did, indeed, buy southern railway securities, and they also purchased, to their later regret, the new bond issues of the southern states. But their southern investments went little further. The North had its own work to look after — industrial expansion, agricultural extension, the building of transcontinental railroads, the development of the mining and ranching West; it consequently had little left to risk in a region where political conditions were disturbed and racial conflict was in the making.

Cotton Culture. Fortunately for the South the world had need of cotton, but to restore production was no easy matter. Seed was lacking, tools and machinery were worn out, horses and mules were scarce, and the labor supply was an unknown quantity. Many southerners, convinced that without slavery the Negroes could never be induced to work, hoped to devise some scheme for sending them back to Africa or to the West Indies; and still more believed that the salvation of the South lay in replacing or supplementing Negro labor with that of immigrants from Europe or elsewhere. But the Negroes would not leave and the immigrants would not come. Some of the planters attempted to revive the old plantation system on the basis of free labor, offering the Negroes wages to return to their former duties. Such transactions were carefully watched by the Freedmen's Bureau, which usually insisted on a written contract, with the amount of wages and the conditions of labor carefully stated. Often it was not the planter, however, who broke the contract, but the freedman, who rarely saw point to working after he had earned a few dollars. Delayed wages were sometimes tried, but with equally indifferent results. Other planters offered laborers a share in the annual proceeds of the plantation, but this system, likewise, proved ineffective. The freedmen resented the necessity of working in gangs, as in slavery times, and even more, the existence of bosses.

The Southern Tenant System. In the end the plantation system had to go, and in a sense the promise of "forty acres and a mule" was realized. The planters found by experience that only when they split up their land into small plots, with a Negro or a white tenant in charge of each, could they obtain satisfactory results. Each tenant had usually to be supplied not only with his mule, but also with his seed, his tools, and his living until the crop was harvested; all this the landlord either furnished directly, or by obtaining credit for his tenants at one of the numerous "country stores" that sprang up all over the South. A crop lien secured both the landlord and the storekeeper against loss. As a rule the tenant turned over from a third to a half of his produce to the landlord as rental, and all the rest went to repay his debts; but by working along on his own time in his own way he produced at least a part of a crop. His status, bound as he was by his crop lien, lay somewhere between slavery and freedom, but it amounted perhaps to as great a change as his limited experience would permit. The first few crops after the war, with the Negroes unsettled and the

Freedmen's Bureau at hand to back them up in fantastic demands, were miserable failures, but by 1869 a cotton crop worth $250 million was marketed. From that time forward the acute poverty of the South began to abate.

The White Farmer. So much attention has been focused upon the Negroes, whether slave or free, that the role of the small white farmer of the South has rarely received the attention it deserves. Even before the Civil War white labor accounted for a considerable part of the South's cotton crop, and after the war the proportion tended to increase. In general the land worked by the small southern farmer in the time of slavery was inferior to that of the great plantations. But after the war the planters were glad to obtain tenants, white as well as black, and they often found it necessary to sell a part, or even all, of their holdings. Independent ownership was stimulated by the low prices that landowners were obliged to accept. Land that had been worth from $20 to $30 an acre before the war sold for $3 to $5 an acre after the war, and sometimes for less. Many whites who had owned poor land before, or no land at all, took advantage of this remarkable opportunity to buy. In ten years, according to the census of 1870, the number of farms in South Carolina had increased from 33,000 to 52,000; in Mississippi, from 43,000 to 68,000; in Louisiana, from 17,000 to 28,000. In the other southern states the figures, while not so striking, show the same general trend. Some of the new landowners were Negroes, but their holdings were generally very small, and most of the land that changed hands went to whites. Some northerners were attracted into the South by the low prices of land, but most of them were unable to adjust themselves satisfactorily to the new environment.

Lincoln's Plan of Reconstruction. Unfortunately, the valiant efforts of the South to work out a new economic system proved to be of far less concern to the national government than the strictly political problem. Even in this field, little "postwar planning" had been undertaken, although Lincoln had been obliged as early as 1862 to appoint military, or provisional, governors for states occupied mainly by Union troops, and to devise a system for the establishment of civil government within their borders. In December, 1863, he set forth in detail a generous plan of reconstruction. With a few exceptions, it promised pardons to all residents of conquered states who would take a prescribed oath of allegiance to the United States, and, whenever in any state as many as one-tenth of the number of persons who had voted in 1860 should take the oath, a civil government was to be inaugurated which the President bound himself to recognize "as the true government of the state." Operating under this plan, three states, Tennessee, Louisiana, and Arkansas, succeeded during the year 1864 in re-creating state governments, and were accorded presidential recognition. The President also recognized a loyal, although decidedly impotent, government in Virginia that throughout the war had maintained a precarious existence at Alexandria.

Lincoln's easy plan for the formation of new, and supposedly loyal, governments in the South was resented by many congressmen. They feared that such magnanimous terms might produce a combination of ex-secessionists and ex-Copperheads that would eventually oust the Republicans from control of the national government. They branded the President's failure to consult Congress on so important a matter as "executive usurpation," and in July, 1864, pushed through Congress the Wade-Davis Bill as a substitute for the President's plan. This bill failed because of a pocket veto, but Lincoln in a formal proclamation described it as "one very proper plan for the loyal people of any state choosing to adopt it." Undoubtedly Lincoln would have made some kind of terms with the congressional opposition had he lived, but at his last Cabinet meeting he expressed his desire to

"reanimate the states" before Congress met again.

Andrew Johnson. Lincoln's death brought to the Presidency a man whom the Republican extremists, or Radicals, felt certain they could use. Andrew Johnson (1808–1875) was both a southerner and a Democrat, but he was not of the ruling caste, and as a fairly typical representative of the poorer whites of the South he was a bitter opponent of the aristocrats. Born in North Carolina, he had migrated at an early age to Greeneville, Tennessee, where he ultimately became the proprietor of a moderately prosperous tailor shop. As a highly effective rough-and-tumble debater, he drifted easily into politics — a Democratic denouncer of the aristocratic Whigs — and for twenty years before he became President he had been a power in Tennessee politics. Although he had voted for Breckinridge in 1860, he had refused to become a party to the destruction of the Union, and alone among the senators from the seceding states had stayed at his desk in the Senate. Johnson's obstinacy and tactlessness were well known, and, except for his devotion to the Union, his political principles were far removed from the majority of northerners who had voted for him. But the Radicals believed that because he shared their hatred of the southern leaders he would support their program.

It was soon clear that Johnson, from the Radical point of view, was quite as untrustworthy as Lincoln. The southern aristocrat, he quickly noted, was at the moment as penniless and powerless as his humblest neighbor. As a southerner, he was convinced that the ex-slave was unprepared for the duties of citizenship, and he cherished as deeply as any aristocrat the right of the states to deal with internal problems without undue interference from the national government. And so he not only kept Lincoln's Cabinet, but he also accepted as legal the loyal governments that Lincoln had recognized in the South, and during the summer of 1865 began a process of reconstruction of his own that was as generous as anything Lincoln had devised.

Johnson's Plan of Reconstruction.   Johnson's plan was to appoint in each of the unreconstructed states a provisional governor — a local man, not an outsider — who would call together a constitutional convention. The delegates to this convention were to be chosen by such of the members of the old white electorate as were now ready and willing to take the oath of allegiance to the United States. The constitutional conventions on assembling were required (1) to invalidate their old ordinances of secession, (2) to abolish slavery, and (3) to repudiate all debts contracted in order to aid the Confederacy in its prosecution of the war; otherwise they were as free as any other such conventions to write into their constitutions whatever they chose. Johnson specifically acknowledged that it was their privilege to decide who should vote and who should hold office, but he let it be known privately that, for the effect such action would have upon the northern Radicals, he hoped that Negroes who could read and write, or who owned a small amount of real estate, would be permitted to vote. With their constitutions rewritten, the states might elect their own governors, legislators, and other officers, and resume their place in the Union. Naturally this plan was enthusiastically accepted by the southern states and was carried through with maximum speed. Before the end of 1865, the President was able to tell Congress that only in Florida and Texas was the work of restoration incomplete, and that in these states it would be finished soon. None of the states, however, saw fit to take Johnson's advice about Negro voting, and most of them chose their old secessionist leaders to represent them again in the Senate and House of Representatives at Washington.

The President's defense of what he had done was presented in a skillful message to Congress written by George Bancroft, the

ANDREW JOHNSON

The southerner who ironically succeeded Lincoln as President, Andrew Johnson, allowed his good intentions toward the South after the Civil War to betray him into much bad politics. His tempestuous character and his freewheeling oratory cost him dear.

historian. In it he maintained, more insistently than Lincoln had thought advisable, that the southern states, as such, had never ceased to exist, but had merely been in a state of suspended vitality. It had been his duty to assist in restoring them to their rightful energy, and this duty he had performed as "gradually and quietly" as possible. Inasmuch as he had found no constitutional warrant to do otherwise, he had left with the states themselves the problem of enfranchisement of the freedmen. As for the delegations that the restored states had sent to Congress, he believed that the adoption of the Thirteenth Amendment warranted their reception, but of this each house of Congress must judge for itself. That Congress had no notion of being bound by the President's action was at once apparent. A "Joint Committee on

Reconstruction," composed of nine representatives and six senators, was promptly created with authority to inquire into the condition of the former Confederate states, and to ascertain whether they were entitled to representation in Congress.

Thaddeus Stevens.　Opposition to the President's policy toward the South was most effectively voiced in the House by Thaddeus Stevens (1792–1868), a Pennsylvania representative whose political career dated back to the Anti-Masonic Party. Stevens had long hated slavery and before the war had opposed all concessions to the slaveholders. His hostility toward the white South continued during and after the war; and his resentment toward Lincoln's easy plan of reconstruction was bitter. The southern states, he held, were no longer states, but only "conquered provinces" with which Congress might deal as it chose; Lin-

THADDEUS STEVENS

The Pennsylvania Republican leader of the national House of Representatives, Thaddeus Stevens was one of the chief architects of Radical reconstruction.

coln's pocket veto of the Wade-Davis Bill was nothing less than "infamous." Lame from birth, old and perilously ill, unmarried and cared for only by a faithful colored housekeeper, Stevens was determined to punish the white South. Congressmen had already learned to fear his lashing tongue, and he proposed to destroy Johnson, whose easy terms of reconstruction he despised.

Charles Sumner.　No less the enemy of Johnson than Stevens was Charles Sumner (1811–1874), the Republican senator from Massachusetts, a Harvard graduate, a student of history and the classics, and a friend of nearly every New Englander who had won distinction in the realm of literature. Honorable and upright to a fault, he was utterly contemptuous of lesser mortals. He had always opposed slavery, and he now opposed the immunity from punishment that presidential reconstruction had offered the white South. In his opinion the seceding states, by their treasonous acts, were guilty of "state suicide." Because they had ceased to exist as states, Congress had the same authority over them that it had always exercised over the territories. A firm believer in political equality for all men, he urged Negro suffrage as a primary condition for the reconstruction of the seceded states.

The "Black Codes."　The state governments set up under Johnson's plan gave unintended assistance to Stevens and Sumner in their war on the President. By enacting "black codes," or "black laws," the restored states had prescribed an inferior legal status for the ex-slaves. At best these laws were meant to protect the Negroes from their own ignorance and helplessness; at worst they were meant to keep them at work and to circumscribe their freedom as much as possible. In the North they were generally denounced as evidence that the South had no notion whatever of living up to the terms of the Thirteenth Amendment. Radicals could also point to the prevalence of racial conflicts in the South, particularly between the lower-class southern whites and the Negroes, whose long-standing contempt for one another was greatly aggravated by emancipation. They complained, too, that violent hatred of the North was freely expressed, and Carl Schurz, whom the President himself had sent on a tour of the South, found that the white South was in no wise repentant.

The Freedmen's Bureau Bill. The first important test of strength between the forces led by the President and those led by Stevens and Sumner came over the Freedmen's Bureau. Should this organization be allowed to live longer than the year after the war for which it had originally been created? The Radicals hoped to continue the Bureau, and through it to make the Negroes into loyal supporters of the national government and the Republican Party. But Johnson with his states'-rights views was ready to turn the whole Negro problem over to the states. On this carefully chosen issue an overwhelming majority in Congress favored the Radicals, so a Freedmen's Bureau Bill such as they desired soon reached the President's desk. As anticipated, he vetoed it, but to the dismay of the Radicals the Senate, with only a few votes to spare, sustained the veto. This development greatly elated Johnson, for he believed now that by use of the veto power he would be able to kill all legislation hostile to his plan of reconstruction. Always tactless, he took occasion to denounce the Radical leaders by name and to cast aspersions on their loyalty. As a result, when a Civil Rights Bill, which declared Negroes to be citizens of the United States and guaranteed them equality before the law, passed Congress and received a veto, many who had formerly supported Johnson turned against him. This time the veto was not sustained, and the bill became a law in spite of the President's opposition. To show its new strength, Congress now revived the Freedmen's Bureau Bill in slightly altered form and passed it over the President's veto. Thus it seemed apparent that the Radicals, if they chose, could undo the President's plan of reconstruction and substitute for it one of their own.

The Fourteenth Amendment. This was exactly what the Joint Committee on Reconstruction had decided to do. After spectacular hearings, it proposed in the early summer of 1866 a Fourteenth Amendment to the Constitution which, after some revision in the Senate, was duly submitted to the states for adoption. The first section of the amendment, which virtually restated the terms of the Civil Rights Bill, declared all persons born or naturalized in the United States to be citizens of the United States, and forbade the states to abridge in any way the privileges and immunities of such citizens, or to "deprive any person of life, liberty, or property without due process of law." The second section, to the disappointment of Stevens, did not require Negro suffrage, but provided that a state which denied the suffrage to any of its male inhabitants over twenty-one years of age, "except for participation in rebellion or other crime," would have its basis of representation in Congress and in the Electoral College correspondingly reduced. The third section was designed to make ineligible for office-holding all ex-Confederate leaders, regardless of any presidential pardons they might have received. The fourth section provided that the debt of the United States, incurred to preserve the Union, should never be questioned, while the debt of the southern states and the Confederacy, incurred to destroy it, should never be paid. A fifth section gave Congress the power to enforce the amendment by appropriate legislation.

With the Fourteenth Amendment presented to the states, the Radical Congress refused to proceed further with its work until after the congressional elections of 1866. Tennessee, which alone among the ex-Confederate states quickly ratified the amendment, was declared fully restored. But Congress left the status of the other ten in doubt, preferring to carry the struggle with Johnson to the electorate. The President eagerly accepted the challenge of the Radicals, made every effort to revive the Union Party, on whose ticket he and Lincoln had been elected, and even took a speech-making "swing around the circle" to Chicago and back. Radicals were equally active and, as events proved, far more effective. They impressed northeastern industrialists with the danger of low-tariff legislation in case the southerners should return to Congress; they charged that ex-Copperheads and ex-secessionists might either repudiate the national war debt or pay it off in depreciated paper currency; they made much fun of the President for his intemperate speeches which were often in bad taste. By the time the election was held, its outcome was no longer in doubt. The Radicals won both houses of Congress by staggering majorities, and the total defeat of the President's program was assured.

Radical Reconstruction. When Congress convened in December, 1866, it promptly laid out a plan of reconstruction far more radical than anything embodied in the Fourteenth Amendment. It proposed to undo as completely as possible all that Lincoln and Johnson had done to restore normal civil government in the ten southern states unrecognized by Congress. Military rule was to be resumed, and the South divided into five military districts with an officer of the United States Army not below the rank of brigadier-general in charge of each. Every general, duly supported by an adequate military force, was ordered to register all the legal voters, excluding those who had ever been disfranchised for disloyalty, and to admit Negroes on the same basis as whites. He was then to call upon these voters to elect a constitutional convention providing for Negro suffrage. If, on submission to the voters, this constitution received a popular majority, the general in

charge was to order the necessary elections to put it into effect; whereupon, if Congress approved the new constitution, and if the legislature of the state adopted the Fourteenth Amendment, and if as many as three-fourths of all the states ratified the Fourteenth Amendment and so made it a part of the national Constitution, then, and not until then, were the representatives and senators of each state to be considered eligible for admission to the two houses of Congress; and then, and not until then, were federal troops to be withdrawn from the state's borders. Furthermore, each of the newly chosen representatives and senators was to take the so-called "ironclad oath" that he had never given voluntary aid to the Confederacy.

The key to this plan of reconstruction was of course Negro suffrage. By giving the Negroes the vote and by denying it to many whites, the Radicals hoped to make sure that the southern states would long remain true to the Republican Party. They feared that without such a provision the Democratic Party might win the ascendancy not only in the South, but in the national government as well. Education of the Negroes in the belief that their freedom depended upon the preservation of Republican rule was well advanced, and the new scheme would give abundant time to complete the process.

Impeachment of Johnson. Although Congress could now count on being able to pass any legislation it chose over the President's veto, the Radicals decided that they had had enough of Johnson, and would use their power to remove him from office. By the Tenure of Office Act, passed early in 1867, Congress made it a misdemeanor, punishable by fine and imprisonment, for the President to remove civil officeholders without the consent of the Senate. This law was designed not only to save from dismissal such Radical officials as had not yet been removed, but also to tempt the President to challenge it, and so to open the way for his impeachment. Johnson was ordinarily extremely scrupulous in the execution of the numerous laws that Congress kept passing over his veto, but he was finally irritated into a near-violation of the Tenure of Office Act. Edwin M. Stanton, the Secretary of War who had served under Lincoln, remained in office under Johnson, but soon went over to the Radicals, for whom he became a kind of spy in the President's Cabinet. Finally the President could tolerate his presence no more, and in August, 1867, asked Stanton to resign. Stanton refused, whereupon Johnson suspended him from office, and as the law required, asked the Senate's consent for his removal. This the Senate refused to give, and Stanton resumed his duties. Thoroughly outraged, Johnson again attempted to remove Stanton from office, although Stanton defiantly refused to yield. The Radicals, now in high glee, voted impeachment charges against the President in the House of Representatives, and as prescribed by the Constitution brought him to trial before the Senate. That the trial was purely political, few denied, but when the vote was taken seven Republican Senators joined with twelve Democrats in voting for acquittal. Thus, by the narrow margin of one vote (35 to 19) the President was left in possession of his office. Technically, he had probably not violated the Tenure of Office Act, for that law seemed to permit the removal of Cabinet members appointed by a *preceding* President, and Lincoln, not Johnson, had appointed Stanton. During the impeachment proceedings, Stanton retired from office, and was succeeded by General J. M. Schofield. But although Johnson had won the struggle over impeachment, he had lost control of reconstruction. From then on the future of the South lay in the hands of the Radical Republicans.

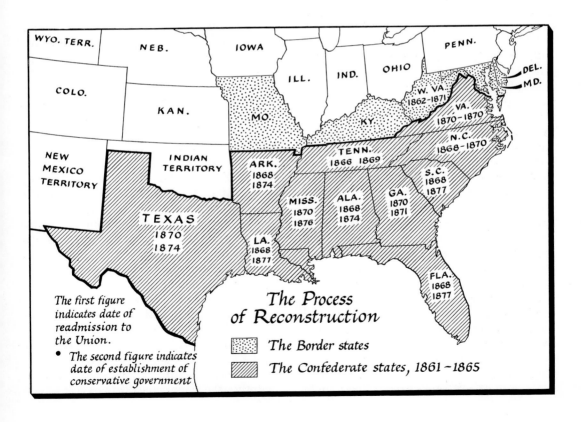

The first figure indicates date of readmission to the Union.

• The second figure indicates date of establishment of conservative government

The Process of Reconstruction

The Border states

The Confederate states, 1861–1865

Military Rule in the South. In conformity with the Reconstruction Acts that Congress had passed over his veto, President Johnson placed a high-ranking army officer in charge of each of the five reconstruction districts of the South. These officers had the power to make arrests, to conduct military trials, and to carry on as they saw fit the ordinary processes of civil government. Their main business was, of course, to organize new state governments according to the plan Congress had laid down. The first step in the process was to register the voters, a task that presented many difficulties. Army officers, Freedmen's Bureau agents, and loyal citizens generally, were made members of the registration boards. Eligible whites, although admonished by their leaders to roll up the largest possible majorities for their race, were reluctant to register but the Negroes presented themselves gladly.

Southern Opinion on Negro Suffrage. At the close of the war, many southerners had had no very great fear of Negro suffrage, believing that the Negroes could be persuaded to vote as their former masters directed. The Negro population was concentrated in the best cotton-growing areas, where before the war the great planters had held sway. In some of these "black counties" the Negroes far exceeded whites in number. It could be maintained, therefore, that in case the few favored whites of the "black counties" were aided by Negro votes, these whites could control the various state governments in complete disregard of the far larger number of whites in the back country. Negro suffrage was thus feared, not only for itself but also for the possible danger of turning the South back to the rule of the prewar plantation owners.

The northern Radicals, however, had taken great pains to wean the Negroes away from allegiance to their former masters. Working mainly through the Union League, a private society organized to disseminate northern propaganda, they taught the freedmen that their former masters were not to be trusted, and that they should rely strictly upon Republican advisers. To make the League more appealing to the Negroes, it was converted into a kind of lodge, with an elaborate ritual and much ostentatious ceremony. With the aid of the northern soldiers stationed in the South and the agents of the Freedmen's Bureau, the League organizers soon had most of the Negroes under their control. Unquestionably they would register and vote as the Radicals desired.

Carpetbag Rule. Slowly and painfully the reconstruction process worked itself out. Since the new electorates included so many Negroes — in five of the ten states more than half of the voters — the conventions chosen in 1867 and 1868 contained in every instance a large bloc of Negro delegates. The leaders, however, turned out to be mainly northerners, men who had come South with the army, or with the Freedmen's Bureau, or merely to fish in troubled waters. Some of these "carpetbaggers," as they were called, were men with a sincere desire to help the Negro; others were interested mainly in personal gain; but practically all were dependable Radicals willing to carry out the wishes of the Radicals in Congress. In each convention there was a considerable number of southern whites, some of whom, called "scalawags," were willing to follow the lead of these northerners. Most southerners tended to look down upon the scalawags, but among them were many "respectable, intelligent, realistic southerners" who saw greater hope for their section in cooperating with the Radicals than in resisting them. The conventions included also many representatives of the numerous poor-white class, whose voice had rarely been heard in state government during antebellum days. Often these native whites joined with the Negro members in efforts to improve conditions for the underprivileged, regardless of race. Consequently, the new constitutions contained many admirable provisions. All of them had racial equality clauses. They also called for far better public school systems than the South had ever known before. Many copied the latest reforms in local government and in the judicial system to be found among the northern states. They democratized the structure of local government and extended additional rights to women. Such reforms, however, were small compensation to many dispossessed southern whites for the prospect of carpetbag rule that the suffrage provisions of every constitution seemed to make certain. Moreover, the traditional, but now disfranchised, leadership of the South, largely conservative, could scarcely welcome the rising power of the lowly poor whites.

Eventually each of the southern states was obliged to accept a carpetbag constitution. The first state to complete the process prescribed by Congress was Arkansas, which in June, 1868, was readmitted to the Union. The last was Georgia, which after much tribulation was reinstated in July, 1870. Seven of the ten states were hurried through in time to make doubly certain the election of a Republican President in 1868, and to send almost solidly Republican delegations to Congress. Reconstruction was now technically over, but the opposition to carpetbag rule in the South was so strong that the federal government dared not withdraw its troops from many of the conquered states.

Congress Humiliates the Supreme Court. The complete triumph that Congress had scored over the President in pushing through its program of reconstruction was paralleled in its humiliation of the Supreme Court. In 1866 that tribunal had held in *Ex parte Milligan* that trials of civilians by military courts were illegal in regions where the civil courts were open for business. This decision cast serious doubt upon the legality of military rule upon which the Radicals proposed to base their plan of reconstruction, and Republican denunciations of the Supreme Court went to violent extremes. To discipline the Court, and also to prevent Johnson from making appointments to it, Congress enacted a law in July, 1866, which provided that the two vacancies among the associate justices should not be filled, and that the number of judges should ultimately become seven instead of nine. Thereafter the Court took pains to avoid as completely as possible all decisions that might offend Congress, although in the case of *Texas v. White* (1869) it went on record as favoring the Johnson theory that the southern states, in spite of their acts of secession, had never legally ceased to exist.

Elections in the South. The first elections in the reconstructed states resulted in the choice of a dubious array of officials. The highest places went mainly to northerners who became residents of the South after the war, and who had frequently seen it for the first time as members of the Union army. Lesser offices were held almost exclusively by Negroes, scalawags, and carpetbaggers. One Negro became lieutenant-governor of Louisiana, another secretary of state in South Carolina. Negroes were numerous in every legislature, and in South Carolina they outnumbered the whites eighty-eight to sixty-seven. Most officeholders were men of little property. In Louisiana only ten members of the legislature were taxpayers; in South Carolina the total taxes paid by the members of both houses were less than $700; in Georgia, they were less than $100. Most of the Negroes and some of the whites chosen to office, including even judicial positions, were illiterate.

Carpetbag Excesses. The inevitable result of entrusting the powers of government to such persons was an orgy of corruption. Private enterprises, such as railroad and canal companies, were expected to pay sizable bribes in order to secure charters, and, indeed, in order to carry on their legitimate business. Public money or public credit was generously voted toward the support of many dubious enterprises. Contracts were let to favorites at ridiculously high figures, and the public servants responsible took a cut of the profits. Public printing in Louisiana during a three-year period cost approximately $1.5 million a year, about $700,000 of which was paid in two of these years to a newspaper belonging to the governor of the state. A single session of the carpetbag legislature in Louisiana cost nearly $1 million, whereas before the war the cost of a session had never been more than one-tenth that amount.

The rule of the carpetbaggers raised tax rates to figures never known before, and piled up debts which most of the southern states felt obliged later on to repudiate; but it must not be forgotten that such political depravity was no monopoly of the South. In New York, for example, during this same period, the Tweed Ring reduced grafting to a science. Of all those who participated in the work of Radical reconstruction the Negroes were the least to blame for its excesses. Only a few of them understood what was being done, and only a few of those who did were shrewd enough to line their pockets with plunder. For the most part they were creatures of the conscience-less rogues who used them.

Contributions of the Carpetbaggers.

It should not be overlooked, however, that there was a brighter side to the rule of the carpetbaggers. They and their allies represented, however crudely, the less privileged classes in southern society, and they inaugurated many policies designed to better the lot of the ordinary man. They supported generously free public schools for the children of both races, although with little regard for available taxable resources. They distributed the tax burden, unreasonable as it became, with better regard to ability to pay than formerly. They voted for poor relief, and the rebuilding of roads, bridges, and public buildings that had been damaged or destroyed during the war.

Most of all, they acquired a taste for democracy that they would not soon forget. The Negroes soon lost the rights they had gained, but the incentive remained, at least with some of them, to win back by merit, privileges they had once enjoyed. As for the poorer whites, they were never again quite as inarticulate as they had been before.

Campaign of 1868.

The later phases of reconstruction were carried through under the administration of General Grant, whom the Republicans nominated for the Presidency, and elected, in 1868. Before the war Grant had been a Democrat, and for a time after the war it was not known which party nomination he would accept. But he had trouble with Johnson, and long before the Republicans held their convention was high in the counsels of the Radicals. On the first ballot every one of the Republican delegates voted for Grant. For Vice-President, the convention chose Schuyler Colfax of Indiana, the Radical Speaker of the House. Throwing off the Unionist disguise they had worn so willingly during the war, the Republicans with this campaign took back their prewar name, and made the carrying through of Radical reconstruction their principal tenet. On Negro suffrage, however, their course was devious. While insisting that it was a necessity in the South, they held that in the North it was a matter for each state to decide for itself. The Fifteenth Amendment was not submitted until after the election. Then, in spite of this plank in the Republican platform, the Radical leaders maintained that the election of Grant amounted to a mandate to write Negro suffrage into the Constitution.

Logically the Democrats should have nominated Johnson, but they turned instead to Horatio Seymour, the able war governor of New York. Opposition to Radical reconstruction was registered unmistakably in their platform, which declared that Congress, instead of restoring the Union, had, "so far as in its power, dissolved it, and subjected ten states, in the time of profound peace, to military despotism and Negro supremacy." The platform also gave its approval to the theory advocated by George H. Pendleton of Ohio that the Civil War bond issues should be paid off in greenbacks, instead of gold, whenever the letter of the law would permit. But the "Ohio idea," as this "soft-money" theory was called, did not meet the approval of Seymour, and was more or less ignored during the campaign. The real issue was Radical reconstruction, and the opposition to what Congress had done was far greater than the electoral returns revealed. Eight states, including New York and New Jersey, voted for Seymour, and in most of the twenty-six that voted for Grant the Democratic minorities were far too large for Republican comfort. In a total popular vote of nearly 6 million, Grant's majority was only about 300,000, and far more than that many Negroes had voted. Of the total white electorate, therefore, clearly Grant was a minority choice. The electoral returns gave Grant 214 votes to Seymour's 80. Both houses of Congress remained in the hands of the Radicals.

Grant the Politician. Some of the very qualities that had made Grant the soldier a success, made Grant the politician a sore trial to his colleagues and to his country. In the army, Grant had learned to stand loyally behind his subordinates, regardless of popular criticism. In politics, this trait sometimes made him the last to recognize that one of his appointees was a rogue. Years of political experience taught him something, and he left office a better politician than when he entered it; but as President he was not a success.

Grant's first Cabinet was an odd assortment of political misfits whom shrewd politicians soon found means to eliminate; not one of Grant's original appointees served longer than a year. By a stroke of good luck, Hamilton Fish of New York, an excellent choice, became Grant's second Secretary of State. Many of his appointments were so bad that the proposal for a federal civil service rapidly gained support. A small but influential group of reformers — such men as E. L. Godkin of the New York *Nation*, George William Curtis of *Harper's Weekly*, Thomas A. Jenckes, a representative from Rhode Island, and Carl Schurz, now United States Senator from Missouri — finally induced Congress in 1871 to set up a Civil Service Commission, of which Curtis became head. But this was done mainly to catch reform votes in the election of 1872, after which the Commission was allowed to die for lack of Congressional appropriations.

The "Ohio Idea." The "sound-money" men who hoped for help from the Grant administration fared far better than the civil service reformers. They claimed that the election of 1868 constituted a mandate to save the country from the "Ohio idea," according to which billions of greenback dollars might conceivably be printed to pay off the national debt. One of the first measures to pass Congress, in March, 1869, pledged the United States to redeem its bonds "in coin or its equivalent," a phrase which the administration and its successors interpreted to mean "in gold." Thus bonds that had been paid for in depreciated greenbacks were to be redeemed in dollars that were worth up to twice as much as the dollars originally lent the government. A refunding act, passed in July, 1870, provided for the systematic refinancing of the national debt on a long-term basis.

What to do with the greenbacks that had been so freely issued during the Civil War, and that were still in circulation, was another serious problem. In Johnson's administration the expedient of reducing them in quantity, in order ultimately to raise their value to a parity with gold, had been tried, but the outcry from the country when commodity prices began to drop was so great that Congress in 1868 called a halt. At the time Grant became President the greenback circulation stood at $365 million, far more than the government had the gold to redeem. For the moment it seemed inexpedient to work for the resumption of specie payments.

The Legal-tender Cases. In February, 1870, the Supreme Court became involved in the matter. In the case of *Hepburn* v. *Griswold*, it reached the unexpected conclusion that the "legal-tender" quality with which Congress had endowed the greenbacks was unconstitutional to the extent that it applied to debts contracted before the passage of the acts in question. The opinion of the Court, delivered by Chief Justice Chase, was reached by a four-to-three vote. But a combination of circumstances enabled the Court to reverse itself the following year. With Johnson out of the way, Congress had promptly raised the number of justices from seven to nine, and on the very day that the Hepburn case was decided, President Grant sent to the Senate the names of two new justices, who soon joined with the minority of the Hepburn decision to affirm by a five-to-four vote the constitutionality of the legal-tender clause. Probably Grant had decided on his nominations without particular reference to the greenback decision, but the prestige of the Court suffered considerably from its speedy change of opinion.

Reduction of Taxes. In the campaign of 1868 the Republicans had definitely committed themselves to the reduction of taxation. When Grant became President many of the war taxes were still in force, so in July, 1870, an act was passed which eliminated most of the "nuisance" taxes, restricted the internal revenues to a small number of articles, such as liquor and tobacco, and greatly reduced the income tax, which, two years later, was abolished entirely. Efforts to lower the tariff, however, met with earnest opposition from those who profited from the high war rates; during Johnson's term Congress had even raised the duties on raw wool, woolen goods, cop-

per, and copper ore. Not until 1872 were the first real reductions achieved. At that time many non-protective duties, such as those on tea, coffee, spices, and various raw materials, were lowered or abolished, and a 10 per cent cut was reluctantly conceded for a few carefully chosen duties on manufactured articles.

It was ironic that Grant, who had shown at the end of the Civil War thorough sympathy with the prostrate South, should have been President during the height of carpetbag rule. With the cooperation of the army assured, detachments of soldiers were always available to put down revolts, real or fancied, and to sustain the carpetbaggers. States that showed signs of going over to the Democrats were apt to be subjected to a congressional investigation, and then dealt with most drastically. On several occasions, for example, military officers deliberately purged southern legislatures of undependable members. Some of the carpetbag governors also made use of Negro militia, whose chief duty, apparently, was to terrorize "disloyal" whites.

The Ku Klux Klan. It was inevitable that southern whites would fight back. As early as 1865 a group of young men who had lately been soldiers in the Confederate army organized, at Pulaski, Tennessee, a secret social society, which, from the Greek word κύκλος, meaning circle, they called the Ku Klux Klan. The society at first spread slowly; but rapid success came after the organization was used to frighten Negroes. Before long, night riders in various disguises, such as ghostly gowns, false faces, and tails, were visiting the cabins of Negroes who asserted their rights, breaking up meetings of the Union League, beating up Negro militiamen, frightening black Republicans away from the polls, and occasionally attacking both scalawags and carpetbaggers. The Klan was soon paralleled by numerous similar organizations such as the Knights of the White Camellia, the Constitutional Guards, the Pale Faces, and the Knights of the Rising Sun. By the year 1869 these orders had covered the South with their activities and had attracted to membership men who would stop at nothing. Murders now replaced whippings as a common proceeding, and the most fiendish acts of torture were common. Horrified at the turn events had taken, and certain that such an opportunity for reprisals would not long be neglected, the responsible heads of the various orders, as early as the spring of 1869, attempted to disband them. But the worst of the "midnight banditti" continued their activities unabated.

Congress replied to the Ku Klux challenge with a series of drastic enforcement acts, which laid down heavy penalties for all found guilty of using force, bribery, or intimidation to prevent citizens from voting, and listed as high crimes subject to severe penalties the various activities of the Klan, such as forming conspiracies, wearing disguises, resisting officers and intimidating witnesses. The President was also authorized to suspend the writ of habeas corpus wherever he deemed such action necessary to suppress "armed combinations" in rebellion against the authority of the United States. Grant singled out for an example nine counties in South Carolina where the lawlessness had been most marked, suspended the writ of habeas corpus within their borders, and brought hundreds of lawbreakers to trial. Federal troops stood by to see that the courts were left free to do their work, and in less than two years federal judges in South Carolina imposed heavy sentences upon eighty-two persons for violation of the acts. The example proved effective, and the number of outrages attributed to the Klan declined sharply from this time on.

Emergence of the "Solid South." Ultimately the attempts of Grant and the Radicals to maintain Republican majorities in the South came to nought. Southerners, bent on the restoration of home rule, learned to stop short of violence in their efforts to restrain the Negroes from the exercise of their newly acquired political rights, but they often found more peaceable means quite as potent. Leading these "redeemers" in many southern states was a new type of southerner interested in industry and commerce. Many of these men had been Henry Clay Whigs before the war and now looked forward eagerly to cooperating with northern capitalists in the profitable work of constructing railroads and industries. Although often referred to as "Bourbons," many of the new southern leaders neither represented the old planter aristocracy nor sought to restore pre-Civil War society. Their eyes were on the city rather than the plantation, upon industry rather than agriculture.

Aiding the redemption movement was the growing pressure of northern opinion which eventually forced Congress to show greater leniency toward the South. In May, 1872, Congress passed an amnesty act that reduced the number of ex-Confederates excluded from the suffrage to about 500. Gradually, in state after state, Democratic majorities took over the administration of government, carpetbaggers were expelled, and great numbers of Negroes ceased voting. Thereafter, a vast majority of southern whites, scalawags along with the rest, felt obliged regardless of important political differences to stand together as members of the Democratic, or "white man's" Party. Thus Radical reconstruction, instead of producing a solidly Republican South, as had been intended, produced a solidly Democratic South.

But the term "Solid South" reflected the facts only of national voting. Within the South sharp lines of cleavage persisted. For while the redeemers continued to obtain general support through talk of home rule and white supremacy, many of their actions were pointed against the poor white almost as much as against the Negro. Many of the redeemers, in fact, supported the Negroes' right to vote and appointed them to minor offices. In return, the Negro vote kept them in power against the challenge of the more radical white Democrats. And once in office, these "business Democrats," or "Conservatives," as they were sometimes called, so sharply reduced taxes that school systems and other state services were greatly curtailed. The length of the southern school term fell off 20 per cent, and illiteracy increased. Southern state constitutions were changed so that many local officers once elected were now appointed, and by gerrymandering, many poor-white farming counties were often underrepresented in the state legislatures. Simultaneously railroads were aided by generous land grants and low taxes, while state regulation of business enterprise met with deep hostility. This "New Departure," as the business-minded movement was sometimes described, greatly distressed many southerners, but their protest was stilled because of their greater opposition to Radical reconstruction.

Liberal Republicanism. By the year 1872 the opponents of Radical reconstruc-

tion within the Republican Party itself had come to be numerous. Known as "Liberals," or "Liberal Republicans," they stood ready to leave the party, if necessary, in order to prevent further efforts to continue carpetbag rule in the South. This movement for reform started in Missouri, as an effort to get rid of some of the unreasonably vindictive provisions that a state constitution, adopted in 1865, had aimed at all citizens who had been southern sympathizers. Such persons were not only denied the right to vote and to hold office, but they might not act as trustees, practice law, teach, preach, or solemnize marriages. In the election of 1870 the Missouri Liberals, with the assistance of the Democrats, drove the Radicals from power and excised the offensive clauses from the state constitution. Soon the movement became national in scope and numbered among its adherents such prominent citizens as Horace Greeley, editor of the New York *Tribune*, Carl Schurz, United States Senator from Missouri, and Charles Francis Adams, son of

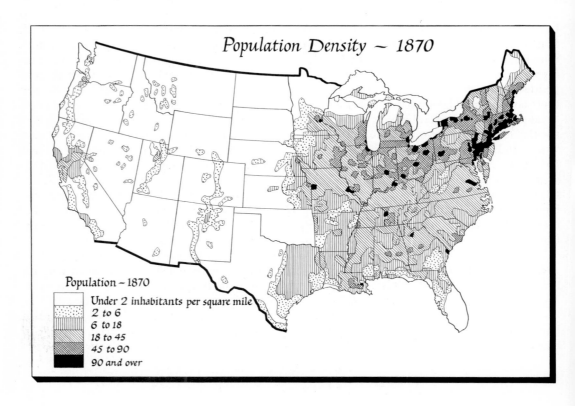

Population Density – 1870

Population – 1870

Under 2 inhabitants per square mile
2 to 6
6 to 18
18 to 45
45 to 90
90 and over

one President and grandson of another. Opposition to "Grantism" went much further with some Liberals than mere denunciation of the administration's southern policy. Civil service reformers hoped for the day when appointments would be made on merit, and tariff reformers were determined that through Liberal auspices they should scale down the high protective duties that had lasted on after the Civil War. A good many Liberals, moreover, were opposed to the increasing and often corrupt connection between big business and government, and hoped for a return to a true *laissez faire* policy.

Election of 1872. When it became apparent that the Radicals intended to renominate Grant, a split in the Republican Party was assured. A national convention, called by the Missouri Liberals, met in Cincinnati, May 1, 1872, and nominated Horace Greeley for the Presidency. Greeley was unfortunately a high-tariff man, so his selection failed to satisfy a large faction among the Liberals who had hoped for tariff reform. Curiously, however, it did not alienate equally the southern Democrats, who remembered that in 1867, when Jefferson Davis was being held under an indictment for treason, Greeley had signed the ex-Confederate's bail bond. It was hard for the northern Democrats to accept an old enemy as their leader, but when the Democratic convention met, it accepted both Greeley and the platform upon which he had been nominated. That document was sufficiently forthright in its criticisms of Radical reconstruction and the spoils system, but it dodged the tariff issue as completely as possible. The Liberal campaign, earnest and purposeful as it was, failed completely to stop Grant. He was not only renominated by the Republicans, but was triumphantly re-elected. Greeley carried two states of the lower South, Georgia and Texas, and four border states, Missouri, Tennessee, Maryland, and Kentucky, but Grant won all the rest. Greeley's death

shortly after the election probably came as the result of his strenuous speech-making tours, his disappointment at the election result, and grief over the death of his wife.

Grant's Foreign Policy. The foreign policy of the Grant administration was far better handled than its domestic affairs. Grant did indeed create a near scandal by his determination to annex the Dominican Republic to the United States, but his efforts in this direction were overruled by the United States Senate. Highly creditable, however, was the settlement of all outstanding disputes between the United States and Great Britain. The most serious of these troubles came from the lax interpretation of neutral duties that had characterized British policy during the Civil War. Soon after that war had ended, the United States had an opportunity to demonstrate that its stricter view of neutrality might be of use to the British. At that time the Fenian Brotherhood, an organization of Irish-Americans, not only planned an invasion of Canada from American soil, but in June, 1866, actually crossed the border in some force and fought a battle with Canadian volunteers. The American government should have forestalled this "invasion," but having failed in that it did the next best thing. It promptly arrested the Fenian leaders, seized their collections of supplies, and strengthened the border garrisons so as to prevent any further such happenings. These events may have had something to do with the increasing willingness of the British to accept responsibility for the depredations committed by the *Alabama* and other Confederate commerce-destroyers, and to arrange for the arbitration of all unsettled controversies.

The Geneva Awards. The tactful diplomacy of Secretary of State Hamilton Fish finally resulted in the signing of the Treaty of Washington in 1871. In this treaty the British government definitely expressed its regret for the "escape" of the

Confederate cruisers, accepted as binding a set of rules that amounted to a clear confession of unneutral action, and agreed to submit the matter of damages to an arbitration tribunal. Meeting at Geneva, the *Alabama* Tribunal awarded damages of $15 million to the United States, a sum so large as to arouse protests in England. Other settlements that grew out of the Treaty of Washington resulted in money payments to Great Britain by the United States for damages suffered by British subjects during the Civil War, and for special favors enjoyed by American fishermen in British North American Waters. And the exact boundary between the United States and Canada in Puget Sound was settled, mostly in favor of the United States, by a referee, the German Emperor.

The Grant Scandals. The scandals that were to make Grant's regime notorious for its corruption had already begun when he took the oath of office for the second time. One of the worst of them, the infamous "gold conspiracy," was engineered in 1869 by two speculators, Jay Gould and James Fisk, with the effective, although unintended, assistance of the President himself. While gold did not then circulate as money, it was in constant demand for adjusting international trade balances. To meet this demand the United States Treasury was accustomed from time to time to sell gold, but Gould managed to persuade Grant that in order to raise farm prices this should be stopped. Knowing that a treasury order to this effect was about to be given, Gould and Fisk "cornered" the existing small supply of available gold, and between September 20 and September 24 drove the price from 140 to 163½. The result was a short but violent stock exchange panic, and serious embarrassment, even bankruptcy, for many legitimate businesses. Finally an emergency order from the President, who at last saw that he had been duped, permitted the Treasury to sell gold, and brought the price down.

Another scandal, which the country learned about in 1872, was brought about by the building of the Union Pacific Railroad, which Congress had chartered during the Civil War. The Credit Mobilier was a construction company, so designed as to permit a few Union Pacific stockholders, who were also the chief stockholders in the Credit Mobilier, to drain off huge profits from construction contracts. Since a principal source of revenue for the railroad was bonds given it as a subsidy from the United States government, an effort was made to "fix" congressmen by selling them Credit Mobilier stock at a generous discount. Oakes Ames, a congressman from Massachusetts, acted as agent for the company and was able to induce many prominent politicians, among them Vice-President Colfax, to accept his favors. The congressional investigation which exposed the scandal tarnished a number of reputations, although to the public the holding of Credit Mobilier stock was seemingly less reprehensible than the attempts made by some congressmen to conceal such holdings.

During Grant's second administration one shocking revelation succeeded another with regularity. Congressmen in 1873 voted themselves a 50 per cent increase in salary, with back pay for two years. Naturally, this "Salary Grab" Act was severely criticized and was almost immediately repealed. The Treasury Department furnished another scandal when in May, 1874, it was disclosed that one John D. Sanborn had collected some $427,000 of overdue revenue, and had received for his services a commission of 50 per cent. To escape formal censure for allowing such a practice, William A. Richardson, Grant's second Secretary of the Treasury, was obliged to resign. Before another year was up, Grant's third Secretary of the Treasury, Benjamin H. Bristow, had uncovered a "Whiskey Ring," composed of revenue officers and distillers who had conspired to defraud the government out of a part of the excise on liquor. Even Grant's private secretary had accepted fa-

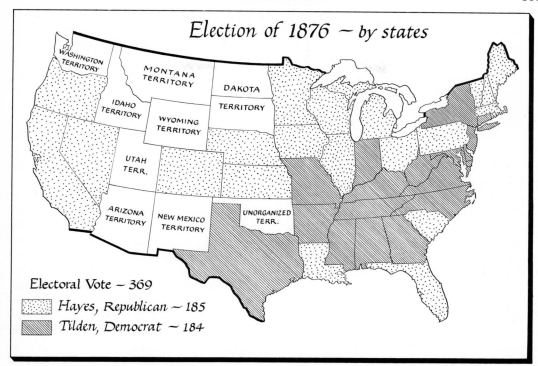

Election of 1876 — by states

Electoral Vote — 369

▓ Hayes, Republican — 185

▨ Tilden, Democrat — 184

vors from the Ring, and the President himself had taken presents that a keener sense of propriety would have led him to refuse. As a climax, Grant's Secretary of War, W. W. Belknap, received through his wife as intermediary a total of $24,450, as the price of keeping in office a post trader at Fort Sill in the Indian Territory. Belknap escaped removal from office by impeachment only by resigning.

The Disputed Election of 1876. The ascendancy of the Republicans, already shaken by the excesses of reconstruction and the scandals of the Grant regime, tottered almost to a fall with the advent of 1873 and the ensuing depression. The elections of 1874 returned a Democratic majority of more than seventy in the House of Representatives, while in the states, North as well as South, Democrats — ex-Copperheads and ex-Confederates — replaced Republicans with great regularity. As the election of 1876 approached, the

nervousness of the Republicans was intense. To many of them the loss of the Presidency seemed almost as bad as to have lost the war. Not daring to select a standard-bearer even slightly tainted with scandal, they turned to the spotless but relatively unknown Rutherford B. Hayes, an able volunteer officer in the Civil War, and three times governor of Ohio. Such a choice was the more necessary because the Democrats seemed certain to nominate Samuel J. Tilden, whose rather hesitant part in the overthrow of the Tweed Ring had made him governor of New York. Tilden's name was thus indelibly connected with political reform, a strong attraction for the Liberal Republicans whose votes the Republicans needed in order to win. More by accident than by plan, both candidates for the Presidency proved to be conservative in their economic views, particularly on the currency. Extremists on the money question gave their votes to a new Independent, or "Greenback," Party. It favored expansion of the currency by the issue of more paper money and nominated Peter Cooper of New York for President. Most voters, however, even if they held soft-money views, were too enthralled by the main contest to take the Greenbackers seriously.

By the time the election was held, the supremacy of the carpetbaggers had been overthrown in all but three of the southern states, South Carolina, Louisiana, and Florida. It was known in advance that every other southern state would vote for Tilden, and on the evening of election day, November 7, it appeared that these three states, too, were safely in the Democratic column. Since New York and several other northern states had gone Democratic, the election of Tilden seemed assured. But the Republican leaders, arguing that thousands of Negroes had been barred from voting in South Carolina, Louisiana, and Florida, claimed them for Hayes who would thus have 185 electoral votes to Tilden's 184. Republican-dominated returning boards in the three unreconstructed states then discounted enough Democratic votes to give Hayes the majority he needed in each, and in December, Republican electors cast the votes of the three states solidly for Hayes, while contesting Democratic groups voted unanimously for Tilden. The electoral contest thus begun rocked the country, and for a time hope of a peaceful settlement seemed faint. Finally Congress decided to refer the double returns to an Electoral Commission of fifteen, five each from the Senate, the House, and the Supreme Court. By a strict party vote, eight to seven, the Commission gave the election to the Republicans. While on the face of the returns it would seem that the election had been "stolen," as the Democrats charged, no doubt many thousands of Negro voters in the South who had wished to vote for Hayes had not dared to vote at all. But the big question remained, would the people, and especially the Democrats, accept the verdict.

Compromise of 1877. Throughout the four month period between the election and inauguration day numerous proposals were made for reconciling the grave dispute. Foremost among southern desires was the end of the reconstruction and the disabilities placed upon the postwar South. Almost as important to many redemption leaders was the need for northern capital and the cooperation of the Federal government to promote their schemes for economic reconstruction of the defeated section. Important northern business leaders as well as Hayes himself were sympathetic. In fundamental outlook, except for the issues settled on the battlefield, there was little that separated the northern Republican leadership from that of the new South. Both groups were conservative, many on both sides were former Whigs, as Hayes had been, most were sound money men, and dedicated to government support of the new industrialism.

Hayes contributed greatly to the spirit of compromise by letting it be known that once in office he would withdraw Federal forces from the South and appoint a southern Democrat to his cabinet. Furthermore, he indicated that he would not overlook white southerners in matters of patronage and that he would support appropriation bills for the reconstruction of southern rivers, harbors, and post offices. Simultaneously a group of northern capitalists, attempting to obtain a large federal subsidy for the construction of the Texas and Pacific Railroad, enlisted the support of many of their southern counterparts for Hayes. Prompted by these inducements and the knowledge that further resistance by their section was impossible, the southern Democratic leaders accepted the compromise and on March 4, 1877, Hayes was inaugurated without serious opposition.

In his inaugural Hayes promised to use every means at his disposal to restore "efficient local self-government" in the South, and promptly thereafter ordered the removal of the remaining federal troops from the South. As Democratic regimes took over in South Carolina and Louisiana, military reconstruction ceased, and the Radical objective to make the South Republican ended in complete failure. Instead, except for a few mountain districts, the South was solidly Democratic and would remain so for almost sixty years. The end of military reconstruction also meant defeat for the Radical Republican effort to assure the freedmen equal public and civil rights.

Negro Segregation. Not all Radicals had supported equal rights for the Negro. At the same time some of them demanded equality in the defeated South, they supported or acquiesced in the continuing inequalities in their own home states in the North. But the support of the northern Radicals was a necessity if the southern freedmen were to preserve most of the civil rights they had gained during reconstruction. Now the President turned their future over to the southern whites. In his continuing efforts to reconcile the sections, Hayes made a southern tour during 1877 where he was enthusiastically applauded, especially after he remarked that the future of the freedmen would be better protected by southern whites than by the "unwanted intrusions" of the Federal government. Hayes attempted to purchase amity between the sections at the expense of the southern freedman. And in the materialist antireform atmosphere of the postwar period the cause of equal rights for Negroes was soon all but forgotten in both North and South. The Civil Rights Act of 1875, which stipulated that all persons irrespective of race were entitled to equal treatment in all public places and facilities, including railroads and hotels, was to be the last Federal civil rights act for over seventy-five years. Even the provisions of that act were substantially narrowed when the Supreme Court in the Civil Rights Cases (1883) held that the Fourteenth Amendment did not restrict private individuals or

companies from discriminating between the races. Further steps toward legalizing Jim Crow legislation were taken by the Supreme Court in *Plessy* v. *Ferguson* (1896) and in *Cumming* v. *County Board of Education* (1899). In the first case regarding railroads and in the second, public schools, the Court held that states and local governments might segregate the races provided the facilities for each were equal. Even before these cases segregation was practiced in many places North and South on an *ad hoc* basis. Afterwards southern state legislation and northern indifference led to discrimination as almost a standard national way of life. Nationwide, unions barred Negroes from membership, or reserved the better jobs for the whites, Negroes were excluded from the better residential districts, almost everywhere they were denied access to hotels and restaurants, and they were relegated to the second balcony in most theaters. In 1900, by southern legislative fiat, segregation was the rule in public transportation, in churches, in theaters, and in sporting events, as well as in the public schools. From North to South Jim Crow was triumphant, and the Negro had become a second-class citizen.

Strangely enough the South did not attempt to disenfranchise the Negro legally until the 1890's. Until then many Negroes voted regularly, largely because the ruling southern conservatives often used their purchased votes to maintain their position against the rising radical challenge of the poor white farming elements. But with the Populist attempt to organize the Negro votes in some states and in others to abolish it, the danger to white supremacy in bidding for Negro votes became apparent to both conservatives and radicals. Consequently both white factions often joined hands and passed poll tax laws and literacy requirements for voting which, when interpreted by local authorities, could deny the voting privilege to the Negro. When the

Supreme Court in *Williams* v. *Mississippi* (1898) declared the literacy requirement constitutional, the Negro was effectively disenfranchised. Thus many of the gains he had stood to win by the outcome of the Civil War had vanished. In the North he was at best a dubious and frequently an unwanted person; in the South he was often without a vote and by law denied the equal educational and social opportunities afforded to even the poorest of his fellow white citizens.

SELECTED BIBLIOGRAPHY

The interpretation of Reconstruction is still a subject of hot dispute among historians. W. A. Dunning, whose works included °*Essays on the Civil War and Reconstruction* (1904), and °*Reconstruction, Political and Economic, 1865–1877* (1907), set the tone for interpretation of the era for nearly two generations. The Dunning "school" was political-minded, emphasizing the evils and hypocrisy of "Radicalism," taking a dim view of Negro competence and aspirations, and finding little good to say about carpetbaggers and scalawags and, for that matter, the Republican Party. Claude Bowers, °*The Tragic Era* (1929), is a lively journalistic treatment, essentially the Dunning thesis for the general reader. Traces of the Dunning line may be found in recent works, such as the scholarly study by E. M. Coulter, *The South During Reconstruction, 1865–1877* (1947); and the popular volume by Hodding Carter, *The Angry Scar* (1959).

Major revisionist works are K. M. Stampp, *The Era of Reconstruction, 1865–1877* (1965); and J. H. Franklin, °*Reconstruction: After the Civil War* (1961). An excellent new survey is J. S. Ezell, *The South since 1865* (1963). °*Reconstruction in the South*, edited by E. C. Rozwenc (1952), provides an excellent selection of conflicting interpretations. Handy documentary collections are J. P. Shenton (ed.), °*The Reconstruction* (1963); and R. N. Current (ed.), °*Reconstruction* (1965). Two recent monographs on Reconstruction are LaWanda and J. H. Cox, *Politics, Principle and Prejudice* (1963); and W. R. Brock, *An American Crisis* (1963), by a British scholar.

Social and economic conditions are treated by Allan Nevins, *The Emergence of Modern America, 1865–1878* (1927). Economic aspects of the era are discussed by two standard

companion volumes: F. A. Shannon, *The Farmer's Last Frontier: Agriculture, 1860–1897* (1945); and E. C. Kirkland, *Industry Comes of Age; Business, Labor and Public Policy, 1860–1897* (1961). An interesting collection of conflicting interpretations is °*The Economic Impact of the American Civil War*, edited by Ralph Andreano (1962). On financial aspects, see E. P. Oberholtzer, *Jay Cooke, Financier of the Civil War* (2 vols., 1907); and R. C. Todd, *Confederate Finance* (1954). Northern inflation is treated in W. C. Mitchell, *A History of the Greenbacks with Special Reference to the Consequences of their Issue, 1862–1865* (1903). An important new study is Irwin Unger, *The Greenback Era* (1964).

The history of the Negro people has become a topic of great interest to recent scholars. A good biography of General O. O. Howard, head of the Freedmen's Bureau, is J. A. Carpenter, *Sword and Olive Branch* (1964). Special studies of importance include: H. H. Donald, *The Negro Freedman* (1952); G. R. Bentley, *A History of the Freedman's Bureau* (1955); V. L. Wharton, °*The Negro in Mississippi, 1865–1890* (1947); G. B. Tindall, *South Carolina Negroes, 1877–1900* (1952); and F. A. Logan, *The Negro in North Carolina, 1876–1894* (1964). W. E. B. DuBois, °*Black Reconstruction in America* (1935), is a bitter Marxist interpretation. Important themes are treated by H. M. Bond, *Negro Education in Alabama* (1939); and O. A. Singletary, °*Negro Militia and Reconstruction* (1957).

The character of the first postwar President is the subject of much controversy. E. L. McKitrick, °*Andrew Johnson and Reconstruction* (1960), contests vigorously the position taken by H. K. Beale, *The Critical Year; A Study of Andrew Johnson and Reconstruction* (1930). While Beale was himself something

° Available in paperback

of a revisionist, he saw the Radicals as economically motivated and insincere in their promises to the Negro. McKitrick sees Johnson as a blundering incompetent whose actions in a fluid situation led to disaster. W. B. Hesseltine, *Lincoln's Plan of Reconstruction* (1960), is an interesting discussion of an important and much-disputed subject. Significant biographies include Lately Thomas, *Sam Ward* (1965); R. N. Current, *Old Thad Stevens* (1942); F. M. Brodie, *Thaddeus Stevens* (1959); H. L. Trefousse, *Benjamin Franklin Wade* (1963); and R. S. West, Jr., *Lincoln's Scapegoat General* (1965), a study of Ben Butler.

Recent important works on legal-constitutional aspects are Jacobus ten Broek, *The Antislavery Origins of the Fourteenth Amendment* (1951); J. B. James, *The Framing of the Fourteenth Amendment* (1956); J. T. Dorris, *Pardon and Amnesty under Lincoln and Johnson* (1953); and H. M. Hyman, *Era of the Oath; Northern Loyalty Tests During the Civil War and Reconstruction* (1954). See also the "classic" treatment by J. W. Burgess, *Reconstruction and the Constitution, 1866–1876* (1902).

The best general surveys of the Grant administration are found in W. B. Hesseltine, *Ulysses S. Grant, Politician* (1935); and Allan Nevins, *Hamilton Fish; The Inner History of the Grant Administration* (1936). Interesting political monographs include C. H. Coleman, *The Election of 1868* (1933); E. D. Ross, *The Liberal Republican Movement* (1919); and P. L. Haworth, *The Hayes-Tilden Disputed Presidential Election of 1876* (1906). Biographies of leaders of the opposition are Stewart Mitchell, *Horatio Seymour of New York* (1938); and G. G. Van Deusen, **Horace Greeley* (1953). A careful study of Pennsylvania politics is E. S. Bradley, *The Triumph of Militant Republicanism* (1964). A stimulating reinterpretation is C. V. Woodward, **Reunion and Reaction; The Compromise of 1877 and the End of Reconstruction* (2nd ed., 1956). Uniquely important is L. D. White, *The Re-publican Era, 1869–1901* (1958), a study of the federal administrative machinery.

The southern states during Reconstruction were studied one by one by members of the Dunning school. Best of this group are J. W. Garner, *Reconstruction in Mississippi* (1901); and C. M. Thompson, *Reconstruction in Georgia* (1915). A monument of early revisionist scholarship is F. B. Simkins and R. H. Woody, *South Carolina during Reconstruction* (1932). Other important revisionist studies are T. B. Alexander, *Political Reconstruction in Tennessee* (1950); and J. H. Whyte, *The Uncivil War; Washington during the Reconstruction* (1958). R. L. Zuber, *Jonathan Worth* (1965), deals with North Carolina in the early years of Reconstruction. The end of Reconstruction is discussed in the major revisionist work of C. V. Woodward, *Origins of the New South, 1877–1913* (1951). An important recent book which challenges the existence of a monolithic northern business community is R. P. Sharkey, *Money, Class and Party* (1959). See also G. R. Woolfolk, *The Cotton Regency; The Northern Merchants and Reconstruction, 1865–1880* (1958). A significant recent monograph is J. F. Stover, *The Railroads of the South, 1865–1900* (1955).

Many works treat of diplomatic themes in the Reconstruction period. On Charles Francis Adams, see the two biographies bearing his name, by C. F. Adams, Jr. (2nd ed., 1917), and M. B. Duberman (1961). Valuable monographs include: L. B. Shippee, *Canadian-American Relations, 1849–1874* (1939); D. F. Warner, *The Idea of Continental Union; Agitation for the Annexation of Canada to the United States, 1849–1893* (1960); Dexter Perkins, *The Monroe Doctrine, 1867–1907* (1937); and C. C. Tansill, *The United States and Santo Domingo, 1798–1873* (1938). On Alaska, see Hector Chevigny, *Russian America, 1741–1867* (1965); Victor Farrar, *The Annexation of Russian America to the United States* (1937); and Frederic Bancroft, *Life of Seward*, Vol. II, already cited.

*John Ferguson Weir, "Forging the Shaft: a Weld-
ing Heat." The Metropolitan Museum of Art,
Gift of Lyman G. Bloomingdale, 1901.*

The

New Nation

· 1877–1897 ·

Labor is prior to, and independent of, capital. Capital is only the fruit of labor, and could never have existed if labor had not first existed.

ABRAHAM LINCOLN

So long as all the increased wealth which modern progress brings goes to build up great fortunes, to increase luxury and make sharper the contrast between the House of Have and the House of Want, progress is not real and cannot be permanent.

HENRY GEORGE

What is the use of being elected or reelected unless you stand for something?

GROVER CLEVELAND

21

FROM HAYES TO HARRISON

In contrast with the meaningful political struggles of the Civil War and Reconstruction period, American politics for the next twenty years after Hayes's inauguration seems relatively unimportant. All too often politicians of both major parties ignored the new and perplexing problems of agriculture, labor, industrial monopoly, and railroad regulation, in order to berate their opponents for positions taken during the years of sectional strife. Reform elements existed in both parties, but only rarely were they able to make their voices effective on the legislative floor or during the political campaigns. For the most part the real goal of party warfare was place and power, which more often than not attracted only second-rate men. Compared to their contemporaries in the world of business and finance, American politicians during the period appear in a most unfavorable light. In part the indecisive character of their role was due to the fact that for only six out of the twenty-two years between 1875 and 1897 did one party control both houses of Congress and the Presidency simultaneously. It might also be said, however, that during these years the politicians rarely gave the American voter significant enough alternatives to warrant a decisive mandate. But the sterility of party politics into which the nation had drifted did not mean any lessening of party interest or party activity. Party loyalties remained strong, party discipline strict, and campaigns were waged as if the very life of the Republic hung in balance.

Rutherford B. Hayes. Rutherford B. Hayes (1822–1893), who succeeded Grant in 1877, never became the leader of his party, but he was by no means a nonentity. Although an able lawyer, he had not, unlike Tilden, served the nation's great corporations. Also unlike Tilden he had volunteered for the war, in which, serving without conspicuous distinction, he had risen to the rank of major general. As Governor of Ohio he had made an excellent record; he was honest, conscientious, and surprisingly nonpolitical. During the Presidential campaign he astonished and delighted reformers by denouncing the spoils system and irritated party regulars by the assertion that "he serves his party best who serves his country best." In other more personal ways he showed his independence. He was a temperance advocate, and his wife's custom of serving nonalcoholic beverages in that hard-drinking age won for her the nickname of "Lemonade Lucy." As President, however, Hayes's principles and good intentions often led him into bad politics. To his Cabinet he appointed four men who had voted for Greeley in 1872. One of them, Postmaster General David M. Key, a Tilden Democrat, owed his appointment to the bargain that had made Hayes President. Hayes had even considered naming the ex-Confederate general, Joseph E. Johnston, as Secretary of War. Such unconventional attitudes, however laudable, did not endear Hayes to Republican regulars, who welcomed cordially his announced determination to become a one-term President.

Second only to his desire to end military reconstruction, Hayes wanted to achieve civil service reform, but to accomplish anything significant along this line he needed a really effective civil service commission, something Congress refused to give him. Nevertheless, Hayes continued to make the best appointments to public office that he could, and his record in this respect was the best of any President's since John Quincy Adams. Early in his administration he engaged in a battle with the Senate over the rule of "senatorial courtesy," according to which every senator of the dominant political party claimed the right to block confirmation of the appointment within his own state of any individual to whom he personally objected. In this fight he won a partial victory. His removal of Chester Alan Arthur, collector of the port of New York, gave great offense to Roscoe Conkling, senator from New York, who succeeded in preventing confirmation of the first man Hayes chose for the place. But with the help of Democratic votes Hayes's second nominee was confirmed.

Resumption. Hayes's tenacious adherence to hard-money views was in keeping with his character. On this issue he was in complete agreement with the leading men of his party, and he approved heartily a law passed early in 1875 which authorized the Secretary of the Treasury to build up a gold reserve preparatory to resumption on January 1, 1879. John Sherman was chiefly responsible for this measure, and as Hayes's Secretary of the Treasury it fell to his lot to carry it into effect. Backed steadfastly by the President, he sold bonds for gold, and ultimately accumulated a gold reserve of $100 million. As this fund grew, confidence that the government would be able on the appointed day to exchange gold dollars for greenbacks grew with it, and the value of the greenback dollar, expressed in terms of gold, also increased. Worth only sixty-seven cents in 1865, the greenback dollars had risen to ninety-six cents in 1877, and well before January 1, 1879, to 100 cents. In 1878 Congress decided that $346 million in greenbacks should remain a permanent part of the national currency, on the assumption that the gold reserve would make every greenback dollar "as good as gold." When the time came for resumption, few cared to make the change. People had become accustomed to greenbacks and continued to use them.

Soft-money Ideas. The steadily appreciating value of the dollar insured profits to moneylenders, particularly those who made long-term loans. For borrowers, however, the situation was far different. The farmer who mortgaged his farm as security for a five-year loan found to his sorrow when the time for payment came that the dollars he had borrowed were worth far less than the dollars with which he had to repay. Dearer dollars also meant lower prices for his wheat, or corn, or livestock. He therefore paid back not only principal and interest, but an additional sum to cover the amount which the dollar had appreciated. Protests against dearer dollars and lower prices came thick and fast, and in the West and the South, where debtors were numerous and creditors few, soft-money ideas, such as Pendleton's "Ohio idea," found favor. In general the Democratic Party was more hospitable to soft-money views than the Republican, but in both parties hard-money men were in the ascendancy. With resumption imminent, the Greenback Party, founded in 1876, won more and more adherents. In the elections of 1878, it polled a million votes, as against its 80,000 of two years before, and elected fifteen members of Congress.

Free Silver. The success of resumption, and the return of prosperity in 1879, tended to discredit Greenbackism, and the high-water mark of 1878 was never attained again. In the meantime, however, a new soft-money panacea had been discovered in what was popularly known as "free silver." The two precious metals used as money, gold and silver, had depended for their value, not upon the fiat of government, but upon commercial demand. By a long-sustained coincidence the relative value of the two metals had been almost constant; it took fifteen or sixteen ounces of silver to equal in value an ounce of gold. In early times the slight fluctuation in the ratio of value between the two metals had been of small concern, but with the progress of modern science the exact amount of silver and gold in all coins could easily be ascertained. Nations therefore made an effort to establish coinage ratios that would harmonize with the existing commercial ratios. Always this was difficult, or even impossible, for the commercial ratio was inevitably a variable, while the coinage ratio established by law was a constant. People who knew the difference hoarded the overvalued coins, and spent those undervalued; or, as Gresham's Law expressed it, the cheap money drove the dear money out of circulation. Paper issues, until 1879 less valuable than either gold or silver, rarely had much difficulty in driving both types of coins out of circulation. Hopeful that the time had come at last

when a metallic currency could be provided for general use, the Secretary of the Treasury obtained from Congress in February, 1873, a new coinage law. This measure took account of the theory, generally observed in European practice, that only one metal should be used as a standard. Accordingly it dropped the silver dollar from the coinage lists, which at the old coinage ratio of sixteen to one contained too much silver to permit it to circulate anyway. This was the notorious "crime of 1873," committed, according to a generation of silver orators, as the result of an "international conspiracy to demonetize silver." Actually, no one would have thought of branding this law as a crime had not the commercial ratio of value between silver and gold begun suddenly to change. This was due primarily to the huge outpourings of silver mines in the American West, although the diminishing demand throughout the world for the use of silver as money may also have been a factor. Whatever the causes, the price of silver declined steadily for the next twenty-five years, a situation which led despairing silver miners to demand as a remedy the "free and unlimited coinage of silver at the ratio of sixteen to one." The silver miners were soon joined by the debtor farmers of the Middle West, and to a lesser extent by those of the South, who had no interest in a higher price for silver, but believed that "free coinage," or "free silver," as they termed the desired policy, would mean a cheaper dollar. Former Greenbackers altered their paper-money arguments to fit this new demand. If the government would only take silver from all who offered it, as it still took gold, coin the silver into silver dollars at the rate of sixteen ounces of silver to one of gold, and put the new silver dollars into circulation, the country would have more money and cheaper money, just as surely as if more greenbacks had been issued. Free silver thus became the adopted child of the Greenbackers and all other inflationists.

The Bland-Allison Act.   The silver issue continued as a constant factor in American politics for the rest of the nineteenth century, and during Hayes's administration the silver forces won what they mistook at first for a considerable victory. By the Bland-Allison Act, passed in 1878 over Hayes's veto, the Secretary of the Treasury was ordered to purchase each month from $2 million to $4 million worth of silver at the market price, and to coin it into silver dollars at the old coinage ratio of sixteen to one. This meant limited rather than unlimited coinage, and since the new silver dollars were made legal tender, if only they could be backed by gold, as were the greenbacks, they would be "as good as gold." In practice Sherman and his successors completely defeated the hopes of the silverites by standing ready at all times to redeem silver dollars, whatever their "intrinsic value," in gold.

Republican Dissensions.   As the time approached for the election of 1880, it became apparent that the Republicans could count upon that most valuable of all political allies, prosperity. The United States enjoyed in 1880 not only a greater volume of foreign trade than had been recorded in any previous year, but also a favorable balance of trade. Farm prices, particularly wheat and cotton, were up, and manufacturers were reaping rich harvests from the markets provided by a steadily increasing population. Confidence replaced the gloom that had characterized the depression years. But could the Republican Party take advantage of the situation? As everyone knew, it was sadly torn by internal strife. At one extreme were the hard-boiled "Stalwarts," led by Roscoe Conkling of New York, who desired to nominate ex-President Grant for a third term. Only a little less conservative were the "Half-Breeds," who regarded James G. Blaine, the "man from Maine," as their leader. There were also many Independents, most of whom preferred Blaine to Conkling, but had little

enthusiasm for either. It was obvious that the day could be saved only by a compromise, which the National Convention after many ballots produced. For President the Republicans chose a "dark horse," James A. Garfield of Ohio, a Blaine man who was satisfactory to the reformers, and for Vice-President, Chester Alan Arthur of New York, Conkling's trusted friend and subordinate.

Democratic Dissensions.   The Democrats, quite as badly divided as the Republicans, were less successful in achieving a united front. The northern and southern wings of the party were still extremely suspicious of each other. Moreover, internal strife existed in both sections. Northern Democrats who had been loyal to the Union during the war had not yet forgiven the "Copperheads," whose desire for peace had almost led them to support the South. Southern Democrats whose devotion to the party stemmed from the leadership of Andrew Jackson had little use for the ex-Whigs and conservative "Bourbons," who now, under the necessity of maintaining white supremacy, called themselves Democrats and sought to monopolize party leadership. So long out of power as to have lost its personality, bereft of intelligent leaders, tainted with treason and with pacifism, the Democratic Party floundered helplessly throughout the campaign. Tilden was too old and too ill to be a candidate, and the nomination went, almost by default, to General Winfield S. Hancock of Pennsylvania, who had won distinction as a Union officer at Gettysburg, and had later pleased the South by the way he conducted himself as military commander of Louisiana during Reconstruction. In politics, however, Hancock was out of his element. As one wag expressed it, he was "a good man, weighing two hundred and fifty pounds." For Vice-President the Democrats chose William H. English of Indiana, a political anachronism who did little to strengthen the party ticket.

Lack of Party Issues. As a matter of fact, the issues that divided the two parties were mainly historical. The Republican Party had come into existence because of the stand it had taken on slavery, and it had survived because of its determination to free the slaves, to save the Union, and to punish the South. Its program was now finished and its excuse for existence had disappeared. The Democrats, for their part, had so long centered their attention upon the issues of slavery, the Civil War, and reconstruction that they failed to observe that the era in which these issues meant anything had rolled by. The platforms of the two parties in 1880 revealed few actual differences on policy and no real awareness of the problems that confronted the nation. The Republican Party existed to oppose the Democratic Party; the Democratic Party existed to oppose the Republican Party. Real issues cut across both parties, and even when recognized, which was rare, tended to be evaded or ignored.

Campaign of 1880. With issues lacking, the campaign centered on the personalities of the candidates. The Republicans, in rejecting the candidacy of General Grant, had freed themselves of the charge of "Bonapartism." Their nominee had been a Union officer in the Civil War, but, like Hayes, he had been a volunteer officer and had won distinction in politics rather than in the army. The Democrats, on the other hand, in their effort to shake off the charge of treason, had nominated a professional soldier. The Democratic platform, written by the Kentucky journalist, Colonel Henry Watterson, called for "a tariff for revenue only." When the Republicans showed a disposition to press this issue, Hancock declared that it was unimportant because the tariff was a "local affair." For this statement he was roundly ridiculed, but he spoke far more truly than he probably knew. Tariff rates are legally levied by Congress, but they have generally been fixed, item by item, because of some local demand.

Election Results. Fought with fury, and as if the result would really be important, the campaign settled nothing much except that Garfield, not Hancock, was to be the next President of the United States. The Republican plurality, out of a total vote amounting to over 9 million, was about 9,000. Neither of the two leading candidates had a majority of all the votes cast, for James B. Weaver of Iowa, the Greenback candidate, polled over 300,000 votes. The Republicans, however, won enough local victories to enable them to recapture the Senate, and to organize the House also. For the first time in six years the Presidency and both houses of Congress were under the control of a single party.

Death of Garfield. But as events proved, the Republicans failed signally to capitalize upon their victory. Their first misfortune was the death of the young and probably able President they had elected. Garfield (1831–1881), like Lincoln, was a product of the American frontier, but he had lived a generation later than Lincoln and had enjoyed advantages, particularly in education, that Lincoln never knew. A volunteer officer in the early years of the Civil War, after 1863 he represented an Ohio district in the lower house of Congress. Here he proved to be a finished debater, a tireless committeeman, and a dependable party regular. His chance at the Presidency came prematurely and unexpectedly, but he had long been marked for preferment. Four months after his inauguration, he was shot by a disappointed office seeker. For weeks he lingered between life and death, but finally on September 19, 1881, he died.

Garfield's death elevated to the Presidency Chester Alan Arthur (1830–1886), a New York politician whose record made him the despair of the reformers. Early in life Arthur became an organization Republican, and his code of ethics, while calling for the strictest personal honesty, tolerated freely the time-honored custom of reward-

THE ASSASSINATION OF PRESIDENT GARFIELD, FROM *HARPER'S WEEKLY*, JULY 3, 1881.

ing the faithful with the spoils of office. As collector of the port of New York he had, as a matter of course, overstaffed his force with party workers, and he never hesitated to call upon his men to do their full political duty during campaigns and on election days. As President, however, he was scrupulously on · guard against criticism. He bore himself with becoming dignity, refused to indulge in a wholesale proscription of Garfield's appointees, and supported civil service reform, and even tariff revision, with wholly unexpected zeal.

Despite the President's best efforts, Congress showed little disposition to inaugurate any disturbing innovations until after the election of 1882. When in that year the electorate returned a decisive Democratic majority to the House of Representatives, the Republican leadership in Congress quickly reacted to this rebuff from the voters. It introduced legislation dealing with both civil service reform and the tariff during the "lame-duck" session that began the month after the election and lasted until the fourth of March following — a

"death-bed repentance," according to the critical Democrats.

Civil Service Reform. On civil service reform the Republicans were obliged to accept the assistance of the Democrats. In fact, it was George H. Pendleton, Democratic senator from Ohio, who introduced and gave his name to the reform measure which an overwhelming bipartisan majority enacted into law in January, 1883. The Pendleton Act authorized the President to appoint three civil service commissioners, not more than two of whom were to belong to the same political party, whose duty it was to provide "open competitive examinations for testing the fitness of applicants" for such public offices as might be "classified." Only the lowest offices were at first classified, but the law provided that the President might extend the classified lists at will to include other executive appointees. President Arthur administered the law in complete good faith. He appointed as the first chairman of the commission Dorman B. Eaton, who as secretary of the Civil

Service Reform Association had been an ardent advocate of reform. During the first year of its existence the commission was given jurisdiction over about 14,000 offices out of a total of 110,000, or about 12.5 per cent.

Changes of national administration from Arthur's time on worked to the advantage of the civil service idea. It happened that Arthur was succeeded by a Democrat, Cleveland; then Cleveland was succeeded by a Republican, Harrison; Harrison in turn was succeeded by a Democrat, Cleveland; and Cleveland, by a Republican, McKinley. Each President, as he was about to retire from office, tended to protect his own appointees by extending the classified lists. Men thus "blanketed" into the civil service were not required to take examinations, but when they died or resigned, their successors received appointments only on recommendation of the commission. By 1893 the number of civil servants under the merit system had reached 45,000; by the

THE "PLUMED KNIGHT"

A Thomas Nast cartoon of November, 1884. The first volume of Blaine's Twenty Years in Congress *appeared during the election year.*

turn of the century it was about 100,000; by the time of the First World War nearly 500,000 — over 60 per cent of federal employees.

Tariff of 1883. Tariff reform was as long overdue as civil service reform, but in practice it proved to be much harder to accomplish. The slight reductions in the Civil War rates obtained in 1872 were practically wiped out in 1875 on the pretext of hard times, and the duties on a few items, such as molasses and sugar, were actually increased. To the reform demands long voiced by David A. Wells, the nation's outstanding expert on the subject, were now added the arguments of such economists as William Graham Sumner of Yale, and Frank W. Taussig of Harvard; also, the public increasingly demanded lower rates. Finally, on the recommendation of President Arthur, Congress created in 1882 a nonpolitical tariff commission which reported back that the existing duties should be cut by as much as 20 per cent. Acting this time without any considerable Democratic collaboration, the Republicans were able to hurry into law before the adjournment of Congress in March, 1883, what one writer has aptly called the "Mongrel Tariff." Partly because of the necessity for haste, partly because of the effective work of the lobbyists, and partly because of the log-rolling tendencies of congressmen themselves, the measure fell far short of the purpose for which it was intended.

The passage of the "Mongrel Tariff" had important political results. Since the Republicans were obliged to defend their handiwork, their party inescapably came to be identified more and more with the policy of protection, while the Democrats, who were inclined to oppose whatever they could in the Republican program, drifted gradually into the advocacy of an out-and-out low-tariff policy. When the Democrats in 1883 took control of the House of Representatives, they ignored the claims of

Samuel J. Randall, a Pennsylvania protectionist who before 1881 had three times been elected Speaker, in favor of a dependable low-tariff advocate, John G. Carlisle of Kentucky.

Election of 1884. The campaign and election of 1884 turned less on the tariff, however, than on the personalities of the two outstanding individuals who contested for the Presidency. The Republicans overlooked the claims of Arthur, who had offended the regulars by vetoing in 1882 an $18 million rivers and harbors ("pork-barrel") bill, and had never been able to live down his past to the complete satisfaction of the reformers. Instead, they nominated their outstanding leader, James G. Blaine (1830–1893), whom Garfield had made Secretary of State, but whose resignation from that office Arthur had not hesitated to accept. Blaine was born in Pennsylvania, but had entered politics in Maine. His background, unlike that of most politicians, was journalism rather than the law. When war broke out in 1861, he did not join the army, but in 1863 entered the House of Representatives and remained there until 1876, when he went to the Senate. A firm believer in the righteousness of Radical Reconstruction, he appealed strongly to a party-loving age. Both on and off the platform he possessed great personal charm, a quality which he used, no less than Henry Clay, to excite the worshipful support of his followers. Both in 1876 and in 1880 far more sentiment had existed for Blaine than for the men the Republicans had nominated, but Blaine's record had offended the reformers, and lesser lights had won the prize. Even now the "Mulligan letters," which revealed that Blaine as a congressman had helped obtain a land grant for an Arkansas railroad from which he hoped to make a financial profit, were flaunted as good reason to keep Blaine in retirement, but the "Blaine or bust" crowd was not to be denied.

Grover Cleveland. The Democrats, as in 1876, nominated a reform governor of New York. Grover Cleveland (1837–1908), who was born in New Jersey, had early moved to New York. After a hard struggle with poverty he had become a practicing lawyer in Buffalo by 1859. During the Civil War, when other young men were joining the army, he borrowed money to hire a substitute because his still meager earnings were needed to support his mother and sisters. In 1863 he received a welcome appointment as assistant district attorney, and in 1870 he became sheriff of Erie County. He revealed qualities of scrupulous honesty and unflinching courage that soon made him a marked man. In 1881, nominated and elected mayor of Buffalo to placate the "better element," he reorganized the city administration, purged it of venal politicians, vetoed dubious measures, and in general endeared himself to reformers. The fame of the "veto mayor" spread, and when in 1882 the New York Democrats needed a candidate for governor with an unimpeachable record, they turned to Cleveland and elected him by a majority of nearly 200,000 votes. As governor, he struggled irritably against a bewildering accumulation of governmental inefficiency or worse, made some progress and many enemies, particularly among the Tammany leaders of New York City.

Election of Cleveland. The nomination of Cleveland guaranteed that a large number of Republican reformers, now called "Mugwumps," would swing their support to the Democratic ticket. Ordinarily this would have insured his election by a fairly wide margin, but flaws were uncovered in his private life which in some minds offset the irreproachable conduct of his public responsibilities. The campaign reached an all-time low in mud-slinging, but the sober second thought of most Americans seemed to coincide with that of a philosophical Mugwump who held that "we should elect Mr. Cleveland to the public office he is so

GROVER CLEVELAND

The first non-veteran to achieve election to the Presidency after the Civil War, Grover Cleveland's record of integrity as mayor of Buffalo and governor of New York paved the way for his nomination and election in 1884.

eminently qualified to fill and remand Mr. Blaine to the private life which he is so eminently fitted to adorn." Cleveland's plurality over Blaine in the country as a whole was only 23,000 and the electoral vote stood 219 to 182. Cleveland carried the solid South, Delaware, Indiana, Connecticut, New Jersey, and New York. The Democrats won control of the House of Representatives by a comfortable margin, but the Republicans retained their majority in the Senate. Benjamin F. Butler, the Greenback candidate, received a total of 175,370 popular votes, and John P. St. John of Kansas, Prohibitionist, 150,369.

Cleveland's effort to inaugurate reforms met many obstacles. He did what he could to protect the Civil Service Commission all he could, and even extended the classified lists, but in order to avoid an outright revolt within his party he was obliged to

yield many non-classified offices to the spoilsmen. He had trouble with the veterans of the Civil War, now organized into a powerful society known as the Grand Army of the Republic, because he opposed their demands for more and larger pensions. Already the Arrears of Pensions Act of 1879 had permitted pensioners, whatever their service disability, to recover back payments for the period between the time of mustering out and the time a given pension was granted. The abuse of this privilege angered the President, but he could do little about it; on the other hand, he could and did veto a "pauper" pension bill that would have given a pension to all who stood in need of it, regardless of disability. He also vetoed hundreds of the private pension bills introduced by lenient congressmen for the benefit of constituents who had seen service, but according to the general law were not entitled to pensions. The President's attitude toward pensions, together with his willingness to restore to the states from which they had come all captured Confederate battle flags, won him the undying hatred of the Union veterans' organization.

Cleveland and the Tariff. Cleveland's chief bid for reform came when he forced both parties to take their stand on the tariff issue. In his annual message of December, 1887, he dealt exclusively with the tariff, presented a well-reasoned, hard-hitting argument against the existing high rates, and, pointing to the annual surplus of about $100 million brought in each year by the Tariff of 1883, declared: "It is a *condition* which confronts us, not a theory." Thus briefed by the President, the Democratic majority in the House of Representatives, with only four dissenting votes, accepted the low-tariff bill presented by Representative Roger Q. Mills of Texas. In response to this Democratic challenge, the Senate Committee on Finance, under the leadership of Republican Senator Allison, presented a sample of what the

Republicans would be glad to do if only they could win control of the government in the election of 1888. As passed by the Republican majority in the Senate, the Allison bill proposed to maintain a generally high level of duties, but it insured a smaller total revenue by resort to prohibitive duties, by the lowering of excises, and by a cut in the duty on sugar. As anticipated, the House would not accept the Senate bill, and the Senate would not accept the House bill. But as Cleveland had foreseen, both parties had been committed to positions that they could not possibly abandon in the coming presidential campaign.

Election of 1888. As was now inevitable, the Democrats renominated Cleveland in 1888, and made tariff reform their principal issue. The Republicans, having lost with Blaine in 1884, turned to one of their lesser figures, Benjamin Harrison of Indiana. The campaign was a revelation to the Republicans, for they learned for the first time how advantageous an issue the tariff could be. Business campaign contributions as insurance against Democratic tariff reductions poured into the Republican coffers in a flood. Republican orators and publicists made much of the necessity of maintaining the high wages of American labor, something that could not be done, they insisted, if the products of low-paid European labor were admitted freely to American markets. When it came to "getting out the vote," party workers, particularly in the doubtful states, scrupled at nothing. The scandals of the election were so open and notorious as to give great impetus to the movement for the "Australian" system of secret voting, which down to this time had made little headway in the United States. Even so, Harrison won the election only because of the electoral college system. In the popular vote Cleveland led by more than 100,000, but Harrison carried the crucial states of New York and Indiana, and so amassed 233 electoral votes to Cleveland's 168.

Benjamin Harrison. Benjamin Harrison (1833–1901) was designed to be, and as President became, "a dignified figurehead." He was at the time of his nomination a successful lawyer of great party regularity who had served one term in the United States Senate. He was in no sense the leader of his party, and James G. Blaine, whom he made his Secretary of State, completely overshadowed him. Harrison was a good platform orator, but cold in his personal relationships. He was as honest as Cleveland, but lacked the latter's forceful nature. During Cleveland's administration the Democratic party leaders, one by one, acknowledged the President's supremacy, whereas Harrison, from the beginning of his administration to its end, had far less to do with charting his party's course than many others of lesser rank.

Harrison's record on civil service reform and pensions was by no means as courageous as Cleveland's. Like President Grant, he allotted many minor offices to his indigent friends and relatives. In making other appointments he solicited and generally accepted the advice of the politicians. His chief contribution to civil service reform was his appointment of Theodore Roosevelt to membership on the Civil Service Commission. In this office, Roosevelt made it his business to see that appointments were made for merit, not as a reward for party service. In consequence he soon fell afoul of the President, whom he came to dislike, and of many of the President's friends, but Harrison was nonetheless obliged to retain the obstreperous commissioner in office, and when in 1893 Cleveland became President again he too retained Roosevelt. The Grand Army of the Republic got exactly what it wanted in a Dependents' Pension Act, which provided that all veterans of the Civil War who had served for as long as ninety days, and who suffered from any disabling mental or physical affliction, should receive pensions of from $6 to $12 a month, according to the degree of their disability.

Widows of veterans and minor children might receive lesser sums. As a result of this law the amount of money appropriated for pensions rose from $89 million in 1889 to $159 million in 1893.

The Republican Program. The main purpose of the Fifty-first Congress was to pass a high protective-tariff law, but to accomplish this strictly partisan end, political strategy of a high order was required. The Republicans had a majority in each house of Congress, but in the House of Representatives the majority was too small for comfort. To expedite the business, the Republican Speaker, Thomas B. Reed of Maine, disregarded traditional practices with impunity. Members present, but not voting, were counted to make a quorum, and a powerful Committee on Rules, of which "Czar" Reed himself was chairman, brought in from time to time whatever special rules were needed to push the Republican program along. To bolster the Republican majority, especially in the Senate, the territories of Wyoming and Idaho were added to the four — North and South Dakota, Montana, and Washington — that the preceding Congress had authorized to take steps toward statehood. Since the voters of this region were predominantly Republican, the control of the Republican Party in Congress was definitely strengthened by their admission. Finally, as a sop to the silver Republicans of the West, who refused to vote for a high tariff until something was done for silver, the Sherman Silver Purchase Act of 1890 was passed. This measure required the Treasury to buy 4.5 million ounces of silver a month at the prevailing market price, the estimated output of all the silver mines in the United States. Not all the silver need be coined, but it was to be paid for in Treasury notes redeemable "in gold or silver coin," and so provided for a substantial addition to the amount of money actually in circulation. An attempt to repeal the Compromise of 1877 by the enactment of a Federal Elections, or "Force Bill," which would again give the national government control of elections in the South, as during Reconstruction, failed; otherwise, the Republicans might have forged a weapon by means of which they could have controlled the national government for many years to come.

The McKinley Tariff. The McKinley Tariff Act, which became law on October 1, 1890, was the Republican answer to the prayers, and the contributions, of the American protectionists. It provided higher duties on manufactured products than the American people had ever known before, including some that were prohibitive, others levied on articles not yet manufactured in the United States, and still others on agricultural items of which the nation produced an abundance and did not import. The reduction of the revenue deemed imperative by both Democrats and Republicans was accomplished in part by the discouraging effect of the high duties on importation, but in larger part by placing raw sugar on the free list. This was in effect an aid to the manufacturers of refined sugar, whose product was still protected though they could now buy raw sugar for less; but it was very disturbing to the sugar producers of Louisiana until the idea of a bounty of two cents per pound on all raw sugar of American origin was included. Thus the sugar schedule, figuratively speaking, succeeded in taking money out of the Treasury with both hands. To please Secretary of State Blaine, a reciprocity clause was included in the McKinley Tariff, although its provisions were much more restricted than Blaine had hoped. The President was authorized to enforce a specified schedule of tariff rates on items listed as free in case the nations that produced them failed to grant equivalent advantages to American exports.

Public reaction to the behavior of the Fifty-first Congress was far from cordial.

The effect of the McKinley Bill on the revenue was disastrous, and to it was added the orgy of spending which Congress permitted itself. The extravagance of its appropriations led the newspapers to describe it as the "billion-dollar Congress," a description strikingly lacking in political appeal. Unfortunate as a Treasury surplus might have been, a deficit, which was even less desirable, appeared to be in sight. Consumers found to their dismay that the higher rates of the McKinley Tariff meant higher prices for what they had to buy. The Force Bill, based as it was upon an attempt to revive sectional antagonisms, was unpopular, North as well as South.

Elections of 1890. Held only a few weeks after the passage of the McKinley Tariff, the congressional elections of 1890 showed how unpopular that measure, and the Congress that passed it, had become. Democratic campaigners did not fail to take full advantage of the opportunity to denounce "Bill McKinley and the McKinley Bill." Merchants and salesmen apologized for high prices on the ground that the new tariff law had made them necessary. By placing tea, coffee, and sugar on the free list, the Republicans had hoped to make much capital of the "free breakfast table," but the fact that the sugar duties were retained for six months after the passage of the bill made this battle cry seem decidedly premature. When the votes were counted, the Republicans discovered that they had received the most emphatic rebuke in the history of their party. In the Senate the Republican majority was narrowed to eight, and would have been wiped out altogether but for the hold-over senators from the newly admitted states. In the House the Democrats had 235 seats, and the Republicans 88, while nine Farmers' Alliance men, or Populists, refused to vote with either of the older parties. The appearance of this group of independents in Congress marked the beginning of an agrarian revolt in the Middle West and the South which, with the assistance it received from the silver mining states of the Far West, created new issues and threatened for a time to bring about a complete realignment of political parties in the United States.

SELECTED BIBLIOGRAPHY

Ray Ginger, *The Age of Excess* (1965), surveys the period 1877–1914; he has also edited a companion volume of source materials, *The Nationalizing of American Life* (1965). A colorful, irreverent survey of this period's politics is Matthew Josephson, *The Politicos, 1865–1896* (1938). James Bryce, *The American Commonwealth* (2 vols., 1888), a classic by a distinguished English observer, examines state and local as well as national affairs; for this period, the first edition should be read. An important newly published source is *Hayes: The Diary of a President, 1875–1881*, edited by T. H. Williams (1964).

Biographical studies of political leaders provide valuable insights, as the era was one of intensely personal politics. In addition to those cited previously, the following are of particular importance: A. C. Flick, *Samuel Jones Tilden* (1939); H. J. Eckenrode, *Rutherford B. Hayes* (1930); Harry Barnard, *Rutherford B. Hayes and His America* (1954); R. G. Caldwell, *James A. Garfield* (1931); G. F. Howe, *Chester A. Arthur* (1935); L. B. Richardson, *William E. Chandler* (1940); and D. S. Muzzey, *James G. Blaine* (1934). Allan Nevins, *Grover Cleveland* (1932), is lengthy and highly friendly; H. S. Merrill, *Bourbon Leader; Grover Cleveland and the Democratic Party* (1957), is brief and more critical. H. J. Sievers, *Benjamin Harrison* (2 vols., 1952–1959), gets down to 1880; a third volume, on the presidency, is promised. Other biographies of interest include; J. R. Lambert, Jr., *Arthur Pue Gorman* (1953); W. A. Robinson, *Thomas B. Reed* (1930); E. B. Thompson, *Matthew Hale Carpenter* (1954); Edward Younger, *John A. Kasson* (1955); O. D. Lambert, *Stephen Benton*

* Available in paperback

Elkins (1955); L. L. Sage, *William Boyd Allison* (1956); D. G. Fowler, *John Coit Spooner* (1961); and David Lindsey, *"Sunset" Cox* (1959). Other interesting new biographies are *"I Am a Democrat,"* a study of David B. Hill by H. J. Bass (1961); and J. W. Nielson, *Shelby M. Cullom* (1962).

Special studies centering on the politics of this period are becoming more numerous. A detailed treatment of a little-known political event is H. J. Clancy, *The Presidential Election of 1880* (1958). Careful works on one major theme are S. P. Hirshon, *Farewell to the Bloody Shirt: Northern Republicans and the Southern Negro, 1877–1893* (1962); and V. P. DeSantis, *Republicans Face the Southern Question: The New Departure Years, 1877–1897* (1959). These recent studies should be compared with Paul Buck, *°The Road to Reunion, 1865–1900* (1937), which traces the process of reconciliation between the white people of the North and South. Studies of southern state politics include A. D. Kirwan, *°Revolt of the Rednecks* (1951), treating Mississippi; and O. H. Shadgett, *The Republican Party in Georgia: From Reconstruction through 1900* (1964).

While the thorny questions of money and tariff are discussed in a number of the works above, see also the following studies: Paul Studenski and H. E. Krooss, *Financial History of the United States* (1952); and Milton Friedman and A. J. Schwartz, *A Monetary History of the United States, 1867–1960* (1963). An important recent general survey is P. P. Van Riper, *History of the United States Civil Service* (1958). A new study of municipal corruption is Seymour Mandelbaum, *Boss Tweed's New York* (1965). The background of the Pendleton Act is fully treated by Ari Hoogenboom, *Outlawing the Spoils* (1962). See also A. B. Sageser, *The First Two Decades of the Pendleton Act* (1935). W. E. Davies, *Patriotism on Parade* (1955), treats the G.A.R. and other patriotic organizations. Useful monographs on veterans and their problems include J. W. Oliver, *History of the Civil War Military Pensions* (1917); and F. H. Heck, *The Civil War Veteran in Minnesota Life and Politics* (1941). Diplomacy under Hayes is dealt with in the biography of his Secretary of State, *William M. Evarts* by C. L. Barrows (1941). Foreign relations in the Garfield-Arthur administration is the subject of D. M. Pletcher, *The Awkward Years* (1962). See also the broad survey of American diplomatic history from 1860 to 1900 by F. R. Dulles, *Prelude to World Power* (1965).

22

THE LAST FRONTIER

The Far West. The exciting events of the Civil War and Reconstruction, followed by the postwar political wrangling, tended to obscure the importance of what was happening on the western frontier. Americans were accustomed to an advancing frontier — there had always been one; but this last western frontier differed markedly from all the rest. It was a frontier of miners and cattlemen, as well as of farmers. It was a strange and inhospitable frontier where the climate ran to extremes in both winter and summer, where the rains were often uncertain, where the conventional materials for fuel and building were extremely scarce, and where distances between habitable places were immeasurably greater than those east of the Mississippi. Moreover, it was all that was left of the area within the continental boundaries for civilization to conquer. The end of the frontier process, which from the beginning had been a kind of common denominator of American history, was in sight.

California Prospectors. Within a few years after the "forty-niners" had invaded California, they and their successors had exhausted practically all of the free gold that the region had to offer. California mining then became a capitalistic enterprise; expensive machinery was required to do the work that formerly anyone with a shovel and a "washpan" had done. As this situation unfolded, some of the adventurers turned to agriculture, others went back to the "States," and still others became "prospectors," men who searched the mountains for signs of gold, and sometimes made a "strike." Not content with having prospected every bleak plateau and hidden valley of the Rocky Mountains, they found their way to such distant regions as South Africa and Australia, and there, too, they discovered gold. Only rarely did one of them acquire wealth, but thanks to their efforts the world's supply of gold was soon doubled.

Colorado. The Pike's Peak gold rush, which occurred just a decade after the rush to California, laid the basis for the state of Colorado. Compared to the forty-niners, the fifty-niners had an easy time of it. The distance from the East to the new gold fields was less than half of that to California. There were no mountains to cross, and the trail to Colorado was well supplied with ferries, merchants, and even stagecoaches. Denver arrived full-grown almost overnight, and within a matter of weeks other mining camps in the "hills," such as Central City and Idaho Springs, achieved sizable proportions. But far sooner than in California the free gold of Colorado gave out, and for a time it seemed that no permanent settlement might result. Some miners stayed on, as in California, to farm; as early as the summer of 1859 radishes, lettuce, onions, and peas brought high prices on the Denver market. Native grasses were cut for hay; claims were staked out and claims clubs formed; irrigation, after the manner of the Mormons in Utah, was introduced. Soon industrial mining replaced the crude efforts of the first comers, and such "valley" towns as Golden, Colorado City, and Pueblo showed signs of permanence. Efforts to follow the example of California in making a new state without going through the customary territorial stage came to nought, although an unauthorized "Territory of Jefferson" existed for a few months. In 1861 Congress made Colorado a territory, and a few years later, in order to obtain more Union senators and representatives in Washington, would have admitted it as a state. This offer, however, was wisely declined, for as late as 1870 the population of Colorado was only 40,000. Admission as the "Centennial State" came finally in 1876. Shortly afterward the exploitation of silver mines around Leadville inaugurated a new and unprecedented era of prosperity.

Nevada. While the rest of the country resounded with the din of Civil War, the mineral empire of the West expanded rapidly. Close on the heels of the Pike's Peak gold rush came a similar rush to the western part of what is now Nevada, where gold had been discovered along the main trail to California. The Comstock Lode, discovered in the spring of 1859, brought in no less than $15 million worth of gold and silver in a single year. Such towns as Carson City and Virginia City flaunted

their wealth in the face of a desert where water was almost as dear as the other liquids miners so liberally consumed. In 1861 Congress made Nevada a territory, and three years later, Nevada accepted the same hasty offer of statehood that Colorado rejected. Unlike most of the mining regions, few areas of Nevada were suitable for agriculture, and the prosperity of the new state was limited to the exploitation of its mineral resources.

Mining Booms in the Northwest. After the opening of Nevada, mining booms came thick and fast. In the vicinity of Lewiston, Idaho, then a part of Washington Territory, gold was found in 1860, and next year the inevitable boom occurred. As new strikes were reported, the miners rushed from place to place founding, as they went, such permanent settlements as Florence and Boise City, but when their claims "played out," they often left as suddenly as they had come. In 1863 the Territory of Idaho was created. By that time also the miners already had crossed the Bitter Root Mountains to lay the foundations of Montana. Such mining centers as Bannack City, Virginia City, Deer Lodge, and Missoula not only drew population away from the farther western camps, but also attracted newcomers from the East, many of whom came up the Missouri River to Fort Benton, which in high water could be reached by steamboats. Among these new arrivals were a number of refugees from the guerrilla warfare that raged along the Kansas-Missouri border during the Civil War, and others who preferred the hazards of the mines to the prospect of being drafted into the army. In 1864 Montana was cut off from Idaho and became a separate territory.

The Far Southwest. During this same period the Far Southwest also had its mining booms. The mineral resources of New Mexico, twin territory with Utah, had long been known, but the Spanish-Mexican

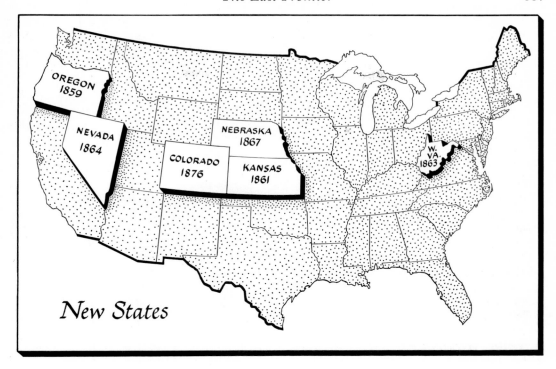

New States

population, located mainly in the upper Rio Grande Valley, subsisted upon agriculture and ignored the mines. The Americans, however, reopened the ancient Indian and Spanish diggings near Tucson and Tubac, and found placer gold in considerable quantities in the valley of the lower Colorado. When in 1862 Colonel James H. Carleton attempted to lead a column of 1,800 California volunteers to the aid of the Union forces in New Mexico, he was plagued by desertions to what he described as "one of the richest gold countries in the world." Thus another mining boom got under way, and in 1863 Congress, following a now established pattern, created the Territory of Arizona out of the western half of New Mexico.

The prosperity of these new mountain territories varied markedly in the years that followed the war. As long as the Comstock Lode continued to yield its riches, Nevada fared best, but by 1880 this

magnificent deposit had been worked out, and the desert cities faded as rapidly as they had bloomed. Stocks in Nevada mines valued at $393 million in 1875 could be bought five years later for $7 million. The economy of Colorado fluctuated according to the availability of mining capital and the intelligence with which it was utilized. In Idaho and Montana the fortune hunters of 1866 numbered probably 30,000 and 40,000 respectively, but the census of 1870 found that only half that many remained. A dozen years later, the opening of rich copper mines near Butte, Montana, ushered in an era of unprecedented prosperity for that region which the exploitation of other base metals, such as lead and zinc, handsomely reinforced. Ultimately the world's largest copper smelters were to be located at Anaconda, Montana. In the Southwest the exhaustion of placer gold brought the Civil War boom to a quick conclusion, and, in the years that followed, the savage

CHEYENNE, WYOMING

A leading rail center, Cheyenne was perhaps the capital of the ranching west.

depredations of the Apaches tended to discourage even the boldest prospectors. Here, as in Montana, copper presently became a more important product than gold. Eventually, however, the prosperity of any territory could be measured by the number of its inhabitants who forsook the mines for the farms or ranches.

The Mining Towns. Social conditions on the mining frontier differed little from place to place. Most mining towns consisted of a single long crooked street that followed, and occasionally crossed, a mountain stream. Most of the houses were hastily improvised, one-room, one-story wooden shacks. Invariably the most pretentious buildings were occupied by saloons and gambling houses. Drunkenness and debauchery were too common to attract much notice, and for a long time individual vengeance provided almost the only punishment that was meted out for crime. Medical help for the sick and injured was of the crudest sort, or, more likely, was altogether missing, and the death rate was high. The romance of the mines, so dear to the heart of the novelist or scenario writer, was built on the slenderest possible basis of fact.

The Mormons. In vivid contrast to the crude mining towns was Utah, the home of the Mormons, as members of the Church of Jesus Christ of Latter Day Saints were generally called. Here the astute Mormon leader, Brigham Young, had foregone the quest of gold and silver in order to develop a planned society based on agriculture. The key to Mormon prosperity was irrigation, which the centralized character of the Mormon establishment enabled Young to introduce with a minimum of difficulty. Determined that the new Zion should grow, he sent missionaries all over Europe and the United States, and founded a Perpetual Emigrating Fund Company to supply converts with the money and services they needed for emigration to the promised land. In the early years some of these newcomers actually pushed handcarts the entire length of the Mormon trail, but well before the Civil War, wagon trains from Salt Lake City provided a better means of transportation, while after 1869 the Union Pacific Railroad solved the problem permanently.

The coming of the railroad meant closer trade relations with the outside world and a considerable modification of the self-sufficient economy that Young had promoted. But despite the growing population, which now began to include many non-Mormons, or "Gentiles," the ascendancy of the Mormon church in economic as well as in religious matters long remained in evidence. The Zion's Cooperative Mercantile Institution, for example, which was incorporated in 1869, engaged in almost every type of merchandising and left most of its competitors far behind. By 1870 the population of Utah was well over 86,000, of whom nearly 13,000 lived in Salt Lake City, a well-planned community with wide streets, comfortable houses, and an impressive Tabernacle, all in marked contrast with the average mining town of crooked streets and vice-infested buildings.

The steady growth of Utah once again brought a strain on the relations of the Mormons with the rest of the country. During the fifties a conflict between the aspiring Mormon theocracy and the federal government had led to the so-called Utah War and indirectly to the Mountain Meadows Massacre. Now the point at issue was the Mormon doctrine of "plural marriages." Hardly more than 3 per cent of the Mormon men had more than one wife, but the existence of polygamy within the nation's borders shocked most Americans and led to serious efforts to end it. Congress passed an "anti-bigamy" act as early as 1862, but it did not become effective until supplemented by the Edmunds Act of 1882, which provided new and severe penalties for polygamists, and the even more drastic Edmunds-Tucker Act of 1887. Under this law federal authorities seized the property of the Mormon church and forced it to pay a high rental even for use of the block on which the Salt Lake Temple stood.

Finally in 1890 Wilford Woodruff, fourth president of the church, suspended the practice of plural marriage for the future, while the federal government gave up further efforts to punish persons who had contracted such marriages before November 1, 1890. In due time the church recovered its property, and polygamy began to disappear. With a population passing 210,000 in 1890, Utah was now judged qualified for statehood, and in 1896 entered the Union.

Staging and Freighting. The business of supplying the Far West with the necessities of life and of transporting to the East the product of the mines soon reached formidable proportions. Stagecoaches and freight wagons made their appearance on the western plains during the fifties, and by the time the Civil War ended few places were too remote for them to reach. As early as 1857, the United States government granted a contract to John Butterfield, whose "Overland Mail" carried the mail to California. During 1860–1861 the firm of Russell, Majors, and Waddell, without a government subsidy, relayed light mail by "pony express" from St. Joseph, Missouri, to Sacramento, California, in less than two weeks. The pony express and the company that backed it were put out of business by the completion of a telegraph line to the Pacific in 1861, but stagecoach connections, with the aid of generous mail contracts, continued to multiply so that by 1866 Ben Holladay, who had a monopoly of most of the western routes, could claim a total of 5,000 miles of stage lines. That same year Holladay sold out to Wells, Fargo, and Company.

Travel by western stage was a memorable experience. The stage itself, with its high, heavy wheels, its wide, thick tires, and its sturdy leather thoroughbraces instead of springs, was no western invention, but rather the product of centuries of experience. It was equipped with three inside seats for passengers, an outside front seat for the driver, and a rear container for baggage. It was drawn by two or more teams of horses. Dangers abounded from the charges of angry buffaloes, from attacks by hostile Indians, from robberies in a region that long had known no law. Passage through these hazards from the Mississippi to the Pacific cost about $200, with corresponding charges for shorter distances.

Freighting on the western plains was no less important than staging. Little of this went through to the Pacific coast, for water transportation was faster and cheaper, but the great interior region opened up by the mines was served, for the most part, by slow-moving freight wagons, drawn by ox teams from such Missouri River towns as Independence, Leavenworth, Nebraska City, and Omaha. After the building of the Union Pacific both the freight wagons and the stages took off into the interior from railroad stations nearest the desired destinations, but in any event huge freight charges had to be paid. High prices gave merchants a chance for correspondingly high profits, and laid the basis for many pioneer fortunes, such, for example, as those amassed by the Creighton brothers of Omaha, and William A. Clark of Montana.

Lawlessness. The traffic of the plains, particularly the cargoes of gold that the stagecoaches took out, led inevitably to many robberies. Gangs of "bad men," drawn together to live by their wits, terrorized the stage routes and took a heavy toll, not only in gold but also in lives. Eventually, in many western states, vigilantes, administering lynch law, put the disorderly elements of society out of business. One might note, indeed, four stages of development of any given mining frontier: (1) peaceful exploitation by the original prospectors; (2) the mining "boom," with its full quota of violence and crime; (3) the establishment of vigilance committees to punish the worst criminals and to intro-

duce a reign of law; and (4) the creation of regular legal governments. In many instances, however, the third and fourth stages were reversed. Legal government in Montana, for example, preceded the work of the vigilantes, and local government throughout the territory was in the hands of the "bad men" until the vigilantes broke their power.

The Black Hills. In 1876, the last great mining boom of the West broke forth in the Black Hills region of southwestern Dakota Territory — a wild, barren region, long suspected of harboring gold. Deadwood, the principal city, lay in the heart of a wilderness and depended for the necessities of life upon stagecoaches and freighters from Bismarck to the east and Cheyenne to the south. Bandits and Indians were plentiful, but Wells, Fargo, and Company carried out the gold in steel-lined, heavily guarded coaches that were not lightly attacked. In a single trip, July, 1877, $350,000 in gold was taken out, and before the stage line surrendered its business to the railroad, the grand total of such shipments had reached $60 million. Deadwood, as the chief supply station for the various mining camps nearby, built up a prosperous trade. Here, too, gathered a notable array of gamblers and outlaws, the backwash of all the mining booms; among them, "Wild Bill" Hickok and "Calamity Jane." Deadwood was more sophisticated than most of the early mining towns and boasted, along with its gambling houses and saloons, several theaters, particularly the *Gem,* which produced numerous plays of merit.

Evolution of Law and Order. For all its tumult, life in the mining camps was founded upon a sound substratum of common sense. Lawlessness eventually gave way to the normal institutions of government. Agriculture, even under the most adverse circumstances, was speedily introduced. Rule-of-thumb arrangements — such, for example, as those which enabled the discoverer of a mine to "stake out his claim," or the first farmer who used the waters of a given stream for irrigation purposes to have a "priority right" over all others — presently received the sanction of law. Women came in, and with them schools, churches, and the amenities of life. Frontier characteristics gradually gave way before the advance of civilization: the individualism of the early miners to the cooperative, capitalistic enterprises that were required to carry on their work; the actual democracy of the boom days to the wide inequalities between those who "struck it rich" and those whose poverty endured; the radicalism of a new society to the conservatism of one that approached middle age. And yet, the social inheritance from the mining frontier could hardly be called negligible. Throughout the region first opened by the mines, the tendency to paint an overbright picture still reflects the chronic optimism of the prospector, and the ease with which the speculative spirit is aroused shows the gambling instinct is not yet quite dead.

The Indians. Among the inevitable complications that resulted from the opening of the mining West was the necessity of developing a new Indian policy for the United States. The old policy of leaving the region west of the "bend of the Missouri" for the exclusive use of the Indians had broken down badly in the decade before the Civil War. Thousands of emigrants, crossing the plains to Oregon, to Santa Fe, to Utah, and to California, came into contact and often into conflict with the Indians. Demands for protection of the trails led to the establishment of army posts in the Indian country at such strategic centers as Fort Kearney and Fort Laramie, and to treaties between the United States and most of the Indian tribes, describing the tribal boundaries and authorizing the government to build both roads and posts wherever it wished. While the Indians received annuities as compensation for the losses they sustained from the white intrusion, they found the new agreements far

THE GOLDFIELD STAGE

Stagecoach travel in the Far West involved many perils, among them the narrow trails over which the "stages" so often had to pass.

from satisfactory and frequently ignored their promises not to molest the emigrants. The requirement of new cessions added still further to the unrest, both for the tribes that had to find new homes and for those who had to make room for unwanted newcomers. The combing of the mountains by prospectors for gold gave the Indians a still further cause for alarm. Altogether, the time was ripe for trouble from the Indians when the Civil War broke out.

The Sioux Outbreak in Minnesota. In 1862 came the first uprising. The Sioux of Minnesota, reduced by land cessions to a narrow and indefensible reserve along the Minnesota River, had long suffered from the dishonesty of traders and government agents. When the regular army garrisons were withdrawn, and their places taken by inexperienced volunteers, the Indians were strongly tempted to seek revenge. Nevertheless, the trouble, when it came, was precipitated by the unauthorized action of a few irresponsible braves who on August 18, 1862, murdered five whites near New Ulm, Minnesota. The white population of the vicinity, sure that a general attack was impending, fled for their lives, while the Indians, no less panicky, divided into two groups, one of which made a hasty retreat to the west, while the other under Little Crow, knowing that the whites would never forgive the murders, took to the warpath, burning farmhouses and villages, and killing men, women, and children by the hundreds. In due time the Indians were met by overwhelming numbers of state militia, decisively defeated, and many of them captured. Of the captives some 400 were tried by court-martial in St. Paul, and thirty-eight of these unfortunates paid the full penalty for their crime at a great hanging bee, held at Mankato, Minnesota, the day after Christmas, 1862. In 1863 the remnants of the Sioux were harassed by an expedition into Minnesota and Dakota, and the entire Sioux holding in Minnesota was confiscated.

The Arapaho and Cheyenne. The rigorous punishment meted out to the Minnesota Sioux failed to deter the Plains Indians from following their example. Among the tribes most affected by the coming of the miners were the Arapaho and Cheyenne, who were persuaded in 1861 to make way for the white advance into Colorado by withdrawing into what was generally known as the Sand Creek Reserve, a barren and gameless tract in the southeastern part of the territory. Sullen and resentful, they began by the spring of 1864 to raid the trails along the South Platte and to push down into Nebraska. Promptly Governor John Evans called out the Colorado militia, but before ordering an attack he urged all peaceable Indians to concentrate in certain designated posts where they would be safe from harm. Not until fall, when the best fighting weather was over, did any considerable number of Indians choose to accept the proffered

sanctuaries, but by that time about 500 of them, including Black Kettle, their leading chief, had reported to Fort Lyons on Sand Creek, and were encamped nearby.

Meanwhile, however, Major General Curtis of the United States Army, in command of the West, had telegraphed, "I want no peace till the Indians suffer more," and Major J. M. Chivington, in command of the Colorado militia, was eager to oblige him. Although bands of Indians were still on the warpath, Chivington chose to ignore them and instead made a surprise attack upon the camp at Sand Creek. At the break of day, November 29, 1864, with about 900 men he fell upon the unsuspecting camp and murdered in cold blood about one hundred men, women, and children. Next year the government made a new treaty with the Arapahos and Cheyennes, pushing them farther to the southeast, but the Senate failed to confirm it, and the homeless Indians were sometimes guilty of attacks on settlers and travelers. Expeditions against them in 1867 and 1868 culminated in another massacre, this time on the Washita, near the Texas border, where Colonel George A. Custer with a detachment of regulars duplicated Chivington's unsavory exploit on November 27, 1868. Black Kettle himself was slain, and his people at length accepted lands assigned to them in the Indian Territory.

The Western Sioux, Apaches, and Comanches. The western Sioux, who ranged north of the Platte and east of the mountains, were deeply disturbed, both by the fate of the Arapahos and Cheyennes, and by the advent of mining activities in Montana. When, in 1865, the government decided to open a road along the Bozeman Trail, from Cheyenne northwestward to the mouth of the Rosebud in Montana, the Sioux determined to resist this invasion of their finest hunting grounds. That year General P. E. Connor, in command of 1,600 men and guided by Jim Bridger, the noted plainsman, marched over part of the route, but was turned back by the Sioux; and in 1866 a second expedition under Colonel H. B. Carrington succeeded only with the greatest difficulty in building Fort Phil Kearny and Fort C. F. Smith to the east of the Big Horn Mountains. Red Cloud, the Indian leader, and his Sioux warriors risked no open fighting, but they continually harassed wood trains sent out from the forts, and otherwise hampered the operations. When finally, two years later, the government made peace with Red Cloud and his warriors, it was on condition that the "country north of the North Platte River and east of the summits of the Big Horn Mountains shall be held and considered to be unceded Indian Territory," and that the forts on the Bozeman Trail should be abandoned. This was one of the few instances in American history in which an Indian treaty registered a white retreat.

To the Southwest two relatively civilized tribes, the Pueblos and the Navajos, inhabited New Mexico and Arizona. They were peaceful farmers and shepherds, but were ready to defend their ancestral lands against white encroachment. The Apaches and Comanches were of a different temper. The Apaches, ranging far throughout eastern Arizona, western Texas, and into Mexico, were famous horsemen and doughty warriors. Their depredations against ranchers, miners, and immigrants reached a climax during the Civil War, but continued intermittently for many years thereafter. North and east of the Apaches were the more numerous Comanches and Kiowas, also expert horsemen, who were a constant menace to whites adventuring on the western plains.

The New Indian Policy. Meanwhile the government had taken steps toward the formation of a new Indian policy. A congressional Committee on the Condition of the Indian Tribes, created in 1865, visited

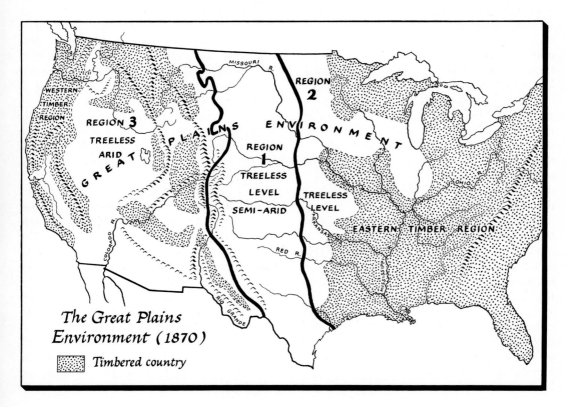

The Great Plains Environment (1870)

Timbered country

the West and discovered how utterly untenable the status of the Indians had become. Its illuminating *Report on the Condition of the Indian Tribes,* made in 1867, led to the creation of an Indian Peace Commission, composed of three generals and four civilians, whose duty it was not only to stop the Indian wars, but also to work out a permanent solution of the Indian problem. The commission held two great meetings, at which treaties were concluded that definitely foreshadowed the reservation system. Confiscation of the western half of the holdings of the Five Civilized Tribes in the Indian Territory, on the ground that the tribes had sided with the Confederacy during the Civil War, made possible the resettlement in that region of the Arapaho, Cheyenne, and other tribes. In the North the Sioux were left in possession of southwestern Dakota, while such minor tribes as the Utes, Shoshonis, and Bannocks were concentrated within appropriate narrow limits. Subsidies in the form of annuities, payments for lands, and outright doles helped the dispossessed Indians to eke out a precarious existence, and unconsciously introduced pauperization as a means of insuring docility.

A new Board of Indian Commissioners, composed of civilians, was created in 1869 to consult with the Bureau of Indian Affairs, which, since 1849, had been a part of the Department of the Interior. Believing that the Indians could eventually be made over into peaceful and contented farmers, the civilian commissioners tried to break down tribal autonomy, and in 1871 induced Congress to abolish the legal fiction of dealing with the tribes by treaty as if they were foreign nations. This was a definite improvement, but the road to integrating the Indian was long and hard.

Later Indian Uprisings. By this time most of the Indian fighting was at an end, although occasional outbreaks occurred as late as 1890. The worst of these was precipitated by the Black Hills gold rush, which brought thousands of whites into the heart of the prime hunting lands reserved for the Sioux. Even before the rush started, military maneuvers had alarmed the Sioux, and many of them had left the reservation. Led by two able braves, Sitting Bull and Crazy Horse, the fugitives ignored all orders to return and fought furiously the troops who were sent to herd them in. During this campaign Colonel Custer and his command of over 200 cavalrymen met the same fate that Custer had meted out to the Indians on the Washita eight years before. Lured into an ambush, Custer and his entire command lost their lives. The campaign, however, could have but one end, and within a short time General Nelson A. Miles had restored order. Crazy Horse was captured, and Sitting Bull fled to Canada. In 1877, a somewhat similar uprising among the Nez Percés of Idaho came to the same inexorable end. Down in New Mexico the Apaches repeatedly gave trouble, and the campaigns against them amounted almost to wars of extermination. Not until 1885, when Geronimo, their principal chief, was captured and exiled to Florida, was a lasting peace established. Trouble broke out again about 1889 with the Sioux in Dakota. A religious frenzy, based upon hope for an Indian Messiah, led to demonstrations by Indian "ghost dancers" that frightened the Indian agents and brought on the needless battle of Wounded Knee (December 29, 1890).

Lands in Severalty. The wars against the Indians, conducted after 1865 exclusively by regular army detachments, were far from popular with the American people, and protests against the inhuman treatment of the tribes grew more and more insistent. The publication in 1881 of Helen Hunt Jackson's *A Century of Dishonor,* with its stinging indictment of the Indian policy, brought public opinion strongly behind all efforts to alleviate the lot of the Indians. Their restriction to reservations, however, was long continued. In 1887 the Dawes Act paved the way for the gradual ending of tribal ownership of lands and the substitution of individual allotments of 160 acres each to heads of families, eighty acres each to single adults or orphans, and forty acres each to dependent children. Only a "trust patent" to the land was given at first, and complete ownership was delayed for twenty-five years. In 1906 the Burke Act gave the Secretary of the Interior a discretionary right to lessen the probationary period and corrected other defects in the original law. Compulsory education for Indian children was introduced in 1891, and full citizenship was conferred in 1924 upon all Indians in the United States. It cannot be said, however, that the government's policy, granted the best of intentions, was a success. More recently the makers of Indian policy have tended to revive the Indian's pride in his tribe and his traditions, on the theory that it is better to make him a good Indian than a poor white man.

The subsidence of the Indian menace during the late sixties and the early seventies paved the way for a new industry on the western plains, the grazing of cattle. The various posts that dotted the western trails, some wholly private, and others developed about a garrisoned fort or an Indian agency, got an early start from the emigrants, who were frequently only too willing to exchange for urgent necessities any livestock they happened to have brought along. It was soon discovered that cattle could fend for themselves on the plains the whole year through, for the wiry "buffalo grass" remained all winter long as nutritious as hay. There was no temptation, however, to increase these herds beyond immediate needs, for the plains still swarmed with buffalo, and outside markets were too distant to be profitable.

The Killing of the Buffalo. Shortly after the Civil War the killing of the buffalo began. Organized hunting parties equipped with repeating rifles killed them by the tens of thousands to obtain "buffalo robes," soon regarded as almost a necessity in the average American home. Others were killed, by Indians and whites alike, for their meat, and still other hunters killed for the sport of it. By 1870 from 5 million to 7 million buffalo still existed, but in the succeeding years the slaughter was terrific; by 1883 probably not more than 1,000 head were left alive.

The passing of the buffalo, unpleasant as it is to contemplate, was not an unmixed evil from the standpoint of white settlers. The government purposely did nothing to prevent the tragedy, for as long as the herds remained intact, the Indians had a sure food supply and could more easily defy control. Some of the later Indian uprisings were caused in part by the Indians' concern at the threatened destruction of their herds, but once the buffalo were gone the end of Indian resistance was at hand. Furthermore, the disappearance of the buffalo, together with the construction of the western railroads and the pacification of the Indians, gave the cattle industry the chance it needed to develop.

Beginnings of the Cattle Industry. In a sense, however, the western cattle industry was already full-grown. Its real beginnings were Mexican, rather than American, and dated back centuries. Both the cattle themselves, and the horses without which the industry would have been vastly different, were the descendants of European stock brought over by the Spaniards in the sixteenth century, and allowed to go wild. Survival of the fittest produced the nineteenth-century cattle that were more noted for their speed and endurance than for tender cuts of beef, many of which had also an incredible spread of horns. The horses, sprung no doubt from Arabian forebears, had developed into sure-footed, quick-witted, wiry broncos, well under 1,000 pounds in weight, but ideally suited for riding. The technique of cattle raising, to the last detail, was worked out in Mexico long before it was introduced on the western plains. The cowboy's saddle, bridle, bit, lariat, and spurs were adaptations, for the most part, of equipment used by Spanish cavalrymen, while the "roundup" and the use of "brands" to indicate ownership were early invented to meet obvious needs. But the industry lacked a market, and until that could be found it remained insignificant.

The Long Drive. Attempts to drive Texas cattle to an outside market were made from the time of the Mexican War, but all such ventures amounted to little until the railroads began to push out across the plains. Then the idea of the "long drive" from somewhere in Texas to a shipping point in Kansas or Nebraska took hold. Abilene, Kansas, a station on the Kansas Pacific, became noted as early as 1867 as a "cow town." Here untold numbers of Texas cattle, driven northward through the Indian Territory, or the "Nation," as cowboys called it, were purchased for the use of the newly established packing houses. Early each year groups of ranchers who wished to participate in a "drive" rounded up their cattle and threw them upon the trail — a route generally known as the "Chisholm Trail," regardless of where it ran. Grazing the cattle as they went, cowboys moved them slowly northward in herds of 2,000 to 3,000 head.

The Cowboy. On the "long drive" the cowboy developed those peculiar characteristics that made him, like the fur trader, the lumberjack, and the prospector, a unique character of the American frontier. He found the revolver indispensable to the protection of his herd, and of great advantage in the actual business of herding. He sang to the cattle, whether to help him bear the loneliness, or to keep the cattle aware of his presence, and thus prevent stampeding. The verses he invented were colorful, they told of the life he led, or rather, its more colorful aspects, and they became as authentic a part of American folklore as the songs of slavery and freedom that the Negroes sang. They contributed, moreover, to the creation of the cowboy legend which was romanticized by fiction writers out of all proportion to the facts.

The advance of the frontier into Kansas and Nebraska drove the "Chisholm Trail" farther and farther west, and determined the location of new cow towns to take the place of those enclosed in settled areas. Dodge City, Kansas, for example, soon replaced Abilene as the leading shipping point for Texas cattle. Settlement interfered with grazing; moreover, the Texas cattle brought with them the germs of the dreaded "Texas fever" to which they themselves had become immune, but which brought almost certain death to northern cattle. Successive quarantine laws were passed that pushed the drive still farther into the West. Also a new market was discovered when the northern plains had been cleared of buffalo. Northern ranchers, eager to expand their herds, paid good prices for the Texas longhorns, bred them up rapidly by the introduction of blooded cattle from the East, and enjoyed a short, but spectacular, prosperity. Texas cattle were driven northward as far as Dakota, Wyoming, and Montana, and even westward into New Mexico, Arizona, Colorado, and Utah.

The Range-cattle Industry. The profits of cattle growing on a well-policed range, for the use of which the government made no charge, and to which, thanks to the railroads, markets were now easily accessible, attracted capital, not only from the American East, but also from Europe, particularly England. Ranching companies, some of them with capital investments of millions of dollars, were formed to crowd more and more cattle upon the range. Access to water was, of course, essential, and each individual or company engaged in the cattle business took care to obtain title to some land so situated. Large "outfits," as the companies were called, sometimes had access to water at many different places, and companies existed that claimed the grazing rights to strips of land no less than a hundred miles long and fifty miles wide.

The law of the range, like the law of the mining camp, was to a great extent invented to meet the needs of the situation. Stockgrowers' associations were formed, at first for mutual protection, but later to work out rules for users of the range that actually had the effect of law. Indeed, the Wyoming Stock-Growers' Association, formed in 1873, came to have more power than the territorial government of Wyoming, which, as a matter of fact, it controlled. The Association promoted community rather than individual roundups, regulated the use of brands and recorded them, discouraged overstocking of the range by refusing membership to outsiders, and made relentless warfare upon all who were suspected of "rustling" (stealing) cattle. Punishment for defiance of the Association was often summary, and without benefit of law.

The Passing of the Cattleman. But the day of the cattleman soon passed. Trouble with rustlers cost the ranchers heavily. Strife with "nesters" (farmers) whose fences interfered with the free access of cattle to water holes not only caused heavy losses in property, but frequently resulted also in loss of life. Cowboys learned to carry wire cutters as part of their equipment; and finally, in self-defense, the cattlemen themselves began to fence the land they used but did not own, only to have their fences branded as illegal and ordered removed by the United States government. But the greatest calamity that befell the cattlemen was the overstocking of the range. By the middle eighties so many cattle had been turned loose to pick up a living from the plains that one severe winter was sure to bring disaster, and instead of one such winter most of the range country saw two, 1885–1886, and 1886–1887. The result was wholesale ruin and bankruptcy and a complete change in the nature of the cattle industry. After this time, ranchers tended more and more to raise hay for winter feed, and in general to carry on farming as well as ranching activities. On many ranges sheep replaced cattle, although not without resort to actual warfare between sheepmen and cattlemen. The close-grazing sheep left the range stripped of grass, so that when sheepmen came to stay cattlemen had to fight or leave. In some of these conflicts, sheepherders were slain, their wagons and supplies burned, and the herds themselves destroyed.

Short-lived as it was, the range-cattle industry left its mark upon the West and upon

A BUCKING BRONCHO

Cowboy costumes and conduct have suffered much embellishment at the hands of fictionists. High adventure was less characteristic of the range than boredom, loneliness, and hard work.

the country as a whole. It did its share to promote the growth of the meat-packing industry. It made clear the absurdity for the Far West of land legislation devised to meet the needs of the eastern half of the continent, and paved the way for important changes based on experience. It bequeathed to the residents of the plains a breezy, slangy language, cowboy costumes, "dude" ranches, and rodeos. It lived persistently in fiction, in the Wild West shows first popularized by "Buffalo Bill" Cody, in the solemn melodies and crude rhymes of the cowboy songs, and in the "westerns" of the movies and television.

The Sod-house Frontier. The mining booms, the building of the western railroads (see pp. 402–406), and the range-cattle industry all played their part in filling in the vast region stretching west from the "bend of the Missouri" to the front ranges of the Rockies. But as with earlier frontiers, it was the farmer with the plow who really converted the "wilderness" into civilization.

At the end of the Civil War the westerly line of farming settlement ran northward from the Indian territory in the south through eastern Kansas and Nebraska, bulged out around Sioux City, dipped far back into northwestern Iowa and then north again through central Minnesota. Within the next twenty-five years waves of immigrants and native farmers combined to effect one of the greatest expansions of agricultural cultivation in the nation's history. During the 1870's over 340,000 new settlers — most of them farmers — entered Kansas alone, and in the following decade Nebraska's population increased by over 250,000. For the time being white settlers were excluded by law, although not in fact, from the Indian territory; but from the southern boundary of Kansas through the Dakota territory in the north the new agricultural frontier pushed inexorably westward. Since this area was largely treeless, pioneers found a substitute for the traditional log cabins in sod houses built from the heavy prairie sod turned up by their

A TYPICAL SOD HOUSE

The scarcity of conventional building materials on the prairies forced farmers to improvise living quarters dug out from the sides of hills or ravines and fronted and roofed with square-cut turf. That their life was not easy is suggested in the rueful ballad, "Starving to Death on a Government Claim."

Frank Baker's my name, and a bachelor I am.
I'm keeping old batch on an elegant plan,
You'll find me out west in the county of Lane,
A-starving to death on a government claim.

My house is constructed of natural soil,
The walls are erected according to Hoyle,
The roof has no pitch, but is level and plain,
And I never get wet till it happens to rain.

Hurrah for Lane county, the land of the free,
The home of the grasshopper, bed-bug, and flea,
I'll holler its praises, and sing of its fame,
While starving to death on a government claim.

LOUISE POUND (ed.), *American Ballads and Songs* (1922), Charles Scribner's Sons.

---

breaking plows; hence the term, "sod-house frontier."

Generous land legislation did its part to induce the restless farmer, the discontented artisan, the newly arrived immigrant, and the former soldier to go West. For a few dollars in fees, the Homestead Act of 1862 made it possible for any American citizen, or any alien who had declared his intention of becoming a citizen, to obtain 160 acres of unoccupied government land by living on it for five years. An act of 1870 provided that any soldier who had fought in the Union army might count his time of service toward the required five-year period. Furthermore, the Pre-emption Act of 1841, which remained on the statute books until 1891, allowed the settler to stake a claim of 160 acres, and after six months' residence to buy it from the government at the minimum price, usually $1.25 an acre. The government even made an effort to adapt its land policy to the conditions of life in the farther West. The Timber Culture Act of 1873, for example, offered additional land to encourage the planting of trees. By taking advantage of the new laws, the enterprising settler could extend his holding far beyond the traditional 160 acres.

Farming on the Plains. This last farmer's frontier was not settled without extreme hardship and much departure from the old techniques of settlement. Where rainfall proved to be inadequate, windmills were often pressed into use, and on the high plains, dry farming and irrigation were employed. Lack of timber posed serious problems not only in housing, but also in fuel and fencing. A solution for the latter problem was supplied by the invention of barbed wire, but, of course, this cost hard money — a great deterrent to most of the newcomers, who had come West with little capital. Even with the aid of technology the Middle Border remained a land of heartbreaking toil where in times of prolonged drought, blizzards, cyclones, and grasshopper scourges, many settlers left their farms and headed East, bankrupt and

discouraged. For the many who were defeated, many more could and did take their
places, and the wavering line of farming
settlement crept westward. Before the turn
of the new century it touched the mountain
barrier in Colorado and eastern Wyoming,

and had even penetrated along the streams
and railroads into the great basin between
the Rockies and the Sierra Nevada. By that
time the last frontier was practically gone,
and the Old West, as the Civil War generation knew it, was rapidly disappearing.

SELECTED BIBLIOGRAPHY

The literature on the American frontier is
exceedingly voluminous; basic works by Turner, Webb, and Billington have already been
cited. A pioneer effort to tell the story of the
end of the frontier is F. L. Paxson, *The Last
American Frontier* (1910); Paxson agrees with
the Turner hypothesis. D. E. Clark, *The West
in American History* (1937), is a useful survey,
rather curiously organized. Contrasting views
on the subject may be found in G. R. Taylor
(ed.), *The Turner Thesis Concerning the
Role of the Frontier in American History* (2nd
ed., 1956); and W. D. Wyman and C. B.
Kroeber (eds.), *The Frontier in Perspective*
(1957). Merle Curti and others, *The Making
of an American Community* (1959), is a detailed study of one Wisconsin county; it bears
out Turner's interpretation. Environmental
differences between the plains and earlier frontiers are explored in J. C. Malin, *The Grass-
lands of North America* (1947). A valuable
administrative history is E. S. Pomeroy, *The
Territories and the United States, 1861–1890*
(1947).

Regional and state surveys are numerous but
of uneven quality. Among those not already
mentioned are: J. W. Caughey, *History of the
Pacific Coast* (1933); H. E. Briggs, *Frontiers
of the Northwest* (1940), a topical treatment
of the upper Missouri Valley; P. F. Sharp,
*Whoop-Up Country; The Canadian-American
West, 1865–1885* (1955); and A. L. Neff, *History of Utah, 1847–1869* (1940). Useful
single-volume state surveys include: R. G.
Cleland, *A History of California: The American Period* (1922); E. C. McReynolds, *Oklahoma* (1954); H. S. Schell, *History of South
Dakota* (1961); and T. C. Blegen, *Minnesota*
(1963). On Montana see two stimulating interpretations: J. K. Howard, *Montana: High,*

Wide, and Handsome (1943); and K. R. Toole,
Montana: An Uncommon Land (1959).

The subject of western mining has recently
been treated in two general works: R. W. Paul,
Mining Frontiers of the Far West (1963); and
W. S. Greever, *The Bonanza West* (1963).
T. A. Rickard, *A History of American Mining*
(1932), is highly technical; G. C. Quiett, *Pay
Dirt* (1936), is journalistic. Among the best
special studies are: G. D. Lyman, *The Saga of
the Comstock Lode* (1934); W. J. Trimble,
The Mining Advance into the Inland Empire
(1914); and M. G. Burlingame, *The Montana
Frontier* (1942). The life of a great Comstock
Lode promoter is treated by R. E. Stewart, Jr.,
and M. F. Stewart, *Adolph Sutro* (1962). Law
and order are discussed in many works, including N. P. Langford, *Vigilante Days and Ways*
(1890); and Wayne Gard, *Frontier Justice*
(1949). Excellent treatments of later rushes
are: Marshall Sprague, *Money Mountain; the
Story of Cripple Creek Gold* (1953); W. T.
Jackson, *Treasure Hill* (1963); and Pierre
Berton, *The Klondike Fever* (1958). A rich
vein is opened by C. C. Spence, *British Investments and the American Mining Frontier,
1860–1901* (1958).

The great transportation problem is dealt
with by O. O. Winther, *The Transportation
Frontier: Trans-Mississippi West, 1865–1890*
(1964). Winther treats one region's transportation problem in *The Old Oregon Country*
(1950). Other themes are developed by R. S.
Bloss, *Pony Express* (1959); and Ellis Lucia,
The Saga of Ben Holladay (1959).

A vivid introduction to the Indian wars is
P. I. Wellman, *Death on Horseback* (2 vols.,
1947). The classic indictment of Indian policy
is H. H. Jackson, *A Century of Dishonor*
(1881). Other valuable works include: G. B.
Grinnell, *The Fighting Cheyennes* (1915);
Stanley Vestal, *Warpath and Council Fire*

* Available in paperback

(1948); C. M. Oehler, *The Great Sioux Uprising* (1959), on the Minnesota war; Mari Sandoz, *Crazy Horse* (1942); Stanley Vestal, *Sitting Bull* (1957); and E. I. Stewart, *Custer's Luck* (1955), the best on a much-written-about episode. Two interesting recent works are Jason Betzinez (with W. S. Nye), *I Fought with Geronimo* (1959), the memoir of an aged Apache; and Oliver Knight, *Following the Indian Wars* (1960), a treatment of war correspondents. On this and other subjects relating to the frontier army, see R. G. Athearn, *William Tecumseh Sherman and the Settlement of the West* (1956). Other recent studies of note include: K. A. Murray, *The Modocs and Their War* (1959); J. J. Mathews, *The Osages* (1961); R. K. Andrist, *The Long Death; The Last Days of the Plains Indians* (1964); and R. M. Utley, *The Last Days of the Sioux Nation* (1963). On the Southwest, see E. E. Dale, *The Indians of the Southwest* (1949); and W. H. Leckie, *The Military Conquest of the Southern Plains* (1963). On the Nez Percé War see the biography of General Miles by V. W. Johnson, *The Unregimented General* (1962); M. D. Beal, *"I Will Fight No More Forever"* (1963); and Francis Haines, *The Nez Percés* (1955).

On Great Plains agriculture, see the now-classic treatment by Everett Dick, *The Sod House Frontier, 1854–1890* (1937), a vivid description of life among the settlers along the Middle Border. Conflict between cattlemen and "nesters" is stressed in Mari Sandoz, *Old Jules* (1935), the biography of her father. A classic, pro-nester account of the Johnson County War is A. S. Mercer, *The Banditti of the Plains* (1894). The political history of an important wheat region is discussed in H. R. Lamar, *Dakota Territory, 1861–1889* (1956).

The best works on the cow country are: E. S. Osgood, *The Day of the Cattleman* (1929); E. E. Dale, *The Range Cattle Industry* (1930); Louis Pelzer, *The Cattlemen's Frontier* (1936); and Lewis Atherton, *The Cattle Kings* (1961). First-hand accounts may be found in: J. H. Cook, *Fifty Years on the Old Frontier* (1923); Andy Adams, *The Log of a Cowboy* (1903); and Lon Tinkle and Allen Maxwell (eds.), *The Cowboy Reader* (1959). Heroic efforts to separate truth from fiction are made by E. D. Branch, *The Cowboy and His Interpreters* (1926); and J. B. Frantz and J. E. Choate, Jr., *The American Cowboy* (1955). Good books on often-distorted subjects are: W. P. Webb, *The Texas Rangers* (1935); and Don Russell, *The Lives and Legends of Buffalo Bill* (1960). On the bison slaughter, see E. D. Branch, *The Hunting of the Buffalo* (1929); and Wayne Gard, *The Great Buffalo Hunt* (1959). The first compilation by the distinguished song-hunter, J. A. Lomax, was his *Cowboy Songs and Other Frontier Ballads* (1910); his work has been ably continued by his son, Alan Lomax.

23

THE ECONOMIC
REVOLUTION

Economic Changes.   During the Civil War and the decades immediately following, there occurred in the United States a series of economic changes that were virtually to revolutionize the life of the nation. The railroads, already expanding rapidly before the Civil War, were extended across the continent to produce a national system of transportation. Almost simultaneously the extension of the telegraph and telephone networks made possible speedy and certain continental communication. The same years witnessed also a spectacular change-over from small factories that had produced only for a local market to great corporate industries that produced for the entire nation. Similarly the banking and financial apparatus upon which all other

business depended began to concentrate in a few strategic centers, with "Wall Street" in New York City as the indispensable center of centers. Inevitably the new industrialism gave rise to urbanization; almost everywhere east of the Mississippi, and even here and there west of it, huge cities appeared into which poured the needed workers, some from rural America, but others from Europe — an avalanche of immigrants whose presence would soon change radically the American pattern of national origins.

The Railroads.   The rapidly expanding railroad system was the key to many remarkable changes. Manufacturers struggled to produce the almost unlimited supplies that the railroads required for their own use, then redoubled their efforts to meet the demands of the new markets that the railroads opened up. Agriculture was equally stimulated, and achieved an ever-widening base of operations, for the railroads assured the early settlement of every remaining frontier. The immigrant tide rose with the increasing number of jobs. Corporation methods of business and finance, first designed to meet the needs of the railroads, were copied and modified by the rest of the business world.

During the Civil War, the railroads enjoyed great prosperity. Rates soared, except where the competition of the Great Lakes and the Erie Canal kept them down, and companies now flourished that had never made profits before. Railroad managers, assured of a wartime abundance of traffic, had shown little interest either in new construction or in improving their equipment. But with the return of peace the time was ripe for the renovation of the old roads and the building of new ones. Capital for the purpose was easily obtained by Jay Cooke and other promoters, who convinced investors, both at home and abroad, that railroad securities were among the safest and most profitable of investments.

The First Transcontinental. The federal government, by its generous subsidies, did much to stimulate the railroad boom. This policy, initiated a number of years before the war but retarded because of southern opposition, was inaugurated in 1862 when Congress chartered the Union and Central Pacific railroads. Proponents of this project could now cite the necessity of connecting California closely enough to the Union to insure its loyalty. The Union Pacific was to build westward from Omaha, the Central Pacific eastward from Sacramento. Each company, after the completion of an initial forty miles of track, was eligible to receive from the government, for each mile of track laid, ten square miles of land in alternate sections, checkerboard fashion, along the right of way; and also, for each mile of track laid, the loan of $16,000, $32,000, or $48,000 (for plains, foothills, or mountain country, respectively) in government bonds.

Generous as these offers seemed, they proved to be inadequate to attract the necessary capital, so in 1864 Congress amended the original terms. The government now

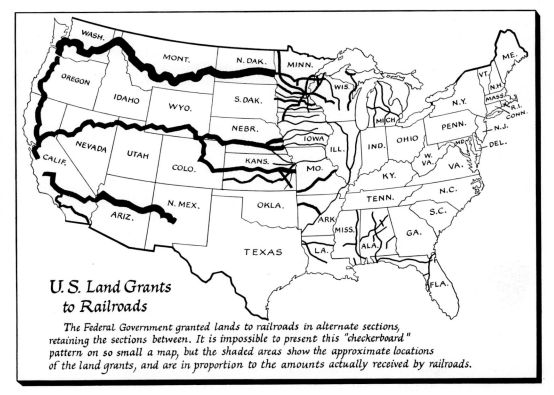

U. S. Land Grants to Railroads

The Federal Government granted lands to railroads in alternate sections, retaining the sections between. It is impossible to present this "checkerboard" pattern on so small a map, but the shaded areas show the approximate locations of the land grants, and are in proportion to the amounts actually received by railroads.

RAILROAD ADVERTISING

Persuasive "flyers" such as this had much to do with bringing homeseekers "across the wide Missouri."

doubled the land grant, accepted a second mortgage for the loans it made, and permitted the companies to borrow private capital, up to the amount of the government loans, on first-mortgage bonds. With these inducements, building soon began in earnest. At first it was stipulated that the eastern boundary of California should be the dividing line between the two roads, but ultimately they were permitted to race for distance, and in 1869, when they met near Ogden, Utah, the Union Pacific had laid 1,086 miles of track and the Central Pacific 689. Problems of construction, particularly in the mountains, taxed the engineering prowess of the builders, while only by resort to the most unusual expedients were they able to recruit and maintain the needed labor. The Union Pacific employed thousands of Irish immigrants, many of them ex-soldiers who under the efficient direction of General Grenville M. Dodge not only built the road, but also on occasion fought off the attacks of hostile Indians. The Central Pacific, after initial difficulties, resorted to the use of Chinese "coolies," or contract laborers. The building of both roads was accompanied by the most flagrant profiteer-

ing.[1] The fortunes of four leading officials of the Central Pacific, Leland Stanford, Collis P. Huntington, Charles Crocker, and Mark Hopkins, began in this way. But unlike the original owners of Union Pacific stock, most of whom sold out their holdings as soon as the road was built, the "Big Four" of the Central Pacific operated their road for many years and took excellent profits from it. Each of them left a fortune of $40 million or more.

Other Railroad Construction.   Railroad building was now almost a national frenzy. Everywhere new rails were being laid, new lines were being planned. The United States itself had chartered two other transcontinentals on terms almost as generous as those given the Union and the Central Pacific, and was soon to charter a third. The Northern Pacific (1864) was designed to connect the head of Lake Superior with Puget Sound; the Atlantic and Pacific (1866), to build southwestward from Springfield, Missouri; the Texas and Pacific (1871), to cross the continent still farther to the south through Texas, New Mexico, and Arizona. These roads received no subsidy in bonds, but they were allowed a double portion of land — twenty sections per mile in the states, and forty in the territories.

National assistance to state-chartered railroads, after the pattern set by the Illinois Central grant of 1850, also continued unabated. The Chicago and Northwestern, the Chicago, Rock Island and Pacific, the Burlington and Missouri River, the Chicago, Milwaukee and St. Paul, the Missouri Pacific, the Atchison, Topeka and Santa Fe, the Kansas Pacific, and many minor western lines all profited, directly or indirectly, from government aid, and built feverishly. In the East and the South there was not only much new building, but, even more important, the consolidation of many lesser lines into systems that rivaled in their magnificent reaches the projected transconti-

[1] See p. 364.

nentals of the West. By 1873 Commodore Vanderbilt, for the New York Central, J. Edgar Thomson, for the Pennsylvania, and Jay Gould, for the Erie, had found ways through to the Midwest. In the South the Chesapeake and Ohio connected Norfolk with Cincinnati, and easy communication through Tennessee linked both Charleston and Norfolk with Memphis. Within five years after the Civil War the South had 2,500 more miles of railroad than ever existed in the old Confederacy, while in the single year 1873, new construction for this area reached a total of 1,300 miles. For the country as a whole, the eight years following the Civil War saw the laying of about 35,000 miles of new track, an increase during the period of almost 100 per cent.

Railroad Improvements. A great variety of improvements kept pace with the new construction. In 1864 George M. Pullman built his first sleeping car, and a few years later he was actively at work on separate dining, drawing-room, and reclining-chair cars. In 1868 George Westinghouse demonstrated on a Pennsylvania passenger train his epoch-making airbrake, a device which contributed greatly to safe rail travel. During these years steel rails were introduced, although it was not until 1877 that the rapid replacement of iron by steel began. As the roadbeds were improved, heavier locomotives and rolling stock were built, and a uniform gauge of four feet, eight and one half inches came into general use. Terminal facilities were greatly improved, and extensive freight yards expedited the traffic in "through freight." Long bridges, after the beginning of work on the Brooklyn Bridge in 1867, became a national passion. In 1869 the Missouri River was bridged at Kansas City, and in 1872 at Omaha. Between 1867 and 1874, James B. Eads built a bridge across the Mississippi at St. Louis. Meantime John A. Roebling, the man who planned the Brooklyn Bridge, had first spanned the Ohio River at Cincinnati.

These great bridges, and numerous lesser ones, enormously enhanced the speed and ease of railroad transportation.

The Panic of 1873. The burst of railroad expansion that had followed the Civil War ended abruptly with the Panic of 1873. On September 18, 1873, the banking firm of Jay Cooke and Company closed its doors in New York, Philadelphia, and Washington. After the Civil War, Cooke had turned his attention to railway securities and again had demonstrated his ability to win the confidence of investors. In attempting to back the Northern Pacific, however, he needed European assistance, but after the outbreak of the Franco-Prussian War in 1870, foreign capital had become increasingly harder to obtain. The result was that Cooke tied up so much of his firm's resources in advances to the railroad that his partners, without his knowledge or consent, finally took the drastic step of closing. Already the business world was nervous, and on the day before Cooke's failure the New York Stock Exchange had experienced a ruinous decline in values. When Cooke's suspension was announced, the Exchange was thrown into a devastating panic, and two days later it closed. Bankruptcies followed, factories shut down, business came to a standstill; a depression that was to last for nearly six years had begun. Thus dramatically did the "boom" that the Civil War unleashed come to an abrupt end.

Causes of the Depression. Conditions in Europe had much to do with bringing on the American depression of the 1870's. The United States had developed close commercial ties with the Old World, and any large-scale reverse abroad was sure to produce repercussions west of the Atlantic. A sharp panic on the Vienna Bourse in May, 1873, inaugurated a general European depression, and the unloading by European investors of their American holdings had helped prepare for the American crash. Chief among the domestic causes of the crisis was the huge overinvestment in railroads accompanied by a wild speculation in railroad securities. During the years preceding 1873, especially in the West, many railroads had built in unpopulated regions where for years operations could be carried on only at a loss, and the securities of such unfortunate roads often became the playthings of speculators. Meanwhile, the amount of capital invested in railroads alone during the period had reached $1 billion, while other huge sums had gone into the development of new American industries. To carry on the expansion American corporations had borrowed $1.5 billion from abroad, with interest charges of $80 million. In order to meet these obligations and to remedy an adverse balance of payments, more gold had to be sent abroad each year than the United States could spare. The new national banks yielded to the temptation to overextend their loans, and in five years preceding the panic lent many times as much money as they took in by way of deposits. Insurance companies were hard hit by the Chicago fire of 1871, which cost them $200 million, and the Boston fire of 1872, which added another $73 million to their outlay.

The Granger Movement. For a period of almost six years after the Panic of 1873 nearly all American business was at low ebb, and new railroad construction almost ceased. Besides having to combat hard times, the railroads were also under vigorous attack for their monopolistic practices. Among the first to protest against railroad extortions were the grain growers of the upper Mississippi Valley, whose dependence upon the railroads was almost complete. Their activities, collectively known as the Granger movement, resulted in the recognition in 1877 by the Supreme Court that the individual states had a right to regulate the railroads that penetrated their territory, a notable extension of governmental authority.

The founder of the Grange, or Patrons of Husbandry, was Oliver Hudson Kelley, a government clerk in Washington who had intended it to be a cultural and social organization, devoted primarily to spreading ideas on scientific farming. Beginning in 1867, the lodge took hold only slowly, in the South as well as in the North, until in the early seventies, when the northwestern farmers seized upon it as a means of attacking the railroads. Granger meetings furnished an ideal forum for the grain growers of the upper Mississippi Valley to speak their minds on the monopolistic tendencies of the railroads. Since the ordinary farmer had no choice but to use the road that ran nearest his farm, competition was a myth. The railroads regularly charged "all the traffic would bear," and dictated at will the terms on which they chose to serve their patrons. Elevators and warehouses, often owned or controlled by the railroads, did likewise; and middlemen, themselves compelled to pay a heavy toll in freight to the roads, were not far behind.

The Granger idea — that the state should regulate the railroads, if necessary to the point of fixing maximum rates — was older than the movement. Toyed with gingerly in Massachusetts, its real beginning was in Illinois, where a new state constitution, adopted in 1870, specifically stated that the General Assembly should pass laws to correct abuses and to prevent unjust discrimination and extortion by railroads in their freight and passenger rates, and by warehouses in their dealings with the public. Armed with this authority the Illinois legislature of 1871 promptly established maximum rates for the transportation of passengers, required that freight charges should be based entirely upon distance traversed, provided regulations for the storing and shipping of grain, and created a state board of railroad and warehouse commissioners to enforce the laws. Against these measures the railroads made a determined, and at first a successful, fight, for on the first test

A GRANGER MEETING IN THE WOODS NEAR WINCHESTER, SCOTT COUNTY, ILLINOIS

From a sketch by Joseph B. Beale reproduced in Frank Leslie's Illustrated Newspaper, *August 30, 1873.*

case the Supreme Court of Illinois held the laws to be unconstitutional. But the Grangers, now thoroughly aroused, promptly voted out of office one of the judges who had held against them and replaced him with a judge who shared their views. The result was that in 1873 a new law, better drawn but designed to effect the same ends, was sustained.

Granger Legislation. Meantime the Grangers, bent on using the power of the state to curb the railroads, had gone into politics throughout the Midwest. Sometimes they were content merely to vote for Republicans or Democrats who agreed with them, but frequently they chose third-party candidates on separate "Anti-Monopoly" or "Independent" or "Reform" tickets. On July 4, 1873, hundreds of Granger audiences gave their approval to a *Farmers' Declaration of Independence,* which repeated in well-worn phraseology the grievances from which farmers suffered, and announced in no uncertain way their determination to find relief. Presently

Granger legislatures had enacted, not only in Illinois, but also in Wisconsin, Minnesota, and Iowa, measures of drastic regulation for railroads and warehouses.

In each instance litigation followed, and the railroads took their cases to the federal courts. The Granger laws, railroad attorneys claimed, were impairments of contracts that the states had already made in granting charters to the railroads, and they provided for the taking of private property without due process of law. But in the spring of 1877, the United States Supreme Court ruled against the railroads in a series of decisions, the most important of which were *Munn* v. *Illinois* and *Peik* v. *the Chicago and Northwestern Railroad.* Thus the "right of a state to regulate a business that is public in nature though privately owned and managed" won striking vindication, and a weapon was forged with which, it was hoped, not only the railroads but other monopolistic enterprises also could be attacked. Most of the early Granger laws were defective and had to be repealed, but the principle on which they were founded endured, and before long railroad and warehouse commissions were at work in nearly every state.

Railroad Building. Hard as times were during the 1870's they could not hold back indefinitely the final conquest of the Far West by the railroads. Sure signs of revived business activity appeared as early as 1878 when the Northern Pacific again prepared to build. Under the leadership of Frederick Billings, a conservative Vermont capitalist, the westward march of the Northern Pacific went forward without incident. In 1881, however, Billings' plans came into conflict with those of Henry Villard, whose Oregon Railroad and Navigation Company controlled the railroad and steamboat lines of the Pacific Northwest. Villard had long sought to induce Billings to agree to some traffic arrangement that would prevent competition between the two systems when the Northern Pacific should be finished, but Billings received all such overtures with cold refusals. Thereupon Villard bought up enough stock to secure complete control of both companies, and organized a holding company, the Oregon and Transcontinental, through which to manage them. He then deposed Billings as president of the Northern Pacific, took the place for himself, and as president of all three corporations achieved the harmony he desired. On the completion of the Northern Pacific in 1883, by way of celebration he ran a "Golden Spike Special" the entire length of the line.

More Transcontinentals. By this time, however, the American public could no longer be thrilled by news that another transcontinental railroad had been finished. In addition to the Union Pacific, completed in 1869, the Southern Pacific was now running trains to the western coast. The Southern Pacific was a California corporation that had shrewdly acquired the right to build within the borders of the state to meet any eastern land-grant railroad.

Owned and managed by the same able group that had built the Central Pacific, it had pushed its lines southward through the state, and was prepared to meet newcomers at Fort Yuma and the Needles, the two points on the border of southern California where the canyon of the Colorado could be crossed. With the aid of territorial charters from Arizona and New Mexico and a state charter from Texas, the Southern Pacific built eastward from Fort Yuma to meet the old Texas Pacific, which it presently absorbed. By January, 1882, it had through trains running over this route from San Francisco to St. Louis, and by February of the next year it had opened up an alternative route through southern Texas to New Orleans. Alert to every opportunity, the Southern Pacific also connected at the Needles with the Atchison, Topeka, and Santa Fe, which had built westward through Kansas on a state land grant, and from Albuquerque to the Needles on the federal grant of the defunct Atlantic and Pacific. In 1884 the owners of the Southern Pacific, who were now in a position to monopolize the railroad business of the Southwest, followed the example of Villard and created a holding company, the Southern Pacific of Kentucky, through which to administer their extensive properties.

Other western railroads extended their lines during these years with the same feverish speed. The Burlington, the Rock Island, the Northwestern, and the Missouri Pacific competed with the transcontinentals and their branches for the exploitation of the Great Plains. The Denver and Rio Grande built heroically through the Colorado mountains, by way of the Royal Gorge of the Arkansas, to connect with the Union Pacific at Ogden. James J. Hill of Minnesota advanced the fortunes of the St. Paul, Minneapolis and Manitoba slowly but surely until, under a new name, the Great Northern, it became in 1893 another transcontinental. North of the United States, in Canada, Donald A. Smith brought the Canadian Pacific to completion in 1885, while south of the United States the Mexican Central, an affiliate of the Santa Fe, had reached Mexico City the year before.

Southern and Eastern Roads. While the most spectacular railroad activities of the period occurred in the trans-Mississippi West, the southern and eastern roads were also busy. In the South the Richmond and West Point Terminal Railway and Warehouse Company, a holding company formed in 1881, laid the foundations for what later became the Southern Railway system. Both northern and English capital poured into its projects. During the booming eighties the railroad mileage in that portion of the South which lay east of the Mississippi River doubled, while to the west of the river the increase was even higher. In the East the great systems that had taken form before the Civil War — the New York Central, the Pennsylvania, the Erie, and the Baltimore and Ohio — built or acquired branch lines, consolidated their holdings, and, when well-managed, made money. Everywhere the introduction of steel rails, improved rolling stock, and new equipment called for enormous expenditures, funds for which the railroads somehow managed to find.

Because of these expensive innovations, statistics on mileage fail to give a complete picture of the railroad development of the period. Nevertheless the statistics are impressive. From 52,000 miles of railroad in 1870 the total mileage in the United States had risen by 1880 to 93,000 and by 1890 to 163,000 — an increase of 70,000 miles in ten years. Construction more than kept pace with the expansion of population. In 1870 the United States had 1,380 miles of railroad per million inhabitants; in 1880 it had 1,858 miles, and in 1890 it had 2,625 miles. By the last-mentioned date the main outlines of the American railroad map were complete; after that date the mileage continued to increase for a time, but such new tracks as were laid served mainly as feeders

for existing lines. The age of railroad pioneering was over.

Railway Consolidations and Abuses. The creation of these great railroad systems was not usually accomplished without the elimination of a multitude of lesser lines. Back in the pre-Civil War era more or less accidental connections had played a considerable part in railroad consolidation. In this way the work of Cornelius Vanderbilt in welding together the New York Central had been greatly facilitated. Panics and periods of depression had also done their bit. During the years following 1857, and even more after 1873, the weaker roads had gone into bankruptcy only to emerge as parts of some stronger, and usually much larger, system. During the depression years of the seventies no less than 450 railroads, fully two-fifths of the roads of the country, had suffered this experience. The holding company idea also greatly facilitated consolidation. Great sectional systems were thus created that could monopolize the business of the region they covered, and at the same time reduce to a minimum the danger of investigation and regulation. Within these areas competition was stifled, and only the interposition of governmental authority could prevent railroad monopolies from charging for their services "all the traffic would bear."

Competing systems, however, could not always be united, and wherever competition existed it tended to become both ruthless and costly. Rebates were given to favored shippers, particularly to those who shipped large quantities of goods long distances. Regions or cities that were served by more than one railroad were granted cut rates, while those dependent upon the services of a single road were overcharged in an effort to make up the losses from the competing rates. More was charged for a short haul where there was no competition than for a longer haul over the same line when competition between the terminal points existed. Such efforts of the

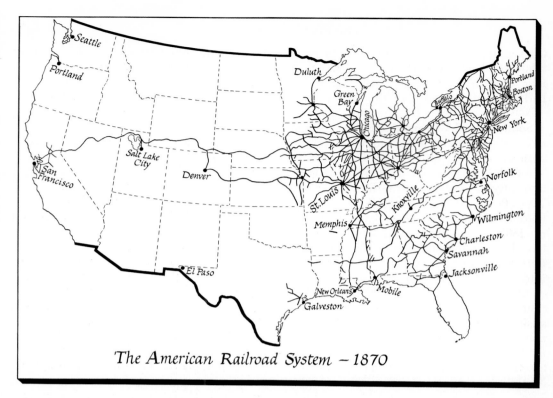

The American Railroad System – 1870

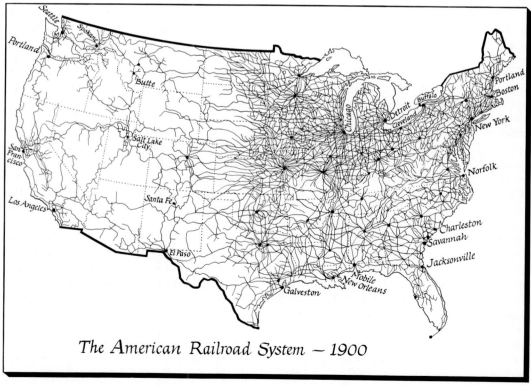

The American Railroad System – 1900

roads to eliminate competition as rate agreements and the pooling of earnings usually came to nothing.

Railroad Regulation. The Granger movement had paved the way for what now became an obvious necessity, the entrance of the national government into the field of railroad regulation. The various state commissions, ill-informed as to the problems that confronted them, and often subservient to the corporations they were supposed to regulate, accomplished comparatively little; by the time a railroad was large enough to need regulation, it was too large for a state commission to regulate it. Local intrastate roads that the commissions could handle were quietly absorbed into powerful interstate systems. While, according to the Granger decisions, the regulatory authority of a state did not necessarily stop at the state's borders, the fact of the matter was that increasingly it did. Finally, in 1886, the Supreme Court of the United States admitted the inadvisability of its earlier ruling permitting states to regulate railroads that extended beyond their borders, and in a case involving the Wabash Railroad and the State of Illinois held in effect that Congress alone had authority to regulate interstate commerce.

Meantime one investigating committee after another had studied the railroad problem. In Granger times a Senate committee, headed by William Windom of Minnesota, had urged unavailingly that a federal bureau of commerce be created. In 1879 the Hepburn committee in New York State submitted evidence of the misconduct of the railroads and inferentially pointed to national regulation as the proper way out. In 1885, the Senate appointed a new investigating committee with a larger range of powers. Headed by Shelby M. Cullom of Illinois, this committee reported in 1886 that three-fourths of the railroad business of the country was interstate in character, hence, under the rule of law laid down in the Wabash decision, beyond the control

of state regulation. Noting the widespread opposition throughout the country to government ownership, the committee recommended regulation by the national government as the preferable alternative.

The ICC. Congress was now ready to act, and in 1887 it established an Interstate Commerce Commission to consist of five members, of whom not more than three might belong to the same political party, to be appointed by the President for six-year terms. The law forbade most of the evil practices uncovered by the various investigating committees, and in a sense made national the current trends in state regulation. Rebates, pools, and discriminations were branded as illegal, and the rule that more could not be charged for a short haul than for a longer one over the same line was established. The commission was authorized to investigate complaints against the railroads and to make decisions which, however, it could enforce only through court action. This provision for a judicial review of its rulings proved to be the undoing of the early commission, for it failed to obtain the judicial backing through which alone its decisions could be made effective. Not until the Presidency of Theodore Roosevelt did the Interstate Commerce Commission become a really effective body.

Telegraph and Cable. While railroads undoubtedly played the principal role in revolutionizing the means of communication on which Americans depended, they were not alone in the field. The electric telegraph, used before the Civil War, now sent news and information to almost every hamlet in the nation. Cable service also steadily improved. The first transoceanic cable, laid in 1858, had soon been destroyed by the use of too strong electric currents, but by 1866, through the persistent efforts of Cyrus W. Field, a better one had been laid, and soon thereafter many others. Americans were thus able to keep in as close touch with London as with New

York, and to be far better informed on world affairs. Improvements in ocean-going steamships also helped, for they facilitated foreign travel for Americans and brought numerous visitors to America from distant shores. Under these circumstances the extremes of provincialism, so common in the United States of an earlier period, began to disappear.

The Telephone.   The telephone was invented by Alexander Graham Bell, an American Scot who taught deaf mutes and was interested in acoustics. Bell was not the first to study the problem of transmitting human speech by electricity, but he did develop the first practicable telephone. The successful launching of the telephone owed much to the organizing genius of Theodore N. Vail, later president of the American Telephone and Telegraph Company. During the eighties telephone systems were introduced into virtually every American city, and by the end of the decade no less than 440,000 instruments were in use. Well before the turn of the century successful long-distance connections had been generally established.

Thomas A. Edison.   In addition to the telegraph and the telephone, electricity soon served many other new uses. Wizard of electrical inventors was Thomas A. Edison (1847–1931), an Ohioan by birth whose formal schooling had been limited to three months, but whose natural ingenuity was superb. In 1879 he made his first really revolutionary invention, a practicable incandescent light. Others had already devised the arc light, which served well enough for street-lighting, but was wholly unsatisfactory for indoor use. In due time business houses and even dwellings were depending for illumination on the new device. The need for central electric power stations offered an opportunity for business expansion so fully appreciated that the number of such stations increased from eight in 1881 to 2,774 in 1898. While

Edison, with his numerous inventions, including among others the phonograph, motion pictures, automatic telegraphy, the stock ticker, and the microphone, ranks as the leading electrical engineer of his time, he was by no means the only one. Some electric railway systems replaced horse cars in the city streets, electric elevators added numbers of stories to the height of skyscrapers, and electric power was being used extensively in industry.

Postal Changes.   Meantime the United States Post Office, regardless of deficits, cheapened its rates and amplified its service. Railroad extensions were followed everywhere by postal extensions. Mail delivery at the door was inaugurated in a few American cities as early as 1871, and thereafter was rapidly bestowed upon smaller and smaller communities. Catalogues and printed circulars were accorded special rates to facilitate general distribution, a tremendous boon to advertisers. The penny postal card, introduced into the United States from Europe in 1873, and the two-cent letter rate, inaugurated in 1883, brought the cost of personal mail service to a minimum. The invention of the typewriter in 1867, by Christopher Latham Sholes, a Milwaukee printer, and its later extensive use in business, added immensely to the volume of the mails. The results of these changes brought the American people closer together, blurred the sharper lines of sectionalism, and assured nationalism. Probably most significant of all, the way was paved for the organization of business along national rather than local or sectional lines. The revolution in means of communication provided a firm foundation for the new industrialism.

The New Industrialism.   The beginning of the new industrialism, as already noted, preceded the Civil War. New machines, both during and after the war, did their part toward pushing it forward. The United States Patent Bureau had granted only

36,000 patents before 1860, but during the three decades from 1860 to 1890 granted approximately 440,000. While by no means all of these inventions were of real significance, some of them were of far-reaching consequence. Americans also borrowed heavily from European ideas and showed their customary skill in adapting them to American needs. There was plenty of work to do. With the population of the country growing rapidly, both from the increase in the native stock and from immigration, the needs of more and more people had to be met. Such newly formed industries as steel and oil had to expand and equip their vast establishments. The use of agricultural machinery, greatly expedited during the war, showed no signs of abatement, and new inventions brought more and more machines to the farmers' attention.

With capital abundant, the United States became a sort of paradise for industrialists. A dependably high tariff assured them of the right to exploit the steadily growing American market, and the constitutional provision against state control of interstate commerce gave them a vast free-trade zone to exploit. Soldiers returning from the war and immigrants streaming in from Europe supplied a comfortable abundance of labor. One by one the high records of production during the war fell below the higher records of the first five years of peace. It became increasingly apparent that the America of the future was to be less rural than urban, more factory than farm.

Leadership of Steel. The best barometer of the new industrialism was steel. Before the Civil War the high cost of steel confined its use to the manufacture of such small articles as tools and cutlery in which quality was demanded regardless of price. That anything so bulky as railroad rails, or the heavy locomotives that ran on the rails, should ever be made of steel rather than of iron seemed utterly fantastic. All this was changed as the result of a remarkable discovery made independently and at about the same time by a Kentuckian, William

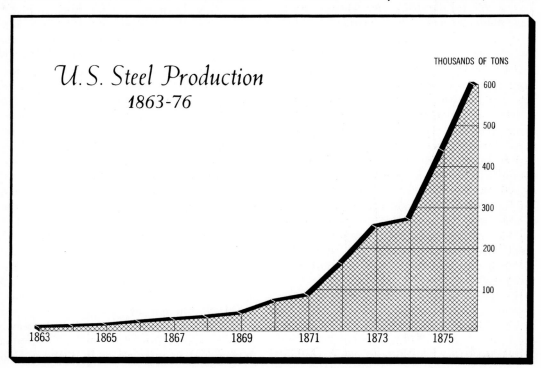

U.S. Steel Production 1863-76

THOUSANDS OF TONS

ANDREW CARNEGIE

The Scottish-born steel manufacturer, whose efforts helped make the United States by the 1890's the greatest steel-producing nation in the world.

Kelly, and an Englishman, Henry Bessemer. Kelly, who made wrought-iron sugar kettles for his neighbors, observed one day that the effect of an air blast on molten iron was to make it white-hot. From this he readily deduced that the molten metal itself contained enough carbon to burn out its impurities, if a strong enough blast of air could be directed against it. Plainly this "air-boiling" process, if it could be made practicable, would tend to eliminate the expensive use of charcoal, and so greatly reduce the cost of refinement. In a series of experiments, carried on between 1851 and 1856, Kelly demonstrated the soundness of his idea.

In 1856, Bessemer, who had been carrying on similar experiments, announced the successful application of a "fuel-less" process and obtained a United States patent on it. In 1866 one Alexander Lyman Holley, by obtaining the right to use both the Bessemer and the Kelly patents, paved the way for a phenomenal development. Within a few years there were dozens of Bessemer steel works in the country, and the price of steel had dropped to a figure that made its use instead of iron entirely practicable. Another new method of producing steel, known as the "open-hearth" process, was introduced into the United States from Europe in 1868 by Abraham S. Hewitt, who shared with his father-in-law, Peter Cooper, control of the New Jersey Steel and Iron Company at Trenton. Ultimately far more open-hearth than Bessemer steel was to be made, but until well toward the end of the century Bessemer steel cost less to produce, and so enjoyed a great advantage. Naturally the steel industry, like the iron industry, tended to concentrate in Pennsylvania, where both iron ore and coal were found in abundance; but by 1873 the Michigan iron mines, little used before the Civil War, were furnishing over half of the ore supply.

Andrew Carnegie. The steel industry was to produce many great names, but none more glamorous than that of Andrew Carnegie (1835–1919), the Scottish immigrant whose career became an almost perfect pattern for the typical American success story. The son of a Dunfermline weaver, young Carnegie was brought to America in 1848 by his parents. He found work, first as a bobbin boy at $1.20 a week in a western Pennsylvania cotton factory, then as a messenger at $2.50 a week in a Pittsburgh telegraph office. Soon he was a telegraph operator, and a little later, the private secretary of Thomas A. Scott, a Pennsylvania Railroad official. From that position to railroading was an easy transition; and then from railroading to bridge-building. Extremely versatile, he pursued many side lines, nearly all of which turned out well. On one of his trips to England he saw steel being made by the Bessemer process, and returned to the United States determined to put "all of his eggs in one basket," the manufacture of steel. By 1873, the date when he opened the J. Edgar Thomson Steel Mills — named after a powerful partner in the enterprise — his career as a steel magnate had begun.

"Rock Oil." No less startlingly new than the steel industry, and almost as revolutionary in its possibilities, was the production and refinement of oil. For centuries petroleum, by seeping to the surface in various parts of the earth, had advertised its existence to mankind, but, strangely enough, no one had seemed to realize that it was of any particular value; much less that, by sinking wells, great pools of it could be tapped. Years before the Civil War enterprising farmers in Pennsylvania were accustomed to skim the substance from Oil Creek, a branch of the Allegheny, and use it to grease their wagons. Some even bottled it and sold it as "Rock Oil,"

a medicine "guaranteed," when externally applied, to cure rheumatism, and good for almost anything, if taken internally. Credit for the first significant use of petroleum as an illuminant belongs to a graduate of Dartmouth College, named George H. Bissell, who was convinced that ultimately he could supplant the old-fashioned tallow candles and whale-oil lamps with something far superior. Bissell leased some land in western Pennsylvania and sent a sample of the oil it produced to Benjamin Silliman, Jr., professor of chemistry at Yale College. In a memorable document, written in 1851, Silliman reported that an excellent illuminant could be made from petroleum, that the cost of refinement would be slight, and that from it a number of important by-products, such as naphtha and paraffin, could also be recovered. Bissell won sufficient support from capitalists to begin operations, and sent Edwin Drake, a minor

STEEL MILLS

The mills at Pittsburgh, Pennsylvania, soon became the leading producers of American steel.

but enthusiastic stockholder, out to Titusville, Pennsylvania, to drill for oil. Drake had observed the methods used in operating the salt wells near Syracuse and Pittsburgh, and successfully followed them in his quest for oil. By August, 1859, "Drake's folly," as the incredulous natives called his venture, was producing oil at the rate of twenty barrels a day.

The Petroleum Industry. When it became apparent that fabulous sums could be made from oil, the venturesome flocked to western Pennsylvania by the thousands. Oil derricks dotted the landscape; crossroads became towns, and towns became cities, almost overnight. Pittsburgh, and other strategic centers, found a new source of wealth in the business of oil refining, while the whole country bought the new kerosene lamps and began to sit up nights. Competition for a while was utterly unrestrained. On this account, and also because of the unpredictable nature of both the supply and the demand, the prices of crude oil and of kerosene varied almost from day to day. Fortunes were lost as well as made. Nevertheless, by 1864 the oil fields around Titusville had expanded to 400 square miles, and by 1872 not only western Pennsylvania, but parts of West Virginia and Ohio also, were included within the 2,000 square miles in the United States devoted to the production of oil. In a dozen years the petroleum industry climbed to a place of high prominence in the nation's business, with huge sales both at home and abroad.

John D. Rockefeller. A central figure in the history of oil refining in the United States is John D. Rockefeller (1839–1937), a native of Richford, New York, who had moved with his parents to Cleveland, Ohio, when he was thirteen years old. Young Rockefeller early exhibited extraordinary business talent. Shrewd, calculating, and thrifty, he made up his mind as early as 1862 that the "coal-oil" business had a future worth sharing. At the end of the war

he gave up his other activities and formed a partnership with Samuel Andrews, an oil refiner who made use of a highly improved process. By this time the two chief western centers for the refining of oil were Pittsburgh and Cleveland, but the advantage, as Rockefeller sensed, lay with Cleveland, which had easy access, both by water and rail, to the East no less than to the West, whereas Pittsburgh, for its eastern market, was wholly dependent upon the Pennsylvania Railroad. Five years later, reinforced by new allies, Rockefeller founded the Standard Oil Company of Ohio, which that year refined 4 per cent of the nation's total output. By 1872, with monopoly as his goal, he had acquired twenty out of the twenty-five refineries in Cleveland and was laying plans for the further conquests that within a decade were to bring him control over 90 per cent of the oil refineries of the country.

The Standard Oil Company. Rockefeller's ruthless methods left him a rich legacy of hatred. The railroads, hard pressed for business during the depression, had little choice but to give him the rebates he demanded. Shippers less favored either were ruined by the unfair competition or sold out to Standard Oil. When it came to the marketing of oil, Rockefeller gave no quarter. The United States was divided into convenient sections, each with its agent and subagents, with every agent under instructions to "sell all the oil that is sold in your district." Railroad records were spied upon by Standard Oil men so that the business of competitive refineries could be stolen. Price cutting was carried to any extreme necessary to put a competitor out of business, and as soon as his defeat was assured the price of oil was set again at a figure as high as or higher than before the price war began. Pipeline companies were gathered up by Standard Oil one by one, usually at its own price. Determined to pay no man profits, Rockefeller built terminal warehouses of his own, established factories to make barrels and other necessary articles, and eliminated hundreds of wholesalers and middlemen. Finally, in order to facilitate centralized control and to insure against unintentional competition among the various Standard properties, the Standard Oil Trust was formed. This device, first adopted in 1879, but revised and more completely applied in 1882, consisted merely of a group of nine trustees to whom was surrendered all the stock of the Standard Oil Company and its various affiliates. Trust certificates were then issued to each Standard stockholder in the proportion of twenty trust certificates for each share of Standard stock. For several years the nine trustees, with Rockefeller at their head, made the decisions for all of the stockholders and all of the companies that were dominated by Standard Oil.

The "New South."   While Standard Oil and numerous comparable businesses were expanding their holdings in the North and West, similar developments had occurred in the "New South." It was apparent to both northerners and southerners that the inadequacy of manufacturing facilities in the South had been one of the major reasons for the section's loss of the war. During Reconstruction and the depressed seventies there was little that enterprising southerners could do to remedy this deficiency. Local capital was all but nonexistent, northern money was employed elsewhere, and what prewar establishments still existed were run down and in need of repairs. But a change in southern atmosphere came rapidly after the breakdown of the Reconstruction governments and the lifting of the national depression. The "redemption" governments that succeeded carpetbag rule were headed by business-minded men, who were eager to cooperate with northern industrialists. They kept taxes low, especially on new industry, made lavish grants of state lands to new enterprises, and leased out state convicts, among whom were many Negroes, to their own and to other business

projects at ridiculously low rates. They also helped obtain the repeal of the Southern Homestead Act of 1866, with its annoying restrictions on the acquisition of federal lands located in the South.

All this favoritism in high places stimulated southern industry. Strongly backed by northern and English capital, southern railroad, lumber, and mining interests embarked on many new ventures, from which among other things the southern people profited much by furnishing essential labor and supplies. Within a period of twenty years, for example, capital estimated at $30 million poured into the southern iron industry, which centered on Birmingham, Alabama, and by the late eighties was producing more pig iron than the entire nation had produced before the Civil War. In the seaboard South perhaps the most spectacular development was the rise of the cigarette industry. Aided by the invention in 1880 of a cigarette-making machine and by the increasing production of bright leaf tobacco, the industry grew rapidly and shifted its center from Virginia to North Carolina. There the Dukes, R. J. Reynolds, and James R. Day paralleled in their own activities the careers of Carnegie and Rockefeller in the North. During the last twenty years of the nineteenth century the southern cotton industry, likewise, made spectacular headway, accounting by 1900 for about half of the cotton mills and half the production of the country. A natural development from the textile industry was the utilization of cotton seed. Long regarded as almost valueless, the oil-rich seed was being processed by the end of the century to obtain edible oils, fertilizers, and animal food. The making of furniture, chemical fertilizers, cement, and brick products helped further to diversify southern industrialism. By 1900 the per capita wealth of the section was estimated at about one-half that of the North, whereas only twenty years earlier it had been about one-third. Nevertheless, since much of the South's industry was still owned by northerners, the colonial nature of its economy was yet to be overcome.

Close observers of business trends during the eighties began to notice the disturbing trend toward monopoly. With nationwide competition at work only the ablest, the most selfish, and the most unscrupulous competitors could survive. In 1880, the nation had 1,990 woolen mills; in 1890, only 1,311. In 1880 it had 1,934 factories that made agricultural implements; in 1890, only 910. During the same decade the number of iron and steel mills decreased by one-third, and the number of leather establishments by three-fourths. In every case, however, the total capital investment and the total output of the industry vastly increased, while ownership, or at least management, was concentrated far more rapidly than even the reduced number of plants would indicate. What the nation was witnessing was the emergence of a large number of near-monopolies, each aspiring to complete control of some important national necessity.

The "Trusts." Public awareness of the situation began with the appearance of an article, "The Story of a Great Monopoly," by Henry Demarest Lloyd, in the *Atlantic Monthly* for March, 1881. A scathing attack on the Standard Oil Company, the article made a deep impression on the public. "This is the original trust," declared a New York committee that in 1888 began the investigation of Standard Oil. "Its success has been the incentive to the formation of all other trusts or combinations. It is the type of a system which has spread like a disease through the commercial system of this country." What the committee charged was fully borne out by the facts. One after another "an incredible number of the necessaries and luxuries of life, from meat to tombstones," had fallen into the hands of some tightly organized little group that frequently by the most unscrupulous and underhanded methods had achieved control. The exact pattern of the Standard Oil

Trust was not always followed, but the results were generally about the same. Sometimes the possession of exclusive patent rights promoted the cause of monopoly and thus made of the liberal patent laws of the United States a kind of subsidy to big business.

The evils of the "trusts," as the public without much discrimination described all big businesses, won much notoriety. Prices were fixed without benefit of competition, and sometimes at higher levels than before the trust was formed. Raw producers were compelled to take what the trust chose to pay, for there was no one else to whom to sell. Labor was forced into line by the closing of troublesome plants and by the circulation of "blacklists" that made it difficult for "agitators" to obtain employment. Politicians were influenced by free passes from the railroads, by campaign contributions, and by outright bribes. Powerful lobbies appeared in Washington and in the several state capitals charged with the duty of winning favors from lawmakers and law enforcers. The Washington lobbyists were sometimes described as the "third house" of Congress. Plants that experience had shown to be well located were enlarged, and others less ideally situated were closed down, without regard for the inevitable unemployment involved or the municipal problems that arose from population changes. Individual freedom suffered blow after blow as the owners of small establishments became the employees of larger ones, and as the chance to enter business independently diminished. Employees were pushed further from the sight and hearing of employers, and could expect less and less personal consideration.

Advantages of the Trusts. And yet the "trusts" were by no means without their good points. Indeed, most business historians have come to believe that the "robber barons" concept of the nineteenth-century industrial leaders was quite mistaken. The time had come when American business, in the interest of the public good, had to be organized along national lines. Much of the competition that the trusts eliminated was sheer waste, and without it prices could be, and often were, reduced. Large-scale businesses were usually far more efficient than the small concerns they supplanted, and were able to make money out of by-products that the smaller operators were forced to throw away. Big business could afford to take heavy initial losses while waiting for ultimate profits. It could bear the cost of advertising and of the slow enlargement of markets. Usually, too, it was better managed, better located, better equipped. Small establishments could not so easily afford to scrap expensive machinery when new inventions made better equipment available. They could not compete with big businesses in paying salaries to the ablest managers. Even without the cutthroat competition to which they were subjected, many of them would have lost out because of their inefficiency.

Legal Status of the Trusts. As public awareness of the trust problem grew, an insistent demand set in that something should be done about it. This meant, to most Americans, that the government should take action against the trusts, but unfortunately governmental action under the existing system was not easily attainable. The Constitution gave the central government only definitely specified powers and left all others to the states. Since the founding fathers had never heard of a trust, the only power to control such organizations that they had lodged with the central government was whatever might be inferred from the right to control interstate commerce. Obviously, the extent to which any such implied power might be exercised would have to be determined by the courts after extensive litigation. The states, on the other hand, had ample power within their several jurisdictions, but their boundaries were too small, for the activities of any important trust extended through many

states. Moreover, the requirement of the national Constitution that each state must give "full faith and credit . . . to the public acts, records, and judicial proceedings of every other state" had embarrassing possibilities. Under the terms of this clause special favors obtained in one state might easily be interpreted to mean special favors in every state. Another constitutional advantage enjoyed by corporations flowed from the Fourteenth Amendment which required that the states might not "deprive any person of life, liberty, or property, without due process of law." In 1886 the Supreme Court, in *Santa Clara County* v. *Southern Pacific Railroad,* reversing an earlier ruling, held that the use of the word "person" in this clause was meant to apply to corporations as well as to individuals. Thus the states, themselves the creators of the corporations, were restrained by the federal government from any measures of taxation or regulation that the courts chose to regard as depriving the corporations of property "without due process of law."

The Sherman Antitrust Act. Attempts to restrain the trusts were made nevertheless. Just as the Grangers had invoked to good advantage the old rule of common law that a common carrier was subject to regulation because it was quasi-public in nature, so now the states fell back upon the common-law prohibition of conspiracy in restraint of trade. During the late eighties state after state passed statutes based on this principle. Finally, Congress also fell into line, and on July 2, 1890, the Sherman Antitrust Act received the President's signature. This measure lacked nothing in vigor of language. It branded as illegal "every contract, combination in the form of trust or otherwise, or conspiracy in restraint of trade or commerce among the several states, or with foreign nations." It defined as a misdemeanor any "attempt to monopolize, or combine or conspire with any other person or persons to monopolize, any part of the trade or commerce among the several states or with foreign nations." Penalties for persons held guilty of violating the act were set at a fine not to exceed $5,000 and imprisonment not to exceed a year, one or both, as the court might prescribe. Furthermore, any person injured by means that the act declared unlawful might recover in court "threefold the damages by him sustained."

Difficulties in Enforcement. Enforcement of these provisions was quite another matter. A number of suits were lodged by the states, and a few decisions unfavorable to the corporations were obtained. Since the technical trust was so clear-cut a violation of both the common law and the statutes, that type of organization was generally discontinued, but in its place new devices to accomplish the same end were speedily invented. Chief among these was the holding company, through which a controlling percentage of the stocks in a great number of enterprises was owned and voted by a single corporation, but many of the trusts chose instead to incorporate as a single great company in the most friendly state they could find. As for penalty provisions of the Sherman Antitrust Act, seven out of the first eight attempts to invoke them went against the government, and in the Knight case (1895) the Supreme Court of the United States held that the mere

purchase of property, even if it made for monopoly and the restraint of trade, was not in itself illegal; further, that manufacture and production (the particular case in question involved the refining of sugar) were no part of interstate commerce. Confronted by this interpretation, the government made little further effort to enforce the act, and lawyers felt free to advise their clients that the Supreme Court of the United States had conceded the legality of private monopoly.

Thus the great interstate railroads and the giant trusts were freed from any effective social control. Their size and power obstructed the self-regulatory operations of competition, the individual states were almost helpless in controlling their actions, and judicial interpretation of the Interstate Commerce and Sherman laws restrained the federal government from intervention in their affairs. The years from 1865 to 1900 became a virtual business paradise. The rising challenge of both organizing labor and the politically-minded farmer were not to be negligible. But in no other modern society had private business been confronted with more economic opportunities and with less social restraint upon its actions. Hailed by most Americans and regularly eulogized by the government, business and business values became for a period the credo of the nation.

SELECTED BIBLIOGRAPHY

An excellent new anthology containing much fresh, lively material on the themes in this chapter is Sigmund Diamond, *The Nation Transformed* (1963). A stimulating, important synthesis is in S. P. Hayes, *The Response to Industrialism, 1885–1914* (1957), which is an overview of the whole period and takes note of political as well as economic developments. The older general accounts, such as I. M. Tarbell, *The Nationalizing of Business, 1878–1898* (1936), are now rather antiquated, in view of

the recent progress of research and reinterpretation. The muckraking and readable work of Matthew Josephson, *The Robber Barons* (1934), has been challenged as one-sided and unappreciative of the constructive work of businessmen and financiers. Significant works in the newer vein include: E. C. Kirkland, *Dream and Thought in the Business Community, 1860–1900* (1956); William Miller (ed.), *Men in Business* (1952); T. C. Cochran, *Railroad Leaders, 1845–1890* (1953); and Julius Grodinsky, *Transcontinental Railroad Strategy, 1869–1893* (1962). On economic

* Available in paperback

thought see the appropriate parts of the monumental work of Joseph Dorfman, *The Economic Mind in American Civilization* (5 vols., 1946–1959). An influential and stimulating monograph is Sidney Fine, *°Laissez Faire and the General Welfare State, 1865–1901* (1956). On the general performance of the economy, see the historical parts in J. A. Schumpeter, *Business Cycles* (2 vols., 1939); and Rendigs Fels, *American Business Cycles, 1865–1897* (1959). On finance, important works include: G. W. Edwards, *The Evolution of Finance Capitalism* (1938); the biography of Jay Cooke by Henrietta Larson (1936); and F. L. Allen, *The Great Pierpont Morgan* (1949).

Two recent short works give an overview of railroad development: A. D. Chandler, Jr., *°The Railroads* (1965); and G. R. Taylor and I. D. Neu, *The American Railroad Network, 1861–1890* (1956). The building of the first transcontinental railroad is the subject of three recent works: W. S. Griswold, *A Work of Giants* (1962); R. W. Howard, *The Great Iron Trail* (1962); and James McCague, *Moguls and Iron Men* (1964). Light on a misunderstood subject is thrown by Carter Goodrich, *Government Promotion of American Canals and Railroads, 1800–1890* (1960). Rich regional studies include: E. C. Kirkland, *Men, Cities and Transportation: A Study in New England History, 1820–1900* (2 vols., 1948); H. H. Pierce, *Railroads of New York, 1826–1875* (1953); and C. N. Glaab, *Kansas City and the Railroads* (1962). A general work on westward extensions is R. E. Riegel, *°The Story of Western Railroads* (1926). On southwestern railroads, see I. G. Clark, *Then Came the Railroads* (1958); and R. C. Overton, *Gulf to Rockies* (1953). Meritorious studies of individual western railroads include: Oscar Lewis, *The Big Four* (1938), a lively anecdotal treatment of the Central Pacific; Nelson Trottman, *History of the Union Pacific* (1923); R. W. Fogel, *The Union Pacific Railroad* (1960), brief but suggestive; V. V. Masterson, *The Katy Railroad and the Last Frontier* (1952); Stuart Daggett, *Chapters on the History of the Southern Pacific* (1922); R. C. Overton, *Burlington West* (1941); and R. G. Athearn, *Rebel of the Rockies; The Denver and Rio Grande Western Railroad* (1962). Biographies include: Julius Grodinsky, *Jay Gould* (1957); M. W. Schlegel, *Ruler of the Reading; The Life of Franklin B. Gowen* (1957); George

Kennan, *E. H. Harriman* (2 vols., 1922); J. B. Hedges, *Henry Villard and the Railways of the Northwest* (1930); and J. G. Pyle, *The Life of James J. Hill* (2 vols., 1917).

On pressures demanding railroad regulation, see S. J. Buck, *°The Granger Movement* (1913). Felix Frankfurter, *°The Commerce Clause under Marshall, Taney and Waite* (1937), is a near-classic. Important new monographs include L. E. Decker, *Railroads, Lands, and Politics* (1964); and Gabriel Kolko, *Railroads and Regulation, 1877–1916* (1965). H. B. Thorelli, *The Federal Antitrust Policy* (1955), is an interesting study by a Swedish scholar.

Convenient introductions to the subject of inventions are found in: Roger Burlingame, *Engines of Democracy* (1940); and F. L. Vaughan, *The United States Patent System* (1956), which stresses conflicts. Biographies of great inventors include: Matthew Josephson, *°Edison* (1959); H. G. Prout, *A Life of George Westinghouse* (1921); and Catherine Mackenzie, *Alexander Graham Bell* (1928). Industries resulting from inventions are the subjects of several excellent books, including: R. N. Current, *The Typewriter and the Men Who Made It* (1954); A. A. Bright, Jr., *The Electric-Lamp Industry* (1949); H. C. Passer, *The Electric Manufacturers, 1875–1900* (1953); and O. E. Anderson, Jr., *Refrigeration in America* (1953).

An important work dealing with the steel industry is Allan Nevins, *Abram S. Hewitt; With Some Account of Peter Cooper* (1935). On Carnegie, see his revealing *Autobiography* (1920); B. J. Hendrick, *The Life of Andrew Carnegie* (2 vols., 1932); and Gail Kennedy (ed.), *°Democracy and the Gospel of Wealth* (1949). On the oil industry, a general survey is H. F. Williamson and A. R. Daum, *The American Petroleum Industry* (2 vols., 1959–1963). The muck-raking classic by I. M. Tarbell, *The History of the Standard Oil Company* (2 vols., 1904), must now be compared with the more sympathetic work of modern scholars, such as: Allan Nevins, *Study in Power; John D. Rockefeller, Industrialist and Philanthropist* (2 vols., 1953); P. H. Giddens, *Standard Oil Company (Indiana)* (1955); R. W. and M. E. Hidy, *Pioneering in Big Business, 1882–1911; History of the Standard Oil Company (New Jersey)* (1955); and G. T. White, *Formative Years in the Far West: A History of Standard*

Oil Company of California and Predecessors through 1919 (1962). Conflicting views are well set forth in Earl Latham (ed.), *⁎John D. Rockefeller; Robber Baron or Industrial Statesman?* (1949). Sample histories of other industries include: R. A. Clemen, *The American Livestock and Meat Industry* (1923); C. B. Kuhlmann, *The Development of the Flour-Milling Industry in the United States* (1929); F. J. Allen, *The Shoe Industry* (1922); A. H. Cole, *The American Wool Manufacture* (2 vols., 1926); and Morton Keller, *The Life Insurance Enterprise, 1885–1910* (1963).

On the growth of industry in the South, see the brief treatment by Holland Thompson, *The New South* (1919). A magnificent guide is T. D. Clark (ed.), *Travels in the New South* (2 vols., 1962). Important special studies include: Broadus Mitchell and C. S. Mitchell, *The Industrial Revolution in the South* (1930); M. A. Potwin, *Cotton Mill People of the Piedmont* (1927); and J. W. Jenkins, *James B. Duke* (1927). Of interest are biographies of the New South's leading journalists: J. F. Wall, *Henry Watterson* (1956); and R. B. Nixon, *Henry W. Grady* (1943). On California industries, see V. P. Carosso, *The California Wine Industry, 1830–1895* (1951); and G. D. Nash, *State Government and Economic Development* (1964).

24

LABOR AND THE NEW IMMIGRATION

Labor Organization. A direct and probably inevitable result of the new industrialism was an increased emphasis on labor organization. As the corporations grew in size and strength, the bargaining power of the individual laborer correspondingly decreased. Concentration gave the employer greater power to oppress, by low wages, long hours, and bad working conditions. But concentration also meant a diminishing number of employers, and a proportionately larger number of employees. By acting together and bargaining collectively, laborers might hope to protect themselves. This they attempted to do through more and stronger trade unions, but even more significantly, by efforts to unite all laborers, of whatever crafts, under one leadership.

Trade Unions. Local labor unions had existed in the United States since the early nineteenth century, but the depression that began in 1837 had been disastrous for labor, and not until the time of the Civil War was much lost ground regained. During the fifties and sixties a few national trade unions were formed, but none of them succeeded in drawing into its ranks any large percentage of those eligible, while attempts at all-labor organizations were even less satisfactory. In August, 1866, at Baltimore, a group of seventy-seven delegates representing a great variety of labor interests formed a National Labor Union which for half a dozen years sponsored annual labor congresses. The N.L.U. was soon drawn into politics, however, lost ground rapidly, and crashed with the Panic of 1873. While it lasted, it gave the movement for an eight-hour day a good start, promoted in a variety of ways the study of labor problems, and furnished an example of concerted action by labor that was not forgotten.

Labor troubles came during the seventies in spite of the fact that labor was as yet imperfectly organized. One of the worst outbreaks occurred in the anthracite coal-mining region of Pennsylvania, where for a dozen years after the Civil War the "Molly Maguires," a secret society of terrorists, carried legitimate protests against miserable working conditions to the worst extremes of violence, and even murder. Finally, in 1877, prosecutions and convictions were obtained that brought the outrages to an end, although the need for united action by the miners had by no means disappeared. The railroad strikes during the summer of 1877 were likewise characterized by much disorder and an unhappy ending. Railroad workers were still unorganized, but a cut of 10 per cent announced by the principal northeastern roads led many men to cease work. The efforts of the strikers, however, were unavailing, for at each center of disturbance federal troops were freely used to break the strike. Another example of labor disaffection appeared in the area surrounding San Francisco Bay. There the chief difficulties were widespread unemployment and the presence of many Chinese who worked for "coolie wages." But the activities of the leading agitators, who at first seemed headed toward revolution, turned instead to the formation of a local Workingmen's Party, which seemed content with writing some of its principles into the new state constitution that California adopted in 1879.

The Knights of Labor.   The need for intelligent leadership, so evident in the labor outbreaks of the seventies, was soon supplied in part by a national organization known as the Noble Order of the Knights of Labor. This society, which was at first a kind of idealistic labor lodge, was founded in 1869 by Uriah S. Stephens, a Philadelphia garment cutter. Unlike its predecessor, the Knights of Labor organized individual workers, rather than uniting existing trade unions; "one big union," to which all workers, skilled or unskilled, should belong, was the ideal. Under these circumstances members of the more exclusive trade unions, who took pride in their craft skills, tended to hold aloof, and for a decade the growth of the Knights was only moderate. After 1878, however, when

Terence V. Powderly (1849–1924) of Scranton, Pennsylvania, became its Grand Master, the order took on new life. Powderly was of Irish origin, born in Carbondale, Pennsylvania. At thirteen years of age he became a switch tender; later as a Scranton machinist he took so prominent a part in the work of the Machinists' and Blacksmiths' Union that he not only lost his job, but also won a place for his name on an employers' blacklist. He was elected mayor of Scranton in 1878 on the Greenback-Labor ticket. When a meeting was held at Reading, Pennsylvania, to reorganize the Knights, Powderly dominated the proceedings, and for the next fifteen years his name and the Knights of Labor were almost synonymous. Powderly, with a tiny salary, traveled at his own expense wherever he felt he could gain more recruits for the Knights. From a membership of only 28,000 in 1880 the organization increased to perhaps as many as 700,000 by 1886.

The program of the Knights was by no means new. They favored the eight-hour day, the "establishment of cooperative institutions productive and distributive," the use of arbitration as a substitute for strikes, and improvements in the legal status of labor. Powderly saw especial virtue in the cooperative idea, and under his urging not less than 135 such ventures were undertaken, some of which endured for a time. But bad management, internal dissension, insufficient funds, and cutthroat competition accounted for the failure of most of them.

In spite of their attempts to avoid them, the Knights became embroiled in a series of violent strikes. In 1884 a recession set in. Companies that took advantage of the opportunity to discharge union men, particularly Knights, were sometimes fought successfully by boycotts, but the chief weapon of labor proved to be the strike. By use of it the Missouri Pacific, early in 1885, was forced to restore a wage cut made without warning and without even the excuse of declining earnings. Public sympathy was almost unanimously with the strikers, and the company in yielding felt obliged to grant its employees time and one-half for overtime, something the strikers had not even asked. In many minor instances during the middle eighties the Knights helped to win such victories.

Strikes of 1886. Sometimes, however, the outcome was far different. In March, 1886, the dismissal of a foreman in the Texas and Pacific car shops, presumably for his membership in the Knights of Labor, provoked another important strike. Under the leadership of Martin Irons, some 9,000 shopmen employed on the Gould system (of which the Texas and Pacific was a part) quit work and attempted by sabotage to make all freight-hauling locomotives unfit for duty. So successful were their efforts that freight traffic along 5,000 miles of railroad in the Southwest was at a standstill; only passenger trains carrying United States mails were permitted to move. At first popular hatred of Jay Gould worked in favor of the strikers, but when food shortages began to be felt and factories had to close down for lack of coal, the public had enough of the strike. Four state governors, strongly backed by public opinion, ordered the strikers to cease interfering with trains, and Powderly himself, led by Gould to believe the railroad would accept arbitration, intervened to call a temporary halt. When Gould later refused arbitration, the strike was resumed with renewed violence, but the public was now so definitely against the strikers that their cause was soon lost.

The Haymarket Riot. Excitement over the southwestern railroad strike had scarcely subsided when the May Day strikes of 1886 claimed the attention of the country. The purpose of these strikes, in which perhaps 340,000 men participated, was to promote the cause of the eight-hour day. Although some labor gains were achieved, an episode that occurred in Chicago, the center of the strike, gave organized labor the most severe setback it had

TERENCE V. POWDERLY

The Grand Master Workman of the Knights of Labor, 1887. During the 1880's the Knights lost out to the American Federation of Labor.

yet received. Chicago was the headquarters of a small group of foreign-born anarchists who welcomed the opportunity to expound to the strikers their principal tenet, the abolition of the state. To promote this end they were ready to advocate, although far less ready to perform, deeds of violence and terror. On the afternoon of May 3, 1886, August Spies, anarchist editor of the *Arbeiter Zeitung*, was addressing a meeting of strikers and sympathizers on a vacant lot not far from the McCormick Harvester Works, when the police attempted to disperse the assembly. In the ensuing melee several strikers were killed or wounded. That night a circular, printed in English and German, called lustily for "Revenge! Revenge! Workmen to arms!" Next day many meetings of protest occurred, the most notable being set for the evening at Haymarket Square, where a crowd of 1,500 assembled to listen to speeches by three leading anarchists. Although the crowd was orderly, the police again appeared and attempted to disperse it. This time, however, the officers of the law were met with a bomb that exploded with terrific violence, killing one policeman and wounding many more. Hard fighting followed, and when the casualties were reckoned it was found that of the policemen seven had lost their lives and over sixty had been seriously wounded, while of the civilians, four were dead and about fifty wounded.

The feeling of blind rage with which the public reacted to the "Haymarket riot" demanded victims. Efforts to find the real culprits, however, proved singularly unavailing. At length, eight well-known anarchists, including Spies, were marked for trial. Evidence that any one of the eight had had anything to do either with making or throwing the bomb was never produced, but seven of the men were given death sentences, and the eighth, imprisonment for fifteen years. The convictions were made on the assumption that these men, by advocating violence, had influenced some unknown person to throw the bomb, but this was merely an assumption. It was clear that the men were convicted because of the opinions they held. In general, the public applauded the sentences and rejoiced when four of the convicted men were hanged. One of the others killed himself with a bomb, and two had their sentences commuted to life imprisonment. A few outraged citizens condemned the whole proceeding as a miscarriage of justice. In 1893, Governor John P. Altgeld pardoned the two men who were serving life sentences, an act of courage that wrecked his political career.

Decline of the Knights. It was ironic that the public saw in the Haymarket riot occasion for further condemnation of the

THE HAYMARKET RIOT, MAY 4, 1886

When the police ordered this mass meeting of workers to disperse, someone threw a bomb into the police ranks which killed one policeman and wounded many others. The police are shown here charging the mob during the riot that followed.

Knights of Labor. Actually the strike for the eight-hour day had been promoted mainly through local trade unions, and Powderly had counseled against it on the ground that the weapon of the strike should not be invoked until all other means of protest had been exhausted. Nevertheless, the Knights had already won a reputation for violence and they received the blame. The control of the central organization over the behavior of the locals disintegrated, and strikes were often undertaken against the advice of the General Executive Board. The result was that skilled workers, alienated by the ruthless way in which the unskilled precipitated conflicts, tended to withdraw from the Knights in order to build up their own trade unions. By 1888 the membership of the Knights of Labor had declined to less than 260,000, and within a few years the order disappeared entirely.

The A. F. of L. Meantime a rival organization, which discarded the "one big union" idea in favor of the federative plan based on shop crafts, had begun to make headway. The American Federation of Labor, founded at Pittsburgh in 1881, began to lengthen its membership list as the Knights declined. While individuals, as such, were excluded from membership, almost any skilled trade union and a few other types, whether national, state, or local, might belong. To protect its individual members against unskilled competition, it sought to limit the number of apprenticeships in each craft. To protect the organization against possible competitors, it warred against what it called "dual unionism." It had no quarrel with capitalism as an economic system, and throughout its history it fought radical movements among its members. Its mission was to insure that labor shared generously in capitalistic enterprise. To this end it formulated a philosophy which it called economic, or day-to-day unionism, to differentiate it from the political unions of Europe. It sought such

practical goals as an eight-hour day, a six-day work week, higher wages, shorter hours, safer and more sanitary working conditions, greater security of job tenure, and the elimination of child labor.

This economic unionism showed little interest in the establishment of cooperatives, and it resisted all efforts to make the Federation over into a separate political party. Instead of going directly into politics, it supported candidates and platforms, of whatever party, provided only that they were favorable to the program of the Federation. While it hoped to see labor win most of its victories peacefully, either by obtaining favorable legislation or by collective bargaining with employers, the Federation was willing in case of necessity to rely on the strike and the boycott. Its organization lent itself admirably to the use of the sympathetic strike, by means of which workers in a related craft might come to the aid of a striking union. A sizable "war chest," supported by a per capita tax levied on members, enabled the Federation's central board of control to aid unemployed strikers and to prolong any conflict it chose to support.

Samuel Gompers. Samuel Gompers (1850–1924) was the central figure in the American Federation. He was born in London, the son of a cigarmaker. At ten he began to learn the shoemaker's trade, but soon gave that up for his father's trade, because the latter was organized. In 1863 he came with his parents to America, and a year later he joined the first cigarmakers' union ever organized in New York City. Eventually he became first the union's secretary and later its president. The training he thus received was significant, for in many ways this local New York cigarmakers' union was a model organization. It followed the British system of benefit payments in case of unemployment, sickness, or death; it tried to encourage skill and intelligence among its members; it gained many of its victories by collective bargaining, by arbitration, and by retaining the good will and respect of employers. Gompers never forgot this early training, and much of the conservatism of his later career may be attributed to it. From 1885 to the time of his death, with the exception of a single year, 1895, he was regularly elected president of the Federation.

Under Gompers' devoted leadership, the Federation scored many successes. It backed the strikes for the eight-hour day with fairly satisfactory results. It supported numerous movements that resulted in the enactment of laws favorable to labor. Partly through its activities, practically every state in the Union was soon equipped with a bureau of labor statistics. It encouraged member unions to set up their own systems for sickness and unemployment benefits, and could soon point to many instances in which its advice had been followed. It promoted efforts to secure adoption by employers of the "closed shop," and to eliminate "yellow dog" contracts, by which workers were obliged to agree prior to employment that they would not join labor unions. From a membership of about 150,000 in 1886 the Federation by 1900 had grown to more than half a million. The A. F. of L.'s greatest strength in its early career lay in the fact that it represented only the favored minority of skilled labor. Skilled craftsmen were more difficult to replace during a strike. Their better pay rates enabled them to build up strike benefit and pension funds. Their common cultural background — the skilled men were predominantly old American or British immigrants — afforded the A. F. of L. unions more solidarity than if they had been composed of unskilled recent immigrants divided by diverse languages and cultures. On the other hand, the A. F. of L. was charged with being concerned with only the aristocrats of labor since unskilled workers were excluded from membership, as well as all skilled workers who did not belong to a union. Political radicals especially disliked the A. F. of L. because of

the organization's conservative social program, its support of capitalism, and its refusal to engage in building a labor party. Moreover, a number of labor organizations, including the four great railway unions, refused to affiliate with the Federation on the ground that they were able to take care of themselves, and were not eager to accept responsibility for others. The railway unions, however, ordinarily could be counted on to cooperate fully with the Federation.

The Homestead Strike.   During the depression-ridden years of the nineties the conservative policies of Gompers and the A. F. of L. were sorely tested. Gompers himself lost office for a year during this period when the armies of unemployed men became increasingly radical and impatient of restraint. An omen of what was to come appeared in 1892 when a violent strike broke out in the steel industry then centered in Pittsburgh, Pennsylvania. The Homestead strike, as this conflict was called, involved on the one hand the Amalgamated Association of Iron and Steel Workers, and on the other hand the powerful Carnegie Steel Company. Carnegie himself was no labor-baiter, and three years before, he had agreed to a satisfactory contract with the union, but at the time trouble broke out in 1892, he had conveniently gone to Europe, leaving the affairs of the company in the hands of Henry Clay Frick, a man who detested organized labor. The chief point at issue between the company and the workers was a proposed reduction in the pay for piecework. The company argued that such a reduction was justified because more efficient machinery had been installed. The worker who made use of the new tools could turn out more pieces than formerly in a given time without any greater expenditure of energy. Thus, according to the employers, a reduction in the piece rate could be made without reducing the worker's daily or weekly earnings. The union, however, refused to be persuaded, and held that the real intent of the company was a wage cut.

When on July 1 the union refused to accept the company's terms, Frick anticipated the strike by closing the Homestead works. Technically, therefore, what followed was the result of a "lockout" rather than a strike. The union at once began to picket the works, while Frick had a wire fence fifteen feet high built around the company's property and ordered 300 guards from the Pinkerton Detective Agency. Fighting between the "Pinkertons" and the strikers on July 6, 1892, resulted in numerous deaths and injuries on both sides. The Pinkertons were no match for the enraged strikers, who captured and disarmed their entire force and ran them out of town. Frick then appealed to the state for protection, and the governor sent enough militia to turn the little mill town into an armed camp. The strikers held out for nearly five months, but at length they were forced to resume work on the company's terms. An important factor in alienating the public from the strikers, whose case at first had aroused considerable sympathy, was the mad attack, not union inspired, by Alexander Berkman, a young anarchist, on the life of Frick. Frick, although seriously injured, soon recovered, and Berkman for his crime spent fifteen years in prison.

The Pullman Strike. Of all the many labor disturbances that punctuated the years of depression after 1893, the Pullman strike of 1894 was by far the most significant. In 1880 George Mortimer Pullman, the inventor and builder of the Pullman sleeping car, had established for the benefit of his employees the "model town" of Pullman on the outskirts of Chicago. This project carried paternalism to an extraordinary length. The company built model dwellings for its employees, and maintained also a company store, a company church, a company school, a company park, and a company theater. The entire village, indeed, was owned and operated by the Pullman Palace Car Company as a business investment — a kind of modern feudalism, so critics were accustomed to say.

Pullman had no use for labor unions, but during the first year of the depression organizers of the American Railway Union made rapid headway with his men. This union was the brain child of Eugene V. Debs, who was later to become the outstanding leader of the Socialist movement in the United States. Debs (1855–1926) was born in Terre Haute, Indiana, of French-Alsatian ancestry. He had worked in the railway shops of his home town when he was fourteen, and at sixteen he had become a locomotive fireman. A passionate defender of the underprivileged and devoted to the union idea, he held high office in the Brotherhood of Locomotive Firemen, and for a time edited *The Locomotive Fireman's Magazine*. He became increasingly impatient, however, with the unaggressive attitude of the railway brotherhoods and the American Federation of Labor, with which the brotherhoods cooperated. Convinced that industrial unions were preferable to trade unions and that railroad men should all be members of one organization, in 1893 he founded the American Railway Union, and such was his persuasiveness that within a year the new union had enrolled 150,000 members.

Railroad Tie-ups. The Pullman strike was precipitated in the spring of 1894 when the Pullman Company, hard hit by the depression, laid off one-third of its men and cut the wages of the rest from 30 to 40 per cent. No reductions, however, were made in the rent charged for company houses nor in the price of goods at the company stores. In protest the men quit work, and with the demand for sleeping cars at a standstill Pullman showed no disposition to call them back. The strikers were on the verge of starvation when the American Railway Union came to the rescue with relief money and with the threat of a boycott against the hauling of Pullman cars. Debs ordered the boycott to be applied on all the western railroads, and the "A.R.U." men obeyed by cutting out Pullman cars from their trains and leaving them on sidetracks. When boycotters were discharged for such acts, the strike became general, and not Pullman cars alone but whole trains stood on sidetracks. From Cincinnati to San Francisco the effects of the strike were felt. Traffic between Chicago and the West was virtually paralyzed, and hoodlums who joined the strikers stooped to every sort of violence, as all the accumulated bitterness and resentment of the unemployed multitudes was poured into the strife.

Federal Troops. The railroad operators, faced by this dangerous situation, would normally have been willing to trust the governor of Illinois — the state most seriously involved — to keep order, if necessary by calling out the militia to aid the civil authorities. But the governor of Illinois happened to be John P. Altgeld, a friend of labor already notorious among conservatives for his pardoning of the Haymarket anarchists. The operators, therefore, demanded that federal troops be brought in, and when Altgeld took no steps in that direction they appealed directly to the President for aid. In spite of any qualms he might have felt about his constitutional power, Cleveland decided that he might intervene on the pretext that the Chicago disorders interfered with the free transport of United States mail. By the Fourth of July 2,000 regulars, including cavalry and field artillery, had moved into the troubled zone, to see that the mails were carried and to break the strike. Altgeld protested vigorously that Cleveland's action was unconstitutional and demanded the immediate withdrawal of the federal troops, but Cleveland stood his ground.

Use of the Injunction. Governmental action against the strikers was not confined to the use of troops, for the federal courts soon took a hand. Debs, who had assumed direct supervision of the strike, was arrested by federal officers on the charge of conspiracy to obstruct the mails, and although released on bail, was enjoined by two federal judges against doing anything to prolong the strike. In direct defiance of this order, Debs urged a group of labor leaders on July 12 to promote a general strike by all the labor organizations of the country. Thereupon he and six others were cited for contempt of court and sentenced to six months in jail. Thus summarily removed from the scene of conflict, Debs was left free to read and to think, and when he emerged from confinement he announced his conversion to socialism. His imprisonment served also to called attention to the fact that the courts were not averse to using the injunction in order to obtain results that could not be guaranteed by the normal procedure of a jury trial. Criticism of "government by injunction" and of the use of the regular army to break strikes was freely expressed.

Governor Waite. That another view of the duty of government could be taken was shown by Governor Davis H. Waite of Colorado, whom Populists, with Democratic assistance, had elected in 1892. Waite did not hesitate to help the striking miners during the "Cripple Creek War" of 1894 instead of giving the customary governmental aid to the employers. When an army of deputy sheriffs made ready to attack the strikers, Waite called out the entire state militia to preserve the peace, and marched his troops between the opposing forces. Waite was a man of no tact and little judgment, but his attitude, like Altgeld's, gave impetus to the forces of labor. Throughout the nineties in Colorado, Idaho, and Montana the Western Federation of Miners battled employers with a violence that bordered on revolution.

"Coxey's Army." That the national government should help solve the problem of unemployment by means of work relief was the contention of "General" Jacob S. Coxey

COXEY'S ARMY ON THE WAY TO WASHINGTON

of Massillon, Ohio, a Greenbacker and a Populist. Coxey advocated that Congress should issue $500 million in legal-tender notes to be expended at the rate of $20 million a month on the building of good roads. Wages of $1.50 per eight-hour day were to be paid to all who needed employment. Coxey also urged that municipalities desirous of making public improvements should be authorized to issue non-interest-bearing bonds equal to half their assessed valuation. These bonds might then be used as security with the Secretary of the Treasury to obtain loans of legal-tender notes to pay for the construction of schools, courthouses, paved streets, and other worthy projects. Both schemes, on the financial side, were highly inflationary in character, but they aimed at a type of governmental activity that in later years became extremely familiar.

In seeking to promote his ideas Coxey hit upon the expedient of presenting, by means of a march of the unemployed on Washington, a "living petition" to Congress. With the assistance of amused and interested newspapermen, he actually got his march started on Easter Sunday, 1894, and on the first of May following "Coxey's Army," 500 strong, entered Washington determined to lay its demands before Congress. At the Capitol Coxey and several of his principal adherents were arrested for disobeying an ordinance to keep off the grass. But Coxey's exploit, which attracted wide newspaper attention, was speedily imitated by other marchers, most of whom were stopped far short of Washington.

Labor in the South. While these exciting events were occurring in the North, within the states of the former Confederacy labor organization was virtually nonexistent, despite the rapid industrial strides being made. Southern labor, in part because of its rural background and in part because of the racial problem, remained docile. Whites from the poorer lands of the piedmont and from the mountains furnished the bulk of the labor supply for the textile mills and such others as required machine operators, while a preponderance of Negroes did the harder work of the mines, the blast furnaces, and the lumber

431

industry. Only in the rarest instances were the two races employed to work side by side at the same tasks. In the textile mills hours of labor were long, sometimes as much as seventy-two hours per week. Nevertheless, one of the chief attractions of the mills to the rural whites was the opportunity for the entire family to be gainfully employed. Wages were low, at first far lower than those paid in the northern mills, but with the head of the house as well as his wife and children at work, his total income was so much larger than he could wrest from a rundown southern farm that the temptation to leave the farm for the factory was almost irresistible.

Most of the southern mills and factories developed along definitely paternalistic lines. The "company" provided houses for the workers, opened stores, and in many instances paid the workers in scrip, good at any time for payments to the company, but redeemable largely for company goods. The company also provided such schools and churches as it deemed desirable, and hired both the teachers and the preachers. To the country people who flocked to the mills these gratuitous acts were accepted without suspicion. They furnished an opportunity for community life before unknown. Throughout the nineteenth century labor organizers in the South were given little encouragement either by employers or by employees. In the twentieth century, however, unionism took strong hold in the South and worked many changes.

Immigration. Closely connected with the labor problem was the new immigration from Europe invading the United States in an increasing tide during the decades that followed the Civil War. The migration of these peoples came in distinct waves. The first great movement had come principally from England during the seventeenth century. Other nationalities, particularly the Dutch along the Hudson, and the Swedes along the Delaware, also had contributed to this early movement. The next great

influx was that of the Scotch-Irish and the Rhineland Germans, or Palatines, in the eighteenth century. The third wave came during the twenty or so years preceding the Civil War, bringing millions of Irish and Germans to the country. The fourth wave occurred immediately after the Civil War and lasted until the First World War. Included in it were all the previous nationalities, but as time went on an increasingly large number arrived also from southern and eastern Europe, who in language and culture differed strikingly from their predecessors.

Despite all the European immigration, the Anglo-American influence remained dominant. Because the English immigrants came first, they set the original patterns in language, literature, law, government, and religion. These traits were greatly modified both by the changed conditions in the New World and by each succeeding wave of newcomers. But since the old stock always greatly outnumbered the new, and held vested positions of power, the non-English immigrants had to learn the English language and conform to Anglo-American customs. Thus the influence of the newcomers, like that of the American environment, simply modified the existing culture and did not substitute a new culture for it. In one form or another, most of the old traditions lived on.

Causes for Immigration. Economic opportunity during and after the Civil War had much influence upon the coming of the immigrants. The demand for cheap labor to man the new industries in most years outran the domestic supply. Western lands also existed for those who had means to reach the West. Official stimulation came by the granting of liberal bounties for those who would serve in the army and by the passage of the act of 1864 which allowed the importation of labor under contracts similar to the indentures of colonial times. Further encouraging immigration, both the federal government and many western states maintained immigration bureaus that vied with the western railroads in issuing pamphlets offering the promise of the new western lands. The new and still competitive steamship companies of the period, quick to see in the immigrant trade a lucrative source of income, offered low trans-Atlantic fares. These low rates were advertised not only by the ship and railroad companies, but by agents who made it their business to induce the discontented everywhere to emigrate. These agents, for a commission, sold the emigrants tickets to the New World, herded them westward to farms if they had the money to buy land, or turned them over to American labor contractors if they had not. Advertisers drew a convincing, but often false, picture of the easy road to wealth in the United States, and for thousands of hard pressed Europeans the appeal promised security and fortune.

In Europe powerful forces goaded many people to emigration. Of all such forces, population pressure was strongest. After 1750 the total population of the Continent increased in 100 years by 85 per cent, or from about 140 million to about 260 million. Within the next fifty years Europe's population increased by another 54 per cent. While most of these people found a living in the rising industrial cities of Europe, many could find no place in their own country either on farm or in factory. Added to the economic urge were other important factors. Dislike of British rule continued as at least a secondary motivation among the Irish, and the revival of reaction that followed the revolutions of 1848 in Germany and central Europe pointed the way to the New World for political nonconformists. Both resentment against the requirement of military service, a situation common to most European countries, and religious motives sent their quotas. The Jews of Russia, which then included most of Poland, were subject to severe discrimination and often to bloody pogroms. After the widespread anti-Jewish

outbreaks beginning in 1881, they came to America in steadily increasing numbers. Even among Christians there were reasons for religious unrest. In most European nations established churches enjoyed special prerogatives that were deeply resented by dissenting sects. There was also widespread criticism of the European clergy's indifference to the public welfare, and to their alleged worldliness. The state of religious freedom existing in the United States militated against persecution while permitting an immigrant group to observe as strict standards of behavior as it desired.

The Uprooted. In spite of the European trend toward urbanization, most of the immigrants were country folk. To some extent the movement to America was only a part of the more general movement from country to city; most went to the cities of their own nation, others to the cities of the New World. The peasants of Europe lived together in villages from which they went out each morning to their fields. The habits and customs of the village were fixed by centuries of tradition; each person knew his status and felt that he belonged to a community. The act of leaving thus involved a complete break with the past. From then on he was one of the "uprooted"; wherever he went he would probably never again feel at home. Conditions on the voyage to America involved bad food, jammed quarters, and much suffering. Upon arriving in the United States the immigrant did not find the warm welcome he had hoped for. Certainly the government did almost nothing to help him.

Many of the people who met the immigrant, including some of his own countrymen, were bent merely on cheating him out of what small sums he still retained. They acted as runners for hotels that swindled him, stole his baggage, cheated him in turning his currency into dollars, sold him railway tickets to nonexistent places, or if they existed, by the most

round-about way. After these confusing experiences, he walked the city streets in search of a job only to find that most employers were eager to take advantage of his ignorance. Under the urging of self-appointed bosses, or *padrones,* as the Italians called them, he usually contracted to do unskilled pick and shovel labor on some construction job. He took whatever wages his boss could get for him and handed over as commission whatever part of his earnings his boss chose to demand.

Immigrants as Farmers. The most favored of the immigrants went back to the land. This was especially true of the Scandinavians and Germans, and to a lesser degree of the Finns, the Dutch, and the Czechs. On their arrival at Chicago they were usually met by "land sharks" eager to sell them worthless or even nonexistent land. But in due time many had learned to be wary, and some were always fortunate enough to find the land they coveted, land that reproduced as nearly as possible the characteristics of the land they had known at home. Friends

and relatives already in America helped the newcomers to settle as close as possible to their own holdings. In general the immigrants preferred to buy or rent land that had already been brought under cultivation. Even so, all was strange and difficult. The soil and crops were different from what they had known, and the American methods of farming required machinery that was costly to purchase and baffling to use. Since towns and villages were few, and American farmers lived in houses widely separated from those of their neighbors, nothing compensated for the community life of the Old World village. Loneliness told heavily upon the whole family, but especially upon the women.

City Immigrants. The great majority had no choice except to remain in the cities, where they had to subsist on meager wages. Able to afford only the cheapest housing, they drifted inevitably into tenement districts and slums where the principal object of owners was to crowd a maximum number of people into a mini-

To the oppressed and impoverished masses of the Old World, America beckoned as perhaps has no other nation before or since. While the lot of the immigrant was often a hard one, there were few restrictions on what he could achieve. The essential harmony with which persons of diverse religions and ethnic strains blended together is movingly recounted in the following excerpt:

Yes, East and West, and North and South, the palm and the pine, the pole and the equator, the crescent and the cross — how the great Alchemist melts and fuses them with his purging flame! Here shall they all unite to build the Republic of Man and the Kingdom of God. Ah, Vera, what is the glory of Rome and Jerusalem where all nations and races come to worship and look back, compared with the glory of America, where all races and nations come to labour and look forward!

Israel Zangwill, *The Melting Pot* (1909)

mum amount of space. New York and Boston, where desirable land was scarce, had perhaps the worst slums, but in every large city conditions were bad enough.

But still the immigrants came. A quarter of a million of them landed on American shores in 1865, and three years later the annual total had reached 326,000, well above the average for the 1850's. By 1873, when more than 460,000 aliens entered the country, the immigrant tide had broken all preceding records. The census of 1870, which counted 38.5 million people in the United States, described 2.3 million of them as immigrants who had arrived during the sixties; while five years later the total number of foreign-born in the population was numbered at 7.5 million. The total for the decade of the seventies, despite the depression, was 2.8 million; while during the eighties all previous records were broken by an influx of 5.2 million, an average of more than half a million immigrants a year. By 1905 the million mark had been reached, and until the outbreak of the First World War in 1914 the avalanche continued.

The "New Immigration." Until the last decade of the nineteenth century, the great bulk of this immigration came, as before the Civil War, from the British Isles and from Germany, but some new trends were in evidence. Immigration from Ireland, although still heavy, was exceeded by the numbers coming from England. The Scandinavian migration also made spectacular gains during the seventies, averaging 25,000 a year. The influx from Germany, which up to the middle eighties furnished about one-third of the total, began at that time to drop off, and by the end of the century it furnished not above one-seventh of the whole. Most significant of all was the really "new immigration" from southern and eastern Europe. From the middle eighties on, the masses from these areas rose as those from northern and western Europe fell. By the later nineties the former exceeded the latter in the proportion of three to two.

Anti-Foreigner Sentiment. The descendants of colonial Americans had long been familiar with immigrants from the British

435

Isles and from Germany, and they found comparatively little difficulty in accustoming themselves to such other northwestern Europeans as the Scandinavians and the Dutch. All these immigrants, despite their initial difficulties, accepted American ways without undue resistance. But Italians and Poles, Russians and Rumanians, Magyars and Bulgars, Czechs and Croats, Slovaks and Slovenes, Jews and Greeks were somehow vastly different. Instead of welcoming amalgamation, they seemed almost to set themselves against it. Because of the language difficulties and for protection, immigrants of a given language group tended to settle together in the cities and to retain tenaciously their native language and customs. In every large city there was an Italian quarter, a Jewish quarter, a Russian quarter, or a Polish quarter. And as the older Americans considered these linguistic enclaves, they became highly critical and resisted the assimilation of the newcomers.

Tenements and Slums. For the shocking living conditions to which they were subjected, the immigrants were scarcely to blame. The builders of the tenements re-

fused to repair them and charged all they could. Neither could the city governments that tolerated such housing conditions be cleared of responsibility. The low rewards of employment drove the immigrants into this sordid and unhealthful way of life. In the immigrant sections life expectancy was low and infant mortality was phenomenally high. What troubled the native Americans was that epidemics might, and sometimes did, start in the unsanitary immigrant sections, then spread to other parts of the city, and even into the country. The immigrants were held responsible, also, for much disorder and violence, although many of the crimes attributed to them were not of their doing.

Religions of the Immigrants. The religions of the immigrants were also criticized. Many of them were devout Roman Catholics, and Protestants were alarmed by any increase in the Catholic population. Catholic immigrants naturally sent their children, when they could afford it, to parochial instead of public schools, and for this they were denounced. In the agricultural Middle West, where cities were

THE SLUMS OF NEW YORK CITY

A native of Denmark, Jacob Riis (1849–1914) worked as a police reporter on two New York newspapers. His books and lectures — based on personal observation — on slum conditions in that city effected many reforms, particularly in the housing codes, and won him the enthusiastic support of Theodore Roosevelt.

When the sun shines the entire population seeks the street, carrying on its household work, its bargaining, its love-making on street or sidewalk, or idling there when it has nothing better to do. . . . Along the curb women sit in rows, young and old alike with the odd head-covering, pad or turban, that is their badge of servitude . . . haggling over baskets of frowsy weeds. . . . Ashbarrels serve them as counters, and not infrequently does the arrival of the official cart en route for the dump cause a temporary suspension of trade. . . . Hucksters and pedlars' carts make two rows of booths in the street itself, and along the houses is still another — a perpetual market doing a very lively trade in its own queer staples, found nowhere on American ground save in "the Bend."

JACOB RIIS, *How the Other Half Lives* (1890). Photograph from Ewing Galloway.

---

deemed evil anyway, the American Protective Association, a secret anti-Catholic order, was formed in 1887 to strengthen the bulwarks of nativism against the foreign invaders. To be a good A.P.A. one had to swear not to employ Catholics and not to vote for Catholics. The order spread from the country to the cities in the 1890's, and claimed a million members by 1896. It was probably responsible for such wild tales as that Catholics were collecting arms in the basements of their churches to use in overthrowing the American government. At least, some A.P.A. chapters gave this as an excuse for themselves collecting arms. In the face of the more exciting silver issue of the nineties, however, the A.P.A. soon lost ground and disappeared. But the temporary popularity of the order revealed a spirit of reckless intolerance that made the immigrant a little skeptical of American boasts of freedom of religion.

Lutherans and Orthodox Catholics. The Roman Catholics were not the only religious group among the immigrants to be made conscious of their religious affiliations. Lutherans, both Scandinavian and German, tended to lean toward the most orthodox opinions of their homelands. This meant, among other things, that each national group was likely to separate from other Lutherans; and the number of separate "synods" multiplied inordinately. The Lutherans antagonized other Protestants by holding services in their native languages and by sending their children to their own parochial schools, where classes were often conducted in a foreign language. The Greek Orthodox Catholics from eastern Europe and the Balkans had religious rites that were foreign to the Americans. The onion-shaped towers of their churches and the ornate robes of their bearded clergy were too exotic to be acceptable to provincial taste.

The Jews. From the very beginning there had been Jews in America but never before in such numbers. The total Jewish population of the United States in 1840 was about 15,000, but by 1880 it was no less than 250,000. At the latter date most Jews had come from Germany, but thereafter most of them came from Russia or from adjacent nations. By 1960 the Jewish population of the country had increased to about 5.5 million. The earlier Jewish immigrants and their descendants tended in general to discard many of their old ways, but many of those who came later retained the traditional Jewish rites and practices. As in Europe, the Jews were urban dwellers and tradesmen, and thus naturally objects of suspicion. The prejudices of the Old World were easily communicated to the New. Soon New York City alone had a million Jews, the largest such concentration of Jewish population anywhere in the world. Actually, the Jews made the adjustment to New World conditions better than most immigrant groups, but they found to their sorrow that they had not left anti-Semitism behind.

Criticism of the Immigrants. Native Americans made much about the danger to the American system of government from the untutored immigrants. It is true that the newcomers, desperately poor and in need of economic security, fell in with the wishes of corrupt city machines. This happened in spite of the many mutual aid societies and associations through which they tried to care for each other during such inescapable emergencies as sickness and death; but the politicians could also help, and the immigrants were in no position to reject aid from any source. Jobs were essential, however tedious and degrading the work, and the local party leader had influence with contractors, especially those who were working on public projects. He could dispense other favors also. If a man found himself or a member of his family in trouble with the law, the party leader could fix it. If he had to have a little cash, the party leader might lend him the money. Christmas gifts for the children could be counted on from party headquarters. One voted as the party leader said. The city machines might wax fat on the graft they collected in return, but to the immigrant the bargain seemed

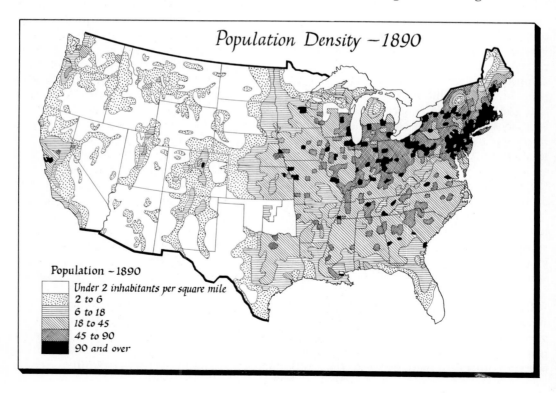

Population Density – 1890

Population – 1890

	Under 2 inhabitants per square mile
	2 to 6
	6 to 18
	18 to 45
	45 to 90
	90 and over

good. A very few immigrants brought with them to the United States radical European political doctrines, and by advocating them persistently gave all immigrants a bad reputation.

Labor and the Immigrant. It might be reasonable to suppose that all labor would stand together, and that the rights of immigrant workers would be no less important to the labor leaders than the rights of native Americans. But for a long time this was not so. The trouble was that the coming of so many immigrants built up the labor supply to such an extent that employers could, and did, keep wages down. Strikes proved unavailing when the jobs of the strikers could readily be filled by immigrants; sometimes immigrants were brought into the country with this very end in view. Unable to speak or read the English language, the strikebreakers were immune from labor propaganda, while wages that seemed low to the native workers seemed high enough to them.

This was particularly true of the French Canadian and Chinese immigrants. During the last three decades of the nineteenth century French Canadians came in large numbers to the mill towns of New England, sometimes with the deliberate encouragement of the mill owners, who used them to break strikes and lower wages. By 1900 there were 134,000 of them in Massachusetts alone, one-sixth of the population of the state, and the proportions in the other New England states were not far behind. The Chinese had entered California during gold-rush days. At first their labor was welcomed, particularly in the building of the western railroads. But by the depression years of the seventies, with thousands of Americans out of work, the attitude toward them became hostile. Even in the East there was fear of the results of cheap Chinese labor. Once in Massachusetts and once in Pennsylvania during the seventies, Chinese coolies were imported from the West and used as strikebreakers.

Labor unions, seeking to obtain higher wages and better working conditions, saw in the horde of immigrants their greatest menace. If the nation's manufacturers could be protected from foreign competition by a tariff, why not the same sort of protection for the American workingman?

Demands for Restriction. The propaganda in favor of restricting immigration grew with the immigrant tide, and by the end of the nineteenth century had reached formidable proportions. The strangeness of the immigrants, their foreign accents, their religious differences, their attitudes toward government, their competition in the labor market, all were held against them. Even immigrants who had arrived earlier deplored those who arrived later. An initial step in the direction of restriction was taken in 1868, with the repeal of the law passed four years before to legalize the importation of labor under contract. But the first really significant triumph of the restrictionists came primarily in response to the insistent demand of the Far West for Chinese exclusion. In 1879 Congress sought to pass a law that would prohibit any ship from bringing to the United States on a single voyage more than fifteen Chinese passengers. This measure was obviously meant to stop the stream of Chinese migration across the Pacific, and was generally regarded as desirable. But the United States had signed a treaty with China in 1868 that gave the two powers mutual rights of immigration and emigration. Ultimately, the Chinese government agreed to give the United States the right to "regulate, limit or suspend but not absolutely prohibit" the immigration of Chinese laborers, and in 1882 a Chinese Exclusion Act, based upon almost complete prohibition, went into effect.

The demand for federal supervision of immigration had by this time grown to such proportions that a general immigration law was almost inevitable. An act of 1882 placed a head tax of fifty cents on immigrants, to be paid by the carrier and used to defray the expense of the immigration service. Idiots, lunatics, persons who were likely to become public charges, and convicts, except those who were guilty only of political crimes, were specifically excluded. To strengthen enforcement, an act of 1891 created the office of "superintendent of immigration" and made possible the establishment of a federal bureau through which the restrictive laws could be made more effective. The new law added to the proscribed lists prostitutes, polygamists, and persons suffering from certain types of diseases.

The Literacy Test. For the most part the restrictions provided in these acts were reasonable and applied equally to all nationals. Demands that legislation be devised to discriminate against immigrants coming from southern and eastern Europe were so insistent, however, that during the 1890's Henry Cabot Lodge, first as a member of the House of Representatives and later as a Senator, took the lead in advocating a literacy test for all prospective immigrants. According to a bill he introduced in 1896, only those who could read and write either their own or some other language might be admitted. The test, he stated frankly, would "bear most heavily upon the Italians, Russians, Poles, Hungarians, Greeks, and Asiatics, and very lightly, or not at all, upon English-speaking immigrants or Germans, Scandinavians and French." Lodge's measure won a majority in both houses of Congress,

but was vetoed by President Cleveland two days before he left office. Cleveland argued cogently that the test proposed was not a test of ability, but only a test of opportunity; it might keep out many who were desirable, and admit many who were not. Similar measures were vetoed later by Presidents Taft and Wilson, but in 1917, during the excitement of the First World War, the literacy test became a law in spite of a second veto by Wilson. Then, shortly after the war ended, Congress adopted a policy of virtual exclusion.

On Bedloe's Island in New York harbor the Statue of Liberty was dedicated in 1886 as a gift of France to the American people. On its base were carved the lines written by Emma Lazarus:

> Give me your tired, your poor,
> Your huddled masses yearning to breathe free,
> The wretched refuse of your teeming shore,
> Send these, the homeless, tempest-tossed, to me:
> I lift my lamp beside the golden door.

That the golden door was even then beginning to close and would within thirty-five years be virtually shut is perhaps one of the great ironies of history. But even though in the future it might be sealed, America would never be able to spend the entire legacy received from the Old World. For the more than 40 million immigrants, together with their varied cultures, have become a part of a new nation dedicated by its own history to the proposition that diversity is better than conformity.

SELECTED BIBLIOGRAPHY

In addition to the general works on labor already mentioned, see the stimulating new impressionistic book by Thomas Brooks, *Toil and Trouble* (1964). A brief documentary collection is *The American Labor Movement*, edited by L. F. Litwack (1962). Useful one-

* Available in paperback

volume texts include: J. G. Rayback, *A History of American Labor* (1959); and Selig Perlman, *A History of Trade Unionism in the United States* (1922). N. J. Ware, *The Labor Movement in the United States, 1860–1895* (1929), remains the best work on the Knights of Labor, but it can now be supplemented by G. N. Grob, *Workers and Utopia; A Study of Ide-*

ological Conflict in the American Labor Movement, 1865–1900 (1961). *The Path I Trod; The Autobiography of Terence V. Powderly,* edited by H. J. Carman and others (1940), is valuable. On Gompers and the American Federation of Labor, see: L. L. Lorwin, *The American Federation of Labor* (1933); Philip Taft, *The A. F. of L. in the Time of Gompers* (1957); Gompers' autobiography, *Seventy Years of Life and Labor* (2 vols., 1925); and Bernard Mandel, *Samuel Gompers* (1963), full and rather critical. Important monographs on trade unionism include: Leo Wolman, *The Growth of American Trade Unions, 1880–1923* (1924); I. B. Cross, *History of the Labor Movement in California* (1935); David Brody, *Steelworkers in America; The Nonunion Era* (1960); C. K. Yearley, *Britons in American Labor, 1820–1914* (1957); and G. S. Mitchell, *Textile Unionism and the South* (1931).

On labor subjects, *The Encyclopedia of the Social Sciences,* edited by E. R. A. Seligman and Alvin Johnson (15 vols., 1930–1935), is quite valuable. Important monographs include: P. H. Douglas, *Real Wages in the United States, 1890–1926* (1930); C. H. Wesley, *Negro Labor in the United States, 1850–1925* (1927); and J. A. Hill, *Women in Gainful Occupations, 1870–1920* (1929).

Labor disputes are the subject of a vast literature. Two general works, both strongly pro-labor, are: Samuel Yellen, *American Labor Struggles* (1936); and Louis Adamic, *Dynamite* (2nd ed., 1934). Significant studies of strife in this period include: W. G. Broehl, *The Molly Maguires* (1964); R. V. Bruce, *1877: Year of Violence* (1959), which treats of the railway uprising; Henry David, *The History of the Haymarket Affair* (1936), a superb work; D. L. McMurry, *The Great Burlington Strike of 1888* (1956), and *Coxey's Army* (1929); and Leon Wolff, *Lockout: The Story of the Homestead Steel Strike* (1965). The Pullman affair is carefully treated in Almont Lindsey, *The Pullman Strike* (1942); see also C. E. Warne (ed.), *The Pullman Boycott of 1894* (1955), for conflicting views on federal intervention. Important works on the leading figures in the Pullman strike include: Ray Ginger, *Eugene V. Debs (The Bending Cross)* (1949); the same author's *Altgeld's America* (1958), which is broader than the title would indicate; H. M. Christman (ed.), *The Mind and Spirit of John Peter Altgeld* (1960),

a collection of Altgeld's papers; and Harry Barnard, *Eagle Forgotten* (1938), the standard life of Altgeld. On the legal aspects of "government by injunction," consult: Edward Berman, *Labor Disputes and the President of the United States* (1924); Felix Frankfurter and Nathan Greene, *The Labor Injunction* (1930); E. E. Witte, *The Government in Labor Disputes* (1932); and the brilliant interpretative study by A. M. Paul, *Conservative Crisis and the Rule of Law; Attitudes of Bar and Bench, 1887–1895* (1960), which is suggestive on other constitutional topics as well.

The saga of the immigrant in America has continued to attract much scholarly interest. In addition to the works already cited, see the general treatment by W. C. Smith, *Americans in the Making* (1939). H. S. Commager (ed.), *Immigration and American History; Essays in Honor of Theodore C. Blegen* (1961), is a collection of provocative papers by leading authorities. M. R. Davie, *World Immigration with Special Reference to the United States* (1936), contains an excellent bibliography. M. T. Bennett, *American Immigration Policies* (1963), is a descriptive history. An interesting collection of writings on immigration policies, stressing divergent viewpoints, is B. M. Ziegler (ed.), *Immigration; An American Dilemma* (1953). See also: W. S. Bernard, *American Immigration Policy* (1950); Charlotte Erickson, *American Industry and the European Immigrant, 1860–1885* (1957), a study of contract labor; G. W. Allport, *The Nature of Prejudice* (1954), a basic work; John Higham, *Strangers in the Land* (1955), a probing study of nativism; and B. M. Solomon, *Ancestors and Immigrants* (1956), an examination of New Englanders' efforts to secure immigration restriction.

Historians have studied almost all national groups, producing a large literature. On immigration from the British Isles, see W. S. Shepperson, *British Emigration to North America* (1957); and W. V. Shannon, *The American Irish* (1964). Thomas Brown, *Irish-American Nationalism* (1965), stresses the late nineteenth century. On Scandinavian immigration, see: K. C. Babcock, *The Scandinavian Element in the United States* (1914); C. C. Qualey, *Norwegian Settlement in the United States* (1938); and G. M. Stephenson, *The Religious Aspects of Swedish Immigration* (1932). On the Jewish migration, see especially Oscar and M. W. Handlin, "A Century of Jewish Immigration to the United States," *American Jewish Yearbook*, 1948–49, pp. 1–85; Samuel Joseph, *Jewish Immigration to the United States from 1881 to 1910* (1914); and Moses Rischin, °*The Promised City; New York's Jews, 1870–1914* (1962). Treatments of other groups of European immigrants include: A. W. Hoglund, *Finnish Immigrants in America, 1880–1920* (1960); Thomas Capek, *The Czechs in America* (1920); R. F. Foerster, *The Italian Emigration of Our Times* (1919); and Theodore Saloutos, *The Greeks in the United States* (1964). An important work on a unique theme is M. L. Hansen and J. B. Brebner, *The Mingling of the Canadian and American Peoples* (1940).

Oriental immigration to the United States is now beginning to receive the serious scholarly attention it deserves. See particularly the economic study by Ping Chiu, *Chinese Labor in California, 1850–1880* (1963); and the more general work by Gunther Barth, *Bitter Strength* (1964), which deals with the period 1850–1870. The following books stress particularly the problems of "exclusion": M. R. Coolidge, *Chinese Immigration* (1909); S. L. Gulick, *The American Japanese Problem* (1914); and E. G. Mears, *Resident Orientals on the American Pacific Coast* (1927).

25

THE POPULIST REVOLT

An Agricultural Revolution. The economic revolution that swept through the United States during and after the Civil War affected agriculture quite as deeply as industry. New machines, mostly powered by horses, reduced the amount of hand labor on the farm to a degree comparable with the changes that steam-powered machines had wrought in the factories. By the end of the century, total expenditures for mechanical harvesters exceeded expenditures for every other type of machine except steam engines. Changes in transportation also contributed to the agricultural revolution. With railroads connecting all parts of the nation, and steamships opening the way to foreign trade, the American farmer found it possible to market more and more of his produce at a distance; but he found, too, that foreign producers were increasingly troublesome competitors. Industrialism in Europe had enlarged the

market there for agricultural commodities, but European importers might also buy from Canada, or Australia, or the Argentine, or even from Egypt and India. Since American farmers produced far more of such items as wheat and cotton than could be consumed at home, prices on the world market determined both the foreign and domestic price.

Despite this situation, the acreage devoted to agriculture in the United States expanded relentlessly. Between 1860 and 1900 both the total number of farms and the acreage tilled in the United States more than doubled. Although some of this expansion was in the South, the major portion was in the North and especially in the West. Over 3.5 million new farms were established in the period, including about 600,000 homesteads. Even more striking was the increase in production of the individual farmer. By increasing the amount of land under cultivation and by adopting machinery and better agricultural methods, the average northern farmer by 1900 was producing about four times the amount of wheat and corn he had produced before the Civil War.

A good many changes accompanied this agricultural revolution. As the plow and the reaper went westward, the older states of the "Middle Border" experienced a sudden increase in population, while newer

443

territories once devoted to cattle raising and mining now became primarily agricultural. Faced with the competition of virgin land, eastern agriculture turned to dairy and truck farming. But perhaps the most significant change for the future of the northern farmer was the conversion to commercial farming; whereas many farmers had previously produced largely for their own consumption, they now produced for sale.

Commercial Farming. Production for sale meant that the farmer now had to purchase in the nearby towns many essentials that he had formerly obtained from his farm. He no longer exchanged wheat for flour at the local mill, but sold his wheat for cash and bought flour and other groceries at the village store. When he moved out of the wooded country to the plains, he also had to buy wire fencing, pumps, windmills, expensive agricultural machinery, and sometimes even fuel. Of necessity he became both a capitalist and a businessman, more and more dependent upon a faraway market. His chronic complaint was that he set no prices. Instead,

New States

those to whom he sold set the prices for what he had to sell, and those from whom he bought set the prices for what he had to buy. Yet to survive he had both to buy and to sell.

Another "New West." Economic conditions in the farming country differed greatly, depending on the fertility of the soil, the availability of markets, the yearly pattern of rainfall. In certain large areas of the West the farmers encountered particularly difficult circumstances. This was true in most of the "Middle Border," a region stretching from the bend of the Missouri to the Rockies, and settled almost entirely after the Civil War. This latest "New West" included Kansas, Nebraska, the Dakotas, and parts of Colorado and Montana. Much of western Missouri, Iowa, and Minnesota was similarly new, while the Indian Territory, in which after 1889 white population was legally permitted, was the newest of all. This New West was the product of railroads, nearly every one of which had received a rich land grant and had used its lands to entice settlers to come in. The railroads sold their lands on easy terms at low prices, and railroad advertisers left nothing undone to display the opportunities of the region they wished to develop. Under their facile pens the legend of the "great American desert" disappeared. Those who could not afford to buy land from the railroads were urged to use their pre-emption rights, to take homesteads, and, as the federal land laws were relaxed, to obtain other hundreds of acres for little or nothing by promising to grow timber, or in regions of slight rainfall, to try irrigation. Veterans of the Civil War, substantial farmers from the upper Mississippi Valley, a few discontented laborers from the cities, and great numbers of European immigrants vied with one another in their rush to obtain cheap lands. What happened can best be told in figures. The combined population of Kansas, Nebraska, and Dakota Territory in 1870 had been only half a million;

ten years later, it was 1.5 million; in 1890, it was over 3 million. And what these states and territories experienced occurred in greater or lesser degree in all the region.

Thanks to easy credit, the New West in a single generation achieved the facilities of a settled materialistic society. Farm mortgages at high interest rates bought farmers the tools, livestock, houses, and barns they needed, to say nothing of the extra acres they were often tempted to buy. Cities grew up that reproduced many of the conditions that their inhabitants had known in the East. Counties, by voting bonds, obtained courthouses and jails, roads and bridges, and even more railroads, privately owned, to be sure, but paid for in no small part by public money. The East believed in the West, was convinced that it would grow, and furnished the capital necessary to build it. Each sizable town — Omaha, Yankton, Atchison, Topeka, Kansas City — became the scene of a real-estate boom.

Western Adversity. The collapse of the western boom began with the summer of 1887, the first of a long series of dry seasons. Settlers who had gone hopefully into western Kansas, Nebraska, and Dakota, or even to Montana or Colorado, learned to their sorrow that they had gone too far. When the drought came, moneylenders changed their minds about the future of the West, and the flow of cash abruptly halted. The same covered wagons that had taken the settlers hopefully west now sometimes turned eastward in defeat and despair. For there was no longer another West to which they could go. Of mountains and deserts and arid plains the government still owned an abundance, but of land suitable for the traditional types of agriculture, perhaps less than 2 million acres remained. Henry George was well aware that such a condition was in sight when he advocated in *Progress and Poverty* (1879) a "single tax" on land. "All who do not possess land," he argued, "are toiling for those who do, and this is the reason why progress and poverty go hand in hand." Most of the people of the New West were unaware of George's theories, and if they had known them, they would not have liked them. What they wanted was a chance to live through the hard years on the land they had taken, without danger of foreclosure by the banks or extortion by the middlemen and the railroads. Convinced that the ills from which they suffered were not of their own making, the farmers of the New West, like those of the New South, were ripe for revolt.

Southern Agriculture. Despite the vast transformation wrought by industrialism in southern life, the South at the end of the nineties, as before the war, was still predominantly agricultural. In every southern state far more people were engaged in agriculture than in any other occupation, while most of the business and professional classes were dependent upon farm income. The New South, like the Old, had few large cities, and its annual output of manufactured goods actually accounted for only about one-eighth of the nation's total output. Southern cotton was still grown after much the same fashion, by nearly the same types of laborers, in approximately the same regions as before the war. The yield had steadily increased. By 1894 the production of cotton in the South exceeded 10 million bales, nearly twice that of the prewar years. Much the same could be said of tobacco, sugar cane, cereals, and livestock, but if the total produce of the South had increased, so also had its population.

A generation after Appomattox, 70 per cent of southern farmers were tenants, and throughout the non-mountainous region the proportion was much higher. A survey of 1880 indicated that only one out of every hundred farmers in Georgia owned the land he tilled. Some of the landless worked for low wages and "rations." More often they fell into one of three large classes:

(1) the cash tenant who paid rent in money or a specified amount of crops, (2) the share tenant who, for the use of the land alone, paid a proportion of the crop produced, usually one-fourth of the cotton and one-third of the corn, and (3) the share cropper who paid a much larger proportion of his crop because he was dependent upon the owner not only for the land but also for food, tools, and animals. Some of the cash and share tenants, usually white, were fairly thrifty; the "croppers," who included most of the country Negroes, were only one step removed from slavery.

The Crop-lien System. One of the many woeful results of the Civil War was the development of the crop-lien system, which came about largely because so many small farmers had no cash to see them through the season until their crops were harvested. Banking facilities in the South had always lagged far behind those of the North. Credit therefore was scarce, and after the war nonexistent in many regions. Faced with these circumstances, the small farmer often bought his food and other supplies on credit from a country store. Gradually the storekeeper, to insure himself against loss, began to take a lien on the crops, and, if possible, also a chattel mortgage. When the farmer happened to be a tenant, the merchant's lien was taken only on his share of the crop. Immediately after the war the landlord and the storekeeper were usually two different people, but as time went on they tended to become one and the same. Legal protection for the merchant was soon added by friendly legislatures. If the farmer's purchases exceeded the value of his crop, he was legally bound to trade year in, year out with the same merchant. Thus entrapped he became a virtual peon. Both the quantity and the kind of goods he bought were subject to some control by the storekeeper. He had to pay whatever price was asked, usually about double that of cash customers, a process often aided by his own inability to read or "figure."

Many other harmful results issued from the crop-lien system. Hopelessly sunk in debt, the farmer often became more and more shiftless. Nor was the merchant, for all his high prices, in too good a financial position. Depending on yearly deliveries of cotton to meet his own obligations, he sometimes found that his debtor croppers had run away before the crop was made, or were lodged in jail. A season of crop failures or of exceptionally low prices might mean disaster. Existing records indicate that while some merchants prospered, many had only a long list of unpaid bills to show for their efforts.

One-crop Agriculture. But for the section as a whole, perhaps the greatest evil of the crop-lien system was its encouragement of one-crop agriculture. Almost everywhere throughout the cotton-growing area the storekeepers tended to insist that their rural debtors raise cotton to the exclusion of all other crops. Being a staple, cotton could be stored without deterioration. It could usually be sold at some price, and it was hard for the farmer in debt to hide it or to use it for his family, as he could use corn and other table crops. Since the merchant had substantial control over what his debtors raised, the growing of corn and other grains decreased rapidly. Even vegetable growing and the raising of small animals were neglected. As a result the southern cotton farmer became dependent upon the storekeeper even for his foodstuffs, and the southern diet became progressively worse. Reliance upon the "three M's" (meat, meal, and molasses) had much to do with the widespread incidence of hookworm, malaria, pellagra, and other diseases. The yearly planting of cotton without crop rotation took its toll of soil, while dependence upon one crop alone meant real want when the price of cotton plummeted.

The One-party System. The one-party system that the Reconstruction period had left as a legacy to the South made it extremely hard for farmers, whether black or white, to improve their lot through political action. Because of the peculiar distribution of the white population, the power of the lower-class rural whites in politics was far less than their numbers would have justified. The best cotton lands lay along the river valleys and close to the sea, precisely the same lands that had grown the cotton of the prewar plantation South. Here the Negroes were concentrated, no longer as slaves but as tenants of a favored few whites. In these "black belts" the landlords and the merchants, supported by the votes of the townspeople and the Negroes they controlled, exercised a disproportionate influence in the politics of any given state. Since the assignment of membership in the legislature and of delegates in nominating conventions was according to population, the representatives of the black counties could practically always outvote the representatives of the white counties. And, since white solidarity demanded unfailing support of whatever Democratic candidates were nominated, the Bourbons or Redeemers of the black belt, eager servants of the industrialists, the landlords, and the merchants, maintained uninterrupted sway. Hardly less than before the Civil War, the South remained in the hands of a favored ruling caste. Discontent with such a system, followed by open revolt against it, was sure to come.

Common Grievances. Common grievances acted powerfully to draw the farmers of the West and the South closer together. The western wheat grower, convinced that unless the price of wheat was as much as a dollar a bushel he could not make money, talked the same language as the southern cotton grower, who held that any price less than ten cents a pound for cotton meant disaster. The northern farm owner who was chronically on the verge of losing his property to the mortgage holder was only a trifle better off than the southern tenant who each year turned over his entire crop to his creditors only to learn that he was still in debt. The West had the greater grievance against the railroads. Debts for lands purchased from them were hard to wipe out, and the high cost of transporting bulky western crops to distant markets ate away an alarming proportion of western farm receipts. But the South, no less than the West, knew how railroad companies watered their stock, granted rebates, evaded taxation, bought favors with free passes, and mixed business with politics. Southern farmers, who sold abroad and would have preferred to buy cheap foreign manufactured goods in return, could see more clearly the disadvantages of the high-tariff system than the farmers of the Northwest, but even the westerners registered their objections to buying in a tariff-protected market and selling against the competition of the whole wide world. Both sections made heated protests against the tolls paid to trusts and middlemen, the inescapable high taxes on farmlands, and the steadily appreciating value of the dollar. And, although the West knew it best, both sections were seriously affected by the rapid disappearance of good cheap lands. The prospect of a re-alliance in the old pre-Civil War pattern between the dominantly agricultural sections of the country was by no means an idle dream.

The Farmers' Alliances. As if to pave the way for a closer union, the distressed farmers of the South and the West had begun during the eighties to organize. Somewhat copying the labor unions, they had banded together into orders of various names and natures. Most important of these organizations were two great sectional "Alliances," the National Farmers' Alliance of the Northwest, and the Farmers' Alliance and Industrial Union of the South. Some of the smaller orders, such as the Grange, which had lasted on in spite of the collapse of the Granger movement, continued to exist; others were absorbed into one or the other of the two dominant organizations, which, commonly called the "Northern" (or "Northwestern") Alliance and the "Southern" Alliance, became the authoritative spokesmen of agricultural discontent.

The Alliances in Politics. Circumstances conspired to drive both Alliances, contrary to their expressed intentions, into politics. The Northern Alliance, like the Southern, made numerous and sometimes successful ventures into cooperative buying and selling, and both orders stimulated among their members a wide variety of social and educational activities. But in spite of all such efforts farm prosperity failed to appear. More and more the conviction grew that the real trouble with agriculture lay in unfair discriminations against it. The railroads, the bankers, the manufacturers, and the merchants were robbing the farmers. Only through governmental intervention could their evil practices be brought to light and corrected. To influence the government, whether state or national, political action was essential.

Alliance Successes. At first the Alliances sought to achieve their ends by control of state governments. In the South the chief business of the Alliance became the capture of the machinery of the Democratic Party, which controlled every state government, and before the elections of 1890 this process was far advanced. In the Northwest the same policy was tried for a time, with the Republican rather than the Democratic Party as the chief objective, but dissatisfaction with the results, together with continuing hard times, led to the nomination in 1890 of many third-party tickets. As yet the name of the new party varied from state to state, but the Kansans, who were affiliated with the Southern Alliance, called their organization the People's Party, a name that won increasing acclaim. "Populist" and "Populism" were natural derivatives. The effectiveness of Alliance activities was mirrored in the election results. In four states, Kansas, Nebraska, South Dakota, and Minnesota, third-party candidates

won the balance of power, although in no case did they obtain outright control. In the South, Alliance gains were even more spectacular. Alliance candidates for governor were elected in North Carolina, South Carolina, and Georgia, while in eight states Alliance-controlled legislatures were chosen. Even in Congress the evidence of agrarian discontent was emphatically recorded. Two third-party senators, William A. Peffer of Kansas and James H. Kyle of South Dakota, were on hand for the opening session of the Fifty-second Congress, while eight third-party representatives from the Northwest voted for Thomas E. Watson of Georgia for Speaker. Watson was the only southern Congressman to admit that he was a third-party man, but among the southern delegations sat perhaps thirty or forty Alliance members, and many others who were drawn to the Alliance by bonds of sympathy.

To the third-party men of the Northwest the logical next step was the formation of a new nationwide party of the people, but to southerners such a course seemed fraught with peril. The Democratic Party of the South was primarily a symbol of white supremacy. If the white voters of the South were divided, Negro voting might become more common, and the supremacy of the white race would be jeopardized. Southern Alliance men preferred, therefore, to work within the framework of the Democratic Party, although there was one great objection to such a course. The southern wing of the party, however strong it might become, could hardly hope to dominate the party as a whole. Through Alliance-controlled southern Democrats, a certain amount of useful state legislation might be achieved, but reforms that depended upon nationwide action would still be out of reach. The so-called "sub-Treasury plan," for example, to which the Southern Alliance was committed after 1889, could never be put into effect without a law of Congress. This plan called for national warehouses in which nonperishable farm produce could be stored and upon which the owners could borrow from the United States government as much as 80 per cent of the "local current value" of their deposits in Treasury notes, issued for the purpose by the United States government, and providing incidentally an unpredictable amount of money inflation.

The People's Party. Southern reluctance was insufficient to restrain the third-party ardor of northwestern Alliance men, who at a series of conventions beginning at Cincinnati in May, 1891, and ending with a nominating convention at Omaha in July, 1892, formally launched the People's Party as a national organization. The Populist platform, written in large part by Ignatius Donnelly of Minnesota, denounced both established parties in vivid rhetoric and called for revolutionary reforms in land policy, in transportation, and in finance. Believing that the value of the gold dollar had been artificially stimulated to the benefit of the creditor class and to the distress of the debtors, the Populists demanded first and foremost an extensive expansion of the currency by silver or paper, or both — in other words, money inflation. As for the transportation issue, they advocated government ownership and operation of the railroads, and also, for good measure, of the telegraph and telephone systems. On the subject of land, they demanded the return to the government by "railroads and other corporations" of all public lands received "in excess of their actual needs," and they condemned alien landownership. Among other reforms favorably mentioned in their platform were the sub-Treasury system, the Australian ballot, a graduated income tax, postal savings banks, shorter hours for labor, the initiative and referendum, election of United States senators by direct vote of the people, and a single term for the President and Vice-President. For their candidates the Populists chose a Union veteran, James B. Weaver of Iowa, for President and James G. Field of Virginia, an ex-Confederate, for Vice-President.

Election of 1892. The Populists, while predicting a victory of the "people" over the "plutocrats" in 1896, hoped in 1892 only to make a good showing. Circumstances arose to exceed their expectations. The Republicans, in spite of the overwhelming rebuke they had received in 1890, had little choice but to renominate the unpopular Harrison and to defend the long list of dubious measures, including the McKinley Tariff, that were associated with his administration. The Democrats, convinced that another battle must be fought over the tariff, turned for a third time to Cleveland. Signs of dissension in both old parties were apparent. Three days before the opening of the Republican Convention, Blaine resigned as Secretary of State and permitted his friends to work openly, if unavailingly, for his nomination. Cleveland, likewise, had met with formidable opposition, both from an eastern faction and from soft-money men of the West and the South. The Populists went into the campaign as the only party willing to take a radical stand on the money question. Their sponsorship of free silver provided, as events proved, the one really exciting issue of the campaign. Cleveland was elected, with 277 electoral votes to Harrison's 145, but for the first time since the Civil War a third party had broken into the Electoral College. Weaver's popular vote of over a million won him 22 electoral votes, all from the silver-mining or farmer-dominated states of the West. Both houses of Congress were safely Democratic, but the Populists rejoiced in the knowledge that they would be represented by a small but faithful few in the Senate as well as in the House.

A casualty of the election was the Farmers' Alliance. In the Northwest it was absorbed into and replaced by the Populist Party. In the South it was torn violently asunder and destroyed by the third-party issue. The smaller faction, convinced that deliverance for the southern cotton farmer was never to be found under the rule of the Democrats, dared the derision of neighbors and the loss of friends to join the Populists. The larger faction, equally certain that white supremacy was still the most important issue, returned to the Democratic Party. Because the southern Populists permitted the race issue to split their party and because a few crackpot Populist leaders in both the West and the South talked at times of a conspiracy of "Jewish international bankers," the charge has been made that the Populists as a whole were racists and anti-Semitic. The facts seem to indicate that in the South they were no more racist than the great majority of white Democrats, and that in the West they were, if anything, less anti-Semitic than their fellow citizens in the East. Although in western rural campaigns an anti-Semitic phrase was used occasionally, more to indict the East than the race, anti-Semitism expressed in act and talk stemmed from the cities, where there were many Jews, and not from the country, where there were almost none.

The Gold Reserve.   There is some reason to suppose that, even before his term of office ended, Harrison had occasion to rejoice in his defeat. A nightmare of his administration had been the condition of the gold reserve. Authorized by the Resumption Act of 1875, and painstakingly assembled by John Sherman during Hayes's administration, this fund had originally amounted to only a little more than $100 million. With that sum the Treasury had successfully resumed specie payments in 1879, although the outstanding issues of greenbacks exceeded the gold reserve by about three dollars to one. Businessmen assumed, however, that as long as there was $100 million in gold in the Treasury, the gold standard was secure. Each year the operation of the Bland-Allison Act of 1878 added somewhat to the burden borne by the gold reserve, for successive Secretaries of the Treasury invariably adopted the policy of backing the silver dollar,

whatever its "intrinsic" value, with gold. But the plentiful revenues and the general prosperity of the eighties steadily increased the gold reserve, until by 1890 the Treasury was able to record that it possessed $190 million in gold, nearly twice the essential minimum.

At this point the financial measures of the Harrison administration began to take effect. In the first place, the McKinley Tariff, as its framers had intended, reduced the annual revenue by about $100 million a year. Secondly, the lavish expenditures of the new administration, particularly for pensions, placed a new and heavy burden upon the Treasury. Thirdly, the Sherman Silver Purchase Act, which replaced the Bland-Allison Act of 1878, not only required the government to purchase nearly twice as much silver as before, but also provided for a new issue of Treasury notes, based on these silver purchases, that all sound-money men agreed must be redeemable in gold rather than in silver. Failure to maintain parity with gold would mean that the silver standard would succeed the gold standard, and the purchasing power of the American dollar would decline to the commercial value of the silver dollar — a drop of nearly 50 per cent.

Condition of the Treasury.   Well before the end of the Harrison administration the condition of the Treasury had begun to excite general alarm. By 1892, the Treasury surplus, which recorded the excess of revenues over expenditures, had almost reached the vanishing point. Far more significant was the fact that the last two years had witnessed heavy withdrawals of gold. Faith that the government could redeem its greenbacks and Treasury notes in gold was obviously shaken, for gold flowed steadily out of the Treasury and paper flowed in. By January, 1893, the gold reserve had dwindled to only $108 million, and the Harrison administration, in order to stave off the inevitable crisis until after March 4, successfully implored the New York banks to exchange $6 million in gold for paper, a sum that kept the gold reserve above the $100 million mark until after Cleveland was inaugurated. But when the Democrats took over the Treasury, they found a gold reserve of only $101 million.

Panic of 1893. By April 21, 1893, within a matter of weeks after the change of government, the gold reserve dropped below the $100 million mark, and the Panic of 1893 was on. Before six months had passed no less than 8,000 business failures, involving liabilities of $285 million, were recorded. Four hundred banks, most of them in the West or South, closed their doors. Railroads followed each other into receivership in a procession that ended only after 156 companies, among them the Erie, the Union Pacific, and the Northern Pacific, had gone into bankruptcy. Panic conditions lasted throughout the summer, after which the country settled down to the long, hard process of waiting out a depression that was to last four full years.

Other reasons than the condition of the Treasury helped bring on the panic and prolong the depression. Well to the front was the long-standing agricultural distress of the West and the South. The purchasing power of the stricken sections had steadily declined, and in consequence the earnings of all businesses that depended on farm markets or the handling of farm goods had suffered. The eighties, too, had been a period of overexpansion in industry. The great transcontinental railroads, the huge industrial trusts, and the building of the urban centers that the new industrialism had made necessary had drained dry the investment resources of the nation. Furthermore, the depression, far from being a strictly American affair, was world-wide. From 1889 on, and particularly after the "Baring panic" of 1890 in England, all Europe had recorded subnormal business conditions; indeed, one reason for the depletion of the American gold reserve was the withdrawal of foreign capital from investment in America in order to bolster the waning fortunes of European enterprise.

Repeal of the Silver Purchase Act. Like all depression Presidents before him, Cleveland did not regard the problem of business recovery as a direct concern of government. The depression was a business problem which business itself was obliged to solve. But the money question was a different matter. Failure to maintain the gold standard would have seemed to Cleveland a breach of public faith. Accordingly, he called Congress at once into special session and asked it to repeal the Sherman Silver Purchase Act, which in his judgment had done much to deplete the gold reserve. He could hardly have thought of a better way to alienate the West and the South, where silver orators were gaining converts every day. The debtor farmers, to whom the gold standard meant low prices and continued agricultural distress, had no desire whatever to save it; for them the fifty-cent dollar had no terrors. The silver interests of the Far West were even more violently opposed to repeal. What silver needed, they insisted, was a larger rather than a smaller subsidy; better still, "the free and unlimited coinage of silver at the ratio of sixteen to one." Congress at length supported Cleveland, but only at the cost of a definite split in the Democratic Party. Enough eastern Republicans joined the eastern Democrats to repeal the Sherman Law, but the confidence of western and southern Democrats in Cleveland was badly shaken.

The President's next move alienated the soft-money men still further. Although silver purchases were discontinued, the drain on the gold reserve was not. By October the amount of gold in the Treasury was less than $82 million, and before the end of the year it was down to $68 million. Faced by this emergency the President, after some hesitation, authorized his Secretary of the Treasury, John G. Carlisle, to invoke the provisions of the still-unrepealed Resumption

Act of 1875, and to buy enough gold to maintain the proper reserve. In January, 1894, an issue of $50 million worth of 5 per cent bonds brought $58 million in gold into the Treasury, but of this sum $24 million was immediately withdrawn, and before the end of the year one more purchase of gold was necessary — an "endless chain," for in each case the gold was hardly in the Treasury before it was drawn out again. To save the situation, Cleveland resorted in February, 1895, to a deal with the Morgan and Belmont banking firms whereby they were permitted to purchase a large issue of 4 per cent gold bonds at a figure far below the price the issue would have brought on the open market. In return for a handsome profit, the bankers agreed to procure half the needed gold from abroad, and to use their influence to prevent further withdrawal of gold from the Treasury. By thus "selling out to Wall Street," Cleveland was able to maintain the gold standard, but his popularity with the debtor South and West had ended.

The Wilson-Gorman Tariff.   Part of the price Cleveland paid for maintaining the gold standard was the defeat of his long-cherished plans for a genuine downward revision of the tariff. Of necessity, or so he thought, he had postponed the tariff battle until after the repeal of the Sherman Act. But once that was done, his prestige with the silver wing of his party was so impaired that in that quarter his commands were no longer respected. Moreover, the alliance of eastern Democrats and eastern Republicans, originally against silver, soon found that it could also function effectively on the tariff. The result was a tariff measure, the Wilson-Gorman Act of 1894, so far removed from the party's pledges that Cleveland called it a "piece of party perfidy" and obstinately refused to sign the bill, although he did permit it to become a law without his signature.

As it passed the House under the leadership of William L. Wilson of West Virginia,

the bill was an honest attempt at tariff reduction. But in the Senate two eastern Democrats, Brice and Gorman, aided and abetted by log-rolling Democrats from every section, and in particular by the "sugar senators" from Louisiana, joined the Republicans to attach 633 amendments to the bill, wholly changing its character. The sugar bounty was not revived, but duties worth $20 million a year to the Sugar Trust were placed on both raw and refined sugar. Throughout the revised measure the low-tariff principle was all but ignored. Reluctantly the House acquiesced in the wrecking of its work, and the President's attempts to intervene proved unavailing. In general the duties of the Wilson-Gorman Tariff were lower than those of the McKinley Tariff, and not far different from those set by the Tariff of 1883. The provision for an income tax, which actually reached the statute books, was declared unconstitutional by the Supreme Court in a five-to-four decision (1895). This was the more remarkable since an income tax had been levied and collected during the Civil War without serious question of its constitutionality.

Labor.   The distress in agriculture that led to the Populist revolt was no more serious than the plight of city workers during the hard years after the Panic of 1893. Industrial depression meant wholesale unemployment, a condition that state and municipal governments were unable to handle effectively and that the national government looked upon as outside its sphere. Strangely, however, the farmers and the laborers, although they claimed a common enemy, found difficulty in uniting forces. For although the Populists included many labor planks in their various platforms to unite "the toiling masses" of city and country, antagonism between the two groups remained strong. Official labor remained suspicious of these "capitalists in shirt sleeves," while the farmer persisted in his distrust of the "sidewalk radicals."

Rise of the Silver Issue. As events turned out, whatever union of the working classes was actually accomplished came primarily on the issue of free silver, and more or less without regard for the wishes of party leaders. Propaganda from mine-owners in the silver states of the Far West flooded the country with denunciations of the "crime of 1873" and with arguments to prove that "the free and unlimited coinage of silver at the ratio of sixteen to one" would restore prosperity. *Coin's Financial School,* a little book written by William H. Harvey and published in 1894, set forth in simple language, and seemingly with unanswerable logic, the doctrines of the silverites. "Professor Coin," as the author called himself, purported to run a school in Chicago for financiers, and the lectures he gave on the money question were recorded in the book. Illustrated with numerous cartoons and diagrams, the book appealed to an enormous audience. Silver orators knew its arguments by heart and spread them far and wide. Soon countless thousands had come to believe that an international conspiracy to set gold above silver was at the root of the economic distress. The restoration of prosperity need not await the enactment of a long and complicated series of reforms. By the simple expedient of restoring silver to its historic status as money, all wrongs would be righted.

Elections of 1894. While the Populists alone were clear cut in their support of free silver, or bimetallism, as it was sometimes called, there were innumerable converts to this "heresy" in both the older parties. As a result the congressional elections of 1894 turned upon hard times and the unpopularity of Cleveland. The Democrats were less responsible for the depression than the Republicans, but it was their misfortune to be in power when the panic broke, and the Republicans drove home the charge that Democratic supremacy and hard times went together. In consequence, the Republicans obtained a two-to-one

COIN'S FINANCIAL SCHOOL

From a cartoon by J. S. Pughe dated June, 1895.

majority in the House of Representatives, greatly reduced the Democratic majority in the Senate, and captured nearly every state government outside the South. The behavior of the Populists during the campaign tended, if anything, to aid the Republicans. In the West the Populists, unable or unwilling to cooperate with the Democrats as fully as in 1892, tended to avoid fusion and to keep "in the middle of the road"; in the South, they unblushingly joined forces with the Republicans. The total Populist vote, however, was more than 40 per cent larger in 1894 than in 1892, and enthusiastic Populists cited the rapid rise of Republicanism before 1860 as evidence of what their party could do by 1896.

William McKinley. That the original Republican plan for 1896 did not contemplate a straight-out endorsement of the single gold standard was apparent from the record of the presidential candidate. William McKinley (1843–1901), author of

WILLIAM McKINLEY

The last Union officer of the Civil War to achieve the Presidency, McKinley was a shrewd and kindly party regular, who became the conservatives' ideal President.

the McKinley Tariff Act of 1890 and governor of Ohio from 1891 to 1895, had no deep convictions on the money question. Indeed, in so far as he had committed himself, he seemed to have taken the silver side. His availability for the Republican nomination in 1896 was further emphasized by his creditable record as a Union officer in the Civil War, by his chivalrous devotion to his invalid wife, by his suave and genial manners, and by his abiding friendship with Marcus Alonzo Hanna, Cleveland industrialist and boss of the Republican Party in Ohio. Hanna had the normal attitude of his class toward tariff protection, but his regard for McKinley was personal no less than political. He early made up his mind that McKinley must be the Republican standard-bearer in 1896, and long before the convention met had rounded up the necessary votes.

The steady drift of the electorate toward the free-silver "heresy" upset the Republican plan for a fence-sitting campaign on the money question. Shrewd observers could easily foretell that, in spite of the strenuous efforts of President Cleveland and the gold-standard Democrats of the Northeast, the Democratic Party would be forced to include in its platform an uncompromising demand for free silver. Confronted by this situation, the Republican leaders, Hanna among them, finally determined to commit their party to the single gold standard. They could not resist a slight gesture, however, in the free-silver direction. The plank finally adopted opposed the free coinage of silver "except by international agreement with the leading commercial nations of the world," and until that could be obtained pledged the party to maintain the existing parity of all money with gold. On the adoption of the gold plank, a small group of "Silver Republicans" bolted the convention, presumably with the intention of joining the Democrats in case the Democratic Party endorsed free silver. But the Republican convention stood its ground, nominated McKinley for President, and adjourned in the hope that Marcus A. Hanna, their new campaign manager, could find the money and the means to restore their party to power.

The action of the Republicans left the Democrats, whose convention met a few weeks later at Chicago, no logical choice but to endorse free silver. The Democratic National Committee, however, was still in the hands of the men who had helped to nominate Cleveland in 1892, and they made a determined effort to halt the trend toward silver. But when their nominee for temporary chairman was defeated by a silverite, 556 to 349, it was apparent that the radicals were in control. The position they took on the money question bore no trace of compromise. "We demand the free and unlimited coinage of both silver and gold at the present legal ratio of sixteen to one without waiting for the aid or consent of any other nation."

William Jennings Bryan. For their candidate they passed by Richard P. Bland, a congressman from Missouri whose ambition for the honor had awakened little enthusiasm, to choose William Jennings Bryan (1860–1925) of Nebraska, a young man whose reputation for persuasive oratory was already well known. Bryan had served two terms in Congress (1891–1895), and had once attracted nationwide attention by a powerful speech on the tariff. During the depression, without actually becoming a Populist, he had adopted several of the Populist doctrines, particularly free silver. As Ignatius Donnelly, the most famous orator of Populism complained, "We put him to school and he wound up by stealing the schoolbooks."

For months before the nominating convention met in 1896, Bryan had been speaking on free silver to western audiences, and had rehearsed many times the ringing phrases that were to bring him fame at Chicago. This opportunity came when he was asked to close the debate on a resolution that would have repudiated free silver and commended the Cleveland administration. Bryan's impassioned "magic words" met the mood of his audience "to the very full." His speech was not a reasoned defense of the silver cause, and was not meant to be. Rather it was a leader's call to action. His closing words, "You shall not press down upon the brow of labor this crown of thorns, you shall not crucify mankind upon a cross of gold," summarized in a sentence all that had gone before. In spite of the fact that more than 150 gold Democrats persistently abstained from voting, Bryan obtained the necessary two-thirds majority after only five ballots. For Vice-President the convention chose Arthur Sewall, a wealthy banker and shipbuilder from Maine.

Plight of the Populists. The plight of the Populists when they learned what the Democrats had done was far from pleasant. The Democratic platform had not only appropriated the silver issue, it had denounced with Populistic fervor the "absorption of wealth by the few"; Cleveland's use of troops in the Pullman strike; and the use of the labor injunction "as a new and highly dangerous form of oppression." It had also called for an income tax and for stricter control of trusts and railroads by the federal government. The Democratic candidate, Bryan, was as dependable on silver as any Populist. The Populist leaders, confident that both the Republicans and the Democrats would be captured by the "gold-bugs," had set the date of their convention later than either of the others, and had hoped to rally all free-silver men and all reformers to their standard. Now they were faced squarely with the problem of sacrificing their party by endorsing the Democratic nominee or aiding the Republicans by dividing the silver

WILLIAM JENNINGS BRYAN

Sometimes called the "Boy Orator of the West," Bryan spoke with magnificent eloquence on such subjects as the protective tariff, which he excoriated, and free silver, which he extolled.

vote. In general, western Populists were willing to accept Bryan and join the Democrats, but to southern Populists such a course, involving, as it did, full surrender to a hated enemy, was painful to contemplate. After a heated battle the Populist convention voted in favor of a compromise. Instead of Sewall, a conservative on most issues other than the silver question, they chose Watson of Georgia for Vice-President, but supported Bryan for President. Their hope that the Democrats would replace Sewall by Watson was unrealized; indeed, the Populist Party practically dissolved during the campaign.

Campaign of 1896. Bryan's superb oratory and the popularity of his cause put the Republicans at an initial disadvantage, but Mark Hanna collected the largest campaign fund ever amassed up to that time, and conducted an elaborate campaign of "education." On the money question, the Republican orators and pamphleteers no doubt had the better of the argument, and they made the most of their advantage. As against the homespun Populist speakers the McKinley forces included most of the nation's financial leaders and economists. Even among the reformers there was some dissent from the free silver hypothesis and some dismay at the overemphasis it received at the expense of the other basic reforms in the Populist and Democratic platforms. Henry Demarest Lloyd, the author of *Wealth Against Commonwealth* (1894), a powerful indictment of the existing economic order, described the free silver movement as a "fake" and called it "the cowbird of the reform movement. It waited until the nest had been built by the sacrifices and labors of others, and then laid its eggs in it, pushing out the others which lie smashed on the ground." But Lloyd, a representative of the more socialistic labor wing of the reform forces, was scarcely accurate in his rueful analysis of the campaign. Free silver was in truth the main amalgam that held the coalition of southern and western farmers, ranchers,

and mine operators together. But there was also truth in the contention of Tom Johnson, perennial mayor of Cleveland, Ohio. He described the election as "the first great protest of the American people against monopoly — the first great struggle of the masses in our country against the privileged classes. It was not free silver that frightened the plutocrat leaders. What they feared, then, what they fear now, is free men."

Election Results. The Republicans undoubtedly picked up many votes as the campaign neared its close, and in the end they won a decisive victory. In general the agricultural South and West supported Bryan, while the industrial Northeast supported McKinley; but McKinley's Northeast extended as far west as Iowa, Minnesota, and North Dakota, while Bryan's solid South and West were broken by such notable Republican exceptions as Maryland, Delaware, West Virginia, Kentucky, California, and Oregon. McKinley received more than 7 million popular votes to 6.5 million for Bryan, while the electoral vote stood 271 to 176. Whatever else the election may have decided, the defeat of Bryan and the downfall of Populism freed the industrial leaders, temporarily at least, from the menace of popular interference with their monopolistic ambitions.

The domestic achievements of the McKinley administration were soon overshadowed by war, but since the Republicans controlled both houses of Congress by decisive majorities, they were able to redeem the promises they had made during the campaign. Under the leadership of Representative Nelson R. Dingley of Maine, a high protective tariff, comparable in its schedules to the McKinley Act, was placed on the statute books. The one faint ray of hope in the measure to low-tariff advocates was a provision for limited reciprocity. The President was authorized to negotiate treaties with foreign nations to scale down the American rates as much as 20 per cent, but the eleven treaties so negotiated were

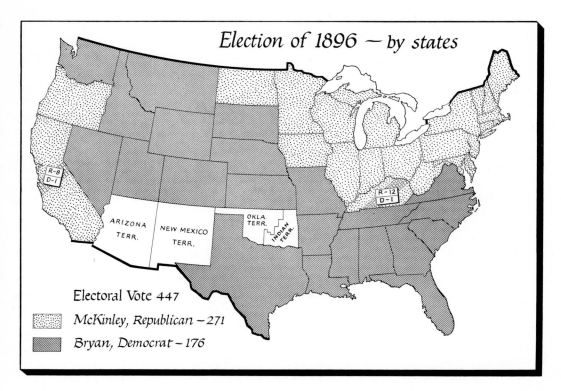

Election of 1896 — by states

R-8
D-1

R-12
D-1

ARIZONA
TERR.

NEW MEXICO
TERR.

OKLA.
TERR.

INDIAN
TERR.

Electoral Vote 447

McKinley, Republican — 271

Bryan, Democrat — 176

all refused ratification by the Senate. Some minor breaches were made in the high-tariff wall by presidential proclamation. To settle the money question, Congress, after a commission to Europe had demonstrated that "international bimetallism" had no chance of success, passed a Gold Standard Act which became law in March, 1900.

The Return of Prosperity. The close coincidence between the return of prosperity and the return of the Republicans to power furnished a valuable weapon to Republican campaigners for many years to come, although good times were on the way back well before the election. It is a curious fact that monetary inflation actually occurred in spite of all the Republicans had done to prevent it, and in a way they had least expected — through an increase in the world's gold supply. For a quarter century before 1890 the amount of new gold mined each year was practically constant. Then a steady increase began which by the end of the nineties reached spectacular proportions. In 1897, approximately twice as much gold was produced

as in 1890; in 1898 nearly two and one-half times as much. The cyanide process by which more gold was extracted from the ore, coupled with new discoveries in Australia, South Africa, and the Klondike, accounted for the increase. Bryan was doubtless right when he first began to assert that the amount of gold in existence was inadequate to transact the world's business, but his arguments were less convincing each succeeding year. Before Bryan became active in politics, American business had to overcome the handicap of a steadily appreciating dollar, which meant also steadily diminishing price levels. By the time Bryan began to run for President, the purchasing power of the dollar had begun to diminish, and prices were on the rise. American agriculture as well as industry responded to the stimulus of gold inflation, while in the East the drought at long last came to an end. Good harvests in America were matched by poor harvests abroad and the price of farm produce rose accordingly. Presently the Spanish-American War, the Philippine Insurrection, and the Boer War added to the boom that had already begun.

SELECTED BIBLIOGRAPHY

The general background of agricultural un-rest is admirably set forth in the 1940 *Yearbook of the United States Department of Agriculture*, which bears the title, *Farmers in a Changing World* (1940). E. G. Nourse, *American Agriculture and the European Market* (1924), calls attention to a fundamental problem not always understood by American farmers. Allan Bogue, *Money at Interest: The Farm Mortgage on the Middle Border* (1955), is an important re-evaluation. Another interesting monograph is A. N. Chandler, *Land Title Origins* (1945).

Two general works of value on the whole subject of farmer protest are: C. C. Taylor, *The Farmers' Movement, 1620–1920* (1953); and F. A. Shannon, °*American Farmers' Movements* (1957), half of which is devoted to readings. A useful brief summary of farmer protest in this period is S. J. Buck, *The Agrarian Crusade* (1920). On political movements, see also: F. E. Haynes, *Third Party Movements since the Civil War, with Special Reference to Iowa* (1916), excellent on the Greenbackers; P. R. Fossum, *The Agrarian Movement in North Dakota* (1925); C. McA. Destler, *American Radicalism, 1865–1901* (1946); and R. V. Scott, *The Agrarian Movement in Illinois, 1880–1896* (1962). Changing points of view with reference to the Populists may be followed in these works: J. D. Hicks, °*The Populist Revolt* (1931); Richard Hofstadter, °*The Age of Reform; From Bryan to F.D.R.* (1955); Norman Pollack, *The Populist Response to Industrial America* (1962); and W. T. K. Nugent, *The Tolerant Populists* (1963), a case study of Kansas. An interesting rejoinder to those who would "over-revise" Populism is C. V. Woodward, "The Populist Heritage and the Intellectual," which may be found in his °*The Burden of Southern History* (1960).

On agrarian protest in the South, see: Theodore Saloutos, °*Farmer Movements in the South, 1865–1933* (1960); and C. V. Woodward, °*Tom Watson, Agrarian Rebel* (1938), a superb biography. There are a number of excellent works on southern Populism and near-Populism: F. B. Simkins, *Pitchfork Ben Tillman* (1944); R. C. Martin, *The People's Party in Texas* (1933); R. C. Cotner, *James Stephen Hogg* (1959), a life of the reform Democratic governor of Texas; D. M. Robison, *Bob Taylor and the Agrarian Revolt in Tennessee* (1935); and Stuart Noblin, *Leonidas LaFayette Polk* (1949), a biography of the North Carolina leader. An interesting treatment of a neglected subject is H. G. Edmonds, *The Negro and Fusion Politics in North Carolina, 1894–1901* (1951); in this connection, see also C. V. Woodward, °*The Strange Career of Jim Crow* (2nd ed., 1957). D. W. Grantham, Jr., *Hoke Smith and the Politics of the New South* (1958), is especially valuable for Georgia.

A convenient summary of the politics of the 1890's is in H. U. Faulkner, °*Politics, Reform and Expansion* (1959), which has a good bibliography. Political studies include G. H. Knoles, *The Presidential Campaign and Election of 1892* (1942); F. E. Haynes, *James Baird Weaver* (1919); J. C. Olson, *J. Sterling Morton* (1942); and Martin Ridge, *Ignatius Donnelly* (1962). An important survey is H. S. Merrill, *Bourbon Democracy of the Middle West, 1865–1896* (1953); the same author's *William Freeman Vilas* (1954) is a case study in Wisconsin Democratic politics. An interesting work on the Democratic Party is J. R. Hollingsworth, *The Whirligig of Politics* (1963). Particularly important for giving the Cleveland administration's side of the story on the financial crisis is J. A. Barnes, *John G. Carlisle* (1931), a rich biography of the Secretary of the Treasury. One of the best books ever written about tariff-making is F. P. Summers, *William L. Wilson and Tariff Reform* (1953). On politics and speculators, see Cedric Cowing, *Populists, Plungers and Progressives* (1965).

The vast literature on the great campaign of 1896 may be sampled in G. F. Whicher (ed.), °*William Jennings Bryan and the Campaign of 1896* (1953). Recently three books on the 1896 campaign have appeared: P. W. Glad, °*McKinley, Bryan and the People* (1964); S. L. Jones, *The Presidential Election of 1896* (1964); and R. F. Durden, *The Climax of Populism* (1965). On the Republican candidate the best books are Margaret Leech, *In the Days of McKinley* (1959); and H. W. Morgan, *William McKinley and His America*

° Available in paperback

(1963). The best work on Mark Hanna is Herbert Croly, *Marcus Alonzo Hanna* (1912). The best books on Bryan are P. W. Glad, *The Trumpet Soundeth; William Jennings Bryan and His Democracy, 1896–1912* (1960); and P. E. Coletta, *William Jennings Bryan, I* (1964–   ), which reaches to 1908. Matthew Josephson, *The President Makers, 1896–1919* (1940), is a liberal and irreverent political survey. R. B. Nye, *Midwestern Progressive Politics* (1951), is useful from this point onward.

Attention should be given to other aspects of protest politics in the period. On the Single Taxers, see the classic statement by Henry George, *Progress and Poverty* (1879); and C. A. Barker, *Henry George* (1955), the standard biography. C. McA. Destler, *Henry Demarest Lloyd and the Empire of Reform* (1963), is the best study on its subject. On the Nationalist Movement the best book is A. E. Morgan, *Edward Bellamy* (1944); but Bellamy's novel, *Looking Backward, 2000–1887* (1887), is of fundamental importance for all its stylistic limitations. The basic guide to Socialism in the United States is the splendid cooperative work edited by D. D. Egbert and Stow Persons, *Socialism and American Life* (2 vols., 1952); its second volume is a massive bibliography put together by T. D. S. Bassett. An able survey of the movement to 1900, in all its significant aspects, is Howard Quint, *The Forging of American Socialism* (1953). Interesting treatments of leading figures and their thoughts may be found in Daniel Aaron, *Men of Good Hope* (1951).

26

SOCIETY IN THE GILDED AGE

The Rise of the City. In 1874 Mark Twain and Charles Dudley Warner published *The Gilded Age,* a satire on the corruption and fortune-chasing of the times that gave its name to the next twenty years. Twain grew up in a Missouri village, and most of his writings involved the people of the Mississippi River countryside. His new book, however, was inspired, at least in part, by the astronomical growth of the industrial city — the most significant development of the post-Civil War era. Before the war America's few great cities had been largely commercial. With some notable exceptions the markets for the goods they produced were in their own immediate surroundings.

The factors that created the national market for manufactured goods, and were in large part responsible for the rise of the metropolis, were numerous. Among the more potent were: (1) the development of the stationary steam engine; (2) the great wave of impoverished European immigrants to supply the manpower needed for mass production; (3) the national network of railroads to convey goods to all parts of the country; and (4) the mentality of the new industrialists that was national rather than provincial, and was willing to take large chances in the hope of large rewards. The goods produced by such a national system, although not necessarily better than those produced by local artisans, were in the end far cheaper both in money and time required for manufacture. The new production was accepted enthusiastically by consumers, and almost every town and city in the nation supported the growth of new factories.

The Urban South and West. While the Northeast led the way in urbanization, other sections were good imitators. The South, during and after Reconstruction, attempted eagerly to supply itself with factories and cities. The new industrialism became almost a religion throughout the reviving section. "Next to God, what this town needs," said an evangelist in the 1890's of Salisbury, North Carolina, "is a cotton mill." The West, too, tried to free itself from its heavy dependence on agriculture, which made no one rich, and to encourage industry, which offered wealth to at least a few. It was not long before every enterprising western city with good railroad or water connections had its factories.

In 1870 only 20.9 per cent of the American population lived in places of eight thousand inhabitants or more; by 1903, 33.1 per cent were so situated. In the East the percentage of city dwellers ran well above this figure; in the South, the Middle West, and the Far West, well below it. But the trend toward urbanization was national, not sectional, and it affected every part of the country. By 1900, 25 million Americans had become city dwellers in a nation that only a few decades earlier had been one largely of farms and woods.

While in every section villages were rapidly becoming towns, and towns cities, in the post-Civil War decades it was the half dozen or so fast-growing metropolitan centers that most attracted attention. Chicago, still a small town of 30,000 in 1850, reached a half million in 1880, and twenty years later had become the second city in the nation with a population of 1.7 million, compared to that of over 3 million for New York. By 1900, Minneapolis and Los Angeles, also, virtually villages at the start of the Civil War, were cities of 200,000 and 100,000, respectively. Birmingham, Alabama, nourished by the coal and iron industry, had grown from nothing in 1871 to 38,000 by 1900. The smaller part of this new population had come from the natural increase of native urban dwellers; perhaps a third more were Americans attracted from native farms and villages. But about 50 per cent of the total urban growth from 1870 to 1900 came from abroad, while in such cities as Chicago and New York the percentage of foreign-born was even higher. In the face of such developments, native-born Americans began to ask whether the nation's traditions and institutions could long be preserved.

Urban Uniformity. The new cities and the rejuvenated old ones showed remarkable similarities. The checkerboard of "squares" in which William Penn had laid out Philadelphia became the favorite American pattern for city development, and each new "addition" strove to be exactly like the rest. Pavements rarely kept up with expansion, and while asphalt and brick won increasing popularity, cobblestone, stone block, wood block, and macadam continued in general use. Telephone, telegraph, and electric light poles and wires, all rare or nonexistent in the seventies, were common by the nineties. Business districts at any given time were everywhere much alike, but in each decade the height of downtown buildings increased. The first of the skyscrapers, made possible by the use of structural steel and iron, was the ten-storied Home Insurance Building of Chicago, completed in 1885. Thereafter city skylines rose, while traffic congestion increased in spite of the best efforts of horsecars, cable cars, and elevated railways to keep pace with it.

The Urban Worker. Behind these externals lay a pattern of life that varied little. City dwellers were employees of industry or trade, dependent upon wages for their daily bread. Wages, judged by present-day standards, were incredibly low; by 1900 American workers, on an average, earned between $300 and $400 a year at a time when a dollar might be worth perhaps only four or five times what it is worth today. The unskilled worker received as little as $1.50 a day for his efforts, but he was often unemployed, and a salary of $4 or $5 a week was not unusual. If one were out of work for long, one begged, borrowed, stole, or starved. The working day was ordinarily ten hours, and the six-day week was taken for granted. Accidents among industrial employees were numerous, and too lightly regarded by employers. The employment of women and children in industry held wages down, but was for many families an absolute necessity. The percentage of women gainfully employed rose from 15 per cent in 1870 to 20 per cent in 1900. Child labor was ruthlessly exploited — in the cotton mills of the South, in the sweatshops of the East, in the packing plants of the West. According to one estimate, there were not less than 10 million people in the United States living in abject poverty.

Poverty existed abundantly in the city even during normal times. In periods of sharp economic reverse, it doubled and trebled and was accompanied by acute distress and actual starvation. The business cycle with its sharp ups and downs had, of course, operated before the Panic of 1873. But during earlier depressions, America was still a land pre-eminently devoted to farming. While the farmer might have had little income during hard times and might even have lost title to his land, he still had been able to provide food and shelter for his family. This was often impossible for the industrial worker in the grim years after 1873, and as a result the stricken cities spawned privation, bread lines, and radicalism.

Tenements and Slums. The long depressions of the seventies and the nineties emphasized the wretched living conditions of the industrial worker in American cities. About 90 per cent of the workers lived in rented quarters, the best of which were none too good and the worst, usually known as tenements, indescribably noisome. Since no major cities had effective building codes and the price of real estate was mounting yearly, owners sought to get as much return from every square inch of property as possible. The usual tenement was a three to six-story structure of brick or wood. Cold water was provided from one tap on the ground floor, and there might be one toilet, often in the cellar, although in the early days it was usually located outside the building. Until the 1890's the tenements were often without fire escapes, and access to the upper floors was by a single staircase. Many of the rooms were miserably lighted, since the next tenement building was but two or three feet away, and many interior rooms had no outside ventilation. A New York housing commission of 1888 found that into one, two, or three of these "small dirty pen-like rooms" were often packed families of ten or fifteen people. In an age ignorant of the simplest sanitary precautions, preventable diseases such as smallpox, typhoid, and typhus took a heavy toll. At any one time during this period three-fourths of the sickness and death in New York City occurred among the less favored half of the population.

The Vulgar Rich. In blatant contrast to the plight of the poor was the vulgar ostentation of the small group of *parvenu* rich. War profiteers, successful speculators, oil men and miners who had "struck it rich" flocked to the cities to display their wealth. Few could approximate the extravagances of the notorious Jim Fisk, but many tried. Fisk, at the height of his glory, had sumptuous offices in "Castle Erie," a huge marble building on Eighth Avenue in New York that also housed his privately owned and operated Grand Opera House. From his theatrical stars and dancers, many of whom were imported, he recruited his own harem. The chief recipients of his favor lived in palaces and drove about in fine carriages. On occasion Fisk would dress himself in the gold lace of an admiral's uniform, and once, when so arrayed, he contrived to receive President Grant. He died on January 7, 1872, from bullet wounds inflicted by Edward S. Stokes, a "business and amatory rival." Stokes, for his crime, was sentenced to four years in the penitentiary at Sing Sing, but he was permitted special privileges, such as driving about at night with the span of horses he kept at a local livery stable.

The Plutocracy. Even more alarming to many thoughtful Americans than the vulgar exploits of men like Fisk and Stokes were the more restrained but perhaps more socially significant actions of "the new plutocracy." To demonstrate their wealth, these people built enormous mansions and attempted to live like the nobility of the Old World. Their entertainments were princely in extravagance. The apogee of such spectacles was probably reached in 1897, when the Bradley Martins rented much of the Waldorf Astoria Hotel and converted it at a cost of over $100,000 into a replica of the Versailles of Louis XIV. The arriving guests, dressed in what they thought the proper costumes for the court of the Sun King, were met by August Belmont, whose suit of gold inlaid armor cost a small fortune. After 1874 when Jennie Jerome, daughter of a Wall Street broker, married Lord Randolph Churchill, many American families of the upper economic stratum sought to insure their place in this incontestable elite by similar international alliances. William Waldorf Astor even settled in England, where by the judicious use of money he soon acquired a seat in the House of Lords. At home his relative, Mrs. William Astor, contented herself by leading American society, or "the four hundred," after the remark of her friend Ward McAllister, who intimated in 1888 that there were only about four hundred people in New York who really counted. Mark Twain's dry comment that we were "all descended from Adam" reflected the dominant sentiment, but it did not dispel the growing fear that the old egalitarian and democratic American traditions were threatened.

City Government. The burgeoning city was regarded as a sinkhole of iniquities by the rural citizens. The diverse character of its population, the great economic and social disparities between its classes, the activities of its very rich and very poor, and the conditions of its slums all excited censure

THE "BREAKER BOYS"

The use of child labor in mining and heavy industries was a major public controversy during the last decade of the nineteenth century. Two opposing points of view are given pungent expression in the following exchange:

George F. Baer, leader of the Pennsylvania anthracite coal interests, tangled with labor lawyer Clarence Darrow at the arbitration commission hearings following the great strike of 1902. Baer said, "The unions are corrupting the children of America by letting them join their illegal organizations." Darrow replied, "If the children had not been at work in the mine they could not have joined the union."

McAlister Coleman, *Men and Coal* (1943), Holt, Rinehart and Winston, Inc.

"THE TAMMANY TIGER LOOSE"

Thomas Nast's portrayal of the mauling of the Republic, one of his most memorable cartoons, was credited with bringing about the downfall of the Tweed Ring. From Harper's Weekly, *November 11, 1874.*

and revulsion. So also did the governments of most cities. After a study of American governments preparatory to writing his famous *The American Commonwealth* (1888), James Bryce called city administration "the one conspicuous failure in the United States." Everywhere from New York to San Francisco the condition seemed the same. In almost every city a corrupt city boss, usually not himself holding office, controlled the elected mayor and the city council, who in turn levied taxes and let clusters of contracts for paving streets, laying sewers, building schools, and other public works. These officials also had the power to grant lucrative utilities franchises to private enterprisers for street railways, the supply of gas, electric power, and water. A long-term franchise — sometimes running for fifty years — giving a monopoly

to a street railway company, with guaranteed incomes double and treble a fair return on the capital invested, offered the chance for millions of dollars in profits, usually to be split between the fortunate capitalist and the corrupt ring of city officials. A good portion of the returns were channeled to the boss, who divided the spoils among his followers in the city wards and precincts. They, in turn, used a part of the funds to help the poor and provide them with cheap entertainment and drink. The rest was pocketed. The precinct and ward captains parceled out city jobs among the faithful and interceded with friendly judges, often members of the machine, when their clients fell afoul the law. Often the local ward boss was the only friend in power whom the poor immigrant had, and the clubhouse of the political machine the only social service agency he knew. For such benevolent activities the machine asked for only one thing, votes on election day; and if gratitude was unlikely to move a citizen, there was usually money to buy his franchise. So the machines repeatedly triumphed at the polls, despite the agonized efforts of reformers.

Tammany and Tweed. As befitted its size and prominence, New York City furnished the country with the outstanding example of municipal corruption. There the Tammany Society, a political organization that dated back to the eighteenth century, controlled the local machinery of the Democratic Party and regularly rolled up huge majorities. When Grant became President of the United States, the "Grand Sachem" of Tammany Hall, as the society was usually called (after its meeting place on Fourteenth Street), was William M. Tweed, a thoroughgoing corruptionist who had worked his way up in politics from membership in a volunteer fire department. By the most barefaced bribery, he and his associates had secured from the state legislature a city charter specifically designed to let them avoid responsibility for their crimes. The principals of the "Tweed Ring" were "Boss" Tweed himself, whose presidency of the board of supervisors of New York County (coterminous with New York City) had obvious possibilities; A. Oakey Hall, the mayor; Peter B. Sweeny, treasurer of both city and county; and Richard B. Connolly, the controller. In 1869 this crew began a series of peculations that mounted year by year until at the height of their power they were dividing among themselves and their confederates 85 per cent of the total expenditures made by the city and county. Tweed received as his share 24 per cent of the "take," and the rest was apportioned by prearranged plan. In one period of thirty months the city and county printing bill ran to over $7 million. It is probable that the loot taken by the Tweed Ring reached $100 million.

At last, scathing editorials in the *New York Times,* and a series of cartoons by Thomas Nast in *Harper's Weekly,* began to take effect, and the public was aroused. The owner of the *Times* was offered a million dollars to quiet his paper, and Nast, a half million to go to Europe and give up his campaign of caricature. Long baffled for lack of direct evidence, the *Times* finally got the proof it needed from an insider with a grievance, a devastating exposure of the Tweed Ring. Under the brilliant leadership of Samuel J. Tilden and Charles O'Conor, the reformers were able by the end of 1872 to drive every member of the ring out of office. Tweed himself died in jail.

Municipal Corruption. Since almost every city had its variation of Tammany Hall, some of the nation's rural-minded reformers came to believe that the city was the natural habitat of corruption and vice. Some serious students of government, like the noted English observer, James Bryce, felt that the explanation lay in the large proportion of immigrants in the urban population. But such explanations were hardly fair either to the city or to the immigrants. For Cincinnati, St. Louis, Minneapolis, and San Francisco, where the older stock of Americans were in the majority, exhibited the same blight. And if the city as an institution was corrupt, it did not hold a monopoly on dishonesty. The Grant administration was known, even before it ended, as the most corrupt that the republic had yet experienced. The number of honest officials in the carpetbag South seems to have been minimal. Yet the scandals that rocked the country were as frequently associated with the North or the West as with the South. The Credit Mobilier, the Whiskey Ring, the frauds in the Indian Service had no southern nor strictly urban connotation. The moral standards of the entire nation during the postwar years sank to a new low.

Moral Laxness. Illustrating the trend of the times was the notorious Beecher-Tilton divorce trial. Henry Ward Beecher was one of the most influential ministers in the country. Discarding the orthodox views of his well-known father, Lyman Beecher, he preached a mixture of the new liberal theology and a strictly orthodox economic and social policy, a combination which pleased not only his own wealthy Brooklyn congregation but many influential Protestant lay and clerical leaders throughout the country. His sermons were reprinted and often cited as the last word in matters where theology and social policy merged. A good portion of the nation was aghast, and the rest perhaps titillated, when in 1875 a member of Beecher's congregation, Theodore Tilton, brought suit against the distinguished clergyman for alienation of his wife's affections, charging adultery. Verbatim accounts of the trial, together with Beecher's letters to Mrs. Tilton, were widely circulated. And although the jury could come to no decision, the effect of the case upon the nation was hardly conducive to the raising of ethical standards.

Business Ethics. A similar lack of ethics permeated business. The pursuit of wealth was in itself notorious, but the devious means men used to gain it hit at the very foundations of American society. In the immediate postwar years this laxity of conduct could be blamed in part on the war, but more important was the utter novelty of large-scale business operations. Before the war most business was small and its activity local. Standards of conduct existed which the prudent businessman, to retain the good will of his customers and the public, felt obliged to recognize. But for national large-scale business no code of ethics had yet been evolved. With monopoly as a goal, the struggle for survival among competitors was intense, and usually only the ruthless had a chance to win. The law offered no restraints, for since such problems had not been faced before, laws to meet them had not been devised. Fur-

thermore, as business organizations grew in size and power, they found that they could, when they chose, have a hand in both the making and the enforcement of laws.

Corporation methods of finance offered an opportunity, rarely long neglected, for astounding frauds in the issuance and manipulation of stocks and bonds. "Wildcat" or "blue-sky" securities were easily sold to a public made gullible by the unprecedented number of fortunes that the "boom" times actually produced. Oil companies were organized that never drilled a well, mining companies that never sank a shaft, railroad companies that never laid a rail — all for the sole purpose of separating careless investors from their savings.

Even the most substantial corporations were frequently led to "water" their stock and to incur bonded indebtedness altogether out of proportion to their assets. Daniel Drew, a hypocritical fraud who hoped to purchase pardon for his sins by making generous pledges, seldom paid, to Drew Theological Seminary, wormed his way into the directorate of the Erie Railway, became its treasurer, and for years manipulated the price of its stock in order to make himself rich. In 1868 Cornelius Vanderbilt, who already controlled the New York Central and the Hudson River railroads, proposed to add the badly rundown Erie to his domain. A battle royal followed in which Drew, supported by his apt "pupils," Jay Gould and Jim Fisk, finally won. To do so, however, Drew and his associates found it necessary to issue 50,000 shares of fraudulent stock, to flee to New Jersey in order to escape arrest, and to bribe the New Jersey legislature to legalize their transaction. But Drew's luck did not hold; by 1876 he was bankrupt with liabilities of over a million dollars.

Not many types of sizable business enterprise came through the cycles of boom and depression with clean records. Three New York savings banks failed in 1872 under scandalous circumstances; while small investors suffered acutely, the former bank officials continued to live in luxury.

During the first eight years of the seventies, twenty-eight New York life insurance companies failed outright, or avoided failure by amalgamation with stronger concerns. Losses to policyholders amounted to a nominal total of $158 million in insurance. Even the solvent companies unblushingly "froze out" aged and undesirable policyholders, usually by increasing rates. In the city, the state, and the nation, in business and in private life, wherever the citizen looked he saw graft, corruption, and unethical conduct.

Rural Life. Still there was a brighter side to American life, even if many failed to see it. For the United States was not merely a nation of corrupt political machines, of slums, and of grafters in low and high places. Most city dwellers were, of course, honest, and more than 60 per cent of the people, as late as 1900, still lived in the country, or in towns of less than 4,000 inhabitants. Practically all of these depended directly or indirectly upon agriculture for their livelihood. Even the cities owed much to the farms, for throughout the nineteenth century an abundant farm demand, restrained from foreign purchases by a protective-tariff policy, absorbed the products of the city factories, and spared American manufacturers the necessity of finding foreign markets as an outlet for their goods. For agriculture, as for industry, these were revolutionary years. New tools were devised, new types of crops were raised to suit city markets, experiments with diversification and standardization were made, a rising price for farmlands was met. Less and less, the farmer farmed according to ritual; more and more he used scientific methods to improve his profits. Caught in the meshes of the prevailing economic system, he made every effort to understand it and to bend it to his needs.

Village Life. Farm life gradually merged with village life. On Saturdays farmers went to town to trade; on Sundays they went to town to church; on other days when work was not too pressing they went to town, with or without excuses. Farmers went to town to retire. Farm boys and girls went to school in town, got jobs in town, and, when they could, went out with the town boys and girls to the pleasures of the city. Farmers and their wives borrowed from the town the conveniences that the town had borrowed from the city. Steadily, the isolation of farm life broke down — a process that the rural free delivery of mail, telephones, electrification, the automobile, and the radio were in due time to accelerate immeasurably.

Country towns and villages enjoyed an importance during most of the nineteenth century that they have since entirely lost. As centers of trade for the surrounding countryside, they could almost count on a steady amount of weekly business. The stores were strung along a single "Main Street" or surrounded a central square on which, in county seats, the courthouse was invariably located. Only in the business districts of the larger towns were the streets paved, and both horses and drivers took mud, ruts, and dust in their stride. The dwellings, at least on one side of the railroad tracks that divided the rich from the poor, were commodious, set well back from tree-lined streets, and surrounded by large lawns. Barns and outbuildings were numerous, for many townspeople kept a horse or two to draw the family "buggy," a cow, a pig to butcher in the fall, and some poultry. There was usually room for fruit trees and a vegetable garden. The incomes of villagers were not large, but they had no need to be to provide a prosperous and pleasant life.

All the town paid deference to the railroad. Over the railroad the town's outside commerce was conducted, and by means of it and the telegraph line that was part of it, contact with the rest of the world was maintained. But resentment against railroad extortion was rife, especially in the West, and campaigns for railroad regulation merged into demands for government ownership. Frequently the railroad companies played leading roles in local as well as in state and national politics.

Crime and misdemeanors were not unknown in the countryside and the village, as any reading of the court files in a county courthouse will attest. Throughout the western part of the Middle West, and especially from West Virginia to Arkansas, the region over which much of the Civil War had been fought, bands of ruffians continued their wartime habits and for years escaped arrest. Most noted of these outlaws was Jesse James, who in 1872 robbed the Kansas City Fair of $10,000, and until the time of his death a decade later kept the Kansas-Missouri border in a state of frightened expectancy.

Rural Religion. On the whole there were only two social classes, usually clustered around three institutions, the saloon, the pool hall, and the church. Although economic standing had little to do with the division, almost invariably the leading professional, business, and tradespeople belonged to the sober, moral, church-going majority, and if they felt the impulse to transgress they usually left for a holiday in the distant city. At the center of the town's social life was the church. On Sundays, services went on all day, with Sunday school at ten, preaching at eleven, children's services in the afternoon, young people's meetings at seven, evening worship with congregational singing at eight. Weekday services included evening prayer meetings, ladies' aid societies, missionary societies, and guilds, all absorbed in money-raising efforts, choir practice, and "revivals." For these protracted meetings, held for several weeks once or twice each year, evangelists were often called in to aid the local pastors, and hundreds were induced to "make their profession of faith." The old emotionalism of the frontier still survived. "Shouting" and "conversion" were for many an intensely exciting experience, and preaching reached the pinnacle of emotion-

alism when "not a dry eye was left in the house." A few country churches, each in its mournful setting of tombstones, still managed to survive, as the long rows of teams tied each Sunday to the church's hitch-racks well attested. Farm families, however, preferred increasingly to attend church in town, and so the country congregations dwindled.

Protestant America, both in the country and in the cities, tended to view hard times as just judgment upon men for their sins. Rivalry with the Roman Catholics and the Jews, whose numbers were being considerably increased by immigration, and competition among the various Protestant denominations themselves, spurred religious workers to greater activity. Leadership was furnished less by the great preachers of the day, such as Henry Ward Beecher and Phillips Brooks, than by the evangelists, among whom Dwight L. Moody, the exhorter, and Ira D. Sankey, the singer, were pre-eminent. In 1875 Moody and Sankey, just returned from a series of successful revivals in the British Isles, began a meeting in Philadelphia that lasted three months, and then went on to New York, Chicago, Boston, and other metropolises. In Chicago for four months their "tabernacle" was crowded daily by an audience of from 5,000 to 10,000 persons. The traditional doctrines of these evangelists, and their imitators, had little direct bearing on the social problems of the time, but they at least extolled the Christian virtues and filled converts with an earnest desire to better the lot of their fellow men.

Practical Christianity. The continued vitality of Protestantism that had sired so many new sects in the past was evidenced by the rapid spread of three organizations devoted to practical Christianity, and the birth and growth of still another important American creed. Far more conscious than the churches of the needs of the time were the Young Men's and Young Women's Christian Associations, both of which dated back to the middle of the century, but began to be really important only during the seventies. They emphasized wholesome recreation, study classes, and even musicals, rather than the inculcation of Christian theology. Immediately effective among the submerged classes was the Salvation Army, which invaded the United States from England in 1879, and soon extended its interest from saving the souls of the down-and-out to an extensive program of social activity.

At the other extreme of religious interpretation was Christian Science, which took its tenets from *Science and Health* (1875), a book by Mrs. Mary Baker G. Eddy. Rejecting medicine, and claiming for the Divine Mind an absolute superiority over matter, the Christian Scientists preached a doctrine which, they claimed, wrought many healings of all types of disease and discord, and notable cures among those whose nerves were unstrung by the increasing tempo of modern life. Its influence also reached over into other denominations and into medicine itself. While Christian Scientists were at pains not to ascribe their cures to the human will, the belief grew among those who made this assumption that a vigorous will had much to do with the attainment of happiness and health.

Roman Catholicism. Religious life was further stimulated by an old group in America, the Roman Catholics. Through the last half of the century the Catholic Church grew rapidly as thousands of its adherents from southern and eastern Europe poured into the country. By 1890 Catholics constituted the largest single religious group in thirteen states. The enhanced stature of American Catholicism was acknowledged by the appointment of James Gibbons, Archbishop of Baltimore, in 1886 as the second American cardinal. Cardinal Gibbons, by upholding firmly the doctrine of the separation of church and state, enabled Catholics to fit their religion

comfortably into the political ideas of their new country. He also took the position that the church should be unified and not separated into ethnic groups, and did much to infuse the Catholic Church with a concern for the social and economic betterment of the laboring classes. Catholicism, in fact, never lost its hold over its communicants in the working classes to the extent that Protestantism did during these years. Nor did this loyalty escape the observation of the anti-Catholic fanatics.

Judaism. For most of the nineteenth century, the Jewish element in the nation's population remained relatively small. From the older colonial Jewish group came much of the impetus for a reform movement that closely paralleled the main developments in Protestantism. Led by Isaac Wise of Cincinnati, Reform Judaism looked toward "Americanization." To a great extent, the importance of traditional dogma was de-emphasized, and many of the old European customs were dropped. Beginning about 1890, however, the quickening stream of Jewish immigration from central and eastern Europe brought opposition to the reform movement. The majority of these newcomers were impoverished and relatively uneducated people who became a force for conservatism. Since many of them continued to preserve their old ways and customs, most of which were utterly strange to native Americans, and clustered together in self-made city ghettos, they became the object of bigotry. Anti-Semitism was almost absent from the nation before 1890. After that it grew rapidly, giving back-handed support to Conservative Judaism and the new Zionism founded in 1897 in Switzerland by Theodor Herzl, which sought to re-establish a Jewish state in Palestine.

Godkin, Curtis, and Schurz. This intensification of religious life in the postwar decades was paralleled by a quickening of social criticism that aimed its shafts not only at corruption and immorality but also at the prevailing spirit of materialism. Edwin Lawrence Godkin, George William Curtis, and Carl Schurz were three important critics. Godkin (1831–1902) was the son of a distinguished British Protestant clergyman, who was also a journalist. After a brief newspaper career in England and Ireland he emigrated in 1856 to America. Nine years later he established *The Nation,* a weekly newspaper, which rapidly became a major intellectual influence. Godkin was a stout defender of sound money and a *laissez faire* economic policy which included free trade. He also fearlessly denounced political corruption and business rascality, and was an ardent supporter of civil service reform. His weekly pronouncements on both politics and society were eagerly awaited by ministers, editors, and minor publicists who pushed the radius of *The Nation*'s influence far beyond the number of its readers.

George William Curtis (1824–1892), a New Englander by birth and intellectual tradition, in 1863 became editor of *Harper's Weekly,* which in the ascendancy it soon gained over men's minds was rivaled only by *The Nation.* Although *Harper's Weekly* appealed to a far wider audience than *The Nation,* possibly because of its broader interests and because of its pictorial representations, including the cartoons of Thomas Nast, it was never as militant or comprehensive in its demands for reform. Curtis' influence, however, was almost as forceful from the lecture platform as from the editor's desk. Scores of audiences heard his speech on "Political Infidelity" and his excoriation of America for its worship of materialism.

But perhaps the most influential reformer was Carl Schurz (1829–1906). German-born and educated, Schurz had to flee from his native country because of his part in the liberal revolutionary movements of 1848–1849. Expelled from France as a radical, he joined the German colony in Wisconsin, where he soon became a leader of the anti-

slavery movement. A major general in the northern forces during the war, he later made an official tour of the South at the behest of President Johnson. Subsequently he was a leader of the Liberal Republicans; for six years, 1869–1875, he represented Missouri in the United States Senate; after that he became Hayes's Secretary of the Interior. Schurz was a born orator, an intense democrat, and an ardent foe of business and political corruption.

Pulitzer and Hearst. By the 1890's two other powerful exponents of a rather different nature had been added to the swelling demand for reform. Joseph Pulitzer and William Randolph Hearst originated the new mass chain newspapers that were to revolutionize urban journalism. They deliberately set the tone of their papers to attract the masses of the cities. An impecunious Hungarian immigrant in 1864, Pulitzer acquired control of the *St. Louis Post-Dispatch* in 1878 and of the *New York World* five years later. Hearst was given the *San Francisco Examiner* by his wealthy father in 1887 and in 1895 acquired the *New York Journal.* Devising a new formula for "yellow journalism" and lowering the prices of his papers substantially, Pulitzer garnished them with a combination of sin, sex, and sensation, together with strident demands for reform. Hearst answered with even more sensationalism and more radicalism. Whatever else they might have done, the two men and their newspapers reached the great city masses and stimulated the growing reform spirit.

In the business and political world the work of Godkin, Curtis, Schurz, and later of Hearst and Pulitzer, had effect also. Scandals were ruthlessly exposed, and sometimes, as in the case of Tweed, the guilty were punished. A governor in Nebraska and a state treasurer in Minnesota were impeached and removed from office. A member of the Kansas legislature laid on the speaker's desk $7,000 that he had been paid to vote for the re-election of Samuel

C. Pomeroy to the United States Senate, and Pomeroy was not re-elected. The Whiskey Ring was put out of business; thievery in the Indian Service was restrained; wholesale attempts to bribe Congress, as in the Credit Mobilier, were not again attempted; a beginning was made with civil service reform; corporation misconduct was exposed; and the people showed a disposition to use the power of government to restrain practices that interfered unjustly with the personal and property rights of individuals.

Urban Reform. Simultaneously both technology and a growing awareness of the evils of urban life were making the city a better place in which to live. The carbon arc electric lamp and Thomas A. Edison's new incandescent bulb, introduced in 1879, not only improved the lighting of the streets but resulted also in a noticeable reduction in crime. The construction of steam elevated railroads in New York during the late sixties, and the perfection of the electric trolley car at the end of the eighties, improved urban transportation. Better paving, concern with pure water, and improved sanitation facilities followed, especially after the great typhoid outbreaks in Philadelphia and Chicago in the eighties and nineties. Frederick Law Olmsted, an architect, had started a campaign before the Civil War to beautify cities and provide places for relaxation through the construction of parks after European models. At the same time playgrounds and playing fields were established where children and adults could enjoy themselves away from dirty and crowded streets.

Along with these developments came the rapid rise of organized sports. Baseball had its origins in what the English called "rounders." As early as 1845 the Knickerbocker Club of New York provided a rule book for the game, but its popularity really dates from the Civil War, during which it was played enthusiastically by the wearers of both the Blue and the Gray. After the

war, its devotees carried it to every part of the nation. During the seventies and eighties it developed into the "great American game," with a complicated system of major and minor leagues. Football, introduced into the United States during the seventies as an adaptation of English Rugby, had by the nineties conquered most of the American colleges and universities. Professional boxing approached the level of respectability when "Gentleman Jim" Corbett won the heavyweight championship in 1892. By this time, too, bicycling had become a fad that women and children as well as men could enjoy. For less strenuous devotees there were such milder activities as lawn tennis, roller skating, and croquet. All classes of people found in sports a satisfying refuge from the workaday world.

By the end of the century at least a start had been made to improve conditions in the city slums. Perhaps more than any other man, Jacob Riis, an immigrant and a New York reporter, paved the way for change by publishing *How the Other Half Lives* (1890). Finally, in 1900 the New York Committee of Fifteen, which included John D. Rockefeller, Jr., Jacob H. Schiff, and George Foster Peabody, made a thorough study of slum housing that led to the first effective New York building law.

Women as Reformers. Along with movements for honesty in politics and for business and urban reform, came a definite upsurge of humanitarianism, led for the most part by a group of educated middle-class women. Women were especially concerned with the settlement house movement, which sought to establish social service institutions in the worst slums of the cities. Among the leaders of the movement that inaugurated social work in the United States were Jane Addams of Hull House in Chicago and Lillian D. Wald of the Henry Street settlement in New York. Women also played an important part in the campaign against alcohol. The evangelical churches, especially the

VARICK STREET, NEW YORK, 1894

A photograph showing how "the other half" lived, from the Jacob A. Riis Collection in the Museum of the City of New York.

Methodist, the Baptist, and the Presbyterian, presented a united front against the "demon rum." They were joined in 1874 by the Women's Christian Temperance Union, for years headed by Frances E. Willard. Both the churches and the lay organization crusaded for temperance instruction in schools, for local option in counties and towns, and for state-wide prohibition. By the end of the eighties the temperance forces could point to only a few victories, but they were confident of more in the future.

Because women seemed to be more easily aroused against intemperance than men, temperance advocates generally favored the "emancipation of women," particularly with the intent of giving them the right to vote. The attainment of suffrage by the illiterate freedmen of the South spurred the women reformers to renewed activity. Led by such intrepid workers as Susan B. Anthony and Elizabeth Cady Stanton, and joined by a few of the professional reformers who before the Civil War had centered their attack upon slavery, the suf-

fragists made a little progress. A few states reluctantly conceded to women the right to vote in school elections, and the two territories of Utah and Wyoming established complete political equality. Eventual victory for woman suffrage was forecast by the increasing freedom with which women attended college, entered such professions as the ministry, the law, and medicine, and organized women's clubs.

Other Reformers. That the zeal for reform characteristic of the generation preceding the Civil War was eclipsed rather than destroyed by that struggle was apparent in a multitude of ways. Dorothea L. Dix put aside her war work to resume her earlier efforts for the improvement of conditions among criminals, paupers, and the insane. In state after state, boards of charities were set up to deal with the problem of relief. State schools for the deaf and blind were established, and occasional efforts were made to deal separately with the problem of juvenile delinquency. Even the humane treatment of animals was advocated, and an American Society for the Prevention of Cruelty to Animals, founded in 1866 by Henry Bergh on the model of the British Royal Society, made rapid progress. The Society interested itself in the well-being of children as well as animals, and did much to rescue the unfortunate from their wretched conditions. All such efforts, however, were at best only piecemeal, and comparatively little thought was given to the underlying causes of insanity, poverty, and crime. Some light was shed on the subject by the work of R. L. Dugdale, *The Jukes: A Study in Crime, Pauperism, Heredity, and Disease* (1877), which traced the history of a feeble-minded and diseased family that had cost the state of New York $1 million since 1800.

Educational Changes. Another trend indicating growing social awareness was the increase in philanthropic activities. Not all the profits of the new industrial age went to individuals. Before the Civil War such a gift as that of Stephen Girard, who left $2 million to found a boys' school in Philadelphia, was so rare as to brand its donor as an eccentric. After the war such gifts became more common. In 1865 Ezra Cornell gave $500,000 to found Cornell University in Ithaca, New York. Two years later George Peabody established the Peabody Fund to improve southern education, and within a few years both Vanderbilt University in Nashville and Johns Hopkins University of Baltimore opened their doors through the generosity of rich donors. Supplemented by the immense outpourings of such philanthropists as John D. Rockefeller, Andrew Carnegie, and Edward Stephen Harkness, the total endowment of colleges and universities in the United States reached an enormous figure.

A new interest in education was signalized in 1867 by the appointment of the first United States Commissioner of Education. Rapid developments followed on all educational levels. In 1873 St. Louis introduced the European institution of the kindergarten. Graded elementary schools, with a separate room and a teacher for each grade, replaced the old one-room school. And the number of high schools grew rapidly. Before the Civil War only about 100 public high schools existed, and most of the training for college was given by private academies. By 1870 the number of high schools had risen to 600, and by 1900, to 6,000.

Higher Education. Educational institutions were revitalized in the period, but the most notable changes took place in the colleges and universities. Even more important than private philanthropy in the stimulation of higher education was the effect of the Morrill Act of 1862, which required of each state, in return for a federal land grant of as many times 30,000 acres as it had senators and representatives, the establishment of at least one college to "teach such branches of learning as are related to agriculture and the mechanic arts." The terms of the act had interesting implications. First, they attacked the prevailing assumption that only the traditional classical subjects were suitable for a college curriculum, and, second, they implied that any able citizen, whatever his intended occupation, might profit from a higher education and that the cost of such was a proper charge on government. Many western state universities rose to quality institutions as a result, and ultimately not less than sixty-nine "land-grant colleges" profited from the terms of the act.

Equally important in the broadening of university horizons was the work of Charles W. Eliot, the brilliant chemist who in 1869, at the age of thirty-five, became president of Harvard University. In a few years Eliot substituted the elective system for the traditional classical curriculum with its emphasis upon languages, mathematics, ethics, rhetoric, and theology. His reform opened the way for the advance of the new social and physical sciences. It also permitted the

FIFTH AVENUE, NEW YORK

Fashionable examples of residential architecture favored by the American well-to-do in the Gilded Age.

introduction of many "bread and butter" courses of varying merit. The elective idea spread like wildfire and evoked both enthusiastic approval and fierce denunciation. But for good and for ill it had come to stay, although most institutions ultimately insisted upon a central core of required "liberal" subjects, especially in the first two years of college.

Among other striking changes of the period was the headway that was made toward equality of opportunity for women in higher education. Women's right to equal treatment in elementary and secondary schools was acknowledged, in theory at least, before the Civil War, but their chances of entering a collegiate institution remained slight, although Mt. Holyoke at South Hadley, Massachusetts, had existed since 1837. In 1865 Vassar opened its doors at Poughkeepsie, New York, to be followed shortly by Wellesley, Smith, Bryn Mawr, and Radcliffe, all in the East. Later, a goodly number of women's colleges were also organized in the West and the South. More important to the advance of women's education, however, was the development of co-education, pioneered by Oberlin, Antioch, and Iowa before the Civil War. The University of Wisconsin set up a special department for women in 1863, and when Ohio State admitted them from its foundation in 1870, the idea was rapidly copied not only by state universities but by private institutions as well.

Colleges for Negroes. Higher education for the Negro made substantial progress in 1867 with the incorporation of Howard University in Washington, and in quick succession such other institutions as Fisk University in Nashville, Straight University in New Orleans, and Shaw University in Raleigh. The Peabody Fund was administered mainly with a view to the improvement of common schools for Negroes, but the Peabody Normal College in Nashville, which it aided generously, also served the cause of education among the whites. In

contrast with most earlier educational institutions, Hampton Normal and Agricultural Institute, which opened at Hampton, Virginia, in 1870 with funds provided by the American Missionary Association sought to emphasize the dignity and importance of skill in labor with the hands, hoping thus to prepare its students as well as possible for the type of work that was actually available to them in the South. Poorer students "worked their way through," and in 1872 Hampton's most distinguished student, Booker T. Washington, arrived with fifty cents in his pocket. Less than ten years later, Washington was chosen to head a school for Negroes at Tuskegee, Alabama, which under his leadership soon rivaled Hampton in its success with the same type of instruction. Critics of industrial education for Negroes complained that it was designed merely to keep the colored race in a permanently inferior status, but in the main Hampton, Tuskegee, and their imitators were applauded for their aims.

The Graduate Schools. Perhaps the best evidence that American scholarship was reaching maturity was the establishment of graduate schools. For a long time, American scholars did their advanced work abroad, less in England than in Germany, where they were more cordially received. When the time came for the establishment of American graduate schools, therefore, they followed the German, not the English, model, and presently the Doctor of Philosophy degree, then virtually unknown in England, was to become in America, as in Germany, the aim of every budding scholar. The first Ph.D. conferred in America was given by Yale in 1861, but the Yale graduate school was not organized until ten years later. By 1872 Harvard had established a graduate school, and in 1876 the Johns Hopkins University set a new precedent by making graduate work its main concern. Before long even the new state universities of the West were emphasizing the importance of research and the training

PROFESSOR BELL'S TELEPHONE

The Centennial Exposition at Philadelphia gave Alexander Graham Bell an opportunity to exhibit his telephone. Dom Pedro, Emperor of Brazil, shown here, stopped to examine the new invention, but the crowds generally passed it by, as little interested in Bell's achievement as they were in Edison's electric light bulb, which most people also ignored.

of scholars, and American universities were seeking to offer opportunities similar to those available in European universities.

The introduction of graduate studies in American universities emphasized research and scholarly writing as qualifications for teachers and as means to advancement. While the teaching of undergraduates may have suffered because of these new interests, in the end the influence of the university and the college upon society grew. In the transition from a raw industrial nation, which was still largely rural in its ways and attitudes, to an urban, scientific, and socially-minded country, the academic philosophers, the social scientists, and the men of the laboratories played an amazing and still undervalued part.

The Centennial Exposition. Probably few Americans were able to take comfort during the dismal seventies from the fact that an educational quickening seemed imminent, or from knowing that their humanitarian instincts were still alive. But a great many had their faith in their country restored by a visit to the Centennial

Exposition, which was held in Philadelphia from May to October, 1876 — the first to be undertaken in the United States. Preparations for it had been begun before 1873, and in spite of bad business conditions the project was not abandoned. The railroads offered reduced rates to Philadelphia and from all over the country the people came. More than 9 million visitors attended, and on a single day as many as 275,000.

Compared with later exhibitions, the Philadelphia Centennial had little to offer. Its success was materialistic rather than artistic. Its architecture was mediocre, and its art exhibits, while representative of the best that the United States could then supply, suffered from the unwillingness of foreign nations — England excepted — to send their treasures to America. But in size the fair was impressive. The Main Building, covering twenty acres of land, was reputed to be the largest building in the world. Machinery Hall housed a magnificent Corliss engine and numerous other symbols of the triumphs of American industry.

When it came to commercial and industrial exhibits, European nations, eager to advance their trade in America, vied with the United States in the richness of their offerings. English furniture and household decorations, German porcelain, French textiles, as well as Japanese bronzes and lacquer wares, and Indian shawls and jewels were displayed. Such exhibits greatly stimulated American interest in foreign lands and travel abroad. But if the Exposition brought one thing home to the observant visitor, it was the fact that the United States now rivaled the European nations in industrial achievement, and that inevitably the future pointed toward an urban, industrial society, a society differing radically from the agrarian culture of the past.

SELECTED BIBLIOGRAPHY

A. M. Schlesinger, Sr., *The Rise of the City, 1878–1893* (1933), is a good general work on urban growth and influence. But it should be supplemented by other interpretative works such as Lewis Mumford, *The Culture of Cities* (1938); C. McL. Green, *American Cities in the Growth of the Nation* (1957); and Blake McKelvey, *The Urbanization of America, 1860–1915* (1963). Among the best studies of individual cities are C. McL. Green, *Washington: Capital City, 1879–1950* (1963); Blake McKelvey, *Rochester* (4 vols., 1949–1961); Bayrd Still, *Milwaukee* (1948); and A. T. Brown, *Frontier Community: Kansas City to 1870* (1963). Important recent monographs treating hitherto unexplored subjects are S. B. Warner, Jr., *Streetcar Suburbs: The Process of Growth in Boston, 1870–1900* (1962); and Stephan Thernstrom, *Poverty and Progress; Social Mobility in a Nineteenth Century City* (1964), a study of Newburyport, Massachusetts. Small town life is treated by Lewis Atherton, *Main Street on the Middle Border* (1954).

The working and home conditions of the poor are well set forth in R. H. Bremner, *From the Depths; The Discovery of Poverty in the United States* (1956); and Roy Lubove, *The Progressives and the Slums: Tenement House Reform in New York City, 1890–1917* (1962). But no student should miss the impassioned works of two notable immigrants: Jacob Riis, *How the Other Half Lives* (1890); and *The Americanization of Edward Bok* (1920). On Jane Addams, see her *Twenty Years at Hull House* (1910); and J. W. Linn, *Jane Addams* (1935). An excellent short work is R. H. Bremner, *American Philanthropy* (1960). See also the classic by Robert Hunter, *Poverty*

(1904). An important new study of social workers is Roy Lubove, *The Professional Altruist* (1965).

Basic works on religion have already been listed. On revivalism in this period, see Gamaliel Bradford, *D. L. Moody* (1927); and W. W. Sweet, *Revivalism in America* (1944). Sibyl Wilbur, *The Life of Mary Baker Eddy* (5th ed., 1923), is the official account of Christian Science; more critical is E. F. Dakin, *Mrs. Eddy* (1929). C. H. Hopkins, *A History of the Y.M.C.A. in North America* (1951); and Sherwood Eddy, *A Century with Youth* (1944), should be consulted for the Y.M.C.A. An excellent survey of the Roman Catholic Church is Theodore Maynard, *The Story of American Catholicism* (1941). Some historical material is also to be found in T. T. McAvoy (ed.), *Roman Catholicism and the American Way of Life* (1960). For the liberal movement, see R. D. Cross, *The Emergence of Liberal Catholicism in America* (1958). The story of the A.P.A. and the growing anti-Catholic movement is best related in D. L. Kinzer, *An Episode in Anti-Catholicism* (1964). David Philipson, *The Reform Movement in Judaism* (2nd ed., 1931), is excellent on the early days of Judaism in the United States.

The literature on reform and reformers is extensive. Two excellent general works are E. F. Goldman, *Rendezvous with Destiny* (1952); and T. H. Greer, *American Social Reform Movements* (1949). Other books of merit are: Arthur Mann, *Yankee Reformers in the Urban Age* (1954); F. M. Stewart, *The National Civil Service Reform League* (1929); and C. W. Patton, *The Battle for Municipal Reform: Mobilization and Attack, 1875–1900* (1940). Joseph Schafer, *Carl Schurz, Militant Liberal* (1930), is the standard biography of one great reformer. D. C. Seitz, *Joseph*

* Available in paperback

Pulitzer (1924); and W. A. Swanberg, *°Citizen Hearst* (1961), are adequate on the two famous publishers. On woman suffrage and temperance, see: Eleanor Flexner, *Century of Struggle; The Woman's Rights Movement in the United States* (1959); Mary Peck, *Carrie Chapman Catt: A Biography* (1944); Alma Lutz, *Susan B. Anthony* (1959); Katharine Anthony, *Susan B. Anthony* (1954); Mary Earhart, *Frances Willard; From Prayers to Politics* (1944); and A. S. Kraditor, *The Ideas of the Woman Suffrage Movement, 1890–1920* (1965).

Good manuals on the general subject of education are: E. P. Cubberly, *Public Education in the United States* (2nd ed., 1934); and E. W. Knight, *Education in the United States* (3rd ed., 1951). A comparison of Edward Eggleston, *°The Hoosier Schoolmaster* (1871), with Herbert Quick, *One Man's Life* (1925), shows how rapidly conditions were changing. L. A. Cremin, *°The Transformation of the School; Progressivism in American Education, 1876–1957* (1961), is excellent. Two works by C. F. Thwing, *A History of Higher Education in America* (1906), and *The American and the German University* (1928), are helpful; the latter shows the Teutonic influence upon American educational development. See also Thomas Woody, *A History of Women's Education in the United States* (2 vols., 1929).

Many of the great universities have produced histories by their own historians, among them: James Gray, *The University of Minnesota, 1851–1951* (1951); M. E. Curti and Vernon Carstensen, *The University of Wisconsin* (2 vols., 1949); Jonas Viles, *The University of Missouri* (1939); Horace Coon, *Columbia* (1947); T. W. Goodspeed, *The Story of the University of Chicago* (1925); E. P. Cheyney, *History of the University of Pennsylvania, 1740–1940* (1940); J. F. Hopkins, *The University of Kentucky: Origins and Early Years* (1951); Hugh Hawkins, *Pioneer: A History of the Johns Hopkins University, 1874–1889* (1960); C. M. Gates, *The First Century at the University of Washington* (1961); C. L. Becker, *Cornell University; Founders and the Founding* (1943); Morris Bishop, *A History of Cornell* (1962); and E. D. Ross, *A History of Iowa State College of Agriculture and Mechanic Arts* (1942). E. D. Ross, *Democracy's College; The Land-Grant Movement in the Formative Stage* (1942), describes the Morrill Act and its results.

On the Negro, see two general works by R. W. Logan, *The Negro in American Life and Thought* (1954), and *°The Negro in the United States* (1957). H. M. Bond, *The Education of the Negro in the American Social Order* (1934), is of lasting significance. A recent and important monograph is August Meier, *Negro Thought in America, 1880–1915* (1964). On the principal Negro leader of this period see Basil Mathews, *Booker T. Washington* (1948); S. R. Spencer, Jr., *°Booker T. Washington and The Negro's Place in American Life* (1955); and Washington's autobiography, *°Up from Slavery* (1901).

27

SCIENCE, SOCIAL IDEAS, AND THE ARTS

৯ *World's Fair of 1893 • Charles Darwin • Social Darwinism • Social Christianity • James and Pragmatism • John Dewey • Pragmatic Education and Law • Reform Darwinism • Henry George • Edward Bellamy • The New Economics • Historians • The Chautauqua Movement • Mark Twain • Henry James • William Dean Howells • Naturalism and Determinism • Poetry and Music • Painting • Architecture*

World's Fair of 1893. In the spring of 1893, only seventeen years after the great Centennial Exhibition in Philadelphia, Chicago opened the World's Columbian Exposition, commemorating the 400th anniversary of the discovery of North America. Here was a further record of the nation's amazing technological and scientific progress, as well as innumerable portents of the shape of things to come. And as the Fair both recorded the past and hinted at the future of material America, it also suggested the revolutionary changes that had been made and were still to come in the realm of ideas and the creative arts. Unlike the Philadelphia Fair, a series of "congresses" accompanied the Columbian Exposition for the purpose of discussing the

most vital scientific, cultural, literary, and religious problems of the day. Imbedded in these conferences is the record of a nation converting from the old comfortable ideas that had worked well in the nineteenth-century agrarian world to new concepts more suitable for an urban, industrial, and scientific civilization.

Charles Darwin. Impregnating many of the conference papers that attacked the older accepted cultural ideas were the spirit and method of the English scientist, Charles Darwin (1809–1882). Darwin was one of several thinkers whose ideas helped bring about the great intellectual upheaval that accompanied the birth of the twentieth-century world. In his book *The Origin of Species* (1859), he used the new scientific method to challenge some of the most ancient and cherished ideas of western civilization. Thus his name became linked with the rise of the new scientific thought. Before writing *The Origin of Species* Darwin had spent years patiently studying animal life in various parts of the world. From his observations he concluded that existing life had not been created by God in six days in the forms it now exhibited, but had evolved slowly over millions of years from the simplest of origins by a process of natural selection. All life was in fierce competition for survival, and those species survived and flourished that were best adapted to their environment. Since the natural environment was continually changing, species likewise had to change or die. This had resulted in the utter extinction of untold numbers of kinds of life, but the fittest — those best adapted to the conditions in which they had to live — had passed on their characteristics to new generations. And thus the struggle for existence had produced over great spans of time entirely new species.

Some of the precepts of Darwinism obviously challenged a literal interpretation of the Biblical story of creation. The result, together with the impact of the new "higher criticism," which subjected the Bible to the test of historical knowledge, started a controversy between "fundamentalist" and "modernist" Christians. But the reasonableness of the evolutionary hypothesis could not be lost indefinitely on a world that owed so much to scientific discovery. Thomas Henry Huxley, the English biologist, and Herbert Spencer, the English philosopher, both of whom visited America, greatly influenced American thinking toward the acceptance of Darwinian concepts, and John Fiske, the American historian, argued that far from undermining religion Darwinism made possible "a higher view of the workings of God and of the nature of Man than was ever attainable before." Prominent clerics, among them Henry Ward Beecher and Lyman Abbott, also attempted to reconcile science and religion. In most churches religion was never quite the same after Darwin. As the modernists gradually won, the result was less and less emphasis upon dogma, upon the Old Testament and original sin.

Social Darwinism. Outside the clergy Darwinism was enthusiastically received for two related reasons. First, its main defenders drew from it a doctrine of progress which exactly suited the spirit of the times. Second, they used it to defend the existing economic and political order. This application of Darwinism to human society was first made by Spencer, who argued that the evolutionary process meant not only ceaseless slow change but also ceaseless slow progress. Moreover, he argued, human society was subject to the same natural laws of fierce competition that governed the destinies of all other species. Man might ignore or violate these laws at his own peril. But if he accepted the "great design" and established the "pure competitive society," then by the workings of the survival of the fittest, the able would rise to the top of the social heap and the unfit would be discarded. The function of government was to keep the peace and perform a few other social functions like distributing the mails, but it should neither help the underprivileged nor restrict the actions of the rich. Thus public education, poor relief, or any system of social insurance was an impediment toward progress and a violation of natural law.

This Spencerian version of *laissez faire* quickly spread through America in the late sixties and early seventies. Clerical leaders, especially the early "modernists" led by Beecher, favored this Social Darwinism, and the universities hailed it. And of course it was cordially embraced by industrialists and financiers. Carnegie even remarked that Spencer was "the man I owe most to." Enamored of the theory that he had been selected by natural law to lead society, Carnegie devised his own "laws of wealth" and published them.

But the most consistent Social Darwinist in America was Professor William Graham Sumner of Yale (1840–1910). Seeing all life, including human society, as engaged in one great grim struggle for existence, he believed that "absolute competition" was the only weapon by which a species sharpened its faculties sufficiently, and pared off enough of its slothful nature, to survive. He was thus scornful of all reformers and implacably opposed to any government intervention in economic life. Such activity was not only harmful, but in the end useless. For the laws of economics were as fixed as those of physics, he argued, and the attempts of reformers to change them were comparable to those of an ant trying to "deflect a mighty river." Sumner celebrated the millionaires as makers of progress. But he was such an outspoken foe of the tariff as a prime example of harmful governmental intervention that he almost lost his position at Yale. In an age dominated by tariff-made monopolies and ridiculous concern for the poor, the "forgotten man" in America, he declared, was the middle-class factory owner or merchant who stood on his own feet in the competitive race and asked neither aid nor restriction.

The emphasis of Social Darwinism on competition and the survival of the fittest had interesting developments in the area of international relations. If what was true of single societies was true of the struggle between nations, then it was obvious that Great Britain, the rapidly rising German Empire, and, of course, the United States had come to world leadership because of a natural, inherent vigor and superiority. Moreover, the continued expansion of these powers at the expense of their weaker and more "unfit" neighbors was in the scheme of things, and in fact hastened progress. Many German and British writers, as well as some Americans, contributed to this Teutonic and Anglo-Saxon myth.

Social Christianity. Although Social Darwinism was extremely popular in the two decades after 1870, counter-developments were already undermining it. By the late 1880's a Protestant religious movement called "the Social Gospel," or "Social Christianity," was challenging the application of biological principles to human society. Christianity had always insisted that man as a moral being was separate from the rest of nature, and Spencer's jump from animals to man was scarcely consistent with this precept. In part, the Social Gospel probably grew from the renewed emphasis on the ethics of Christianity by clergymen who, as modernists, had discarded much of the older supernaturalism. Among the chief concerns of the followers of the Social Gospel was the plight of the poor. Central to the new doctrine was the belief that the church should become an active leader in a movement for social and economic reform that would implant the ethics of Christ in the factory and the market place. Washington Gladden, Shailer Matthews, and Lyman Abbott — one of the editors of the influential *Outlook* — were among the moderate clerical leaders of the Social Gospel. Their aim was a Christian capitalism dominated by ethical considerations. More radical were George D. Herron, until 1899 Professor of Applied Christianity at Iowa College, and Walter Rauschenbusch of the Rochester Theological Seminary, who believed that the abolition of private property was the only basis on which a "Christian democracy" could be established.

A movement with similar aims got under way in the Roman Catholic Church, especially after Pope Leo XIII issued in 1891 an encyclical pointing to the critical problem created by vast wealth and attendant poverty among the masses, and called upon both church and state to find a remedy. With the blessings of James Cardinal Gibbons, Father John A. Ryan, born and raised in Populist North Dakota, took up the challenge. Within a short time he had formed a considerable group of like-minded people intent on using the Catholic Church as an instrument of social justice.

Although the advocates of the Social Gospel probably remained a minority among the clergy, their efforts had a profound effect on the reform movement in the first years of the twentieth century, and especially on the character of modern Protestantism. Social Christianity achieved one of its more immediate ends by bringing back to the fold many workingmen who had been alienated by the seeming indifference of the church to their plight. And it started the development through which the social service agencies of the church became a major part of its activities.

James and Pragmatism. Simultaneously with the growth of Social Christianity, William James (1842–1910), professor of psychology and philosophy at Harvard, and brother of the novelist Henry James, was developing his philosophy of pragmatism. His *Principles of Psychology* (1890) was a pathmaking book, and his later volumes were even more important. His association at Harvard with Chauncey Wright and Charles Sanders Peirce introduced him to the speculations of these two men about chance and indeterminism in the universe. By the time he was a mature scholar, James was opposed to the closed deterministic universe of the nineteenth century, including that of Darwin. Instead, he emphasized the importance of chance, human thought, deed, and free will. Man was a relatively free agent in James's unpredictable universe. James's philosophy gave no final answers about the universe, how it operated, or where it was going. Pragmatism was centered on man, principally on the thought process and its relation to events. For James, thought was never separate from the act, but was a part of it. Indeed the validity of the thought could be tested not by reference to some theological or philosophical system but by the action it inspired and the consequences of that action.

John Dewey. James's most illustrious follower, John Dewey (1859–1952), spent most of his adult life as a professor at Chicago and Columbia Universities. Like James, Dewey was a convinced democrat and an ardent reformer. He believed intensely that through intelligence man could partly control his natural environment and build a democratic society far more productive of human happiness than any culture had yet produced. He developed his own variety of pragmatism which he called

WILLIAM JAMES

Long a professor at Harvard University, James made a substantial contribution to scientific knowledge by his perceptive approach to psychology.

"instrumentalism." Far more than James, he insisted that thought of any value inspired action, since it was only by using thought as an instrument of action that man arrived at what was true. In accordance with his own philosophy, Dewey was an activist all his life. His more formal philosophic thought may be found in a series of scholarly books starting with *Experience and Nature* (1925).

Both James's and Dewey's varieties of pragmatism have been severely criticized for emphasizing action to the virtual exclusion of ethical and aesthetic considerations. Their pragmatism also practically ignored the vast speculative systems of the past and questioned the value of history as an aid to discovering what was true for the present. But the most damaging criticism was that pragmatism included no stable system of human values. By insisting that truth was to be measured largely by the consequences of a belief, pragmatism came close to admitting that the end justified the means.

481

Pragmatic Education and Law. Unlike James, Dewey became a public figure very early in his career, and his continuing preoccupation with current issues gave pragmatism an immediate popularity that few philosophies have enjoyed. Despite its critics, the public welcomed Dewey's doctrine, perhaps because so much in it was ingrained in the American mind. The practical and experimental approach, the emphasis upon the present and the future, the rather cavalier treatment of the past, and especially the emphasis upon the free and creative role of man — all these views were close to actual American experience. More specifically, pragmatism-instrumentalism had profound effects on American education. Dewey's doctrine of "learning by doing" was first applied in Chicago, and its widespread acceptance by "progressive" educators started a debate that still continues.

Dewey's instrumentalism also had an impact upon law, for it undermined the assumption that judges decided a case according to a set of immutable principles. In 1881 Oliver Wendell Holmes, Jr. (1841–1935), a close friend of James, published his *Common Law*. Holmes, after 1902 a justice of the United States Supreme Court, held that the great decisions of American constitutional law had not been reached mainly by applying logic to the immutable principles of the Constitution; instead "The felt necessities of the time, the prevalent moral and political theories, intuitions of public policy avowed or unconscious, even the prejudices which judges share with their fellow men, have had a good deal more to do than the syllogism in determining the rules by which men should be governed." Doctrinaire pragmatists went even further, maintaining that if justice were to be served, any legal decision had to be considered for its social and economic effects. Thus in 1908, Louis D. Brandeis made judicial history when in presenting a brief in the case of *Muller* v. *Oregon* he cited the opinion of experts that the hours women worked affected their health and

therefore the health of the whole community. On the basis of the social facts presented, the Supreme Court overturned previous decisions and held the Oregon ten-hour law constitutional. Brandeis himself became a Supreme Court Justice in 1916.

The effect of pragmatism on areas outside education and the law is more difficult to measure. But its assumption that man was free to act, its refusal to accept dogma, its experimental and tentative spirit, its emphasis on facts and results, and its bent toward democratic reform supported or at least encouraged the reforming spirit of many intellectual rebels.

Reform Darwinism. Some who rejected Social Darwinism showed the influence of pragmatism. Others were moved as much by the ethical impulse of the Social Gospel. At the same time a logical attack against the conservative position was drawn from Darwinism itself. As a method, Darwinism had stressed the importance of empirical research and thus encouraged the rising social scientists to take a hard look at the facts before they made sweeping judgments about society. In effect Social Darwinism sanctioned unrestrained private enterprise and the pursuit of gain as beneficent social goals. The thirty years following the Civil War, with two depressions and ever-increasing rural misery, did not bear out that view. In the light of the facts it was natural for empirically-minded social critics to reach the opposite conclusion, that cooperation and social planning might best benefit America. Once made, these assumptions could be defended even from Darwinism. For this "reform Darwinism" stressed both the element of change and the importance of environment in the theory of evolution. If change was the rule for the animal kingdom, why not also for human society? And if environment was so important in creating new species, why could not human nature be altered by change in the social environment? Reform

Darwinists ardently believed so, and set about to prove it.

Among the earliest and most vigorous advocates of reform Darwinism was Lester Ward (1841–1913). Born of a poor Illinois family and hardened by manual labor, Ward educated himself and in 1906 secured a professorship at Brown University. Through his writings he founded American sociology, and gave it a reforming bias which it long retained. Central to Ward's thought was a sharp distinction between the life of the species and human society. The former, he argued, was controlled by blind "genetic" or inherited forces, which were neither logical nor efficient. Ward pointed out the enormous wastage in nature and the misshapen varieties of life it brought forth. On the other hand, the evolution of human society was the result of man's intellectual ability to produce change and "to shape the environmental forces to his own advantage."

Ward's books attracted little public notice, possibly because of the author's difficult style. But their point of view influenced a whole generation of sociologists, among the more important of whom were Albion Small and Edward A. Ross. Small was the editor of the *American Journal of Sociology* for thirty years after its founding in 1895. "The entire spirit of sociology," he wrote, "is a deep loyal impulse of social service. Its whole animus is constructive, remedial and ameliorative." Ross argued for a sociology based upon a "real Darwinism" with reform as its objective. In *Sin and Society* (1907), which contained a preface written by Theodore Roosevelt, Ross demanded "an annual supplement to the Decalogue" so that the majority of citizens would appreciate the fact that sin evolved along with society, and that tax dodging was "larceny," child labor "slavery," and adulteration of foods "murder."

Henry George. In 1879, Henry George (1839–1897) published his influential *Progress and Poverty*. George spent most of his young life working as a printer and a journalist in San Francisco where he watched a virtual frontier trading post transformed into a sophisticated urban society. At the same time he saw both wealth and poverty rapidly compounded. What caused this paradox, George asked himself, and found the answer in the fast growing monopoly of land in the hands of a few, with constantly increasing land rents and land value. The individual owners, however, had little to do with the process. What gave land its value was the growth of the society upon it, and the number of people using it and needing it. The difference between the values of urban and rural land was a social and an "unearned" increment. Therefore George proposed a "single tax" upon this unearned increment which would pay all the costs of government, and at the same time destroy the monopoly of land by making it too expensive to hold in large quantities. This basic monopoly gone, equal opportunity would return and the monopoly problem, George believed, would be solved. *Progress and Poverty* attracted a huge reading audience, and single-tax societies flourished not only in the United States but in many foreign countries as well. But perhaps in the long run George's most important influence lay in the questions he raised about the existing social system. Nearly every important reformer in the next thirty years read his book, and a large number of them confessed that their interest in changing the social system was ignited by reading *Progress and Poverty*.

Edward Bellamy. Edward Bellamy (1850–1898), in his attack on reigning social beliefs, was animated by much the same religious and egalitarian ethics that had moved Henry George. A New Englander and a professed Christian, he was so incensed by church defenses of the industrial system that he refused to attend services and forbade his children to attend. Socialism, he finally came to believe, was the only system in which an industrial society could practice and preserve Christian ethics. He embodied his themes in *Looking Backward* (1888), a novel describing a utopia in which private ownership of production had been peacefully abolished and everyone lived in a sort of great industrial army. Although both young men and women were obliged to work at manual labor a certain number of years, throughout this highly technical society there was a great amount of individual choice and an absence of coercion. *Looking Backward* was hardly an artistic triumph, but as a tract for the times it was an overwhelming success. Inspired by Bellamy's "Nationalism," hundreds of thousands of Americans read the book and organized clubs to work for the inception of the new state. During the turbulent nineties the movement died almost as quickly as it had grown, but Bellamy's short-lived success clearly indicated that many Americans, thoroughly disenchanted with the *laissez-faire* industrial society as it then existed, demanded change. *Looking Backward* also introduced an ethical socialism which, stripped of its Marxist overtones of materialism, violence, and class warfare, was acceptable to many of the book's readers.

The New Economics. George and Bellamy were publicists rather than economists and had arrived at their economic ideas in a most informal way. Meanwhile a group of young professional economists were also challenging the validity of the prevailing *laissez-faire* concepts. The leaders of this group, Richard T. Ely of Johns Hopkins and Wisconsin, Simon Patten of Pennsylvania, and John R. Commons of Wisconsin, acted from similar assumptions. Instead of viewing man as a competitive animal, they saw him as an ethical creature, "full of noble instincts," as Patten believed, "and swift accurate reactions to duty. . . ." Both Ely and Commons were lay leaders in the Social Gospel movement, and all three firmly believed in man's ability to reorder nature and human society through the agency of the state. In founding the American Economic Association in 1885, these young rebels wrote into its credo a denunciation of *laissez faire* as "unsafe in politics and unsound in morals." They also spelled out their aspirations for the state: "We regard the state," their document read, "as an educational and ethical agency whose positive aid is an indispensable condition to human progress."

Perhaps the most original of all the young economists of the period was Thorstein Veblen (1857–1929). Son of a Norwegian immigrant to Wisconsin, Veblen studied formal economics both at Yale under Sumner and later at Johns Hopkins. A natural rebel against conventions and a self-confessed "disturber of the intellectual peace," Veblen was not able to obtain a university position until he was almost forty, and his unconventional morals and ideas, together with his difficult personality, made his short academic career a stormy one. Veblen's books were not widely read. They were too iconoclastic, too ironic in spirit, and too prolix in style to interest even most scholars. But some of his ideas became influential, and the most original of his phrases passed into the common vocabulary.

Veblen contended that he was not a reformer but that he depicted the American economy exactly as it existed. But in his "descriptive studies" he denied practically all the fundamental postulates of Social Darwinism. He argued that basically most men were moved by an "instinct of workmanship," which if untrammelled, would result in efficient, aesthetically pleasing production. But in the dominating "pecuniary society," the businessman, as distinct from the pure industrialist, was animated almost entirely by the "acquisitive instinct" which he satisfied by manipulating the price system by which he thus throttled and debased productive facilities. Veblen saw increasing friction in the advancing industrial society between the men who wanted to produce and the small capitalist class that was interested solely in accumulating wealth. The end product, he predicted, would probably be revolution and dictatorship. The alternative he offered was a society run by an educated elite of engineers and technicians. In *The Theory of the Leisure Class* (1899) Veblen ridiculed the customs and mentality of the rich. And he related his concepts of "conspicuous consumption" and "pecuniary emulation," involving the search for status symbols, to similar phenomena in "other savage and barbarous societies."

Historians. Evolutionary science, especially in its claim to have established a law of development for the species and its emphasis upon environment, also influenced the teaching and writing of American history. The search for a causal law in history similar to the law of natural selection produced a number of works that stimulated historical thought. Herbert Baxter Adams' racist views were optimistic. The democratic seed that had been planted in the early German forests, Adams argued, reached its flowering in the Anglo-Saxon civilization of the United States. The conclusions of Brooks and Henry Adams, grandsons of the sixth President, were extremely pessimistic. For Brooks, civilization in the past had alternated between a masculine, military, creative phase and a feminine, pecuniary, sterile one. Equating the civilization of the United States in 1890 with the latter phase, Brooks forecast disaster. His brother Henry, who had already written his brilliant *History of the United States during the Administrations of Jefferson and Madison* (1889–1891), took an equally pessimistic view of America's future.

More profound in their influence on American historical thought were the historians who sought in the immediate environment an explanation of the development of American society. Charles A. Beard (1874–1948) led the group who emphasized economic factors as most important in determining men's political and social views. In *An Economic Interpretation of the Constitution* (1913) Beard attempted to show a close relationship between the personal economic interests of the founding fathers and their votes in the Constitutional Convention. The work drew excited denunciations from the nation's conservatives and equally warm praise from its radicals. Although Beard's findings were later questioned by historians, his economic approach has continued to influence the writing of American history down to the present.

But of all the environmentalists Frederick Jackson Turner (1861–1932) left the most persistent imprint on subsequent historical thought. Born in post-frontier Wisconsin, Turner had seen the Indian and the forest disappear before the pioneer's plow, and the pioneer replaced in turn by the farmer. At the Chicago World's Fair history conference in July, 1893, Turner read what probably still remains the single most influential paper in American historical writing, "The Significance of the Frontier in American History." Pointing out that "the germ theory of politics" had been sufficiently emphasized, and that the evolution of institutions along the Atlantic coast was, after all, a fairly "familiar phenomenon," he urged historians of the United States to study the West as well as the East.

American social development has been continually beginning over again on the frontier. This perennial rebirth, this fluidity of American life, this expansion westward with its new opportunities, its continuous touch with the simplicity of primitive society, furnish the forces dominating American character. The true point of view in the history of this nation is not the Atlantic coast, it is the Great West.

Turner's words were heeded, and soon a veritable cult of the West had sprung up among the writers of American history. He had spoken at the right time, for, as he noted, the federal Census Bureau had announced in 1890 that the continuous

frontier line in the United States had disappeared. As he spoke at Chicago, Turner stood at a great time divide: behind him were the frontier and the farmer; ahead, industry and the city. By the logic of his own environmentalism, the influence of the former was bound to wane, that of the latter to wax.

The Chautauqua Movement. New ideas reached the people, not only by way of books, magazines, and newspapers, but also through an institution unique to the period, the Chautauqua, so called from an assembly, originally promoted by the Methodists, that met regularly beginning in 1874 at Lake Chautauqua, New York. At first concerned mainly with the development of better Sunday Schools, the sessions expanded in length to as much as two months, and in content to include a great variety of educational and recreational interests. Soon, similar assemblies, operating

in imitation of the original, appeared throughout the United States and Canada. Early in the twentieth century the traveling Chautauqua caught on, with programs of perhaps a week or so in length arranged by lecture bureaus for a sequence of towns, or "circuits," as they were commonly called. Ordinarily these meetings were held in a big tent, and for most small and some larger towns in every section of the country the Chautauqua furnished the chief excitement of any given summer. As with the earlier Lyceum, the Chautauqua provided a platform for the nation's ablest lecturers, and in addition a setting for concerts, recitals, and even theatricals. The Chautauqua movement continued well into the 1920's, but gave way in the end to the automobile, the movies, the radio, and the depression. While it lasted, it served well the end of planting deep in the minds of the people the thoughts of its intellectual leaders.

Touring Chautauqua companies brought culture and education to millions of rural and small town Americans during the years 1875–1925. Well-known speakers, including the matchless Mark Twain, enthralled audiences whose previous exposure to "serious culture" had been slight.

For the most part local Chautauquas are held for a short period, . . . the average being probably ten days. . . . A large tent usually serves as the audience room, . . . men of the type of William Jennings Bryan, Robert M. LaFollette and Richmond Pearson Hobson speak. . . . Whether from the country or from the town, the audience soon becomes impatient with anything technical or academic, . . . and quickly avails itself of the open-sided tents . . . to make their escape. But, with a skilled speaker, they will sit for an hour or two, apparently unmindful of the intense heat or the uncomfortable benches. . . . On [one] program was excellent vocal and orchestral music, two of the leading political speakers of the country, a famous preacher, a half dozen clean entertainments, and much more that a discerning committee of men who were interested in the uplift of the community could provide.

PAUL M. PEARSON, "The Chautauqua Movement," *The Annals of the American Academy of Political and Social Science* (1912)

Mark Twain. Before the Civil War almost all of the country's first-rate authors had come from the Atlantic seaboard, with a majority from New England and New York. But after 1870 almost the reverse occurred. Creative writers came from every portion of the country, and fewer came from New York and New England than from any other major section.

The best evidence that the eastern monopoly of talent had been broken was the spectacular literary career of Samuel Langhorne Clemens, more familiarly known as Mark Twain (1835–1910). Brought up in the small village of Hannibal, Missouri, on the Mississippi River, Twain spent his youth in a variety of pursuits including those of river steamboat pilot, gold miner, newspaper editor, and public lecturer. It was as a humorist that he offered his first popular book, *The Innocents Abroad* (1869), and he returned to the role repeatedly in novels, short stories, and numerous public lectures. But Twain is most widely remembered for his accounts of boyhood along the Mississippi River in *Tom Sawyer* (1876) and, especially, *Huckleberry Finn* (1884), one of the great novels of American literature. As in many humorists, there was an ambivalence in Twain. Intensely disliking the materialistic spirit of the new industrialism, he was also attracted to its glitter and its rewards. While he continually satirized the *nouveau riche* and their lack of taste and manners, he himself lost heavily in speculative attempts to establish a fortune. Although celebrating the western spirit, he lived most of his adult life in the East. An ardent democrat, his sardonic estimate of human nature is revealed in a superb short story, "The Man Who Corrupted Hadleyburg." As he became older, his pessimism grew, and few bleaker notes were struck in American literature than in his *The Mysterious Stranger* (1916), published posthumously.

MARK TWAIN

Samuel Langhorne Clemens was the first westerner to gain prominence in the world of literature.

Henry James. In two of his works, *The Innocents Abroad* and *A Connecticut Yankee at King Arthur's Court* (1889), Twain brought Americans in humorous juxtaposition with the peoples of the Old World, but much more serious in attempting an international comparison were the works of another American, Henry James (1843–1916). Born in New York, James spent much of his life abroad, and unlike his philosopher brother William, never felt really at home in America. He was repelled by the American lack of refinement, by the crass materialism of his age, and by an atmosphere which he felt was thoroughly uncongenial to artistic and creative pursuits. After a fruitless try at the law in 1882, he settled in England permanently. James admired the English upper classes for their subtle intellectual sophistication, their devotion to literature and the arts, and their cultivated manners.

But James never became entirely detached from his birthright. One of his major themes was the interaction in the encounter between the cultured and morally complex European and the innocent, rather gauche, vigorous, and often puritanical American as depicted in two of his earlier books, *Daisy Miller* (1879) and *The Europeans* (1878). For a period in his middle life James drew his inspiration almost entirely from his new-found home in England. Then in *The Ambassadors* (1903) and *The Golden Bowl* (1904), he went back to a study of the impact of Europe and Europeans upon the American character and mind. It was mostly in these later works, by his acute inquiry into the minds of his characters, that James established his reputation and started a major trend in modern American writing, the psychological and stream-of-consciousness novel.

William Dean Howells. More congenial to American taste at the time, both in his choice of subject matter and in his treatment of characters, was William Dean Howells (1837–1920). Born in an Ohio village, Howells became a magazine editor in both Boston and New York. As an editor he acquainted Americans with the twin schools of naturalism and determinism, then flourishing in France and Russia. The naturalists, responding to the urban and democratic tides, argued that writers should forget the upper classes and concentrate on the lives of the masses, depicting them, even those from the lower depths, as faithfully as possible. The determinists, Darwinian in emphasis, tried to show that man's life, mind, and character were all products of his environment, and that free will was mostly a fantasy.

While it was probably his discovery and aid of able young writers that won Howells the title of "the dean of American literature," he was something of a pathbreaker in his own novels. In *The Rise of Silas Lapham* (1885) and *A Hazard of New Fortunes* (1890), he became the first American writer to deal seriously with some of the central social problems of his times. Concerning himself with the class and individual tensions released by the movement of Americans from village to city, by the newly rising rich, and by the new place of women in society, he became the originator of American realism. Yet his own preference for upper-middle-class characters, and his squeamishness about sex and violence, prevented him from advancing far along the road to naturalism.

Naturalism and Determinism. Far more uninhibited than Howells were four men of the next generation. Stephen Crane (1871–1900) and Frank Norris (1870–1902) both died quite young; Jack London (1876–1916) lived to the age of forty; but Theodore Dreiser (1871–1945) pursued a long literary life. Most of the new forces and trends in literature can be seen in the work of this quartet. In their novels and short stories realism shaded into naturalism, and they were frank in discussing the darker side of life. Crane in *The Red Badge of Courage* (1895) captured brilliantly the mental strain of a young soldier going into battle for the first time. Norris in *The Octopus* (1901) portrayed the plight of the California wheat farmer exploited by the railroad. London realistically drew a host of characters from the waterfront bum to the working stiff of the western wheat fields. Norris, and especially Dreiser, emphasized the social environment in the shaping of their characters. By introducing violence into their plots all four writers violated the moral and literary canons of their time. Dreiser's *Sister Carrie* (1900) not only depicted the squalid life of a slum girl and her attachments to several dubious males, but also in the end saw her attain money and a respectable career. So shocked was America that the book was withdrawn from sale for several years. In *The Iron Heel* (1908), London described the coming class war and the rise of a particularly violent dictatorship. Before the

advent of this group most of America's writers had been drawn from the more or less comfortable middle class. And although Crane and Norris followed that pattern, Dreiser came from a Catholic working-class family in Indiana and Jack London was born a waif on the Oakland, California, waterfront.

Poetry and Music. The years between 1870 and 1914 also witnessed the rebirth of American poetry and the rise of women as serious literary artists. Emily Dickinson (1830–1886) in New England and Sidney Lanier (1842–1881) in the South were writing finely wrought verse immediately after the Civil War, and Edward Arlington Robinson (1869–1935) became the first significant American poet of the twentieth century. The emergence of Ellen Glasgow

WILLIAM DEAN HOWELLS

Editor, novelist, and social critic, Howells was long the dean of American writers.

(1874–1945) and Edith Wharton (1862–1937) as important novelists was a revolution of the sexes in American letters. Ellen Glasgow's studies of decaying Virginia aristocracy, of the unmannered and uncultured rising lower classes, of the southern feminine tradition which she deplored, and of the disfigurement of city and countryside by industry all have much to say about the modern South. Edith Wharton's books are equally critical of life among old New York families. As literary craftsmen neither woman had a superior in the years before the First World War.

Despite the country's rich Germanic heritage, serious native music was practically nonexistent during the nineteenth century mainly for want of an appreciative public. Before the Civil War the New York Philharmonic was the only orchestra giving regular concerts. Within the next fifty years, however, most major cities established symphony orchestras, and within a short time there were flourishing groups in Boston, Philadelphia, Pittsburgh, Cleveland, Chicago, Minneapolis, San Francisco, and Los Angeles.

Painting. Painters and sculptors labored under much the same difficulties as musicians. Few of the new millionaires were men of taste and those who did collect art favored the recognized European masters. This was unfortunately also true at first of the Metropolitan Museum in New York, established in 1870, and of similar public galleries subsequently organized elsewhere. Most artists of ability sought their training in Europe and some of these decided either to remain abroad or else to return to Europe after they had tried unsuccessfully to find favor and patronage in their native country.

Mary Cassatt, of Philadelphia, was trained in France and chose to stay there, and both James McNeill Whistler and John Singer Sargent eventually settled in England, where Whistler, especially, acquired a reputation both for his fog-shrouded riverscapes and his belligerent thrusts at hostile critics. The three expatriates were much influenced by the reigning French school of impressionism, as were the majority of their colleagues working at home. But George Inness, Thomas Eakins, Winslow Homer, and Albert Pinkham Ryder were doing nonderivative and genuinely American work which by its originality and its aesthetic appeal eventually won them fame. Almost ignored in his own time, Ryder, in particular, has attracted the attention of modern critics because of his eerie, dreamlike, symbol-laden canvases which seem to point toward the post-impressionist and abstract art of the twentieth century.

Something of a landmark in American painting occurred in 1908 when a group of Philadelphia artists, labeled by critics the "Ashcan School," held a show in New York which elicited widespread public discussion. The Philadelphia group, most of whom had to work at illustrating to make a living, were led by Robert Henri, John Sloan, and Robert Prendergast, and the controversy which arose involved both their manner of painting and what they chose to paint. Influenced perhaps both by photography and by a cult of scientific naturalism akin to that then developing in the novel, they included among their subjects dirty streets and trash-filled alleys depicted with a precision that dismayed the more romantic critics who held that only the beautiful should be painted, and that there was nothing beautiful about urban slums. The camera-like realism of the group was soon forgotten, but their liberal ideas about what made suitable subjects for painting were extremely influential. And the public discussion which the "Ashcan" exhibition excited indicated a new-found American interest in painting that augured well for the future.

Architecture. American architecture after the Civil War was the epitome of inutility, ugliness, and banality. Some of the bumptious spirit of the gilded age with its ignorance of standards and lack of taste was expressed by the architects of the period, but many of the models for the most atrocious edifices came from abroad. Most of the public and private buildings of the period, which borrowed simultaneously from almost every historic style and then added an improbable mélange of decorated towers, turrets, balconies, and ornamented ginger-bread, are now gone. Hastening their departure was Henry Hobson Richardson (1838–1886), who began to design public buildings after the Romanesque style which had preceded the Gothic movement in early medieval Europe. With their spare and clean exteriors, and their well-lighted and functional interiors, such buildings were a welcome relief from the monstrosities of the age before. During the nineties a brief return to the columned and porticoed classical school, a movement popularized by the pseudo-classical buildings of the Chicago Fair, was headed by Stanford White. Ralph Adams Cram, another leading New York architect of the time, preferred a simplified Gothic for his structures. But even though the buildings of both men were far superior to those of the seventies, they exhibited a lack of originality and a failure to comprehend that the new industrial and urban age demanded a new type of building.

Meanwhile modern technology made possible radical changes in the building art. The employment of steel by John and Washington Roebling in the beautifully designed Brooklyn Bridge completed in 1883 illustrated both the great utility and the aesthetic possibilities of this new material. It was shortly discovered that with the use of a steel skeleton, and later of steel reinforced concrete, the weight of a building no longer demanded bearing walls of massive thickness. Together with the invention of the electric elevator, the new steel and concrete shell greatly raised the permissible height limit, and the American skyscraper was made possible.

LOUIS HENRI SULLIVAN: *Architect*

In the Wainwright Office Building in St. Louis (1890), Sullivan, the most original American architect of his time, emphasized vertical as well as horizontal lines. Unlike most of his colleagues, Sullivan eschewed useless ornamentation in favor of good basic design.

By his buildings great in influence and power; his drawings unsurpassed in originality and beauty; his writings rich in poetry and prophecy; his teachings persuasive and eloquent; his philosophy where, in "Form Follows Function," he summed up all truth in Art, Sullivan has earned his place as one of the great architectural forces in America.

Inscription on a monolith in Graceland Cemetery erected to Sullivan by the architects and builders of Chicago

491

Simultaneously with these developments a school of Chicago architects was advocating a new style of building to conform to the peculiar needs and spirit of the age. At the center of this group was Louis H. Sullivan (1856–1924) with his doctrine that "form follows function." Sullivan first applied his dictum in 1890 by designing the Wainwright office building in St. Louis, a structure equally free from the traditional thick walls and from elaborate ornamentation. One of the world's great creative architects was Sullivan's student, Frank Lloyd Wright (1869–1959). Wright was a fierce opponent of the new skyscraper on the grounds that in a continent so broad, buildings should be parallel, not vertical, to the earth. At his two schools, Taliesin East and Taliesin West, Wright argued for an organic architecture in harmony with the site and using native materials. Long unhonored in his own country, Wright probably contributed as much to modern building as any western European architect.

Although Wright was vehemently opposed to skyscrapers, and though many critics have damned such buildings for creating urban congestion and for removing man further from his natural habitat of earth, sunshine, and air, they are considered by many foreigners to be the most typical expressions of modern American civilization. In many ways perhaps they are. For these long clean pencils of steel and concrete, symphonies of science, engineering, and design, are at once a historic symbol of American society's triumph over a raw continent, and at the same time towering tokens of an undisclosed collective future.

SELECTED BIBLIOGRAPHY

Useful surveys of the thought of this period are H. S. Commager, *The American Mind* (1950); and M. G. White, *Social Thought in America* (2nd ed., 1957). An examination of one segment is R. G. McCloskey, *American Conservatism in the Age of Enterprise* (1951). A valuable anthology is *Late Nineteenth Century Liberalism,* edited by Louis Filler (1962).

The general impact of Darwin and Darwinism is clearly shown in Perry Miller (ed.), *American Thought: Civil War to World War I* (1954). For the impact of evolution on social ideas see: Richard Hofstadter, *Social Darwinism in American Thought* (2nd ed., 1955); and Gail Kennedy (ed.), *Democracy and the Gospel of Wealth* (1949). On religion and science see Sidney Warren, *American Freethought, 1860–1914* (1943); and E. A. White, *Science and Religion in American Thought; The Impact of Naturalism* (1952). The Social Gospel movement and the influence of industrialism and urbanism on religion are well studied in: C. H. Hopkins, *The Rise of the Social Gospel in American Protestantism, 1865–1915* (1940); Henry May, *Protestant Churches and Industrial America* (1949); and

A. I. Abell, *The Urban Impact on American Protestantism, 1865–1900* (1943). J. A. Ryan, *Social Doctrine in Action* (1941), the autobiographical account of the priest who led a similar movement in the Roman Catholic Church, should be supplemented by A. I. Abell, *American Catholicism and Social Action: A Search for Social Justice, 1865–1950* (1960).

R. B. Perry, *The Thought and Character of William James* (2 vols., 2nd ed., 1948), is the standard biography of the father of pragmatism; a single-volume abridgement is available in paperback. Sidney Hook, *John Dewey* (1939), is the best study of James's important disciple. Max Lerner (ed.), *The Mind and Faith of Justice Holmes* (1943); and M. A. D. Howe (ed.), *The Holmes-Pollock Letters* (2 vols., 1942), are good for Holmes's influence on American legal thinking. Samuel Chugerman, *Lester F. Ward; The American Aristotle* (1939); and Joseph Dorfman, *Thorstein Veblen and His America* (1934), are excellent biographies. For the early history of the economics profession, see R. T. Ely, *Ground under Our Feet* (1938). W. G. Sumner, *Social Darwinism,* edited by Stow Persons (1963); and W. G. Sumner, *What Social Classes Owe*

* Available in paperback

to Each Other (1883), are the best introduction to Sumner's thinking. The development of sociological thought is well brought out in Charles Page, *Class and American Sociology: From Ward to Ross* (1940).

A British scholar's view of American historical writing is H. H. Bellot, *American History and American Historians* (1952). An intriguing new study is Jurgen Herbst, *The German Historical School in American Scholarship* (1964). Interesting analyses are in W. T. Hutchinson (ed.), *The Marcus W. Jernegan Essays in American Historiography* (1937). Modern controversies about the writings of Turner and Beard have produced a voluminous literature; see, for example, Lee Benson, *°Turner and Beard* (1960); and B. C. Borning, *The Political and Social Thought of Charles A. Beard* (1962). On Henry Adams the basic biography is by Ernest Samuels (3 vols., 1948–1964). But see also Elizabeth Stevenson, *°Henry Adams; A Biography* (1955); W. H. Jordy, *°Henry Adams, Scientific Historian* (1952); and R. A. Hume, *Runaway Star* (1951). These should be supplemented with Adams' own *°Education of Henry Adams* (1918), which is at once an autobiography and a seminal book for an understanding of the period. For Brooks Adams, see A. F. Beringause, *Brooks Adams; A Biography* (1955). Southern historiography is treated by W. H. Stephenson, *Southern History in the Making* (1964).

Among the more general works on the literature of the period Van Wyck Brooks, *New England: Indian Summer* (1940), and *The Confident Years; 1885–1915* (1952), should be read, along with Edmund Wilson (ed.), *°The Shock of Recognition* (2nd ed., 1955); Alfred Kazin, *°On Native Grounds* (1942); and Maxwell Geismar, *°Rebels and Ancestors* (1953). For individual authors, see: Van Wyck Brooks, *°The Ordeal of Mark Twain* (2nd ed., 1933); B. A. Marks (ed.), *°Mark Twain's "Huckleberry Finn"* (1959); H. N. Smith, *Mark Twain* (1962); L. J. Edel, *Henry James* (3 vols., 1953–1962); F. O. Matthiessen, *°Henry James, The Major Phase* (1944); John Berryman, *°Stephen Crane* (1950); E. H. Cady, *The Road to Realism* (1956), and *The Realist at War* (1958), on William Dean Howells; Ernest Marchand, *Frank Norris* (1942); R. H. Elias, *Theodore Dreiser* (1949); W. A. Swanberg, *Dreiser* (1965); and Irving Stone, *°Jack London: Sailor on Horseback* (1938). A useful anthology is M. R. Stern and S. L. Gross (eds.), *American Literature Survey: Nation and Region, 1860–1900* (1962). R. W. Schneider, *Five Novelists of the Progressive Era* (1965), treats Howells, Crane, Norris, Dreiser, and Churchill.

An interesting treatment of painting is Jerome Mellequist, *The Emergence of an American Art* (1942). L. H. Sullivan, *°Autobiography of an Idea* (1924); and F. L. Wright, *An Autobiography* (1943), are two superb personal statements by world-influential architects. An important re-evaluation is C. W. Condit, *The Chicago School of Architecture* (1964). Excellent works on individuals include: Lloyd Goodrich, *Thomas Eakins* (1933); F. F. Sherman, *Albert P. Ryder* (1920); and H. R. Hitchcock, *The Architecture of H. H. Richardson and His Times* (1936), and *In the Nature of Materials, 1887–1941; The Buildings of Frank Lloyd Wright* (1942). See also Lewis Mumford, *°The Brown Decades* (1931).

Maurice B. Prendergast, "Central Park — 1901."
Courtesy of the Whitney Museum of American
Art, New York City.

World Power

and

Reform

· 1897–1921 ·

He has marked the American people as His chosen Nation to finally lead in the regeneration of the world. This is the divine mission of America, and it holds for us all the profit, all the glory, all the happiness possible to man.

ALBERT J. BEVERIDGE

A square deal for every man! This is the only safe motto for the United States.

THEODORE ROOSEVELT

America asks nothing for herself except what she has a right to ask for humanity itself.

WOODROW WILSON

28

THE PATH OF EMPIRE

American Isolation. Until the final decades of the nineteenth century the foreign policy of the United States reflected primarily the interest of the American people in westward expansion. Washington's policy of isolation was designed to keep the new nation free from any European entanglements that might distract it from its main business — the conquest of a continent. The Monroe Doctrine which warned European governments to keep out of American affairs was merely the converse of the same proposition. The War of 1812 and the war with Mexico were both expansionist wars, and the Civil War was fought, in considerable part, to decide whether the North or the South should have the advantage in the formation of new western states. During all these years the country cared little about the activities of other nations so long as they made no moves to block American expansion. American political development was self-centered and introspective. American eco-

nomic development was a frantic struggle to exploit the rich natural resources of the continent, and to satisfy, mainly by domestic production, the needs of a rapidly growing people. Since no major foreign threat existed, American diplomacy during the quarter-century after the Civil War was episodic and inconsequential.

By the last decade of the century a change had set in. The era of continental expansion was over, the United States was full grown, the time-honored frontiering process was at an end. Good free and cheap lands were nearing exhaustion. American industry was maturing; already its mines and factories were able to supply the needs of the domestic market, with a margin left over for sale abroad. American capital had increased to the point that considerable sums now were invested abroad. National self-sufficiency meant that the energy and attention of the nation could now be diverted outside its borders. As a result, the American government felt called upon to play an important part in international affairs.

Blaine's Foreign Policy. James G. Blaine, twice Secretary of State (1881, 1889–1892) attempted to widen the sphere of American influence to include, in fact as well as in theory, all of the Americas. Toward European nations with an interest in the western hemisphere he adopted an almost belligerent attitude. While serving under Garfield he made a blustering, but unavailing, demand that the British government give up its rights under the Clayton-Bulwer Treaty of 1850 to joint control of any interoceanic canal that should be built. During his second term he tried to establish a kind of prescriptive right for the United States to the fur-seal fisheries of the Bering Sea. Most important of all, he sought consistently to promote the cause of "Pan-Americanism."

Blaine's fondest dream was to induce Latin America to enter a kind of informal federation, with the United States as an interested and friendly "elder sister" at its head. Through such a union Blaine hoped to eliminate wars between the smaller American nations and to promote better commercial relationships between them and the United States. In pursuit of this goal he received in Washington on October 2, 1889, the representatives of nineteen independent American republics. Nothing could be accomplished on the important subject of arbitration, but the First Pan-American Congress, as this meeting came to be called, discussed at length such important problems as the standardization of sanitary regulations, the building of an intercontinental railroad, and the adoption of uniform weights and measures, including a common silver coin. One permanent result of the congress was the establishment of an international union of American republics, with headquarters in Washington.

Hawaii and Samoa. It is also possible to discern in Blaine's foreign policy an effort to reserve the Pacific as a region for future American exploitation. Blaine cultivated good relations with Japan, and at the same time managed to keep on friendly terms with China in spite of the deepening antagonism between the two great Oriental nations. Nor was Blaine displeased when Americans in Hawaii staged a revolution in 1893, with annexation to the United States as their goal. Not until McKinley became President was annexation actually accomplished (1898), but Blaine favored it and hoped for it. Blaine also sought to retain for the United States a foothold in the Samoan Islands, first tentatively marked out as early as 1872. Both Germany and Great Britain had rival interests in the Samoas, however, and a conference of the three contending parties, held in Berlin early in 1889, worked out a tripartite protectorate, which lasted until 1899. The islands were then divided between the United States and Germany, while Great Britain was indemnified for her withdrawal by title to the Gilbert and Solomon Islands, which had formerly belonged to Germany.

Chile. While Blaine's policy in the Pacific was later to pay substantial dividends, his plans for Pan-Americanism fell far short of their goals. The United States minister to Chile, a Blaine appointee, openly took sides in a Chilean revolution, and even more unfortunately gave his support to the side that lost. While feeling against the United States was still high in Chile, American sailors on shore leave at Valparaiso became involved in street fighting that cost two of them their lives and others serious injuries. By threat of military reprisals, the United States collected an indemnity of $75,000 for this "outrage," and built up an immeasurable amount of ill will throughout Latin America. These incidents undid nearly everything Blaine had accomplished. Under the terms of the McKinley Act he negotiated a few useful trade treaties, and the First Pan-American Congress set a precedent that was later to become significant, but for the most part Blaine's high hopes of international accord among the Americas were long to remain unrealized.

The Venezuelan Controversy. That the aggressive nature of American diplomacy was neither a personal policy of Blaine's nor an exclusively Republican policy was made evident shortly after Harrison left office by Cleveland's handling of the Venezuelan boundary dispute. The boundary line between Venezuela and British Guiana lay in a tropical wildernesss and had never been properly delimited. Long a subject of desultory controversy, the argument became intense when gold was discovered in the disputed territory. To Cleveland the prospect of the British government enforcing its will upon Venezuela, as the American government had recently enforced its will upon Chile, was extremely disquieting. He had made up his mind that any action which resulted in the seizure of territory that properly belonged to an American nation would constitute a clear violation of the Monroe Doctrine. In his message to Congress of 1894, he therefore expressed his hope that the matter would be arbitrated, and Congress by resolution promptly echoed his sentiments. The British government, however, refused to submit the whole question to arbitration, although pointing out that it had long been willing to arbitrate within certain specified limits. This attitude satisfied neither Cleveland nor his aggressive Secretary of State, Richard Olney, who in a belligerent statement of June 20, 1895, declared that "the United States is practically sovereign upon this continent, and its fiat is law."

The British were at first in no mood to back down, and Cleveland plainly threatened war. Eventually, however, a plan of arbitration satisfactory to the United States was accepted, and Americans boasted about their diplomatic triumph. Undoubtedly the British about-face was due to other circumstances than American pressure. In particular, a telegram of congratulation, sent by Kaiser Wilhelm II of Germany to Paul Kruger, the anti-British Boer leader in South Africa, foreshadowed the fact that the future enemy of Great Britain was to be Germany, rather than the United States. Indeed, friendship with the United States became from this time forward a paramount objective of British diplomacy. Despite the strong stand that the United States had taken on behalf of a Latin-American republic, most Latin-American nations still mistrusted the motives of the "Colossus of the North," and hemispheric relations continued strained.

Cuba. Great Britain was not the only European power whose concern with American affairs led to diplomatic difficulties with the United States. Spain still held a remnant of her once great American empire, notably the two islands of Cuba and Puerto Rico. Cuba had long been a storm center in Spanish-American relations. Before the Civil War southern expansionists had coveted the island; after the war Cuban insurrectionists had repeatedly sought to involve the United States in their struggles. For ten years, from 1868 to 1878, the island was in constant turmoil, and in 1895 another revolt broke out. This second insurrection came about in no small part as a result of American tariff legislation. The McKinley Act of 1890, which admitted raw sugar free of duty and compensated American growers by a bounty, had enormously stimulated the Cuban sugar industry. Much new foreign capital was poured into Cuban plantations, and for a brief period the island enjoyed unusual prosperity. When, in 1894, the Wilson-Gorman Act again made raw sugar dutiable, Cuban sugar prices declined sharply, and the era of prosperity vanished as rapidly as it had come. Hard times and unemployment provided a convenient setting for insurrection against Spanish rule.

Nature of the Cuban Revolt. It is an exaggeration to speak of the disorder in Cuba that broke out in 1895 as a revolution, although citizens of the United States tended to view it in that light. Maximo Gomez, the Cuban leader, was never able to maintain a government or even to keep an army in the field. He was an insurrectionist rather than a genuine revolutionary, and his chief weapon was devastation. Small guerrilla bands, often operating by night, destroyed sugar mills and laid waste plantations belonging to Spanish loyalists. Carrying on at first almost without military equipment, the Cuban *insurrectos* were soon receiving aid from other Cubans who resided in the United States, and from American sympathizers. In New York a Cuban junta, which called itself the Cuban government, sold bonds, and with the proceeds bought and shipped arms to the insurrectionary forces.

Spanish Methods of Warfare. Spanish methods of dealing with the insurrection were both brutal and effective. "Butcher" Weyler, the Spanish commander in Cuba, by using "corrals" of barbed wire and blockhouses to separate the more peaceful sections of the island from the more warlike, and by herding all suspects into *reconcentrado* camps, was well along with the task of restoring order when the Cuban situation began to make the headlines in American newspapers. Reporters told of the bad conditions they saw, and Americans who resided in Cuba or who visited the island corroborated the newspaper accounts. The American public began to feel that the government of the United States should take a hand in the situation. Both Cleveland and McKinley tried hard to keep the peace, and the latter had only this object in mind when he made strong representation to the Spanish government "against the uncivilized and inhuman" conduct of Weyler's campaign. The Spanish government, conscious of its inability to defend Cuba, made every effort to comply with McKinley's requests, even ordering the abandonment of the *reconcentrado* policy and the recall of Weyler. In fact, the American minister to Spain informed Washington that the Spanish officials, if given a little time, would agree to whatever demands the United States cared to make.

The Approach of War. Chances for a peaceful settlement declined as a result of

THE HEARST PRESS

Lurid headlines such as these clearly placed the blame for the Maine *disaster on the Spanish, and helped bring the sales of the* Journal *to over a million copies a day.*

two untoward incidents. The first was the publication of a private letter written by de Lôme, the Spanish minister in Washington, to a friend in Cuba. This letter, purloined from the mails and published in the newspapers, described McKinley as a "spineless politician." De Lôme's recall was immediately demanded. The other unfortunate incident was the destruction of the battleship *Maine* in Havana harbor, February 15, 1898, with heavy loss of life. That the Spanish government could have promoted such a catastrophe at a time when its officials were making every effort to placate the United States seems incredible, but the American public jumped immediately to the conclusion that Spain was responsible. As the press thundered "Remember the Maine," the American demands on Spain became more and more peremptory.

It is possible that McKinley might have averted war had he decided to make a firm stand for peace. He would have received the cordial support of Marcus A. Hanna and many other leading capitalists who feared the economic unsettlement that war might bring. But McKinley knew that opposition to following the lead of the plutocrats on this, or any other matter, was already rife among the young Republicans, and he believed that only by yielding to the popular clamor for war could he be certain of holding his party together. In spite of the fact that on April 9 the Spanish government ordered the cessation of hostilities in Cuba and gave in to the American contentions on every essential point, the President on April 11 sent a war message to Congress. Six days later Congress by joint resolution demanded that Spain withdraw from Cuba and authorized the President to use the military and naval forces of the United States to effect that end. Expressly disclaiming any attempt to annex Cuba, the resolution went on to claim that the people of the island were "and of right ought to be free and independent."

Spanish-American War. The outbreak of hostilities in 1898 came not because of any failure of American diplomacy, but because the American people wanted a war. President McKinley merely bowed to the popular clamor. In part at least this demand was inspired by Americans who wanted protection for their investments in Cuba, now totaling more than $50 million. But in larger part it arose from the public as a whole. It is significant that while American business generally opposed war, many journalists, politicians, admirals, and even clergymen were demanding intervention in Cuba in the name of nationalism, manifest destiny, and humanity. The spirit of empire was in the air. The great European powers had already divided up much of Africa and Asia and were rapidly fore-

closing upon the rest. Darwinism, as applied to the life of nations by Admiral Alfred Thayer Mahan and Senator Henry Cabot Lodge, urged expansion as the inevitable manifestation of the survival of the fittest. At the other extreme, preachers argued for imperialism as a means of christianizing and civilizing the less favored peoples of the earth. And it should not be forgotten that Americans had lived through a harrowing depression and an election in which radical social changes had been proposed and one social class had fought another. What was better calculated to restore national unity in this "psychic crisis" than a foreign venture which promised little in the expenditure of blood and much in glory?

Perhaps the American craving for heroics was in part a legacy of the Civil War. For over thirty years that struggle had colored American thought and action. Veterans of the Civil War were honored for their war records, and in politics particularly they fared better than the men who had stayed at home. As the old soldiers grew older, they forgot the ugliness of war and recalled only its excitement and adventure. Young Americans had grown to manhood on a steady diet of Civil War glorification. They envied the boys in blue or gray, and felt cheated that they had had no chance to win distinction for themselves. Older Americans took pride in the great new nation that they had seen emerge, but their faith was somehow tinctured with doubt. Had the United States really arrived as a nation, or was it only on its way? If the United States could win a war, who could deny it the high station among the nations of the world to which it aspired?

The American Navy. As the American people entered the war, they were extremely conscious and proud of their new navy — "The great white fleet." The construction of steel ships had begun during the eighties, and even during the depressed nineties more and more units were added to the navy. By that time Admiral Mahan had begun the publication of a series of books which seemed to demonstrate that the influence of sea power on a nation's destinies, particularly in wartime, was decisive. Mahan made important converts, among them Theodore Roosevelt, whom McKinley appointed Assistant Secretary of the Navy in 1897. In office Roosevelt made a fetish of naval efficiency and insisted above all else on target practice. Ten days after the *Maine* went down, he took advantage of his superior's absence from Washington to put the entire navy on a war footing. It was possibly due to Roosevelt's planning, also, that Commodore George Dewey was in command of an American squadron in Asiatic waters — in striking distance of the Spanish fleet in Manila Bay — when war broke out. The stronger portion of the American navy, however, was mobilized off Chesapeake Bay under command of Captain William T. Sampson.

The Army.   Though the navy was well prepared for war, the army was not. Its 27,000 officers and men were scattered over the country in small garrisons; it lacked a central planning board comparable to the present general staff; and its ranking officers had age rather than efficiency to commend them. The second line of defense, the National Guard of the states, was of uncertain size and merit, but capable of expansion in case of need. Everyone took it for granted, however, that in a really important war, a volunteer army, organized along the lines of the Union army in the Civil War, would do most of the fighting. And yet Congress, for all its impatience to get on with the war, did little to make ready for the conflict before it came. Although $50 million was appropriated for the national defense in March, 1898, it was not until late in April, after the war resolutions had been passed, that extensive army increases were authorized. At that time Congress voted to expand the regular army

to 62,597 men, and to create a volunteer army of 125,000. While most of the volunteers were to be raised through the states, Congress also authorized the President to accept directly into the national service three regiments of volunteer cavalry. This provision was included primarily to enable Theodore Roosevelt to lead a regiment into battle. With the help of Captain Leonard Wood, an officer in the medical corps, Roosevelt brought together a motley array of ex-cowboys, college athletes, and adventurers to form the "First United States Volunteer Cavalry," or, as they were generally called, the "Rough Riders."

Dewey at Manila.   The first blow of the war was struck by Commodore Dewey at

ADMIRAL GEORGE DEWEY

A national hero by virtue of his victory at Manila Bay, Dewey was promoted to Admiral of the Navy, a rank which an appreciative Congress created especially for him.

THE BATTLE OF MANILA BAY, AS PORTRAYED IN A RUSSIAN PRINT.

Manila Bay, into which the American commander had led his little fleet of four cruisers and three minor war craft on the early morning of May 1. There, in leisurely fashion, Dewey methodically destroyed the Spanish ships, which their commander, Admiral Montojo, who knew full well what was in store for him, had thoughtfully stationed at some distance from the defenses of Manila so that the city might be spared the danger of shellfire, and in shallow water where as many as possible of his men might escape. The Spanish losses in this one-sided battle included 381 killed, besides numerous wounded, while not an American was killed and only seven or eight were wounded.

Popular rejoicing in the United States when the news arrived from Manila Bay was unrestrained, but Dewey's position was in reality far from comfortable. He had possession of the Bay, but not one foot of land. He lost no time in urging the American government to send an expeditionary force to his aid, but the requested land forces did not arrive until the end of July.

When finally General Wesley Merritt arrived with a force of nearly 11,000, the city of Manila was captured with little more than token resistance. By that time both the Spanish and the Americans were less worried about each other than about the presence of a large army of Philippine insurgents under Emilio Aguinaldo, whom the Spanish had once exiled, but whom Dewey had brought back home. Curiously, the surrender of Manila to the Americans occurred August 14, with both parties to the agreement unaware of the fact that on the other side of the world, two calendar days before, an armistice had been signed with a view to ending all hostilities.

The Atlantic Theater. Events in the Atlantic theater had moved less swiftly than in the Pacific, but the outcome was no less decisive. The first concern of the American fleet was to intercept and destroy a Spanish squadron, known to have set sail from the Cape Verde Islands on April 29 for American waters. But the Spanish commander, Cervera, succeeded in reaching the port of Santiago de Cuba without being sighted. There he was presently blockaded by Admiral Sampson's entire fleet. Unwilling to risk his ships to the mines and fortifications of the harbor's entrance, Sampson, like Dewey before him, asked for a land expedition to come to his aid. The plans of the army, prepared by Major General Nelson A. Miles, were to take Puerto Rico during the summer, and later, when the danger from tropical diseases would be less, to make a frontal assault on Havana. All this had now to be changed, and an expeditionary force had to be dispatched to Santiago with little time for preparation. Amidst literally indescribable confusion, some 6,000 troops including Theodore Roosevelt's Rough Riders embarked at Tampa Bay, Florida, on June 14, and six days later appeared off Santiago. From their first meeting, General William R. Shafter, in command of the army, and Admiral Sampson, in command of the navy, misunderstood each other completely. Nevertheless, the troops somehow got

ashore several miles to the east of the harbor and began an advance that by the first days of July had led them to the storming of San Juan Hill, close to the city's last defenses. By this time, however, the American striking force was almost spent, and the officers in command scarcely knew whether to advance or retreat.

Naval Battle of Santiago. As events proved, the Spanish were even more thoroughly demoralized than the Americans. Their army was short of ammunition and the city was on the verge of famine. Ultimate surrender was inevitable. Under orders from Madrid, Admiral Cervera made an attempt to escape with his squadron from the harbor, but American shells set his wooden-decked ships afire, and one after another they had to be beached. When the fight was over, the Spanish had lost every ship and had suffered casualties of 400 killed and wounded; the American fleet was practically unharmed, with only one man killed and one man wounded.

AMERICAN ARTILLERY IN PUERTO RICO

The action sketches of the noted artist-illustrator, Frederick Remington, graphically captured for American readers the excitement of the war.

The War Ends. With Cuba's naval protection gone and communications with Spain cut, there was nothing left for the Spanish government to do but to sue for peace. This it did through the French embassy at Washington, which opened negotiations for an armistice on July 13. Three days later, General Toral, in command of the Spanish forces at Santiago, signed articles of capitulation with Shafter. By this time General Miles, lest he be too late, was beginning his expedition to Puerto Rico, which, lacking opposition, proved to be a model of efficiency in comparison with the Santiago campaign. The chief purpose of the expedition was to enable the United States to establish a valid claim to the island, for the French ambassador soon learned that before the United States would make peace, Spain must agree to withdraw entirely from the western hemisphere. Spanish sovereignty over Cuba must be relinquished, and all the rest of the Spanish West Indies must be ceded to the United States. On the other side of the world the American government demanded the cession of Guam and possession of the city, harbor, and bay of Manila, pending determination in the treaty of the "control, disposition, and government" of the Philippines. In view of these somewhat extraordinary territorial demands, the United States promised to waive for the time being "any demand for pecuniary indemnity." On these terms an armistice was signed on August 12, and the war was over.

Peace Negotiations. Commissioners from the United States and Spain met in Paris, October 1, 1898, to work out the details of peace. The American delegation consisted of William R. Day, chairman, who was required to resign as Secretary of State to accept the assignment, three leading senators, of whom one was a Democrat, and a prominent Republican newspaper editor. McKinley's instructions gave the commissioners no option as to the expul-

AMERICAN TROOPS IN CUBA, CHEERING THE SURRENDER AFTER THE SIEGE OF SANTIAGO.

sion of the Spanish Empire from America, but the Spanish delegation argued plausibly that, inasmuch as there was no government in Cuba worthy of the name, the island should be ceded directly to the United States, which would thereby become responsible for the Cuban debt. The Americans refused this dubious offer. They agreed that the United States should occupy the island temporarily, but they successfully insisted that Spain should assume the island's debt. The most heated dispute was over the Philippine Islands, which McKinley informed the American commissioners they must somehow obtain. Since the demand seemed utterly unjustified on military grounds, Spanish protests were long drawn out, and in the end the Spanish commissioners won an extraordinary concession. Without exactly explaining why it was to be done, the United States agreed to "pay to Spain the sum of $20 million within three months after the exchange of the ratifications of the present treaty." On December 10, 1898, the treaty was finally signed, and the President submitted it to the Senate for ratification.

Ratification of the Treaty. For a time there was danger that the necessary two-thirds majority could not be obtained. Led by the resourceful William Jennings Bryan, "anti-imperialists" gave battle throughout the country against the acquisition of the Philippines. Not only Democrats, but also many prominent Republicans objected strenuously to the terms of the treaty, and when the time came several voted against ratification. Speaker Thomas B. Reed resigned his seat in the House and retired from politics rather than stand with his party on such an issue. Andrew Carnegie went to Washington to lobby against the treaty. Strange as it may seem, the man who finally saved the treaty was Bryan. Some attribute this move to his conviction that free silver would not provide the Democrats with a winning issue in 1900, and his desire to supplement free silver with anti-

imperialism. Others argue that he was eager to prevent imperialism from becoming the principal issue, and wished only to hold the field open for free silver. Whatever his motives, Bryan urged that the proper policy for the moment was to accept the treaty, and then to demand that the Philippines be set free. Without his efforts it seems certain that the administration would have lost.

The United States as a World Empire. The United States emerged from the Spanish-American War as a world power. Its possessions included Alaska, Hawaii, the Philippines, Puerto Rico, Guam, and a number of minor islands, apart from the temporary occupation of Cuba. Of these possessions Alaska and Hawaii seemed most easily assimilable. Alaska the United States had owned since 1867, but only since 1896, when gold was discovered in the Klondike, a nearby district in Canada, had the possibilities of "Seward's Folly" been realized. Thereafter, the discovery of gold and other valuable mineral deposits in Alaska had proved the acquisition to be an extremely profitable investment. Hawaii likewise furnished a worthwhile addition to American economic resources, particularly because of its production of sugar. In governmental organization both Alaska and Hawaii became territories of the United States after the traditional pattern, although statehood for both seemed distant.

Freedom for Cuba. The Spanish cessions presented many perplexing problems. Cuba had to be occupied and provided with a government before it could be set free. Under General Leonard Wood as governor, and with the assistance of many American medical men, notably Majors William C. Gorgas and Walter Reed, the pacification and sanitation of the island was soon accomplished. As an incident to this task the mosquito carrier of yellow fever was identified and the pestilence it spread brought under control. By 1901 the

Cubans had formed a constitution, patterned after the Constitution of the United States, and were ready to begin self-rule. However, they were first required by the United States to subscribe to the historic "Platt Amendment," which seriously limited the sovereignty of the new republic. By its terms Cuba might not make any treaty impairing its independence, it must keep its debt within its capacity to pay, it must permit the United States to intervene with force in case that should be necessary to keep order, it was obligated to grant the United States two naval stations, one of which, Guantanamo, is still held, and it must carry out the plans of sanitation the United States had begun. When an insurrection broke out in Cuba in August, 1906, the United States exercised its right of intervention. For more than two years the American occupation continued. On several other occasions the United States made use of its right of intervention, but in every instance stopped short of annexation, although many Americans and a few Cubans argued for it.

The Philippines.　The problem of Cuba was negligible compared to the problem of the Philippines, for in annexing the latter the United States acquired also a full-scale insurrection. The Philippine population, which was a mixture of native peoples and immigrants from the Asiatic mainland, included about 7 million Spanish-speaking and Roman Catholic Filipinos, besides about three-quarters of a million uncivilized Igorrotes and Moros. Under Spanish rule the islanders had suffered from neglect, exploitation, and oppression, and when the Spanish-American War broke out, Filipino insurgents already were seriously challenging Spanish supremacy. At first the Filipinos had assumed naively that the American promise of freedom for Cuba carried with it by implication the promise of freedom for the Philippines. When they learned that the United States had no such intentions, they turned in full force against

the new invaders, and for almost three years fought hard for their independence. Not until October 1, 1901, did the United States find it possible to announce the complete suppression of the insurrection, although for many months conditions in the Philippines failed to justify the statement.

Puerto Rico.　The occupation of Puerto Rico involved fewer perplexities than confronted American officials either in the Philippines or in Cuba. The population of the island was less than a million, nearly two-thirds of whom were white, and the rest of Negro extraction. There had been no revolution and no war damage of consequence. American rule was accepted without enthusiasm, but without protest. Even under the military regime rapid strides were made toward better sanitation, the construction of roads, and the reordering of public finance. So smooth was the transition that as early as April 12, 1900, Congress passed the Foraker Act establishing a civil government for Puerto Rico, the first to be accorded any of the new possessions. The pattern of government thus set for the dependencies was similar to that of the traditional American territory, but with more limited privileges of self-government. Furthermore, residents of the island were not accorded full American citizenship, but were described as citizens of Puerto Rico. An act of March 2, 1917, however, provided the island with the customary territorial government and declared its inhabitants citizens of the United States. Still later, in 1950, the Puerto Ricans were granted the right to adopt a constitution and establish a government of their own. The island was now described as a self-governing commonwealth voluntarily associated with the United States. Its people elected their own governor and legislature, and on local matters its government was completely autonomous.

Election of 1900.　Republican successes in the elections of 1898 denoted little more than general satisfaction at the victories won by Americans in the war with Spain, but the presidential election of 1900 was a pitched battle, with the forces favoring annexation of the Philippines lined up solidly on one side, and those opposed on the other. The Republicans, with William McKinley once again their standard-bearer, and with Theodore Roosevelt, the hero of San Juan Hill, as their candidate for Vice-President, rejoiced in the "new and noble responsibility" that had come to the American people, and asserted that "no other course was possible" in the Philippines than the one that they had taken. The Democrats also renominated their leader of the preceding campaign, William Jennings Bryan; but for second place they had no war hero, only the time-worn Vice-President of Cleveland's second administration, Adlai E. Stevenson of Illinois.

Imperialism the Paramount Issue. Throughout the campaign the debate on imperialism held the center of the stage. The arguments were not new; they had all been used while the Treaty of Paris was before the country. Nor was the decision ever in doubt. McKinley, as the cartoonists so graphically portrayed, always had his "ear to the ground," and he was convinced that he had read the public mind aright. Nevertheless, Democratic orators dwelt long upon the inconsistency of a democracy such as the United States fighting to suppress the ambitions of another people to be free. They cast William McKinley in the role of George III, and Aguinaldo, the Filipino insurgent leader, in that of George Washington. They pointed out the practical difficulties involved in annexation. The United States was wholly without experience in the governing of colonies. How could it hope to solve the problems of a distant and "alien race"? A great navy and a great army would be necessary to protect the new possessions. Once the United States had depended upon the Atlantic Ocean and the Pacific Ocean for its

defense. But with Asiatic possessions American military might must be expanded to reach far across the seas.

Republican politicians had no difficulty in justifying all that had been done. The Philippines, they claimed, offered an inviting missionary field. The United States had at last an opportunity to extend the blessings of American civilization. The Filipinos were not yet capable of governing themselves; freedom would mean only anarchy and misrule, or perhaps conquest by some predatory commercial nation, such as Germany or France. The United States had become a great power, and it must accept the responsibilities of greatness. The Philippines were pictured as a rich land inviting lucrative investments, but more important, as a steppingstone to the "illimitable markets" of China and the Orient. Besides, the United States needed colonies to become a truly great nation. Other great nations had colonies and were engaged in a mad scramble for more.

Election Results. But imperialism was not the only issue of the campaign. More important to many people were the old issues of free silver and the tariff. Cartoonists made merry with the "hold-your-nose-and-vote" crowd who in the confusion could not escape voting for something they heartily disliked, or against something they heartily approved. Shrewdly, Republican campaigners rang the changes on prosperity, and pressed home the point with such slogans as "The Full Dinner Pail." A well-filled Republican campaign chest helped even more. When the votes were counted, it appeared that Bryan had carried only the normally Democratic states of the South and four silver states in the Far West. Even Nebraska deserted him. The popular vote stood 7.2 million for McKinley to 6.3 million for Bryan and the electoral vote, 292 to 155. Both houses of Congress were Republican by substantial majorities, and, except in the South, Republican candidates for state office were generally the victors.

Although some authorities deny that the voters sanctioned the new colonial acquisitions, in so far as an election could decide anything, the country apparently had given its approval to imperialism, the gold standard, and a high protective tariff.

A problem of imperialism as yet unsettled at the time of the election was how to reconcile the exigencies of empire with the Constitution of the United States. According to the treaty of cession, "the civil rights and political status of the native inhabitants" were left to the determination of Congress. It was not yet clear whether Congress was compelled to extend the liberties guaranteed by the Constitution to its island possessions, or whether the freedom of Congress in this respect was as much subject to the Constitution in the new territory as in the old. In other words, as the public phrased the question, does the Constitution follow the flag?

From the first, Congress assumed that it was free from all embarrassing constitutional restraints. In the Foraker Act, for example, it levied a tariff against Puerto Rican imports into the United States equal to 15 per cent of the regular Dingley rates. If Puerto Rico had become a part of the United States this provision was clearly contrary to the constitutional requirements that "all duties, imports, and excises shall be uniform throughout the United States." Obviously, therefore, Congress did not regard the island as a part of the United States in the constitutional sense, nor did the President who signed the law.

The "Insular Cases." In a series of five-to-four opinions on what came generally to be known as the "Insular Cases," the Supreme Court decided in 1901 not to interfere with the stand that Congress and the President had taken. The first of these cases, *De Lima* v. *Bidwell*, was brought by an importer of Puerto Rican sugar against the collector of the port of New York who *before* the enactment of the Foraker Act, but *after* the acquisition of Puerto Rico by

the United States, had charged the full Dingley duties. In this case the Court held that the money collected must be refunded, for Puerto Rico was no longer foreign territory. In another case, however, *Downes* v. *Bidwell*, where the collections had been made *after* the passage of the Foraker Act and according to its terms, the Court held that a refund was unnecessary, for Puerto Rico was not exactly a part of the United States. To eight justices these decisions seemed utterly contradictory, for the result was achieved by Mr. Justice Brown changing sides and voting in the second decision with the four justices who had constituted the minority in the first. The second decision, that Puerto Rico and the other dependencies were "territory appurtenant — but not a part — of the United States," stood. In another case, *Hawaii* v. *Mankichi*, the Court decided that in the period after annexation, but before the passage of an organic act of government, the inhabitants of the Hawaiian Islands could not claim the right of trial by jury as secured by the Fifth and Sixth Amendments. To the consternation of many constitutional scholars, the Court held that the "rights alleged to be violated . . . are not fundamental in their nature."

American Colonial Policy. Cuba was set free, or at least relatively free, although the United States might easily have retained the island as a dependency. Even the Philippines were promised ultimate independence; on this issue the two parties differed merely as to when independence should be granted. Philippine policy, therefore, worked toward increasing autonomy regardless of the party in power. McKinley sent William Howard Taft to the Philippines to institute civil government, and under his able administration the foundations of self-rule were laid. By 1907 the Filipinos were electing the lower house of their legislature; by 1916, under the terms of the Jones Act, they were permitted virtual autonomy, although during the twenties, with the Republicans again in the ascendancy, some of the privileges were lost. And eventually, after World War II, they achieved independence.

Philippine Civilization. American occupation of the Philippines carried with it also many other familiar aspects of American culture. One of the most important innovations was the American public-school system. In 1898 perhaps 5,000 Filipino children were in school; by 1920, over a million. At first American teachers were placed in charge, but adequately trained Filipinos, many of them educated in the United States, were soon available to take over the work. By 1920 the number of American teachers had dwindled to 300, but the English language rivaled the Spanish as the most generally understood tongue in the islands. American sanitation also reached the Philippines. Smallpox and cholera were stamped out, lepers were isolated in colonies and treated, and the infant death rate was sharply reduced. Good roads were built, and rail and water transportation was improved. Most significant of all, the modified tariff barriers that had at first restricted trade between the Philippines and the United States soon gave way to virtual free trade, thus opening the rich American markets to Philippine sugar, coconut oil, rice, tobacco, and hemp. The result of this favored economic status was a degree of prosperity such as the Philippines had never known before. Whatever their political differences, the economic ties that bound the islands to the United States became closer with each succeeding year.

The "Open Door." While trade helped to sustain good relations between the United States and the Philippines, it also threatened to involve America seriously for the first time with the Oriental mainland. Possession of the Philippines made the United States, whether it so desired or not, a power in Asia with an interest in whatever went on there. But the great powers

of Asia, with the exception of Japan, were also the great powers of Europe. By 1895 Great Britain, France, Russia, and the Netherlands dominated most of the non-Chinese Orient. And within a few years it was apparent that they, together with Japan and Germany, were intent upon completing the process with a division of China. "Spheres of influence" were already marked out, in which the various nations enjoyed special "concessions" and which they obviously hoped to absorb. Great Britain held Hong Kong; Japan, Korea; Germany, a ninety-nine year lease on the port of Kiao-chau, together with special rights in the entire Shantung peninsula; France, Kwangchau Bay; and Russia, Port Arthur together with special privileges in Manchuria. If the process of dismembering China were completed, the old American trade with China would rapidly diminish and the imperialist hope that the Philippines would act as a way station for a greatly expanded commerce with the Orient would entirely dissolve. On the other hand, how could the United States maintain her traditional isolation from Europe and still further her position and aspirations in the Far East?

To counter the trend, Secretary of State Hay seized upon a British suggestion and asked the great powers to agree to an "open door" in China. Each power was invited by notes of September 6, 1899, (1) to respect the trading privileges of all other nations within its sphere of influence, (2) to permit Chinese officials to collect the existing tariff under which the United States was a most favored nation, and (3) to avoid discrimination against the nationals of other countries in port dues and in railroad rates. From every state except Great Britain Hay received something less than a commitment to abide by the doctrine. The others all stated that while they were in favor of the open door in principle, they could not agree to act under it until all others had accepted. Thereupon Hay blandly announced that since all had

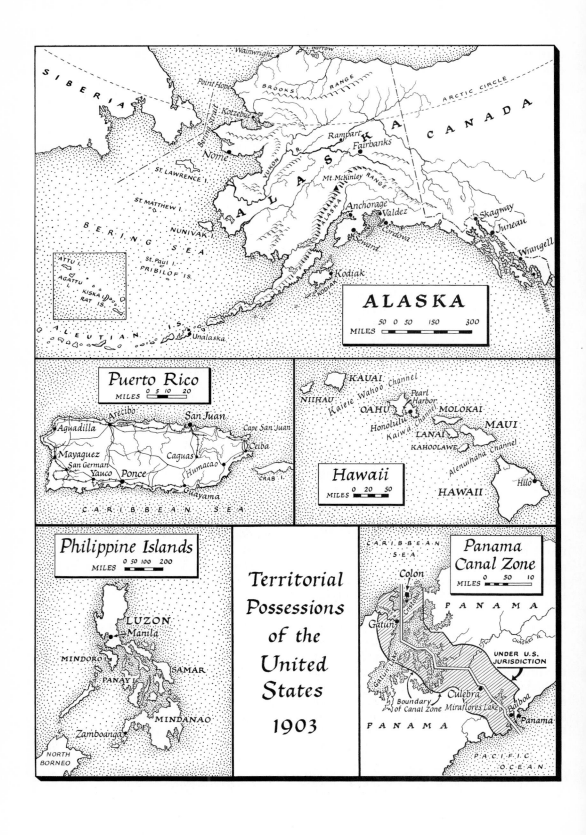

Territorial
Possessions
of the
United
States
1903

agreed in principle, the United States now considered the policy approved. But events soon proved that very little had been changed.

The outbreak of the Boxer Rebellion in the spring of 1900 furnished an excellent pretext for the European powers to pursue their ends. This nationalist movement, led by a Chinese patriotic society called the Boxers, was directed at all foreigners and foreign property. With the Chinese police unable or unwilling to restore order, many foreigners were killed, and eventually the whole foreign diplomatic corps was surrounded and besieged in Peking. Armed intervention by the foreign powers was now inevitable, and after much negotiation a joint international expeditionary force was sent to Tientsin, where it set out for Peking to relieve the besieged diplomats on August 16, 1900. Most well-informed men took it for granted that the affair would end in the complete partition of China. That it did not was due largely to the position of the United States, supported by Great Britain and eventually Germany. While the fighting was still in progress, Secretary of State Hay stated that it was a cardinal point of American policy to "preserve Chinese territorial and administrative entity," together with the "open door" for the commerce of all nations. Subsequently Hay obtained an agreement among the participating nations to accept a money indemnity from China rather than the territorial cessions which some of them would have strongly preferred.

The United States recognized no political alliance, with China or any other nation, but the Boxer negotiations betrayed clearly how significantly the acquisition of empire had altered the basic assumptions of American diplomacy. The decision to take part in an international military expedition was hard to reconcile with the traditional policy of no entangling alliances, while the demand for the preservation of Chinese territorial integrity, in view of the rapacious desires of some of the world's greatest nations, was an even more startling innova-

tion. To guarantee this latter end, the American government would have to rely either upon military force, a course which the American people would probably oppose, or, more likely, upon diplomatic maneuverings toward a balance of power in the Orient. Either course would involve a virtual abandonment of long-established traditions.

Minor Possessions. Recounting the spoils of imperialism, Americans were aware that certain minor possessions also formed a part of their new empire. American sovereignty extended to Guam, some 1,500 miles east of the Philippines, to American Samoa, and to numerous uninhabited Pacific islets over which no other nation had chosen to raise its flag. Until otherwise directed, these possessions remained under the absolute control of the President as commander-in-chief of the army and navy. Under his authority, the United States Navy, aided in each case by a local advisory legislature, administered both Guam and American Samoa until well after the Second World War. By an act of Congress, approved August 1, 1950, Guam became an unincorporated territory of the United States, and thereafter its administration was vested in the Department of the Interior. By an order of July 1, 1951, President Truman transferred the administration of American Samoa also to the Department of the Interior. Both the Guamanians and the American Samoans became American citizens.

The United States also acquired two other tiny colonies as a result of the decision to build a canal across the Isthmus of Panama. The Canal Zone, ten miles wide, obtained by treaty with Panama in 1903, came to be inhabited principally by government employees, and was eventually left to the government of Congress, the President, and the national courts. The Virgin Islands, acquired by purchase from Denmark in 1917, were deemed of value for the proper defense of the Canal. To govern the impoverished 25,000 inhabitants, most of whom were of Negro descent, the President was authorized to appoint a governor, subject to the approval of the Senate. The Danish code of laws, already in force, was retained. President Truman, in 1950, appointed the first Virgin Islander to the governorship, while by a revised Organic Act of 1954, local legislative authority was vested in a unicameral legislature composed of eleven senators.

Imperial Defense. Just as the opponents of imperialism had predicted, the United States could not avoid rapid military expansion. If there was to be an American empire, that empire had to be defended. Under Elihu Root as Secretary of War the United States Army underwent a reorganization so thorough that the scandals and inefficiency marring the prosecution of the war against Spain could not soon be repeated. In keeping with modern practice a general staff was created to take the place of the senior major general in command of the army, and to lay plans for the proper defense of the United States and its possessions. By means of the Army War College (1901), and other service schools, an attempt was made to carry on the military education of officers after they had been commissioned. The size of the army was not greatly increased, but a new militia law, designed to make of the National Guard a more efficient second line of defense, was passed in 1903. Even more striking than the reorganization of the army was the rapid expansion of the navy, to which over a long period one or two new battleships were added every year.

Decline of Interest in Colonies. Quite as striking a fact as the sudden acquisition of a colonial empire by the United States was the equally sudden subsidence of the expansionist urge. After the first excitement, interest in the newly acquired possessions diminished, and the public showed not the slightest appetite for more. When the United States entered the First World War in 1917, one of the certainties, unchallenged by any political party, was that the American nation would not emerge with more colonies. From the financial point of view colonial empire proved to be almost a total loss; the Philippines in particular cost the government huge sums, and brought little profit to anyone. This, perhaps, need not have been so; other nations took a heavy toll from their possessions. But neither the American government nor the American people showed great aptitude along this line. Americans with a taste for foreign trade and investments were not lacking, and in the sense of expanding commercial interests, American imperialism was by no means dead. But American traders made as good profits, if not better, in lands outside rather than inside the American empire. Discouraging, too, was the discovery that distant possessions meant involvement in world politics and the consequent danger of war.

SELECTED BIBLIOGRAPHY

An influential reinterpretation of the background for expansion is Walter LaFeber, *The New Empire* (1964). E. R. May, *Imperial Democracy; The Emergence of America as a Great Power* (1961), is a fresh examination of several of the main subjects of this chapter. Notable discussions of foreign relations of this period are in G. F. Kennan, *American Diplo-

macy, 1900–1950* (1951); R. E. Osgood, *Ideals and Self-Interest in America's Foreign Relations* (1953); and Hans Morgenthau, *In Defense of the National Interest* (1951). These may be contrasted with the more idealistic approach of F. R. Dulles, in his *The Imperial Years* (1956), and *America's Rise to World Power, 1898–1954* (1955). A convenient documentary collection is D. M. Smith (ed.), *Major Problems in American Diplomatic His-*

* Available in paperback

tory (1964). The expansionist sentiment that dominated some American thinking during these years is the subject of J. W. Pratt, *Expansionists of 1898* (1936); and it also receives attention in Frederick Merk, *Manifest Destiny and Mission in American History* (1963). See also the important survey by S. F. Bemis, *The Latin American Policy of the United States* (1943).

The best analysis of Harrison's foreign policy is A. F. Tyler, *The Foreign Policy of James G. Blaine* (1927); while Henry James, *Richard Olney and His Public Service* (1923), is a friendly examination of Cleveland's aggressive Secretary of State. Valuable also is G. R. Dulebohn, *Principles of Foreign Policy under the Cleveland Administrations* (1941). On the navy, see: W. D. Puleston, *Mahan* (1939); R. S. West, Jr., *Admirals of the American Empire* (1948); and G. C. O'Gara, *Theodore Roosevelt and the Rise of the Modern Navy* (1943).

On some of the episodes of pre-Spanish War imperialism, see: G. H. Ryden, *The Foreign Policy of the United States in Relation to Samoa* (1933); H. C. Evans, Jr., *Chile and Its Relations with the United States* (1927); and A. L. P. Dennis, *Adventures in American Diplomacy, 1896–1906* (1928). The literature on Hawaii is large; among the best works for this period are S. K. Stevens, *American Expansion in Hawaii, 1842–1898* (1945); and F. H. Conroy, *The Japanese Frontier in Hawaii, 1868–1898* (1953). Discussions of Anglo-American relations are contained in: H. C. Allen, *Great Britain and the United States* (1955); L. M. Gelber, *The Rise of Anglo-American Friendship, 1898–1906* (1938); and C. S. Campbell, Jr., *Anglo-American Understanding, 1898–1903* (1957).

A short, lively account of the Spanish-American War, magnificently illustrated, is Frank Freidel, *The Splendid Little War* (1958). The most entertaining account of American intervention in Cuba is Walter Millis, *The Martial Spirit* (1931). A brief survey is provided by H. W. Morgan, *America's Road to Empire; The War with Spain and Overseas Expansion* (1965). The role of newspapermen in promoting the war is well set forth in J. E. Wisan, *The Cuban Crisis as Reflected in the New York Press* (1934).

The debates over the question of Empire are well covered in a collection edited by T. P. Greene, *American Imperialism in 1898* (1955). Claude Bowers, *Beveridge and the Progressive Era* (1932), recounts the thinking and activities of a leading imperialist. The anti-imperialist argument is given in Merle Curti, *Bryan and World Peace* (1931); W. M. Armstrong, *E. L. Godkin and American Foreign Policy, 1865–1900* (1957); M. A. D. Howe, *Portrait of an Independent, Moorfield Storey* (1932); and G. F. Hoar, *Autobiography of Seventy Years* (1903). Elmer Ellis, *Mr. Dooley's America: A Life of Finley Peter Dunne* (1941), is the biography of a political humorist who viewed the whole imperialistic venture with considerable misgivings. On the Treaty of Paris, see: C. E. Hill, *Leading American Treaties* (1922); W. S. Holt, *Treaties Defeated by the Senate* (1933); and Royal Cortissoz, *Life of Whitelaw Reid* (1921).

J. W. Pratt, *America's Colonial Experiment* (1950), is a convenient summary. Much has been written on individual dependencies and protectorates, including: J. P. Nichols, *Alaska* (1924); E. S. Pomeroy, *Pacific Outpost; American Strategy in Guam and Micronesia* (1951); L. H. Evans, *The Virgin Islands* (1945); and B. W. and J. W. Diffie, *Porto Rico* (1931). On Cuba, see: R. H. Fitzgibbon, *Cuba and the United States, 1900–1935* (1935); D. A. Lockmiller, *Magoon in Cuba* (1938); and D. F. Healy, *The United States in Cuba, 1898–1902* (1963). On the Philippines, important works include: G. L. Kirk, *Philippine Independence* (1936); A. S. Pier, *American Apostles to the Philippines* (1950); and Leon Wolff, *Little Brown Brother* (1961), a severely critical account of the putting-down of the Philippine insurrection.

A. W. Griswold, *The Far Eastern Policy of the United States* (1938), is standard and reliable. Tyler Dennett, *John Hay* (1933), and *Americans in Eastern Asia* (2nd ed., 1941), are useful for the Open Door policy. Recent monographs include: C. S. Campbell, Jr., *Special Business Interests and the Open Door Policy* (1951); Charles Vevier, *The United States and China, 1906–1913* (1955); and two works by P. A. Varg, *Open Door Diplomat: The Life of W. W. Rockhill* (1952), and *Missionaries, Chinese and Diplomats* (1958). W. A. Williams, *The Tragedy of American Diplomacy* (2nd ed., 1962), is leftist and highly critical of "open door imperialism."

29

WORLD POLITICS

Toward World Power. By 1900 the United States had acquired an empire that stretched some 10,000 miles across the surface of the earth. By that fact alone it was forced to concern itself within the next fifteen years not only with Latin-American affairs, but also with East Asian politics, and even with the balance of power in Europe. Superficially, the nation was well prepared to play an important role in world politics. By all statistics of population, trade, iron and steel production, naval power, and even size of empire, America was one of the world's great powers. But then, as in the past, it lacked one important requisite for achieving world greatness: the inclination of its people. True, Americans were willing to keep and protect the empire they had won in 1898, but after the first excitement had diminished, they

showed little desire to extend it. In fact, they often forgot the nation had an empire, and thus with composure could berate European, and particularly British, imperialism without admitting that America had indulged in the same game. No matter what new conditions obtained, the traditional cautious policy of isolationism was to die hard.

The Roosevelt Foreign Policy. The American people might still believe that nothing had changed in the nation's foreign policy, but the President and the Department of State knew better. Six months after his second inauguration William McKinley visited the Pan-American exposition at Buffalo, and on September 5, 1901, made a speech in which he emphasized the end of American commercial isolation and the importance of reciprocity as a means of promoting foreign trade. Next day, during a reception, he was shot by an anarchist. After his death on September 14, 1901, he was succeeded by his youthful Vice-President.

On the surface, at least, Theodore Roosevelt (1858–1919) seemed completely at odds with the American people in their desire for a cautious foreign policy. He had contributed much to the imperialist wave culminating in the Spanish-American War. As President he often acted as his own

Secretary of State and he still advocated the strenuous life for nations as well as for individuals. War at times was good, he believed, and preferable to loss of national honor. Every expansion of a great civilized power meant "a victory for law, order and righteousness." Roosevelt sensed the growing international insecurity of his age, and was continually worried about America's defenses. Although one might expect an extremely active and perhaps adventurous foreign policy from such a man, he acted precipitately only when American security was involved, and then only when the adversary was a small country. In general, his public speeches on foreign policy were the essence of propriety.

Roosevelt was not altogether happy with the American Far Eastern policy that he had inherited, and in some ways his actions constituted a retreat from the principles of the previous administration. He firmly believed in holding and defending the Philippines, but near the end of his term, he regretted their acquisition and wished there were some honorable way of getting rid of them. He also supported the principle of commercial opportunity in China, without risking serious conflict, and at times he doubted the wisdom of having committed the United States to maintain Chinese territorial integrity.

After the suppression of the Boxers and the restoration of order in China, the withdrawal of the expeditionary forces was carried out according to agreement by all the nations except Russia, who remained in Manchuria, with a view to exacting further concessions from China. To block Russian ambitions only the Japanese were prepared to act. Japanese students of western civilization had reached the conclusion that the growing population of Japan could be supported only by the rapid expansion of manufacturing. But Japan lacked an adequate supply of the two greatest essentials for a manufacturing nation, coal and iron, both of which China possessed in abundance. Access to these commodities, as well as to Chinese markets for Japanese goods, the Russian program might make impossible. With their economic "life-line" thus endangered, Japanese statesmen made deliberate plans for the expulsion of Russia from Manchuria. On January 30, 1902, Japan signed a treaty of alliance with Great Britain, which stipulated that if either signatory were attacked by more than one power, the other must come to its aid. This alliance permitted the British to concentrate their naval strength in European waters where German naval power was on the rise, and left Japan free to drive the Russians out of Manchuria.

Russo-Japanese War. The Russo-Japanese War of 1904 was soon over. It was fought on Chinese soil, although China, strongly supported by the United States, succeeded in remaining neutral. Before the war and during its early stages, the American government naturally favored Japan, for the Russians rather than the Japanese had endangered the "open door" policy. Roosevelt looked upon Japan as a "counterpoise" against Russia and felt that Japan was "playing our game" when it destroyed Russian sea power. But after a series of Japanese victories in Manchuria, Roosevelt became worried that the war would result in Japan taking over Russia's interests in the province instead of freeing it from foreign influence. Consequently, when the President was asked to mediate the struggle, he declined to do so before he had obtained the promise of Japan to respect the "open door" policy in Manchuria and return the province to China. With this achieved, Russian and Japanese delegates met at Roosevelt's invitation at the Portsmouth Naval Yard, New Hampshire, on August 9, 1905, to discuss peace. Largely because of Roosevelt's pressure the Japanese gave up their demands for an indemnity and Russia agreed to a cession of one-half of the island of Sakhalin. Both sides agreed to evacuate Manchuria, and Japan got a firmer hold on Korea and took over from Russia the South Manchuria Railroad.

Japanese-American Relations. Although Roosevelt labored to save the "open door" in Manchuria, he agreed to its being shut in Korea. Two things were apparent by 1905: first, that Japan probably could not be stopped in its penetration of Korea except by force; second, that the Philippines might become a logical place for Japanese expansion in the future. Since Roosevelt believed it impractical, if not impossible, to stop Japan in Korea, the next best thing was to acknowledge the inevitable and obtain compensation. In July, 1905, William Howard Taft negotiated an executive agreement in Tokyo by which the United States recognized Japanese "suzerainty" over Korea in return for a Japanese disavowal of any aggression in the Philippines. Four months later the United States legation was removed from Seoul, and thereafter Korean questions were conducted through the Japanese foreign office.

Notwithstanding Roosevelt's generous gesture, relations between Japan and the United States grew critical after the Peace of Portsmouth. Besides objecting to the peace treaty, the Japanese people had other grievances. They resented the American patrol of the sealing waters off the Pribilof Islands, which had resulted in the killing of five Japanese nationals in July, 1906. Even more disturbing was the treatment of Orientals on the American side of the Pacific. Japanese immigration into California was increasing, and their presence gave rise to the same race prejudice that had manifested itself earlier against the Chinese. In October, 1906, the San Francisco School Board issued an order requiring ninety-three Japanese school children in the city to attend a separate school. Japan's national pride, quickened by her victory over Russia, was wounded, and the Japanese government sent strongly worded protests to Washington. Roosevelt was furious at the "infernal fools" in California,

as was most of the East Coast. After strong and persistent pressure, he succeeded in obtaining a repeal of the school measure, promising in return to put an end to the unwanted immigration. Following a series of negotiations, the famous "Gentlemen's Agreement" was adopted, whereby the Japanese government promised to stop the emigration of its laborers to the United States mainland, and Roosevelt denied entrance to continental United States to Japanese immigrants not coming directly from Japan. The agreement thus permitted the continuation of Japanese immigration into Hawaii, where they constituted the principal labor force on the sugar plantations.

The Root-Takahira Agreement. Fearful that his conciliatory action might be interpreted as a sign of weakness, Roosevelt now decided to dispel any such misunderstandings by sending the American fleet, now the second largest in the world, around the globe by way of Japan. Both ships and men were given an enthusiastic welcome in Tokyo and the voyage, in addition to displaying America's newborn naval power to the world, set the stage for a short period of better relations with Japan. This period culminated in the signing of the Root-Takahira Agreement on November 30, 1908. The executive agreement was not a treaty but merely bound the Roosevelt administration and the then current government in Japan. By its terms both powers agreed (1) to maintain the status quo in the Pacific area and to respect each other's possessions there, (2) to maintain the "open door" in China, and (3) to maintain the "independence and integrity of China." There has been much subsequent argument over just what the Root-Takahira Agreement meant. On the surface it looked as if the United States had won a sweeping victory in getting a Japanese promise to respect the Philippines, and to support the principles of the "open door" and the integrity of China. But the first part of the agreement might also be interpreted as an

American acknowledgment of the special economic and political position of Japan in Manchuria and North China, which, of course, was a reversal of American Far Eastern policy.

Railroad Politics in Manchuria. Whatever the actual intent of the Root-Takahira Agreement, the Japanese apparently interpreted it as giving them a free hand to develop their already large interests in Manchuria. Not to be outdone by Japan, Russia likewise stepped up her activity in North China. Both countries, in their attempts to get economic and political control of desired territory, relied upon the holding of treaty ports and the construction of railroads in the interior. In 1895 there were only 200 miles of Chinese railroads, but by 1913 there were 6,000 miles. Most of the new railroad construction was in Manchuria, where the Chinese population was smallest, and thus more easily subject to economic domination by the foreign powers.

William Howard Taft, who became President March 5, 1909, knew the Far East well and had many friends there, among whom was Willard Straight, the American Consul General at Mukden. Straight urged the President to checkmate Japan in Manchuria by promoting American investments there. Taft and his Secretary of State, Philander C. Knox, accepted this idea and made every effort to implement it, but American bankers were reluctant to risk their money in an unfamiliar region. A great international consortium of private capital that Knox sought to bring about for the purchase of all the Japanese and Russian railroads in Manchuria lacked foreign as well as American backing, and came to nought. Taft's other efforts to use "dollars for bullets" in Far Eastern diplomacy, which included the backing of another consortium which would stabilize the Chinese currency and promote industrialization in Manchuria, were equally barren of results, and when Wilson became President in 1913 the policy of "dollar diplomacy" was abruptly discontinued.

The American position in the Far East was still further undermined by the growing threat to peace in Europe. Fear of Germany led Great Britain to strengthen her alliances, and to give her acquiescence to the Japanese penetration into North China. After the Anglo-Russian entente of 1907, Great Britain sought to bring Russia and Japan closer together in order to present a common front against Germany and Austria in case of war. Spurred by the Knox proposal to internationalize the railroads of Manchuria, Japan and Russia actually did reach agreements in 1910 and 1912, much to the delight of Great Britain. Secretly the two powers divided Manchuria and Mongolia between themselves and promised to resist the efforts of any other nation to exploit these provinces either commercially or politically. Thus, after 1912, the United States stood isolated in the Orient and virtually helpless either to maintain the integrity of China or to preserve the "open door."

Anglo-American Relations. While American diplomacy in the Far East achieved little lasting success, it enjoyed a gratifying record of successful accomplishments in the western hemisphere. Here the United States had a better understanding of the problems that arose, and it ordinarily had no such powerful antagonists to deal with as in the Orient. Events soon proved that on most matters of consequence in the western hemisphere the United States could count on British support. In the settlement of the dispute over the Alaskan boundary, in 1903, the British government showed more concern for the maintenance of cordial relations with the United States than for pleading the cause of Canada, a component part of the empire. By a reinterpretation of the treaty line of 1825, agreed upon by Great Britain and Russia, the Canadians laid claim to a corridor across the Alaskan panhandle that would have given them access to the ocean from the gold fields of the Klondike. Irate at such claims, Theodore Roosevelt threatened to use force to maintain American sovereignty in the disputed region. Such action was not necessary, however, for on an Anglo-American commission of six — three Americans, two Canadians, and an Englishman — the British representative voted consistently with the Americans, much to the displeasure of the Canadians.

The Panama Canal. The British also gave way to American desires in the matter of constructing a canal through Central America, a project that seemed almost a necessity if the new American possessions were to be protected. Such a waterway would reduce the trip from New York to San Francisco by almost two-thirds, and in the event of war would save many precious days in transferring the fleet from one ocean to the other. Unfortunately, the Clayton-

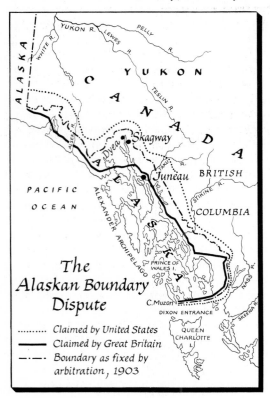

The Alaskan Boundary Dispute

.... Claimed by United States
———— Claimed by Great Britain
—·—·— Boundary as fixed by
          arbitration, 1903

Bulwer Treaty of 1850 gave the British equal rights with the Americans in the construction of any such canal, but Great Britain, after some reluctance, yielded to the American insistence on a strictly American canal. The first Hay-Pauncefote treaty of February 5, 1900, implementing the new agreement, was defeated in the Senate because of a clause prohibiting the United States from fortifying the canal, but a second treaty, concluded on November 18, 1901, omitted the obnoxious clause. The only reservations the British insisted upon were that the canal be "free and open to the vessels of commerce and of war of all nations . . . on terms of entire equality," that there be no discriminations "in respect of the conditions or charges of traffic."

Hay's success in the canal undertaking was probably due more to the inclinations of the British than to his own undoubted ability. Under heavy diplomatic attack from the major European nations and isolated in an increasingly hostile world, Great Britain was seeking dependable friends. A strong United States in the Caribbean might protect British interests there, freeing British sea power to concentrate nearer home against the rising German navy. Within a few years, Great Britain tacitly acknowledged American supremacy in the Caribbean by reducing her naval and land forces to a mere token. As in the Panama Canal negotiations and in the Alaskan boundary dispute, British diplomacy seemed pointed toward American friendship, even at considerable cost. While the American public in general distrusted Great Britain and disdained British friendship, the American government welcomed the British gestures.

Of the four routes available for a canal only two were seriously discussed, one through Panama, then a province of Colombia, where a French canal company had previously gone bankrupt in attempting to dig a waterway, and the other through Nicaragua. A presidential group, known as the Walker Commission, and the House of

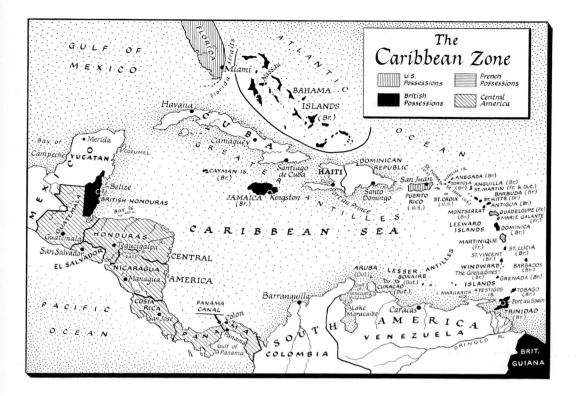

Representatives, influenced by the possibility of building a water-level canal and by the extremely high price of $109 million which the French company had set for its concession in Panama, both voted for the Nicaraguan route. Alarmed by these developments, the French company reduced its asking price to $40 million and sent a remarkable representative to the United States in the person of Philippe Bunau-Varilla. Bunau-Varilla was joined in his task of persuading the American government to reverse itself in favor of the Panama route by Nelson W. Cromwell, a New York attorney who had contributed $60,000 to the Republican campaign fund of 1900. Led by Mark Hanna, the Senate on June 28, 1902, voted for the Panama route, but instructed the President to negotiate with Nicaragua in the event that a right of way through Panama could not be secured in "a reasonable time."

Canal Diplomacy. Using the threat of the Nicaraguan alternative, Secretary Hay drove a sharp bargain with Tomas Herran, the Colombian representative at Washington. The United States was to receive a canal zone six miles wide across the Isthmus in return for a cash payment of $10 million and a yearly annuity of $250,000. Within this zone, stretching from Panama City to Colón, but not including those cities, the United States was to have virtually sovereign rights. The treaty contained one other most remarkable provision: Colombia agreed not to negotiate with the French company, and thus forfeited a chance to obtain part of the $40 million which the French company was to receive from the United States. The United States Senate promptly ratified the treaty, but the Colombian government, resenting both the terms and the manner in which they had been imposed, refused to ratify. Apparently, the chief Colombian objection to the treaty lay in its monetary clauses. Since the French concession expired in October, 1904, at which time all such interests and property in Panama would revert to Colombia, by waiting a short time Colombia might claim the entire $40 million. But the Department of State warned Colombia that it would consider any modification of the treaty "a breach of faith," and there the matter rested.

Up to this time President Roosevelt had not been strongly prejudiced for either the Panama or the Nicaragua route, but with Colombia's refusal, he became a zealous advocate of the Panama route. To influence the President further, the ingenious Bunau-Varilla sent him a newspaper containing a story of a possible revolution in Panama against Colombian control. This hint was all that Roosevelt needed. The predicted revolution in Panama was both fomented and financed in New York City by officers of the French company, but its success was unquestionably due to the cooperation of the American navy. By an old treaty the United States had recognized the "rights of sovereignty and property" which Colombia held in Panama. By the same instrument both countries agreed to protect the right of free transit across the Isthmus. Obviously, the latter clause was aimed at an intrusion of any third power and was not meant to confer upon the United States the right to obstruct the passage of Colombian troops. On October 30, 1903, however, the commander of the U.S.S. *Nashville* was ordered in case of rebellion to seize the Panama Railroad and "to prevent the landing of any armed force with hostile intent" within fifty miles of Panama. On November 2, the *Nashville* steamed into Colón. Since the only possible route by which Colombia could bring troops to Panama was by sea, the revolution took place the next day without the usual accompaniment of violence. Three days later, Secretary Hay accorded diplomatic recognition to the new republic.

With Colombia disposed of, and with Bunau-Varilla appointed the first minister of Panama to the United States, a new treaty, the Hay-Bunau-Varilla Treaty, quickly cleared the way for construction of the canal. The United States acquired a zone five miles wide on each side of the canal, an area which she could fortify at will. Panama received an initial payment of $10 million and $250,000 a year, beginning nine years after date. The size of the annual payments was raised in 1922 and again in 1955, when it amounted to almost $2 million a year. But as subsequent events proved, the Panamanians were still not satisfied. The United States guaranteed the independence of Panama, but the principles of the Platt amendment, including the right of intervention, were applied to the new republic.

The actual building of the canal was a magnificent feat. At first sanitation threatened to be an even greater problem than excavation, but the efforts of Colonel W. C. Gorgas in making the canal zone a safe place in which to live were soon successful. Administrative difficulties hampered work for a while, but Roosevelt at length made Major George W. Goethals, an army engineer, chairman of the canal commission, and extracted a promise from the other members never to disagree with the chairman. After that, work proceeded satisfactorily, and on August 15, 1914, the first ocean steamer passed through the canal. The cost of building it ran to $275 million, which the government raised by floating bonds, together with another $113 million for fortifications; but the receipts during the first fifteen years of operations were large enough to meet the interest in full. Roosevelt considered the building of the Panama Canal the greatest achievement of his administration.

Roosevelt defended his Panama action on the grounds that the canal was desperately needed by the world and that in delaying its construction Colombia had been, in effect, an enemy of civilization. All the canal negotiations were conducted "by the highest, finest and nicest standards of public and governmental ethics." Years later, however, he publicly boasted, "I took Panama." The American people were apparently delighted with the Panama action, while the great European imperial nations were united in their criticism. Latin-American countries, of course, bitterly condemned this "rape" of a sister republic and expressed a widespread distrust of American intentions.

Later Relations. To counter the rising wave of anti-Americanism in Latin America, the United States made three unsuccessful efforts to appease Colombia for the loss of Panama by the payment of an indemnity. The first two offers of money payments were refused by Colombia, and the third, negotiated by Bryan, while acceptable to Colombia because it contained an apology for the action taken, was turned down by the United States Senate, where Roosevelt's friends objected to this slur on his name. Another diplomatic problem related to the Canal was occasioned by the Congressional Act of 1912 exempting American coastwise shipping from payment of tolls. Great Britain immediately objected on the grounds that the exemption violated a clause of the Hay-Pauncefote Treaty opening the Canal to the vessels of "all nations" on terms of "entire equality." The British protest pointed out that the exemption would result in placing the entire costs for the Canal and its maintenance on foreign shipping. Both Taft and Congress, however, refused to consider repeal of the tolls act, and discrimination continued until June, 1914, when President Wilson successfully insisted on its abolition. Unrevealed at the time, it appeared later that what the President wanted was British support for his Mexican policy, and that the price the British government demanded for such support was the repeal of the tolls act.

The "Big Stick" Policy. The Canal, built in part to defend the continent, became a major concern of American strategists. As a lock canal it was vulnerable to attack, and because it was surrounded on all sides by weak and unstable states, the United States became increasingly preoccupied with means to defend its "big ditch" against rising European imperial ambitions. Diplomatically, the obvious instrument for defense of the Canal was the Monroe Doctrine, which consequently took on a new significance. In the region surrounding the Canal the United States became far more aggressive, and virtually sought to control the whole Caribbean area. Years before he became President, Theodore Roosevelt had quoted an old African adage: "Speak softly and carry a big stick, and you will go far." Later this statement was resurrected and fittingly applied to his Caribbean policy. This "big stick" policy was spectacularly implemented in the Venezuela crisis of 1902 and in the Dominican affair of 1903–1904.

THE PANAMA CANAL IN CONSTRUCTION

The engineering marvel of its day, construction on the canal was followed eagerly by the American public. This view is of a section of the Gatun Locks.

Despoiled for years by civil wars and acquisitive dictators, Venezuela in 1900 was burdened by a huge European debt on which it was currently paying neither interest nor principal. After all peaceful efforts to obtain a settlement had been blocked by the Venezuelan dictator, Cipriano Castro, the interested European powers determined on armed intervention. But before cooperating, Germany significantly asked what the attitude of the United States would be toward the joint project. The American government replied that the Monroe Doctrine applied only to territory and did not prohibit policing action for the collection of valid debts. Two years later, however, after Great Britain, Germany, and Italy had instituted a blockade of Venezuelan ports, Roosevelt began to doubt the desirability of any type of European policing action in the western hemisphere. German resort to the bombardment of a Venezuelan port and village no doubt influenced him, but he also feared that policing actions might result in America, as they had in China, in territorial

"IS THIS WHAT WE WANT?"

The "big stick" policy did not lack for critics, as this New York World *(August 1, 1904) cartoon on Roosevelt in Santo Domingo clearly indicates.*

IS THIS WHAT WE WANT?

seizures. When the Venezuelan President suggested arbitration, Roosevelt transmitted the proposal to the blockading powers, who accepted it. The case was referred to the Hague Tribunal, which settled the dispute satisfactorily in 1904.

Roosevelt Corollary to the Monroe Doctrine. The Dominican Republic soon provided another opportunity for the President to clarify his interpretation of the Monroe Doctrine. From 1882 to 1899 Ulysses Heureau, an extravagant and ruthless dictator, had ruled that unhappy nation, borrowing heavily on its credit at ruinous rates of interest. By the time of his assassination the resources of the small country, including the customs duties and railroad receipts, were pledged for years ahead. When a revolution broke out in 1903 several European powers threatened to land troops, but the new Dominican President, believing that one intruding nation was preferable to many, asked instead for United States intervention. For over a year Roosevelt delayed. Then, fearing that extensive European intervention might be the prelude to annexation, he acted. Even as troops were landing, Secretary of War Root justified the course by stating, "What we will not permit the great Powers of Europe to do, we will not permit any American Republic to make it necessary for the great Powers of Europe to do." President Roosevelt later amplified Root's remarks in his annual message to Congress in December, 1904. After assuring all Latin-American nations that they need not fear American interference if they maintained internal order and kept their international obligations, Roosevelt stated his famous corollary to the Monroe Doctrine:

> Chronic wrongdoing, or an impotence which results in a general loosening of the ties of civilized society, may in America, as elsewhere, ultimately require intervention by some civilized nation, and in the Western Hemisphere the adherence of the United States to the Monroe Doctrine may force

the United States, however reluctantly, in flagrant cases of such wrongdoing or impotence, to the exercise of an international police power.

Caribbean "Dollar Diplomacy.". The practical terms of the corollary were worked out in the Dominican Republic, where under the shadow of American troops an agreement was signed making the country a virtual protectorate of the United States. By its provisions a United States official was to collect Dominican customs and to apportion them according to a fixed ratio between current expenses and payment of debt. The Dominican government agreed not to increase its debt nor change its customs rates without consent of the United States. Although the Senate failed to approve it, this arrangement continued in force by executive agreement until 1907 when a treaty was ratified containing substantially the same terms.

During the Taft administration American control of the Caribbean was further extended. Secretary Knox pushed intervention into the financial affairs of Central American states to its next logical step. If unpaid European loans to Central America constituted a menace to American interests, why not transfer such loans to American banks? Both public policy and the private banking interests of the nation could thereby be served at the same time. Accordingly, after a revolution in Nicaragua had deposed another dictator, Knox negotiated an executive agreement with the new government providing for the transfer of the national debt from European to American banks. To guarantee the loans would be paid, the same American control of Nicaraguan income was established as existed in the Dominican Republic.

Wilson's Caribbean Policy. Although Woodrow Wilson verbally denounced dollar diplomacy and temporarily abandoned it in the Orient, his administration continued the Roosevelt-Taft formula throughout the Caribbean. For years the United States had been interested in obtaining from Nicaragua exclusive rights in the construction of a canal through its territory. Knox first obtained the privilege in 1913, but the Senate refused to accept the agreement. A year later Wilson's Secretary of State, William Jennings Bryan, negotiated the Bryan-Chamorro Treaty containing all of Knox's concessions, and also giving the United States the exclusive right to lease sites for naval bases on both the Atlantic and the Pacific shores of Nicaragua. This time the Senate ratified.

With the outbreak of the First World War, defense of the Caribbean became even more a concern of the United States. Revolution and anarchy in Haiti ended in 1915 with the landing of American marines and the organization of an American protectorate more extensive in its scope than the one in Nicaragua. A year later a United States military government was instituted in the Dominican Republic against the express wish of the Dominican government. The purchase of the Virgin Islands from Denmark for $25 million in 1917 rounded out the American empire in the Caribbean. Thus by 1917 the United States had come to dominate the Caribbean area.

Motives of American Control. The charge has often been made that United States penetration in the Caribbean after 1900 was primarily motivated by economic reasons. According to this theory, the main end of the Roosevelt-Taft-Wilson policy in this area was to further the investment of surplus American dollars. The motives of any national policy are invariably complex, and the forces arising out of a maturing American capitalism unquestionably helped fashion the United States Caribbean policy in the opening years of the twentieth century. But that is far from saying that economic forces were as important in determining action as were the political considerations of national defense and security. The impoverished Dominican Republic, where Roosevelt first reluctantly intervened, was scarcely an important spot for United States trade and investment. By 1913 American investments there totaled a mere $4 million, and American trade $11 million. Conversely, in Mexico, where significant American investments were imperiled, the Wilson administration refused to intervene.

The Mexican Revolution. For many years before 1910 Mexico had been ruled by the iron-handed dictator, Porfirio Diaz. Supported by the church, the army, and the large landholders, the Diaz regime had been responsible for the breaking up of a communal land system and the creation of a large class of landless peasants. The impoverished masses earned a meager living on the great estates or in the foreign-controlled industries which the dictator assiduously cultivated. By 1910 American investments in Mexico amounted to perhaps $1 billion, representing control of approximately 78 per cent of the mines, 72 per cent of the smelters, and 58 per cent of the oil production. The controlling capital in the rest of the Mexican industries was largely European, particularly British. While the wealth of Mexico was thus being channeled to foreigners and a few favored Mexicans, the masses of the people were held in the bondage of illiteracy and poverty. In 1910, however, a long-smoldering revolution broke out under the leadership of Francisco Madero, a man educated in the United States and with democratic inclinations. Supported by the peasantry and a small group of middle-class merchants, the revolutionary movement broke Diaz's power and placed Madero in the Presidency. This popular movement aimed at the destruction of feudalism and the creation of a democracy, at a redivision of the land among the people, and at drastic curtailment, if not extinction, of the foreign ownership of the nation's wealth. The movement culminated in the Constitution of 1917, of which clause 27 significantly declared that ownership of all the lands, waters, and subsurface wealth of Mexico was vested in the nation and might be expropriated at the need of the nation.

In taking these first steps toward the construction of a modern state, Mexico soon found the way a rough one. After May, 1911, Madero was unable to keep order, since many of his local leaders were more addicted to looting than to reform. Thus he was peculiarly vulnerable to the counterrevolutionary forces made up of the feudal elements in Mexico and the representatives of foreign capital, including members of the diplomatic corps in Mexico City. Among the leaders of this latter faction was Henry Lane Wilson, the American ambassador and a sympathetic friend of American and British investors. Led by a strong man, Victoriano Huerta, the counterrevolutionists seized the government in February, 1913, and threw Madero in jail, where he was murdered a few days later. Publicly congratulating Huerta on his coup, Ambassador Wilson urged that the United States recognize the new government as the major powers of Europe had already done. Recognition by the United States would have greatly strengthened Huerta's position and probably secured his success against the popular forces now being led by Pancho Villa, Emiliano Zapata, and Venustiano Carranza. But Taft refused to act during his last few weeks in power and turned the whole problem over to the incoming President, Woodrow Wilson.

The Mobile Doctrine. On the basis of precedent, recognition of an existing Latin-American government would have been almost automatic. Moreover, since the Huerta government seemed likely to restore order and protect property, most European nations promptly recognized the regime. But Woodrow Wilson made it evident that he was utterly opposed to "that scoundrel Huerta" and to his "despotism" in Mexico. The President recalled Ambassador Wilson and sent John Lind to Mexico City as his special envoy. Lind was instructed to obtain an armistice among the warring factions in Mexico and to gain their consent to a free election in which all the candidates might enter save Huerta. The winner of the election was to be declared President and accorded recognition by the United States. When this plan proved impracticable, American citizens were warned to leave Mexico, and an arms embargo was instituted against all the warring parties, including the Huerta government. The American-Mexican policy, Wilson announced, would be one of "watchful waiting." Then, to rebuke powerful American elements demanding intervention and even the possible annexation of Mexico, the President in a speech delivered at Mobile, October 27, 1913, formulated his so-called Mobile Doctrine. "The United States," he declared flatly, "will never again seek one additional foot of territory by conquest."

"Watchful Waiting." "Watchful waiting" was easier to defend as an ideal than to live up to in practice. When Wilson announced his Mobile Doctrine, strong detachments of the regular army were already mobilized along the Mexican border, and impressive naval units were stationed in Mexican waters. These measures, the first of which was taken before Taft left office, were regarded as essential for the protection of American territory from Mexican marauders, and for the assistance of American citizens desirous of escaping from Mexico to the United States. Wilson's determination to be rid of Huerta led him also to lift the embargo on Huerta's opponents, while retaining it against Huerta. Finally, on the pretext that Huerta had failed to apologize properly for the arrest at Tampico of a group of American sailors, Wilson asked and obtained of Congress permission to take necessary military measures to bring Huerta to terms. On April 22, 1914, American marines and bluejackets took Vera Cruz, occupied the customs house, and prevented the landing of munitions for Huerta from a German ship.

Eighteen Americans and many more Mexicans were killed in the clash. Huerta promptly handed the American charge d'affaires at Mexico City his passport, and the United States prepared for war.

The Niagara Conference. The complete wrecking of "watchful waiting" was prevented by the action of the three leading Latin-American nations, Argentina, Brazil, and Chile, who promptly offered mediation. This Wilson as promptly accepted, and instead of the war a conference was held at Niagara Falls, Canada, in which representatives of the United States and the two leading Mexican factions participated. The Niagara recommendations were of little consequence, but the conference at least afforded the United States an opportunity to welcome the assistance of other American nations in solving the Mexican problem, and, by postponing military action, made possible the peaceful elimination of Huerta, who now realized that he could not win. In July, 1914, Huerta resigned and left the country; in August, Carranza, the favorite of the United States as the best hope of peace, entered the capital. In November of the same year the American occupation of Vera Cruz was terminated, but not until the summer of 1915 did the United States accord Carranza's government full recognition. Arms that Carranza was permitted to purchase in the United States helped the new President to restore order, much to the disgust of other revolutionary factions to whom American manufacturers were forbidden to sell. Carranza's chief opponent, Villa, vented his rage at the United States for this affront by twice crossing the border in 1916 and murdering American citizens. With the consent of Carranza an American military expedition under the command of Brigadier-General John J. Pershing advanced into Mexico in search of Villa, but it failed to catch him, and was presently withdrawn at Carranza's insistence.

Wilson, both at the time and later, was

subjected to severe criticism for his initial interference in the Huerta affair, and for his policy of "watchful waiting." But American involvement in the Mexican revolution had actually begun with the activities of Henry Lane Wilson well before Woodrow Wilson became President of the United States. Ambassador Wilson had tried as hard to commit his government to the support of Huerta as President Wilson tried to bring about the Mexican usurper's downfall. Wilson's subsequent policy on the whole served the cause of peace. It resulted in the loss of several hundred American lives, and perhaps $200 million worth of property, but it fell far short of outright military intervention. In general, it seems reasonable to conclude that Wilson's readiness to intervene in the Caribbean whenever serious European complications threatened, coupled with his reluctance to use a strong policy in Mexico, constitute rather convincing evidence that the over-all American Caribbean policy was dictated largely by strategic considerations, and only secondarily by the need of supporting private American investments.

The Peace Movement. While the United States, before 1914, still believed in its historic policy of isolation and tried in general to hold aloof from European political disputes, many thoughtful Americans had begun to fear that the nation's new overseas commitments might conceivably result in involvements that would lead to war. It did not require much logic to deduce that the surest way to keep the United States out of war was to keep war out of the world, and a strong movement for world peace began. The first Hague Conference, called by the Tsar of Russia in 1899, had already struggled with this problem and had recommended three means for settling disputes without resort to war: (1) through good offices and mediation, which, when offered by a third party to powers at war or about to go to war, must not be considered an unfriendly act; (2)

through international commissions of inquiry, for which so many precedents existed, particularly in the relations between Great Britain and the United States; and (3) through submission to a new court of arbitration to be established at The Hague. Not only did the United States accept the recommendations of the Hague Conference, but President Roosevelt submitted the first case for the Hague Tribunal to decide — an old and unimportant controversy with Mexico — and agreed to the decision.

At the second Hague Conference, held in 1907, the United States began a persistent campaign to commit the nations of the world to the settlement of their disputes by peaceful means. The American delegation worked strenuously, although unavailingly, for the creation of an international court of justice, to which cases could be referred for adjudication. The conference, and a subsequent one at London, drew up a set of rules for the conduct of war on land and sea, but both failed of ratification. Even the United States refused to support a ban on poison gas in armed combat. More fruitful was a model arbitration treaty which all the nations of the world were urged to follow. While Roosevelt was President, Secretary Root negotiated twenty-five treaties providing for the reference of disputes between the signatory nations to the Hague Tribunal, but these agreements were weakened by excluding all questions of "national honor or of grave national interests," precisely the kind of differences that caused most wars. President Taft was also an earnest advocate of arbitration, and during his administration Secretary Knox obtained two treaties, with Great Britain and France respectively, of a more general nature than their predecessors; but unfortunately the United States Senate amended them to death.

Wilson's Secretary of State, Bryan, had spoken to Chautauqua audiences all over the country on the subject of peace, and regarded his cabinet appointment as a direct invitation to further the cause of arbitration. More successful than any of his predecessors, he obtained the ratification of no less than thirty arbitration treaties. Bryan believed that war, if postponed until the period of acute tension had ended, could be averted. His treaties provided for the arbitration by international commissions of all disputes "of whatever character and nature." While the arbitration proceedings were in progress, the participating nations might neither increase their armament nor resort to war. It is worthy of note that by 1914 Bryan had obtained treaties of this nature with every one of the European nations allied against Germany in the First World War, while Germany, Austria, and Turkey had rejected his proposals.

The Algeciras Conference. In general, the United States sought during these prewar years to avoid any direct participation in European diplomacy, but Theodore Roosevelt no doubt involved his country far more deeply in European affairs than most Americans realized when he took part in the settlement of the Moroccan crisis of 1905–1906. This threat to European peace was precipitated when the German Emperor made a threatening speech at Tangier in March, 1905. By a secret understanding Great Britain and France had agreed to support each other in their determination to dominate Egypt and Morocco. But in Morocco the French intentions ran squarely against an old treaty which Germany and even the United States had signed, the terms of which guaranteed a commercial open door in the North African country to all nations. War appeared likely when Germany demanded an international conference on the subject and France refused to agree. After much belligerent talk from each side, the Kaiser asked the United States, as the foremost defender of the open-door principle, to help promote the conference, and this Roosevelt eventually did. But in his instructions to Henry

ELIHU ROOT

Outstanding as an organizer of the new American Empire, Root was first Secretary of War, then Secretary of State in Theodore Roosevelt's Cabinet.

White, the representative of the United States at the conference, the President directed that nothing should be done to break up the Anglo-French entente, and that White should help France "get what she ought to have."

When the conference finally took place at Algeciras, Spain, in January, 1906, it decided against the open-door principle and accorded to France a victory on all important points. For one of its decisions, that the port of Casablanca should not be turned over to Germany, Roosevelt took personal credit. He deeply distrusted Germany and was strongly opposed to the establishment of such a German outpost so close to the western hemisphere. Of more lasting importance, by consistently supporting Great Britain and France, Roosevelt served notice on Germany that in the future she would probably be outvoted in any similar world conference. Without knowing at the time how partisan the United States had been at Algeciras, many Americans were plainly uneasy about the affair. In ratifying the Algeciras convention the Senate emphasized this feeling by stating that the United States took no responsibility for the enforcement of the pact, and further that the action did not in any way change the historic American policy "which forbids participation by the United States in settlement of political questions which are entirely European in their scope."

Roosevelt's successors retreated somewhat from the advanced position he had taken and showed a greater reluctance to break with long-established tradition. Taft notably abstained from interfering either in the second Moroccan incident of 1911 or in the Turko-Italian war that followed. To him these matters were not of "direct political concern" to the American nation. Woodrow Wilson followed the same course during the Balkan wars of 1913. Except for the Algeciras episode the United States thus clung to its traditional isolation from purely European disputes until after the outbreak of the First World War.

SELECTED BIBLIOGRAPHY

H. K. Beale, *Theodore Roosevelt and the Rise of America to World Power* (1956), is a series of valuable lectures; the author's untimely death cut short a projected multivolume biography. H. F. Pringle, *Theodore Roosevelt* (1931), was for many years the most influential biography; it is severely critical in tone, especially in foreign policy. W. H. Harbaugh, *The Life and Times of Theodore Roosevelt* (*Power and Responsibility*) (1961), is an excellent study, more friendly than Pringle, yet not uncritical. G. W. Chessman, *Governor Theodore Roosevelt* (1965), is a full-scale study of a neglected episode in T. R.'s life. G. E. Mowry, *The Era of Theodore Roosevelt, 1900–1912* (1958), is a general survey of the period; it contains chapters on foreign policy and a full bibliography. Of great scholarly importance is *The Letters of Theodore Roosevelt*, superbly edited by E. E. Morison and others (8 vols., 1951–1954). A brief, brilliant reinterpretation is *The Republican Roosevelt* (1954) by J. M. Blum, one of those who worked on the *Letters* project. Useful for foreign affairs in T. R.'s second term is P. C. Jessup, *Elihu Root* (2 vols., 1938); see also the brief life by R. W. Leopold, *Elihu Root and the Conservative Tradition* (1954).

On relations with Japan, see: P. J. Treat, *Diplomatic Relations between the United States and Japan, 1895–1905* (2 vols., 2nd ed.,

1938); A. L. P. Dennis, *The Anglo-Japanese Alliance* (1923); and J. A. White, *The Diplomacy of the Russo-Japanese War* (1964). Useful special studies include: T. A. Bailey, *Theodore Roosevelt and the Japanese-American Crises* (1934); R. W. Paul, *The Abrogation of the Gentlemen's Agreement* (1936); and Roger Daniels, *The Politics of Prejudice: The Anti-Japanese Movement in California and the Struggle for Japanese Exclusion* (1962). An interesting monograph on a related subject is E. H. Zabriskie, *American-Russian Rivalry in the Far East, 1895–1914* (1946).

On Canadian relations there are a number of good books, among them, R. C. Brown, *Canada's National Policy, 1883–1900* (1964); C. C. Tansill, *Canadian-American Relations, 1895–1911* (1943); and P. E. Corbett, *The Settlement of Canadian-American Disputes* (1937). Allan Nevins, *Henry White* (1930), sheds light on the subject of the Alaskan boundary dispute. An important episode in the Taft administration is treated in L. E. Ellis, *Reciprocity, 1911* (1939).

On inter-American problems, interesting fresh material may be found in T. F. McGann, *Argentina, the United States, and the Inter-American System, 1880–1914* (1957). Generally useful on the Caribbean region are: J. F. Rippy, *The Caribbean Danger Zone* (1940); W. H. Callcott, *The Caribbean Policy of the United States, 1890–1920* (1942); and C. L. Jones, *The United States and the Caribbean*

* Available in paperback

(1929). Also valuable are: H. C. Hill, *Roosevelt and the Caribbean* (1927); E. T. Parks, *Colombia and the United States* (1935); and A. P. Whitaker, *The United States and South America, The Northern Republics* (1948). A recent defense of American policies is D. G. Munro, *Intervention and Dollar Diplomacy in the Caribbean, 1900–1921* (1964).

The literature on the Panama Canal is extensive. Among the more important diplomatic studies are: N. J. Padelford, *The Panama Canal in Peace and War* (1942); M. W. Williams, *Anglo-American Isthmian Diplomacy, 1815–1915* (1916); and W. D. McCain, *The United States and the Republic of Panama* (1937). On the building of the canal see: J. B. and Farnham Bishop, *Goethals* (1930); J. M. Gibson, *Physician to the World; The Life of General William C. Gorgas* (1950); and M. P. DuVal, Jr., *And the Mountains Will Move* (1947), which emphasizes the engineering problems.

On Mexican relations, a valuable general survey is H. F. Cline, **The United States and Mexico* (2nd ed., 1963). A popularly written, highly critical biography is Carleton Beals, *Porfirio Diaz* (1932). Interesting sidelights are contained in Edith O'Shaughnessy, *Intimate Pages of Mexican History* (1920). Case studies are set forth in D. M. Pletcher, *Rails, Mines and Progress: Seven American Promoters in Mexico, 1867–1911* (1958). Special studies treating Wilson's Mexican policy include: G. M. Stephenson, *John Lind of Minnesota* (1935); C. C. Clendenen, *The United States and Pancho Villa* (1961); R. E. Quirk, **An Affair of Honor; Woodrow Wilson and the Occupation of Vera Cruz* (1962), and **The Mexican Revolution, 1914–1915* (1960). See also J. M. Callahan, *American Foreign Policy in Mexican Relations* (1932); and Harold Nicolson, *Dwight Morrow* (1935). Important studies include: Ernest Gruening, *Mexico and Its Heritage* (1928); Frank Tannenbaum, *Mexico, the Struggle for Peace and Bread* (1950); and Anita Brenner, *The Wind That Swept Mexico* (1943).

On the Algeciras Conference, see E. N. Anderson, *The First Moroccan Crisis, 1904–1906* (1930). J. B. Scott, *The Hague Peace Conferences of 1899 and 1907* (2 vols., 1909), may now be supplemented by the new monograph by C. DeA. Davis, *The United States and the First Hague Peace Conference* (1962).

30

THE PROGRESSIVE
MOVEMENT

ও *The Reform Spirit* · *The Muckrakers* · *Conservatism and Progressivism* · *City and State Reform* · *Theodore Roosevelt as President* · *The Trust Problem* · *Railroad Regulation* · *The Pure Food Act* · *Labor and the Square Deal* · *Conservation* · *The Panic of 1907*

The Reform Spirit. The years from 1900 to 1916 saw the rise of a reform movement in the United States that affected every aspect and every level of American life. Just as in the Jacksonian period, the spirit of reform captured the public conscience. Some of the momentum of this reform movement came from the Populists, whose party had practically disappeared by the turn of the century, but many of whose principles were espoused alike by Bryan Democrats and Roosevelt Republicans. Unlike the Populist schemes, which were almost solely supported by farmers, the reforms of the progressive age were backed by large sections of labor, by many wealthy individuals, businessmen, and in particular by the urban middle classes. Why so many well-to-do people should lend themselves to reform may seem inexplicable at first glance. But the years after the Civil War

had seen the spectacular rise of big business, which not only dominated many parts of the government but also threatened the existence of many small businesses. Simultaneously, the growing labor unions and a rising support for European socialism threatened the small owner from another direction. At the turn of the century small businessmen, members of the free professions, and the white collar classes in general were also extremely uneasy about their social as well as their economic position. The rise of the great trusts had been accompanied by the rise in the social power and prestige of their owners. Onetime independent lawyers, newspaper editors, and scores of other professionals, including many politicians, were now employees of the reigning capitalists. This "status revolution" had not taken place without resentment. Might not reform, the dispossessed professional and small businessman asked, curb the power of the great corporations and the corporate magnate, and also stop the inroads of unions and of socialism among the working people? In part the progressive movement was an attempt to preserve the status of this middle segment, not only economically but socially and politically as well. Thus in a way the reform movement was conservative, since it was directed toward retaining individual values in an increasingly organized society.

Important business groups also contributed to the reform impulse with a view to securing a more equitable and efficient economy, one more in harmony with the urban and industrial world of the twentieth century. Many shippers, large and small, were in favor of railroad regulation to insure equal rates and service between the geographical sections of the country as well as between individual shippers. Middle-western and western bankers supported the demand for monetary reform in part to decrease their dependence upon eastern banks and in part to insure a more adequate supply of credit during stringent times. Some easterners were in favor of curbing the reckless western exploitation of natural resources by national conservation legislation. And much local urban reform dealing with utilities and public health was supported by business classes in the interest of social efficiency. The development of social Christianity, the emphasis that Darwinism gave to environment, and the rising power of women in social and moral questions also help explain the reform spirit of the American middle classes in a reasonably prosperous age.

The Muckrakers. The new awakening also owed much to the "muckrakers," a group of energetic journalists who made it their chief concern to discover and exploit in popular articles the seamy side of business and political behavior. They were given their name by Roosevelt, who was by no means unsympathetic to their work, but who compared the most sensational of them to the character in *Pilgrim's Progress* "who could look no way but downward with the muckrake in his hands." A vehicle was available for the muckrakers in the new popular magazines: *McClure's, Cosmopolitan, Everybody's, American, Pearson's, Munsey's, Arena,* and a number of others. Through these journals Ida M. Tarbell exposed the "History of the Standard Oil Company," Lincoln Steffens, "The Shame of the Cities," Thomas Lawson, "Frenzied Finance," Charles Edward Russell, "The Beef Trust," Ray Stannard Baker, "The Railroads on Trial," and so on through an almost interminable list of titles. Numerous writers of muckraking tendencies, including Winston Churchill, David Graham Phillips, William Allen White, and Upton Sinclair, produced popular novels which inquired into politics, labor conditions, and social questions. Of particular importance in securing the passage of the Pure Food Act was Sinclair's *Jungle* (1906), which graphically and in nauseating detail described the unsanitary conditions in the great Chicago meat packing houses.

Conservatism. During the last half of the nineteenth century a majority of Americans had believed that social health depended upon a minimum of governmental interference with business and the individual. According to this theory the "natural law" of competition operating in a free market would send the able and virtuous men to the top, while the misfits would sink to the bottom. Since they were able, the group at the top naturally assumed that they should dominate the government either directly or through their agents. Anything that threatened this rule either in the economic or the political sphere was considered socially bad. In denouncing the unions as evil, during the coal strike of 1902, the capitalist George F. Baer was quite sincere when he told the workers they should put their trust in the "Christian men to whom God in His infinite wisdom has given control of the property interest of the country." Men of such beliefs naturally felt increasingly that the government should help the economic and moral laws along by granting such aid as tariffs to aspiring businessmen. In broad terms, such was the conservative view at the turn of the century.

The Progressive Creed. The Populists had believed that this sort of governmental friendliness to big business and neutrality to the rest of the people was as unfair individually as it was harmful socially. They favored instead a government representative of — and dominated by — a majority of the people who would use it to assist them in troubled times. With this Populist view the progressives agreed. However much they differed on the means to achieve their ends, practically all of them insisted that government should clearly reflect the majority will and that the often corrupt business control over government should be broken. Most progressives also felt that the most ruthless economic activity of big business ought to be curbed and that opportunity for the small businessman, the farmer, and the laborer to make their way up in the world should be increased. Women and children, and other groups who could not fend for themselves in a harsh, competitive urban world, should be protected. The more morally minded among them even insisted that men should be restrained from gambling and drinking. To secure these ends, progressives believed, the state should intervene as a regulatory and protective agency.

There was, of course, much difference of opinion among progressives as to the limits of governmental interference in the life of its citizens. Some insisted that the government need only break up the monopolies by antitrust laws. Others, at the opposite extreme, accepted many socialistic ideas that had first been brought to America from Europe far back in the nineteenth century. Because opportunity was widespread in America, such socialistic ideas had long had scant appeal. During the early nineties a Socialist Labor Party, founded by Daniel De Leon, made a few converts. But it was not until the formation of the more conservative Social Democratic or Socialist Party, which nominated Eugene V. Debs for President in 1900, that the movement had any real influence.

Municipal Reform. Reforms in municipal government marked the beginnings of the progressive movement. The Tammany machine in New York was no worse than many others, only better advertised. Lincoln Steffens' articles made the "shame of the cities" better known than ever before, but reformers had already arisen to correct the situations Steffens described. In Toledo Samuel M. Jones, better known as "Golden Rule" Jones, made successful war upon the private-contract system and advocated the municipal ownership of public utilities. In most American cities transportation, gas, electricity, and water facilities were then owned by private concerns doing business under long-term franchises secured from the city government. Since the returns from such monopolies were enormous, bribery and corruption often accompanied their granting. The "gas and water socialism" of the reform mayors was often inspired as much by the desire for clean government as by a demand for more economical and efficient service. Elected to office in 1897, Jones was repeatedly re-elected, and in 1904 was succeeded by his friend and disciple, Brand Whitlock, who continued the good work. In Cleveland Thomas L. Johnson became mayor in 1901. A convinced "single-taxer," he secured among other reforms a long-overdue reassessment of property values, municipal control of the streetcar system, and a three-cent fare. Under his regime Cleveland could claim to be the "best governed city in the United States," a claim that Milwaukee, under the Socialist leadership of Emil Seidel and Daniel W. Hoan, soon challenged.

To many thoughtful critics the reform of city government could best be promoted by a change in the system. City administration was primarily a business affair; why should it be hampered by a form of government patterned after that of the United States? Why should the Democrats and the Republicans run opposing tickets for city offices? In 1901 the city of Galveston,

Texas, which the year before had been destroyed by a tidal wave, was in desperate need of efficient government, and tried to obtain it by turning over its administration to a commission of five, each of whom headed up a separate department of city affairs. Soon many other cities were experimenting with the "commission form" of government, and Staunton, Virginia, developed an even more reasonable scheme, the "city manager" plan. This system sought to duplicate the methods of the business corporation. The elected board or commission employed a manager, who ran the city with the same freedom of action that was normally accorded a business executive. Soon hundreds of American cities, large and small, were being administered, usually more efficiently than before, by commissions and city managers. But thousands adhered to the old systems, and in all too many instances to the old ways.

The most spectacular of the reforms of this period occurred in the realm of state, rather than city, government. Reformers observed that the state governments were almost completely in the control of whatever big business corporations happened to be most powerful in their particular part of the country. Well-oiled party machines did the bidding of the state "boss," and the "boss" in turn supported the business interests that furnished the oil for his machine. Speaking before the New York Constitutional Convention of 1915, Elihu Root remarked:

> Mr. Platt ruled the state; for nigh upon twenty years he ruled it. It was not the governor; it was not the legislature; it was Mr. Platt. And the capital was not here [at Albany]; it was at 49 Broadway. . . . The ruler of the state during the greater part of the forty years of my acquaintance with the state government has not been any man authorized by the constitution or by law. . . . The party leader is elected by no one, accountable to no one, bound by no oath of office, removable by no one. . . . I don't criticize the men of the invisible government. . . . But it is all wrong.

ROBERT MARION LA FOLLETTE

After serving as governor of Wisconsin, La Follette was elected in 1905 to the United States Senate, and served there until the time of his death.

For a reformer to be elected to a governorship under such conditions was in itself a revolution; once in office his only chance of remaining there was to break the power of the machine.

Robert M. La Follette. Outstanding among the reform governors of the period was Robert M. La Follette (1855–1925) of Wisconsin, a man whose influence upon the course of political events during his lifetime was more widespread than that of many Presidents. "Fighting Bob," as he came to be called, had entered politics, without benefit of machine assistance, as a county prosecutor, soon after his graduation from the University of Wisconsin in 1879. In 1884 he was nominated and elected for the first of three successive terms in the national House of Representatives. He was an indefatigable canvasser, delighted in controversy, and developed political speechmaking to a fine art. Like many another Republican he was defeated in the national elections of 1890. His ambitions for a career in state politics, however, might easily have been gratified but for a controversy with the all-powerful Senator Philetus Sawyer, who was both a politician and a lumber baron. According to the La Follette version of the story, Sawyer attempted through La Follette to bribe the judge — a Democratic brother-in-law of La Follette — before whom a fraud case was to be tried. Deeply incensed, La Follette made the whole matter public, and helped the state recover the funds of which it had been defrauded.

From that time on La Follette was a crusader for reform. Determined to win the governorship, he was repeatedly denied the nomination in spite of a growing popular sentiment in his favor; not until 1900 was he able to line up a majority of the convention delegates. Thereafter he built up a most successful machine of his own dedicated to reform. Elected, and twice re-elected, he forced through reluctant legislatures laws for the more effective taxation of the railroads and other corporations; for the establishment of direct primaries through which the people, not boss-ridden conventions, could select their own candidates for office; for prohibiting state officials from accepting free passes from railroads; and for the conservation of the natural resources of the state in forests and water power. In his quest of good government he enlisted the aid of experts from the University of Wisconsin, whose new president, Charles R. Van Hise, was his close personal friend. He was instrumental, also, in the creation of a Legislative Reference Bureau through which legislators might obtain expert advice on the drafting of bills.

Other Crusaders. The "Wisconsin idea," which fundamentally aimed at freeing the state from business domination through venal party bosses and turning over public administration to popularly chosen leaders willing to seek the advice of experts, exactly suited the temper of the times. Governors in other states duplicated in varying degrees the La Follette record in Wisconsin. In Missouri Joseph W. Folk won public attention as a circuit attorney by successfully prosecuting the corrupt ring of St. Louis "boodlers" that for years had fattened on municipal graft. As governor for four years after 1905, he sought with moderate success to repeat in the state arena what he had done for his home city. In New York Charles Evans Hughes became a national figure while serving as counsel for a legislative investigating committee that was examining the methods of the New York life insurance companies. Hughes's sensational disclosures brought about abrupt and sweeping changes in the insurance business and led to his election as governor in 1906. In California the star of Hiram Johnson began to rise. As early as 1902 he attracted attention as a member of the staff of prosecuting attorneys in charge of some San Francisco "boodling" cases. In 1908 he secured the conviction of Abe Ruef, grafting municipal boss, after the original prosecutor had been shot in the line of duty. In 1910 Johnson was elected governor, and determined above all else to end the domination of the state by the political minions of the Southern Pacific Railroad. The roll of reform governors included also A. B. Cummins of Iowa, John A. Johnson of Minnesota, and many lesser lights, while numerous private individuals, such as William S. U'Ren of Oregon, crusader for "the Oregon system," also battled for reform in state government.

The Direct Primary. The most fundamental of the political reforms effected during these years was the substitution of the direct primary for the convention system of making nominations. Under the old system, the original caucuses or "primaries" by which convention delegates were chosen were attended by only a small fraction of the voters, certainly never more than 15 per cent, and a large proportion of these were local officeholders and aspirants to office. This made it easy for the machine to secure a working majority of the delegates to almost every convention, and to put through the "slate" of nominees agreed upon by the leaders in advance. The direct primary, however, substituted voting at the polls by secret ballot for the caucus-convention system and thus reduced the chances of machine manipulation. Within a comparatively short time after the passage in 1903 of the Wisconsin primary law, similar laws had been enacted by nearly every state in the Union. The results were gratifying to the reformers. The new laws greatly promoted the possibility of successful popular uprisings against corrupt machines, and because of them in state after state men were elected to office who under the old system would never have had a chance.

Initiative, Referendum, and Recall. The initiative and referendum were twin measures of popular government that might be used as clubs over legislatures unresponsive to the popular will. By these devices laws could be initiated by petition, and voted on by ballot. The use of the referendum for constitutional provisions and for such local legislation as the flotation of bond issues was by no means new, but its application to ordinary lawmaking, coupled with the power of popular initiative, was decidedly an innovation. The initiative and referendum were first adopted in South Dakota in 1898, but obtained their best test in Oregon, where from 1902 to 1910 no less than thirty-two measures were referred to the people for a vote. In Oregon, too, the recall, a measure by which faithless officials, on petition of a stipulated number or percentage of the voters, were required to stand for re-election at special elections, was given a thorough trial. Indeed, "the Oregon system" came to be the term most commonly used to describe the innovations in popular government. Largely because of U'Ren's effective leadership, Oregon adopted the Australian ballot in 1891, a registration law in 1899, the initiative and referendum law in 1902, the direct primary in 1904, a sweeping corrupt-practices act in 1908, and the recall in 1910. Within a decade nearly twenty states had the initiative and referendum, and nearly a dozen the recall. Acceptance of "the Oregon system" moved in general from west to east, and in the older states often met unyielding opposition.

Direct Election of Senators. Even the federal government was affected by state reforms. Preferential primaries were introduced whereby the voters might express their choices for United States senators. These laws assumed that in senatorial elections state legislatures would be guided solely by the popular mandate, and regardless of personal or party considerations would elect the primary winner to the senatorship. The movement for direct election of United States senators dated far back into the nineteenth century, and had won warm support not only from the Populists, but from many conservative citizens as well. Four times, in 1894, 1898, 1900, and 1902, the House of Representatives had supported a constitutional amendment for the direct election of senators, but each time the Senate had refused to concur. Meantime the scandals involved in legislative elections became increasingly flagrant. At best, state legislation in years when a senator was to be chosen tended to be treated as of secondary importance; at worst, open bribery was resorted to by individuals and corporations bent on the success of a candidate friendly to their interests.

Undoubtedly the framers of the Constitution had intended that the upper chamber should represent not merely the individual states, but also the wealth of the nation. They had built better than they knew. By the twentieth century the United States Senate could be spoken of, without great exaggeration, as a "millionaire's club." Men of great wealth aspired to a seat in it as a crowning evidence of success. Corporations with privileges to protect made every effort to secure a senatorship for one of their directors, or at least for one of their attorneys. Party bosses themselves often sought and obtained election to the Senate. The general level of intelligence in the upper chamber was high — has perhaps never been higher — but the senators, so critics insisted, represented the vested interests of the country rather than the people as a whole. In 1906 David Graham Phillips wrote a series of articles for *Cosmopolitan,* entitled "The Treason of the Senate." Although his language was so violent that it brought forth a denunciation by Theodore Roosevelt in which the President first used the term "muckraker," Phillips' facts were accurate, and the old system for the selection of senators began to totter. Naturally the Senate refused, as long as it dared, to risk the results of popular election. But the preferential primaries, which eventually were adopted by more than half the states, brought about by indirection the change that the Senate had tried to avoid. Further, as popularly chosen senators took their seats, the opposition to direct election was broken down. By 1912 the Senate submitted to the inevitable and agreed to the Seventeenth Amendment, which a year later became a part of the Constitution.

The reforms of the Roosevelt era in state and city government also helped those who wished to enlist the aid of the law in the improvement of social conditions. No longer so deferential to the rich man's point of view, and unhampered by the constitutional limitations that restricted the activities of the national government, the states crowded their statute books with laws that had rarely or never been obtainable before. A large part of the new legislation was designed to promote the "square deal" for labor, but other important subjects, particularly the prohibition of the liquor traffic, were considered.

Labor Legislation. Perhaps the most important of the new labor laws was the series of employer's liability, or workmen's compensation, acts that followed Maryland's first feeble attempt at such legislation in 1902. These acts were designed to reverse the old common-law rule that a workman had to prove negligence on the part of his employer in order to obtain compensation for injuries, and that even this might be insufficient if he himself, or any "fellow-servant," had been guilty of contributory negligence. The new principle, which by 1921 had been accepted in all but six states, was that in hazardous occupations the employer was liable for all injuries that occurred to his employees while they were at work. As a result of the new laws, millions of dollars were soon paid out each year in benefits to injured workmen or their families.

Efforts were made also to increase the protection given to women and children in industry. Most of the states eventually adopted laws forbidding in certain types of industry the employment of children under fourteen years of age, while laws for compulsory school attendance accomplished the same purpose in another way. Opposition from the southern textile industries caused some of the southern states to lag either in the enactment or in the enforcement of child-labor laws, and as early as 1906 a movement was begun to give Congress authority over child labor by a constitutional amendment. Such an amendment was actually submitted in 1924, but it failed of ratification. Laws limiting the number of hours per day that women and children might be employed, and fixing minimum-wage schedules that they must be paid, were also enacted by some states. Attempts to extend these same principles to employed men met with stronger opposition, but a few successes were recorded.

In the whole field of labor legislation the United States still lagged far behind European nations.

Prohibition. Attempts by prohibitionists to abolish the liquor traffic date to a much earlier period, but the era of successful activity began with the formation of the Woman's Christian Temperance Union in 1874 and, in particular, the Anti-Saloon League in 1893. The latter received the active support of all the evangelical sects, and was maintained by the funds its agents were permitted to collect at regular church services. Its methods came to be quite as ruthless as those of the politicians with whom it had to deal. It knew only one test for fitness to hold office. If a man favored the liquor traffic, the Anti-Saloon League was against him. With a budget that by 1903 had reached $400,000 a year, the League was in a position to hire hundreds of organizers and to maintain scores of offices. For a generation, under the leadership of Wayne B. Wheeler and William H. Anderson, it made "wet" or "dry" take precedence over nearly every other issue in state and local politics. Between a low license fee and a higher one, the League favored the higher. Between a high license and "local option," whereby a town or county might vote to exclude saloons, it supported local option. Between local option and state-wide prohibition, it was for state-wide prohibition. And between state-wide prohibition and national prohibition, it advocated national prohibition. Never too squeamish about its methods or political bedfellows, it took what it could get.

It got a great deal. Its first successes were mainly confined to the rural districts and were obtained by local option, but before Roosevelt left office four southern states had voted "dry," and within the next few years many others, northern as well as southern, were to follow. By the First World War, nearly half the people of the United States lived in "dry" territory, while in three-fourths of its total area the saloon had been outlawed. The ratification of the Eighteenth Amendment to the Constitution in 1919 merely completed a process that had been long under way.

Woman Suffrage. Woman suffrage was a companion reform to prohibition. If women obtained the vote, so prohibitionists reasoned, they would with certainty aid the temperance cause. In 1869 the Territory of Wyoming had conferred the suffrage on women, and by 1911 six western states, Wyoming, Colorado, Utah, Idaho, Washington, and California, had accepted the innovation *in toto*, while many other states gave women the right to vote in certain elections. Like the prohibitionists, the suffragists hoped to crown their efforts by obtaining an amendment to the Constitution that would end the denial of the suffrage to women, and, while adding state after state to their lists of converts, they continued to work on Congress. An outbreak of "militancy," borrowed from "suffragettes" in Great Britain, may have had something to do with bringing Congress to yield in 1919. The Nineteenth Amendment became a part of the Constitution in 1920.

The movements for prohibition and woman suffrage were attended by a great variety of reforms designed to promote the public health and happiness. New building codes were devised, and public parks and playgrounds were multiplied. Renewed efforts were made to wipe out gambling and prostitution. Special courts were established to deal with juvenile delinquency. Divorce laws were relaxed. Legal discriminations against women, aside from the suffrage, were almost everywhere abolished. Most of these laws, like prohibition and the labor codes, depended for their constitutionality upon the "police power"; that is, the right of the state to do whatever might be necessary to promote the health, happiness, and morality of its citizens. Such laws frequently interfered seriously with the full freedom of individuals and led to an enormous amount of litigation. The courts, almost invariably hostile in the beginning, eventually relented, and in nearly every instance granted a grudging approval to the measures that the public desired.

Theodore Roosevelt.   Just as this broad reform movement was getting under way, Theodore Roosevelt (1858–1919) became President at the death of McKinley on September 14, 1901. Well-born, well-educated, well-to-do, the new President in his youth had disdained the life of a rich man's son, and in 1881, as a representative in the state legislature of New York, had entered politics "at the bottom of the ladder." A few years later, however, he considered rejecting a political career and began to spend part of each year on a Dakota ranch. But in 1886 he consented to make the hopeless race as Republican candidate for mayor of New York. His defeat was assuaged by his appointment by President Harrison to the Civil Service Commission, where for six years he did outstandingly effective work. In 1895, he became president of the New York Police Board, where again he acquitted himself well. In spite of his active political life, he wrote extensively, sometimes of his ranch and hunting exploits, but more often books of American history and biography. He re-entered national politics in 1896 by campaigning enthusiastically for McKinley, and after McKinley's inauguration served as Assistant Secretary of the Navy. As a war hero Roosevelt was elected governor of New York in 1898 and Vice-President in 1900. Never a dependable party regular, and given to impetuous statements and sometimes actions on all manner of questions, the new President was immediately suspect to the more conservative element of his party, who disliked his mystical nationalism, his often expressed sympathy for the disinherited, and his obvious preference for men of letters, artists, and soldiers to the businessman or financier. They were

also apprehensive about his gradually evolving view that the state should protect large segments of the population against ruthless competition and his Jacksonian conviction that the President, representing all the people, should take a major part in the formulation of such legislative policy. Roosevelt was no radical. But whether from a fear of rising socialism or of a dominant corporate collectivism, or simply from his own sense of justice, he became convinced that many changes had to be made in American political life. Conservatives, of course, could be expected to oppose most of these views; indeed, some of them had helped to make him Vice-President as a means of insuring an end to his political career.

Roosevelt as President.   To the confusion of his critics, Roosevelt took over his new duties in perfect good taste and even promised "to continue absolutely unbroken the policies of President McKinley." Especially reassuring was his decision to retain McKinley's Cabinet, for whatever his faults, McKinley had proved himself to be an able judge of men. Two of the advisers on whom Roosevelt was to depend most, John Hay, Secretary of State, and Elihu Root, Secretary of War, were already in the Cabinet, while a third, William Howard Taft, had been picked by McKinley for the difficult task of inaugurating civil government in the Philippines. Roosevelt even sought with some success to appease Mark Hanna, now Senator from Ohio, although, as both knew, the personal gulf between them was very wide. It was inevitable that eventually Roosevelt was to be his own President. For the most part McKinley had been content to follow public opinion, but aggressive leadership was an integral part of the Roosevelt personality. Fortunately the new President embodied to a remarkable degree the interests and prejudices of the average American. When he sought to lead there was no dearth of followers.

The Trust Problem Again. Economics was definitely not Roosevelt's forte, but he would have been blind indeed if he had not recognized in the emergence of "big business" a problem of fundamental importance to his administration. In one industry after another great corporations, successfully claiming the rights of persons before the law, had grown to monopolistic proportions. The total capital of million-dollar corporations had increased from $170 million in 1897 to $5 billion in 1900, and to $20.5 billion in 1904. Railway mergers, such as the one by which E. H. Harriman brought the Union Pacific and the Southern Pacific together in 1900, had become the order of the day. Concentration in industry was effected both by means of "horizontal" combinations, through which several industries of the same kind were united, and by means of "vertical" combinations, through which business of allied interests joined forces. Of the latter type was the United States Steel Corporation, the first of America's billion-dollar companies, which J. P. Morgan helped knit together in 1901. What happened to steel happened also in greater or lesser degree to tobacco, petroleum, sugar, copper, beef, starch, flour, whiskey, and innumerable other commodities. Among the rulers of these great corporations there was a close community of interest, and since most of the mergers were arranged by financiers, a few great banking firms, notably the house of Morgan, came to occupy a commanding position in the nation's business structure.

Northern Securities Case. Roosevelt's first action against the trusts was taken in February, 1902, when his Attorney General announced that suit was being brought under the terms of the Sherman Antitrust Act to dissolve the Northern Securities Company, through which the year before a merger of three northwestern railroads, the Great Northern, the Northern Pacific, and the Chicago, Burlington & Quincy, had been attempted. If the government could

AMERICAN WOMEN DEMAND THE VOTE

Dr. Anna Howard Shaw (1847–1919), a physician and Methodist minister who was president of the National American Woman Suffrage Association from 1904 to 1915, favored dignified and orderly methods in the fight for the right to vote. Her views are clearly expressed in the following passage from her autobiography:

There has never been any sympathy among American suffragists for the militant suffrage movement in England, and personally I am wholly opposed to it. I do not believe in war in any form; and if violence on the part of men is undesirable in achieving their ends, it is much more so on the part of women; for women never appear to less advantage than in physical combats with men. As for militancy in America, no generation that attempted it could win. No victory could come to us in any state where militant methods were tried. They are undignified, unworthy — in other words, unAmerican.

ANNA HOWARD SHAW, *The Story of a Pioneer* (1915), Harper and Row

induce the Supreme Court to support it in this instance, Roosevelt believed that he might later make the Sherman Act a more effective weapon in arresting the trend toward monopoly. The organizers of the Northern Securities Company, James J. Hill and J. P. Morgan, believed that they had remained within the letter of the law, but a decision of the Supreme Court, reached in 1904, by abandoning the reasoning of the Knight case, held otherwise. According to the majority of the Court the Northern Securities Company was a violation of free competition within the meaning of the Sherman Act, and must be dissolved. The decision did not stop business consolidation since the business community soon found other ways to cooperate, but the psychological effect upon the public was profound.

Gleeful at having induced the Court to reverse itself, and acclaimed by the public as a "trust-buster," Roosevelt went ahead with other prosecutions. A total of twenty-five indictments were brought by the Department of Justice during his administration, and in a few instances the government scored victories. Eventually Roosevelt

came to distinguish between "good trusts," which showed a proper concern for the welfare of the consumer, and "bad trusts," which sought only selfish ends. The latter he prosecuted, the former he let alone. The Supreme Court, in "the rule of reason" it adopted in 1911, came to about the same conclusion. Only when the monopolistic actions of trusts "unreasonably" interfered with interstate commerce would the Court hold against them. By allowing itself this wide latitude, the Court was free to ignore mere "bigness," while at the same time punishing the misuse of power that great size made possible.

But this more selective use of the Sherman Act failed to achieve the desired results. As the government proceeded against one trust after another, monopolies still seemed to grow. Long before Roosevelt left office he had de-emphasized "trust-busting" by asking for federal incorporation and regulation of all interstate business.

Railroad Regulation. Roosevelt's efforts to obtain regulatory laws from Congress most nearly approached success with

> *The 26th President's avocations were legion: he was by turn a historian, rancher, naturalist, conservationist, soldier, and politician. But it was his championship of the rights of individual Americans against the growing power of trusts and monopolies which gained him the enthusiastic support of his reform-minded contemporaries.*

A democracy can be such in fact only if there is some rough approximation to similarity in stature among the men composing it . . . a simple and poor society can exist as a democracy on a basis of sheer individualism. But a rich and complex industrial society cannot so exist; for some individuals, and especially those artificial individuals called corporations, become so very big that the ordinary individual is utterly dwarfed beside them, and cannot deal with them on terms of equality. It therefore becomes necessary for these ordinary individuals to combine in their turn, first in order to act in their collective capacity through that biggest of all combinations called the Government, and second, to act, also in their own self-defense, through private combinations, such as farmers' associations and trade unions.

THEODORE ROOSEVELT, *An Autobiography* (1913), Charles Scribner's Sons

reference to the railroads. The Interstate Commerce Commission, established in 1887, but hampered repeatedly by court decisions, had been singularly ineffective, and without a new grant of powers it could never hope to cope with the great mergers that had taken place since its creation. First, the rebate evil was curbed by the Elkins Act of 1903, which was supported even by many railroad companies. Then a new Department of Commerce and Labor was set up, with a fact-finding Bureau of Corporations designed to ferret out questionable corporation practices. Finally, with strong presidential support, the Hepburn Act, which added immeasurably to the power and prestige of the Interstate Commerce Commission, became law in 1906. No longer did the commission have to go to court to enforce an order; now the carrier had either to accept the rates set by the commission or go to court itself. Furthermore, the law also extended the jurisdiction of the commission to include other common carriers; and it empowered the commission to prescribe a uniform system of bookkeeping for all railroads, a provision of fundamental importance in the regulation of rail rates. Within a few years, under the operation of the new law, the "I.C.C." had not only effected drastic reductions in rates, but it had also won the respect of the public, the courts, and the carriers themselves, who increasingly tended to accept its decisions as final.

Food and Drugs. The railroads were not the only trusts to feel the force of national regulation. The meat packers, the food processors, and the producers of drugs and patent medicines had much to explain when the muckrakers got through with them. Precedents for federal action in this field were not altogether lacking, for laws dating back to the eighties required inspection by the Bureau of Animal Industry of all meat exports. This requirement was extended by a law of 1906 to meats destined for interstate commerce, and a Pure Food and Drug Act, passed the same year, placed some restrictions, but not nearly enough, on the producers of prepared foods and patent medicines. An amendment to this act, passed in 1911, prohibited also the use of misleading labels, but events proved that the gullible public bought about as freely when the unpleasant truth was printed on the label as when it was not. The real problem, fraudulent advertising, still remained. All such regulation, when undertaken by the federal government, depended for its validity upon the powers of Congress over interstate commerce, and the exact line of demarcation between state and national authority could be drawn only by the courts. Roosevelt, annoyed at the existence of this "twilight zone," strongly favored resolving all doubts in favor of the national government.

The "Square Deal." An apt phrase maker, Roosevelt insisted on a "square deal" for labor, capital, and the public — a phrase that gave him the advantage of an attractive label for his labor policy. Naturally the rapid development of industrial concentration aroused the fears of labor, and as the strength of organized capital grew, the strength of organized labor grew also. By 1905 the American Federation of Labor claimed for its affiliates a total membership of 2 million, with perhaps 600,000 unaffiliated but cooperating union members. Under the circumstances a test of strength between labor and capital was almost inevitable. It came, reasonably enough, in the coal-mining region of Pennsylvania, where in spite of deplorable labor conditions the operators were stubbornly determined to resist reform. Demanding recognition of their union, a wage increase of 20 per cent, and an eight-hour day, the anthracite coal miners quit work on May 12, 1902, and at a cost of perhaps $1 million to all concerned held their lines intact until October 23. John Mitchell, the strike leader, kept his men from violence and won much sympathy for the strikers' cause. George F. Baer, who spoke for the operators, was far less skillful in handling public opinion. He insisted from the first that the companies would not even so much as meet with the union representatives, and refused an invitation to attend a White House conference with the labor leaders.

Fully conscious of the widespread suffering that the coal shortage was sure to bring, Roosevelt used his influence with both sides in favor of a compromise solution. He found the miners ready enough to talk terms, but the operators remained obdurate. Only after the President had threatened to send in a "first-rate general" with sufficient federal troops "to dispossess the operators and run the mines as a receiver" would the owners consent to governmental mediation. Even so the operators agreed to accept the findings of a commission appointed by the President only if sociologists and not union men were to represent the labor viewpoint. Thereupon work was resumed at the mines; Roosevelt appointed a union leader as an "eminent sociologist" to the commission, and in March, 1903, a decision was announced that generally favored the miners. Thus the President had obtained his "square deal" for labor.

Nor was this all. Repeatedly the President recommended to Congress legislation favorable to labor, such as the protection of women and children in industry, limitations on the use of injunctions in labor disputes, and employer's liability laws for workers on interstate railroads. Only the latter recommendation received the favorable action of Congress, and the first such law, passed in 1906, was annulled by the Supreme Court. A law of April, 1908, met the Court's objections. Perhaps Roosevelt's thinking on the labor problem was not too far in advance of his times. Although he believed that unions were "beneficial," he was stoutly opposed to the closed shop and to labor intervention into politics. But his actions in the 1902 coal strike represented a distinct change from those of his predecessors in office, and his actions constituted an important precedent by assuming that the public was an interested third party in any large strike.

Roosevelt and the Negro Problem. Roosevelt's real concern for the more unfortunate groups in society was reflected again in his handling of the race problem. Early in his administration he shocked southern whites by inviting Booker T. Washington, the great Negro educator, to dine with him at the White House. Although the white South admired Washington as a leader of his race, it was a long time before it could forgive Roosevelt for this disregard of the color line. Nor did it like his determination not to distinguish between whites and Negroes in appointments to office. Indianola, Mississippi, got a Negro postmistress, and Charleston, South Carolina, a Negro collector. He showed, too, the utmost contempt for the "lily-white" Republican organizations in the South which vied with the Democrats in their determination to keep Negroes out of politics. On the other hand, he was as impetuous as any southerner might have been in his handling of the "Brownsville affair." Because a few Negro soldiers, absent from their barracks without leave, had been charged with shooting up the town of Brownsville, Texas, three companies of Negro troops were dishonorably discharged from the service. Subsequent investigations seemed to prove that most of the troops were innocent, but Roosevelt left office without having admitted his mistake.

Conservation. A policy especially dear to Roosevelt's heart was the conservation of the nation's natural resources. Since the nation's birth its public lands had been a national treasure of incalculable worth. Now the best of these had been used up; although at the turn of the century more than 500 million acres still remained open to settlement, only a small fraction of this vast area could ever be farmed in the traditional American way. Moreover, even after the lands had passed into private or corporate hands the tendency had been to exploit them rather than to preserve their fertility. Millions of acres, particularly in the East and the South, had been thoroughly despoiled or could be farmed only by the lavish use of fertilizer. What had happened to the lands had happened also in varying degrees to other natural resources. Four-fifths of the nation's forests had been chopped down without thought of replacement, and many of the remaining had been acquired by a few large lumber companies bent on rapidly exploiting them. Mineral resources, too, metals, coal, gas, and oil, had been used with the utmost wastefulness. Water-power sites had been allowed to pass into the hands of private companies who had developed their possibilities for profit, without regard for the destruction of beauty or prevention of floods. By the turn of the century pessimists were beginning to foretell the exhaustion of the nation's rich resources and the extension of the poverty of the Old World to the New.

During Roosevelt's administrations conservation activities were many and varied. The Reclamation Act of 1902 put the federal government into the business of building the dams, tunnels, flumes, and ditches necessary for irrigation projects. An Inland Waterways Commission, appointed in 1907, stressed the interrelation of all conservation problems and urged the President to call a national conference on conservation, to which representatives from all sections and from both parties should be invited. As a result, on May 13, 1908, Roosevelt met with a distinguished assembly of notables. From the conference he obtained support for such important policies as the protection of the water supply of navigable streams, the control of forest fires, regulation for the cutting of timber on government lands, the granting of surface titles to public lands separate from the right to exploit the minerals that lay below the surface, and the withdrawal from sale of lands bearing coal, oil, natural gas, and phosphate. On Roosevelt's order, the Secretary of the Interior added to the forest lands already in public reserves some 80 million acres of coal lands, 1.5 million acres of lands adjacent to water-power sites, and nearly 5 million acres of phosphate lands.

There was a direct relationship between Roosevelt's policy of governmental inter-

ference in the affairs of business and his policy of conservation. In the former he brought businessmen face to face with the specter of effective governmental regulation; in the latter he served notice that in certain spheres, previously left open to private initiative, the government either would act itself or would permit individuals to act only on terms laid down by the government in advance. The day of rampant individualism was almost ended.

Roosevelt's Election. As President, Roosevelt enjoyed a tremendous personal popularity. To a phenomenal degree he exhibited many of the traits and ideals that the average American most admired. His leadership had much to do with the overwhelming victories scored by the Republicans in the four elections (1902, 1904, 1906, 1908) held during his administration, and his nomination and election in 1904 was a great personal triumph. To oppose him the Democrats turned that year to a conservative New York judge, Alton B. Parker,

known for his friendliness to business interests. Clinching the Democratic bid for Wall Street support, Parker came out openly for the gold standard and completely repudiated Bryan's record on free silver. Nevertheless, he suffered a worse defeat than Bryan had in 1896 and in 1900, with the electoral vote 336 for Roosevelt and 140 for Parker. Elated by the returns, Roosevelt immediately issued a dramatic statement that he must have regretted later many times. "The wise custom which limits the President to two terms regards the substance and not the form, and under no circumstances will I be a candidate for or accept another nomination."

The Panic of 1907. Roosevelt's second administration came near disaster with the Panic of 1907, which many claimed was the result of his unwarranted attacks on business. His prosecutions of the trusts and his attempts to regulate the railroads, hostile critics declared, endangered legitimate profits; the "square deal" encouraged labor

RUINED LAND: *The Copperhill-Ducktown Area in Tennessee*

The widespread abuse of America's land and water resources has been, and still remains, a national disgrace. Partly through the efforts of conservationists such as Edwin Way Teale, the distinguished author-naturalist, an aroused public increasingly has demanded and received corrective state and federal legislation.

. . . like a pleasant dream sliding into a nightmare, the country swiftly changed. . . . All around us dead hills, red, raw, ribbed by erosion, stood stark in the sunshine. Hardly two miles from dense woodland we were in the midst of a moonscape on earth. . . . What had produced this desert in the midst of a green landscape? . . . Not far from the village of Ducktown copper was unearthed. . . . In the early days of copper mining, it was a custom to roast the ore under large log fires. . . . This eliminated the sulphur. As . . . the demand for wood mounted . . . the forests receded in an expanding circle. . . . In times of dry weather, almost daily fires ran across the open spaces . . . flames swept the earth bare of vegetation. . . . the clouds of sulphur-dioxide gas that rose from the roasting piles . . . attacked the grass and plants and bushes that remained . . . [and] entered the soil. . . . Erosion . . . did the rest. Left behind, like a red flayed carcass, were the raw hills. . . . They formed a nightmare region, symbolic of all the erosion-ridden fields . . . man has created on this continent.

Reprinted by permission of Dodd, Mead & Company from *North with the Spring* by EDWIN WAY TEALE. Copyright, 1951, by EDWIN WAY TEALE

---

to make unreasonable demands; and conservation called a halt to the lucrative exploitation of natural resources. Roosevelt was deeply sensitive to the criticism that his policies were undermining confidence, but he claimed that the fault lay with business, not with him. Eventually he decided that the Panic of 1907 was purely "psychological," and intentionally produced by "malefactors of great wealth," bent on discrediting his policies.

Undoubtedly an important factor in bringing on the Panic of 1907 was the wholesale multiplication of securities in the early years of the century. United States Steel, for example, was capitalized at a sum far in excess of the total capital of the companies it incorporated. These securities were often sold at higher prices than were justified by the earning power of the corporations represented, and investor disillusionment was inevitable. Another factor was the inelasticity of the currency and credit. The United States government had no way of providing an extra supply of money to meet an emergency. The total amount of gold and silver, national bank notes, and Treasury notes that composed the money of the country was relatively fixed. If confidence lagged and money was hoarded, a shortage was certain. Much the same thing was true of credit, which was limited primarily by the ability and willingness of a few great New York bankers to lend. Practically every financial institution in the country was connected in one way or another with the Wall Street bankers, and was subject to their control. They thus constituted a kind of "money trust" that almost at will could grant or withhold the credit necessary to keep the nation's business moving.

The Panic began on October 22, 1907, with a run on the Knickerbocker Trust Company, the third largest bank in New York City. Disastrous runs occurred also on other New York banks, and stock exchange values plunged rapidly. To help meet the emergency, George B. Cortelyou, Secretary of the Treasury, deposited

$25 million of Treasury funds with hard pressed New York banks, while the President, at the suggestion of J. P. Morgan, promised the United States Steel Corporation immunity from prosecution so that it could absorb the Tennessee Coal and Iron Company. This, Morgan told Roosevelt, was necessary to save an important New York bank from collapse and thus stave off a major disaster. The storm was soon over, and the depression that followed was short-lived compared to those which followed the Panic of 1873 and 1893. Congress, however, was convinced that the Panic might have been averted altogether, or that its worst effects might have been avoided, had the banking and currency system of the United States been on a sounder footing, and in 1908 passed the Aldrich-Vreeland Act empowering the national banks of the country for a period of six years to issue emergency currency in times of financial stringency. This was but a stopgap measure. The most important part of the act was the creation of a National Monetary Commission to investigate the currency systems of the world and to lay plans for a thoroughgoing reform in the American system.

SELECTED BIBLIOGRAPHY

The character of the Progressive Movement has recently been a controversial topic among historians. A good sampling of conflicting views may be found in *The Progressive Era, edited by Arthur Mann (1963). A near-classic statement of what may be termed the "advanced progressive" position is in B. P. De-Witt, The Progressive Movement (1915). Disillusionment with the movement and nearly all its works is expressed in John Chamberlain, *Farewell to Reform (1932). R. H. Wiebe, Businessmen and Reform (1962), is a careful study of the way businessmen divided on the various issues of the era. A provocative new work, which seems to set the whole movement on its head, is Gabriel Kolko, The Triumph of Conservatism (1963); if Kolko is right — something few scholars are willing to concede — then a full-scale reinterpretation is in order. Two recent anthologies are Richard Hofstadter, *The Progressive Movement (1963), brief; and Otis Pease, The Progressive Years (1962), full and rich. H. U. Faulkner has written two surveys of the period: The Quest for Social Justice (1931), and The Decline of Laissez Faire (1951). Fascinating details are gathered in the massive work by the journalist Mark Sullivan, Our Times (6 vols., 1926–1935).

On the Muckrakers, see C. C. Regier, The Era of the Muckrakers (1932); Louis Filler, *Crusaders for American Liberalism (1939); and D. M. Chalmers, *The Social and Political Ideas of the Muckrakers (1964). Two excellent samplers are *The Muckrakers, edited by A. M. and Lila Weinberg (1961); and Harvey Swados, *Years of Conscience (1962). Important autobiographies are those of Lincoln Steffens (2 vols., 1931), of which an abridgement is available in paperback; Upton Sinclair (1962); and R. S. Baker, American Chronicle (1945). A full-length biography of S. S. McClure is Peter Lyon, Success Story (1963). Important muckraking works are: *The World of Lincoln Steffens, edited by Ella Winter and Herbert Shapiro (1962); R. S. Baker, *Following the Color Line (1908); and D. G. Phillips, *The Treason of the Senate (1906).

On socialism, D. A. Shannon, The Socialist Party of America (1955), is a fine work, notable for its appreciation of regional differences. Ira Kipnis, The American Socialist Movement, 1897–1912 (1952), contains valuable detail, but is marred by its left-wing bias. H. W. Morgan, Eugene V. Debs: Socialist for President (1962), stresses campaigns; *American Socialism, 1900–1960, is an anthology edited by Morgan (1964). Richard Drinnon, Rebel in Paradise; A Biography of Emma Goldman (1961), is a sympathetic life of a remarkable anarchist agitator. A rich collection of radical materials is J. L. Kornbluh (ed.), Rebel Voices: An I.W.W. Anthology (1964).

On LaFollette and the Wisconsin leadership in reform, there are several admirable books. His detailed *Autobiography (1913) is of

* Available in paperback

fundamental importance. A full-length biography written by his widow and his daughter, B. C. LaFollette and Fola LaFollette, *Robert M. LaFollette, 1855–1925* (2 vols., 1953), is based upon his papers. More critical in tone is R. S. Maxwell, *LaFollette and the Rise of the Progressives in Wisconsin* (1956). Charles McCarthy, *The Wisconsin Idea* (1912), is the statement of an enthusiastic LaFollette supporter, while McCarthy's own part is told in E. A. Fitzpatrick, *McCarthy of Wisconsin* (1944). Biographies of some LaFollette enemies include R. N. Current, *Pine Logs and Politics; A Life of Philetus Sawyer, 1816–1900* (1950); and R. S. Maxwell, *Emanuel L. Philipp, Wisconsin Stalwart* (1959).

Progressive efforts in the states are examined in many books. Among the more important are: W. A. Flint, *The Progressive Movement in Vermont* (1941); R. E. Noble, Jr., *New Jersey Progressivism before Wilson* (1946); G. E. Mowry, °*The California Progressives* (1951); and H. L. Warner, *Progressivism in Ohio* (1964). The battle for municipal reform may be followed in Lincoln Steffens' muckraking classic °*The Shame of the Cities* (1904), as well as in some notable · memoirs, including: T. L. Johnson, *My Story* (1911); Brand Whitlock, *Forty Years of It* (1914); and F. C. Howe, *The Confessions of a Reformer* (1925). An important scholarly work on municipal reform is W. E. Bean's delightful *Boss Ruef's San Francisco* (1952).

On prohibition, the best account of how the movement achieved success is P. H. Odegard, *Pressure Politics: The Story of the Anti-Saloon League* (1928), a classic in political science. J. R. Gusfield, *Symbolic Crusade* (1963); and J. H. Timberlake, *Prohibition and the Progressive Movement, 1900–1920* (1963), are important new monographs. The principal scholarly state studies are: J. B. Sellers, °*The Prohibition Movement in Alabama* (1943); D. J. Whitener, *Prohibition in North Carolina*

(1945); G. M. Ostrander, *The Prohibition Movement in California* (1957); and N. H. Clark, *The Dry Years* (1965), on Washington state.

A sympathetic account of a controversial organization is A. K. Steigerwalt, *The National Association of Manufacturers, 1895–1914* (1964). Also on business history see such works as: I. M. Tarbell, *The Life of Elbert H. Gary* (1925); Herbert Croly, *Willard Straight* (1924); and J. A. Garraty, *Right-Hand Man; The Life of George W. Perkins* (1960). Important criticisms of the economic order include: H. D. Lloyd, °*Wealth against Commonwealth* (1894); and three works by Thorstein Veblen, °*The Theory of the Leisure Class* (1899), °*The Theory of Business Enterprise* (1904), and °*The Instinct of Workmanship* (1914). On Roosevelt and labor, see: H. L. Hurwitz, *Theodore Roosevelt and Labor in New York State, 1880–1900* (1943); R. J. Cornell, *The Anthracite Coal Strike of 1902* (1957); and Elsie Glück, *John Mitchell, Miner* (1929). Interesting works showing the need for pure food and drug reform are: J. H. Young, *The Toadstool Millionaires* (1961); O. E. Anderson, Jr., *The Health of a Nation; Harvey W. Wiley and the Fight for Pure Food* (1958); and Upton Sinclair's classic muckraking novel, °*The Jungle* (1906).

General introductions to conservation include: C. R. Van Hise, *The Conservation of Natural Resources in the United States* (2nd ed., 1915); and D. C. Coyle, *Conservation* (1957), a popular survey. S. P. Hays, *Conservation and the Gospel of Efficiency; The Progressive Conservation Movement, 1890–1920* (1959), is a provocative reinterpretation. Other important works include: M. M. Vance, *Charles Richard Van Hise* (1960); and John Ise, *Our National Park Policy* (1961). On the "scientific management" movement of this period, see Samuel Haber, *Efficiency and Uplift* (1964).

31

TAFT AND WILSON

The Election of 1908 · Taft as President · The Payne-Aldrich Tariff · Rise of Insurgency and the Progressive Party · Election of 1912 · Woodrow Wilson · Tariff and Financial Legislation · Business and Labor Policy · Wilsonian and Jeffersonian Democracy

The Republicans Nominate Taft. During his problems with the Panic of 1907, Roosevelt was confronted with the more personal consideration of his decision about the presidential election of 1908. Had no other questions been involved, Roosevelt undoubtedly would have continued in the office which was his again almost for the asking. But in 1904 he had announced that he would abide by the "wise custom" which had limited his predecessors to eight years. Beyond this promise he had grave scruples about the continuance of a President in office. Although emphatic in his approval of a strong executive, to avoid the dangers of a possible dictatorship he believed no less strongly in limiting the duration of the President's power.

In order to head off the possibility that his devotees might draft him, Roosevelt decided to work actively for the nomination of his able Secretary of War and close personal friend, William Howard Taft (1857–1930) of Ohio. Taft was a huge man weighing 350 pounds, good-natured, affa-

ble, with an infectious chuckle. His political ascent had been principally by the appointive route. A graduate of Yale, he became successively a judge in the superior court of Ohio, federal solicitor-general, federal judge, commissioner to the Philippines and governor-general, and finally Secretary of War. An able administrator and Roosevelt's favorite envoy abroad, he seemed to have an almost ideal training for the Presidency. His personal inclinations lay toward the Supreme Court, but more than once he felt obliged to reject the appointment he craved to attend unfinished business. Effectively supported by the President, Taft was nominated on the first ballot by a Republican convention that would have preferred to name Roosevelt.

Bryan Again. The Democrats, disastrously defeated four years before with the conservative Parker, renominated Bryan, who was still young, vigorous, and hopeful, and whose devoted adherents gave him the same unstinted support that Henry Clay and James G. Blaine had once enjoyed. In 1906 he had made a trip around the world and returned with his self-confidence restored. Ready at last to admit that free silver was a dead issue, he proposed in August, 1906, a new program for curbing the trusts. Corporations were to be barred from contributing to campaign funds, interlocking directorates prohibited, and a federal license of all interstate businesses required. To solve the railroad problem he reverted to the Populist remedy of government ownership, "not as an immediate issue, but as an ultimate solution of the controversy." The difficulty with Bryan's program was that it so resembled Roosevelt's; well before election time Congress had passed and Roosevelt had signed a measure forbidding corporations to contribute toward the election of national officers, while Bryan still temporized on the railroad question.

Election of 1908. The real issue in the lackadaisical campaign of 1908 was whether Bryan or Taft could be better trusted to carry out the Roosevelt policies. In the end Taft won by an electoral vote of 321 to 162. Later, not without a show of justice, Bryan complained that the Republicans had enjoyed an unfair advantage in the campaign. Taft, the progressive disciple of Roosevelt, carried the West, while Taft, the conservative jurist, carried the East. Forty-six states participated in the election of 1908, for in 1907 the majority party in Congress had at last decided that Republican supremacy was well enough established to risk the admission of Oklahoma, an almost certain Democratic state. A similar offer to admit New Mexico and Arizona as one state failed because of the opposition of Arizona.

Taft as President. With Roosevelt in the Presidency, the country felt satisfied that the reform spirit still prevailed in national affairs. The accession of Taft, it was confidently predicted, would bring little change. Unfortunately, Taft was unable to live up to the reputation that Roosevelt had made for him. An able constitutional lawyer, he had more respect for the legislative independence of Congress than Roosevelt, and often it was Congress rather than the President who determined the course of national policy. Nor was Taft a disciple of the "strenuous life." Unlike Roosevelt, who

was never happier than in the midst of an "elegant row," the new President tended to avoid political warfare. Soon Taft began to make mistakes, not a few of which stemmed from his lack of practical political experience.

The Payne-Aldrich Tariff. Taft's first failure was with tariff reform, a question which Roosevelt had advised him to avoid. True to a promise made during the campaign, Taft called Congress into special session for March 15, and by April 9 the Payne Bill, providing for moderate reductions, had passed the House. When the bill reached the Senate, it was sponsored by Senator Aldrich of Rhode Island, chairman of the Senate Committee on Finance, and rewritten to fit the high-protectionist views of the multimillionaire industrialists, of whom Aldrich was one. But Aldrich's plans for a quick passage of the bill were frustrated by a little group of middle-western Republican insurgents, led by La Follette, who had entered the Senate in 1906. Determined that the bill should not be passed before the public could find out how complete a betrayal it was of the Republican campaign pledges, La Follette and his confederates studied it by night and debated it by day. They were unable to prevent its passage, but ten of them joined with the Democrats in refusing to vote for it. The measure, known as the Payne-Aldrich Bill, at length was approved by the President, who later described it as the best tariff bill that the Republican Party had ever passed. A large segment of public opinion, however, held quite otherwise.

The Ballinger Controversy. Circumstances soon made it appear that on the subject of conservation the new President was no more to be trusted than on the tariff. Taft's Secretary of the Interior, R. A. Ballinger, felt obliged to restore to private entry some water-power sites in Montana and Wyoming and some coal lands in Alaska. This action was vigorously protested by one of his subordinates, Louis R. Glavis, and by the chief of the forestry service, Gifford Pinchot. After careful investigation, Taft decided that there was nothing improper in Ballinger's actions, and for their insubordination dismissed both Glavis and Pinchot from office. But to the ever more hostile public, it appeared that the President, however well-founded his action, had lined up with the anti-conservationists.

Insurgency in the House. Meantime insurgency had broken out in the House, where a small group of progressive-minded Republicans had discovered that with Democratic cooperation they could outvote the Republican regulars. This power they determined to use against the autocratic Speaker Joseph G. Cannon of Illinois, an ultra-conservative who consistently and effectively blocked all progressive legislation. Ably led by Representative George W. Norris of Nebraska, they presented an amendment to the House rules designed to take the appointment of the Rules Committee out of the control of the Speaker and to make it elective by the House. With every parliamentary device in his possession, Cannon fought back, but eventually the Insurgent-Democratic combination won out. When the next Congress met, the rules were still further amended. All committees were made elective, with the Ways and Means Committee acting as a committee on committees. The changes were fundamental. No longer could it be said that the Speaker, next to the President, was the most powerful American official; moreover, the chief agency for maintaining party discipline in the House was destroyed. Members felt free to vote as their consciences or their constituents might direct, regardless of party pressure. By the spring of 1910 the group of middle-western Republican senators who had opposed the tariff bill were in direct conflict with the President. They openly criticized Taft's stand on the tariff, on the Ballinger-Pinchot controversy, and on numerous other issues.

Taft in return denied them patronage and even attempted without success to defeat some of them in the Republican primaries.

With the Republican party on the verge of a disastrous split, the interest of the public in Theodore Roosevelt's reaction became intense. Almost immediately after Taft's inauguration Roosevelt left the country for a hunting expedition in Africa. His return to New York on June 18, 1910, set off a huge public celebration. It was soon apparent that the old cordiality between Roosevelt and Taft was gone, although in the campaign of 1910 Roosevelt made every effort to heal the breach in the party and to bring about a Republican victory. But the disillusioned electorate could see no other way to rebuke the Republican conservatives than by voting the Democratic ticket. As a result, the House of Representatives fell to the Democrats by a large majority, and the Republicans controlled the Senate by so slender a vote that the dozen or more insurgents held the balance of power. In the states the trend was equally pronounced. The normally Republican strongholds of New York, Ohio, Massachusetts, Connecticut, and New Jersey went Democratic by large majorities.

As a whole the election was intended to rebuke the Taft administration, but in many ways it was undeserved. Taft actually had carried out the Roosevelt policies with considerable success. He had secured a revision of the tariff, which, however inadequate, was something that Roosevelt had not even dared to attempt. He had vigorously prosecuted the trusts. In sponsoring the Mann-Elkins Act of 1910, he had greatly increased the powers of the Interstate Commerce Commission. By permitting the government purchase of privately owned timber tracts in the Appalachians, by withdrawing oil lands from entry — another thing Roosevelt had never done — and also by obtaining from Congress the authority that Roosevelt lacked for withdrawing coal lands, he had served the cause of conservation. Other measures enacted during his administration included the division of the Department of Commerce and Labor into two departments; the establishment of a Bureau of Mines; the improvement of the public land laws; and the enactment of postal-savings and parcel-post laws.

Much of Taft's unpopularity may be attributed to his political ineptitude, and much of it merely to misfortune. Even his most praiseworthy actions were regularly misunderstood and denounced. When he promoted a Democrat, Associate Justice White, to be Chief Justice of the Supreme Court, the Republican regulars were offended, and when he chose Governor Hughes of New York as associate justice, Republican progressives accused him of seeking to sidetrack a possible competitor for the 1912 nomination. When reciprocity with Canada, on which Taft had set his heart, was repudiated by Canada after acceptance by the United States, Taft was blamed. When Taft's Secretary of State proposed to follow the same tactics in Nicaragua and Honduras that Roosevelt had used in Haiti, he was accused of "dollar diplomacy."

The La Follette and Roosevelt Candidacies. The original program of the Republican insurgents was to capture the Republican Party. This was made clear as early as January 23, 1911, when a group of them, meeting at Senator La Follette's house in Washington, formed the National Progressive Republican League and drew up an extensive program of reform. On the assumption that Roosevelt still would not consider a third term, they rallied around La Follette as the "logical man" to defeat Taft for renomination. To the intense disappointment of La Follette, who claimed that he had been used only as a "stalking-horse," Roosevelt announced on February 24, 1912, that he was ready to throw his "hat in the ring." From this day on the La Follette candidacy was a lost

cause, and the progressive wing of the party turned with enthusiasm to Roosevelt.

It soon developed that the ex-President, for all his popular appeal, had entered the campaign too late. The party machine was in the hands of the conservatives, who were determined to renominate Taft. They had already lined up many of the southern delegations which, because they were so largely composed of federal officeholders, could always be trusted to follow the will of the President, and they now made haste to gather in the rest. Where the old convention system of choosing delegates was in force, the party regulars almost invariably controlled and obediently delivered their delegations to Taft. But wherever the new system of preferential primaries existed, Roosevelt generally won; indeed, several states quickly adopted such laws in order to promote his chances. In the Republican Convention in Chicago on June 18, it was apparent that the Roosevelt forces were approximately 100 votes short of a majority. To make up this deficiency, they had brought contests involving about 250 seats, some fairly reasonable and others merely for the "moral effect." But the convention, effectively controlled by the conservatives, decided nearly all the contests in favor of Taft, who was nominated on the first ballot, although 107 delegates voted for Roosevelt, and 344 sat silent in protest.

The Progressive Party. Even before the Republican Convention met it was obvious that Roosevelt was in no mood to accept defeat. If he lost the Republican nomination, he would run anyway. Six weeks after the Chicago meeting a convention of the new Progressive Party met, again in Chicago, to select Roosevelt as its standard-bearer. Its symbol to match the Republican elephant and the Democratic donkey was the "bull moose," an animal Roosevelt much admired. An enthusiastic audience of 20,000 people heard the Progressive leader denounce both old parties as "husks, with no real soul within either," and demand a new party "to speak out wisely and fearlessly on the vital issues of the day."

On a great variety of issues the new party did speak out. Its program, called the "New Nationalism," demanded increases in the powers of the federal government to regulate large business interests and to provide for society's weak and unfortunate members. Its policy on trusts recognized corporations as "an essential part of modern business," and in lieu of dissolving them demanded effective regulation through "a strong federal administration commission." It proposed a federal securities commission to supervise the issuance of stocks and bonds. It called for an immediate revision of the tariff in favor of the consumer, a land monopoly tax, and the government ownership of Alaskan railroads. It endorsed, too, all the current reforms such as the direct primary, woman suffrage, an easier way to amend the Constitution, better working

THE BULL MOOSE CAMPAIGN

conditions in the factories, the prohibition of child labor, the better regulation of labor by women, minimum-wage standards, and an eight-hour day in continuous twenty-four-hour industries. Such pronouncements delighted social workers and gave the new party a crusading character. With a fervor reminiscent of Populism the Progressive Convention sang "Onward, Christian Soldiers," and quoted Roosevelt's challenge to the Taft forces at Chicago: "We stand at Armageddon and we battle for the Lord."

Meanwhile, the Democrats, convinced that the Republican split would insure their triumph at the polls in November, met in Baltimore, July 25, to choose their candidate from a long list of favorite sons. After the tenth ballot J. Beauchamp (Champ) Clark of Missouri, Speaker of the House, seemed the certain nominee. But Bryan, still the dominant personality in the party, switched from Clark to Governor Woodrow Wilson of New Jersey on the fourteenth ballot. The Tammany delegation from New York had voted for Clark since the tenth ballot, and Bryan's explanation of his conduct was that he could not support anyone who owed his nomination to Tammany. On the forty-sixth ballot the convention finally chose Wilson.

The Campaign of 1912. The campaign provided plenty of excitement. Roosevelt and Taft, throughout the primary contests and on into the election campaign, belabored each other as only two friends fallen out can do. Wilson proved to be an admirable public speaker, and defended his "New Freedom," as he called his program, with a felicity that won him many votes. Assailing Roosevelt's concept of a powerful regulatory state, Wilson predicted that it would lead to the rule of exploiting monopolies sanctified by government. What was needed, Wilson believed, was the destruction of "illicit competition" by big business through the forceful use of the antitrust law and a return to the "old competitive democratic principles."

The results of the election were what all astute observers were able to foresee. Wilson, with fewer popular votes than Bryan had received in any of his three defeats, amassed an electoral vote of 435 to Roosevelt's 88 and Taft's 8. With the Democrats equally victorious in the House of Representatives and the Senate, the new President would be assured also of a comfortable working majority in Congress. In most of the state contests the Democrats also scored victories, the cleanest sweep their party had made since before the Civil War. The reform policies of Roosevelt, which Taft had sought with only partial success to continue, were left to be carried to fruition by a Democratic President.

Woodrow Wilson. Woodrow Wilson (1856–1924), upon whom this task devolved, had an unusual preparation for the Presidency. The son of a prominent southern clergyman, he gave up law to become a college professor, and as a political scientist at Princeton University achieved international recognition. Like so many progressive leaders of both parties, Wilson started his political life as a conservative. He had defended the open shop in the nineties, was opposed to the Populists, and as late as 1908 felt that both Bryan and Roosevelt were dangerous radicals. On the expansion of the presidential power, however, he agreed with Roosevelt completely. Deeply impressed with the vast powers wielded by the prime ministers in Great Britain and elsewhere, he became convinced that the principle of executive leadership must somehow be grafted upon the American system. "The President," wrote the professor, "is at liberty, both in law and conscience, to be as big a man as he can. His capacity will set the limit." As President of Princeton, Wilson made an effort to democratize the university that was unappreciated by his governing board. When the Democratic "boss" of New Jersey, in search of window dressing for his ticket, offered Wilson a nomination as governor

in 1910, he accepted gladly, campaigned effectively, and was elected.

To the consternation of the party bosses, Wilson, once in office, insisted on carrying out the pledges of the party platform. Turning against the people who had nominated him, the governor put into effect the doctrine of executive leadership he so long had taught. By appealing to the people both directly and through the press, he soon had the legislature doing his bidding. It passed measures to establish employer's liability, to punish corrupt practices, to control public utilities, and to reform the election machinery. These victories in a state that had long been known as the "home of the trusts" made Wilson a marked man. Adroitly presented to the public outside New Jersey by Colonel Edward M. House of Texas, he had become by 1912 the favorite candidate of the progressive wing of his party.

Wilson's View of the Presidency. Wilson was determined to be a prime-minister type of President, and with this end in view he included in his cabinet as Secretary of State the man whose influence with the western and southern wings of the Democratic Party was still second to none, William Jennings Bryan. Other similar appointments were made to achieve party cohesiveness. Breaking a century old precedent, Wilson appeared in person to read his messages to Congress, took the people into his confidence, and made the most of newspaper publicity. Using his influence directly upon congressmen in personal interviews, he accorded patronage favors to his supporters, while denying them to others. Behind the scenes he relied heavily upon the advice of Colonel House, with whom he discussed most matters of consequence, and Joseph P. Tumulty, his faithful private secretary, a shrewd and practical politician.

The Underwood-Simmons Tariff. Wilson's first efforts were directed toward the downward revision of the tariff which his predecessor had failed to achieve. Under steady pressure from the White House, the Underwood-Simmons Tariff Act was ready for the President's signature on October 3, 1913. Neither a free-trade nor a low-tariff measure, its schedules of duties were on the average about 10 per cent lower than those of the Payne-Aldrich Tariff, and it placed a hundred new items, mostly raw materials or foodstuffs, on the free list. What these duties might have done for business and for the revenue had times remained normal will never be known, for the outbreak of war in Europe drastically reduced importations. The revenue sacrificed forced the government to fall back on the income tax, made possible by the adoption of the Sixteenth Amendment, and provided for in the Underwood-Simmons Act. A tax of 1 per cent was charged against all incomes in excess of $3,000, or, in the case of married couples, $4,000; while on incomes above $20,000 a surtax, beginning with an additional 1 per cent, was gradually stepped up to a maximum of 6 per cent on incomes above $500,000. At the time these rates were devised the possibilities of the income tax were only faintly realized, but within a few years it became the federal government's chief instrument for revenue.

The Federal Reserve Banking System. On the heels of the tariff act came banking and currency reform on a scale never before attempted in the United States. The National Monetary Commission reported in 1912 that the only sure cure for the financial ills from which the country suffered would be a centralized banking system, substantially a third Bank of the United States. The subject was also investigated during the second half of the Taft administration, this time by a committee of the Democratic House of Representatives, headed by A. P. Pujo of Louisiana. The Pujo Committee balked at the idea of creating the same kind of bank that a great

Democratic President, Andrew Jackson, had felt obliged to destroy. Under Wilson's leadership, Congress eventually hit upon the expedient of creating a series of sectional banks, held together only by a Federal Reserve Board. This board, which Wilson thought of as analogous to the Interstate Commerce Commission, was to consist of seven members, two of whom, the Secretary of the Treasury and the Comptroller of the Currency, were to be members *ex officio,* while the others were to be appointed by the President and confirmed by the Senate for ten-year terms. One of the nonpolitical members was to be designated governor of the board. The United States was to be divided into twelve districts, each of which would contain some metropolitan center in which a Federal Reserve Bank would be established. The new banks were not to do business with individuals, but were to be strictly "bankers' banks," with which every national bank was required to deposit its reserve, and which state banks might also so use at their option.

The hope of the men who framed the measure was that in times of crisis the strength of the total reserves could be mobilized to sustain any one bank. The law also provided for a new type of currency, Federal Reserve notes. These new notes were based upon the commercial loans made by member banks to businessmen. Thus the total amount of bank notes in circulation could vary with the amount of business being conducted in the country, and so overcome the inelasticity of the currency, a chronic complaint under the old system. As the system developed, it was also hoped that through the sale or purchase of government bonds and through changing the rediscount rate, the Federal Reserve Board could alter the amount of credit in the country and thus help to prevent wild speculative booms and sharp depressions. The Glass-Owen Federal Reserve Act, as it was known, received Wilson's signature on December 23, 1913.

When the Federal Reserve System was first proposed, the bankers of the country regarded it with extreme suspicion, and the fact that Secretary Bryan openly supported it was well calculated to exaggerate their fears. But before the measure reached final passage, the bankers had begun to see its advantages, and within a short time most of them were enthusiastic. Although by 1929 only about one-third of the banks of the country were members of the Federal Reserve, their combined assets accounted for more than four-fifths of the nation's banking resources.

Wilson's Trust Policy. When Wilson appeared before Congress on January 20, 1914, to direct attention to the trust problem, he had information available that his predecessors had lacked. Wilson knew, better than either Taft or Roosevelt had known, the hopelessness of trying merely to turn big business into little businesses. Such efforts were like trying to turn back the clock. What Wilson now sought of Congress was a clear definition of what was fair and unfair in business activity, and a more complete recognition of the fact that the government through proper agencies should have the right to enforce the regulations of Congress. Before the mid-term election of 1914, Congress had enacted two significant measures, the Clayton Anti-Trust Act and the Federal Trade Commission Act. The Clayton Act added various new prohibitions to the already long list of forbidden corporation practices, and the Federal Trade Commission Act created a new board of five members to investigate the origin and management of corporations, and to seek the assistance of the courts in ending such "unfair methods of competition in commerce" as it might discover. Some progress was made with the enforcement of these laws during Wilson's first administration, but the work thus begun was adversely affected by the entrance of the United States into the First World War. During that struggle little attempt was made to enforce the restrictions of the Clayton Act, and after the Republicans returned to power in 1921, there was little desire to enforce them.

A "Magna Charta" for Labor. The attitude of the Wilson administration toward labor was clearly revealed by the incorporation of what labor called its "Magna Charta" in the Clayton Act. One section of the act specifically exempted labor and agricultural corporations from prosecution under the terms of the antitrust laws, while another section limited the use of the injunction in labor disputes, prescribed trials by jury in contempt cases, and legalized such labor weapons as strikes, picketing, peaceable assembly, boycotts, and the collection of strike benefits. The framers of the Sherman Antitrust Act had probably not meant to extend its provisions to labor unions, but in the Danbury Hatters decision of 1908 (*Loewe* v. *Lawler*, 208 U.S., 274) the Supreme Court had read that interpretation into the law. Judicial obstacles had also been placed in the way of nearly

TAFT AND WILSON

Here the twenty-seventh and twenty-eighth Presidents of the United States meet at Wilson's first inauguration.

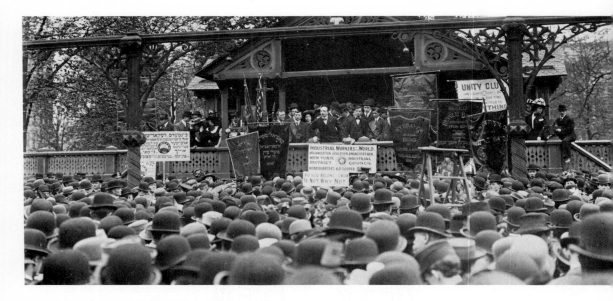

AN INDUSTRIAL WORKERS OF THE WORLD (I.W.W.) MEETING

Known as the "Wobblies," the members of this militant labor organization often engaged in outright warfare with mineowners and others of the managerial class.

every other labor practice, and "government by injunction" had become a fact. The provisions of the Clayton Act were therefore hailed as a great boon to labor, but during the reactionary years of the twenties many of these guarantees were nullified by the courts.

The friendliness of the Wilson administration toward labor was manifested in other ways. A Children's Bureau in the new Department of Labor sought to extend at least advice on the care of the nation's youth. Twice the administration approved national legislation to prohibit child labor, but each time the Supreme Court declared the measure unconstitutional. The La Follette Seaman's Act required better physical conditions for ships' crews and ended the tyrannical control of sea captains over their men. Such measures fell far short of the goals of America's small but active number of radicals. The most extreme of these groups was the Industrial Workers of the World, the "I.W.W." or "Wobblies," whose strength was recruited in the Pacific Northwest. The objectives of the "Wobblies" were frankly revolutionary,

and their anarchistic methods resulted in the passage of criminal syndicalist laws by sixteen states that seriously crippled their activities. Finally, the United States government completed their destruction by bringing to trial some 113 I.W.W. leaders, most of whom were convicted and given long jail sentences.

Rural Credits.   In his inaugural address Wilson had stressed the needs of agriculture and particularly the need of rural credits. The Federal Reserve Act authorized short-term loans up to six months on farm mortgages, but the pressure for long-term loans, by means of which the purchase of farm lands could be financed, grew steadily more insistent. After two years' consideration, Congress finally agreed to the Federal Farm Loan Act of 1916, which created a farm loan system patterned closely on the model of the Federal Reserve System. A central board consisting of the Secretary of the Treasury and four appointive members was given general control over a dozen Federal Farm Land Banks operating in as many different districts. In deference to the wishes of private moneylenders, who objected to the government's monopolizing the business of supplying rural credits, the law provided also for the establishment of joint-stock land banks, privately financed. By 1930 the two types of banks created by the Federal Farm Loan Act had together lent over $2 billion to farmers at interest rates of from 5 to 6 per cent.

"Dollar Matching." Before the exigencies of war halted the course of domestic reform the Wilson administration inaugurated another notable policy. Gifts from the federal government to aid the states in education and internal improvements were almost as old as the Constitution, but throughout the nineteenth century these grants had been made primarily in the form of land or the receipts from land sales. When Wilson became President this source of supply had so nearly approached exhaustion that some new form of subsidy had to be found. It was discovered in the form of income tax revenue, which was collected from a comparatively small fraction of the population, most of whom lived in the Northeast, although the earnings upon which the income tax was paid were drawn from all over the nation. The larger, poorer, and less densely populated states of the West and the South had come to believe that by some means the government should attempt to redistribute among all the states the heavy earnings being piled up in the urban areas. And the South and the West controlled the Democratic Party.

The new type of federal grants in aid of education began in 1914 with the passage of the Smith-Lever Act, which provided that the government should match, dollar for dollar, the contributions of cooperating states in a program of agricultural education for working farmers by county agents. The supervision of this program was given to the Department of Agriculture, working through the land-grant colleges. This measure was followed in 1917 by the Smith-Hughes Act, which appropriated funds, again on a dollar-matching basis, for edu-

cation in commercial, industrial, and domestic-science subjects in schools of less than college grade. A board of vocational education, created by the act, was given the right to pass on the merits of the projects for which the various states proposed to use their allotments.

Federal Highways Act. The Federal Highways Act of 1916 applied the dollar-matching principle to road building. The automobile, at first condemned because it tore up the roads, soon led to a demand for better roads that overtaxed the resources of the states. In such an emergency it was only natural to turn to the federal government for aid, and Democrats who remembered Jackson's war on the Bank soon demonstrated that they had quite forgotten his Maysville veto. Aid was needed for a Lincoln Highway, just marked out from coast to coast, for a Dixie Highway from the Great Lakes to the Gulf, and for many similar projects. Yielding to the general pressure, Congress appropriated $5 million the first year for distribution among the

New States

states. Size, population, and existing mail routes were all factors in determining the amounts to be allotted to each. Every dollar contributed by the federal government had to be matched by the state which received it, and federal control must be accepted in all actual expenditures. The dollar-matching principle, together with its attending federal control, was rapidly extended during the First World War and during the New Deal period, and accounted for much of the increase in the influence and power of the federal government over that of the states.

Wilsonian v. Jeffersonian Democracy. The contrast between Wilson's Jeffersonian demand for a new freedom in his election campaign of 1912 and his later legislative program is marked. Instead of limiting the power of the federal government, as the Wilsonians suggested they might do in their attack upon the Progressive program, they greatly increased it. With Hamiltonian thoroughness, the Wilsonians had devised a great national banking system that gave the national government extensive power in regulating the currency and credit sys-

tem of the entire nation. In their attempts to "restrain men from injuring one another," they circumscribed the area in which private industry regulated its activities. In protecting the rights of labor and children, they seriously limited the freedom of individuals to do as they pleased. In concerning themselves with the public welfare, they assumed wide paternalistic privileges for the national government. By 1915, the Wilsonians had enacted much of the Bull Moose program of "New Nationalism."

A partial explanation of the inconsistency of Wilson and his supporters lay in their devotion to the twin Jeffersonian ideals of equal opportunity for all men and individual freedom as well. By 1914 the two ideals were to a degree incompatible in a world of big business and big cities. By limiting individual freedom in certain ways, the Wilsonians hoped to strengthen equality of opportunity for all. As so often before in history, the responsibility of office forced the Wilsonians to compromise their theory with hard facts. Wilson had compromised by 1914 on domestic issues; in the future this man of peace was to do so again in foreign policy.

SELECTED BIBLIOGRAPHY

Indispensable is H. F. Pringle, *The Life and Times of William Howard Taft* (2 vols., 1939), based upon the Taft papers and highly sympathetic. The biographies of leading conservatives give some insight into the minds of the opponents of reform. In addition to those on Root, already noted, see: Everett Walters, *Joseph Benson Foraker* (1948); N. W. Stephenson, *Nelson W. Aldrich* (1930); and W. R. Gwinn, *Uncle Joe Cannon* (1955). A detailed study of Massachusetts is R. M. Abrams, *Conservatism in a Progressive Era* (1964). There are two important biographies of H. L. Stimson: H. L. Stimson and McGeorge Bundy, *On Active Service in Peace and War* (1948); and E. E. Morison, *°Turmoil and Tradition* (1960). The standard biography

* Available in paperback

of the progressive New York governor and future Chief Justice is M. J. Pusey, *Charles Evans Hughes* (2 vols., 1951).

The literature on the Ballinger-Pinchot controversy continues to grow. The fullest account of the affair is in E. R. Richardson, *The Politics of Conservation* (1962). Pinchot's side is argued in A. T. Mason, *Bureaucracy Convicts Itself* (1941). See also M. N. McGeary, *Gifford Pinchot, Forester-Politician* (1960); and M. L. Fausold, *Gifford Pinchot, Bull Moose Progressive* (1961).

Two dependable guides to the Progressive revolt against Taft, both based upon wide research, are K. W. Hechler, *Insurgency; Personalities and Politics of the Taft Era* (1940); and G. E. Mowry, *°Theodore Roosevelt and the Progressive Movement* (1946). G. W. Norris, *°Fighting Liberal* (1945), is a very thin autobiography. By far the best study of the Nebraska insurgent is Richard Lowitt, *George W. Norris*, I (1963–   ), which reaches to 1912. *The Autobiography of William Allen White* (1946) is rich and vivid; it may be supplemented by Walter Johnson, *William Allen White's America* (1947). Other important biographies of progressives include: A. T. Mason, *Brandeis* (1946); T. R. Ross, *Jonathan Prentice Dolliver* (1958); E. F. Goldman, *Charles J. Bonaparte* (1943); L. G. Geiger, *Joseph W. Folk of Missouri* (1953); and C. O. Johnson, *Borah of Idaho* (1936). An interesting collection of pronouncements is Theodore Roosevelt, *The New Nationalism* (1910). A detailed and opinionated work, which lays most of the blame for the failures of the Progressive Party on the head of George Perkins, is A. R. E. Pinchot, *History of the Progressive Party, 1912–1916*, edited by H. M. Hooker (1958).

Woodrow Wilson and the Progressive Era, 1910–1917 (1954), by A. S. Link, is a fine introduction, with a superb bibliography. Professor Link is engaged in the production of a full-length biography, based upon multi-archival research. Five volumes of his *Wilson* have appeared since 1947; their intensive treatment covers the first term. A full-length study by Arthur Walworth, *Woodrow Wilson*, is now available in a single volume (2nd ed., 1965). Recent brief biographies are J. A. Garraty, *Woodrow Wilson* (1956); and J. M. Blum, *Woodrow Wilson and the Politics of Morality* (1956).

The history of the first Wilson administration is treated by F. L. Paxson, *Pre-War Years, 1913–1917* (1936). A brilliant brief survey of these years is contained in W. E. Leuchtenburg, *The Perils of Prosperity, 1914–32* (1958). Wilson's 1912 speeches were edited and published soon after the campaign as *The New Freedom* (1913). An interesting collection of materials focusing upon the apparently divergent attitudes of the major 1912 candidates upon a single issue is E. C. Rozwenc (ed.), *Roosevelt, Wilson and the Trusts* (1950).

The Wilson cabinet proved to be particularly fruitful in autobiography. See especially W. G. McAdoo, *Crowded Years* (1931); D. F. Houston, *Eight Years with Wilson's Cabinet* (2 vols., 1926); Josephus Daniels, *The Wilson Era; Years of Peace, 1910–1917* (1944); and

The Cabinet Diaries of Josephus Daniels, edited by E. D. Cronon (1963). J. M. Blum, *Joe Tumulty and the Wilson Era* (1951), is an informative biography of Wilson's principal secretary. Sidney Ratner, *American Taxation* (1942), is especially good on the income tax. On the Federal Reserve, see P. M. Warburg, *The Federal Reserve System* (2 vols., 1930). On the trust problem, see G. C. Henderson, *The Federal Trade Commission* (1924); and D. D. Martin, *Mergers and the Clayton Act* (1959). Wilson's petroleum policy is the subject of J. L. Bates, *The Origins of Teapot Dome* (1963). A case study of the crisis over the confirmation of Justice Brandeis is A. L. Todd, *Justice on Trial* (1964).

A number of works on the labor movement have already been cited. Labor historians have produced many interesting studies of this period in recent years. Among these are: Hyman Weintraub, *Andrew Furuseth* (1959); J. O. Morris, *Conflict within the AFL, 1901–1938* (1958); Marc Karson, *American Labor Unions and Politics, 1900–1918* (1958); Marguerite Green, *The National Civic Federation and the American Labor Movement, 1900–1925* (1956); M. J. Nadworthy, *Scientific Management and the Unions, 1900–1932* (1955); and J. P. Felt, *Hostages to Fortune: Child Labor and Reform in New York State* (1964).

Recently historians have begun to concern themselves with the intellectual currents of the Progressive Era. Two comprehensive analyses reaching rather different conclusions have recently appeared: D. W. Noble, *The Paradox of Progressive Thought* (1958); and Charles Forcey, *The Crossroads of Liberalism; Croly, Weyl, Lippmann and the Progressive Era, 1900–1925* (1961). Daniel Levine, *Varieties of Reform Thought* (1964), is brief and lucid. Henry May, *The End of American Innocence: A Study of the First Years of Our Own Time, 1912–1917* (1959), is a reinterpretation of the period based upon very wide reading. Basic works with which intellectual historians must concern themselves include: Herbert Croly, *The Promise of American Life* (1909); Walter Rauschenbusch, *Christianity and the Social Crisis* (1907); Walter Weyl, *The New Democracy* (1912); L. D. Brandeis, *Other People's Money* (1914); and two books by Walter Lippmann, *A Preface to Politics* (1913), and *Drift and Mastery* (1914).

32

WILSON'S FOREIGN POLICY

War in Europe. On July 28, 1914, the American ambassador to France, Myron T. Herrick, warned Washington that the rift between Austria and Serbia was out of control and that most of Europe was already mobilizing for a general war. Neither the President nor most of his officials were prepared for the startling news. In taking over the Presidency, Wilson obviously had little expectation of becoming a diplomat. Preoccupied with domestic reforms, he had not so much as mentioned foreign affairs either in his inaugural address or in his first message to Congress. For the majority of Americans the news from abroad was dumfounding. Engrossed in their own affairs, they had little comprehension of the true state of European national rivalries or of the great system of alliances that threatened to turn any local quarrel into a general conflict.

For years Europe had depended on a "balance of power" between two large blocks of contending nations to keep the peace. On one side were Germany, Austria, and Italy, whose agreements on military cooperation dated back to the days of Bismarck; on the other were Great Britain, France, and Russia, ancient enemies driven together by the rising power of Germany. France and Russia had been allies since 1891, but the *entente* that bound Great Britain to France dated no further back than 1904, while the agreement between Great Britain and Russia came as late as 1907. Each set of partners made every effort to bring over the lesser nations of Europe to its side. Some, like Switzerland, Belgium, the Netherlands, and the Scandinavian countries, maintained a rigid neutrality, but others more or less unofficially chose sides. The Triple Alliance, led by Germany, could count with some certainty on the support of Bulgaria and Turkey, while the Triple Entente, led by Great Britain, was on friendly terms with Spain and Portugal, and hoped for support from Greece and Serbia.

Imperial Rivalry. Competition for empire was one of the forces bringing these powers into conflict all over the world. England, France, and Russia had old established empires to which they had added substantially in the last quarter of the nineteenth century. Germany and Italy also

560

wanted a "place in the sun," but they had entered the competition too late to obtain the share of spoils to which they felt themselves entitled. The Triple Entente, Germany believed, was created only to draw about her a "ring of iron" that would prevent the legitimate fulfillment of her desires. Imperial rivalry went further, however, than the mere acquisition of colonies. In the commercial exploitation of nonindustrial nations lay an equally inviting field. Rivalry for concessions in China, Persia, Morocco, Turkey, and the Balkans — everywhere that money could be invested and profits taken — was acute, with sometimes one nation ahead and sometimes another.

The Balkans. In no region was the atmosphere more tense than in the Balkans and the Near East. Here, in addition to the ever-present activities of the British and the Germans, the Austrians, the Italians, and the Russians all claimed special interests based on proximity, while the Russian government, as a cloak for its ambition to secure free access to the Mediterranean, assumed the additional role of protector to Greek Orthodox Christians and to the peoples of Slavic extraction. In 1908 Austria had annexed Bosnia and Herzegovina, two Serbian provinces handed her for administration in 1878, after the Russo-Turkish War. In 1911 Italy had fought a war with Turkey to secure her conquest of Tripoli; and in 1912–1913 the Balkan states had fought two wars among themselves, as a result of which both Turkey and Bulgaria had lost much territory to Greece, Serbia, and Rumania. For months before the war broke out the Balkan situation had European diplomats on edge.

Nationalism. Another factor in the situation was the exaggerated nationalism that the nineteenth century had bequeathed to the twentieth. Historically European nations were peopled by mixed populations, with no valid title to racial "purity," and

their nationalism owed more to a common language and history than to "race." Each nation prided itself upon its cultural heritage, perverted its history to make its glories seem greater, and aroused the patriotism of its people to the highest possible pitch. It became, therefore, a matter of national pride to draw within the boundaries of any given nation all who spoke its language or shared its culture. France looked forward to the time when Alsace-Lorraine, taken from her by Germany in 1871, should be again a part of France; Italy dreamed of drawing all of Dalmatia within her borders; nearly every Balkan nation claimed a part of every other; subject nations like the Poles and the Czechs longed to be free. Austria-Hungary, a polyglot of nationalities, was threatened by her every neighbor.

The dangers of the situation were compounded by the rampant militarism that affected every European nation. Universal military training had long been a policy of all the great powers of Europe except Great Britain, and most of the lesser ones. Huge standing armies made every nation an armed camp, with preparedness a national watchword. Her island character saved Great Britain from the necessity of keeping pace in land armament, but she prided herself on the overwhelming strength of her navy. Germany's expressed intention of challenging British supremacy on the high seas not only aroused Great Britain to new shipbuilding, but also led her to abandon her position of "splendid isolation," and actively to seek allies. On this account she had ended her rivalries with France and Russia, had made an alliance with Japan, and had sought earnestly to win the friendship of the United States.

House's Peace Mission. Among the few Americans who realized that an international war might break out at any moment was Colonel Edward M. House, the intimate adviser of the President, who in the spring of 1914 went to Europe to promote the reduction of land and naval armaments.

COLONEL EDWARD M. HOUSE

A nonmilitary Texas colonel and a shrewd politician, Colonel House was Wilson's close adviser at home and his frequent representative abroad.

House visited the Kaiser and talked with him for half an hour, established close connections with Sir Edward Grey and others in England, and had a try at Paris only to be frustrated there by a cabinet crisis. Everywhere he found "militarism run stark mad," but the British told him they were ready to talk reduction, and he so reported to the Kaiser. On June 28, 1914, shortly before he sailed for the United States, he learned that the heir to the Austrian throne, Archduke Franz Ferdinand, and his wife had been assassinated at Sarajevo, in the province of Bosnia, but neither House nor his English hosts appeared to realize that this Balkan incident would lead to war.

Immediate Causes of the War. The incidents that led directly to the outbreak of war seemed trifling to Americans. The assassination appeared to be the work of superpatriotic young Bosnian Serbs who disliked the Archduke's plan for making the "dual monarchy" of Austria and Hungary into a "triple monarchy" that would extend to the Slavs in the empire a right of participation comparable to that enjoyed by the Austrians and the Magyars. The success of such a plan would delay the creation of a greater Serbia, and it was apparently with this thought in mind that the fatal shots were fired. Naturally the Austrian government took a serious view of the situation, the more so because it claimed, probably with good reason, that the Serbian government had known of the plot and had made no real effort to prevent its execution. On the assumption that Serbian officials were in reality responsible for what had happened, the Austrian government decided upon punitive measures against its diminutive neighbor, and on July 5 obtained from the German Kaiser his unqualified permission to go ahead. On July 23 an Austrian ultimatum was delivered to Serbia. The Serbian reply, when it came, was deemed "evasive," and Austria began to mobilize for war.

The ramifications of the European network of alliances now came quickly into play. Russia, fearing that Austria's real intention was annexation rather than punishment, supported Serbia's plea that the affair should be settled by the Hague Tribunal. Some such settlement was also strongly urged by Great Britain and Italy, but Austria remained obdurate. Germany now also made every effort to localize the affair, but refused to abandon her ally. On July 28 Austria declared war on Serbia, and on the following day Russia began mobilization. At this point the German Kaiser telegraphed frantically to his kinsman, the Tsar, to use his influence for peace, and the Tsar ordered that mobilization should be confined strictly to the Austrian frontier. But years of European military planning now served effectively to prevent last minute reconsiderations. The great distances of the Russian countryside made a partial mobilization ineffective and the Russian military leaders easily persuaded the Tsar to reverse himself. On July 30 he gave the command for general mobilization. Thereupon the German government delivered an ultimatum to Russia, requiring the cessation of mobilization within twelve hours. When this demand was disregarded, Germany on August 1 declared war on Russia.

France was the ally of Russia, and Germany now demanded to know in eighteen hours what France intended to do. Bound by her treaty with Russia, and ready to have a try at getting back Alsace-Lorraine, France replied that she would consult her own interests. Thereupon, on August 3, Germany declared war on France and began at once to move troops toward the Belgian frontier. The German plan of campaign was to avoid the heavily fortified Franco-German frontier, demand passage through neutral Belgium, and by forced marches outflank and destroy the French army before the anticipated Russian invasion of eastern Germany could do any vital damage — a plan that failed, for the Belgians resisted valiantly and the French reformed their lines and eventually held the invaders at bay. Germany, despite her treaty to protect Belgian neutrality, thereupon declared war on Belgium. Great Britain, meantime, had been debating her obligations to France, which might mean less than aid in time of war, but the attack on Belgium, whose neutrality she, too, was pledged to defend, forced her decision. On August 5 she declared war on Germany.

American Neutrality. The breath-taking speed with which Europe thus plunged into the abyss of war left Americans aghast. The American course, however, was clear. Neutrality, since the days of George Washington, had become an American tradition. On August 4 the President issued the first of a series of proclamations of neutrality, while two weeks later he urged the American public to be "neutral in fact as well as

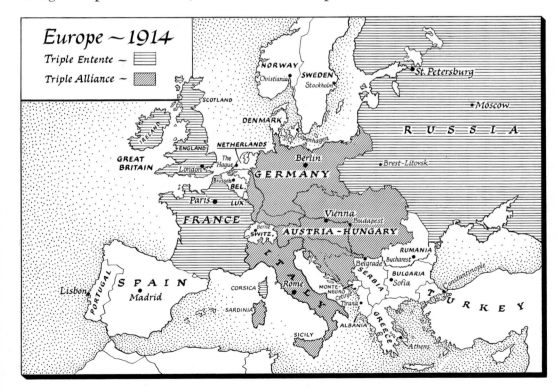

Europe ~ 1914

Triple Entente —
Triple Alliance —

in name. . . ." Wilson's neutral course met with national approval. This was Europe's war, not America's, and with the help of a sizable army of war correspondents the American public prepared to stand by and watch while the fire burned itself out.

German-Americans. But neutrality in thought and deed soon proved to be easier preached than practiced. The census of 1910 showed over 13 million people of foreign extraction in the United States, and when one added persons with one or both parents born abroad, the figure amounted to over 32 million. Understandably, many of these people had a double loyalty: they were loyal to the United States but also sympathetic toward the country from which their ancestors had come. Some whose family memories ran back to the Central Powers, as Germany and her associated nations came to be known, were outspoken in their bias. Joined by a group of Irish-Americans, who hated Britain, by some professional Anglophobes, and by a few other Americans who admired German efficiency and industrial skill, they constituted a minority group favorable to German success. The people of German extraction among them were soon known as "hyphenated Americans," a term not applied to citizens of British descent who were ardently in favor of British success.

Sympathy for the Allies. This apparent discrimination stemmed from the fact that at the very outbreak of the war the bulk of popular sympathy was for the "Allies," as the nations opposed to Germany and Austria were called. Austria and Germany had issued the first declarations of war; they were apparently the aggressors. Germany's violation of her treaty with Belgium, called by one German diplomat a "scrap of paper," was hard to overlook. The rapid progress of German troops through Belgium and northern France and their harsh treatment of enemy civilians produced a deep feeling of sympathy for the underdogs in the fight. But perhaps even more influential in the pro-Allied bias of the American people was their cultural solidarity with the people of the British Empire. A common language and literature, together with many kindred institutions, fostered a feeling of community with the British. This was especially true among the more educated and articulate American citizens. Most American college graduates had studied English literature, English government, and English history; few had comparable courses in the institutions and literature of Germany and Austria. The British Isles had long been America's greatest overseas customer, and most of the strings binding the New York financial community to the rest of the world ran to London. The obvious friendliness of British foreign policy toward the United States since the Spanish-American War had borne fruit. While German expansion had appeared to threaten American interests both in the Caribbean and the Pacific, Great Britain's policy seemed to be pointed toward a trans-Atlantic understanding. But if the majority of Americans were sentimentally inclined toward Britain and France, they were also ardent neutrals, and remained intent upon insulating the United States from the carnage taking place across the Atlantic.

Attitude of American Officials. American sympathy for the British was perhaps even stronger among the makers of public opinion and policy than among the masses. Although Wilson sincerely desired to keep America neutral, he himself inclined toward the British viewpoint. This attitude probably owed less to his ancestry, which was Scottish and Scotch-Irish, than to his interest in English history and admiration of the English parliamentary system. Despite his inclination to the Allied side, however, the President was not a partisan. Three months after the start of the war Wilson felt that neither side was entirely culpable and that the most desirable conclusion would be a negotiated peace, adding, however, that a peace dictated by the Allies would probably "not hurt greatly the interests of the United States."

A part of the President's sympathy for the Allied cause probably reflected the sentiments of his advisers. With few exceptions they were thoroughly pro-Allied in spirit. Not one favored the German side. Leading this pro-Allied group in Washington were the influential Colonel House, Secretary of the Treasury McAdoo, and Robert Lansing, State Department Counselor, who became Secretary of State after Bryan's resignation. Abroad the nation was represented by men of the same general point of view. Myron T. Herrick in France, James W. Gerard in Berlin, and Brand Whitlock in Belgium all were unneutral in spirit. Walter Hines Page in London was so rabidly pro-English that he became less an ambassador than a propagandist for the British cause, even though retaining his official position.

Propaganda. Given this initial bias, the Allies made effective use of propaganda to sell their cause to the American public. Sir Gilbert Parker, a Canadian novelist familiar with the United States, headed the American section of the official British propaganda institute in London. There thousands of editorials and pamphlets were ground out for American consumption, and a free news service for American newspapers was established. The cutting by the British navy of all trans-Atlantic cables connecting the United States with the Central Powers served to reinforce the American bias, for although German accounts continued to reach the United States through wireless stations, much of the war news came through London where it was given a British slant. Allied propagandists made effective use of the German destruction of the historic library at Louvain in Belgium and the shooting of the English nurse, Edith Cavell, as a spy. But perhaps most effective in convincing Americans that the Germans were pursuing a policy of terror

INTERNAL SECURITY: *World War I*

Fingerprinting German nationals in New York, an indication of the suspicion under which all "enemy aliens" were held.

toward noncombatants was the May, 1915, report of the official British Commission on alleged German outrages. This commission was headed by Lord Bryce, scholar and long-time friend of the United States. Although many of the report's accounts of German atrocities against civilians were later disproved, Bryce's name on the document gave it a ring of authenticity and persuaded many Americans to accept its findings as true.

German propaganda efforts actually preceded those of the British, and for a time at least were moderately effective. Headed by the American poet, George Sylvester Viereck, and by the German embassy in Washington, the campaign was well financed and reached to every part of the country. But after the launching of the German unrestricted submarine campaign and the sinking of the passenger liner *Lusitania*, public opinion definitely turned against the Central Powers. Perhaps as a kind of substitute Germany then sought to minimize the growing American trade with the Allies by sabotaging industrial plants and trade facilities in America. As early as January, 1915, a railroad bridge in Maine, over which artillery sold to Canada was to be moved, was destroyed. There followed a series of explosions on ships moving out of American harbors bound for Britain and in American munitions plants, as well as an unsuccessful effort to blow up the Welland Canal. Fortunately, the identity of the foreign agents, among whom was the Austrian ambassador, implicated in these and other similar activities, was proved. While these incidents did little to stop trade to the Allies, they did create a fresh wave of anti-German feeling throughout the country. Perhaps the most significant result of both the British and the German propaganda campaigns was that after two years of intense effort, they failed to persuade most Americans to become active partisans for either side. To this extent the campaigns failed or were mutually cancelling, and propaganda proved an uncertain weapon.

Economic Ties with the Allies. The war trade between America and the Allies, which the Germans tried to reduce by sabotage, was an extremely important factor itself in conditioning the American mind. For months before the outbreak of war, the United States had been in the grip of an advancing depression. In 1914 alone 16,000 business firms went bankrupt, and in the major cities of the nation thousands of workingmen were unemployed. But within a few months after August, 1914, the economic situation quickly changed for the better due to the enormous purchases of the Allied powers. American exports to all Allied nations increased from $824 million in 1914 to almost $2 billion in 1915. By the following year they had jumped to $3.2 billion. Labor, business, agriculture, and, in fact, almost the whole American economy had a stake in these overseas markets, but after the British disaster in 1915 due to a lack of artillery shells, an increasing portion of this trade was in munitions. "The Allies," the British Foreign Minister, Lord Grey, later wrote,

"became dependent for an adequate supply on the United States." At the same time, because of the British control of the seas, Germany's trade with the United States virtually vanished.

At the very start of the war a few Americans questioned the wisdom of selling war materials to the belligerent nations. Many neutral European countries had ceased doing so, and it was argued that because the British controlled the seas so completely, such trade would be restricted to the Allied Powers, and thus would endanger America's neutrality. Accordingly, Senator Hitchcock of Nebraska introduced an embargo measure in December, 1914. But even Secretary of State Bryan felt that an embargo after war was declared would be unneutral, and when businessmen, farmers, and laborers alike protested, the proposal was soundly beaten. In commenting on trade with the Allies, the *Financial Annalist* was simply voicing the sentiments of the majority of all American classes: "We need it for the profits it will bring."

Loans to the Allies. Lending money to the Allies was another question. As early as August 10, 1914, J. P. Morgan and Company, later appointed the American purchasing agent for the Allied nations, inquired about the government's attitude toward such loans. Declaring that "money is the worst of all contraband because it commands everything else," Bryan vehemently opposed any private American loans to warring powers. But as American shipments increased to staggering figures, the Allied nations soon began to run short of international exchange. By the end of 1915 it appeared that Great Britain and France would either have to reduce their purchases or float huge loans in the United States. Both Secretary of the Treasury McAdoo and Secretary of State Lansing favored large-scale loans, as did many other Americans who saw the new prosperity endangered by a possible curtailment of Allied purchasing. Unquestionably the swing of American opinion toward Great Britain and France after the sinking of the *Lusitania* was also important in the revision of policy. In September, 1915, it became known in New York that the administration would not oppose loans to the Allies. Within a short time the first loan of $500 million was made, a large part of it taken by corporations engaged in production for the Allies. Later Allied loans were floated by popular subscription, and by April, 1917, Great Britain, France, and Russia together had borrowed $2.3 billion in the United States, of which the larger part went to pay for Allied purchases and consequently never left American shores. Cut off from all such purchasing, Germany had small need for American exchange. By 1917 the German loans from American lenders were a paltry $27 million.

Evidence produced by the so-called Nye Committee of 1934 indicated that the New York financial community was heavily committed to Allied victory. Undoubtedly this Wall Street position had its influence among businessmen, a portion of the press, and perhaps a few high American officials. But the assumption that Wall Street influence was mainly responsible for changing the Administration's mind and thus shoving America toward war cannot be supported by evidence. After the loans were made, Wilson became even more neutral in his attitude toward the European struggle, a position he did not change until after the resumption of Germany's unrestricted submarine warfare in January, 1917.

Whatever the government's attitude, the intimate trading and financial connections between the Allies and the United States had serious repercussions both abroad and at home. For one thing, they made an Allied victory and perhaps even Allied continuance in the war dependent upon a steady stream of ammunition and supplies from the United States. This situation did not go unnoticed in Germany, and it furnished a weapon to the military faction, who demanded and got from their leaders the unrestricted use of submarines on the high seas.

International Law and the War. To protect American neutrality while carrying on the war trade, the American government relied upon the rights of neutrals as prescribed by international law. As early as 1625, Hugo Grotius published the first book on international law, *De Jure Belli ac Pacis.* The rules of international law, which grew with the times, had nothing more behind them than custom and the common consent of sovereign states. There was a law of peace that was rarely broken, and a law of war that was rarely kept. Invariably in time of war disputes broke out as to what the law really was and how it should be construed. The rights of neutrals were particularly subject to debate. Twentieth-century attempts to obtain agreement on the meaning of the rules or to amend them met with no success. Neither the code of land warfare adopted by the Second Hague Conference, nor the Declaration of London on naval warfare, was fully ratified. Promptly on the outbreak of the war Wilson asked the belligerents to adhere to the Declaration of London, and the Central Powers agreed to do so if the Allies would bind themselves similarly. But the British feared the limitations on sea power contained in the proposed rules and refused to accept them. The United States, therefore, in defending its neutrality had nothing better to depend on than the jumbled mass of precedents and opinions that had accumulated since the time of Grotius, many of them utterly unrelated to the conditions of modern warfare.

Relations with Great Britain. It was immediately apparent that the British had no notion of allowing the vast amount of American goods being shipped overseas to fall into the hands of its enemies. The products of American farms and factories were coveted by both sides, and the United

States was eager to sell. All this was entirely satisfactory to the British, with the single important exception that they were determined to prevent anything of value from reaching the Central Powers. To accomplish their purpose the British had only to use their naval strength, but, unlike the Germans, they did what they could to reconcile wartime necessities with the rules of international law. For authority in dealing with neutral trade, they invoked three well-recognized belligerent rights: (1) the stoppage of trade in contraband goods, (2) the doctrine of continuous voyages, and (3) the blockade.

In each instance, however, British policy affronted the neutrals. The British definition of contraband — that is, goods that might be of direct (absolute contraband) or indirect (conditional contraband) use to the enemy — was so generous as to include every commodity that the Central Powers might wish to import. This, the State Department claimed, was going too far. Further, British ships inspected trade between the United States and such neutrals as bordered on Germany, or on any of her allies, to make sure that none of it was ultimately intended for the enemy. If that was deemed to be the case, the trip was regarded as one continuous voyage which might be interrupted anywhere in its progress. This, too, was protested, although in the Civil War the United States had done practically the same thing to prevent British commodities from reaching the South. Finally, a Ministry of Blockade was set up, which took good care that all shipping found anywhere on the high seas was carefully scrutinized to prevent the Central Powers' obtaining anything that the British did not wish them to have. Such a blockade, the United States maintained, was illegal. It was enforced at long distance; it was applied against neutral as well as against belligerent coasts; and it was unenforceable against the countries that bordered on the Baltic Sea, because there the German navy was supreme.

The protests lodged by the United States against Great Britain also included vigorous denunciations of the British practice of taking neutral ships to Allied ports to be searched. The old rules contemplated search on the high seas, but with modern shipping such a practice was difficult, and after submarine warfare began, extremely dangerous. Sometimes American ships were held up for months in Allied ports. The British practice of searching American mail, both to and from Europe, also drew vigorous protest. Exports from the Central Powers were given as scant courtesy as imports, and for long periods American industry was shut off from supplies obtainable only from Germany, such as dyestuffs, drugs, and sugar-beet seed.

As early as September 26, 1914, the American government officially protested a British proposal to lengthen their list of contraband goods. Such action, "so prejudicial to neutral rights," the American note warned, might engender "bitter feeling" between the two nations. After each succeeding extension of British blockade practices, Washington regularly protested. But both Wilson and Lansing admitted later that many of the notes, none of which had the character of an ultimatum, had been toned down so as not to embarrass the British. From 1915 on, the Allied governments bought almost the total supply of American exports at high prices. The amount of goods consigned to the Central Powers and seized by the British was both relatively small and almost wholly owned by foreigners before it left American shores. In general, American officials studiously built up a case against Great Britain for future claims and as carefully refrained from pushing their demands to lengths that would precipitate a serious quarrel with the British.

The close community of interests thus developed between the United States and the Allies was an object of great concern to the Germans, who were handicapped by their inability to trade with America, and was of scarcely less concern to many German sympathizers in the United States itself. Some of the latter, including Senator William J. Stone of Missouri, chairman of the Senate Committee on Foreign Relations, favored a complete embargo on the sale of military supplies, particularly ammunition, outside the national borders, but the State Department maintained with unimpeachable logic that such trade was not a violation of neutrality. If Germany could not buy in the United States, it was the fault of the British navy, not of the American government.

Submarine Warfare. Germany's most effective means of retaliation against the pressure of Allied sea power proved to be the submarine, a type of craft her engineers had brought to extraordinary efficiency. On February 4, 1915, in protest against the British stoppage of food shipments to Germany, the German government drew a "war zone" about the British Isles, and announced its intention to sink on sight every enemy merchantman within the area. The United States was warned to keep American shipping out of the danger zone lest by mistake American ships and lives be lost. Against this new type of warfare the American government lodged an immediate protest. Its illegality was obvious even to the German government, which defended it only on the ground of retaliation for illegal actions by the Allies, and the willingness of neutrals to acquiesce in them. The war-zone decree could not be defended as a blockade, for a blockade, to be binding on neutral nations, must effectively stop a major part of the shipping plying to and from the blockaded ports, whereas German submarines could not hope to intercept more than an occasional ship. Visit and search by a submarine to ascertain the character of the ship and the nature of its cargo would be a virtual impossibility. Sinking on sight defied all the rules that required the attacking warship to provide for the safety of noncombatant passengers and crews. Reciting the evidence that the war-zone decree was illegal, Wilson's note of protest warned that in case American ships or lives were lost the German government would be held to a "strict accountability."

The *Lusitania*. The threat to American neutrality posed by the submarine blockade led Wilson to dispatch Colonel House to Europe on a "quest for peace." House cherished the chimerical hope that he might persuade the British to give up their blockade and the Germans their submarine attacks on merchantmen — the very weapons by which the two leading contenders hoped to win the war. Naturally his quest was fruitless. On May 7, 1915, the British passenger liner, *Lusitania*, on which he had sailed to Europe a few weeks before, was torpedoed without warning and sunk off the Irish coast on her way to England. More than 1,100 persons lost their lives, including 128 Americans. The sinking was a clear violation of neutral rights. Warning had not been given by a shot across the ship's bow, or in any other manner prescribed by sea usage. The fact that an advertisement in a New York paper had warned passengers of what might happen if they sailed on the *Lusitania* seemed to prove that the act was premeditated; no known rule of international law provided for a newspaper warning, and the advertisement was generally regarded as a hoax. The fact that the *Lusitania* carried ammunition intended for Allied use was equally irrelevant. The Germans had a perfect right to capture and confiscate the ship, even to sink it, but according to the existing rules they should first have found out by search what its cargo contained and made satisfactory provision for the safety of noncombatants.

American opinion on the *Lusitania* disaster was not entirely unanimous. Theodore Roosevelt, the most bitter of the anti-German leaders in the United States, described the attack on the *Lusitania* as an

THE *LUSITANIA* WARNING

Published in a New York newspaper, the Lusitania *warning had no standing in international law, but seemed to show clearly the intent of the German government.*

OCEAN STEAMSHIPS.

CUNARD

EUROPE VIA LIVERPOOL

LUSITANIA

Fastest and Largest Steamer
now in Atlantic Service Sails
SATURDAY, MAY 1, 10 A.M.
Transylvania, Fri., May 7, 5 P.M.
Orduna, - - Tues.,May 18, 10 A.M.
Tuscania, - - Fri., May 21, 5 P.M.
LUSITANIA, Sat., May 29, 10 A.M.
Transylvania, Fri., June 4, 5 P.M.

Gibraltar—Genoa—Naples—Piraeus
S.S. Carpathia, Thur., May 13, Noon

NOTICE!

TRAVELLERS intending to
embark on the Atlantic voyage
are reminded that a state of
war exists between Germany
and her allies and Great Britain
and her allies; that the zone of
war includes the waters adjacent to the British Isles; that,
in accordance with formal notice given by the Imperial German Government, vessels flying
the flag of Great Britain, or of
any of her allies, are liable to
destruction in those waters and
that travellers sailing in the
war zone on ships of Great
Britain or her allies do so at
their own risk.

IMPERIAL GERMAN EMBASSY

WASHINGTON. D. C., APRIL 22, 1915.

"act of piracy," and demanded immediate war. Many agreed with him, particularly along the Atlantic seaboard where the importance of keeping open the sea lanes to Europe was most keenly felt, but in the West and the South there was a tendency to ask why American citizens needed to venture into the danger zone. Should the American government not prevent such incidents in the future by prohibiting its nationals from sailing on belligerent merchant ships, or on ships carrying munitions? Bryan himself took this attitude, which easterners called "provincial," and he would have been willing even to submit the *Lusitania* incident to arbitration. He signed the first note of protest that Wilson wrote, but the next one was too much for him, and he resigned from the cabinet rather than be party to a policy which in his judgment might easily lead to war. The same sentiment appeared in Congress, where only the vigorous intervention of the President prevented the passage of the McLemore-Gore resolutions, forbidding American citizens to travel on belligerent merchantmen except at their own peril.

Germany Backs Down. The *Lusitania* incident led to a diplomatic correspondence between the United States and Germany that lasted all through the summer of 1915. Wilson's statement, made in a public address just before his first note was sent, "There is such a thing as a man being too proud to fight," seemed to betoken an attitude of weakness, but in three successive notes he argued the case with Germany, taking stronger ground each time. The submarine, he held, used as Germany was using it, was an illegal weapon, and any repetition of the *Lusitania* offense would be regarded as a "deliberately unfriendly" act. This was a threat of war, as the German ambassador to the United States, Count von Bernstorff, well knew, but the offense was repeated on August 19, 1915, when the *Arabic* was sunk with the loss of two American lives. Thereupon von Bernstorff, acting on his own initiative, promised the American State Department in writing that liners would not be sunk "without warning and without safety to the lives of noncombatants, provided that the liners do not try to escape or offer resistance." Eventually the German government agreed to von Bernstorff's promise. Wilson had scored a signal diplomatic triumph, but only by the threat of war. When, either by accident or intent, a few more sinkings occurred, notably the *Sussex,* on March 24, 1916, Wilson in a spectacular appearance before Congress renewed his threat and forced from the German government a reiteration of its promise. This promise, called the "Sussex Pledge," was given only on the condition that the United States would force the Allies to abide by international law. But for nine months, whether because it feared the United States or because it had discovered a need for more submarines, the German government kept its qualified promise.

Preparedness. In part, at least, to implement his threats, Wilson now put himself at the head of a strong campaign for military preparedness that, in spite of much pacifist protest, was sweeping the country. In his annual message to Congress of December, 1915, he called emphatic attention to the need for strengthening the national defenses. Early in 1916 he toured the country to speak for preparedness, and on Flag Day, June 14, led a preparedness parade down Pennsylvania Avenue. His determination to make the United States ready for war was strengthened by the failure of another mission by Colonel House to Europe, this time to offer the Allies a "plan to compel peace." The idea was that Wilson, with Allied foreknowledge, should demand the cessation of hostilities and a conference of the belligerents to discuss peace terms. If the proposals of the Allies — to be agreed upon in advance after consultation with the United States — were not accepted by Germany, then the United

States would "probably" join the Allied war effort. Wilson's use of the word "probably," as an afterthought, no doubt wrecked the plan, and the war went on. With the failure of the plan the President was even more fearful that the United States might be drawn into the war and more determined to be ready for it.

The battle of Jutland, fought May 31-June 1, 1916, gave Americans a rude jolt. In that engagement the German High-Seas Fleet boldly challenged the British Grand Fleet in the North Sea and inflicted such serious damage upon it as to serve warning that British command of the seas might soon be threatened. Already the Chicago *Tribune,* persistent champion of a foreign policy based on national self-interest, had warned its readers of the dire consequences to the United States in case the British fleet should be destroyed. If this should happen, the *Tribune* argued, every item of American foreign policy "would have to be scrutinized in the light of unknown conditions," and the nation's future might be gravely imperiled. To forestall such a calamity, many Americans, including apparently some of the makers of *Tribune* policy, were ready to form a definite alliance with Great Britain and enter the war.

Opposition to preparedness now lost ground steadily in Congress, for even those who were unwilling to concede that the British navy was the first line of defense for the United States were aware of the dangers to America that might come from German control of the seas. A National Defense Act authorizing the increase of the standing army to 175,000, and the National Guard to 450,000, became law early in June. Even more important was the Naval Appropriation Act, passed two months later, which provided for the immediate construction of four dreadnoughts and four battle cruisers. The total appropriation carried in this measure ran to $313 million, the largest sum Congress had ever voted at any one time for naval purposes. Three capital ships, the *Nevada,* the *Pennsylvania,* and the *Oklahoma,* had just been completed. To further promote the national defense Congress created a Council of National Defense, to consist of six Cabinet officers and seven unpaid civilian experts, as well as a United States Shipping Board, which might build, or otherwise acquire, and operate a fleet of merchantmen.

Election of 1916. The campaign of 1916 occurred during the months immediately following Wilson's diplomatic victory over Germany. That Wilson would be a candidate to succeed himself was taken for granted. The congressional elections of 1914 had found most of the Progressives back in the Republican fold, but that year the Democrats had emerged triumphant in a straight-out two-party contest. The reason for this, as everyone knew, was Woodrow Wilson. When the Democratic Convention met in St. Louis, June 14, it renominated Wilson by acclamation and in its platform recorded complete approval of every action the administration had taken.

In a shrewd effort to unite all forces opposed to Wilson, the Republicans turned for their candidate to Associate Justice Charles Evans Hughes of the United States Supreme Court. With the discretion permitted to justices, Hughes had not openly taken sides for or against Germany, for or against intervention in Mexico, for or against preparedness. Nor had he been involved in any way in the disastrous Republican split of four years before. His background as governor of New York was presumably satisfying to the progressive wing of the party, and his decisions as associate justice had caused the conservatives no alarm. Hughes's availability was so obvious that the Republicans, meeting at Chicago on June 7, named him on the first ballot, although he had done nothing to advance his candidacy and had not even said that he would accept the nomination. All went as planned. Roosevelt, by declining a Progressive nomination and supporting Hughes, dealt a deathblow to the party

he had founded. Pro-Germans who thought Wilson had been unfair to Germany, anti-Germans who condemned his soft treatment of wanton aggressors, pacifists who were for peace at any price, war advocates who demanded, sometimes in the same breath, intervention in both Mexico and Europe, all rallied to the Republican standard. The day Hughes resigned from the Supreme Court to accept the proffered nomination he might have been elected, for then all factions could have claimed him as their own.

As the campaign progressed, the President's chances improved. His followers argued, truthfully enough, that he had "kept us out of war," forgetting, perhaps, that he had made a threat that might draw the nation in. Many Progressives who had supported Roosevelt in 1912 were ready to change their allegiance to Wilson, for under his dynamic leadership a comprehensive program of domestic reform had been achieved. Wilson got the "breaks" of the campaign. When a "hyphenated American" sent a telegram to Wilson denouncing him for unfairness to Germany, the President's reply was tart: "I would feel deeply mortified to have you or anybody like you vote for me. Since you have access to many disloyal Americans and I have not, I will ask you to convey this message to them."

The Adamson Act. Hughes, on the other hand, was obliged to conduct a campaign of carping criticism, while not being free to take sides on anything. He had only one stroke of luck. The railway brotherhoods chose Labor Day immediately preceding the election as a desirable time to strike for recognition of the basic eight-hour day and time and a half for overtime. Such a strike would have throttled business and seriously hampered the President's efforts to speed preparedness. Faced by this emergency, Wilson asked Congress to prevent the strike by enacting into law the demands of the brotherhoods. Congress

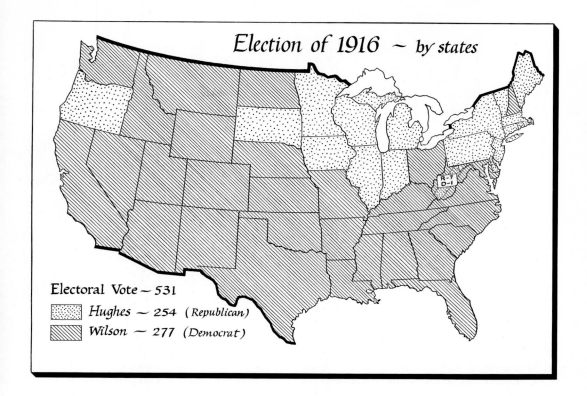

Election of 1916 ~ by states

R-7
D-1

Electoral Vote — 531

Hughes — 254 (Republican)

Wilson — 277 (Democrat)

obeyed with the passage of the Adamson Act. Here Hughes had some ground for criticism and he made the most of it, but when he was asked if he would favor the repeal of the law, he could only reply, "You can't repeal a surrender."

On election night it appeared certain that Hughes had won. He had carried the East almost solidly, plus every state in the Old Northwest except Ohio. But the returns from the South and the farther West told a different story. The solid South was conceded to the Democrats, but Wilson also carried every state west of the Mississippi except Minnesota, Iowa, South Dakota, and Oregon, which he lost by slender margins. In the electoral college the vote stood 277 to 254, the closest division since 1876. Again the Democrats captured both houses of Congress. Significantly the protest vote of nearly a million that had been cast for Eugene V. Debs, the Socialist candidate in 1912, dropped to 585,113 for Allen Benson in 1916.

Wilson's Bid For Peace. Deeply impressed by the popularity of the slogan, "He kept us out of war," Wilson made another attempt shortly after the election to bring the war to an end. In a note released December 20, 1916, he asked the fighting powers for "an avowal of their respective views" as to terms upon which the war might be concluded. Both sides, he observed, claimed to be fighting for "virtually the same" things. Perhaps if they would state their war aims more precisely, the differences between them would not be too great to bridge. Anticipating Wilson's offer, and with the military situation running strongly in their favor, the German authorities had already let it be known on December 12 that they were willing to enter a peace conference. They thus made Wilson's call for a statement of war aims appear to be a reinforcement of their own offer. The Allies indignantly rejected the idea of treating with a victorious Germany, but, although deeply offended that Wilson

should have made a move for peace at a time when Germany was winning, they replied at length to his inquiry. Peace, they said, must carry with it the restitution of conquered territories, full reparations for damages done, and guaranties that nothing of the kind would happen again. The Germans refused to state specific aims, reserving for themselves full freedom of action at the council table.

Reading these replies, Wilson believed that there could be no hope of a lasting peace if either side were permitted to have its way. On January 22, 1917, in an address before the Senate, he began to argue the case for "peace without victory," hoping that eventually the warring nations would heed his words. Such a peace as the victor might impose upon the vanquished, he said, "would be accepted in humiliation, under duress, at an intolerable sacrifice . . . Only a peace between equals can last." He even outlined the terms of what he thought would constitute a just peace: equality of rights for small and great nations; universal recognition of the principle that governments derive their just powers from the consent of the governed; the right of every great people to have an outlet to the sea; the freedom of the seas "in law and in fact";

the limitation of armaments; the avoidance by all nations of entangling alliances. Already he had made known his belief that there must be a league to enforce peace, and he told the Senate that if such a peace as he had outlined could be made the United States must do its part to maintain it.

The Submarine Again. These were brave words, but before they were spoken the German government had already decided upon the policy which was to rob them of their effect. Convinced by its admiralty that unrestricted submarine warfare would speedily destroy enough shipping to isolate Great Britain and force her to sue for peace, the German government announced on January 31, 1917, that its submarines would sink on sight all ships found within specified war zones, whether neutral or belligerent. Its promise to the United States not to sink without warning and without making provision for the safety of noncombatants it withdrew on the ground that the United States had failed to stop the illegal practices of the Allies. Wilson had no choice now but to break off diplomatic relations with Germany.

For a time it seemed that the President was seeking a formula short of outright war

574

WOODROW WILSON

Aloof, scholarly, often pedantic, Woodrow Wilson nevertheless became one of the great leaders of popular democracy. The son of a Presbyterian minister, his religious convictions ran deep, and his public addresses, always distinguished by clarity of thought and expression, gained added force by their moral fervor.

The way to success in America is to show you are not afraid of anybody except God and His judgment. If I did not believe that, I would not believe in democracy. . . . If I did not believe that the moral judgment would be the last and final judgment in the minds of men, as well as at the tribunal of God, I could not believe in popular government.

From a speech given in Philadelphia, July 4, 1914

---

to resolve the situation. He spoke of "armed neutrality," and asked Congress to grant him authority to provide American merchantmen with guns for their defense. A "little group of willful men," as the President called them, filibustered this measure to death, but the needed authority was found in an unrepealed law of 1797, and American merchantmen were armed. Wilson professed to believe that the Germans would never carry out their threats, but when, on March 18, German submarines sank three ships with loss of American lives, war became inevitable.

Why America Fought. Despite the prominence of the submarine issue, many factors worked together to draw the United States into the war. Undoubtedly the diplomatic impasse over submarine warfare did in fact precipitate hostilities; but other considerations also influenced the American people. How closely the American economy was geared to Allied trade became apparent when the German submarine threat of January, 1917, brought about a sudden stoppage of shipments from Atlantic ports. Thoroughly frightened by the German sinkings, neutral shipping refused to put to sea. Belligerent merchantmen continued to come and go, but they were utterly unable to handle the traffic that cluttered the docks and warehouses of the eastern seaboard and tied up the railroads with unloaded freight as far west as Pittsburgh. Without American shipping to move American goods overseas, the United States faced a severe economic reverse. And Great Britain faced the loss of the war.

In the spring of 1917 the Germans seemed to have victory within their grasp. German offensives in the East had been overwhelmingly successful; Allied offensives were invariably followed by "strategic retreats." Nearly all of Belgium and a large part of northern France lay in German hands. The Russians had lost most of Poland, while Rumania was no sooner in the war on the Allied side than her army was defeated and her territory occupied. Much of Serbia had long since been overrun. Austria, Bulgaria, and Turkey seemed completely subservient to the German will. Germany had lost her colonies, and she was beginning to suffer from the Allied blockade, but with the assistance of the submarine she had good reason to believe that her road to victory was clear. From its inception unrestricted submarine warfare took a terrific toll. For weeks one ship out of every four that left British ports failed to return. Neutral shipping tended more and more to stay out of the war zone. Even if the British navy remained afloat, Great Britain was faced with the threat of being starved into submission.

The Balance of Power. It now seems apparent that the one outcome of the war completely unacceptable to most Americans was a German victory. No doubt they would have preferred Wilson's "peace without victory" to American intervention in the war, provided that such a peace would have left Great Britain strong and her navy still able to control the eastern Atlantic. But they feared the consequences of substituting Germany for Great Britain as an Atlantic neighbor. From its infancy the United States had relied upon the balance between the British navy on the one hand and the continental armies of Europe on the other as a sure means of protection for the western hemisphere from European invasion. Always the two forces had checkmated each other. Continental armies could threaten the security of the British Isles if the British navy should be committed too far away from home, while the British navy could make the huge continental armies ineffective beyond European shores.

Within the American government many officials freely admitted their uneasiness at the thought of a German victory. After the outbreak of war both Lansing and House warned Wilson repeatedly that such a victory, by destroying British sea power, would threaten American security. "It is safer and surer and wiser for us to be one of many enemies," Lansing wrote in 1916, "than to be in the future alone against a victorious Germany." Anglo-American accord had made possible the location of some of the new American navy in the Pacific, as a guarantee against the danger of Japanese aggression. Germany, coveting Latin America as a field for colonial expansion, had been long restive under the restraints of the Monroe Doctrine. If

Germany drove the British navy from the Atlantic, what would be her next move? As if to provide an answer to this question, intercepted dispatches that the British secret service had turned over to the American government revealed that on March 1, 1917, the German Foreign Minister, Alfred Zimmermann, had offered Mexico an alliance if war occurred between the United States and Germany, on condition "That we shall make war together and together make peace. We shall give generous financial support, and it is understood that Mexico is to reconquer the lost territory in New Mexico, Texas, and Arizona." Further, the President of Mexico was to urge Japan to shift from the Allies to the Central Powers, presumably in return for what spoils Japan might desire at the expense of the United States. After the news of the "Zimmermann plot" reached the public, an American declaration of war on Germany was almost a certainty.

Wilson Asks for War. Wilson called Congress into special session for April 2, and on the evening of that day read his call to arms. Everything else had been tried, he claimed, and now the only recourse was war. The President disclaimed any desire to fight against the German people, and distinguished between them and their government. That government, however, had challenged the security of democracy throughout the world. The United States was glad to fight, he said,

> for the ultimate peace of the world and for the liberation of its people, the German peoples included; for the rights of nations great and small and the privilege of men everywhere to choose their way of life and of obedience. The world must be made safe for democracy. Its peace must be planted upon the tested foundations of political liberty.

The response of Congress to the President's eloquent appeal was not unanimous, but it was convincing. On April 4 the

Senate passed the war resolution by a vote of 82 to 6, and on April 6 the House concurred by a vote of 373 to 50. Diplomatic relations with Austria-Hungary were promptly broken, but war was not declared until December 7. Against Germany's other allies, Turkey and Bulgaria, the United States issued no declarations of war. Claiming that the war against Germany was being fought on behalf of neutral rights generally, the United States urged other neutrals also to join in the crusade. As a result several Latin-American nations and China entered the war on the Allied side. Long before, Japan and Portugal had joined the Allies in order to fulfill their treaties with Great Britain, while Italy by generous promises and Greece by threats had also been brought into the Allied camp. Thus the war became in fact as well as in name a World War.

The "War to End War." President Wilson was an idealist who rarely talked or thought about foreign affairs in terms of "power politics." To have done so would have been inconsistent with his character and ethical outlook, although his actions, as for example in his Caribbean policy,

were not always in harmony with his words. His argument that "we entered the war as the disinterested champions of right" was a rationalization. The United States entered the war because so many Americans felt that continued neutrality would imperil the future security of the nation. But Wilson's high principles had a strong appeal for the masses. He touched a magic chord when he said, "The world must be made safe for democracy." With Russia then in the throes of a democratic revolution, a fair case could be made for the assertion that the war was a conflict between autocracies and democracies. As long as autocracy with its attendant militancy existed in any of the great nations, there could be little reason to hope for a just and lasting peace. In line with this argument, the war became in Wilson's mind and words not only a war to make the world safe for democracy, but also a "war to end war." With these emotional overtones ringing in their ears, the American people went to war in a mood of the highest idealism. They fought — or at least great numbers of them so believed — for the survival of democracy and for peace on earth.

SELECTED BIBLIOGRAPHY

The leading works on the background of the European conflict are S. B. Fay, *The Origins of the World War* (2 vols., 2nd ed., 1930); and B. E. Schmitt, *The Coming of the War, 1914* (2 vols., 1930). While Fay and Schmitt do not agree completely, both contend that some blame should go to each side. H. E. Barnes, *The Genesis of the World War* (3rd ed., 1929), a pioneer "revisionist" book, puts most of the blame on France and Russia. Conflicting interpretations are gathered in *The Outbreak of the First World War*, edited by D. E. Lee (2nd ed., 1963). See the recent brief interpretation by Laurence Lafore, *The Long Fuse* (1965). Dependable over-all sur-

veys which reflect the thinking of their times are: C. J. H. Hayes, *A Brief History of the Great War* (1920); B. H. Liddell Hart, *The Real War, 1914–1918* (1930); and Cyril Falls, *The Great War* (1959). A vivid new study which depicts the horror of the war's opening weeks is B. W. Tuchman, *The Guns of August* (1962). A valuable new analysis, based upon multi-archival research, is Marion Siney, *The Allied Blockade of Germany, 1914–1916* (1957).

E. R. May, *The World War and American Isolation, 1914–1917* (1959), is a superb survey and analysis, based upon European as well as American sources; it is generally pro-Wilson in its conclusions. A. S. Link, *Wilson the Diplomatist* (1957), is a rich series of lectures

° Available in paperback

by the leading Wilson scholar of today. Interesting discussions of Wilson's diplomacy may be found in: Harley Notter, *The Origins of the Foreign Policy of Woodrow Wilson* (1937); E. H. Buehrig, *Woodrow Wilson and the Balance of Power* (1955); and *Wilson's Foreign Policy in Perspective,* a group of five stimulating centennial essays, edited by E. H. Buehrig (1957). A fascinating account of one crucial episode is B. W. Tuchman, °*The Zimmermann Telegram* (1958).

Charles Seymour defends the Wilson position on neutrality and intervention in *American Diplomacy during the World War* (1934), and *American Neutrality, 1914–1917* (1935). The same is true of the polemical work by N. D. Baker, *Why We Went to War* (1936), and of the scholarly legal study by A. M. Morrissey, *The American Defense of Neutral Rights, 1914–1917* (1939). Seymour, Baker, and Miss Morrissey emphasize the German submarine as the decisive factor in bringing about American intervention. Edwin Borchard and W. P. Lage, *Neutrality for the United States* (2nd ed., 1940), one of the many books designed to keep this nation out of another world war, argues that the United States was not truly neutral in 1914–1917, and that the submarine was something of an excuse for formal entry into the war. Criticism of American neutrality was first effectively stated in C. H. Grattan, *Why We Fought* (1929). It was continued by C. C. Tansill in *America Goes to War* (1938), which is marred by Anglophobia. Walter Millis, *Road to War, America, 1914–1917* (1935), is the most clearly written of all the revisionist works; Millis seems not to have objected so much to American intervention as to the way it came about. A recent re-evaluation is S. R. Spencer, Jr., *Decision for War, 1917* (1953). Conflicting interpretations are gathered together in °*America's Entry into World War I,* edited by H. J. Bass (1964). An excellent recent synthesis is D. M. Smith, *The Great Departure; The United States and World War I, 1914–1920* (1965).

On American involvement with the war, *The Intimate Papers of Colonel House,* edited by Charles Seymour (4 vols., 1926–1928), provides a running commentary from the pen of an insider. B. J. Hendrick, *Life and Letters of Walter H. Page* (3 vols., 1922–1925), reveals clearly the strongly pro-British sympathies of the American Ambassador to the Court of St. James. Robert Lansing, *War Memoirs of Robert Lansing, Secretary of State* (1935), a valuable source, may now be supplemented by the scholarly analysis of D. M. Smith, *Robert Lansing and American Neutrality, 1914–1917* (1958). See also the recent monograph on Lansing's Japanese policy, *Vain Endeavor* (1962), by B. F. Beers.

For the side of the Central Powers, see Konstantin Dumba, *Memoirs of a Diplomat* (1932); and J. H. von Bernstorff, *My Three Years in America* (1920). The experiences of the American Ambassador in Berlin are recounted in J. W. Gerard, *My Four Years in Germany* (1917). The plight of German-Americans has been well studied in Carl Wittke, *German-Americans and the World War* (1936); and C. J. Child, *The German-Americans in Politics, 1914–1917* (1939).

H. C. Peterson, *Propaganda for War* (1939), examines closely and critically the effects of British propaganda in the United States. See also the broader work by H. D. Lasswell, *Propaganda Techniques in the World War* (1927). On Anglo-American relations see also: Armin Rappaport, *The British Press and Wilsonian Neutrality* (1951); and L. W. Martin, *Peace Without Victory; Woodrow Wilson and the British Liberals* (1958). The attitude of an influential anti-preparedness Congressman may be found in A. M. Arnett, *Claude Kitchin and the Wilson War Policies* (1937).

33

THE FIRST WORLD WAR

Creating the American Army · War Finance · Mobilizing Opinion · Industrial Mobilization · Home Front · The A.E.F. · Contributions to Victory · The Fourteen Points · The Armistice · Election of 1918 · The Peace of Paris · Senate Rejection of the League of Nations

The American Army. Before the entrance of the United States into the war most Americans probably believed that geographic conditions would limit American participation primarily to naval and financial aid. A succession of missions to Washington from the Allied governments soon proved that the Allies needed everything — money, ships, supplies, men — if the Central Powers were to be defeated. Nor could they wait. The United States must act quickly and efficiently.

Since the allies desperately needed fresh fighting men, the plans of the General Staff for raising an army were immediately speeded up. Convinced that the principle of volunteering, upon which both Great Britain and the United States had mainly relied in earlier wars, was now inadequate, the military leaders persuaded Congress to approve in May, 1917, a Selective Service Act. This measure operated to produce a pool of able-bodied men between the

ages of eighteen and forty-five, from which 2.81 million were finally selected for service. For the training of the men thirty-two camps and cantonments, mainly located in the South, were hastily constructed. Even more difficult than the problem of obtaining the men was the problem of supplying the army with competent officers. For the higher ranks, officers of the regular army and the National Guard were promoted, but for the lower grades the army depended upon the graduates of hastily organized officers' training camps from which "ninety-day wonders" were soon being turned out.

Financing the War. Financing the war would have been difficult enough had the United States had only her own expenditures to consider, but she had also largely to finance her Allies. Economists urged a "pay-as-you-go" system, with taxation of wartime profits and earnings furnishing most of the revenue, but such a system was a practical impossibility. For one thing, money was needed immediately, and newly devised taxes would take months, or even years, to produce the needed funds. Congress therefore resorted to loans as well as taxes. Five huge bond issues were floated, the first four known as "Liberty Loans," and the last, after the fighting had ended, as the "Victory Loan." The total amounts so subscribed reached over $21.4 billion, and drew upon the savings of over 65 million individuals. Each loan was accompanied by a great "drive," in which every conceivable device was used to induce the public to subscribe. The bonds were issued in denominations as low as $50 and $100, and their purchase, on the installment plan if need be, was made almost a test of loyalty. Orators harangued theater, church, and school audiences on the iniquities of the Germans and the necessity of the war. Individuals suspected of being pro-German were compelled to prove their patriotism by particularly generous contributions; corporations with large payrolls put pressure on their employees to subscribe; thrift stamps and war-savings certificates tapped even the savings of children. Unfortunately all the securities marketed by the government were negotiable, and because the government refused to buy them back ahead of maturity dates, they depreciated materially in value. Speculators made excellent prof-

its; worse still, the bonds served to promote rather than restrict inflation. Prices rose rapidly, and the government made no serious attempt to hold them down.

The income tax, with its surtax feature, offered an easy means of expanding national revenue. The Revenue Act of 1916 had already doubled the normal income tax, but the War Revenue Act of 1917 doubled it again, bringing it to 4 per cent, and taxed incomes as low as $1,000. The graduated surtax and the tax on corporation earnings were also raised, and a new graduated excess profits tax took from 20 to 60 per cent of business earnings exceeding the average for the years 1911–1913. The excise taxes on liquor and tobacco were steeply increased, and a host of "nuisance taxes" introduced — on railroad and sleeping-car tickets, theater tickets and club dues, telephone and telegraph messages, and numerous other "luxuries." These were the beginning; still higher taxes were written into the Revenue Acts of 1918 and 1919.

A PARADE OF DRAFTEES

These groups of soldiers-to-be are awaiting their turn to join a march up Fifth Avenue, New York. Such parades were a common practice during the recruiting period.

A LIBERTY LOAN CHOIR SINGING "AMERICA" ON THE CITY HALL STEPS IN NEW YORK

"America" (My Country 'tis of Thee) was then more generally in use than at present. Not until 1931 did Congress designate "The Star Spangled Banner" as the national anthem.

All together the United States raised a total of $11.3 billion from taxation, less than one-third of the total expenditures from April, 1917, to October, 1919 — $35.4 billion — of which $9.5 billion was lent to the Allies.

Public Opinion on the War. The raising of huge armies, the flotations of unprecedentedly large loans, and the ruthless expansion of taxation required the support of a thoroughly aroused public opinion. When war was declared in 1917, the action was unquestionably approved by a majority of the people as well as by a majority of Congress. But a small minority, composed of ardent isolationists, pacifists, Socialists, and pro-Germans, were bitterly opposed to the war. Many of them were in complete agreement with Senator La Follette, who in casting his vote against the war resolution maintained, "I say Germany has been patient with us," or with Morris Hillquit, the Socialist, who asserted, "The country has been violently, needlessly, and criminally involved in war."

Restriction of Civil Liberties. It was deemed essential, if the sacrifices necessary to win the war were to be borne, that public opinion should support the government with virtual unanimity. Accordingly, Congress passed the Espionage Act of June 15, 1917, which levied stiff penalties on persons making false statements that might obstruct the prosecution of the war, incite disloyalty, or hinder recruiting. It also authorized the Postmaster-General to bar from the mails any printed matter violating the act. In the Trading-with-the-Enemy Act of October 6, 1917, the Post Office was granted further power to set up a virtual censorship on foreign-language newspapers. By far the most stringent of all wartime measures against dissent was the Sedition Act of May 16, 1918, aimed at persons uttering disloyal, scurrilous, or abusive language about the Constitution, the government of the United States, the armed forces, and the flag, or language calculated to interfere with war production.

Despite the fact that relatively few serious acts of disloyalty occurred, the federal government was vigorous in its use of the Espionage and Sedition Acts. Over 1,500 persons were arrested for disloyal utterances, among them the gentle Eugene V. Debs, who for years had led the Socialist cause in the United States. Some of the proceedings were against actual pro-Germans, but most, as in the Debs' trial, were against economic and political radicals who supported the Socialist position that the war was imperialistic and a direct result of capitalism.

War and the Constitution. An even more direct blow to freedom of discussion was struck by Postmaster-General Burleson, who not only curtailed the mailing privileges of radical and foreign-language newspapers, but also on occasion ordered the suppression of publications which happened to contain criticism of administration policy. An edition of *The Nation* was held up because it carried the caption "Civil Liberties Are Dead," and an issue of *The Public* was confiscated because it suggested that the wartime taxes on large incomes were too low. In the unnecessarily drastic use made of the Espionage and Sedition Acts, the authorities probably reflected faithfully an insistent public demand for repression of all dissent. The harm done to freedom of speech and of the press illustrates the cruel dilemma of a democracy at war. "When a nation is at war," Associate Justice Holmes stated, "many things that might be said in time of peace are such a hindrance to its effort that their utterance will not be endured so long as men fight, and that no court could regard them as protected by any constitutional right." The Court's admission that the Constitution was suspended when the nation was faced with a "clear and present danger" thus placed enormous responsibility upon the good sense and moderation of administrators.

The Creel Committee. In its attempt to achieve national solidarity, however, the Wilson administration relied more upon persuasion than coercion. Just eight days after the declaration of war, the President created the Committee on Public Information, naming as its head George Creel, an editor and free-lance writer. The Creel Committee, as it was soon called, early conceived of itself as having a double function — not only to keep the American public informed about the progress of the war, but also to formulate and state the official view of why the nation went to war and what it was fighting for. The Committee was thus both a newsgathering agency and a propaganda machine. Obtaining many of its ideas from a previously established British organization, it offered free to national publishers a day-to-day account of the war's progress. It turned out a stream of persuasive books, pamphlets, and throwaways on a great variety of subjects. It also organized a bureau of speakers to carry oral messages to practically every important audience. At the end of the war Creel estimated that the Committee had issued over 75 million pieces of propaganda and that 75,000 volunteer speakers had addressed 7.5 million separate audiences.

The Creel thesis on the origins of the war was a simple one taken over from the Allies. It pictured a militarized and Prussianized German state seeking to dominate the world, having carefully planned the war years in advance of Sarajevo. The war was thus against autocracy and "to make the world safe for democracy." Later the Creel Committee fully adopted Wilson's war aims and spread the word both at home and abroad that the United States was seeking no material gains, but was rather waging a war to end war, and to secure eternal peace. Such oversimple explanations of the struggle could hardly be precisely accurate. Nor could such broad aspirations be achieved. But during the struggle most Americans accepted them as true, and the will to victory was strengthened accordingly.

Council of National Defense. Neither the political nor the economic organization of the United States was fitted to meet the emergencies of war, and drastic changes had to be made in both. Fortunately the defense measures of 1916 had provided for a planning board known as the Council of National Defense. The six members of this council were cabinet officers with an abundance of other work to do, but they were supplemented by an Advisory Commission of seven civilians, also provided for in the law. Headed by Daniel Willard, a railroad president, and assisted by as many "dollar-a-year" volunteers as it could use, the Council soon became a kind of civilian general staff. Largely through the plans it devised, the government of the United States was reorganized for wartime efficiency while industry, agriculture, labor, and every other form of American economic life were forced to operate with the single-minded purpose of winning the war. Temporarily both the freedom of capital and individual rights were sacrificed to the larger necessity of a military victory.

The Wartime Government. Before the war was over, six great wartime agencies had taken over the chief responsibility for adjusting American economic life to the necessities of the struggle. The oldest of these was the United States Shipping Board, created in 1916. Through its Emergency Fleet Corporation it worked valiantly, and with considerable success, to build ships faster than the submarines could sink them. A second agency, the Food Administration, had as its responsibility the supply of food, both for soldiers and for noncombatants, overseas. Food Administrator Herbert Hoover preached the "gospel of the clean plate," persuaded the American people to accept "wheatless" and "meatless" days, and encouraged all who could to plant "war-gardens." More important still, Hoover's Grain Corporation set high prices for wheat that led to a remarkable expansion of the nation's wheat acreage, with a corresponding increase in production. A Fuel Administration dealt

similarly with the pressing coal and oil problem; a Railroad Administration took over all the railroads of the country and operated them as if they were a single system; a War Trade Board licensed foreign trade and took care that American commodities did not reach the enemy; and a War Industries Board, most powerful of all, took full command of American production. Under Bernard Baruch as chairman, the W.I.B. told manufacturers at will what materials they could use and what materials they must save. It could order them to undertake totally new endeavors. It could determine priorities, and so give or withhold both the raw materials and the transportation upon which every manufacturer depended. It could, and did, fix prices. Of great assistance in working out the orders of the War Industries Board was the War Finance Corporation, operating with a $500 million revolving fund granted by Congress and such other sums as it could borrow, which lent to businesses that needed encouragement, and restrained vigorously all nonessential demands for capital.

Long before the war was won, the government of the United States was exercising powers that in ordinary times would have been deemed incompatible with democracy. The six great "war boards" were responsible to the President alone. Beginning in March, 1918, the heads of these boards met with him weekly as a kind of war cabinet. Such legislation as they required, Congress ordinarily promptly supplied. The most sweeping of these grants was contained in the Overman Act, signed May 20, 1918, by which the President, until six months after the war ended, was given free rein "to utilize, coordinate, or consolidate any executive or administrative commissions, bureaus, agencies, offices, or officers" at will; to create new agencies and abolish old ones, and to use funds voted for any purpose in whatever way he judged to be most efficacious. Working closely together under the President, and assured of support by state councils of defense locally

maintained, the war boards all but supplanted the ordinary civil authorities. The
American economic system of 1918 was a
virtual state capitalism in which most of the
power of decision resided with the federal
government.

If a change had occurred in the locus of
economic control, little had taken place in
the personality of the controllers. The war
boards were necessarily staffed with businessmen and industrialists, many of whom
offered their services to the government on
a dollar-a-year basis while retaining their
permanent positions in private industry.
Whatever the resulting favoritisms, it was
generally acknowledged that the system
performed near miracles in the production
of vital war goods. According to the
German General Ludendorff, American industrial production, as much as any other
single factor, accounted for the Allied victory.

Labor and the War. The support of
organized labor for the war was greatly
promoted by the efforts of Samuel Gompers, one of the seven members of the
Advisory Commission, whose insistence that
the war must not be used to depreciate
wages or labor standards became a governmental policy on the understanding that organized labor would not embarrass the
government by "basic strikes." Indeed, the
draft, which took many men out of the
labor market, and the cessation of immigration, which cut off an historic source of
supply, led to a labor scarcity that drove
wages to unprecedented heights. By 1918
the average worker was earning nearly
twice as much as in 1914, and even allowing for the mounting costs of living, his
wages were fully 20 per cent higher than
when hostilities began. High wages and
steady employment also meant prosperity
for the labor unions, whose membership
rose during the war by no less than 37 per
cent. To facilitate the mobility of labor the
government expanded the United States

Employment Service of the Labor Department, and to fill labor shortages it encouraged the use of women in industry. To
keep labor disputes at a minimum, a War
Labor Conference Board, created early in
1918, laid down the rules that should govern the relationship of capital and labor,
and a National War Labor Board, under
the co-chairmanship of William Howard
Taft and Frank P. Walsh, acted as a court
of last resort in labor matters.

The Standard of Living. Perhaps even
more important than the war's immediate
effects were the enduring changes it created in American society. The enormous
demands upon American farmers and manufacturers stimulated intensely the productive resources of the nation. The number of
acres under cultivation increased by 10 per
cent between 1914 and 1920, the production of mines about 30 per cent, total manufactures about 35 per cent. While much
of this gain was temporarily sent abroad,
the resulting increase in basic productive
facilities presented the possibility of a sizable elevation in the national standard of
living during the postwar years. Even
more dramatic was the impact of the war
upon America's international economic
position. As late as 1914 the United States
had been a debtor nation, that is, the government and citizens of the United States
owed more to Europeans than the latter
owed to them. But the costs of the war
had forced European capital to withdraw
from America and elsewhere in the world.
Into this void American investors had
stepped. They not only bought out European holdings in America and in many
colonial areas, but also lent large sums in
Europe itself. Whereas Great Britain,
France, and Germany had formerly been
the chief investors across international
boundaries, the United States with almost
$20 billion lent abroad at the end of the
war had become the foremost creditor nation of the world.

Despite government statistics it is impossible to say precisely how the increase in national wealth during the war was divided among the various classes of Americans. Certainly most manufacturers and the owners of large capital fared well — income tax returns in 1918 indicated that over 25,000 people in the United States had a yearly income of over $1 million, exactly four times as many as before the war — and the farmer and the laborer took a relatively larger proportion of the national income than they had before. But because of inflation, salaried workers and people living on fixed incomes suffered. The war effected other major changes in American society. Because of the urgent need for labor in manufacturing establishments, southern Negroes migrated to northern cities in vast numbers. The war also speeded up the American woman's invasion of factory and office. By the end of 1917 almost 2 million women were working in manufacturing establishments alone.

The "Home Front."

Undoubtedly the most unlovely feature of the home front was the ugly intolerance bred by the war. Americans of foreign extraction suffered from it more acutely than any others, especially those who had been pro-German in the period of neutrality. Most of the acts of intolerance were not acts of the government, but of the people. The German language, which before the war had been more widely taught in America than any other foreign language, was all but eliminated from the public schools and was drastically restricted in the colleges. Printing, preaching, teaching, even talking in German were treated as if criminal offenses, and sometimes made so. Musicians of Teutonic origin, such as Frederick Stock and Fritz Kreisler, were publicly humiliated. It was as Wilson himself had said on the eve of war: "Once lead this people into war and they'll forget there ever was such a thing as tolerance. To fight you must be brutal and ruthless, and the spirit of ruthless brutality will enter into every fiber of our national life, infecting Congress, the courts, the policemen on the beat." Conformity, as the President had foreseen, became the only true virtue, and the man who refused to conform had to pay a severe penalty.

The Navy in the War.

For actual combat duty the navy preceded the army to Europe by many months. Indeed, Rear Admiral William S. Sims, who was chosen for overseas command, was in London before the United States entered the war, and by May 4 the first detachment of American destroyers had crossed the Atlantic. Ultimately 300 warships, large and small, and 75,000 officers and men were serving in all the overseas detachments of the American navy. Their activities extended from the vicinity of the British Isles to the Mediterranean. The American naval forces made no effort to operate separately, but became to all intents and purposes a part of the British Grand Fleet. American ships were used, among other things, to enforce the very rules of blockade against which the United States as a neutral had protested so vigorously.

The greatest single concern of the combined navies when the United States entered the war was the defeat of the submarine. This was eventually accomplished by a variety of means. American insistence had much to do with the laying of a mine barrage across the opening of the North Sea, between the Orkney Islands and the coast of Norway. This, and a similar mine barrage across the Straits of Dover, seriously crippled submarine activities. Cruising destroyers, armed with improved means of detection, also hunted down the "U-boats," and sank them with depth charges. By the end of the war nearly half the German submarine flotilla had been destroyed. American ships likewise played a leading role in convoying merchantmen and troop-

"THE BRIDGE TO FRANCE"

This American merchantman is unloading a cargo of hay, iron, and canned goods at St. Nazaire, France, 1918.

ships through the danger zone, thereby cheating the submarines of their prey.

The A.E.F. The frantic pleas of the Allies for American troops in France led the General Staff to decide that troops would have to be sent overseas only partly trained and partly equipped. The rest of the work could be done over there. Mainly as a token of good intentions General John J. Pershing was ordered to France in May, 1917, as head of the American Expeditionary Force, and next month the first of the American detachments began to arrive. The American plan called for more than the mere transporting of troops. Already the facilities of France and her allies were being taxed to the limit to support their own armies, and the American contingent must be a help, not a burden. Accordingly, the Americans created their own docks, railroads, freight yards, hospitals, barracks, warehouses, and all other such facilities. Over 5 million tons of supplies were sent abroad by the United States before the armistice was signed. The records show that more than 2 million men were trans-

ported overseas. Not all these were fighting men, but from this number Pershing formed forty-two combat divisions.

From the first General Pershing insisted upon the creation of a separate American command. In this he was opposed by the Allies, who wished to use the American troops as replacements, to be brigaded with French or British units. But Pershing was adamant. Convinced that three years of defensive fighting had weakened the Allied armies for effective offensive tactics, he finally forced the Allied leaders to give in, albeit reluctantly. The American army thus became a wholly independent unit, although Pershing lent troops at times to the hard pressed French forces. In the 1918 spring fighting before Paris, especially at Château-Thierry early in June, the Americans gave a good account of themselves. Surprised and pleased, Marshal Foch, Allied commander-in-chief in France, now cooperated more willingly in the creation of a separate American command. Pershing was never able to supply from American sources all the *matériel* of war necessary for the operations of a complete army. The ordnance, the tanks, and the airplanes he used were in considerable part of Allied manufacture. But the men were all Americans, and they did Pershing's bidding, subject only to the supreme command of Foch. Before the war ended, American troops held one-fourth of the battle line, even more than the British.

Saint-Mihiel. Pershing's first action as an independent commander was the reduction of the Saint-Mihiel salient, where the German line protruded sharply across the Meuse River southeast of Verdun. With some French assistance, but following his own plans, he attacked both flanks of the salient and in two days he had rolled the Germans back. Half a million American troops participated in the battle; they suffered 7,000 casualties and took 16,000 German prisoners. Had they been permitted to do so the Americans would have pushed

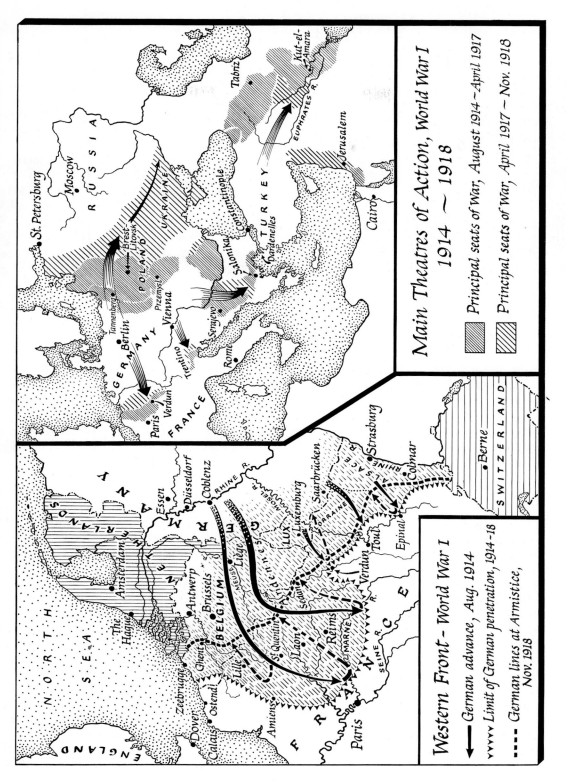

Main Theatres of Action, World War I
1914 ~ 1918

Principal seats of War, August 1914 ~ April 1917

Principal seats of War, April 1917 ~ Nov. 1918

Western Front - World War I

German advance, Aug. 1914

Limit of German penetration, 1914-18

German lines at Armistice, Nov. 1918

"OVER THERE"

Some Allied troops are shown here negotiating the churned-up mud of a battlefield in France.

ahead toward Metz, across the German frontier, but Haig, who headed the British forces, favored a different strategy, and Foch listened to Haig instead of Pershing. The American army was shifted to the west, and directed down the Meuse River and through the Argonne Forest toward Sedan. The war ended before Sedan was taken, but by November 11, Pershing explained later, the American troops "had cut the enemy's main line of communications, and nothing but surrender or an armistice could save his army from complete disaster."

The Meuse-Argonne Sector. The advance of the American army in the Meuse-Argonne sector was only a part of the larger campaign by which Foch smashed his way to victory through the supposedly impregnable Hindenburg Line, behind which the Germans had taken refuge. Three other major offensives, the Ypres-Lys, the Somme, and the Oise-Aisne sector, preceded and accompanied the American drive. With the Allied forces acting for once in complete coordination, an Allied

movement was begun north of Salonika against Bulgaria, another against the Turks in Palestine, and a third against the Austrians in Italy. Everywhere the Allied arms were successful. Before the end of September, Bulgaria was out of the war; Turkey quit in October; Austria surrendered early in November; on November 11 Germany, too, with her armies everywhere in full retreat gave up the fight.

American participation in the war was not wholly confined to the fighting in France. In July, 1918, an American regiment was sent to Italy, and in October two American divisions were lent to the French for use in Belgium. More debatable was the part played by American troops in Allied maneuvers against Bolshevist Russia. Without a declaration of war against Russia, 5,000 Americans fought with the Allies in the Archangel-Murmansk campaign that lasted from September, 1918, to May, 1919, while 10,000 Americans joined an Allied expedition to Vladivostok and eastern Siberia that lasted until January, 1920.

The Russian Revolution. The United

States watched with tremendous interest the revolutionary experiment in Russia. As soon as possible after the overthrow of the Tsar in March, 1917, an American mission headed by Elihu Root, former Secretary of State, and Major General Hugh L. Scott, chief of staff of the United States Army, was sent to Petrograd to assist the new government and to encourage it in the continued prosecution of the war against Germany. But the wheel of revolution in Russia turned rapidly to the left, and before the end of the year Nicolai Lenin and Leon Trotsky, leaders of the most extreme advocates of Communism, the Bolsheviki, had climbed to power with the secret assistance of German gold, and on the promise to the Russian people of peace. Late in December, 1917, at Brest-Litovsk, they agreed to end the war on German terms. Finland had declared its independence in July, 1917, and when the Treaty of Brest-Litovsk was finally signed in March, 1918, Poland, Lithuania, and the Ukraine were also separated from Russia, a preparatory step to their assimilation by Germany. The defection of Russia was of great help to Germany, and the repudiation by the Bolsheviki of all foreign debts by no means improved the feelings of the Allies. Naturally they wished to bring to power in Russia a government that would resume the war against Germany and agree to meet its financial obligations. The military activities on Russian soil, in which the United States participated, although ultimately unsuccessful, were directed to this end.

America's Contribution to Victory. The military contribution of the United States to the winning of the war was not inconsiderable. An army of 3.5 million men was raised, of whom 1.4 million saw active service overseas. The "Yanks" captured 44,000 prisoners, took 1,400 guns, and brought down 755 enemy airplanes. The American contribution in the air was somewhat disappointing. In spite of the activities of the Aircraft Production Board and the creation

of a new "Liberty engine," "the eyes of the army went aloft in foreign planes." But the armed forces had trained 11,000 aviators by the time of the armistice, and 4,300 of them were in France. American casualties, considering the short period of time Pershing's troops were engaged, were heavy — heavier, probably, than in corresponding French and British units where the troops were better trained and the utmost caution was exerted to conserve their dwindling man power. The total number of American deaths reached 125,000, but of these less than half were battle casualties. Compared with the 1.7 million of the Russians, the 1.6 million of the Germans, the 1.4 million of the French, the 900,000 of the British, and the 800,000 of the Austrians, American losses were slight, and were sustained during only about six months of actual fighting, while for the European belligerents the war lasted over four years. Excellent health precautions practically eliminated such diseases as dysentery and typhoid, while skillful surgery and hospitalization returned five-sixths of those wounded to their regiments. The worst scourge came from influenza which took as heavy a toll from civilians as from soldiers.

Unity of Command and Supply. The United States could claim credit for much else. Pershing was quick to point out that the Allies needed above all else a unified command. American insistence, together with the threat of an imminent German victory, helped pave the way for the assumption of supreme command in France by Marshal Foch. The Americans introduced another almost equally important reform — a unified system of supply. Their idea was that all resources — shipping, food, munitions, and other supplies — should be pooled and drawn upon as needed. General Charles G. Dawes, Pershing's purchasing agent, was chiefly responsible for the inauguration of this change. Finally, there came the ideal of a peace so evenhanded in its justice toward all nations, great and small, victor and vanquished, that the causes of war would be forever abolished. Long before the entrance of the United States into the war, Wilson had been urging such a settlement, and before its close his doctrines had gained an almost miraculous ascendancy over world opinion. What he stated in general terms every nation translated into the specific terms its national aspirations demanded. A "peace of justice" meant something quite different to each nation, but in every case it meant something worth fighting for. If this war should be the war that would end all war, the goal was doubly worth the effort. Wilson's idealism became a two-edged sword. It provided the Allies with a unified purpose in the war and served also to break down enemy morale. Why fight against a peace of justice?

The Debate on War Aims. Wilson's interest in a peace of justice had been stated clearly in his "peace without victory" speech of January, 1917. After the entrance of the United States into the war, he modified his stand only by insisting on a complete victory over the autocratic rulers of the Central Powers, but for the *people* of Germany and of her allies, as distinguished from their *governments,* he still adhered to generous terms. In reply to Pope Benedict XV's proposal in August, 1917, for a negotiated peace, Wilson stated that the United States wished neither punitive damages, nor the dismemberment of empires, nor the establishment of exclusive economic leagues after the war, but only the abolishment of autocratic rulers. That his ideas conflicted with the semi-secret treaties on the postwar world that the Allies had agreed to among themselves, the President must have known. These treaties planned a victor's peace rather than a peace of justice, but Wilson seemed to believe that he could rally the masses of the world to his cause, and that in the end his views would prevail. Wilson gave classic statement to these views in a speech delivered before Con-

gress in January, 1918. If the world were to become "a fit and safe place to live in," the peace should embody these "Fourteen Points":

1. Open covenants of peace openly arrived at.
2. Freedom of navigation upon the seas, alike in peace and in war.
3. Equality of trade conditions among all nations consenting to the peace.
4. Guaranties that national armaments will be reduced.
5. The adjustment of colonial claims in the interests of the populations concerned.
6. The evacuation of all Russian territory.
7. Belgium must be evacuated and restored.
8. French territory should be freed and restored, and the wrong of Alsace-Lorraine should be righted.
9. Readjustment of Italian frontiers along clearly recognizable lines of nationality.
10. The peoples of Austria-Hungary should be accorded opportunity for autonomous development.
11. Rumania, Serbia, and Montenegro should be evacuated and restored, and Serbia accorded an access to the sea.
12. The Turkish portions of the Ottoman Empire should be assured a secure sovereignty, but other nationalities under Turkish rule should have autonomy.
13. An independent Polish state with free and secure access to the sea.
14. A general association of nations for mutual guaranties of political independence and territorial integrity.

Wilson's program was not merely the product of his own thinking. Some of it was suggested to him by the "Inquiry," a group of scholars assembled by Colonel House to provide the State Department with the specific data it would need at the peace conference. Wilson spoke for himself and for the government he headed, but he could not speak officially for the nations he usually referred to as the "Associates" of the United States in the war.

Defeat of Germany. The German defeat, when it came, was complete in a strictly military sense. Later the German people were persuaded to believe that they had laid down their arms in the hope of a just peace when they might have fought on indefinitely. But they were badly beaten, and their commanding officers knew it. Their allies had been defeated, one by one. Their supposedly impregnable Hindenburg Line had cracked. Their submarine campaign had failed. Their services of supply were breaking down. Their troops, in full retreat, were, for the most part, thoroughly demoralized. Revolution, born less of Wilson's promises than of military disaster, was incipient. Generals Ludendorff and Hindenburg informed the Kaiser in September that the war was lost, and that peace must be made at once. It was the hopelessness of the military situation and the certainty of Allied victory that led the German government, seeking the best peace terms in sight, to ask Wilson for an armistice on the basis of the Fourteen Points. The impending collapse of the military front, not merely unrest at home, forced Germany to sue for peace.

The Armistice. Negotiations for an armistice were begun early in October, 1918, by a new German Chancellor, Prince Max of Baden, reputedly a liberal, who professed to Wilson that he spoke "in the name of the German government and the German people." Even so, the pre-armistice negotiations were long drawn out. Wilson's Fourteen Points were accepted by the Allied leaders only after elaborate interpretations and amendments, to all of which the Germans were obliged, because of the military situation, to consent. Wilson's second point, the "freedom of the seas," was ruled out altogether at the insistence of the British. Moreover, it was expressly stipulated that full compensation must be made for all damage done to invaded territories "by land, by sea, and from the air." When the German envoys signed the armistice, they knew that they were obtaining substantially less than the Fourteen Points, but

ARMISTICE DAY, 1918

The end of hostilities overseas led to thousands of such hysterical demonstrations as the one pictured here, on Broad Street, New York.

they realized also that failure to sign meant only the substitution of unconditional surrender for what was left of the Wilson program. Even so, the armistice was not actually signed until the German fleet at Kiel had mutinied, the Kaiser had been forced to abdicate, and leaders who owed no allegiance to the former "autocratic rulers" were in complete control. With the signing of the armistice, November 11, 1918, the war came to an end.

Military Terms of the Armistice. The military terms of the armistice were severe and no nation with the faintest hope of victory would have accepted them. The German army must retire to the left bank of the Rhine, surrendering huge stores of military supplies and railroad equipment; the bridgeheads at Cologne, Coblenz, and Mainz must be occupied by Allied troops; Allied prisoners of war and deported

591

inhabitants of occupied territory must be returned without reciprocity; the German submarines and battle fleet must be taken to a neutral or Allied port for internment (the Germans took their ships to Scapa Flow as required, but ultimately scuttled them); and the predatory treaties of Brest-Litovsk and Bucharest, with Russia and Rumania respectively, must be canceled. Further, the Allies were at liberty to requisition such German property as their armies of occupation might need, and to maintain the blockade of Germany that they had set up during the war.

Election of 1918. Wilson, meantime, had suffered a disastrous political setback at home. In the mid-term elections of 1918 the Republicans won the House of Representatives by a majority of twenty votes, and the Senate by a bare majority. Wilson himself may have contributed to the Democratic defeat by an appeal on October 25 for a Democratic majority in Congress through which alone, he maintained, he could hope to carry on his policies. Since Wilson had previously demanded that politics be purged from the war effort, the Republicans skillfully turned this statement into a charge that they had not supported the war, and may have gained many votes as a result. Wilson's propaganda for an early and just peace had small appeal for such "bitter-enders" as Theodore Roosevelt, and the fact that he had led the country into the war at all was equally offensive to the pacifists and the German-Americans. To critics of his war policy were added those who disliked the liberal legislation of his first administration, his surrender to labor in the Adamson Act, and his attitude toward Mexico. Finally, after six long years of separation from the spoils of office, Republican politicians were alert to every opening that would facilitate their return to power, and they directed their campaign with skill.

Paris was decided upon as the place for making a peace treaty. Unwisely, perhaps,

Wilson chose to represent the United States in person at the Conference, and to take along with him a delegation that would in no way interfere with his wishes. The group included only one Republican and no representative at all from the Senate, whose assent would be necessary for treaty ratification. The President's party reached France December 13, 1918, but the Paris Peace Conference did not actually convene until January 18, 1919. In the meantime Wilson paid official visits to Paris, London, and Rome, and inspected some of the battle-fields of the war. Everywhere he was received with wild enthusiasm by the people and with every show of hospitality by the heads of the Allied governments, although many of them regretted the necessity of having to deal with him personally.

The Paris Peace Conference. The Paris Peace Conference was an extraordinary gathering. All the Allies were represented, including such nonparticipating belligerents as China and Brazil, but Russia and Germany for good reason were denied any voice in the proceedings. Russia had withdrawn from the war, and it was clear that the problem of reconciling conflicting Allied opinions would be serious enough without a German delegation ready to take every advantage of Allied disagreements. The Conference was too large to carry on the actual negotiations, and met only for plenary sessions to confirm what had already been agreed on behind the scenes. All matters of consequence were settled by the "Big Four," Clemenceau of France, Lloyd George of England, Orlando of Italy, and Wilson. Of this group, Wilson was still committed in principle to what was left of the Fourteen Points after the pre-armistice negotiations. But Clemenceau, Lloyd George, and Orlando considered themselves equally bound by the secret treaties which the Allies had negotiated with each other early in the war. These treaties promised France Alsace-Lorraine, the Saar Basin, and an independent government for the rest of German territory west of the Rhine. Great Britain was to receive most of the German colonies, and a free hand in Egypt, Persia, and Mesopotamia. Italy was assured the Trentino, the southern Tyrol, and control of the Adriatic. Rumania had been assigned Transylvania and other territorial acquisitions. Japan was to succeed Germany in Shantung and in the islands of the Pacific. Russia, who had forfeited her claims by withdrawing from the war, was to have been given Constantinople and the Dardanelles. To the Allies these terms signified their rightful spoils of victory, and they proposed to obtain as many of them as they could.

The Treaty of Versailles. Wilson had hoped that the influence of an aroused world opinion would enable him to persuade the Allies to forget their harsh terms, but in the end he won only a compromise. When delegates from the new German republic agreed to this treaty on June 28, they surrendered Alsace-Lorraine to France, gave Poland generous blocks of territory including a corridor to the sea along the Vistula, and ceded border rectifications to Belgium and Denmark. The German colonies were handed over to the Allied countries, not for outright annexation, but under a League of Nations mandate system that in practice amounted to the same thing. The Saar Basin, Germany's richest coal-mining area, was turned over to French exploitation for fifteen years, during which time it was to be under the political control of an international commission. Reparations for the damages done by the German armies had been agreed to in the pre-armistice terms, but the Conference was unable to fix upon the amount due and left this to be decided by a Reparations Commission after peace was restored.

In some ways harder for the Germans to bear than the reparations bill (most of which was never paid anyway) was the assertion in the treaty that their country and her allies were responsible "for causing all the loss and damage to which the Allied and Associated governments have been subjected as a consequence of the war." This "war-guilt" clause, they maintained, quite indefensibly placed full blame upon the Central Powers for the outbreak of war in 1914.

The Treaty of Versailles also provided for the disarmament of Germany. Her standing army was reduced to 100,000 men and conscription was abolished; frontier fortifications not in Allied hands were to be razed; the manufacture, importation, or exportation of war materials was virtually prohibited; and the German navy was reduced to insignificance. The treaty promised, however, that the Allies would themselves soon take steps toward disarmament.

The League of Nations. Harsh as these terms were, they did not satisfy Clemenceau, who conceded even this much only on condition that there be a separate alliance between Great Britain, the United States, and France to repel jointly any future German attacks on France. Wilson consented to the alliance, but the Senate refused to accept so forthright a departure from the American tradition of nonintervention in European affairs. Wilson pinned his hope for future peace, however, less on the proposed alliance than upon the League of Nations, which by his persistent efforts the Allies were at length induced to include in the Treaty of Versailles. Through this organization, he hoped, many of the injustices of the treaty could be righted later when wartime fevers had abated. The Covenant of the League described three principal agencies: (1) a permanent Secretariat with headquarters soon to be established in Geneva, Switzerland; (2) a Council of nine members (later enlarged), to consist of one representative from each of the great powers, France, Great Britain, Italy, Japan, and the United States, and four others to be chosen by the Assembly; (3) an Assembly in which every member nation was to have a representative and a vote. The members of the League agreed by the famous Article X "to respect and preserve as against external aggression the territorial integrity and existing political independence" of all other members, and to recognize the right of every member nation to bring problems that might disturb the peace to the attention of the Assembly or the Council. Peace was to be achieved primarily by arbitration or adjudication, and the establishment of a permanent court of international justice was contemplated; but disputes not so adjusted were to be submitted for settlement either to the Council or to the Assembly. Against nations making illegal war the Council could impose drastic economic sanctions, and if it deemed military measures necessary to check aggressors, it could make appropriate recommendations to members of the League.

The Peace of Paris. The Treaty of Versailles was only one of many treaties that taken together may properly be called the Peace of Paris. Wilson's tenth point expressly stated that he wished to see the place of Austria-Hungary among nations "safe-guarded and assured," but the disintegration of that unfortunate power had been so complete that its resurrection was beyond possibility. Each of the many national groups composing the old Empire was now determined to be free, except, possibly, the German-speaking portion of Austria, which would have preferred union with Germany. But the Treaty of Saint-Germain, signed September 10, 1919, with the new "Republic of Austria," forbade any such development. The Treaty of Trianon with Hungary was not signed until June 4, 1920. It cut down the domain of the old Magyar kingdom to an irreducible minimum. The Treaty of Neuilly with Bulgaria, signed November 27, 1919, trimmed off in similar fashion the borders of Germany's smallest ally, and the Treaty of Sèvres with Turkey, signed August 10, 1920, left little non-Turkish territory to the Turks.

Through these and numerous supplementary treaties the "Balkanization" of central Europe was completed. The states that had aided the Allies were rewarded by territorial gains; those that had supported the Central Powers were punished by territorial losses. Numerous new states appeared on the map of Europe: Finland, Estonia, Latvia, Lithuania, Poland, Czechoslovakia, Yugoslavia, Albania. Everywhere the problem of "minorities" threatened the permanence of peace, for boundary lines that would separate every nationality from every other simply could not be drawn. Even the victors were not wholly satisfied. During the Peace Conference Wilson had insisted that the Italians were not entitled to Fiume on the east coast of the Adriatic, and as a result the Italian delegation had left the Conference. Ultimately they came back, and by a coup Italy later obtained the coveted port. But the Italians never forgave Wilson, although he consented to the inclusion within Italian borders of the Austrian Trentino on the ground that Italy needed it for a defensible northern frontier. As unattainable as precise boundaries between national groups was the hope, seemingly cherished by every state, of achieving economic self-sufficiency. Instead of creating a world community, as Wilson had hoped, the Peace of Paris accelerated in many ways the old forces of nationalism.

The completed Peace of Paris was severely criticized in many quarters. In Germany it was looked upon as a hypocritical violation of the promised peace of justice based upon the Fourteen Points. The "Diktat of Versailles" became a hated phrase throughout the defeated country and was used to whip up the coming wave of German nationalism. Many victorious Allies denounced the Peace for not giving them all they had been promised in the secret treaties of 1915 and in Wilson's Fourteen Points. Nationalists everywhere denounced the peace for being too lenient toward the defeated, and idealists, especially in the United States, considered the settlement much too harsh. Not a few American liberals were also opposed to the Paris settlement because they feared that the peace and the League would serve merely to freeze the world on the basis of the *status quo* and against any future wave of national and social revolutions.

Despite the faults of the Versailles Treaty, it is improbable that a much better peace could have been obtained at Paris in 1919. In a world dominated by fear, hate, and intolerance, the European allies were demanding some reward for their years of suffering and some security for their future. As usual, the material rewards were not enough to satisfy all the victorious claimants. And the road to security was a debatable one. To a Frenchman who had seen his country invaded and devastated twice in his lifetime, reliance upon a League of Nations had to grow out of faith rather than experience. Had the peoples of Europe instead of their governments made peace, the settlement would have been much harsher, judging by the vengeful slogans popular in all nations from Britain to Italy. But such a so-called practical and realistic peace would have alienated Wilson and the majority of Americans who were halfway expecting a millennium, but who were in the last analysis not willing to pay for it by pledging their own armed strength to France or even to the League to stop further aggression.

The treaty was a compromise between European memories and American expectations, between theoretical justice and the realities of the time. It was a much more moderate peace than the one Germany exacted from Russia at Brest-Litovsk. Much can be said for Lloyd George's observation that the chief trouble was not with the peace written at Versailles but with its administration afterwards when the United States was absent from the world's councils. It may well have been, as Wilson commented about the Far Eastern settlement, the best that could be wrung "from a dirty past." Certainly most of the forward-looking ele-

ments incorporated in the peace were there because of the American President's long and dogged struggles in Paris.

The Senate and the Treaty. The seeds of future wars were strewn throughout the Peace of Paris, but Wilson hoped that the League of Nations might prevent their growth. Unfortunately, he was soon to discover that for this innovation he was unable to win the support of his own government. After the election of 1918, with the Republicans in control of the Senate, Henry Cabot Lodge of Massachusetts became chairman of the Senate Committee on Foreign Relations, to which the treaty was referred. Throughout his public life Lodge had been a conservative, an ardent Republican partisan, and a nationalist who in foreign affairs had strongly supported the extension of American power. He was opposed to practically everything Wilson stood for in the peace and disliked the President personally — a feeling cordially reciprocated by Wilson. Once Lodge had believed that a world organization might be able to preserve the peace, but by 1918 he had changed his mind. He was not willing publicly to join the "bitterenders," such as La Follette of Wisconsin, and Johnson of California, who were adamant against any world organization. But he did feel that securing world peace was impossible "by any of the methods proposed." As a knowing politician, however, Lodge recognized the popular support for the League over the country. Accordingly, he announced that he was for a League, but not Wilson's League. His strategy was to "Republicanize the treaty" by attaching to it a series of reservations or interpretations, most of which would have reduced America's obligations to the world organization. By such a course he hoped to keep unity between the pro- and anti-League factions of his own party and also claim credit for the final result. If the treaty were accepted with his amendments it would then be in part a Republican treaty; if it were rejected, much of the blame for its defeat could be placed upon Wilson and the Democrats. Either result, Lodge calculated, would aid the Republican Party and damage Wilson and the Democrats in the coming presidential election. To help insure such results, Lodge ignored the moderates in his party and contrived the appointment to his committee of four bitterly anti-League and anti-Wilson Republicans.

As the final struggle over the treaty took shape, the Senate was divided into three main groups. (1) A dozen determined "irreconcilables" who were against any American participation in the League. Most of them were middle-western and western Progressives, devoted to the concept of a "little America" divorced from the world and thus able to devote most of its energies to domestic reform. They were as much opposed to expanding the nation's private financial power abroad as they were to extending its political power, whether alone or in concert with the members of the League. A few of this group, however, were not isolationists, but rather extreme nationalists who were eager to expand American business and financial strength and, if necessary, its political commitments, but who strongly opposed American acceptance of any obligations to an international authority. (2) A group of about thirty-five Republican "reservationists," some sincerely committed to the League principle, but many more only moderately so, and not to the extent of either violating their nationalist sentiments or hurting their party's chances in the 1920 elections. (3) And finally some forty-six Democrats, most of whom were willing to follow loyally Wilson's leadership.

Unfortunately, the President himself had opened the way to a partisan struggle by refusing to take to Paris any pro-League Republicans of national stature. Moreover, on his return to the United States he continued to ignore such powerful Republican friends of the League as Taft, Root, and Hughes. Throughout the long fight Wilson never attempted to conciliate the opposition. He was convinced that the people, if sufficiently aroused, could force their rulers to heed the popular will. The Senate might prefer not to ratify the treaty, but in the end, he remarked, it would have "to take its medicine."

Accordingly, when the Lodge group sought to add crippling interpretations to the treaty, a process described by some observers as "death by strangulation," the President took his case to the people on an extensive speaking tour to the West Coast. His health already shattered by illness in Paris, he broke down physically under the strain and was obliged to return to Washington, where he suffered a severe stroke. For months thereafter the country was virtually without a President and the League without its champion. Although the exact degree of Wilson's incapacity is still in dispute, visitors were barred from his sick room, and his wife became the only intermediary between the President, his cabinet officers, and the Senate.

Eventually the Lodge Committee proposed fifteen reservations to the treaty — to outmatch by one Wilson's Fourteen Points. The Republican majority stood ready to ratify, but the Democratic minority following Wilson's own recommendation declined, although it was well known that the leading European powers would have preferred ratification with the reservations to no ratification at all. Many votes were taken, and the treaty was twice before the Senate. On the final vote, March 20, 1920, the Senate was ready to accept the treaty by a vote of forty-nine to thirty-five with the reservations attached. This was less than the necessary two-thirds, but a change of seven votes would have meant ratification. Before the vote was taken Wilson asked the Democrats to stand by him and vote down the treaty with Republican reservations. Voting against the treaty were the "bitter-end" isolationists and many of Wilson's closest supporters, Democratic regulars, who were willing to accept the treaty precisely as it stood, but in no other form. Thus the treaty failed, with an overwhelming majority of the Senate favoring its adoption, although some wanted it with reservations, and others only without. As one historian has summarized the result, men on both sides consistently voted their party instead of their conscience.

Who really killed the treaty? Some observers believed that if Wilson had been more pliable a compromise could have been reached, but others insisted that the reservations were designed to kill the treaty, and would have been progressively stronger had they been acceptable to the President. Certainly Lodge soon took the lead in promoting a strictly unilateral policy by the United States in world affairs. With his faculties seriously impaired, Wilson failed to understand the completeness of his defeat and thought that the American people, who were rapidly drifting back into isolationism, were still with him. When Congress by joint resolution sought to declare the war with Germany at an end, he interposed his veto, charging that such a course would amount to an "ineffaceable stain upon the gallantry and honor of the United States." The election of 1920, he maintained, must be made a "solemn referendum" to decide whether the American people would accept or reject the obligations required by the treaty and the League.

It seems apparent that the United States by its refusal to support the League of Nations destroyed whatever chance there was to prevent another general war. Had the American nation shown itself willing to accept the responsibilities of world leadership, it is possible that the return to international anarchy might have been forestalled. Conceivably, also, the mistakes and the injustices of the treaty, of which there were many, might have been resolved through instrumentalities provided for in the League. But when the richest and most powerful of all the nations refused to cooperate in any effective way for the maintenance of peace, the possibility of another world war became a probability. Essentially what the United States had done in Europe was to help create an alliance of power that won the war and wrote the peace, and one that was necessary for its continued enforcement. By refusing to support that peace afterwards, it materially weakened the victors and strengthened the vengeful defeated. During the fight on the League, Wilson had recorded his conviction that, in case his efforts failed, the war would have to be fought all over again. A generation later the war that Wilson had predicted came to pass and changed the shape of the world.

SELECTED BIBLIOGRAPHY

The best single volume on American participation in the war is F. L. Paxson, *America at War, 1917–1918* (1939). Two recent books stressing military aspects are Laurence Stallings, *The Doughboys* (1963); and Frank Freidel, *Over There* (1964). L. P. Ayres, *The War with Germany* (1919), is a valuable statistical study; T. G. Frothingham, *The American Reinforcement in the World War* (1927), is a clear and satisfactory account. For interesting studies of experiments that never amounted to much, see D. F. Trask, *The United States in the Supreme War Council* (1961); and L. E. Gelfand, *The Inquiry* (1963).

The mobilization of American resources to win the war has received much attention. W. F. Willoughby, *Government Organization in War Time and After* (1919), is a valuable survey of the federal agencies created for the prosecution of the war. Activities of the WIB are discussed in M. L. Coit, *Mr. Baruch* (1957); and Baruch's autobiography, *Baruch: The Public Years* (1960). On price controls, see Herbert Stein, *Government Price Policy in the United States during the World War*

* Available in paperback

(1939); and G. P. Adams, Jr., *Wartime Price Control* (1942), which relates the experience of the first war for the benefit of another wartime generation. On food, see Herbert Hoover, *Years of Adventure, 1874–1920* (1951), the first volume of his *Memoirs;* and W. C. Mullendore, *History of the United States Food Administration, 1917–1919* (1941). On the financing and cost of the war, see J. M. Clark, *The Costs of the World War to the American People* (1931). F. R. Dulles, *The American Red Cross, A History* (1950), narrates the contribution of that illustrious organization.

Josephus Daniels, *The Wilson Era; Years of War and After, 1917–1923* (1946), is the reminiscence of the Secretary of the Navy. For the role of Daniels' energetic assistant see Frank Freidel, *Franklin D. Roosevelt: The Apprenticeship* (1952), the first of a multivolume biography of the highest quality. The relation between these two colorful characters is explored further in Jonathan Daniels, *The End of Innocence* (1954). Maritime aspects are also dealt with by: E. E. Morison, *Admiral Sims and the Modern American Navy* (1942); Louis Guichard, *The Naval Blockade, 1914–1918* (1930); and T. A. Bailey, *The Policy of the United States toward the Neutrals, 1917–1918* (1942). Two biographies of the Secretary of War are: Frederick Palmer, *Newton D. Baker; America at War* (2 vols., 1931); and C. H. Cramer, *Newton D. Baker* (1961). J. J. Pershing, *My Experiences in the World War* (2 vols., 1931), is an excellent memoir; the best biography is Frederick Palmer, *John J. Pershing, General of the Armies* (1948). D. A. Lockmiller, *Enoch A. Crowder* (1955), deals with the founder of "selective service."

An excellent account of society on the Home Front is in P. W. Slosson, *The Great Crusade and After, 1914–1928* (1930). On the part played by labor, see John Steuben, *Labor in Wartime* (1940). An interesting monograph on Pacific Northwest labor in wartime is H. M. Hyman, *Soldiers and Spruce* (1963). On the mobilization of public opinion in favor of the war, see two books by the head mobilizer, George Creel, *How We Advertised America* (1920), and *Rebel at Large* (1947). On the same subject, see J. R. Mock, *Censorship, 1917* (1941); J. R. Mock and Cedric Larson, *Words that Won the War* (1939); and G. F. Bruntz, *Allied Propaganda and the Collapse of the German Empire in 1918* (1938).

H. C. Peterson and G. C. Fite, *Opponents of War, 1917–1918* (1957), is a horrifying catalogue of the abuses of liberty in wartime; perhaps no other work portrays so vividly the hysteria of the Home Front. See also the classic account by Zechariah Chafee, Jr., *Free Speech in the United States* (1941). An account of one hideous episode is E. M. Rudwick, *Race Riot at East St. Louis, July 2, 1917* (1964). On some radical victims, see P. F. Brissenden, *The I.W.W.* (2nd ed., 1920); Oscar Ameringer, *If You Don't Weaken* (1940); R. L. Morlan, *Political Prairie Fire; The Nonpartisan League, 1915–1922* (1955); William Preston, Jr., *Aliens and Dissenters* (1963); and Donald Johnson, *The Challenge to American Freedoms* (1963). R. S. Bourne, *War and the Intellectuals, is a collection of essays by a dissenter, brought together by Carl Resek (1964).

On the Paris Peace Conference and the Treaty of Versailles, a massive summary is *A History of the Peace Conference of Paris,* edited by H. W. V. Temperley (6 vols., 1920–1924). A recent study is Ferdinand Czernin, *Versailles, 1919* (1964). R. S. Baker, *Woodrow Wilson and World Settlement* (3 vols., 1922), gives a valuable inside picture in immense detail. Interesting memoirs include: J. T. Shotwell, *At the Paris Peace Conference* (1937); D. H. Miller, *The Drafting of the Covenant* (2 vols., 1928); and Harold Nicolson, *Peacemaking, 1919 (1933).

Controversy over the Peace Conference has persisted ever since. Two collections of writings well illustrating the diverse points of view are T. P. Greene (ed.), *Wilson at Versailles (1957); and I. J. Lederer (ed.), *The Versailles Settlement (1960). Much of the early controversy was touched off by J. M. Keynes's savage indictment, *The Economic Consequences of the Peace* (1919); an impassioned rejoinder is Étienne Mantoux, *The Carthaginian Peace; or the Economic Consequences of Mr. Keynes* (1946). Paul Birdsall, *Versailles Twenty Years After* (1941), is a careful reevaluation. Special studies of Wilsonian peace diplomacy include: L. A. R. Yates, *The United States and French Security, 1917–1921* (1957); L. L. Gerson, *Woodrow Wilson and the Rebirth of Poland, 1914–1920* (1953); R. H. Fifield, *Woodrow Wilson and the Far East* (1952); R. W. Curry, *Woodrow Wilson and Far Eastern Policy, 1913–1921* (1957); and

A. J. Mayer, *Wilson vs Lenin; Political Origins of the New Diplomacy* (1959).

On the establishment of the League of Nations, see the comprehensive treatment by D. F. Fleming, *The United States and the League of Nations, 1918–1920* (1932). An important study of the American background of the League idea is R. J. Bartlett, *The League to Enforce Peace* (1944). T. A. Bailey, *Woodrow Wilson and the Lost Peace* (1944), and *Woodrow Wilson and the Great Betrayal* (1945), are brilliantly written and have had an enormous influence on historians. Although he himself holds internationalist views, Bailey places much of the blame for the defects of the peace and the failure of the treaty on Wilson. J. C. Vinson, *Referendum for Isolation* (1961), is a calm study of the defeat of the League. On Wilson's chief Senate opponent, see J. A. Garraty, *Henry Cabot Lodge* (1953), judicious and objective. On the sad last years of Wilson, see the moving account by Gene Smith, *When the Cheering Stopped* (1964).

*Thomas Hart Benton, "Boom Town." From the
Collection of The Memorial Art Gallery of the
University of Rochester.*

Prosperity

and

Depression

· 1921–1939 ·

The country is not in good condition.

CALVIN COOLIDGE

That high and increasing standards of living and comfort should be the first considerations in public mind and in government needs no apology.

HERBERT HOOVER

I pledge you, I pledge myself, to a new deal for the American people.

FRANKLIN D. ROOSEVELT

34

THE SEARCH FOR NORMALCY

ैऽ Warren G. Harding • The Washington Conference • The Kellogg-Briand Pact • "Americanism" • Radicalism and Violence • Immigration Restriction • European War Debts • Business and Agricultural Depression • The Coolidge Prosperity Formula • The Farm Problem • Elections of 1924 and 1928

Election of 1920. The election of 1920 was hardly the "solemn referendum" on the Treaty and the League for which Wilson had hoped. It was rather a referendum on the Wilson administration as a whole, and ever since the election of 1918 the prospect of a Republican victory had been growing. The country was no longer in a reform mood. It resented having had to fight a war, was tired of the long debate over the Treaty of Versailles, and was eager for a return to what Senator Warren G. Harding of Ohio described as "normalcy." The death of Theodore Roosevelt in 1919 removed the logical Republican candidate from the scene. Subsequently a self-defeating contest between Governor Frank O. Lowden of Illinois, General Leonard Wood, and Senator Hiram Johnson of California paved the way for the nomination of Harding, a reservationist during the fight on the Treaty of Versailles and always a dependable party

regular. Harding's limited talents made it seem certain that the charge of "executive usurpation" would never be brought against him. For Vice-President the Republicans chose Calvin Coolidge of Massachusetts, whose national reputation was made when he called out the state militia in 1919 to suppress a Boston police strike. To oppose this ticket the Democrats nominated James M. Cox, Governor of Ohio, for President, and Franklin D. Roosevelt, Wilson's Assistant Secretary of the Navy, for Vice-President. On the League of Nations issue the Democratic candidates supported Wilson's record. But the Republican platform was vague on this issue, and the Republican candidates were even more vague. Such League advocates as Hughes, Root, and Taft maintained that the election of Harding would be the surest way to get the United States into the League, while such irreconcilables as Johnson of California and Borah of Idaho were equally certain that Harding would keep the nation out of the League. Exactly what the public was thinking on this particular issue when it went to the polls is still debated, but the election returns gave Republican candidates a decisive victory. Harding's popular majority was over 7 million, and in the electoral college he received 404 votes to Cox's 127. He was assured also of a strong Republican majority in both houses of Congress.

Harding. Warren Gamaliel Harding (1865–1923) had obtained most of his education as editor of the Marion, Ohio, *Daily Star*. From journalism he had drifted easily into politics. Always associated with the most conservative wing of his party, he had made the nominating speech for Taft against Roosevelt in the convention of 1912. Defeated for the governorship of Ohio in 1910, Harding won election to the United States Senate in 1914, his first important office. A genial and handsome man, he was well liked by his associates, and thoroughly imbued with the common man's vanities and prejudices. He was, however, almost totally ignorant of the intricacies of important public issues and had a rather dubious sense of moral values. He read little and habitually expressed his thoughts in clichés. Quite aware of his intellectual limitations, he took comfort in the belief that as President he could command the judgment of the best minds of his party. Determined to be a good President, Harding solicited the advice of experts on major problems, but on minor questions he often listened to his poker playing and drinking companions, many of whom came from the seamier side of politics and had even less of a sense of moral discrimination than the President.

Harding showed his curious ability to mix the good with the bad in his major appointments. His selections of Hughes as Secretary of State and Hoover as Secretary of Commerce were above reproach, but they were offset by the appointment of Albert B. Fall of New Mexico, a notorious anticonservationist, as Secretary of the Interior, and Harry M. Daugherty, whose legal talents were at best mediocre, as Attorney-General. For Secretary of the Treasury Harding decided upon Andrew W. Mellon, one of the richest men in the United States, an understandable, but not wholly defensible, choice. Outside the Cabinet the President's lack of discrimination persisted. He made ex-President Taft Chief Justice of the Supreme Court, a deserved compliment, but he turned over the newly organized Veterans' Bureau to a nonentity, Charles R. Forbes, who eventually was imprisoned for fraud. In general, the new President regarded political offices as the rightful spoils of victory, and to members of the unsavory "Ohio gang" that followed him to Washington went many jobs and favors.

The Return to Isolation. The new President, despite his votes as Senator for the Treaty of Versailles with reservations, and his temporizing during the campaign, chose to interpret his election as a mandate against ratification. The Treaty of Versailles, he maintained, was dead. Following a July, 1921, joint resolution of Congress, which once more declared the war at an end, the American Department of State began negotiations with Germany that led to a separate treaty, signed August 25, 1921, and later duly ratified. By this document the United States obtained every possible advantage of the Treaty of Versailles, but accepted none of its responsibilities. The Department of State also negotiated and the Senate ratified similar peace treaties with Austria and Hungary, together with treaties establishing normal relations with the "succession states" of Central Europe and with Turkey. As for Soviet Russia, the new administration agreed with the stand taken by the Wilson administration that the United States should have no diplomatic relations with a government that was determined. "to conspire against our institutions," and "whose diplomats will be the agitators of dangerous revolt." For a time the Department of State seemed also to extend this policy of non-recognition to the League of Nations, an extreme position from which it eventually retreated. In describing Republican diplomatic policy, however, the customary term "isolation" needs clarification. Under Harding and his Republican successors the United States refused to cooperate formally with the League in collective action to maintain world peace, but the nation did not withdraw from world politics, as has so often been stated; indeed, in many ways it was far more aggressive in making international political agreements than it had ever been before.

The Washington Conference. At the International Conference on the Limitation of Armaments, convened in Washington on Armistice Day, November 11, 1921, and often called the Washington Conference, the Harding administration concluded naval and political agreements profoundly affecting the future balance of power in Asia and the whole world. Every possible device was employed to build up this Conference as the Republican counterpart of the Wilsonian program. It was persistently spoken of as the "Peace Conference," although it was nothing of the kind. The real purposes of the Conference were (1) to end the unhealthy and expensive naval rivalry among Great Britain, the United States, and Japan that had resulted from the building programs undertaken during the war; (2) to induce Great Britain to give up her alliance with Japan in return for continued American friendship; and (3) to negotiate a settlement of Far Eastern affairs that would check the aggression of Japan in China.

In the protracted negotiations preceding the naval agreement, each nation, as could have been predicted, sought to promote a disarmament program that would maintain its own power and decrease that of its potential enemies. Nevertheless, in the end five powers, the United States, the British Empire, Japan, France, and Italy, agreed to limit their strength in capital ships to total tonnages that bore to each other roughly the ratios of 5:5:3:1.7:1.7, respectively. Consent could not be obtained, however, to extend this agreement to lesser craft. But the limitations adopted at least resulted in tremendous budgetary savings for the nations concerned. In 1927 at the suggestion of President Coolidge, a conference met at Geneva to discuss the limitation of

auxiliary ships, but failed to reach an agreement. In 1930 at London, a conference called by President Hoover fared somewhat better. Some limitations were imposed on the building of lesser craft, Japan was appeased by a more generous quota, and the naval holiday was extended to 1936. But Japan served notice in 1934 that after 1936 she would no longer be bound by any limitations, and after that date the race for naval supremacy was vigorously renewed. The United States was significantly handicapped in this contest by an article of the London agreements which bound the United States, the British Empire, and Japan to maintain the *status quo* with respect to "fortifications and naval bases in the Pacific" except in the Japanese "home islands." Taken together with the ship ratios, this provision left Japan relatively stronger in the Far East, and the United States and Great Britain relatively weaker. The extraordinary significance of this development was not fully realized until after the Japanese attack on Pearl Harbor.

The Four-Power Pact. The Washington Conference resulted in the drafting of two other noteworthy treaties, one signed by four powers, and the other by nine. The Four-Power Pact, agreed to by the United States, the British Empire, France, and Japan, paved the way for the abrogation of the Anglo-Japanese Alliance, which had become distasteful to both Great Britain and the United States. The new pact aimed to preserve peace in the Pacific by pledging the contracting powers mutually to respect one another's rights "in relation to their insular possessions and insular dominions in the region," and to refer potential disputes to a joint conference. The four powers also bound themselves to "communicate with one another fully and frankly" on the action to be taken in case their rights were "threatened by the aggressive action of any other power." Had the pact ever been taken seriously, it might have constituted almost as decisive a de-

THE WASHINGTON CONFERENCE, 1921

Left to right the participants in the Conference who are shown here are: J. S. Garrett, Secretary General of the Conference; Jonkheer H. A. Van Karne-Beek, Netherlands; Sao Ke Alfred Sze, China; Arthur James Balfour, United Kingdom; Charles Evans Hughes, United States; Aristide Briand, France; Carlo Schanzer, Italy; Baron de Cartier de Marchienne, Belgium; Prince Ivesato Tokugawa, Japan; Viscount D' Alte, Portugal.

parture from the American policy of isolation as if the United States had entered the League of Nations.

The Nine-Power Pact. The Nine-Power Pact related to "principles and policies to be followed in matters concerning China," and was signed by the United States, Belgium, the British Empire, China, France, Italy, Japan, the Netherlands, and Portugal. The situation in the Far East had changed materially as a result of the first World War. In 1915 Japan had in effect repudiated the doctrine of the open door by presenting to China twenty-one demands for special privileges, many of which China was forced to concede. In 1917, by the Lansing-Ishii Agreement, Japan once more gave lip service to the open door, but won from the United States recognition "that territorial propinquity creates special rela-

tions between countries." At the Paris Peace Conference, Japan insisted on being awarded the German concessions in Shantung, although the Japanese delegates promised Wilson that Japan would eventually withdraw from the peninsula, which, at least in a military sense, she did. Japan was also given a mandate over the German island of Yap in the northern Pacific. The purpose of the Nine-Power Pact was to reconcile this situation, as nearly as possible, with the open door for world trade in China and the integrity of the Chinese Republic. The new treaty administered a strong rebuff to Japanese policy, for it pledged the signatory powers to respect Chinese sovereignty, to aid China in maintaining an effective government, to use their influence in favor of "equal opportunity for the commerce and industry of all nations" in China, and to "refrain from

605

taking advantage of conditions in China to seek special rights." But the treaty provided no means of restraint to an offending power, and Japan was soon violating all these pledges with impunity.

The World Court. Republican efforts to promote world peace were not limited to military agreements. The idea of a permanent court of international justice had been advocated by the American delegation to the Second Hague Conference in 1907, and was far more closely identified with Republican than with Democratic policy. When, therefore, under Article XIV of the League of Nations Covenant, plans were drawn in 1922 for such a court, there seemed no good reason why a Republican administration should not give the new institution its blessing. Indeed, Elihu Root had assisted in drafting the World Court protocol, and John Bassett Moore, America's foremost authority on international law, was slated for a place on its bench of eleven (later fifteen) judges. The only difficulty in the way of American participation seemed to lie in the fact that the judges were to be chosen by the Council and Assembly of the League of Nations, but it was proposed that, for this purpose only, the United States might have a voice in the proceedings. Certain that public opinion was "overwhelmingly in favor of participation," President Harding urged American adherence to the Court, only to be rebuffed by the Senate, in which the irreconcilables were able to prevent any action being taken. Fearing that adherence to the Court would be the entering wedge to further involvement in European political problems, much the same group that defeated the League in the Senate now voted down the Court. Subsequent efforts to secure its adoption were equally fruitless.

The Washington naval and political agreements and the arguments used against World Court participation clearly indicated the distinctions to be drawn between the Wilsonian and the new Republican foreign policies. The Republican program was not isolationist in the sense of seeking to achieve a hermit state but, rather, ultranationalistic in the sense of refusing to countenance a formal and constitutional tie with the other nations of the world, a tie which would in theory commit American armed forces to a cooperative maintenance of peace, particularly when peace was threatened by the leading European powers. Foreshadowing the future, Republican policy was far less timorous in Asia than it was in Europe. But even with nations of the Old World the new Republican leadership eagerly sought political and economic agreements, provided they were adjudged to be in the real and immediate interests of the United States, and did not bind the nation to collective punitive actions. The economic, technological, and social facts of the twentieth century, despite men's opinions or prejudices, conspired to draw the nations of the world closer together. By necessity many agencies of the League became world forums for the discussion of international problems intimately affecting the United States. To participate, representatives of the United States, at first unofficially, but later on terms of complete equality, sat in on the nonpolitical discussions of League committees, such as the conference on the control of the world opium traffic. Despite their desire to remain politically uncommitted even some of the most ardent American nationalists believed that some international action was necessary if the danger of another great world war were to be diminished. As a way out of their dilemma this group advanced the plan to maintain international peace by securing from every nation a simple pledge that it would not resort to war. Their chief leader was Senator William E. Borah of Idaho, a consistent opponent of both the League and the World Court, who called his plan "the outlawry of war." Most politicians, including President Coolidge, regarded the "outlawry" scheme as completely impractical and even unconstitutional. But the 1925 European

Pact of Locarno, by which Germany, Belgium, France, Great Britain, and Italy undertook not to attack each other except for purposes of defense or to fulfill their obligations under the League of Nations, heartened the "outlawry" advocates in the United States.

When in 1927 Premier Aristide Briand of France urged a treaty between the United States and France similar to the Locarno agreements, the "outlawry" enthusiasts were quick to take advantage of their opportunity. They persuaded the Secretary of State, Frank B. Kellogg of Minnesota, who had succeeded Hughes in 1925, to expand the scope of the negotiations. The eventual result was a world meeting where, on August 27, 1928, fifteen nations including Japan, Italy, and Germany solemnly signed the Pact of Paris. By signing, the nations promised to abstain from war as a "solution of international controversies," and renounced it "as an instrument of national policy in their relations with one another."

Ultimately sixty-two nations adhered to the Kellogg Pact; but the futility of all such declarations unless implemented by sanctions against aggressors was soon to be demonstrated. Neither Congress nor the American people were willing to accept the obligation to use force against an aggressor nation within or without the League structure. This was made clear by the Senate action in approving the Pact of Paris. The Senators ratified the Pact with only one dissenting vote, but only after adopting "interpretations" insisting that the action did not curtail America's right of self-defense, that no obligations incompatible with the Monroe Doctrine had been assumed, and that the United States was not bound to take action against states breaking the treaty.

"Americanism." The extent of the popular desire to avoid any entangling foreign obligations can perhaps be measured by a phenomenal postwar preoccupation with "Americanism." During the war the term "hyphenated Americans" had been used to describe people with double loyalties, both to their new country and to the country of their origin. Reflecting the new wave of nationalism, the term "one hundred per cent American" was coined to designate people whose attachment to traditional American ways, beliefs, and institutions was absolute. The term, of course, automatically cast suspicion upon many recent immigrants and other unassimilated minority groups. Public opinion favored restrictive legislation to halt the entry of these groups into the United States. Immigration had necessarily been small during the war, but the close of hostilities soon proved conclusively that something more drastic than a literacy test would be necessary if the distressed multitudes of Europe were to be prevented from seeking refuge in America. In the year ending June 30, 1921, over 800,000 immigrants came to the United States, and in spite of the attempt at restriction, nearly two-thirds of them came from southern and eastern Europe.

The growth of radicalism and violence in the postwar years was attributed, with or without justification, to the immigrants, and was used as one argument in favor of restrictive legislation. During April, 1919, over thirty bombs were found in the mails addressed to prominent Americans who had expressed opposition to Communism. Then on September 16, 1920, a fearful explosion in front of the J. P. Morgan and Company offices on Wall Street killed thirty-eight people and injured hundreds of others. This outrage and the founding of the American Communist Party in the spring of 1920 convinced many people that action had to be taken against the further introduction of aliens with subversive ideas.

Immigration Restriction. In response to the insistent demand for immigration restriction, Congress in 1921 passed an Emergency Immigration Act that assigned to each nation an immigrant quota consisting of not more than 3 per cent of the number of its nationals resident in the United States according to the census of 1910. Immigrants from other American nations were exempted from the quota system, but in 1922 an amendment required that all aliens resident in a western hemisphere country must have lived there not less than five years before being freed from the quota restrictions.

The law of 1921 was meant merely as a temporary stopgap while the details of the new immigration policy were being worked out, and in 1924 Congress passed another immigration act. This time the quota was set at 2 per cent of the nationals resident in the United States in 1890, thereby reducing still further the numbers eligible for admission, particularly from southern and eastern Europe. The law also provided that after July 1, 1927, the total annual number of immigrants was to be limited to 150,000, with quotas based upon "national origins" to be determined from a study of the census of 1920. The difficulty in determining the national origins of the American people completely baffled the committee of cabinet members charged with that duty, and not until 1929 were its halfhearted recommendations put into effect. A most unfortunate clause of the 1924 act barred all aliens ineligible for citizenship, a provision specifically aimed at the Japanese, who deeply resented the special discrimination. The gentlemen's agreement of 1907 had worked well enough that there was no good reason for its unilateral repeal; furthermore, since under the quota system Japanese immigration would have been limited to a mere trickle, this was an unnecessary affront to a proud and sensitive people. Whatever their imperfections, the new quotas insured that an overwhelming proportion of the few immigrants permitted to enter the United States originated in the countries first contributing to its settlement. Great Britain and Northern Ireland, for example, were permitted to send 65,721 immigrants annually,

while the Italian quota was only 5,802. Moreover, the effect of the act was already evident in 1930 when the census revealed that the proportion of foreigners resident in the United States had ceased to increase.

The spirit of intolerance which marked the rising public insistence on immigration restriction pervaded the domestic scene as well and was directed toward any group which the older nativist groups disliked or feared: the radical, the Catholic, the Jew, and the Negro. Enticed during the war by high wages, large numbers of Negroes had migrated from the South to northern cities, only to find much of the same discrimination that they had left in the South. Friction over jobs, housing, and the use of public facilities led to appalling race riots in East St. Louis in 1917, in Chicago, Oklahoma City, Springfield, Ohio, and many other northern cities in 1919. The loss of life and property in the northern cities was severe. Meanwhile, the rate of lynchings, which had dropped to thirty-five in 1917, shot up to seventy-six in 1919, and there were demands from both North and South that the Negro "be put in his place."

The Ku Klux Klan. This climate of fear and hatred gave rebirth to the Ku Klux Klan, a movement dedicated to organized intolerance, and similar in many ways to European Fascism. This latter-day Klan, which was founded in November, 1915, near Atlanta, Georgia, by William J. Simmons, was only a small and harmless southern organization until 1920–1921, when both its national officers and its purposes changed. Many simple-minded people were undoubtedly attracted to the Klan by its theatrical and mysterious ritual, its outlandish costumes, and its spectacular parades and rallies. Others may have believed in the sincerity of its stated program, which stressed patriotism and Christian morality. But one of its major purposes was to organize hatred against Catholic, Jew, Negro, immigrant, and radical. It spread palpably untrue stories about these groups and, particularly in the Middle West and the South, intimidated many individuals by burning fiery crosses before their homes or warning them out of the community. These threats it supplemented by whippings, tar-and-featherings, and even murder. Invading politics, the Klan sought to control public offices with the purpose of discharging Catholic teachers and other public employees it disliked. At the crest of its strength in 1924–1925, it had enrolled about 5 million members, making its officers wealthy and its power for evil enormous. Fortunately its excesses and the return of sanity to many of its members sent it into rapid decline. But the basic intolerance that had spawned the Klan exhibited itself anew in the famous Sacco-Vanzetti case of 1920, which resulted years later in the execution of two Italian aliens, primarily because of their radical ideas.

America and the World. In spite of the continuing devotion of most Americans to the idea of nationalism in world politics, the role of the United States in international affairs intensified during the later twenties. As a result of the war, the nation had expanded its industrial facilities enormously; it had discovered unsuspected possibilities in agricultural production; and it had accumulated out of its profits huge sums for new investment, much of which was now being placed abroad. The new industrial capacity increasingly required both foreign markets and a variety of foreign materials, such as nickel, tin, and nitrates, that it did not produce at home. What the United States really needed was a peaceful world generally committed to the open door through which trade would flow unobstructed. That American statesmen of the twenties failed to achieve this goal was not surprising. They were faced at home by a determined support of nationalist principles and a deep-seated belief in the protective-tariff system; they

were faced abroad by the jealousies and hatreds engendered by the war and the peace, feelings compounded by the conviction that the American people had escaped most of the war's ravages, but had taken most of its profits.

Among the most perplexing of the problems confronting the American government during this period was the collection of the loans by which it had so largely financed the Allied cause after 1917 and the work of reconstruction after the war. To the American people these intergovernmental loans seemed no different from the loans of one individual to another, and

KU KLUX KLAN PARADE

This unusual photograph, taken in Tulsa, Oklahoma, September 21, 1923, shows both horses and riders fully hooded. To the left of the Klansmen is former Sheriff "Bill" McCullough, who tried in vain to stop the parade, and back of him the uniformed police, who marched alongside the column.

their repayment was regarded as a matter of simple honesty. For Europeans the war was a common endeavor, in which each nation had given all it had to give. The United States had entered the conflict late, its casualty list was short, and it should not grudge the dollars it had spent. Most of the money lent had been expended in the United States, and goods rather than gold had been sent abroad. Nor could European nations hope to build up large balances in America by the shipment of goods; the high American tariff forestalled that. To the war-heated imaginations of European critics "Uncle Sam" became "Uncle Shylock," and hostile feeling ran high.

Nevertheless, in 1922 Congress created a World War Foreign Debt Commission which opened negotiations with the various Allied nations and ultimately reached refunding agreements with fifteen of them. American policy called for settlements in accordance with ability to pay; hence the interest charges ranged from as low as .4 per cent for Italy to the normal 3.4 per cent required of Great Britain and the more solvent states. The British settlement was effected as early as June, 1923, and the others during the next few years. Opposition to repayment reached its maximum in France, where the costly work of reparation threatened to bankrupt the government, and strained severely relations between the two countries, but an agreement was signed in April, 1926, which set the interest rate at 1.6 per cent, and allowed a period of sixty-two years for payment. The grand total of all the funded debts was fixed at more than $11.5 billion, with three-fourths of the amount owed by Great Britain ($4.6 billions), France ($4.02 billions), and Italy ($2.04 billions). Repayments by December 31, 1930, amounted to about $2.5 billion, of which more than 70 per cent came from Great Britain. Next year, following the Hoover moratorium, a few nations met their obligations, but thereafter payments from all nations except Finland virtually ceased.

Reparations. Inevitably the problem of war debts became closely intertwined with the problem of German reparations. If Germany could meet her obligation to the Allies, then the Allies could make their payments to the United States. Any connection between these two problems was vigorously denied by the American government, but its existence in fact, if not in theory, was quite clear. The difficulties experienced by Germany in paying the enormous sums required by the Reparations Commission in 1921 led to two efforts at readjustment, one in 1924, and another in 1929. In each case the commission of experts entrusted with the negotiations was headed by an American, the first by Charles G. Dawes, and the second by Owen D. Young. The Dawes Plan reduced the sums required from Germany each year, arranged for a foreign loan to support the German monetary system, and required French withdrawal from the Ruhr Valley, a district into which France had sent her troops in 1922 because of German failure to meet reparations payments. For four years, in large part by borrowing in the United States, Germany was able to meet the new payments, but by 1928 she was again in trouble. The Young Plan proposed another set of annuities to run for a period of fifty-nine years, the capitalized value of which would amount to only about $10 billion, approximately the sum due from the Allies to the United States. Further, it stipulated that additional reductions might be made proportional to any readjustments in the inter-Allied war debts; in other words, if the United States reduced its demands, the Allies would reduce theirs. But the Young Plan, too, overtaxed either the willingness or the ability of Germany to pay, and after 1931 all reparation payments were discontinued. Altogether Germany had paid the Allies about $4.5 billion, more than half of which had been borrowed from American investors.

Latin-American Problems. American investments also acted as important counters in policy toward Latin America. After only a few days in office, Harding submitted to the Senate for ratification a treaty proposing payment of $25 million to Colombia for damages incurred by Theodore Roosevelt's actions in seizing the Canal Zone. This same treaty had previously been defeated by the Republicans, but now that American and British oil interests were competing for Colombian concessions, one of Roosevelt's closest friends, Senator Henry Cabot Lodge, explained his change of mind by stating that "the question of oil is one that is vital to every great maritime nation" and that the nation should stand behind its overseas investors. The treaty was ratified April 20, 1921, by a vote of 69–19, and subsequently the American oil interests won a coveted concession.

Two 1925 Mexican laws also threatened America's increasing economic stake in Latin America. The first, passed by the Calles government, permitted aliens to acquire lands in Mexico only if they agreed to renounce the protection of their own governments, and the second declared that, since all mineral and other subsoil rights were the "inalienable and imprescriptable property of the nation," alien concessionaires must renew their rights on these terms. Further difficulties with Mexico were posed by that government's anticlerical laws which confiscated Church property and expelled foreign clerics. Faced with a demand by many American investors for armed intervention, President Coolidge sought to lessen the tension by sending his personal friend, Dwight W. Morrow, to Mexico, to find a peaceful solution to the controversy. Morrow succeeded in persuading the Mexican government to soften both the antiforeign and the anticlerical laws. Although the concessions were not entirely satisfactory to American investors, the willingness of Washington to accept this settlement helped abate the widespread Latin-American animosity toward the United States incurred during the Roosevelt, Taft, and Wilson administrations.

Coolidge's reluctance to use arms in support of American investors was accompanied by other concrete indications that the United States was retreating from its earlier aggressive Caribbean and Central American policy. In 1924 President Coolidge ordered the evacuation of marines from the Dominican Republic and in 1925 from Nicaragua, although they were sent back to Nicaragua again after another revolutionary outbreak. However, in 1933 the marines were withdrawn from all the independent Central American countries. But long before that date the United States had disavowed the old Roosevelt corollary to the Monroe Doctrine. By the Clark Memorandum of December 17, 1927, but not officially published until 1930, the United States disclaimed the right of intervention into the affairs of its sister American republics. It still guaranteed their independence and their territorial integrity from extra-hemisphere aggression, but otherwise their internal and external affairs were their own business. Thus by act and by profession the Coolidge-Hoover administrations laid the groundwork for the Good Neighbor policy of the New Deal.

The Harding Scandals. There is no evidence that Harding had any other connection with the scandals that disgraced his administration than his bad judgment of men. One set of scandals revolved around Attorney-General Daugherty, whose position as chief law-enforcement officer of the United States provided infinite possibilities for illegal actions. A friend of Daugherty, Colonel Thomas W. Miller, became Alien Property Custodian, with wide powers in restoring or retaining the possessions of aliens seized by the United States during the war. Ultimately Miller was dismissed from office, and was jailed on conviction of having taken a bribe. Daugherty's closest friend, next to Harding, was Jess Smith, who in a single case took $50,000 to arrange a settlement before Miller. Smith committed suicide. Daugherty's association with such characters naturally

WARREN G. HARDING

Almost as impressive in personal appearance as Washington, the twenty-ninth President conspicuously lacked the ability to fulfill effectively the duties of his high office.

made him suspect, but when finally brought to trial for conspiring to "defraud the United States," he was saved from conviction by a hung jury. Another focus of scandal was the Veterans' Bureau. Forbes, its chief, soon made deals with contractors in the building of hospitals and the purchase and sale of supplies at great personal gain but at heavy loss to the government. His closest adviser, Charles F. Cramer, committed suicide; Forbes resigned, but was eventually convicted of defrauding the government, and was imprisoned.

Most sensational of the Harding scandals was that of Albert B. Fall, Secretary of the Interior, who asserted that certain oil lands, held as naval reserves by the Navy Department, should be in his custody, and was able to persuade the Secretary of the Navy to agree to the transfer. In return for a personal "loan" of $100,000, Fall turned over the right to exploit the Teapot Dome reserve in Wyoming to the Sinclair oil interests, and for a much larger sum, the Elk Hills reserve in California to the Doheny group. Fall was ultimately exposed by a senatorial investigating committee headed by Senator Thomas J. Walsh of Montana, and in 1929 he was convicted of having taken a bribe, and sent to jail for a year. But the two multimillionaires to whom he had sold out, Harry F. Sinclair and Edward L. Doheny, won acquittals in the criminal cases lodged against them. In civil suits, however, their leases were annulled by the Supreme Court on the ground of "fraud," "collusion" and "conspiracy."

Death of Harding. Harding never realized the full truth about the scandals that marred his administration, but he knew enough by 1923 to make him sick at heart, and his acute distress at the misconduct of his friends may have had something to do with his physical collapse and death at San Francisco, August 2, 1923, on his way back from a trip to Alaska. During the administration of Harding's successor, Calvin Coolidge, the revelation of fraud in high places gradually came to an end. Meanwhile public interest had already centered first on a sharp postwar economic recession and then on a note of domestic prosperity that was to continue until 1929.

"Normalcy." The search for "normalcy" in international relations, which took the form of a retreat to nationalism, was paralleled by an endeavor of the nation's political leaders to turn back the clock as far as possible in domestic affairs. Even before Harding took office, the unusual wartime powers of the President had been withdrawn, the war boards through which the economic life of the nation had been mobilized for action had been virtually scrapped, and the army had been sent home. These were but symbols. For many years thereafter in all matters that concerned the relationship of government and business, the efforts of those in authority were directed toward restoring the old American system of private enterprise with a minimum of governmental interference.

Business Depression. The return of peace was soon followed by a sharp business recession. A bad break in the stock market during October, 1919, served warning of evil days to come, and by the summer of 1920 economic distress was everywhere apparent. Undoubtedly the most important cause was the failure of Europe to continue its heavy purchases of American goods. This was due in part to the unexpectedly rapid recovery of European agriculture, but there were other factors also. For months after the armistice the government of the United States continued the policy of lending to its associates in the war, but by 1920, confessing its inability to "assume the burdens of all the earth," it was making no new loans. Foreign exchange, influenced by the enormous debts owing the United States, dropped precipitately; in February, 1920, the English pound was worth only about $3 compared to prewar value of nearly $5, French and Belgian francs previously worth about twenty cents, only seven or eight cents, and the German mark, formerly about twenty-five cents, only two or three cents. European purchasers found it practically impossible to pay the prices for American goods, the more so because the high American tariff, raised again in 1921, made it hard for them to exchange what they could produce for what they needed to buy. The American public added to the general distress by indulging in a "buyers' strike" against abnormally high retail prices that, among other things, reduced the importation of Japanese silk, and in turn, the ability of the Japanese to buy American cotton.

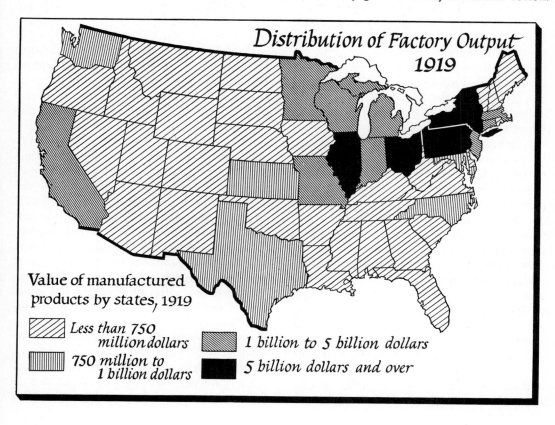

Distribution of Factory Output 1919

Value of manufactured products by states, 1919

Less than 750 million dollars

750 million to 1 billion dollars

1 billion to 5 billion dollars

5 billion dollars and over

The years 1920 and 1921 saw a general slackening in nearly every kind of business. Retailers and wholesalers who had bought at high prices found their shelves stocked with goods that no one wished to buy. Manufacturers who had made heavy purchases of high-priced raw materials were confronted by wholesale cancellation of orders. Railroad earnings went down, and banks were forced to contract their loans. Stocks and bonds slumped disastrously, and speculators were particularly hard hit. A total of 8,881 business failures, with liabilities of $295 million, occurred in 1920, and 19,652, involving $755 million, in 1921. With nearly 3.5 million men out of work the country faced for the first time in many years a serious problem of unemployment.

Depression in Agriculture. The suffering in agriculture was even more acute than in industry. The European market upon which American farm prosperity had come to depend seemed irretrievably lost. Not only did European producers raise a greater percentage of the farm products their countries needed, but European purchasers turned also to other sources of supply. Meat from the Argentine, wheat from Canada, Australia, and Russia, cotton from Egypt and India tended increasingly to supplant imports from the United States. Even the American market failed the farmers, for the changed food habits of the people called for far less wheat and meat per capita than had been consumed earlier in the century. The American farmer, equipped with gasoline-driven tractors, harvested larger crops than ever before. During the three years following the disastrous break of 1920, production of nine basic field crops equaled or surpassed that of the preceding three years. Naturally, the bottom dropped out of farm prices. With wheat at the lowest figure in twenty-five years, cotton at five cents a pound, and other farm commodities correspondingly deflated, the cost of production for most farmers far exceeded the proceeds from sales. The dizzy boom in farm land values accompanying the war and the first months of peace collapsed with a frightening crash.

Low prices, unpaid mortgages, and constant foreclosures conspired inevitably to drive the farmers together. During and immediately after the war the National Non-Partisan League of North Dakota, an organization designed to bring the entire resources of the state to the aid of the farmer, scored remarkable, although only temporary, successes. More permanent were such farm orders as the American Farm Bureau Federation, representing the more prosperous farmers, the American Society of Equity, the Farmers' Union, and the old Grange, which in these troubled times took on new life. Largely as a result of their endeavors, a bipartisan "Farm Bloc" was formed in both houses of Congress to work together as a unit for whatever measures might benefit the farmers, and against anything that might injure them.

Coolidge Prosperity. It was against this economic background of hard times that the Harding-Coolidge administration took form. Nearly every item of legislation and nearly every administrative policy was devised with this situation in mind. The depression had to be broken and prosperity restored. Whatever the causal relationships, there can be no doubt that, at least with the exception of agriculture, the depression did wear itself out in a minimum of time, and that good times did return. The Republicans, as the party in power, took full credit for what had happened, and the public came to regard the name of Harding's successor, Calvin Coolidge, as synonymous with prosperity. President Coolidge (1872–1933), no less than Harding, was a devotee of "normalcy." During a long career of officeholding, he had done little to excite either opposition or approval. Born in Vermont, he studied law at Amherst College, and began to practice in 1897 at Northampton, Massachusetts. After holding numerous local offices he became lieutenant-governor of Massachusetts in 1916, and governor in 1919. In these offices, and as President, Coolidge was conscientious, abstemious of speech, and utterly uninterested in reforms. He accepted the Harding Cabinet, made changes reluctantly only under heavy pressure, and carried forward the work of the Harding administration without any perceptible change in direction. His political philosophy was summed up by his statement that liberalism, or the desire to change things, was compounded of equal parts of ignorance and the envy of other people's possessions. Four-fifths of society's troubles, he commented, would be solved "if we would only sit down and keep still."

The Recovery Program. The Harding-Coolidge formula for business recovery was never precisely stated in a political document, but it soon became fully apparent. First of all came economy in federal expenditures, a policy that under Harding was tolerated as a political necessity, but under Coolidge accurately reflected the presidential state of mind. Economy, said Coolidge in his 1924 inaugural address, "is idealism in its most practical form." Under the terms of a Budget Act, passed in June, 1921, a Director of the Budget, appointed by the President, was required to scrutinize all requests for congressional appropriations, to eliminate duplications, and to pare down excesses. Estimates so obtained were then submitted to Congress, where in each house a single Committee on Appropriations determined the final recommendations. Budget directors took their duties seriously, and effected considerable savings, particularly by cutting down on naval and military appropriations, but had to face mounting bills for pensions and veterans' relief. Nevertheless, whereas expenditures due to the war and its aftermath had absorbed 94 per cent of the national budget in 1920, they accounted for only 86 per cent in 1924. Throughout the

early twenties, however, state and local expenditures mounted even more rapidly than federal spending declined. It is difficult to believe, therefore, that there was the direct relationship between "Coolidge economy" and the return of prosperity that Republican politicians were wont to claim.

The Veterans' Bonus. After 1925 even federal expenditures began to rise. One reason for this was the passage in 1924, over President Coolidge's veto, of a Veterans' Bonus Bill, which promised "adjusted compensation" to veterans of the war. This act granted each veteran paid-up insurance to fall due twenty years later. The amount owing each soldier was computed on the basis of $1.25 for each day overseas, and $1 for each day in service at home. While the grant was not made in cash, each veteran was permitted to borrow up to 22.5 per cent of the face value of his policy, and the avalanche of borrowings that set in materially increased the expenditures of the government.

Reduction of Taxes. A second item in the recovery program was the reduction of taxes, particularly those that "penalized success" by robbing business of its "legitimate profits." Not content with the repeal of the excess-profits tax and the surtax reductions that Congress included in the Revenue Law of 1921, Secretary of the Treasury Mellon pressed insistently for further reductions. "High rates," he maintained, "tend to destroy individual initiative and seriously impede the development of productive business. . . . Ways will always be found to avoid taxes so destructive in their nature and the only way to save the situation is to put taxes on a reasonable basis."

Mellon was unable to persuade Congress to reduce the maximum surtax as rapidly as he had hoped, but in the Revenue Act of 1924 the rate was brought down from 50 to 40 per cent, and two years later to 20 per cent. Other reductions did away with most of the wartime excise taxes, radically reduced the normal income tax rates, modified the estate tax, and abolished the gift tax. A considerable proportion of the funds thus released for private use went into highly speculative investments. Had the tax rates been permitted to remain at higher levels, it is reasonable to suppose that the speculative craze of the later twenties might have been avoided. As it was, Mellon was able to lower the obligations of the United States during the decade of the twenties from about $24 billion to about $16 billion.

Government Withdrawal from Business. A third item in the Republican recovery program was the systematic elimination of government from competition with private business. Business, Coolidge declared on many occasions, "should be unhampered and free" because the prosperity and welfare of the whole nation depended upon its operation. The Transportation Act of 1920, although passed by the Republican Congress before Wilson left office, was in full accord with the policies adopted during the Harding-Coolidge regime. Under its terms the railroads of the country were handed back to their owners, with generous indemnification for whatever damages they had suffered during the period of government operation. The Jones Merchant Marine Act of 1920 dealt in similar terms with the shipping that the government had built or acquired for special wartime service. A Merchant Fleet Corporation was created with authority to operate the ships as long as necessary, to lay out new lanes for American overseas commerce, and to turn over the ships and the routes at minimum cost to private companies as fast as American purchasers could be found. The intent, never fully realized, was to get the government out of the shipping business. Possibly the most striking case in point was the refusal of the administration to countenance any plan for the effective governmental operation of the Muscle Shoals power development in Alabama, begun during the war years to aid in the production of nitrates. In a single stretch of thirty-seven miles the Tennessee River falls 134 feet. To make use of this power the government planned a series of dams and two nitrate plants. One of the nitrate plants was in operation by 1918, but the Wilson Dam was not completed until 1925, when the wartime need for nitrates had long passed. To Senator Norris of Nebraska and others who were undismayed by the prospect of a government-owned business, the Muscle Shoals development seemed to offer an ideal opportunity for the production of cheap power, but Congress was persuaded to offer the whole property for sale. The only qualified bidder was Henry Ford, whose offer involved so heavy a loss to the government that it could not be accepted. A small amount of power was leased to the Alabama Power Company for distribution in the surrounding territory, but for the most part the potentialities of this development remained unexploited until the time of the New Deal.

Restraints on Regulation. The distaste of the administration and its supporters for governmental interference in business went much further, and called also for a drastic reduction in the amount of federal regulation. Legislation to accomplish this end would have been difficult to obtain from the more liberally-minded Congress, but the same purpose was achieved by indirect means. One by one the great regulatory bodies created by preceding administrations were packed with the friends of the very businesses they were supposed to regulate. The Interstate Commerce Commission was in effect handed over to the railroads, the Federal Trade Commission to the trusts, and the Federal Reserve Board to the bankers. For good measure the Tariff Commission was delivered into the custody of the protectionists. In criticism of a series of such Coolidge appointments, Senator Norris had this to say:

The effect of these appointments is to set the country back more than twenty-five years. It is an indirect but positive repeal of Congressional enactments, which no Administration, however powerful, would dare to bring about by any direct means. It is the nullification of federal law by a process of boring from within.

Aids to Business. Not content with removing, or at least vitiating, governmental checks and restraints in private enterprise, the administration in a great variety of ways gave business direct and substantial aid. The rationalization for such aid was sometimes called the percolator theory of national economics. This line of reasoning ran that if the top levels of business were kept prosperous then much of this prosperity would seep down to benefit the middle and the working classes. The most traditional means of accomplishing this end was by protective tariffs, and these Congress promptly supplied through two measures, the Emergency Tariff Act of 1921, and the Fordney-McCumber Act of 1922. The new laws raised tariff rates to the highest levels yet known, and particularly insured the new chemical, optical, and drug industries started by the war, hence called "war babies," against the threat of foreign competition. But government assistance to business went much further than the tariff. For the shipping industry and the new aircraft corporations the government provided generous subsidies. For individuals and companies with a taste for foreign investment, the State Department promised to lend a hand by exposing weak foreign securities, and whether because of this, or in spite of it, American capital sped abroad in a seemingly endless stream. For the better promotion of foreign trade the Department of Commerce extensively and expensively reorganized its foreign service. For the benefit of domestic producers the Bureau of Standards offered elaborate facilities for testing, and recommended standard types in all sorts of manufactured articles from bricks to automobile tires.

Secretary of Commerce Hoover who was tireless in his efforts to promote greater efficiency in business was generally credited with having "elevated a relatively unimportant cabinet position to one of major rank."

The Disciplining of Labor. The return of the Republicans to power was accompanied by a drastic change in the attitude of the national government toward labor. Organized labor had been greatly strengthened by the war. The restraints imposed upon labor by the desire of all classes to win the war were removed by the return of peace. The mounting cost of living gave rise to the charge that wages, high as they were, had not risen correspondingly. Furthermore, the long period of prosperity had unfitted labor psychologically to accept such readjustments as the restoration of peacetime conditions made inevitable. In 1919 strike after strike broke out. Among the most notable were a general strike in Seattle that was calmed down only by the intervention of outside labor leaders, a strike in the steel industry that lasted months before its failure was admitted, and a series of strikes among the coal miners and the textile workers.

The presence of many radicals among the strike leaders made labor generally unpopular with the public, and paved the way for an hysterical outburst against the "reds." The Department of Justice, under Attorney-Generals A. Mitchell Palmer and Daugherty, waged war against radicals and deported or jailed many of them. The federal courts, whose decisions on the legality of many labor policies were of fundamental importance, remained markedly conservative. To Harding in his brief term of office fell the selection of four members of the United States Supreme Court and the men he chose were all conservatives. Taft, in fact, remarked that he had been picked as Chief Justice "to reverse a few decisions." Less apparent, but hardly less important, was the careful attention given by Attorney-General Daugherty to the records of all proposed appointees to the lower courts and to subordinate positions in the Department of Justice. Before he left office in 1924 he was thus able to give a lasting conservative cast to the administration of justice in the United States. Characteristic of the stiffening attitude of the courts toward labor was the sweeping injunction Daugherty obtained in 1922 from Federal Judge J. H. Wilkerson of Chicago, a Harding appointee, when a strike of the railroad shopmen seriously disrupted interstate commerce. Wilkerson's injunction forbade "not merely violence but picketing of all sorts, strike meetings, statements to the public, the use of union funds to carry on the strike, and the use of any means of communication by the leaders to direct it." The fact that this harsh judgment was sustained on appeal demonstrated the hollowness of the hope that the Clayton Anti-Trust Act had furnished an enduring "Magna Charta for Labor."

Persistence of Progressivism. Despite the deep conservative urge of the Republican leadership during the twenties, neither the Harding nor the Coolidge administration was able to cancel the purely legislative gains of the progressive years. Through judicial interpretation and administrative rulings much of the reform vitality was temporarily sapped. But the basic legislation of the progressive years was not repealed and little new legislation of a reactionary nature was passed. This was largely due to the temper of Congress wherein a large group of Republican middlewestern and western agrarian progressives combined with opposition-minded southern Democrats to organize the so-called Farm Bloc, which was to hold the balance of legislative power over most of the period. Few members of this progressive group were forward-looking in the sense that they wished to face and solve the myriad problems of the new industrial and urban age.

In foreign affairs most of them opposed any effective international cooperation for world peace. But their deep allegiance to the old progressive ideology impelled them to stop Secretary Mellon's demand for the repeal of the inheritance tax, to ameliorate his basic reductions of income tax rates, to prevent a wholesale raiding of natural resources by the petroleum and electric power interests. In matters affecting agriculture they proposed and passed through Congress several important measures which anticipated, at least in principle, the New Deal agricultural program.

Farm Relief. The Harding-Coolidge agricultural policy opposed most of the middlewestern and southern demands for farm relief. The Farm Bloc had little difficulty in obtaining as a part of the Emergency Tariff Act of 1921 increased duties on wheat to protect northwestern farmers against importation from Canada, and additional protection for such farm products as meat, wool, and sugar. But these duties could not seriously affect the prices of commodities of which the United States had an "exportable surplus." The Farm Bloc was instrumental also in the passage of the Capper-Volstead Act of 1922 that encouraged cooperative marketing, and the Intermediate Credits Act of 1923, which created a system of banks designed to provide farmers with credits for not less than six months nor more than three years. But remedies more radical than tariff protection and easier credits were consistently opposed. The McNary-Haugen Bill, an ingenious measure designed to raise the domestic price of certain farm crops by creating a governmental agency which could buy up and "dump" the surplus on foreign markets, was before Congress for several years beginning in 1924, and in 1927 passed both houses of Congress only to be vetoed by President Coolidge as "economically unsound." Another scheme for agricultural relief, the export debenture plan, proposed to place export bounties on

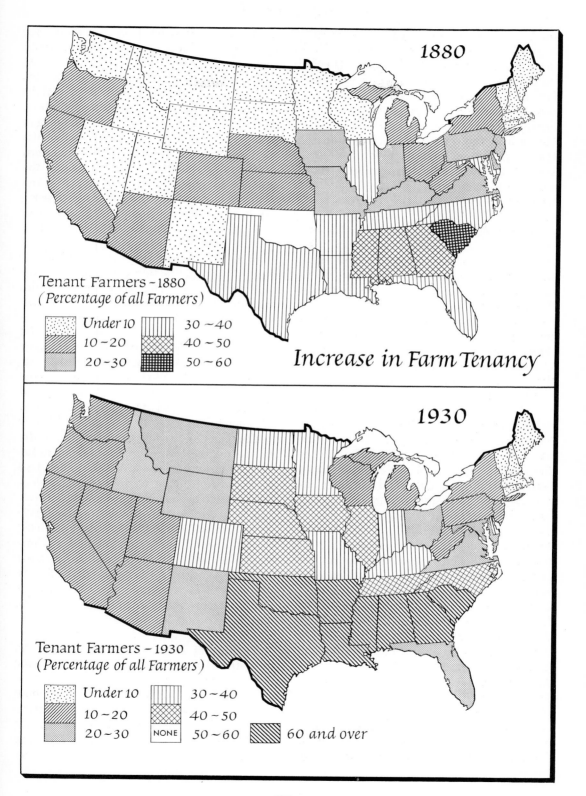

1880

Tenant Farmers – 1880
(*Percentage of all Farmers*)

Under 10		30 ~40	
10 ~ 20		40 ~ 50	
20 ~ 30		50 ~ 60	

Increase in Farm Tenancy

1930

Tenant Farmers – 1930
(*Percentage of all Farmers*)

Under 10		30 ~ 40	
10 ~ 20		40 ~ 50	
20 ~ 30	NONE	50 ~ 60	60 *and over*

specified agricultural commodities, to be paid by the United States in the form of debentures receivable for customs. On the assumption that these debentures would be purchased at a discount by importers, proponents of the plan argued that the bounty to the farmers would come directly out of the protective tariff. But this attempt, aimed no less than the McNary-Haugen Bill "to get the farmer up on stilts" along with the tariff-protected manufacturer, failed even to pass Congress.

Election of 1924. In contrast to the unhappy state of American agriculture, the recovery of business from the depression that had gripped the country when Harding was inaugurated was phenomenal. By the time Coolidge became President the tide had turned, and in the campaign of 1924 the Republicans could count on prosperity as their best talking point. Steady gains were reported in iron and steel, in the automobile industry, in the building trades, and among wholesalers and retailers. Dividends that had vanished during the depression were resumed by a large number of corporations in 1923 and 1924, while occasional stock dividends demonstrated still more conclusively that times had changed. Even railroad earnings increased, and all signs pointed to even better times ahead.

With prosperity working for them, the Republicans entered the campaign of 1924 full of confidence. Their nomination for President went naturally to Coolidge, whom the public had come to regard as a kind of personification of prosperity. The Democrats, as if determined to make their defeat a certainty, staged a long-drawn-out contest in their convention between William G. McAdoo, Wilson's Secretary of the Treasury and Railroad Administrator, and Alfred E. Smith, the idol of the New York City Democrats. The Ku Klux Klan had infected much of the South and West with its prejudice, and because Smith was a Roman Catholic, Klan-conscious delegates

refused to support him. Neither Smith nor McAdoo could win the two-thirds majority required for nomination, and on the 103rd ballot the convention turned to John W. Davis of West Virginia and New York, a brilliant but conservative lawyer whose connection with the firm of J. P. Morgan and Company completely disqualified him in the eyes of labor and the western liberals. To compound this blunder the convention chose for Vice-President Governor Charles W. Bryan of Nebraska, brother of William Jennings Bryan, who had little but his name to recommend him for the post, but whose name alone was enough to alienate the eastern conservatives. With such a ticket, nominated after such a fight, the Democrats had not the slightest chance of winning. A Progressive ticket, supported by the discontented elements of organized labor, by discouraged farmers of the Middle West, and by most of the Socialists, was headed by Robert M. La Follette of Wisconsin, a progressive Republican, and Burton K. Wheeler of Montana, a liberal Democrat, for Vice-President.

The election was a Coolidge landslide. In the popular vote the Republican ticket won a plurality of more than 7 million and a majority of about 2.5 million. The electoral college gave Coolidge 382 votes, Davis 136, and La Follette 13. All of the Davis votes came from the South and La Follette carried only his own state, Wisconsin. Congress was again safely Republican in both houses. A warning, however, that all was not as well as it seemed was contained in the fact that nearly 5 million voters had cast their ballots for La Follette.

Election of 1928. The election of 1928 gave the Republicans another vote of confidence. There was much talk of another nomination for Coolidge, but the President announced in 1927 that he did not "choose to run," and the Republican choice fell upon Herbert Hoover. However high his standing among business leaders, the nomination of the Secretary of Commerce was far from satisfactory to the still unprosperous farmers of the Middle West, and to appease them Senator Charles E. Curtis of Kansas was nominated as Vice-President. The Democrats, with obvious reluctance, yielded to the pressure of the powerful Democratic city machines, and nominated Alfred E. Smith, with what comfort could be found for the rural South and West in the nomination of Senator Joseph T. Robinson of Arkansas for Vice-President. Smith was a Catholic, a "wet," and a Tammany man. Robinson was a "dry" from a state that had few Catholics and no large cities. But no one was deceived. The ticket of Smith and Robinson, despite its "one hundred per cent American" names, represented primarily the descendants of recent immigrants who made up the bulk of the voting population in all the great cities of the East.

Hoover's Victory. Hoover's predictable victory was due primarily to four factors: (1) the belief which he assiduously cultivated that the continuance of Republican rule meant the continuance of prosperity; (2) the prejudice of rural America against a corrupt political machine based on immigrant votes from which Smith had risen; (3) the deep-seated opposition of many American Protestants to a Catholic in the Presidency; and (4) the determination of the evangelical churches to retain prohibition, which Smith denounced and Hoover called a "noble experiment." "Hoover Democrats," voting the Republican ticket in large numbers, shattered the solid South; for the first time since Reconstruction the Republicans carried Virginia, North Carolina, Tennessee, Florida, and Texas. Smith also lost his own state, New York, and every western and border state.

But significant for the future complexion of the parties, Smith carried Massachusetts and Rhode Island and polled heavy totals in other urban regions where minority groups were dominant. The electoral vote stood 444 to 87, and the popular vote 21.3 million to 15 million. Naturally the Hoover landslide carried with it overwhelming Republican majorities in Congress and in most of the states. The heavy protest vote that had been cast for La Follette four years before had dwindled to a mere quarter of a million votes for Norman Thomas, the Socialist candidate.

SELECTED BIBLIOGRAPHY

Brief general surveys which treat this period include D. A. Shannon, *Between the Wars: America, 1919–1941* (1965); and G. E. Mowry, *The Urban Nation: 1920–1960* (1965). J. D. Hicks, *The Republican Ascendancy, 1921–1933* (1960), deals with all major aspects of the 1920's and contains a full bibliography. Another useful survey is H. U. Faulkner, *From Versailles to the New Deal* (1950). In a special category is F. L. Allen, *Only Yesterday* (1931), a sparkling book which has long set the tone for interpretation of America in the 1920's. For the transition to the period, see J. D. Hicks, *Rehearsal for Disaster* (1961); and F. L. Paxson, *The Great Demobilization and Other Essays* (1941). An interesting new monograph is C. A. Chambers, *Seedtime of Reform* (1963), which shows the role of social work in the 1920's.

W. M. Bagby, *The Road to Normalcy; The Presidential Campaign and Election of 1920* (1962), is a scholarly work, based upon archival research. Frank Freidel, *Franklin D. Roosevelt: The Ordeal* (1954), contains an excellent account of the 1920 campaign. Important memoirs include J. M. Cox, *Journey Through My Years* (1946), by the Democratic standard-bearer; and W. H. Hays, *The Memoirs of Will H. Hays* (1955), by the masterful Republican National Chairman. Running commentaries from a master of political invective are contained in H. L. Mencken, *On Politics (A Carnival of Buncombe)*, edited by Malcolm Moos (1956).

* Available in paperback

Harding is only now beginning to get much scholarly attention. Andrew Sinclair, *The Available Man* (1965), is a perceptive short life based on some of Harding's papers; other biographies are expected shortly. Lively and colorful is the journalistic work by S. H. Adams, *°Incredible Era; The Life and Times of Warren Gamaliel Harding* (1939), which devotes much attention to scandals. The best study of one major episode is Burl Noggle, *°Teapot Dome* (1962). A valuable monograph on an obscure subject is D. C. Swain, *Federal Conservation Policies, 1921–1933* (1963). A fascinating account of how Harding made one decision is D. J. Danelski, *°A Supreme Court Justice Is Appointed* (1965), which studies the naming of Pierce Butler. Another work on the court in this period is A. T. Mason, *William Howard Taft: Chief Justice* (1965).

On foreign policy, see the brief survey by Allan Nevins, *The United States in a Chaotic World; 1918–1933* (1950). The careers of Secretaries of State are recounted in Dexter Perkins, *Charles Evans Hughes and American Democratic Statesmanship* (1956); L. E. Ellis, *Frank B. Kellogg and American Foreign Relations, 1925–1929* (1961); and R. H. Ferrell, *Frank B. Kellogg and Henry L. Stimson* (1963). An interesting and provocative synthesis is Selig Adler, *°The Isolationist Impulse: Its Twentieth Century Reaction* (1957).

The literature on continuing diplomatic problems of the 1920's is very large, and can only be treated briefly here. On the League and Court issues, see D. F. Fleming, *The United States and World Organization, 1920–1933* (1938); and F. P. Walters, *A History of the League of Nations* (1952). On the Far East, consult F. R. Dulles, *Forty Years of American-Japanese Relations* (1937); Dorothy Borg, *American Policy and the Chinese Revolution, 1925–1928* (1947); and G. E. Wheeler, *Prelude to Pearl Harbor: The United States Navy and the Far East, 1921–1931* (1963). G. F. Kennan, *Soviet-American Relations, 1917–1920* (2 vols., 1956–   ), is a monumental work still incomplete. Kennan has also done a brief, semi-documentary book, *°Soviet Foreign Policy, 1917–1941* (1960). Louis Fischer, *The Life of Lenin* (1964), is superb. On one crucial episode, see J. A. White, *The Siberian Intervention* (1950); and B. M.

Unterberger, *America's Siberian Expedition, 1918–1920* (1956). See also the survey by W. A. Williams, *American-Russian Relations; 1781–1947* (1952), which is sympathetic with the Soviet position.

On the Washington Conference, the best study is J. C. Vinson, *The Parchment Peace: The United States Senate and the Washington Conference, 1921–1922* (1955). The best work on the naval aspects is Harold and Margaret Sprout, *Toward a New Order of Sea Power* (1940). Herbert Feis, *The Diplomacy of the Dollar: First Era, 1919–1932* (1950), is a valuable study by an expert with a flair for writing clear prose. On the knotty problems of war debts and reparations, see B. H. Williams, *Economic Foreign Policy of the United States* (1929). On the Peace Pact, the best book is R. H. Ferrell, *Peace in Their Time; The Origins of the Kellogg-Briand Pact* (1952). J. C. Vinson, *William E. Borah and the Outlawry of War* (1957); and J. E. Stoner, *S. O. Levinson and the Pact of Paris* (1942), are also useful.

There are two good biographies of Coolidge: W. A. White, *A Puritan in Babylon* (1938); and C. M. Fuess, *Calvin Coolidge* (1940); plus a selection from his press conferences, *The Talkative President*, edited by H. H. Quint and R. H. Ferrell (1964). A. T. Mason, *Harlan Fiske Stone* (1956), is a fine study of the man Coolidge appointed to direct the clean-up in the Justice Department and later elevated to the Supreme Court. Another first-rate biography is W. T. Hutchinson, *Lowden of Illinois* (2 vols., 1957). Interesting studies of the 1928 campaign are: E. A. Moore, *A Catholic Runs for President* (1956); R. C. Silva, *Rum, Religion and Votes* (1962); and V. D. Bornet, *Labor Politics in a Democratic Republic* (1964). A fine brief life is Oscar Handlin, *°Al Smith and His America* (1958). Samuel Lubell, *°The Future of American Politics* (2nd ed., 1956), contains a shrewd analysis of the implications of the 1928 campaign. A model state monograph is J. J. Huthmacher, *Massachusetts People and Politics, 1919–1933* (1959).

The standard survey of economic history is George Soule, *Prosperity Decade, 1917–1929* (1947). An interesting monograph is G. G. Schroeder, *The Growth of Major Steel Companies, 1900–1950* (1953). An acute analysis of the thinking of business leaders is J. W. Prothro, *The Dollar Decade* (1954). On transportation, see W. N. Leonard, *Railroad Consolidation under the Transportation Act of 1920* (1946). A basic study of importance here is H. G. Moulton, *The American Transportation Problem* (1933). On the merchant marine and its problems see especially P. M. Zeis, *American Shipping Policy* (1938).

On agriculture, see the splendid survey by M. R. Benedict, *Farm Policies of the United States, 1790–1950* (1953). A major work on the beginning of the long farm depression is J. H. Shideler, *Farm Crisis, 1919–1923* (1957). Theodore Saloutos and J. D. Hicks, *°Twentieth Century Populism (Agricultural Discontent in the Middle West, 1900–1939)* (1951), traces the history of the principal farm orders from their formation and shows their effect on the political life of states and nation. On the Farm Bureau, the laudatory official history by O. M. Kile, *The Farm Bureau Through Three Decades* (1948), should be contrasted with the highly critical treatment of Grant McConnell, *The Decline of Agrarian Democracy* (1953). On farm relief, see H. E. Socolofsky, *Arthur Capper* (1962); J. D. Black, *Agricultural Reform in the United States* (1929); and G. C. Fite, *George N. Peek and the Fight for Farm Parity* (1954).

Irving Bernstein, *The Lean Years; A History of the American Worker, 1920–1933* (1960), is an important study which takes some of the gloss off the vaunted prosperity decade. Philip Taft, *The A. F. of L. from the Death of Gompers to the Merger* (1959), is the second volume of a major work. Other studies in labor history include: David Brody, *°Labor in Crisis: The Steel Strike of 1919* (1965); C. E. Warne (ed.), *°The Steel Strike of 1919* (1963); S. D. Alinsky, *John L. Lewis* (1949); Matthew Josephson, *Sidney Hillman* (1952); and Benjamin Stolberg, *Tailor's Progress* (1944), on the I.L.G.W.U.

R. K. Murray, *°Red Scare; A Study in National Hysteria, 1919–1920* (1955), is a fine

summary. See also Stanley Coben, *A. Mitchell Palmer* (1963), a careful study of the man in charge of the Red Scare. R. L. Friedheim, *The Seattle General Strike* (1964), is scholarly and analytical. Two important works by Theodore Draper, *°The Roots of American Communism* (1957), and *°American Communism and Soviet Russia* (1960), treat the history of the movement to 1930 in brilliant fashion; see also Irving Howe and Lewis Coser, *°The American Communist Party* (1957). The major biographies of Norman Thomas by M. B. Seidler (1961), and Harry Fleischman (1964), are rather uncritical. Best works on the decade's foremost radical cause are Felix Frankfurter, *°The Case of Sacco and Vanzetti* (1927); and G. L. Joughin and E. M. Morgan, *°The Legacy of Sacco and Vanzetti* (1948).

On the progressive movement of the 1920's, see K. C. MacKay, *The Progressive Movement of 1924* (1947); and B. K. Wheeler and P. F. Healy, *Yankee from the West* (1962). On the Muscle Shoals controversy, see P. J. Hubbard, *Origins of the TVA* (1961). Books about notable progressives of the period include: O. G. Villard, *Fighting Years* (1939); Michael Wresgin, *Oswald Garrison Villard* (1965); Harry Barnard, *Independent Man; The Life of Senator James Couzens* (1958); Howard Zinn, *La Guardia in Congress* (1959); and Arthur Mann, *La Guardia: A Fighter Against His Times, 1882–1933* (1959).

On the Negro, Gunnar Myrdal, *°An American Dilemma; The Negro Problem and Modern Democracy* (2 vols., 2nd ed., 1964), is a work of unusual excellence; it is summarized by Arnold Rose, *°The Negro in America* (1948). Interesting studies of Negro leaders are E. M. Rudwick, *W. E. B. DuBois* (1960); and E. D. Cronon, *°Black Moses* (1955), on Marcus Garvey. J. M. Mecklin, *The Ku Klux Klan* (1924), a good contemporary study, may now be supplemented by D. M. Chalmers, *Hooded Americanism* (1965); and C. C. Alexander, *The Ku Klux Klan in the Southwest* (1965).

35

THE URBAN MASS CULTURE

ह‍ *The Consumer Society · The Automobile · The Airplane · Advertising · The Movies · Radio · Journalism · Book Publication · The New American Woman · Prohibition · Gangsterism · The Wickersham Commission · Educational Changes · Religious Trends · Catholicism and Judaism · Foreign Opinion of the U.S.A.*

A Consumer Society. The 1920's witnessed an abrupt end to the wave of reform which had swept the country in the first two decades of the century. Reformers and the causes they advocated did not, of course, disappear entirely. But the attention of the public was directed increasingly toward more material things. Less talk was heard about the old "enemies of the people"; much less consideration was given to moral and ethical improvement; and the old idealistic calls for a more democratic and egalitarian society were muted. Instead public attention was centered upon the new consumer goods pouring from the factories, the booming stock market, rising profits and wages, and upon the new and mushrooming amusement industries. As the will to collective social action lessened, a new cult of individualism arose which emphasized the right of the individual to profit and enjoy himself irrespective of old

social institutions, conventions, and indeed the law itself. The great revolt of the twenties was aimed as much against conventional American attitudes and morals as against Wilsonian internationalism and reform.

What caused the great shift in sentiment? Disillusionment with the results of the war as compared with Woodrow Wilson's promises was a factor, as was the threat — real or imagined — of foreign Communism and domestic radicalism. But the chief reason for the slackening of the reformist drive was undoubtedly the economic prosperity of the twenties. Although not all parts of the economy responded to the general upward spiral, industrial production rose by 60 per cent. Profits, rents, returns on investments and real wages followed. The average work week was cut by as much as eight hours, and the public was also given the opportunity to buy goods on the installment plan. For the first time many workers had adequate food and shelter, even some luxuries, and the hours of leisure in which to enjoy them. With such rewards at hand or promised in the immediate future, it would be foolish to disturb the prospects with unsettling talk of reform and government regulation. Indeed, Big Business, the old whipping boy of the Populists and the Progressives, now seemed to be the principal source of the new richer life.

But perhaps even more important in explaining the new American attitudes was the rapid urbanization of the country and the development of a new type of industrialism. By 1920 more than one half of the population lived in towns and cities, and during the next decade that preponderance grew rapidly as 6 million more left the countryside for the cities. If Frederick Jackson Turner was right in assuming that the frontier and the availability of free land had profoundly changed American character and institutions, then it was reasonable to suppose that the urbanization of America would produce changes equally great. A second powerful influence was the birth and incredibly rapid development of a new technology geared to the mass production of consumer articles. Hitherto much industrial production had been in capital goods, railroads, bridges, and factories — a consumption pattern which influenced individual Americans only indirectly. But during the twenties most of the new industries produced consumer

goods intended for direct sale to the masses. Out of the relationships and institutions built around this new activity came forces that were to make stupendous changes in society, changes dictated not only by the revolutionary character of the new production but also by the tastes and wants of mass consumers. Of these new industries perhaps the most potent was automobile manufacturing.

The Automobile. Founded largely on European ideas and inventions, the American automobile industry produced only 4,000 cars in 1900, and its growth remained modest until World War I. But during the war and after, production boomed, and by 1928 over 26 million automobiles and trucks were operating in the United States. By that time the General Motors Corporation had surpassed the United States Steel Corporation in earnings, and the total automotive industry, together with its subsidiary industries, such as petroleum, rubber, and glass, employed more men and utilized

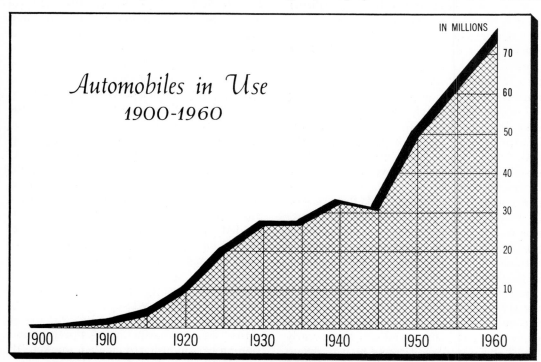

Automobiles in Use
1900-1960

IN MILLIONS

more raw materials than any other single sector of the economy.

Many men contributed to the inspiring growth of this new industry, but none was of greater significance than Henry Ford (1863–1947). Beginning at Detroit in 1893, Ford was making a dependable car by the turn of the century, and by 1914 had produced a half million of his famous "Model T." Ford made no change in his basic designs from 1909 to 1927. The car was ugly, it came in only one color, black, but it ran and it was cheap. Ford's greatest contributions to industrial change were not so much his mechanical ideas as his revolutionary concepts of production and distribution. In 1913 he established an efficient production line, and from then on he unrelentingly pursued the policy of standardized machine production, lower prices, and higher wages. It was only by continually lowering the price of his car and raising the wages of his workers, Ford stated, that he could sell to the millions. Ford was an industrial autocrat with many strange ideas. In his early days he was anti-Semitic; and he was always suspicious of education and culture. But he did lower the price of his car from $950 in 1909 to $290 in 1924, at the same time reducing the working hours of his men and raising their wages substantially above those paid by other industries.

The fierce price competition between Ford and his most formidable competitor, the General Motors Corporation, founded in 1908 by William C. Durant, reduced the major motor companies from over forty in 1910 to essentially three by 1927. Low retail prices created the desperate necessity of producing and selling in volume if profits were to be made. This in turn made advertising increasingly important, and eventually led to the sale of automobiles on extended credit. During the 1920's 60 per cent of all automobiles were sold on credit. The salesman and the sales organization became as important as the producer and the factory. Eventually the state of competition in the industry led it to the calculated promotion of obsolescence. By 1931 the industry was purchasing and destroying functioning cars in order to create a market. By

Despite his enormously successful use and perfection of mass production techniques, which soon enabled him to price his famous "Model T" within reach of most middle-class Americans, Ford's management of his huge enterprise seemed both casual and arbitrary to many of his contemporaries.

So far as a close observer can discover, Ford . . . acts wholly upon inspiration. In reply to a direct question he disclaimed any systematic theory of organization or administration, or any dependence upon scientific management, and seemed to lay emphasis wholly upon the personal equation. As he put it, "I know what kind of help I want and I look around until I find the man I am sure will give it." He has thus built up about himself not so much an organization as a staff of aides — all ranking as equals, none in command of any one department, all ranking any titular departmental head, each eager both to meet any suggestion Ford advances or to volunteer suggestions for his decision, each as likely as the other to be put in charge of any shop-betterment idea Ford may conceive, because he observes no discrimination in lines of service. This alone makes the Ford establishment unusual, to say the least, in its direction. It also makes the establishment his own absolutely throughout, though, as he said, leisurely looking out of his office window, "I have no job here — nothing to do."

H. L. ARNOLD AND F. L. FAUROTE, *Ford Methods and the Ford Shops* (1915)

---

that time also the necessity to promote more sales had led to the habit of introducing a "new model" every year. Even Ford was forced in 1927 to introduce a new higher-priced model to meet the competition.

The automobile age brought many changes. Public demand spurred the rapid construction of paved intercity roads, a development which destroyed the old isolation surrounding the farm, produced great problems for state governments, and was eventually to transform the transportation of both passengers and freight. The automobile also was to have profound effects upon the growth of cities. And in a less obvious way it influenced even the dress and moral standards of the public. Of equal importance to society was the automotive industry's introduction of new ways of doing business, techniques which other mass consumer industries soon made use of.

The Airplane. The amazing success of the automobile industry gave rise to the hope, not soon to be realized in full, of the early development of commercial aviation. American aviation began in 1903 when Orville and Wilbur Wright first made successful flights with power-driven planes at Kitty Hawk, North Carolina. In 1914 the industry was still in its infancy, but when the war ended in 1918 the United States had twenty-four aircraft plants capable of producing 21,000 aircraft a year. But cancellation of war contracts virtually wrecked the new industry, while both the Army and the Navy refused to concede to air power the significance it merited, even after General "Billy" Mitchell's bombers sank a surrendered German battleship, the *Ostfriesland,* and other target craft, in a test demonstration.

Meantime, "gypsy" fliers, who made a precarious living by taking passengers on "joy rides," kept the public air-conscious and prepared the way for commercial transportation; "stuntfliers" also revealed its possibilities, particularly for long-distance flights. The Atlantic was crossed by way of the Azores as early as May, 1919; from Newfoundland to Ireland in June of the same year; and from Great Britain to New York by a British dirigible the following July. But the achievement that most caught the country's fancy was the solo flight of youthful Charles A. Lindbergh, who took off from Roosevelt Field, Long Island, on May 20, 1927, and thirty-three hours later landed successfully near Paris. The fact that he was not the first to fly the Atlantic in no wise diminished Lindbergh's fame. By order of President Coolidge, he was brought home on a warship, and rose immediately to the status of the nation's greatest hero. Later in the month two army pilots reached Honolulu from California, while in June, 1931, another American aviator, Wiley Post, flew around the world in less than eight days' time.

Advertising.   The mass production-consumption process was accompanied by a revolution in advertising and an increased emphasis on salesmanship and public relations. In 1902 the annual advertising revenue of the *Saturday Evening Post* amounted to about $300,000. Twenty years later it was over $28 million. To swell consumption, credit became progressively easier to obtain and the term of payment longer, for even the lowest priced articles. Three out of four radios produced in the decade were sold on credit.

Under this barrage of inducements to buy, old habits of personal thrift began to crumble. Successful salesmen were everywhere lionized and the sales process itself became a national craze. One sold not only goods but ideas, religion, and especially oneself; and all too often the new arts of persuasion embraced deception and downright fraud. This mass-oriented, consumer-conscious, and sales-stimulated capitalism also developed the very natural inclination to produce what the market wanted. Consumer likes and dislikes were studied intensively, and the successful manufacturer produced articles of the kind, shape, and color he correctly guessed the masses desired.

The Movies.   This dictation of national standards by the common man through the operation of the mass consumption process was least harmful in the production of material goods. True, aesthetic standards might decline, but beyond this little harm was done. But when the same process was applied to the cultural and educational institutions of the nation, much more was at stake. The results perhaps were clearest in the new motion picture and radio industries. The invention of motion pictures antedates the turn of the century. From the first "peep shows," which treated the viewer to only a brief episode, up to World War I progress was slow. In 1914 David W. Griffith made "The Birth of A Nation," an epic picture that centered on the Civil War and Reconstruction. Griffith's budget of over $100,000 for the production, his use of crowd scenes and mass action, and his new camera techniques were revolutionary. The public responded with enthusiasm, and by 1918 the movie industry had become big business with headquarters in southern California. Soon its products were being distributed not only in the United States but throughout the world. By 1922, 40 million tickets were being sold weekly, and reigning movie stars were better known than most politicians. "Movie magazines," the introduction of the "talking picture" in 1927, and the use of color further enhanced the popularity of films. By 1937, 75 million people were crowding into the nearly 90,000 theaters weekly; of this audience more than one-third were minors, and one-sixth were under fourteen years of age.

As the motion picture industry assumed big business proportions it inevitably reflected big business attitudes. A few large Hollywood companies accounted for most of the films made and competed with each other for control of the market. Box office receipts became the chief criterion of excellence, and the producers catered shamelessly to the public taste. Production costs became so lavish, and the promise of massive profits from "smash hit" pictures so alluring, that producers were constantly preoccupied with censoring from their films subject matter that might offend any significant part of the world market. Since the major part of a movie audience was adolescent in taste if not in years, pictures had to be patterned to the adolescent mind. Because the public, in its dreams of escape or attainment, wanted happy endings, tragedy as a plot theme was all but excluded. And since the treatment of any controversial subject was apt to reduce the potential market, or so the producers thought, the average movie avoided such questions. The moving pictures of the 1920's and 1930's thus were almost equally removed from life and from art. Their value in lifting the cultural level of the nation was almost nonexistent; the quality of their influence on public ethics and morality was dubious.

Radio. Another new influence upon American life was furnished by the radio. Wireless telegraphy and telephony were known before the outbreak of World War I, and during that struggle they proved to be of such tremendous military value that revolutionary improvements were made within a few years' time. By 1920 the manufacturers of radio supplies were beginning to present programs as a means of promoting the sales and use of their products, and it was from this practice that radio broadcasting developed. The pioneer station in this endeavor was KDKA of Pittsburgh, which broadcast the returns of the election of 1920. Soon many broadcasting stations, generously supported by advertisers, were competing for control of the air, and to prevent complete chaos Secretary Hoover maintained an informal system of licensing in the Commerce Department. In 1927 Congress established a Federal Radio Commission of five members with the right to license broadcasting stations, and to determine the power, wave lengths, and hours of operation to be allotted to each. This act, which made the granting

of wave-lengths contingent upon the licensees conducting stations in the public interest and gave the Commission power to revoke licenses, served in practice to moderate the grosser abuses of an instrument that provided strong means of swaying public opinion and of affecting public taste. In 1939 the industry formulated a much debated code which sought to exclude all broadcasts on controversial public issues except such as pertained to traditional politics. By the Mayflower decision of 1941, however, the Federal Communications Commission, created by an act of Congress in 1934, challenged the right to ban broadcasts on such issues and subsequently instituted proceedings against stations which censored labor news and suppressed other controversial discussion.

CHARLES CHAPLIN

Time has enhanced rather than diminished the reputation of this gifted character actor. Oxford University gave him an honorary degree in 1962.

LISTENING TO THE RADIO

In its earliest manifestation, the radio aroused a degree of wonderment and concern unknown to the sated listeners of a later period.

Radio, like the movies, became big business. By the 1940's there were radios in almost every American home. By that time, also, 730 of the 900 privately owned stations had been organized into four nationwide networks, the advertising receipts of which were enormous. In newscasting and in presenting political campaigns, the radio industry was at its best. Constrained to impartiality, it granted equal time to political candidates, and the entire nation was able to hear for the first time paramount public questions debated by aspiring office seekers. Radio probably also presented the news with less bias and distortion than did some of the nation's newspapers. Occasionally, industries of national scope, like the United States Steel Corporation, which did not sell directly to the public, performed a significant service by subsidizing broadcasts of operas or symphony concerts. Radio was responsible for much of the astonishing rise in the appreciation of serious music. But the great majority of advertisers were interested in appealing to the mass market, and they naturally supported the programs which captured the largest audiences. As a result the cultural

level of radio, like that of the film, tended to reflect the tastes and intellectual level of the majority of its listeners.

However debatable were the effects of the movies and radio upon popular culture and taste, the stimuli to consume they gave to the crowd was all but incalculable. The movies gave to viewers the sight and almost the very sense of participation in the world of the rich and of the supremely leisured. And the pitchmen of the radio commercial reached almost every ear in the nation with the incessant plea to buy, with cash if convenient, with credit if not, the lush life and the luxury goods depicted on the screen. With this assault a "revolution in expectancy" began that called into question the validity of the old national virtues of thrift, industry, and sobriety.

Journalism. Just as films and radio felt the great influence of the masses, so did the more traditional means of communication. The introduction of the first tabloid newspaper, the *New York Daily News,* in 1919, revolutionized journalism. Most of these new "picture papers," as the *News* and its imitators were called, omitted all reference to serious cultural endeavors, played down important world news, and concentrated on sex, sin, and scandal. Their circulation grew enormously, and their success probably had much to do with the demise of such quality newspapers as the *New York World,* sold in 1931 to the Scripps-Howard chain. Developments in magazines tended to follow those in newspapers. The decade saw a spectacular rise of "the pulps," a name derived from the cheap wood-pulp paper on which such magazines were printed. Their stock in trade was detective and "true confession" stories, in which the heroine, who had departed from the paths of virtue, repented and told all. With gaudily colored covers and liberally sprinkled with pictures as shocking as the law permitted, such periodicals competed with the movie and sporting magazines for public custom.

Book Publication. Nor did book publishing escape the pull of the times. Sensational fiction was produced in quantity, the publisher of one such book announcing it as "intimate as a boudoir, as amusing as a peephole and as suggestive as a bill of fare." Even the old and decorous art of biography stooped to obtain mass approval. By stressing the defects and the unconventional actions of such national heroes as George Washington and Benjamin Franklin, a group of popular writers in the early twenties started the "debunking" tradition. From debunking, such authors later in the decade turned to biographies of the more scandalous characters of the past. But perhaps the most significant development in the popular book trade was the movement making book publishing into a big business. Although the selections of the Literary Guild and the Book-of-the-Month Club, both organized in 1927, were books far above the average in quality, this application of mass merchandising techniques to the literary trade set a trend toward quantity as a substitute for quality. Soon most advertising and publicity skills were enlisted in the hope of making commonplace novels into "best sellers."

The New American Woman. One of the most startling revolutions in twentieth-century American society was the change in the status and importance of women. The growing power of women as a class was foreshadowed well before the 1920's, particularly in their demands for political equality and moral reform. During the twenties, however, women as a group seemed to lose their taste for reform, and apparently decided to enjoy the masculine world as it was. Throughout the decade one masculine sanctuary after another fell. Women invaded the business world *en masse.* As typists, secretaries, and even executives their numbers soon changed the entire nature of the office. Whereas in the early years of the century perhaps 2 million women were working, 10 million

earned a weekly salary by 1913, and by 1955 that figure had jumped to 27 million, or over 30 per cent of the entire working force of the nation. Nor were women inactive in politics. Two states elected women governors in the 1920's, "Ma" Ferguson in Texas and Nellie Tayloe Ross in Wyoming.

The typical "flapper," the name given to the new young woman of the twenties, tried to match men in almost every activity and accomplishment of life. She cut her hair in a boyish bob, discarded the corset, and shortened her skirt from ankle to knee. A flattened bosom, a lowered belt line, and

TEACHING OLD DOGS NEW TRICKS

The gay and carefree 1920's witnessed the emergence of the "flapper," whose style of dress and conduct shocked some oldsters, but inspired others to attempt equal excesses. Cover of Life Magazine, *February 18, 1926. Designed by John Held, Jr.*

FEBRUARY 18, 1926   Teaching old Dogs new tricks   PRICE 15 CENTS

a strict diet changed her appearance into something remotely resembling the adolescent male. She drank bootleg liquor, smoked cigarettes, appeared in "beauty contests," and discussed with her dates the latest theories of sex. Whether she was any more responsible than men for the changing relations between the sexes is debatable, for signs of the rapidly changing morality were in the air of postwar America. The old standards no longer elicited reverence from either sex. In fifteen years the number of divorces had doubled, and a survey of marriages in 1929 indicated that over half were "unhappy" and that 15 per cent of husbands and wives queried felt that adultery was "normal" and presumably not harmful. Some social critics viewed this change in sexual morality as not at all

PRE-PROHIBITION ADVERTISING

The Eighteenth Amendment allowed the liquor interests to continue in business a full year after its ratification — with understandable results.

disastrous for society. Others saw it as the portent of the collapse of civilization. But harmful or not, there was no gainsaying that women had achieved a status somewhat near to equality with men, and also that they had had a major role in changing the old standards of middle-class morality and taste.

Prohibition. Certainly Americans of both sexes helped to destroy respect for law by their defeat of the "noble experiment" of prohibition. The rock on which prohibition foundered was enforcement. It was one thing to outlaw the existing liquor traffic, but quite another to prevent its replacement by illicit venders of liquor. The Eighteenth Amendment made no great change in the national appetite for strong drink, and a large minority of the population felt outraged by what they considered to be an attack on their personal liberty. This was particularly true of the city populations in which the immigrant element constituted so important a part. Others who had never drunk before were impelled out of sheer defiance or perversity to do what the law forbade. Americans since colonial times had never felt obliged to obey a law that they did not like; indeed, many argued that the only way to defeat an obnoxious law was to prove that it could not be enforced. Thus a market for liquor still existed, and to supply it a whole new industry came into being. The ways of the "moonshiners," who had long hidden their stills in the mountains to avoid the payment of revenue, were extensively imitated; "rum-runners" brought a steady stream of cargoes from abroad to unpatrolled sections of the American coast; smugglers crossed the border from Mexico and from Canada; chemical formulas, sometimes undependable, were used to "renovate" industrial alcohol by the removal of denaturants; private citizens set up toy stills, manufactured "home-brew" and "bathtub gin," or turned the unfermented juice of the grape into more or less palatable wine.

The Volstead Act, which defined intoxicating beverages as those containing as much as .5 per cent alcohol, and created the machinery for enforcement, imposed upon federal officials an impossible task. "Bootleggers" had already gained valuable experience in the states where prohibition had preceded the Eighteenth Amendment. They knew how easily the problem of distribution could be solved and they were adept at bribery and deception. Against these experts the Prohibition Bureau, which until 1927 was outside the civil service, mobilized a miscellaneous army of petty politicians and their friends. Furthermore, the entrance of the national government into the field of enforcement led the states to relax their efforts. Former wet states in many instances repealed the limitations they had once placed on liquor dealers, while dry states cheerfully resigned to federal agents the task of matching wits with the bootleggers. The United States Department of Justice found itself suddenly swamped with a type of business it had never known before, and prohibition cases clogged the federal courts. Thirty-five hundred civil cases and 65,000 criminal cases were brought within a period of less than two years.

Gangsterism. Illicit liquor soon made possible one of the nation's biggest and most profitable businesses. Since it operated wholly outside the law, all restraints were eliminated, and competitors traded bloody blows. Backed by gangs of thugs, the gangsters fought furiously for the enormous profits of monopoly, and in most large cities a well-recognized king of the underworld emerged, to whom, while his reign lasted, the whole business paid tribute. Deaths among the gangsters were numerous, but trials for these murders were rare and convictions still rarer. The gang leaders, successfully defended by highly paid criminal lawyers, not only sneered openly at the prohibition agents, but also systematically instituted one new "racket" after another. Gambling, prostitution, the trade in narcotics, and other illegal activities came naturally within the orbit of the "racketeers," but even the most legitimate of businesses were not immune. Operators of any small business might be compelled to pay heavily for "protection" — against the protectors themselves! Failure to meet the racketeers' demands meant smashed windows, flattened tires, burned delivery trucks, bombed stores, and for the most obdurate, sudden death. Racketeering was at its worst in Chicago and New York, but few large cities escaped its ravages, and the whole nation paid tribute, directly or indirectly, to the power of gangland.

The Wickersham Commission. With conditions fast becoming unbearable, a Law Enforcement Commission of eleven members was appointed by President Hoover in 1929 to conduct an investigation. Headed by George W. Wickersham, who had been Attorney-General under Taft, the Commission recognized the hopelessness of adequate enforcement, but recommended that prohibition be continued. In the summer of 1932 President Hoover, in spite of the impending campaign, admitted that some changes in the existing system would have to be made, while the Democratic platform went the whole length of demanding repeal. Following the triumphant Democratic victory at the polls, Congress acted. In February, 1933, the repeal amendment was submitted, and by the end of the year it was a part of the Constitution.

Educational Changes. Faced with the increasing materialism and lawlessness of the twenties, new reformers arose, many of whom placed their hopes on education as a remedy. America responded with generous support. Compulsory school attendance up to sixteen or even eighteen years of age became required by law in most states, and each year saw thousands of new, well-equipped school buildings opened. By

1928 it was estimated that the United States gave as much to education in taxes and gifts as the rest of the world combined. In 1900 only one child in ten had entered high school, and only one in thirty-three had entered college. By 1931, 50 per cent went to high school, and one in seven continued to college, most of the increase coming in postwar years. But even if the nation was not quite aware of it, quantity did not guarantee quality. The great numbers crowding into the high schools created a demand that the old educational aims be radically changed to fit the needs, the intellectual capabilities, and the tastes of the majority. This condition and the respect given John Dewey's theories of "education for life" radically shifted the emphasis away from cultural courses toward a more practical and vocational type of education. Moreover, the more zealous educational reformers demanded that the educational process be democratized so that every child, irrespective of his mental endowment, be promoted along with the rest.

Colleges and universities all too often fell prey to the same anti-intellectual forces that were victorious in the lower schools. There were, of course, many excellent innovations and improvements, particularly in the establishment of graduate professional schools. But along with these encouraging developments came more dubious additions — courses in "accident prevention," "mental hygiene," and "charm," together with such a bewildering proliferation of offerings in "physical culture" as to defy analysis. College athletics became big business during the twenties, with football receipts in 1929 amounting to over $20 million. And often it seemed that the major efforts of both students and faculties were being utilized in distinctly nonintellectual pursuits.

Religious Trends. Besides the family and education, the other great social institution that traditionally bound society together was the church. But during the twenties, on the surface at least, religion seemed to be either at a standstill or in retreat. Although immediately after the war the churches were suffused with vitality, the disillusionment over the peace, the materialism of the twenties, the growing spirit of extreme nationalism at home and abroad, and the disposition of the age to derogate ethics and things of the spirit cast a pall over many religious activities. By 1926 many churches admitted extreme difficulties in obtaining funds to support their foreign missionary work. The fundamentalist revival, as shown in the anti-evolution laws in the South and particularly in the trial of John T. Scopes, lost the church much support from a generation increasingly interested in science. The "monkey trial," as it was called, took place in the small town of Dayton, Tennessee, but through the press it quickly attracted a world-wide audience. Scopes, a high school science teacher, was arrested for violating the state Anti-Evolution Law. To his defense came Clarence Darrow, one of the nation's most brilliant trial lawyers. The star witness for the prosecution was William Jennings Bryan, whose World Fundamental Association had been influential in placing the law on the books of Tennessee and other southern states. The resulting battle between Bryan and Darrow epitomized the cultural conflict being waged in the country. In a very personal way Bryan remained the champion of rural America still dedicated to the old virtues and beliefs, whereas Darrow represented a new spirit of doubt and challenge arising from the cities. Scopes was found guilty by the local jury, but the national consensus was that Bryan had been made to appear naive, and that such laws had no place on the statute books.

The continuing battle between the modernist or liberal Christians and the fundamentalists was also internally disruptive. For the first time in its history, the Episcopal Church in 1925 deposed a bishop for heresy, and a few years later funda-

THE SCOPES TRIAL

William Jennings Bryan, witness for the prosecution, and Clarence Darrow, counsel for the defense, are shown here at the famous "monkey trial" in Dayton, Tennessee.

mentalists among the Presbyterians drove the nationally known minister Harry Emerson Fosdick from his pulpit in New York City for being too liberal in his interpretation of the Scriptures. In the preceding twenty years, many churches had won the respect of many alienated workingmen by their emphasis upon the Social Gospel. Attacked during the twenties by both economic and religious conservatives, the Social Gospel movement lost much of its vitality. Instead of answering the charge that the doctrines of the Social Gospel would lead to anarchy and revolution, its onetime supporters increasingly turned from day-to-day economic issues to the more congenial problems of prohibition and world peace. In light of the failure of prohibition, and the coming depression of 1929, this dominance of "the pew over the pulpit," as one minister described it, was perhaps unfortunate. It was significant

that, save for Father Coughlin's radio organization of the Social Justice movement, the churches were remarkably silent during the great depression.

Despite the gloomy prediction that organized religion was in permanent eclipse, there were many indications that the church retained its essential vitality. One such sign was the ecumenical movement, the subject of numerous conferences during the twenties and the thirties. Led by a group of minister-scholars in the Union Theological Seminary of New York — and supported by the powerful modernist *Christian Century* magazine — the campaign for a United Protestant church increasingly gained support. The Federal Council of the Churches of Christ established in 1908 continued active, and the even more inclusive organization of the National Conference of Christians and Jews was organized in 1931.

Catholicism and Judaism. The steady growth of the Roman Catholic Church during the twenties and thirties, despite the immigration restrictions of the early twenties which cut off a principal source of its membership, was also evidence of continuing strong religious life. The bigotry of the Ku Klux Klan and the defeat of Al Smith for the Presidency caused, according to one Catholic writer, an abiding inferiority complex among many Catholics. Certainly this sense of not being quite accepted by the majority as American had undone some of Cardinal Gibbons' early work, and perhaps accounted for the increased activity of Catholics in founding their own schools and cultural organizations. In 1928 Ludwig Lewisohn published *The Island Within,* in which the Jewish hero, Arthur Levy, because of increased antagonism, gave up a lifelong attempt to identify with the gentile majority, concluded that the barriers to integration were insurmountable, and dedicated the rest of his life to his people and their separate characteristics.

The majority in America had themselves to blame during the twenties for much of the rising sense of separatism among minority religious groups. But with the depression and the rise of Fascism in Europe, the tide turned. The repeal of prohibition tended to identify large immigrant and "wet" Catholic groups with the majority in America. The New Deal's evident tolerance of all groups further cemented unity. The Fascist persecution in Europe created sympathy for the Jews, and brought to America large groups of Jewish and Catholic intellectuals who enriched both the cultural life of the nation and its religious tradition. American religion was far from moribund, but in 1929 at least it was difficult to be optimistic about its future.

Foreign Opinion of the U.S.A. By 1929 many foreign intellectuals were aware that the vital industrial and economic power of the United States was rapidly making it a great force among the world's nations.

Consequently, they came in droves, surveyed the scene, and subsequently published their estimates of American culture. A few liked what they saw. André Siegfried, the Frenchman, saw much to criticize but also much to praise. The Irish poet George William Russell, known to the literary world as A.E., characterized the American people as youthful, competent and kindly, full of enormous energy, "evolving a beauty and elegance of their own." But most Europeans held a different opinion. Many recognized that the United States with its emphasis upon mass production, high wages, and mass credit and consumption had developed a new type of economic society. Some even acceded to the proposition that this sort of democratic, capitalistic distribution of goods was the answer to the challenge of socialist Russia. But they objected strenuously to a society in which the taste of the masses, the desire for profits, and the advertising cliché often set the cultural norms. It was a culture that had little in common with the established and aristocratic societies of Europe, and one which, by its enormous appeal to the common man everywhere, threatened to invade countries abroad. To such a threat the response of the European intellectual was predictable: America was a "Babbitt warren," dedicated to materialism, where the primitive tastes of the collective man were rapidly eradicating all traces of refinement, elegance, and artistic creativity.

That there was much to be critical about, none could deny. But what most Europeans and many Americans overlooked was the promise held out by mass democratic education, and the fact that even then, above the culture of the masses, a large and vital segment of the population was devoted to the pursuit of artistic creation and the cultivation of the mind and of the spirit. Since the educative process is slow and America's crusade for mass higher education had barely started before World War I, the full fruits of this radical experiment could not be harvested for generations.

Even so, in the America of the twenties art and music were rapidly gaining assurance and maturity, writers were creating a literature that was to leave its mark on all of western culture, and the student of society had never felt so free to criticize a culture with a view to its reconstruction. If self-criticism is the mother of social transformation, then the American culture of the future was in for some remarkable changes.

SELECTED BIBLIOGRAPHY

A collection of contemporary materials, illustrating many aspects of life in this period, is *The Twenties, edited by G. E. Mowry (1963). Some of the spirit of the age can be found in such works as Laurence Greene, *The Era of Wonderful Nonsense* (1939); Charles Merz, *The Great American Bandwagon* (1928); and Lloyd Morris, *Postscript to Yesterday; America: The Last Fifty Years* (1947). R. S. and H. M. Lynd, *Middletown* (1929), is a brilliant sociological study of everyday life in Muncie, Indiana. *Recent Social Trends in the United States* (2 vols., 1933), by President Hoover's Research Committee on Social Trends, is indispensable.

T. C. Cochran, *The American Business System; A Historical Perspective: 1900–1955* (1957), examines the basic trends of business which affected society. D. L. Cohn, *Combustion on Wheels* (1944); Allan Nevins and F. E. Hill, *Ford* (3 vols., 1954–1963); Keith Sward, *The Legend of Henry Ford* (1948); and C. L. Dearing, *American Highway Policy* (1941), cover the automobile and related industries. But see also the excellent collection of readings on the automobile industry, *Giant Enterprise*, edited by A. D. Chandler, Jr. (1964).

For the mass media in general, see Bernard Rosenberg and D. M. White (eds.), *Mass Culture* (1957); and Otis Pease, *The Responsibilities of American Advertising, 1920–1940* (1958). Gilbert Seldes, *Seven Lively Arts* (1924), *The Great Audience* (1950), and *The Public Arts* (1956), are essential to a discussion of mass media and culture. Among the welter of books on the movies perhaps Lewis Jacobs, *The Rise of the American Film* (1939), is the most historical and scholarly. But Leo Rosten, *Hollywood* (1941); Nathan Leites and Martha Wolfenstein, *Movies* (1950); and M. D. Huettig, *Economic Con-*

trol of the Motion Picture Industry* (1944), should also be consulted. For radio see Federal Council of the Churches of Christ in America, *Broadcasting and the Public* (1938); and P. F. Lazarsfeld, *The People Look at Radio* (1946). Among the better works on jazz are Barry Ulanov, *A History of Jazz* (1952); and Rudi Blesh and Harriet Janis, *They All Played Ragtime* (1950). For the great changes in American morals and the new status of women, see B. B. Lindsey and Wainwright Evans, *The Revolt of Modern Youth* (1925); and *Civilization in the United States: An Inquiry by Thirty Americans,* edited by H. E. Stearns (1922).

On prohibition, an excellent contemporary study is the Federal Council of the Churches of Christ in America, *The Prohibition Situation* (1925). An interesting recent survey by an Englishman is Andrew Sinclair, *The Era of Excess (Prohibition)* (1962). Two popular accounts are Charles Merz, *The Dry Decade* (1931); and Herbert Asbury, *The Great Illusion* (1950). Virginius Dabney, *Dry Messiah: The Life of Bishop Cannon* (1949), is an eloquent attack upon this prominent dry leader.

John Dewey, *The School and Society* (1899), and *Democracy and Education* (1916), present the author's thesis that social utility should be the principal aim of education. See also E. H. Wilkins, *The Changing College* (1927); J. E. Kirkpatrick, *The American College and Its Rulers* (1926); R. C. Angell, *The Campus* (1928); and R. B. Fosdick, *The Story of the Rockefeller Foundation* (1952). H. K. Beale, *A History of Freedom of Teaching in American Schools* (1941), and *Are American Teachers Free?* (1936), are rather pessimistic.

For religious trends in the period, D. B. Meyer, *The Protestant Search for Political Realism* (1960), traces the decline of Social Christianity and the growth of pessimism in

* Available in paperback

Protestantism. P. A. Carter, *The Decline and Revival of the Social Gospel, 1920–1940* (1956); and R. M. Miller, *American Protestantism and Social Issues, 1919–1939* (1958), are written from other viewpoints. H. W. Schneider, *Religion in 20th Century America* (2nd ed., 1964), is a good general survey. K. K. Bailey, *Southern White Protestantism in the Twentieth Century* (1964), is an important analysis. N. F. Furniss, *The Fundamentalist Controversy, 1918–1931* (1954), concerns the clash between modernists and traditionalists. Gail Kennedy (ed.), *Evolution and Religion, The Conflict Between Science and Theology in Modern America* (1957), is one of the better cultural volumes in the Amherst Series. The Scopes trial is excellently handled in Ray Ginger, *Six Days or Forever?* (1958); and S. N. Grebstein (ed.), *Monkey Trial; The State of Tennessee vs. John Thomas Scopes* (1960). On the great Dayton antagonists, see Irving Stone, *Clarence Darrow for the Defense* (1941); Clarence Darrow, *The Story of My Life* (1932); and L. W. Levine, *Defender of the Faith* (1965), a superb study of Bryan's last decade.

36

IDEAS AND THE FINE ARTS
IN THE MACHINE AGE

ಶ Scientific Indeterminism • Freud • Euro-
pean Pessimism • H. L. Mencken • Walter
Lippmann • Reinhold Niebuhr • An Intel-
lectual Class • Cultural Alienation • The
Reform Tradition • Flight to the Left •
Cultural Nationalism • A Basic Pessimism
• Literature • F. Scott Fitzgerald • Sinclair
Lewis • Hemingway • Faulkner • Drama
and Poetry • Painting • Music

As it had during the nineteenth and
early twentieth centuries, science continued throughout the 1920's and 1930's
to exert a profound influence upon men's
minds. Beginning about 1910 some basic
assumptions about how the world was constructed and how it moved had changed.
Most of the great scientists of the eighteenth and nineteenth centuries had assumed that the physical world operated
with the regularity of a machine, with few
or no deviations from established patterns.
Darwin had seen similar law and regularity in the animal and plant worlds, which
changed according to a law of the survival
of the fittest with environment the controlling force. Both Herbert Spencer and

Karl Marx applied such mechanical thinking to human society, and subsequently the
most radical behaviorist psychologists contended that individual man was simply a
product of the forces that operated on him.
John B. Watson, in his Behaviorism (1914),
argued that man's conduct was almost completely a reaction to his environment.
Given a newborn baby, Watson declared,
he could make almost anything out of the
child. Behaviorist doctrines were popular
throughout the twenties. But by that time
a great change had occurred in the thinking of a major group of creative scientists.

Scientific Indeterminism. In 1905 Albert Einstein published his law of relativity. It was soon followed by Max
Planck's quantum theory of the action of
light waves, and Werner Heisenberg's discovery that atoms move in unpredictable
patterns, which led to his formulation of
the principle of indeterminism. Meanwhile biologists had concluded that many
new forms of plant and animal life resulted
from erratic mutations. Henri Bergson, the
influential French philosopher, insisted that
the life of the species was not entirely
governed by physical environment, but
was creative and unpredictable, and that

life itself contained a force accounting for much of the change. All these new hypotheses contradicted the mechanistic theory of the universe. Scientists still saw law in the universe, but many of these laws they now believed to be mathematical, statistical, and probable rather than mechanistic and absolute.

Other scientific findings indicated that a great part of the universe was beyond the reach of man's five senses, that there were realms that he could neither see, feel, hear, taste, nor smell. Once again science had diminished man's stature compared to that of the universe around him. But although the new indeterminism forced man to admit anew his own vast limitations, it also again allowed the exercise of creative intelligence, intiuitive and moral powers, and free will.

Sigmund Freud. At first only a few intellectuals felt the impact of the new science, but by the 1920's the results were more generally apparent, and by the 1930's popular books were disseminating its findings. Along with the new scientific outlook, the theories and writings of a group of European thinkers had a profound influence upon the American mentality. Most important were the psychoanalytical theories of the Viennese physician, Sigmund Freud (1856–1939). At the heart of Freud's doctrine was the concept that the human personality was largely motivated by the conflict between the subconscious mind and the super-ego, the first being the instinctual drives, particularly sex, and the second the moral and ethical conditioning of society. This inner conflict often engendered strains in the human personality, inducing irrational dreams, and, in acute cases, violent and self-destructive action. Since the individual could seldom recognize the nature of the forces that set up strains within him, only the properly trained psychoanalyst, by interpreting his actions in the light of the individual's past, could make them understandable. This

explanation, plus the therapy of "confession" would, according to Freud's theory, provide a catharsis after which the individual could live more rationally with both himself and society.

Freud's emphasis upon sex as the dominant instinctual drive was distasteful to many. But psychoanalysis worked in some cases, and the Viennese physician's theories rapidly gained acceptance, particularly by the postwar generation. Freud became something of an idol to certain intellectual and literary cults. The novels and short stories of Sherwood Anderson and the plays of Eugene O'Neill in particular reflected his theories. Since popular and badly distorted accounts of Freudianism — of which there were many — seemed to excuse self-indulgence, Freud also became something of a demi-god for pleasure lovers. But in the long run his theories made important contributions to mental therapy, helped clear away the remnants of Victorian cant and hypocrisy, and were used by many churches and universities. Freud's doctrines were essentially optimistic since they held out hope of treatment and cure for the warped personality.

European Pessimism. During those same years Americans read and pondered the more pessimistic writings of other European intellectuals. Early in the decade, Oswald Spengler's *Decline of the West* was translated and had a surprising sale in the United States. By a complicated historical analysis, Spengler proved to his own satisfaction that western culture was doomed. To him the days of western art, religion, and even democracy were numbered. The fact that the publication of Spengler's book coincided with the rise of Fascism in Europe lent force to his thesis.

Even more influential was the work of the Spanish philosopher, José Ortega y Gasset. His *Revolt of the Masses,* first published in English in 1932, was a brilliant and trenchant attack on modern democracy and mass culture. Society always had been divided, he argued, between a creative, artistic, intelligent minority, and the unproductive multitudes. When the masses should become dominant, society, culture, art, and even freedom itself were doomed.

A short time later (1935), the ideas of the Italian engineer, economist, and sociologist, Vilfredo Pareto, added further to the gloom. Pareto sought to prove that the majority of men were not logical, nor did they respond to rational appeals, but rather to emotions, sentiments, and myths.

H. L. Mencken. Much of the deeply pessimistic European thought was paralleled in the United States by a similar intellectual group. Whether H. L. Mencken (1880–1956) was a pessimist, a nihilist, or a mischievous and extremely witty iconoclast, is difficult to say. Mencken had a gift for the cutting phrase, and his lack of veneration for almost every American institution found a ready response among intellectuals. His scorn was mainly turned against Puritanism and the prohibitionist mentality of the "Bible belt," the term he used to designate the South and the Middle West, and against the cultureless, money-grabbing businessmen. Few things were spared his irony and sarcasm. For him, most men were beneath contempt, idiots, knaves, and cowards who had "not moved an inch in a thousand years." He scorned reformers, and he held no brief for democratic government, which he termed "mobocracy" and "government by orgy." Theologians and professors he considered rather worse than politicians. The American people he characterized as "the most timorous, sniveling, poltroonish, ignoramus mob of serfs and goose-steppers ever gathered under one flag in Christendom since the end of the Middle Ages. . . ." Obviously Mencken was no worshiper of the doctrine of progress; to him, truth was unascertainable, and most of society's problems insoluble.

In 1924, along with George Jean Nathan,

Mencken established the *American Mercury,* a monthly magazine that did much to maintain standards of taste and quality in music, arts, and letters, however violent its views on American mores. At the peak of Mencken's popularity, the *New York Times* referred to him as "the most powerful private citizen in America." Despite such high praise, Mencken's influence failed to survive the decade. He had no constructive program to offer his readers, and with the coming of the depression his negative attitudes lost him most of his following.

Walter Lippmann. Much more influential on the American mind for the next

HENRY L. MENCKEN

Caustic critic of American folkways and general disturber of the peace, Mencken did much to shock Americans out of their instinctive complacency and to prepare them for the harsh realities of the 1930's.

forty years was Walter Lippmann (1889–
). Born in New York City, he grad-
uated from Harvard in 1909, and began a
career in journalism that was to make him
the one modern equivalent in power and
influence to America's great editors of the
past. As an editor and daily columnist,
Lippmann had measurable impact on the
political and economic life of the nation.
Author of an influential series of books,
starting with *A Preface to Politics* (1913),
Lippmann was at first supremely confident
that man, by the use of his rational powers,
could build a society in which reason and
the arts would flourish. But after 1918 he
grew steadily more pessimistic. Liberalism,
he finally confessed, had been the "defender and the liberator" of the underdog,
but had supplied no guide for the masses
when they were free. Once rid of authority and the old moral values, the masses
of the modern state responded only to
self-interest, thereby deifying the "rule of
the second best," and threatening to obliterate the cultural and aesthetic heritage of
the past. To forestall the encroaching
anarchy he saw in both international relations and domestic economic institutions,
Lippmann sought some means to balance
the power of the masses with that of self-
interested groups, and thus to blunt the
conflict between them. During the thirties
he talked of a "compensated economy" or
a "free collectivism" in which the state
would not dictate but would "balance,
equalize, neutralize, offset and correct the
private judgments of masses of individuals." Increasingly he looked to the past
for institutional sanctions by which the
baser appetites of individuals might be
mitigated. In *The Good Society* (1936),
he urged his generation to develop once
more a sense for the historic values of western civilization.

Reinhold Niebuhr. Much the same
kind of change took place in the ideas of
Reinhold Niebuhr, who as one of the leading speculative theologians of the time had
a profound effect on Protestant thought.
Born in Missouri in 1892, Niebuhr took a
degree at Yale and occupied a Detroit pas-
torate from 1915 to 1928, when he joined
the faculty of the Union Theological Seminary in New York City. Niebuhr at first
was dedicated to the Social Gospel, and
his theology was wholly optimistic in its
estimate of man and his capabilities. During the twenties, however, he changed
sharply, and though he remained a social
radical, he eventually became the chief
defender of an unorthodox but thoroughly
conservative theology. In his book *Does
Civilization Need Religion?* (1928), he was
still relatively hopeful for mankind although he admitted that he had lost most
of his earlier optimism. As Niebuhr
watched society he was increasingly convinced that individual man was "essentially perverse," though not totally corrupt.
But man in the mass was infinitely worse
than the individual, since the group or the
state had no conscience. From these "new
barbarians" little improvement could be
expected. Instead of progress, there would
be simply change, which would have as
much potential for frightfulness as for happiness. Existing society was in a process
of total decay which "threatened the whole
world with disaster." The one chance for
reconstruction lay in a return to faith.
Only if men took "the leap of faith" into
religious belief was there a chance of re-
pairing what had been so severely damaged
by rationalism. To the scientifically ori-
ented twentieth century, Niebuhr's demand
for mysticism and irrationalism sounded
like total heresy, but he had a profound
and continuing influence upon many
clergymen.

John Dewey was one of the few outstanding intellectuals in the period who
did not fall prey to either an embracing
pessimism or irrationalism. He contended
that human intelligence could construct the
good society by the use of the instrumental and scientific approach. But even
Dewey was disheartened as he saw what

happened when mass society embraced industrialism. In 1922 he wrote that the nation had reached "the point of reverence for mediocrity; for submergence of individuality in mass ideals and creeds." Five years later he admitted that the kind of knowledge and insight needed to organize a humane, collective democracy was still not yet in existence.

An Intellectual Class. Precisely at this time, when pessimism was darkest, the United States produced its first large coherent group of self-conscious intellectuals. Recruited chiefly from the prosperous urban middle class, its members were attracted to the large cities where artists, novelists, dramatists, magazine editors, literary critics, and essayists formed colonies like that in Greenwich Village in New York City. There they established organizations where they discussed their ideas, magazines like *The Masses* and the *Seven Arts,* and theatrical groups like the Washington Square Players. The *Seven Arts* published the first writings of Eugene O'Neill, Sherwood Anderson, and Van Wyck Brooks. As these bright young people and scores of others came together, they dissolved their old ties with the middle-class culture into which they had been born and identified themselves with this new intellectual class. Like most such new classes of highly articulate people they rebelled against the past; but few groups have been as consistently critical of and as thoroughly alienated from their own society as were American intellectuals from 1920 to the present. They delighted in attacking the conservative canons of art and music, and nineteenth-century morals. In the famous Armory Art Show of 1913, they shocked conservative aesthetic taste by introducing the country to the post-impressionist, Fauvist, and cubist movements in French art, while in their writings, they depicted squalid and erotic aspects of life with an explicitness which even Theodore Dreiser had never dared to use.

The Intellectual and Mass Culture. Optimistic during the prewar years when they had hoped to reconstruct society in accordance with their own taste, the new intellectual class was sobered by America's entrance into the war and rendered pessimistic by the disillusioning peace which concluded it. Postwar society completed their disillusionment and enhanced their sense of alienation. Even though the Wilson administration had censored the anti-war activities of some intellectuals, it had still largely identified with them by using them in its war and peace effort. But the Harding, Coolidge, and Hoover administrations gave them no recognition. At the apex of postwar society the intellectual saw the businessman, who had persuaded the country to accept his materialist values. "Advertising instead of truth," one of them angrily wrote, "cash instead of art, machines instead of men." The intellectuals looked with equal revulsion at the new mass culture. Even before the war Randolph Bourne, essayist and critic, had sensed the threat inherent in a culture of the masses. He was gleeful, he wrote, at the demise of nineteenth-century standards, but he was not happy about the "low-brow snobbery" taking their place. When the full tide of the new mercantile culture burst upon the intellectuals, their scorn knew no bounds.

Cultural Alienation. As the intellectuals looked about them in the postwar world, they deplored the advances of industrialism and urbanism. In 1922 there appeared a volume edited by Harold E. Stearns, entitled *Civilization in the United States; An Inquiry by Thirty Americans,* among whom were many of the nation's leading commentators and critics. They covered most aspects of American culture, and almost to a man their reports were tracts of disappointment, indictment, and despair. Thus there arose in many of the creative minds of the period a sense of alienation from their own culture which led some to become exiles in Europe. Among the most eminent of these expatriates were two poets: T. S. Eliot, who went to England and eventually became a British citizen; and Ezra Pound, who made his home in Italy. By far the largest group lived in Paris. Ernest Hemingway, Glenway Wescott, and Gertrude Stein were a few of the creative writers who expressed their opinion of their native culture by preferring what they found along the banks of the Seine. For those who stayed at home there were other ways of living apart. One was to turn one's back upon the majority, forget about causes, and live in a world of individual taste. Herbert Croly, who had so confidently written about *The Promise of American Life*, promised that he would make "no more dashes into the political jungle" but content himself with the moral regeneration of individual man. Another escape from the dreary landscape of the present was to make art the nucleus of life. This extreme aestheticism exalted the artist and scorned or disregarded everything else. Floyd Dell of Greenwich Village announced that for him "art was more important than the destinies of nations, and the artist a more exalted figure than the prophet."

Academicians also registered their disgust at the prevailing tendencies of a mass culture. For years Harvard professors Paul Elmer More and Irving Babbitt had preached the doctrine of righteousness, restraint, taste, and order. Now joined by Norman Foerster of the State University of Iowa, they published the credo of a "New Humanism," which rejected the materialist, scientific, and mechanical world of the twenties and sought a society in which human and spiritual values were emphasized. Something of the same spirit, though with a sectional twist, was obvious in the southern agrarian movement. In the book entitled *I'll Take My Stand* (1930), Allen Tate, Robert Penn Warren, and John Crowe Ransom, among others, argued for a return to the old agrarian and feudal South in which a cultured elite presided over the great majority of farmers and artisans.

The Reform Tradition. The urge to form a cultural elite, profoundly conservative in its implications, was felt by only a minority as yet. During the twenties and thirties most intellectuals probably looked to the left rather than to the right. The first issue of *The Masses* in 1913 proclaimed that it was a revolutionary and not a reform magazine. Some of this spirit of cultural rebellion was naturally directed toward political ends. *The Masses* closed down when it became involved in an antiwar program after 1917. But *The New Republic*, founded in 1914 by Herbert Croly, remained throughout the period a flourishing journal of reform and protest. *The Nation*, which under Oswald Garrison Villard exposed progressive and radical democracy, also became a vehicle for the rebel spirit. Despite the efforts of these magazines and their contributors, the influence of "Babbittry," Sinclair Lewis' term for the mores of small town business and the business mentality in both politics and culture, became more and more pervasive.

Flight to the Left. As the twenties wore on, some intellectuals, disappointed with the increasing weakness of the reform tradition, began to search for more radical solutions. The path to the extreme left had already been blazed by John Reed, a young Harvard graduate who left Greenwich Village to become a Communist, died in Moscow in 1920, and was buried in the Kremlin. Few American-born intellectuals were connected with the origin and stormy early career of the Communist Party at the start of the decade. But after the disillusionment of the Sacco-Vanzetti case, some of them began to look toward Moscow. After 1929, when it looked as if the whole world was moving toward totalitarianism, the leftward drift became even stronger. Among other celebrated literary figures, Lincoln Steffens, Edmund Wilson, John Dos Passos, and Theodore Dreiser had about as many kind words for the Soviet system as they had sharp criticisms of their own. Though it is doubtful that more than a very few of the highest American creative and critical talents ever formally joined the Communist Party, the pull of the far left was strong. The pages of *The New Masses,* a frankly Marxist magazine edited by Joseph Freeman, were studded with well-known names. During the thirties, the pronouncements of the American Writers Conferences became increasingly leftist.

By the late thirties many of the exiles began to return. The depression probably played a part in inspiring this movement. But perhaps the New Deal, with its positive policies of relief and reconstruction and great social experiments, did even more. Its Federal Writers Project, and similar organizations for the drama, music, and the dance, not only gave jobs to scores of unemployed artists, but also imbued the population at large with a taste for the arts that remained after the depression had run its course. From the days of the "brain trust" on, the New Deal employed thousands of intellectuals in its planning and administrative agencies. Never before in the nation's history had the intellectual so much reason for identifying himself with the ruling power.

Cultural Nationalism. Among the many intellectual exiles returning from Europe in the thirties was Harold Stearns. In *America Now* (1938), he edited a second evaluation of American culture, which had little of the pessimism of his earlier book. Some of its contributors even made claims for American supremacy in culture and the arts. As the menace of Hitlerian Germany became more evident, patriotic sentiments multiplied. By 1940 many former critics of American society had become its ardent defenders. John Dos Passos, Archibald MacLeish and Van Wyck Brooks, among others, were now attacking the literature of the twenties instead of the society which produced it. In particular they criticized the antiwar sentiment, the debunking, and the satirical novels as having destroyed the nation's cultural institutions.

A Pessimistic Literature. The returning intellectuals did not come back to the same culture they had rebelled against. Almost every volume of fiction bore testimony to the break with past conventions and beliefs and an acceptance of pessimism about man and his future. In the literature of the twenties the hero was more often than not a victim and a passive figure, less a man of action than one acted upon by nature and society. Men were "just another race of animals whose behavior," wrote Edmund Wilson, critic and novelist, "was fixed by their environment and by the cells which they had had from their parents. . . ." For such pawns of biological fate there could be little censure but also little hope. "Madam," one of Hemingway's characters said, "there is no remedy for anything in life." Such a philosophy indicated the evident erosion of the old faith in human nature and in progress.

Moreover, most American literature of the twenties was completely apolitical and almost asocial. Writers were not interested in economics, politics, or society, but instead were preoccupied with individual character. This was the age of the new "hardboiled intelligentsia," who would rather have been "accused of a crime than a sentiment." Accordingly, creative literature was almost entirely lacking in sentiment and even ethics. Many of the principal characters were like John O'Hara's, of whom one critic wrote that since they had no values they had little pride and they could not be insulted.

Since the tension set up between man's desires and his ethics had been the stock in trade of older novelists, these new practitioners had to find other ways to interest readers. Usually they relied on conflict between people without ethics fighting for material or sensual gain. The frank treatment of sex, a trend before the war, now became general and often wearisome. The

F. SCOTT FITZGERALD

Talented and uninhibited, Fitzgerald embodied perhaps more fully than any other writer the spirit of disillusionment that characterized the "lost generation."

new woman was often depicted with the same sensual appetites as man, as in Faulkner's *Wild Palms,* Hemingway's *To Have and Have Not,* and John O'Hara's *Butterfield 8.* Along with sex went perversion and often glorification of violence. The writers of the twenties and thirties buried Victorian morality as deeply as the reforming progressives had interred Victorian economics.

The literary attack upon traditional morality also brought rural life under criticism. Beginning with Edgar Lee Masters' *Spoon River Anthology* and Sherwood Anderson's *Winesburg, Ohio,* both published before 1920, the "revolt from the village," as Sinclair Lewis phrased it, was in full evidence. Although villages and small towns had produced many of their literary colleagues, these writers depicted them as the abode of frustration and abnormality. The businessman also was an object of attack, as was the middle class in general. But many writers ignored bourgeois so-

ciety, especially in its more normal aspects, while agreeing in general with the sentiments of a Floyd Dell character that "Middle class life in America is dull enough in reality without having to endure it in books too."

Literature and the Depression. The depression had a sharp but temporary influence on American letters. Compared with the individualist novels of the early twenties, the novels of the thirties tended to depict undifferentiated characters who were less people than types. In Dos Passos' massive trilogy, *U.S.A.,* for example, capitalists, politicians, labor leaders, and crooks abound, and although the novel presents a brilliant panorama of life in America, it has no protagonist. A mass of factual detail was substituted for the symbolic event and all too often zeal for social mission took the place of style. At their best, the social and proletarian novels of the thirties had many commendable qualities, but most were formless and uninspired political tracts, devoid of any craftsmanship or creativeness.

Although artists attacked American society during these years as one dominated by a materialist, business, and anticultural mentality, they ironically proved the contrary by their own artistic production. For at no time in the past had the nation produced so large a group of brilliant novelists, poets, dramatists, and painters, nor had art been received with such acclaim. Before the war William Butler Yeats had sensed the coming cultural flowering. "The fiddles," he wrote, "are tuning as it were all over America." Looking back, W. H. Auden, the English poet, remarked that American novelists "produced the only significant literature between the two great wars." Only by comparison with literature were the achievements in the other creative arts less spectacular.

F. Scott Fitzgerald. Perhaps the most representative writer of the postwar generation was F. Scott Fitzgerald (1896–

SINCLAIR LEWIS

A steady procession of novels by Lewis caricatured Americans and American life with painstaking attention to detail.

1940). Minnesota born and Princeton educated, Fitzgerald published his first book, *This Side of Paradise,* in 1920. This novel brilliantly chronicled the new generation of selfish, rebellious, cynical, and pleasure-loving youth. Fitzgerald for the next ten years of his life lived the career of one of his jazz age heroes in one great party carried on in Paris, in Italy and on the Riviera. His best work, *The Great Gatsby* (1925), revealed his consciousness that his way of life was dissipating his talent and splendid vitality. He returned home, finished *Tender Is The Night* (1934), and died before he could complete *The Last Tycoon,* his last work. Fitzgerald's sharp characterization, his insight into the motivations of his generation, and his memorable prose assure him a lasting place in American letters.

Sinclair Lewis. Sinclair Lewis (1885–1951), also born in Minnesota, published his first successful novel in 1920. This book, *Main Street,* was an attack against the small-minded materialism of the typical midwestern small town of Gopher Prairie. With the eye of a consummate journalist, Lewis portrayed the town's bleak ugliness and its lack of culture. In *Babbitt* (1922), he examined the life of the businessman of the Middle West in much the same satiric spirit, and in the process coined a new word. An enormously popular novelist, Lewis, in other important novels, dealt with a hypocritical evangelist, *Elmer Gantry* (1927), an aspiring scientist, *Arrowsmith* (1925), and a likable manufacturer of automobiles, *Dodsworth* (1929). In 1930 he became the first American writer to win the Nobel prize for literature. He was, however, scarcely a man of genius. Timely as his novels were, his characters are curiously flat and one-dimensional, and his subjects, if not his themes, now appear dated.

Ernest Hemingway. Another midwestern novelist was Ernest Hemingway (1896–

ERNEST HEMINGWAY

The novels and short stories of this skilled craftsman profoundly influenced the writing of the English language both in the United States and elsewhere.

EUGENE O'NEILL

Son of an actor, and close student of psychology, Eugene O'Neill became the outstanding playwright of his age. He won two Pulitzer prizes in the 1920's and the Nobel prize for literature in 1936.

1961). Born in a Chicago suburb, Hemingway served in the ambulance corps of the Italian army during the war and later became a newspaper reporter in Paris. His first novel, *The Sun Also Rises* (1926), was an uncompromising picture of the hedonistic life of the expatriates. There followed *A Farewell to Arms* (1929), a brilliant war novel, and a series of short stories, which include some of his finest pieces. Hemingway's fiction deals mostly with tough, cynical activists who live dangerously and heroically. Hemingway's central figures are pessimists who expect and receive little from life and society; they battle strenuously and accept final defeat with stoic calm and dignity. Attracted by the Spanish character, Hemingway strongly sympathized with the Loyalists during the Civil War. In 1940 he wrote *For Whom the Bell Tolls,* a statement of man's commitment to the heroic individual virtues stressed in his earlier works. His

clean, spare prose, precise description, and acute ear for dialogue have left a heritage that the literary tradition will not soon exhaust.

William Faulkner. Of the many able writers the South produced in the twentieth century, the most notable was William Faulkner (1897–1962). Born in New Albany, Mississippi, Faulkner returned to life at Oxford in his native state after service in World War I. He first attracted attention with *Sanctuary* (1931), a sensational novel of dubious merit. His real literary fame was won by a series of novels which examined the relationship between the decaying aristocracy and the poor white classes of his mythical Yoknapatawpha County. *The Sound and the Fury* (1929) and *As I Lay Dying* (1930) won critical acclaim; his subsequent novels, such as *The Hamlet* (1940), *The Town* (1957), and *The Mansion* (1959), rapidly increased his reputation and won him a Nobel prize. Faulkner's prose is often extremely complex, and his search for the threads of guilt and expiation in the human mind makes his books difficult and obscure. But few have written about the modern South with such power and understanding.

Another southern writer of great promise was Thomas Wolfe (1900–1938). Born and reared in North Carolina, Wolfe took a master's degree at Harvard and taught for a while in New York. His prose came out as if a torrent, especially in his four autobiographical novels, starting with *Look Homeward, Angel* (1929), and ending with *You Can't Go Home Again* (1940). But in his short life he was never able to discipline either himself or his writing, and his critical position has never been secure.

Drama and Poetry. Eugene O'Neill (1888–1953) won critical acclaim in the 1920's with *The Emperor Jones.* In rapid succession he wrote other plays of more enduring worth, which together won him a Nobel prize in 1936. Full of Freudian themes and often borrowing heavily from Greek tragedies, O'Neill's plays were grim and pessimistic accounts of man against nature, against the gods, and against himself. But despite the heavy prose and complex symbolism, his plays have a power acknowledged on both sides of the Atlantic.

Close to O'Neill in theme, temper, and tone was Robinson Jeffers (1887–1962), who wrote a series of long poems beginning with *Tamar* in 1924. Sometimes stressing the irrational and darkly compelling sexual forces in man, Jeffers celebrated the overwhelming amoral vitality of natural forces. In the stellar galaxies he saw harmony and law; in society little but confusion, passion, and defeat.

In a more popular vein were the middle-western poets, Carl Sandburg and Vachel Lindsay. Both often used folk myths as their themes, but Sandburg was essentially a free-verse poet of the industrial city. The foremost poet of these years was Robert Frost (1875–1963), a countryman with a love and deep understanding of both nature and man. Frost's finely wrought and deceptively simple poems were in part a protest against the formlessness of much modern art and in part a warm testament to the old natural and human verities.

Painting. During these years painting also came of age. Most of the rebellious and talented group which had participated in both the Ashcan exhibitions and the Armory show of 1913 were still productive during the twenties and the thirties. They were joined after the war by a new generation of painters who attained maturity during the twenties and the thirties. By that time American painting was fully abreast of European post-impressionist developments, ranging from cubism through expressionism to pure abstraction. The older realist tradition was carried on by a group of midwestern artists led by Grant Wood of Iowa, Thomas Hart Benton of

Missouri, and John Steuart Curry of Kansas, who painted the everyday scenes of the region with a precision of detail that rivaled the camera. Also close to the realist tradition were the works of Eugene Speicher, Charles Burchfield, Reginald Marsh, and Yasuo Kuniyoshi, who sought to make the real more convincing by intelligent selection and invention. Stuart Davis and Georgia O'Keeffe, among others, sought their effects through the geometric organization of color and space. But more and more painters rejected realism to become devotees of a highly personalized expressionism which tended toward the mystical, the irrational, and the subjective. Among the leading painters in this latter group were Max Weber, whose glowing colors were reminiscent of old stained glass, and Arthur Dove, whose vision led him into a magical world of his own.

AMERICAN GOTHIC

This example of stark realism, by Grant Wood, is redolent of the Middle West, in which the artist lived.

LEOPOLD STOKOWSKI

American appreciation of serious music was greatly stimulated in the twentieth century by the acquisition from abroad of such distinguished artists as Leopold Stokowski, for decades conductor of the Philadelphia Symphony Orchestra.

As in literature, the creative and materialistic world of the middle classes was more and more avoided. The artist chose his models from the lower classes. And more often than not he chose to portray the warty, wrinkled, and distorted forms of humanity rather than those akin to classical modes. Freudian symbols appeared almost as much in painting as in writing. And the stream-of-consciousness in writing was perhaps paralleled in painting by a subjectivism which at times created a world of color and form mysteriously its own.

Music. In Aaron Copland and Samuel Barber the nation produced its first notable composers. But of far more significance was the increasing nationwide support for the reproduction of serious music, whether in concert halls or on phonograph records. Throughout the twenties and thirties America attracted for its many thriving symphony orchestras numerous renowned conductors from abroad. Arturo Toscanini's engagement in 1927 by the New York Philharmonic was paralleled by Philadelphia's earlier acquisition of Leopold Stokowski, Boston's of Serge Koussevitsky, and Minneapolis' of Dimitri Mitropoulos. Their coming indicated an interest in good music and a willingness to support it that was as remarkable for the time as it was portentous for the future. Despite the lamentation of critics, especially those of the 1920's, America in 1940 was no longer a cultural wasteland.

SELECTED BIBLIOGRAPHY

The relationship of modern scientific thought with society is dealt with in two of A. N. Whitehead's more popular books: °*Science and the Modern World* (1925), in which the philosopher includes a chapter on God along with one on relativity; and °*Adventures of Ideas* (1933). Other useful works are Bernard Barber, °*Science and the Social Order* (1952); M. G. White, °*Social Thought in America* (2nd ed., 1957); Gail Kennedy (ed.), °*Pragmatism and American Culture* (1950); and A. A. Roback, °*History of American Psychology* (1952). But see also Wolfgang Kohler, °*Gestalt Psychology* (2nd ed., 1947), which emphasizes the impact of behaviorism. Oscar Cargill, *Intellectual America; Ideas on the March* (1941), shows the growth of Freud's influence in the United States. See also Benjamin Nelson (ed.), °*Freud and the Twentieth Century* (1957); and the brief life by Giovanni Costigan, *Freud* (1965). For Spengler and Ortega y Gasset the best introduction is their own works. Edgar Kemler, °*The Irreverent Mr. Mencken* (1950), should be supplemented by Maxwell Geismar, °*The Last of the Provincials* (2nd ed., 1949); William Manchester, °*Disturber of the Peace* (1950); and Alistair Cooke (ed.), °*The Vintage Mencken*

° Available in paperback

(1955). Two major works by Walter Lippmann are *The Phantom Public* (1925), and *A Preface to Morals* (1929). An interesting memoir is Reinhold Niebuhr, *Leaves From the Notebook of a Tamed Cynic* (1929).

C. F. Ware, *Greenwich Village, 1920–1930* (1935); and Allen Churchill, *The Improper Bohemians* (1959), discuss the rise of a self-conscious intellectual class. A major recent study, notable for its insight, is Christopher Lasch, *The New Radicalism in America, 1889–1963: The Intellectual as a Social Type* (1965). The feeling of alienation of the intellectual from his native culture may be found in practically every book written on the arts and literary criticism during the twenties. Malcolm Cowley, *Exile's Return* (2nd ed., 1951); J. W. Krutch, *The Modern Temper* (1929); and Lionel Trilling, *The Liberal Imagination* (1950), all emphasize the air of gloom which characterized the creative mind in the decade. For the new humanism see Irving Babbitt, *Democracy and Leadership* (1924); and Norman Foerster (ed.), *Humanism and America* (1930). For the southern agrarian position, see Donald Davidson and others, *I'll Take My Stand* (2nd ed., 1962). Granville Hicks (ed.), *Proletarian Literature in the United States: An Anthology* (1935); and V. F. Calverton, *The Liberation of American Literature* (1932), illustrate the literary shift to the left. The critical works of Edmund Wilson, particularly *Travels in Two Democracies* (1936), *The Shores of Light* (1953), and *American Earthquake* (1958); and the novels of John Dos Passos will give the student a better appreciation of the rising radical temper. H. E. Stearns (ed.), *America Now* (1938); and John Dos Passos, *The Ground We Stand On* (1941), should be contrasted with earlier writings by the same authors.

Important literary works include Malcolm Cowley (ed.), *After the Genteel Tradition* (1937), a collection of critical works on recent American novelists; F. J. Hoffman, *The Twenties* (1955); Van Wyck Brooks, *Days of the Phoenix* (1957); and W. B. Rideout, *The Radical Novel in the United States, 1900–1954* (1956). A good anthology is *American Literature Survey: The Twentieth Century*, edited by M. R. Stern and S. L. Gross (1962). Among the best biographical works on leading literary figures are Arthur Mizener, *The Far Side of Paradise* (1951), and Andrew Turnbull, *Scott Fitzgerald* (1962), excellent lives of Fitzgerald; C. H. Baker, *Hemingway, the Writer as Artist* (3rd ed., 1963), and Philip Young, *Ernest Hemingway* (1952); Arthur and Barbara Gelb, *O'Neill* (1962), and B. H. Clark, *Eugene O'Neill* (5th ed., 1947). Mark Schorer's fine biography, *Sinclair Lewis* (1961); and Ernest Hemingway's memoir, *A Moveable Feast* (1964), are indispensable for an understanding of the literary 1920's. Faulkner is evaluated by Malcolm Cowley in his introduction to *The Portable Faulkner* (1946). An understanding of Thomas Wolfe as a person and a writer can be gleaned from Elizabeth Nowell, *Thomas Wolfe* (1960).

J. I. H. Baur, *Revolution and Tradition in Modern American Art* (1951); *Art in America; A Complete Survey*, edited by Holger Cahill and A. H. Barr, Jr. (2nd ed., 1935); and Martha Cheney, *Modern Art in America* (1939), are good general works covering the developments in modern art. Jacques Schnier, *Sculpture in Modern America* (1948), is a broad survey. On music, J. T. Howard, *Our Contemporary Composers; American Music in the Twentieth Century* (3rd ed., 1946), is comprehensive. But see also Aaron Copland, *Our New Music* (1941), by one of the nation's first really gifted composers. F. L. Wright, *When Democracy Builds* (1945), and *On Architecture* (1941), are important statements by a great architect. G. C. Manson, *Frank Lloyd Wright* (1958), is a biographical study. *Built in USA, 1932–1944*, edited by Elizabeth Mock (1944), contains a good visual record of the nation's building achievements during the period. Grace Overmyer, *Government and Arts* (1939), is devoted to a study of the WPA cultural projects. J. A. Kouwenhoven, *Made in America: The Arts in Modern Civilization* (1948), contains material on the field of commercial design, in which the United States has made major contributions.

37

THE GREAT DEPRESSION

Hoover. When Herbert Hoover (1874–1964) took office on March 4, 1929, the great majority of Americans fully expected his administration to be a notable one. Few Presidents have entered office with such a record of solid achievement behind them in so many varied pursuits. Hoover was born in Iowa, the son of Quaker parents. Left an orphan at an early age, he worked his way through college and ultimately graduated in mining engineering from Stanford University. In his work he saw much of the world, and as a promoter he amassed a fortune. Living in England at the outbreak of the First World War, he was a natural choice to head overseas relief work, and served as chairman, first of the American Relief Commission, and later of the Commission for the Relief of Belgium. In these offices, as Food Administrator during American participation in the First World War, and as Secretary of Commerce he had demonstrated repeatedly his extraordinary ability as an administrator. On the basis of his record Hoover was no reactionary either in domestic or in foreign affairs. He had supported Theodore Roosevelt during the campaign of 1912 and throughout the war years was a firm Wilsonian internationalist. His work in Belgian relief had earned him a reputation as a great humanitarian. During the short depression of 1921 he proposed, as Secretary of Commerce, if conditions became worse, a national program of public works to relieve public unemployment. It was reasonable, therefore, to suppose in 1929 that he could expect the support not only of his own party regulars, but also that of a good many independents and progressive Democrats as well.

The Hoover administration, however, was certain to encounter difficulties even if it had been blessed with good times. The new President was fundamentally a business executive rather than a politician, and showed little skill in appeasing the leaders of his party, many of whom were jealous of his success. His cabinet, headed by Henry L. Stimson, formerly governor-general of the Philippines, was undistinguished, and added little to his political strength. Mellon was kept on as Secretary of the Treasury, less because Hoover wanted him than because of the esteem in which he was held by the business interests of the country; all the others, including the Secretary of State, were virtually unknown to the general public. Prohibition was sure to be a nightmare, and farm relief a persistent puzzle. Furthermore, tariff revision, the political ruination of many preceding administrations, was imminent. During the campaign Hoover had promised the farmers an increase in agricultural duties. He hoped to escape a general tariff revision, but a more experienced politician would have foreseen that once tariff tampering had begun, there would be little chance of limiting its scope.

Hoover's program for the relief of agriculture was enacted into law well before the panic days of October, 1929, but the depression in agriculture was of long standing. The Agricultural Marketing Act, signed June 15, 1929, was designed to help agriculture help itself by means of voluntary cooperation. Proponents of the measure believed that with appropriate federal encouragement the farmers could work together through cooperatives by applying the same principles of orderly production and distribution that governed the activities of prudent manufacturers. They could thus find means to curtail production when necessary, to shift to different crops as demand changed, and to eliminate wasteful and expensive methods of marketing. The act created a Federal Farm Board of eight members, and provided it with a $500 million revolving fund from which it could lend to cooperatives, and to such stabilization corporations as it might set up for the purpose of buying, storing, and selling surpluses.

The Federal Farm Board began operations at once, with Alexander Legge of the International Harvester Company as its chairman. Its efforts to stimulate the formation of cooperatives were successful, and loans for this purpose during the first year of its operation amounted to over $165 million. These activities contributed significantly to the orderly marketing of nearly

HERBERT HOOVER

Like two of his predecessors, Martin Van Buren and Grover Cleveland, Hoover was a "depression" President; but by using the power of the national government in an effort to defeat the depression, he set a new precedent and paved the way for the New Deal.

every type of crop produced in the United States. Much sound advice was also distributed as to the curtailment of crops where the market was glutted, although other governmental agencies, particularly the Department of Agriculture and the agricultural colleges, considerably confused the situation by explaining to the farmers how more and more of the same commodities might be grown on less but better fertilized soil.

Stabilization Activities. It soon became apparent that something far more drastic than cooperative marketing was necessary if the rapid downward trend of prices for wheat and cotton was to be stopped. Accordingly, in 1930, a Grain Stabilization Corporation and a Cotton Stabilization

Corporation were set up, each with authority to buy in the open market in order to raise prices. As long as governmental purchases continued, the effect on the price of wheat and cotton was good, but after a year or two the Stabilization Corporations found themselves in possession of vast stores of produce that they were unable to market.

When necessity obliged them to cease their purchases, the price of wheat dropped to fifty-seven cents a bushel, and the price of cotton to five cents a pound. The Federal Farm Board ended its brief career in 1933 with total losses of about $184 million. In its final report the Board concluded that agriculture could not return to a healthy state without some radical limitation of farm production.

The Hawley-Smoot Tariff. Meantime, Congress had plunged eagerly into the revision of the tariff that Hoover had promised. Representative Willis C. Hawley of Oregon, chairman of the House Ways and Means Committee, introduced on May 7, 1929, a bill that did not far exceed the limited recommendations of the President. But a log-rolling generosity at once developed which resulted in numerous amendments of the original bill, and ultimately provided for a scale of duties far higher than those of the record-breaking Fordney-McCumber Act of 1922. The Senate Finance Committee, headed by Reed Smoot of Utah, altered the bill in detail, but not greatly in principle. A few insurgents sought to improve the measure by including within it the export debenture plan for the relief of agriculture, and a flexible schedule clause which would have given the President authority to act on changes recommended by the Tariff Commission; but these provisions, largely because of pressure from the President, finally were stricken out. The Hawley-Smoot Tariff, as it came from the conference committee, accepted in the main the higher rates proposed by either house, and raised the

general level of protection by about 7 per cent.

In spite of a rising volume of criticism directed against the measure, Hoover signed it. It was not what he had wished, and he did not disguise his disappointment; but neither did he heed the petition of more than a thousand economists who urged that he veto the bill, pointing out that the measure was certain (1) to raise prices for the consumer; (2) to encourage wasteful and unnecessary concerns to remain in business; (3) to limit the exportation of products, both from farm and factory, by restricting imports; (4) to yield no benefits to the farmers whose prices were fixed by what the exportable surplus would bring; and (5) to insure reprisals from foreign countries whose trade would be adversely affected. One of the first of the predicted reprisals came from Canada, which promptly increased the rates on most of its important imports from the United States, and others came thick and fast. In 1932 Great Britain, whose devotion to free trade had long been slipping, veered completely over to the protective-tariff policy. For the establishment of these higher trade barriers in the face of world-wide depression the United States bore a leading responsibility.

Background of the Great Depression. Hoover was scarcely well seated in the presidential chair when the Great Depression began, and his administration, like Cleveland's second, became indelibly associated in the public mind with hard times. The Great Depression was preceded by a long period of speculation, this time mainly in stocks and bonds. The prosperity of the twenties was to a remarkable extent corporation prosperity. Few individuals owned great businesses; Henry Ford was an outstanding exception. Most "big businesses" were jointly owned by hundreds or thousands of stockholders, whose investments might vary from a $100 share to values running to many millions. Throughout the prosperous twenties stocks multiplied at an increasing tempo. The fact that business was actually owned by millions of investors was regarded with satisfaction by President Hoover and others as proof that it was essentially democratic, but any careful examination of corporation statistics showed that a comparatively small number of investors owned the greater part of the stock. Moreover, the direction of a given industry lay inevitably with the few insiders who represented the largest holdings. In a sense the control of business was less democratic than ever before. With investments so widely diffused, the individual with a 3 per cent holding might be as powerful as the majority stockholder of an earlier age. Thus, the ownership of property had been divorced from the power to control it, and the way was open for the few at the top of corporations to utilize the property of the many for their own purposes.

Stock Speculation. While many of those who purchased stocks were genuinely interested in obtaining sound investments, many others operated only as speculators, buying when prices were low, and selling when they rose. Some bought "on margin," depositing only enough money with their brokers to cover the probable range of fluctuation. They were sure to encounter difficulties if their guesses went wrong. This speculative demand for stocks was to a great extent responsible for the generally high price level of securities during the later twenties. Often the actual earning power of a given stock was far too low to justify the price at which it sold; valuations of twenty-five times the total earnings were by no means uncommon. Optimists refused to be alarmed at the situation and insisted that the high prices paid for securities were merely an evidence of the healthy condition of American enterprise. Investors had faith in the

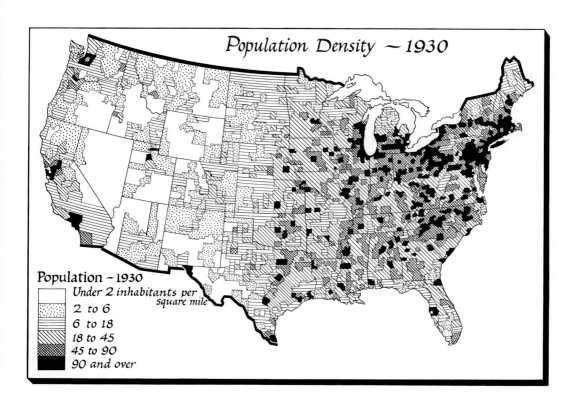

Population Density ~ 1930

Population ~ 1930

	Under 2 inhabitants per square mile
	2 to 6
	6 to 18
	18 to 45
	45 to 90
	90 and over

soundness of business and were willing to back it with their dollars. Even the Federal Reserve Board, at least indirectly, supported speculation, for it kept the supply of credit plentiful even when much too much of the easy money was being used in outright stock speculations. Between September, 1927, and September, 1929, borrowings for speculation on the New York Stock Exchange rose from $3.3 billion to $8.5 billion. Prices of stocks, as one misguided observer noted, soared upward to "what looks like a permanently high plateau." One issue never known to pay a dividend climbed steadily from $40 to $450 a share.

In the midst of all this madness a few pessimists warned that the business cycle might not be as obsolete as many seemed to believe, and that a crisis was probably close at hand. Too much of the country's credit was being diverted into stock-exchange notes, and industry, as a result of the easy money, was being tempted to overexpand. Who was to buy all the goods that producers could make? Already the building boom of the earlier twenties was on the decline, automobile sales were off, and oil production far exceeded the demand. But these wise protests were brushed aside by optimists in high places who assured investors that all was well. Two days before the market crashed, Charles E. Mitchell, president of the National City Bank of New York, asserted unequivocally: "I know of nothing fundamentally wrong with the stock market or with the underlying business and credit structures."

Panic of 1929. The stock market collapse came in October, 1929, when British interest rates were raised to 6.5 per cent in order to repatriate needed capital that had been attracted to the United States by the high speculative profits. As a result many European holdings were thrown on the market, and prices began to sag. Frightened at the prospect, and no longer

able to borrow at will, American speculators also began to unload. On Thursday, October 24, 1929, 12.8 million shares changed hands and until October 29, when the sales reached 16.4 million shares, the frantic selling continued. During the month of October the value of stocks listed on the New York Stock Exchange declined from $87 billion to $55 billion, or about 37 per cent. And this, it developed, was only the beginning. In spite of repeated assurances from high authorities, both in government and finance, that prosperity lay "just around the corner," no less than nine similar declines to "new low levels" were recorded within the next three years. By the first of March, 1933, the value of all stocks listed on the New York Stock Exchange was set at only $19 billion, less than one-fifth the inflated values of October 1, 1929.

In spite of optimistic efforts to maintain that the stock-market collapse was purely a paper loss which would not seriously undermine the fundamental soundness of American business, it was soon evident that a period of unparalleled depression had begun. The catastrophic fall in stock prices brought a sharp deflationary movement. Stock brokers called upon speculators to pay back the sums they had borrowed, banks made the same demands upon brokers and upon many businessmen who had used stocks as collateral for their loans. Since many were unable to pay, bankruptcies added to the credit stringency. Merchants refused credit to buyers of their wares and drastically reduced their inventories of goods. Prices dropped sharply; foreign trade fell off; factories curtailed production, and many closed their doors never to reopen them; real-estate values (but not mortgages) declined; new construction, except on government works, practically ceased; banks went under; worst of all, wages were cut drastically, and unemployment began to mount. By the end of 1930, 6 or 7 million workers were out of jobs; two years later the number had doubled. Nor was the United States alone in its distress. No longer able to secure American loans, foreign nations fell likewise into the abyss of depression; indeed, many of them, like Germany, had not far to fall. Once again the people of the United States were to learn by experience that whatever seriously affected one great nation was bound to affect all.

Causes of the Depression. Efforts to account for the plunge from prosperity to adversity soon demonstrated conclusively that no one factor, but a great number working together, produced such startling results. Economists were able to reach substantial agreement as to the principal causes of the depression, but they were by no means in harmony as to the importance of each cause. Among other disturbing influences they cited the following:

1. *Agricultural overexpansion,* both in the United States and elsewhere. American farmers produced more wheat, cotton, corn, livestock, and other commodities than they could sell at satisfactory prices, and to some extent the same condition existed in much of the rest of the world. Agricultural surpluses piled up at home and abroad with devastating effect on the price of each new crop. Farm purchases steadily declined, for farmers had less and less with which to buy. Payments on the heavy mortgage burden assumed in more prosperous times still further curtailed the farmers' buying power, and drove many of them to tenancy.

2. *Industrial overexpansion.* The American industrial plant had been overbuilt during the boom, and could not be operated at maximum capacity. There were too many factories and too much machinery. Industry was geared to produce far more than it could sell. Automobiles, for example, had been turned out in steadily increasing numbers during the twenties to supply a new market. But now every American family that could afford an automobile (and many that could not) had one or sometimes more than one. With 26.5 million motor cars in operation by 1929, the market for automobiles was confined largely to replacements. The same condition existed in housing. Rapid building during the twenties had caused the lumber industry and others producing building materials to overexpand their markets.

3. *The increasing effectiveness of machines.* Ingenious labor-saving devices made possible greater production with comparatively less labor. Fewer men produced more goods. "Technological unemployment" might not be permanent, but the men who were thrown out of work by the new machines had to seek other jobs, and they sometimes failed to find them. Thus the buying power of labor was diminished. The new machines might make more goods, but whose wages were to pay for them? Introduction of labor-saving devices was rarely paralleled by increased wages, a shortening of the labor day and the labor week, and a diminishing use of women and children in industry.

4. *Capital surpluses were too high.* As a prominent banker, Frank A. Vanderlip, expressed it, "Capital kept too much and labor did not have enough to buy its share of things." This was more easily possible because of the monopolistic nature of much American business, which so greatly facilitated the control of prices. Throughout the boom years the tendency of business was to take too high profits, and to reinvest the capital thus accumulated in order to produce still more goods, which in return might produce still more profits. A wider distribution of earnings, particularly if paid out in the form of higher wages, might well have stimulated purchasing power and diminished the danger of ultimate collapse.

5. *The overexpansion of credit,* both for productive and consumptive purposes. Money was plentiful and cheap throughout the twenties, and the policy of the Federal Reserve Board and the Coolidge administration was to keep it so. At the personal

insistence of President Coolidge in 1927 the Federal Reserve Board eased credit restrictions. A year later when the New York Stock Exchange announced that brokers' loans amounted to $4 billion, the highest figure in history, both Secretary of Commerce Hoover and Governor Young of the Federal Reserve Board argued for the curtailment of easy money and credit. They were joined by a group of conservative bankers who thought even then that there was too much speculation in stocks. But it was not until after Hoover took office that the Board reversed itself and started to tighten credit. By that time it was too late to ward off disaster. It had been too easy to borrow, whether for business expansion, for speculation, or for the satisfaction of personal desires. There was too much installment buying, and too much of the national income was diverted into interest payments. In keeping with the speculative spirit of the times, purchasers cheerfully mortgaged their futures to obtain goods that would often be consumed before they could be paid for. The Coolidge policy had definitely encouraged both speculation and purchasing on credit.

6. *Banking and Financial Ethics.* After the Democratic victory of 1932, a Senate Committee headed by Ferdinand Pecora began an investigation of the ethics and practices during the golden twenties of the great New York banks and investment companies. To a large extent such institutions controlled the American financial structure, and their ethics were bound to be reflected throughout the country. Among the officers of many such institutions the committee found a complete disregard for the welfare of depositors and the economic health of the country; in some they found outright fraud, chicanery, and theft. The officers of some great banks had used their depositors' money to operate. enormous speculations in the stock market, and had divided the profits among themselves and a small group of powerful political figures. Heading the "Cut in List," or

the favored group of outsiders, of J. P. Morgan and Company, for example, were the names of Calvin Coolidge, John W. Davis, General Pershing, Owen J. Roberts, Newton D. Baker, and Bernard M. Baruch. Other great bankers had sold worthless foreign bonds to their correspondent banks throughout the country, simply to collect the commission on the sales. Such sharp practices and others even more venal weakened the entire country's financial structure to such an extent that it was extremely vulnerable to the harsh demands of the depression.

7. *International trade was out of balance.* European nations, with their economies badly shattered by the war, had depended mainly on funds borrowed from American investors to pay for imports and to stabilize foreign exchange. The only way they might have repaid these obligations was by shipping goods to the United States. But the Fordney-McCumber Tariff of 1922, followed by the Hawley-Smoot Tariff of 1930, definitely lessened any such possibility. The debtor nations of Europe in self-defense were obliged to adopt high-tariff policies, and by various other expedients to stimulate whatever industries were necessary to cut down their reliance on foreign goods. During the years 1922–1927 the production of British-made automobiles, for example, was increased from 49 per cent of the domestic supply to 86 per cent. Thus the United States, blindly committed to the protective principles of an earlier age, stood to lose both its export business and a good share of the money by which this business had been sustained. Many manufacturers understood the situation, and did their best to prevent the adoption of tariffs that in the long run were certain to bring disaster, but most citizens were slow to recognize that international trade was a "two-way street," and were quite unprepared for the collapse that followed the withdrawal of American credits.

Even more fundamental perhaps was the

division of the world between rich nations, usually advanced industrially, and poor undeveloped nations trying to pay their way with agricultural and other primary products. Just as agricultural prices had fallen so drastically in the United States, so also had the world prices of primary commodities and metals. Thus a significant share of the market for manufactured goods was reduced at the same time the world's industrial capacity was rapidly increasing. In the world, as in the United States, most industrial producers were too rich and the buyers too poor to keep the international machinery of exchange operating.

8. *Political unrest throughout the world,* particularly in Europe, Asia, and South America, also added to the difficulties in sustaining prosperity. Intergovernmental debts, whether funded or not, constituted a continuing threat both to trade and to international good feelings. The reparations problem remained unsettled. Most countries were overburdened with governmental debts, and few national budgets were in the balance. The War and the Peace of Paris bore a share of responsibility for the economic disarray. The break-up of the Austro-Hungarian Empire destroyed the economic unity of much of the Danube basin. The old patterns of trade and commercial intercourse were further obstructed by the nationalistic aspirations of the new states. With major cities like Vienna cut off from their hinterlands and farmers deprived of urban markets, economic confusion was the only possible result.

Finally, it can also be argued, a fortuitous element accentuated the depression. In most sharp downward movements of the economy during recent times some activities failed to fall along with all the others. Thus while farm prices and factory production were going down, home construction and international trade might be stationary or were increasing in tempo, thus helping to cushion the total impact of the decline. But in 1929–1933 almost every line of economic activity seemed to be falling precipitately at the same time. Instead of a cushioning effect, one factor accentuated the other to produce in sum a frightening crisis.

Hoover Fights the Depression. Undoubtedly, President Hoover was greatly shocked by the advent of the Great Depression. During the campaign of 1928 he had promised the electorate a "final triumph over poverty" if only the country were "given a chance to go forward with the policies of the last eight years." But instead of the promised prosperity, there was adversity on every hand. Faced by this situation, Hoover deemed it his duty as President to aid business in fighting its way back to recovery. For a time he directed his efforts mainly toward obtaining the voluntary cooperation of business and labor leaders in measures of self-help. At a series of conferences in Washington he talked against the curtailment of buying power that must inevitably follow the reduction of payrolls, and urged that "the first shock" of the depression "must fall on profits and not on wages." He insisted that wage scales ought not for the moment to be lowered at all, and succeeded in committing many industries to a policy of expansion in spite of the unsettled economic conditions. But "business as usual" soon proved to be a difficult formula for executives to maintain in the face of declining receipts and mounting inventories. In spite of good intentions, wages did go down and unemployment figures began to mount.

RFC, HLB. As the economy continued to fall, Hoover began to inaugurate more radical policies. Early in 1930 he asked and obtained from Congress huge sums to be used in the erection of public buildings, the improvement of rivers and harbors, and the building of federal roads. By these and similar expenditures, voted later, he sought to take up the slack of unemployment. Before he left office, more than $2.25 billion had been appropriated for

A NEW YORK "HOOVERVILLE"

These 1932 shacks, built by unemployed men near West and Charlton Streets, New York, were typical of the living quarters that appeared on innumerable vacant city lots throughout the nation.

such purposes. For a long time, however, the President opposed any more direct effort by the national government to deal with the problem of unemployment. Direct relief, he maintained, was a function of the states, the municipalities, and voluntary organizations. He argued that the granting of huge sums by the national government would be too impersonal and would subject local communities to the control of "a remote bureaucracy." It was not the function of the national government, he wrote, "to relieve individuals of their responsibilities to their neighbors." But as conditions steadily worsened after 1930, it was apparent that states, cities, and private charities had failed to build up reserves for relief purposes and that their current resources were woefully inadequate. The Pennsylvania Department of Public Welfare reported that one out of every three persons in the state was dependent upon charity and that all the public and private funds together were only

equal to supporting the destitute at the barest minimum for two to five months of every year. Eventually even Hoover had to admit that only the national government had the resources in taxes and credit necessary to meet the existing emergency. Even so, the President was still opposed to direct grants to citizens or even federal gifts to the states. Instead he asked Congress for funds from which loans could be made to states that were no longer able to finance their own relief expenditures, and in spite of the growing strain on the budget these appropriations were made.

To administer these and other necessary loans, Congress created a Reconstruction Finance Corporation, patterned somewhat after the War Finance Corporation of the Wilson administration. The RFC, with Charles G. Dawes of Chicago as its first president, lent freely not only to the states but also to banks, agricultural credit corporations, life-insurance companies, and other financial organizations, and to the hard pressed railroads. Though the public complained bitterly that distressed individuals were deprived of such help, many corporate bankruptcies were thus forestalled or delayed. Loans actually disbursed before Hoover left office amounted to nearly $2 billion.

For the benefit of homeowners who were about to lose their property, Hoover encouraged the passage of the Home Loan Bank Act of July 22, 1932. Under its terms a series of banks were established to discount home mortgages, and thus provide a service similar to that rendered by the Federal Reserve Banks in the commercial field. The large appropriations necessary to carry these various measures into effect unbalanced the national budget by many billions of dollars long before the "New Deal" was inaugurated.

Not all the actions of the Hoover administration in its efforts to deal with the depression were concerned with internal affairs. When in March, 1931, France refused to permit Germany and Austria to unite in a customs union, a train of events was set in motion which led to the almost complete collapse of European finance. Until that time the depression had remained primarily an American affair, but from then on its worldwide character was abundantly apparent. The finances of central Europe sank first, but eventually every European nation was affected, including Great Britain, which in September, 1931, was forced to abandon the gold standard. American investors in foreign securities, particularly those of Germany, were hard hit, and American trade with Europe was more drastically curtailed than ever before.

Hoover's Moratorium. Believing that the huge burden of intergovernmental debts constituted one of the chief impediments to world trade, and therefore to recovery, Hoover in June, 1931, advocated a moratorium for one year on both the principal and interest of all such obligations. This action was deeply resented by France,

who wished to continue her collections from Germany, and it was far from popular in the United States; but in due time it was accepted by the fifteen governments involved and went into effect. At the Lausanne Conference of 1932, the European powers attempted to solve the debt riddle for all time by granting Germany a three-year moratorium on reparations, and by establishing a new low figure, $714 million, as the amount to be paid. All this, however, was contingent upon the willingness of the United States to cancel its war debts. Many American businessmen, believing that private debts from abroad could be more readily collected if the public debt were out of the way, favored cancellation, but neither Hoover nor his successor, Roosevelt, conceded this point. Reparation payments were never resumed by Germany, and when the moratorium ended in 1932 only six governments, Great Britain, Czechoslovakia, Italy, Finland, Latvia and Lithuania, met their obligations to the United States. The next year all these nations, except Finland, made only small token payments, and after that no payments at all. Finland, which paid in full every year, even after its territory was invaded by Russia in the winter of 1939–1940, won much acclaim in the United States, but the sums involved were small. In 1934 Congress passed the Johnson Act, which prohibited Americans from purchasing the securities of any nation in default on its debt to the United States. By this time the debts in fact, if not in law, had ceased to be, and their restraining influence upon the course of international trade could not have been great.

Politics and Social Conditions. The effect of the depression upon the political fortunes of Herbert Hoover and his party was disastrous. As a result of the mid-term election of 1930, the Senate was almost evenly divided between Republicans and Democrats, and the House was Democratic by a small margin. With conditions steadily deteriorating during the next two years, serious rumblings of discontent sounded throughout the country. Meeting in annual convention, the usually conservative American Federation of Labor made a startling declaration: "We shall use our might to compel the plain remedies withheld by those whose misfeasance caused our woe." In the Middle West farmers were beginning to organize. Here and there armed men met and turned back sheriffs intent upon serving foreclosure writs, while others barricaded roads to stop the delivery of farm produce to the cities until agricultural prices rose.

The Bonus Expeditionary Force. Recalling the grim days of 1893, "General" Jacob S. Coxey again attempted to lead an army of unemployed on Washington. Much more impressive was the march of 15,000 destitute war veterans on the capital, demanding the passage of the Patman Bonus Bill which proposed immediate payment of the soldiers' bonus in cash. The President exerted himself to defeat the bill, and the angry veterans were dispersed only

THE BONUS ARMY

Unemployed veterans of World War I converged on Washington in the summer of 1932 as a "Bonus Expeditionary Force" (BEF). Some of the men are shown here demonstrating on the Capitol steps.

when federal troops under General Douglas MacArthur, on the President's orders, met them with fixed bayonets and tanks. Though impolitic, Hoover's opposition to the bonus bill was certainly defensible. But his use of troops against the unarmed and impoverished veterans was met with a nationwide wave of angry criticism and offered as proof that his administration had little compassion for or understanding of the plight of the nation's poor.

Election of 1932.   That the Republicans were faced with a serious defeat in 1932 seemed clear, but the Republican Convention had no choice other than to renominate Hoover and to stand on its record. Both Hoover and Curtis were renominated, and the Hoover policies were accorded unstinted praise. President Hoover, however, in announcing that the government would assume responsibility for the nation's economic situation, promised greater loans to business and a much larger program of public works. But he was still stoutly opposed both to direct federal grants to the unemployed and to the federal control of agricultural production. Denouncing the federal bureaucracy which both measures would involve, he declared: "Not regimented mechanisms, but free men is our goal."

The Democrats, after a lively contest, emerged with Franklin D. Roosevelt, popular two-term governor of New York, as their candidate for President, and John Nance Garner, Speaker of the House, as their candidate for Vice-President. The Democratic platform blamed the Republicans for the depression, called for a drastic reduction in government expenses, a balanced federal budget, a sound currency, and the "removal of government from all fields of private enterprise." It promised, however, federal aid to the states to care for the needy, a state system of unemployment and old-age insurance, the effective control of the farm crop surplus, and an enlarged public-works program. During

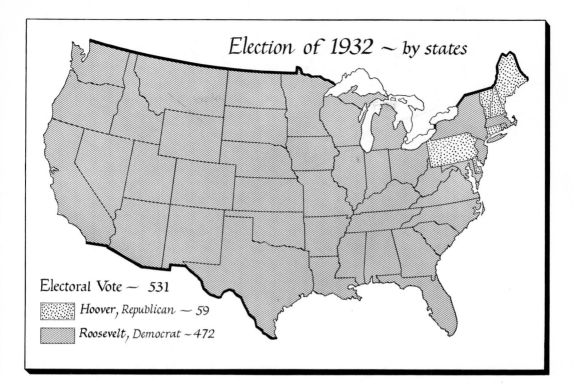

Election of 1932 ~ by states

Electoral Vote — 531

Hoover, Republican — 59

Roosevelt, Democrat ~472

the campaign most of Roosevelt's speeches sounded as contradictory as the Democratic platform. He attacked Hoover for his spending programs, yet he proposed relief for the unemployed and a huge program of public works and reforestation. Without being specific he was for crop reduction, but he labeled as "a cruel joke" the Hoover farm board's advice to the farmers to allow 20 per cent of their wheat land to lie idle and to plow up every third row of their cotton. In only one or two speeches did he do more than hint at what was to come. But his call for a New Deal in government, his promises to remember the "forgotten man," and his personal charm and sense of confidence won the voters in droves.

When the returns were in, it was apparent that Hoover had been as badly defeated as Smith had been four years before. The electoral vote stood 472 to 59, and the popular vote, 22.8 million to 15.7 million. Hoover carried only six states, Maine, New Hampshire, Vermont, Connecticut,

Delaware, and Pennsylvania. Both houses of Congress went overwhelmingly Democratic, and in the states the Democratic landslide carried into office many candidates who had regarded their names on the party ticket as either a courtesy or a joke.

The Communist Party. In general, the dissatisfied elements of society supported Roosevelt, but the existence of a small, more radical minority was revealed by the vote of 884,781 for Norman Thomas, the Socialist candidate, and 102,991 for William Z. Foster, the Communist. The American public had long been accustomed to the Socialist Party organized at the turn of the century by Eugene V. Debs. The Socialist vote in 1932 was in fact smaller than it had been in 1912. But the Communist Party running under its own label was something entirely different. First organized in 1919, the Communists remained a small, ineffective splinter group for almost a decade. Their attempts to invade

A COMMUNIST PARADE

Union Square, New York, was the scene of this May Day, 1930, parade. The depression and attendant unemployment made many converts to the Communist cause.

the labor movement were met by the determined opposition of the A. F. of L., and their 1924 endorsement of La Follette was repudiated by the Wisconsin senator. Seeking to capitalize on both economic distress and racial tensions, the Party announced itself openly for the first time in 1932. In addition to issuing literature calling for the violent overthrow of capitalism and the capitalist state, the party also nominated for the first time in American history a Negro, James Ford, as its Vice-Presidential candidate. After the election, the party adopted the "popular front" tactics by which it sought to play down its revolutionary mission and, by cooperating with radical and liberal groups, to use them for its own purposes. As in Europe, this "boring from within" technique was to be more successful than the more open stand taken in the twenties. With the more favorable climate of the depression years, the party made small but impressive gains among certain sectors of the labor movement and among radical intellectuals. These successes were also aided by the

tolerant attitude of a good many liberals and by the fact that the Communist Party was the only one in the early years of the new decade consistently to denounce Fascism. Nevertheless, the small Communist vote in 1932 indicated that after three years of unemployment and privation the public was still overwhelmingly committed to democracy and the democratic way of life.

The Banking Crisis. Before the adoption of the Twentieth Amendment, both a defeated President and the old Congress continued in power from the November elections until March 4 of the following year. This "lame duck" session was extremely embarrassing in the winter of 1932–1933 because of the enormity of the problems confronting the defeated President. Hoover tried to enlist the aid of the President-elect, but Roosevelt refused to commit himself on his future plans, particularly with regard to balancing the budget, a promise which Hoover felt might help restore confidence in the rapidly deteriorating financial situation. And since the harassed outgoing President received no support from either the financial community or the Democratic Congress, government practically came to a standstill in the interim before inauguration day.

Meanwhile the increasing public pessimism led to a banking crisis of unparalleled gravity. Unemployment was at its worst during the winter of 1932–1933, and was estimated at anywhere from 13 million to 17 million. Production in one great industry after another dropped to almost negligible proportions. Fear that the financial structure of the country was endangered showed in the mounting totals of gold exported and of gold and currency hoarded; by the middle of February, the disappearance of bullion and currency from the American economy amounted to about $30 million a day. In Detroit, where the drastic curtailment of automobile production had created a peculiarly difficult situation, the banks held on grimly, but by the middle of February they were near the breaking point. Loaded down with frozen assets and drained of their deposits by frightened customers, they escaped collapse only when the governor of the state on his own authority extended the holiday period by eight days, and then obtained from the legislature the right to prolong it if need be still further. With the Michigan banks suspended, the panic spread to one state after another, and nearly every state executive declared a long bank holiday. By inauguration day, bank deposits were temporarily unusable, bills remained unpaid, and credit was virtually unobtainable. The circulatory system of capitalism had stopped, and no one knew what the next day would bring.

Franklin D. Roosevelt. Few Presidents have been met with as immediate and as terrifying a crisis as that confronting Roosevelt on his first day in office. The extraordinary times obviously demanded an extraordinary man, and that Franklin Delano Roosevelt (1882–1945) soon proved himself to be. Born to a comfortable fortune, as his distant relative, Theodore Roosevelt, had been, he was a graduate of Groton and Harvard, had been frequently abroad, spoke French almost as fluently as English, and had been admitted to the bar. In 1905 he had married his sixth cousin, Eleanor Roosevelt, a favorite niece of the President; and, like the other Roosevelts, they became the parents of a large family. Young Roosevelt, although a Democrat by birthright, never disguised his admiration for the President whose name he bore, and tended consciously or unconsciously to pattern after him. In 1910 he was a member of the New York legislature, and won the undying enmity of the Tammany machine by his fight against its candidate for the United States Senate, William F. Sheehan. Partly because his name was Roosevelt, and partly because he knew about ships, he became Assistant Secretary of the Navy under Woodrow Wilson, a post of great

responsibility which he filled with ability during the First World War. In 1920 he was the unsuccessful Democratic candidate for Vice-President, and after the campaign made preparations for a business career. The transformation of Roosevelt from a retired minor politician to a dynamic leader of men began when, in August, 1921, an attack of infantile paralysis left him hopelessly crippled in both legs. By an unsurpassed exhibition of will power he fought his way back to health and even learned to walk again, although not without firm support. Utterly unconquered in spirit, he read widely, corresponded with the leaders of the Democratic Party, and dedicated himself to its rebuilding along progressive lines. In 1928, despite the Hoover landslide, he was elected governor of New York, and two years later he was triumphantly re-elected. As governor he inaugurated few policies of note before the depression struck, but his insistence that the state should provide for the hungry and the jobless, his proposal for a state unemployment insurance system, his abil-

RUN ON A BANK

Scenes of this kind were all too common in the early years of the depression; indeed, bank failures in many of the smaller towns had occurred with great frequency throughout the prosperous 1920's.

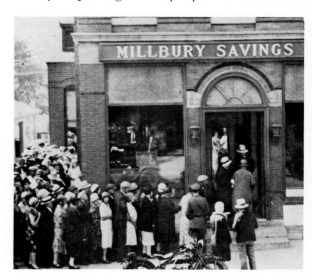

ity to deal adroitly with all matters affecting human nature, his unfailing good humor, and his consuming interest in new ideas made him a marked man.

Roosevelt's "Brain Trust." However unwilling he might have been to accept responsibility before he took office, the new President showed no such hesitation after March 4, 1933. His cabinet included none of the great names — Owen D. Young, Newton D. Baker, John W. Davis, Alfred E. Smith, and the like — pressed upon him by those who doubted his ability, and showed his evident determination to be his own master. All observers agreed that the little coterie of "bright young men" surrounding the President, called by the public the "brain trust," would have much more to do with the shaping of his policies than the somewhat nondescript cabinet, headed by Senator Cordell Hull of Tennessee, that he had constructed. During his campaign he had relied heavily upon the assistance of his "brain trust," which included among others three Columbia University professors, Raymond Moley, Rexford Guy Tugwell, and Adolph A. Berle, Jr. From these advisers, scorned as theorists by "hard-headed" businessmen and "hard-boiled" politicians alike, he obtained many of the ideas he now proposed to translate into deeds.

The President proved his leadership during the banking crisis. The day after inauguration Roosevelt closed every bank in the country, and by the time he had assembled Congress in special session on March 9 he had ready for instant passage an Emergency Banking Act. Before the day was over, the law received the President's signature, breaking all known records. This measure authorized the Secretary of the Treasury to call in all gold, whether in the shape of coin, bullion, or gold certificates; it provided for the examination and reopening of all banks deemed sound, and for a system of "conservators" to take charge of all others; and it authorized an extensive issue of emergency currency to be used if necessary in halting runs. By March 13, banks which federal examiners found solvent began to reopen, and the government's guaranty of their stability proved sufficient to restore public confidence. Only $15 million of the new emergency currency had to be used, and millions of dollars that the banks had paid to anxious depositors during the crisis began to flow back. Some 3,000 banks, scattered throughout the country, were either reopened under conservators or were not reopened at all, but there was no longer any reason to doubt the essential soundness of the banking structure, and business proceeded as usual.

Presidential Leadership. During the next few weeks the President had occasion again and again to demonstrate his capacity for effective leadership. Relying on the support of public opinion, he showed an unerring sense of the dramatic. Whether in a radio appeal to the nation or in a personally delivered message to Congress, he seldom failed to time his pronouncements exactly and irresistibly. He held frequent conferences with the representatives of the press, took them freely into his confidence, made them like him, and obtained through them a steady stream of favorable publicity. Like Theodore Roosevelt and Woodrow Wilson before him, he had no scruples about the constitutional right of the Executive to direct the course of legislation. His energetic "brain-trusters," sometimes without much help from congressional committees, drafted the laws that Congress was called upon to pass. Whenever he could he used the same tactics on legislators that he used on newspapermen, but he was entirely capable of sterner measures. Farley, his patronage broker, kept books on every congressman, and it was an open secret that those who voted with the President could hope to have their recommendations for appointments honored, while those who voted against him could not. The President knew that the best time to get his program

through was while the country still regarded the steps taken as essential to meet
an emergency, and while congressmen,
with their hunger for patronage unap-
peased, were unwilling to interrupt the
"honeymoon" period with which each new
administration begins. To forestall long
debates over bothersome details he frequently induced Congress to delegate much
discretionary authority to the President
himself, or to some executive officer. Thus
many of the New Deal measures were
passed in more or less skeleton form, with
the details to be filled in later by the President and his advisers. Operating in this
hasty fashion, the special session of Congress enacted into law within a hundred
days many of the principal policies of the
New Deal.

Direction of the New Deal. The Emergency Banking Act foretold at the very
outset the direction in which the New Deal
was to go. With the whole financial system in a state of collapse, the President
might have turned toward the left, with
social revolution somewhat after the Russian pattern as his goal. Had he directed
Congress to nationalize the banking system, a long step toward the state ownership
and administration of all industry and finance would have been taken. He might
also have turned to the right, toward what,
in contrast with Communism, was currently called Fascism, and drew its inspiration from the exploits of Mussolini in Italy.
His goal then would have been to preserve
the private-profit system at the expense, if
need be, of democracy. But neither Communism nor Fascism had any deep rooting
in America, and one seemed as unlikely as
the other to attract the democratically inclined Roosevelt.

There is no evidence that Roosevelt considered either way. What he proposed was
a middle course, more in line with American precedents. The business of the nation was to be left in private hands, but
with controls set up by the government
to prevent the ever-recurring booms and

crises from which capitalism had suffered
so long. Extreme individualism had already been limited by extensive governmental regulation; what Roosevelt had in
mind was to extend regulation to the point
where it would result in a planned economy. Underlying much of New Deal
thought was the assumption that private
capitalism had failed to provide a good
national life and therefore the state had
to assume the role of directing the nation's
economic destiny. Since a favored few
had been taking too much out of the
national pot and the great majority not
enough, it was the duty of the government
to reapportion the national income by
"soaking the rich" with high income and
business taxes and using the proceeds for
less fortunate groups. All of these ends,
Roosevelt believed, might be accomplished
by greatly increasing the regulatory powers
of the government through the democratic
method and without destroying the basic
rights of the individual. Beyond this broad
theory of a planned economy Roosevelt
had few fixed ideas. By nature he was a
politician and an experimenter. When his
advisers made a proposal that seemed desirable on either political or social grounds,
he would support them, even if many of
their suggestions seemed to be working at
cross purposes. Whatever final shape his
program might take, the President was determined to provide relief for the unemployed, to help the farmer, to promote by
every means at his disposal the restoration
of prosperity, and so to reform the American system that another such depression
would not occur.

The London Economic Conference.
Very early in his administration the President was called upon to decide whether
he could achieve these objectives and at
the same time carry on a program of international cooperation. Apparently he at
first thought that the two were not incompatible. He accepted, seemingly without
reservation, the commitments of his predecessor with respect to American participa-

tion in the World Economic Conference to be held in London during the summer of 1933. He even showed some disposition to extend the scope of the conference to include the revision of war debts, and he appointed as head of the American delegation the Secretary of State, Cordell Hull, who was devoted to tariff reduction and the reopening of world trade.

But a month after the Conference had opened and had seemingly made progress toward an international agreement to stabilize world currencies and to reduce tariff barriers, thus freeing world trade, Roosevelt abruptly changed his mind and announced that he would seek recovery in America through the establishment of a "sound internal economic system." Appar-

ently his "brain trust" had convinced him that he could not effectively intervene radically in the free market at home to support and regulate prices and wages, and at the same time attempt to reestablish a free international market. Whatever the motives that led the President to his decision, it was a fact that the program of legislation he had pushed through Congress was based on the assumption that the United States must "go it alone." For the moment international cooperation was to be sidetracked and economic isolation given a trial. Since American assistance was fundamental in the development of any world program, there was nothing left for the London Conference to do but wind up its affairs and go home.

SELECTED BIBLIOGRAPHY

The most balanced survey of the Hoover Administration is H. G. Warren, *Herbert Hoover and the Great Depression* (1959), necessarily based upon published materials since Mr. Hoover refused to open his papers to scholars. The second and third volumes of *The Memoirs of Herbert Hoover* (1952) reveal a great deal about the author's mind. Semiofficial works by friends of the administration, and valuable as sources are: W. S. Myers (ed.), *The State Papers and Other Public Writings of Herbert Hoover* (2 vols., 1934); W. S. Myers and W. H. Newton, *The Hoover Administration; A Documented Narrative* (1936); and R. L. Wilbur and A. M. Hyde, *The Hoover Policies* (1937). See also *The Memoirs of Ray Lyman Wilbur, 1875–1949*, edited by E. E. Robinson and P. C. Edwards (1960). Wilbur, an old Hoover friend and President of Stanford University, served as Secretary of the Interior.

Broadus Mitchell, *Depression Decade: From New Era to New Deal, 1929–1941* (1947), is a survey of economic history, critical in tone. Walter Johnson, *°1600 Pennsylvania Avenue; Presidents and the People, 1929–1959* (2nd

ed., 1963), is political history by a liberal who believes in a strong presidency and finds the Hoover record a dismal one. The first volume of A. M. Schlesinger, Jr., *The Age of Roosevelt*, which bears the subtitle, *°The Crisis of the Old Order* (1957), is a superbly written if somewhat distorted backdrop for the New Deal, of which the author is perhaps the leading scholarly partisan.

Dixon Wecter, *The Age of the Great Depression, 1929–1941* (1948), is a comprehensive and well-written survey of social history. F. L. Allen, *°Since Yesterday; The Nineteen-Thirties in America, September 3, 1929–September 3, 1939* (1940), is a sprightly examination of social phenomena. A rich collection of documents gathered by D. A. Shannon, *°The Great Depression* (1960), illustrates the impact of the depression upon the people. Another valuable book of readings is C. A. Chambers (ed.), *°The New Deal at Home and Abroad, 1929–1945* (1965). A lively book on the stock market debacle is J. K. Galbraith, *°The Great Crash, 1929* (1955). An important new work on monetary problems is Milton Friedman and Anna Jacobson, *°The Great Contraction, 1929–33* (1965). A sympathetic account of one of the chief casualties

° Available in paperback

of the crash is Forrest McDonald, *Insull* (1962). There are two good studies of the Hawley-Smoot Tariff: E. E. Schattschneider, *Politics, Pressures and the Tariff* (1935), a valuable inside picture of the making of the tariff; and J. M. Jones, *Tariff Retaliation* (1934), an examination of its international implications. On Hoover's problems with the veterans, see W. W. Waters, *B.E.F.; The Whole Story of the Bonus Army* (1933). On a major public work project of the era, see P. L. Kleinsorge, *The Boulder Canyon Project* (1941).

In addition to the books on Secretary Stimson already cited, see the highly critical short study by R. N. Current, *Secretary Stimson, A Study in Statecraft* (1954). A fine scholarly work is R. H. Ferrell, *American Diplomacy in the Great Depression; Hoover-Stimson Foreign Policy, 1929–1933* (1957), based upon multi-archival research and objective in tone. W. S. Myers, *The Foreign Policies of Herbert Hoover, 1929–1933* (1940), is semiofficial and rather dull. A good survey of an area in which the administration had some success is Alexander DeConde, *Herbert Hoover's Latin-American Policy* (1951). On the Manchurian problem, see H. L. Stimson, *The Far Eastern Crisis; Recollections and Observations* (1936); but compare it with S. R. Smith, *The Manchurian Crisis, 1931–1932* (1948), a scholarly work. Excellent background material is to be found in Owen Lattimore, *Manchuria, Cradle of Conflict* (2nd ed., 1935). For the lasting importance of the Stimson Doctrine, see Robert Langer, *Seizure of Territory, The Stimson Doctrine and Related Principles in Legal Theory and Diplomatic Practice* (1947). Critical in tone is R. N. Stromberg, *Collective Security and American Foreign Policy* (1963).

A superb account of the 1932 campaign is in Frank Freidel, *The Triumph* (1956), the third volume of his *Franklin D. Roosevelt.* Still useful is R. V. Peel and T. C. Donnelly, *The 1932 Campaign, An Analysis* (1935), by shrewd contemporary observers. While Freidel treats Roosevelt's governorship with insight, see also the topical study by Bernard Bellush, *Franklin D. Roosevelt as Governor of New York* (1955). An important analysis of urban politics of the period is contained in Alex Gottfried, *Boss Cermak of Chicago* (1962), a biography of a Democratic leader who was assassinated soon after leading his party to victory. On the tangled New York City politics of this period see Herbert Mitgang, *The Man Who Rode the Tiger* (1963), a life of Samuel Seabury.

On American Communism, the literature is vast and not always reliable. Excellent scholarly works not already cited include: Nathan Glazer, *The Social Basis of American Communism* (1961); R. L. Roy, *Communism and the Churches* (1960); R. W. Iversen, *The Communists and the Schools* (1959); and Daniel Aaron, *°Writers on the Left* (1961). Of the memoirs of ex-Communists, two of the most interesting are J. A. Wechsler, *The Age of Suspicion* (1953); and Granville Hicks, *Where We Came Out* (1954). Sensational in tone are Eugene Lyons, *The Red Decade* (1941); and Martin Dies, *The Trojan Horse in America* (1940). See also A. R. Ogden, *The Dies Committee* (2nd ed., 1945), for a critical account of a famous investigation of "un-American activities." A sprightly, critical, and well-informed history of the Comintern to 1939 is Franz Borkenau, *°World Communism* (2nd ed., 1962).

38

THE NEW DEAL

Relief, Recovery, and Reform. It was soon apparent that the New Deal had set itself the triple task of relief, recovery, and reform. The legislation of the "hundred days," hastily conceived as it was, pointed toward one or more of these objectives. Inconsistencies were frequent; relief sometimes got in the way of recovery, and recovery in the way of reform. But occasionally, also, reform measures promoted recovery, and recovery almost always helped solve the problem of relief. Whatever their contradictions and interactions, the three goals remained constant, and they were never long forgotten. From time to time changes were based on experience, or even on political expediency, but they were invariably defended as merely a better way of accomplishing what the New Deal had set out to do. Most of the

New Deal measures cost money, and the Economy Act, signed by the President on March 20, 1933, was soon recognized as an empty gesture. The savings made under its terms were only temporary, and were soon overbalanced by the extraordinary expenditures undertaken for relief, recovery, and reform.

Relief. In its attack on the relief problem the New Deal amplified what the Hoover administration had already begun. But the New Deal attitude toward relief was far more humanitarian and comprehensive than that of the preceding administration. From the first, Roosevelt insisted that no one should go hungry and that all considerations about social and political theory should be secondary to that objective. If local authorities could not provide food and shelter, then the national government would do it directly or indirectly without pausing to consider the costs and the long-term political or economic effects of such action. Secondly, the New Deal insisted that, if at all possible, jobs should be provided the needy and a direct dole paid only in cases of emergency. Roosevelt's consistent humanitarian spirit was exemplified by his declaration that no government could long afford to run a deficit "in the books of human fortitude." Through the Federal Emergency Relief Administration, created May 12, 1933, contributions instead of RFC loans were made available to the states for relief purposes. The law permitted local authorities to provide either work relief or an outright dole, but since in practice the dole was far more economical than "made work," it was used unsparingly. By the end of 1934 about one-sixth of the population of the country was on relief. At the head of the FERA was Harry Hopkins, a professional social worker who had been in charge of relief activities in New York while Roosevelt was governor. Hopkins believed work relief preferable to the dole for psychological reasons, and under his urging the President established the Civil Works Administration in October, 1933, as a branch of the FERA. Through the CWA an effort was made to provide emergency jobs for workers who might otherwise have spent the winter on relief. The CWA actually gave millions of men the first employment they had had for years, but the organization was so hastily devised that it was shot through with inefficiency, and partly on this account was discontinued the following spring.

Relief: WPA. As year after year went by with no really significant falling-off in the relief rolls, federal relief workers became convinced that the situation must be dealt with on a more or less permanent basis. In harmony with these views, the new Relief Act of April 8, 1935, required the government to provide "work relief, and to increase employment by providing useful projects." For this purpose a total of nearly $5 billion was appropriated on the understanding that federal relief officials would help devise work projects, would prescribe rules for the selection of workers, and would regulate the conditions of labor. During the summer of 1935 the FERA handed over to a new Works Progress Administration, established in July under the direction of the energetic Hopkins, the task of providing work for all employables. The wage to be paid on all such projects was a "security wage," lower

than that afforded by private employment but higher than the sums paid for direct relief. The WPA also undertook to provide the unemployed with the kind of work they were best fitted to do. By this time the many trifling projects of the FERA and the CWA had brought "made work" into ill-repute, and had even provided it with a name, "boondoggling," but under WPA the nature of the work projects undertaken steadily improved. For the unskilled laborers, who constituted the great majority of relief workers, jobs were found on such projects as the construction of country roads and city streets, the improvement of parks and playgrounds, and the building of flood-control or irrigation dams. Carpenters, plasterers, masons, plumbers, and other skilled laborers were used to erect or repair schoolhouses, libraries, city halls, courthouses, and other public buildings. Even the "white-collar" classes were not neglected, and projects were devised to aid artists, writers, actors, musicians, architects, and many others possessed of more or less professional abilities. At one time about 80 per cent of the nation's top-ranking artists were on the WPA rolls. Few aspects of American life were unaffected by the activities of the WPA. Supplementary to its program was the work of the National Youth Administration, through which needy high school and college students were enabled to earn small sums for noninstructional assistance to their teachers, while equally needy young people who were not in school were provided with useful part-time jobs.

Over a six-year span the WPA spent $11.3 billion, of which $4 billion were spent on roads and streets, $1 billion on public buildings, $1 billion on publicly owned utilities, and $2.5 billion on community projects, which included schools and recreation facilities. By 1941 the WPA had employed at one time or another 8 million different individuals, or about one-fifth of all workers in the country. The average number of WPA workers varied from

2 million in 1937 to well over 3 million in November, 1938, an election month. The WPA was terminated by the war in 1944, but as late as 1940, in the midst of the re-armament boom, it still had 2 million workers on its rolls. The WPA was per-haps the most attacked of all New Deal agencies, partly because of its size and the extent of its operations. Labor leaders were critical because it paid lower wages than the "going rate," and conservatives because it was far more expensive than the dole. The Republicans charged, at times with good reason, that the relief rolls were being used by the administration for po-litical purposes. But scarcely a community had not benefited by repaired or newly constructed public buildings, improved streets and highways, new parks, play-grounds, and swimming pools, together with other more or less permanent contri-butions to the convenience and comfort of the public.

Relief: CCC. A relief project particu-larly cherished by the President was the Civilian Conservation Corps, created in 1933. The purpose of this organization was to establish conservation camps in every part of the country providing work for un-married young men between the ages of eighteen and twenty-five. The CCC soon had more than 250,000 youths at work un-der army officers clearing forests, planting trees, improving roads, and preventing floods. Enlistments were for one year. The men received $1 a day each in addition to medical care and maintenance, but were required to allot $25 a month to depen-dents or relatives. Most of them were im-mensely improved in health and morale as a result of their experience. The CCC lasted until well after the entrance of the United States into the Second World War.

Pump Priming and Recovery. The sec-ond broad objective of the New Deal was to get the economic wheels turning again so that jobs would be available for all those able to work, business would be prof-itable, and agricultural prices would rise. Government spending on a vast scale, or, as it later came to be called, "pump prim-ing," was to be a main instrument in the attempt at recovery. Consequently the RFC established during Hoover's adminis-tration was given greatly increased powers to lend huge sums to private industry, as well as to public agencies, at very low rates of interest. Starved for credit, the business world eagerly accepted billions in govern-mental loans, and eventually repaid most of them with interest. Supplementing this lending policy was a program of direct spending on public construction. The Pub-lic Works Administration, created in the opening days of the New Deal, was sup-plied by Congress with $3.3 billion to build post offices, harbors, and dams in the hope that such a large construction pro-gram would provide much new business for heavy industries and for the construc-tion trades. Actually, the PWA developed slowly, partly because of the rigid honesty of its administrator, Secretary of Interior Harold L. Ickes, and partly because de-tailed plans for large projects took time to provide. Not until the business recession of 1937–1938 did the PWA become im-portant. But by 1939 it had sponsored projects in all but three counties within the United States at an estimated cost of nearly $6 billion. And unquestionably the PWA helped the country recover from the 1937–1938 recession in much the same way that the other spending programs aided more general recovery.

John Maynard Keynes. Much of the theoretical base for New Deal pump prim-ing was advanced by John Maynard Keynes, an eminent but unorthodox Eng-lish economist, in a pamphlet, "The Means to Recovery," published shortly after Roose-velt became President. Keynes derided as obsolete the customary emphasis upon balancing the national budget, and argued instead that the best means of curing the depression lay in generous public spending. Whenever private spending became inadequate to keep industry functioning at capacity, Keynes believed that the government should step in with public spending. Keynes was not a socialist, and his ideas were as much anathema to the Marxists as to the rugged individualists. The purpose of government spending in his view was to promote private initiative by providing it with the means to forge ahead. While regarding expenditures for productive enterprise as preferable, he admitted that even expenditures for direct relief would help. "The object must be to raise the total expenditure to a figure which is high enough to push the vast machine in American industry into renewed motion." Deficit financing, under depression conditions, he regarded as a positive good, for in effect it would multiply several times over the amounts made available by public appropriation. The government should take any steps necessary to make credit cheap and abundant, keep interest rates down, and even, on occasion, lower taxes. In the long run any policy that expanded employment and increased the national income was justifiable, and to the extent that it succeeded would even contribute to the collection of more taxes and the balancing of the national budget.

A Managed Economy.   Keynes had also written extensively about the need for modern states to intervene radically in the economy for the purpose of directing the national output toward greater social utility. And though Roosevelt apparently was not directly influenced by the English economist, very early in the depression the President indicated his belief that a managed economy was necessary to achieve an equitable national life. In his speech of September 23, 1932, at the Commonwealth Club of San Francisco, the most philosophical of his campaign addresses, he stated that the main task before the country was not the further "discovery or exploitation

HARRY L. HOPKINS AND HAROLD L. ICKES

Roosevelt's chief relief administrator, Hopkins helped devise much of the New Deal's social legislation. He was often in conflict with the pugnacious Ickes, who served FDR ably as Secretary of the Interior and administrator of the PWA.

of natural resources or necessarily producing more goods," but rather the job of "adjusting production to consumption, of distributing wealth and products more equitably." Although he then declared that the government should assume powers to direct the economy "only as a last resort," by 1933 he clearly felt that the time had come when it was necessary, if recovery were to be achieved, for the government to become a major partner in the shaping of the economy.

Recovery: The NRA.   Quite the most ambitious of the New Deal efforts to restore prosperity was the National Recovery Administration of 1933, under the terms of the National Industrial Recovery Act. The NRA, some of the ideas for which originated in the National Chamber of Commerce, was the chief New Deal effort to devise a planned economy. As the depression deepened, many businesses sought to survive by slashing prices and by cutthroat selling. The purpose of the NRA was to permit industry and commerce to govern themselves in order to suppress "unfair competition," to apportion markets, limit production, and, to a degree, eliminate price competition. In return for such privileges, quite contrary to the antitrust laws, business had to agree to shorten working hours, raise wages, and attempt to increase employment. Codes of "fair competition" were to be devised by the different types of manufacturers, mine operators, common carriers, utility corporations, merchants, and every other type of business, according to which each group would standardize its behavior. If such codes were drawn so as not to create a monopoly or eliminate small business, they were to be approved by the NRA administrator, and the standards set in each code were to have the force of law throughout the industry. For all businesses not organized under their own code authority, the President issued a blanket code, which abolished child labor, fixed a thirty-five hour week for ordinary labor with a minimum wage of forty cents an hour, and a forty-hour week for white-collar jobs with minimum wages of twelve to fifteen dollars a week. Labor had little voice in the making of the codes, and the interest of consumers was entirely ignored. Organized labor, however, was not neglected in the NRA and in the long run was to profit more by virtue of Section 7(a) of the act, to be discussed later, than any other group in the economy.

Under the energetic leadership of General Hugh S. Johnson, the NRA made a valiant effort to live up to the high hopes of those who sponsored it. But soon difficulties in the enforcement of the NRA codes appeared. "Chiselers" who ignored the rules put the honest dealer at a serious disadvantage. Wartime compulsion was lacking, and the hope that the code authorities set up by each business group could secure the obedience of all members proved illusive. Small business complained that the codes favored large industries, and a few important establishments, in-

cluding the Ford Motor Company, refused entirely to cooperate. Business was extremely irritated at organized labor, which had regained much of its strength and used the strike persistently in trying to enforce its demands. Finally General Johnson, following a tempestuous outbreak against labor for its failure to do its part, as he saw it, resigned in September, 1934, and the following May the United States Supreme Court in a unanimous opinion found the law under which the NRA had been operating to be unconstitutional. The decision of the Court, that too much authority had been delegated by Congress to the President, and that the existing emergency gave Congress no authority that it would not have otherwise, angered the President, but he acknowledged the Court's authority, and the whole NRA organization was rapidly dismantled.

Recovery and Labor.   Despite the New Deal's concern for workingmen, Roosevelt's initial plans for recovery from the depression paid scant attention to the trade unions. Thus his original proposals for the NRA had not included any labor provisions beyond those permitting him to set minimum wage and maximum hour provisions. To obtain the necessary votes in Congress, the historic Section 7(a) had to be added to the NRA bill. This section declared that labor had "the right to organize and bargain collectively through representatives of their own choosing." To implement the radical new labor policy, the President established a National Labor Board whose functions were taken over by the much more powerful National Labor Relations Board established by Congress in the summer of 1934. Under the stimulus of Section 7(a) and protected by a series of pro-labor decisions of the National Labor Relations Board, many unions which had been long dormant were reinvigorated in 1934–1935, with a consequent swelling of membership rolls and the outbreak of numerous strikes for union recognition, higher wages, and shorter hours. The renewed union activity drew bitter criticism from business interests and probably also helped persuade the President that a strong labor movement by its insistence on higher wages and shorter hours would aid recovery. After the NRA was declared unconstitutional, the administration actively supported the National Labor Relations Act, designed to soften the blow sustained by labor in the loss of Section 7(a).

The Wagner Labor Act and the NLRB. The Wagner Act, as the new labor bill was called after its sponsor, Senator Robert Wagner of New York, became with later modifications the basic federal statute controlling national labor relations. As such it was one of the New Deal's most important measures and one of the most controversial. Adding to the permissive grant of power to unions given by Section 7(a), the act placed the power of the government actively behind the organization of unions by enjoining all employers from certain types of anti-union activity. As well as declaring the refusal of an employer "to bargain collectively with representatives of his employees" as an unfair labor practice, it also denied the employer the right to "interfere with, restrain or coerce employees," to contribute financial or other support to so-called company unions, and to encourage or discourage membership in any union by hiring or firing practices. The act also provided for the creation of a National Labor Relations Board empowered to hold elections among workers for the purposes of collective bargaining, to hold investigations on an employee's charge of an unfair labor practice, and to issue cease and desist orders if in its judgment the charges were valid. The NLRB so zealously set about its function to implement the Wagner Act — one of its rulings denied to employers the right to criticize publicly any union activity and thus curtailed the basic right of free speech — that it excited widespread criticism and at times even

incurred Roosevelt's displeasure. Its solicitous attitude, however, enabled the union movement to make almost revolutionary gains.

The C.I.O. One result of the revitalized unionism was the division of organized labor into two competing organizations. Through the early days of the New Deal the American Federation of Labor adhered to the traditional Gompers policy of organizing most of its member unions on the basis of craft or skill. Even in the new mass production industries, where automatic machinery had made obsolete many individual skills and where most employees were simply production workers, the A.F. of L. insisted on dividing these new recruits among its old trade unions, which, on the whole, were governed by conservative-minded leaders preoccupied with problems of the skilled artisans. Charges were made, with some justice, that union leaders had lost touch with the problems of the mass-production worker and that the old organization introduced many divisive and often competing union organizations into one shop, whereas a single industrial union could meet and bargain with management as an effective mobilized unit.

John L. Lewis, militant head of the United Mine Workers, one of the few industrially organized unions, took the lead in the formation of a Committee for Industrial Organization to promote the unionization of industries as units and not in accordance with specified trades or skills. Lewis was opposed by the A.F. of L., but, with the support of his own and several other powerful unions, he sent organizers into many of the great mass-production industries, such as automobiles, steel, textiles, rubber, aluminum, plate glass, and furniture. In most instances the C.I.O. plan of organization met a long-felt need, old unions took on new life, and new unions were founded as needed. For cooperating with Lewis in his endeavors ten unions

THE SIT-DOWN STRIKE

The new weapon of labor warfare won substantial victories for the strikers, particularly in the automobile industry. This scene is in an automobile assembly plant.

were expelled in 1936 from the A.F. of L., and as a result the C.I.O. assumed a separate identity. Claiming to represent a membership of nearly 4 million workers as against the 5 million A.F. of L., the C.I.O. changed its name in November, 1938, to the Congress of Industrial Organizations, and elected Lewis as its first president.

The "Sit-down." The methods by which the C.I.O. had risen to such great importance involved among other things the use of a weapon new to American labor history, the "sit-down" strike. Workers, instead of first leaving the factories and then picketing them to prevent the employment of "scabs," simply retained in idleness the posts they ordinarily held, and forcibly resisted removal. This technique was successfully employed in C.I.O. strikes against two leading automobile companies, the General Motors Corporation and the Chrysler Corporation. In both instances, with the assistance of Governor Frank Murphy of Michigan, agreements were finally

reached to vacate the plants on condition that the C.I.O. union be recognized as the bargaining agent for its members, while later negotiations won other concessions. The United States Steel Corporation, long the despair of labor leaders, in March, 1937, quickly accorded the C.I.O. Steel Workers' Organizing Committee full bargaining authority for all its employees. Most of the other "Big Steel" companies also capitulated, but the "Little Steel" companies fought back. Strikes that began in May, 1937, spread rapidly through Pennsylvania, Ohio, and Illinois, and were accompanied by much disorder. Quick action of the employers prevented sit-down strikes, and without this weapon the unions lost the first round in the struggle. The steel companies, also, as the Senate Civil Liberties Committee's investigation of the strike revealed, had enrolled private armies equipped with modern arms and had liberally employed labor spies and strikebreakers. Shocked by these facts, public sentiment eventually supported the unions, and subsequent action by the NLRB ultimately brought a union victory in 1941.

Continued conflict between capital and labor after 1936 wearied the public and irritated the President. Many other Americans were alienated by the growing violence of C.I.O. activities and by certain strikes which they attributed to Communist agitators. The increasing disenchantment with organized labor, as well as a desire to protect non-union labor, prompted the search for other solutions to the wage problem and aided the passage of the Fair Labor Standards Act of 1938. By this act a national minimum wage and a maximum work week were set for restricted groups. The original minimum wage was set at twenty-five cents an hour and the maximum work week at forty-four hours, to be reduced to forty hours by 1940. Subsequent legislation after World War II raised the minimum wage and greatly extended the groups of workers covered. An amendment of 1961, for example, set a minimum of $1.25 an hour to become effective in 1963. Few permanent acts of the New Deal were more revolutionary than the "Wages and Hours Act," which introduced government regulation into the very basis of the free market mechanism.

Agricultural Recovery. Parallel to the New Deal program for industry and labor was an equally comprehensive plan for the rehabilitation of agriculture. Striking out along what the President himself called "a new and untrod path," the Agricultural Adjustment Act of May 12, 1933, sought a remedy for the chronic overproduction that had for so long kept farm prices down. Frankly recognizing that the export market was too unreliable to be a factor in their planning, the framers of the act proposed to restrict the American output, if need be, to what the United States alone could consume. By careful supervision of production, the real income of farmers was to be brought back to the average levels of the five years preceding the First World War.

An Agricultural Adjustment Administration was set up with authority to buy and hold surpluses, and to contract with the producers of specified basic commodities for whatever cooperation might be needed to insure crop control. Since the farmers were to be paid generously for their cooperation, what agriculture would receive was, in effect, a double subsidy, one of direct money payments on the basis of the contracts signed, and the other through higher prices for crops harvested. The cost involved in the crop-restriction program was to be met by a tax levied against the processors of farm produce, who in turn would pass the burden along to the consumers. The farmer, if this elaborate scheme of economic planning worked, would find himself at last on a parity with other economic groups. Basic commodities at first brought within the scope of the act were cotton, wheat, corn, hogs, rice, tobacco, and milk, but a year later the list was greatly lengthened.

Organized in the Department of Agriculture under Secretary Henry A. Wallace, the AAA experimented with crop-reduction programs, at first in cotton, wheat, corn, and hogs, then in numerous other farm products. As anticipated, benefit payments cut down production and brought up prices, although the prolonged drought of the western half of the Mississippi Valley probably affected the situation as much as, or more than, the AAA. So devastating was the drought in some western states that many farmers had little to live on except the money they received from the government under their crop-reduction programs; furthermore, windstorms that swept through the western "dustbowl" threatened to render much land permanently useless. Caustic criticism of the AAA program was inevitable. Crop reduction, at a time when drought conditions threatened the country with shortages, was difficult to defend, and in many instances had to be modified. Farmers whose lifelong habits had been based upon growing more on their lands found it hard to adjust to an economy of growing less. They signed the contracts and accepted the benefit payments because they needed the money, but they resented the system. Processors complained bitterly at the heavy taxation forced upon them, and found themselves seriously handicapped in competing for foreign markets. Consumers paid steeply increased prices for nearly everything that came from the farm.

The AAA Invalidated. In spite of these criticisms the country was hardly prepared for the drastic action of the United States Supreme Court that announced January 6, 1936, in a six-to-three decision, that the AAA was unconstitutional. Justice Roberts of the Court held that there was nothing in the Constitution to justify federal control of agricultural production, and that, in attempting to deal with the strictly local business of farming, Congress had invaded a right reserved to the states. Since the processing taxes and benefit payments existed only as means to an illegal end, the Court held that they, too, were invalid. The implications of this decision disturbed the minority of the Court, which in a dissenting opinion of Justice Stone warned the majority that "courts are not the only agency of government that must be assumed to have capacity to govern." Nor could agricultural economists quite understand how farming could be classified as a strictly local business when most farm prices, if unregulated, would depend upon nationwide and even upon worldwide conditions.

RA, FCA. In wrecking the AAA the Supreme Court did not destroy the entire New Deal structure for dealing with agriculture. A new Farm Credit Administration, established in March, 1933, had taken over every federal agency that had anything to do with agricultural credits. By 1934 it was lending on an average rate of $5 million a day. Much of this credit was used to refinance mortgages that might otherwise have been foreclosed, but loans for production and for marketing were also supplied. As a further aid in dealing with the mortgage problem, the Frazier-Lemke Moratorium Act of 1935 delayed foreclosure proceedings for a three-year period, provided a court of law would give its approval, both to the propriety of the delay and to the adequacy of the rental to be paid. For the benefit of farmers who were still keeping up the unequal struggle against marginal or sub-marginal lands the Resettlement Administration was formed in April, 1935. Its chief purpose was to buy up land from which farmers could not ordinarily make a living, and then to "resettle" the dispossessed owners in "healthy rural communities." The RA was less successful than its proponents had hoped, and eventually, renamed the Farm Security Administration, it turned its attention chiefly to helping tenant farmers become land owners.

Soil Conservation. The hostility of the Supreme Court was sufficient to put an end to the NRA, which had begun to break down anyway, but the critical condition of agriculture required that some substitute be found immediately for the AAA. As a stopgap measure, designed mainly to save the situation until something better could be devised, Congress enacted in February, 1936, the Soil Conservation and Domestic Allotment Act. Instead of the control of production at which the AAA had aimed, the primary objective of the new act was to be soil conservation. Direct payments to farmers were to be continued, but henceforth they were to be made in return for cooperation with the government in an elaborate program for the promotion of soil fertility, the prevention of erosion, and the more economic use of farm land. By placing restrictions on the planting of soil-depleting crops, some effort was made to control the production of such basic commodities as cotton, wheat, and corn, but by 1937 the cotton yield reached 18.9 million bales, or about three times the amount the country used annually, while most other crops showed a wide margin over the nation's ability to consume. Furthermore, with the processing tax now declared illegal, the subsidy had to come directly out of the Treasury.

The New AAA. Finally, in 1938 Congress enacted a new Agricultural Adjustment Act retaining the soil-conservation and benefit-payment features of the preceding program, and making provisions to limit the acreage allotments of wheat, cotton, corn, tobacco, and rice crops in accordance with probable needs. It also authorized the making of storage loans as a means of holding agricultural surpluses off the market; and it sanctioned resort to marketing quotas in emergencies, provided that two-thirds of the growers of the commodity concerned recorded their approval in a referendum vote. All this was a part of an elaborate effort to raise the income of farmers to "parity," that is, to the same ratio with the incomes of other groups that had existed in the five years prior to 1914; to make doubly sure of this goal the sum of $212 million was appropriated in 1939 for "parity payments" to help bridge the gap between current prices and "parity prices." For the benefit of wheat growers, a Federal Crop Insurance Corporation was established in the Department of Agriculture from which guaranties could be obtained to the amount of 50 or 75 per cent of normal yields. Payments of losses and premiums were to be made either in wheat or in its cash equivalent.

Although participation in the AAA program was kept purely voluntary, the generous subsidies were hard for farmers to resist. About 5.25 million agricultural producers working through 3,000 county conservation associations and many more subordinate committees, took part in the 1939 program. Nearly three-fourths of the crop

THE GREAT DEPRESSION

In the 1930's America was stricken by the greatest depression in its history. Prolonged droughts compounded the misery, especially in the agricultural Southwest. Nobel Prize winner John Steinbeck, in his moving novel, The Grapes of Wrath, *unforgettably recreates the anguish of a dispossessed farm family on the move.*

And then the dispossessed were drawn west — from Kansas, Oklahoma, Texas, New Mexico; from Nevada and Arkansas families, tribes, dusted out, tractored out. Carloads, caravans, homeless and hungry; twenty thousand and fifty thousand and a hundred thousand and two hundred thousand. They streamed over the mountains, hungry and restless — restless as ants, scurrying to find work to do — to lift, to push, to pull, to pick, to cut — anything, any burden to bear, for food. The kids are hungry. We got no place to live. Like ants scurrying for work, for food, and most of all for land.

JOHN STEINBECK, *The Grapes of Wrath* (1939), The Viking Press land of the nation was involved. An "ever normal granary" was promoted by loans on warehouse surpluses amounting approximately to nine cents per pound on cotton, sixty cents per bushel on wheat, and fifty-seven cents per bushel on corn. By this device both producer and consumer hoped to be protected against shortages and price fluctuations. The marketing quota provisions of the act were also promptly invoked to protect the prices of cotton and of several types of tobacco, while nearly 170,000 wheat growers, some of them in drought-threatened areas where there was little prospect of a crop, took out federal crop insurance. The cost of all this to the government exceeded $500 million annually in the prewar years and $2 billion to $3 billion after World War II.

HUEY P. LONG

Long's promise to give every American an income of $5,000 a year appealed to the unemployed masses and gave Roosevelt grave concern. Here the controversial Senator from Louisiana is shown in one of his most belligerent moods.

Reform: Social Security. The third great objective of Roosevelt's New Deal was to reform existing institutions so that the possibility of another great depression would be minimized, and, in case another similar disaster was experienced, much of the personal distress of the thirties would be avoided. One of the most comprehensive New Deal reforms, and one which unquestionably touched more Americans than any other, was in the broad field of social security. In an act of August 14, 1935, Congress established the Social Security Board, providing for old-age annuities, unemployment insurance, and more adequate care for the needy, the dependent, and the disabled. Until 1935 protection against these hazards had been a private matter, a not illogical situation as long as the country was largely agricultural. But now with a majority of the population living in cities and dependent upon a weekly pay check, the necessity for some such legislation was apparent. Medical efficiency promoted longevity, while employers increasingly tended to keep down the average age of the men on their payrolls. Technological unemployment and business readjustments threw many people out of work, and all the efforts of the New Deal had failed to provide complete reemployment. The aged, confronted by a seemingly hopeless situation, listened attentively to the fantastic promises of Doctor F. E. Townsend of California, who urged a 2 per cent transaction tax to provide pensions up to $200 per month for everyone over sixty who would quit work and spend the money as fast as it came in. The unemployed looked with equal favor upon the program urged by Congressman Ernest Lundeen of Minnesota, who advocated payments of not less than $10 per week to all jobless persons over eighteen years of age. The discontented were impressed by the blandishments of Huey P. Long, who, first as governor of Louisiana and later as United States Senator, promoted the organization of a "Share-Our-Wealth Society," which set as its goal an income of not less than $5,000 a year for every American family. With so many extremists making headway, it seemed essential that the government take immediate steps to provide a workable system of social security.

The Social Security Act was called "the most complex measure ever considered by Congress." (1) By the familiar dollar-matching device it enabled the federal government to assist the states in the care of unemployables. It particularly encouraged state provision for old-age pensions, for the care of dependent children, and for assistance to the needy blind. (2) It authorized grants to promote through state agencies the rehabilitation of the physically disabled, the care of mothers and children, and the improvement of the public health. Its most notable provisions, however, set up (3) an elaborate federal-state system of unemployment compensation, and (4) a strictly federal system of old-age insurance.

Unemployment Compensation. The plan for unemployment compensation required that each state desiring to cooperate with the federal government establish for the purpose an appropriate administrative agency. Because of the widely divergent conditions in different parts of the nation, the states were permitted considerable latitude in devising regulations to meet local requirements. Funds for the support of the program were provided by a federal tax on employers' payrolls. Toward this tax, however, employers were permitted to write off as tax credits all payments up to 90 per cent of the federal tax made toward the support of a federally approved state unemployment system.

By the summer of 1937 all states and territories had complied with the requirements of the Social Security Act, and the next year the payment of benefits began. Although the law excluded from its operation all government employees, farm laborers, domestic servants, casual workers, and the employees of charitable organiza-

tions, probably half the working population of the country came under its protection. In 1939 the Social Security Board took over the United States Employment Service, and thereafter attempted to coordinate job insurance with job placement. Anyone without work was required to register at his local employment office, which must try to help him find another job. If, after a specified waiting period, he remained unemployed, benefit payments were authorized. These payments at first amounted to from $5 to $15 a week, and continued until the worker had either exhausted all his wage credits, or had reached the maximum period permitted by law, usually three or four months; provided that in the meantime he had failed to find another job.

Old-age Insurance. The Social Security Act provided for monthly payment benefits to qualified workers in industry and commerce who retired from employment at the age of sixty-five. The same groups were excepted from its operations as were denied the advantages of unemployment compensation. Payments of from $15 to $80 a month, depending upon the total amount of wages earned by the beneficiary after 1936, were to begin on January 1, 1942, and were to continue until the time of death, with lump-sum settlements payable to the estates of those who died before reaching the age of sixty-five. Funds for carrying out the program were to be obtained by an income tax on employees, deducted from their wages by employers, and an excise tax on payrolls. Equal sums were collected from employers and employees, at first amounting to a total of two per cent of the worker's income. All payments were made to a Trust Fund established by the Treasury, and it was expected that over a period of years the receipts and payments would be in approximate balance. By the time the promised payments began, some 25.5 million people were eligible for retirement benefits. Experience with the social security program led Congress to amend the original legislation repeatedly during the next two decades. These amendments increased substantially both the number of people covered and the benefits obtainable. That the social security system had materially blunted the financial problems of old age, unemployment, and disability was scarcely open to question.

The Housing Problem.   Another type of New Deal reform was that designed to eliminate city slums and provide better housing for the underprivileged. Coupled with this problem was the need of saving large numbers of homeowners from losing their property through mortgage foreclosures. To meet these needs government credit was for a time extended through the Home Owners' Loan Corporation, the purpose of which was to refinance home mortgages, and through locally established Federal Savings and Loan Associations, to provide funds for new building. When its lending ceased in 1936, the HOLC had acquired mortgages totaling $3 billion and had helped some million homeowners. Another agency, the Federal Housing Administration, established in 1934, undertook to insure home mortgages of which it approved up to 80 (later 90) per cent of the appraised value of the property. This left private capital to provide the money, but the FHA took most of the risk. The most ambitious of the efforts to deal with housing came with the establishment of the United States Housing Authority in 1937. The purpose of this agency was to aid local communities to remedy their "shortage of decent, safe, and sanitary dwellings for families of low income." As a result of USHA activities, nineteen low-rent apartment houses had been constructed by the end of 1939 in thirteen different cities, and loans of more than $500 million for the use of 155 communities had been approved.

Financial   Reforms.   An   important group of New Deal reforms, and one most

bitterly opposed by business interests, was a series of financial regulatory measures aimed at correcting pre-1930 abuses and excesses. These measures made the government so potent in directing the nation's financial mechanism that the stock and commodity markets ever since have responded as much to the political news from Washington as they have to purely economic stimuli. Kindred reform measures also directly affected the nation's prime interstate and oceanic carriers, the production and distribution of electric power, and the terms of international trade by alteration of the tariff rates.

Among the major financial measures was the Glass-Steagall Act of 1933 which, in addition to guaranteeing small depositors against bank failures, divorced commercial and investment banking; permitted national banks to establish branch banks; gave the Federal Reserve Board the right to place severe restrictions upon banks lending too freely for speculative purposes; forbade loans from their own banks to the executive officers of Federal Reserve Banks; and expanded the Federal Reserve System to include industrial and savings banks. Two years later, the old Federal Reserve Board was replaced by a Board of Governors of seven members appointed by the President, with widely expanded powers.

Currency Reform.   The President also seemed determined to experiment with a managed currency which would have the same buying power at all times. To the dismay of many conservatives, he promptly took the United States off the gold standard and secured from Congress a Gold Repeal Resolution which invalidated the gold clauses employed in many public and private contracts. Gold exports were forbidden; gold coin, gold bullion, and gold certificates were taken out of circulation; and a price fixed by the government was paid for all gold newly mined in the United States or offered for sale from abroad. A few months later, under the terms of a new Silver Purchasing Act, the Treasury began to purchase silver, ostensibly to increase the supply of silver in the national monetary stocks. The effect of these measures upon the purchasing power of the dollar was far less marked than the President and his monetary advisers had anticipated, although the United States was soon in possession of most of the world's supply of gold and silver. As long as this treasure remained impounded, there seemed to be no grave threat of currency inflation, except by congressional issues of paper money. Against this latter evil, however, the President took a firm and successful stand.

The SEC. Another Roosevelt reform was an attempt to deal with the problems of speculative investment. A Federal Securities Act, signed on May 27, 1933, insisted that the vendors of securities be made to tell the public the truth about what they had to sell, and imposed heavy penalties for the interstate circulation of fraudulent advertising, through the mails or otherwise. The next year another act established the Securities and Exchange Commission to take over from the Federal Trade Commission the administration of these regulations. While it was beyond the power of the SEC to guarantee the purchasers of securities against loss, it could and did compel the disclosure of such information as might enable investors to form intelligent opinions. The SEC was authorized also to restrict buying on margin or the purchase of stock on credit, to license stock exchanges, and to regulate their practices so as to stimulate legitimate trading and discourage mere gambling.

The Hull Trade Agreements. On the old question of tariff reform, the New Deal made considerable headway. Wisely refraining from the customary effort at direct revision downward, it left the Hawley-Smoot Tariff in force, but proposed through a series of reciprocal trade agreements to

FRANKLIN DELANO ROOSEVELT

The most controversial of American Presidents, Roosevelt, by his charm, eloquence, and genuine compassion for the plight of America's "little men," won the unswerving devotion of the masses.

It is not too early . . . to predict that Franklin D. Roosevelt will be added to the list of great Presidents. The challenging nature of his times, the airy eagerness with which he met every challenge, the breadth of his view of presidential power, his leadership of the forces of domestic reform and the forces of international freedom, his influence on the presidency — all these factors lead most historians to prophesy greatness for his name. Those millions who still denounce Mr. Roosevelt lavishly may as well face the hard fact bravely that Roosevelt had his own rendezvous with history, and that history will be kind to him. It is kind to almost all Presidents, but especially to those who wield their vast powers with boldness and imagination in response to the "felt necessities of the time."

CLINTON ROSSITER, "The Presidents and the Presidency," *American Heritage* (1956)

683

bring duties on imports down to more reasonable levels. By this means, the customary "logrolling" by Congressmen representing constituents with special interests was avoided. A Trade Agreements Act, passed in June, 1934, authorized the President for a three-year period to negotiate agreements with other countries for the mutual lowering of tariff rates. Without referring the matter to Congress for consent, he might lower the existing duties by as much as 50 per cent, provided only that the free list not be disturbed. The exercise of this grant of authority, which was repeatedly renewed, fell at first to Secretary of State Cordell Hull, a lifelong devotee of the low-tariff principle. In five years Hull concluded more than twenty agreements, including two with Great Britain and Canada that were particularly comprehensive. Perhaps three-fourths of the exports and imports of the United States were affected, and as a result of the improved trade relations thus made possible, good will toward the United States mounted rapidly, especially among the nations of Latin America.

Railroad Coordination. Partly to promote recovery, but partly also with a view to reform, the New Deal instituted drastic changes in the control of transportation. The railroads in particular required attention, for the competition of automobiles, trucks, and pipelines, with such inevitable loss of business as accompanied the depression, had brought them to the brink of ruin. To assist in planning for their future, an Emergency Railroad Transportation Act was passed June 16, 1933. This measure provided for a federal coordinator of transportation whose duty was to eliminate wasteful competition, to coordinate train service, and to effect needed economies. RFC loans were used freely to buy new railroad equipment and to permit improvements in service. In this way many roads obtained the funds to experiment with streamlined, air-conditioned trains, drawn by diesel-electric or steam-electric locomotives. The intelligent leadership of Joseph B. Eastman, federal coordinator appointed by the President, had much to do with the fact that the railroads, on the entrance of the United States into the Second World War, were able to deal with the emergency without being taken over by the government.

The Merchant Marine. The New Deal frankly accepted the theory that a strong merchant marine was essential to the national defense. The Merchant Marine Act of 1936 declared: (1) that the United States should have shipping adequate to maintain normal flow of water-borne commerce "at all times"; (2) that this shipping should be "capable of serving as a naval and military auxiliary in time of war"; (3) that it should be owned so far as possible by American citizens and should operate under the American flag; (4) that it should be "composed of the best-equipped, safest, and most suitable types of vessels." The act supplanted the old Shipping Board and its subsidiary Merchant Fleet Corporation with a new Maritime Commission, one duty of which was to determine the ocean lanes which American ships should ply, and another, to work out, in full cooperation with the Navy Department, a "long-range program for replacements and additions to the American Merchant marine." So successful was the Maritime Commission in its endeavors that, when the Second World War broke out, the total American tonnage was two-thirds the British, and far in excess of any other. It was also vastly improved in serviceability.

Electric Power and TVA. Although the electrical power industry had made great technical advances during the twenties, it had shown little sense of obligation to the public. Local distributing companies were ruthlessly combined into interstate giants which were promptly gathered up by holding companies which in turn were often controlled by top holding companies to the enormous profit of a few financial manipulators. Efforts of the New Deal to obtain a "death sentence" for all public utility holding companies failed, but Congress did give the Securities and Exchange Commission authority to limit their operations.

A dramatic approach to the problem of securing the maximum social benefits from electrical power was made through the creation of the Tennessee Valley Authority, a public corporation whose activities eventually extended far beyond the production of electric power. In this area the Roosevelt administration was ready to go much further than mere regulation and to experiment with actual government ownership and operation. Effectively guided by Senator George W. Norris of Nebraska, it singled out the Tennessee Valley for its first great project. This region, ramifying into seven states — Tennessee, Kentucky, Alabama, Mississippi, Virginia, North Carolina, and Georgia — and embracing some 40,000 square miles, seemed to offer an ideal testing ground for New Deal theories on social and economic planning. It counted among its residents a high proportion of the underprivileged, whom cheap power was expected to benefit; and it possessed vast natural resources, most of them inadequately exploited or being allowed to degenerate. Since the government had already spent huge sums upon the Muscle Shoals development, it was believed that here, if anywhere, results might speedily be obtained.

In May, 1933, Congress authorized the President to appoint a board of three directors, known as the Tennessee Valley Authority, to control the mighty project. The TVA was authorized to construct dams for the improvement of navigation and the control of floods; to develop new forms of fertilizer and to promote their use; to build and operate hydroelectric plants and to distribute the power they generated; and to take such other steps as it might see fit to promote the agricultural and industrial

development of the region. The TVA was quickly organized, and with the Muscle Shoals plant as a starting point was soon supplying cheap electric power to a limited area. With the help of PWA funds it pushed rapidly the construction of six new dams, the largest of which, the Norris Dam, was completed in 1936. By 1940 TVA power was being generated at four dams, and was used both to carry forward new construction and to provide cheap power for residential and commercial consumers. By June, 1939, according to TVA estimates, the Authority was serving about 180,000 customers, either directly or indirectly, and its acquisition later in the year of facilities belonging to the Tennessee Electric Power Company added perhaps 150,000 more.

Varieties of TVA Endeavor. The work of the TVA spread as time went on into many fields. It carried on an elaborate program for water control, and the consequent checking of erosion; it produced great quantities of fertilizer, and tested its effectiveness in most of the states of the Union; it experimented with low-cost housing for its employees; it promoted actively the use of the Tennessee River for commercial navigation; it extended the advantages of electricity to many farmers through a program of rural electrification; and it cooperated generously with local authorities in providing public-health services, particularly with a view to checking the ravages of malaria and tuberculosis. Friends of the competitive system bitterly criticized the TVA as a socialistic and monopolistic enterprise endowed with unfair advantages. As a tax exempt agency it had a built-in advantage over private tax-paying business. Moreover, as was pointed out, it removed property from the local tax rolls and thus raised the rates on privately owned property. TVA's contributions to the general welfare were not invariably appreciated by the people they were meant to help, but the evidence seemed conclusive that conditions of life

in the Tennessee Valley had been enormously improved by the work of the TVA. Other hydroelectric developments under the New Deal, such as the Grand Coulee and Bonneville Dams on the Columbia, Boulder (Hoover) Dam on the Colorado, and Fort Peck Dam on the upper Missouri, were not accompanied by the extensive program of social betterment promoted by the TVA, but they were all intended to provide whatever benefits to society might accrue from an unlimited flow of cheap power.

Opposition to the New Deal. Naturally the extensive program of change under the New Deal aroused intense opposition. The policy of spending as freely to defeat the depression as the nation would spend to defeat an enemy in time of war provoked critics to the direst prophecies. When Hoover took office the national debt had stood at more than $17 billion; when he left office, at nearly $21 billion. But the New Deal expenditures by 1940 had doubled the debt of 1933, and the $45 billion limit set by Congress during the First World War soon had to be raised.

Moreover, the New Deal tax bill, frankly labeled by some of its proponents as one designed to "soak the rich," had raised income taxes to their highest peacetime levels. How long could the nation continue to "soak" the rich and to spend so lavishly without danger of bankruptcy? To many observers the socialistic tendencies of the New Deal seemed even worse than the spending. With the government in complete control of nearly every aspect of the nation's economic life, what was to become of "rugged individualism"? More baldly stated, how could private business continue to make profits in the face of crippling taxes, governmental regulation and competition, and an arrogance on the part of labor which the government had seemingly promoted? Roosevelt, as the personification of the New Deal, although highly esteemed by those who liked it, was intensely hated by those who did not. Well-to-do himself, he was denounced as a "traitor to his class," who, in order to curry favor with the masses, stood ready to destroy his own kind. He was accused, too, of building up a powerful federal bureaucracy to keep the Democratic Party in power.

TVA was one of the New Deal's most far-reaching and notably successful experiments in combined economic-social planning. As such it attracted the attention of numerous foreign visitors to the United States. Madame Odette Keun, a French writer and journalist, was one such observer.

For the TVA is wrapped heart and soul in the evolution of the mountaineers. How to transform their thinking and their agricultural customs and adapt them to present conditions; how to develop their economic life, keeping them from the servitude of factories for which they are physically and mentally unsuited . . . how to preserve their independent spirit and their culture . . . and yet teach them responsibility to society and give them a significant and useful role in the community; this is the task TVA has undertaken. It is especially for these mountaineers and their brothers in the valley that it elaborated its agricultural program, invented its fertilizer, created its Agricultural Industries Division, founded its educational and training courses. . . . Its goal is to secure for them a more intelligent, dignified and assured existence. . . .

Excerpt from ODETTE KEUN, *A Foreigner Looks at the TVA* (1937). From O. Handlin (ed.), *This Was America*, Harvard University Press.

Election of 1936. Whatever the reasons back of the returns, early elections soon made it clear that the New Deal had great public appeal. In the state and congressional elections of 1934, the Democrats won again, as in 1932, by a landslide. In the campaign of 1936 the Republicans were in a quandary to find a suitable presidential candidate, due to the shortage of talented officeholders. Their choice finally fell upon Governor Alfred M. Landon of Kansas, one of the few Republican governors to escape the Democratic sweeps. While surprisingly liberal, the Republican candidate and his platform were to the right of the Democrats. The Democrats, fully confident of victory, renominated their ticket of 1932, and elected it by another devastating landslide. Only two states, Maine and Vermont, voted for Landon. The electoral vote stood 523 for Roosevelt to 8 for Landon, and the popular vote 27.7 million to 16.6 million. Not since James Monroe was re-elected in 1820 with but a single opposing electoral vote had an election been so one-sided. In both houses of Congress the Democratic majorities became so large as to threaten dissension.

Among the many postelection observations of analysis, one stood out pre-eminently. It was apparent that the "vertical" lines of cleavage between the parties, so characteristic of nineteenth-century American politics, had given way to a "horizontal" division, which placed the more favored economic groups in the Republican column and the less favored elements in the Democratic. This was revealed with some clarity by the campaign contributions which for the Republicans amounted to about $9 million dollars, and for the Democrats to about $5.5 million dollars. A great majority of union labor, as well as the Catholic, Negro, and Jewish minorities, had voted for Roosevelt. As a consequence the New Deal carried every large city in the country, giving the Democratic party more of an urban tinge than it had ever had before.

Roosevelt Attacks the Supreme Court. Roosevelt's overwhelming victory in 1936 no doubt furnished in part the explanation for an attack on the Supreme Court that the President launched shortly after his second inauguration. Before the election

687

he had not hesitated to express his irritation with decisions based upon precedents set in "horse-and-buggy days," but he had studiously refrained from attacking the Court during the campaign. Now, with 60 per cent of the nation's voters behind him, what might have been hazardous before seemed safe enough. That the Court majority was bitterly hostile to the New Deal seemed obvious. Out of nine important decisions involving New Deal measures, the government scored victories in only two, and in one of these the majority was only five to four. Not a single member of the Court had been appointed by Roosevelt. Of the nine members of the Court, six were more than seventy years of age, and of these six, five were consistently conservative.

There were two ways in which reform of the Court could be effected: (1) by an amendment to the Constitution, which might either require retirement at a given age or set limits to the doctrine of judicial review; (2) by a law of Congress to provide for an increase in the number of justices, thus permitting the President to "pack" the Supreme Court with new appointees of less conservative views. Determined somehow to discipline the Court, the President chose the latter alternative, but he coupled with it an ingenious provision for calling attention to the advanced age of some of the justices. The measure he urged on Congress would have set the age of seventy for the voluntary retirement of Supreme Court justices, and for each member of the Court who reached that age and failed to retire the President might appoint an additional justice until a maximum Court of fifteen members had been reached. The measure also provided for an extensive reorganization of the lower federal courts with a view to expediting business and increasing efficiency.

The President was quite unprepared for the furor that his "court-packing" bill evoked. Many Democrats professed to believe with the Republicans that a basic safeguard of American liberty was endangered, and that the President aspired to create a dictatorship. In the Senate, where the administration forces chose to stage the initial contest, Burton K. Wheeler of Montana, a left-wing Democrat in every other respect, led the opposition with infinite resourcefulness. Wheeler claimed to hold no brief for the Court as constituted, but whatever change was to be made, he asserted, should be made by constitutional amendment. In the end the President for the first time on a matter of major importance failed to carry Congress with him. Astutely led by Chief Justice Hughes, the Court itself took a major part in the proceedings; by a series of decisions favorable to the New Deal, it materially weakened the President's case. Also, Justice Willis Van Devanter, senior member of the Court in point of service and a conservative, announced his determination to take speedy advantage of the act which Congress passed March 1, 1937, granting full pay to retiring justices over seventy years of age. Finally, the sudden death of Senator Joseph Robinson, administration floor leader in charge of the Court bill, put an end to the President's hopes. Congress passed a bill which instituted some of the reforms Roosevelt had called for in the lower courts, but it left the Supreme Court intact.

Nevertheless the President soon got what he wanted most, a court less conservative in character, which would no longer stand in the way of New Deal objectives. Had he been less impatient, he might have obtained the same result with far less bitterness and party dissension. Eventually Roosevelt appointed more justices to the United States Supreme Court than any other President since Washington, and the new members he selected were invariably ardent New Dealers.

The Recession of 1937. The Supreme Court fight was barely ended when a downward trend in business, called by

Democrats a recession and by Republicans a new depression, provided the administration with another major problem. The slump came unheralded and caught most New Dealers along with everyone else unawares. It was caused in no small part by the attempt of the national government to curtail expenditures, a fact which supported the argument of Roosevelt's opponents that there had been no real recovery, but only a continuous process of pump priming. New Dealers, on the other hand, charged that capital itself had gone on strike, and that business contraction in the interest of maintaining high price levels was a principal cause of the trouble. After initial hesitation, the administration moved to halt the decline. The Board of Governors of the Federal Reserve System promptly reversed the deflationary policy it had been pursuing since the summer of 1936, and the "second New Deal," at which Congress had balked while the Court battle went on, was instituted early in 1938.

This included much additional pump priming, particularly through the WPA, the PWA, the RFC, and the USHA; the creation of a new AAA, already described, for the revival of agriculture; and somewhat belatedly (1939) a wide grant of power to the President to reorganize the federal departments of government in the interest of greater efficiency. The conviction that methods of price control had been devised in monopolistic industries led also to an attempt to enforce the moribund antitrust laws. Since the days of the ill-starred NRA these regulations had been more or less in abeyance, but the President now chose Thurman W. Arnold of Yale to be Assistant Attorney-General, and charged him with the duty of reviving them.

Elections of 1938. The "Roosevelt Recession," together with the unpopularity of the President's fight on the Supreme Court, left the New Deal vulnerable politically for the first time, and the elections of 1938

THE NINE OLD MEN

This vicious cartoon from The New Masses *caricatures the members of the Supreme Court that turned thumbs down on much New Deal legislation. Brandeis is third from the left and Stone second from the right.*

accurately recorded the shifting of public opinion. Anti-Roosevelt Democrats took a greater part than formerly in party councils, and, in spite of a demand from the President that some of his severest critics in Congress be "purged," most of them were triumphantly renominated and re-elected. The election left both houses of Congress in Democratic hands, but Republican gains included 79 seats in the House and 8 in the Senate. Moreover, after the elections it was soon apparent that many southern Democrats were no longer willing to support certain New Deal reforms. Instead they increasingly combined with middlewestern Republicans to form a conservative and antiurban coalition that was to persist for years. Many states now returned to their former Republican allegiance, electing Republican governors, or legislatures, or both. Noteworthy among these change-overs were Pennsylvania, Massachusetts, Connecticut, Michigan, Wisconsin, and Minnesota. Although 1938 marked still another Democratic victory, there was no denying that the political tide had turned. The future for conservatism and the Republican Party was much more promising.

The New Deal Balance Sheet. By 1938 the New Deal, which had been in power for six years, had made an indelible imprint upon American life. It had committed the federal government to provide for its citizens whenever economic adversity threatened the livelihood of any sizable number of them; it had attempted to manage production and prices of farm goods by subsidy and regulation; it had interfered in the financial and business life of the country to an extent hitherto undreamed of in peacetime; it had intervened in the day-to-day relations of capital and labor; it had engaged in government construction, some of which competed outright with private capital and the quantity of which had never before been equaled in American history. In doing so much, it had greatly augmented the power of the federal government, particularly that of the executive branch, had minimized the power of the states, and had even invaded some of the rights which the Constitution seemed to reserve to private citizens. The sum of these activities meant in part a final farewell to *laissez faire,* a tremendous increase in the size and power of the federal bureaucracy, and the raising and spending of unprecedented sums in peacetime.

Division of the National Income. Despite New Deal spending, taxation, and regulation, the various economic groups seemed to be getting about the same share of the national wealth in 1939 as they had in 1929. According to one study, the proportion of the national income represented by wages and salaries had risen during the period from 65.5 per cent to 68.2 per cent, and that of individual profits from 15.6 to 15.7 per cent, while interest and rents had declined from 11.5 per cent to 10.1 per cent, and corporation dividends from 7.4 per cent to 6 per cent. The farmer's real income in the period probably increased more than that of any other group, while people living on fixed incomes suffered most. At the beginning of 1939 there were still 8 million to 10 million unemployed in the United States, while millions of families continued to live below what the Department of Labor called a subsistence level. Unemployment in the United States did not disappear, and the per capita national income did not rise to its 1929 level, until the war spending of the forties began to affect the national economy. But in recreating confidence in the business and financial structure during these dreary years, the Roosevelt policies had served an essential purpose. By providing jobs to the unemployed and feeding the destitute, the New Deal obviously prevented any great drift of public opinion to either the extreme left or right. Its contribution to American life through the construction of roads, streets, schools, parks, swimming pools, and playgrounds was incalculable. One art historian has recently written that no government since that of Periclean Athens had so stimulated architecture, painting, and music. But probably the greatest achievement of the New Deal was to recreate a feeling of confidence in the American people that the government at Washington was really their government, and that it could be used just as energetically to fight the enemies of the good life within the country as to fight an enemy attack from without.

After the elections of 1938 the New Deal program called for little additional reform, but looked rather toward defending the advances already made. Some of this growing caution unquestionably stemmed from the President's awareness that the country and Congress were in no mood for continued domestic innovations, and some of it from his growing preoccupation with foreign affairs. For by 1938 most well-informed statesmen recognized that civilization was faced with the imminent danger of a second world war.

SELECTED BIBLIOGRAPHY

The finest survey of this period is provided by W. E. Leuchtenburg, *Franklin D. Roosevelt and the New Deal, 1932–1940* (1963). An excellent double-biography is A. B. Rollins, Jr., *Roosevelt and Howe* (1962). R. G. Tugwell, *The Democratic Roosevelt* (1957), is rich in insight. Dexter Perkins, *The New Age of Franklin Roosevelt, 1932–1945* (1957), is a brief overview, generally sympathetic and stressing foreign policy. D. W. Brogan, *The Era of Franklin D. Roosevelt* (1950), is lively and well-informed, the work of a Britisher who knows American politics. Basil Rauch, *The History of the New Deal, 1933–1938* (1944), is a pioneer effort at synthesis, highly sympathetic. John Gunther, *Roosevelt in Retrospect* (1950), is popular, anecdotal and "pro." A hostile view of F.D.R. and his work is E. E. Robinson, *The Roosevelt Leadership, 1933–1945* (1955), a book by a conservative whose hero is Hoover. J. M. Burns, *Roosevelt: The Lion and the Fox* (1956), stresses domestic politics of the first two terms and seems to argue that Roosevelt could have achieved more if he had been less opportunistic. Two scholarly studies of Roosevelt's thinking, both stressing his consistency, are D. R. Fusfeld, *The Economic Thought of Franklin D. Roosevelt and the Origins of the New Deal* (1956); and T. H. Greer, *What Roosevelt Thought* (1958).

A. M. Schlesinger, Jr., *The Coming of the New Deal* (1958), and *The Politics of Upheaval* (1960), II and III in his monumental *The Age of Roosevelt*, cover domestic affairs in the first administration. Interesting collections which bring out some of the varying interpretations of the period are E. C. Rozwenc (ed.), *The New Deal* (2nd ed., 1959); and Morton Keller (ed.), *The New Deal* (1963). An excellent volume of readings is *The New Deal and the American People*, edited by Frank Freidel (1964). The active part played by the President himself is apparent from *The Public Papers and Addresses of Franklin D. Roosevelt*, compiled by S. I. Rosenman (13 vols., 1938–1950).

New Dealers have provided us with an abundance of memoirs. *The Secret Diary of Harold L. Ickes* (3 vols., 1953–1954), gives a running account, often gossipy and petty, of events from 1933 to Pearl Harbor. Fascinating details are given in *The Journals of David E. Lilienthal* (2 vols., 1964). J. M. Blum, *From the Morgenthau Diaries* (2 vols., 1959–   ), is an able distillation of a great mass of data compiled by the Secretary of the Treasury. Frances Perkins, *The Roosevelt I Knew* (1946), is the warm and friendly reminiscence of the Secretary of Labor. S. I. Rosenman, *Working with Roosevelt* (1953), tells a great deal about the preparation of the President's speeches. R. L. Moley, *After Seven Years* (1939), the earliest important memoir is harsh in its judgment, as is J. A. Farley, *Jim Farley's Story; The Roosevelt Years* (1948). Eleanor Roosevelt published a number of volumes of reminiscences, including *This Is My Story* (1937), and *This I Remember* (1949). Other memoirs include Grace Tully, *F.D.R., My Boss* (1949), by one of the President's private secretaries; E. J. Flynn, *You're the Boss* (1947), by the boss of the Bronx; M. S. Eccles,

* Available in paperback

Beckoning Frontiers (1951); and Francis Biddle, *In Brief Authority* (1962). R. E. Sherwood, °*Roosevelt and Hopkins* (2nd ed., 1950), based upon the Hopkins Papers, is brilliantly written but thin on the prewar period.

On relief, the standard work is D. S. Howard, *The WPA and Federal Relief Policy* (1943), full and richly detailed. See also S. F. Charles, *Minister of Relief; Harry Hopkins and the Depression* (1963). On recovery, a comprehensive discussion is in the Brookings Institution, *The Recovery Program in the United States* (1936). J. M. Keynes, °*General Theory of Employment, Interest and Money* (1936), is presented in simplified form by Joan Robinson, *Introduction to the Theory of Employment* (1937). Important works by Keynes's chief American apostle are A. H. Hansen, *Full Recovery or Stagnation?* (1938), and *Fiscal Policy and Business Cycles* (1941). L. S. Lyon and others, *The National Recovery Administration* (1935), is an early assessment; on the NRA see also H. S. Johnson, *The Blue Eagle from Egg to Earth* (1935); and Sidney Fine, *The Automobile under the Blue Eagle* (1963). The social situation in one city is clearly presented in R. S. and H. M. Lynd, °*Middletown in Transition* (1937).

On labor, a collection of essays by various authorities, *Labor and the New Deal*, edited by Milton Derber and Edwin Young (1957), is a good introduction. Irving Bernstein, *The New Deal Collective Bargaining Policy* (1950), traces administration policy to the passage of the Wagner Act. Walter Galenson, *The CIO Challenge to the AFL; A History of the American Labor Movement, 1935–1941* (1960), is a massive work by a competent scholar. Contemporary accounts of the labor split include Benjamin Stolberg, *The Story of the CIO* (1938); Edward Levinson, *Labor on the March* (1938); and Herbert Harris, *Labor's Civil War* (1940). An interesting memoir is John Brophy, *A Miner's Life*, edited by J. O. P. Hall (1964). See also: Irving Howe and B. J. Widick, *The UAW and Walter Reuther* (1949); C. R. Walker, *American City* (1937), on the great Minneapolis strike of 1934; and B. W. Newell, *Chicago and the Labor Movement; Metropolitan Unionism in the 1930's* (1961). A provocative discussion of some notable labor and radical figures is in Murray Kempton, *Part of Our Time* (1955). A good study of a leading Catholic friend of

labor is F. L. Broderick, *Right Reverend New Dealer, John A. Ryan* (1963).

On agriculture, see two careful evaluations of New Deal farm policies and their long-range implications: M. R. Benedict, *Can We Solve the Farm Problem?* (1955); and M. R. Benedict and O. C. Stine, *The Agricultural Commodity Programs; Two Decades of Experience* (1956). Russell Lord, *The Wallaces of Iowa* (1947), gives a sympathetic view of the Secretary of Agriculture. Wallace's successor is treated in Dean Albertson, *Roosevelt's Farmer: Claude R. Wickard in the New Deal* (1961). Other useful scholarly studies on agriculture include C. M. Campbell, *The Farm Bureau and the New Deal* (1964); and Wilma Dykeman and James Stokely, *Seeds of Southern Change: The Life of Will Alexander* (1962). Special studies of New Deal community projects are P. K. Conkin, *Tomorrow a New World* (1959), an over-all analysis; and E. C. Banfield, *Government Project* (1951), a case study of a single attempt in Arizona, rich in human interest. Bernard Sternsher, *Rexford Tugwell and the New Deal* (1964), is a verbose study of a leading agricultural reformer.

Conservative criticisms of the New Deal's alleged "regimentation" may be found in Herbert Hoover, *The Challenge to Liberty* (1934). The story of the leading right-wing group of the period is well told by George Wolfskill, *The Revolt of the Conservatives: A History of the American Liberty League, 1934–1940* (1962). D. R. McCoy's forthcoming biography of Landon is eagerly awaited. Interesting short studies of dissident groups are in D. R. McCoy, *Angry Voices; Left-of-Center Politics in the New Deal Era* (1958), which treats the Coughlin crusade, but not the Socialists or Communists. On Coughlin, see especially C. J. Tull, *Father Coughlin and the New Deal* (1965); on Lemke, see E. C. Blackorby, *Prairie Rebel* (1963).

On banking and currency, see A. W. Crawford, *Monetary Management under the New Deal* (1940); E. A. Goldenweiser, *American Monetary Policy* (1951); and A. D. Gayer (ed.), *The Lessons of Monetary Experience* (1937). A lively survey of monetary panaceas is J. E. Reeve, *Monetary Reform Movements* (1943). Two good monographs on Treasury policy are G. G. Johnson, Jr., *The Treasury and Monetary Policy, 1933–1938* (1939); and

A. S. Everest, *Morgenthau, the New Deal, and Silver* (1950).

The trade agreements program has been treated in a number of works, among them G. L. Beckett, *The Reciprocal Trade Agreements Program* (1941); and J. M. Letiche, *Reciprocal Trade Agreements in the World Economy* (1948). On railroad coordination, see C. M. Fuess, *Joseph B. Eastman, Servant of the People* (1952), a good documented biography of the program's administrator. Interesting books on housing include M. W. Straus and Talbott Wegg, *Housing Comes of Age* (1938); and Nathan Straus, *Seven Myths of Housing* (2nd ed., 1945).

The literature on TVA is large and chiefly laudatory. Views of two of its administrators are set forth in D. E. Lilienthal, *TVA; Democracy on the March* (2nd ed., 1953); and G. R. Clapp, *The TVA: An Approach to the Development of a Region* (1955). C. H. Pritchett, *The Tennessee Valley Authority, A Study in Public Administration* (1943), a favorable view, should be contrasted with the more critical Philip Selznik, *TVA and the Grass Roots* (1949). A rich study which examines efforts to establish a Connecticut Valley Authority is W. E. Leuchtenburg, *Flood Control Politics; the Connecticut River Valley Problem, 1927–1950* (1953). On rural electrification, see K. E. Trombley, *The Life and Times of a Happy Liberal; A Biography of Morris Llewellyn Cooke* (1954); and F. W. Muller, *Public Rural Electrification* (1944).

The best work on social security is E. E. Witte, *The Development of the Social Security Act* (1962). Other good books on this subject include Abraham Epstein, *Insecurity* (2nd ed., 1938), which points out the limitations of the act; and Lewis Meriam, *Relief and Social Security* (1946). An excellent scholarly study is Abraham Holtzman, *The Townsend Movement* (1963).

The controversy over the Supreme Court produced a vast amount of writing. Among the works paving the way for the attempted reform of the Court was the celebrated muckraking book by Drew Pearson and R. S. Allen, *The Nine Old Men* (1936). R. H. Jackson, *The Struggle for Judicial Supremacy* (1941), gives some of the background; it should be compared with the biography of Jackson by E. C. Gerhart, *America's Advocate* (1958). Joseph Alsop and Turner Catledge, *The 168*

Days (1938), is a lively journalistic account of the Court fight. A good collection of sources and diverse interpretations is A. H. Cope and Fred Krinsky (eds.), *Franklin D. Roosevelt and the Supreme Court* (1952). An assessment by E. S. Corwin, *Constitutional Revolution, Ltd.* (2nd ed., 1946), may be compared with the larger study by C. H. Pritchett, *The Roosevelt Court* (1948).

One aspect of the ideology of the later New Deal is developed by T. W. Arnold, *The Folklore of Capitalism* (1937). The most comprehensive analysis of the 1937–1938 recession is K. D. Roose, *The Economics of Recession and Revival* (1954). On TNEC, a competent survey is David Lynch, *The Concentration of Economic Power* (1946). Other valuable special studies include R. F. de Bedts, *The New Deal's SEC* (1964); and B. D. Karl, *Executive Reorganization and Reform in the New Deal* (1963).

State politics of the New Deal era is the subject of a number of scholarly studies. On the New Deal South, see the brilliant analysis by V. O. Key, *Southern Politics in State and Nation* (1949); A. P. Sindler, *Huey Long's Louisiana: State Politics, 1920–1952* (1956); W. D. Miller, *Mr. Crump of Memphis* (1964); and Frank Freidel, *F.D.R. and the South* (1964). On California, see *I, Candidate for Governor and How I Got Licked* (1935), a colorful first-hand account of the EPIC campaign by Upton Sinclair; and R. E. Burke, *Olson's New Deal for California* (1953). On the Minnesota Farmer-Labor movement, see G. H. Mayer, *The Political Career of Floyd B. Olson* (1951). On New York, see the critical study of La Guardia's mayorality by Charles Garrett, *The La Guardia Years* (1961); and Allan Nevins, *Herbert H. Lehman and His Era* (1963).

On Canadian-American affairs, see J. M. Callahan, *American Foreign Policy in Canadian Relations* (1937); and J. B. Brebner, *The North Atlantic Triangle* (1945). A general treatment of the Good Neighbor policy is E. O. Guerrant, *Roosevelt's Good Neighbor Policy* (1950). A first-rate monograph on one vital area is E. D. Cronon, *Josephus Daniels in Mexico* (1960). On Puerto Rico, a good survey to 1938 is Thomas Mathews, *Puerto Rican Politics and the New Deal* (1960); a vivid report by the Governor of the later period is R. G. Tugwell, *The Stricken Land* (1947).

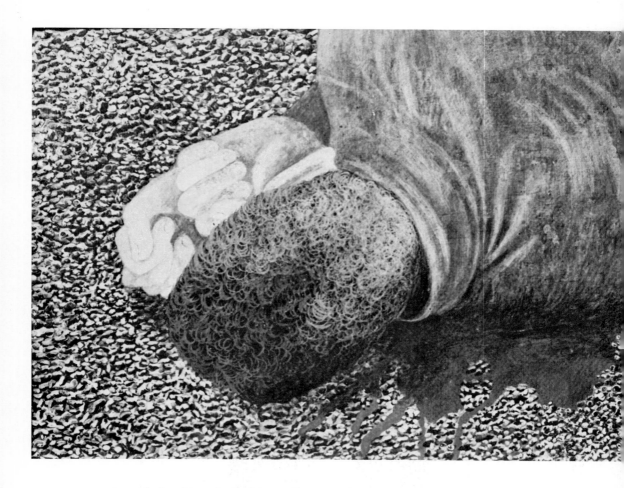

Ben Shahn, "Death on the Beach — 1945." From the collection of Rosalie Berkowitz, Courtesy of The Downtown Gallery.

The Price of

Leadership

· 1939–1965 ·

Why should I not make an agreement in good faith today and unhesitatingly break it tomorrow if the future of the German people demands it?

ADOLF HITLER

An iron curtain has descended across the continent.

WINSTON CHURCHILL

This limited test ban, in our most careful judgment, is safer by far for the United States than an unlimited nuclear arms race.

JOHN F. KENNEDY

39

WORLD CRISIS

The Russian Revolution. In the two decades after the First World War Americans who had enthusiastically supported the struggle "to make the world safe for democracy" suffered many disappointments. The failure of the United States to accept responsibility for anything that happened outside its borders was in itself disillusioning. But even more distressing was the discovery that democracy, both in Europe and in Asia, was on the wane; that dictatorships of such magnitude as modern times had never known were being created; that the arbitrary will of autocrats to war, against which Wilson had hoped the League of Nations would insure the world, was present in an increasingly aggravated form. The League of Nations was duly organized, but its weakness in the face of the appalling problems that confronted it soon became painfully apparent. The League was little used,

contrary to Wilson's hopes, to eradicate some of the more glaring political and economic injustices written into the Peace of Paris, but rather more as a policeman to maintain the terms of the war settlement. Thus for the defeated nations and for those which had not obtained all they had hoped to get from the peace, it stood in the way of their national ambitions and was often treated as an enemy. Moreover, without the United States and particularly after the rise of the nationalist dictatorships, the League was a policeman with questionable power. What the League might have been had the United States chosen to be one of its leading members is a matter of conjecture. But the strength it was able to muster without American assistance was insufficient to stem the tide that led to war.

The first of the great upheavals was the Russian revolution of March, 1917, against the Tsarist government. After a few months' existence, the democratic regime headed by Kerensky was overthrown by the Communists led by Lenin and Trotsky. By the end of 1922, the two had organized the Union of Soviet Socialist Republics as a revolutionary nation committed to the radical doctrines of Karl Marx and Friedrich Engels. They seized and socialized most of the private property in the state, liquidated their enemies, and established a "dictatorship of the proletariat" whose power rested with the small ruling group — or Presidium — of

696

the Communist Party, the only political organization allowed to survive.

An original tenet of Communist policy was that national revolution was only a prelude to world revolution. With this goal in mind Lenin founded in 1919 the Third International or Comintern with headquarters in Moscow. Communist leaders in most nations looked to this central agency for guidance and support. The success of the Russian revolution spurred Communist activity everywhere, and from 1918 on the fear of other successful, Communist-inspired revolutions throughout the world was a persistent factor in the foreign and domestic policies of many states. But after the death of Lenin in 1924 and the accession of Josef Stalin as his successor, Russian policy for a time veered away from world revolution and emphasized the building of socialism in Russia alone. Trotsky, a believer in immediate world revolution, was exiled, and three successive "five year plans" were undertaken to make Russia industrially and agriculturally self-sustaining, and thus able to defend herself in case of war. This new Russian posture allayed somewhat the fears of most capitalist nations, and in 1934 Russia was invited to become a member of the League of Nations, where for the next four years she was a leader in arguing for collective security against potential aggression. Until the Roosevelt administration, the United States persistently refused to recognize the Soviet Union, in part because of its repudiation of all pre-1919 debts, but mostly because the stated purpose of its government was the overthrow of institutions most Americans held dear. After the outbreak of the Great Depression, many Americans argued that there was more to be gained than lost by resuming diplomatic relations. And after the Roosevelt administration received assurances from the Soviet government that it would refrain from "agitation and propaganda within the United States," recognition was accorded in November, 1933. Despite the growing acceptability of the Soviet

LENIN AND STALIN

The dual leadership of the original Bolshevik revolt ended with the death of Lenin, the exile of Trotsky, and the elevation of Stalin to supreme control. Later, when Bulganin and Khrushchev succeeded Stalin, Bulganin was soon dropped. What will happen to the present team?

government in international circles, mutual suspicion between the western democratic nations and the Communists remained, generated on the one side by Russia's continued support of Communist revolutionary parties throughout the world, and on the other by the Soviet fear that the capitalist countries were bent upon destroying Communism everywhere.

The Rise of Italian Fascism. The year 1922 witnessed the rise of another European dictator, Benito Mussolini. Aided by the chaotic condition of the existing democratic regime in Italy and the possibility of a Communist revolution, Mussolini and his Black Shirt followers through the threat of force took over the government and rapidly proceeded to destroy democratic institutions. Since Fascism, as Mussolini called his movement, posed no immediate threat

697

to capitalism — indeed, free unions and strikes were outlawed — and since he designated international Communism as the chief enemy of Fascism, he obtained a good deal of sympathy from the propertied classes in all countries. By instituting a relatively efficient government able to keep order, the Fascists also won considerable international support. But in the realm of foreign affairs, Mussolini's flamboyant nationalism, his encouragement of Italian militarists, and his expansionist claims on the Mediterranean, the Balkans, and Africa boded ill for the continued peace of southern Europe.

Because of the relatively backward state of Italian industrialism, and the poverty of both the land and its people, Fascist Italy by itself was scarcely a major threat to the peace of Europe. But the National Socialist or Nazi revolution in Germany was something far different. The continued weakness of the German Weimar democratic republic, the desire to revenge the defeat of 1918, the hope of recovering the lost German territories, the rising threat of Communism, and finally the withering effects of the great depression all played into the hands of Adolf Hitler, who, with a shrewd combination of force, rabble rousing, and politics, made himself chancellor of Germany in February, 1933. Soon, the last vestige of democracy was wiped out, and the nazification of the state was complete. Henceforth Hitler was Germany's only "Führer," and a powerful secret police suppressed the slightest show of criticism. Germany, like Russia and Italy, had become a totalitarian dictatorship; in every instance the individual existed for the state, not the state for the individual.

Nazism. The Nazi ideology, like the Fascist, was less noted for common sense and consistency than for its appeal to the prejudices that Hitler found about him. The Nazis adopted in full the "stab-in-the-back" legend that Germany had been betrayed in 1918, not defeated, and demanded the complete overthrow of the Versailles settlement. This was held to be Germany's due, not merely because of injustices in the treaty, but because Germans, as members of the master race, had superior rights. Racism, more than anything else, was basic in the Nazi philosophy. The "Nordic," or "Aryan," race, of which the Germans were held to be the only really pure strain, was born to command; all other "races," Latin, Slav, Semite, Negro, Oriental, existed merely to take orders. Racial purity, in the Nazi scheme of things, was supremely important; mixtures with "impure" blood were an intolerable affront to the race. The Jewish "race," of all races, was the most reprehensible. It was both parasitic and unassimilable, the source of most of the woes of the world. Acting on these principles, the Nazis ordered the most fiendish persecutions of the Jews on the slightest pretexts.

Closely akin to racism was German nationalism; internationalism to the Nazis was the quintessence of evil. Communism, which looked forward to world revolution, was the worst of all, but such international institutions as the Roman Catholic Church, the Masonic order, and the League of Nations came likewise under the ban. Furthermore, the German nation must have room to grow — *Lebensraum*. To fulfill its mission it must expand its borders to include the "heartland" of the European continent. To this end Hitler demanded an increase in the German birth rate — there should be 250 million Germans instead of only 80 million. The German colonies, too, must be returned, and German power recognized throughout the world.

The Rise of Japanese Militarism. While the safety of democracy in Europe and America was being thus imperiled, news of alarming developments came also out of Asia. Although the government of Japan had been changed late in the nineteenth century to harmonize somewhat with Occidental practices, the theory of popular sovereignty had always been effectively excluded. The state was in a sense a theocracy, for the Emperor was worshiped as the Son of Heaven, and such privileges of government as were extended to the people were held to be merely gifts emanating from the divine will. In actual practice the Emperor was subject to the control of a small group of "elder statesmen" and privy councilors, whose advice he dared not reject. A parliament in the form of a two-house Diet existed, but the Cabinet was responsible only to the Emperor, and a peculiarly independent status was assigned to the ministers of War and Navy. Invariably these men were selected from among the highest-ranking active officers of the branches concerned.

During the First World War, Japan had enjoyed an unusual prosperity. Her military contribution to the defeat of the Central Powers had been comparatively slight, but she had profited greatly from the sale of war goods to the Allies and from their use of her excellent fleet of merchantmen. After the war, American purchases of Japanese silk staved off economic disaster, but the Great Depression cut down American buying power and seriously imperiled Japanese prosperity. This situation played directly into the hands of the nation's powerful military leaders, who had long maintained that Japan need only essay the role of conqueror to get whatever she needed. War would bring plunder, and was thus an end in itself, but the military leaders had much civilian support for the theory that Japanese expansion was an economic necessity.

First on the list was Manchuria. Japanese bankers and industrialists were already entrenched there, but they were eager for the economic monopoly that conquest would bring them. After Manchuria much of China might be taken, and, if the time was propitious, the European and American dominions in eastern Asia and the Indies. Various terms were used to cloak the Japanese designs. Whether known as a "Monroe Doctrine for Asia," or the "New Order," or the "Co-Prosperity Sphere," what the Japanese leaders really wanted was a Far East exclusively dominated politically, economically, and socially by Japan.

Manchukuo. The Manchurian "incident" of 1931 was the beginning of a procession of events that led directly toward the Second World War. On the faintest pretexts, Japanese troops occupied large sections of Manchuria, organized it into the satellite state of Manchukuo, and set a puppet Emperor on its throne. Because this act of aggression constituted a direct violation of the Kellogg-Briand Peace Pact, the United States refused to recognize Manchukuo. But since the Hoover administration refused to support Secretary Stimson's policy with economic or military pressure, even to the extent of promising to cooperate with proposed sanctions of the League of Nations, America's protests had no effect upon the Japanese expansionists. When the League of Nations voiced mild disapproval, Japan summarily gave notice of her intent to withdraw from the League.

THE NEW FASCIST CORPS

Benito Mussolini, in a typical pose, reviews the passing parade on the twentieth anniversary of Italy's entrance into World War I.

The Chinese "Incident." One result of Japanese aggression was to unite the faction-torn Chinese for self-defense. Even the deeply antagonistic Nationalists under Chiang Kai-shek and the Communists under Chang Hsueh-liang found ways of cooperating under Chiang Kai-shek as Generalissimo. When, therefore, the Japanese decided in 1937 to prosecute an undeclared war against China, their troops were confronted by organized opposition. But the Chinese were no match for the well-trained and well-supplied Japanese armies, who soon had under their control most of the Chinese seacoast and much of the adjacent interior. While the Japanese refused to admit that the China "incident" was a war, the League of Nations seemed to regard it as such, and after much delay recommended that the various member nations extend what aid they could to China. Over the Burma Road, which by 1938 American-trained engineers had completed with the use of Chinese labor, China was able to import some useful war materials, and eventually both the British and the American governments extended credits to China. An incident of the war was the destruction on December 12, 1937, by Japanese bombers, of an American gunboat, the *Panay*. The act seemed deliberate, but the American public was apathetic and the apologies of the Japanese government were accepted.

Ethiopia. Meantime, the dictatorships in Europe were also on the march. In 1935, Mussolini began a war of conquest against Ethiopia, with the avowed intent of adding that African kingdom to his empire. This venture was so fraught with peril for the peace of Europe that for a time it seemed as if the League of Nations might employ effective economic sanctions to prevent it. If Italy could be kept from obtaining oil, it appeared that war could not go on. But the League finally backed down. It applied sanctions, but not the oil sanctions that alone were well calculated to achieve results. The British navy, upon which the

main brunt of enforcing the sanctions would have fallen, was inadequately prepared for war, and no state wanted to risk the disruption of world trade, which was just recovering from depression levels. Mussolini went ahead, practically unimpeded, with his plan of conquest, drove the Ethiopian monarch, Haile Selassie, into exile, and on May 9, 1936, announced that the Italian King had also assumed the title of Emperor.

The Spanish Civil War. Inflated with one victory, Mussolini soon sought another. When in 1936 a revolt broke out in Spain against the democratic government of the Spanish Republic, Mussolini sent his "legions" to the aid of the revolutionary leader, General Francisco Franco, whose Fascist tendencies were unmistakable. Aid for Franco came also from Germany, and help for the "Loyalists," as the government forces were called, came from Russia. The civil war in Spain was widely recognized as a dress rehearsal for the coming world war, but the democratic nations were unwilling to do anything effective for the Loyalists, who, after a bitter and bloody struggle, were defeated. In General Franco, the new dictator of Spain, both Hitler and Mussolini recognized a kindred spirit and a potential ally.

Appeasement. Only those who wished to be deceived could believe that Hitler's rise to power in Germany would not still further unsettle the peace of Europe. In 1933, Germany gave notice of her withdrawal from the League of Nations; two years later, after the required plebiscite, she took back the Saar Basin; next year, in 1936, German troops reoccupied and remilitarized the Rhineland; two years after that they occupied Austria and incorporated that formerly independent state into Hitler's "Third Reich." The portion of German *Lebensraum* next coveted by Hitler was Czechoslovakia, which Germany now almost completely surrounded, but the Führer chose at first to demand only the Sudetenland, a strip along the Czech-German border mainly inhabited by Germans. To retain this region, which was essential to her defense, Czechoslovakia was ready to fight. Russia had already promised her aid in repelling a Nazi invasion, but in the end Czechoslovakia was betrayed by nations she had thought were her friends, France and England. Among the peoples of the western democracies pacifism had become passion; any settlement seemed better to them than war. Accordingly, their governments were probably in accord with the weight of public opinion when they proposed to keep Germany at peace by a policy of "appeasement." Prime Minister Chamberlain of Great Britain and Premier Daladier of France met with Hitler and Mussolini at Munich in September, 1938, to find a solution short of war. They found it by demanding that Czechoslovakia yield to Hitler's requests in return for a solemn German promise that this would be Hitler's last expansion in Europe. But in March, 1939, all of Czechoslovakia was occupied by Hitler. Not to be outdone, Mussolini the very next month transported an army across the Adriatic and took possession of Albania.

Rome-Berlin Axis. By this time the bond of friendship which had formed between Hitler and Mussolini, soon after the former's accession to power, was also extended to Japan. The objection of all three nations to the spread of Communism found expression in the Anti-Comintern Pact signed by Germany and Japan in 1936, and adhered to by Italy in 1937. Then in May, 1939, immediately following the Czechoslovakian and Albanian incidents, Germany and Italy concluded also a ten-year military alliance — the "Rome-Berlin Axis." The agreement pledged that if either power should become involved in war, the other would come to its aid "with all its military forces, on land, sea, and in the air." Rumor had it that the next expansionist effort of the Axis Powers would be the acquisition of Tunisia by Italy.

End of Appeasement. What Mussolini had done in the Balkans, Great Britain and France were prepared to discount, but Hitler's absorption of Czechoslovakia, in complete disregard of his promise that the Sudetenland would be his final conquest, brought appeasement to an end. That Hitler intended to press on with his program of expansion was at last clear to all. From Lithuania he demanded, and received, Memel. From Poland he demanded under threat of war consent to the restoration of the free city of Danzig to the Reich, and to the building of a German highway and railroad across the Polish Corridor. With British and French opinion now running strongly against further appeasement, Prime Minister Chamberlain, with the full support of the French government, as well as his own, promised Poland all possible aid should her independence be threatened. Similar guarantees were soon given Greece and Rumania, and an Anglo-Turkish pact provided for mutual assistance "in the event of aggression leading to war in the Mediterranean area." France began to patch up her differences with Turkey over Syria, and even the United States showed concern. President Roosevelt, in a message of April 16, 1939, to the Axis dictators, asked them for assurance that they would not invade thirty named states. The recipients of the message treated it with a display of ridicule, which did little to reassure an anxious world.

The Russian-German Accord. Throughout these proceedings the great enigma had been Russia. That the signers of the Anti-Comintern Pact had anything but hatred for the Soviet system could hardly be doubted; they made it plain on every possible occasion that they intended to destroy it. But the western democracies had also had their suspicions of Russia; was not the Comintern as much dedicated to their destruction as

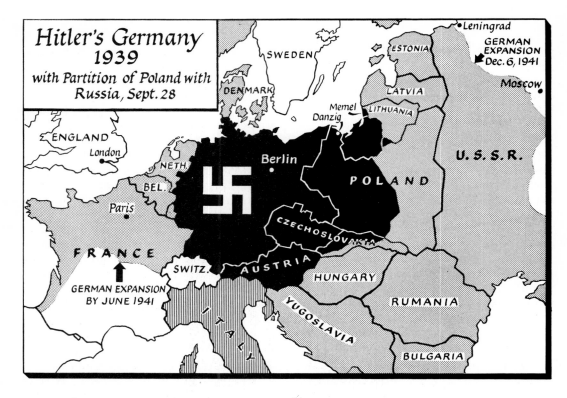

**Hitler's Germany
1939**
*with Partition of Poland with
Russia, Sept. 28*

SWEDEN

DENMARK

ENGLAND
London

NETH.

BEL.

Paris

FRANCE

SWITZ.

GERMAN EXPANSION
BY JUNE 1941

ITALY

Berlin

AUSTRIA

Memel
Danzig

Leningrad
GERMAN
EXPANSION
Dec. 6, 1941

Moscow

ESTONIA

LATVIA

LITHUANIA

U.S.S.R.

POLAND

CZECHOSLOVAKIA

HUNGARY

YUGOSLAVIA

RUMANIA

BULGARIA

to that of the Axis Powers? During the negotiations that preceded Munich, Russia had been deliberately slighted. In that conference, which decided the fate of Czechoslovakia, one of Russia's near neighbors, no Russian had been permitted a voice. Talk was rife that Britain and France were building up Nazi Germany as a counterweight to Soviet Russia, and that a war to the death between Germany and Russia was their real objective. However this may have been, both Great Britain and France seemed, by March, 1939, to be eager for Russian collaboration, and a special British envoy was sent to Russia to negotiate an Anglo-Soviet pact. Throughout the summer of 1939, while Hitler voiced more and more threats against Poland, these negotiations continued, but without results. Then, to the amazement of most of the world, came the announcement that Russia and Germany had agreed late in August to a commercial pact for the exchange of German manufactured goods for Russian raw materials, and to a nonaggression pact by which each nation would respect the territory and sov-

ereignty of the other. Thus reinforced, Hitler went ahead in a three weeks' *Blitzkrieg* to conquer two-thirds of Poland, leaving the rest of that unhappy country to Russia.

The Second World War. In response to the frantic demands of Poland, Great Britain and France on September 3, 1939, declared war on Germany, but they were able to do nothing to restrain the rapid Nazi drive. Both nations mobilized fully; the British re-established the blockade they had found so effective in the First World War, and the French manned their touted Maginot Line. But for more than half a year there was little real fighting in the West, and the situation came to be called a "phony war." Stalin, however, took quick advantage of the opportunity to overrun Russia's former Baltic provinces, Latvia, Lithuania, and Estonia. His efforts to invade Finland, however, met with stiff resistance. The tenacity with which the Finns defended their borders against the vastly superior foe excited amazement. But the odds against the Finns were too great, and in March, 1940, the Finnish government made peace. By the terms agreed upon, the Finnish boundaries were "rectified," but her independence was left intact.

The Fall of France. In April, 1940, the "phony war" in the West came to a sudden end. Hitler's armies overran Denmark and Norway, the former without resistance, and the latter in spite of all the help that Allied ships and troops could give. In May the Nazi *Blitzkrieg* struck Belgium and Holland with devastating fury, and by the end of June it had brought them, as well as France, to surrender. Two weeks before France admitted defeat, Mussolini brought Italy into the war on Hitler's side, while the lesser nations of Europe that had not yet been conquered made every effort to curry favor with the victorious Germans. To most observers the invasion of England appeared imminent. The army that the British had landed on the Continent was able, almost miraculously, to withdraw at Dunkirk, but it had lost practically all its equipment and appeared to be easy prey for the conquering foe. Only the royal air and naval forces blocked the way. Fully mindful of this fact, the British navy took prompt action to keep as many French warships as possible out of Hitler's hands. British naval forces attacked, and in large part destroyed, the French squadron at Oran in North Africa on July 3, 1940, and persuaded a similar squadron at Alexandria to remain immobilized.

In desperate but still defiant mood, the British prepared to carry on the war alone. "I have nothing to offer," said the new Prime Minister, Winston Churchill, "but blood, toil, tears, and sweat." As if to help redeem this pledge the German *Luftwaffe* began an aerial bombardment of Great Britain in August that destroyed large sections of London, as well as many other British cities, and lasted through the entire fall and winter. In fallen France, now ready to concede a German victory, a government subject to German dictation was set up at Vichy, with southeastern France and the overseas empire, theoretically at least, under its control. The Chief-of-State, aged Marshal Pétain, struggled with only slight success to maintain the fiction of French independence. Most of the other conquered countries established exile governments in London, where also a faction of "Free French," under the leadership of General Charles de Gaulle, claimed to represent France. Thus the British Isles remained one of the last bastions of freedom throughout once democratic Europe. Great Britain with her empire, in fact, now stood alone against the organized might of the dictators. Upon her hung the fate not only of Europe but also of Africa and Asia.

The "Good Neighbor" Policy. The New Deal that Roosevelt had inaugurated in the United States at about the time Hitler came to power in Germany was primarily concerned with domestic affairs. But it was not overlooked that danger to the American continent existed from the aggressor nations of Europe and Asia. Partly on this account the traditional American interest in securing Latin-American friendship was greatly intensified under Roosevelt. He quickly let it be known that his policy toward Latin America was to be that of the "good neighbor." He sent Secretary Hull to the Pan-American Conference in Montevideo, and cordially approved the doctrine on which the Conference agreed, that "no state has the right to intervene in the internal or external affairs of another." In 1936, he journeyed 7,000 miles by sea to Buenos Aires in order to open a special Inter-American Conference for the Maintenance of Peace, and told delegates that non-American states seeking "to commit acts of aggression against us will find a Hemisphere wholly prepared to consult together for our mutual safety and our mutual good."

Cuba. A practical demonstration of how the "good neighbor" policy might be expected to operate was given in the case of Cuba, which dared at last to attempt the overthrow by revolution of its current

HITLER SALUTES HIS TROOPS

The occasion for this Berlin parade was the re-enactment, July 4, 1936, of the historic march through Weimar on the tenth anniversary of the first Nazi Party Congress.

dictator, Gerardo Machado. The depression which began in 1929 became particularly acute in Cuba after the passage in 1930 of the Hawley-Smoot Tariff, which increased the rates on sugar imported into the United States. Machado, a tyrant who had maintained himself in office since 1924, should normally have been one of the first casualties of the depression. But American investors in Cuban securities liked him, for he consistently made the interest payments due on the huge sums that the Cuban government had borrowed in the United States. Out of deference to their wishes the Hoover administration had so strongly supported Machado that the Cubans dared not revolt. When Roosevelt became President, he let it be known that Machado could expect no further backing from the American government. As a result the dictator was promptly driven from office. Unfortunately, however, the government succeeding him lasted only three weeks, when another revolution occurred. Undoubtedly American pressure was applied from this time forward to insure the establishment of an orderly and competent government in the island, but no American troops were landed, and American interests were watched over exclusively by recognized diplomatic agents. For the first time since the Spanish-American War a serious revolutionary outbreak in Cuba came to an end without military intervention by the United States. Furthermore, on May 29, 1934, a treaty between the United States and Cuba formally abrogated the Platt Amendment, which for a generation had rankled the Cubans. That same year a reciprocal trade treaty materially reduced the tariff on Cuban exports to the United States and checked the decline of Cuban-American trade.

Other evidence that the "big stick" policy was really at an end accumulated rapidly. By an agreement reached in August, 1934, the financial receivership which the United

States maintained in Haiti was greatly liberalized, and the last detachment of American marines was ordered to leave the republic. About the same time negotiations were begun with Panama to abolish the special privileges that that nation had been forced to accord the United States, and after a long delay this, too, was accomplished. But the real test of the Good Neighbor policy came in Mexico, where many citizens of the United States still held major investments, particularly in the extractive industries. The drastic Mexican law of 1938 expropriating all foreign-held oil properties was met with investor-inspired demands for stern action and, if necessary, the use of force. Roosevelt, however, refused to scuttle the Good Neighbor policy, and a potentially explosive situation was solved by mild if protracted diplomatic negotiations.

The Philippines. In a part of the world far distant from Latin America, the early New Deal's anti-imperialist policy and the growing menace to world peace also affected American relations with the Philippines, which were scheduled to obtain complete independence on July 4, 1946. In accordance with the Tydings-McDuffie Act of 1934, they had become an autonomous Commonwealth with a President of their choosing and an elective National Assembly. Except for control over foreign relations and a few other specified restrictions, the Philippine nationalists had obtained practically all the political liberty they sought, but they were still far from happy. They knew full well that the economic prosperity of the islands had been built upon freedom of trade with the United States, a privilege that was now to be gradually withdrawn. They knew also that independence would carry with it the obligation of self-defense, and in Japan they recognized a dangerous enemy. Fully alive to the Japanese threat, President Manuel Quezon in 1935 asked and obtained from President Roosevelt the services of Douglas

MacArthur, retiring Chief-of-Staff of the United States Army, who worked to create a native constabulary strong enough to hold any foreign invader at bay, pending the anticipated assistance of the United States naval and military forces.

Canada. The Roosevelt administration also made a systematic effort to draw Canada more closely into the fraternity of American nations. This was somewhat facilitated by the greater independence which Canada enjoyed, after the First World War, within the British Empire. The United States and Canada had exchanged ministers since 1927 and were thus able to carry on their diplomatic relations directly instead of by way of London. Neither Hoover nor Roosevelt was able to obtain ratification of the St. Lawrence Waterway Treaty, negotiated in 1932, which would have made possible a deep-sea channel from the Gulf of St. Lawrence to the Great Lakes, but Roosevelt, on a visit to Canada in 1938, reminded his hearers that the Monroe Doctrine applied as much to the territory north of the United States as to the territory south of it. "I give you assurance," he said, "that the people of the United States will not stand idly by if the domination of Canadian soil is threatened by any other empire." That Roosevelt meant what he said became evident two years later when he conferred on measures of joint defense with Prime Minister Mackenzie King of Canada at Ogdensburg, New York. By this time Canada was at war with Germany and Italy, while the United States, at least in theory, was a neutral. Nevertheless, the heads of the two governments agreed to set up a defense board, consisting of four or five members from each country, the business of which would be to "commence immediate studies relating to sea, land, and air . . . defense of the north half of the Western Hemisphere." On both sides of the border this declaration was hailed as the practical equivalent of a military alliance.

"Continental Solidarity." The rapid descent toward war in Europe led Roosevelt to renewed emphasis upon "continental solidarity" and "hemispheric defense." When the Pan-American Conference met in Lima, December 10, 1938, the United States was acutely conscious of the inroads being made by German and Italian propaganda in Latin-American states, and sought to unite the republics of the New World in a common defense against "aggressor nations." The agreement which Secretary Hull was able to obtain was not nearly as binding as the American government had hoped, but it affirmed that the peoples of America still had faith in "absolute adherence to the principles of international law," and that they would work together to defend the peace of the continent. When war actually broke out, delegates from the various American republics met at Panama, October 1, 1939, to consider a common policy of neutrality. After several days' deliberation they issued a declaration which asserted that the "waters adjacent to the American continent" must be "free from the commission of any hostile act by any non-American belligerent nation." Two months later an engagement between German and British naval units off the coast of Uruguay demonstrated conclusively that something stronger than words would be required to keep the war far removed from American shores. By the spring of 1940 the assistance that Hitler's armies received from Nazi sympathizers in Norway, the Netherlands, Belgium, and France led to a new wave of concern throughout the Americas. Fear that some such situation might exist within their own countries led many Latin-American governments to affirm more strongly their desire to cooperate fully with the United States.

The occupation of the Dutch West Indies by the Allies after the defeat of the Netherlands brought no protest from the United States, but when France was compelled to sue for peace, notice was promptly served on Germany that the United States, under the terms of the Monroe Doctrine, could permit no transfer of American colonies from one European nation to another. The President also advocated that the Pan-American Conference, scheduled to meet in Havana on July 20, 1940, should adopt a new rule for territorial readjustments in the American hemisphere. On behalf of the United States he formally renounced all territorial aspirations, and he urged that the American republics should act together, each having equal voice, in determining what postwar rearrangements would be permitted in the New World. He suggested further that the system he favored for the Americas might well be applied in other continents also. Instead of Asia for the Japanese and Europe for the Germans, let each of the nations of Asia have an equal voice in Asiatic affairs, and each of the nations of Europe an equal voice in European affairs.

Act of Havana. Neither Europe nor Asia was in a position to heed the President's advice, but at the Havana Conference the patient diplomacy of Secretary Hull bore significant fruit. The Act of Havana was adopted which forbade the transfer of any European colony to another non-American power, and stated that if any such transfer were attempted the colony in question would pass immediately under the joint control of the American states. To provide for the government of the colony a committee of twenty-one, to consist of one member for each American nation, might be summoned at will by any of the participating nations, and as an assurance against impotence this committee was to be considered fully constituted "from the date of the appointment of two-thirds of its members." Furthermore, actions might be taken with the approval of two-thirds of the members present, while a special emergency declaration gave the United States the support for the Monroe Doctrine from the other American nations that it long had craved:

If the necessity for emergency action be deemed so urgent as to make it impossible to await action of the committee, any of the American republics, individually or jointly with others, shall have the right to act in a manner required for its defense or the defense of the continent.

Roosevelt's insistence that the United States must take the lead in preparing for the defense of all the Americas found little opposition within the nation, but many Americans, after reflecting on the results of the "war to end war" which they had entered in 1917, were convinced that the proper course of conduct for the United States was to maintain its neutrality, come what might. This sentiment was greatly strengthened by the rather sensational hearings of a Senate committee, headed by Senator Gerald P. Nye of North Dakota, which in 1934 began to examine the record of the munitions industries during and after the First World War. Extreme isolationists began to demand insistently that Congress enact neutrality laws so strict as to preclude all possibility of American involvement in case war again broke out in Europe.

"Collective Security." Opposed to this point of view were the believers in "collective security," who maintained that the world had become too small for any nation so large and influential as the United States to remain aloof from what was going on. If war came it might easily engulf the United States, but even if the United States failed to take part, it would still be intimately affected. Normal lines of trade would be broken up; the basis for a new world depression would be laid; and in a thousand other ways the United States would feel the impact of hostilities. The proper course, therefore, was to prevent war. Let the United States join with peace-loving nations to curb aggressors and to compel peace. Negative neutrality was not enough. War must be prevented.

As early as 1933, when Hitler rose to power in Germany and began his program of rearmament, Roosevelt made it clear that, whatever other Americans might think,

the President of the United States leaned strongly in the direction of collective security. In an address to the nations of the world issued May 16, 1933, the day before Hitler was to make an expected warlike statement to the Reichstag, Roosevelt urged the adoption of the MacDonald plan for the elimination of weapons designed primarily for aggressive warfare. If the nations would agree not to possess or use these weapons, then the "frontiers and independence of every nation" would become secure. A few days later, Norman H. Davis, American representative at an international conference on disarmament held in Geneva, told the delegates that, provided a satisfactory treaty could be arranged, the United States would be willing to consult with the other nations in case of a threat to peace. Further, should any disciplinary measures be undertaken against an aggressor nation, the United States "would refrain from any action tending to defeat such collective effort," that is, from insisting on its rights as a neutral.

A Quarantine of Aggressors. The disarmament conference died a lingering death, and many Americans were relieved that Roosevelt was not obliged to live up to the pledges he had made. The President, nevertheless, demonstrated repeatedly that he had not changed his mind about either the Fascist peril to the world or the best way to meet it. After the German occupation of the Rhineland, Roosevelt denounced those nations which had reverted "to the old belief in the law of the sword" and which had adopted the "fantastic conception" that they alone were chosen to be the masters of human destiny. In a direct reference a year later to the German pogroms against the Jews, he stated bluntly that he could hardly believe "that such things could occur in twentieth-century civilization." Speaking before the Pan-American Union in 1939, he characterized the methods of Germany and Italy as those of the Huns and Vandals. Roosevelt's classic utterance on collective security, prompted by Japanese and Italian operations in China and Ethiopia, came on October 5, 1937, during an address delivered in Chicago:

> It seems to be unfortunately true that the epidemic of world lawlessness is spreading. When an epidemic of physical disease starts to spread, the community approves and joins in a quarantine of the patients in order to protect the health of the community against the spread of the disease. . . . War is a contagion, whether it be declared or undeclared. It can engulf states and peoples remote from the original scene of hostilities. We are determined to keep out of war, yet we cannot insure ourselves against the disastrous effects of war and the dangers of involvement. . . . There must be positive endeavors to preserve peace. America hates war. America hopes for peace. Therefore, America actively engages in the search for peace.

Naval Expansion. The American search for peace did not stand in the way of active naval expansion, particularly after the breakdown of all plans for disarmament. In January, 1938, the President asked Congress to appropriate a billion dollars for naval defense. A month later he asked for another huge increase in appropriations and that a start be made on a two-ocean navy. The following year he proposed doubling the military budget with a good part of the increase going to the air force. Except for the Presidential request to fortify the island of Guam, Congress agreed to the major parts of these military proposals. From the point of view of those who believed in collective security the navy was necessary if the United States was to have any influence in restraining "warmongers," while from the point of view of the isolationists it was necessary to defend American borders against a warmongering world.

Neutrality Legislation. The advocates of collective security were probably a small minority in the United States, and Roosevelt found it expedient from time to time to tone down or even to disavow, at least temporarily, his own sentiments. In this instance Congress, rather than the President, represented the dominant public opinion. By a series of neutrality laws it attempted to eliminate all opportunities for the United States to be drawn into a non-American conflict. The first of these acts, passed in 1935 during the Italian attack on Ethiopia, required the President to impose an embargo upon the shipment of arms to belligerent nations, and authorized him to prohibit Americans from traveling upon the ships of belligerents. The second act, passed the following year, added a prohibition against the flotation of loans in the United States by any non-American belligerent. An even more comprehensive act became law in May, 1937. American merchant ships might not carry munitions to belligerents nor arm themselves against attack. Certain discretionary powers were also bestowed upon the President. He might forbid American ships to transport commodities of any kind to a belligerent nation; he might require all shipments to be made on a strictly "cash and carry" basis; and he might exclude enemy warships, submarines, and armed merchantmen from the use of American ports. These acts went far toward eliminating all the various causes of conflict that had led the United States into war in 1917. By them notice was also pointedly served upon European nations that the American people were no longer willing to defend the principles of neutrality for which they once had fought.

While the President found these laws distasteful, he showed considerable facility in adapting them to his own views on foreign policy. He recognized the existence of a state of war between Italy and Ethiopia, and declared the embargo on arms in force. This was advantageous to Ethiopia, which could not have purchased arms in America in any event, and an intended handicap to Italy, which might have done so. Secretary Hull also attempted to persuade American shippers to embargo voluntarily other products to Italy, especially scrap iron and oil. Pointing out that American shipments of goods to Italian Africa had increased twenty times, he stated bluntly that such shipments were "directly contrary to the policy of this government." Since Japan had not declared war against China, he refused to recognize the hostilities in the Orient as war, presumably to enable the Chinese to continue their purchases of American munitions. To Spain, where civil war existed, but with the Italians and Germans helping the insurgents and the Russians helping the Loyalists, he applied the embargo, much to the discomfiture of the Loyalists, who had the money with which to buy. The operations of the neutrality legislation actually aided the Fascists during the Spanish war, since American trade continued with Italy, who, although not officially at war, actively supported the Fascist leader, General Franco.

Roosevelt Urges Changes. Foreseeing clearly the trend of events in 1939, the President asked Congress to modify the Neutrality Act of 1937 by removing the mandatory feature of the embargo on arms to belligerents. It was the President's idea that the American government should be left free to follow traditional practice on this subject. No doubt he believed that the cause of peace would be served if the European dictators knew in advance that their opponents would be able to buy arms in the United States. But Congress was recalcitrant; the most the President could obtain was a promise from Congressional leaders that neutrality legislation would be the first order of business at the next session. Thus on September 1, 1939, when Hitler began his supreme effort to dominate Europe, the United States by its own actions found itself unable to aid embattled world democracy. Like the British before Munich, the American people wanted contradictory things: peace, a democratic world, and a world secure from aggression. They had not faced the paradoxical fact of history that peace comes only to the strong and to a people willing to fight for it if necessary.

Following the German invasion of Poland, the President called a special session of Congress to revise the Neutrality Act. Meeting on September 21, 1939, it now agreed to permit the export of war goods on a "cash and carry" basis. But the prohibition of loans to participants was continued, American ships were barred from carrying passengers or war materials to belligerents, and travel by American citizens on the vessels of belligerents was forbidden. Neutral nations, thus bereft of a powerful champion of neutral rights, looked on helplessly while German submarines sank their ships.

Most Americans probably believed during the "phony war" period that the European struggle would and should end in a stalemate. But after the fall of France they had to face the strong possibility of a Hitler victory. What then would happen to the New World? A surprising number of Americans were willing to take their chances. The first consideration, such persons believed, was that the United States must at any cost keep out of the war. Led by such adamant isolationists as Senator Wheeler and Colonel Charles A. Lindbergh, and supported by the Hearst newspapers and the *Chicago Tribune,* they gave their sympathy and contributions to an America First Committee, which sought to discredit intervention. Opponents of the extreme isolationist view rallied similarly to the support of a Committee to Defend America by Aiding the Allies, headed for a time by the Kansas editor, William Allen White. Among those whose sympathies lay with this committee was the President of the United States. It was he who persuaded Congress to permit the shipment of American-made munitions to the enemies of Germany and Italy; furthermore, he had deliberately returned to the manufacturers as supposedly "outmoded" such military items as airplanes, knowing full well that they would promptly be shipped to the Allies.

America Arms. Only a small minority of Americans, whatever their opinions on neutrality, opposed the further strengthening of American defenses. Obviously, with Japan determined to press her "new order" in Asia and Hitler on the loose in Europe, the United States needed a two-ocean navy. Even the Panama Canal was vulnerable if an enemy nation managed to obtain a nearby base for aircraft operation. Also, the revolutionary methods of land warfare used by the Germans had to be considered. Their attacks depended on the airplane, the tank, and other mechanized vehicles, equipment which the United States conspicuously lacked. It seemed clear to most Americans, whether isolationists, interventionists, or mere neutrals, that the least the nation should do was to perfect its armament with all possible speed, even if radicals and pacifists insisted that preparedness was only a prelude to war. Congress gave unhesitating support to the defense program. By the end of September, total appropriations for defense had reached the gigantic sum of $13 billion. To facilitate further large-scale borrowing, the national debt limit was raised to $49 billion. Additional income and excise taxes were also voted, in defiance of the tradition that new taxes were not to be thought of in an election year. To furnish political supervision over the activities of army and navy, the President broke precedents right and left by making Henry L. Stimson, Secretary of State under Herbert Hoover, his Secretary of War, and Frank Knox, Republican vice-presidential candidate in 1936, his Secretary of the Navy. To put the industrial machine on a war basis, the President set up first a Defense Advisory Commission, then, when difficulties developed, an Office of Production Management. He showed some reluctance, however, to place the whole problem of production under one man's control, although William S. Knudsen, president of General Motors, headed both boards.

Unwilling to risk the delay involved in raising an army by volunteering, the President urged Congress to adopt a Selective Service Act. This plan met with the most determined opposition by the few isolationist Democrats and the great majority of the Republican members of both Houses. But by the middle of September, 1940, preparedness leaders in Congress were victorious. The new measure required all men between the ages of twenty-one and thirty-five inclusive to register for a year of military training, and on October 16 approximately 17 million citizens presented themselves for the draft. From this number the army planned to call into service during the first year about 800,000 men, and to replace them with a similar number each succeeding year. Each class, at the end of its period of training, was to remain subject to recall for emergency service during a ten-year period. Congress might also at any time declare the nation in peril, and hold the men in training under arms indefinitely. As the nation increased its cooperation with beleaguered Britain and the danger of war increased, the terms of the draft law were stiffened. The first class called had not yet completed its year of training when the President asked Congress to authorize the retention of all draftees in service for as much as eighteen months beyond the period for which they had originally been called. Congress complied on August 18, 1941, but only after a bitter legislative struggle, and then only by a majority of one vote in the House of Representatives. Four months later the requirement of registration was extended to include all men from 18 to 64 years of age, with service liability limited to those from 20 to 45. Meantime the National Guard, as the nation's second line of defense, had long since been called into service.

Measures "Short of War." President Roosevelt, and a steadily increasing number of other Americans, believed the defense of the United States should be further promoted by effective measures "short of war" to help the British war effort. When it became known that the British navy was perilously short of destroyers, whereas the

United States was not, pressure arose to sell "outmoded" American destroyers to the British, just as previously military airplanes had been sold to the Allies. Although specific legislation seemed to bar such action, the President was advised by Attorney-General Jackson that his powers as Commander-in-Chief of the army and navy would permit him to exchange obsolete destroyers for such naval bases as he might deem essential to the defense of the United States. Accordingly, the President announced early in September that the United States had leased from the British government for a period of ninety-nine years eight bases, one each in Newfoundland, Bermuda, the Bahamas, Jamaica, St. Lucia, Trinidad, Antigua, and British Guiana. When these advanced positions were fully equipped, it was supposed that the Atlantic coastline of the United States, as well as the Panama Canal, would be completely safeguarded against attack from the east. In return for this "dismemberment of the British Empire," as the Axis Powers chose to term the deal, fifty American destroyers were turned over to British crews. It seemed evident that the hard pressed British, now fighting gamely against incessant attacks from the air as well as the constant threat of invasion by sea, could count on further aid from the United States when the need arose.

The Presidential Campaign. With foreign relations so critical and with the necessity of hastening the national defense program so obvious, many observers regarded the necessity of holding a presidential election in 1940 as almost a calamity, but the Constitution was inexorable on this point. As events proved, this was no ordinary election. Shattering all precedents, the Democrats renominated Roosevelt for a third term, and chose Secretary of Agriculture, Henry A. Wallace, as his running mate. The Republicans, convinced that the leading contenders for their nomination lacked the popular appeal necessary to defeat the President, turned to an ex-Democrat and a

Lewis in The Milwaukee Journal

"THE SPHINX SPEAKS, BUT SAYS —"

Roosevelt's reluctance to admit that he would be a candidate for a third term led to such amiable cartoons as the one here reproduced.

businessman, Wendell L. Willkie of Indiana. Both party platforms promised aid to Great Britain; both promised to keep the United States out of war. But platforms, as everybody knew, meant only what the candidates chose to make them mean. Charged with the intention of leading the United States into the war, Roosevelt replied: "I have said this before, but I shall say it again and again and again: Your boys are not going to be sent into any foreign war. . . . The purpose of our defense is defense." Willkie made a strenuous campaign, stressing that in a democracy no one man should be considered indispensable, but the voters preferred in the crisis to stand by the President. About 50 million voters went to the polls, the largest number in American history up to that time. Of these nearly 55 per cent voted for Roosevelt, who carried 38 states with 449 electoral votes, while Willkie carried only 10 states with 82 electoral votes. Both houses of Congress and a majority of the state governments remained safely Democratic.

711

SELECTED BIBLIOGRAPHY

Roosevelt's foreign policy is treated briefly and favorably by Allan Nevins, *The New Deal and World Affairs* (1950). Bitterly hostile are the principal revisionist treatments, C. A. Beard, *American Foreign Policy in the Making, 1932–1940* (1946); and C. C. Tansill, *Backdoor to War; The Roosevelt Foreign Policy, 1933–1941* (1952). A spirited reply to Beard is Basil Rauch, *Roosevelt: From Munich to Pearl Harbor* (1950). The fullest account of American foreign policy in the immediate prewar years may be found in two books by W. L. Langer and S. E. Gleason, *The Challenge to Isolation, 1937–1940* (1952), and *The Undeclared War, 1940–1941* (1953); the authors are friendly to the administration and have been dubbed "court historians" by the revisionists. A useful summary, a bit more critical in tone, is D. F. Drummond, *The Passing of American Neutrality, 1937–1941* (1955). An important source is Cordell Hull, *The Memoirs of Cordell Hull* (2 vols., 1948). See also the immensely detailed study by J. W. Pratt, *Cordell Hull* (2 vols., 1964).

The history of events in Europe leading up to the Second World War has produced a vast literature. G. A. Craig and Felix Gilbert (eds.), *The Diplomats, 1919–1939* (1953), is an interesting collection of essays by specialists. Hajo Holborn, *The Political Collapse of Europe* (1951), emphasizes the break-up that followed the First World War and the failure of the United States to understand its significance. E. H. Carr, *The Twenty Years' Crisis, 1919–1939* (2nd ed., 1946), is an influential interpretation by a British liberal who is critical of his government's policies. F. L. Schuman, *Europe on the Eve* (1939), and *Night over Europe* (1941), give a vivid summary of diplomatic events from 1933 to 1940, from the viewpoint of a strong supporter of collective security. A. J. P. Taylor, *The Origins of the Second World War* (1961), is an attempt at revisionism which sees the war as a ghastly mistake brought about by blunderers on both sides.

Interesting interpretations by a leading American diplomat are in G. F. Kennan, *Russia and the West under Lenin and Stalin*

(1961). On American policy toward the Soviet Union, consult R. P. Browder, *The Origins of Soviet-American Diplomacy* (1953); and J. E. Davies, *Mission to Moscow* (1941). On Germany, see especially Alan Bullock, *Hitler* (2nd ed., 1962), a superb biography, based upon the most extensive research. W. L. Shirer, *The Rise and Fall of the Third Reich* (1960), is a massive summary by an American journalist. Interesting works on Fascist Italy include Ivone Kirkpatrick, *Mussolini* (1964); and William Ebenstein, *Fascist Italy* (1939). *The United States and the Italo-Ethiopian Crisis*, edited by Brice Harris, Jr. (1965), is a collection of varying interpretations.

On Spain, see the superb new study by Gabriel Jackson, *The Spanish Republic and the Civil War, 1931–1939* (1965). Hugh Thomas, *The Spanish Civil War* (1961), is written with clarity and objectivity. A good study of the background of the civil war is Gerald Brenan, *The Spanish Labyrinth* (2nd ed., 1950). On American policy toward Spain, see F. J. Taylor, *The United States and the Spanish Civil War, 1936–1939* (1956); Allen Guttmann, *The Wound in the Heart* (1962); and *American Neutrality and the Spanish Civil War*, edited by Guttmann (1963).

Keith Feiling, *The Life of Neville Chamberlain* (1946), an official biography, states the case for its controversial subject. J. W. Wheeler-Bennett, *Munich: Prologue to Tragedy* (1948), is scholarly and perspicacious. A collection of documents and varying interpretations is F. L. Loewenheim, *Peace or Appeasement?* (1965). On Anglo-American relations, see Forrest Davis, *The Atlantic System* (1941); and Herbert Nicholas, *Britain and the U.S.A.* (1963).

On the Far East, see especially Dorothy Borg, *The United States and the Far Eastern Crisis of 1933–1938* (1964). Surveys of American policy include T. A. Bisson, *American Policy in the Far East, 1931–1941* (1941); and C. A. Buss, *War and Diplomacy in Eastern Asia* (1941). Important testimony presented by the American Ambassador to Japan is J. C. Grew, *Turbulent Era* (1952). J. K. Fairbank, *The United States and China* (2nd ed., 1958), is a general survey by a leading American scholar.

* Available in paperback

R. A. Divine, *The Illusion of Neutrality* (1962), is a competent monograph dealing with the struggles over neutrality legislation. The best work on the Nye Committee is J. E. Wiltz, *In Search of Peace* (1963). But see also W. S. Cole, *Senator Gerald P. Nye and American Foreign Relations* (1962). Dorothy Detzer, *Appointment on the Hill* (1948), is the reminiscence of a leading pacifist lobbyist. Herbert Feis, *Seen from E. A.* (1947), relates some of the difficulties encountered by the State Department in operating under the neutrality laws. Another work of value, rather critical in tone, is L. C. Gardner, *Economic Aspects of New Deal Diplomacy* (1964).

The battle between isolationists and interventionists may be followed in two competent monographs: Walter Johnson, *The Battle against Isolation* (1944), an account of the Committee to Defend America by Aiding the Allies; and W. S. Cole, *America First; The Battle against Intervention, 1940–1941* (1953). A frank study of the Chairman of the Senate Foreign Relations Committee is F. L. Israel, *Nevada's Key Pittman* (1963).

On Wendell Willkie and the 1940 campaign, see M. E. Dillon, *Wendell Willkie* (1952), which gives the most attention to his pre-1940 career; Joseph Barnes, *Willkie* (1952); and D. B. Johnson, *The Republican Party and Wendell Willkie* (1960), a scholarly study. Roland Young, *Congressional Politics in the Second World War* (1956), is based chiefly upon Congressional documents. Robert Sobel, *The Origins of Interventionism; The United States and the Russo-Finnish War* (1960), is an interesting monograph which argues for the importance of its subject. See also J. A. DeNovo, *American Interests and Policies in the Middle East, 1900–1939* (1963).

The outbreak of war with Japan has been the subject of many works, a number of which can be sampled in a convenient anthology, *°Pearl Harbor; Roosevelt and the Coming of the War*, edited by G. M. Waller (2nd ed., 1965). See also R. A. Divine, *°The Reluctant Belligerent* (1965). Herbert Feis, *°The Road to Pearl Harbor; The Coming of the War between the United States and Japan* (1950), is scholarly and favorable to the administration; Walter Millis, *This Is Pearl!* (1947), is a more popular treatment from the same point of view. Bitterly critical of Roosevelt and Hull is the revisionist work by C. A. Beard, *President Roosevelt and the Coming of the War, 1941* (1948). A more temperate revisionist work which criticizes Roosevelt and Hull for their alleged inflexibility is P. W. Schroeder, *The Axis Alliance and Japanese-American Relations, 1941* (1958). A vivid reconstruction of events in Hawaii on December 7, 1941, is Walter Lord, *°Day of Infamy* (1957). But see also the splendid work of Roberta Wohlstetter, *Pearl Harbor* (1962).

40

THE SECOND WORLD WAR

The Lend-Lease Act. However the election results of 1940 are interpreted, Roosevelt believed that his foreign policy had received the emphatic endorsement of the American people. Thus fortified, the President reasserted his determination to give all possible aid to Britain, and set "four freedoms" as the American goal for the postwar world — freedom of speech, freedom of religion, freedom from want, freedom from fear. He also submitted to Congress a plan whereby the government should lend, lease, or otherwise transfer military equipment to nations resisting aggressors. This measure, which amounted to a declaration of partial war, was fought for weeks by the isolationists in and out of Congress. Replying to the President's argument that Lend-Lease would not lead to war but rather would prevent it, Senator Wheeler charged that the Act constituted the New Deal triple-A foreign policy: it would "plow

under every fourth American boy" and give the President the dictatorial power "to conduct undeclared war anywhere in the world." Aiding the Montana Senator in his attack were a few Democratic colleagues, together with the great majority of Republicans in both houses. By exerting all his influence, however, Roosevelt secured the passage of the Act on March 11, 1941. Subsequently, Congress appropriated $7 billion to finance the Act, and almost immediately shipments of vital materials were on their way abroad.

Anglo-American Cooperation. Even after the passage of the Lend-Lease Act, the majority of Congress and the American people were opposed to declaring war. By the spring of 1941, however, most of the high navy and army officials had concluded that American security demanded the nation's participation in the struggle against the dictators. More and more the President was leaning in that direction, but he was too shrewd a politician to lead a divided country into a struggle that would demand above all unity of purpose and action. He therefore minimized the talk of active war, while continuing to do everything in his power to aid the countries resisting aggression.

In line with this policy, Axis, Danish, and French ships in American ports were seized.

An executive agreement, reached April 10, 1941, between Secretary of State Hull and the Danish minister to Washington (who had refused to cooperate with his Nazi-dominated government), gave the United States permission to make military use of the island of Greenland. During the next few weeks of steadily mounting tension the President turned over fifty tankers to the British government, closed the Axis consulates in the United States, and, following the sinking in the South Atlantic of an American merchantman, proclaimed a state of "unlimited national emergency."

Meanwhile a virtual Anglo-American alliance had been consummated. During the debate on the Lend-Lease Act a full-dress meeting of the British and American general staffs had taken place in Washington. Rapidly thereafter the two nations pooled their military intelligence and worked out elaborate plans for joint action. By September, 1941, American army transports were carrying thousands of British troops from Canada to Egypt where they were sorely needed in the critical battle for the Nile. Most of the above acts were performed by executive action and some were kept from the public. But whether the people realized it or not, the last pretense of American neutrality had evaporated.

Meantime Hitler, after a winter of diplomatic preparation, made ready in the spring of 1941 to march his armies into the Balkans. Hungary, Rumania, and Bulgaria agreed to cooperate with his regime. The government of Yugoslavia was like-minded, but the Yugoslav army revolted and staged a brave but hopeless struggle against the invaders. Next the Greeks, whom Mussolini had been seeking in vain to conquer since the fall of 1940, were overwhelmed. The little British army sent to their aid from Egypt was driven out, and, after a short stand in Crete, was forced back to North Africa. There the British commander, General Sir Archibald Wavell, had recently pushed the Italians far to the west along the coast of Libya, but now the British hold on the eastern Mediterranean was tenuous indeed. Anticipating a German push to the oil fields of the Middle East, British and "Free French" forces, early in June, 1941, occupied Syria, but their chances of resisting a Nazi attack in force seemed slender.

Hitler Attacks Russia. Then on June 22, with Hungary, Rumania, and Finland as allies, Hitler attacked Russia. Washington and London were not unprepared for the turn of events; both, in fact, had warned Russia repeatedly that such an attack was a certainty. Despite all past differences, the United States and Great Britain received the U.S.S.R. to the anti-Nazi cause with cordiality. From Churchill came the prompt announcement: "Any man or state who fights against Naziism will have our aid. Any man or state who marches with Hitler is our foe." And from Roosevelt came the assurance that supplies would soon be flowing from the United States to Russia under the terms of the Lend-Lease Act. To the surprise of most experts who recalled the Red Army's sorry showing against the Finns, the Russians offered sustained military resistance to the invading armies. Although the Germans and their allies took much territory, the collapse they had confidently expected failed to occur. In the winter of 1941–1942, the Russian armies for several months even held the offensive and regained some of the ground they had lost.

The Atlantic Charter. With Russia, a totalitarian nation, fighting on the Allied side, the question of war aims was raised repeatedly. To answer this question, and also to give dramatic emphasis to the solidarity of Anglo-American opinion, President Roosevelt and Prime Minister Churchill met at an undisclosed point in the Atlantic, and on August 14, 1941, issued over their joint signatures the so-called Atlantic Charter. This document disclaimed for Great Britain and the United States any desire for territorial, or other, aggrandizement, or for any territorial changes not in accord with the wishes of the people concerned. It asserted the right of all peoples to choose the form of government under which they wished to live, and promised to promote equal access for all states, "great or small, victor or vanquished," to the raw materials of the world. Other named objectives included improved labor conditions; the unhindered use of the high seas; and the disarmament of aggressor nations as a step toward the abandonment of the use of force in international relations.

By this time the increasing tempo of submarine attacks had brought the "Battle of the Atlantic" to a crisis. Since a substantial number of freighters being sunk carried lend-lease materials, many Americans demanded that the United States join with Great Britain in convoying merchant fleets overseas. High officials of the navy also favored this policy as a prelude to actual hostilities. Admiral Stark considered "every day of delay in our getting into war as dangerous." But Roosevelt, leading a still undecided nation, ordered only that American ships and aircraft should "patrol" the western 2,000 miles of the Atlantic in order to advise the British as to the whereabouts of Axis craft. The President denied on May 27, 1941, that American ships were engaged in a "shooting war," but he promised that they would take whatever action was necessary to insure the delivery of war goods to Great Britain. He announced also, on July 7, 1941, that units of the United States navy had arrived in Iceland to supplement and ultimately replace the British forces already there; soon afterward he ordered the navy to keep open the sea lanes between Iceland (only 700 miles from the British coast) and the United States. The effectiveness of these actions brought speedy Axis retaliation. German submarines had already sunk eight American freighters when, on September 4, 1941, an American destroyer was attacked while trailing a German submarine. Thereupon the President ordered destroyers to shoot submarines on sight. In mid-October another destroyer

was hit, and eleven of her crew were killed. That same month, a second destroyer was torpedoed and sunk, with the loss of seventy-six of her crew. After these attacks, Congress, by a measure signed November 17, authorized the arming of American merchant ships and freed them from the remaining restrictions of the neutrality laws, which thus far had kept them outside "combat zones." The United States was by now engaged in a naval war, and complete participation seemed close at hand.

Japanese Threat to Asia.   The final denouement, however, was to come from another quarter. In the Far East the irreconcilable differences between the Japanese "new order" and the American "open door" had long been in evidence. Secretary Hull, throughout his administration, had refused to recognize the conquests of Japan in China, and on July 26, 1939, he notified the Japanese government that the long-standing commercial treaty between Japan and the United States would be abrogated. This move was generally believed to anticipate an embargo on munitions shipments to Japan, but no such action was taken, and the conquest of China went on. In the summer of 1940, however, the United States forbade the export of essential war materials to any foreign country, without license, but by this time Japan was poised for action. From the puppet French government, the Japanese extorted the right to occupy the northern part of French Indo-China, and in September, 1940, their troops took possession. The United States now countered with a complete embargo on the exportation of iron and steel scrap, except to Great Britain and the nations of the western hemisphere. But against this action, the Japanese government had a trump card to play. Within a few hours it announced that a joint economic, political, and military alliance had been formed by Germany, Italy, and Japan.

The threat posed by the "Rome-Berlin-Tokyo Axis" was not lost on informed Americans. During the Sino-Japanese War the government of Japan had become unmistakably dictatorial in character, and in 1940 took on the earmarks of the totalitarian state. Japan's next move would obviously be made with the support of the European members of the Axis. Hatred for British and American agents and diplomats in the Far East had long been freely exhibited; would the Japanese, under Axis protection, now try to drive the West out of eastern Asia?

Interest in the Atlantic theater blinded many Americans to the perilous situation in the Far East, but when Japan, in July, 1941, obtained permission from Vichy-France to occupy all of French Indo-China, the American State Department knew that trouble was at hand. Japanese troops pouring into this area posed a grave threat to the Philippine Islands, as well as to the British and Dutch possessions in the Far East, the main source of the world's tin and rubber supply. In protest, therefore, the American government on July 24 froze all Japanese assets in the United States, an action which the Dutch and British governments quickly paralleled. During the protracted discussions that followed, it was evident that neither nation would retreat from its respective position. The most the Japanese were willing to offer was a promise that they would not advance beyond Indo-China, provided the United States agreed to supply Japan with its needs for gasoline and oil, restore normal commercial relations between the two countries, guarantee the delivery to Japan of strategic supplies from the Netherlands Indies, and give no further aid to China. The American answer was presented by Secretary Hull on November 26, 1941. It included demands that Japan withdraw from both China and French Indo-China, recognize the government of Chiang Kai-shek, and abide by the principles of nonaggression and commercial equality. In return the United States promised to resume normal commercial relations with Japan and to release frozen Japanese assets in America.

Pearl Harbor. In October General Hideki Tojo had become head of a Japanese government controlled by the military, whose position was clearly indicated by its continued build-up of Japanese forces in Indo-China. Such actions, of course, discounted completely all hopes of a peaceful settlement, even though on November 15, 1941, a special Japanese envoy, Saburo Kurusu, arrived in Washington with what purported to be new Japanese proposals. Indeed, while the peace conversations were still in progress at Washington, early on the morning of December 7, a Japanese carrier-borne air force attacked the great American naval base at Pearl Harbor, in Hawaii. So complete was the surprise that most American aircraft were destroyed on the ground, leaving the American battle fleet at the mercy of the foe. Nineteen of the 86 American ships in the harbor were seriously hit, 5 capital ships were sunk or put out of action, and there were 4,575 killed, wounded, or missing. Had the Japanese been able to bring with them troops to effect a landing, they might well have taken Hawaii.

PEARL HARBOR

On December 7, 1941, "a day which will live in infamy," the Japanese attacked Pearl Harbor. Here a rescue crew is shown beside the USS West Virginia.

The day after Pearl Harbor, Congress, with only one dissenting vote, recognized the existence of a state of war between the United States and Japan, while Japan issued its overdue declaration of war against the United States and the British Empire. Within a few days, Germany and Italy, acting on their commitments to Japan, declared war against the United States, while Congress, by a unanimous vote in both houses, responded with similar declarations against the Axis powers in Europe. Thus the total war that most Americans had hoped to avoid at last became a fact. Many other American nations were soon involved in the conflict. Some of them, notably Mexico and Brazil, went the whole length of declaring war; by July, 1943, only one American power, Argentina, had failed at least to sever diplomatic relations with the Axis.

After the shock of Pearl Harbor had abated, the charge was often made that Roosevelt had cunningly placed the Japanese in such a position that their only alternative was to attack the United States. Only by this circuitous route, this argument ran, could the President achieve his chief goal of getting the United States into the European war. Not a shred of evidence exists to support the charge. Only the mistaken calculation of the Japanese army leaders set off the train of events that led to direct American participation in both the Orient and Europe.

The War in 1942.   For many months the war in the Pacific went badly for the United Nations, as the Allies now began to call themselves. The attack on Pearl Harbor was followed immediately by attacks on the Philippine Islands, Wake Island, Guam, Hong Kong, Malaya, and Thailand. The Thai government offered practically no resistance, Guam fell on December 11, Wake Island, December 24, and Hong Kong on Christmas Day, 1941. In the Philippines General MacArthur, whose forces during the last phases of the dispute with Japan

had been somewhat augmented by troops from the United States, made a valiant stand on the Bataan peninsula and the island of Corregidor. But the assistance from the United States navy on which his campaign was predicated was not forthcoming. Bataan capitulated on April 9, 1942, and Corregidor on May 6, 1942. Well before the end came, MacArthur, in response to an insistent demand from both the United States and Australia, left the Philippines by stealth to take command of the Allied forces in Australia. Meantime Japanese troops overran Malaya, captured Singapore, conquered Burma, and except for a few precarious footholds forced the United Nations completely out of the East Indies. With the Burma Road closed, aid to China decreased to almost nothing, and the Allies fell back upon India and Australia as bases of operation.

Elsewhere in the world the position of the United Nations was equally depressing. Operating off the Atlantic coast line and in the Caribbean, German submarines sank hundreds of American freighters during the first months of 1942 and produced an acute gasoline and oil shortage along the Atlantic seaboard. Far more important was the threatened collapse in the summer of 1942 of the United Nations' entire position in Russia and North Africa. By that time the German General Erwin Rommel was within seventy miles of Alexandria, threatening the British defense of the Suez Canal and the Middle East. By August German armies were fighting in the streets of Stalingrad on the Volga, thus threatening to cut off all of southern Russia and its vital oil supplies.

Stung to desperation by the unbroken procession of defeats, the people of the United States settled down with determination to create a war machine adequate to cope with their enemies. During 1942 Congress authorized increases in the size of the army and navy, and by 1945 America had over 12 million men under arms. The navy, which had only 4,500 ships in 1941, was by 1945 increased to 90,000 ships and landing craft. Included in this vast fleet were 23 battleships, 20 large carriers, 78 small carriers, and 72 cruisers. For the first time in the nation's history women were recruited in numbers for the fighting forces, some 100,000 volunteering for service in the Women's Army Corps (WAC) and over 80,000 in the naval counterpart, the WAVES. To house, equip, and supply this great force was in itself an enormous task. But in addition, the nation had to maintain and even increase the flow of lend-lease goods to its allies, and, of course, provide for the civilian population.

War Government. Early in 1942 the War Production Board headed by Donald M. Nelson, together with numerous other boards and agencies created as events required, paved the way for a war government not unlike the one developed in the First World War. The Defense Plant Corporation, for example, spent over $16 billion in construction of government-owned factories to produce vitally needed materials and products, chief among which was synthetic rubber to replace the nation's Far Eastern natural rubber supply lost to the Japanese. To conserve existing rubber, low speed-limits for automobile traffic, as well as tire- and gasoline-rationing, were accepted as necessary evils. The chief means by which the WPB sought to accelerate war production were (1) by prohibiting the manufacture of a long list of civilian products containing iron and steel, (2) by a system of priorities directing essential materials and products to manufacturers and consumers, and (3) by a kind of national budgeting of steel, aluminum, and copper through what was called the Controlled Materials Plan. Just as the nation's basic metals were rationed among manufacturers according to war needs, so were many consumer products rationed among civilians. Since employers were competing fiercely for a dwindling labor supply, wages were set by the Office of Price Administration, as were rents and the prices of practically all

MASS MILITARY PRODUCTION

Chrysler Corporation built and operated this Detroit plant for the Ordnance Corps during World War II, producing nearly 25,000 tanks of twelve different models on five assembly lines.

basic commodities and services. Taxes rose astronomically, yet the people responded willingly to the plea that they invest at least 10 per cent of their incomes in war bonds.

By such means American energy was turned from peacetime pursuits to production for war. Hundreds of completely new war factories were built, and old plants were converted for the making of weapons. Shipyards increased their capacity enormously, and by the end of the war some of them were turning out a standardized merchant ship by almost production-line methods. Labor generally forgot its internal conflicts and carried on with only infrequent strikes. Farmers provided a steady flow of lend-lease foodstuffs abroad, while supplying adequately army and civilian needs both overseas and at home. By 1944 American industry accounted for over one-half the world's total war production, while at the same time maintaining the prewar civilian standard of living. By the end of 1942 a million American soldiers poured overseas to the British Isles, to Australia and New Zealand, to East Africa and Egypt, the spearhead of what was to become the most highly mechanized and the best equipped force in the world.

Well before the end of 1942 the tide of battle had begun to turn. While the Russians were grinding the German offensive to a stop at Stalingrad and the British were chasing the Afrika Korps westward, the United States had chalked up a series of costly but important naval victories in the Coral Sea, off Midway, and in the Solomon Islands. The initiative seemed definitely to have passed from the Japanese to the Allies on August 7, 1942, when the marines took Tulagi harbor and the airfield on Guadalcanal. Still disappointed in the progress made, the American people gave the Roosevelt administration a stinging rebuke on election day, November 3, by reducing substantially the Democratic majorities in both House and Senate, and by overthrowing Democratic control in many states.

Invasion of North Africa. Four days later, came the news that a huge Anglo-American armada had landed troops in French North Africa, with the avowed intention of occupying the entire North African seacoast of the French Empire, both Mediterranean and Atlantic. This daring operation had been planned at a meeting of Churchill and Roosevelt in Washington the preceding June, but the secret was well kept, and the Axis Powers were taken completely by surprise. Without serious loss 500 transports, supported by 350 warships, brought the invasion forces to their destination. General Dwight D. Eisenhower, in supreme command of operations on land, got his troops ashore with little serious fighting except at Casablanca and Oran. Although the Vichy-French government dared not condone the Allied invasion, some of its representatives in North Africa deliberately aided the invaders. The Allies had expected to make General Henri Giraud, a high-ranking French officer who had escaped from

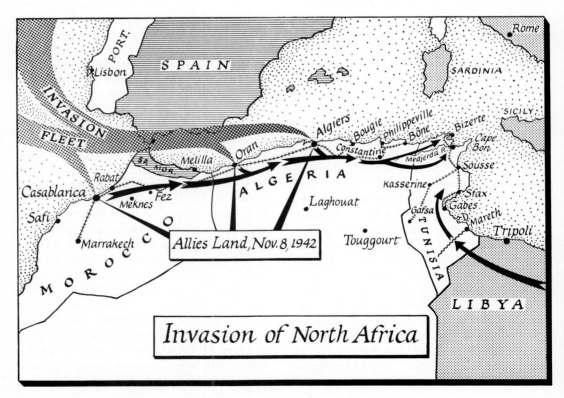

Invasion of North Africa

imprisonment in Germany, the chief French official in North Africa, but this plan did not meet the approval of the Free French leader in London, General Charles de Gaulle, who outmaneuvered both Giraud and the Allied leaders, and himself assumed control. The subjection of the Vichy government to Germany now became more abject than ever. The southeastern half of France, which up to the time of the North African invasion had not been occupied by German troops, was quickly taken over, and the remnant of the French fleet at Toulon was scuttled to avoid capture by German land forces.

Tunisia. Obviously the Allied governments had hoped that their African conquests would extend to Tunisia before that colony could be occupied by the Axis, but in this they were disappointed. Early in 1943, German and Italian divisions under General Jurgen von Arnim were concentrated in Tunisia for a last-ditch fight, in which General Erwin Rommel's famous Afrika Korps, still retreating from Egypt, was expected to join. The final struggle came in May, 1943, when the British Eighth Army under General Sir Bernard Montgomery closed in from the east, and British, French, and American troops from the west. Von Arnim and Rommel were able to join forces, but were promptly and disastrously defeated. All of Tunisia, including the cities of Tunis and Bizerte, was occupied by the victorious Allied troops, who, during the final phases of the campaign, took well over 200,000 prisoners, among them von Arnim himself. Before the final collapse, Rommel had left Africa for Europe, but practically all the Axis troops which he and von Arnim had commanded were killed or captured.

Italy. The next great goal of Allied endeavor was Sicily, which Eisenhower's forces invaded on July 10, 1943, and conquered in less than six weeks. Before this task was completed, King Victor Emmanuel, assisted by elements in the Fascist Grand Council, forced Mussolini out of power, and set up a new government under Marshal Pietro Badoglio as premier. Badoglio's aim was peace, but the Italian peninsula was invaded before he accepted Eisenhower's terms of unconditional surrender and turned over the entire Italian navy to the Allies. Stiff German resistance held the Allies back many months in Italy, but at length, on June 4, 1944, Rome was taken. The chief strategic purpose of the North African and Italian campaign was to clear the Mediterranean of enemy sea and air power, and this end was fully accomplished. By the fall of 1944, with Italy now recognized as a "co-belligerent," Allied arms had reached the valley of the Po.

The Second Front. Since 1942 a joint British-American staff had laid plans for an invasion of Germany through the heart of Europe, but the exact place of this "second front" had been a subject of long debate. Prime Minister Churchill and his military aides consistently argued for a thrust into the "soft underbelly" of Europe and up through the Balkans, freely admitting that one of their aims was to seal eastern Europe off from the advancing Communists. The American command, however, insisting that political arguments be subordinated to the fundamental military task of crushing Germany, successfully held out for a direct cross channel attack against Hitler's "fortress Europa." On June 6, 1944, the long-awaited "second front" was launched from England across the Channel to the coast of Normandy. To conduct this campaign Eisenhower and Montgomery were transferred from Italy. Despite miserable weather and the lack of harbors, the invasion was completely successful, and the reconquest of France began. On August 24–25, Paris was occupied by Allied troops amidst riotous demonstrations of joy by its inhabitants. To reinforce the Channel invaders, another expedition landed August 15 on the Mediterranean coast of France, and worked its way northward with extraordinary rapidity.

EISENHOWER AND MONTGOMERY

As Eisenhower's subordinate in the battle for Germany, Montgomery obeyed orders reluctantly, and in his postwar memoirs severely criticized his chief.

When winter set in, nearly all of France and Belgium had been freed, part of the Netherlands had been cleared of enemy troops, and Allied armies were fighting on German soil. Somewhat belatedly, the British and American governments recognized de Gaulle's "Free French" Committee as the provisional government of France. For Belgium and the Netherlands, governments-in-exile, long since functioning in England, had only to be transferred to the Continent.

On the Sea and in the Air. In the air and on the seas the German situation grew steadily more desperate. The attempt of the *Luftwaffe* to bomb the British into submission had not only failed completely; it had brought devastating retaliation. While the Germans were able to make only "nuisance" raids over England, British and American bombers attacked German, German-held, and Italian cities by night and day. Harbor installations, airfields, war factories, railway yards, power plants, bridges, dams, and entire cities were subjected to almost continuous bombing. After the Allied landings on the French coast had been

effected, a German secret weapon, the robot bomb, inflicted considerable casualties upon the civilian population of southern England, but it failed completely to halt the invasion. On the high seas, where German submarines had long taken a heavy toll, new devices for detecting and destroying them diminished drastically their effectiveness and all but eliminated them as a factor in the war. Lend-lease supplies flowed in a steady stream to Russia, while communications with the British Isles and the Mediterranean approached peacetime conditions.

Meantime on the eastern front the Germans, after losing at Stalingrad in 1942, retreated steadily before growing Russian strength. Not only were they forced to abandon all Russian territory, but they were also driven out of Bulgaria, Rumania, and Finland, each of which, like Italy, joined the Allies. By the end of 1944, Russian troops had invaded Poland, Hungary, Yugoslavia, Czechoslovakia, and East Prussia, while British forces were well along with the reconquest of Greece, and "partisans"

"D" DAY, JUNE 6, 1944

Eisenhower gives his last instructions to American paratroopers who will drop on the invasion coast in France.

THE RUINS OF BERLIN

Strikingly similar to the ruins of Richmond after the American Civil War is this scene at the Nollendorf Platz in Berlin, July 30, 1945. The fact that the debris has been cleared from the street tends only to emphasize the totality of the destruction.

under Marshal Tito were aiding in the liberation of Yugoslavia. The utter hopelessness of the German situation seemed plain to all except the Nazi leaders.

Many optimists, including General Eisenhower, had dreamed of victory in 1944, but as winter set in, the Allied campaigns, both eastern and western, slowed to a halt. To make matters worse, the Germans under Field Marshal Karl von Rundstedt launched a terrific and utterly unanticipated counterattack in the Belgium-Luxembourg sector that for a time seriously threatened the Allied position. But as the old year ended, the Allies, mainly through the efforts of General George S. Patton's Third American Army, brought the German drive to a standstill and regained the initiative.

Conquest of Germany. The time had now come for the careful synchronization of Allied activities on the eastern and the western fronts. In the eastern theater, the Russians delayed their customary winter offensive until January 12, 1945. Then they struck forcefully with five huge armies, and the German defenses were smashed from the Baltic to the Carpathians. By the end of February, Russian troops were on German soil only thirty-one miles from Berlin. In the west, Eisenhower was somewhat delayed by the von Rundstedt offensive, but by early March, Allied troops had penetrated into nearly every stronghold of the famed West-wall, taking prisoners by the hundreds of thousands. Many Germans succeeded in withdrawing across the Rhine, but on March 7, owing to the failure of the retreating forces to destroy a bridge at Remagen, they were followed by American soldiers in considerable numbers. The bridge soon collapsed, but from newly established bridgeheads Allied forces in great strength pushed forward through the very heart of the Reich. The "scorched-earth" policy that the Nazi leaders had ordered, together with the persistent bombing of German cities and the devastation incidental to military operations, left much of Germany in ruins.

No reliable evidence exists to indicate that Roosevelt had agreed to Russian troops occupying Berlin in advance of the troops of other nations. But the Anglo-American advance was halted when it might easily have reached Berlin ahead of the Russians. General Eisenhower took full responsibility for the decision, justifying it on the grounds that Berlin had no military value. For the same reason he also called back an American advance on Prague, thus enabling the Russians to occupy another capital city and dominate the reconstruction of another country. By the end of April, when the Russian and American forces met on the banks of the Elbe River, victorious Russian armies had occupied all of the various Nazi satellite nations in eastern Europe, the German armies in northern Italy had surrendered, and Mussolini had lost his life at the hands of a Milanese mob. The Russians fought their way street by street through the rubble of Berlin, and took possession of what was left of the stricken city. Hitler himself committed suicide and shortly afterward Admiral Karl Doenitz, to whom Hitler had transferred his authority, notified the Allies that Germany was ready to surrender. On May 8, 1945, the Allied victory in Europe, "V-E Day," was officially proclaimed.

The Pacific. By this time the Allies dominated the Pacific. In mid-November, 1942, the Japanese tried to oust the Americans from Guadalcanal, but failed, in large part because of naval defeats administered by American squadrons operating under the command of Admiral William F. Halsey. Japanese efforts to push across New Guinea in order to strike at Australia were also frustrated. After that, the bitter fighting necessary to clear the way back to the Philippines could begin. By this time the American navy had recovered from its losses at Pearl Harbor, and with each succeeding month its strength increased. In the cold and fog of the Aleutians, where the Japanese had held two American islands, Kiska and Attu, since June, 1942, the Americans struck at Attu, May 11, 1943, and soon took the island. The Japanese then abandoned

Kiska. The next great effort of the American navy was to drive the Japanese from the islands of the mid-Pacific. In November, 1943, marine and army forces successfully invaded several atolls in the Gilberts, among them Tarawa, where the fighting was particularly bloody. Kwajalein in the Marshalls was taken early in 1944.

It was now plain that the strategy of Admiral Chester W. Nimitz, commander-in-chief of the Pacific fleet, called for a direct advance across the Pacific to Asiatic waters. No effort was made to clear every island occupied by the Japanese, but important bases, with airfields that could dominate wide stretches of ocean, were taken and strongly held. By June, 1944, the advance had reached Saipan in the Marianas, 1,500 miles from Tokyo and 1,600 miles from Manila. Frightened by the approaching danger, the Japanese sent carrier-based planes to attack the American ships off Saipan, but the attackers suffered heavily, while American planes in turn inflicted severe damage upon the enemy fleet. The bloody but successful conquest of Saipan was followed in the next month by the occupation of Guam and Tinian. Bomber attacks could now be made from these bases, as well as from China, upon Formosa and the Japanese homeland, and the exploit of the *Hornet,* which had sent its planes in April, 1942, to attack Tokyo, was repeated by the land-based planes from Saipan, November 23, 1944. From this time on, the destruction of Japanese cities and industrial targets proceeded mercilessly.

Iwo Jima and Okinawa. To shorten the bombing range to Japan, two more islands were taken by American land and naval forces early in 1945. The first, Iwo Jima, a tiny islet in the volcano group midway between Guam and Tokyo, provided the Japanese with three airfields and a radar station. Enemy intelligence was thus able to detect flights of Tokyo-bound American planes. So great was the nuisance value of this island that on February 19, 1945, two

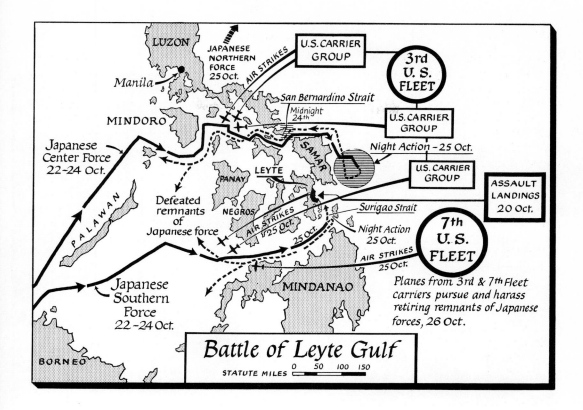

Battle of Leyte Gulf

STATUTE MILES   0   50   100   150

LUZON

Manila

JAPANESE NORTHERN FORCE 25 Oct.

AIR STRIKES

U.S. CARRIER GROUP

3rd U.S. FLEET

MINDORO

San Bernardino Strait

Midnight 24th

U.S. CARRIER GROUP

Japanese Center Force 22–24 Oct.

SAMAR

Night Action – 25 Oct.

U.S. CARRIER GROUP

LEYTE

PANAY

PALAWAN

Defeated remnants of Japanese force

NEGROS

AIR STRIKES 25 Oct.

25 Oct.

Surigao Strait

Night Action 25 Oct.

ASSAULT LANDINGS 20 Oct.

7th U.S. FLEET

AIR STRIKES 25 Oct.

MINDANAO

Japanese Southern Force 22–24 Oct.

Planes from 3rd & 7th Fleet carriers pursue and harass retiring remnants of Japanese forces, 26 Oct.

BORNEO

---

divisions of marines, supported by a prodigious show of naval force, undertook its conquest. The entrenched Japanese fought back furiously; the battle lasted a month, and American casualties reached 20,000, but the coveted terrain was won.

The last major amphibious operation in the advance on Japan began on Easter Sunday, April 1, when Okinawa, largest island in the Ryukyus, only 370 miles from Japan, was invaded. Fourteen hundred ships and upwards of 100,000 American soldiers and marines participated in the action. The Americans got ashore easily, but in southern Okinawa, toward which the Japanese retreated and reformed, the enemy staged a desperate and unexpectedly prolonged resistance. During this engagement Japanese *Kamikaze*, specially trained pilots who deliberately sought to smash their bomb-laden planes into the American ships, first made their appearance in large numbers. Enough of them succeeded in their suicidal missions to inflict serious losses upon the American

fleet. But by the middle of June, the Americans were in complete control of the island, and the doom of Japan was sealed. American bombers, operating from convenient airfields and from the decks of a host of task-force carriers, now burned and blasted the Japanese islands at will.

MacArthur's Return to the Philippines. Meantime, the campaign of MacArthur to retake the Philippines had made notable progress. His forces bypassed the principal Japanese bases, and by "leapfrog" tactics landed at unexpected, and sometimes undefended, points along a predetermined route. By January, 1944, he had begun to advance in this fashion along the northern shores of New Guinea, and well before the end of the year he was ready to launch the actual invasion of the Philippines. On October 20, he landed with a large army on the island of Leyte, and began the reconquest he had promised earlier to the peoples of America and the Philippines. To protect

MacArthur's movements, a heavy naval concentration under Admiral Halsey was obliged to fight one of the greatest sea-actions of history, for the Japanese at last decided that they must risk a major portion of their fleet. In the waters adjacent to Leyte, beginning on October 25, the Americans fought off the Japanese in a series of complicated and extensive actions so costly to the enemy as to reduce the Japanese navy to "fifth-rate" status.

After the battle of Leyte, organized resistance disintegrated slowly but surely. In January, 1945, MacArthur put ashore a formidable force at Lingayen Gulf, and began the fateful march to Manila. Japanese resistance was light at first, but the approaches to the capital were stubbornly defended, and not until February 3 could American troops enter it. After that, the Japanese staged within the city a last-ditch fight that

lasted for weeks. Meantime Mindanao and certain lesser islands had been successfully invaded. Japanese hopes were waning fast, but stiff fighting continued on many of the islands until the end of the war.

The Asiatic Mainland. While the war in the Pacific was thus being planned and fought, Allied forces were attempting to block the Japanese from further conquests on the mainland of Asia. The task could hardly have been more difficult. With India as a base, some Allied aid to the Chinese was soon being flown in over the Himalayas, but it was never enough. Bad relations between the government of Chiang Kai-shek and the armed communist bands controlling much of North China added to the turmoil in that unhappy nation. Meager American air forces, operating under General Joseph W. Stilwell, aided Chiang's

> *Concerned by the fact that both German and American scientists were on the verge of developing what has come to be known as the atomic bomb, Albert Einstein (1879–1955), the physicist whose own research laid the foundation for this discovery, sent the following letter to President Roosevelt, informing him of this fact and of its awesome implications.*

Some recent work by E. Fermi and L. Szilard, which has been communicated to me in manuscript, leads me to expect that the element uranium may be turned into a new and important source of energy in the immediate future. Certain aspects of the situation which has arisen seem to call for watchfulness and, if necessary, quick action on the part of the administration. I believe therefore that it is my duty to bring to your attention the following facts. . . .

In the course of the last four months it has been made probable through the work of Joliot in France, as well as Fermi and Szilard in America — that it may become possible to set up a nuclear reaction in a large mass of uranium, by which vast amounts of power and large quantities of new radium-like elements, would be generated. Now it appears this could be achieved in the immediate future.

This new phenomenon would also lead to the construction of bombs, and it is conceivable, though much less certain — that extremely powerful bombs of a new type may thus be constructed. A single bomb of this type, carried by boat and exploded in a port, might very well destroy the whole port, together with some of the surrounding territory.

ALBERT EINSTEIN to FRANKLIN D. ROOSEVELT, October 11, 1939

---

armies, but in spite of their best efforts Japanese troops were able to penetrate into Chinese territory almost at will.

Probably, Stilwell's principal achievement lay in clearing the Japanese from northern Burma so as to open a new supply route — the Ledo Road — from India to China. Using Chinese troops, he nearly completed this task when, in the fall of 1944, he was relieved of his command and recalled to the United States. This action was taken at the insistence of Chiang Kai-shek, with whom Stilwell had had numerous personal differences over the training and disposition of Chinese troops. American engineers went on with the road, however, and in January, 1945, the first motor caravan crossed it into China. Allied successes farther to the south in Burma, under the leadership of Lord Louis Mountbatten, were also heartening, but in spite of the achievements in

Burma the war ended with the Japanese still in control of their principal gains on the mainland of Asia.

The Atomic Bomb. Nevertheless, the Japanese ability to continue the war was waning fast. Far-ranging American submarines, joining their successes to those of American surface forces, helped to drive the Japanese navy and merchant marine almost completely from the seas. In consequence, connections between the home islands and the overexpanded "Co-Prosperity Sphere" broke down. In late May, 1945, Stalin informed the United States that certain Japanese officials had already talked to the Russians about terms for a possible peace. But it was also known that most Japanese militarists were intent upon avoiding unconditional surrender, even if that meant a last-ditch stand on the Japanese home islands. Consequently American plans for "softening up" the resistance to an invasion of the Japanese home island of Kyushu went on. With a view to shortening the war and saving hundreds of thousands of lives that a direct invasion of Japan might have cost, President Truman authorized the use of the secret and terrible weapon that Allied scientists had put at his disposal, the atomic bomb. The first atomic bomb was dropped on Hiroshima, August 6, 1945. Shortly thereafter, a similar bomb was dropped on Nagasaki. The results were cataclysmic — a single bomb proved more devastating than the concentrated action of a thousand ordinary bombers equipped with full loads of ordinary explosives. The development of the atomic bomb was the result of cooperative efforts by numerous American, British, Canadian, and European scientists, who, with the full backing of their governments, had pooled their resources in a successful effort to split the atom. Although the bomb may have short-ened the war materially, many Americans regretted that their government had resorted to it before making greater efforts to induce Japan, who was already beaten, to surrender. A majority of the scientists contributing to the development of the bomb argued that its demonstration on some deserted spot should have preceded its actual use. In view of Japan's evident growing desire for peace, some military men felt that the unconditional surrender terms might have been modified. The fateful decision was made not only to save lives and to end the war quickly, but also to enable the United States to concentrate its efforts on the resuscitation of a devastated Europe. The dropping of the bomb hurt American prestige throughout the world and continues to do so, but the awesome destruction of Hiroshima and Nagasaki made clear, perhaps as only an actual example could have done, how totally catastrophic another major war would be.

Japanese Surrender. For some months it was understood by the British and American chiefs of state that Russia intended eventually to enter the war against Japan. With the end so near, the Russian government found it inexpedient to delay longer, and on August 9, following a formal declaration of war, issued the day before, Russian troops began to advance against light opposition into Manchuria. Faced by this new threat, and assured by the President of the United States that only surrender could save Japanese civilization from total annihilation by the further use of atomic bombs, Japan gave up. As early as August 10, the Japanese news agency, Domei, broadcast that Japan was willing to accept the terms of unconditional surrender, as defined by the Allies at Potsdam, Germany, the preceding month, provided only that Emperor Hirohito's sovereignty would not be questioned. The President of the United States, replying for the Allies, stated the willingness of the nations at war with Japan to retain the Emperor for the time

THE BIG THREE AT POTSDAM

Mr. Churchill, President Truman, and Generalissimo Stalin link hands outside Churchill's Potsdam residence, where Churchill entertained with a dinner party on July 23, 1945.

being, on condition that he take orders from an Allied supreme commander, to be resident in Japan. This offer the Japanese government accepted, and by August 14 the war was over. The documents of surrender were not actually signed until the formal surrender of September 1. Thereafter the occupation of Japan by American forces proceeded rapidly, and General MacArthur, acting through the Emperor, became the real ruler of Japan. September 2, 1945, was officially designated V-J Day by the President, but by this time the chief celebrations were over.

The Home Front. The solidarity of the "home front" during the years of American participation in the Second World War was virtually unbroken. The Japanese attack on Pearl Harbor, followed by declarations of war against the United States by both Germany and Italy, left little room for opposition to the war, even among isolationists. Few Americans of German or Italian descent were prepared to apologize for the behavior of Hitler or Mussolini, while not one Japanese on the Pacific Coast and in Hawaii, for all the suspicion with which they were regarded, was ever found guilty of sabotage or espionage. Communists in the United States were violently antiwar and isolationist during nearly two years of American neutrality, but after Hitler's attack on Russia, the "party line" reversed itself, and when the United States entered the war, American Communists gave their government consistent support. Some Socialists, led by Norman Thomas, a few clergymen, and a small number of conscientious objectors furnished about all the opposition there was to the war. Under the circumstances, there was little persecution of nonconformists.

Americans of Japanese Ancestry. The one notable blot on the American record of tolerance was the treatment of the Japanese in Hawaii and on the Pacific Coast. In the Hawaiian Islands between 30 and 40

A RELOCATION CAMP FOR JAPANESE

Japanese Americans, both immigrants and American-born, are in this group arriving at the Alien Reception Center at Manzanar, California. Called "potential enemies" because of their race, 112,000 of them lived through World War II virtually as prisoners.

per cent of the population were of Japanese ancestry; hence it was not possible to remove them to the mainland, as was actually suggested, without completely disrupting the economic life of the Islands. But the political rights of Hawaiians, regardless of race, color, or nationality, were almost totally abrogated during the war. Military law replaced civilian government, and army officers discharged the duties normally assigned to judges and police magistrates. Only with the greatest difficulty did the Hawaiians regain their normal rights, and to guard against any repetition of unpleasantnesses associated with army rule, they began immediately after the war a movement for statehood. On the Pacific Coast, even in California where they were most numerous, the Japanese constituted only a tiny fraction of the total population. But under military orders, they were herded into interior "relocation camps." Conditions in the camps were far from satisfactory, but in general the Japanese "evacuees" conducted themselves well. Despite the discrimination against their ancestry, many Americans of Japanese descent, both from Hawaii and from the mainland, served with distinction in the Army of the United States. After the war, the "relocation camps" were broken up, and their inmates were allowed to return to whatever remained of their normal life.

Cost of the War. Perhaps the American people inherited a lighter burden of intolerance from the Second than from the First World War, but the cost in dollars, lives, and social dislocation was much heavier. Expenditures for the Second World War reached about $300 billion, more than eight times as much as the nation spent on the First World War. The cost in lives was about 393,000, at least three times as many as in 1917–1918, although far fewer in proportion to the amount of fighting done. The difference was due to better training before battle action and greater medical efficiency. Of the total 15.2 million people mobilized by the United States, over 1 million were reported as casualties. But even these figures were a small part of the total human costs of the war. Just how many soldiers and civilians on both sides of the line perished will probably never be known. Some 80 million men had been mobilized by all the powers, and of this number at least 15 million had been killed. In addition, countless civilians had died from the violence, disease, and hunger accompanying probably the greatest tragedy known to history.

The cost in dollars of the war was met in large part by borrowing, although heavy taxation made it possible to finance about 40 per cent of war expenditures from current income. Income taxes were made applicable to nearly everyone, and the public was encouraged to invest in bonds by regular payroll deductions if necessary. Eight special "drives," with a tremendous fanfare of advertising, sought to tap the nation's savings, particularly those of the small investor. Unlike the bonds of the First World War, which were all transferable and were frequently sold at a discount by hard pressed investors, the savings bonds of the Second World War were nontransferable, and were redeemable by the government on demand. Thus purchasers who had overbought, or who found that for any reason they could not hold their bonds, were spared the heavy losses that in the previous war had overtaken the buyers of "Liberty Bonds." But no safeguards were possible against the legacy of high taxation which the war would leave for many generations.

Allied Unity. The unity of effort that the Allies had attained during the war seemed to offer hope for the achievement of a successful world organization. There had been frequent conferences held by heads of states, their foreign ministers, and their military advisers. As early as August, 1942, Prime Minister Churchill visited Stalin in Moscow, with the American Ambassador to Russia representing the United States. After the invasion of North Africa, Churchill and Roosevelt met at Casablanca, North Africa, in January, 1943, to lay further plans. They conferred with de Gaulle and Giraud, and they hoped that Stalin and Chiang Kai-shek would join them, but the latter two claimed that it was impossible to leave their countries at that time. Out of this conference came much undisclosed planning and an official announcement that only by "unconditional surrender" could the Axis nations obtain peace. At a conference of foreign ministers, held in Moscow during October, 1943, definite plans were laid for the second front in France, and for some kind of world organization to follow the war. Next came a conference of Churchill, Roosevelt, and Chiang Kai-shek in Cairo in November, 1943, and immediately thereafter the first meeting of both Churchill and Roosevelt with Stalin, at Teheran. So complete were the plans worked out at the Cairo and Teheran meetings that more than a year elapsed before the conferees got together again. Then, early in February, 1945, the "Big Three," Churchill, Roosevelt, and Stalin, accompanied by large retinues of military and governmental advisers, met at Yalta in the Crimea. This conference not only agreed on the "timing, scope and co-ordination" of the last campaign against Germany, but also authorized the calling of the San Francisco Conference, where the United Nations was to be organized, and established many of the basic principles of the coming peace that were to shape the future.

Of vast significance to the peace of the world was the attitude of the Russian leaders. During the war they had seemingly renounced their policy of world revolution; but would this attitude carry over into the making and the keeping of the peace? President Roosevelt, knowing full well that Russian cooperation would be essential to world stability, had made every effort to win the confidence of the Russian leaders. He had accorded the most bountiful lend-lease aid to Russia; he had supported the early launching of a second front in France to relieve the pressure on the Russian armies to the East; and he had opposed a British-sponsored campaign in the Balkans to which Russia vehemently objected, and which, if successful, would have seen British and American troops rather than Russian in control of the Balkans and much of Central Europe at the end of the war.

Yalta. The climax of Roosevelt's overtures to Russia came at Yalta. As part of the price necessary to win Stalin's cooperation, he acceded to the Russian demand that three of the Russian Soviet republics should be accorded membership in the United Nations. Also, as a gesture of conciliation, both to Russia and to American sentiment, he agreed to the principle of the great-power veto in all important acts of the Security Council. In European boundary settlements, Roosevelt conceded to Russia the right to annex all of eastern Poland, and to Poland the right to make compensatory an-

nexations at the expense of Germany. These things, the President believed, he could not have prevented, even if he had tried. For in spite of frequent grave criticism leveled at the Yalta agreements it must be remembered that, at the time they were being made, Russia was in a far stronger position to exact concessions in Eastern Europe than were its western allies. Things might have been vastly different had Roosevelt prior to this time been willing to defy his military advisers, and to support Churchill's plan for the invasion of the Balkans and Central Europe simultaneously with, or even before, launching the attack on France. But this is all in the realm of speculation. The fact was that when the Yalta Conference convened, Russian troops were already far into Germany, and by February 20, 1945, they had advanced to within thirty miles of Berlin, whereas on the western front the ground lost by the German offensive under von Rundstedt had just been recovered and Allied troops were over 200 miles from Berlin. At this same time Russian occupation forces held all of Poland, eastern Czechoslovakia, and most of Hungary, and Tito's Communist Partisans were driving the Germans out of Yugoslavia, while the American invasion of Italy seemed hopelessly stalled in the Apennines. Moreover, Roosevelt secured from Russia in return for the Polish concessions a pledge that the then Russian-dominated Polish temporary government would be "reorganized on a broad democratic basis" and that "free elections" would be held in the immediate future under the supervision of the three governments. The Polish formula, in fact, was extended at Yalta to all the "liberated areas," with the three governments promising the rights of the Atlantic Charter to all liberated peoples and agreeing to assist the liberated states in the establishment through "free elections" of governments "broadly representative of all democratic elements in the population."

On the Far East, Roosevelt's attitude was determined by his military advisers, who urged him to pay almost any price in order to obtain assurance that Russia would join in the war against Japan. The atomic bomb had not yet been proved, and the prospect of direct invasion of the Japanese homeland seemed grim indeed. Roosevelt therefore agreed to conditions that would make Russia dominant in Manchuria at the end of the war, and in addition promised the Soviets the southern half of Sakhalin and the Kuril Islands. The concessions made to Russia in Manchuria were granted without the knowledge or consent of the Chinese government. In return, Stalin promised again — he had said the same thing to Cordell Hull in 1943 — that "in two or three months after Germany has surrendered the Soviet Union shall enter the war against Japan." He also promised to conclude a treaty of friendship with the nationalist government of China, which meant forsaking the Chinese Communists.

The Yalta Conference also ratified a plan — which had been in process of development ever since Teheran — for the eventual division of Germany into three zones of military occupation, one each for the British, American, and Russian forces. Later, at Potsdam, the French were awarded a zone. Berlin, the capital, although located deep in the Russian zone, was to be an international area under joint three- (later four-) power control. The seeds of future conflict were liberally strewn among the Yalta decisions, especially as they concerned Berlin and the divided rule of Germany. But on the whole, the Yalta decisions were not nearly as unfavorable to the West as many American critics have subsequently claimed. Had Russia lived up to the European agreements, the West would have won far more than its military position in 1945 would have warranted. Had Winston Churchill's advice been taken, however, and had American troops been permitted to capture Berlin and Prague, the postwar map of eastern Europe might have been radically different. But American leaders had forgotten that military power has always been as important in shaping a peace as in winning a war.

Election of 1944. Nearly a year before the end of the war, the people of the United States were obliged to hold a presidential election. The war was going well, and its successful prosecution had in most minds a long priority over domestic policies. But the Constitution required an election. Except for the existence of war, there is little reason to suppose that Roosevelt would, or could, have run for a fourth term, but the need of his continued leadership during the crises was, for those who trusted him, a sufficient reason for renominating him. He had little opposition in the Democratic convention, but the Democratic city bosses joined forces with the southern conservatives to oust Henry A. Wallace as Vice-Presidential candidate in favor of Senator Harry S. Truman, of Missouri, an inconspicuous regular who had headed effectively a Senate committee on the investigation of the national defense program. The Republicans had expected a hard-fought campaign for the nomination between Governor Thomas E. Dewey, of New York, and Wendell Willkie, but when Willkie lost in the Wisconsin primary, he withdrew, and the nomination went to Dewey on the first ballot.

The campaign was notable for the wide range of agreement between the two candidates. Both endorsed, in the main, the social legislation of the New Deal. Both urged international organization after the war for the maintenance of peace. But for the fourth time Roosevelt won a decisive victory. The President led in 36 states with 432 electoral votes, while Dewey led in 12 states with only 99 electoral votes. The Democrats also retained their majority in the Senate, greatly improved it in the House, and won a majority of the governorships. Aside from registering the confidence of the majority in Roosevelt's military leadership, the election demonstrated clearly that the American people were far more ready than they had been twenty-five years earlier to accept an important role in international affairs. Isolationism might rise again, but for the moment that historic

American policy seemed dead. The defeat of numerous outstanding isolationists and ex-isolationists made certain that the new Congress would be receptive to any plan of postwar cooperation that offered a reasonable hope of world peace.

Death of Roosevelt. During the campaign, the health of President Roosevelt had become a matter of considerable concern to the American public. The cares of office had obviously aged him. Lines on his face had deepened, he had lost weight, and he was noticeably less willing to exert himself to stand or walk. He suffered from colds and bronchial infections, and frequently took extended rests. But he had waged a vigorous campaign and had convinced the country that he was capable of carrying on, or so the election returns seemed to show. On April 12, 1945, however, he died suddenly at his winter home in Warm Springs, Georgia, of a massive cerebral hemorrhage. Like Woodrow Wilson, he was a casualty of the conflict in which he played so major a part. His death cast a gloom over America and the free world that even the imminence of victory could not completely erase.

SELECTED BIBLIOGRAPHY

The best survey is A. R. Buchanan, *The United States and World War II* (2 vols., 1964); it contains a carefully selected bibliography. There are several single-volume histories of the Second World War, including W. P. Hall, *Iron out of Calvary* (1946); and H. C. O'Neill, *A Short History of the Second World War* (1950). On the war as a whole, Winston Churchill, *The Second World War* (6 vols., 1948–1953), is a brilliant interpretation. Two interesting critiques by military historians are H. W. Baldwin, *Great Mistakes of the War* (1950); and J. F. C. Fuller, *The Second World War* (1949). K. R. Greenfield (ed.), *Command Decisions* (1959), contains perceptive analyses by historians.

Among the memoirs of leading American participants the following are of particular importance: D. D. Eisenhower, *Crusade in Europe* (1948); O. N. Bradley, *A Soldier's Story* (1951); M. W. Clark, *Calculated Risk* (1950); E. J. King and W. M. Whitehill, *Fleet Admiral King, A Naval Record* (1952); J. W. Stilwell, *The Stilwell Papers*, edited by T. H. White (1948); H. H. Arnold, *Global Mission* (1949); A. A. Vandegrift and R. B. Asprey, *Once a Marine* (1964); and Douglas MacArthur, *Reminiscences* (1964). There is no memoir of General Marshall, but F. C. Pogue has published the first volume of his *George C. Marshall* (1963), which covers 1880–1939.

A brilliant treatment of the naval side is

* Available in paperback

S. E. Morison, *The Two-Ocean War* (1963), an abridgment of his *History of United States Naval Operations in World War II* (14 vols., 1947–1960). John Toland, *But Not in Shame* (1961), is a competent survey of the early months of the war. Other books of merit include E. B. Potter (ed.), *The Great Sea War* (1960); Robert Leckie, *Strong Men Armed* (1962); J. A. Iseley and P. A. Crowl, *The U.S. Marines and Amphibious War* (1951); and Robert Sherrod, *History of Marine Corps Aviation in World War II* (1952). Other valuable works dealing with the navy include R. G. Albion and others, *Forrestal and the Navy* (1962); A. A. Rogow, *James Forrestal* (1964); and Armin Rappaport, *The Navy League of the United States* (1962), a study of the unofficial navy pressure group.

A brief survey of a tangled situation is Gaddis Smith, *American Diplomacy during the Second World War* (1964). An even broader treatment is John Snell, *Illusion and Necessity: The Diplomacy of Global War, 1939–1945* (1963). Herbert Feis, *Churchill — Roosevelt — Stalin: The War They Waged and The Peace They Sought* (1957), is a superb survey of wartime diplomacy by a former State Department officer who had access to archival materials. Feis continued his work with two shorter books: *Between War and Peace: The Potsdam Conference* (1960), and *Japan Subdued* (1961). See also W. H. McNeill, *America, Britain, and Russia: Their Cooperation and Conflict, 1941–1946* (1953). Willard

Range, *Franklin D. Roosevelt's World Order* (1959), gathers together the President's expressed thinking about the international situation throughout his life. W. D. Hassett, *Off the Record with F.D.R., 1942–1945* (1958), contains vivid impressions of the wartime President, as recorded by his secretary. W. D. Leahy, *I Was There* (1950), is the memoir of a leading figure. Shrewd, objective analyses by careful scholars are in J. L. Snell (ed.), *The Meaning of Yalta: Big Three Diplomacy and the New Balance of Power* (1956). A collection which brings out divergent viewpoints is *The Yalta Conference, edited by R. F. Fenno, Jr. (1955). Other important works on wartime diplomacy include W. L. Langer, *Our Vichy Gamble* (1947); and Herbert Feis, *The Spanish Story* (1948). Relations between Roosevelt and General de Gaulle are explored in D. S. White, *Seeds of Discord* (1964); and Milton Viorst, *Hostile Allies* (1965).

Eliot Janeway, *The Struggle for Survival: A Chronicle of Economic Mobilization in World War II* (1951), is a lively overview, critical in tone. A substantial study of the key Congressional body is D. H. Riddle, *The Truman Committee* (1964). Records of some of the important wartime agencies are available as follows: D. M. Nelson, *Arsenal of Democracy* (1946); E. R. Stettinius, Jr., *Lend-Lease, Weapon for Victory* (1944); H. M. Somers, *Presidential Agency: OWMR, The Office of War Mobilization and Reconversion* (1950); and F. C. Lane and others, *Ships for Victory* (1951). See also the general survey by D. L. Gordon and Royden Dangerfield, *The Hidden Weapon: The Story of Economic Warfare* (1947). Elias Huzar, *The Purse and the Sword: Control of the Army by Congress through Military Appropriations, 1933–1950* (1950), is a valuable monograph. W. W. Wilcox, *The Farmer in the Second World War* (1947), is illuminating. One hideous wartime episode is treated by Robert Shogan and Tom Craig, *The Detroit Race Riot* (1964).

On Americans of Japanese ancestry, there are several excellent books. D. S. Thomas and others, *Japanese-American Evacuation and Resettlement* (3 vols., 1946–1954), tells the painful story of Japanese internment on the Pacific Coast. Interesting books on the Hawaiian situation include A. W. Lind, *Hawaii's Japanese* (1946); and Gwenfread Allen, *Hawaii's War Years, 1941–1945* (1950).

Later phases of the European war are treated in a number of the works cited in the last bibliography. Charles de Gaulle, *War Memoirs* (3 vols., 1955–1960), are of first importance. B. L. Montgomery, *Memoirs* (1958), is generally critical of the British field marshal's associates and superiors. Alan Moorehead, *Montgomery: A Biography* (1946), is a friendly, well-written book; Chester Wilmot, *The Struggle for Europe* (1952), by an Australian journalist, is also pro-Montgomery, and critical of the American leadership. Albert Norman, *Operation Overlord* (1952), is by General Bradley's staff historian. On American operations in France see S. L. A. Marshall, *Night Drop* (1962); and Cornelius Ryan, *The Longest Day* (1959), the best on the invasion as a whole. Two excellent books on the Battle of the Bulge are R. E. Merriam, *The Battle of the Bulge (Dark December)* (1947); and John Toland, *Battle* (1959). The character and personality of General Patton have recently been evaluated in two books: Fred Ayer, Jr., *Before the Colors Fade* (1964); and Ladislas Farago, *Patton* (1964). A brilliant study of the mythical German stronghold and its consequences is R. G. Minott, *The Fortress That Never Was* (1964). A special study of great interest is Walter Rundell, Jr., *Black Market Money* (1964). H. R. Trevor-Roper, *The Last Days of Hitler* (3rd ed., 1956), carefully sifts the evidence on what finally happened to Hitler.

Among the many books on later phases of the war in the Pacific are C. V. Woodward, *The Battle for Leyte Gulf* (1947); and R. F. Newcomb, *Iwo Jima* (1965). E. M. Zacharias, *Secret Missions* (1946), sheds light on the disintegration of the Japanese will to fight. R. J. C. Butow, *Japan's Decision to Surrender* (1954), is a careful work based upon Japanese sources. Paul Kecskemeti, *Strategic Surrender: The Politics of Victory and Defeat* (1958), studies the surrender of the three Axis countries.

Among the many works treating the atomic bomb, the following are of particular interest here: J. P. Baxter, *Scientists Against Time* (1946); R. C. Batchelder, *The Irreversible Decision* (1961); R. G. Hewlett and O. E. Anderson, Jr., *The New World, 1939–1946* (1962); and L. R. Groves, *Now It Can Be Told* (1962), the reminiscence of the general in charge of the Manhattan Project.

41

THE TRUMAN ERA

Truman. The death of Roosevelt threw
the heavy burden of reconverting the
United States to peace and reconstructing
the war-torn world upon Harry S. Truman
(1884–   ). As Roosevelt was the embodiment of the extraordinary American,
Truman to most of his fellow countrymen
seemed to personify the typical ordinary
American. He was from a small town in
Missouri, and had served honorably as a
National Guard officer in the First World
War. He had gone into politics because he
needed a job. As an organization Democrat,
he was not above accepting a county judge-
ship at the hands of "Boss" Thomas Pendergast, a blatant corruptionist who controlled
the destinies of the Democratic Party in
Kansas City and aspired to control the state.
In Missouri a county judge is an administrative officer; Truman was neither a lawyer
nor a "judge" in the usual sense. But he had
under his control the expenditure of huge
sums of money, particularly in the construction of highways and public buildings,
and not the faintest suspicion of dishonesty
was ever attached to any of his acts. At
Pendergast's suggestion, he was nominated
for the Senate in 1934, won as any other
Democrat won that year, and was re-elected
in 1940. His emergence as a senatorial investigator who was willing on occasion
even to point out the shortcomings of the
President gave him much favorable publicity. When Henry Wallace was denied the
Vice-Presidential renomination, Truman,
partly because he was almost the only mid-
dlewesterner acceptable to all factions of
his party, won the unsolicited post that a
few months later was to make him President.

The first great concern of the new President was to carry through to a successful
conclusion the United Nations Conference
on International Organization, already
called by the United States, Great Britain,
Russia, and China to meet in San Francisco, April 25, 1945. Roosevelt promoted
the holding of this conference before the
war came to an end, and had promised to
open it in person.

The San Francisco Conference. To facilitate the creation of the new world organization, Great Britain, Russia, China,
and the United States had held a meeting
in the autumn of 1944 at Dumbarton Oaks
in Washington and had agreed upon a set
of tentative proposals. In many respects
the new plan was similar to that of the

SIGNING THE UNITED NATIONS CHARTER

In San Francisco, June 26, 1945, Secretary of State Edward R. Stettinius (seated) put his signature to the document that joined the United States with forty-nine other nations in the creation of the United Nations. Twenty years later the UN membership had grown to one hundred and fourteen.

League of Nations, but it contained nothing comparable to the historic Article X to which the United States Senate had so violently objected; it gave greater authority to the smaller Security Council (representing five great powers and six selected others) and less to the larger Assembly, thereby eliminating a principal cause for delay and indecisiveness in the actions of the League; it made more feasible the use of force against would-be aggressors, and put less trust in disarmament; it proposed as an integral part of the plan a Permanent Court of International Justice; and it presumed that the Charter, unlike the Covenant, would be entirely separate from any treaty of peace. Invited to the Conference at San Francisco were all of the nations, now more than fifty, that had joined in the hostilities against the Axis powers. At the Conference the smaller nations greatly influenced the results, although none of the fundamentals of the Dumbarton Oaks proposals was altered. Whatever the faults and virtues of the Charter, it was widely ratified, and in the United States Senate met negligible opposition.

Other Conferences. Exhibiting the general spirit of world cooperation of the Dumbarton Oaks and San Francisco conferences was a series of important international agreements already reached on a wide variety of subjects. At Bretton Woods in New Hampshire, a conference held in July, 1944, proposed an International Bank for Reconstruction and Development, with a parallel organization, the International Monetary Fund, to maintain stability in the exchange values of national currencies. Somewhat earlier a United Nations Relief and Rehabilitation Administration (UNRRA), a Food and Agriculture Organization of the United Nations, and a Provisional International Civil Aviation Organization had been set up. Within the Americas a conference at Chapultepec, Mexico, did much to cement intracontinental solidarity.

The United Nations. The process of putting the San Francisco Charter into effect began at London on January 10, 1946, when the General Assembly opened its first session. A week later the Security Council met at London. On its recommendation, the Assembly chose Trygve Lie, a Norwegian, as the first Secretary-General of the United Nations. After much debate, New York City was chosen as the permanent headquarters of the new world organization.

It soon became apparent that the Security Council, under existing regulations, could never become the effective instrument that at least some of the framers of the United Nations Charter had hoped. The chief difficulty lay in the provision which permitted each great power to veto any important action that might be proposed. When Roosevelt and Churchill agreed to this crippling provision they could hardly have foreseen the ruthlessness with which one nation, Russia, would exercise the veto power. During the first seven years of the life of the United Nations, the Russian veto was interposed no less than fifty times, and by the early 1960's the number had exceeded one hundred. In practice, the Russian use of the veto power frequently made the United Nations quite ineffective.

UN Agencies. In spite of the discouraging effect of the Russian vetoes, the United Nations was able to provide most of the machinery for world cooperation that had been contemplated by the San Francisco Charter. This involved the creation of several important subordinate bodies. (1) The Economic and Social Council consisted of eighteen members elected by the Assembly. This Council in turn set up or took over from the old League of Nations a wide variety of commissions through which to operate and to seek advice. It also sponsored such previously created international bodies as the United Nations Education, Scientific, and Cultural Organization (UNESCO). (2) A Trusteeship Council of twelve members had a somewhat ill-defined measure of authority over mandates and over territory detached from a defeated nation. "Strategic areas," however, such as the former Japanese mandates in the Pacific which were handed over to the United States for administration, were to be directly under the Security Council. (3) An International Court of Justice, with fifteen judges chosen by the Security Council in conjunction with the Assembly, was to hear such cases in dispute between nations as might be referred to it. The establishment of a Military Staff Committee, to advise the Security Council on the means by which armed force might be used to carry out United Nations decisions, was rendered impossible by Russian lack of cooperation. For a time a "Little Assembly," consisting of one representative from each member nation, although unauthorized by the United Nations Charter, served as a kind of substitute for the larger and more cumbersome Assembly, when the latter was not in session, but the "Little Assembly" had no real authority, and was promptly boycotted by Russia and her satellites.

UN Peace Efforts. The record of the United Nations on the preservation of peace during its first few years of existence gave little reason for optimism. Its first sessions were confronted by Iranian protests against the continued Russian military occupation of Iranian territory, and perhaps the evidence that the majority of the Security Council sympathized with Iran may have had something to do with the decision of the Soviet leaders to recall their troops. Charges made by the Ukraine that British troops in Greece threatened the peace of the Balkans were denied by the Greeks, who charged in turn that Albania, Bulgaria, and Yugoslavia were supporting Greek Communist insurgents in their attempt to overthrow the Greek government. A United Nations Commission investigated the situation, but a Russian veto prevented action being taken on its report, and the guerrilla fighting continued. Efforts of the United Nations to intervene in the Dutch-Indonesian dispute, as will be noted, were more successful. Russian intransigence prevented the Security Council from appointing a governor of Trieste, as provided for under the terms of the peace treaty with Italy. Thus Trieste remained under joint Anglo-American control until 1954, when Yugoslavia and Italy, after prolonged negotiations, agreed on its division between them.

Demobilization. Despite initial setbacks, however, the American public remained optimistic about the chances for world cooperation. Russia, it was true, was dedicated to world revolution, but up to the end of the war Stalin's interest in cooperation had seemed genuine. He had abolished the Comintern, he had stopped the war on religion, and he had seemed willing to compromise on details at Yalta, even promising that the future of much of eastern Europe would be settled by democratic elections. In addition to these fair prospects the United States held a monopoly on the atomic bomb, the threat of which was worth untold divisions of armed strength.

The rapid demobilization of American armed forces, taken in conjunction with the growing realization that the United States would not use the atomic bomb again except under the most critical conditions, may have been a serious mistake. The existence of a well-trained army and a powerful navy could have given the nation much additional diplomatic strength during the impending sparring among the Allies for a peace settlement. But public insistence was too strong to be denied, and by December, 1945, the military forces were disintegrating at the rate of over 1.5 million a month, and by the next spring the Selective Service Law had to be extended for a year in order to keep military personnel even to the needed minimum. This was the second peacetime conscription act in American history, but world conditions have necessitated its operation ever since. At the end of the year the army numbered only 670,000 men, the navy, 395,000, and the marine corps, 83,700.

The Disintegration of Peace. Meantime, in international affairs, the hope that the victorious Allies could work together successfully in the pursuit of peace had been all but demolished. Just two weeks after her Yalta pledge to establish democratic governments in the liberated nations, Russia began the establishment of a Communist dictatorship in Rumania. Within another two weeks it was also clear that the Soviets would follow the same tactics in Poland. At the Potsdam Conference, during July and August, 1945, Russia's intentions toward eastern Europe became even more evident. Wherever the Russian army dominated, Communist states subservient to Moscow were to be the order of the new day. As Churchill remarked at Potsdam, an "iron fence" was being built around them.

Minor Peace Treaties. One of the Potsdam agreements stipulated that the peace treaties for Germany and Austria should not be undertaken until settlements had been reached on Italy, Finland, Hungary, Bulgaria, and Rumania. After much bickering, the task of drawing these treaties was turned over to a council of the foreign ministers of the appropriate great powers, while changes in the treaties so drafted might be suggested by a general peace conference representing all the Allies, to be held in Paris in May, 1946. It was during the course of these negotiations that President Truman and his new Secretary of State, James F. Byrnes, at last came to the conclusion that concessions to the Russians rarely, if ever, brought any concession in return. The American negotiators, with strong British and French backing, began to stand their ground against the Russians with such firmness that they were accused by Russian sympathizers in the United States of shifting to a "get-tough-with Russia" attitude. Chief among these critics was Henry A. Wallace, who had become Secretary of Commerce in President Roosevelt's cabinet after the election of 1944, and had been retained by President Truman. In a speech delivered in New York on September 12, 1946, Wallace criticized

American foreign policy, and urged that the United States give Russia a free hand in eastern Europe. President Truman, after some hesitation, dismissed Wallace from his cabinet and gave the Byrnes policy his full support.

After almost interminable negotiations, the five treaties were at last officially signed in Paris on February 10, 1947. The war-making potential of all five former German satellites was reduced to insignificance, heavy reparations were assessed against them, and all except Bulgaria were obliged to make extensive territorial readjustments. Italy, once Germany's closest associate, ceded land to France, Greece, Albania, and Yugoslavia, and turned over the administration of her colonies to the four principal Allies. Even before the end of the war she had been forced to restore freedom to her two conquered provinces, Ethiopia and Albania. Among the Allied powers the principal gainer from these treaties was Yugoslavia, a nation in which the Communists under Marshal Tito had already achieved complete control. Yugoslavia's territory was increased, her reparations bill topped the Allied list, and her right to arm remained unrestricted. In thus strengthening this strategically located satellite, the Russians apparently hoped to win a springboard for their expected jump to full control of the Mediterranean.

Germany and Austria. The restoration of peaceful relations with the minor enemy states had proved to be difficult, but with Germany and "liberated" Austria the task was to remain for years an impossibility. Germany was broken into four zones of military occupation, one for each of the "Big Four" powers, and the city of Berlin, although supposedly under joint four-power control, was similarly subdivided. The government of Germany as a whole was to be in the hands of an Allied Control Council composed of the four high commanding officers of the several zones. The conquered nation was to be administered as "a single economic unit," but all decisions of the Council had to be unanimous. Unfortunately, the western powers neither asked nor received from Russia guarantees of uninterrupted access to Berlin, although the only way they could reach the city was through the Russian zone. This agreement was made at a time when it was assumed that Russian good will was the only guarantee needed. A similar four-divisional plan was worked out for Austria, and for Austria's capital city, Vienna, but there was one extremely important difference, the existence of an independent Austrian government, which eventually won the recognition of all four great powers. The Russians, however, in contrast with the trustful attitude of the western powers in the case of Berlin, obtained formal consent from the other powers to their maintenance of "communication lines" with Austria through both Hungary and Rumania. This gave the Russian government the opportunity to keep military forces not only in Austria but in the two neighboring states also, even after peace treaties with them had been signed and ratified.

The occupation of Austria proceeded with relatively minor difficulties, but the occupation of Germany presented an interminable procession of virtually insoluble problems. Germany in defeat was without a government, its cities and industries were in ruins, it was overrun with "displaced persons," and it was in no mood even to try to help itself. Fortunately, the Allied Control Council reached agreement on about fifty major measures before the Russian policy of non-cooperation set in. The Allies also worked out a plan for the trial of those Germans who were principally responsible for the war and were still alive. After ten months of hearings the international court constituted for the purpose sentenced eleven "war criminals" to be hanged, and eight others to long prison terms. Three of the defendants were freed, and one of the condemned, Göring, escaped execution by suicide. Later, many less not-

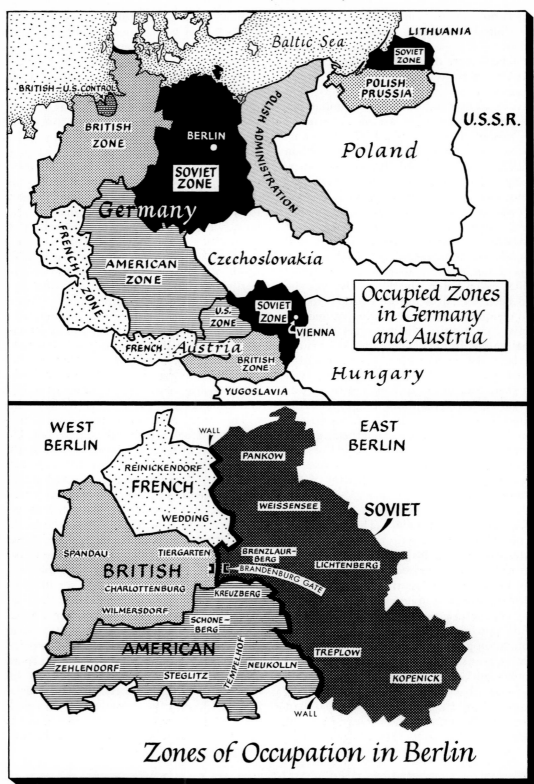

Occupied Zones in Germany and Austria

Zones of Occupation in Berlin

able criminals were also brought to trial, and many convictions were obtained.

"Bizonia" and "Trizonia." As time wore on, it became evident that Russian policy toward Germany had shifted. At the Potsdam Conference, all the great powers, Russia included, had wished to keep Germany decentralized, as the best available means of preventing the revival of the nation's military might, but eventually the Soviet leaders concluded that they might better profit from a highly industrialized Germany with a political system that would insure its subordination to Russia. For this program the western powers naturally showed scant sympathy. Working against odds to keep their sections together economically, the British and Americans first consolidated their zones for administrative purposes into a "Bizonia," which the addition of the French zone presently made a "Trizonia." The break between East and West grew more marked with each succeeding month. Finally, in March, 1948, when the Russians refused all further participation in the Allied Control Council, almost the last vestige of governmental unity disappeared.

The net result of Russian intransigence was the creation of two Germanies, one to the west under the sponsorship of the western democracies, and one to the east under Soviet control. Unhampered by Russian vetoes, the western powers in the next few years proceeded rapidly with the restoration of western Germany, while the Russians strove to build up a Communist-dominated industrial and military power in eastern Germany. Similarly, there evolved two Berlins, a western-occupied West Berlin, and a Russian-occupied East Berlin.

China. On the other side of the world, in eastern Asia, the road to peace was quite as long and tortuous as in Europe. In China the end of the war, instead of bringing peace, brought only a life-and-death conflict between the Nationalist government of Chiang Kai-shek and an increasingly power-ful Communist faction which Russian backing had built up in Manchuria and northern China. In an effort to restore peace the government of the United States, in December, 1945, sent General George C. Marshall on a special mission to China to bring the warring factions together into one government. But the Marshall mission, in spite of the brief armistice it facilitated, failed utterly, and the war continued. On Marshall's recommendation, the United States reduced drastically its aid to Chiang's government and adopted a "plague-on-both-your-houses" attitude toward the fighting factions. In the months that followed, the Communists went from one triumph to another until by the spring of 1949 the Nationalist armies were in full rout, and Chiang himself had fled to Formosa.

Korea. In Korea, as in China, the peace presented almost insuperable obstacles. At the Cairo Conference of 1943, Roosevelt, Churchill, and Chiang Kai-shek had pledged themselves to establish an independent Korea, but at the end of the war the United States and Russia divided that unhappy nation between them at the thirty-eighth parallel for military occupation. The professed intent of the two powers was the establishment of a native Korean government, but mutual distrust prevented any such development. Finally, during the summer of 1948, two Korean governments appeared, a Korean People's Republic in the northern zone, modeled on the Soviet pattern, and a Republic of Korea in the southern zone, with a democratic constitution, under the presidency of Syngman Rhee.

Japan. In Japan, American occupation had gone more smoothly than had at first been expected. The retention of the Emperor and the early creation of a Japanese government reduced to a minimum the problems of the American occupation forces. The Japanese people were cooperative; MacArthur gave the orders, and the Japanese government carried them out.

Despite some efforts to give the Japanese occupation the appearance of joint Allied operation, it remained primarily an American affair. As in Germany, the war leaders were brought to trial, and eventually seven of them, including Tojo, the wartime premier, were executed. Efforts were made to break up large landed estates in the interest of a wider distribution of holdings, to dissolve the large corporations, to develop labor organizations after the western pattern, and to institute extensive educational reforms. But all these measures failed dismally to restore stable economic conditions in Japan, and the very survival of the nation seemed to depend upon the steady importation of unpaid-for supplies from the United States. After the outbreak of the Korean war in 1950, the Japanese economy greatly benefited from the war purchases made by the United States.

Ever since March, 1947, when General MacArthur reported that a peace treaty might be made with Japan, the United States had worked toward that end. But for the next three years the opposition of Russia and Nationalist China blocked the proposal. Finally, in September, 1951, a peace conference was assembled at San Francisco where the occupation was declared at an end. In a treaty ratified by the Senate in March, 1952, Japan agreed to give up all claims to its former empire in the Kurils, Formosa, the Pescadores, Korea, and China. It further agreed to honor all its former debts, while the victors relinquished all reparations. A subsequent agreement between the Japanese government and the United States, made possible by the treaty, provided for American military bases within the Japanese home islands. To mollify the objections of New Zealand, Australia, and the Philippines, who feared to rearm Japan, the United States had previously concluded a defensive agreement with each of these countries. The American military bases so gained, together with those established on the former Japanese islands, now held as trust territories by the United States, gave

this nation a great armed potential as well as widespread obligations throughout East Asia.

The Philippines. In spite of the vastly changed conditions resulting from the war, the United States finally gave the Philippine Islands their independence on July 4, 1946, although on terms that the Filipinos accepted with some reluctance. The American government took pains to provide for the creation of an effective Philippine army, and for the retention by the United States of important military and naval bases. In economic matters, a Philippine Trade Act paved the way for the gradual institution of American tariffs on goods imported from the Philippines, after an eight-year period of free trade on the quota basis. Congress also voted a total of $720 million to compensate the Philippine government and the owners of private property in the Islands for the war damage they had suffered. These acts, however, failed to solve the pressing internal problems of the Philippine Republic. The prewar sugar-coconut-to-bacco economy, which had profited the landlord-merchant class a great deal, but the ordinary peasant very little, had been shattered by the war. Many of the peasants were loath to go back to it; and some of them, under the leadership of a left-wing pro-Communist organization known as the Hukbalahap, went the whole distance of open revolt. The success of Ramon Magsaysay, Secretary of Defense after 1950, in his campaign against the "Huks," coupled with his promises of reform, led to his election to the Philippine presidency in 1953. While in general the Filipinos made considerable economic progress, thanks in no small part to American aid, they suffered much from the venality and inefficiency of their political leaders. The death in a plane crash of Magsaysay, who was an exception to the rule, was a great misfortune.

India, Burma, Malaya. It was apparent that most of the colonial peoples in Asia

U.S.S.R.

Magadan

SEA OF OKHOTSK

Irkutsk
Lake Baikal

Nikolayevsk

SAKHALIN
(SOV. UN.)

OUTER MONGOLIA

AMUR R.

KURILE IS.
(SOV. UN.)

Harbin

Changchun

MANCHURIA

INNER MONGOLIA

Mukden

HOKKAIDO

Vladivostok

SEA OF JAPAN

Peiping

Tientsin

Darien

Wonsan

HONSHU

TIBET

CHINA

Tsingtao

Seoul

KOREA

HWANG HO

Yellow Sea

Tokyo

Nanking

Osaka

JAPAN

Nagasaki

SHIKOKU

Shanghai

KYUSHU

YANGTZE

Changsha

Wenchow

RYUKYU IS.

Foochow

Canton

BURMA

Amoy

FORMOSA

Hanoi

Macao (PORT.)

Hong Kong

HAINAN

Rangoon

FRENCH INDO-CHINA

LUZON

THAILAND

Bangkok

PHILIPPINE ISLANDS

Manila

China, Japan and Eastern Asia

Saigon

South China Sea

MINDANAO

MALAY STATES

N. BORNEO

Palau Is.

Truk

SARAWAK

Celebes Sea

CAROLINE ISLANDS

Singapore

BORNEO

CELEBES

Halmahera

SUMATRA

NEW GUINEA

Rabaul

Jakarta

I N D O N E S I A

JAVA

INDIAN OCEAN

Darwin

had no intention of going back to the old system of subservience to white dominion. They had seen the white man defeated and humiliated, and they had lost their awe and fear of the Europeans. What they wanted when the Japanese were driven out was self-rule, such as the United States eventually granted to the Philippines. In recognizing this new spirit among colonial peoples, Great Britain was not far behind the United States. In India, the task was less one of getting the British out than of getting the Hindus and Moslems to agree on a plan of self-government. Finally a divided India emerged with two new nations, India, dominated by the Hindus, and Pakistan, dominated by the Moslems, both claiming membership in the British Commonwealth of Nations. In Burma, where there was less internal friction, complete independence was granted. In Malaya, although British control continued for a time, two autonomous governmental units were organized, but in 1963 Britain welcomed the birth of the new state of Malaysia, which included not only the federated Malay states but parts of Borneo, and for a short time Singapore.

Indo-China, Indonesia. Unfortunately the willingness of the United States and Great Britain to grant home rule to their dependencies was not fully shared by other European nations who had possessions in the Orient. In the populous Dutch East Indies the returning European overlords met a determined Indonesian independence movement, and sharp fighting broke out. After mediation by the United Nations and protracted negotiations, the Dutch government unwillingly recognized the new Republic of Indonesia in December, 1949. The new state, comprising some 75 million people, eventually included all of the old Dutch East Indies possessions. Even more grudgingly the French ultimately retired from Indo-China. After almost continuous fighting against both local nationalists and Communists, who drew much of their strength from Red China, France in 1950

belatedly granted autonomy to the three native states, Vietnam, Cambodia, and Laos. But by that time local Communists, under the leadership of Ho Chi Minh, had become a major threat, and despite American aid totaling $2 billion the French had to capitulate at the Geneva Conference of May, 1954. By the terms of the Geneva agreement France withdrew from all of Indo-China, gave northern Vietnam to Ho's Communists, and recognized the complete independence of South Vietnam, Cambodia, and Laos.

This great European withdrawal from South Asia, however, did not bring peace to the area. India and Pakistan continued to quarrel over the disposition of Kashmir. Indonesia, despite its steadily worsening economic condition, became increasingly imperialistic and threatened the new state of Malaysia. And in almost every south Asian country, the Communists, whether chiefly inspired and aided by Moscow or by Peking, constituted a continuous threat to internal order.

The Truman Doctrine and the "Cold War." Meanwhile Communist actions in Europe clearly indicated that the hope for "One World," inspired by wartime collaboration of Great Britain, Russia, and the United States, and by the establishment of the United Nations, was for the indefinite future an illusion. Wherever the Red army exercised control, either by direct occupation or by its heavy shadow across an international border, free governments disappeared. By one means or another Communist minorities took over in Poland, Yugoslavia, Bulgaria, Hungary, and finally even Czechoslovakia. The Russian zones in Germany and Austria were separated from other zones of occupation by heavy Red army patrols, and were stripped of their resources. From the Baltic to the Adriatic an "iron curtain" had descended, behind which the Soviet leaders could in safety and secrecy consolidate their gains and plan further expansion. In Italy and

France they galvanized Communist minorities into action, preparatory to taking over those governments. In Turkey they served notice that directly or indirectly the Soviets must control the Dardanelles. In Greece they made every effort to promote a Communist revolution that would establish Russian influence on the shores of the Mediterranean. Obviously the Russians were bent upon creating "One World," but that was to be a Communist world. And if democracy and freedom were to be saved, then the United States as the only western nation with adequate strength had to confront the Communist challenge.

It was the Greek situation which finally led the United States to take a positive stand against the Russian program of aggression, and thus to begin the so-called cold war between the two great world powers. When the British government, in line with its general policy of retrenchment, announced that it could no longer maintain a garrison in Greece, the United States determined that the time had come to take a stand. The government of Greece had little to recommend it, except its anti-Communism, but it was at least subject to improvement. If the Communists came in, then down would come the "iron curtain," and the liberties of one more "liberated" country would disappear. Faced by this situation, President Truman, on March 12, 1947, sent a message to Congress calling for immediate American aid for both Greece and Turkey. The United States, the President declared, "must assist free peoples to work out their own destinies in their own way." To give strength to his words the President recommended that Congress vote $300 million for aid to Greece and $100 million for aid to Turkey. The Truman Doctrine, as this revolutionary demand came to be called, aroused much discussion in the United States. A small minority, headed by Henry A. Wallace, denounced it, while others regretted that the American nation had acted alone instead of through the United Nations. But the appropriations passed Congress substantially as the President requested, with Senator Arthur Vandenberg, a Republican, championing the President's cause. American policy toward Europe had by this time achieved a bipartisan status, except for left-wing criticism, in its opposition to Russian imperialism. As further evidence of the nonpartisan character of his policy, Truman in January, 1947, had replaced Secretary Byrnes as Secretary of State, with General George C. Marshall, a man who had never been in politics and had never expected to be.

The Marshall Plan. Marshall soon supplemented the Truman Doctrine with what was sometimes called the "Marshall Plan," or "European Recovery Plan." It seemed clear that American aid to one or two hard pressed nations would never serve to turn back the Communist tide. Governments

GENERAL GEORGE C. MARSHALL

Marshall was not only the principal American strategist during World War II, but also served his country later, first as Secretary of State, then as Secretary of Defense.

struggled heroically to restore their war-torn economies, but the results generally were disheartening. Europe as a whole needed to be helped back to its normal economic life. If that could be done, the chief appeal of Communism would disappear. In an address delivered at Harvard University on June 5, 1947, Secretary Marshall called upon European nations first to get together to see what they could do to help themselves, and then to state in concrete terms what additional aid they would need from the United States to accomplish the task. The Marshall Plan, which proposed to supply the needed funds, was enthusiastically received throughout all western Europe, but Russia and her satellites, to whom it was also open, pointedly refused to have anything to do with it and branded it an instrument of American imperialism.

Background of ERP. The European Recovery Plan (ERP) was by no means the first contribution of the United States toward the rehabilitation of the war-torn world. Lend-lease totals had recorded some $48.5 billion worth of American assistance in return for reverse lend-lease worth $7.8 billion, but in the postwar settlements the sums due to the United States were reduced to millions rather than billions, although Russia steadfastly refused to negotiate a settlement of any sort. Further, to take the place of lend-lease funds, to which the British economy had been closely geared during the war, the United States Congress, late in 1945, voted to lend the British government a total of $4 billion with an interest charge of only 2 per cent, and with repayments in fifty equal installments, beginning in 1951. American aid to recovery had also included substantial contributions (about $11 billion) to the United Nations Relief and Rehabilitation Administration (UNRRA), which was created in 1943 and until 1947 distributed aid freely on both sides of the iron curtain. The tendency of Communist governments "to feed their political supporters and starve their political enemies," however, together with charges of graft and maladministration, notably in China, led the United States to discontinue its support of UNRRA in favor of direct relief "done by the United States unilaterally . . . and not as a member of an international organization." Thus in a sense the Marshall Plan grew out of American experience with postwar relief.

ECA Begins Work. As a result of the American overtures, sixteen nations of western Europe sent their representatives to Paris in July, 1947, and reported what they could do to help themselves and what they would need from the United States — a gigantic $19 billion, to be spread over a four-year period. Scaled down to $17 billion, the program thus devised was accepted in principle by the United States, and in April, 1948, Congress voted $5 billion as the first annual appropriation for ERP. To administer the program, an Economic Cooperation Administration (ECA) was set up, with Paul G. Hoffman, a Republican business executive, as chief. Soon billions of American dollars were pouring into Europe and being invested in the restoration of railroads, in hydroelectric projects, new steel mills, cheap housing for the bombed-out masses, and agricultural machinery. By 1949 western Europe's agricultural and industrial production, due in large part to Marshall funds, had regained its 1939 figure. Evidence that ERP had also served, as was intended, to check the spread of Communism was not long in coming. The governments of France and Italy now eliminated all Communists from their cabinets, and despite the strikes and violence this entailed, stood their ground steadfastly. In Italy a free election, which the Communists felt sure they could win, showed 70 per cent of the electorate against the Communists, and only 30 per cent in favor of their "Popular Front."

Communist Seizure of Czechoslovakia. In the face of this growing strength of free Europe the Russians did not remain idle. The establishment of the Cominform in September, 1947, was apparently intended, at least in part, to offset the Truman Doctrine and the Marshall Plan. In February, 1948, with complete Russian support and connivance, the Communists seized power in Czechoslovakia, where until that time a multi-party government had been permitted to exist. Efforts were also made to discipline the Communist dictator of Yugoslavia, Marshal Tito, whom the Cominform in June, 1948, accused of deviation from the party line. But Tito, although fully cognizant of the hazards of his course, stood his ground and refused to be intimidated. During the next two years, in fact, while not renouncing his devotion to Communism, he moved ever closer to an understanding with the West.

The Berlin Blockade. But the outstanding action taken by Russia to show her displeasure with the western world related to Germany. In the summer of 1948, despairing of ever reaching any further agreements on German affairs with the Russian authorities, the western occupation powers announced their intention of establishing a native German government for West Germany, and issued a new currency for use throughout all Trizonia and West Berlin. On the pretext that this currency reform would "place Berlin's economy and her working population in an untenable situation which only can be solved by Berlin's close connection with the eastern part of Germany," the Soviet authorities laid down a blockade against all movement of supplies from the West into Berlin. Since there were in the western-occupied section of the city some 2 million people whose lives might depend on the continued importation of food from the West, it seemed clear that the Soviet intent was to force the western powers out of Berlin by the threat of wholesale starvation. With the western powers eliminated, nothing further would stand in the way of Russian control of the entire capital city — an important step toward a united Communist Germany under Russian domination.

The "Air Lift." At this juncture a firm British-American exercise of their rights to go overland to Berlin, by the use of force, if necessary, might have repaired the early damage done by not securing an unequivocal right of transit at Potsdam. It might also have saved the free world much future trouble. But the two governments avoided a direct confrontation with Russia by the use of aircraft. The air lanes to Berlin were still open, and the western powers at once undertook to fly in the supplies necessary to feed the beleaguered Germans. New airfields were opened up, and soon coal to keep the people warm and even to keep the factories going was reaching Berlin by air. Hundreds of airplanes were brought from the United States to participate in the operation, and both British and American military pilots got superb training, the possible significance of which the Russians could hardly have overlooked. General Lucius D. Clay, the United States Military Governor in Germany, stated clearly the American position when he said, "They can't drive us out by any action short of war." The Russians did everything else they could think of. They withdrew their representative from the four-power Berlin city government, set up a separate police in their section of the city, excluded personnel of the lawful city government from the City Hall, which was within their area, and installed a German Communist of their own choosing as mayor. But in spite of all this, the air lift continued; furthermore, the western occupation authorities, not to be outdone by the Russians, clamped down a counter-blockade on trade between Trizonia and Soviet-dominated eastern Germany.

Effect on Germany. The air lift did much to make friends among the Germans for all who participated in it, particularly for the Americans who bore so large a proportion of the expense and furnished so many of the planes. With the assurance that they were not to be abandoned, the German leaders accepted the Allied invitation to work out a new constitution for the 45 million Germans living in the western occupational zones, with the result that a new Federal Republic, with Bonn as its capital, came into existence.

Finally, in the spring of 1949, the Russian leaders revealed that they were now willing to lift their blockade, if at the same time the western powers would end their counterblockade and agree to a meeting of the Council of Foreign Ministers to discuss the whole German question. Since the western powers had been willing to accept such an arrangement all along, the deal was quickly closed. All blockades were lifted May 12, 1949, and the Foreign Ministers began what proved to be a fruitless meeting on May 23. The West Germans, under their new constitution, however, achieved self-government with Konrad Adenauer, a Christian Democrat, as their first Chancellor, while the Russians set up in their zone the satellite German Democratic Republic.

North Atlantic Treaty Organization. Perhaps the most notable result of the Russian blockade and the air lift was its effect in influencing the United States to cement a permanent military alliance with non-American powers. Before the Berlin blockade, but after the fall of Czechoslovakia to the Communists, Britain and France joined with the Benelux countries to create a system of regional defense, a course of action authorized by the United Nations charter. When the United States indicated its willingness to enter such an organization, negotiations began which ended on March 15, 1949, with the signing of the North Atlantic Treaty by twelve nations — Belgium, Canada, Denmark, France, Great Britain, Iceland, Italy, Luxembourg, the Netherlands, Norway, Portugal, and the United States. Two years later Greece and Turkey also joined. The North Atlantic Treaty Or-

ganization, or NATO as it was popularly called, provided for the mutual defense of all its members against armed attack over a period of twenty years. The members also agreed to develop a common general staff to work out plans for the common armament and defense of the participating nations. The United States, it was generally understood, would make sizable financial contributions for equipping this North Atlantic army and would contribute military and naval forces.

Neither the North Atlantic Treaty nor the $1.5 billion called for in 1949 by the State Department to aid in equipping this international army was agreed to without protracted debate in Congress. A wing of the Republican Party led by Senator Robert A. Taft insisted that the defense of Europe by troops against a possible Russian attack was at best a dubious gamble. Instead of wasting American strength on such a plan, Taft argued, we should build up our own strength at home and deter Russia from an attack by overwhelming air power. Opposition also arose throughout Europe to the expenditures of money for rearmament at the expense of recovery.

Containment. Despite such dissensions, the United States Senate approved the North Atlantic Treaty on July 21, 1949, by a vote of 82–13, and Congress subsequently appropriated $1.3 billion for its implementation. After General Dwight D. Eisenhower was appointed commander-in-chief of the new forces in December, 1950, with headquarters in France, the North Atlantic Army began to take shape. Along the Mediterranean area a combined British and American naval and air force stood guard, aided by Turkish and Greek land forces. With the United States thus committed to a mutual defense of western Europe for at least twenty years, American land, air, and naval power dotted the map in a great arc from the Middle East to Norway. The purpose of this extensive deployment of American forces, an administration spokesman said, was to "contain" Communism and stop its penetration of Europe, the Middle East, and Africa. Although the Truman policy of "containment," as it rapidly came to be called, met bitter criticism from ardent American nationalists as defeatist and resigned to the surrender of eastern Europe to the Communists, it was accepted by the majority of the public as the only alternative to another major war.

Inflation. Higher wages, justifiably or not, resulted in higher prices, and pushed along the pronounced trend toward inflation that had set in immediately after the war came to an end. Price controls had been accepted as necessary evils as long as the war lasted; but with the fighting finished, the public echoed the impatience of businessmen for a return to "business as usual." Believers in price controls argued that if the great backlog of purchasing power built up during the war were turned loose, the resulting competition for the limited amount of goods available would produce a violent inflation of prices. But their opponents, led by the National Association of Manufacturers, held that, if controls were taken off, prices might rise temporarily, but would decline eventually as the volume of goods increased. The people were clearly tired of government restraints, and over the protest of President Truman Congress emasculated the act under which the Office of Price Administration had operated. Finally, yielding to irresistible pressure, the President announced by radio on October 14, 1946, that all controls, except on rents, would have to go. The effect was startling. By the end of the year the consumers' price index was 55.5 per cent higher than in August, 1939, and 31.7 per cent higher than in December, 1945. And prices had just begun to rise, for with each round of wage increases there came inevitably a wave of price increases.

Elections of 1946. Upon entering office, Truman had promised to carry on the pro-gressive policies of his predecessor. But that proved to be not entirely possible despite Democratic control of Congress through 1946. A definable drift toward conservatism, both in Congress and in the country at large, was already apparent under Roosevelt. When he died, the reform movement lost its great leader, and the revolt of conservatives against Presidential direction became more marked with each passing year. The Republicans won the Congressional elections of 1946 by a landslide, 241 to 188 in the House, and 51 to 45 in the Senate. State and local elections showed a similarly strong Republican trend.

The Eightieth Congress. If a Democratic Congress and a Democratic President could not get along together, there was even less to hope for from a Democratic President and a Republican Congress. The Eightieth Congress was determined to make a record on economy and on tax reduction. The President could not restore appropriations that Congress had lopped off, however essential he might deem them, but he could, and did, veto a tax-reduction bill. The continued high tax rates were far from popular, but at the end of the year the President was able to point with pride at the achievement of a balanced budget for the first time in many years. Next year, however, he was unable to prevent substantial tax reductions, and the budget was unbalanced again. An even worse breach between the legislative and the executive branches came with the passage of the Taft-Hartley Labor-Management Relations Act, which made substantial amendments to the Wagner-Connery Act of 1935. The new law included many provisions most unpalatable to organized labor. It permitted employers to sue unions for breach of contract and for damages due to jurisdictional strikes; it prohibited the closed shop; it required a sixty day "cooling off" period before strikes and lockouts that might disturb the national economy; it forbade unions to contribute to political campaign funds; and it required union officials to swear that they were not Communists, or else the organizations they represented would be ineligible for such assistance as they might otherwise receive from the National Labor Relations Board. Furthermore, it protected the states in their right to enact "right to work," or open shop, laws. This measure was vetoed by the President, but was repassed by overwhelming majorities in each house to become a law in June, 1947.

Atomic Energy Act. In this atmosphere of quarreling, one of the few positive measures that the Eightieth Congress was able to produce was legislation for the domestic control and development of atomic energy. A five-man commission was created, with exclusive authority over the development of this fateful new source of energy, and to head it the President chose David E. Lilienthal, for many years the efficient head of TVA. Under the commission American scientists went ahead to unlock further the secrets of nuclear energy, and to make their findings useful for peaceful as well as warlike purposes. But more than a few people, including many of the participating scientists, were uneasy over the implications for democracy of the need to keep ultra-secret the evolution of such a huge government corporation. Fortunately, a few members of Congress had easy access to the innermost developments of this portentous creation.

1948 Elections. As the presidential election of 1948 neared, the Republicans felt certain of victory, especially since it looked for a time as if the Democratic votes would be split between three bitterly contesting candidates. But to win, the Republicans had first to heal the breach existing in their own party between the liberal and internationalist eastern faction led by Governor Thomas E. Dewey of New York, and the more conservative and nationalist group of midwesterners headed by Senator Robert A. Taft of Ohio. Possible compromise candidates were the very popular General Dwight D. Eisenhower, and ex-Governor Harold E. Stassen of Minnesota, who appealed to the younger, more liberal element in the party. But after Eisenhower removed himself from consideration and accepted the presidency of Columbia University, Dewey won the nomination. The Republican platform, while by no means ready to abandon all the social gains made during the Roosevelt era, urged that greater responsibility be given to the states in such matters as housing, conservation, public health, and security for the aged. It favored also "minimum" governmental controls over business, and lauded the free-enterprise system as the "mainspring of material well-being and political freedom." On the moot labor problem, it pledged the party to protect "both workers and employers against coercion and exploitation." The conservatism of these pronouncements was thinly veiled and reflected well the point of view of the Republican majority in the Eightieth Congress.

The Democrats entered the contest with little hope of victory. Despite Truman's advocacy of many liberal measures in the spring of 1948, many old New Dealers were disenchanted with "the little man from Missouri." Truman's spring speeches in support of civil rights and reform also served to widen the impending split between the conservative southern wing of the party and the more radical groups from the northern cities. In addition, Henry Wallace had early announced the formation of a third party in opposition to the "get tough with Russia" program, which he claimed would lead the nation to war, and it was assumed that the new party would draw most of its support from former Democratic voters.

Democratic Despair. Despite considerable Democratic discontent with Truman's leadership, he was nominated without serious opposition. The chief excitement in the Democratic convention came from a successful effort, led by Mayor Hubert H. Humphrey of Minneapolis, to write into the

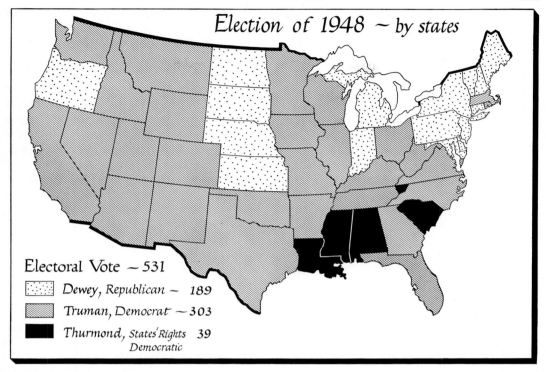

Election of 1948 ～ by states

Electoral Vote ― 531

- [::::] Dewey, Republican ― 189
- [////] Truman, Democrat ―303
- [■■] Thurmond, States'Rights 39
  Democratic

platform a plank calling on Congress to support the President "in guaranteeing these basic and fundamental rights: (1) the right of full and equal political participation, (2) the right of equal opportunity of employment, (3) the right of security of person, and (4) the right of equal treatment in the services and defense of our nation." Although heatedly opposed by most southern delegates, the platform as finally adopted carried the drastic civil-rights plank. It also denounced unsparingly the record of the Eightieth Congress, called for the repeal of the Taft-Hartley Act, and advocated an extension of Social Security benefits, an increase in the minimum wage, more adequate federal legislation on housing, and strong federal support of farm prices. On foreign policy the two platforms were in fundamental agreement. Both supported the United Nations while condemning the intemperate use of the veto by Russia. Both endorsed the foreign-aid program, although the Republicans wished to be more gener-

ous to China than the Democrats had been. Both favored full recognition of the new Jewish state of Israel. Both accepted the policy of reciprocal-trade agreements as a means of regulating the tariff.

As the campaign got under way, all signs still pointed to Republican victory. Republican chances were increased by the defection of the extreme states'-rights faction of the Democratic Party. Offended by the civil-rights plank in their party platform, the "Dixiecrats" held a rump convention at Birmingham and nominated a separate States' Rights Democratic ticket, headed by Governor J. Strom Thurmond of South Carolina. It was apparent that Thurmond would carry at least three or four states in the Lower South. All the various public-opinion polls predicted confidently the election of Dewey, who campaigned as if he were a sure winner.

The Democrats Win. Truman, on the other hand, conducted a vigorous campaign, almost unaided. He called a special session of the Republican-dominated Eightieth Congress to meet in July, right after the nominations, and asked it to put through legislation to halt rising prices, to meet the housing crisis, to protect civil rights, and to take various other steps called for by both platforms. When it adjourned without acting on his suggestions, he toured the country condemning it for its failure to deliver on promises in the Republican platform and branding it the worst Congress the nation had ever had. The election results were the greatest political upset in American history. The Republicans went down to a resounding defeat. Truman failed to capture a popular majority, but in the electoral college the vote stood Truman 303, Dewey 189, and Thurmond 39. In the congressional and state elections the Democratic victory was even more decisive. Both houses of Congress were overwhelmingly Democratic, and Democratic governors were chosen in most of the States.

The "Fair Deal." Buoyed up by his triumph, which he rightly considered to be a personal one, Truman presented the Eighty-first Congress in January, 1949, with a demand for an extensive program of reform. Promptly labeled the "Fair Deal," this program called for the repeal of the Taft-Hartley Act, generous federal aid to education and public health, low-cost housing, an extension of the Social Security system, and a comprehensive federal law protecting civil rights throughout the nation. In the same month he described the nation's foreign policy as one based upon three points — resistance to Russian expansion, support of the United Nations, and continued large-scale aid to provide both military and internal economic strength to the nations resisting aggression. To these the President recommended the addition of a fourth point, a $45 million program of technical aid and investment by the government and private business for the undeveloped and colonial regions of the world.

Through the development of sound economies and a rising living standard in primitive areas, Truman argued, the threat of internal Communist growth could be radically diminished.

Whatever hope the administration had for the passage of the program was dashed by a revival of the conservative trend in the country and a rapidly growing split in the Democratic Party between northern progressives and southern conservatives. Almost immediately a congressional coalition of southern Democrats and Republicans was formed to defeat the major parts of the "Fair Deal." All the President could secure of his domestic program was a modest extension of the Social Security system, an increased program of federal housing, and a revision of the Fair Labor Standards Act, raising the legal minimum wage.

While agreeing with the first three points of Truman's foreign policy, Congress virtually vetoed the Point Four program, as it became known, by appropriating only $10 million for the rehabilitation of backward areas. The mid-term congressional elections of 1950 brought defeat to many northern progressive Democrats. From that time on the conservative coalition made up of southern Democrats and Republicans became the real majority in Congress, and the administration was on the defensive. Only a presidential veto killed the so-called Tidelands Oil Bill, which would have given to the coastal states the control of the tidelands and the resources they contained. A similar veto, however, failed to stop the passage of the McCarran Immigration Act, which, though raising the total immigration quotas slightly, placed such a bewildering number of restrictions on immigrants and even visitors that many friendly countries protested.

A Balance of Terror. Simultaneously with the rejection of the "Fair Deal" the administration's foreign policy was being threatened by increasing pressures from Russia. Undoubtedly contributing to the Communists' aggressive spirit was Russia's acquisition of the atomic bomb. Soon after the end of World War II both the United States and the United Nations had established bodies to make recommendations for the international control of atomic energy. As the July, 1946, American tests at the Bikini atoll demonstrated, a small number of such bombs could devastate an entire nation and possibly end civilization itself. Within a few months the American government presented a plan calling for the creation of an International Atomic Development Authority with wide powers to further the peaceful uses of the frightening new source of energy and to prevent its warlike employment anywhere in the world. The agency was to have unrestricted privileges of inspection in all nations, and its actions were not to be subjected to the usual veto power of the United Nations. Once a world authority was functioning, the United States promised to destroy all of its atomic weapons. Russia agreed to an international authority provided the United States at once destroyed its stockpile of weapons, the authority's inspection powers be radically limited, and each major nation retain its veto. Such conditions made agreement impossible, and the reason for the Russian position became amply clear on September 23, 1949. On that day President Truman announced that "within recent weeks an atomic explosion has occurred within the U.S.S.R." From that moment on the United States lost some of its power to influence world affairs, and a "balance of terror," as Churchill phrased it, began.

With the acquisition of atomic weapons Russia became even more aggressive. Disarmament talks in Paris among the Big Four powers ended in December, 1951, without achievement. By September, 1952, Russia had cast its fifty-first veto in the United Nations, while elsewhere throughout the world it actively encouraged the armed expansion of Communism. While by the spring of 1950 western Europe seemed secure against the Russian threat, East Asia was another matter. The Communist gov-

ernment of China had consolidated its power, while the Nationalist Chinese under Chiang Kai-shek held only the island of Formosa. In January, 1950, Russian recognition and support of the Vietminh Communist faction in Indo-China converted a jungle police action into a full-sized war between the Communists and the French forces supporting the French-recognized Vietnam government. By the end of 1952, 400,000 men, including over 200,000 French and French-colonial troops, were engaged in a desperate armed struggle to preserve the former French colonies in Indo-China from the Communist forces. At the same time, the Russian-inspired war in Korea threatened to bring the democratic world face to face with a second great war for survival.

After the division of Korea at the end of the Second World War, Americans sponsored the formation of a United Nations commission to supervise the selection of a constitutional convention for the entire peninsula. When Russian occupation authorities refused to permit the commission to enter North Korea, a Korean Republic organized in the American-controlled zone was recognized in 1948 by the United Nations as the official government for the entire country. The following year both Russia and the United States withdrew their troops from the divided peninsula, but not until both powers had established an armed native force in their respective zones. Thereafter both the Syngman Rhee government in the south and the Communist government in the north claimed to be the legal government of a unified Korea. The situation became ominous when a United Nations commission appointed to investigate the danger of war on the peninsula was refused admission to the northern territory.

The Korean War. The meaning of the North Korean desire for secrecy became clear when on June 25, 1950, Communist forces in large numbers crossed the thirty-

TRAPPED MARINES IN KOREA

Units of the First Marine division, encircled near the Changjin area early in December, 1950, make their way through the snow with a litter patient to a cleared strip for air evacuation.

eighth parallel on the pretext that the South Koreans had invaded their territory. It was immediately apparent that the South Koreans were no match for their well-armed adversaries. Before the Communist assault on South Korea, American policy in East Asia had been ill-defined. A policy statement of the United States State Department could have been interpreted in Moscow as a rejection of the use of American forces on the mainland of East Asia, and thereby may have contributed to the attack. Confronted by the invasion, however, the President and Secretary of State Dean Acheson acted with dispatch. Within hours the Council of the United Nations had approved an American resolution ordering the North Koreans to retire, and on June 27, 1950, the Council authorized the use of armed force to stop aggression. Since the Russians were absent from the Security Council meetings, in protest against the refusal of the Council to seat a delegate of the Chinese Communist government, the

Council escaped an interminable debate and the inevitable veto.

On June 26, 1950, the day before the Council action, President Truman, without a formal resolution by Congress, which was not in session, authorized General Douglas MacArthur to support the South Koreans, and on the following day, after the Council action, MacArthur became the commander of a United Nations armed force. Most of the men making up the international army then and later were Americans, although units from Great Britain, Canada, Australia, and Turkey soon joined, as did small detachments from other nations. By late 1952 the South Korean forces, supplied and armed by the United States, were holding from one-half to three-quarters of the battle line. After some weeks of preparation, the United Nations forces stabilized the collapsing South Korean front and then began a counteroffensive, which by early October, 1950, had driven to the old border at the thirty-eighth parallel.

The Chinese Problem. Authorized by the United Nations General Assembly to proceed into North Korea, MacArthur within the following month had virtually defeated the enemy and was confidently predicting that American soldiers would be home by Christmas. In a few days, however, the entire character of the war changed. On November 25, 1950, Chinese Communist troops crossed the Yalu River in force and threatened the dispersed United Nations forces with a major disaster. After serious losses and a retreat far back into South Korea, the United Nations lines gradually were reformed. Thereafter the weary struggle up the peninsula began again, but this time against a major foe capable of hurling countless numbers of men into battle and generously supplied with Russian arms.

With the entry of the Chinese into the war, a major policy debate took place in the United States, which at times threatened to disrupt the administration's bipartisan foreign policy, and even to break up the united front of the western European states struggling against Russian imperialism. For some time many Republicans had bitterly criticized the Truman-Acheson policy for loss of China to the Communists. They became more insistent after China joined the war, and especially after a serious dispute between the administration and General MacArthur over the advisability of bombing Chinese airfields and cities and the use of the Chinese Nationalist troops on Formosa. MacArthur declared that both these measures were necessary to win the war and discounted the chance that Russia would intervene, thus converting the Korean conflict into a world war, with its threat of atomic destruction. The administration, on the other hand, steadfastly supported its own "limited war" concept. Moreover, since most of the European nations were adamant against an extension of the war, such a course would not have won the support of the United Nations. In the words of Chief-of-Staff General Omar Bradley, a full-scale Chinese war would have been "the wrong war, at the wrong place, at the wrong time and with the wrong enemy."

Irked at this decision, MacArthur several times made public his views, indiscretions that led finally to his dismissal by President Truman. Immediately MacArthur became the hero of the Republican group and was welcomed enthusiastically by a large public when he returned to the United States. Then followed a series of dramatic hearings before the Senate Military Affairs Committee, which underlined the growing Republican distrust of the administration's policy of containment of Communism rather than aggressive action, its preoccupation with the defense of Europe at the alleged expense of Asia, and of the United Nations, since that organization almost unanimously concurred in the decision to fight a limited war.

Peace Talks. Hampered by the decision not to bomb the Chinese military bases, the United Nations forces nevertheless recovered from their defeat in the early months of 1951, and by June had once again won most of South Korea from the enemy. Then, after a hint by Russia that a compromise truce might be arranged in Korea, formal peace negotiations began at Kaesong on July 10, 1951. Months were spent in haggling, and the talks were broken off only to be resumed at Panmunjom, where Chinese insistence that all prisoners of war be repatriated by force, if necessary, voided any hope of immediate peace.

By the time Eisenhower took office, the Korean negotiators had agreed upon most matters of importance except the vexing problem of what to do with prisoners of war, in particular, the 46,000 Chinese and North Koreans taken by the United Nations forces who did not want to return to their own countries. After a long period of disheartening negotiations it was agreed that the prisoners on both sides of the line would have the final right to return or stay, and that their complicated repatriation would be supervised by representatives of five neutral powers. The truce, officially signed on July 27, 1953, divided Korea substantially as it had been divided before the war, at the same time expressing the pious hope that a united Korea might be created in the future by negotiation. Both sides promised to respect a demilitarized zone between the two halves of the country and not to augment armaments, conditions which were to be supervised by the representatives of the neutral powers.

War Mobilization. The Korean War turned out to be a far greater venture than anyone could have foreseen when it started in June, 1950. To provide the necessary manpower for the conflict and simultaneously expand America's armed forces, draft calls were increased, and Congress against its will was forced to extend the Selective Service Act until 1955. The demands of the Korean War, added to the already booming rearmament program, also placed a strain upon the American economy. By 1952 America's defense budget had risen to the astronomical figure of $50 billion. As shortages of critical materials appeared, and as prices of goods in short supply mounted, the President again asked Congress for emergency powers. After much debate the Defense Production Act of September, 1950, was passed, granting to the President the power to impose price and wage controls and to ration strategic materials by a priority system. In January, 1952, Mobilization Director Charles E. Wilson ordered prices and wages frozen at the then current levels, but not before inflation had again raised the price level substantially. And as taxes again rose to pay the bills for the national effort, the country seemed to be reliving the days of the Second World War.

Results of the War. At the outset the United States furnished the bulk of the troops on the United Nations side, but as the war went on Republic of Korea forces, armed, trained, and equipped mainly by the Americans, came to exceed those of all other participants combined: R.O.K., 460,000; U.S., 250,000; Others, 40,000. Casualties were extremely high and followed somewhat the same proportions. They included, killed in combat: R.O.K., 71,500; U.S., 25,000; Others, 2,500. In addition, the number of wounded reached about 250,000, while those missing or captured were counted at above 83,000. Among the missing were at least 8,500 Americans, many of whom could be presumed to be dead. Estimates of civilian South Koreans who had lost their lives in the war ran as high as 400,000, with far more than that number left homeless, and perhaps 100,000 orphans. The cost of the war to the United States alone reached $22 billion, but the losses of South Korea, where, for example, 75 per cent of the mines and textile mills had been destroyed, were almost incalculable. North Korean losses were even greater in proportion than those suffered by the South Koreans; the population of North Korea, some said, had declined from 8 million to 4 million. Chinese casualties had probably exceeded a million.

In return for all this ghastly expenditure of "blood and treasure," it was possible to count some gains. Much had been learned about air fighting, particularly with jet planes, although at heavy cost, for each side shot down nearly a thousand of its opponent's planes. The program of preparedness in the western world, languishing when the war began, had taken on a new life: now the United States alone had an army of 3.6 million men, and the NATO forces in Europe had been substantially increased. A major war, daily threatening to become a world war, had been limited, and neither side had used atomic weapons. An international army of sorts had fought in Korea under the aegis of the United Nations, perhaps pointing the way to the distant future when peace might be maintained by a world government supported by adequate police power. Communist aggression in this instance had been futile, since the battle lines came to rest in Korea about where they had started. But the Korean War was never a popular one in the United States. Many citizens questioned whether it would have been necessary had American foreign policy been different. Many others deplored the fact that American entrance into the struggle had been achieved by the President without formal action by Congress. And practically everyone regretted the stalemate at the end. These widespread queries and doubts, and the sense of frustration with a peace that was not a peace, were to have profound impact upon the American state of mind and upon internal policies.

SELECTED BIBLIOGRAPHY

E. F. Goldman, *The Crucial Decade — And After — America, 1945–1960* (1961), is a lively general survey, liberal in viewpoint. Herbert Agar, *The Price of Power: America since 1945* (1957), is particularly good on foreign policy. An excellent documentary collection is *The United States in the Contemporary World, 1945–1962*, edited by R. L. Watson, Jr. (1965). Interesting surveys of American foreign policy may be found in J. W. Spanier, *American Foreign Policy since World War II* (2nd ed., 1962); and N. A. Graebner, *Cold War Diplomacy, 1945–1960* (1962), which includes important documentation. A careful analysis is C. O. Lerche, Jr., *The Cold War . . . and After* (1965).

H. S. Truman, *The Memoirs of Harry S. Truman* (2 vols., 1955–1956), is a peppery and revealing reminiscence, chiefly devoted to foreign policy. Jonathan Daniels, *Man of Independence* (1950), is a friendly biography by a Truman associate. Excellent background on Dewey is in Warren Moscow, *Politics in the Empire State* (1948). D. A. Shannon, *The Decline of American Communism* (1959), contains a good critical account of the Wallace campaign, and is especially valuable for its description of Communist maneuvers. K. M. Schmidt, *Henry A. Wallace: Quixotic Crusade, 1948* (1960), is a full-length study, rather friendly to its subject. For contrast, see Dwight Macdonald, *Henry Wallace* (1948).

J. F. Byrnes, *All in One Lifetime* (1958), is the memoir of Truman's first Secretary of State; it should be compared with his earlier

reminiscence, *Speaking Frankly* (1947). Rich and exciting is the memoir of Robert Murphy, *Diplomat Among Warriors* (1964). On the San Francisco Conference, see R. B. Russell, *A History of the United Nations Charter: The Role of the United States, 1940–1945* (1958). Hajo Holborn, *American Military Government* (1947); and Wolfgang Friedmann, *The Allied Military Government of Germany* (1947), are useful. An interesting work by German journalists is J. J. Heydecker and Johannes Leeb, *The Nuremberg Trial*, translated and edited by R. A. Downie (1962). See also the earlier analysis by Sheldon Glueck, *The Nuremberg Trial and Aggressive War* (1946). Two worthwhile monographs are J. F. Golay, *The Founding of the Federal Republic of Germany* (1958); and W. P. Davison, *The Berlin Blockade: A Study in Cold War Politics* (1958). An excellent and detailed study is J. E. Smith, *The Defense of Berlin* (1963), which covers 1945–1962.

Herbert Feis, *The China Tangle* (1953), is a rich, balanced account of events in China during and immediately after the Second World War. On American policies in the Far East in the early postwar years, see Maurice Zinkin, *Asia and the West* (2nd ed., 1953); H. M. Vinacke, *The United States and the Far East, 1945–1951* (1952); and K. S. Latourette, *The American Record in the Far East, 1945–1951* (1952). A recent scholarly work is Tang Tsou, *America's Failure in China, 1941–50* (1964). There are several helpful accounts of postwar Japan, among them: J. B. Cohen, *Japan's Economy in War and Reconstruction* (1949); E. M. Martin,

* Available in paperback

The Allied Occupation of Japan (1948); and R. A. Fearey, *The Occupation of Japan — Second Phase: 1948–1950* (1950). See also the broader works of E. O. Reischauer, *°The United States and Japan* (2nd ed., 1965); and D. M. Brown, *Nationalism in Japan* (1955). A careful study is F. S. Dunn, *Peace-Making and the Settlement with Japan* (1963). R. H. Fifield, *The Diplomacy of Southeast Asia, 1945–1958* (1958), is a useful summary of a highly complicated situation.

On Latin America, see Laurence Duggan, *The Americas: The Search for Hemisphere Security* (1949); and J. L. Mecham, *The United States and Inter-American Security, 1889–1960* (1961). R. J. Alexander, *Communism in Latin America* (1957), is full and rich. Edwin Lieuwen, *°Arms and Politics in Latin America* (2nd ed., 1961), is an excellent critical appraisal of a perennial problem.

On the return to peacetime conditions in the United States there are a number of useful studies. R. G. Martin, *The Best Is None Too Good* (1948), centers on the problems of veterans. Two stimulating works edited by S. E. Harris are *Economic Reconstruction* (1945), and *Saving American Capitalism* (1948). The diversity of viewpoints on the subject is well brought out in *°Industry-wide Collective Bargaining; Promise or Menace?* (1950), a collection edited by C. E. Warne. A rather optimistic view is set forth in A. J. Goldberg, *°AFL–CIO: Labor United* (1956). A critical analysis of the position of the labor movement following the reunion, and the passage of "right to work" laws in several states, is Sidney Lens, *°The Crisis of American Labor* (1959).

On the United Nations and its efforts to keep the peace of the world, there is an ever-growing list of books. V. M. Dean, *The Four Cornerstones of Peace* (1946), is an early, well-informed account of the formation of the United Nations. An interesting appraisal is H. G. Nicholas, *°The United Nations as a Political Institution* (2nd ed., 1963). A good area study is J. A. Houston, *Latin America in the United Nations* (1956). On postwar assistance to war-damaged nations, see *UNRRA: The History of the United Nations Relief and Rehabilitation Administration*, edited by George Woodbridge (3 vols., 1950), an official history. Special aspects of the work of the UN are treated in C. E. Toussaint, *The*

Trusteeship System of the United Nations (1956); and Theodore Besterman, *UNESCO: Peace in the Minds of Men* (1951).

The establishment of Israel has been treated in many works. A good introduction is Joseph Dunner, *The Republic of Israel: Its History and Its Promise* (1950). Accounts by members of the Anglo-American Commission are R. H. S. Crossman, *Palestine Mission: A Personal Record* (1947); and Bartley Crum, *Behind the Silken Curtain* (1947). Gerald De Gaury, *The New State of Israel* (1952), is a discussion of pressing problems. An important scholarly work is Samuel Halperin, *The Political World of American Zionism* (1961).

Much has also been written on the deterioration of American-Russian relations and the coming of the Cold War. Two early analyses are Sumner Welles, *Where Are We Heading?* (1946); and Walter Lippmann, *The Cold War* (1947). T. A. Bailey, *America Faces Russia* (1950), is a general survey of American-Russian relations by a leading diplomatic historian. D. F. Fleming, *The Cold War and Its Origins, 1917–1960* (2 vols., 1961), puts much of the blame on the Truman administration. W. B. Smith, *My Three Years in Moscow* (1950), is an American Ambassador's memoir. Two works by Hugh Seton-Watson, *°The East European Revolution* (3rd ed., 1956), and *The Pattern of Communist Revolution* (1953), are instructive. Other discussions of interest include A. Z. Carr, *Truman, Stalin and Peace* (1950); and V. M. Dean, *The United States and Russia* (1948).

The development of bipartisan foreign policy can be traced in A. H. Vandenberg, *The Private Papers of Senator Vandenberg*, edited by A. H. Vandenberg, Jr., and J. A. Morris (1952). H. B. Westerfield, *Foreign Policy and Party Politics: Pearl Harbor to Korea* (1955), traces the ups and downs of bipartisanship; in this connection see also R. A. Dahl, *°Congress and Foreign Policy* (1949). Recent studies of the South and foreign policy are C. O. Lerche, Jr., *The Uncertain South* (1964); and A. O. Hero, Jr., *The Southerner and World Affairs* (1965). On the Marshall Plan see H. S. Ellis, *The Economics of Freedom: The Progress and Future of Aid to Europe* (1950); and H. B. Price, *The Marshall Plan and Its Meaning* (1955). H. L. Hoskins,

The Atlantic Pact (1949), is clear and to the point on NATO.

L. M. Goodrich, *Korea: A Study of U.S. Policy in the United Nations* (1956), is a good introduction to the problem. The best general study of the war yet to appear is T. R. Fehrenbach, *This Kind of War* (1963). J. A. Field, Jr., *History of United States Naval Operations: Korea* (1962), is official. The activities of the marines are recounted in Andrew Geer, *The New Breed* (1952). The gifted military historian S. L. A. Marshall has published two vivid books on the Korean War: *The River and the Gauntlet* (1953), on the Yalu retreat; and *Pork Chop Hill* (1956). Eugene Kinkead, *In Every War but One* (1959), is a study of military morale in Korea;

for a contrasting interpretation, see A. D. Biderman, *March to Calumny* (1963). The MacArthur dismissal is discussed at length in two recent scholarly works: J. W. Spanier, *The Truman-MacArthur Controversy and the Korean War* (1959); and Trumbull Higgins, *Korea and the Fall of MacArthur* (1960). Richard Rovere and A. M. Schlesinger, Jr., *The General and the President, and the Future of American Foreign Policy* (1951), is a lively and readable defense of the administration. Louis Smith, *American Democracy and Military Power: A Study of Civil Control of the Military Power in the United States* (1951), deals with constitutional aspects of the problem. W. H. Vatcher, *Panmunjom* (1958), is a careful study of the armistice negotiations.

42

THE EISENHOWER YEARS

Russia's ability to manufacture the atomic bomb, the uncertain course of the Korean War, and a number of sensational Communist "spy" trials between 1949 and 1951 led to much controversy over the issue of loyalty. This agitation had important effects upon domestic politics and threatened for a time to change the direction of foreign policy.

The Loyalty Issue. That the purpose of Communist Party leadership was to overthrow the government of the United States by force and violence was the verdict of a federal jury in New York, which in the fall of 1949 convicted eleven outstanding Communists on this charge. Critics of labor maintained that Communists had won actual control of many unions, and were deliberately fomenting labor unrest. Deeply concerned by these accusations, conservative labor leaders, such as Philip Murray, President of the CIO, made every effort to root out Communist officeholders. Similar

charges against college and university faculties led to some dismissals, and to an increasing tendency to require special loyalty oaths of teachers. There were charges, too, that Communists had worked their way into the federal government, particularly into the State Department. The outstanding case in this connection was that of Alger Hiss, who had held a position in the State Department from 1936 to 1947, had attended the Yalta meeting of the Big Three, and had been secretary-general of the San Francisco Conference which had drawn up the United Nations Charter. Hiss, on the basis of revelations made by Whittaker Chambers, a confessed ex-Communist, was convicted of perjury in January, 1950, and was sentenced to five years in prison for having sworn that he was not a Communist. The very next month Dr. Klaus Fuchs, a naturalized British citizen who had worked with both the British and the American teams on atomic research, confessed to British authorities that he had turned over to Russian agents vitally important secrets relating to the atomic bomb. He was promptly tried, convicted, and sentenced. Others accused of helping reveal atomic secrets to Russia included Julius Rosenberg, an engineer, and his wife Ethel, who were convicted of treason, and after a long delay were executed in June, 1953.

McCarthy and McCarran. Inevitably the anti-Communist issue found its way into politics. Senator Joseph R. McCarthy, a Republican from Wisconsin, charged that there were large numbers of Communist sympathizers and bad security risks in the State Department, and demanded that Secretary of State Acheson be made to resign. McCarthy's charges were without evidence, but were nevertheless echoed by those anxious to discredit the Truman administration. Further responding to the anti-Communist feeling, Congress in September, 1950, passed the McCarran Internal Security Act, which required all Communist and Communist-front organizations to register with the Attorney-General, forbade aliens who had ever been Communists to enter the country, discriminated in naturalization proceedings against Communists who had already entered, and empowered the government to hold Communists and Communist-sympathizers in detention camps during time of war. The bill was vetoed by the President as an unreasonable attack on civil rights, but Congress promptly passed it over his veto.

Amidst this furor an acrimonious debate broke out over American foreign policy. It began on December 20, 1950, with a radio-television address by Herbert Hoover. The venerable ex-President urged that the threat of Communism could best be met by strengthening the defenses of the Western Hemisphere, particularly with reference to sea- and air-power. He cautioned the nation against sending its armies on vain missions to police the various threatened areas of the world. European nations, he asserted, were not doing enough to protect themselves, and were relying altogether too much on American aid. As for the Far East, Japan should be encouraged to rearm in its own defense, and the non-Communist nations should not commit their "sparse ground forces" in a hopeless test of strength with Red China. Hoover's isolationism was promptly attacked by Secretary Acheson, who likened it to "sitting quivering in a storm cellar waiting for whatever fate others may wish to prepare for us." John Foster Dulles, although a Republican, was equally outspoken. He saw no need to "crawl back into our own hole in a vain hope of defending ourselves against the rest of the world," and pointed out that "solitary defense is never impregnable."

Troops to Europe. In Congress the debate centered on the intention of the administration to send more troops from the United States to Europe. The appointment late in 1950 of General Eisenhower to head the NATO forces in western Europe, followed by the establishment of a Supreme Headquarters of the Allied Powers in Europe (SHAPE) near Paris, made it essential for the United States to reach a decision on this vital issue. Senator Taft agreed with ex-President Hoover that sea- and air-power were the primary essentials for the protection of the United States, and doubted the constitutional right of the President to send troops to fight in Europe under the authority of the North Atlantic Treaty. Finally, however, when General Eisenhower testified before the Senate Foreign Relations Committee that four more American divisions were needed to insure the success of the NATO army, the Senate gave way. It adopted a qualifying resolution, however, that no additional ground troops should be sent to Europe without congressional approval, a resolution which, of course, had not the force of law.

European Union. The process of achieving western unity in the cause of mutual defense proved to be long and arduous. The United States had demanded that the nations of Europe furnish their fair share of NATO manpower, a commitment that they accepted in principle. But the American government also insisted that West Germany be permitted to rearm in order to participate in the general defense, a frightening thought to the nations, particularly France, which had so recently suffered from

German militarism. Furthermore, many West Germans had had their fill of war, and were opposed to rearmament. A French proposal, designed to avoid the creation of a separate German army, suggested the possibility of a unified European Defense Community (EDC), to consist of France, Italy, West Germany, and the Benelux countries, with the military resources of all members joined under a single command. But this idea, reasonable and proper as it seemed to most Americans, ran counter to Europe's nationalistic spirit and was never ratified by all the NATO members. Nevertheless, at American insistence, plans for German rearmament and participation in NATO defense went forward.

On the economic front progress toward European unity was more encouraging. A hopeful indication of future cooperation came with the formation on August 1, 1952, at Luxembourg, of the European Coal and Steel Community (ECSC), or as it was also known, the Schuman Plan. This French-inspired organization created a single market for coal and steel throughout Italy, France, West Germany, and the Benelux countries. ECSC acted as a powerful stimulant to economic prosperity in the nations concerned, and led eventually to two other important steps toward European union, the Common Market, designed to break down customs barriers among the ECSC powers, and Euratom, a unified organization to promote the industrial use of atomic energy. By treaties signed at Rome, March 25, 1957, and promptly ratified by the six powers concerned, the new European Community, with ECSC, the Common Market, and Euratom all closely intertwined, became a fact. Free trade advantages to the member nations would eventually become comparable to those enjoyed by the various states within the United States. At the time Great Britain might also have joined, but the special trade privileges guaranteed to the Commonwealth nations prevented this development, and the British government countered with the creation of a

similar European Free Trade Association (EFTA), generally called the "Outer Seven," consisting of Great Britain, Switzerland, Austria, Portugal, and the three Scandinavian countries. Hopes for the combination of the two trade areas, while deeply cherished, were dashed when President de Gaulle of France, in January, 1963, refused to countenance the admission of Great Britain to the Common Market.

Politics at Home. Meantime, in the realm of domestic politics, a majority of the American people had turned against the Democratic administration. The decline of Truman's popularity was first apparent in the Congressional elections of 1950. The unpopular Korean War and the resulting high taxes and inflation, together with the charge that the administration had been soft on Communists, had resulted in sizable Democratic losses in both the Senate and the House of Representatives. Subsequently the discovery of shadowy deals, or even downright corruption, in certain governmental departments, notably the Internal Revenue Bureau, gave the Republicans a new and important issue. Following a House investigation, the Internal Revenue Bureau dismissed 114 employees, while the President, who had at first discounted the idea that serious wrongdoing existed, launched an investigation of his own.

Campaign of 1952. By this time the presidential campaign of 1952 was well under way. With a Republican triumph generally conceded, attention focused on the fight for the Republican nomination. Senator Robert A. Taft, ever since his resounding re-election in 1950, had been the favorite candidate of the conservative, nationalistic element in the party. He was early in the field and by the first of the year seemed to be well along toward an easy victory. But for some time the more liberal wing of the party had been endeavoring to obtain support for General Eisenhower.

Its task was made easier by Eisenhower's statement from Europe on January 7, 1952, that he was a Republican, and that he would accept the nomination provided he did not have to campaign for it. That the public in general wanted Eisenhower was hardly open to doubt, but the Taft forces did not yield readily, and to make possible an Eisenhower victory the convention had to set aside a long-established rule that allowed delegates temporarily seated, but whose seats were being contested, to vote on the merits of other contestants. Only this action made it possible for Eisenhower to win on the first ballot. To appease the losers, Senator Richard M. Nixon of California, who had acquired some reputation as a Red investigator, was given the Vice-Presidential nomination.

President Truman's announcement on March 29, 1952, that he would not be a candidate for re-election, left the battle for the Democratic nomination wide open. Senator Estes Kefauver of Tennessee went to the convention with strong support because of the national reputation he had built up by televising the findings of his crime investigation committee. On the third ballot, however, the nomination went to Governor Adlai E. Stevenson of Illinois, who had consistently refused to be a candidate. Perhaps more than any other Democratic leader, Stevenson represented the ideal compromise between the liberal Democrats of the North and the states'-rights Democrats in the South.

On foreign policy, as in 1948, there was little to choose from in the two platforms, except for emphasis. The Republicans again stressed the great importance of Asia in American diplomacy, and denounced the Democrats for their failure to support Nationalist China more effectively. This failure to act, plus Acheson's subsequent vacillating policy, the Republicans charged, had led directly to the Korean War. The Republicans also deplored the "negative, futile, and immoral policy of containment" sponsored by Truman and Acheson, and

implied that they would be much more positive in their struggle against Communism, both at home and abroad.

On domestic issues there were more forthright differences. Standing on the New Deal record, the Democrats promised to preserve and extend the reforms of the past twenty years, to repeal the Taft-Hartley Act, and to extend public power projects. A civil-rights plank promised to secure by federal legislation the rights of all citizens to equal employment, personal security, and equal voting privileges. The Republicans, while not challenging the basic reforms of the New Deal, favored greater local and state control in such matters as public power and the administration of federal lands. They promised also to "restore" to the states control over the tidelands and their resources, to amend but not repeal the existing labor laws, and to aid the states in securing civil liberties by "supplemental" legislation. They charged, too, that the Democrats had countenanced corruption, wasted public funds, and had not taken firm enough measures against subversive civil servants.

In this campaign television for the first time played an important part in national politics. Millions of Americans watched both conventions on TV, and saw both Eisenhower and Stevenson in action as the campaign progressed. Practically unknown outside his state before the campaign, Stevenson found in television an important ally. His quickness of mind, his facility with words, and his dry humor won him many adherents, particularly among intellectuals.

The Eisenhower Victory. Eisenhower went out of his way to unite the warring Republican factions. He had obviously been in substantial agreement with the Truman-Acheson foreign policy, but now he worked closely with Senator Taft, declared that he and Senator McCarthy "shared the same purpose," and gave isolationist Republicans who were candidates

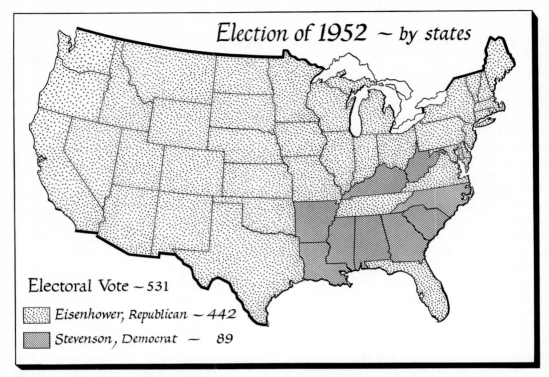

Election of 1952 — by states

Electoral Vote — 531

Eisenhower, Republican — 442

Stevenson, Democrat — 89

for office the same unreserved support that he gave internationalists. Accenting Democratic corruption, he promised to clean the "top to bottom mess" in Washington, and to "rout the pinks." He assailed the Truman foreign policy as being too timid in both Asia and Europe, and promised to secure freedom for the enslaved peoples of Europe "by peaceful means." During the last week of the campaign he promised that, if elected, he would go to Korea, a statement interpreted by many voters to mean that he had a plan to end the Korean War. To the knowing, only the size of the Eisenhower majority was surprising. His distinguished military record, attractive personality, and, above all, his expressed intention of uniting contending factions not only in the Republican Party, but in the country as a whole, appealed strongly to most Americans, and practically insured his election. The Republican candidate won by 33.9 million to 27.3 million popular votes, and 442 to 89 electoral votes. Along with the Presidency the Republicans won a majority in the House of 221 to 213, and by the slenderest

possible margin, a majority in the Senate. Thus for the first time in twenty years the party found itself master in Washington.

Eisenhower. Dwight D. Eisenhower (1890–   ) was born in Denison, Texas, but his parents moved to Abilene, Kansas, when he was only a year old. He was graduated from West Point in 1915. For several years he served as special assistant to General Douglas MacArthur, went with him to Manila, and helped work out plans for defense of the Philippines. During the Louisiana war maneuvers of 1941, the excellence of his planning marked him for promotion, and immediately after Pearl Harbor General Marshall called him to Washington, where he became head of the War Plans Division, then chief of the Operations Division. When finally it was decided that Marshall should stay in Washington, Eisenhower was the natural choice for commander of the United States forces in Europe, and in December, 1943, he became Supreme Allied Commander. His military successes, coupled with his skill in dealing with the great variety of nationalities placed under his command, made him a leading world figure. After the war, President Truman appointed him Chief of Staff to succeed Marshall, a position he surrendered in 1948 to become president of Columbia University. But he was still subject to call for military duty, and in December, 1950, the President sent him on a second mission to Europe, this time as head of the NATO defense forces. Again he was very successful and again he had a major voice in making the Truman foreign policy, despite the later strictures he was to cast upon it.

Modern Republicanism.   After the election Eisenhower paid his promised visit to Korea, only to discover, if he had not known it before, that the road to peace in that unhappy land was still beset by many obstacles. On his return he settled down to the task of selecting the personnel of his administration. In forming his cabinet he continued his campaign policy of seeking to heal the breach in the Republican Party between the conservative nationalists on the one hand, and the liberal internationalists on the other.

In office Eisenhower proved to be somewhat less conservative than he had seemed as a candidate. What he apparently had in mind was the modernization of Republican conservative doctrines by a strong infusion of the New Deal-Fair Deal interest in social welfare and equal opportunity for all, while at the same time emphasizing firmly the advantages of private over public enterprise, and calling for the elimination as far as possible of government competition with private business, and the reduction of government controls over the nation's economic life. In dealing with Congress, however, he was unwilling to use effectively his tremendous personal popularity to put through his program of "modern Republicanism." Fortunately many Democrats, despite their irritation with his strongly partisan 1952 campaign record, saw eye to eye with him on important legislative matters, and supported him when their help was needed. What developed was a kind of bipartisan "government of the middle," in which the moderates of both parties maintained control, to the despair of both the conservative Republicans and the liberal Democrats.

EISENHOWER AND HIS CABINET

The group includes also Henry Cabot Lodge (extreme left), Harold Stassen (extreme right), and Vice-President Richard M. Nixon (opposite Eisenhower).

Congressional Conservatism. In general, however, the President did better with the conservative aspects of his program than with those involving liberal ideas. Congress promptly enabled him to redeem his pledge to return Pacific and Gulf Coast off-shore oil lands to the adjacent states, an action generally favored by the oil interests. The Reconstruction Finance Corporation, to the satisfaction of private bankers, was allowed to die, and the price and wage controls instituted during the Korean War were eliminated. Federal power projects suffered from the President's preference for a "partnership" policy with local and usually private authorities. He also went along with Secretary of Agriculture Benson's proposal to reduce agricultural price supports, but despite both lowered price supports and sharp acreage reductions, the surplus in basic crops continued throughout the Eisenhower years as an unsolved economic, social, and political problem.

Portions of the presidential program that carried a New Deal flavor met a decidedly mixed reaction from Congress. The President failed to obtain the revision of the Taft-Hartley Act that he had promised during the campaign, and his recommendations for federal aid to schools, for a national prepaid health insurance plan, and for a long-term highway development program were unavailing. The housing appropriations made by Congress likewise bore little resemblance to his requests. He did persuade Congress, however, to continue the tariff-reduction authority granted him under the Reciprocal Trade Act. He also won congressional assent to American participation in the completion of the Great Lakes — St. Lawrence Seaway, a project for which Hoover, Roosevelt, and Truman had sought in vain to win favorable action. The changed attitude of Congress resulted in large measure from the decision of the Canadian government to construct the Seaway alone, along an all-Canadian route, if the United States continued its refusal to share in the work.

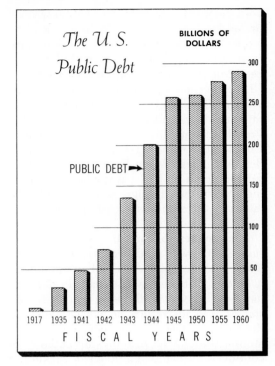

The U. S. Public Debt

BILLIONS OF DOLLARS

PUBLIC DEBT →

300
250
200
150
100
50

1917 1935 1941 1942 1943 1944 1945 1950 1955 1960

FISCAL YEARS

Budget-Balancing. In theory the Republicans were also adamant for a reduction in both federal expenditures and taxes, for achieving a balanced budget, and for stopping inflation. The Treasury, therefore, set about funding the federal debt on a long-term basis at higher interest rates, and the President recommended substantial cuts in the $79 billion budget inherited from the Truman administration. Since almost two-thirds of the total budget went for defense purposes, severe reductions had to be made in the military appropriations. Opponents argued that there had been no corresponding lessening in the need for national defense, and that the primary purpose of the President and his business-minded Secretary of Defense, Charles E. Wilson, former head of General Motors, was only to keep taxes down and balance the budget. The presidential decision to cut the air force drastically, despite the persistence of the cold war, aroused particularly vigorous criticism. Many Republicans had high hopes that foreign aid could also be substantially reduced, and some reductions in this item were made, although increases in allotments to Asiatic countries wiped away some of the savings made by awarding lower sums to Europe. The reduction of taxes also proved to be a thorny problem. A 10 per cent cut in income taxes was made and there were reductions also in excise taxes. A full-dress tax revision measure that became law in August, 1954, afforded some relief to individuals, but did more to help corporations. The Eisenhower administration achieved its first balanced budgets in 1956 and 1957, but a severe recession during the latter year put it back in the red again. Meantime the national debt continued to grow, reaching a total of nearly $285 billion by 1959, and inflation continued, although at a reduced rate.

Internal Security. True to its promise in the 1952 election, the administration sought to step up the campaign for internal security against Communists and enemy agents operating in the United States. In particular, it attempted to weed out what it called "security risks" from the ranks of federal employees.

Under the Truman administration employees had been dismissed only if the government had reasonable grounds for considering them disloyal. The new regulations under Eisenhower were much more comprehensive; an employee might be dismissed as a "security risk" because he drank too much or talked too much, because he was related to or had associated with a Communist, or because he had expressed opinions in the past that happened to coincide with the Communist position. Under the new regulations some 2,600 employees were dismissed by October, 1954. Since only a handful of the total number dismissed were even accused of subversion, the administration opened itself to the charge that it was destroying the morale of the federal service and the very essence of the civil-service principle in order to justify unwarranted

SENATOR JOSEPH R. McCARTHY

His unsubstantiated and reckless attacks on the loyalty of many prominent Americans made this Republican senator's name a synonym for demagoguery.

Frequently hearsay evidence is accepted as the truth and is used to smear a government employee in such a way that he cannot defend himself. That is what the Communists do, what McCarthy did, what the so-called Un-American Activities Committee in the House did. It simply cannot be squared with the Bill of Rights. . . . The McCarthys, the McCarrans, the Jenners, the Parnell Thomases, the Veldes have waged a relentless attack, raising doubts in the minds of the people about the loyalty of most employees in government. If the same methods and standards were applied to private institutions, like banks, for instance, the discovery of one or two dishonest tellers or bookkeepers would be used to condemn all the employees and officers of all banks.

HARRY S. TRUMAN, *Memoirs*, Vol. 2, pp. 271, 285. Doubleday and Co., Inc. © 1956 Time Inc.

calumnies made during the preceding election campaign.

Meanwhile, various committees of Congress were continuing their own un-American activities investigations. Of these the most conspicuous were the House Committee on Un-American Activities presided over by Harold H. Velde of Illinois, and the Senate Governmental Operations Committee headed by Joseph R. McCarthy of Wisconsin. These committees, and others like them set up by the several states, investigated people in all walks of life, and while publicly exposing some Communists, at times they also violated the basic civil liberties of many individuals. As the zeal to investigate mounted, and as people were branded as disloyal often on ridiculously flimsy evidence, a reaction occurred. Some of McCarthy's charges on television — particularly those which intimated that Presidents Truman and Eisenhower were guilty of laxity toward Communism — strained credulity to the breaking point; others brought him into conflict with the army authorities, and led to an undignified television hearing that further reduced his public stature. Finally, in December, 1954, the Senate voted 67 to 22 to sustain a charge against him of conduct unbecoming a senator. When McCarthy died suddenly in 1957, the worst aspects of McCarthyism were already over.

Elections of 1954, 1956, and 1958. Although Eisenhower retained his phenomenal personal popularity, his administration was never able to command a controlling majority of Congress after the 1954 elections. Despite the vigorous 1954 campaign by Vice-President Nixon, keyed largely to the charge that the Democrats were "soft on Communism," the Republican Party lost control of both houses of Congress. After recovering from two serious illnesses, Eisenhower did manage to win a second spectacular victory over Stevenson in 1956. But as commentators pointed out, his re-election to the Presidency by an even greater number of votes than he had won in 1952 was

more in the nature of "a popularity contest" than it was a political decision. For while the President was winning re-election, his party suffered further losses in the House, in the Senate, and in the governorship races among the states. This improbable trend was further emphasized in the Congressional elections of 1958, when the Democrats again increased their margins of control in both houses of Congress and among the state governments. Obviously, the increasing amount of independent voting loosened a sense of party responsibility and made it difficult for a President to obtain congressional assent to his legislative program. It also testified to a growing conviction by many voters that the national parties no longer afforded a clear alternative and that the only real choice was between individual candidates. This belief was nurtured by the close similarity between the programs of the national parties; perhaps, too, it was due to the continued control of Congress by the alliance between southern Democrats and conservative Republicans, mostly from the Middle West, that seemed triumphant no matter which party won the formal elections.

Foreign Affairs: Asia. During the campaign of 1952, John Foster·Dulles, who was to become Eisenhower's Secretary of State, had bitterly criticized the Truman-Acheson policy of "containment" and had promised if the Republicans were successful, a more "positive" foreign policy. In line with this promise the President soon "deneutralized" Formosa, "unleashing" Chiang Kai-shek from Truman's restrictions which barred him from attacking the Chinese mainland. But since Chiang had not nearly the strength required for such an attack, this "unleashing" resulted in exactly nothing. For a time it also seemed as if the United States under the urging of Dulles might directly intervene in the French struggle against the Communists in Indo-China, where, despite enormous American aid, French forces had suffered one defeat after another. By early 1954 the French situation had become desperate, and when Eisenhower refused to support them with American fighting forces, the French agreed to attend the Geneva Peace Conference of April, 1954, at which Red China was represented. The settlement divided Indo-China into Communist and non-Communist independent states, most of which were so weak that without support, it was evident, they would fall prey to the southward march of Red China. Although, out of deference to Dulles' feelings, the United States did not attend the conference, it agreed tacitly to abide by the agreement, and thus concurred in the division of Indo-China.

To shore up crumbling East Asia the Secretary of State took another leaf from the Truman book, and hastily organized a pact to contain Communism there. The resulting South East Asia Treaty Organization (SEATO), officially subscribed to at Bangkok in February, 1955, by Pakistan, the Philippines, Thailand, Australia, New Zealand, France, Great Britain, and the United States, was designed to do for East Asia what NATO was doing for western Europe. But SEATO never did create an organized defense force, and its members, in case of Communist aggression, were bound only to consult. Furthermore, such important Asian nations as India, Burma, Indonesia, and Ceylon not only refused to join, but regarded the new organization with disfavor as an undue interference by the West in Asiatic affairs. In April, 1955, the Conference of Asiatic and African nations held at Bandung, Indonesia, further emphasized a growing antiwestern spirit. This conference, in which Red China's premier Chou En-lai played a major role, adopted a strongly worded resolution against the "neo-colonialism" of the West, while saying nothing about Communist aggression.

During Eisenhower's second administration American-Chinese relations again approached the boiling point when, late in August, 1958, Red China opened a bombardment of the supply lines that bound

two small offshore islands, Quemoy and Matsu, to Formosa. These islands, regarded by Chiang Kai-shek as an essential stepping-stone for his return to the continent, were now garrisoned by about one-third of Chiang's troops. Their protection, Eisenhower asserted, was increasingly important to the defense of Formosa, and Secretary Dulles warned the Peking government not to seek their recovery. With the American Seventh Fleet under orders to keep supply lines open from Formosa to within three miles of the beleaguered shores, the risk of open warfare between Red China and the United States seemed great. Verbally, Nikita Khrushchev, who had succeeded to power in the Soviet Union shortly after the death of Stalin in 1953, came strongly to the aid of his Chinese ally, and to save the situation Dulles finally induced Chiang to announce that he would not use force in his attempt to regain the mainland. The United States, in return, reassured Chiang that Red China would never be permitted to reconquer Formosa. Although this diplomatic exchange amounted in effect to a recognition of the fact that there were two Chinas, one on the mainland and one on Formosa, the United States still insisted that Red China must not be recognized officially, and that Chiang's government must represent China in the United Nations. Despite continued bombardments, the offshore islands remained in Chiang's possession.

The Middle East. Secretary Dulles' plans for a positive policy against Communist encroachment were as ineffective in the Middle East as they had been in East Asia. In the Middle East the sources of conflict could hardly have been more numerous. Local potentates bargained with a number of international oil companies for profits, and the various companies, supported by their home governments, competed vigorously among themselves. Heated antagonisms existed between the East and the West, an inevitable legacy of the colonialism which World War II had practically wiped away in the region. Compounding the tension was Arab nationalism, which was accentuated by the birth of the state of Israel and the way it had come into being by a division of Palestine.

Hitler's persecution of the Jews had given great impetus to the Zionist movement for the creation of a Jewish homeland in Palestine, and the British government, which since 1922 had held a mandate over the "Holy land," had pledged itself by the Balfour Declaration of 1917 to promote this end. When the war began to go against him, Hitler invoked what he called the "final solution" of the Jewish problem, the liquidation of all Jews within his domain. His orders, carried out seemingly without serious protest from the German people, led to the slaughter of nearly 6 million Jews, mostly in extermination centers set up for the purpose. Faced by this grim alternative, Jewish refugees fled by every possible means toward Palestine, and continued the migration even after the war ended. The influx of so many Jews frightened and angered the local Arabs, who could count on the support of such neighboring Arab states as Trans-Jordan, Egypt, Iraq, Saudi Arabia, Syria, and Lebanon. Both Great Britain and the United States, because of their need for Arabian oil, were reluctant to offend the intensely anti-Jewish Arab rulers, and British policy was pro-Arab, even to the setting of drastic limitations on the number of Jews to be admitted to Palestine, limitations that the ingenuity of the refugees found many ways to circumvent. At length, with violence between Arabs and Jews on the increase, the British government requested the Assembly of the United Nations to study the problem. This was done, but the resulting report failed to bring the contending factions any closer to peace.

State of Israel. British action finally brought the situation to a head. Despairing of its ability to maintain peace, and unwill-

ing to bear the continued expense involved, the British government announced early in 1948 that it was withdrawing from Palestine. When in May the British High Commissioner actually left, the Jews proclaimed the independent state of Israel, as of midnight, May 14–15. The new state received immediate recognition from the United States and the Soviet Union, but its Arab neighbors promptly attacked it with what military might they could muster. In the fighting that followed, the outnumbered Jews outfought the Arabs, and made it clear that the state of Israel was there to stay. The United Nations, trying to do something to stop the fighting, at length decided through the General Assembly to authorize the five great powers to send a mediator to Palestine. For this task the powers chose Count Folke Bernadotte of Sweden, who in June, 1948, achieved a truce, only to be assassinated by Jewish extremists who wished the war to continue until the new nation should dominate all Palestine. Despite this untoward incident and much irregular fighting, a provisional settlement involving the establishment of a Jewish state was gradually worked out, largely through the efforts of Count Bernadotte's American successor, Dr. Ralph Bunche. Early in 1949 even the British government capitulated to the inevitable, and accorded recognition to Israel. The Arab states, however, persistently refused to recognize Israel and united in a boycott against their new neighbor. This economic war, together with the presence in the neighboring Arab states of about 800,000 Arab refugees, and almost daily marauding by small groups on both sides of the border, dimmed the hope of any real peace and confronted the world with the prospect of a major upheaval that might come at any time.

The rise of Israel added just one more conflicting interest for American policy to resolve in the Middle East. In domestic politics the numerous Jewish votes inclined American sentiment toward Israel. But the great American international oil companies held important oil concessions in Saudi Arabia, Kuwait, and Iran, which, together with large British and Dutch companies, produced most of the oil consumed by America's European NATO allies. Moreover, Arab nationalism had to be pacified lest it look to Russia. Consequently, the American policy in the Middle East since Truman's presidency had been one of forestalling any Communist intercession in the region while attempting to work out an agreement between Israel and the Arab states. Although agreement proved impossible, development loans were made to both the Jews and the Arabs, and the Communist threat was hopefully countered by another Dulles-inspired international pact, the Middle East Treaty Organization (METO) with Great Britain, Pakistan, Iran, Iraq (who withdrew in 1959), and Turkey as adherents, and the United States as an unofficial benefactor.

Egypt. This precarious Middle Eastern balance, always in danger of disruption, was destroyed by the precipitate action of Egypt. After the British had finally withdrawn from Egypt early in the 1950's, Colonel Gamal Abdel Nasser emerged as the strong man of the new Egyptian republic. Claiming that the Israeli government was arming against him, and that the West would not give him arms enough to meet the challenge, he made a bargain with Czechoslovakia to exchange Egyptian cotton for Russian-type arms. Apparently Nasser had in mind not only the extinction of Israel, but also the creation of an all-Arab federation with himself at its head. He gave every possible aid to the nationalist movements in French North Africa, and in his propaganda developed a strongly anti-western line. One of Nasser's favorite projects was the Aswan High Dam on the upper Nile River, from the building of which he expected great things for the Egyptian economy. Toward the financing of this $1.3 billion undertaking, the United States had agreed to supply $56 million,

Great Britain $14 million, and the International Bank for Reconstruction and Development $200 million. But Nasser, hoping to play the East against the West in his search for additional funds, let it be known that he was considering a Soviet proposal to finance the project. In consequence, the United States precipitately withdrew its offer, after which both Great Britain and the International Bank withdrew theirs. Thereupon Nasser, in angry retaliation, announced on July 26, 1956, the nationalization of the Suez Canal, the income from which would be used for building the High Dam.

Suez Canal. Most outraged by Nasser's coup were Great Britain and France. The British government owned 44 per cent and private French shareholders over 43 per cent of the Canal stock, so profits were involved, although not for long, since the Canal Company's concession was due to

TITO AND NASSER

These two independent leaders, Tito of Yugoslavia and Nasser of the United Arab Republic, greet each other cordially, September 24, 1960, at the Yugoslav United Nations headquarters in New York.

expire in 1968. The graver dangers were that Nasser, under Soviet influence, might not only stop the flow of vital oil through the Canal to western Europe, but also by his all-Arab, anti-Israel crusade bring on a third world war. For a time American restraint kept the British and the French from military intervention, but early in November, 1956, a Franco-British force took Port Said and began to occupy all Egyptian territory adjacent to the Canal. At the same time, the Israelis launched a spectacularly successful attack on Egyptian troops in retaliation, the Israelis claimed, for constant border outrages. The evidence of Anglo-Franco-Israeli collusion was clear, but the British and French claimed that they had acted only to maintain uninterrupted transit through the Canal, as their treaty rights permitted.

Knowing that the course of action they had chosen would be regarded with disfavor by the United States, the anti-Egyptian allies had not consulted the American government in advance, assuming, apparently, that it would accept a *fait accompli.* But instead the Eisenhower administration, working mainly through the United Nations where the Soviet and neutralist blocs gave it enthusiastic support, demanded and obtained an immediate end to hostilities, together with the speedy withdrawal of all the attacking forces. If the withdrawal was not effected immediately, moreover, the Soviets threatened they would come to Egypt's aid with rockets. In the end it was arranged that small United Nations detachments, drawn exclusively from the armies of minor powers, should police the troubled areas while the invaders got out. Meantime Nasser, whose forces had shown up badly in the fighting, vented his rage by blocking the Canal with sunken ships, while at the same time Arab sabotage, particularly in Syria, ended the westward flow of oil through three out of four of the Middle East's great pipelines. Somewhat belatedly, the American government put into effect an emergency plan, worked out by the American oil companies, long before, which temporarily helped supply American oil to meet the needs of western Europe. After several months the Canal was reopened strictly on Nasser's terms, the pipelines were in part repaired, and oil began to flow westward again.

The Eisenhower Doctrine. Following his rift with the United States, Sir Anthony Eden, whose health was seriously impaired, resigned as Prime Minister, and was succeeded by Harold Macmillan. But neither the British nor the French governments would accept further responsibility for the Middle East, and the United States had little choice but to fill the "vacuum of power" it had helped to create. In recognition of this development, Congress, at the President's insistence, gave its approval to what was generally called the Eisenhower Doctrine, according to which the American government agreed to support against external Communist aggression any Middle Eastern power that asked for American help. Congress also granted the President, at his request, a special fund of $200 million to use against Communist expansion in the Middle East. The most significant application of the Eisenhower Doctrine came in July, 1958, when Lebanon, following an antiwestern takeover in neighboring Iraq, appealed to Eisenhower for help. Thereupon the President ordered 9,000 American marines and paratroopers to the vicinity of Beirut, with appropriate air and naval protection. Two days later the British landed troops in Jordan. Despite a series of threats from Khrushchev and anguished outcries from Nasser, the American troops remained in Lebanon until October, when the crisis seemed to have ended. After 1958, the peace in the Middle East remained in precarious balance. METO never really matured into a full-fledged alliance, and the enmity between Arab and Jew did not abate. Moreover, Russian aid and military equipment was welcomed not only in Egypt but in various other Arab states.

THE HUNGARIAN REVOLT

Students and workers such as these staged the October, 1956, revolt in Hungary, which Soviet arms so ruthlessly suppressed. American assistance, probably counted on by the rebels, failed to materialize.

Hungarian Revolt. Any remaining illusion that the way to a real peace with Russia was to be relatively easy was shattered by the events in Hungary during the autumn of 1956. There, as in Poland, Khrushchev's speeches denouncing Stalin's crimes of self-glorification, wholesale murder, and mass repression had ignited anti-Russian movements. In Poland the new Soviet rulers made terms with the revolt, permitting a Communist government somewhat independent of Moscow to take over.

But in Hungary, where a sudden revolt won widespread support within the Hungarian army, there was bitter fighting and ruthless suppression. Death totals, estimated as high as 50,000, and not all Hungarian, occurred before Russian troops and tanks were able to win an uneasy peace. More than 150,000 refugees fled to neighboring Austria, from which the nations of the western world made energetic efforts to transport them as immigrants. By a decisive vote in which many neutralist nations joined the western bloc, the United

Nations Assembly voiced in vigorous resolutions its censure of Russian behavior. But the Soviet government, unlike the invaders of Egypt, persisted in its course, blamed American propaganda for all the trouble in Hungary, and through its puppet government in Budapest refused even to grant United Nations investigators permission to enter the stricken nation. President Eisenhower publicly expressed his sympathy with the heroic fight of the Hungarians for freedom, but denied that the American government had in any way sought to promote a revolt that was foredoomed to failure. One result of the ruthless Russian policy in Hungary was that the NATO alliance, which had shown signs of falling apart, began to draw together again.

Germany and NATO. Previous to the ugly events in Hungary many people throughout western Europe had become increasingly anxious about Secretary Dulles' aggressive language. The Secretary of State's declaration that the United States

773

would no longer fight Communism in local wars, but would rely on "massive retaliatory power" was generally interpreted as a threat of an atomic attack on Russia in case Russian aggression continued. The support of some Republicans for a policy of "liberation" of states already overrun by the Communists also added to the tension. Distrust of American diplomatic leadership cost the United States much support throughout Europe, and there was much discussion, originating particularly in France, of the possibility of constituting western Europe as a "third force" to be used as an intermediary between Russia and the United States. The re-election of the pro-American government of Konrad Adenauer in West Germany proved to be a counterweight to the "third force" proponents. By cooperating fully with the American insistence on German rearmament, Adenauer succeeded in winning not only practically full sovereignty for his Federal Republic but also membership in NATO, for which he agreed to supply eventually twelve divisions of troops. The suppression of the Hungarian people ended for a time further discussion by American leaders of liberating eastern European nations. But Europe's fear of atomic devastation, in case of another world war, preserved its desire to obtain a greater voice in the determination of western policy. This was especially true after the development of space rockets, which made the whole continent vulnerable to attack.

Space Exploration. The so-called "space race" was inaugurated in October, 1957 when the Soviets announced that their scientists had put a 184-pound artificial satellite, Sputnik I, into circulation around the earth. A month later Sputnik II appeared, about six times as large, and carrying a live dog. Soviet propagandists found in this triumph conclusive evidence that their scientists had far outstripped those of the United States, or any other country, while Americans, long given to assuming their nation's pre-eminence in scientific achieve-

ment, were deeply humiliated. Actually American progress in space exploration was not as laggard as the public at first seemed to think, for on January 31, 1958, the United States sent up its first small satellite, Explorer I, weighing only 30.8 pounds, but containing instruments that, among other things, discovered the Van Allen radiation belt, a find of great significance. Other American satellites soon followed, but in the race to penetrate space the Soviets long continued their lead. They were first to orbit the moon and the sun, and to hit the moon.

U.S. Defenses. American anxiety over Soviet successes in space reflected not only disappointment that the United States was not first in this aspect of technological development but also real concern for the national defense. In order to cut down on military expenditures, the Eisenhower administration had subordinated reliance on expensive conventional methods of warfare to dependence on atomic weapons, from which the nation could get "more bang for a buck." Secretary of Defense Wilson had his doubts about basic research, which to him meant "when you don't know what you are doing," and saw little virtue in heavy expenditures on a missile program when air power of proved capacity stood ready to carry American nuclear weapons anywhere in the world. From air bases that ringed the Communist nations American bombers could more cheaply provide the "massive retaliation" that would hold Red aggression in leash. On the other hand, the Russians, from the end of the Second World War on, had seemingly been more perceptive than the Americans about the importance of research in rocketry and missiles. The Soviet government had made every effort to "capture," or recruit, German scientists engaged in this work, and had probably absorbed far more such talent than came to the United States. But American "missilemen," despite discouragement and shortage of funds, continued their efforts, even if in rival programs.

If a nation had the rocketry to lift a satellite into space, a reasonable deduction was that it could also land missiles at will almost anywhere on the planet. The U.S.S.R., with its intermediate range ballistic missile (IRBM) program already well along, claimed as early as August 26, 1957, to have tested successfully an intercontinental ballistic missile (ICBM), and by January, 1959, Khrushchev declared publicly that he had these weapons in mass production. But meantime the United States had not been idle. A stepped-up IRBM program soon yielded the air force "Thor," the army "Jupiter," and the navy "Polaris," the latter designed for use by submerged submarines. By 1960 these weapons were paralleled by the "Minuteman," the "Titan," and the "Atlas," all in the ICBM class. Supplemented as they were by air-borne nuclear bombs, they successfully maintained the "balance of terror," upon which alone, it seemed, the peace of the world must depend.

The effectiveness of the new atomic weapons, whether bombs or warheads for rockets and lesser projectiles, could be determined only by actual tests, which until 1958 the atomic powers carried out in remote and unpopulated regions. But scientists were quick to observe that the results of these explosions could not be localized, for the radioactive debris they produced drifted far and wide in the stratosphere, and if sufficiently multiplied would eventually descend as "fall-out" to endanger health, or even life, anywhere on the planet. Conscious of world opinion on the subject, and possibly convinced also of Russian leadership in the atomic race, the U.S.S.R. announced March 30, 1958, that it would suspend further testing if the other atomic powers would do likewise. Much wrangling followed as to the exact cut-off time for the testing, each side attempting to finish its experiments before agreeing to a terminal date. But in October, 1958, a Geneva Conference at last got around to discussing proposals to avoid future contamination of the earth. Here again there was wide disagreement over the western demand for inspection, and for a time it looked as if nothing could be accomplished except for the temporary suspension of tests. But eventually in 1963, both sides agreed to a ban on above ground testing of the bombs. Even so France and China, both of whom were feverishly attempting to develop their own atomic weapons, were not parties to the agreement. Consequently all life on earth was still under the threat of severe damage or even extermination by man-made radioactive fallout.

Eisenhower's Personal Diplomacy. In April, 1959, Secretary Dulles, to whom the President had delegated almost complete authority over foreign policy, resigned in ill-health, and died the following month. From that date Eisenhower retained much of the power to direct foreign affairs and embarked upon a course of personal diplomacy in an effort to achieve something near world peace before his administration ended. During the spring of 1959 the tensions were great. The previous autumn Russia had served an ultimatum on the West declaring that if Berlin were not made a demilitarized free city within six months, she would sign a separate peace treaty with East Germany, leaving the Soviet satellite free to deny the western powers access to the city. After the West absolutely refused to negotiate on the basis of an ultimatum, there subsequently occurred many feverish high level negotiations. Eisenhower himself visited Great Britain, France, and Germany, and Vice President Nixon journeyed to Russia. Then, on August 3, 1959, President Eisenhower announced that Khrushchev had accepted his invitation to confer with him in the United States.

Khrushchev's visit to the United States the following month went off without incident. He spent a weekend with Eisenhower at Camp David in the Maryland mountains, and while the conferees reached no agreement on disputed issues, they parted amicably enough. Khrushchev got his way about the summit conference, for which official preparations began the following December, but he had long since given up his insistence on a specific time limit for the Berlin settlement he demanded.

Few observers had expected the summit conference to end world tensions, but the manner of its collapse was totally unforeseen. Two weeks before the date set for it to open the Soviets shot down over central Russia a United States U-2 reconnaissance plane, and captured its pilot, who confessed that he was on a spy mission. After numerous contradictory statements, the American government took full responsibility for the flight and for others of the same kind that had preceded it, but despite the supercharged international atmosphere both President Eisenhower and Premier Khrushchev showed up in Paris, May 16, 1960, for the "Big Four" summit conference. Thereupon Khrushchev, who might understandably have refused to appear, used the conference instead for a vituperative denunciation of both the United States and President Eisenhower, and then scuttled the conference by refusing to deal further with the President unless he offered impossible apologies.

Earlier in the year Eisenhower had made a goodwill tour to Latin America; later he visited the Philippines, Okinawa, South Korea, and Hawaii. Left-wing demonstrations against a proposed visit to Japan were so violent, however, that the Japanese Premier was obliged to withdraw the invitation, while Khrushchev angrily canceled well-matured plans for the President to visit the Soviet Union.

Decline of Colonialism. During the waning months of Eisenhower's administration another important issue served to aggravate tensions between the Communist nations and the West. In September, 1960 at a spectacular meeting of the United Nations, Khrushchev angrily demanded that the "imperialist nations" free all their colonies without delay. Actually the western powers were far along with this task, especially in Africa, the last of the colonial continents. France had freed Tunisia and Morocco as early as 1956, and two years later had called General de Gaulle to the presidency of a Fifth Republic, clothed with virtually dictatorial powers to deal with the explosive Algerian situation. De Gaulle gave the various French colonies the right to remain French, to secede completely from the "French Community," or to become self-governing states within it comparable to the nations of the British Commonwealth. All of them chose one of the last two alternatives, and were soon well on the way toward some degree of independence. Great Britain, likewise, continued with the liquidation of its empire. Only Portugal remained obdurate. Even Belgium, which had long ruled the Belgian Congo with an iron hand, pulled out prematurely, leaving its former colony in near anarchy. Here the United Nations, in an effort to restore some semblance of order, followed its post-Suez precedent, and sent in a police force recruited in the main, this time, from other African powers. The UN action greatly irritated Khrushchev, who was working for a Communist takeover in the Congo, and it explained in part his hostility to the new United Nations Secretary-General, Dag Hammarskjöld. As in the case of the Israeli border defenders, the Communist bloc refused to pay anything toward the upkeep of the new military force that Hammarskjöld had called into being. Hammarskjöld lost his life in an airplane accident over Africa, September 18, 1961, and was succeeded by U Thant of Burma. Meantime, additional admissions to the United Nations, mostly from Africa, had brought its membership by the end of 1960 to ninety-nine (soon to be larger), nearly twice the original number, and had shifted the balance of power in the Assembly from the West to "uncommitted" Asian and African nations that refused to follow the lead of either Washington or Moscow.

Since 1953 Dulles had strongly contended against such "neutralism," as it came to be called, implying that those countries who were not positively for the West were against it. But following the lead of India, most of the new nations of Asia and Africa preferred to remain neutral and seek favors from both sides. Thus the Dulles-Eisenhower foreign policy had not only failed to achieve anything more positive than the Truman-Acheson "containment" formula; it had actually witnessed the loss of ground to the Communists in Asia and the growth of neutralism there and elsewhere. Moreover, Eisenhower, instead of ending his administration with the long step toward peace that he had envisioned, left office with world tensions undiminished.

Election of 1960.   It was with this back-

ground of international turmoil that the presidential campaign and election of 1960 occurred.   Chief interest centered in the selection of a Democratic candidate for President, since it was generally assumed that Vice-President Nixon would head the Republican ticket.   The principal Democratic aspirants were three prominent United States Senators, Hubert Humphrey of Minnesota, John F. Kennedy of Massachusetts, and Lyndon B. Johnson of Texas. In July the Democratic convention met in Los Angeles, and on the first ballot Kennedy won the nomination with only a few votes to spare.   To strengthen the ticket Kennedy chose Johnson, whose following among the delegates was next largest, as his running mate.   The Democratic platform demanded greater government action to stimulate the national economy, with an annual 5 per cent increase in the gross national

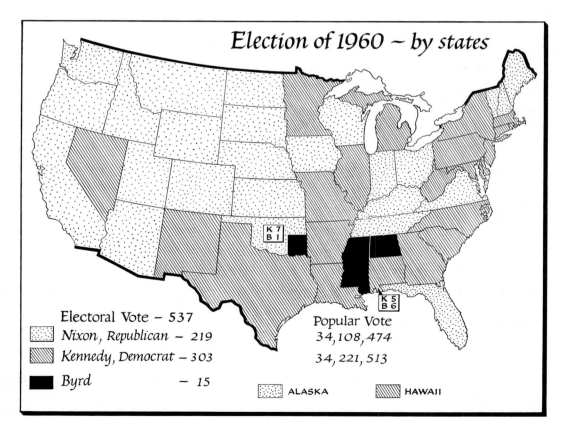

Election of 1960 – by states

Electoral Vote – 537
Nixon, Republican – 219
Kennedy, Democrat – 303
Byrd – 15

Popular Vote
34,108,474
34,221,513

ALASKA   HAWAII

product as the goal; more generous welfare measures and a minimum wage of $1.25 per hour; "not less than 90 per cent of parity" for agricultural income; a vigorous defense of racial equality; generous foreign aid to underdeveloped nations; and above all a strengthening of the national defenses.

The Republican convention, held two weeks later in Chicago, was in comparison a somewhat tame affair. Nixon was nominated for President without incident, and at his suggestion the delegates chose Henry Cabot Lodge, United States Ambassador to the United Nations, for Vice-President. Due to the intervention of Governor Nelson A. Rockefeller of New York, the platform contained a more aggressive stand on civil rights than the original platform makers had intended, and specific advocacy of an intensified missile program regardless of cost. It also called for "a crash research program" to develop new uses for farm products, the extension of "business-like methods" to government operations, and promises on foreign aid and economic growth not very different from those of the Democrats.

As usual, the campaign turned more on personalities than on issues, although Kennedy hammered hard on the need for greater economic growth to outdistance the rising power of the U.S.S.R., and to forge ahead along what he called "the new frontier." A series of four Nixon-Kennedy television debates, or more accurately "confrontations," furnished the chief excitement of the campaign. Probably from 65 to 75 million Americans watched and listened while the Senator and the Vice-President replied to questions asked by a panel of news reporters, and commented also on the views expressed by each other. Kennedy handled himself well enough to render ridiculous the aspersions Republicans had cast on his immaturity, and the debates undoubtedly won him many votes. Kennedy's Roman Catholic religion was a factor in the campaign, and undoubtedly cost the Democratic candidate millions of votes in the predominantly Protestant and rural sections of the South and West. But in the urban industrial areas, where Catholics were most numerous, the religious issue certainly helped him.

Election results were surprisingly close. In a total popular vote of nearly 69 million, Kennedy outdistanced Nixon by only 113,000 votes, while in the electoral college he received 303 votes to Nixon's 219. The Democrats, aided by strong Negro and Jewish as well as Catholic backing, won relatively narrow victories in the eastern seaboard states, in the Deep South, and in Illinois, but lost most of the Middle West, including Ohio, the border states, and the Far West, including California. Both houses of Congress remained Democratic by substantial margins, but the conservative southern delegations held the balance of power in each. The narrowness of the Democratic victory was regarded with some misgivings by both foreign and domestic observers, and served somewhat to undermine the mandate with which Kennedy took office.

SELECTED BIBLIOGRAPHY

One of the best approaches to the Eisenhower period is by way of the numerous memoirs which have already appeared. The President's own reminiscences, *The White House Years* (2 vols., 1963–1965), are a convenient

* Available in paperback

starting point, for they reveal much of the character of their author; the first volume is subtitled *°Mandate for Change*. Richard Nixon, *°Six Crises* (1962), contains some revealing memories of the Vice-President, although it is not a full-scale autobiography. Sherman Adams, *°Firsthand Report* (1961), is the reminiscence of the controversial Secretary to the President. L. L. Strauss, °*Men and Decisions* (1962), is the memoir of the Chairman of the Atomic Energy Commission, whose nomination for a cabinet post was rejected by the Senate. E. T. Benson, *Cross Fire* (1962), is the rather sour recollection of the ultra-conservative Secretary of Agriculture. J. W. Martin and R. J. Donovan, *My First Fifty Years in Politics* (1960), is the autobiography of the former Speaker of the House, who was deposed from the minority leadership during Eisenhower's second term. E. J. Hughes, °*The Ordeal of Power* (1963), is an "inside" account by an able journalist who sought to make the administration more liberal.

An interesting collection of evaluations is °*Eisenhower as President*, edited by Dean Albertson (1963). Divergent journalistic sketches are M. J. Pusey, *Eisenhower, the President* (1956), by a warm admirer; and Marquis Childs, *Eisenhower: Captive Hero* (1958), by a liberal critic. A valuable behind-the-scenes report on the first term is R. J. Donovan, *Eisenhower: The Inside Story* (1956). R. H. Rovere, *Affairs of State: The Eisenhower Years* (1956), is a collection of witty running critiques by a liberal journalist.

Serious scholarly works on Eisenhower's domestic policies are already beginning to appear. The passage of the Landrum-Griffin Act is studied by A. K. McAdams, *Power and Politics in Labor Legislation* (1964). A critical account of the urban renewal program is Martin Anderson, *The Federal Bulldozer* (1964). Substantial monographs on two major issues are E. R. Bartley, *The Tidelands Oil Controversy* (1953); and Aaron Wildavsky, *Dixon-Yates; A Study in Power Politics* (1962). W. R. Willoughby, *The St. Lawrence Waterway: A Study in Politics and Diplomacy* (1961), is based upon documentation from both sides of the border. A valuable study of an issue which took twenty years to resolve is W. J. Block, *The Separation of the Farm Bureau and the Extension Services* (1960).

A. T. Mason, °*The Supreme Court from Taft to Warren* (1958), is a running commentary on the trend of decision-making. Scholarly studies of the Supreme Court under Warren include C. H. Pritchett, *Congress versus the Supreme Court, 1957–1960* (1961); and W. F. Murphy, *Congress and the Court*

(1962). The loyalty issue is debated in a collection of contemporary writings brought together in °*Loyalty in a Democratic State*, edited by J. C. Wahlke (1952). A careful scholarly work is R. S. Brown, Jr., *Loyalty and Security; Employment Tests in the United States* (1958). C. H. Pritchett, *Civil Liberties and the Vinson Court* (1954), brings out the division within the Supreme Court. An interesting collection of materials is Allen Guttmann and B. M. Ziegler (eds.), °*Communism, the Courts and the Constitution* (1964). Highly critical of the work of investigating committees are R. K. Carr, *The House Committee on Un-American Activities* (1952); and R. H. Rovere, °*Senator Joe McCarthy* (1959). The Hiss trial and the issues it raised are discussed temperately in Alistair Cooke, *A Generation on Trial: U.S.A. v. Alger Hiss* (2nd ed., 1952). A fascinating memoir is Whittaker Chambers, *Witness* (1952). Highly critical is the study by H. L. Packer, *Ex-Communist Witnesses* (1962).

J. R. Beal, *John Foster Dulles* (1957), is a semiofficial biography. N. A. Graebner, *The New Isolationism* (1956), devotes much attention to domestic forces promoting foreign commitments which the author considers unrealistic. Among the many volumes appraising administration foreign policies, the following are samples: C. B. Marshall, *The Limits of Foreign Policy* (1954); T. I. Cook and Malcolm Moos, *Power through Purpose: The Realism of Idealism as a Basis for Foreign Policy* (1954); and H. L. Roberts, °*Russia and America: Dangers and Prospects* (1955). The views of an experienced "realist" are set forth in G. F. Kennan, °*The Realities of American Foreign Policy* (1954), and *Russia, the Atom and the West* (1958), the latter being particularly critical of Dulles. C. W. Mills, °*The Causes of World War Three* (1958), is a bitter critique of American policy from something like a unilateralist viewpoint. G. A. Almond, °*The American People and Foreign Policy* (2nd ed., 1960), is a useful survey. C. M. Eichelberger, *U.N.: The First Fifteen Years* (1960), is an optimistic interpretation by a veteran supporter of collective security. J. C. Campbell, °*Defense of the Middle East: Problems of American Policy* (2nd ed., 1960), summarizes events after 1945. Understandably bitter about American policy in the Suez affair is Anthony Eden, *Memoirs* (3 vols., 1960–1965); see also Herman Finer, *Dulles over Suez* (1964), a savage indictment. Hugh Seton-Watson, *°Neither War Nor Peace: The Struggle for Power in the Postwar World* (2nd ed., 1962), is a convenient summary of events near the close of the Eisenhower period.

H. A. Kissinger, *°Nuclear Weapons and Foreign Policy* (1957), is by an influential military theoretician; it explores the possibilities dispassionately. T. K. Finletter, *Power and Policy: U.S. Foreign Policy and Military Power in the Hydrogen Age* (1954), is the analysis of a former Democratic Secretary of the Air Force. M. D. Taylor, *Uncertain Trumpet* (1960), is a critique of what its author, a former Army Chief of Staff, considered excessive reliance upon nuclear weapons. Herman Kahn, *On Thermonuclear War* (2nd ed., 1960), is a controversial study of what is possible after the bombs start to fall. See also the dispassionate study by Robert Gilpin, *American Scientists and Nuclear Weapons Policy* (1962).

A perceptive analysis of politics midway through the Eisenhower period is Samuel Lubell, *The Revolt of the Moderates* (1956), based upon the energetic author's careful sampling of public opinion. The best books on Adlai Stevenson are K. S. Davis, *A Prophet in His Own Country* (1957); and S. G. Brown, *Conscience in Politics* (1961). T. H. White, *°The Making of the President, 1960* (1961), is a superb dramatic account of the campaign of 1960; the author's partiality for Kennedy does not mar the work's value. Of the many books on the Republican candidate, the most substantial is Earl Mazo, *°Richard Nixon* (1959), by a rather admiring journalist. An elaborate collection of studies of the Nixon-Kennedy confrontations is *The Great Debates,* edited by Sidney Kraus (1962).

43

THE AFFLUENT SOCIETY

The New American. When André Sieg-fried, the French historian, revisited the United States in 1955, he was astounded by the changes of the last thirty years. The "old Americans" had been displaced by a "new type," who was in a sense "a stranger to western Europeans." In the 1920's popu-lation experts had predicted that the new immigration restrictions plus the then steadily declining birth rate would cause the total population to level off sometime around 1965–1970, after which no great changes would be experienced. Instead, the birth rate after 1940 had rocketed. This, together with increasing longevity, brought a spectacular jump in population. The birth rate had been 17 or 18 per thousand in the 1930's; during the fifteen years after the Second World War it varied from 21 to 25.8 per thousand. Meanwhile life expec-tancy, which had gone up from 49 years in

1900 to 68 years in 1950, was still increas-ing. By the 1960 census the population numbered 179 million compared with 151 million in 1950; the ten years' gain of 18.5 per cent was the largest relative gain since the first decade of the century.

The postwar gains were all the more striking because immigration had con-tributed little to the totals. The proportion of foreign born in the country dropped from 13.6 per cent in 1900 to less than 6 per cent in 1955, with the result that unless the nation changed its immigration policy, peo-ple of foreign birth were due almost to disappear. The population of 1955 was almost a homogeneous one, from which the large immigrant groups of fifty years before had practically disappeared. By 1960 the "melting pot" had done most of its work. American surnames might represent a medley of European nations, but increas-ingly American citizens thought of them-selves only as Americans. Through inter-marriage among the descendants of dif-ferent immigrant groups, and with the older American stock, many an American citizen who on one side of his family stemmed only recently from Europe, was eligible on the other side for membership in the oldest American nativist genealogical societies. But for whatever reason, the average American who went to Europe in 1960, no matter what his family origins had been, felt he was a foreigner.

Population Movements. Despite the population changes of the 1950's, many old American traits and customs nonetheless persisted. Both the geographical and the social mobility of the population had struck foreign commentators very early in the nation's history. But during the 1940's and 1950's people moved about as they never had done before. The war, prosperity, the almost universal ownership of automobiles, and the beckoning of new opportunities were all causes of this folk-wandering. The drift of the population from the farm to the city — an old trend — was further accelerated. In 1900, 60 per cent of the population was classed as rural; by 1960, the figure had dropped to about 33 per cent.

Curiously, however, the rapid growth of the city did not result in a commensurable amount of urban political influence. Many southern and middle-western states remained without great cities. Yet despite the smallness of their populations, the vote of their two United States Senators equaled those of the senators from New York or California. In nearly every state, whether urban or rural, redistricting lagged far behind the changes in population, and in both state legislatures and in Congress, the power of the rural voters at election time was much greater than their numbers justified. It was possible in many such states for representatives from rural districts containing only 20 to 40 per cent of the population to block the will of the urban majority. Finally in June, 1964, the Supreme Court in one of its rare decisions dealing directly with politics, *Reynolds* v. *Sims,* declared that such unequal representation denied equal rights to all citizens and ordered a redistribution of legislative seats. This decision and the resulting redistricting augured important changes in American politics.

While the farmer and the villager continued their moves to the city, a part of the city populace had begun an exodus to the country — or at least to the suburbs. The staggering increase in city ground rents, taxes, crime, dirt, air pollution, and noise caused many urban dwellers to look to the countryside for quiet, fresh air, cheap living, and a healthier environment for their children. Suburban centers mushroomed, and by midcentury about one-sixth of the total population lived in these new social units. Suburban life came in time to have important effects upon those who lived it. The hours which the average "exurbanite" spent in commuting meant that he had less time to devote to his family. The cleavage between the place where he lived and the place where he worked meant at best divided loyalties. The social and political results of grouping together numbers of like-minded people, often in rows of almost identical houses, are still unclear. More detectable, however, is the effect of the suburban movement upon the city itself. While the population of the metropolitan area surrounding a city increased rapidly, that of the city itself as a political unit often went down. According to the 1960 census, seven of the ten largest cities in the country had either lost or had failed to gain in popu-

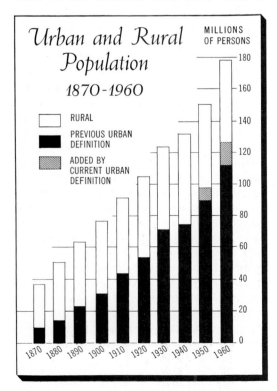

Urban and Rural Population 1870-1960

MILLIONS OF PERSONS

RURAL

PREVIOUS URBAN DEFINITION

ADDED BY CURRENT URBAN DEFINITION

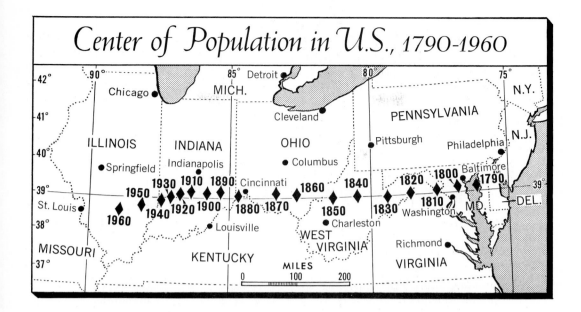

Center of Population in U.S., 1790-1960

lation. Moreover, the cities lost to their satellite suburbs mainly younger and more vigorous people from the higher economic levels. What effect this had upon the quality of urban leadership was still undetermined, but the loss in business and taxes was already apparent. By 1960 the center of many cities seemed to be dying of slow rot, and the ability of municipalities to continue to maintain essential services was questionable. While urban renewal was widely discussed, and there were striking evidences of it in a few cities such as Philadelphia, Boston, and St. Louis, the predicted flow of population back to urban centers was as yet but a trickle.

One other characteristic of the postwar population movement was the widespread urge to settle in more moderate climates. The census of 1960 indicated that the postwar rush to Florida, California, Texas, and the other Southwest and Pacific Coast states was accelerating. California, with an increase of over 5 million people in the ten year span, led the movement, and its total population of over 18 million by 1964 exceeded that of New York. Following at an appreciable distance in total growth were Florida, New York, Texas, Ohio, Michigan, and Illinois. Something of the change in

political power occasioned by the shift in population can be seen in the redistribution of seats in the House of Representatives following the 1960 census. The Far West, together with Hawaii and Alaska, gained twelve seats, while the East lost six, and the Middle West and the South three each.

The rapid increase in the population caused many problems. After the decade of the thirties, when the birth rate had been low, the new increase meant that a far greater proportion of the population was concentrated at both ends of life, among the young and the old. Millions of new school-age children put vast demands on an already burdened educational system, and the lengthened life span meant more pressure by the aged for pensions, better medical care, and social institutions. In 1900 only 4 per cent of the population had been over sixty-five years of age. In 1955 this percentage had more than doubled, and estimates for 1975 indicated that 21 million people, or fully 10 per cent of the population, would be over the retirement age of sixty-five. For the twenty years following 1960 the burden thus placed upon the producing element of the population in their middle years was to be increasingly heavy.

783

The Postwar Economy. Economists of the thirties were as wide of the mark in their predictions as the population experts. Recalling the twenties, many had predicted a sharp primary depression immediately after the war and the possibility of an even greater one sometime thereafter. By the early 1960's nothing of that order had occurred. Instead, the economic machine had poured out an unequaled volume of goods. Production during the Second World War was amazing; by 1945 it was about two-thirds greater than it had been in 1939, and the country had achieved the remarkable feat of producing most of the world's munitions and improving its own standard of living at the same time. By 1945–1946 a huge war-born backlog of purchasing power, estimated at $150 billion, stimulated a boom that lasted for more than fifteen years with only a few short and minor setbacks. By 1955 it was estimated that the American productive machine, with only 6 per cent of the world's population at its disposal, was yielding almost 50 per cent of the world's goods. Since only 5 to 6 per cent of this total product was exported, the result was untold riches for the American consumer. After 1955, however, the economy's rate of growth declined as compared with those of Western Europe and Japan.

This huge outpouring of goods had not come about without striking changes in the structure, control, and character of the nation's industrial institutions, including a greatly increased concentration of corporate power and production in the hands of a relatively few giant organizations. In 1950 the Federal Trade Commission reported that the historic evolution of industry toward larger and fewer units of control had accelerated even beyond the prewar rate. The same kind of evolution was taking place in banking, in merchandising, and in the service industries. Increasingly the corporation numbering its employees in the thousands became the standard unit of business from the extractive industries to the merchandising outlets. Bigness gave rise to trade associations, and by 1950 over 12,000 such organizations were issuing regulations barring cutthroat competition and fixing fair

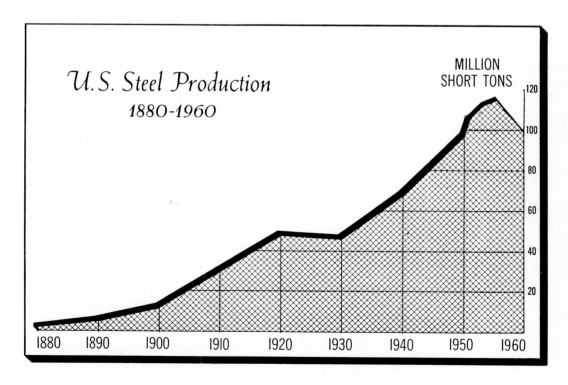

U.S. Steel Production 1880-1960

MILLION SHORT TONS

standards of business conduct. Under such conditions price competition in the classical sense tended to disappear. Administered prices arrived at by tacit agreement among two or three of the larger companies often set a pattern for the whole industry.

A New Business Attitude. However gigantic, the postwar corporation seldom used its strength openly in an antisocial way. Occasionally, as in the case of the General Electric and Westinghouse price-fixing scandal, some corporate managers were jailed. But the new attitude was that the consuming public should at all costs be pleased. As industrial units grew larger, the whims and tastes of the masses were increasingly catered to. Market research bureaus and public relations experts attempted to keep corporation executives informed as to public preferences. The fundamental gospel of postwar business was mass production, and in order to insure the requisite mass consumption, business generally attempted to hold unit prices down. Most American companies preferred making pennies on millions of units rather than dollars on a few thousand. The constantly increasing cost of labor spurred industry to adopt labor-saving devices wherever possible. By the early 1960's "automation" had gone so far that some factories and offices were run by a handful of skilled workers operating a bewildering number of sophisticated machines. Increased labor costs and the huge capital charges for the new automatic machines were partially responsible for a steady rise in prices; in spite of the higher prices the margin of profit — the difference between the cost of production and the selling price — declined throughout the period. By 1960 or soon after some industries were in trouble because of the "profit squeeze."

The Managerial Society. In part the change in the attitude of business toward the public was caused by the chastening effects of the great depression of the 1930's and New Deal regulation, but it was probably as much due to the effect of the new kind of businessman who ran the modern corporation. Large industries steadily recruited college and university-trained men. Knowledgeable in economics and related subjects, many of this new managerial class had a heightened sense of social responsibility and responded more freely to the public good than the old corporate managers. Nor was business so largely dependent upon Wall Street bankers, for many postwar corporations financed most of their operations out of their own earnings. Simultaneously, the traditional pressure of the stockholders for large dividends was weakened. In the American Telephone and Telegraph Company, for example, over a million individuals held shares, and the maximum holding did not exceed 0.1 per cent of the total. With ownership so widely diffused, the control of such companies lay not so much with a few leading stockholders as in former days, as with management itself.

The new spirit of this "managerial revolution" was well expressed by the officials of the American Telephone and Telegraph Company, who stated publicly in the mid-fifties that they no longer represented the stockholders but were "trustees" for four important groups, the suppliers, the workers, the stockholders, and the public. Their function as trustees was to see that each of the four groups obtained a "fair" return for their goods, their money, or their work. To the interesting question of who would manage the managers, one economist replied that "public consensus" would provide a proper check on their use of arbitrary power. But much more real as a check upon business activities was the increasing role of government in the total economic life of the country. To an extent unimaginable in the 1920's, government regulated corporations through a maze of complex devices. It set minimum wage rates; it limited the advertising claims of corporations; it partially controlled their supply of credit;

it bulked ever larger in wage negotiations; and through a multiplicity of taxes it not only helped determine the rate of profit but also gained a knowledge of corporation activities that insured even more precise regulation whenever it was deemed necessary.

Welfare Unionism. The labor union was another check upon the abuse of power by big business. Resuscitated by the New Deal, unions grew rapidly in the postwar years, and by 1955, 25 per cent of the nation's workers, or about 17 million, belonged to labor organizations. Except in the more rural regions, the open shop had practically disappeared by 1960. The power of the unions was indicated by the increasing number of "fringe benefits" which they had secured in addition to higher wage scales; collective medical plans, numerous insurance programs, and liberal retirement provisions beyond those provided by the social security agency were features of the new "welfare unions." Unions often engaged in political activities and in some

heavily industrialized states gained much power. But the record was not all one way. The Taft-Hartley Act and the right-to-work laws, passed mostly in agricultural states, were instrumental in checking the growth and influence of trade unionism. Also crippling to unionism were the 1958–1959 revelations of extensive graft and corruption on the part of certain union leaders. The congressional investigations in those years, and the subsequent trial and conviction of James Hoffa, national leader of the teamsters' union, indicated undemocratic procedures in many unions, and in some, outright gangsterism. Despite the fact that in the sixties the percentage of union members in the total working force was diminishing, the long-term record of postwar unionism was on balance a favorable one. There had been no mass violence during a strike since the Little Steel Strike of 1937. Although some major work stoppages had hurt national production severely, the phenomenal increase in production during these years plus the remarkable rise in workers' real incomes was evidence that the

> *A striking phenomenon of American life, which first appeared in the twenties but came into full fruition following World War II, was the growth of suburban America. Many of its attendant political, economic, and social problems remain unsolved.*

An air-view of America in the mid-1950s compared with one a decade earlier would show a wholly different picture of people and place. . . . The formerly open spaces were being rapidly filled in; the movement of population was out of the small towns and cities into the unsettled areas between them. . . . Its product was the suburb and the greater cluster city.

The meaning of what was happening was that America was resettling itself, wherever it could, looking for open spaces and "grass for the children to walk on," and better schools, and a garage for the car, and a closer-knit community. As the automobile was brought within the reach of most, and TV carried urban culture into every home, the suburbs could afford to stretch further away from the metropolitan center. . . . Americans were too much in a hurry to wait for a plan or for rationality, and too bent on profit to waste any open spaces. . . .

MAX LERNER: *America As A Civilization* (1957), Simon and Schuster, Inc.

labor union played an important and valuable part in the national economy.

The Middle-Class Worker. Whatever the exact causes, the top three-quarters of the working class fared far better than ever before. According to the United States Department of Commerce, the national average family income in 1955 was $5,600 a year and that of non-farm families $6,300 a year. Only 15 per cent were below the assumed subsistence level of $2,000, and only 20 per cent of families had incomes of less than $3,000. Over 30 per cent of families had incomes of $5,000. These averages rose steadily as the decade progressed. By 1960, 41 per cent of families were earning more than $5,000 a year. By that time also the forty-hour week was standard in industry.

The ordinary worker, far from harboring proletarian sentiments, thought of himself as middle class. Although the quantity of available housing never seemed quite to catch up with the demand, he was usually adequately housed. Housing projects in the cities had eliminated many of the pestilen-tial tenements of a half century earlier. During the decade of the forties the net gain in housing units for the nation as a whole reached 8.5 million, and the housing boom continued into the fifties with new construction at the rate of about a million units a year. The Federal Housing Administration continued to underwrite mortgages, and much additional assistance came through such federal agencies as the Veterans Administration. The proportion of working-class families who lived in respectable houses or apartments, equipped with good kitchens, central heating, adequate plumbing, electrical refrigerators, telephones, and comfortable furniture, was far greater than it had ever been before; even farm houses, except in the more primitive areas, were acquiring such modern conveniences. Large numbers of working-class families could afford to wear good clothes, own an automobile and a television set, attend movies, buy a house on the installment plan, take out insurance, and enjoy vacations. In spite of all this, recent statistics show that the lowest quarter of the nation's working population had not made economic gains comparable to those of the majority. Wage rates for unskilled labor remained comparatively low; moreover, unskilled labor accounted for an increasingly large percentage of the unemployed working force.

On the farm, rural electrification and the gasoline engine had considerably diminished the back-breaking duties of an earlier generation. In 1935, 90 per cent of the farms in the United States had no electricity; by 1954 the figures were reversed. In 1935 a farmer had to pay from ten to seventeen cents per kilowatt hour for electric current; in 1954 it cost him on the average only a little over three cents. The variety of labor-saving tools which came into use included such innovations as corn- and cotton-picking machines, milking machines, combines that harvested and threshed the grain in one operation, and tractors to supply power for every variety of machine used in the fields. "Stoop-labor," as in the production of sugar beets and vegetables, still existed, but in a constantly reducing ratio. In fact, there were only

O'HARE FIELD, CHICAGO

The extraordinary impact of the airplane on American society is apparent from this air view of one of the busiest airports in the world.

8 million farm laborers in 1950 in comparison with 9.5 million in 1940, although during the decade agricultural production had risen 25 per cent.

The Upper Economic Classes. The United States had certainly not achieved the "classless society" which had been the dream of some revolutionists, but except for a few of the "big rich," the disparity of incomes between those in the upper brackets and those in the lower brackets had begun to show a remarkable diminution. High taxes accounted in large part for this state of affairs. Most really large earned income tended to drop to modest proportions after taxes. For example, under the 1959 tax levies a married couple with no dependents had to pay a $20,120 income tax on a $50,000 income, and a $53,640 tax on a $100,000 income. And although these rates were lowered by about 10 per cent in the 1964 revenue act, they were still high enough to level off salaried income. Many states also levied income taxes, while estate, property, sales, and "nuisance" taxes took additional tolls. There were still many loopholes, however, which benefited the taxpayer — particularly the wealthy one — such as the low tax on capital gains (25 per cent), tax-exempt state and municipal bonds, and the 27.5 per cent allowance for depletion of mineral resources. Salaries, too, could be augmented by liberal expense accounts, especially when they provided free automobiles, long vacations, and lavish entertainment, in addition to a sizable surplus often untaxed. It was evident that many wealthy people were escaping from the high tax rates while the salaried man or the wage earner paid his full quota. A study in 1962 of the ownership pattern concluded, moreover, that during the fifties the share of the national wealth owned by a few of the very wealthy had increased significantly.

A Countervailing Society. The abundance produced by business, and its widespread distribution among all classes, elicited much admiration. The new business system was described as a people's capitalism and a democratic capitalism, and was claimed to be more effective in raising the entire economic level of the · nation than any other system, past or present. Despite all this euphoria, some authorities raised serious questions. They were not convinced that the "countervailing power" of business, labor, and government would check each other to the extent that some economists, notably John K. Galbraith, seemed to think. What would happen, they asked, if business and labor got together, or government and business? How could government then assure the unorganized part of the population relative economic justice? By the 1950's the Department of Defense had become by far the greatest single customer for many of the nation's great corporations, with military expenditures amounting to as much as $70 billion a year. What would happen in the event of a genuine peace, and a consequent reduction in government spending? Other critics saw the massive emphasis of the system on distribution and salesmanship as an encouragement of false materialistic values and a menace to thrift, truth, and a good many other of the older national virtues. A still more serious question concerned the nation's ability to survive in face of the long-term competition of Soviet Russia. In *The Affluent Society* (1958) Galbraith argued that the nation was spending far too much of its energies on the private and not nearly enough on the public sector of the economy — too much on consumers' goods and not enough on schools, universities, and the scientific research upon which national existence depended in the Atomic Age. Whether an economic system so thoroughly committed to mass production and consumption could change its emphasis without a major crisis remained to be seen.

The Negro and Civil Rights. The more egalitarian-minded segment of American society was in the postwar years also concerned with another problem, the granting of equal civil rights to minorities, especially to the Negro. In 1950 there were about 15 million Negroes in the United States, of whom 9 million lived in the South, and the rest were mostly concentrated in the larger cities of the North and West. To varying degrees, racial discrimination still existed in all sections of the country. But almost everywhere substantial progress had been made toward equal treatment. The number of Negroes lynched each year had dropped from a humiliating total of 106 in 1900 to zero in 1952. The civil and political disabilities from which the Negro had suffered were also on the decline. In 1948 the Supreme Court ruled that the "white covenants," by which property owners in the North had excluded Negroes from residential districts, could not be judicially enforced. And although fierce resistance against Negro admission to white districts persisted in many northern cities, at least the legal pattern had been established that discrimination in housing could not be maintained by legal action. The increasing Negro voting power in the North had much to do with breaking down the restrictions on Negro suffrage in the South. By 1958, well over a million Negroes, representing one-quarter of those of voting age, were registered to vote in eleven southern states. Throughout the rural districts in the deep South, however, the great majority of Negroes as late as 1960 was still denied the ballot, and despite federal legislation there was every indication that local opposition to Negro voting remained adamant. Discrimination against Negroes in the use of theaters, hotels, hospitals, and restaurant facilities was, especially in the North, beginning to give way. Segregation of Negroes in the armed forces was officially abandoned in 1951; thereafter the number of Negroes winning commissions and promotions in all branches of the service steadily increased. Probably most important of all, discrimination against the race in education had received a serious blow.

Following a trend already well established, the Supreme Court ruled, May 17, 1954, in *Brown* v. *Board of Education* that

Ten.
"I'm ~~Eight~~ I Was Born On The Day Of The Supreme Court Decision"

First appeared May, 1962

INTEGRATION

This controversial subject has attracted the attention of many cartoonists, but not all have had the perspicacity shown here by Herblock.

the old judicial doctrine of "separate but equal" facilities for the races would no longer satisfy the requirements of the Constitution, and that Negroes must everywhere be permitted to attend the same public schools as whites. This unanimous opinion was delivered by the new Chief Justice, Earl Warren, whom President Eisenhower had appointed in 1953. Accordingly the Court ordered the integration of schools to take place everywhere "with all deliberate speed." In the District of Columbia segregation was immediately abolished by order of the school board, and in a few states officials moved voluntarily toward compliance with the court decision. But most southern governors and legislatures sought by various means to circumvent this radical step. By 1960 only 765 of the 2,838 schools in the seventeen southern and border states were

desegregated. Civil disorder manifested itself particularly in Little Rock, Arkansas, in September, 1957, when Governor Orval Faubus challenged the federal authority, and again in 1960 in New Orleans when Governor James Davis sought to obstruct the orders of the local school board and those of a federal judge. After much hesitation, President Eisenhower ordered federal troops to Little Rock with instructions to enforce integration, and in New Orleans both local police and federal marshals were needed to prevent possible serious rioting. In 1959 Virginia slowly started to desegregate in a few districts, but only after much delay and an attempt to close all the public schools in the state and convert them into segregated private institutions. After Virginia's tardy action it seemed certain that the upper South would eventually follow, although in many rural districts throughout the deep South the struggle for school integration was bitterly resisted by the white population. Had it not been for an important group of southern moderates, these years of transition might have been far more turbulent than they were. But a large number of southern clergymen and educators, supported by many of the section's most influential newspapers, urged compliance with the law. Their courageous action turned a possible large-scale tragedy into a relatively peaceful, if "deliberate," social movement.

Political and Economic Equality. Meanwhile, in 1957, the Eisenhower administration had asked for a sweeping civil rights law. After much negotiation and debate Congress, under the leadership of Senator Lyndon B. Johnson of Texas, finally passed a compromise measure which did, however, include some federal protection for Negro voting rights in the South. In 1960 the national platforms of both parties contained strong civil rights planks, and during the campaign all four top candidates, including Senator Johnson, strongly supported the stand of their parties. And although there was considerable disagreement in the South with these developments, it seemed reasonably clear in 1960 that the Negro in both the South and the North had at least made a start toward achieving substantial legal equality. The final test, however, as to whether America could solve its race problems without much disorder and bloodshed was still to come, and at the start of the sixties no man could reasonably tell what the results would be.

In spite of these reform measures, the economic status of Negroes remained far less satisfactory than that of whites. Whatever security the need of their labor had once given them in the rural South was undermined by the increasing use of farm machinery. For thousands there was no alternative but flight to the industrial centers. There they soon learned that the Negroes were almost invariably the first to be fired and the last to be hired. During the depression of the 1930's the relief measures of the New Deal had proved to be a boon to the Negroes, and resulted, incidentally, in a wholesale drift to the Democratic Party. Fortunately, the rising tide of prosperity that characterized the forties lifted the Negroes along with the rest of the population. Their incomes tended to be substantially lower than those of the whites, their living conditions less satisfactory, and their jobs less secure, but in comparison with their earlier economic status, they had made progress. No longer were they all in the lowest income brackets. Many had lifted themselves from the bottom fifth of the "spending units" to the fourth, third, and even second fifths. The rise in their economic status was reflected in a variety of other ways. Illiteracy among them had declined from 44.5 per cent in 1900 to 11 per cent in 1950. More and more of them attended colleges or universities — a total of 74,526 in 1950, according to United States Office of Education statistics, though this figure was probably far too low since many institutions kept no records that distinguished between white and Negro students.

Also, they were increasingly well organized and more militant to secure and safeguard their rights, particularly through such organizations as the National Association for the Advancement of Colored People. In the South, Negro leaders organized their people for social action with such restraint and decorum as to elicit widespread admiration.

Development of Mass Culture. During the postwar economic boom the development of mass culture continued. As the wage level went up and the hours of work went down, public demand converted the amusement and leisure-time industries into big business. More and more the national heroes of the masses were drawn from the entertainment industries. The typical folk hero was no longer the hero of work or achievement, but the "hero of leisure" — the baseball star, the television "personality," the football player, the movie "queen." As the national image of such great men as Washington, Lincoln, and Edison dimmed, a variety of ever-changing soon-forgotten, and rather improbable characters became the temporary idols of the crowd. Reacting to the same forces which impelled other businesses, the agencies devoted to public information and amusement tended to combine into monolithic organizations. A cause for real concern was the drift of the daily newspaper toward monopoly. Whereas, in 1909, 2,600 papers had been published in the nation's 1,300 largest cities, by 1945 only 1,750 remained. In only one out of twelve cities were there competing papers, and in ten entire states not one city had a rival daily newspaper. That this growing monopoly of the press was not as serious as it might have been a few decades earlier was due to the development of radio and television. Barred from general use before 1947 because of technical and financial difficulties, television developed rapidly after that date. At its best, in the presentation of current affairs or of drama, television was superb. But as with radio, its dependence on advertisers, who naturally wished to appeal to the largest possible market, usually meant that the programs were tailored to the masses, and that subjects of intellectual and cultural worth were largely ignored.

Fragmentation of the Cultural Market. To a degree the success of television led to improvement in the quality of both movies and radio. Because of the strong appeal of television to the mass market, these other media were hard hit financially. Seeking a way out of their difficulties, both radio and movies began to produce programs of superior merit for much smaller, specialized audiences. Some radio stations offered day-long programs of serious music, for example, and adult and experimental films were made with a frequency which would have been unheard of in the industry's heyday.

A similar fragmentation of the national mass market was producing like results in the publishing industry. With costs increasing, the publisher after 1950 no longer depended solely upon the hard-backed national best seller to produce a profitable year. Cheap paperbound books were sold in huge quantities in every kind of outlet. Among this number were trashy works full of sensationalism and violence, but many titles of great literary and intellectual worth achieved enormous sales in the new inexpensive formats.

"The Lonely Crowd." No society, perhaps, had ever been probed and analyzed more thoroughly than that of America since the Second World War. Among a host of serious studies of what was wrong with it, one of the most widely read was David Riesman's *The Lonely Crowd* (1950). Riesman's thesis was that the intensely individualistic American had become so much a creature of conformity that he was no longer an independent individual. The once "inner directed personality" had become "other directed," bent by the standards of the mass media, society's stereotypes, and the state. The eminent psychiatrist, Erich Fromm, contended that the average citizen was engaged in a massive escape from freedom, since he could no longer endure the solitary agony of making a free choice. And Walter Lippmann in *The Public Philosophy* (1955) wrote of the "inner barbarians" who were in but not of the culture to which they belonged, and who threatened the very existence of the rational and cultured state. Undeniably, the American over the years had become more and more a conformist in actions, dress, amusements, and many other things. Given the degree of centralization which existed in the culture, this was understandable, and in part even desirable. In the mechanistic and highly technical society of the mid-twentieth century the anarchistic individual of the frontier would probably have been a menace. But whether the American mind was conformist to such a degree as was sometimes charged is debatable. The very existence of so many and such eloquent critics seemed to argue that it was not, as did also, for example, the national debate over the purposes and ends of the educational system.

Educational Changes. After the Second World War the American faith in education was, if anything, stronger than ever. In 1940 the average citizen left school after 9.3 years of training; by 1957 the comparable figure was 11.3 years. Some sort of high school education had become almost universal, and by 1960 a large part of the youthful population was attending either a junior college or a four-year college or university. Increasingly, success in almost any line of work seemed to call for a higher education. But as the numbers thronging the schools increased, so did the criticism directed at the elementary and secondary schools for their failure in teaching the basic techniques of reading, writing, and arithmetic, and for their unwillingness to segregate the superior students from the mass so that abler minds would be stimulated instead of stultified. Especially after the first "Sputnik" challenged American scientific accomplishments, the whole education system became a subject for national discussion and concern. Such criticism, and the growing competition for places in colleges and universities, had some good results in elementary and secondary schools. A higher standard of work was demanded from the abler students, who were more and more frequently taught separately from their slower colleagues; advanced subjects such as science and foreign languages were introduced at an earlier age than formerly, and nonintellectual activities were, in an increasing number of communities, stripped from the curriculum. Colleges and universities also reacted to criticism, but their problem was easier because increased enrollments enabled many of them to establish more highly selective entrance requirements. The federal government extended indirect aid to education and research at the college and university level through the newly established National Science Foundation, while the national platforms of both parties in the 1960 election promised aid to secondary schools.

Rising Religious Interests. The period following the Second World War, unlike the 1920's, was one of rising interest in religion and church-going. By 1959 the largest number of Americans in history, 109 million, or 63 per cent of the total population, claimed membership among some 250 varieties of churches. But even though 70 million were not church members, religion itself was no longer a subject of debate, for few of this number were actually antagonistic to churches and their work. Among the most prominent developments in American Protestantism were an emphasis upon ritual, a de-emphasis on practical Christianity, and a growing interest in doctrine. This was certainly true among the Protestant clergy, among whom the movement toward neo-orthodoxy, or the stressing of certain classical Christian dogmas, was gaining popularity. Possibly the return of many Jews to

the orthodox synagogues and the growth of a Jewish cultural movement also indicated a conservative trend.

On the other hand, the most popular evangelist of the period, Billy Graham, who had started life as a fundamentalist, became less literal in his interpretation of the Scriptures and more of a religious modernist as his audiences and his fame increased. Whether the attitudes of the different sects were hardening toward one another, as one historian claimed, is a debatable question. In the early part of the period, when the power of Roman Catholicism seemed to be flourishing, Protestantism for a short time grew notably apprehensive. President Truman's 1951 proposal to appoint an ambassador to the Vatican was met with such a storm of criticism that the plan was shelved. At about the same time *The Christian Century* ran a long series of articles appraising the rising power of the Catholic Church. The questions of whether the state should advocate birth control and subsidize the parochial schools continued to divide some Protestants from some Catholics. On the other hand, the ecumenical movement among the Protestant sects was stronger during the 1950's than it had been before the war. The growing number of union churches, and the estimated 300,000 marriages a year which crossed Protestant, Catholic, and Jewish religious barriers, were also counter-evidence. Finally, although the tendency to vote along religious lines was certainly apparent in some areas during the 1960 presidential election, the fact remained that a professed Catholic had been elected President in a country dominated by a large Protestant majority.

Renewed Pessimism. The world-shattering events between 1939 and 1960 had a profound effect upon American thought. The collapse of western Europe before the dictatorships, the use by the police states of torture and genocide as studied policy, the chaotic condition of the world after the war, and the atomic "balance of terror" during the period of the cold war, all left indelible marks upon the nation's intelligentsia. Gone almost entirely from their thought was the nineteenth-century faith in ordered progress. Gone also was the once fervently held belief in the essential goodness of man. Even some of his stoutest defenders from the humanist and rationalist traditions were now willing to concede that man was an ambivalent creature whose capacity for good was equaled by his capacity for evil. Also a thing of the past was the one-time complete confidence that man could control his destiny. In such an atmosphere of pessimism, the hopefulness that had inspired the optimistic political credos of the nineteenth and early twentieth centuries disappeared; America's best minds were now less concerned with future reform than with devising formulas which would preserve the gains of the past. Many held that the root cause of much of the social disorder in the past fifteen years had been the ascendancy of the masses. Such thinkers held that the creation of an educated elite based upon merit and ability might help to redress the balance. A good many former leftists, including Max Lerner and Edmund Wilson, talked in such terms. So did former moderates like Reinhold Niebuhr, Walter Lippmann, and Raymond Moley, the old New Deal brain-truster. Elton Mayo put the case rather strongly in his *Human Problems of an Industrial Civilization* (1960). Such a creative minority, he believed, was necessary to compel the masses to accept the "rational" solutions required for survival. Many of the same people and others of more conservative tastes believed that a reconstruction of natural law, as a check on the passions and blind self-interest of the mob, was a necessary condition for the perpetuation of western civilization. But these men had no answer to the question how either the elite or natural law could excite in the masses the necessary reverence and obedience without recourse to the violent methods of the police states.

The New Conservatism. The same gloomy atmosphere, plus the realization that many of the old goals of equality and abundance had been reached, gave birth to a political movement mostly made up of intellectuals and university professors who called themselves the New Conservatives. The very name reflected a precipitate change in the political climate. For years conservatism had been in such ill repute that few intellectuals and fewer politicians dared assume a conservative label. As in many such movements the new conservatism was made up of various kinds of people and many shades of doctrine. At its extreme right was a group who apparently wanted to restore the social order of the nineteenth century. This "radical right," clustered around the John Birch Society, organized and headed by a Boston candy manufacturer, was relatively few in numbers but well organized and financed. It advocated the repeal of the income tax and most of the New Deal welfare programs, the "enfranchisement" of private business from federal regulation, the cessation of all aid to foreign countries, and the withdrawal of the United States from the United Nations. A little less extreme were a number of former leftists including Max Eastman, John Dos Passos, John Chamberlain, and Whittaker Chambers, the former Communist who had figured prominently in the Alger Hiss affair. Most such people were grouped around the *National Review*, an ultra-conservative magazine. William Buckley, its editor, stood at the extreme right in the new movement. In one of his books, *Up From Liberalism* (1959), he commented that "all that is finally important in human experience is behind us . . . the crucial explorations have been undertaken. . . ."

Most of the intellectual and academic supporters of the new movement were more moderate in their views than those connected with the John Birch Society or the *National Review*. But in general the attitude of the New Conservative toward human nature was ambivalent. He was friendly toward traditional religion, hostile to the more outspoken claims of rationalism, and insistent that man as an individual was a creature of free will and thus bore a major responsibility for his actions, good and bad. In political terms he was a foe of class action, of social planning, and of the belief that all men were potentially good. He viewed the traditional individual freedoms of the press, of speech, and of worship as interconnected, but more often than not he stressed the primacy of economic freedom as the one without which the others could not long exist. No friend of security, because he was sure it led to a leveling process in society, he claimed to be a defender of the creative individual in the arts, literature, and thought, as well as in economic activity. And to that extent he was an elitist, but his hoped-for elite was one based upon ability rather than upon simple inheritance of either name or money.

A Changed Liberalism. Not all intellectuals by any means were ready to join the New Conservative movement away from rationalism and experiment toward reliance upon more ancient approaches and institutions. Walter Lippmann, for one, still believed that the major troubles of the past fifty years had not been occasioned by the rationalistic approach to problems but rather by the irrational answers which governments had given to the problems confronting them. Other intellectuals suggested that what was needed was a fueling up rather than a dampening down of the democratic revolutionary tradition. And still others had no regrets about the individual losing himself in the economic or social class. In fact, they saw the class as the only efficient instrument of bargaining in a mass society and believed that the conflict between classes was the only way in which freedom might be preserved. In much the same way that John K. Galbraith hoped that a rough economic justice might issue from the countervailing power and conflict between the major economic groups

in the country, the liberal historian Arthur M. Schlesinger, Jr., believed that the competition between classes for leverage on the government was the only insurance left for the preservation of freedom and justice.

Postwar Literature. American literature after the Second World War was marked by no such burst of originality as that which had characterized the rebellious and experimental writers of the 1920's and 1930's. Indeed, several of the great innovators of the earlier period were still the major figures of the later. The popularity of Scott Fitzgerald and Sinclair Lewis had waned in the 1930's, but Hemingway remained a bestseller until his death in 1961, and Faulkner produced several important novels between 1945 and his death in 1962 in which the brooding sense of tragedy was only gradually mellowed. Moreover, there were few authentic new voices to speak for their time as Fitzgerald had done for the Jazz Age, Hemingway for the "lost generation," or Lewis and Faulkner in their different ways for the Midwest and the South. American literature after the Second World War was dispiritedly similar to what had gone before. Most authors exhibited the same desire to escape from existing society and its problems, but displayed little of the high indignation or bitter disillusionment of the writers of the twenties. Most novels about the Second World War were not so much pacifistic, as they were preoccupied with the helplessness of the individual or even the group when caught up in such a maelstrom. Much of this same air of individual hopelessness persisted in later literary works. There was no satirist in the tradition of Sinclair Lewis. Nor was there any flight to London, Paris, or Reno. The only retreat for the average writer was to a peculiar world of his own creation, a world of the mind and the imagination, where the individual was free from most social restraints. In this private world, often rather nebulous, the characters were sometimes little more than social symbols, like Truman Capote's buyer of human dreams. Even when fictional characters were depicted more realistically, they were seldom concerned with the important, or even the mundane, issues of society. Few were social rebels, and when they did rebel they did so in curious ways. James Gould Cozzens said he had no thesis in his novels, except that man was caught by "relentless inexorable forces" and that he got "a very raw deal from life." In Cozzens' writings the precept that freedom was the knowledge of necessity is repeated again and again. The standard hero in much postwar writing was not a protagonist but a victim of circumstances, depicted in such a way that he compelled sympathy.

Another persistent theme was the loneliness of the individual and his inability to communicate with his fellows. In the writings of Carson McCullers, Truman Capote, and Tennessee Williams, the thesis of David Riesman's *The Lonely Crowd* is illustrated again and again. The creative mind seems to have felt that as the masses of men became increasingly literate, they developed a mute and stultifying sameness, and became incapable of sympathetically identifying themselves with their fellows. The lonely hero of modern fiction lived in an irrational, amoral universe, where cause and effect had lost their once intimate and logical relationship, and where chance or caprice seemed often to be the prime mover. This growing belief in irrationalism may have contributed to the lack of structure in both the modern novel and the play.

The New Writers. The weight of criticism was perhaps responsible to some extent for the paucity of creative writers comparable in talent to those of the twenties and thirties. But while there were few literary giants in the postwar years, there were some highly skilled craftsmen. Among the most capable was Truman Capote (1924–   ), whose haunting and imaginative works were peopled with sensitive and ill-adjusted individuals like those in *The Grass Harp* (1953), searching for human

values in a disinterested world. Carson McCullers (1917–   ), another gifted southern writer, in *The Heart Is a Lonely Hunter* (1940), *The Member of the Wedding* (1946), and *The Ballad of the Sad Café* (1951), examined the spiritual isolation of both young and old, and even the crippled, in contemporary society. Nelson Algren (1909–   ) recruited as his central characters worthless, nameless derelicts from the lowest depths of the Chicago and New Orleans slums. Like Frankie Machine in *The Man with the Golden Arm* (1949), a dealer in a gambling den and a dope addict, they carry their loneliness and guilt to the grave. "For me," wrote Tennessee Williams (1914–   ), the country's most important dramatist, "the dominating premise had been the need for understanding and tenderness and fortitude among individuals trapped by circumstances." Williams' people, often from the contemporary South, are usually trapped by Freudian relationships which they can neither understand nor control.

Exceptional in modern fiction are the characters of James Gould Cozzens (1903–   ), who are drawn from the professional classes, and have a sense of responsibility to their fellows and to their profession. In Cozzens' irrational world, where the strongest of men are frail in the face of their passions and of circumstances, and where present good often sires the evil of the future, the principal virtues are fortitude and stoicism. Exceptional also to the norms of modern fiction were the outlook and the characters of J. D. Salinger (1919–   ) and of Saul Bellow (1915–   ). After the publication of *The Catcher in the Rye* (1951), a veritable cult grew up around Salinger. In *Henderson the Rain King* (1959), *The Adventures of Augie March* (1953), and *Herzog* (1964), Bellow's heroes are buffeted by the impersonal world and by fellow human beings, but they are not simply victims of circumstance; they are not limited in stature but can grow in any direction and to any dimension. Moreover, they are accountable for their actions, many of which are significant.

State of American Culture. If most of the nation's creative writers, like its ablest essayists, theologians, and social commentators, were deeply pessimistic about the state of man and the cultural future of the country, their opinions were not shared by the great mass of the people. Indeed, as far as the general cultural climate of America was concerned, the pessimism of the intellectuals did not square wholly with the facts. For in the midst of many banal books, bad movies, and worse television programs, there was every indication in the early 1960's that the general cultural upswing that had been so marked in the twenties and the thirties was still in motion. With the death of the New Deal the federal government no longer subsidized the arts, but during the forties and the fifties universities and colleges had more than offset this loss. At almost every important state and private educational institution artists and musicians had been added to the faculty. Many universities had respectable art museums, and university presses were turning out many important publications every year. Creative writing, the dance, the theater, the moving picture, and television had been made legitimate subjects of study, and it is possible that the growth in popularity of both the ballet and the little theater during the fifties was directly related to earlier activities of the kind at institutions of higher education. Before 1920 the string quartet was practically unknown in the United States. By 1950 scores of chamber music groups, some with worldwide reputations, flourished in America. By the same date thirty-two professional symphony orchestras, several of them among the best in the world, were playing regular schedules in the major cities.

A good many things in the country could justly be criticized during the 1950's. But in looking at both sides of the ledger the American people had little reason to despair about their society. In the course of the years they had constructed a decent democratic political system, which for the first time in world history had virtually removed

TENNESSEE WILLIAMS

This gifted contemporary playwright has probably delved deeper into the human psyche than any other dramatist since Eugene O'Neill.

the masses from poverty. No advanced state, including those of the "classless" variety, had progressed much further toward a more equitable division of goods among its citizens. It was still relatively easy to move up the social and economic scale. Extensive educational and cultural facilities were among the best and were becoming increasingly accessible. Despite the portrayal of social misfits by novelists, the average American had no reason to regard his fellow citizen as anything remotely approaching a monster. Measured by the size and extent of its charities, no country was more benevolent to its own unfortunates or to those of the rest of the world. For a nation of heterogeneous peoples, many of whose forefathers had landed on American shores with little or nothing, and who had been recruited mostly from the underprivileged and unwanted folk of Europe, this record was not a bad one.

SELECTED BIBLIOGRAPHY

Among the more general works on recent American society which can be read with profit are: F. L. Allen, °*The Big Change* (1952), an optimistic survey of the new America; J. K. Galbraith, °*The Affluent Society* (1958), much more critical; D. W. Brogan, °*The American Character* (2nd ed., 1956), an informed British estimate; W. L. Warner, °*American Life: Dream and Reality* (1953), by a sociologist; an interesting compilation by James Burnham (ed.), *What Europe Thinks of America* (1953); and Max Lerner, °*America as a Civilization: Life and Thought in the United States Today* (1957), a large collection of both complacent and critical essays.

Among the best appraisals of American economic institutions is J. K. Galbraith, °*American Capitalism* (2nd ed., 1956), an optimistic scholarly study. A. A. Berle, °*Power Without Property* (1959), contains a study of the changing interior relationships in America's large corporations, as does also the earlier Peter F. Drucker, °*The New Society: The Anatomy of the Industrial Order* (1950). A. A. Berle, °*The Twentieth Century Capitalist Revolution* (1954), can also be read with profit. C. W. Mills, °*The Power Elite* (1956), contains a trenchant but perhaps overdrawn analysis of the power relationships among big wealth, big business, and big government. Michael Harrington, °*The Other America: Poverty in the United States* (1962), is a valuable corrective to more optimistic accounts of the economy. For a biting account of the new middle classes see C. W. Mills, °*White Collar* (1951); his *The New Men of Power* (1948) contains a critical appraisal of modern labor leaders.

Among the many recent books on the problems of the Negro in the South and elsewhere, T. D. Clark, *The Emerging South* (1961), explores the region's recent changes. B. M. Ziegler (ed.), °*Desegregation and the Supreme Court* (1958); Don Shoemaker (ed.), *With All Deliberate Speed* (1957); H. H. Humphrey (ed.), °*School Desegregation* (1964); and Benjamin Muse, *Ten Years of Prelude* (1964), are centered on the results of the Supreme Court's famous decision. James Bald-

win, °*Nobody Knows My Name* (1961); and L. E. Lomax, °*The Negro Revolt* (1962), are commentaries by able Negroes. Brooks Hays, *A Southern Moderate Speaks* (1959); Dan Wakefield, °*Revolt in the South* (1961); and J. M. Dabbs, *Who Speaks for the South?* (1965), are observations by informed whites. M. L. King, °*Stride Toward Freedom: The Montgomery Story* (1958), is by one of the principal southern Negro leaders. Stimulating treatments of the civil rights problem are in C. E. Silberman, *Crisis in Black and White* (1964); and Samuel Lubell, *White and Black* (1964). A careful study of the civil rights bills of 1956–7 is J. W. Anderson, *Eisenhower, Brownell and the Congress* (1964). An interesting study of an important problem is Ray Marshall, *The Negro and Organized Labor* (1965). Impassioned indictments of segments of the white South are J. W. Silver, *Mississippi: The Closed Society* (1964); and Howard Zinn, *The Southern Mystique* (1964).

One of the nation's more perceptive students of mass culture, Dwight Macdonald, sees some hope for the future in the fragmentation of the cultural market; see his essay, "Masscult and Midcult," in his *Against the American Grain* (1962). For treatments of various cultural media see Hortense Powdermaker, °*Hollywood; The Dream Factory* (1950); and Russell Lynes, °*The Tastemakers* (1954). More perceptive and more general criticism of recent American society can be obtained from David Riesman and others, °*The Lonely Crowd* (1950), which argues that the American personality has changed greatly in the past fifty years; Walter Lippmann, °*The Public Philosophy* (1955), that the nation must regain a sense of its past and must renew its devotion to its common ideals; Erich Fromm, *Escape from Freedom* (1941), that modern society has found freedom too much of a burden; and W. H. Whyte, Jr., °*The Organization Man* (1956), which discusses the effects of modern business organization upon the individual personality of the businessman.

Recent educational changes are discussed in Paul Woodring, *A Fourth of a Nation* (1957); Jacques Barzun, °*The House of Intellect* (1959); and Arthur Bestor, *Educational*

° Available in paperback

Wastelands (1953), and *The Restoration of Learning* (1955). Will Herberg, *°Protestant, Catholic, Jew* (1955), stresses the withering in America of theological differences among the creeds; Paul Blanshard, *°American Freedom and Catholic Power* (1949), is an attack upon the Catholic Church. John Cogley (ed.), *°Religion in America* (1958), contains a good many thoughtful essays by representatives of various creeds. An intriguing sociological study is E. D. Baltzell, *The Protestant Establishment* (1964).

The tenets of the new conservatism are sharply if somewhat arbitrarily defined in W. F. Buckley, Jr., *°Up From Liberalism* (1959); and in more political terms by Barry Goldwater, *°The Conscience of a Conservative* (1960). M. M. Auerbach, *The Conservative Illusion* (1959), is a well-reasoned critique; and Daniel Bell, *°The End of Ideology* (1960), is a highly stimulating inquiry into present political values. A. M. Schlesinger, Jr., *°The Vital Center* (1949), argues for the new liberalism. Malcolm Cowley, *°The Literary Situation* (1954), discusses with perception the state of twentieth-century literature and contains much information on contemporary authors.

44

THE NEW FRONTIER

Kennedy. John Fitzgerald Kennedy (1917–1963), the son of Joseph P. Kennedy, a Boston multimillionaire who had held high office during the New Deal, attended Harvard University, from which he graduated in 1940. At the outbreak of World War II, he entered the armed forces and served with distinction as a naval officer in the South Pacific. In 1946 he won election for the first of three terms to the national House of Representatives, and in 1952, despite the overwhelming Eisenhower landslide, he was elected to the United States Senate. Four years later at the Democratic Convention in Philadelphia he came within a few votes of winning his party's nomination for Vice-President. Re-elected to the Senate in 1958, he immediately opened an aggressive, well-financed campaign for the 1960 Democratic nomination for President.

Personal considerations were to play a great part in Kennedy's career as President. He was independently wealthy, a traditional ground for public suspicion. He was the first Roman Catholic ever to achieve the American Presidency, which displeased some Americans as much as it pleased others. As a Congressman, he had supported the use of federal funds in aid of parochial schools (although as President he was to reverse this position). During his Senate career he had avoided taking a stand on the movement to censure Senator McCarthy, an attitude loudly deplored by the liberal wing of his party. The author of several books — his *Profiles in Courage* won the 1957 Pulitzer prize for biography — he could be represented as an intellectual, a label that had cost Stevenson the support of many ordinary citizens in 1952 and 1956. But these political liabilities, if such they were, were matched by the new President's keen wit and youthful vigor, supplemented by the considerable charm of his attractive wife and family.

From the opening days of his administration, Kennedy raised the hopes of those who advocated a fresh approach in both domestic and foreign affairs. His appointments in general did not follow the traditional pattern of rewards for political service, although his selection of Adlai E. Stevenson to be Ambassador to the United Nations might be so construed. For key positions in his administration he chose some Republicans, such as Allen W. Dulles, whom he continued as Director of the Central Intelligence Agency, and C. Douglas Dillon,

Eisenhower's Undersecretary of State, whom he made Secretary of the Treasury. Other appointees, like Robert S. McNamara, the youthful president of the Ford Motor Company, who became Secretary of Defense, were from industry and without experience in politics. For Secretary of State he passed over several more prominent candidates to select Dean Rusk, president of the Rockefeller Foundation. As his Attorney-General he named his own younger brother, Robert, despite the outcries of nepotism that arose from both parties. Most of Kennedy's other appointees were relatively youthful liberals who had already demonstrated their abilities in business, education, or government.

The Kennedy style was apparent in the new President's relations with the public. In his speeches and news conferences he relied less upon histrionics and personality than upon informed, tightly reasoned, vigorous prose. Despite frequent flashes of humor, he often displayed an earnestness of purpose that was almost somber. He made no attempt to disguise his preference for men of intellectual and cultural attainments over those who had achieved success in business or industry, as for example in assigning a prominent part in the inaugural ceremonies to Robert Frost, the poet, or in giving a dinner for Nobel Prize winners, or in recommending to Congress the creation of a medal of honor for outstanding contributors to American life and culture. In foreign policy his willingness to take risks that he deemed necessary won general approval. Liberals who had once doubted his dedication to progressive principles responded cordially to his domestic program. By the autumn of 1963 his standing with the people was such that his re-election in 1964 was generally conceded. But this was not to be, for his life was cut short by one of the most tragic events in recent history.

The Assassination. In the hope of strengthening his political position in the South, where the stand he had taken against

THE KENNEDY FUNERAL

The elaborate ceremonies that preceded the President's interment were viewed on television by countless numbers, both within and without the United States. The flag-draped casket containing the President's body is shown here in the Capitol Rotunda in Washington.

Negro segregation had cost him many friends, President Kennedy scheduled a "non-political" speech for Dallas, Texas, on November 22, 1963. As he rode in an open limousine with Mrs. Kennedy from the Dallas airport into the center of the city, rifle shots rang out. The President was mortally wounded, and the Governor of Texas, John B. Connally, Jr., who was riding in the same car as the President, was seriously injured. The assassin, Lee Harvey Oswald, a neurotic with leftwing sympathies, was soon apprehended, but was himself killed two days later by an overwrought citizen of Dallas. As soon as the President's death was announced, Vice-President Johnson, who was riding behind the President in the fateful motorcade, took the oath of office as President and immediately returned to Washington to assume the duties of the Presidency. Throughout the nation the emotional reaction to the assassination of President Kennedy was intense; regardless of their political views, the American people grieved openly and without restraint.

Johnson. Fortunately the new President was able to meet the emergency. Ten years older than his predecessor and with more than twice his length of service in national politics, Johnson had shared in most important decisions of the Kennedy administration and could assure the nation and the world that an informed and experienced hand was at the helm. He retained every member of the Kennedy cabinet and all other administrative heads and emphasized repeatedly that he would work for the goals that Kennedy had sought, both at home and abroad. Foremost among these aims was the strong civil rights measure to which Kennedy had committed his administration. Johnson's forthright support of civil rights legislation reassured, and was meant to reassure, those who had feared that the new President's southern background and his close friendships with many southern politicians might make a difference.

Lyndon Baines Johnson (1908–) was born near Stonewall, Texas, the descendant of Texas frontiersmen. After completing high school at the age of fifteen, Johnson worked at a number of different jobs before entering Southwest State Teachers College at San Marcos, Texas, in 1926. After his graduation four years later, he taught for a time in the Texas public school system. In 1932 he became secretary to Congressman Richard M. Kleberg. Thus introduced to Washington, Johnson was not long in finding his true vocation. Under Franklin D. Roosevelt he became director in 1935 of the Texas NYA program and two years later was elected to Congress, where he remained for five additional terms. During World War II he saw service for several months in the South Pacific as a member of the Naval Reserve, but returned to his seat in the House at the request of President Roosevelt. In 1948, after a hard-fought campaign, he won election to the Senate by a slender majority. Before the end of his first term he was minority leader, and after his reelection in 1954, which he won decisively, he was chosen majority leader.

In many ways the new President differed markedly from his predecessor. A typical southwesterner, he was in his personal relations democratic, hospitable, and informal. Although not as impressive as Kennedy in his formal public appearances, he was exceptionally effective in direct dealings with politicians. Regarded generally as a conservative before the election of 1960, he nevertheless cherished a deep concern for the welfare of the ordinary farmer, the city worker, and the various minority groups. Although a man of principle, he was a realist and was not afraid to compromise; to him politics was "the art of the possible."

Peace Efforts. The eagerness of the new administration to promote the cause of peace was foreshadowed by Kennedy's advocacy during the campaign of 1960 of a Peace Corps through which individual Americans might volunteer to serve their nation abroad in nonmilitary missions. Launched by executive order, March 1, 1961, and placed on a statutory basis by Congress the following September, the Peace Corps achieved far greater success than its critics had anticipated. By the end of its first sixteen months 3,642 volunteers had been sent abroad, and only 77 had failed to serve out their full terms of enlistment. The acceptance of Peace Corps men and women by the less privileged peoples to whom they were sent grew as they demonstrated their effectiveness in such fields as education, sanitation, agriculture, and home economics. It was evident well before Kennedy's death that the Corps could count on indefinite retention.

The United States also responded cordially to the call of the Sixteenth Assembly of the United Nations for new talks on disarmament. The Assembly created a committee of eighteen nations, the four nuclear powers and fourteen others, to take part in the negotiations. President de Gaulle of France saw no hope in disarmament and refused to cooperate, but delegates from the remaining seventeen nations met in Geneva in 1962 and again in 1963. Unfortunately the negotiators achieved only a reiteration of the well-known Soviet and American positions. The Soviets advocated the total abolition of all armies and weapons over a four year period. The United States countered with a detailed and well-coordinated plan for equally complete disarmament over a period of nine years, but with careful controls and on-the-spot inspection. But the Soviets insisted that inspection was only another name for espionage, something they did not propose to tolerate, and on this stumbling block the conference failed.

Foreign Affairs. Perhaps the most significant foreign development of the Kennedy years was the growing rift between the Soviet Union and China. The cause of this split, the Chinese declared, was Khrushchev's departure from the Marxist-Leninist doctrine that capitalism could be overthrown only by violence. Two weeks before Kennedy took office the Soviet leader had outlined in a major address a new approach to East-West relations. Since an atomic war might well wipe out both the Communist and the free nations, such a conflict, Khrushchev declared, must not occur. Instead, Communism should seek its goal of world domination by the steady subversion of existing "imperialist" nations, by promoting national uprisings, and by waging guerrilla wars for the liberation of subject peoples. This Russian policy of "peaceful co-existence," as Khrushchev sometimes termed it, seemed to Chou En-lai and his adherents a complete betrayal of the Communist cause. They considered victory to be impossible without direct conflict, and argued that Khrushchev had become a "partner of the imperialists." Undoubtedly the split ran deeper than mere differences in ideology. The two nations had conflicting claims along the Siberian-Chinese border, and both sought exclusive domination of the Communist parties in the new nations of Asia and Africa. These practical considerations greatly exacerbated the ideological warfare and led the Soviets as early as 1958 to order the withdrawal of all aid to China. A by-product of the Soviet absorption in the dispute with China was the effort made by various satellite states of eastern Europe to seek greater independence from their Russian overlords. Rumania, for example, was no longer content

LYNDON BAINES JOHNSON

The remarkable facility shown by Kennedy's successor in obtaining from Congress legislation that a large majority of the people wanted assured his nomination and election to the Presidency "in his own right" (1964). But many who voted for him then condemned the stern measures he ordered later in Vietnam and the Dominican Republic.

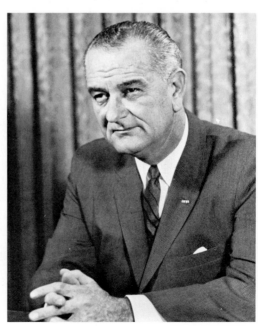

merely to produce raw materials and food-stuffs for the Soviet industrial complex, and in an effort to further trade with the West signed several commercial agreements in 1964 with western nations. Similar evidences of unrest and national independence were apparent elsewhere, especially in Poland and Hungary.

Among the free nations, the unity that the threat of Russian aggression had once inspired was also weakening. In this retreat France under General de Gaulle led

THE SPACE PROGRAM

At Cape Canaveral (later Cape Kennedy), American astronauts were soon duplicating, and in some ways surpassing, the achievements of Soviet cosmonauts. Astronaut Alan B. Shepard, Jr., is shown here walking toward the missile that would project him into space, May 5, 1961.

the way. He early announced his intention to develop a French atomic bomb, and French scientists continued their activities in this direction after achieving their first explosion in the Sahara Desert in 1960. France, de Gaulle believed, should be the "third force" around which the nations of continental Europe should gather as a counterbalance to the two Anglo-Saxon powers, Great Britain and the United States, and Russia. In January, 1963, he vetoed Great Britain's application to join the European Common Market (EEC), and subsequently he signed a treaty with West Germany calling for the closest cooperation on defense and many other matters of consequence. De Gaulle's policy ran directly counter to the American concept of a united Europe in close alliance with the United States and threatened the stability of NATO as the central factor in the European power structure. Moreover, de Gaulle took an independent and usually anti-American line in urging neutrality for Southeast Asia, in recognizing Red China, and in assiduously attempting to build up French influence in South America. With the last-mentioned objective in view, he paid a prolonged visit to Latin America in 1964.

National Defense. In order to cope with such a rapidly shifting world, the Kennedy administration made important changes in the nation's defense policy. Convinced by conversations with Khrushchev, held at Vienna in June, 1961, that the Soviet leader was determined to carry out his promised support for "uprisings" against existing non-Communist governments, President Kennedy reversed the Eisenhower policy of almost total dependence on the atomic bomb as a deterrent. In line with Secretary McNamara's ruling that there should be no more arbitrary ceilings on defense spending, Congress increased substantially the strength of the army and navy and retained many air force contingents previously scheduled for deactivation. To dampen further the Communist interest in "bush wars," the President let it be known that the United States itself would resort to guerrilla warfare, if that should be necessary to prevent Communist takeovers; also that he would not hesitate to use atomic weapons should the defense of the free world require it.

During the campaign of 1960 there had been much talk of the "missile gap" that was supposed to exist between the United States and the Soviet Union. The Democrats charged that in the interest of economy the Eisenhower administration had permitted the Soviets to forge ahead in the development of intercontinental missiles, while the Republicans, somewhat more accurately, denied the accusation. Whatever the merits of the argument, the Kennedy administration immediately raised the budget figures both for long-range missiles and for the so-called "space race." In July, 1961, the United States scored a spectacular achievement by launching an Atlas E missile and dropping it in a designated target area 9,050 miles away in the Indian Ocean. But the following September the Soviets also launched long-range missiles and guided them for 7,500 miles into the central Pacific area. As both sides continued to claim superiority, one thing seemed quite certain: either nation had the facilities to drop atomic warheads almost anywhere within the boundaries of the other.

Space Exploration. The race between the United States and the Soviet Union in space exploration accented sharply the military and political rivalry of the two nations. President Kennedy had been in office only a few months when he announced that the American government should commit itself to the project of "landing a man on the moon and returning him safely to earth." Experts held that the ultimate cost of this undertaking might be as high as $40 billion, but Congress approved it and voted initial funds for the project to the National Aeronautics and Space Administration. In this area of competition, however, the Soviets

were seemingly a long lap ahead. On April 12, 1961, they announced that they had placed a manned spaceship, Vostok I, in orbit, and that its cosmonaut, Yuri Gagarin, after circling the earth, had landed his craft successfully. On August 6 following, another Soviet satellite, Vostok II, carried its pilot seventeen times around the earth and brought him down alive. Soviet scientists also placed one cosmonaut in orbit, August 11, 1962, and another into a nearly identical orbit the next day, then brought both men down safely on August 15. Their later accomplishments included putting a man and a woman into space at the same time but in separate space ships, and sending three men together into orbit.

In contrast with these achievements, the United States could point to substantial, if less spectacular gains. It had to its credit two sub-orbital flights, one by Alan B. Shepard, Jr., on May 5, 1961, and another by Virgil I. Grissom on July 21 following. A more significant American space triumph came on February 20, 1962, when John H. Glenn, Jr., circled the earth three times, and in so doing gave the morale of the United States and all the free world a much-needed boost. Glenn's success was duplicated May 24 by Scott Carpenter, while Walter M. Shirra, Jr., on October 3, 1962, orbited the earth six times. The American space flights, unlike those of the Soviets, took place amidst a maximum of publicity. Millions of television viewers witnessed both the launching of the rocket and the recovery of the astronaut. Further American successes, particularly the 1963 flight of a space craft to the planet Venus and the even more spectacular close-up televised photographing of the moon's surface, gave increased insurance that American efforts in the space race were not lagging.

The Problem of Cuba. The renewed emphasis that the Kennedy administration had given to America's conventional military defenses proved to be exceedingly fortunate, for in October, 1962, the nation was confronted in Cuba with one of its gravest crises since the Korean War. The Cuban Revolution of 1959 in its early days was supported by most of the progressive elements of the island, and won American sympathy. The Eisenhower administration early indicated its benevolent attitude toward the revolutionists by stopping arms shipments to the discredited Batista regime months before either Great Britain or France took similar action. During this period Fidel Castro, the revolutionary leader, announced that his intentions were to supplant the existing dictatorship with a democratic regime, but once in power he rapidly exhibited radical leftist tendencies. His government confiscated privately held land and factories, nationalized most foreign holdings, launched a violent campaign against religion, and summarily executed or jailed thousands of Cuban citizens. As it became increasingly evident that Communist influence would dominate the new regime, thousands of Cuban refugees made their way to the United States. Awakened at last to the real character of the Castro government, the United States froze Cuban credits in America and attempted to isolate it diplomatically and economically from the rest of the world.

The United States was also involved in an attempt by Cuban refugees to overthrow the Castro government. From Miami and other refugee centers volunteers for this undertaking had trained in Guatemala, and on April 17, 1961, they landed, about 1,500 strong, at the Bay of Cochinos (Pigs) on the south-central coast of Cuba. The invaders, as events proved, had totally inadequate military supplies and little air cover. They were no match for Castro's tanks and jet aircraft, and within a few days all who survived were captives. Unfortunately Castro's charge that the United States was responsible for the invasion proved to be true. During the Eisenhower administration, the Central Intelligence Agency had planned and promoted it, with the approval of the United States Joint Chiefs of Staff

as to the military means to be employed. One of the first decisions Kennedy had to make as President was whether to proceed with the plans or cancel them. Despite the vigorous opposition of some of his advisers, Kennedy and a majority of his staff favored the project. The President was charged later with contributing to its failure by proscribing the direct use of American planes as air cover, but the inability or unwillingness of the Cuban population to rise up against Castro, as the invaders had expected, was probably even more important. The President was as deeply humiliated by the Cuban fiasco as his predecessor had been over the U-2 incident the year before, but like Eisenhower, Kennedy assumed full responsibility for the blunder.

After the Bay of Pigs episode, Castro threw off all pretense and admitted openly that Cuba had become a Communist state, the first, but he vowed not the last, in the western hemisphere. Soon he was receiving substantial assistance, both civilian and military, from the Soviet Union. Many Americans counseled some form of United States intervention, perhaps a blockade that would prevent Soviet shipments and personnel from reaching Cuba, but the President refused to be stampeded into any action that might result in war. The main concern of the United States, he seemed to think, was the prevention of any exportation of the Communist system from Cuba to other Latin-American republics. In the fall of 1962, however, he learned that the Cuban government was receiving from the Soviets not only defensive weapons, as he had been led to believe, but also missiles and bombers capable of destroying most United States and Caribbean cities and the Panama Canal. As a result he announced, October 22, 1962, in a televised broadcast, a "quarantine" against the delivery to Cuba of any such weapons and ordered the navy and the air force to make it effective. He further warned that an attack by Cuban-based missiles on American targets would be construed as an attack coming from the Soviet

Union itself, and that retaliation by the United States would follow immediately. The Organization of American States, formed in 1948 to promote hemispheric solidarity, voted 20 to 0 to back up the position the President had taken, and most of the European allies of the United States took a similar stand. Hope ran high that through the United Nations, or some other diplomatic channel, open warfare could be averted, but the President insisted that, as a condition of negotiation, the missile sites already being built in Cuba must be dismantled. If this were not done by the Soviets and the Cubans, with appropriate international inspection, the President indicated that the United States might have to do the job itself. Around-the-clock activity in the Pentagon, together with the massing of military and naval forces in case the President should order an invasion, left no doubt that he meant business. The air force, moreover, was prepared to destroy the missile sites by bombing, if necessary.

To the relief of all the world, Khrushchev, faced by the tough American stand, gave in. Soviet ships on the way to Cuba with military equipment turned back rather than face the American blockade. Khrushchev also promised to remove all offensive weapons and to permit inspection to prove that they were gone. In return he asked only that the United States lift its blockade and agree not to invade Cuba, a concession that the President was willing to make, but only on evidence that the Soviets had converted their words into deeds. When Secretary-General U Thant of the United Nations visited Havana to arrange for the implementation of the Soviet-American agreement, however, he found Castro completely unwilling to permit the inspection that Khrushchev had promised. Confronted by this situation, the United States resorted to air flights over Cuba, from which it learned that all missiles designed for offensive use were being dismantled and returned to Russia, and that Soviet forces in Cuba were being evacuated. With this

assurance, the quarantine was lifted, but Castro's behavior continued to keep the Cuban problem in the news. He demanded that the United States surrender to him its Guantanamo naval base, and he stepped up his efforts to foment revolution in other Latin-American countries. The American hope that stringent trade restrictions would cripple the Castro government grew dim when other free-world nations refused to cooperate, and led many extremists to advocate direct military and naval intervention by the United States as the only means to achieve the desired end.

The Test-ban Treaty. After the Cuban confrontation, which had brought the United States and the Soviet Union so frighteningly near the brink of war, the two nations showed an unmistakable interest in the prevention of similar incidents for the future. In order to "reduce the danger of accidental war," they agreed on April 5, 1963, to establish a "hot line" between Moscow and Washington, by means of which the responsible leaders of the two nations could communicate with each other directly and at a moment's notice. Also, they joined with Great Britain in subscribing, on July 25, 1963, to a "test-ban" treaty signed at Geneva, which forbade atomic testing in the air, in space, and under water. Such an agreement had earlier proved to be impossible because of differences over the amount of inspection required to insure honest observation of the treaty, but since all atomic explosions of consequence, except those made underground, could now be detected almost anywhere in the world, the three nations got together on the points on which they could agree. In any event, underground explosions would release little, if any, of the harmful "fall-out" that came from tests made on or above the surface of the earth. The test-ban agreement was ratified not only by the three principal atomic powers (albeit with some opposition in the United States Senate), but by many other nations also; not, however, by France or Red China.

Following the test-ban agreement, Khrushchev still promised the western leaders that he would continue "to step on your corns," but in practice he was somewhat less aggressive. He showed a greater degree of willingness to cooperate with the West on scientific and cultural matters; he made no new rude demands on the subject of Berlin and the German problem; he showed little interest in promoting Red China's bid for supremacy in Southeast Asia. In August, 1964, he even urged an extension of "the international confidence" built up since the signing of the test-ban treaty, and advocated other agreements in "various international spheres." Meanwhile, Soviet satellite leaders, including Cuba's Castro, notably muted their clamor against the "wicked imperialists." The hopes of the western nations for a *détente,* during which a war-weary world might seek further to resolve its differences, were dimmed perceptibly when the Soviet Presidium suddenly ousted Khrushchev, October 14, 1964, and replaced him with Leonid L. Brezhnev as First Secretary of the Communist Party, and Aleksei N. Kosygin as Premier. But the new Soviet team, during its first few months in power, showed little disposition to reverse the trend to which Khrushchev had seemingly committed his country.

Latin America. The conditions which had brought about the Cuban revolution reflected with considerable accuracy the entire Latin-American problem that the Kennedy-Johnson administration had to face. Because of the much graver situations in Europe and Asia, the United States in the years that followed the Second World War had paid relatively little attention to the Latin part of its own hemisphere. Whereas billions of dollars in United States funds had provided economic assistance for other parts of the world, Latin America had received little American aid. While the region had not suffered from war damage, its archaic and usually corrupt governments, often controlled by a small clique of ruling

families, had served quite as effectively to hold back economic progress. Educational and health facilities for the masses were almost nonexistent, and most of the wealth was concentrated in the hands of a favored few. A relatively static economic structure, combined with one of the world's highest birth rates, tended to intensify the already existing massive poverty. In the revolutionary-minded world of the 1960's, the way was thus opened for upheavals on a continental scale.

The presence of a Russian-backed Communist regime in Cuba had a profound effect upon all the governments of Latin America, many of which feared that their very existence was imperiled. Among their underprivileged masses, "Fidelista" sympathizers were numerous, and the incentive for revolution against the ruling classes was great. Faith in the United States as the defender of the continent was also at low ebb, particularly after the abortive Cuban invasion. To meet this new emergency, the American government proposed an Alliance for Progress, reminiscent of the European Recovery Plan that had worked so well. At an Inter-American Economic and Social Council meeting, held in Punta del Este, Uruguay, in August, 1961, the United States urged the Latin-American nations to institute the reforms it deemed necessary to head off Communism and promote democracy. Most of Latin America stood in desperate need of both the will and the means to promote such essentials as land reform; better taxation systems; adequate housing, health, and sanitation facilities; and sensible labor-management relations. In what came to be called the Declaration of Punta del Este, to which the United States and all the Latin-American republics except Cuba subscribed, the United States promised to supply a "major part" of the $20 billion in outside capital needed to institute the program. The Latin-American nations agreed in return to devote to it "a rapidly increasing share of their resources." But it was easier to plan the Alliance for

Progress than to make it work. Within months after Punta del Este, President Quadros of Brazil had resigned, President Velasco Iberra of Ecuador and President Frondizi of Argentina had been forced out of office, and the Trujillo regime in the Dominican Republic had fallen. Elsewhere in Latin America, moreover, political uneasiness was widespread, and the unwillingness of the economic overlords to give up their prerogatives was painfully apparent.

How could the stability and the will necessary even to inaugurate the Alliance for Progress be achieved? A visit by President and Mrs. Kennedy to Mexico in the summer of 1962 revealed that cordial relations existed between the two North American republics, a fact further emphasized by the settlement reached a year later of the El Chamizal border dispute. From Venezuela also came the heartening news that President Rómulo Betancourt, despite much Castro-inspired terrorism, had succeeded in holding office to the end of his term in 1964 and in turning over the government in orderly fashion to his legally elected successor. But such political order was more often the exception than the rule. In Honduras a military coup expelled the President and set up a new government. In Haiti an unprincipled dictator, François Duvalier, unconstitutionally continued himself in power. In Panama rioting broke out against the United States along the borders of the Canal Zone, and for a time diplomatic relations between the two countries were broken off. In the Dominican Republic, the new government set up under Juan Bosch after the fall of Trujillo gave way seven months later to a military junta. When, in April, 1965, rebellion broke out in turn against this regime, the United States took the long-renounced step of "sending in the marines," the first such action against a neighboring republic in over thirty years. Early detachments were dispatched ostensibly to protect the lives of Americans and other foreigners caught in the fighting zone, but the heavy reinforce-

ments that followed were admittedly sent to prevent a Communist takeover, such as had happened in Cuba. Soon the United States had more than 30,000 military personnel in the troubled area. The reaction of Latin America to unilateral intervention by the "Colossus of the North" was one of intense hostility and boded little good for the future. The Washington authorities sought, however, with great earnestness and some success to induce the Organization of American States to take a hand in the three-cornered dilemma.

Berlin. Meanwhile, tension between East and West over Berlin had caused great anxiety. Angered by the steady stream of refugees that flowed at the rate of about 20,000 a month from East Germany through Berlin to the West, the Communist authorities on August 13, 1961, closed off East Berlin from the rest of the city and erected a concrete and barbed-wire wall along the border to keep would-be escapees at home. While a few individuals still managed to get through to freedom, the principal escape route for refugees from Communist rule was now blocked. Elsewhere along its western borders, the Soviet Union and its satellites had long since constructed similar barriers against the flight of their supposedly "happy people" to the West. Although the Allied powers vigorously protested the action of the Communists in so dividing Berlin, they studiously avoided an armed clash that might lead to war and confined their efforts to the protection of the territory they held. President Kennedy, however, at once sent then Vice-President Johnson to West Berlin with a pledge that the United States would not retreat before the new Communist menace; at the same time 1,500 additional United States troops, supported by British and American armed vehicles, were moved into the city. Khrushchev's demands that West Berlin be turned into a free city, that Allied troops be withdrawn, and that East Germany be recognized by the western powers were all rejected, despite the

THE BRANDENBURG GATE

The Communist rulers of East Germany, to stop the flight of so many of their supposedly "happy" people through Berlin to West Germany, erected barbed-wire and concrete barriers to shut off their section of the divided city. The Berlin Wall thus became a monument to the discontent of East Germans with Communist rule.

Soviet premier's threats. President Kennedy, by way of emphasizing further his unwillingness to be intimidated, called into service enough National Guard and Reserve units to enable him to send 45,000 more men to Europe and to ready more troops for combat service. The Berlin wall still stood, but to some westerners its creation seemed to be a major Communist blunder, an admission to the world that Communism could not stand competition with a free society. President Kennedy emphasized further the intent of the United States to stand firm in the defense of West Berlin by visiting the city himself in July, 1963, and electrified a vast audience by the assertion, *Ich bin ein Berliner.*

Cyprus. The United States was again involved in Europe when fighting broke out in 1963 between the Greek and Turkish inhabitants of Cyprus, an island in the eastern Mediterranean that had won its independence from Great Britain in 1959. Threats by both Greece and Turkey to intervene on behalf of their Cypriot kinsmen imperiled the solidarity of the NATO alliance, which the United States felt obliged at all costs to preserve. In considerable part through the efforts of the American Undersecretary of State, George Ball, a temporary truce was arranged. United Nations troops, admitted for the purpose, kept the contending factions apart, but the readiness of Archbishop Makarios, the Greek President of Cyprus, to accept aid from Moscow aroused many misgivings in the West.

Africa. The situation in Africa, where European powers were engaged in a precipitate retreat from colonialism, gave both Khrushchev and the Chinese Reds another troubled area in which to operate. One after another most of the former African colonies of Great Britain and France had emerged as independent nations, with new native governments, armies of their own, and membership in the United Nations. French efforts to retain Algeria were a demonstrated failure long before either the French government or the French people awoke to the fact. Finally, in the spring of 1962, President de Gaulle signed an agreement with the Algerian rebels that was designed to introduce virtual independence, but with close ties to France. Angry Algerian "colons," as the local descendants of Europeans were called, aided by a secret army under the leadership of renegade French officers, still kept the country aflame, but in the summer of 1962 the French withdrew, and the Algerians took over. Unlike the British and the French, the Portuguese, who also had African colonies, refused to make any concessions to their dependencies and held on to them by brute force. In Angola the terror was particularly alarming, and attracted much unfavorable attention in the United Nations.

The Congo. Equally disturbing were the chaotic conditions that continued in the Congo. There, after the Belgian withdrawal, the contest finally settled down to a test of endurance between what passed for a central government at Leopoldville, of which Cyrille Adoula became prime minister in 1961, and the Katanga provincial government at Elisabethville, headed by Moise Tshombe. In an effort to restore order, the United Nations intervened with military force, but the factional fighting continued. To add to the confusion the Soviets attempted to support incipient governments, the first under Patrice Lumumba, who was murdered, and the second under Antoine Gizenga, a local leader in the eastern part of the country. Since the Soviet Union, its satellites, and France steadfastly refused to pay their assessments for maintaining United Nations forces in the Congo, the steady drain on the world organization's budget threatened it with bankruptcy. This condition was eventually relieved by an American loan of $100 million to the UN, and the evacuation in late 1963 of all UN forces in the Congo. Further revolts, one

aided by the Chinese Reds, so imperiled the country that in July, 1964, Moise Tshombe, who meantime had been defeated and driven into exile, was recalled as prime minister, but Congo conditions still remained unsettled.

Southeast Asia. By supporting the United Nations in its attempt at pacification, the United States was able to avoid direct intervention in the Congo, but was less fortunate in Southeast Asia. There, because of constant guerrilla activity by Communist forces, the accord arrived at by the Geneva Conference of 1954 broke down. In Laos, due chiefly to the ineffectiveness of the Laotian government, American military aid proved to be virtually useless, and led the Kennedy administration to work instead for the preservation of Laotian neutrality. Communist pressure continued, however, and in April, 1964, Prince Souvanna Phouma, the neutralist prime minister, visited Peking to seek help in restraining it. Meantime the second of the French succession states, Cambodia, renounced all American aid late in 1963, and appeared

THE WAR IN VIETNAM

American "advisers," equipped with helicopters and a variety of military vehicles, participated much more actively in the fighting than their designation implied.

also to be making the best bargain it could with Red China. In South Vietnam the American government made a determined effort to prevent the further spread of Communism into Southeast Asia. After official investigations by Vice-President Johnson and by General Maxwell D. Taylor, the United States sent great quantities of military equipment, including helicopters, to aid the South Vietnamese government in counter-guerrilla warfare. Along with the *matériel* of war, it sent a steady stream of American military "advisers," technicians, pilots, and ground troops, numbering altogether over 45,000 by mid-1965. By this time nearly 400 Americans had lost their lives in the struggle.

Unfortunately the ability of the South Vietnamese people to resist the Viet Cong, as they called their opponents, was hampered by a succession of military coups that toppled first Ngo Dinh Diem, the only really strong leader they produced, then a succession of make-shift governments. Nor were many other anti-Communist countries willing to support the American efforts in South Vietnam, a fact that became painfully evident after a meeting of SEATO representatives at Bangkok in April, 1964. Some of the Allied powers, France in particular, blamed the American government for disregarding the 1954 Geneva agreement to neutralize the area, and urged adherence to that policy as the only way to prevent a complete Communist takeover.

Despite many disheartening setbacks, the American forces stayed on in South Vietnam. Early in August, 1964, when some North Vietnamese P-T boats attacked American destroyers in Tonkin Bay, President Johnson ordered a retaliatory air attack on certain specified naval installations along the North Vietnamese coast, although disclaiming at this time any intention of escalating the war. But in February, 1965, convinced that Viet Cong successes in the South were due chiefly to the infiltration of men and supplies from the North, he ordered continued air strikes on military installations, transportation routes, and bridges in North Vietnam. This action aroused heated protests, not only in the Communist world, but also among the Allies and within the United States itself, where demands for an end to the war became more and more vehement.

According to many observers, the President's real objective in thus stepping up the war was to make possible a negotiated peace. They so interpreted his avowed willingness to open "unconditional discussions" with any power or powers (presumably North Vietnam and Red China) interested in ending hostilities. The United States, he promised, would invest a billion dollars in the economic development of Southeast Asia, including North Vietnam, if only stable conditions in that area could be restored. When his offer elicited no response, however, he asked and received from Congress an appropriation of $700 million for the further defense of South Vietnam.

Domestic Affairs. During the campaign of 1960, Kennedy had promised that under a Democratic administration the economic growth of the United States would surge forward at a far more rapid rate than during the Eisenhower years. But before he could concern himself with growth the new President had to face the problems of a business recession which reached a disheartening low just as he took office. With the number of jobless standing at 6.9 per cent of the working population, Congress agreed to a temporary thirteen week extension of unemployment benefits, approved an area development program that Eisenhower had twice vetoed, liberalized social security payments, extended the minimum wage protection to an additional 3.6 million workers, and provided for an increase in the minimum wage, within a two year period, from $1 an hour to $1.25. These measures, together with substantial federal expenditures on highways, aided materially in promoting recovery.

With the end of the recession in sight, the President set about securing the "New Frontier" that he had asked for in his campaign. During his first two years his efforts were virtually blocked in this endeavor, in part by the long-standing congressional coalition of southern Democrats and conservative Republicans, and in part by the critical position of the country in international finance. For the time being the President himself was unwilling to promote the kind of deficit spending that some of his pre-election supporters had expected, not only because he was eager to prevent inflation, but also because of the unfavorable balance of payments that had developed in the country's foreign accounts. As a result of European and Japanese recovery, the United States no longer sold more abroad than the combined totals of what it bought and what it sent abroad for military purposes, economic aid, tourist expenditures, and investment. Instead of the relatively even balance of payments that before 1958 had long kept about $22 billion worth of gold in the United States Treasury, the balance had turned strongly in favor of Europe, with persistent American losses that by 1962 had brought the Treasury's gold resources down to less than $17 billion. Since about two-thirds of this gold was earmarked to back federal reserve notes, the United States actually had available less than $6 billion for use in international settlements. The Kennedy administration could not, therefore, run the risk of an inflationary spiral that might further reduce the nation's gold supply and lower the value of the dollar. The most conspicuous success that the President won from his refractory Congress was the passage in 1962 of a foreign free trade bill that gave him unprecedented freedom in adjusting American tariffs to competitive needs.

Reform Programs. The Kennedy administration was able to take a few other steps toward reform. The Federal Power Commission, the majority of its members

Kennedy appointees, undertook with some success to bring natural gas producers under more effective control. The Food and Drug Administration, as a result of investigations begun by Senator Kefauver's Antitrust and Monopoly Subcommittee, scored several successes, including legislation that greatly strengthened the safeguards surrounding the production, testing, and sale of medicines. Meanwhile, Attorney-General Robert Kennedy launched antitrust suits against corporations deemed guilty of price-fixing and illegal mergers. He was encouraged by the decision of a federal judge in January, 1961, which held twenty-nine electrical companies guilty of price-fixing and other illegal practices. Fines of $2 million were levied against the offending corporations, and several of their high executives were sent to prison for their activities.

The Kennedy administration also intervened in a threatened national steel strike to obtain an agreement maintaining the existing wage scale with some additional fringe benefits, together with what it regarded as an understanding that the companies would not raise the price of steel products. The agreement was designed to stop the inflationary pay-raise, price-rise cycle that had so long prevailed in major industries. But as soon as the wage contract was safely signed, the United States Steel Corporation, in what seemed to the President, the workers, and most of the public an act of bad faith, raised the price of steel by $6 a ton. When most of the other steel companies followed suit, Kennedy in a televised press conference angrily denounced those who had instigated the price increases for their "irresponsible defiance" and "ruthless disregard" of the nation's welfare. The increase, he said, was not only inflationary, but would add a billion dollars to the nation's defense costs and would impair the ability of American firms to compete in the world market. Roger M. Blough, head of United States Steel, defended the action and stated that the higher prices would stand. But the President let it be known that military contractors would thereafter shift as much as possible of their steel purchases to firms maintaining the old price. After two steel companies announced that they would not raise their prices and a third reversed its action, United States Steel and the others capitulated. The incident revealed not only the power of the federal government as a prime purchaser, but also the extent to which it had moved into the market mechanism establishing the level of wages and prices.

The 1962 mid-term elections indicated popular approval of the new administration. In Congress, the Democrats won four additional seats in the House and held their own in the Senate, the first time since 1934 that any party in power had not suffered a mid-term reverse. Possibly because of this vote of confidence, the President, in January, 1963, called upon Congress to enact an extensive program of domestic legislation, including a $10 billion tax cut to encourage business and diminish unemployment, the further extension of social security and public health benefits, and the establishment of a Community Corps, comparable to the Peace Corps, to enroll and train young Americans "out of school and out of work."

Taxes and Civil Rights. The new Congress, despite its overwhelmingly Democratic majorities, seemed little disposed to give the President what he wanted, largely because conservative southern Democrats held most of the important committee assignments in both houses. Attention tended to focus on foreign aid, the tax cut, and civil rights. The continuance of the foreign aid program, which had cost the United States $100 billion since 1945, was denounced as a gigantic giveaway, shot through with inefficiency and mismanagement, which served mainly to insure a balance-of-payments deficit for the United States. Left unsaid was that it served directly few Congressional constituents. The tax cut, which normally should have pleased the

business community, was less welcome because it proposed to close certain valued loopholes and was not to be accompanied by a corresponding cut in expenditures. It was intended to produce a deficit which, however, according to the economists who advised the President, would stimulate business and prevent another of the periodic recessions that had so regularly marked the preceding decade. The civil rights program, to the anger of most southern Democrats, proposed that the national government should interfere with the rights of the states to deal as they chose with the Negro problem.

What was often called "the Negro revolution" was an outstanding phenomenon of the year 1963 — the 100th anniversary of the freeing of the slaves. Undoubtedly the grim persistence of economic hardship for so large a proportion of the race was the chief motivating force behind this movement. The Negroes had come a long way since slavery, but the great majority of them remained in the lowest income bracket or in the ranks of the unemployed. This condition was the more keenly felt because of the social and political discriminations from which they suffered, particularly in the states of the old Confederacy, where some of them were still denied even the right to vote. In the North, although they were granted full political rights, they usually had to live in segregated areas and to send their children to schools that were segregated in fact, if not in law. They were at a disadvantage, too, in the competition for employment; some labor unions even denied them the privilege of membership, and almost invariably they were still "the last to be hired and the first to be fired."

During the first two years of his administration President Kennedy had not requested any significant civil rights legislation. Early in March, 1961, however, he created a Committee on Equal Employment Opportunity, with Vice-President Johnson at its head, which solicited and obtained anti-discrimination pledges from leading defense contractors. The Department of Justice also won from the Interstate Commerce Commission a ruling against segregation in southern bus terminals. The responsibility for this decision was shared in some degree by the Congress of Racial Equality (CORE), which had promoted "freedom rides" by representatives of both races into the deep South and had precipitated incidents at Birmingham, Alabama, and Jackson, Mississippi, which won sympathy for the Negro cause throughout most of the nation.

Except in Mississippi and South Carolina, school desegregation made slow but steady gains, although the percentage of Negroes attending schools with whites remained extremely low. Negroes were encouraged, however, by Kennedy's willingness to name members of their race to high office. He appointed two Negroes to federal judgeships, another to be Ambassador to Norway, and he made Dr. Robert C. Weaver Administrator of the Housing and Home Insurance Agency. But when, early in 1962, the President sought to create a Department of Urban Affairs, with a seat in the Cabinet to which he intended to appoint Weaver as its first Secretary, the conservative coalition in Congress promptly turned the measure down. The President's hope of easing racial tension in the South also received a rude jolt when Governor Ross R. Barnett of Mississippi personally intervened to prevent registration at the University of Mississippi of a Negro student, James H. Meredith, whose admission had been ordered by a federal court. To obtain compliance with the court order, the President sent in scores of federal marshals and, shortly thereafter, army units. In the rioting that accompanied Meredith's appearance on campus, two persons were killed and many others injured, but Meredith was duly registered and began to attend classes.

Martin Luther King. Encouraged by such resolute action on the part of the federal government, Negro leaders now stepped up their campaign for equality in both the North and the South. Outstanding among them was Martin Luther King, Jr., a well-educated Baptist minister who preached peaceful resistance, somewhat after the Gandhi pattern that had helped free India. He won his first victory at Montgomery, Alabama, where he led a yearlong boycott, beginning in December, 1955, against a local bus company for its discrimination against Negroes in the seating of passengers. The company, to save itself from bankruptcy, eventually gave in. During the next few years racial demonstrations of one kind or another erupted in all parts of the nation; most notable was the epidemic of "sit-ins" and "freedom rides" in the deep South. Participants in these activities scrupulously avoided violence and cheerfully incurred arrest for their refusal to abide by local rules and customs; King himself went to jail at Albany, Georgia, in December 1961, and twice more the following year. Early in 1963 he recruited thousands of Negroes to parade peacefully in favor of equal rights at Birmingham. The dispersal of these marchers by the Birmingham police, who made free use of police dogs and fire hoses, aroused massive sentiment in favor of the Negro cause throughout the nation and the world. For his success in obtaining greater rights for the Negroes by nonviolent means, Martin Luther King was awarded the 1964 Nobel Peace Prize.

Increasingly the Negro protest began to insist on drastic economic readjustments. Organizations such as CORE and the National Association for the Advancement of Colored People (NAACP) everywhere demanded that more and better jobs be available to Negroes. The climax of the Negro revolt came with the Washington March, August 28, 1963, in which some 200,000 Negroes and white sympathizers from all over the nation participated, walking in orderly fashion from the Washington Monument to the Lincoln Memorial. Not a single deed of violence marred the demonstration.

KENNEDY AND THE WASHINGTON MARCH

The President is shown here posing in mirthful mood with some of the leaders of the Washington March. Second from the left is the Reverend Martin Luther King. Next to the President is Walter Reuther, exploding in laughter. Second from the right, visible only from the eyes up, is Vice-President Johnson.

Meanwhile, southern extremists continued to fight nonviolence with violence. Negro homes and churches were bombed, and several Negro leaders and white civil rights workers were murdered in cold blood.

Revulsion against these wild deeds undoubtedly aided the Negro cause, both in the North and in most of the South. Previously indifferent individuals and corporations made a sincere effort to add Negroes to their payrolls. One of the difficulties they encountered was that so few Negroes had the skills they needed for the positions to which they aspired; some employers met this problem with on-the-job training, a requirement also for many of the whites they hired. The need for better educational opportunities for Negroes was apparent, and more and more school boards recognized the necessity for desegregation and for new types of vocational education. Measures designed to end or ameliorate racial dis-

crimination in housing also won increasing attention and occasional adoption. Perhaps most important of all was the decision of President Kennedy to lend urgency to his demand for civil rights legislation. Seeking support for the bill before Congress, he made his fateful trip to Dallas.

Johnson and Congress. On taking over the Presidency, Lyndon Johnson found the main features of the Kennedy legislation hopelessly stalled in Congress, but he knew better than most politicians how to prod that body into action. He kept Congress in session, despite its desire to adjourn for the holidays, until it had passed the long-delayed foreign aid bill, not at the $4.5 billion figure President Kennedy had recommended, but at $3 billion, all the existing majority in Congress would grant. He also used his influence to pry the Kennedy tax reduction bill out of the committees that were blocking it and through both houses of Congress. He achieved this goal in part by cutting the proposed Kennedy budget from over $100 billion to well under that sum, thus satisfying some critics who demanded tax cuts should be accompanied by reduced spending. Well before he became President, crippling amendments had eliminated most of the reforms from the original bill, but Congress, responding to public as well as presidential pressure, enabled Johnson, early in 1964, to sign an $11.5 billion tax cut into law.

The President's next major effort was to expedite passage of the civil rights bill, long held up in the House of Representatives. Proud of the fact that Congress, while he was Senate majority leader, had passed the first civil rights legislation since Reconstruction, he pushed hard for action on the pending bill. The proposed measure sought (1) to promote the freer registration of voters, (2) to forbid discrimination in such public facilities as hotels, restaurants, and stores, (3) to authorize action by the Attorney-General against school segrega-

tion and other discriminatory practices, and (4) to create a federal agency for the enforcement of equality in job opportunity. Early in 1964 the House passed the measure, substantially as Kennedy in his time had agreed to it. In the Senate, however, it met a determined southern filibuster, the longest in that body's history. But after eighty-seven days of wearisome talk, the necessary two-thirds majority for cloture was made possible by the adoption of a series of Republican-sponsored amendments, designed to increase moderately the power of local governments in the administration of the measure. On June 10, 1964, for the first time in its history, the Senate voted 71 to 29 for cloture on a civil rights measure, thus assuring the passage of the bill. Forty-four Democrats and 27 Republicans voted for cloture, 23 Democrats and 6 Republicans against it.

The administration scored similar successes with the minor measures it sponsored. By the time Congress adjourned for the autumn campaign, it had passed measures to increase the pay of Congressmen, federal

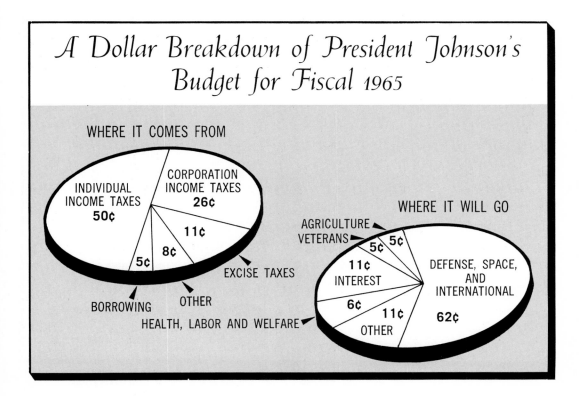

A Dollar Breakdown of President Johnson's Budget for Fiscal 1965

judges, and civil servants, to give financial aid to state and local governments attempting to provide adequate mass transportation for the burgeoning cities, and to create within government-owned lands wilderness sanctuaries that eventually might include as many as 60 million acres. Altogether, the Congressional record for significant legislation was one of the most impressive since New Deal days. Since in good part this record was due to Johnson's remarkable legislative ability, he faced with confidence the campaign of 1964, in which it was obvious that he would be the Democratic candidate to succeed himself.

Election of 1964.   With the Democratic nomination a foregone conclusion, election interest centered at first on whom the Republicans would nominate. After the defeat of Nixon in 1960, the general expectation was that Nelson A. Rockefeller, the moderately liberal Governor of New York, would win the nomination, but his popu-

larity with the voters was seriously marred by his divorce in 1962, and his remarriage the following year to the recently divorced mother of four young children. Rockefeller campaigned earnestly, despite this handicap, and entered a number of primaries. His chief opponent was Senator Barry M. Goldwater of Arizona, the idol of the ultra-conservative wing of the party and one of the six Republicans who had voted against the civil rights bill. Goldwater had long maintained that the Republicans should give up the practice of nominating moderate candidates on compromise platforms, and, in his own words, should give the voters "a choice not an echo." Failure to assert their conservatism, he insisted, was the principal cause of Republican defeats; the people would vote conservative if only they were given the opportunity. In his book, *The Conscience of a Conservative* (1960), and elsewhere, he urged the curtailment of governmental authority, particularly at the federal level, in the interest of

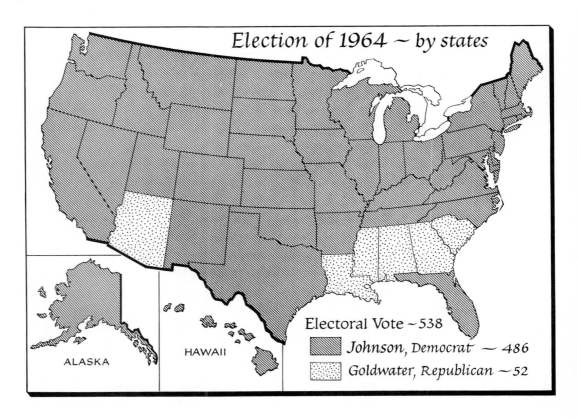

Election of 1964 ~ by states

ALASKA

HAWAII

Electoral Vote ~ 538

Johnson, Democrat — 486

Goldwater, Republican — 52

greater freedom for the individual. He opposed federal aid for education, federal price supports for agriculture, and federal expenditures for such projects as TVA. While claiming that he was personally against racial discrimination, he would leave to the states the protection of civil rights. In the activities of labor unions, he saw a challenge to individual liberty that must be curbed. In foreign affairs, he found little virtue in American aid to other governments and advocated that the United States should withdraw its recognition of the Soviet Union, take a tough line toward all Communist powers, and leave the United Nations in the event that that body should vote to admit Red China. He seemed also to believe that the United States should make use of its superior military power however and whenever it saw fit to do so.

During the first weeks of the campaign, the general expectation was that Rockefeller and Goldwater would cancel each other out and that the party nomination would go to some "non-candidate," of whom there were several. But in a year when the Republican nomination was not expected to mean much at best, Goldwater gathered up the delegates in the non-primary states with little opposition, and by a thin margin defeated Rockefeller in the important California primary. A last minute effort by Governor William Scranton of Pennsylvania to head off the Goldwater nomination was unavailing, and the San Francisco Convention, July 15, 1964, chose the Arizona Senator on the first ballot. For second place on the ticket, Goldwater chose another ultraconservative, William E. Miller of New York, Chairman of the Republican National Committee. Goldwater views also dominated the report of the platform committee, and the convention shouted down all efforts to liberalize it by amendments from the floor.

The Democratic Convention, meeting in Atlantic City the following month, nominated Johnson as expected, and accepted his recommendation of Senator Hubert H. Humphrey of Minnesota as its candidate for Vice-President. The platform warmly supported the record of the Kennedy-Johnson administration, in which Humphrey had also played an important part.

The tone of the campaign that followed was set by a sentence in Goldwater's acceptance speech: "Extremism in the defense of liberty is no vice; moderation in pursuit of justice is no virtue." This statement, which was widely interpreted to mean that the end justifies the means, aroused unbounded enthusiasm among the radical-rightist members of such organizations as the John Birch Society and the Ku Klux Klan, but promoted serious misgivings on the part of many Republican moderates, some of whom flatly refused to endorse the party ticket. Goldwater's opposition to the atomic test-ban treaty and his advocacy of greater truculence in dealing with the Soviet Union frightened many voters into thinking that he was "trigger-happy," and might precipitate a major war. His hostility toward TVA, his objections to farm subsidies, his opposition to "medicare," and his uncertain attitude toward social security, which during the New Hampshire primary he had said should be "voluntary," all told against him. Also of importance was the defection from the Republican Party of many business and industrial leaders who regarded Johnson as both prudent in economic matters and basically friendly toward business. A few days before the election three overseas developments probably helped the President: (1) The Labour Party in a British national election won a bare majority; (2) Red China exploded a nuclear bomb; and (3) the Soviet Presidium ousted the supposedly all-powerful Khrushchev. Faced by the uncertainties that these events produced, most of the voters thought it safer to stand by the President.

Indeed, Johnson won the election almost by default. With peace and prosperity working for him, and Goldwater frightening more people than he convinced, the President made few specific promises and urged merely the continuance of the program he had begun, a program that would

820 *The Price of Leadership*

lead eventually to an undefined "great society." Forty-four states and the District of Columbia cast 486 electoral votes for Johnson and Humphrey, while six states cast only 52 votes for Goldwater and Miller. Five of the Republican states were South Carolina, Georgia, Alabama, Mississippi, and Louisiana, all of which changed from their normally Democratic posture solely because they liked Goldwater's idea of leaving the defense of Negro rights to the states; if the Negroes of these states had had full freedom to vote it seems probable that Johnson would have carried all of them. The sixth state was Arizona, which Goldwater won by a slender margin. The popular vote in the nation at large stood at about 43 million to 27 million. Goldwater also carried down to defeat many Republicans who under normal circumstances would have won easily. In the national House of Representatives the Democrats increased their lead by about forty seats, and in the Senate by two. Among the new members to appear in Congress after the election was Robert F. Kennedy, the former Attorney-General, who had resigned from the Cabinet to win nomination and election to the Senate from New York. At home the election administered a resounding rebuke to the extreme rightists, and abroad it made clear to all concerned that the United States would stand firmly by the policies it had developed after the Second World War.

The New Congress. During the early months of 1965, the President's foreign program, particularly with respect to Vietnam and the Dominican Republic, came in for increasing criticism, but few were able to argue with him effectively on domestic affairs. His goal of the "great society," as he termed it, appealed to the overwhelming majority of Americans and found favor with the new Congress, which liberal Democrats with the aid of a few liberal Republicans dominated easily. Johnson's long experience as a legislator now stood him in good

stead; he knew how to line up the votes for the measures he desired, and he did not hesitate to make the most of his advantage. Relying on the reports of study groups he had appointed for the purpose, he outlined in his first message to the new Congress an ambitious program.

> I propose we begin a program in education to ensure every American child the fullest development of his mind and skills. I propose we begin a massive attack on crippling and killing diseases. I propose we launch a national effort to make the American city a better and more stimulating place to live. I propose we increase the beauty of America and end the poisoning of our rivers and the air we breathe. I propose we carry out a new program to develop regions of our country now suffering from distress and depression. I propose we make new efforts to control and prevent crime and delinquency. I propose we eliminate every remaining obstacle to the right and opportunity to vote. I propose we honor and support the achievements of thought and the creation of art.

On these and other items he soon dispatched special messages to Congress in support of bills drafted to accomplish the ends he had in mind. And soon, one after another, the bills he advocated began to pass. On March 9, 1965, he signed the Appalachia Aid Act, which appropriated $1.1 billion to fight poverty in the backward mountain areas from southern Pennsylvania far down into the deep South. On April 11, 1965, he signed an Elementary and Secondary Education Act, appropriating $1.3 billion in aid for schools where the children of low-income bracket families were concentrated, with incidental benefits to parochial as well as public schools. Most important of all, he demanded a Voting Rights Bill to provide a simple, uniform standard for voting in federal elections, and to make impossible the ingenious efforts, so common in some of the southern states, to prevent Negroes from voting. While this measure was before Congress, Negro demonstrations called attention to Selma, Alabama, as an example of discriminatory conduct, and 25,000 civil rights enthusiasts, both Negro and white, from all over the nation participated in a protest march on the capitol at Montgomery, March 25, 1965. The murder after the march of a white participant, Mrs. Viola Liuzzo of Detroit, Michigan, the mother of five children, gave emphasis to the need for federal intervention.

That the Voting Rights Bill and most of the other measures Johnson favored would pass was generally conceded. "Just look at him," wrote one observer. "He got the education bill through without a murmur from the religious lobbies. When the voting rights bill was made the pending business of the Senate, not a single Southerner raised a voice in objection. Medicare is a shoo-in. It's incredible — they give him all he asks for."

The strong consensus of opinion that made possible the success of the Johnson legislative program did not conceal, however, the troubled spirit of the American people. They were unhappy about the role they were being called on to play in foreign affairs. They were worried at the existence of poverty in the midst of unparalleled prosperity. They were concerned over the racial and sectional differences that divided them. They were annoyed by the tumult that both right-wing and left-wing elements felt obliged to raise. But they still believed that their way of life would survive and that the problems of today would at least grow no worse tomorrow. They were learning that they must accept as normal the world of threats and dangers that lay about them, just as other nations less favored by geographic isolation had always had to do. They were coming to terms with the fact that their pre-eminence precluded them from being loved; what they did for the less favored peoples of the world would have to be its own reward. They were beginning to understand that the price of leadership comes high and that they had no choice but to pay it.

SELECTED BIBLIOGRAPHY

The most substantial biography of Kennedy yet to appear is J. M. Burns, *John Kennedy: A Political Profile* (2nd ed., 1961), the work of a leading political scientist. A magnificent commemorative work is *The Kennedy Years,* edited by Harold Faber and others (1964). Popular and friendly in tone are William Manchester, *Portrait of a President* (1962); and Hugh Sidey, *John F. Kennedy, President* (1964). A rather acid biography of Joseph P. Kennedy is R. J. Whalen, *The Founding Father* (1964). Works by John F. Kennedy include *Profiles in Courage* (1956), a series of sketches of Senators whose fighting spirit captivated the young Senator Kennedy; *The Strategy of Peace,* a campaign collection of speeches edited by Allan Nevins (1960); and *To Turn the Tide,* presidential pronouncements edited by J. W. Gardner (1962). Two posthumous works are

* Available in paperback

The Burden and the Glory, a collection of speeches edited by Allan Nevins (1964); and *A Generation of Immigrants* (1964), brief and moving. A collection of Kennedy's news conferences is *Kennedy and the Press,* edited by H. W. Chase and A. H. Lerman (1965).

The most revealing memoirs of the Kennedy era published so far are A. M. Schlesinger, Jr., *A Thousand Days* (1965), and T. C. Sorensen, *Kennedy* (1965). *The Presidential Election and Transition, 1960–1961,* edited by P. T. David (1961), is a collaborative study. Helen Fuller, *Year of Trial* (1962), is a liberal journalist's survey of Kennedy's first year in office. An interesting discussion by a presidential assistant is T. C. Sorensen, *Decision-Making in the White House* (1963). Economic policies are discussed in two works by a Kennedy friend, Harvard economist S. E. Harris: *The Economics of the Political Parties* (1962), and *The Economics of the Kennedy Years and a Look Ahead* (1964). Critical in tone are

B. D. Nossiter, *The Mythmakers* (1964), by a liberal; and Milton Friedman, °*Capitalism and Freedom* (1964), by a conservative. A well-informed account of relations between Kennedy and business is Hobart Rowen, *The Free Enterprisers* (1964).

The Kennedy assassination and its immediate consequences were treated in a number of books, the most successful of which was *Four Days* (1964), a magnificent pictorial report put out by United Press International and *American Heritage*. A basic source is °*The Assassination of President Kennedy*, the official report of the Warren Commission (1964).

The best introduction to the career of Lyndon B. Johnson is the sympathetic work of his columnist friend W. S. White, °*The Professional* (1964). An uncritical biography of Johnson's great sponsor, Speaker Rayburn, is C. D. Dorough, *Mr. Sam* (1962). Some of the Johnson flavor comes through in a campaign selection of his speeches and writings, *A Time for Action* (1964). A lively journalistic treatment of Johnson's first hundred days in office is Michael Amrine, *This Awesome Challenge* (1964). An interesting and well-informed political analysis is Douglass Cater, *Power in Washington* (1964); soon after its publication Cater joined Johnson's staff. The best biography of the new Vice-President is Winthrop Griffith, *Humphrey* (1965), friendly but not worshipful. See also two works by Humphrey: *War on Poverty* (1964), and °*The Cause of Mankind* (1964).

On the 1964 campaign, the best journalistic study is T. H. White, *The Making of the President, 1964* (1965). But see also R. H. Rovere, *The Goldwater Caper* (1965), a collection of periodical pieces by a liberal; and R. D. Novak, *The Agony of the G.O.P. 1964* (1965), an "inside" report by a well-informed columnist. N. A. Rockefeller, °*The Future of Federalism* (1962), is a lecture series by a Republican liberal, at the time an aspirant for the 1964 nomination. °*The Radical Right*, edited by Daniel Bell (1963), is a collection of essays by liberal academics. Complementary volumes, edited by Congressmen, are James Roosevelt, °*The Liberal Papers* (1962); and M. R. Laird, °*The Conservative Papers* (1964). An interesting summing-up by a veteran radical is Norman Thomas, *Socialism Re-examined* (1964). Important domestic themes of the

Kennedy-Johnson era are explored in: S. A. Levitan, *Federal Aid to Depressed Areas* (1964); Richard Harris, *The Real Voice* (1964), an excellent work on the Kefauver drug industry investigation; and Anthony Lewis, *Gideon's Trumpet* (1964), a superb account of one man's struggle for his right to have the services of an attorney.

Discussions of foreign policy continue to crowd publishers' lists. Major works include T. K. Finletter, °*Foreign Policy: The Next Phase, The 1960's* (2nd ed., 1960); H. A. Kissinger, °*Necessity for Choice* (1961), and *The Troubled Partnership* (1965); Norman Cousins, °*In Place of Folly* (2nd ed., 1962); T. W. Wilson, Jr., *Cold War and Common Sense* (1962); W. W. Rostow, *The View from the Seventh Floor* (1964); and J. W. Fulbright, °*Old Myths and New Realities* (1964). On the progress of the North Atlantic Treaty Organization, contrast the official report by H. L. Ismay, *NATO: The First Five Years, 1949–1954* (1955), with the later critical analysis by R. E. Osgood, *NATO: The Entangling Alliance* (1962). On American relations with western Europe, see Walter Lippmann, *Western Unity and the Common Market* (1962); E. S. Furniss, °*France: Troubled Ally* (1960); and A. P. Whitaker, °*Spain and Defense of the West: Ally and Liability* (1961). The foreign aid program is assessed by Herbert Feis, *Foreign Aid and Foreign Policy* (1964); and F. M. Coffin, *Witness for Aid* (1964).

A handy introduction to once-remote areas of the world is G. A. Lensen, °*The World beyond Europe* (1960). J. M. Maki, °*Government and Politics in Japan* (1962), is a competent survey. R. P. Newman, °*Recognition of Communist China?* (1961); and H. S. Quigley, *China's Politics in Perspective* (1962), are lively and informative. An enormous work on Red China is Edgar Snow, *The Other Side of the River* (1962), by a veteran left-wing journalist. Two useful introductions to another troubled area are C. A. Buss, °*Southeast Asia and the World Today* (1958), which contains documents; and Richard Butwell, °*Southeast Asia Today — And Tomorrow* (1961). Pierre Rondot, °*Changing Patterns of the Middle East* (1961), is helpful. A competent survey is W. N. Brown, *The United States and India and Pakistan* (2nd ed., 1963).

Among the many recent books on Africa, the following are of particular interest for an understanding of the region and of American policy toward it: G. M. Carter, °*Independence for Africa* (1960); Arnold Rivkin, °*Africa and the West: Elements of Free-World Policy* (1962); G. W. Shepherd, Jr., °*The Politics of African Nationalism: Challenge to American Policy* (1962); and Walter Goldschmidt (ed.), °*The United States and Africa* (2nd ed., 1963). A specialized study is C. F. Gallagher, *The United States and North Africa* (1963).

A. A. Berle, Jr., °*Clear and Present Danger: Latin America and U.S. Policy* (1962), is a brief assessment by a Kennedy adviser who is a former American Ambassador to Brazil. Tad Szulc, °*The Winds of Revolution: Latin America Today — and Tomorrow* (1962), is a well-informed discussion by a liberal journalist. H. L. Matthews, *The Cuban Story* (1961), is the account of an early journalist-supporter of Castro; it may be contrasted with the much more critical analysis by Theodore Draper, °*Castro's Revolution: Myths and Realities* (1962). A competent critical account of one dramatic episode is K. E. Meyer and Tad Szulc, °*The Cuban Invasion, Chronicle of a Disaster* (1962). See also Haynes Johnson and others, °*The Bay of Pigs* (1964). An interesting documentary collection is °*The "Cuban Crisis" of 1962*, edited by D. L. Larson (1963). A sweeping expose of the C.I.A. is David Wise and T. B. Ross, *The Invisible Government* (1964).

Appendix

The Declaration of Independence

IN CONGRESS, JULY 4, 1776,

THE UNANIMOUS DECLARATION OF THE THIRTEEN UNITED STATES OF AMERICA.

WHEN, in the course of human events, it becomes necessary for one people to dissolve the political bands which have connected them with another, and to assume, among the powers of the earth, the separate and equal station to which the laws of nature and of nature's God entitle them, a decent respect to the opinions of mankind requires that they should declare the causes which impel them to the separation.

We hold these truths to be self-evident, that all men are created equal; that they are endowed by their Creator with certain unalienable rights; that among these, are life, liberty, and the pursuit of happiness. That, to secure these rights, governments are instituted among men, deriving their just powers from the consent of the governed; that, whenever any form of government becomes destructive of these ends, it is the right of the people to alter or to abolish it, and to institute a new government, laying its foundation on such principles, and organizing its powers in such form, as to them shall seem most likely to effect their safety and happiness. Prudence, indeed, will dictate that governments long established, should not be changed for light and transient causes; and, accordingly, all experience hath shown, that mankind are more disposed to suffer, while evils are sufferable, than to right themselves by abolishing the forms to which they are accustomed. But, when a long train of abuses and usurpations, pursuing invariably the same object, evinces a design to reduce them under absolute despotism, it is their right, it is their duty, to throw off such government and to provide new guards for their future security. Such has been the patient sufferance of these colonies, and such is now the necessity which constrains them to alter their former systems of government. The history of the present King of Great Britain is a history of repeated injuries and usurpations, all having, in direct object, the establishment of an absolute tyranny over these States. To prove this, let facts be submitted to a candid world:—

He has refused his assent to laws the most wholesome and necessary for the public good.

He has forbidden his governors to pass laws of immediate and pressing importance, unless suspended in their operation till his assent should be obtained; and, when so suspended, he has utterly neglected to attend to them.

He has refused to pass other laws for the accommodation of large districts of people, unless those people would relinquish the right of representation in the legislature; a right inestimable to them, and formidable to tyrants only.

He has called together legislative bodies at places unusual, uncomfortable, and distant from the depository of their public records, for the sole purpose of fatiguing them into compliance with his measures.

He has dissolved representative houses repeatedly for opposing, with manly firmness, his invasions on the rights of the people.

He has refused, for a long time after such dissolutions, to cause others to be elected; whereby the legislative powers, incapable of annihilation, have returned to the people at large for their exercise; the state remaining, in the meantime, exposed to all the danger of invasion from without, and convulsions within.

He has endeavored to prevent the population of these States; for that purpose, obstructing the laws for naturalization of foreigners, refusing to pass others to encourage their migration hither, and raising the conditions of new appropriations of lands.

He has obstructed the administration of justice, by refusing his assent to laws for establishing judiciary powers.

He has made judges dependent on his will alone, for the tenure of their offices, and the amount and payment of their salaries.

He has erected a multitude of new offices, and sent hither swarms of officers to harass our people, and eat out their substance.

He has kept among us, in time of peace, standing armies, without the consent of our legislatures.

He has affected to render the military independent of, and superior to, the civil power.

He has combined, with others, to subject us to a jurisdiction foreign to our Constitution, and unacknowledged by our laws; giving his assent to their acts of pretended legislation:

For quartering large bodies of armed troops among us:

For protecting them by a mock trial, from punishment, for any murders which they should commit on the inhabitants of these States:

For cutting off our trade with all parts of the world:

For imposing taxes on us without our consent:

For depriving us, in many cases, of the benefit of trial by jury:

For transporting us beyond seas to be tried for pretended offences:

For abolishing the free system of English laws in a neighboring province, establishing therein an arbitrary government, and enlarging its boundaries, so as to render it at once an example and fit instrument for introducing the same absolute rule into these colonies:

For taking away our charters, abolishing our most valuable laws, and altering, fundamentally, the powers of our governments:

For suspending our own legislatures, and declaring themselves invested with power to legislate for us in all cases whatsoever.

He has abdicated government here, by declaring us out of his protection, and waging war against us.

He has plundered our seas, ravaged our coasts, burnt our towns, and destroyed the lives of our people.

He is, at this time, transporting large armies of foreign mercenaries to complete the works of death, desolation, and tyranny, already begun, with circumstances of cruelty and perfidy scarcely paralleled in the most barbarous ages, and totally unworthy the head of a civilized nation.

He has constrained our fellow citizens, taken captive on the high seas, to bear arms against their country, to become the executioners of their friends, and brethren, or to fall themselves by their hands.

He has excited domestic insurrections amongst us, and has endeavored to bring on the inhabitants of our frontiers, the merciless Indian savages, whose known rule of warfare is an undistinguished destruction of all ages, sexes, and conditions.

In every stage of these oppressions, we have petitioned for redress, in the most humble terms; our repeated petitions have been answered only by repeated injury. A prince, whose character is thus marked by every act which may define a tyrant, is unfit to be the ruler of a free people.

Nor have we been wanting in attention to our British brethren. We have warned them, from time to time, of attempts made by their legislature to extend an unwarrantable jurisdiction over us. We have reminded them of the circumstances of our emigration and settlement here. We have appealed to their native justice and magnanimity, and we have conjured them, by the ties of our common kindred, to disavow these usurpations, which would inevitably interrupt our connections and correspondence. They, too, have been deaf to the voice of justice and consanguinity. We must, therefore, acquiesce in the necessity which denounces our separation, and hold them, as we hold the rest of mankind, enemies in war, in peace, friends.

We, therefore, the representatives of the United States of America, in general Congress assembled, appealing to the Supreme Judge of the world for the rectitude of our intentions, do, in the name, and by the authority of the good people of these colonies, solemnly publish and declare, that these united colonies are, and of right ought to be, free and independent states: that they are absolved from all allegiance to the British Crown, and that all political connection between them and the state of Great Britain is, and ought to be, totally dissolved; and that, as free and independent states, they have full power to levy war, conclude peace, contract alliances, establish commerce, and to do all other acts and things which independent states may of right do. And, for the support of this declaration, with a firm reliance on the protection of Divine Providence, we mutually pledge to each other our lives, our fortunes, and our sacred honor.

The Constitution of the United States

WE the people of the United States, in order to form a more perfect union, establish justice, insure domestic tranquillity, provide for the common defense, promote the general welfare, and secure the blessings of liberty to ourselves and our posterity, do ordain and establish this Constitution for the United States of America.

ARTICLE I

SECTION 1

All legislative powers herein granted shall be vested in a Congress of the United States, which shall consist of a Senate and House of Representatives.

SECTION 2

1. The House of Representatives shall be composed of members chosen every second year by the people of the several States, and the electors in each State shall have the qualifications requisite for electors of the most numerous branch of the State legislature.

2. No person shall be a representative who shall not have attained to the age of twenty-five years, and been seven years a citizen of the United States, and who shall not, when elected, be an inhabitant of that State in which he shall be chosen.

3. Representatives and direct taxes[1] shall be apportioned among the several States which may be included within this Union, according to their respective numbers, which shall be determined by adding to the whole number of free persons, including those bound to service for a term of years, and excluding Indians not taxed, three fifths of all other persons.[2] The actual enumeration shall be made within three years after the first meeting of the Congress of the United States, and within every subsequent term of ten years, in such manner as they shall by law direct. The number of representatives shall not exceed one for every thirty thousand, but each State shall have at least one representative; and until such enumeration shall be made, the State of New Hampshire shall be entitled to chuse three, Massachusetts eight, Rhode Island and Providence Plantations one, Connecticut five, New York six, New Jersey four, Pennsylvania eight, Delaware one, Maryland six, Virginia ten, North Carolina five, South Carolina five, and Georgia three.

4. When vacancies happen in the representation from any State, the executive authority thereof shall issue writs of election to fill such vacancies.

5. The House of Representatives shall choose their speaker and other officers; and shall have the sole power of impeachment.

SECTION 3

1. The Senate of the United States shall be composed of two senators from each State, chosen by the legislature thereof,[1] for six years; and each senator shall have one vote.

2. Immediately after they shall be assembled in consequence of the first election, they shall be divided as equally as may be into three classes. The seats of the senators of the first class shall be vacated at the expiration of the second year, of the second class at the expiration of the fourth year, and of the third class at the expiration of the sixth year, so that one third may be chosen every second year; and if vacancies happen by resignation or otherwise, during the recess of the legislature of any State, the executive thereof may make temporary appointments until the next meeting of the legislature, which shall then fill such vacancies.[1]

3. No person shall be a senator who shall not have attained to the age of thirty years, and been nine years a citizen of the United States, and who shall not, when elected, be an inhabitant of that State for which he shall be chosen.

4. The Vice President of the United States shall be President of the Senate, but shall have no vote, unless they be equally divided.

5. The Senate shall choose their other officers and also a president pro tempore, in the absence of the Vice President, or when he shall exercise the office of the President of the United States.

[1] Revised by the 16th Amendment.
[2] Revised by the 14th Amendment.

[1] Revised by the 17th Amendment.

6. The Senate shall have the sole power to try all impeachments. When sitting for that purpose, they shall be on oath or affirmation. When the President of the United States is tried, the chief justice shall preside: and no person shall be convicted without the concurrence of two thirds of the members present.

7. Judgment in cases of impeachment shall not extend further than to removal from office, and disqualifications to hold and enjoy any office of honor, trust or profit under the United States: but the party convicted shall nevertheless be liable and subject to indictment, trial, judgment and punishment, according to law.

SECTION 4

1. The times, places, and manner of holding elections for senators and representatives, shall be prescribed in each State by the legislature thereof; but the Congress may at any time by law make or alter such regulations, except as to the places of choosing senators.

2. The Congress shall assemble at least once in every year, and such meeting shall be on the first Monday in December, unless they shall by law appoint a different day.

SECTION 5

1. Each House shall be the judge of the elections, returns and qualifications of its own members, and a majority of each shall constitute a quorum to do business; but a smaller number may adjourn from day to day, and may be authorized to compel the attendance of absent members, in such manner, and under such penalities as each House may provide.

2. Each House may determine the rules of its proceedings, punish its members for disorderly behavior, and, with the concurrence of two thirds, expel a member.

3. Each House shall keep a journal of its proceedings, and from time to time publish the same, excepting such parts as may in their judgment require secrecy; and the yeas and nays of the members of either House on any question shall, at the desire of one fifth of those present, be entered on the journal.

4. Neither House, during the session of Congress, shall, without the consent of the other, adjourn for more than three days, nor to any other place than that in which the two Houses shall be sitting.

SECTION 6

1. The senators and representatives shall receive a compensation for their services, to be ascertained by law, and paid out of the Treasury of the United States. They shall in all cases, except treason, felony, and breach of the peace, be privileged from arrest during their attendance at the session of their respective Houses, and in going to and returning from the same; and for any speech or debate in either House, they shall not be questioned in any other place.

2. No senator or representative shall, during the time for which he was elected, be appointed to any civil office under the authority of the United States, which shall have been created, or the emoluments whereof shall have been increased during such time; and no person holding any office under the United States shall be a member of either House during his continuance in office.

SECTION 7

1. All bills for raising revenue shall originate in the House of Representatives; but the Senate may propose or concur with amendments as on other bills.

2. Every bill which shall have passed the House of Representatives and the Senate, shall, before it becomes a law, be presented to the President of the United States; if he approves he shall sign it, but if not he shall return it, with his objections to that House in which it shall have originated, who shall enter the objections at large on their journal, and proceed to reconsider it. If after such reconsideration two thirds of that House shall agree to pass the bill, it shall be sent, together with the objections, to the other House, by which it shall likewise be reconsidered, and if approved by two thirds of that House, it shall become a law. But in all such cases the votes of both Houses shall be determined by yeas and nays, and the names of the persons voting for and against the bill shall be entered on the journal of each House respectively. If any bill shall not be returned by the President within ten days (Sundays excepted) after it shall have been presented to him, the same shall be a law, in like manner as if he had signed it, unless the Congress by their adjournment prevent its return, in which case it shall not be a law.

3. Every order, resolution, or vote to which the concurrence of the Senate and the House

of Representatives may be necessary (except on a question of adjournment) shall be presented to the President of the United States; and before the same shall take effect, shall be approved by him, or being disapproved by him, shall be repassed by two thirds of the Senate and House of Representatives, according to the rules and limitations prescribed in the case of a bill.

SECTION 8

The Congress shall have the power

1. To lay and collect taxes, duties, imposts, and excises, to pay the debts and provide for the common defense and general welfare of the United States; but all duties, imposts, and excises shall be uniform throughout the United States;

2. To borrow money on the credit of the United States;

3. To regulate commerce with foreign nations, and among the several States, and with the Indian tribes;

4. To establish a uniform rule of naturalization, and uniform laws on the subject of bankruptcies throughout the United States;

5. To coin money, regulate the value thereof, and of foreign coin, and fix the standard of weights and measures;

6. To provide for the punishment of counterfeiting the securities and current coin of the United States;

7. To establish post offices and post roads;

8. To promote the progress of science and useful arts, by securing for limited times to authors and inventors the exclusive right to their respective writings and discoveries;

9. To constitute tribunals inferior to the Supreme Court;

10. To define and punish piracies and felonies committed on the high seas, and offenses against the law of nations;

11. To declare war, grant letters of marque and reprisal, and make rules concerning captures on land and water;

12. To raise and support armies, but no appropriation of money to that use shall be for a longer term than two years;

13. To provide and maintain a navy;

14. To make rules for the government and regulation of the land and naval forces;

15. To provide for calling forth the militia to execute the laws of the Union, suppress insurrections and repel invasions;

16. To provide for organizing, arming, and disciplining the militia, and for governing such part of them as may be employed in the service of the United States, reserving to the States respectively, the appointment of the officers, and the authority of training the militia according to the discipline prescribed by Congress;

17. To exercise exclusive legislation in all cases whatsoever, over such district (not exceeding ten miles square) as may, by cession of particular States, and the acceptance of Congress, become the seat of the government of the United States, and to exercise like authority over all places purchased by the consent of the legislature of the State in which the same shall be, for the erection of forts, magazines, arsenals, dockyards, and other needful buildings; and

18. To make all laws which shall be necessary and proper for carrying into execution the foregoing powers, and all other powers vested by this Constitution in the government of the United States, or in any department or officer thereof.

SECTION 9

1. The migration or importation of such persons as any of the States now existing shall think proper to admit, shall not be prohibited by the Congress prior to the year one thousand eight hundred and eight, but a tax or duty may be imposed on such importation, not exceeding ten dollars for each person.

2. The privilege of the writ of habeas corpus shall not be suspended, unless when in cases of rebellion or invasion the public safety may require it.

3. No bill of attainder or ex post facto law shall be passed.

4. No capitation, or other direct, tax shall be laid, unless in proportion to the census or enumeration hereinbefore directed to be taken.[1]

5. No tax or duty shall be laid on articles exported from any State.

6. No preference shall be given by any regulation of commerce or revenue to the ports

[1] Revised by the 16th Amendment.

of one State over those of another: nor shall vessels bound to, or from, one State be obliged to enter, clear, or pay duties in another.

7. No money shall be drawn from the treasury, but in consequence of appropriations made by law; and a regular statement and account of the receipts and expenditures of all public money shall be published from time to time.

8. No title of nobility shall be granted by the United States: and no person holding any office of profit or trust under them, shall, without the consent of the Congress, accept of any present, emolument, office, or title, of any kind whatever, from any king, prince, or foreign State.

Section 10

1. No State shall enter into any treaty, alliance, or confederation; grant letters of marque and reprisal; coin money; emit bills of credit; make anything but gold and silver coin a tender in payment of debts; pass any bill of attainder, ex post facto law, or law impairing the obligation of contracts, or grant any title of nobility.

2. No State shall, without the consent of the Congress, lay any imposts or duties on imports or exports, except what may be absolutely necessary for executing its inspection laws: and the net produce of all duties and imposts laid by any State on imports or exports, shall be for the use of the treasury of the United States; and all such laws shall be subject to the revision and control of the Congress.

3. No State shall, without the consent of the Congress, lay any duty of tonnage, keep troops, or ships of war in time of peace, enter into any agreement or compact with another State, or with a foreign power, or engage in war, unless actually invaded, or in such imminent danger as will not admit of delay.

ARTICLE II

Section 1

1. The executive power shall be vested in a President of the United States of America. He shall hold his office during the term of four years, and, together with the Vice President, chosen for the same term, be elected as follows:

2. Each State shall appoint, in such manner as the legislature thereof may direct, a number of electors, equal to the whole number of senators and representatives to which the State may be entitled in the Congress: but no senator or representative, or person holding an office of trust or profit under the United States, shall be appointed an elector.

The electors shall meet in their respective States, and vote by ballot for two persons, of whom one at least shall not be an inhabitant of the same State with themselves. And they shall make a list of all the persons voted for, and of the number of votes for each; which list they shall sign and certify, and transmit sealed to the seat of the government of the United States, directed to the president of the Senate. The president of the Senate shall, in the presence of the Senate and House of Representatives, open all the certificates, and the votes shall then be counted. The person having the greatest number of votes shall be the President, if such number be a majority of the whole number of electors appointed; and if there be more than one who have such majority, and have an equal number of votes, then the House of Representatives shall immediately choose by ballot one of them for President; and if no person have a majority, then from the five highest on the list the said House shall in like manner choose the President. But in choosing the President, the votes shall be taken by States, the representation from each State having one vote; a quorum for this purpose shall consist of a member or members from two thirds of the States, and a majority of all the States shall be necessary to a choice. In every case, after the choice of the President, the person having the greatest number of votes of the electors shall be the Vice President. But if there should remain two or more who have equal votes, the Senate shall choose from them by ballot the Vice President.[1]

3. The Congress may determine the time of choosing the electors, and the day on which they shall give their votes; which day shall be the same throughout the United States.

4. No person except a natural born citizen, or a citizen of the United States, at the time of the adoption of this Constitution, shall be eligible to the office of President; neither shall any person be eligible to that office who shall not have attained to the age of thirty-five

---

[1] Voided by the 12th Amendment.

years, and been fourteen years a resident within the United States.

5. In case of the removal of the President from office, or of his death, resignation, or inability to discharge the powers and duties of the said office, the same shall devolve on the Vice President, and the Congress may by law provide for the case of removal, death, resignation, or inability, both of the President and Vice President, declaring what officer shall then act as President, and such officer shall act accordingly, until the disability be removed, or a President shall be elected.

6. The President shall, at stated times, receive for his services a compensation, which shall neither be increased nor diminished during the period for which he shall have been elected, and he shall not receive within that period any other emolument from the United States, or any of them.

7. Before he enter on the execution of his office, he shall take the following oath or affirmation: — "I do solemnly swear (or affirm) that I will faithfully execute the office of President of the United States, and will to the best of my ability, preserve, protect and defend the Constitution of the United States."

Section 2

1. The President shall be the commander in chief of the army and navy of the United States, and of the militia of the several States, when called into the actual service of the United States; he may require the opinion, in writing, of the principal officer in each of the executive departments, upon any subject relating to the duties of their respective offices, and he shall have power to grant reprieves and pardons for offenses against the United States, except in cases of impeachment.

2. He shall have power, by and with the advice and consent of the Senate, to make treaties, provided two thirds of the senators present concur; and he shall nominate, and by and with the advice and consent of the Senate, shall appoint ambassadors, other public ministers and consuls, judges of the Supreme Court, and all other officers of the United States, whose appointments are not herein otherwise provided for, and which shall be established by law: but the Congress may by law vest the appointment of such inferior officers, as they think proper, in the President alone, in the

courts of law, or in the heads of departments.

3. The President shall have power to fill up all vacancies that may happen during the recess of the Senate, by granting commissions which shall expire at the end of their next session.

Section 3

He shall from time to time give to the Congress information of the state of the Union, and recommend to their consideration such measures as he shall judge necessary and expedient; he may, on extraordinary occasions, convene both Houses, or either of them, and in case of disagreement between them with respect to the time of adjournment, he may adjourn them to such time as he shall think proper; he shall receive ambassadors and other public ministers; he shall take care that the laws be faithfully executed, and shall commission all the officers of the United States.

Section 4

The President, Vice President, and all civil officers of the United States, shall be removed from office on impeachment for, and conviction of, treason, bribery, or other high crimes and misdemeanors.

ARTICLE III

Section 1

The judicial power of the United States shall be vested in one Supreme Court, and in such inferior courts as the Congress may from time to time ordain and establish. The judges, both of the Supreme and inferior courts, shall hold their offices during good behavior, and shall, at stated times, receive for their services, a compensation, which shall not be diminished during their continuance in office.

Section 2

1. The judicial power shall extend to all cases, in law and equity, arising under this Constitution, the laws of the United States, and treaties made, or which shall be made, under their authority; — to all cases affecting ambassadors, other public ministers and consuls; — to all cases of admiralty and maritime jurisdiction; — to controversies to which the United States shall be a party;[1] — to contro-

1 Revised by the 11th Amendment.

versies between two or more States; — between citizens of different States; — between citizens of the same State claiming lands under grants of different States, and between a State, or the citizens thereof, and foreign States, citizens or subjects.

2. In all cases affecting ambassadors, other public ministers and consuls, and those in which a State shall be party, the Supreme Court shall have original jurisdiction. In all the other cases before mentioned, the Supreme Court shall have appellate jurisdiction, both as to law and to fact, with such exceptions, and under such regulations as the Congress shall make.

3. The trial of all crimes, except in cases of impeachment, shall be by jury; and such trial shall be held in the State where the said crimes shall have been committed; but when not committed within any State, the trial shall be at such place or places as the Congress may by law have directed.

Section 3

1. Treason against the United States shall consist only in levying war against them, or in adhering to their enemies, giving them aid and comfort. No person shall be convicted of treason unless on the testimony of two witnesses to the same overt act, or in confession in open court.

2. The Congress shall have power to declare the punishment of treason, but no attainder of treason shall work corruption of blood, or forfeiture except during the life of the person attainted.

ARTICLE IV

Section 1

Full faith and credit shall be given in each State to the public acts, records, and judicial proceedings of every other State. And the Congress may by general laws prescribe the manner in which such acts, records and proceedings shall be proved, and the effect thereof.

Section 2

1. The citizens of each State shall be entitled to all privileges and immunities of citizens in the several States.[1]

2. A person charged in any State with treason, felony, or other crime, who shall flee from justice, and be found in another State, shall on demand of the executive authority of the State from which he fled, be delivered up to be removed to the State having jurisdiction of the crime.

3. No person held to service or labor in one State under the laws thereof, escaping into another, shall, in consequence of any law or regulation therein, be discharged from such service or labor, but shall be delivered up on claim of the party to whom such service or labor may be due.[2]

Section 3

1. New States may be admitted by the Congress into this Union; but no new State shall be formed or erected within the jurisdiction of any other State; nor any State be formed by the junction of two or more States, or parts of States, without the consent of the legislatures of the States concerned as well as of the Congress.

2. The Congress shall have power to dispose of and make all needful rules and regulations respecting the territory or other property belonging to the United States; and nothing in this Constitution shall be so construed as to prejudice any claims of the United States, or of any particular State.

Section 4

The United States shall guarantee to every State in this Union a republican form of government, and shall protect each of them against invasion; and on application of the legislature, or of the executive (when the legislature cannot be convened) against domestic violence.

ARTICLE V

The Congress, whenever two thirds of both Houses shall deem it necessary, shall propose amendments to this Constitution, or, on the application of the legislatures of two thirds of the several States, shall call a convention for proposing amendments, which in either case, shall be valid to all intents and purposes, as part of this Constitution when ratified by the legislatures of three fourths of the several States, or by conventions in three fourths thereof, as the one or the other mode of ratification may be

---

[1] Elaborated by the 14th Amendment, Sec. 1.

[2] See the 13th Amendment, abolishing slavery.

proposed by the Congress; Provided that no amendment which may be made prior to the year one thousand eight hundred and eight shall in any manner affect the first and fourth clauses in the ninth section of the first article; and that no State, without its consent, shall be deprived of its equal suffrage in the Senate.

ARTICLE VI

1. All debts contracted and engagements entered into, before the adoption of this Constitution, shall be as valid against the United States under this Constitution, as under the Confederation.[1]

2. This Constitution, and the laws of the United States which shall be made in pursuance thereof; and all treaties made, or which shall be made, under the authority of the United States, shall be the supreme law of the land; and the Judges in every State shall be bound thereby, anything in the Constitution or laws of any State to the contrary notwithstanding.

3. The senators and representatives before mentioned, and the members of the several State legislatures, and all executives and judicial officers, both of the United States and of the several States, shall be bound by oath or affirmation to support this Constitution; but no religious test shall ever be required as a qualification to any office or public trust under the United States.

ARTICLE VII

The ratification of the conventions of nine States shall be sufficient for the establishment of this Constitution between the States so ratifying the same.

Done in Convention by the unanimous consent of the States present the seventeenth day of September in the year of our Lord one thousand seven hundred and eighty-seven, and of the independence of the United States of America the twelfth. In witness whereof we have hereunto subscribed our names.

[1] See the 14th Amendment, Sec. 4, for additional provisions.

AMENDMENTS

First Ten Amendments submitted by Congress Sept. 25, 1789.
Ratified by three-fourths of the States December 15, 1791.

ARTICLE I

Congress shall make no law respecting an establishment of religion, or prohibiting the free exercise thereof; or abridging the freedom of speech, or of the press; or the right of the people peaceably to assemble, and to petition the government for a redress of grievances.

ARTICLE II

A well regulated militia, being necessary to the security of a free State, the right of the people to keep and bear arms, shall not be infringed.

ARTICLE III

No soldier shall, in time of peace be quartered in any house, without the consent of the owner, nor in time of war, but in a manner to be prescribed by law.

ARTICLE IV

The right of the people to be secure in their persons, houses, papers, and effects, against unreasonable searches and seizures, shall not be violated, and no warrants shall issue, but upon probable cause, supported by oath or affirmation, and particularly describing the place to be searched, and the persons or things to be seized.

ARTICLE V

No person shall be held to answer for a capital, or otherwise infamous crime, unless on a presentment or indictment of a grand jury, except in cases arising in the land or naval forces, or in the militia, when in actual service in time of war or public danger; nor shall any person be subject for the same offense to be twice put in jeopardy of life or limb; nor shall be compelled in any criminal case to be a witness against himself, nor be deprived of life, liberty, or property, without due process of law; nor shall private property be taken for public use without just compensation.

ARTICLE VI

In all criminal prosecutions, the accused shall enjoy the right to a speedy and public trial, by an impartial jury of the State and district wherein the crime shall have been committed, which district shall have been previously ascertained by law, and to be informed of the nature and cause of the accusation; to be confronted with the witnesses against him; to have compulsory process for obtaining witnesses in his favor, and to have the assistance of counsel for his defense.

ARTICLE VII

In suits at common law, where the value in controversy shall exceed twenty dollars, the right of trial by jury shall be preserved, and no fact tried by a jury shall be otherwise reëxamined in any court of the United States, than according to the rules of the common law.

ARTICLE VIII

Excessive bail shall not be required, nor excessive fines imposed, nor cruel and unusual punishments inflicted.

ARTICLE IX

The enumeration in the Constitution of certain rights shall not be construed to deny or disparage others retained by the people.

ARTICLE X

The powers not delegated to the United States by the Constitution, nor prohibited by it to the States, are reserved to the States respectively, or to the people.

ARTICLE XI

Submitted by Congress March 5, 1794. Ratified January 8, 1798.

The judicial power of the United States shall not be construed to extend to any suit in law or equity, commenced or prosecuted against one of the United States by citizens of another State, or by citizens or subjects of any foreign State.

ARTICLE XII

Submitted by Congress December 12, 1803. Ratified September 25, 1804.

The electors shall meet in their respective States, and vote by ballot for President and Vice President, one of whom, at least, shall not be an inhabitant of the same State with themselves; they shall name in their ballots the person voted for as President, and in distinct ballots, the person voted for as Vice President, and they shall make distinct lists of all persons voted for as President and of all persons voted for as Vice President, and of the number of votes for each, which lists they shall sign and certify, and transmit sealed to the seat of the government of the United States, directed to the President of the Senate; — The President of the Senate shall, in the presence of the Senate and House of Representatives, open all the certificates and the votes shall then be counted; — The person having the greatest number of votes for President, shall be the President, if such number be a majority of the whole number of electors appointed; and if no person have such majority, then from the persons having the highest numbers not exceeding three on the list of those voted for as President, the House of Representatives shall choose immediately, by ballot the President. But in choosing the President, the votes shall be taken by States, the representation from each State having one vote; a quorum for this purpose shall consist of a member or members from two thirds of the States, and a majority of all the States shall be necessary to a choice. And if the House of Representatives shall not choose a President whenever the right of choice shall devolve upon them, before the fourth day of March next following, then the Vice President shall act as President, as in the case of the death or other constitutional disability of the President. The person having the greatest number of votes as Vice President shall be the Vice President, if such number be a majority of the whole number of electors appointed, and if no person have a majority, then from the two highest numbers on the list, the Senate shall choose the Vice President; a quorum for the purpose shall consist of two thirds of the whole number of Senators, and a majority of the whole number shall be necessary to a choice. But no person constitutionally ineligible to the office of President shall be eligible to that of Vice President of the United States.

ARTICLE XIII

Submitted by Congress February 1, 1865. Ratified December 18, 1865.

SECTION 1

Neither slavery nor involuntary servitude, except as punishment for crime whereof the party shall have been duly convicted, shall exist within the United States, or any place subject to their jurisdiction.

SECTION 2

Congress shall have power to enforce this article by appropriate legislation.

ARTICLE XIV

Submitted by Congress June 16, 1866. Ratified July 28, 1868.

SECTION 1

All persons born or naturalized in the United States, and subject to the jurisdiction thereof, are citizens of the United States and of the State wherein they reside. No State shall make or enforce any law which shall abridge the privileges or immunities of citizens of the United States; nor shall any State deprive any person of life, liberty, or property, without due process of law; nor deny to any person within its jurisdiction the equal protection of the laws.

SECTION 2

Representatives shall be apportioned among the several States according to their respective numbers, counting the whole number of persons in each State, excluding Indians not taxed. But when the right to vote at any election for the choice of electors for President and Vice President of the United States, representatives in Congress, the executive and judicial officers of a State, or the members of the legislature thereof, is denied to any of the male inhabitants of such State, being twenty-one years of age, and citizens of the United States, or in any way abridged, except for participation in rebellion, or other crime, the basis of representation therein shall be reduced in the proportion which the number of such male citizens shall bear to the whole number of male citizens twenty-one years of age in such State.

SECTION 3

No person shall be a senator or representative in Congress, or elector of President and Vice President, or hold any office, civil or military, under the United States, or under any State, who having previously taken an oath, as a member of Congress, or as an officer of the United States, or as a member of any State legislature, or as an executive or judicial officer of any State, to support the Constitution of the United States, shall have engaged in insurrection or rebellion against the same, or given aid or comfort to the enemies thereof. But Congress may by a vote of two thirds of each House, remove such disability.

SECTION 4

The validity of the public debt of the United States, authorized by law, including debts incurred for payment of pensions and bounties for services in suppressing insurrection or rebellion, shall not be questioned. But neither the United States nor any State shall assume or pay any debt or obligation incurred in aid of insurrection or rebellion against the United States, or any claim for the loss or emancipation of any slave; but all such debts, obligations, and claims shall be held illegal and void.

SECTION 5

The Congress shall have power to enforce, by appropriate legislation, the provisions of this article.

ARTICLE XV

Submitted by Congress February 27, 1869. Ratified March 30, 1870.

SECTION 1

The right of citizens of the United States to vote shall not be denied or abridged by the United States or by any State on account of race, color, or previous condition of servitude.

SECTION 2

The Congress shall have power to enforce this article by appropriate legislation.

ARTICLE XVI

Submitted by Congress July 12, 1909. Ratified February 25, 1913.

The Congress shall have power to lay and collect taxes on incomes, from whatever source derived, without apportionment among the several States, and without regard to any census or enumeration.

ARTICLE XVII

Submitted by Congress May 16, 1912. Ratified May 31, 1913.

The Senate of the United States shall be composed of two senators from each state, elected by the people thereof, for six years; and each senator shall have one vote. The electors in each State shall have the qualifications requisite for electors of the most numerous branch of the State legislature.

When vacancies happen in the representation of any State in the Senate, the executive authority of such State shall issue writs of election to fill such vacancies: *Provided,* That the legislature of any State may empower the executive thereof to make temporary appointments until the people fill the vacancies by election as the legislature may direct.

This amendment shall not be so construed as to affect the election or term of any senator chosen before it becomes valid as part of the Constitution.

ARTICLE XVIII[1]

Submitted by Congress December 17, 1917. Ratified January 29, 1919.

After one year from the ratification of this article, the manufacture, sale, or transportation of intoxicating liquors within, the importation thereof into, or the exportation thereof from the United States and all territory subject to the jurisdiction thereof for beverage purposes is hereby prohibited.

The Congress and the several States shall have concurrent power to enforce this article by appropriate legislation.

This article shall be inoperative unless it shall have been ratified as an amendment to the Constitution by the legislatures of the several States, as provided in the Constitution, within seven years from the date of the submission hereof to the states by Congress.

[1] Repealed by the 21st Amendment.

ARTICLE XIX

Submitted by Congress June 5, 1919. Ratified August 26, 1920.

The right of citizens of the United States to vote shall not be denied or abridged by the United States or by any State on account of sex.

The Congress shall have power by appropriate legislation to enforce the provisions of this article.

ARTICLE XX

Submitted by Congress March 3, 1932. Ratified January 23, 1933.

SECTION 1

The terms of the President and Vice President shall end at noon on the 20th day of January, and the terms of Senators and Representatives at noon on the 3d day of January, of the years in which such terms would have ended if this article had not been ratified; and the terms of their successors shall then begin.

SECTION 2

The Congress shall assemble at least once in every year, and such meeting shall begin at noon on the 3d day of January, unless they shall by law appoint a different day.

SECTION 3

If, at the time fixed for the beginning of the term of the President, the President-elect shall have died, the Vice President-elect shall become President. If a President shall not have been chosen before the time fixed for the beginning of his term, or if the President-elect shall have failed to qualify, then the Vice President-elect shall act as President until a President shall have qualified; and the Congress may by law provide for the case wherein neither a President-elect nor a Vice President-elect shall have qualified, declaring who shall then act as President, or the manner in which one who is to act shall be selected, and such person shall act accordingly until a President or Vice President shall have qualified.

SECTION 4

The Congress may by law provide for the case of the death of any of the persons from whom the House of Representatives may choose a President whenever the right of choice shall have devolved upon them, and for the case of the death of any of the persons from whom the Senate may choose a Vice President whenever the right of choice shall have devolved upon them.

SECTION 5

Sections 1 and 2 shall take effect on the 15th day of October following the ratification of this article.

SECTION 6

This article shall be inoperative unless it shall have been ratified as an amendment to the Constitution by the legislatures of three-fourths of the several States within seven years from the date of its submission.

ARTICLE XXI

Submitted by Congress February 20, 1933. Ratified December 5, 1933.

SECTION 1

The Eighteenth Article of amendment to the Constitution of the United States is hereby repealed.

SECTION 2

The transportation or importation into any State, Territory, or possession of the United States for delivery or use therein of intoxicating liquors in violation of the laws thereof, is hereby prohibited.

SECTION 3

This article shall be inoperative unless it shall have been ratified as an amendment to the Constitution by conventions in the several States, as provided in the Constitution, within seven years from the date of the submission thereof to the States by the Congress.

ARTICLE XXII

Submitted by Congress March 12, 1947. Ratified March 1, 1951.

No person shall be elected to the office of the President more than twice, and no person who has held the office of President, or acted as President, for more than two years of a term to which some other person was elected President shall be elected to the office of the President more than once.

But this article shall not apply to any person holding the office of President when this article was proposed by the Congress, and shall not prevent any person who may be holding the office of President, or acting as President, during the term within which this article becomes operative from holding the office of President or acting as President during the remainder of such term.

This article shall be inoperative unless it shall have been ratified as an amendment to the Constitution by the legislatures of three-fourths of the several states within seven years from the date of its submission to the states by the Congress.

ARTICLE XXIII

Submitted by Congress June 16, 1960. Ratified April 3, 1961.

SECTION 1

The District constituting the seat of Government of the United States shall appoint in such manner as the Congress may direct:

A number of electors of President and Vice-President equal to the whole number of Senators and Representatives in Congress to which the District would be entitled if it were a State, but in no event more than the least populous State; they shall be in addition to those appointed by the States, but they shall be considered, for the purpose of the election of President and Vice-President, to be electors appointed by a State; and they shall meet in the District and perform such duties as provided by the twelfth article of amendment.

SECTION 2

The Congress shall have power to enforce this article by appropriate legislation.

ARTICLE XXIV

Submitted by Congress August 27, 1962. Ratified January 23, 1964.

SECTION 1

The right of citizens of the United States to vote in any primary or other election for President or Vice-President, for electors for President or Vice-President, or for Senator or Representative in Congress, shall not be denied or abridged by the United States or any State by reason of failure to pay any poll tax or other tax.

SECTION 2

The Congress shall have the power to enforce this article by appropriate legislation.

The States of the Union

(with dates of ratification of the Constitution or admission to the Union)

1.	Delaware	Dec. 7, 1787	26.	Michigan	Jan. 26, 1837
2.	Pennsylvania	Dec. 12, 1787	27.	Florida	Mar. 3, 1845
3.	New Jersey	Dec. 18, 1787	28.	Texas	Dec. 29, 1845
4.	Georgia	Jan. 2, 1788	29.	Iowa	Dec. 28, 1846
5.	Connecticut	Jan. 9, 1788	30.	Wisconsin	May 29, 1848
6.	Massachusetts	Feb. 6, 1788	31.	California	Sept. 9, 1850
7.	Maryland	Apr. 28, 1788	32.	Minnesota	May 11, 1858
8.	South Carolina	May 23, 1788	33.	Oregon	Feb. 14, 1859
9.	New Hampshire	June 21, 1788	34.	Kansas	Jan. 29, 1861
10.	Virginia	June 25, 1788	35.	West Virginia	June 19, 1863
11.	New York	July 26, 1788	36.	Nevada	Oct. 31, 1864
12.	North Carolina	Nov. 21, 1789	37.	Nebraska	Mar. 1, 1867
13.	Rhode Island	May 29, 1790	38.	Colorado	Aug. 1, 1876
14.	Vermont	Mar. 4, 1791	39.	North Dakota	Nov. 2, 1889
15.	Kentucky	June 1, 1792	40.	South Dakota	Nov. 2, 1889
16.	Tennessee	June 1, 1796	41.	Montana	Nov. 8, 1889
17.	Ohio	Mar. 1, 1803	42.	Washington	Nov. 11, 1889
18.	Louisiana	Apr. 30, 1812	43.	Idaho	July 3, 1890
19.	Indiana	Dec. 11, 1816	44.	Wyoming	July 10, 1890
20.	Mississippi	Dec. 10, 1817	45.	Utah	Jan. 4, 1896
21.	Illinois	Dec. 3, 1818	46.	Oklahoma	Nov. 16, 1907
22.	Alabama	Dec. 14, 1819	47.	New Mexico	Jan. 6, 1912
23.	Maine	Mar. 15, 1820	48.	Arizona	Feb. 14, 1912
24.	Missouri	Aug. 10, 1821	49.	Alaska	Jan. 3, 1959
25.	Arkansas	June 15, 1836	50.	Hawaii	Aug. 21, 1959

Other Governmental Units

(with appropriate dates)

District of Columbia	Created, July 16, 1790; governmental status fixed, June 11, 1878
Guam	Acquired by treaty, Dec. 10, 1898; becomes unincorporated territory, Aug. 1, 1950
Philippine Islands	Acquired by treaty, Dec. 10, 1898; become independent, July 4, 1946
Puerto Rico	Acquired by treaty, Dec. 10, 1898; achieves commonwealth status, July 3, 1952
American Samoa	Acquired by treaty, Dec. 2, 1899; transferred from Navy to Interior, July 1, 1951
Panama Canal Zone	Acquired by treaty, Nov. 8, 1903; government defined, Aug. 24, 1912
Virgin Islands	Acquired by treaty, Aug. 4, 1916; U.S. takes possession, March 31, 1917

Presidents, Vice-Presidents, and Cabinet Members

President	Vice-President	Secretary of State	Secretary of Treasury	Secretary of War
17. Andrew Johnson....1865 Unionist Tennessee		W. H. Seward....1865	Hugh McCulloch....1865	E. M. Stanton....1865 U. S. Grant....1867 L. Thomas....1868 J. M. Schofield....1868
18. Ulysees S. Grant....1869 Republican Illinois	Schuyler Colfax....1869 Republican Indiana Henry Wilson....1873 Republican Massachusetts	E. B. Washburne....1869 Hamilton Fish....1869	Geo. S. Boutwell....1869 W. A. Richardson....1873 Benj. H. Bristow....1874 Lot M. Morrill....1876	J. A. Rawlins....1869 W. T. Sherman....1869 W. W. Belknap....1869 Alphonso Taft....1876 J. D. Cameron....1876
19. Rutherford B. Hayes....1877 Republican Ohio	William A. Wheeler....1877 Republican New York	W. M. Evarts....1877	John Sherman....1877	G. W. McCrary....1877 Alex. Ramsey....1879
20. James A. Garfield....1881 Republican Ohio	Chester A. Arthur....1881 Republican New York	James G. Blaine....1881	Wm. Windom....1881	R. T. Lincoln....1881
21. Chester A. Arthur....1881 Republican New York		F. T. Frelinghuysen....1881	Chas. J. Folger....1881 W. Q. Gresham....1884 Hugh McCulloch....1884	R. T. Lincoln....1881
22. Grover Cleveland....1885 Democratic New York	T. A. Hendricks....1885 Democratic Indiana	Thos. F. Bayard....1885	Daniel Manning....1885 Chas. S. Fairchild....1887	W. C. Endicott....1885
23. Benjamin Harrison....1889 Republican Indiana	Levi P. Morton....1889 Republican New York	James G. Blaine....1889 John W. Foster....1892	Wm. Windom....1889 Charles Foster....1891	R. Proctor....1889 S. B. Elkins....1891
24. Grover Cleveland....1893 Democratic New York	Adlai E. Stevenson....1893 Democratic Illinois	W. Q. Gresham....1893 Richard Olney....1895	John G. Carlisle....1893	D. S. Lamont....1893
25. William McKinley....1897 Republican Ohio	Garret A. Hobart....1897 Republican New Jersey Theodore Roosevelt....1901 Republican New York	John Sherman....1897 Wm. R. Day....1897 John Hay....1898	Lyman J. Gage....1897	R. A. Alger....1897 Elihu Root....1899
26. Theodore Roosevelt....1901 Republican New York	Chas. W. Fairbanks....1905 Republican Indiana	John Hay....1901 Elihu Root....1905 Robert Bacon....1909	Lyman J. Gage....1901 Leslie M. Shaw....1902 G. B. Cortelyou....1907	Elihu Root....1901 Wm. H. Taft....1904 Luke E. Wright....1908

President	Vice President	Secretary of State	Secretary of Treasury	Secretary of War
27. William H. Taft........1909 Republican Ohio	James S. Sherman......1909 Republican New York	P. C. Knox..........1909	F. MacVeagh.........1909*	J. M. Dickinson......1909 H. L. Stimson........1911
28. Woodrow Wilson.........1913 Democratic New Jersey	Thomas R. Marshall....1913 Democratic Indiana	Wm. J. Bryan........1913 Robert Lansing......1915 Bainbridge Colby....1920	W. G. McAdoo........1913 Carter Glass........1918 D. F. Houston.......1920	L. M. Garrison......1913 N. D. Baker.........1916
29. Warren G. Harding......1921 Republican Ohio	Calvin Coolidge.......1921 Republican Massachusetts	Chas. E. Hughes.....1921	Andrew W. Mellon....1921	John W. Weeks.......1921
30. Calvin Coolidge........1923 Republican Massachusetts	Charles G. Dawes......1925 Republican Illinois	Chas. E. Hughes.....1923 Frank B. Kellogg....1925	Andrew W. Mellon....1923	John W. Weeks.......1923 Dwight F. Davis.....1925
31. Herbert Hoover.........1929 Republican California	Charles Curtis.......1929 Republican Kansas	Henry L. Stimson....1929	Andrew W. Mellon....1929 Ogden L. Mills......1932	James W. Good.......1929 Pat. J. Hurley......1929
32. Franklin D. Roosevelt...1933 Democratic New York	John Nance Garner.....1933 Democratic Texas Henry A. Wallace......1941 Democratic Iowa Harry S. Truman......1945 Democratic Missouri	Cordell Hull........1933 E. R. Stettinius, Jr...1944	Wm. H. Woodin.......1933 Henry Morgenthau, Jr...1934	Geo. H. Dern........1933 H. A. Woodring......1936 H. L. Stimson.......1940
33. Harry S. Truman........1945 Democratic Missouri	Alben W. Barkley......1949 Democratic Kentucky	James F. Byrnes.....1945 Geo. C. Marshall....1947 Dean G. Acheson.....1949	Fred M. Vinson......1945 John W. Snyder......1946	Robt. H. Patterson...1945 K. C. Royall........1947 *
34. Dwight D. Eisenhower....1953 Republican Kansas	Richard M. Nixon.....1953 Republican California	John Foster Dulles...1953 Christian A. Herter...1957	George M. Humphrey...1953 Robert B. Anderson...1957	
35. John F. Kennedy........1961 Democratic Massachusetts	Lyndon B. Johnson.....1961 Democratic Texas	Dean Rusk...........1961	C. Douglas Dillon...1961	
36. Lyndon B. Johnson......1963 Democratic Texas	Hubert H. Humphrey...1965 Democratic Minnesota	Dean Rusk...........1963	C. Douglas Dillon...1963 Henry H. Fowler.....1965	

*Lost cabinet status in 1947

Cabinet Members (continued)

	ATTORNEY-GENERAL	POSTMASTER-GENERAL	SECRETARY OF NAVY	SECRETARY OF INTERIOR	SECRETARY OF AGRICULTURE
17.	James Speed.....1865 Henry Stanbery...1866 Wm. M. Evarts...1868	Wm. Dennison...1865 A. W. Randall...1866	Gideon Welles.....1865	John P. Usher...1865 James Harlan...1865 O. H. Browning...1866	Cabinet status since 1889.
18.	E. R. Hoar......1869 A. T. Ackerman...1870 Geo. H. Williams...1871 Edw. Pierrepont...1875 Alphonso Taft....1876	J. A. J. Creswell..1869 Jas. W. Marshall..1874 Marshall Jewell..1874 James N. Tyner...1876	Adolph E. Borie...1869 Geo. M. Robeson...1869	Jacob D. Cox......1869 C. Delano.......1870 Zach. Chandler...1875	
19.	Chas. Devens.....1877	David M. Key....1877 Horace Maynard.1880	R. W. Thompson...1877 Nathan Goff, Jr...1881	Carl Schurz......1877	
20.	W. MacVeagh....1881	T. L. James.....1881	W. H. Hunt......1881	S. J. Kirkwood...1881	
21.	B. H. Brewster....1881	T. O. Howe.....1881 W. Q. Gresham...1883 Frank Hatton....1884	W. E. Chandler...1881	Henry M. Teller..1881	
22.	A. H. Garland....1885	Wm. F. Vilas....1885 D. M. Dickinson..1888	W. C. Whitney.....1885	L. Q. C. Lamar...1885 Wm. F. Vilas....1888	N. J. Colman.....1889
23.	W. H. H. Miller...1889	J. Wanamaker....1889	Benj. F. Tracy.....1889	John W. Noble...1889	J. M. Rusk......1889
24.	R. Olney........1893 J. Harmon.......1895	W. S. Bissell.....1893 W. L. Wilson....1895	Hilary A. Herbert..1893	Hoke Smith.....1893 D. R. Francis....1896	J. S. Morton.....1893
25.	J. McKenna......1897 J. W. Griggs.....1897 P. C. Knox......1901	James A. Gary...1897 Chas. E. Smith..1898	John D. Long.....1897	C. N. Bliss......1897 E. A. Hitchcock..1899	James Wilson...1897
26.	P. C. Knox......1901 W. H. Moody....1904 C. J. Bonaparte..1907	Chas. E. Smith...1901 Henry C. Payne..1902 Paul Morton.....1904 Robt. J. Wynne..1904 G. B. Cortelyou..1905 G. von L. Meyer.1907	John D. Long.....1901 Wm. H. Moody...1902 Paul Morton.....1904 C. J. Bonaparte..1905 Victor H. Metcalf..1907 T. H. Newberry..1908	E. A. Hitchcock..1901 J. R. Garfield...1907	James Wilson...1901

OTHER MEMBERS

Secretary of Commerce and Labor
Established Feb. 14, 1903.

George B. Cortelyou.........1903
Victor H. Metcalf..........1904
O. S. Straus...........1907
Chas. Nagel........1909

(Department divided, 1913.)

Secretary of Commerce

W. C. Redfield....1913
Joshua W. Alexander.....1919
H. C. Hoover.....1921
H. C. Hoover.....1925
W. F. Whiting....1928
R. P. Lamont....1929
R. D. Chapin....1932
D. C. Roper.....1933
H. L. Hopkins....1939
Jesse Jones.....1940
Henry A. Wallace.1945
W. Averell Harriman......1946
Charles W. Sawyer......1948
Sinclair Weeks....1953
Lewis L. Strauss..1958
Frederick H. Mueller.......1959
Luther H. Hodges.......1961
John T. Connor..1964

Secretary of Defense
Established July 26, 1947.

James V. Forrestal.1947
Louis A. Johnson..1949
George C. Marshall.......1950
Robert A. Lovett..1951
Charles E. Wilson.1953
Neil H. McElroy..1957
Thomas S. Gates, Jr...........1959
Robert S. McNamara.....1961

Secretary of Health, Education, and Welfare
Established April 1, 1953.

Oveta Culp Hobby.1953
Marion B. Folsom.1955
Arthur S. Flemming........1958
Abraham A. Ribicoff.........1961
Anthony J. Celebrezze......1962
John W. Gardner.........1965

Attorney General	Postmaster General	Secretary of Navy	Secretary of Interior	Secretary of Agriculture	*Secretary of Labor*
27. G. W. Wickersham..1909	F. H. Hitchcock..1909	G. von L. Meyer..1909	R. A. Ballinger..1909 W. L. Fisher....1911	James Wilson...1909	Established March 4, 1913.
28. J. C. McReynolds..1913 Thos. W. Gregory.1914 A. M. Palmer...1919	A. S. Burleson...1913	Josephus Daniels..1913	F. K. Lane......1913 J. B. Payne......1920	D. F. Houston...1913 E. T. Meredith..1920	W. B. Wilson....1913 J. J. Davis......1921
29. H. M. Daugherty..1921	Will H. Hays.....1921 Hubert Work....1922 Harry S. New....1923	Edwin Denby......1921	Albert B. Fall....1921 Hubert Work....1923	H. C. Wallace....1921	W. N. Doak.....1930
30. H. M. Daugherty..1923 Harlan F. Stone..1924 John G. Sargent...1925	Harry S. New....1923	Edwin Denby......1923 Curtis D. Wilber..1924	Hubert Work......1923 Roy O. West.....1928	H. M. Gore......1924 W. M. Jardine..1925	Frances Perkins..1933
31. Wm. D. Mitchell..1929	Walter F. Brown.1929	Chas. F. Adams....1929	Ray L. Wilbur...1929	Arthur M. Hyde..1929	L. B. Schwellenbach.....1945
32. H. S. Cummings..1933 Frank Murphy....1939 Robt. H. Jackson..1940 Francis Biddle.....1941	James A. Farley..1933 Frank C. Walker.1940	Claude A. Swanson.1933 Chas. Edison......1940 Frank Knox......1940 James V. Forrestal.1944	Harold L. Ickes..1933	H. A. Wallace....1933 C. R. Wickard...1940	M. J. Tobin......1948
33. Tom C. Clark....1945 J. H. McGrath...1949 James P. McGranery.....1952	Robt. E. Hannegan......1945 Jesse L. Donaldson...1947	James V. Forrestal..1945 *	Harold L. Ickes..1945 Julius A. Krug..1946 O. L. Chapman..1951	C. P. Anderson..1945 C. F. Brannan....1948	M. P. Durkin..1953 James P. Mitchell.1953
34. Herbert Brownell, Jr...1953 Wm. P. Rogers....1957	Arthur E. Summerfield..1953		Douglas McKay..1953 Fred A. Seaton..1956	Ezra T. Benson...1953	Arthur J. Goldberg....1961
35. Robt. F. Kennedy.1961	J. Edward Day...1961 J. A. Gronouski..1963		Stewart L. Udall..1961	Orville L. Freeman......1961	W. Willard Wirtz. 1962
36. Robt. F. Kennedy.1963 Nicholas Katzenbach.....1964	J. A. Gronouski..1963 Lawrence F. O'Brien.........1965		Stewart L. Udall.1963	Orville L. Freeman......1963	

*Lost cabinet status in 1947

Population of the United States, 1790-1960

DIVISION AND STATE	1790	1800	1810	1820	1830	1840	1850	1860	1870
UNITED STATES.....	3,929,214	5,308,483	7,239,881	9,638,453	*12,866,020	*17,069,453	23,191,876	31,443,321	39,818,44
GEOGRAPHIC DIVISIONS									
New England......	1,009,408	1,233,011	1,471,973	1,660,071	1,954,717	2,234,822	2,728,116	3,135,283	3,487,92
Middle Atlantic....	952,632	1,402,565	2,014,702	2,699,845	3,587,664	4,526,260	5,898,735	7,458,985	8,810,80
South Atlantic.....	1,851,806	2,286,494	2,674,891	3,061,063	3,645,752	3,925,299	4,679,090	5,364,703	5,853,61
East South Central.	109,368	335,407	708,590	1,190,489	1,815,969	2,575,445	3,363,271	4,020,991	4,404,44
West South Central.	....	....	77,618	167,680	246,127	449,985	940,251	1,747,667	2,029,96
East North Central.	....	51,006	272,324	792,719	1,470,018	2,924,728	4,523,260	6,926,884	9,124,51
West North Central	....	....	19,783	66,586	140,455	426,814	880,335	2,169,832	3,856,59
Mountain..........	....	....	....	....	....	....	72,927	174,923	315,38
Pacific...........	....	....	....	....	....	....	105,871	444,053	675,12
NEW ENGLAND									
Maine...........	96,540	151,719	228,705	298,335	399,455	501,793	583,169	628,279	626,91
New Hampshire....	141,885	183,858	214,460	244,161	269,328	284,574	317,976	326,073	318,30
Vermont..........	85,425	154,465	217,895	235,981	280,652	291,948	314,120	315,098	330,55
Massachusetts.....	378,787	422,845	472,040	523,287	610,408	737,699	994,514	1,231,066	1,457,35
Rhode Island......	68,825	69,122	76,931	83,059	97,199	108,830	147,545	174,620	217,35
Connecticut.......	237,946	251,002	261,942	275,248	297,675	309,978	370,792	460,147	537,45
MIDDLE ATLANTIC									
New York........	340,120	589,051	959,049	1,372,812	1,918,608	2,428,921	3,097,394	3,880,735	4,382,75
New Jersey........	184,139	211,149	245,562	277,575	320,823	373,306	489,555	672,035	906,09
Pennsylvania......	434,373	602,365	810,091	1,049,458	1,348,233	1,724,033	2,311,786	2,906,215	3,521,95
SOUTH ATLANTIC									
Delaware..........	59,096	64,273	72,674	72,749	76,748	78,085	91,532	112,216	125,01
Maryland..........	319,728	341,548	380,546	407,350	447,040	470,019	583,034	687,049	780,89
Dist. of Columbia...	....	14,093	24,023	33,039	39,834	43,712	51,687	75,080	131,70
Virginia...........	747,610	880,200	974,600	1,065,366	1,211,405	1,239,797	1,421,661	1,596,318	1,225,16
West Virginia......	....	....	....	....	....	....	....	....	442,01
North Carolina.....	393,751	478,103	555,500	638,829	737,987	753,419	869,039	992,622	1,071,36
South Carolina.....	249,073	345,591	415,115	502,741	581,185	594,398	668,507	703,708	705,60
Georgia...........	82,548	162,686	252,433	340,989	516,823	691,392	906,185	1,057,286	1,184,10
Florida...........	....	....	....	....	34,730	54,477	87,445	140,424	187,74
EAST SOUTH CENTRAL									
Kentucky.........	73,677	220,955	406,511	564,317	687,917	779,828	982,405	1,155,684	1,321,01
Tennessee........	35,691	105,602	261,727	422,823	681,904	829,210	1,002,717	1,109,801	1,258,52
Alabama..........	....	....	....	127,901	309,527	590,756	771,623	964,201	996,99
Mississippi........	....	8,850	40,352	75,448	136,621	373,651	606,526	791,305	827,92
WEST SOUTH CENTRAL									
Arkansas..........	....	....	1,062	14,273	30,388	97,574	209,897	435,450	484,47
Louisiana.........	....	....	76,556	153,407	215,739	352,411	517,762	708,002	726,91
Oklahoma.........	....	....	....	....	....	....	....	....	....
Texas............	....	....	....	....	....	....	212,592	604,215	818,57
EAST NORTH CENTRAL									
Ohio..............	....	45,365	230,760	581,434	937,903	1,519,467	1,980,329	2,339,511	2,665,26
Indiana...........	....	5,641	24,520	147,178	343,031	685,866	988,416	1,350,428	1,680,63
Illinois...........	....	....	12,282	55,211	157,445	476,183	851,470	1,711,951	2,539,89
Michigan..........	....	....	4,762	8,896	31,639	212,267	397,654	749,113	1,184,05
Wisconsin.........	....	....	....	....	....	30,945	305,391	775,881	1,054,67
WEST NORTH CENTRAL									
Minnesota.........	....	....	....	....	....	....	6,077	172,023	439,70
Iowa..............	....	....	....	....	....	43,112	192,214	674,913	1,194,02
Missouri..........	....	....	19,783	66,586	140,455	383,702	632,044	1,182,012	1,721,29
North Dakota......	....	....	....	....	....	....	....	....	2,40
South Dakota......	....	....	....	....	....	....	....	....	11,77
Nebraska..........	....	....	....	....	....	....	....	28,841	122,99
Kansas...........	....	....	....	....	....	....	....	107,206	364,39
MOUNTAIN									
Montana..........	....	....	....	....	....	....	....	....	20,59
Idaho............	....	....	....	....	....	....	....	....	14,99
Wyoming..........	....	....	....	....	....	....	....	....	9,11
Colorado..........	....	....	....	....	....	....	....	34,277	39,86
New Mexico.......	....	....	....	....	....	....	61,547	93,516	91,87
Arizona...........	....	....	....	....	....	....	....	....	9,65
Utah.............	....	....	....	....	....	....	11,380	40,273	86,78
Nevada...........	....	....	....	....	....	....	....	6,857	42,49
PACIFIC									
Alaska............	....	....	....	....	....	....	....	....	....
Washington........	....	....	....	....	....	....	....	11,594	23,95
Oregon...........	....	....	....	....	....	....	13,294	52,465	90,92
California.........	....	....	....	....	....	....	92,597	379,994	560,24
Hawaii...........	....	....	....	....	....	....	....	....	....

* Includes 5,318 persons in 1830 and 6,100 in 1840 on public ships in U.S. service, not credited to any division or state.

DIVISION AND STATE	1880	1890	1900	1910	1920	1930	1940	1950	1960
UNITED STATES.....	50,155,783	62,947,714	75,994,575	91,972,266	105,710,620	122,775,046	131,669,275	150,697,361	179,323,175
GEOGRAPHIC DIVISIONS									
New England......	4,010,529	4,700,749	5,592,017	6,552,681	7,400,909	8,166,341	8,437,290	9,314,453	10,509,367
Middle Atlantic....	10,496,878	12,706,220	15,454,678	19,315,892	22,261,144	26,260,750	27,539,487	30,163,533	34,168,452
South Atlantic.....	7,597,197	8,857,922	10,443,480	12,194,895	13,990,272	15,793,589	17,823,151	21,182,335	25,971,732
East South Central.	5,585,151	6,429,154	7,547,757	8,409,901	8,893,307	9,887,214	10,778,225	11,477,181	12,050,126
West South Central.	3,334,220	4,740,983	6,532,290	8,784,534	10,242,224	12,176,830	13,064,525	14,537,572	16,951,255
East North Central.	11,206,668	13,478,305	15,985,581	18,250,621	21,475,543	25,297,185	26,626,342	30,399,368	36,225,024
West North Central	6,157,443	8,932,112	10,347,423	11,637,921	12,544,249	13,296,915	13,516,990	14,061,394	15,394,115
Mountain.........	653,119	1,213,935	1,674,657	2,633,517	3,336,101	3,701,789	4,150,003	5,074,998	6,855,060
Pacific............	1,114,578	1,888,334	2,416,692	4,192,304	5,566,871	8,194,433	9,733,262	14,486,527	21,198,044
NEW ENGLAND									
Maine...........	648,936	661,086	694,466	742,371	768,014	797,423	847,226	913,774	969,265
New Hampshire....	346,991	376,530	411,588	430,572	443,083	465,293	491,524	533,242	606,921
Vermont..........	332,286	332,422	343,641	355,956	352,428	359,611	359,231	377,747	389,881
Massachusetts......	1,783,085	2,238,947	2,805,346	3,366,416	3,852,356	4,249,614	4,316,721	4,690,514	5,148,578
Rhode Island......	276,531	345,506	428,556	542,610	604,397	687,497	713,346	791,896	859,488
Connecticut......	622,700	746,258	908,420	1,114,756	1,380,631	1,606,903	1,709,242	2,007,280	2,535,234
MIDDLE ATLANTIC									
New York........	5,082,871	6,003,174	7,268,894	9,113,614	10,385,227	12,588,066	13,479,142	14,830,192	16,782,304
New Jersey........	1,131,116	1,444,933	1,883,669	2,537,167	3,155,900	4,041,334	4,160,165	4,835,329	6,066,782
Pennsylvania......	4,282,891	5,258,113	6,302,115	7,665,111	8,720,017	9,631,350	9,900,180	10,498,012	11,319,366
SOUTH ATLANTIC									
Delaware.........	146,608	168,493	184,735	202,322	223,003	238,380	266,505	318,085	446,292
Maryland.........	934,943	1,042,390	1,188,044	1,295,346	1,449,661	1,631,526	1,821,244	2,343,001	3,100,689
Dist. of Columbia...	177,624	230,392	278,718	331,069	437,571	486,869	663,091	802,178	763,956
Virginia..........	1,512,565	1,655,980	1,854,184	2,061,612	2,309,187	2,421,851	2,677,773	3,318,680	3,966,949
West Virginia......	618,457	762,794	958,800	1,221,119	1,463,701	1,729,205	1,901,974	2,005,552	1,860,421
North Carolina....	1,399,750	1,617,949	1,893,810	2,206,287	2,559,123	3,170,276	3,571,623	4,061,929	4,556,155
South Carolina.....	995,577	1,151,149	1,340,316	1,515,400	1,683,724	1,738,765	1,899,804	2,117,027	2,382,594
Georgia..........	1,542,180	1,837,353	2,216,331	2,609,121	2,895,832	2,908,506	3,123,723	3,444,578	3,943,116
Florida...........	269,493	391,422	528,542	752,619	968,470	1,468,211	1,897,414	2,771,305	4,951,560
EAST SOUTH CENTRAL									
Kentucky.........	1,648,690	1,858,635	2,147,174	2,289,905	2,416,630	2,614,589	2,845,627	2,944,806	3,038,156
Tennessee........	1,542,359	1,767,518	2,020,616	2,184,789	2,337,885	2,616,556	2,915,841	3,291,718	3,567,089
Alabama.........	1,262,505	1,513,401	1,828,697	2,138,093	2,348,174	2,646,248	2,832,961	3,061,743	3,266,740
Mississippi.......	1,131,597	1,289,600	1,551,270	1,797,114	1,790,618	2,009,821	2,183,796	2,178,914	2,178,141
WEST SOUTH CENTRAL									
Arkansas..........	802,525	1,128,211	1,311,564	1,574,449	1,752,204	1,854,482	1,949,387	1,909,511	1,786,272
Louisiana.........	939,946	1,118,588	1,381,625	1,656,388	1,798,509	2,101,593	2,363,880	2,683,516	3,257,022
Oklahoma*.......	....	258,657	790,391	1,657,155	2,028,283	2,396,040	2,336,434	2,233,351	2,328,284
Texas............	1,591,749	2,235,527	3,048,710	3,896,542	4,663,228	5,824,715	6,414,824	7,711,194	9,597,677
EAST NORTH CENTRAL									
Ohio.............	3,198,062	3,672,329	4,157,545	4,767,121	5,759,394	6,646,697	6,907,612	7,946,627	9,706,397
Indiana..........	1,978,301	2,192,404	2,516,462	2,700,876	2,930,390	3,238,503	3,427,796	3,934,224	4,662,498
Illinois...........	3,077,871	3,826,352	4,821,550	5,638,591	6,485,280	7,630,654	7,897,241	8,712,176	10,081,158
Michigan.........	1,636,937	2,093,890	2,420,982	2,810,173	3,668,412	4,842,325	5,256,106	6,371,766	7,823,194
Wisconsin........	1,315,497	1,693,330	2,069,042	2,333,860	2,632,067	2,939,006	3,137,587	3,434,576	3,951,777
WEST NORTH CENTRAL									
Minnesota........	780,773	1,310,283	1,751,394	2,075,708	2,387,125	2,563,953	2,792,300	2,982,483	3,413,864
Iowa............	1,624,615	1,912,297	2,231,853	2,224,771	2,404,021	2,470,939	2,538,268	2,621,073	2,757,537
Missouri..........	2,168,380	2,679,185	3,106,665	3,293,335	3,404,055	3,629,367	3,784,664	3,954,653	4,319,813
North Dakota.....	36,909	190,983	319,146	577,056	646,872	680,845	641,935	619,636	632,446
South Dakota.....	98,268	348,600	401,570	583,888	636,547	692,849	642,961	652,740	680,514
Nebraska.........	452,402	1,062,656	1,066,300	1,192,214	1,296,372	1,377,963	1,315,834	1,325,510	1,411,330
Kansas...........	996,096	1,428,108	1,470,495	1,690,949	1,769,257	1,880,999	1,801,028	1,905,299	2,178,611
MOUNTAIN									
Montana.........	39,159	142,924	243,329	376,053	548,889	537,606	559,456	591,024	674,767
Idaho............	32,610	88,548	161,772	325,594	431,866	445,032	524,873	588,637	667,191
Wyoming.........	20,789	62,555	92,531	145,965	194,402	225,565	250,742	290,529	330,066
Colorado.........	194,327	413,249	539,700	799,024	939,629	1,035,791	1,123,296	1,325,089	1,753,947
New Mexico.......	119,565	160,282	195,310	327,301	360,350	423,317	531,818	681,187	951,023
Arizona..........	40,440	88,243	122,931	204,354	334,162	435,573	499,261	749,587	1,302,161
Utah............	143,963	210,779	276,749	373,351	449,396	507,847	550,310	688,862	890,627
Nevada..........	62,266	47,355	42,335	81,875	77,407	91,058	110,247	160,083	285,278
PACIFIC									
Alaska...........	....	....	....	....	....	....	....	....	226,167
Washington.......	75,116	357,232	518,103	1,141,990	1,356,621	1,563,396	1,736,191	2,378,963	2,853,214
Oregon...........	174,768	317,704	413,536	672,765	783,389	953,786	1,089,684	1,521,341	1,768,687
California........	864,694	1,213,398	1,485,053	2,377,549	3,426,861	5,677,251	6,907,387	10,586,223	15,717,204
Hawaii...........	....	....	....	....	....	....	....	....	632,772

* Includes population of Indian territory: 1890, 180,182; 1900, 392,060.

European Immigration Into the United States,

Country	1841–50	1851–60	1861–70	1871–80	1881–90
Austria ⎫ Hungary ⎭			7,800	72,969	353,719
Belgium	5,074	4,738	6,734	7,211	20,177
Bulgaria					
Czechoslovakia					
Denmark	539	3,749	17,094	31,771	88,132
Finland					
France	77,262	76,358	35,986	72,206	50,464
Germany	434,626	951,667	787,468	718,182	1,452,970
Greece	16	31	72	210	2,308
Italy	1,870	9,231	11,725	55,759	307,309
Netherlands	8,251	10,789	9,102	16,541	53,701
Norway ⎫ Sweden ⎭	13,903	20,931	109,298	⎧ 95,333 ⎨ ⎩ 115,922	176,586 391,776
Poland	105	1,164	2,027	12,970	51,806
Rumania				11	6,348
Russia	551	457	2,512	39,284	213,282
Spain	2,209	9,298	6,697	5,266	4,419
Portugal	550	1,055	2,658	14,082	16,978
Switzerland	4,644	25,011	23,286	28,293	81,988
Turkey (in Europe)	59	83	129	337	1,562
United Kingdom ..	1,047,763	1,338,093	1,042,674	984,914	1,462,839
England	32,092	247,125	222,277	437,706	644,680
Ireland	780,719	914,119	435,778	436,871	655,482
Scotland	3,712	38,331	38,769	87,564	149,869
Wales	1,261	6,319	4,313	6,631	12,640
Not Specified ...	229,979	132,199	341,537	16,142	168
Yugoslavia					
Other Europe	79	5	8	1,001	682
Total Europe	1,597,501	2,452,660	2,065,270	2,272,262	4,737,046

From *Statistical Abstract of the United States.*

1841-1960

1891–1900	1901–10	1911–20	1921–30	1931–40	1941–50	1951–60
592,707	2,145,266	⎰453,649	32,868	*	24,860	67,106
		⎱442,693	30,680	7,861	3,469	36,637
18,167	41,635	33,746	15,846	4,817	12,189	18,575
160	39,280	22,533	2,945	938	375	104
		3,426	102,194	14,393	8,347	918
50,231	65,285	41,983	32,430	2,559	5,393	10,984
		756	16,691	2,146	2,503	4,925
30,770	73,379	61,897	49,610	12,623	38,809	51,121
505,152	341,498	143,945	412,202	117,621	226,578	477,765
15,979	167,519	184,201	51,084	9,119	8,973	47,608
651,893	2,045,877	1,109,524	455,315	68,208	57,661	185,491
26,758	48,262	43,718	26,948	7,150	14,860	52,277
95,015	190,505	66,395	68,531	4,740	10,100	22,935
226,266	249,534	95,074	97,249	3,960	10,665	21,697
96,720		4,813	227,734	17,026	7,571	9,985
12,750	53,008	13,311	67,646	3,871	1,076	1,039
505,290	1,597,306	921,201	61,742	1,356	548	584
8,731	27,935	68,611	28,958	3,258	2,898	7,894
27,508	69,149	89,732	29,994	3,329	7,423	19,588
31,179	34,922	23,091	29,676	5,512	10,547	17,675
3,626	79,976	54,677	14,659	737	580	2,653
659,954	865,015	487,589	550,804			
216,726	388,017	249,944	157,420	21,756	111,252	156,171
388,416	339,065	146,181	220,591	13,167	25,377	57,332
44,188	120,469	78,357	159,781	6,887	16,131	32,854
10,557	17,464	13,107	13,012	735		2,589
67						
		1,888	49,064	5,835	1,576	8,225
122	665	8,111	22,983	8,865	7,734	12,076
3,558,978	8,136,016	4,376,564	2,477,853	348,289	621,704	1,325,345

* With Germany after 1938.

Picture Credits

In the following page-by-page list of credits, page numbers appear in bold face. The following abbreviations have been used for a few sources from which a great many illustrations have been obtained: Bettmann — The Bettmann Archive; Culver — Culver Service; Cushing — Charles Phelps Cushing; L. of C. — Library of Congress; N.-Y. Hist. Soc. — Courtesy of the New-York Historical Society, New York City; N.Y.P.L. — New York Public Library.

FRONT END PAPER — Engraving by James Peake, "A Design to represent the beginning and completion of an American Settlement or Farm," from *Scenographia Americana,*" 1768, Courtesy of the New York Public Library.
BACK END PAPER — Photo by Rus Arnold, Chicago skyline, 1965.

13 N.Y.P.L. **15** Brown Brothers. **18** Topsfield Historical Society. **28** N.Y.P.L. **30** The Charleston Library Society, South Carolina. **42** Culver. **50** Cushing. **67** Bettmann. **68** National Portrait Gallery, London. **69** Bettmann. **74** Valentine Museum. **77** Chicago Historical Society. **79** N.-Y. Hist. Soc. **80** Historical Pictures Service, Chicago. **84** Brown Brothers. **87** Art Collections of the University of California, Berkeley. **88** Vinton Freedley. **89** Culver. **98** N.Y.P.L. **102** American Antiquarian Society. **104** Courtesy Harry Shaw Newman, The Old Print Shop, New York. **114** Courtesy of The Bowdoin College Museum of Fine Arts. **115** Board of Regents of Gunston Hall. **117** N.Y.P.L. **119** Museum of Fine Arts, Boston. **128** Culver. **133** Thomas Jefferson Memorial Foundation, Inc. **134** The Peabody Museum of Salem. **151** Culver. **153** William L. Clements Library, Ann Arbor. **154** William L. Clements Library, Ann Arbor. **155** N.-Y. Hist. Soc. **159** Yale University Art Gallery, Mabel Brady Garvan Collection. **160** Photograph from the Smithsonian Institution. **163** Harris & Ewing. **172** E. E. Ayer Collection at The Newberry Library. **181** Owned by the American Antiquarian Society, on loan at the Worcester Art Museum. **181** Owned by the Worcester Art Museum. **183** The Huntington Library, San Marino, California. **186** Bettmann. **196** Museum of Fine Arts, Boston. **200** Bettmann. **204** Ladies Hermitage Ass'n. **209** L. of C. **214** American Antiquarian Society. **219** University of Texas Archives. **221** Culver. **230** Brown Brothers. **235** Culver. **236** Museum of the City of New York. **239** McCormick Collection, Wisconsin State Historical Society. **243** L. of C. **250** N.-Y. Hist. Soc. **252** Historical Pictures Service, Chicago. **253** Virginia State Library. **254** Bettmann. **257** Culver. **267** L. of C. **270** Utah State Historical Society. **273** Southwest Museum, Los Angeles. **280** The Transportation Museum, University of Michigan. **284** Courtesy, Eldredge Collection, The Mariners Museum, Newport News, Virginia. **286** Courtesy Harry Shaw Newman, The Old Print Shop, New York. **289** L. of C. **291** Bettmann. **304** The Meserve Collection. **305** Culver. **327** Ansco Historical Collection **344** Culver. **352** Brown Brothers. **377** N.Y.P.L. **378** Culver. **380** L. of C. **388** Courtesy of the National Archives. **391** Nevada Historical Society. **397** Brown Brothers. **398** Nebraska State Historical Society. **404** Union Pacific Railroad Photo. **407** N.Y.P.L. **414** Keystone View Co. **415** Brown Brothers. **425** Brown Brothers. **426** Brown Brothers. **431** L. of C. **434** Culver. **453** Bettmann. **454** N.-Y. Hist. Soc.

455 Culver. **463** George Eastman House. **464** L. of C. **472** Photograph by Jacob A. Riis, The Jacob A. Riis Collection, Museum of the City of New York. **473** Photograph by Byron, The Byron Collection, Museum of the City of New York. **475** Bettmann. **481** Brown Brothers. **486** Courtesy Carl E. Backman. **488** N.-Y. Hist. Soc. **491** Courtesy The Museum of Modern Art, New York. **501** Brown Brothers. **502** Harvard University Library. **503** L. of C. **504** U.S. Signal Corps Photo No. 111–SC–9441 in The National Archives. **522** N.Y.P.L. **527** Brown Brothers. **533** Brown Brothers. **539** Courtesy of the Women's Archives, Radcliffe College. **540** Brown Brothers. **544** Soil Conservation Service — USDA. **552** Brown Brothers. **555** Culver. **556** Brown Brothers. **565** Bettmann. **570** Culver. **574** United Press International Photo. **580** The National Archives. **581** Photo from European. **586** The National Archives. **588** Bettmann. **591** Brown Brothers. **609** Wide World Photos. **612** Harris & Ewing. **624** Brown Brothers. **628** Courtesy of Westinghouse. **629** N.-Y. Hist. Soc. **633** Culver. **641** Brown Brothers. **646** Courtesy of Scribners. **647** Courtesy of Scribners. **648** Acme. **649** Courtesy of The Art Institute of Chicago. **650** Wide World Photos. **653** Handy Collection. **660** Acme. **664** United Press International Photo. **665** International News Photo. **673** Wide World Photos. **676** USDA. **679** USDA. **680** Wide World Photos. **683** Acme. **686** TVA. **689** Brown Brothers. **697** Sovfoto. **699** Brown Brothers. **704** Brown Brothers. **711** R. A. Lewis in *The Milwaukee Journal.* **717** Official United States Navy Photograph. **719** Chrysler Corporation. **722** top, OWI photo no. 208–N–28560 in the National Archives; bottom OWI photo no. 208–N–28568 in the National Archives. **723** Wide World Photos. **726** upper left, Official U.S. Air Force Photo; upper right, Albert Einstein College of Medicine, Yeshiva University; bottom, U.S. Strategic Bombing Survey photo no. 243–H–269 in the National Archives. **728** Wide World Photos. **729** Wide World Photos. **736** Wide World Photos. **745** Brown Brothers. **754** Wide World Photos. **765** Harris & Ewing. **767** Wide World Photos. **771** Wide World Photos. **786** San Francisco Chamber of Commerce. **788** Metro News Service. **790** Herblock, *The Washington Post.* **797** Photo by Angus Beau, Courtesy New Directions. **801** Wehner Wolff, from Black Star. **803** The White House. **804** United Press International Photo. **810** Monkmeyer Press Photo Service. **811** Wide World Photos. **816** Wide World Photos.

List of Maps and Charts

List of Maps and Charts

Index of Place Names on Maps

Index of Place Names on Maps

Index of Place Names on Maps

Index of Place Names on Maps

Index of Illustrations

Index of Illustrations

Index of Illustrations

General Index

General Index

xliii

General Index

Chiang Kai-shek, Chinese Nationalist, 700; Hull asks Japan to recognize, 717; bad relations with Communists, 726; differences with Stilwell, 727; World War II conferences, 730; flees to Formosa, 741; holds Formosa, 753; unleashed by Eisenhower, 768

Chicago, originally Fort Dearborn, 151; railroad terminal, 280; hopes for transcontinental, 297; anti-Douglas demonstration, 298; 1860 Rep. Conv'n, 306; fire of 1871, 406; strike center (1886), 425; railroad strike, 430; treatment of immigrants, 434; Dem. Conv'n (1896), 455; growth of, 461; Moody and Sankey revival, 468; typhoid outbreak, 471; Hull House, 471; World's Fair, 478, 485; accepts progressive education, 482; symphony orchestra, 490; Rep. and Prog. Conv'ns (1912), 551; race riots in, 608; racketeering in, 633; 1960 Rep. Conv'n, 778

Chicago and Northwestern R.R., state-chartered, 404; transcontinental competition, 408

Chicago, Burlington & Quincy R.R., merger with G.N. and N.P., 539

Chicago, Milwaukee and St. Paul R.R., state-chartered, 404

Chicago, Rock Island and Pacific R.R., state-chartered, 404; transcontinental competition, 408

Chicago Times, suspended, 336

Chicago Tribune, on U.S. foreign policy, 571; supports isolationism, 709

Chickamauga, battle of, 325

Chickasaw Indians, lands sought by whites, 200

Child labor, lessened by free schools, 237; prevalence of, 240; in "gilded age," 462; progressives on, 532; legislation on, 536; Sup. Ct. on, 556; abolished by NRA, 674

Children's Bureau, established 556

Chile, Blaine's policy toward, 497; offers mediation, U.S.-Mexico, 525

China, opens ports to U.S., 292; markets of, 507; U.S. Open Door policy, 509; Boxer Rebellion, 511; Russo-Japanese War, 515; Root-Takahira agreement, 516; Manchurian railroads, 517; imperial rivalry in, 561; represented at Paris (1919), 592; at Washington Conf., 604–606; coveted by Japan, 699; attacked by Japan, 700; FDR on, 707; Japanese conquests in, 716; in World War II, 726–727; joins in call for U.N. Conf., 735; Communist conquest, 741; opposes peace with Japan, 742; misuse of UNRRA funds, 746; U.S. parties on, 751; intervenes in Korea, 755; war losses, 756; Hoover's opinion on, 761;

foreign policy, 769; differences with Soviet Union, 803; recognized by de Gaulle, 804; refuses to sign test-ban agreement, 807; ambitions in Southeast Asia, 808; Vietnam war, 812; proposed admission to U.N., 819

Chinese, used on railroad constr'n, 404; Calif. opposition to, 424, 516; used as strikebreakers, 439

Chinese Exclusion Act (1882), 439

Chisholm Trail, long drive route, 396

Chisholm v. Georgia, Sup. Ct. decision, 128

Chivington, Maj. J. M., Sand Creek attack, 392

Choctaw Indians, lands coveted by whites, 200–201

Chou En-lai, Chinese premier, 769; criticizes Khrushchev, 803

Christian Century, urges church union, 635; on rising power of Catholics, 793

Christian Science, new religious sect, 469

Christianity, accepted by slaves, 249; an advantage of slavery, 256; European critics of, 433; practical emphasis, 468; Amer. influence on, 469; influenced by Darwinism, 478–479; "Social Gospel," 480; modernist controversy, 634–635; Mencken's views on, 641; Niebuhr on, 642; rising interest in dogma, 793. See also Religion, names of denominations

Chrysler Corporation, sit-down strike, 676

Church of England. See Anglican Church

Churches. See Religion, names of denominations

Churchill, Lord Randolph, marries Jennie Jerome, 463

Churchill, Winston, U.S. writer, 531

Churchill, Winston S., Brit. Prime Minister, 703; promises aid to USSR, 715; meets FDR, 720; favors attack on southern Europe, 721; World War II conferences, 730–731; urges Allies capture of Berlin and Prague, 732; agrees to U.N. veto, 737; on "iron fence," 738; on "balance of terror," 753

Cincinnati, O., founded by Symmes, 102; shipyards, 283; Liberal Republican conv'n in, 363; railroad connections, 405; railroad strike, 430; Populist conv'n (1891), 449; city gov't, 465

Cities, in colonial South, 30; significance of, 39; as melting pots, 40; transportation between, 42; described, 43–44; in 1800, 134; lyceums in, 236; promoted by railroads, 281; in postwar South, 344; promoted by industrialism, 402; affected by railroad rates, 409; increasing migration to, 433;

immigrants in, 434–435; Jews in, 438; along Middle Border, 445; in the "gilded age," 460–461; tenements and slums, 462; city gov't, 463–465; morality, 466; critics of, 531; gov't reforms, 532–533; in 1920's, 625; opposition to prohibition, 632; gangsterism in, 633; intellectuals on, 643; vote for FDR (1936), 687; favor Kennedy (1960), 778; growth of suburbs, 782–783; Negro minorities in, 789; newspaper consolidations in, 791; plans for mass transportation, 818. See also under individual names

City manager plan, origins of, 533

Civil Liberties Com. (U.S. Senate), investigates steel strikes, 676

Civil rights, in North during Civil War, 336; under 14th Amendment, 353; Act of 1875, 367; during World War I, 581; Truman on, 750; Dem. stand on, 751, 763; effect of McCarthyism on, 768; Rep. demands for (1960), 778; Negro demands for equality, 789–790; Johnson's commitment to, 802; Kennedy program on, 814–816; Johnson's record on, 817

Civil service, under Jackson, 203; reform effects, 359; aspirations for, 363; Hayes's record on, 373; Pendleton Act, 377; progress of reform, 378; effect of McCarthyism on, 767

Civil Service Commission, headed by Curtis, 359; headed by Eaton, 377; Cleveland's efforts to protect, 380; Theodore Roosevelt a member, 381, 538

Civil War, efforts to prevent, 309–310; Sumter fired on, 313; division of forces, 314; lack of preparedness, 315; armies of, 316; conscription, 317; Bull Run, 318; the blockade, 319; western theater, 321; battles in East, 322; Antietam to Gettysburg, 324; Vicksburg to Chickamauga, 327; Appomattox, 328; behind the lines, 329–332; diplomacy, 333–335; wartime politics, 335–337; significance of the war, 338–339; on Kans.-Mo. border, 386; promotes railroad prosperity, 403; glorification of, 500; "Birth of a Nation," 628

Civil Works Administration (1933), 671

Civilian Conservation Corps (1933), 672

"Claims clubs," to enforce squatters' rights, 205; in mining west, 386

Clark, George Rogers, during Amer. Rev., 88; proposed Miss. River expedition, 125

Clark, J. Beauchamp (Champ), Speaker, 552

xliv

General Index

1

General Index

Thoreau, Henry, transcendentalist, 230; sketch of, 231

Three-fifths Compromise, in Phila. Conv'n., 111

Thurmond, J. Strom, Dixiecrat cand., 751, 752

Tidelands Oil Bill, vetoed by Truman, 725; favored by Republicans, 763; passed under Eisenhower, 766

Tidewater, in colonial South, 28, 29

Tientsin, U.S. expeditionary force to, 511

Tilden, Samuel J., nominated for Pres't, 365; defeated, 366; compared with Hayes, 372; prosecutes Tweed Ring, 465

Tilton, Theodore, accusations against Beecher, 466

Timber Culture Act (1873), 399

Tin, from Far East, 717

Tinian, taken by U.S., 724

Tippecanoe, Harrison's victory at, 148

Tito, Marshal (Josep Broz), Yugoslav leader, 723; successes of, 731; achieves complete control, 739; independent of USSR, 747

Titusville, Pa., oil center, 289, 416

Tobacco, grown in Va., 13–14; in Carolinas, 20; in island colonies, 23; staple in Tidewater, 28; grown along Hudson, 36; enumerated article, 61; importance in 1800, 134; dependence of Va. and Ky. on, 248; improved methods of culture, 251; growing production of, 286; post-Civil War development, 417; in New South, 445; Philippine product, 509; manufacturers' trust, 539; under AAA, 677

Tocqueville, Alexis de, *Democracy in America*, 188

Tojo, Hideki, Japanese premier, 717; trial and execution, 742

Tokyo, visited by Taft, 516; Rome-Berlin-Tokyo Axis, 716; attacked by U.S. bombers, 724

Toledo, O., canal terminal, 200; under "Golden Rule" Jones, 532

Toleration, withheld in Mass. Bay Colony, 16; granted in Rhode Island, 17; in Md., 20; in Pa., 22; Oglethorpe on, 23; in New Eng., 35; in New York, 36; in Phila., 50

Toleration Act, in Md., 20

Tolls Controversy, Panama Canal dispute, 521

Tonkin Bay, naval action, 812

Toombs, Robert, in Congress (1850), 274

Topeka, Kans., antislavery settlement, 298; real estate boom, 445

Topeka Constitution, Kans. document, 299

Toral, Gen. José, surrenders Santiago, 504

Tordesillas, Demarcation Line signed, 8

Tories, British partisans in Amer. *See* Loyalists

Tory Party, in Eng., favors the South, 334

Toscanini, Arturo, conductor, 650

Toulon, French fleet scuttled, 721

Tourism, affects balance of payments, 813

Town government, in New Eng., 32

Townsend, Dr. F. E., on old age pensions, 680

Townshend, Charles, Brit. Chancellor of the Exchequer, 75

Townshend Duty Act, proposed, 75; repealed, 76

Townships, in Middle Colonies, 38; land survey units, 100

Trade, in Middle Ages, 5–6; rivalry over, 9; Eng. trading companies, 10; New Eng., 16, 33; slave trade, 24; in tobacco, 28; plantation imports, 29; Middle Colonies, 39; intercolonial, 42; under Navigation Acts, 61–64; regulation by taxes, 75; importance of Brit. connection to, 78; during Amer. Rev., 86, 97; postwar handicaps, 102; expanding, 105; during French Rev. wars, 125–126; Mississippi River (1800), 134; comm'l restrictions on, 144–147; during War of 1812, 153; after the war, 158; effect of Jackson's diplomacy on, 218; after Panic of 1837, 221; intersectional, 255; over Santa Fe trail, 262; promoted by railroads, 282; during Civil War, 321; regulations of, 411; transportation changes, 443; Open Door policy, 509; U.S. with Mexico, 524; wartime, 566–569; blocked by submarines, 575; postwar, 613–614; after 1929, 656; during 1920's, 658–659; World Econ. Conf. on, 668; Hull trade agreements, 684; U.S.-Cuban, 704; effect of neutrality laws on, 708–710; effect on balance of payments, 813. *See also* Commerce

Trade Agreements Act (1934), 684

Trade associations, after World War II, 784

Trade Unions. *See* Labor

Trading Companies, promote Eng. trade, 9; colonial foundations, 19

Trading-with-the-Enemy Act (1917), 581

Trafalgar, Brit. sea victory, 144

Transcendentalism, Emersonian philosophy, 230; promotes reform, 242

Transcontinental railroads, proposed, 296; rejected by Congress, 305; aided by gov't, 339, 403–404; completion of, 408

Trans-Jordan (Jordan), Arab state, 770

Trans-Mississippi West, slavery in, 169; increasing Amer. interest in,

172; Indian removal to, 208; railroads in, 408–409

Transportation, intercolonial, 42; nat'l support of, 160–161; Adams-Clay program for, 198; the canal age, 199–200; federal aid to, 209; early railroads, 279–283; river and ocean, 283; effects of improvements, 287; during Civil War, 330, 333; federal aid to, 339; in postwar South, 344; in early Far West, 389–390; railroad expansion, 402–411; pipelines, 416; of immigrants, 433; effect of changes in, 443; Populist views on, 449. *See also* Canals, Railroads, Roads

Transportation Act of 1920, returns railroads to owners, 616

Transylvania, promised to Rumania, 593

Transylvania Co., formed, 70; proposed colony, 71

Treasury, Dep't. of the, created, 117; during removal of deposits, 216; agents in South, 345; Grant scandal in, 364; accumulated gold reserve, 373; purchases of silver, 375; maintains gold standard, 450–452; supports N.Y. banks (1907), 545–546; calls in gold, 666

Treasury, U.S., receipts under Jackson, 210; surplus in, 217; effect of distribution on, 218; Sub-Treasuries established, 222; issues National Bank notes, 331; issues "shinplasters," 332; during gold conspiracy, 364; purchases silver, 382; drain on after 1890, 383; declining gold reserve, 450–452; drained by farm subsidies, 679; under Eisenhower, 766; balance of payments problem, 813

Treaties, Utrecht (1713), 24; Peace of Paris (1763), 69; Oswego (1766), 70; Franco-Amer. alliance (1778), 86; Paris (1783), 90, 102; Fort Stanwix (1784), 120; Fort McIntosh (1785), 120; Fort Greenville (1795), 121; Jay's with Great Brit. (1794), 126; Pinckney's with Spain (1795), 127; Conv'n of 1800, 130; La. Purchase (1803), 138; Fort Jackson (1813), 154; Ghent (1814), 155; Rush-Bagot (1817), 156; Adams-Onís (1819), 165, 263; Indian Springs (1827), 201; for Indian renewal, 208; Webster-Ashburton (1824), 225–227; U.S.-Texas (1844), 265; Guadalupe Hidalgo (1848), 269; Clayton-Bulwer (1850), 273; with Siam (1856), 292; Washington (1871), 363; with China (1868), 439; Paris (1898), 505; Portsmouth (1905), 513; Hay-Pauncefote (1900, 1901), 518; Hay-Herran (1903), 519; Hay-Bunau-Varilla (1903), 520; Bryan-Chamorro (1908),